The Alternative Service Book 1980

The Alternative Service Book 1980

Services authorized for use in the Church of England in conjunction with The Book of Common Prayer

together with The Liturgical Psalter

Clowes
SPCK
Cambridge University Press

The Alternative Service Book 1980
together with The Liturgical Psalter

Designed by Keith Murgatroyd FSIAD, PPSTD
Set in Palatino type by Eyre & Spottiswoode Ltd,
Her Majesty's Printers, at Thanet Press, Margate

This edition printed and bound in Great Britain by William
Clowes (Beccles) Ltd, Beccles and London, and jointly
published by

Cambridge University Press
The Pitt Building, Trumpington Street, Cambridge, CB2 1RP

William Clowes (Publishers) Ltd
16 Commerce Way, Colchester, CO2 8HH

SPCK: The Society for Promoting Christian Knowledge
Holy Trinity Church, Marylebone Road, London NW1 4DU

British Library Cataloguing in Publication Data
Church of England. *Liturgy and ritual*
The Alternative Service book, 1980, with the liturgical psalter
I. Title   II. Liturgical psalter.
264'.03   BX 5147.03

CONTENTS

The Preface 9

Preface

The Church of England has traditionally sought to maintain
a balance between the old and the new. For the first time
since the Act of Uniformity this balance in its public worship
is now officially expressed in two books, rather than in one.
The Alternative Service Book (1980), as its name implies, is
intended to supplement the Book of Common Prayer, not to
supersede it. The addition of a date to its title may serve as a
reminder that revision and adaptation of the Church's
worship are continuous processes, and that any liturgy, no
matter how timeless its qualities, also belongs to a particular
period and culture.

It is a remarkable fact that for over three hundred years and
despite all attempts at revision, the Book of Common Prayer
has remained the acknowledged norm for public worship in
the Church of England, as well as a model and inspiration for
worship throughout most of the Anglican Communion.

Rapid social and intellectual changes, however, together
with a world-wide reawakening of interest in liturgy, have
made it desirable that new understandings of worship
should find expression in new forms and styles. Christians
have become readier to accept that, even within a single
church, unity need no longer be seen to entail strict
uniformity of practice. The provision of alternative services
is to be welcomed as an enrichment of the Church's life
rather than as a threat to its integrity. As long ago as 1906 a
Royal Commission reported that 'the law of public worship
in the Church of England is too narrow for the religious life
of the present generation'. Three-quarters of a century later
it can be said with even greater certainty that the gospel of
the living Christ is too rich in content, and the spiritual needs
of his people are too diverse, for a single form of worship
to suffice.

There are few parts of the Church which have not been affected by the recent phase of liturgical revision. The Church of England set up its own Liturgical Commission in 1955, and subsequently authorized new services for experimental use under the Prayer Book (Alternative and Other Services) Measure, 1965. Since then the Commission has prepared revised forms, sometimes in as many as three distinct series, for almost every aspect of the Church's worship. Those which are judged to be most generally useful are here gathered together in a single book. Its publication marks a pause in a programme of liturgical business which has occupied, first the Convocations and the House of Laity, and latterly the General Synod, for more than fifteen years.

This new book of services is the first fully authorized alternative to the Book of Common Prayer. Under the terms of the Worship and Doctrine Measure, 1975, from which such services now derive their legal status, the Book of Common Prayer retains its authority as a doctrinal standard. According to Canon A5, 'The doctrine of the Church of England is grounded in the holy Scriptures, and in such teachings of the ancient Fathers and Councils of the Church as are agreeable to the said Scriptures. In particular such doctrine is to be found in the Thirty-nine Articles of Religion, the Book of Common Prayer, and the Ordinal.' New forms of worship do not erode the historical foundations of the Church's faith, nor render respect for them any less appropriate than it was before.

Nevertheless, Christians are formed by the way in which they pray, and the way they choose to pray expresses what they are. Hence those who seek to know the mind of the Church of England in the last quarter of the twentieth century will find it in this book as certainly as in those earlier formulations. Few books can have had their origin in so much, and such detailed, public debate. With the exception of the Psalter and the readings at the Holy Communion, the wording of every part of the book has been subject to repeated scrutiny by the General Synod.

But words, even agreed words, are only the beginning of worship. Those who use them do well to recognize their transience and imperfection; to treat them as a ladder, not a goal; to acknowledge their power in shaping faith and kindling devotion, without claiming that they are fully adequate to the task. Only the grace of God can make up what is lacking in the faltering words of men. It is in reliance on such grace that this book is offered to the Church, in the hope that God's people may find in it a means in our day to worship Him with honest minds and thankful hearts.

The Calendar
and
Rules to Order the Service

It is provided in Canon B6 'Of Sundays and other Days of Special Observance' that it is lawful for the General Synod to approve Holy Days which may be observed generally or provincially, and, subject to any directions of the Convocation of the province, for the Ordinary to approve Holy Days which may be observed locally.

THE SEASONS

9th Sunday before Christmas (5th before Advent)
8th Sunday before Christmas (4th before Advent)
7th Sunday before Christmas (3rd before Advent)
6th Sunday before Christmas (2nd before Advent)
5th Sunday before Christmas (1st before Advent)

1st Sunday in Advent (4th before Christmas)
2nd Sunday in Advent (3rd before Christmas)
3rd Sunday in Advent (2nd before Christmas)
4th Sunday in Advent (1st before Christmas)

Christmas Eve
Christmas Day
1st Sunday after Christmas
2nd Sunday after Christmas

The Epiphany of our Lord
1st Sunday after the Epiphany
2nd Sunday after the Epiphany
3rd Sunday after the Epiphany
4th Sunday after the Epiphany
5th Sunday after the Epiphany
6th Sunday after the Epiphany

9th Sunday before Easter (3rd before Lent)
8th Sunday before Easter (2nd before Lent)
7th Sunday before Easter (1st before Lent)

Ash Wednesday
1st Sunday in Lent (6th before Easter)
2nd Sunday in Lent (5th before Easter)
3rd Sunday in Lent (4th before Easter)
4th Sunday in Lent (3rd before Easter)
5th Sunday in Lent (2nd before Easter)
Palm Sunday (1st before Easter)
Monday in Holy Week
Tuesday in Holy Week
Wednesday in Holy Week
Maundy Thursday
Good Friday
Easter Eve

Easter Day
Monday in Easter Week
Tuesday in Easter Week
Wednesday in Easter Week
Thursday in Easter Week
Friday in Easter Week
Saturday in Easter Week
1st Sunday after Easter
2nd Sunday after Easter
3rd Sunday after Easter
4th Sunday after Easter
5th Sunday after Easter
Ascension Day
Sunday after Ascension Day (6th after Easter)

Pentecost (Whit Sunday)
Trinity Sunday
2nd Sunday after Pentecost (Trinity 1)
3rd Sunday after Pentecost (Trinity 2)
4th Sunday after Pentecost (Trinity 3)
5th Sunday after Pentecost (Trinity 4)
6th Sunday after Pentecost (Trinity 5)
7th Sunday after Pentecost (Trinity 6)
8th Sunday after Pentecost (Trinity 7)
9th Sunday after Pentecost (Trinity 8)
10th Sunday after Pentecost (Trinity 9)
11th Sunday after Pentecost (Trinity 10)
12th Sunday after Pentecost (Trinity 11)
13th Sunday after Pentecost (Trinity 12)
14th Sunday after Pentecost (Trinity 13)
15th Sunday after Pentecost (Trinity 14)
16th Sunday after Pentecost (Trinity 15)
17th Sunday after Pentecost (Trinity 16)
18th Sunday after Pentecost (Trinity 17)
19th Sunday after Pentecost (Trinity 18)
20th Sunday after Pentecost (Trinity 19)
21st Sunday after Pentecost (Trinity 20)
22nd Sunday after Pentecost (Trinity 21)
Last Sunday after Pentecost

PRINCIPAL HOLY DAYS

Easter Day, Ascension Day, Pentecost (Whit Sunday)
Christmas Day, the Epiphany
Maundy Thursday, Good Friday
Every Sunday in the year

FESTIVALS AND GREATER HOLY DAYS

1 Jan	The Naming of Jesus, *or*
	The Circumcision of Christ
25	The Conversion of St Paul
2 Feb	The Presentation of Christ in the Temple
19 Mar	St Joseph of Nazareth, Husband of the Blessed Virgin Mary
25	The Annunciation of our Lord to the Blessed Virgin Mary
25 Apr	St Mark the Evangelist
1 May	St Philip and St James, Apostles
14	St Matthias the Apostle
11 June	St Barnabas the Apostle
24	The Birth of St John the Baptist
29	St Peter the Apostle
3 July	St Thomas the Apostle
22	St Mary Magdalen
25	St James the Apostle
6 Aug	The Transfiguration of our Lord
24	St Bartholomew the Apostle
8 Sept	The Blessed Virgin Mary
21	St Matthew the Apostle
29	St Michael and All Angels
18 Oct	St Luke the Evangelist
28	St Simon and St Jude, Apostles
1 Nov	All Saints
30	St Andrew the Apostle
26 Dec	St Stephen the first Martyr
27	St John the Evangelist
28	The Holy Innocents

The Festival of the Patron Saint or Title of a church

The Dedication Festival of a church, being the anniversary of the date of its dedication or consecration (or the first Sunday in October if that date is unknown)

Ash Wednesday

Monday, Tuesday, and Wednesday in Holy Week

Easter Eve

Monday to Saturday in Easter Week

LESSER FESTIVALS AND COMMEMORATIONS

Diocesan, local, or other commemorations may be added to these lists.

The collect, psalms, and readings 'Of any Saint' may be used when no others are appropriate.

13 Jan	Hilary, Bishop of Poitiers, Teacher of the Faith, 367
17	Antony of Egypt, Abbot, 356
21	Agnes, Virgin, Martyr, 304
24	Francis de Sales, Bishop, Teacher of the Faith, 1662
26	Timothy and Titus, Companions of St Paul
27	John Chrysostom, Bishop of Constantinople, Teacher of the Faith, 407
28	Thomas Aquinas, Priest, Teacher of the Faith, 1274
30	Charles I, King, Martyr, 1649
3 Feb	Saints and Martyrs of Europe
21	Saints and Martyrs of Africa
23	Polycarp, Bishop of Smyrna, Martyr, c155
27	George Herbert, Priest, Pastor, Poet, 1633
1 Mar	David, Bishop, Patron Saint of Wales, c601
2	Chad, Bishop of Lichfield, Missionary, 672

7 Mar	Perpetua and her Companions, Carthage, Martyrs, 203
8	Edward King, Bishop of Lincoln, Teacher, Pastor, 1910
17	Patrick, Bishop, Patron Saint of Ireland, c460
20	Cuthbert, Bishop of Lindisfarne, Missionary, 687
	Thomas Ken, Bishop of Bath and Wells, 1711
21	Thomas Cranmer, Archbishop of Canterbury, Martyr, 1556
29	John Keble, Priest, Pastor, Poet, 1866
8 Apr	Saints and Martyrs of the Americas
9	William Law, Mystic, Non-juror, 1761
21	Anselm, Archbishop of Canterbury, Teacher of the Faith, 1109
23	George, Patron Saint of England, Martyr, 4th century
29	Catherine of Siena, Mystic, 1380
2 May	Athanasius, Bishop of Alexandria, Teacher of the Faith, 373
8	Julian of Norwich, Mystic, c1417
19	Dunstan, Archbishop of Canterbury, 988
24	John and Charles Wesley, Priests, Poets, Teachers of the Faith, 1791, 1788
25	The Venerable Bede, Priest, Monk of Jarrow, 735
26	Augustine, first Archbishop of Canterbury, 605
31	The Visit of the Blessed Virgin Mary to Elizabeth
1 June	Justin, Martyr at Rome, c165
5	Boniface, Bishop, Missionary, Martyr, 754
9	Columba, Abbot of Iona, Missionary, 597
14	Fathers of the Eastern Church
	Basil the Great, Bishop of Caesarea, Teacher of the Faith, 379
22	Alban, first Martyr of Britain, c209
28	Irenaeus, Bishop of Lyons, Martyr, c200
6 July	Thomas More, Martyr, 1535
11	Benedict, Abbot of Monte Cassino, c550
26	Anne, Mother of the Blessed Virgin Mary

29 July	William Wilberforce, Social Reformer, 1833
4 Aug	Dominic, Priest, Friar, 1221
5	Oswald, King of Northumbria, 642
10	Laurence, Deacon, Martyr, 258
11	Clare of Assisi, Virgin, 1253
13	Jeremy Taylor, Bishop of Down and Connor, Pastor, Teacher, 1667
20	Bernard, Abbot of Clairvaux, 1153
28	Augustine, Bishop of Hippo, Teacher of the Faith, 430
31	Aidan, Bishop of Lindisfarne, Missionary, 651
	John Bunyan, Author, 1688
3 Sept	Gregory the Great, Bishop of Rome, Teacher of the Faith, 604
13	Cyprian, Bishop of Carthage, Martyr, 258
14	Holy Cross Day
20	Saints and Martyrs of Australia and the Pacific
25	Lancelot Andrewes, Bishop of Winchester, 1626
27	Vincent de Paul, Founder of the Vincentian Order, 1660
4 Oct	Francis of Assisi, Friar, 1226
6	William Tyndale, Translator of the Bible, 1536
10	Paulinus, Bishop, Missionary, 644
13	Edward the Confessor, King of England, 1066
15	Teresa of Avila, Mystic, 1582
17	Ignatius, Bishop of Antioch, Martyr, c107
29	James Hannington, Bishop of East Equatorial Africa, Missionary, Martyr, 1885
31	Saints and Martyrs of the Reformation Era
2 Nov	Commemoration of All Souls
3	Richard Hooker, Teacher of the Faith, 1600
8	Saints and Martyrs of England
11	Martin, Bishop of Tours, 397
13	Charles Simeon, Pastor, Preacher, 1836
16	Margaret of Scotland, Queen, Wife, Mother, 1093
17	Hilda, Abbess of Whitby, 680
	Hugh, Bishop of Lincoln, 1200

20 Nov	Edmund of East Anglia, King, Martyr, 870
2 Dec	Nicholas Ferrar, Deacon, Founder of the Little Gidding Community, 1637
3	Saints and Martyrs of Asia
	Francis Xavier, Missionary, 1552
6	Nicholas, Bishop of Myra, c326
7	Ambrose, Bishop of Milan, Teacher of the Faith, 397
14	John of the Cross, Mystic, Teacher of the Faith, 1591
29	Thomas Becket, Archbishop of Canterbury, Martyr, 1170
30	Josephine Butler, Social Reformer, Wife, Mother, 1907
31	John Wyclif, Theologian, Reformer, 1384

SPECIAL DAYS OF PRAYER AND THANKSGIVING

Christmas Eve and Easter Eve are days of preparation for Christmas Day and Easter Day.

Ember Days are the Wednesdays, Fridays, and Saturdays within the weeks before the Third Sunday in Advent, the Second Sunday in Lent, and the Sundays nearest to the Festivals of St Peter, and St Michael and All Angels. On these days prayer is offered for all who serve the Church in its various ministries, both clerical and lay, and for all who are to be ordained or commissioned to those ministries. Ember Days may also be observed on such days as are directed by the Bishop.

Rogation Days are the Monday, Tuesday, and Wednesday after the Fifth Sunday after Easter. On these days prayer is offered for God's blessing on the fruits of the earth and the labours of men.

The Thursday after Trinity Sunday may be observed as a day of Thanksgiving for the Institution of Holy Communion.

Harvest Thanksgiving.

The Eve of St Andrew's Day (29 November) may be observed as a day of Intercession and Thanksgiving for the Missionary Work of the Church.

DAYS OF DISCIPLINE AND SELF-DENIAL

Ash Wednesday, Good Friday.

The other weekdays in Lent.

All the Fridays in the year except:
(a) Christmas Day and the Epiphany.
(b) all Festivals and Greater Holy Days falling outside Lent.
(c) the Fridays after Christmas Day and Easter Day.

A TABLE OF MOVEABLE FEASTS AND HOLY DAYS

Advent Sunday is the fourth Sunday before Christmas Day.

Ash Wednesday is the first day of Lent, and falls in the seventh week before Easter.

Holy Week is the week before Easter Day, and includes Palm Sunday, Maundy Thursday, Good Friday, and Easter Eve.

Ascension Day is forty days after Easter Day.

Pentecost (Whit Sunday) is seven weeks after Easter Day.

Trinity Sunday is eight weeks after Easter Day.

THE DATE OF EASTER
unless other provision is made

1981 April 19	2004 April 11
1982 April 11	2005 March 27
1983 April 3	2006 April 16
1984 April 22	2007 April 8
1985 April 7	2008 March 23
1986 March 30	2009 April 12
1987 April 19	2010 April 4
1988 April 3	2011 April 24
1989 March 26	2012 April 8
1990 April 15	2013 March 31
1991 March 31	2014 April 20
1992 April 19	2015 April 5
1993 April 11	2016 March 27
1994 April 3	2017 April 16
1995 April 16	2018 April 1
1996 April 7	2019 April 21
1997 March 30	2020 April 12
1998 April 12	2021 April 4
1999 April 4	2022 April 17
2000 April 23	2023 April 9
2001 April 15	2024 March 31
2002 March 31	2025 April 20
2003 April 20	

A TABLE OF MOVEABLE FEASTS
ACCORDING TO THE DATE OF EASTER

Sundays after Christmas (/leap year)	Sundays after Epiphany (/leap year)	Sunday 9 before Easter (/leap year)	Ash Wednesday (/leap year)	Easter Day
2	1	18/19 Jan	4/5 Feb	22 Mar
2/1	1	19/20	5/6	23
1	1/2	20/21	6/7	24
1	2	21/22	7/8	25
1/2	2	22/23	8/9	26
2	2	23/24	9/10	27
2	2	24/25	10/11	28
2	2	25/26	11/12	29
2/1	2	26/27	12/13	30
1	2/3	27/28	13/14	31
1	3	28/29	14/15	1 Apr
1/2	3	29/30	15/16	2
2	3	30/31	16/17	3
2	3	31/1 Feb	17/18	4
2	3	1/2 Feb	18/19	5
2/1	3	2/3	19/20	6
1	3/4	3/4	20/21	7
1	4	4/5	21/22	8
1/2	4	5/6	22/23	9
2	4	6/7	23/24	10
2	4	7/8	24/25	11
2	4	8/9	25/26	12
2/1	4	9/10	26/27	13
1	4/5	10/11	27/28	14
1	5	11/12	28/29	15
1/2	5	12/13	1 Mar	16
2	5	13/14	2	17
2	5	14/15	3	18
2	5	15/16	4	19
2/1	5	16/17	5	20
1	5/6	17/18	6	21
1	6	18/19	7	22
1/2	6	19/20	8	23
2	6	20/21	9	24
2	6	21/22	10	25

Ascension Day	Pentecost (Whit Sunday)	Sundays after Pentecost	Sunday 9 before Christmas	Advent Sunday
30 Apr	10 May	23	25 Oct	29 Nov
1 May	11	23	26	30
2	12	23	27	1 Dec
3	13	23	28	2
4	14	23	29	3
5	15	22	23 Oct	27 Nov
6	16	22	24	28
7	17	22	25	29
8	18	22	26	30
9	19	22	27	1 Dec
10	20	22	28	2
11	21	22	29	3
12	22	21	23 Oct	27 Nov
13	23	21	24	28
14	24	21	25	29
15	25	21	26	30
16	26	21	27	1 Dec
17	27	21	28	2
18	28	21	29	3
19	29	20	23 Oct	27 Nov
20	30	20	24	28
21	31	20	25	29
22	1 June	20	26	30
23	2	20	27	1 Dec
24	3	20	28	2
25	4	20	29	3
26	5	19	23 Oct	27 Nov
27	6	19	24	28
28	7	19	25	29
29	8	19	26	30
30	9	19	27	1 Dec
31	10	19	28	2
1 June	11	19	29	3
2	12	18	23 Oct	27 Nov
3	13	18	24	28

RULES TO ORDER THE SERVICE

1   (a) The readings and all else which is proper to the service of
the nine Sundays before Christmas, Christmas Day, the
First and Second Sundays after Christmas, the Epiphany,
the Presentation of Christ, Ash Wednesday, the Sundays of
Lent, the days of Holy Week and Easter Week, the Sundays
after Easter, Ascension Day, the Sunday after Ascension
Day, Pentecost, Trinity Sunday, and All Saints' Day, are
said on their appointed days and are not replaced by the
service of any other days, subject to the following
exceptions:

(i) when All Saints' Day falls on the Eighth Sunday before
Christmas, it takes precedence over the Sunday.

(ii) the Festival of the Patron Saint or Title or the Dedication
Festival of a church may be observed on the Ninth to the
Fifth Sundays before Christmas inclusive, on the First and
Second Sundays after Christmas, and on every Sunday after
Easter except the First.

(b) At Baptisms, Confirmations, Ordinations, and
Marriages, on days for which provision is made in this rule,
unless the Bishop directs otherwise, the readings of the day
are used, and the collect of the day is said.

2   Principal Holy Days, Festivals, and Greater Holy Days are
observed with their own proper service of Morning and
Evening Prayer, and may also be observed with a celebration
of Holy Communion with their own proper readings and all
else which pertains to the service.

3   When a Festival or Greater Holy Day falls on one of the days
to which reference is made in Rule 1, it is transferred to the
first available day, except that when the Festivals of Saint
Joseph and the Annunciation fall on a Sunday in Lent they
are transferred to the preceding Saturday. When the
Festivals of Saint Joseph and the Annunciation are both to be
transferred to the week after the First Sunday after Easter,

the Festival of the Annunciation is transferred to the Monday and the Festival of Saint Joseph to the Tuesday.

4   When a Festival or Greater Holy Day falls on a Sunday other than those to which reference is made in Rule 1, it is observed on the Sunday, and the readings and all else proper to the Sunday are omitted for that year.

5   The service of Evening Prayer appointed for a Festival or Greater Holy Day is normally used on the evening of the Festival or Greater Holy Day itself, but if circumstances require, it may be used instead on the evening before the Festival or Greater Holy Day. For Christmas Day, the Epiphany, Easter, Ascension Day, Pentecost, and All Saints' Day, provision is made for Evening Prayer on the previous day.

6   The Lesser Festivals and Commemorations may be observed with their appropriate collects, psalms, and readings; but if they fall on a Principal Holy Day, a Festival or Greater Holy Day (whether transferred or not), Ash Wednesday, one of the days of Holy Week or Easter Week, or Ascension Day, they are not observed. When a Lesser Festival or Commemoration is observed as the Feast of the Patron Saint or Title of a church, it may be treated as a Festival or Greater Holy Day.

7   When a Festival or Greater Holy Day falls on an Ember Day or a Rogation Day, the service of the Festival or Greater Holy Day is used, and when a Lesser Festival or Commemoration falls on an Ember Day or Rogation Day, the service of the Lesser Festival or Commemoration is to be preferred: in such circumstances, prayers suitable to Embertide or Rogationtide may be said during the intercessions at Holy Communion and after the last collect at Morning and Evening Prayer.

8 The collect, psalms, and readings appointed for the Harvest Thanksgiving may replace those appointed for the day, but not on the Festivals of Saint Matthew, Saint Michael and All Angels, or Saint Luke.

9 On weekdays, the collect of the previous Sunday is said, unless other provision is made; on the weekdays following Christmas Day, the Epiphany, Ash Wednesday and Ascension Day, it is replaced by the collects of these Holy Days; and, subject to Rule 6, on a Lesser Festival or Commemoration, it is replaced by the collect appointed for that day. The collects of Christmas Day and Easter Day are not said on Christmas Eve and Easter Eve respectively.

10 The Proper Thanksgiving of Advent is said from Advent Sunday until Christmas Day; of Christmas, until the Epiphany; of the Epiphany, until the Ninth Sunday before Easter; of Lent, from Ash Wednesday until Palm Sunday; of Passiontide, on Palm Sunday and the six days following; of Easter, until Ascension Day; of Ascension Day, until Pentecost; of Pentecost, for six days after; except that they are replaced by the Proper Thanksgiving of Maundy Thursday, the Presentation of Christ in the Temple, the Annunciation, the Festivals of Saints, and the Dedication of a Church, on their appointed days. In this Rule the word 'until' is used exclusively.

A TABLE OF TRANSFERENCES
required or excluded by the Rules

St Joseph or the Annunciation	falling on a Sunday in Lent or on any day between Palm Sunday and the First Sunday after Easter, both inclusive	must be transferred
St Mark	falling on Easter Day or any day to the First Sunday after Easter inclusive or on any Sunday in Eastertide	must be transferred
St Philip and St James or St Matthias	falling on Ascension Day or a Sunday	must be transferred
St Barnabas	falling on Pentecost or Trinity Sunday	must be transferred
St Simon and St Jude or St Andrew	falling on a Sunday	must be transferred
St Stephen St John Holy Innocents and the Naming of Jesus	falling on the Sunday after Christmas Day	must be transferred
All other Festivals	falling on a Sunday	may not be transferred

General Notes

1. **Distinctions in the Text** Sections of services with numbers in blue may be omitted. Where a number of options are included in a mandatory part of a service, the rubric governing the options is numbered in black, but the texts themselves are numbered in blue. Texts in bold type are to be said by the congregation.

2. **Saying and Singing** Where rubrics indicate that a section is to be 'said', this must be understood to include 'or sung' and vice versa.

3. **Posture** Wherever a certain posture is particularly appropriate, it is indicated in the left-hand margin. At all other points local custom may be established and followed.

4. **Biblical Passages** The sentences, psalms, and readings may be read in any duly authorized version.

5. **Prayer Book Texts** Where parts of a service are sung to well-known settings, the traditional words for which they were composed may be used.

6. **The Lord's Prayer** On any occasion the Lord's Prayer may be used in its modern form (as in Holy Communion Rite A p. 142), or in its modified form (as in Holy Communion Rite B p. 196), or in its traditional form (as in the Book of Common Prayer).

7. **Collects** On any occasion when more than one collect is provided (pp. 398 ff.), only one need be used.

8. **Collect Endings** In the case of any collect ending with the words 'Christ our Lord', the Minister may at his discretion add the longer ending:
   'who is alive and reigns with you and the Holy Spirit, one God, now and for ever.'

9. **Hymns** Various points are indicated for the singing of hymns; but, if occasion requires, they may be sung at other points also.

10 Chanting Psalms and Canticles

(a) Breath is to be taken at asterisks, and at the end of lines except where the pointing clearly forbids it, or when the sign ⏝ is used to indicate a 'carry-over.'

A shorter break, or 'mental comma', made without taking breath, is indicated by an extra space between words.

(b) The centred dot indicates how the syllables within a bar are to be divided, when there are more than two.

(c) The sign † indicates use of the second half of a double chant.

(d) A double space between verses indicates that a change of chant is appropriate.

(e) The final 'ed' should not be pronounced as a separate syllable unless marked with an accent (e.g. blessèd).

(f) Verses enclosed within square brackets may be omitted.

(g) The Jewish doxologies which conclude Books 1 to 4 of the Psalter (see Psalms 41, 72, 89, 106) are enclosed within brackets. When a Christian doxology is used, they may be omitted.

Sentences

INTRODUCTORY SENTENCES

These sentences may be used at Morning or Evening Prayer, or at Holy Communion, on any day during the seasons or occasions indicated. Other sentences will be found with the Sentences, Collects and Readings (pp. 398 ff.).

Ninth Sunday before Christmas to Saturday before Advent
In many and various ways God spoke of old to our fathers by the prophets; but in these last days he has spoken to us by a Son. *Hebrews 1.1, 2*

Deliverance for the righteous shall come from the Lord: he is their strength in time of trouble. *Psalm 37.40*

Advent Sunday to Christmas Eve
The glory of the Lord shall be revealed, and all mankind shall see it. *Isaiah 40.5*

Listen to the word of the Lord, all nations: make it known to the ends of the earth that the Lord has ransomed us. *Jeremiah 31.10*

Now is our salvation nearer than when we first believed. *Romans 13.11*

When the Lord comes, he will bring to light things now hidden in darkness, and will disclose the purposes of the heart. *1 Corinthians 4.5*

Christmas Day to Eve of Epiphany
To us a child is born, to us a son is given. *Isaiah 9.6*

I bring you news of great joy, a joy to be shared by the whole people. Today in the town of David a Saviour has been born to you; he is Christ the Lord. *Luke 2.10, 11*

God's love for us was revealed when God sent his only Son into the world, so that we could have life through him. *1 John 4.9*

Epiphany to Epiphany 6
From the rising of the sun to its setting my name is great
among the nations, says the Lord of hosts. *Malachi 1.11*

The Word became flesh. He came to dwell among us, and we
saw his glory. *John 1.14*

Jesus said, I am the light of the world. He who follows me
will not walk in darkness, but will have the light of life.
John 8.12

God has shone in our hearts to give the light of the
knowledge of his glory in the face of Jesus Christ.
2 Corinthians 4.6

The grace of God has dawned upon the world with healing
for all mankind. *Titus 2.11*

Ninth Sunday before Easter to Shrove Tuesday
Jesus said, Come to me, all whose work is hard, whose load
is heavy; and I will give you rest. *Matthew 11.28*

Ash Wednesday to Saturday before Lent 5
Remember your mercies, Lord, your tenderness from ages
past: do not let our enemies triumph over us. *Psalm 25.1, 6*

The sacrifice of God is a broken spirit: a broken and contrite
heart he will not despise. *Psalm 51.17*

Compassion and forgiveness belong to the Lord our God,
though we have rebelled against him. *Daniel 9.9*

Lent 5 to Wednesday in Holy Week
Jesus said, For their sake I consecrate myself, that they also
may be consecrated by the truth. *John 17.19*

God shows his love for us in that while we were still sinners
Christ died for us. *Romans 5.8*

God forbid that I should glory, save in the cross of our Lord
Jesus Christ, by whom the world is crucified unto me, and I
unto the world. *Galatians 6.14*

Jesus Christ died for all, so that living men should live no longer for themselves, but for him who died and was raised to life for them. *2 Corinthians 5.15*

Christ himself bore our sins in his body on the tree, that we might die to sin and live to righteousness. By his wounds we have been healed. *1 Peter 2.24*

Easter Day to Eve of Ascension

The Lord has risen. Alleluia! *Luke 24.34*

Minister	Christ is risen.
All	**He is risen indeed. Alleluia!** *Luke 24.34*

Christ our Passover has been sacrificed for us: therefore let us keep the feast. (Alleluia!) *1 Corinthians 5.7*

Praise be to the God and Father of our Lord Jesus Christ! In his great mercy he has given us new birth into a living hope by the resurrection of Jesus Christ from the dead. *1 Peter 1.3*

Ascension Day to Eve of Pentecost

Christ has gone up on high. Alleluia! *Ephesians 4.8*

We have a great high priest who has passed through the heavens, Jesus the Son of God. (Alleluia!) *Hebrews 4.14*

Since we have a great high priest who has passed into the heavens, Jesus the Son of God, let us with confidence draw near to the throne of grace. *Hebrews 4.14, 16*

Pentecost

Jesus said, You will receive power when the Holy Spirit comes upon you; and then you will be my witnesses. *Acts 1.8*

God's love has been shed abroad in our hearts through the Holy Spirit he has given us. *Romans 5.5*

Trinity Sunday

By day and by night around the throne they sing: Holy, holy, holy is the Lord God almighty: he was, he is, and he is to come. *Revelation 4.8*

After Pentecost
Our help is in the name of the Lord, who made heaven and earth. *Psalm 124.8*

Seek the Lord while he may be found; call upon him while he is near. *Isaiah 55.6*

Jesus said, Know that I am with you always, to the end of time. *Matthew 28.20*

God is spirit, and those who worship him must worship in spirit and in truth. *John 4.24*

If the Spirit is the source of our life, let the Spirit also direct our course. *Galatians 5.25*

When anyone is united to Christ, there is a new world; the old order has gone, and a new order has already begun. *2 Corinthians 5.17*

God was in Christ reconciling the world to himself. *2 Corinthians 5.19*

In everything make your requests known to God in prayer and petition with thanksgiving. *Philippians 4.6*

To God, the only God, who saves us through Jesus Christ our Lord, be glory and majesty, dominion and power, before all time and now and for ever. *Jude 25*

Saints' Days
Since we are surrounded by so great a cloud of witnesses, let us lay aside every weight, and the sin which clings so closely, and let us run with perseverance the race that is set before us. *Hebrews 12.1*

The righteous will be remembered for ever; the memory of the righteous is a blessing. *Psalm 112.6; Proverbs 10.7*

Blessed are the pure in heart, for they shall see God. *Matthew 5.8*

Blessed Virgin Mary
A virgin shall conceive and bear a son, and his name shall be called Emmanuel. *Matthew 1.23*

Mary said: Behold, I am the handmaid of the Lord; let it be to me according to your word. *Luke 1.38*

Dedication
Truly the Lord is in this place: this is no other than the house of God; this is the gate of heaven. *Genesis 28.16, 17*

Martyrs
Precious in the sight of the Lord is the death of his saints. *Psalm 116.15*

These are they who have passed through the great tribulation; they have washed their robes and made them white in the blood of the Lamb. *Revelation 7.14*

Rogation and Harvest
The earth and all that is in it is the Lord's; let the heavens rejoice, and let the earth be glad. *Psalms 24.1; 96.11*

Times of Thanksgiving
Give thanks to the Lord, and call upon his name; tell the nations all that he has done. *Psalm 105.1*

Let the nations be glad and sing; for God judges the people with righteousness and governs the nations upon earth. *Psalm 67.4*

Times of Trouble
God is our refuge and strength, an ever present help in trouble. *Psalm 46.1*

Unity
Christ is our peace, who has made us one, and has broken down the barrier which divided us. *Ephesians 2.14*

General
Seek the Lord while he may be found; call upon him while he is near. *Isaiah 55.6*

God is spirit, and those who worship him must worship in spirit and in truth. *John 4.24*

In everything make your requests known to God in prayer and petition with thanksgiving. *Philippians 4.6*

Through Jesus let us continually offer up to God the sacrifice of praise, that is, the tribute of lips which acknowledge his name. *Hebrews 13.15*

To God, the only God, who saves us through Jesus Christ our Lord, be glory and majesty, dominion and authority, before all time and now and for ever. *Jude 25*

POSTCOMMUNION SENTENCES

In addition to those provided in the Collects and Readings (pp. 398 ff.), the following sentences may be used at Holy Communion on any day during the seasons indicated.

Ninth Sunday before Christmas to Saturday before Advent
Jesus said, I have not come to abolish the law and the prophets, but to fulfil them. *Matthew 5.17*

As in Adam all die, so in Christ shall all be made alive.
1 Corinthians 15.22

Advent Sunday to Christmas Eve
Repent, for the kingdom of heaven is close at hand.
Matthew 3.2

Christmas Day to Eve of Epiphany
The bread of God is he who comes down from heaven and gives life to the world. *John 6.33*

Epiphany to Epiphany 6
The light shines in darkness, and the darkness has not overcome it. *John 1.5*

Ninth Sunday before Easter to Shrove Tuesday
Hear what the Spirit says: To him who conquers I will grant to eat of the tree of life, which is in the paradise of God.
Revelation 2.7

Ash Wednesday to Saturday before Lent 5
My eyes are even fixed on the Lord, for he releases my feet
from the snare: turn to me and take pity on me, for I am
wretched and alone. *Psalm 25.15*

Lent 5 to Wednesday in Holy Week
As we eat this bread and drink this cup, we proclaim the
death of the Lord until he comes. *1 Corinthians 11.26*

Easter Day to Ascension Eve
Jesus said, He who eats my flesh and drinks my blood has
eternal life, and I will raise him up at the last day. *John 6.54*

Friday after Ascension to Saturday before Pentecost
He has ascended to the heavens, with captives in his train:
he has given gifts to men. (Alleluia!) *Ephesians 4.8*

After Pentecost
Man shall not live by bread alone, but by every word that
proceeds from the mouth of God. *Matthew 4.4*

Jesus said, Be assured, I am with you always, to the end of
time. *Matthew 28.20*

Jesus said, Whoever would save his life will lose it; and
whoever loses his life for my sake, he will save it. *Luke 9.24*

Jesus said, If anyone serves me, he must follow me; and
where I am, there shall my servant be also. *John 12.26*

All of us, in union with Christ, form one body, and as parts
of it we belong to one another. *Romans 12.5*

Hear what the Spirit says: Behold, I stand at the door and
knock. If anyone hears my voice and opens the door, I will
come in to him and eat with him, and he with me.
Revelation 3.20

Morning Prayer and Evening Prayer

NOTES

1 **Interchangeability** Either form of Morning Prayer and of Evening Prayer may be used on Sundays or weekdays; but the full form is recommended for use on Sundays.

2 **Sentences** Sentences for use on Sundays, other Holy Days and special occasions are included with the collects and readings (pp. 398 ff.). There is a further selection on pages 37-42.

3 **Penitence** Sections 3-7 (pp. 48, 49), 26-30 (pp. 61, 62), 63-67 (pp. 82, 83), may be used at a later point in the service after the collects.

4 **The Absolution** In the absence of a priest, 'us' and 'our' are said instead of 'you' and 'your' at sections 6, 29, and 66.

5 **Venite** The whole of Psalm 95 may be said instead of the form at sections 9 and 53.

6 **The Psalms** The psalms to be read each day are as appointed in Table 1 (pp. 985 ff.), or Table 2 (p. 1050).

7 **The Readings** The readings should be announced in the order: book, chapter, verse.

8 **Readings at Holy Communion** If Holy Communion is to follow immediately, two or three readings may be used. When three readings are used, the New Testament reading will be read at sections 13 or 36, and the Gospel after sections 15 or 38. The Sermon will follow the Gospel.

9 **Canticles in Advent and Lent** Saviour of the World and the last five verses of Te Deum are particularly suitable for use in Advent and Lent.

10 **The Litany** The Litany (pp. 99-102) may be said instead of sections 17-23 or 40-46 followed by the Lord's Prayer, the Collect of the Day, and the Grace.

Sentences

GENERAL

Seek the Lord while he may be found; call upon him while he is near. *Isaiah 55.6*

God is spirit, and those who worship him must worship in spirit and in truth. *John 4.24*

In everything make your requests known to God in prayer and petition with thanksgiving. *Philippians 4.6*

Through Jesus let us continually offer up to God the sacrifice of praise, that is, the tribute of lips which acknowledge his name. *Hebrews 13.15*

To God, the only God, who saves us through Jesus Christ our Lord, be glory and majesty, dominion and authority, before all time and now and for ever. *Jude 25*

TIMES OF THANKSGIVING

Give thanks to the Lord, and call upon his name; tell the nations all that he has done. *Psalm 105.1*

Let the nations be glad and sing; for God judges the people with righteousness and governs the nations upon earth. *Psalm 67.4*

TIMES OF TROUBLE

God is our refuge and strength, an ever present help in trouble. *Psalm 46.1*

Morning Prayer

1 **Stand**
The minister may say

> We have come together as the family of God
>   in our Father's presence
> to offer him praise and thanksgiving,
> to hear and receive his holy word,
> to bring before him the needs of the world,
> to ask his forgiveness of our sins,
> and to seek his grace,
> that through his Son Jesus Christ
> we may give ourselves to his service.

2 A SENTENCE OF SCRIPTURE may be said (see p. 46) and A HYMN may be sung.

3 The minister may say

> If we say we have no sin, we deceive ourselves,
> and the truth is not in us. If we confess our sins,
> God is faithful and just, and will forgive us our
> sins, and cleanse us from all unrighteousness.

or the sentences for Ash Wednesday to Lent 5 may be used.

4 The minister may say

> Let us confess our sins to almighty God.

5 **Kneel**
All
> **Almighty God, our heavenly Father,**
> **we have sinned against you and against our**
>   **fellow men,**
> **in thought and word and deed,**
> **through negligence, through weakness,**
> **through our own deliberate fault.**

We are truly sorry
and repent of all our sins.
For the sake of your Son Jesus Christ, who
   died for us,
forgive us all that is past;
and grant that we may serve you in newness
   of life;
to the glory of your name. **Amen.**

6   Priest   Almighty God,
                who forgives all who truly repent,
                have mercy upon *you*,
                pardon and deliver *you* from all *your* sins,
                confirm and strengthen *you* in all goodness,
                and keep *you* in life eternal;
                through Jesus Christ our Lord. **Amen.**

7   Instead of section 5 one of the alternative Confessions may
    be used (pp. 165, 166).

8   **Stand**
    Minister   O Lord, open our lips;
    People   **and our mouth shall proclaim your praise.**

    Minister   Let us worship the Lord.
    People   **All praise to his name.**

    All   **Glory to the Father, and to the Son,**
                 and to the Holy Spirit:
                 as it was in the beginning, is now,
                 and shall be for ever. Amen.

9   VENITE, or JUBILATE, or THE EASTER ANTHEMS (which
    shall always be used on Easter Day)

    VENITE
1   **O come let us sing | out · to the | Lord:**
       let us shout in triumph to the | rock of | our sal | vation.

2 Let us come before his | face with | thanksgiving:
    and cry | out to · him | joyfully · in | psalms.

3 For the Lord is a | great | God:
    and a great | king a · bove | all | gods.

4 In his hand are the | depths · of the | earth:
    and the peaks of the | mountains · are | his | also.

†5 The sea is his and | he | made it:
    his hands | moulded | dry | land.

6 Come let us worship and | bow | down:
    and kneel be | fore the | Lord our | maker.

7 For he is the | Lord our | God:
    we are his | people · and the | sheep of · his |
    pasture.

8 If only you would hear his | voice to | day:
    for he | comes to | judge the | earth.

9 He shall judge the | world with | righteousness:
    and the | peoples | with his | truth.

Glory to the Father and | to the | Son:
    and | to the | Holy | Spirit;
as it was in the be | ginning is | now:
    and shall be for | ever. | A | men.

JUBILATE

1 O shout to the Lord in triumph | all the | earth:
    serve the Lord with gladness
    and come before his | face with | songs of | joy.

2 Know that the Lord | he is | God:
    it is he who has made us and we are his
    we are his | people · and the | sheep of · his |
    pasture.

3 Come into his gates with thanksgiving
    and into his | courts with | praise:
    give thanks to him and | bless his | holy | name.

4 For the Lord is good * his loving mercy | is for | ever:
    his faithfulness through | out all | gener | ations.

Glory to the Father and | to the | Son:
　　and | to the | Holy | Spirit;
as it was in the be|ginning is | now:
　　and shall be for | ever. | A|men.

THE EASTER ANTHEMS

1　Christ our passover has been | sacri·ficed | for us:
　　so let us | cele|brate the | feast,

2　not with the old leaven of cor|ruption · and | wickedness:
　　but with the unleavened | bread of · sin|cerity · and |
　　truth.

3　Christ once raised from the dead | dies no | more:
　　death has no | more do|minion | over him.

4　In dying he died to sin | once for | all:
　　in | living · he | lives to | God.

5　See yourselves therefore as | dead to | sin:
　　and alive to God in | Jesus | Christ our | Lord.

6　Christ has been | raised · from the | dead:
　　the | firstfruits · of | those who | sleep.

7　For as by | man came | death:
　　by man has come also the resur|rection | of the | dead;

8　for as in | Adam · all | die:
　　even so in Christ shall | all be | made a|live.

Glory to the Father and | to the | Son:
　　and | to the | Holy | Spirit;
as it was in the be|ginning is | now:
　　and shall be for | ever. | A|men.

10　THE PSALMS appointed
　　Each psalm or group of psalms ends with

Glory to the Father and | to the | Son:
　　and | to the | Holy | Spirit;
as it was in the be|ginning is | now:
　　and shall be for | ever. | A|men.

11 **Sit**
THE FIRST READING, from the Old Testament

At the end the reader may say

This is the word of the Lord.
All   **Thanks be to God.**

Silence may be kept.

12 **Stand**
BENEDICTUS, or A SONG OF CREATION,
or GREAT AND WONDERFUL

BENEDICTUS (The Song of Zechariah)

1 **Blessèd be the Lord the ˈ God of ˈ Israel:**
    for he has come to his ˈ people · and ˈ set them ˈ free.

2 **He has raised up for us a ˈ mighty ˈ saviour:**
    born of the ˈ house · of his ˈ servant ˈ David.

3 **Through his holy prophets he ˈ promised · of ˈ old:**
    that he would save us from our enemies
    from the ˈ hands of ˈ all that ˈ hate us.

4 **He promised to show ˈ mercy · to our ˈ fathers:**
    and to reˈmember · his ˈ holy ˈ covenant.

5 **This was the oath he swore to our ˈ father ˈ Abraham:**
    to set us ˈ free · from the ˈ hands of · our ˈ enemies,

6 **free to worship him withˈout ˈ fear:**
    holy and righteous in his sight ˈ all the ˈ days of ·
    our ˈ life.

7 **You my child shall be called the prophet of the ˈ**
    Most ˈ High:
    for you will go before the ˈ Lord · to preˈpare his ˈ way,

8 **to give his people knowledge ˈ of salˈvation:**
    by the forˈgiveness · of ˈ all their ˈ sins.

9 **In the tender compassion ˈ of our ˈ God:**
    the dawn from on ˈ high shall ˈ break upˈon us,

10   to shine on those who dwell in darkness and the ˥
     shadow · of ˥ death:
         and to guide our feet ˥ into · the ˥ way of ˥ peace.

     Glory to the Father and ˥ to the ˥ Son:
         and ˥ to the ˥ Holy ˥ Spirit;
     as it was in the be˥ginning is ˥ now:
         and shall be for ˥ ever. ˥ A˥men.

A SONG OF CREATION
On weekdays vv. 4-17 may be omitted.

1   **Bless the Lord all cre**˥**ated** ˥ **things:**
        sing his ˥ praise · and ex˥alt him · for ˥ ever.

2   **Bless the** ˥ **Lord you** ˥ **heavens:**
        sing his ˥ praise · and ex˥alt him · for ˥ ever.

3   **Bless the Lord you** ˥ **angels · of the** ˥ **Lord:**
        bless the ˥ Lord all ˥ you his ˥ hosts;

4   bless the Lord you waters a˥bove the ˥ heavens:
        sing his ˥ praise · and ex˥alt him · for ˥ ever.

5   **Bless the Lord** ˥ **sun and** ˥ **moon:**
        bless the ˥ Lord you ˥ stars of ˥ heaven;

6   bless the Lord all ˥ rain and ˥ dew:
        sing his ˥ praise · and ex˥alt him · for ˥ ever.

7   **Bless the Lord all** ˥ **winds that** ˥ **blow:**
        bless the ˥ Lord you ˥ fire and ˥ heat;

8   bless the Lord scorching wind and ˥ bitter ˥ cold:
        sing his ˥ praise · and ex˥alt him · for ˥ ever.

9   **Bless the Lord dews and** ˥ **falling** ˥ **snows:**
        bless the ˥ Lord you ˥ nights and ˥ days;

10 bless the Lord ˥ light and ˥ darkness:
        sing his ˥ praise · and ex˥alt him · for ˥ ever.

11 **Bless the Lord** ˥ **frost and** ˥ **cold:**
        bless the ˥ Lord you ˥ ice and ˥ snow;

12 bless the Lord ˥ lightnings · and ˥ clouds:
        sing his ˥ praise · and ex˥alt him · for ˥ ever.

13 O let the earth | bless the | Lord:
　　bless the | Lord you | mountains · and | hills;

14 bless the Lord all that | grows · in the | ground:
　　sing his | praise · and ex|alt him · for | ever.

15 Bless the | Lord you | springs:
　　bless the | Lord you | seas and | rivers;

16 bless the Lord you whales and all that | swim · in the |
　　waters:
　　sing his | praise · and ex|alt him · for | ever.

17 Bless the Lord all | birds · of the | air:
　　bless the | Lord you | beasts and | cattle;

18 bless the Lord all | men · on the | earth:
　　sing his | praise · and ex|alt him · for | ever.

19 O People of God | bless the | Lord:
　　bless the | Lord you | priests · of the | Lord;

20 bless the Lord you | servants · of the | Lord:
　　sing his | praise · and ex|alt him · for | ever.

21 Bless the Lord all men of | upright | spirit:
　　bless the Lord you that are | holy · and |
　　humble · in | heart.

Bless the Father the Son and the | Holy | Spirit:
　　sing his | praise · and ex|alt him · for | ever.

GREAT AND WONDERFUL

1 Great and wonderful are your deeds Lord |
　　God · the Al|mighty:
　　just and true are your | ways O | King · of the | nations.

2 Who shall not revere and praise your | name O | Lord?
　　for | you a|lone are | holy.

3 All nations shall come and worship | in your | presence:
　　for your just | dealings · have | been re|vealed.

To him who sits on the throne | and · to the | Lamb:
　　be praise and honour glory and might
　　for ever and | ever. | A|men.

13 **Sit**
   THE SECOND READING, from the New Testament

   At the end the reader may say

        This is the word of the Lord.
   All   **Thanks be to God.**

   Silence may be kept.

14 A SERMON may be preached here, or at the end of the
   service.

15 **Stand**
   TE DEUM, or GLORIA IN EXCELSIS or, in Lent, SAVIOUR
   OF THE WORLD

   TE DEUM
   Verses 14-18 may be omitted.
 1 **You are ˡ God · and we ˡ praise you:**
     you are the ˡ Lord and ˡ we acˡclaim you;

 2 **you are the eˡternal ˡ Father:**
     all creˡation ˡ worships ˡ you.

 3 **To you all angels * all the ˡ powers of ˡ heaven:**
     cherubim and seraphim ˡ sing in ˡ endless ˡ praise,

 4 **Holy holy holy Lord * God of ˡ power and ˡ might:**
     heaven and ˡ earth are ˡ full of · your ˡ glory.

 5 **The glorious company of apˡostles ˡ praise you:**
     the noble fellowship of prophets praise you
     the white-robed ˡ army · of ˡ martyrs ˡ praise you.

 6 **Throughout the world the holy ˡ Church acˡclaims you:**
     Father of ˡ majesˡty unˡbounded;

†7 **your true and only Son * worthy of ˡ all ˡ worship:**
     and the Holy ˡ Spirit ˡ advocate · and ˡ guide.

 8 **You Christ are the ˡ King of ˡ glory:**
     the eˡternal ˡ Son · of the ˡ Father.

9   When you became man to | set us | free:
      you did not ab|hor the | Virgin's | womb.

10   You overcame the | sting of | death:
      and opened the kingdom of | heaven · to | all be|lievers.

11   You are seated at God's right | hand in | glory:
      we believe that you will | come and | be our | judge.

12   Come then Lord and | help your | people:
      bought with the | price of | your own | blood;

13   and bring us | with your | saints:
      to | glory | ever|lasting.

(†) 14   Save your people Lord and | bless · your in|heritance:
      govern and up|hold them | now and | always.

15   Day by | day we | bless you:
      we | praise your | name for | ever.

16   Keep us today Lord from | all | sin:
      have mercy | on us | Lord have | mercy.

17   Lord show us your | love and | mercy:
      for we | put our | trust in | you.

18   In you Lord | is our | hope:
      let us not be con|founded | at the | last.

GLORIA IN EXCELSIS

1   Glory to | God · in the | highest:
      and | peace · to his | people · on | earth.

2   Lord God | heaven·ly | King:
      al|mighty | God and | Father,

3   we worship you we | give you | thanks:
      we | praise you | for your | glory.

4   Lord Jesus Christ only | Son · of the | Father:
      Lord | God | Lamb of | God,

5   you take away the | sin · of the | world:
      have | mercy | on | us;

6   you are seated at the right hand ǀ of the ǀ Father:
     re ǀceive ǀ our ǀ prayer.

7   For you a ǀlone · are the ǀ Holy One:
     you a ǀlone ǀ are the ǀ Lord,

8   you alone are the Most High
     Jesus Christ with the ǀ Holy ǀ Spirit:
     in the glory of God the ǀ Father. ǀ A ǀmen.

SAVIOUR OF THE WORLD

1   Jesus saviour of the world * come to us ǀ in your ǀ mercy:
     we look to ǀ you to ǀ save and ǀ help us.

2   By your cross and your life laid down
     you set your ǀ people ǀ free:
     we look to ǀ you to ǀ save and ǀ help us.

3   When they were ready to perish you ǀ
     saved · your dis ǀciples:
     we look to ǀ you to ǀ come to · our ǀ help.

4   In the greatness of your mercy loose us ǀ from our ǀ
     chains:
     forgive the ǀ sins of ǀ all your ǀ people.

5   Make yourself known as our saviour and ǀ
     mighty · de ǀliverer:
     save and ǀ help us · that ǀ we may ǀ praise you.

6   Come now and dwell with us ǀ Lord Christ ǀ Jesus:
     hear our ǀ prayer · and be ǀ with us ǀ always.

(†) 7 And when you ǀ come in · your ǀ glory:
     make us to be one with you * and to ǀ share the ǀ
     life of · your ǀ kingdom.

16   THE APOSTLES' CREED

All   I believe in God, the Father almighty,
           creator of heaven and earth.

           I believe in Jesus Christ, his only Son,
           our Lord.

He was conceived by the power of the
        Holy Spirit
and born of the Virgin Mary.
He suffered under Pontius Pilate,
was crucified, died, and was buried.
He descended to the dead.
On the third day he rose again.
He ascended into heaven,
and is seated at the right hand
        of the Father.
He will come again to judge the living
        and the dead.

I believe in the Holy Spirit,
the holy catholic Church,
the communion of saints,
the forgiveness of sins,
the resurrection of the body,
and the life everlasting. Amen.

17 **Kneel**
The minister may say

	Lord, have mercy upon us.
People	**Christ, have mercy upon us.**
Minister	Lord, have mercy upon us.

18 **All** **Our Father in heaven,**
hallowed be your name,
your kingdom come,
your will be done,
on earth as in heaven.
Give us today our daily bread.
Forgive us our sins
as we forgive those who sin against us.
Lead us not into temptation
but deliver us from evil.

For the kingdom, the power, and the glory
        are yours
now and for ever. Amen.

19   These versicles and responses may be said.

Minister   Show us your mercy, O Lord;
People   **and grant us your salvation.**

Minister   O Lord, save the Queen;
People   **and teach her counsellors wisdom.**

Minister   Let your priests be clothed with righteousness;
People   **and let your servants shout for joy.**

Minister   O Lord, make your ways known upon the earth;
People   **let all nations acknowledge your saving power.**

Minister   Give your people the blessing of peace;
People   **and let your glory be over all the world.**

Minister   Make our hearts clean, O God;
People   **and renew a right spirit within us.**

20   THE COLLECT OF THE DAY

21   THIS COLLECT may be said.

O God, the author of peace
and lover of concord,
to know you is eternal life,
to serve you is perfect freedom.
Defend us your servants
from all assaults of our enemies;
that we may trust in your defence,
and not fear the power of any adversaries;
through Jesus Christ our Lord. **Amen.**

22 ONE OF THESE COLLECTS is said.

Almighty and everlasting Father,
we thank you that you have brought us safely
to the beginning of this day.
Keep us from falling into sin
or running into danger;
order us in all our doings;
and guide us to do always
what is right in your eyes;
through Jesus Christ our Lord. **Amen.**

or

Eternal God and Father,
you create us by your power
and redeem us by your love:
guide and strengthen us by your Spirit,
that we may give ourselves in love and service
to one another and to you;
through Jesus Christ our Lord. **Amen.**

23 Here may be read the State Prayers, occasional prayers and
thanksgivings, or other forms of prayer. The prayers may
conclude with one of the Endings (p. 107). A sermon may be
preached, hymns may be sung, and the service may end
with a blessing.

Evening Prayer

24 **Stand**
The minister may say

> We have come together as the family of God
>   in our Father's presence
> to offer him praise and thanksgiving,
> to hear and receive his holy word,
> to bring before him the needs of the world,
> to ask his forgiveness of our sins,
> and to seek his grace,
>   that through his Son Jesus Christ
> we may give ourselves to his service.

25 A SENTENCE OF SCRIPTURE may be said (see p. 46) and
A HYMN may be sung.

26 The minister may say

> If we say we have no sin, we deceive ourselves,
> and the truth is not in us. If we confess our sins,
> God is faithful and just, and will forgive us our
> sins, and cleanse us from all unrighteousness.

or the sentences for Ash Wednesday to Lent 5 may be used.

27 The minister may say

> Let us confess our sins to almighty God.

28 **Kneel**
All
> **Almighty God, our heavenly Father,**
> **we have sinned against you and against our**
> **fellow men,**
> **in thought and word and deed,**
> **through negligence, through weakness,**
> **through our own deliberate fault.**
> **We are truly sorry**
> **and repent of all our sins.**

For the sake of your Son Jesus Christ, who
    died for us,
forgive us all that is past;
and grant that we may serve you in newness
    of life;
to the glory of your name. Amen.

29   Priest   Almighty God,
    who forgives all who truly repent,
    have mercy upon *you*,
    pardon and deliver *you* from all *your* sins,
    confirm and strengthen *you* in all goodness,
    and keep *you* in life eternal;
    through Jesus Christ our Lord. **Amen.**

30   Instead of section 28 one of the alternative Confessions may
be used (pp. 165, 166).

31   **Stand**
Minister   O Lord, open our lips;
People   **and our mouth shall proclaim your praise.**

Minister   Let us worship the Lord.
People   **All praise to his name.**

All   **Glory to the Father, and to the Son,
and to the Holy Spirit:
as it was in the beginning, is now,
and shall be for ever. Amen.**

32   PSALM 134, or O GLADSOME LIGHT,
or THE EASTER ANTHEMS

PSALM 134

1   **Come bless the Lord all you | servants · of the | Lord:
you that by night | stand · in the | house of · our | God.**

2   **Lift up your hands toward the holy place and |
bless the | Lord:
may the Lord bless you from Zion
the | Lord who · made | heaven · and | earth.**

Glory to the Father and | to the | Son:
　　and | to the | Holy | Spirit;
as it was in the be|ginning is | now:
　　and shall be for |ever. |A|men.

O GLADSOME LIGHT

1　O gladsome light, O grace
　　Of God the Father's face,
　　The eternal splendour wearing;
　　Celestial, holy, blest,
　　Our Saviour Jesus Christ,
　　Joyful in thine appearing.

2　Now, ere day fadeth quite,
　　We see the evening light,
　　Our wonted hymn outpouring;
　　Father of might unknown,
　　Thee, his incarnate Son,
　　And Holy Spirit adoring.

3　To thee of right belongs
　　All praise of holy songs,
　　O Son of God, lifegiver;
　　Thee, therefore, O Most High,
　　The world doth glorify,
　　And shall exalt for ever.

Other translations of the original may be used.

THE EASTER ANTHEMS

1　Christ our passover has been | sacri·ficed | for us:
　　so let us | cele|brate the | feast,

2　not with the old leaven of cor|ruption · and | wickedness:
　　but with the unleavened | bread of · sin|cerity · and |
　　truth.

3　Christ once raised from the dead | dies no | more:
　　death has no | more do|minion | over him.

4　In dying he died to sin | once for | all:
　　in | living · he | lives to | God.

5   See yourselves therefore as | dead to | sin:
        and alive to God in | Jesus | Christ our | Lord.

6   Christ has been | raised · from the | dead:
        the | firstfruits · of | those who | sleep.

7   For as by | man came | death:
        by man has come also the resur|rection | of the | dead:

8   for as in | Adam · all | die:
        even so in Christ shall | all be | made a|live.

     Glory to the Father and | to the | Son:
        and | to the | Holy | Spirit;
     as it was in the be|ginning is | now:
        and shall be for | ever. | A|men.

33   THE PSALMS appointed
     Each psalm or group of psalms ends with

     Glory to the Father and | to the | Son:
        and | to the | Holy | Spirit;
     as it was in the be|ginning is | now:
        and shall be for | ever. | A|men.

34   **Sit**
     THE FIRST READING, from the Old Testament

     At the end the reader may say

                 This is the word of the Lord.
     All   **Thanks be to God.**

     Silence may be kept.

35   **Stand**
     MAGNIFICAT, or BLESS THE LORD

     MAGNIFICAT (The Song of Mary)
1   **My soul proclaims the | greatness · of the | Lord:**
        my spirit re|joices · in | God my | saviour;

2   for he has looked with favour on his | lowly | servant:
      from this day all gener|ations · will | call me |
      blessèd;

†3   the Almighty has done | great things | for me:
      and | holy | is his | name.

4   He has mercy on | those who | fear him:
      in | every | gener|ation.

5   He has shown the | strength · of his | arm:
      he has scattered the | proud in | their con|ceit.

6   He has cast down the mighty | from their | thrones:
      and has | lifted | up the | lowly.

7   He has filled the hungry with | good | things:
      and the rich he has | sent a|way | empty.

8   He has come to the help of his | servant | Israel:
      for he has re|membered · his | promise · of | mercy,

9   the promise he | made · to our | fathers:
      to Abraham | and his | children · for|ever.

      Glory to the Father and | to the | Son:
      and | to the | Holy | Spirit;
      as it was in the be|ginning is | now:
      and shall be for | ever. | A|men.

BLESS THE LORD

1   Bless the Lord the | God of · our | fathers:
      sing his | praise · and ex|alt him · for | ever.

2   Bless his holy and | glori·ous | name:
      sing his | praise · and ex|alt him · for | ever.

3   Bless him in his holy and | glori·ous | temple:
      sing his | praise · and ex|alt him · for | ever.

4   Bless him who be|holds the | depths:
      sing his | praise · and ex|alt him · for | ever.

5   Bless him who sits be|tween the | cherubim:
      sing his | praise · and ex|alt him · for | ever.

6 **Bless him on the ˈ throne of · his ˈ kingdom:**
  sing his ˈ praise ˸ and exˈalt him · for ˈ ever.

7 **Bless him in the ˈ heights of ˈ heaven:**
  sing his ˈ praise · and exˈalt him · for ˈ ever.

  Bless the Father the Son and the ˈ Holy ˈ Spirit:
  sing his ˈ praise · and exˈalt him · for ˈ ever.

36 **Sit**
THE SECOND READING, from the New Testament

At the end the reader may say

                This is the word of the Lord.
All   **Thanks be to God.**

Silence may be kept.

37 A SERMON may be preached here, or at the end of
the service.

38 **Stand**
NUNC DIMITTIS, or THE SONG OF CHRIST'S GLORY,
or GLORY AND HONOUR

NUNC DIMITTIS (The Song of Simeon)
 1 **Lord now you let your servant ˈ go in ˈ peace:**
   your ˈ word has ˈ been fulˈfilled.

 2 **My own eyes have ˈ seen the · salˈvation:**
   which you have prepared in the ˈ sight of ˈ
   every ˈ people;

(†) 3 **a light to reˈveal you · to the ˈ nations:**
   and the ˈ glory · of your ˈ people ˈ Israel.

   Glory to the Father and ˈ to the ˈ Son:
   and ˈ to the ˈ Holy ˈ Spirit;
   as it was in the beˈginning is ˈ now:
   and shall be for ˈ ever. ˈ Aˈmen.

THE SONG OF CHRIST'S GLORY

1 **Christ Jesus was in the** | **form of** | **God:**
  but he did not | **cling · to e** | **quality · with** | **God.**

2 **He emptied himself * taking the** | **form · of a** | **servant:**
  and was | **born · in the** | **likeness · of** | **men.**

3 **Being found in human form he** | **humbled · him** | **self:**
  and became obedient unto death | **even** |
  death · on a | **cross.**

4 **Therefore God has** | **highly · ex** | **alted him:**
  and bestowed on him the | **name a · bove** | **every** | **name,**

5 **that at the name of Jesus every** | **knee should** | **bow:**
  in heaven and on | **earth and** | **under · the** | **earth;**

6 **and every tongue confess that Jesus** | **Christ is** | **Lord:**
  to the | **glory · of** | **God the** | **Father.**

Glory to the Father and | **to the** | **Son:**
and | **to the** | **Holy** | **Spirit:**
as it was in the be | **ginning is** | **now:**
and shall be for | **ever.** | **A** | **men.**

GLORY AND HONOUR

1 **Glory and** | **honour · and** | **power:**
  are yours by | **right O** | **Lord our** | **God:**

2 **for you cre** | **ated** | **all things:**
  and by your | **will they** | **have their** | **being.**

3 **Glory and** | **honour · and** | **power:**
  are yours by | **right O** | **Lamb · who was** | **slain;**

4 **for by your blood you ransomed** | **men for** | **God:**
  from every race and language * from | **every** |
  people · and | **nation,**

5 **to make them a** | **kingdom · of** | **priests:**
  to stand and | **serve be** | **fore our** | **God.**

To him who sits on the throne | **and · to the** | **Lamb:**
be praise and honour glory and might * for ever and |
ever. | **A** | **men.**

All   I believe in God, the Father almighty,
             creator of heaven and earth.

             I believe in Jesus Christ, his only Son,
                 our Lord.
             He was conceived by the power of the
                 Holy Spirit
             and born of the Virgin Mary.
             He suffered under Pontius Pilate,
             was crucified, died, and was buried.
             He descended to the dead.
             On the third day he rose again.
             He ascended into heaven,
             and is seated at the right hand
                 of the Father.
             He will come again to judge the living
                 and the dead.

             I believe in the Holy Spirit,
             the holy catholic Church,
             the communion of saints,
             the forgiveness of sins,
             the resurrection of the body,
             and the life everlasting. Amen.

40   **Kneel**
     The minister may say

                  Lord, have mercy upon us.
     People   **Christ, have mercy upon us.**
     Minister   Lord, have mercy upon us.

41   **All**   Our Father in heaven,
                  hallowed be your name,
                  your kingdom come,
                  your will be done,
                  on earth as in heaven.
                  Give us today our daily bread.
                  Forgive us our sins
                  as we forgive those who sin against us.

> **Lead us not into temptation**
> **but deliver us from evil.**
>
> **For the kingdom, the power, and the glory**
> **are yours**
> **now and for ever. Amen.**

42 These versicles and responses may be said.

> Minister   Show us your mercy, O Lord;
> **People**   **and grant us your salvation.**
>
> Minister   O Lord, save the Queen;
> **People**   **and teach her counsellors wisdom.**
>
> Minister   Let your priests be clothed with righteousness;
> **People**   **and let your servants shout for joy.**
>
> Minister   O Lord, make your ways known upon the earth;
> **People**   **let all nations acknowledge your saving power.**
>
> Minister   Give your people the blessing of peace;
> **People**   **and let your glory be over all the world.**
>
> Minister   Make our hearts clean, O God;
> **People**   **and renew a right spirit within us.**

43 THE COLLECT OF THE DAY

44 THIS COLLECT may be said.

> O God,
> the source of all good desires,
> all right judgements, and all just works:
> give to your servants that peace
>   which the world cannot give;
> that our hearts may be set to obey
>   your commandments,
> and that freed from fear of our enemies,
> we may pass our time in rest and quietness;
> through Jesus Christ our Lord. **Amen.**

45   THIS COLLECT is said.

> Lighten our darkness,
> Lord, we pray;
> and in your mercy defend us
> from all perils and dangers of this night;
> for the love of your only Son,
> our Saviour Jesus Christ. **Amen.**

46   Here may be read the State Prayers, occasional prayers and thanksgivings, or other forms of prayer. The prayers may conclude with one of the Endings (p. 107). A sermon may be preached, hymns may be sung, and the service may end with a blessing.

Morning Prayer or Evening Prayer with Holy Communion Rite A

47

	MP	EP
Penitence	1-7 optional	24-30
Versicles	8	31
Psalms	9, 10	32, 33
1st Reading	11	34
Canticle	12 optional	35 optional
2nd Reading	13	36
Canticle	15	38
Apostles' Creed	16	39 optional
Collect of the day	20	43
Daily Collect(s)	21 optional, 22	44 optional, 45

	HC
General Intercession	
or	
Prayer for the Church and World	20, 21, 81
Penitence (if not used above)	23-29, 80
The Peace	30-31
The Preparation of the Gifts	32-35
The Eucharistic Prayer	36-41
The Communion	42-49, 66, 85
After Communion	50-56, 77, 86

The Shorter Form of Evening Prayer is not suitable for combination with Holy Communion.

Canticles at Morning Prayer and Evening Prayer

48 When it is desired to say two varying canticles at Morning
    and Evening Prayer on weekdays, they may be appointed
    as follows.

Day	Morning Prayer	Evening Prayer
Monday	Great and wonderful	Magnificat
	Te Deum	Glory and honour
Tuesday	Song of creation	Bless the Lord
	Saviour of the world	Song of Christ's glory
Wednesday	Benedictus	Magnificat
	Te Deum	Nunc dimittis
Thursday	Song of creation	Easter Anthems
	Gloria in excelsis	Song of Christ's glory
Friday	Benedictus	Bless the Lord
	Saviour of the world	Glory and honour
Saturday	Great and wonderful	Easter Anthems
	Gloria in excelsis	Nunc dimittis

49 If Benedictus is used invariably as the first canticle at
    Morning Prayer on weekdays, the following order may be
    observed for the second.

Monday	Te Deum
Tuesday	Song of creation
Wednesday	Te Deum
Thursday	Gloria in excelsis
Friday	Saviour of the world
Saturday	Great and wonderful

50 If Magnificat is used invariably as the first canticle at Evening
    Prayer on weekdays, the following order may be observed
    for the second.

Monday	Nunc dimittis
Tuesday	Bless the Lord
Wednesday	Nunc dimittis
Thursday	Song of Christ's glory
Friday	Glory and honour
Saturday	Easter Anthems (Lent, Saviour of the world)

Morning Prayer (Shorter Form)

51 **Stand**
A SENTENCE OF SCRIPTURE may be said (see p. 46).

(see p. 46)

52 Minister   O Lord, open our lips;
People   **and our mouth shall proclaim your praise.**

    Minister   Let us worship the Lord.
    People   **All praise to his name.**

    All   **Glory to the Father, and to the Son,**
    and to the Holy Spirit:
    as it was in the beginning, is now,
    and shall be for ever. Amen.

53 VENITE, or JUBILATE, or THE EASTER ANTHEMS (which shall always be used on Easter Day)

VENITE

1 **O come let us sing ǀ out · to the ǀ Lord:**
    let us shout in triumph to the ǀ rock of ǀ our sal ǀ vation.

2 **Let us come before his ǀ face with ǀ thanksgiving:**
    and cry ǀ out to · him ǀ joyfully · in ǀ psalms.

3 **For the Lord is a ǀ great ǀ God:**
    and a great ǀ king a·bove ǀ all ǀ gods.

4 **In his hand are the ǀ depths · of the ǀ earth:**
    and the peaks of the ǀ mountains · are ǀ his ǀ also.

†5 **The sea is his and ǀ he ǀ made it:**
    his hands ǀ moulded ǀ dry ǀ land.

6 **Come let us worship and ǀ bow ǀ down:**
    and kneel be ǀ fore the ǀ Lord our ǀ maker.

7 **For he is the ǀ Lord our ǀ God:**
    we are his ǀ people · and the ǀ sheep of · his ǀ pasture.

8   If only you would hear his | voice to | day:
       for he | comes to | judge the | earth.

9   He shall judge the | world with | righteousness:
       and the | peoples | with his | truth.

Glory to the Father and | to the | Son:
       and | to the | Holy | Spirit;
as it was in the be | ginning is | now:
       and shall be for | ever. | A | men.

JUBILATE

1   O shout to the Lord in triumph | all the | earth:
       serve the Lord with gladness
       and come before his | face with | songs of | joy.

2   Know that the Lord | he is | God:
       it is he who has made us and we are his
       we are his | people · and the | sheep of · his |
       pasture.

3   Come into his gates with thanksgiving
       and into his | courts with | praise:
       give thanks to him and | bless his | holy | name.

4   For the Lord is good * his loving mercy | is for | ever:
       his faithfulness through | out all | gener | ations.

Glory to the Father and | to the | Son:
       and | to the | Holy | Spirit;
as it was in the be | ginning is | now:
       and shall be for | ever. | A | men.

THE EASTER ANTHEMS

1   Christ our passover has been | sacri · ficed | for us:
       so let us | cele | brate the | feast,

2   not with the old leaven of cor | ruption · and | wickedness:
       but with the unleavened | bread of · sin | cerity · and |
       truth.

3   Christ once raised from the dead | dies no | more:
       death has no | more do | minion | over him.

4　　**In dying he died to sin ⏐ once for ⏐ all:**
　　　　in ⏐ living · he ⏐ lives to ⏐ God.

5　　**See yourselves therefore as ⏐ dead to ⏐ sin:**
　　　　and alive to God in ⏐ Jesus ⏐ Christ our ⏐ Lord.

6　　**Christ has been ⏐ raised · from the ⏐ dead:**
　　　　the ⏐ firstfruits · of ⏐ those who ⏐ sleep.

7　　**For as by ⏐ man came ⏐ death:**
　　　　by man has come also the resur ⏐ rection ⏐ of the ⏐ dead;

8　　**for as in ⏐ Adam · all ⏐ die:**
　　　　even so in Christ shall ⏐ all be ⏐ made a ⏐ live.

　　　　Glory to the Father and ⏐ to the ⏐ Son:
　　　　and ⏐ to the ⏐ Holy ⏐ Spirit;
　　as it was in the be ⏐ ginning is ⏐ now:
　　　　and shall be for ˻ ever. ˻ A ⏐ men.

54　THE PSALMS appointed
　　Each psalm or group of psalms ends with

　　　　Glory to the Father and ⏐ to the ⏐ Son:
　　　　and ⏐ to the ⏐ Holy ⏐ Spirit;
　　as it was in the be ⏐ ginning is ⏐ now:
　　　　and shall be for ˻ ever. ˻ A ⏐ men.

55　**Sit**

　　THE FIRST READING, from the Old Testament
　　THE SECOND READING, from the New Testament
　　Silence may be kept.

56　**Stand**

　　On Sundays, one of the following CANTICLES
　　On weekdays, as follows

　　Monday TE DEUM
　　Verses 14-18 may be omitted.

1　　**You are ⏐ God · and we ⏐ praise you:**
　　　　you are the ⏐ Lord and ⏐ we ac ⏐ claim you;

2　　**you are the e ⏐ ternal ⏐ Father:**
　　　　all cre ⏐ ation ⏐ worships ⏐ you.

3   To you all angels * all the ┃ powers of ┃ heaven:
       cherubim and seraphim ┃ sing in ┃ endless ┃ praise,

4   Holy holy holy Lord * God of ┃ power and ┃ might:
       heaven and ┃ earth are ┃ full of · your ┃ glory.

5   The glorious company of ap ┃ostles ┃ praise you:
       the noble fellowship of prophets praise you
       the white-robed ┃ army · of ┃ martyrs ┃ praise you.

6   Throughout the world the holy ┃ Church ac ┃claims you:
       Father of ┃ majes ┃ty un ┃bounded;

7   your true and only Son * worthy of ┃ all ┃ worship:
       and the Holy ┃ Spirit ┃ advocate · and ┃ guide.

8   You Christ are the ┃ King of ┃ glory:
       the e ┃ternal ┃ Son · of the ┃ Father.

9   When you became man to ┃ set us ┃ free:
       you did not ab ┃hor the ┃ Virgin's womb.

10   You overcame the ┃ sting of ┃ death:
       and opened the kingdom of ┃ heaven · to ┃ all be ┃lievers.

11   You are seated at God's right ┃ hand in ┃ glory:
       we believe that you will ┃ come and ┃ be our ┃ judge.

12   Come then Lord and ┃ help your ┃ people:
       bought with the ┃ price of ┃ your own ┃ blood;

13   and bring us ┃ with your ┃ saints:
       to ┃ glory ┃ ever ┃lasting.

14   Save your people Lord and ┃ bless · your in ┃heritance:
       govern and up ┃hold them ┃ now and ┃ always.

15   Day by ┃ day we ┃ bless you:
       we ┃ praise your ┃ name for ┃ ever.

16   Keep us today Lord from ┃ all ┃ sin:
       have mercy ┃ on us ┃ Lord have ┃ mercy.

17   Lord show us your ┃ love and ┃ mercy:
       for we ┃ put our ┃ trust in ┃ you.

18   **In you Lord | is our | hope:**
      let us not be con | founded | at the | last.

Tuesday A SONG OF CREATION (short version)
1   **Bless the Lord all cre | ated | things:**
      sing his | praise · and ex | alt him · for | ever.

2   **Bless the | Lord you | heavens:**
      sing his | praise · and ex | alt him · for | ever.

3   **Bless the Lord you | angels · of the | Lord:**
      bless the | Lord all | you his | hosts;

18   **bless the Lord all | men · on the | earth:**
      sing his | praise · and ex | alt him · for | ever.

19   **O People of God | bless the | Lord:**
      bless the | Lord you | priests · of the | Lord;

20   **bless the Lord you | servants · of the | Lord:**
      sing his | praise · and ex | alt him · for | ever.

21   **Bless the Lord all men of | upright | spirit:**
      bless the Lord you that are | holy · and |
      humble · in | heart;

      bless the Father the Son and the | Holy | Spirit:
      sing his | praise · and ex | alt him · for | ever.

Wednesday BENEDICTUS (The Song of Zechariah)
1   **Blessèd be the Lord the | God of | Israel:**
      for he has come to his | people · and set | them | free.

2   **He has raised up for us a | mighty | saviour:**
      born of the | house · of his | servant | David.

3   **Through his holy prophets he | promised · of | old:**
      that he would save us from our enemies
      from the | hands of | all that | hate us.

4   **He promised to show | mercy · to our | fathers:**
      and to re | member · his | holy | covenant.

5   **This was the oath he swore to our | father | Abraham:**
      to set us | free · from the | hands of · our | enemies,

6   free to worship him with ˈout ˈ fear:
      holy and righteous in his sight ˈ all the ˈ days of ·
      our ˈ life.

7   You my child shall be called the prophet of the ˈ
    Most ˈ High:
      for you will go before the ˈ Lord · to pre ˈpare his ˈ way,

8   to give his people knowledge ˈ of sal ˈvation:
      by the for ˈgiveness · of ˈ all their ˈ sins.

9   In the tender compassion ˈ of our ˈ God:
      the dawn from on ˈ high shall ˈ break up ˈon us,

10   to shine on those who dwell in darkness and the ˈ
    shadow · of ˈ death:
      and to guide our feet ˈ into · the ˈ way of ˈ peace.

    Glory to the Father and ˈ to the ˈ Son:
      and ˈ to the ˈ Holy ˈ Spirit;
    as it was in the be ˈginning is ˈ now:
      and shall be for ˈ ever. ˈ A ˈmen.

Thursday GLORIA IN EXCELSIS

1   Glory to ˈ God · in the ˈ highest:
      and ˈ peace · to his ˈ people · on ˈ earth.

2   Lord God ˈ heaven ·ly ˈ King:
      al ˈmighty ˈ God and ˈ Father,

3   we worship you we ˈ give you ˈ thanks:
      we ˈ praise you ˈ for your ˈ glory.

4   Lord Jesus Christ only ˈ Son · of the ˈ Father:
      Lord ˈ God ˈ Lamb of ˈ God,

5   you take away the ˈ sin · of the ˈ world:
      have ˈ mercy ˈ on ˈ us;

6   you are seated at the right hand ˈ of the ˈ Father:
      re ˈceive ˈ our ˈ prayer.

7   For you a ˈlone · are the ˈ Holy One:
      you a ˈlone ˈ are the ˈ Lord,

8   you alone are the Most High
     Jesus Christ with the | Holy | Spirit:
        in the glory of God the | Father. | A | men.

Friday, or any day in Lent SAVIOUR OF THE WORLD

1   **Jesus saviour of the world * come to us | in your | mercy:**
        we look to | you to | save and | help us.

2   **By your cross and your life laid down**
     you set your | people | free:
        we look to | you to | save and | help us.

3   **When they were ready to perish you |**
     saved · your dis | ciples:
        we look to | you to · come to · our | help.

4   **In the greatness of your mercy loose us | from our |**
     chains:
        forgive the | sins of | all your | people.

5   **Make yourself known as our saviour and |**
     mighty · de | liverer:
        save and | help us · that | we may | praise you.

6   **Come now and dwell with us | Lord Christ | Jesus:**
        hear our | prayer · and be | with us | always.

7   **And when you | come in · your | glory:**
        make us to be one with you * and to | share the |
        life of · your | kingdom.

Saturday GREAT AND WONDERFUL

1   **Great and wonderful are your deeds Lord |**
     God · the Al | mighty:
        just and true are your | ways O | King · of the | nations.

2   **Who shall not revere and praise your | name O | Lord?**
        for | you a | lone are | holy.

3   **All nations shall come and worship | in your | presence:**
        for your just | dealings · have | been re | vealed.

     To him who sits on the throne | and · to the | Lamb:
        be praise and honour glory and might
        for ever and | ever. | A | men.

All

I believe in God, the Father almighty,
creator of heaven and earth.

I believe in Jesus Christ, his only Son,
   our Lord.
He was conceived by the power of the
   Holy Spirit
and born of the Virgin Mary.
He suffered under Pontius Pilate,
was crucified, died, and was buried.
He descended to the dead.
On the third day he rose again.
He ascended into heaven,
and is seated at the right hand
   of the Father.
He will come again to judge the living
   and the dead.

I believe in the Holy Spirit,
the holy catholic Church,
the communion of saints,
the forgiveness of sins,
the resurrection of the body,
and the life everlasting. Amen.

58 **Kneel**
All

Our Father in heaven,
hallowed be your name,
your kingdom come,
your will be done,
on earth as in heaven.
Give us today our daily bread.
Forgive us our sins
as we forgive those who sin against us.
Lead us not into temptation
but deliver us from evil.

For the kingdom, the power, and the glory
   are yours,
now and for ever. Amen.

59   THE COLLECT OF THE DAY

60   ONE OF THESE COLLECTS is said.

> Almighty and everlasting Father,
> we thank you that you have brought us safely
> to the beginning of this day.
> Keep us from falling into sin
> or running into danger;
> order us in all our doings;
> and guide us to do always
> what is right in your eyes;
> through Jesus Christ our Lord. **Amen.**

or

> Eternal God and Father,
> you create us by your power
> and redeem us by your love:
> guide and strengthen us by your Spirit,
> that we may give ourselves in love and service
> to one another and to you;
> through Jesus Christ our Lord. **Amen.**

61   Here may be read the State Prayers, occasional prayers and
thanksgivings, or other forms of prayer. The prayers may
conclude with one of the Endings (p. 107). A sermon may be
preached, hymns may be sung, and the service may end
with a blessing.

Evening Prayer (Shorter Form)

62   **Stand**
A SENTENCE OF SCRIPTURE may be said (see p. 46).

63   The minister may say

> If we say we have no sin, we deceive ourselves,
> and the truth is not in us. If we confess our sins,
> God is faithful and just, and will forgive us our
> sins, and cleanse us from all unrighteousness.

Or the sentences for Ash Wednesday to Lent 5 may be used.

64   The minister may say

> Let us confess our sins to Almighty God.

65   **Kneel**
All   **Almighty God, our heavenly Father,**
we have sinned against you and against our
**   fellow men,**
in thought and word and deed,
through negligence, through weakness,
through our own deliberate fault.
We are truly sorry
and repent of all our sins.
For the sake of your Son Jesus Christ, who
**   died for us,**
forgive us all that is past;
and grant that we may serve you in newness
**   of life;**
to the glory of your name. Amen.

66   Priest   Almighty God,
who forgives all who truly repent,
have mercy upon *you*,
pardon and deliver *you* from all *your* sins,
confirm and strengthen *you* in all goodness,

and keep *you* in life eternal;
through Jesus Christ our Lord. **Amen.**

67   Instead of section 65 one of the alternative Confessions may
      be used (pp. 165, 166).

68   **Stand**
      Minister   O Lord, open our lips;
      People   **and our mouth shall proclaim your praise.**

      Minister   Let us worship the Lord.
      People   **All praise to his name.**

      All   **Glory to the Father, and to the Son,**
                  and to the Holy Spirit:
                  as it was in the beginning, is now,
                  and shall be for ever. Amen.

69   THE PSALMS appointed
      Each psalm or group of psalms ends with

      Glory to the Father and | to the | Son:
          and | to the | Holy | Spirit;
      as it was in the be |ginning is | now:
          and shall be for |ever. |A |men.

70   **Sit**
      THE READING, from the New Testament

      Silence may be kept.

71   **Stand**
      On Sundays, one of the following CANTICLES
      On weekdays, as follows

      Monday MAGNIFICAT (The Song of Mary)
  1   **My soul proclaims the | greatness · of the | Lord:**
          my spirit re |joices · in | God my | saviour;

  2   **for he has looked with favour on his | lowly | servant:**
          from this day all gener |ations · will | call me |
          blessèd;

†3   the Almighty has done | great things | for me:
        and | holy | is his | name.

4   He has mercy on | those who | fear him:
        in | every | gener | ation.

5   He has shown the | strength · of his | arm:
        he has scattered the | proud in | their con | ceit.

6   He has cast down the mighty | from their | thrones:
        and has | lifted | up the | lowly.

7   He has filled the hungry with | good | things:
        and the rich he has | sent a | way | empty.

8   He has come to the help of his | servant | Israel:
        for he has re | membered · his | promise · of | mercy,

9   the promise he | made · to our | fathers:
        to Abraham | and his | children · for | ever.

Glory to the Father and | to the | Son:
    and | to the | Holy | Spirit;
as it was in the be | ginning is | now:
    and shall be for | ever. | A | men.

Tuesday BLESS THE LORD

1   Bless the Lord the | God of · our | fathers:
        sing his | praise · and ex | alt him · for | ever.

2   Bless his holy and | glori·ous | name:
        sing his | praise · and ex | alt him · for | ever.

3   Bless him in his holy and | glori·ous | temple:
        sing his | praise · and ex | alt him · for | ever.

4   Bless him who be | holds the | depths:
        sing his | praise · and ex | alt him · for | ever.

5   Bless him who sits be | tween the | cherubim:
        sing his | praise · and ex | alt him · for | ever.

6   Bless him on the | throne of · his | kingdom:
        sing his | praise · and ex | alt him · for | ever.

7   Bless him in the | heights of | heaven:
        sing his | praise · and ex | alt him · for | ever.

Bless the Father the Son and the | Holy | Spirit:
sing his | praise · and ex | alt him · for | ever.

1 **Lord now you let your servant | go in | peace:**
your | word has | been ful | filled.

2 **My own eyes have | seen the · sal | vation:**
which you have prepared in the | sight of |
every | people;

(†) 3 **a light to re | veal you · to the | nations:**
and the | glory · of your | people | Israel.

Glory to the Father and | to the | Son:
and | to the | Holy | Spirit;
as it was in the be | ginning is | now:
and shall be for | ever. | A | men.

1 **Christ Jesus was in the | form of | God:**
but he did not | cling · to e | quality · with | God.

2 **He emptied himself * taking the | form · of a | servant:**
and was | born · in the | likeness · of | men.

3 **Being found in human form he | humbled · him | self:**
and became obedient unto death | even |
death · on a | cross.

4 **Therefore God has | highly · ex | alted him:**
and bestowed on him the | name a · bove | every | name,

5 **that at the name of Jesus every | knee should | bow:**
in heaven and on | earth and | under · the | earth;

6 **and every tongue confess that Jesus | Christ is | Lord:**
to the | glory · of | God the | Father.

Glory to the Father and | to the | Son:
and | to the | Holy | Spirit;
as it was in the be | ginning is | now:
and shall be for | ever. | A | men.

Friday GLORY AND HONOUR

1 **Glory and | honour · and | power:**
   are yours by | right O | Lord our | God:

2 **for you cre|ated | all things:**
   and by your | will they | have their | being.

3 **Glory and | honour · and | power:**
   are yours by | right O | Lamb · who was | slain;

4 **for by your blood you ransomed | men for | God:**
   from every race and language * from | every |
   people · and | nation,

5 **to make them a | kingdom · of | priests:**
   to stand and | serve be|fore our | God.

   To him who sits on the throne | and · to the | Lamb:
   be praise and honour glory and might
   for ever and | ever. | A|men.

Saturday THE EASTER ANTHEMS
or, in Lent, SAVIOUR OF THE WORLD (p. 79)

1 **Christ our passover has been | sacri·ficed | for us:**
   so let us | cele|brate the | feast,

2 **not with the old leaven of cor|ruption · and | wickedness:**
   but with the unleavened | bread of · sin|cerity · and |
   truth.

3 **Christ once raised from the dead | dies no | more:**
   death has no | more do|minion | over him.

4 **In dying he died to sin | once for | all:**
   in | living · he | lives to | God.

5 **See yourselves therefore as | dead to | sin:**
   and alive to God in | Jesus | Christ our | Lord.

6 **Christ has been | raised · from the | dead:**
   the | firstfruits · of | those who | sleep.

7 **For as by | man came | death:**
   by man has come also the resur|rection | of the | dead;

8   for as in | Adam | all | die:
        even so in Christ shall | all be | made a | live.

    Glory to the Father and | to the | Son:
        and | to the | Holy | Spirit;
    as it was in the be | ginning is | now:
        and shall be for | ever. | A | men.

72   **Kneel**
      All   **Our Father in heaven,**
                hallowed be your name,
                your kingdom come,
                your will be done,
                on earth as in heaven.
                Give us today our daily bread.
                Forgive us our sins
                as we forgive those who sin against us.
                Lead us not into temptation
                but deliver us from evil.

                For the kingdom, the power, and the glory
                  are yours
                now and for ever. Amen.

73   THE COLLECT OF THE DAY may be said.

74   THIS COLLECT is said.

                Lighten our darkness,
                Lord, we pray;
                and in your mercy defend us
                from all perils and dangers of this night;
                for the love of your only Son,
                our Saviour Jesus Christ. **Amen.**

75   Here may be read the State Prayers, occasional prayers and
    thanksgivings, or other forms of prayer. The prayers may
    conclude with one of the Endings (p. 107). A sermon may be
    preached, hymns may be sung, and the service may end
    with a blessing.

The Canticles
(Book of Common Prayer)

VENITE

1 O come, let us sing unto the Lord:
    let us heartily rejoice in the strength of our salvation.

2 Let us come before his presence with thanksgiving:
    and shew ourselves glad in him with psalms.

3 For the Lord is a great God:
    and a great King above all gods.

4 In his hand are all the corners of the earth:
    and the strength of the hills is his also.

5 The sea is his and he made it:
    and his hands prepared the dry land.

6 O come, let us worship, and fall down:
    and kneel before the Lord our Maker.

7 For he is the Lord our God:
    and we are the people of his pasture, and the sheep
    of his hand.

8 Today if ye will hear his voice, harden not your hearts:
    as in the provocation, and as in the day of temptation in
    the wilderness;

9 When your fathers tempted me:
    proved me, and saw my works.

10 Forty years long was I grieved with this generation, and said:
    It is a people that do err in their hearts, for they have not
    known my ways.

11 Unto whom I sware in my wrath:
    that they should not enter into my rest.

Glory be to the Father, and to the Son:
    and to the Holy Ghost;
As it was in the beginning, is now, and ever shall be:
    world without end. Amen.

JUBILATE

1 O be joyful in the Lord, all ye lands:
   serve the Lord with gladness, and come before his
   presence with a song.

2 Be ye sure that the Lord he is God:
   it is he that hath made us and not we ourselves; we are
   his people, and the sheep of his pasture.

3 O go your way into his gates with thanksgiving, and into
   his courts with praise:
   be thankful unto him, and speak good of his name.

4 For the Lord is gracious, his mercy is everlasting:
   and his truth endureth from generation to generation.

   Glory be to the Father, and to the Son:
   and to the Holy Ghost;
   As it was in the beginning, is now, and ever shall be:
   world without end. Amen.

BENEDICTUS

1 Blessed be the Lord God of Israel:
   for he hath visited, and redeemed his people;

2 And hath raised up a mighty salvation for us:
   in the house of his servant David;

3 As he spake by the mouth of his holy prophets:
   which have been since the world began;

4 That we should be saved from our enemies:
   and from the hands of all that hate us;

5 To perform the mercy promised to our forefathers:
   and to remember his holy Covenant;

6 To perform the oath which he sware to our
   forefather Abraham:
   that he would give us;

7 That we being delivered out of the hands of our enemies:
   might serve him without fear;

8 In holiness and righteousness before him:
   all the days of our life.

9   And thou, child, shalt be called the Prophet of the Highest:
        for thou shalt go before the face of the Lord to prepare
        his ways;

10   To give knowledge of salvation unto his people:
        for the remission of their sins,

11   Through the tender mercy of our God:
        whereby the dayspring from on high hath visited us;

12   To give light to them that sit in darkness, and in the shadow
        of death:
        and to guide our feet into the way of peace.

Glory be to the Father, and to the Son:
    and to the Holy Ghost;
As it was in the beginning, is now, and ever shall be:
    world without end. Amen.

BENEDICITE

1   O all ye Works of the Lord, bless ye the Lord:
        praise him, and magnify him for ever.

2   O ye Angels of the Lord, bless ye the Lord:
        praise him, and magnify him for ever.

3   O ye Heavens, bless ye the Lord:
        praise him, and magnify him for ever.

4   O ye Waters that be above the Firmament, bless ye the Lord:
        praise him, and magnify him for ever.

5   O all ye Powers of the Lord, bless ye the Lord:
        praise him, and magnify him for ever.

6   O ye Sun and Moon, bless ye the Lord:
        praise him, and magnify him for ever.

7   O ye Stars of Heaven, bless ye the Lord:
        praise him, and magnify him for ever.

8   O ye Showers and Dew, bless ye the Lord:
        praise him, and magnify him for ever.

9   O ye Winds of God, bless ye the Lord:
        praise him, and magnify him for ever.

10   O ye Fire and Heat, bless ye the Lord:
         praise him, and magnify him for ever.

11   O ye Winter and Summer, bless ye the Lord:
         praise him, and magnify him for ever.

12   O ye Dews and Frosts, bless ye the Lord:
         praise him, and magnify him for ever.

13   O ye Frost and Cold, bless ye the Lord:
         praise him, and magnify him for ever.

14   O ye Ice and Snow, bless ye the Lord:
         praise him, and magnify him for ever.

15   O ye Nights and Days, bless ye the Lord:
         praise him, and magnify him for ever.

16   O ye Light and Darkness, bless ye the Lord:
         praise him, and magnify him for ever.

17   O ye Lightnings and Clouds, bless ye the Lord:
         praise him, and magnify him for ever.

18   O let the Earth bless the Lord:
         yea, let it praise him, and magnify him for ever.

19   O ye Mountains and Hills, bless ye the Lord:
         praise him, and magnify him for ever.

20   O all ye Green Things upon the earth, bless ye the Lord:
         praise him, and magnify him for ever.

21   O ye Wells, bless ye the Lord:
         praise him, and magnify him for ever.

22   O ye Seas and Floods, bless ye the Lord:
         praise him, and magnify him for ever.

23   O ye Whales, and all that move in the Waters,
      bless ye the Lord:
         praise him, and magnify him for ever.

24   O ye Fowls of the Air, bless ye the Lord:
         praise him, and magnify him for ever.

25   O all ye Beasts and Cattle, bless ye the Lord:
         praise him, and magnify him for ever.

26 O ye Children of Men, bless ye the Lord:
    praise him, and magnify him for ever.

27 O let Israel bless the Lord:
    praise him, and magnify him for ever.

28 O ye Priests of the Lord, bless ye the Lord:
    praise him, and magnify him for ever.

29 O ye Servants of the Lord, bless ye the Lord:
    praise him, and magnify him for ever.

30 O ye Spirits and Souls of the Righteous,
    bless ye the Lord:
    praise him, and magnify him for ever.

31 O ye holy and humble Men of heart, bless ye the Lord:
    praise him, and magnify him for ever.

32 O Ananias, Azarias, and Misael, bless ye the Lord:
    praise him, and magnify him for ever.

    Glory be to the Father, and to the Son:
    and to the Holy Ghost;
    As it was in the beginning, is now, and ever shall be:
    world without end. Amen.

TE DEUM

1 We praise thee, O God:
    we acknowledge thee to be the Lord.

2 All the earth doth worship thee:
    the Father everlasting.

3 To thee all Angels cry aloud:
    the Heavens, and all the Powers therein.

4 To thee Cherubin and Seraphin:
    continually do cry,

5 Holy, Holy, Holy:
    Lord God of Sabaoth;

6 Heaven and earth are full of the Majesty:
    of thy glory.

7   The glorious company of the Apostles:
      praise thee.

8   The goodly fellowship of the Prophets:
      praise thee.

9   The noble army of Martyrs:
      praise thee.

10 The holy Church throughout all the world:
      doth acknowledge thee;

11 The Father:
      of an infinite Majesty;

12 Thine honourable, true:
      and only Son;

13 Also the Holy Ghost:
      the Comforter.

14 Thou art the King of Glory:
      O Christ.

15 Thou art the everlasting Son:
      of the Father.

16 When thou tookest upon thee to deliver man:
      thou didst not abhor the Virgin's womb.

17 When thou hadst overcome the sharpness of death:
      thou didst open the kingdom of heaven to all believers.

18 Thou sittest at the right hand of God:
      in the Glory of the Father.

19 We believe that thou shalt come:
      to be our Judge.

20 We therefore pray thee, help thy servants:
      whom thou hast redeemed with thy precious blood.

21 Make them to be numbered with thy Saints:
      in glory everlasting.

22 O Lord, save thy people:
      and bless thine heritage.

23 Govern them:
        and lift them up for ever.

24 Day by day:
        we magnify thee;

25 And we worship thy name:
        ever world without end.

26 Vouchsafe, O Lord:
        to keep us this day without sin.

27 O Lord, have mercy upon us:
        have mercy upon us.

28 O Lord, let thy mercy lighten upon us:
        as our trust is in thee.

29 O Lord, in thee have I trusted:
        let me never be confounded.

MAGNIFICAT

1   My soul doth magnify the Lord:
        and my spirit hath rejoiced in God my Saviour.

2   For he hath regarded:
        the lowliness of his hand-maiden.

3   For behold, from henceforth:
        all generations shall call me blessed.

4   For he that is mighty hath magnified me:
        and holy is his name.

5   And his mercy is on them that fear him:
        throughout all generations.

6   He hath shewed strength with his arm:
        he hath scattered the proud in the imagination of
        their hearts.

7   He hath put down the mighty from their seat:
        and hath exalted the humble and meek.

8   He hath filled the hungry with good things:
        and the rich he hath sent empty away.

9   He remembering his mercy hath holpen his servant Israel:
        as he promised to our forefathers, Abraham and his
        seed, for ever.

     Glory be to the Father, and to the Son:
        and to the Holy Ghost;
     As it was in the beginning, is now, and ever shall be:
        world without end. Amen.

NUNC DIMITTIS

1   Lord, now lettest thou thy servant depart in peace:
        according to thy word.

2   For mine eyes have seen:
        thy salvation,

3   Which thou hast prepared:
        before the face of all people;

4   To be a light to lighten the Gentiles:
        and to be the glory of thy people Israel.

     Glory be to the Father, and to the Son:
        and to the Holy Ghost;
     As it was in the beginning, is now, and ever shall be:
        world without end. Amen.

Prayers for Various Occasions

1 **THE LITANY**

Sections I and VI must always be used, but a selection of appropriate suffrages may be made from Sections II, III, IV and V.

I

Let us pray.

God the Father,
have mercy on us.

God the Son,
have mercy on us.

God the Holy Spirit,
have mercy on us.

Holy, blessed, and glorious Trinity,
have mercy on us.

II

From all evil and mischief;
from pride, vanity, and hypocrisy;
from envy, hatred, and malice;
and from all evil intent,
Good Lord, deliver us.

From sloth, worldliness, and love of money;
from hardness of heart
and contempt for your word and your laws,
Good Lord, deliver us.

From sins of body and mind;
from the deceits of the world, the flesh,
    and the devil,
Good Lord, deliver us.

From famine and disaster;
from violence, murder, and dying unprepared,
Good Lord, deliver us.

In all times of sorrow;
in all times of joy;
in the hour of death,
and at the day of judgement,
Good Lord, deliver us.

By the mystery of your holy incarnation;
by your birth, childhood, and obedience;
by your baptism, fasting, and temptation,
Good Lord, deliver us.

By your ministry in word and work;
by your mighty acts of power;
and by your preaching of the kingdom,
Good Lord, deliver us.

By your agony and trial;
by your cross and passion;
and by your precious death and burial,
Good Lord, deliver us.

By your mighty resurrection;
by your glorious ascension;
and by your sending of the Holy Spirit,
Good Lord, deliver us.

III

Hear our prayers, O Lord our God.
Hear us, good Lord.

Govern and direct your holy Church; fill it with
love and truth; and grant it that unity which is
your will.
Hear us, good Lord.

Give us boldness to preach the gospel in all the
world, and to make disciples of all the nations.
Hear us, good Lord.

Enlighten your ministers with knowledge and
understanding, that by their teaching and their
lives they may proclaim your word.
Hear us, good Lord.

Give your people grace to hear and receive your word, and to bring forth the fruit of the Spirit.
Hear us, good Lord.

Bring into the way of truth all who have erred and are deceived.
Hear us, good Lord.

Strengthen those who stand; comfort and help the fainthearted; raise up the fallen; and finally beat down Satan under our feet.
Hear us, good Lord.

IV

Guide the leaders of the nations into the ways of peace and justice.
Hear us, good Lord.

Guard and strengthen your servant Elizabeth our Queen, that she may put her trust in you, and seek your honour and glory.
Hear us, good Lord.

Endue the High Court of Parliament and all the Ministers of the Crown with wisdom and understanding.
Hear us, good Lord.

Bless those who administer the law, that they may uphold justice, honesty, and truth.
Hear us, good Lord.

Teach us to use the fruits of the earth to your glory, and for the good of all mankind.
Hear us, good Lord.

Bless and keep all your people.
Hear us, good Lord.

V

Help and comfort the lonely, the bereaved, and the oppressed.
Lord, have mercy.

Keep in safety those who travel, and all who are in danger.
Lord, have mercy.

Heal the sick in body and mind, and provide for the homeless, the hungry, and the destitute.
Lord, have mercy.

Show your pity on prisoners and refugees, and all who are in trouble.
Lord, have mercy.

Forgive our enemies, persecutors, and slanderers, and turn their hearts.
Lord, have mercy.

Hear us as we remember those who have died in the peace of Christ, both those who have confessed the faith and those whose faith is known to you alone, and grant us with them a share in your eternal kingdom.
Lord, have mercy.

VI

Give us true repentance;
forgive us our sins of negligence and ignorance and our deliberate sins;
and grant us the grace of your Holy Spirit
to amend our lives according to your holy word.
**Holy God,
holy and strong,
holy and immortal,
have mercy upon us.**

One of the prayers (sections 13 and 14), and the Lord's Prayer may be added.
When the Litany is said instead of the Prayers at Morning or Evening Prayer, the Lord's Prayer, the Collect of the Day, and the Grace are added here.

STATE PRAYERS

2   Almighty God, the fountain of all goodness,
bless our Sovereign Lady, Queen Elizabeth, and
all who are in authority under her; that they may
order all things in wisdom and equity,
righteousness and peace, to the honour of your
name, and the good of your Church and people;
through Jesus Christ our Lord. **Amen.**

3   Almighty God, the fountain of all goodness,
bless, we pray, Elizabeth the Queen Mother,
Philip Duke of Edinburgh, Charles Prince of
Wales, and all the Royal Family. Endue them
with your Holy Spirit; enrich them with your
heavenly grace; prosper them with all
happiness; and bring them to your everlasting
kingdom; through Jesus Christ our Lord. **Amen.**

4   Almighty and everlasting God, the only worker
of great marvels, send down upon our bishops
and other pastors and all congregations
committed to their care the spirit of your saving
grace; and that they may truly please you, pour
upon them the continual dew of your blessing.
Grant this, O Lord, for the honour of our
advocate and mediator, Jesus Christ. **Amen.**

A GENERAL INTERCESSION

5   O God, the creator and preserver of all
mankind, we pray for men of every race, and in
every kind of need: make your ways known on
earth, your saving power among all nations.
(Especially we pray for . . .)
Lord, in your mercy
hear our prayer.

We pray for your Church throughout the world:
guide and govern us by your Holy Spirit, that
all who profess and call themselves Christians

may be led into the way of truth, and hold the
faith in unity of spirit, in the bond of peace, and
in righteousness of life. (Especially we pray for . .
Lord, in your mercy
hear our prayer.

We commend to your fatherly goodness all who
are anxious or distressed in mind or body;
comfort and relieve them in their need; give them
patience in their sufferings, and bring good
out of their troubles. (Especially we pray for . . .)
Merciful Father,
accept these prayers
for the sake of your Son,
our Saviour Jesus Christ. Amen.

A GENERAL THANKSGIVING

6
    Almighty God, Father of all mercies,
we your unworthy servants give you most
    humble and hearty thanks
for all your goodness and loving kindness
to us and to all men.
We bless you for our creation, preservation,
    and all the blessings of this life;
but above all for your immeasurable love
in the redemption of the world by our
    Lord Jesus Christ,
for the means of grace, and for the hope of glory.
And give us, we pray, such a sense of all
    your mercies
that our hearts may be unfeignedly thankful,
and that we show forth your praise,
not only with our lips but in our lives,
by giving up ourselves to your service,
and by walking before you in holiness
    and righteousness all our days;
through Jesus Christ our Lord,
to whom, with you and the Holy Spirit,
    be all honour and glory,
for ever and ever. Amen.

A PRAYER OF DEDICATION

7   This may be used at the end of Morning or Evening Prayer,
or at a service of Ante-Communion.

> **Almighty God,**
> **we thank you for the gift of your holy word.**
> **May it be a lantern to our feet,**
> **a light to our paths,**
> **and a strength to our lives.**
> **Take us and use us**
> **to love and serve all men**
> **in the power of the Holy Spirit**
> **and in the name of your Son,**
> **Jesus Christ our Lord. Amen.**

CONCLUDING PRAYERS

8   Almighty God, you have given us grace at this
time with one accord to make our common
supplication to you; and you have promised that
when two or three are gathered together in your
name you will grant their requests. Fulfil now, O
Lord, the desires and petitions of your servants,
as may be most expedient for them, granting us
in this world knowledge of your truth, and in
the world to come, life everlasting. **Amen.**

9   Heavenly Father, you have promised through
your Son Jesus Christ, that when we meet in his
name, and pray according to his mind, he will be
among us and will hear our prayer. In your love
and wisdom fulfil our desires, and give us your
greatest gift, which is to know you, the only true
God, and Jesus Christ our Lord; who is alive and
reigns with you and the Holy Spirit, one God,
now and for ever. **Amen.**

10   Be with us, Lord, in all our prayers, and direct our way toward the attainment of salvation; that among the changes and chances of this mortal life, we may always be defended by your gracious help; through Jesus Christ our Lord. **Amen.**

11   Almighty and eternal God, sanctify and govern our hearts and bodies in the ways of your laws and the works of your commandments; that under your protection, now and ever, we may be preserved in body and soul; through Jesus Christ our Lord. **Amen.**

12   Guide us, Lord, in all our doings with your gracious favour, and further us with your continual help; that in all our works begun, continued, and ended in you, we may glorify your holy name, and by your mercy attain everlasting life; through Jesus Christ our Lord. **Amen.**

13   Almighty God, the fountain of all wisdom, you know our needs before we ask, and our ignorance in asking; have compassion on our weakness, and give us those things which for our unworthiness we dare not, and for our blindness we cannot ask, for the sake of your Son, Jesus Christ our Lord. **Amen.**

14   Almighty God, you have promised to hear the prayers of those who ask in your Son's name; we pray that what we have asked faithfully we may obtain effectually; through Jesus Christ our Lord. **Amen.**

ENDINGS

15   The grace of our Lord Jesus Christ, and the love of God, and the fellowship of the Holy Spirit be with us all evermore. **Amen.**

16   Now to him who is able to do immeasurably more than all we can ask or conceive, by the power which is at work among us, to him be glory in the Church and in Christ Jesus throughout all ages. **Amen.**

17   The Lord be with you
and also with you.

Let us bless the Lord.
Thanks be to God.

BLESSINGS

18   The Lord bless you and watch over you,
the Lord make his face shine upon you
and be gracious to you,
the Lord look kindly on you
   and give you peace;
and the blessing of God almighty,
the Father, the Son, and the Holy Spirit,
be among you and remain with you always.
Amen.

19   The love of the Lord Jesus
draw you to himself,
the power of the Lord Jesus
strengthen you in his service,
the joy of the Lord Jesus fill your hearts;
and the blessing of God almighty,
the Father, the Son, and the Holy Spirit,
be among you and remain with you always.
Amen.

Subject Index of Prayers

Abbots   *861*
Affliction, support in   *413, 504, 512, 678, 698, 817*
Angels   *802*
Authority, those in   *709*

Baptism   *227, 236-8, 244, 248, 249, 463, 570, 648, 918*
Bishops   *395, 855*

Church   *558, 643, 780, 794, 807*
Church work   *558*
Civic occasions   *974*
Communion, after   *552*
Confirmation   *227, 236-8, 253, 258, 259, 503, 508, 658,*
   703, 717

Death   *308, 320, 322-4, 329, 331, 334-6, 413, 570, 573, 574*
Death to sin   *570, 573, 574, 612, 648*
Departed   *308, 320, 322-4, 329, 331, 334-6, 835*
Discipleship   *467, 486, 508, 512, 526, 552, 602, 617, 658, 728,*
   768, 800, 819
Discipline   *504, 570*
Dying   *933*

Ember Days   *878, 879*
Everlasting life   *422, 426, 483, 526, 570, 573, 574, 612, 722,*
   810, 819

Family life   *213, 216, 218, 221, 296-300, 455*
Faith   *408, 640, 658, 717, 728*
Following saints   *754, 768, 775, 810, 817*
Forgiveness   *495, 499, 558, 622, 787, 817*
Freedom   *59, 653*

God's Word   *426, 754, 766, 794*
Good works   *742, 775*
Government   *709*
Grace to do good works   *480, 607, 668, 673, 688, 713, 742*
Guidance   *455, 460, 480, 574, 703, 717, 909*

Harvest   *890*
Healing   *490, 787, 804*
Holy Spirit   *60, 467, 630, 635, 653, 663, 668, 673, 909*
Humility   *422, 526, 552, 683, 688*

Jews 558
Judgement, the Last 422, 483
Judgement, for right 635, 775

Love 668, 673, 713, 745
Love of God and his commandments 617, 713, 717, 745

Marriage 213, 216, 287, 296-300
Meetings 99-102, 105, 106, 622, 640, 960
Ministry 432, 552, 558, 643, 688, 878, 879
Mission 450, 467, 552, 558, 643, 693, 752, 754, 794, 815, 907

Nations of the world 490, 558, 653, 709
New life 476, 480, 573, 574, 602, 607, 612, 648
New Year 60, 617, 703, 728

Obedience 437, 463, 504, 683, 790, 815

Parish clergy 380, 381, 558, 949, 954
Parliament 709
Peace 69, 495, 499, 512, 673, 722, 912
Prayer, acceptance of 622
Protection 59, 60, 70, 678, 703, 802
Purity 508, 733

Queen, the 103

Reconciliation 693
Repentance 499, 508, 777
Reverence 398, 640
Rogation Days 884, 885
Royal Family 103

Sacred ministry 380, 381, 395, 432, 558, 771, 878, 879,
    949, 954
Saints 810, 837, 871
Salvation 413, 472, 490, 504, 763, 787
Scripture 426, 766, 794
Service 467, 552, 558, 602, 607, 643, 653, 688
Sick 490, 929
Sickness, in time of 472, 512, 517, 526, 607, 617, 678, 698
Sinners 495, 499, 504, 570, 612, 622
Social responsibility 970

The Order for Holy Communion

also called The Eucharist

and The Lord's Supper

Rite A

NOTES

1 **Preparation** Careful devotional preparation before the service is recommended for every communicant.

2 **The President** The president (who, in accordance with the provisions of Canon B12 'Of the ministry of the Holy Communion', must have been episcopally ordained priest) presides over the whole service. He says the opening Greeting, the Collect, the Absolution, the Peace, and the Blessing; he himself must take the bread and the cup before replacing them on the holy table, say the Eucharistic Prayer, break the consecrated bread, and receive the sacrament on every occasion. The remaining parts of the service he may delegate to others. When necessity dictates, a deacon or lay person may preside over the Ministry of the Word.

When the Bishop is present, it is appropriate that he should act as president. He may also delegate sections 32-49 to a priest.

3 **Posture** When a certain posture is particularly appropriate, it is indicated in the margin. For the rest of the service local custom may be established and followed. The Eucharistic Prayer (sections 38, 39, 40, and 41) is a single prayer, the unity of which may be obscured by changes of posture in the course of it.

4 **Seasonal Material** The seasonal sentences and blessings are optional. Any other appropriate scriptural sentences may be read at sections 1 and 50 at the discretion of the president and 'Alleluia' may be added to any sentence from Easter Day until Pentecost.

5 **Greetings** (section 2 etc.) In addition to the points where greetings are provided, at other suitable points (e.g. before the Gospel and before the Blessing and Dismissal) the minister may say 'The Lord be with you' and the congregation reply 'and also with you'.

6   **Prayers of Penitence** These are used either after section 4 or section 23 (but see Note 22 below for occasions when the Order following the pattern of the Book of Common Prayer is used).

7   **Kyrie eleison** (section 9) This may be used in English or Greek. Alternative versions are set out in section 79.

8   **Gloria in excelsis** (sections 10 and 73) This canticle may be appropriately omitted during Advent and Lent, and on weekdays which are not Principal or Greater Holy Days. It may also be used at sections 1 and 16.

9   **The Collect** (section 11) The Collect may be introduced by the words 'Let us pray' and a brief bidding, after which silence may be kept.

10   **Readings** Where one of the three readings is to be omitted, provision for this is found in Table 3 of the Alternative Calendar and Lectionary according to the season of the year.

11   **The Gospel in Holy Week** (section 17) From Palm Sunday to the Wednesday in Holy Week, and on Good Friday, the Passion Gospel may be introduced: 'The Passion of our Lord Jesus Christ according to N', and concluded: 'This is the Passion of the Lord'. No responses are used.

12   **The Sermon** (section 18) The sermon is an integral part of the Ministry of the Word. A sermon should normally be preached at all celebrations on Sundays and other Holy Days.

13   **Proper Prefaces** The Proper Prefaces are set out in section 76. They are obligatory when this is indicated in the seasonal propers but may be used on other suitable occasions. The Sunday Prefaces (31), (32), and (33) are for use with the Fourth Eucharistic Prayer and the Order following the pattern of the Book of Common Prayer.

14 **Second Eucharistic Prayer** (section 39) The three paragraphs beginning 'For he is your living Word' and ending 'a people for your own possession' may be omitted if a Proper Preface is used.

15 **Acclamations** These are optional. They may be introduced by the president with the words 'Let us proclaim the mystery of faith' or with other suitable words or they may be used without introduction.

16 **Manual Acts** In addition to the taking of the bread and the cup at section 36 the president may use traditional manual acts during the Eucharistic Prayers.

17 **Words of Invitation** (section 45) The words provided are to be used at least on Sundays and other Holy Days, and those in section 85 may be added. On other days those in section 85 may be substituted.

18 **The Blessing** (section 54) In addition to the blessings provided here and in section 77 the president may at his discretion use others.

19 **Notices** Banns of marriage and other notices may be published after section 2, section 19, or section 53.

20 **Hymns, Canticles, the Peace, the Collection and Presentation of the Offerings of the People, and the Preparation of the Gifts of Bread and Wine** Points are indicated for these, but if occasion requires they may occur elsewhere.

21 **Silence** After sections 6, 13, 15, 17, 18, 26, before sections 42 and 51, and after the biddings in section 21, silence may be kept.

22 **The Order following the pattern of the Book of Common Prayer** (sections 22 and 57-75) When this Order is being followed the Prayers of Penitence should not be used at section 4, as they are requisite at section 59. The Order provided should then be followed in its entirety.

23 **Ministry to the Sick** When Holy Communion is ministered to the sick, the Laying on of Hands or Anointing may follow the Absolution (section 28); the alternative Eucharistic Prayer for use with the sick (section 84) may be used; and the service may be shortened if the needs of the patient require it.

24 **A Service without Communion** When there is no communion, the minister reads the service as far as the Absolution (section 28), and then adds the Lord's Prayer, the General Thanksgiving, and/or other prayers (see section 86) at his discretion, ending with the Grace. When such a service is led by a deacon or lay person, 'us' is said instead of 'you' in the Absolution.

The Order for
Holy Communion
Rite A

THE PREPARATION

1   At the entry of the ministers AN APPROPRIATE
    SENTENCE may be used; and A HYMN, A CANTICLE,
    or A PSALM may be sung.

2   The president welcomes the people using these or other
    appropriate words.

	The Lord be with you	or The Lord is here.
All	**and also with you.**	**His Spirit is with us.**

or Easter Day to Pentecost

	Alleluia! Christ is risen.
All	**He is risen indeed. Alleluia!**

3   This prayer may be said.

All   **Almighty God,**
            to whom all hearts are open,
            all desires known,
            and from whom no secrets are hidden:
            cleanse the thoughts of our hearts
            by the inspiration of your Holy Spirit,
            that we may perfectly love you,
            and worthily magnify your holy name;
            through Christ our Lord. Amen.

PRAYERS OF PENITENCE

4   THE PRAYERS OF PENITENCE (sections 5-8) may be said
     here, or after section 23; if they are said here, sections 6-8 are
     always used.
     Alternative confessions may be used (see section 80).

5   THE COMMANDMENTS (section 78) or the following
     SUMMARY OF THE LAW may be said.

    Minister   Our Lord Jesus Christ said: The first
               commandment is this: 'Hear, O Israel, the Lord
               our God is the only Lord. You shall love the Lord
               your God with all your heart, with all your soul,
               with all your mind, and with all your strength.'
               The second is this: 'Love your neighbour as
               yourself.' There is no other commandment
               greater than these.
    All   **Amen. Lord, have mercy.**

6   The minister invites the congregation to confess their sins in
     these or other suitable words (see section 25).

               God so loved the world that he gave his only
               Son Jesus Christ to save us from our sins, to be
               our advocate in heaven, and to bring us to
               eternal life.

               Let us confess our sins, in penitence and faith,
               firmly resolved to keep God's commandments
               and to live in love and peace with all men.

7   **All**   **Almighty God, our heavenly Father,**
               we have sinned against you and against our
                  fellow men,
               in thought and word and deed,
               through negligence, through weakness,
               through our own deliberate fault.
               We are truly sorry,
               and repent of all our sins.

For the sake of your Son Jesus Christ, who
    died for us,
forgive us all that is past;
and grant that we may serve you in newness
    of life
to the glory of your name. Amen.

8   President   Almighty God,
    who forgives all who truly repent,
    have mercy upon *you*,
    pardon and deliver *you* from all *your* sins,
    confirm and strengthen *you* in all goodness,
    and keep *you* in life eternal;
    through Jesus Christ our Lord. **Amen.**

---

9   KYRIE ELEISON may be said (see also section 79).

    Lord, have mercy.
    Lord, have mercy.

    Christ, have mercy.
    Christ, have mercy.

    Lord, have mercy.
    Lord, have mercy.

10   GLORIA IN EXCELSIS may be said.

    All   **Glory to God in the highest,**
    and peace to his people on earth.

    Lord God, heavenly King,
    almighty God and Father,
    we worship you, we give you thanks,
    we praise you for your glory.

Lord Jesus Christ, only Son of the Father,
Lord God, Lamb of God,
you take away the sin of the world:
have mercy on us;
you are seated at the right hand of the Father:
receive our prayer.

For you alone are the Holy One,
you alone are the Lord,
you alone are the Most High,
Jesus Christ,
with the Holy Spirit,
in the glory of God the Father. Amen.

11   The president says THE COLLECT.

THE MINISTRY OF THE WORD

12   Either two or three readings from scripture follow, the last of
      which is always the Gospel.

13   **Sit**
      OLD TESTAMENT READING

      At the end the reader may say

                  This is the word of the Lord.
      All   **Thanks be to God.**

14   A PSALM may be used.

15   **Sit**
      NEW TESTAMENT READING (EPISTLE)

      At the end the reader may say

                  This is the word of the Lord.
      All   **Thanks be to God.**

16   A CANTICLE, A HYMN, or A PSALM may be used.

17   **Stand**
      THE GOSPEL. When it is announced

      All   **Glory to Christ our Saviour.**

      At the end the reader says

                       This is the Gospel of Christ.
      All   **Praise to Christ our Lord.**

18   **Sit**
      THE SERMON

19   **Stand**
      THE NICENE CREED is said on Sundays and other Holy
      Days, and may be said on other days.

      All   **We believe in one God,**
                       the Father, the almighty,
                       maker of heaven and earth,
                       of all that is,
                       seen and unseen.

                       We believe in one Lord, Jesus Christ,
                       the only Son of God,
                       eternally begotten of the Father,
                       God from God, Light from Light,
                       true God from true God,
                       begotten, not made,
                       of one Being with the Father.
                       Through him all things were made.
                       For us men and for our salvation
                       he came down from heaven;
                       by the power of the Holy Spirit
                       he became incarnate of the Virgin Mary,
                       and was made man.
                       For our sake he was crucified under
                       Pontius Pilate;
                       he suffered death and was buried.

On the third day he rose again
in accordance with the Scriptures;
he ascended into heaven
and is seated at the right hand of the Father.
He will come again in glory
to judge the living and the dead,
and his kingdom will have no end.

We believe in the Holy Spirit,
the Lord, the giver of life,
who proceeds from the Father and the Son.
With the Father and the Son he is worshipped
    and glorified.
He has spoken through the Prophets.

We believe in one holy catholic
    and apostolic Church.
We acknowledge one baptism for the
    forgiveness of sins.
We look for the resurrection of the dead,
and the life of the world to come. Amen.

THE INTERCESSION

20   INTERCESSIONS AND THANKSGIVINGS are led by the
      president, or by others. The form below, or one of those in
      section 81, or other suitable words, may be used.

21   This form may be used
      (a) with the insertion of specific subjects between the
      paragraphs;
      (b) as a continuous whole with or without brief biddings.

      Not all paragraphs need be used on every occasion.
      Individual names may be added at the places indicated.
      This response may be used before or after each paragraph.

      Minister   Lord, in your mercy
      All   hear our prayer.

Let us pray for the Church and for the world,
and let us thank God for his goodness.

Almighty God, our heavenly Father, you
promised through your Son Jesus Christ to hear
us when we pray in faith.

Strengthen *N* our bishop and all your Church in
the service of Christ; that those who confess your
name may be united in your truth, live together
in your love, and reveal your glory in the world.

Bless and guide Elizabeth our Queen; give
wisdom to all in authority; and direct this and
every nation in the ways of justice and of peace;
that men may honour one another, and seek the
common good.

Give grace to us, our families and friends, and to
all our neighbours; that we may serve Christ in
one another, and love as he loves us.

Comfort and heal all those who suffer in body,
mind, or spirit . . .; give them courage and hope
in their troubles; and bring them the joy of your
salvation.

Hear us as we remember those who have died in
the faith of Christ . . .; according to your
promises, grant us with them a share in your
eternal kingdom.

Rejoicing in the fellowship of (*N* and of) all your
saints, we commend ourselves and all Christian
people to your unfailing love.

Merciful Father,
All   **accept these prayers
for the sake of your Son,
our Saviour Jesus Christ. Amen.**

22   The Order following the pattern of the Book of Common
Prayer continues at section 57.

PRAYERS OF PENITENCE

23   THE PRAYERS OF PENITENCE (sections 24-28) are said
      here, if they have not been said after section 4; if they are said
      here, sections 26-28 are always used.
      Alternative confessions may be used (see section 80).

24   THE COMMANDMENTS (section 78) or the following
      SUMMARY OF THE LAW may be said.

> **Minister**   Our Lord Jesus Christ said: The first
> commandment is this: 'Hear, O Israel, the Lord
> our God is the only Lord. You shall love the Lord
> your God with all your heart, with all your soul,
> with all your mind, and with all your strength.'
> The second is this: 'Love your neighbour as
> yourself.' There is no other commandment
> greater than these.
>
> **All**   **Amen. Lord, have mercy.**

25   The minister may say

> God so loved the world that he gave his only
> Son Jesus Christ to save us from our sins, to be
> our advocate in heaven, and to bring us to
> eternal life.

or one or more of these SENTENCES.

> Hear the words of comfort our Saviour Christ
> says to all who truly turn to him:
> Come to me, all who labour and are heavy
> laden, and I will give you rest. *Matthew* 11.28

> God so loved the world that he gave his only
> Son, that whoever believes in him should not
> perish but have eternal life. *John 3.16*

Hear what Saint Paul says:
This saying is true and worthy of full
acceptance, that Christ Jesus came into the
world to save sinners. *1 Timothy 1.15*

Hear what Saint John says:
If anyone sins, we have an advocate with the
Father, Jesus Christ the righteous; and he
is the propitiation for our sins. *1 John 2.1*

26	Minister	Let us confess our sins, in penitence and faith, firmly resolved to keep God's commandments and to live in love and peace with all men.

27 **All**   **Almighty God, our heavenly Father,**
          we have sinned against you and against our
             fellow men,
          in thought and word and deed,
          through negligence, through weakness,
          through our own deliberate fault.
          We are truly sorry,
          and repent of all our sins.
          For the sake of your Son Jesus Christ, who
             died for us,
          forgive us all that is past;
          and grant that we may serve you in newness
             of life
          to the glory of your name. Amen.

28 President Almighty God,
          who forgives all who truly repent,
          have mercy upon *you*,
          pardon and deliver *you* from all *your* sins,
          confirm and strengthen *you* in all goodness,
          and keep *you* in life eternal;
          through Jesus Christ our Lord. **Amen.**

29   All may say

We do not presume
to come to this your table, merciful Lord,
trusting in our own righteousness,
but in your manifold and great mercies.
We are not worthy
so much as to gather up the crumbs under
    your table.
But you are the same Lord
whose nature is always to have mercy.
Grant us therefore, gracious Lord,
so to eat the flesh of your dear son
    Jesus Christ
and to drink his blood,
that we may evermore dwell in him
and he in us. Amen.

The alternative prayer at section 82 may be used.

THE MINISTRY OF THE SACRAMENT

THE PEACE

30   **Stand**

The president says either of the following or other suitable
words (see section 83).

Christ is our peace.
He has reconciled us to God
    in one body by the cross.
We meet in his name and share his peace.

or   We are the Body of Christ.
In the one Spirit we were all baptized into
    one body.
Let us then pursue all that makes for peace
and builds up our common life.

He then says

>   The peace of the Lord be always with you
> **All**   **and also with you.**

31   The president may say

>   Let us offer one another a sign of peace.

and all may exchange a sign of peace.

THE PREPARATION OF THE GIFTS

32   The bread and wine are placed on the holy table.

33   The president may praise God for his gifts in appropriate
words to which all respond

>   **Blessed be God for ever.**

34   The offerings of the people may be collected and presented.
These words may be used.

>   **Yours, Lord, is the greatness, the power,**
>   **the glory, the splendour, and the majesty;**
>   **for everything in heaven and on earth is yours.**
>   **All things come from you,**
>   **and of your own do we give you.**

35   At the preparation of the gifts A HYMN may be sung.

THE EUCHARISTIC PRAYER

THE TAKING OF THE BREAD AND CUP AND THE GIVING OF THANKS

36 The president takes the bread and cup into his hands and replaces them on the holy table.

37 The president uses one of the four EUCHARISTIC PRAYERS which follow.

---

38 **FIRST EUCHARISTIC PRAYER**

President The Lord be with you or The Lord is here.
All **and also with you.** **His Spirit is with us.**

President Lift up your hearts.
All **We lift them to the Lord.**

President Let us give thanks to the Lord our God.
All **It is right to give him thanks and praise.**

President It is indeed right,
it is our duty and our joy,
at all times and in all places
to give you thanks and praise,
holy Father, heavenly King,
almighty and eternal God,
through Jesus Christ your only Son our Lord.

For he is your living Word;
through him you have created all things from
   the beginning,
and formed us in your own image.

Through him you have freed us from the
   slavery of sin,
giving him to be born as man and to die upon
   the cross;
you raised him from the dead
and exalted him to your right hand on high.

Through him you have sent upon us
your holy and life-giving Spirit,
and made us a people for your own possession.

PROPER PREFACE, when appropriate (section 76)

Therefore with angels and archangels,
and with all the company of heaven,
we proclaim your great and glorious name,
for ever praising you and saying:

All **Holy, holy, holy Lord,
God of power and might,
heaven and earth are full of your glory.
Hosanna in the highest.**

This ANTHEM may also be used.

**Blessed is he who comes in the name of
the Lord.
Hosanna in the highest.**

President Accept our praises, heavenly Father,
through your Son our Saviour Jesus Christ;
and as we follow his example and obey
his command,
grant that by the power of your Holy Spirit
these gifts of bread and wine
may be to us his body and his blood;

Who in the same night that he was betrayed,
took bread and gave you thanks;
he broke it and gave it to his disciples,
saying,
Take, eat; this is my body which is given
for you;
do this in remembrance of me.
In the same way, after supper
he took the cup and gave you thanks;
he gave it to them, saying,
Drink this, all of you;
this is my blood of the new covenant,
which is shed for you and for many for the
forgiveness of sins.

Holy Communion A/131

Do this, as often as you drink it,
in remembrance of me.

All   **Christ has died:**
Christ is risen:
Christ will come again.

President   Therefore, heavenly Father,
we remember his offering of himself
made once for all upon the cross,
and proclaim his mighty resurrection and
     glorious ascension.
As we look for his coming in glory,
we celebrate with this bread and this cup
his one perfect sacrifice.

Accept through him, our great high priest,
this our sacrifice of thanks and praise;
and as we eat and drink these holy gifts
in the presence of your divine majesty,
renew us by your Spirit,
inspire us with your love,
and unite us in the body of your Son,
Jesus Christ our Lord.

Through him, and with him, and in him,
by the power of the Holy Spirit,
with all who stand before you in earth
     and heaven,
we worship you, Father almighty,
in songs of everlasting praise:

All   **Blessing and honour and glory and power**
be yours for ever and ever. Amen.

Silence may be kept.

The service continues with THE LORD'S PRAYER at section
42 on p. 142.

| President | The Lord be with you or The Lord is here. |
| **All** | **and also with you.**   **His Spirit is with us.** |

| President | Lift up your hearts. |
| **All** | **We lift them to the Lord.** |

| President | Let us give thanks to the Lord our God. |
| **All** | **It is right to give him thanks and praise.** |

President   It is indeed right,
it is our duty and our joy,
at all times and in all places
to give you thanks and praise,
holy Father, heavenly King,
almighty and eternal God,
through Jesus Christ your only Son our Lord.

The following may be omitted if a Proper Preface is used.

For he is your living Word;
through him you have created all things from
the beginning,
and formed us in your own image.

Through him you have freed us from the
slavery of sin,
giving him to be born as man and to die upon
the cross;
you raised him from the dead
and exalted him to your right hand on high.

Through him you have sent upon us
your holy and life-giving Spirit,
and made us a people for your own possession.

PROPER PREFACE, when appropriate (section 76)

Therefore with angels and archangels,
and with all the company of heaven,
we proclaim your great and glorious name,
for ever praising you and saying:

All	Holy, holy, holy Lord, God of power and might, heaven and earth are full of your glory. Hosanna in the highest.

This ANTHEM may also be used.

> Blessed is he who comes in the name of
> the Lord.
> Hosanna in the highest.

President	Hear us, heavenly Father, through Jesus Christ your Son our Lord, through him accept our sacrifice of praise; and grant that by the power of your Holy Spirit these gifts of bread and wine may be to us his body and his blood;

> Who in the same night that he was betrayed,
> took bread and gave you thanks;
> he broke it and gave it to his disciples,
>   saying,
> Take, eat; this is my body which is given
>   for you;
> do this in remembrance of me.
> In the same way, after supper
> he took the cup and gave you thanks;
> he gave it to them, saying,
> Drink this, all of you;
> this is my blood of the new covenant,
> which is shed for you and for many for the
>   forgiveness of sins.
> Do this, as often as you drink it,
> in remembrance of me.

All	Christ has died: Christ is risen: Christ will come again.

President   Therefore, Lord and heavenly Father,
            having in remembrance his death once for all
               upon the cross,
            his resurrection from the dead,
            and his ascension into heaven,
            and looking for the coming of his kingdom,
            we make with this bread and this cup
            the memorial of Christ your Son our Lord.

            Accept through him this offering of our duty
               and service;
            and as we eat and drink these holy gifts
            in the presence of your divine majesty,
            fill us with your grace and heavenly blessing;
            nourish us with the body and blood of your Son,
            that we may grow into his likeness
            and, made one by your Spirit,
            become a living temple to your glory.

            Through Jesus Christ our Lord,
            by whom, and with whom, and in whom,
            in the unity of the Holy Spirit,
            all honour and glory be yours, almighty Father,
            from all who stand before you in earth
               and heaven,
            now and for ever. **Amen.**

Silence may be kept.

The service continues with THE LORD'S PRAYER at section
42 on p. 142.

President	The Lord be with you or The Lord is here.
All	**and also with you.** **His Spirit is with us.**

President	Lift up your hearts.
All	**We lift them to the Lord.**

President	Let us give thanks to the Lord our God.
All	**It is right to give him thanks and praise.**

President   Father, we give you thanks and praise
through your beloved Son Jesus Christ,
your living Word through whom you have
     created all things;

Who was sent by you, in your great goodness,
     to be our Saviour;
by the power of the Holy Spirit he took flesh
and, as your Son, born of the blessed Virgin,
was seen on earth
and went about among us;

He opened wide his arms for us on the cross;
he put an end to death by dying for us
and revealed the resurrection by rising to
     new life;
so he fulfilled your will and won for you a
     holy people.

PROPER PREFACE, when appropriate (section 76)

Therefore with angels and archangels,
and with all the company of heaven,
we proclaim your great and glorious name,
for ever praising you and saying:

All   **Holy, holy, holy Lord,**
God of power and might,
heaven and earth are full of your glory.
Hosanna in the highest.

This ANTHEM may also be used.

> **Blessed is he who comes in the name of
> the Lord.
> Hosanna in the highest.**

President   Lord, you are holy indeed, the source of
        all holiness;
grant that, by the power of your Holy Spirit,
and according to your holy will,
these your gifts of bread and wine
may be to us the body and blood of our Lord
        Jesus Christ;

Who in the same night that he was betrayed,
took bread and gave you thanks;
he broke it and gave it to his disciples,
        saying,
Take, eat; this is my body which is given
        for you;
do this in remembrance of me.
In the same way, after supper
he took the cup and gave you thanks;
he gave it to them, saying,
Drink this, all of you;
this is my blood of the new covenant,
which is shed for you and for many for the
        forgiveness of sins.
Do this, as often as you drink it,
in remembrance of me.

All   **Christ has died:
Christ is risen:
Christ will come again.**

President   And so, Father, calling to mind his death on
        the cross,
his perfect sacrifice made once for the sins
        of all men,
rejoicing at his mighty resurrection and
        glorious ascension,
and looking for his coming in glory,
we celebrate this memorial of our redemption;

We thank you for counting us worthy
to stand in your presence and serve you;
we bring before you this bread and this cup;

We pray you to accept this our duty
and service,
a spiritual sacrifice of praise and
thanksgiving;

Send the Holy Spirit on your people
and gather into one in your kingdom
all who share this one bread and one cup,
so that we, in the company of all the saints,
may praise and glorify you for ever,
through him from whom all good things come,
Jesus Christ our Lord;

By whom, and with whom, and in whom,
in the unity of the Holy Spirit,
all honour and glory be yours, almighty Father,
for ever and ever. **Amen.**

Silence may be kept.

The service continues with THE LORD'S PRAYER at section
42 on p. 142.

President	The Lord be with you	or The Lord is here.
All	**and also with you.**	**His Spirit is with us.**

President   Lift up your hearts.
All   **We lift them to the Lord.**

President   Let us give thanks to the Lord our God.
All   **It is right to give him thanks and praise.**

President   It is indeed right,
              it is our duty and our joy,
              at all times and in all places
              to give you thanks and praise,
              holy Father, heavenly King,
              almighty and eternal God,
              creator of heaven and earth,
              through Jesus Christ our Lord:

PROPER PREFACE, when appropriate (section 76)

The following is used when no Proper Preface is provided.

              For he is the true high priest,
              who has loosed us from our sins
              and has made us to be a royal priesthood
                 to you,
              our God and Father.

              Therefore with angels and archangels,
              and with all the company of heaven,
              we proclaim your great and glorious name,
              for ever praising you and saying:

All   **Holy, holy, holy Lord,**
              God of power and might,
              heaven and earth are full of your glory.
              Hosanna in the highest.

This ANTHEM may also be used.

**Blessed is he who comes in the name of
the Lord.
Hosanna in the highest.**

President   All glory to you, our heavenly Father:
in your tender mercy
you gave your only Son Jesus Christ
to suffer death upon the cross for
    our redemption;
he made there
a full atonement for the sins of the
    whole world,
offering once for all his one sacrifice
    of himself;
he instituted,
and in his holy gospel commanded us
    to continue,
a perpetual memory of his precious death
until he comes again.

Hear us, merciful Father, we humbly pray,
and grant that by the power of your
    Holy Spirit
we who receive these gifts of your creation,
this bread and this wine,
according to your Son our Saviour Jesus
    Christ's holy institution,
in remembrance of the death that he suffered,
may be partakers of his most blessed body
    and blood;

Who in the same night that he was betrayed,
took bread and gave you thanks;
he broke it and gave it to his disciples,
    saying,
Take, eat; this is my body which is given
    for you;
do this in remembrance of me.
In the same way, after supper
he took the cup and gave you thanks;
he gave it to them, saying,

Drink this, all of you;
this is my blood of the new covenant,
which is shed for you and for many for the
forgiveness of sins.
Do this, as often as you drink it,
in remembrance of me.

All   **Christ has died:**
Christ is risen:
Christ will come again.

President   Therefore, Lord and heavenly Father,
in remembrance of the precious death
and passion,
the mighty resurrection and glorious ascension
of your dear Son Jesus Christ,
we offer you through him this sacrifice of
praise and thanksgiving.

Grant that by his merits and death,
and through faith in his blood,
we and all your Church may receive forgiveness
of our sins
and all other benefits of his passion.
Although we are unworthy, through our
many sins,
to offer you any sacrifice,
yet we pray that you will accept this,
the duty and service that we owe;
do not weigh our merits, but pardon
our offences,
and fill us all who share in this
holy communion
with your grace and heavenly blessing.

Through Jesus Christ our Lord,
by whom, and with whom, and in whom,
in the unity of the Holy Spirit,
all honour and glory be yours, almighty Father,
now and for ever. **Amen.**

Silence may be kept.

THE COMMUNION

THE BREAKING OF THE BREAD AND THE GIVING OF THE BREAD AND CUP

42 THE LORD'S PRAYER is said either as follows or in its traditional form.

President As our Saviour taught us, so we pray.
All **Our Father in heaven,**
hallowed be your name,
your kingdom come,
your will be done,
on earth as in heaven.
Give us today our daily bread.
Forgive us our sins
as we forgive those who sin against us.
Lead us not into temptation
but deliver us from evil.

For the kingdom, the power, and the glory
are yours
now and for ever. Amen.

43 The president breaks the consecrated bread, saying

We break this bread
to share in the body of Christ.
All **Though we are many, we are one body,**
because we all share in one bread.

44 Either here or during the distribution one of the following anthems may be said.

Lamb of God, you take away the sins of
the world:
have mercy on us.

Lamb of God, you take away the sins of
the world:
have mercy on us.

**Lamb of God, you take away the sins of
the world:
grant us peace.**

or **Jesus, Lamb of God: have mercy on us.
Jesus, bearer of our sins: have mercy on us.
Jesus, redeemer of the world: give us
your peace.**

45 Before the distribution the president says

Draw near with faith. Receive the body of our
Lord Jesus Christ which he gave for you, and his
blood which he shed for you.

Eat and drink in remembrance that he died for
you, and feed on him in your hearts by faith with
thanksgiving.

Additional words of invitation may be used (see section 85).

46 The president and people receive the communion. At the
distribution the minister says to each communicant

The body of Christ keep you in eternal life.
The blood of Christ keep you in eternal life.

or   The body of Christ.
The blood of Christ.

The communicant replies each time **Amen,** and then
receives.

Alternative words of distribution may be found in section 66.

47 During the distribution hymns and anthems may be sung.

48   If either or both of the consecrated elements be likely to prove insufficient, the president himself returns to the holy table and adds more, saying these words.

> Father, giving thanks over the bread and the cup according to the institution of your Son Jesus Christ, who said, Take, eat; this is my body (and/or Drink this; this is my blood), we pray that this bread/wine also may be to us his body/blood, to be received in remembrance of him.

49   Any consecrated bread and wine which is not required for purposes of communion is consumed at the end of the distribution or after the service.

AFTER COMMUNION

50   AN APPROPRIATE SENTENCE may be said and A HYMN may be sung.

51   Either or both of the following prayers or other suitable prayers are said (see section 86).

52   President   Father of all, we give you thanks and praise, that when we were still far off you met us in your Son and brought us home. Dying and living, he declared your love, gave us grace, and opened the gate of glory. May we who share Christ's body live his risen life; we who drink his cup bring life to others; we whom the Spirit lights give light to the world. Keep us firm in the hope you have set before us, so we and all your children shall be free, and the whole earth live to praise your name; through Christ our Lord. **Amen.**

or

53 **All**   **Almighty God,**
                    we thank you for feeding us
                    with the body and blood of your Son
                        Jesus Christ.
                    Through him we offer you our souls and bodies
                    to be a living sacrifice.
                    Send us out
                    in the power of your Spirit
                    to live and work
                    to your praise and glory. Amen.

THE DISMISSAL

54 The president may say this or an alternative BLESSING
(section 77).

        The peace of God, which passes all
        understanding, keep your hearts and minds in
        the knowledge and love of God, and of his Son
        Jesus Christ our Lord; and the blessing of God
        almighty, the Father, the Son, and the Holy
        Spirit, be among you, and remain with you
        always. **Amen.**

55 President   Go in peace to love and serve the Lord.
    All   **In the name of Christ. Amen.**

    or

    President   Go in the peace of Christ.
    All   **Thanks be to God.**

From Easter Day to Pentecost 'Alleluia! Alleluia!' may be
added after both the versicle and the response.

56 The ministers and people depart.

The Order following the pattern of the Book of Common Prayer

(continued from section 22)

57   The priest prepares the bread and wine on the holy table, the offerings of the people may be presented, and A HYMN may be sung.

58   THE COMMANDMENTS (section 78) or the following SUMMARY OF THE LAW may be said.

Minister   Our Lord Jesus Christ said: The first commandment is this: 'Hear, O Israel, the Lord our God is the only Lord. You shall love the Lord your God with all your heart, with all your soul, with all your mind, and with all your strength.' The second is this: 'Love your neighbour as yourself.' There is no other commandment greater than these.

All   Amen. Lord, have mercy.

59   The priest invites the congregation to confess their sins in these or other suitable words (see section 25). Alternative confessions may be used (section 80).

Let us confess our sins, in penitence and faith, firmly resolved to keep God's commandments and to live in love and peace with all men.

60   All   Almighty God, our heavenly Father, we have sinned against you and against our fellow men, in thought and word and deed, through negligence, through weakness, through our own deliberate fault. We are truly sorry, and repent of all our sins. For the sake of your Son Jesus Christ, who died for us,

forgive us all that is past:
and grant that we may serve you in newness
of life
to the glory of your name. Amen.

61   Priest   Almighty God,
who forgives all who truly repent,
have mercy upon *you*,
pardon and deliver *you* from all *your* sins,
confirm and strengthen *you* in all goodness,
and keep *you* in life eternal;
through Jesus Christ our Lord. **Amen.**

62   The priest says these SENTENCES.

Hear the words of comfort our Saviour Christ
says to all who truly turn to him:
Come to me, all who labour and are heavy
laden, and I will give you rest. *Matthew 11.28*

God so loved the world that he gave his only
Son, that whoever believes in him should not
perish but have eternal life. *John 3.16*

Hear what Saint Paul says:
This saying is true and worthy of full
acceptance, that Christ Jesus came into the
world to save sinners. *1 Timothy 1.15*

Hear what Saint John says:
If anyone sins, we have an advocate with the
Father, Jesus Christ the righteous; and he
is the propitiation for our sins. *1 John 2.1*

63   Priest   Lift up your hearts.
         All   **We lift them to the Lord.**

         Priest   Let us give thanks to the Lord our God.
         All   **It is right to give him thanks and praise.**

Priest	It is indeed right,
	it is our duty and our joy,
	at all times and in all places
	to give you thanks and praise,
	holy Father, heavenly King,
	almighty and eternal God,
	through Jesus Christ your only Son our Lord.

PROPER PREFACE, when appropriate (section 76)

Therefore with angels and archangels,
and with all the company of heaven,
we proclaim your great and glorious name,
for ever praising you and saying

All   **Holy, holy, holy Lord,**
God of power and might,
heaven and earth are full of your glory.
Hosanna in the highest.

64   **All**   **We do not presume**
to come to this your table, merciful Lord,
trusting in our own righteousness,
but in your manifold and great mercies.
We are not worthy
so much as to gather up the crumbs under
     your table.
But you are the same Lord
whose nature is always to have mercy.
Grant us therefore, gracious Lord,
so to eat the flesh of your dear Son
     Jesus Christ
and to drink his blood,
that we may evermore dwell in him
and he in us. Amen.

65   Priest   Almighty God, our heavenly Father,
in your tender mercy
you gave your only Son Jesus Christ
to suffer death upon the cross for
     our redemption;
he made there

a full atonement for the sins of the
    whole world,
offering once for all his one sacrifice
    of himself;
he instituted,
and in his holy gospel commanded us
    to continue,
a perpetual memory of his precious death
until he comes again.

Hear us, merciful Father,
we humbly pray,
and grant that we who receive these gifts of
    your creation,
this bread and this wine,
according to your Son our Saviour Jesus
    Christ's holy institution,
in remembrance of the death that he suffered,
may be partakers of his most blessed body
    and blood;

Who in the same night that he was betrayed,
Here the priest takes the paten.
took bread and gave you thanks;
he broke it, *Here he breaks the bread.*
and gave it to his disciples, saying,
Take, eat;
Here he lays his hand on all the bread.
this is my body which is given for you;
do this in remembrance of me.
In the same way, after supper
Here he takes the cup.
he took the cup and gave you thanks;
he gave it to them, saying,
Drink this, all of you;
*Here he lays his hand on all the vessels of wine to be
consecrated.*
this is my blood of the new covenant,
which is shed for you and for many for the
    forgiveness of sins.
Do this, as often as you drink it,
in remembrance of me. **Amen.**

66   The priest and people receive the communion. At the
      distribution the minister says to the communicants the
      following words, or those in sections 45 and 46.

            The body of our Lord Jesus Christ, which was
            given for you, preserve your body and soul to
            eternal life. Take and eat this in remembrance
            that Christ died for you, and feed on him in your
            heart by faith with thanksgiving.

            The blood of our Lord Jesus Christ, which was
            shed for you, preserve your body and soul to
            eternal life. Drink this in remembrance that
            Christ's blood was shed for you, and be thankful.

67   If either or both of the consecrated elements be likely to
      prove insufficient, the priest himself returns to the holy table
      and adds more, and consecrates according to the form in
      section 65, beginning, 'Our Saviour Christ in the same
      night . . .,' for the bread, and at 'In the same way, after
      supper our Saviour . . .,' for the cup.

68   Any consecrated bread and wine which is not required for
      purposes of communion is consumed at the end of the
      distribution or after the service.

69   THE LORD'S PRAYER is said either as follows or in its
      traditional form.

      Priest   As our Saviour taught us, so we pray.
      **All   Our Father in heaven,
                 hallowed be your name,
                 your kingdom come,
                 your will be done,
                 on earth as in heaven.
                 Give us today our daily bread.
                 Forgive us our sins
                 as we forgive those who sin against us.**

**Lead us not into temptation
but deliver us from evil.**

**For the kingdom, the power, and the glory
are yours
now and for ever. Amen.**

70   One or other of the following prayers or one of those at
     sections 52 and 53 is used.

71   Lord and heavenly Father, we your servants
     entirely desire your fatherly goodness
     mercifully to accept this our sacrifice of praise
     and thanksgiving, and to grant that, by the
     merits and death of your Son Jesus Christ, and
     through faith in his blood, we and all your
     Church may receive forgiveness of our sins and
     all other benefits of his passion.

     And here we offer and present to you, O Lord,
     ourselves, our souls and bodies, to be a
     reasonable, holy, and living sacrifice, humbly
     beseeching you that all we who are partakers of
     this holy communion may be fulfilled with your
     grace and heavenly benediction.

     And although we are unworthy, through our
     many sins, to offer you any sacrifice, yet we pray
     that you will accept this, the duty and service
     that we owe, not weighing our merits but
     pardoning our offences, through Jesus Christ
     our Lord; by whom and with whom, in the unity
     of the Holy Spirit, all honour and glory are yours,
     Father almighty, now and for ever. **Amen.**

     or

72   Almighty and everliving God, we heartily thank
     you that you graciously feed us, who have duly
     received these holy mysteries, with the spiritual
     food of the most precious body and blood of

your Son our Saviour Jesus Christ, and assure
us thereby of your favour and goodness towards
us and that we are true members of the mystical
body of your Son, the blessed company of all
faithful people, and are also heirs, through
hope, of your eternal kingdom, by the merits of
the most precious death and passion of your
dear Son. And we humbly beseech you,
heavenly Father, so to assist us with your grace,
that we may continue in that holy fellowship,
and do all such good works as you have
prepared for us to walk in; through Jesus Christ
our Lord, to whom, with you and the Holy
Spirit, be all honour and glory, now and for
ever. **Amen.**

73   GLORIA IN EXCELSIS or A HYMN may be sung.

All   **Glory to God in the highest,**
            and peace to his people on earth.

            Lord God, heavenly King,
            almighty God and Father,
            we worship you, we give you thanks,
            we praise you for your glory.

            Lord Jesus Christ, only Son of the Father,
            Lord God, Lamb of God,
            you take away the sin of the world:
            have mercy on us;
            you are seated at the right hand of the Father:
            receive our prayer.

            For you alone are the Holy One,
            you alone are the Lord,
            you alone are the Most High,
            Jesus Christ,
            with the Holy Spirit,
            in the glory of God the Father. Amen.

| 74 | Priest | The peace of God, which passes all understanding, keep your hearts and minds in the knowledge and love of God, and of his Son Jesus Christ our Lord; and the blessing of God almighty, the Father, the Son, and the Holy Spirit, be among you, and remain with you always. **Amen.** |

75   The ministers and people depart.

Appendices

PROPER PREFACES

Suitable for use with all Eucharistic Prayers (sections 38, 39, 40, and 41) and the Order following the pattern of the Book of Common Prayer (section 63).

Advent
1 And now we give you thanks because in his coming as man the day of our deliverance has dawned; and through him you will make all things new, as he comes in power and triumph to judge the world.

2 And now we give you thanks because you prepared the way of your Son Jesus Christ by the preaching of your servant John the Baptist, who proclaimed him as the Lamb of God, our Saviour.

The Incarnation
3 And now we give you thanks because by the power of the Holy Spirit he took our nature upon him and was born of the Virgin Mary his mother, that being himself without sin he might make us clean from all sin.

4 And now we give you thanks because in the incarnation of the Word a new light has dawned upon the world; you have become one with us that we might become one with you in your glorious kingdom.

5 And now we give you thanks because in coming to dwell among us as man, he revealed the radiance of your glory, and brought us out of darkness into your own marvellous light.

6 And now we give you thanks because in choosing the blessed Virgin Mary to be the mother of your Son you have exalted the humble and meek. Your angel hailed her as most highly favoured; with all generations we call her blessed, and with her we rejoice and magnify your holy name.

7 And now we give you thanks because in his earthly childhood you entrusted him to the care of a human family. In Mary and Joseph you give us an example of love and devotion to him, and also a pattern of family life.

Lent
8 And now we give you thanks because through him you have given us the spirit of discipline, that we may triumph over evil and grow in grace.

The Cross
9 And now we give you thanks because for our sins he was lifted high upon the cross, that he might draw the whole world to himself; and, by his suffering and death, became the source of eternal salvation for all who put their trust in him.

10 And now we give you thanks because for our salvation he was obedient even to death on the cross. The tree of shame was made the tree of glory; and where life was lost, there life has been restored.

Maundy Thursday
11 And now we give you thanks because when his hour had come, in his great love he gave this supper to his disciples, that we might proclaim his death, and feast with him in his kingdom.

The Blessing of the Oils
12 And now we give you thanks because by your Holy Spirit you anointed your only Son to be servant of all and ordained that he should enter into his kingdom through suffering. In your wisdom and love you call your Church to serve the world, to share in Christ's suffering and to reveal his glory.

The Resurrection
13 And now we give you thanks because you raised him gloriously from the dead. For he is the true Paschal Lamb who was offered for us and has taken away the sin of the world. By his death he has destroyed death, and by his rising again he has restored to us eternal life.

14 And now we give you thanks because in his victory over the grave a new age has dawned, the long reign of sin is ended, a broken world is being renewed, and man is once again made whole.

15 And now we give you thanks because through him you have given us eternal life, and delivered us from the bondage of sin and the fear of death into the glorious liberty of the children of God.

16 And now we give you thanks because through him you have given us the hope of a glorious resurrection; so that, although death comes to us all, yet we rejoice in the promise of eternal life; for to your faithful people life is changed, not taken away; and when our mortal flesh is laid aside, an everlasting dwelling place is made ready for us in heaven.

The Ascension
17 And now we give you thanks because you have highly exalted him, and given him the name which is above all other names, that at the name of Jesus every knee shall bow.

Pentecost: Baptism and Confirmation
18 And now we give you thanks because by the Holy Spirit you lead us into all truth, and give us power to proclaim your gospel to the nations, and to serve you as a royal priesthood.

Trinity Sunday
19 And now we give you thanks because you have revealed your glory as the glory of your Son and of the Holy Spirit: three persons equal in majesty, undivided in splendour, yet one Lord, one God, ever to be worshipped and adored.

The Transfiguration
20 And now we give you thanks because the divine glory of the incarnate Word shone forth upon the holy mountain; and your own voice from heaven proclaimed your beloved Son.

St Michael and All Angels

21 Through him the archangels sing your praise, the angels fulfil your commands, the cherubim and seraphim continually proclaim your holiness; the whole company of heaven glorifies your name and rejoices to do your will. Therefore we pray that our voices may be heard with theirs, for ever praising you and saying:

All   **Holy, holy, holy Lord . . .**

All Saints' Day

22 And now we give you thanks for the hope to which you call us in your Son, that following in the faith of all your saints, we may run with perseverance the race that is set before us, and with them receive the unfading crown of glory.

Apostles and Evangelists

23 And now we give you thanks because your Son Jesus Christ after his resurrection sent forth his apostles and evangelists to preach the gospel to all nations and to teach us the way of truth.

Martyrs

24 And now we give you thanks that in the witness of your martyrs who followed Christ even to death you revealed your power made perfect in our human weakness.

Saints' Days

25 And now we give you thanks for the work of your grace in the life of Saint *N* and that by the same grace you lead us in the way of holiness setting before us the vision of your glory.

Dedication

26 And now we give you thanks for your blessing on this house of prayer, where through your grace we offer you the sacrifice of praise, and are built by your Spirit into a temple made without hands, even the body of your Son Jesus Christ.

Marriage
27 And now we give you thanks because you have made the union between Christ and his Church a pattern for the marriage between husband and wife.

Ordination
28 And now we give you thanks because within the royal priesthood of your Church you ordain ministers to proclaim the word of God, to care for your people and to celebrate the sacraments of the new covenant.

Unity
29 And now we give you thanks because of the unity that you have given us in your Son and that you are the God and Father of us all, above all and through all and in all.

Baptism
30 And now we give you thanks because through baptism we have been buried with Christ so that we may rise with him to the new life.

Suitable for use with the Fourth Eucharistic Prayer (section 41) and the Order following the pattern of the Book of Common Prayer (section 63).

Sundays
31 And now we give you thanks because you are the source of light and life; you made us in your image, and called us to new life in him.

32 And now we give you thanks because on the first day of the week he overcame death and the grave and opened to us the way of everlasting life.

33 And now we give you thanks because by water and the Holy Spirit you have made us in him a new people to show forth your glory.

Advent
Christ the Sun of Righteousness shine upon you and scatter
the darkness from before your path; and the blessing . . .

Christmas
Christ, who by his incarnation gathered into one all things
earthly and heavenly, fill you with his joy and peace; and the
blessing . . .

or

Christ the Son of God, born of Mary, fill you with his grace to
trust his promises and obey his will; and the blessing . . .

Epiphany
Christ the Son of God gladden your hearts with the good
news of his kingdom; and the blessing . . .

Ash Wednesday to Lent 4
Christ give you grace to grow in holiness, to deny
yourselves, take up your cross, and follow him; and the
blessing . . .

Lent 5 and Holy Week
Christ crucified draw you to himself, to find in him a sure
ground for faith, a firm support for hope, and the assurance
of sins forgiven; and the blessing . . .

Easter
The God of peace, who brought again from the dead our
Lord Jesus, that great shepherd of the sheep, through
the blood of the eternal covenant, make you perfect in every
good work to do his will, working in you that which is
well-pleasing in his sight; and the blessing . . .

or

The God of peace, who brought again from the dead our Lord Jesus, that great shepherd of the sheep, make you perfect in every good work to do his will; and the blessing . . .

or

God the Father, by whose glory Christ was raised from the dead, strengthen you to walk with him in his risen life; and the blessing . . .

or

God, who through the resurrection of our Lord Jesus Christ has given us the victory, give you joy and peace in your faith; and the blessing . . .

Ascension
Christ our king make you faithful and strong to do his will, that you may reign with him in glory; and the blessing . . .

Pentecost
The Spirit of truth lead you into all truth, give you grace to confess that Jesus Christ is Lord, and to proclaim the word and works of God; and the blessing . . .

Trinity Sunday
God the Holy Trinity make you strong in faith and love, defend you on every side, and guide you in truth and peace; and the blessing . . .

Saints' Days
God give you grace to follow his saints in faith and hope and love; and the blessing . . .

or

God give you grace to follow his saints in faith and truth and gentleness; and the blessing . . .

or

God give you grace to share the inheritance of his saints in glory; and the blessing . . .

Unity

Christ the Good Shepherd, who laid down his life for the sheep, draw you and all who hear his voice to be one within one fold; and the blessing . . .

General

The God of all grace who called you to his eternal glory in Christ Jesus, establish, strengthen and settle you in the faith; and the blessing . . .

or

God, who from the death of sin raised you to new life in Christ, keep you from falling and set you in the presence of his glory; and the blessing . . .

or

Christ who has nourished us with himself the living bread, make you one in praise and love, and raise you up at the last day; and the blessing . . .

or

The God of peace fill you with all joy and hope in believing; and the blessing . . .

78 **THE COMMANDMENTS**

Either A:

Minister	Our Lord Jesus Christ said, If you love me, keep my commandments; happy are those who hear the word of God and keep it. Hear then these commandments which God has given to his people, and take them to heart.
	I am the Lord your God: you shall have no other gods but me. You shall love the Lord your God with all your heart, with all your soul, with all your mind and with all your strength.
All	**Amen. Lord, have mercy.**

Minister	You shall not make for yourself any idol. God is spirit, and those who worship him must worship in spirit and in truth.
All	**Amen. Lord, have mercy.**

Minister	You shall not dishonour the name of the Lord your God. You shall worship him with awe and reverence.
All	**Amen. Lord, have mercy.**

Minister	Remember the Lord's day and keep it holy. Christ is risen from the dead: set your minds on things that are above, not on things that are on the earth.
All	**Amen. Lord, have mercy.**

Minister	Honour your father and mother. Live as servants of God; honour all men; love the brotherhood.
All	**Amen. Lord, have mercy.**

Minister	You shall not commit murder. Be reconciled to your brother; overcome evil with good.
All	**Amen. Lord, have mercy.**

Minister	You shall not commit adultery. Know that your body is a temple of the Holy Spirit.
All	**Amen. Lord, have mercy.**

Minister	You shall not steal. Be honest in all that you do and care for those in need.
All	**Amen. Lord, have mercy.**

Minister	You shall not be a false witness. Let everyone speak the truth.
All	**Amen. Lord, have mercy.**

Minister	You shall not covet anything which belongs to your neighbour. Remember the words of the Lord Jesus: It is more blessed to give than to receive. Love your neighbour as yourself, for love is the fulfilling of the law.
All	**Amen. Lord, have mercy.**

or B:

Minister	God spoke all these words, saying, I am the Lord your God (who brought you out of the land of Egypt, out of the house of bondage). You shall have no other gods before me.
All	**Amen. Lord, have mercy.**

Minister	You shall not make for yourself a graven image (or any likeness of anything that is in heaven above, or that is in the earth beneath, or that is in the water under the earth; you shall not bow down to them or serve them; for I the Lord your God am a jealous God, visiting the iniquity of the fathers upon the children to the third and the fourth generation of those who hate me, but showing steadfast love to thousands of those who love me and keep my commandments).
All	**Amen. Lord, have mercy.**

Minister	You shall not take the name of the Lord your God in vain (for the Lord will not hold him guiltless who takes his name in vain).
All	**Amen. Lord, have mercy.**

Minister	Remember the sabbath day, to keep it holy. (Six days you shall labour, and do all your work; but the seventh day is a sabbath to the Lord your God; in it you shall not do any work, you, or your son, or your daughter, your manservant, or your maidservant, or your cattle, or the sojourner who is within your gates; for in

six days the Lord made heaven and earth, the sea, and all that is in them, and rested the seventh day; therefore the Lord blessed the sabbath day and hallowed it.)

All   **Amen. Lord, have mercy.**

Minister   Honour your father and your mother (that your days may be long in the land which the Lord your God gives you).

All   **Amen. Lord, have mercy.**

Minister   You shall not kill.

All   **Amen. Lord, have mercy.**

Minister   You shall not commit adultery.

All   **Amen. Lord, have mercy.**

Minister   You shall not steal.

All   **Amen. Lord, have mercy.**

Minister   You shall not bear false witness against your neighbour.

All   **Amen. Lord, have mercy.**

Minister   You shall not covet (your neighbour's house; you shall not covet your neighbour's wife, or his manservant, or his maidservant, or his ox, or his ass, or) anything that is your neighbour's.

All   **Lord, have mercy on us, and write all these your laws in our hearts.**

79   KYRIE ELEISON

Section 9 may be said in one of the following forms.

Lord, have mercy (upon us.)   Kyrie eleison.
Lord, have mercy (upon us.)   **Kyrie eleison.**
Lord, have mercy (upon us.)   Kyrie eleison.

Christ, have mercy (upon us.)	**Christe eleison.**
Christ, have mercy (upon us.)	Christe eleison.
Christ, have mercy (upon us.)	**Christe eleison.**
Lord, have mercy (upon us.)	Kyrie eleison.
Lord, have mercy (upon us.)	**Kyrie eleison.**
Lord, have mercy (upon us.)	Kyrie eleison.

80 **ALTERNATIVE CONFESSIONS**

Either A:

All **Almighty God, our heavenly Father,
we have sinned against you and against our
    fellow men,
in thought and word and deed,
in the evil we have done
and in the good we have not done,
through ignorance, through weakness,
through our own deliberate fault.
We are truly sorry,
and repent of all our sins.
For the sake of your Son Jesus Christ, who
    died for us,
forgive us all that is past;
and grant that we may serve you in newness
    of life
to the glory of your name. Amen.**

or B:

All **Almighty God, our heavenly Father,
we have sinned against you,
through our own fault,
in thought and word and deed,
and in what we have left undone.
For your Son our Lord Jesus Christ's sake,
forgive us all that is past;
and grant that we may serve you in newness
    of life
to the glory of your name. Amen.**

or C:

All   Father eternal, giver of light and grace,
we have sinned against you and against our
   fellow men,
in what we have thought,
in what we have said and done,
through ignorance, through weakness,
through our own deliberate fault.
We have wounded your love,
and marred your image in us.
We are sorry and ashamed,
and repent of all our sins.
For the sake of your Son Jesus Christ, who
   died for us,
forgive us all that is past;
and lead us out from darkness
to walk as children of light. Amen.

81   ALTERNATIVE FORMS OF INTERCESSION

Either A:

Minister   Let us pray for the whole Church of God in
Christ Jesus, and for all men according to their
needs.

O God, the creator and preserver of all
mankind, we pray for men of every race, and in
every kind of need: make your ways known on
earth, your saving power among all nations.
(Especially we pray for . . .)
Lord, in your mercy
All   **hear our prayer.**

Minister   We pray for your Church throughout the world:
guide and govern us by your Holy Spirit, that
all who profess and call themselves Christians

may be led into the way of truth, and hold the faith in unity of spirit, in the bond of peace, and in righteousness of life.
(Especially we pray for . . .)
Lord, in your mercy

All **hear our prayer.**

Minister We commend to your fatherly goodness all who are anxious or distressed in mind or body; comfort and relieve them in their need; give them patience in their sufferings, and bring good out of their troubles.
(Especially we pray for . . .)
Merciful Father,

All **accept these prayers
for the sake of your Son,
our Saviour Jesus Christ. Amen.**

or B:

Minister In the power of the Spirit and in union with Christ, let us pray to the Father.

Hear our prayers, O Lord our God.
All **Hear us, good Lord.**

Minister Govern and direct your holy Church; fill it with love and truth; and grant it that unity which is your will.
All **Hear us, good Lord.**

Minister Give us boldness to preach the gospel in all the world, and to make disciples of all the nations.
All **Hear us, good Lord.**

Minister Enlighten your ministers with knowledge and understanding, that by their teaching and their lives they may proclaim your word.
All **Hear us, good Lord.**

Minister	Give your people grace to hear and receive your word, and to bring forth the fruit of the Spirit.
All	**Hear us, good Lord.**

Minister	Bring into the way of truth all who have erred and are deceived.
All	**Hear us, good Lord.**

Minister	Strengthen those who stand; comfort and help the faint-hearted; raise up the fallen; and finally beat down Satan under our feet.
All	**Hear us, good Lord.**

Minister	Guide the leaders of the nations into the ways of peace and justice.
All	**Hear us, good Lord.**

Minister	Guard and strengthen your servant Elizabeth our Queen, that she may put her trust in you, and seek your honour and glory.
All	**Hear us, good Lord.**

Minister	Endue the High Court of Parliament and all the Ministers of the Crown with wisdom and understanding.
All	**Hear us, good Lord.**

Minister	Bless those who administer the law, that they may uphold justice, honesty, and truth.
All	**Hear us, good Lord.**

Minister	Teach us to use the fruits of the earth to your glory, and for the good of all mankind.
All	**Hear us, good Lord.**

Minister	Bless and keep all your people.
All	**Hear us, good Lord.**

Minister	Help and comfort the lonely, the bereaved, and the oppressed.
All	**Lord, have mercy.**
Minister	Keep in safety those who travel, and all who are in danger.
All	**Lord, have mercy.**
Minister	Heal the sick in body and mind, and provide for the homeless, the hungry, and the destitute.
All	**Lord, have mercy.**
Minister	Show your pity on prisoners and refugees, and all who are in trouble.
All	**Lord, have mercy.**
Minister	Forgive our enemies, persecutors, and slanderers, and turn their hearts.
All	**Lord, have mercy.**
Minister	Hear us as we remember those who have died in the peace of Christ, both those who have confessed the faith and those whose faith is known to you alone, and grant us with them a share in your eternal kingdom.
All	**Lord, have mercy.**
Minister	Father, you hear those who pray in the name of your Son: grant that what we have asked in faith we may obtain according to your will; through Jesus Christ our Lord. **Amen.**

82 ALTERNATIVE PRAYER OF HUMBLE ACCESS (section 29)

Most merciful Lord,
your love compels us to come in.
Our hands were unclean,
our hearts were unprepared;
we were not fit
even to eat the crumbs from under your table.
But you, Lord, are the God of our salvation,
and share your bread with sinners.
So cleanse and feed us
with the precious body and blood of your Son,
that he may live in us and we in him;
and that we, with the whole company of Christ,
may sit and eat in your kingdom. Amen.

83 A SELECTION OF OTHER INTRODUCTORY WORDS TO THE PEACE (section 30)

Advent, Christmas, Epiphany
Our Saviour Christ is the Prince of Peace; of the increase of
his government and of peace there shall be no end.

Lent
Being justified by faith, we have peace with God through
our Lord Jesus Christ.

Easter, Ascension
The risen Christ came and stood among his disciples and
said, Peace be with you. Then they were glad when they saw
the Lord.

Pentecost
The fruit of the Spirit is love, joy, peace. If we live in the
Spirit, let us walk in the Spirit.

Saints' Days
We are fellow-citizens with the saints, and of the household
of God, through Christ our Lord who came and preached
peace to those who were far off and those who were near.

President   The Lord be with you or The Lord is here.
All   and also with you.   His Spirit is with us.

President   Lift up your hearts.
All   We lift them to the Lord.

President   Let us give thanks to the Lord our God.
All   It is right to give him thanks and praise.

President   It is indeed right,
           it is our duty and our joy,
           to give you thanks, holy Father,
           through Jesus Christ our Lord.

           Through him you have created us in your image;
           through him you have freed us from sin
               and death;
           through him you have made us your own people
               by the gift of the Holy Spirit.
           Hear us, Father,
           through Christ your Son our Lord,
           and grant that by the power of your
               Holy Spirit
           these gifts of bread and wine
           may be to us his body and his blood.

           Who in the same night that he was betrayed,
           took bread and gave you thanks;
           he broke it and gave it to his disciples,
               saying,
           Take, eat; this is my body which is given
               for you;
           do this in remembrance of me.
           In the same way, after supper he took the cup
           and gave you thanks;
           he gave it to them, saying,
           Drink this, all of you;
           this is my blood of the new covenant

which is shed for you and for many for the
    forgiveness of sins.
Do this as often as you drink it, in
    remembrance of me.

Therefore, Father,
proclaiming his saving death and resurrection
and looking for his coming in glory,
we celebrate with this bread and this cup
his one perfect sacrifice.

Accept through him, our great high priest,
this our sacrifice of thanks and praise,
and grant that we who eat this bread and
    drink this cup
may be renewed by your Spirit and grow into
    his likeness.

Through Jesus Christ our Lord,
by whom, and with whom and in whom,
all honour and glory be yours, Father,
now and for ever. **Amen.**

85   **ADDITIONAL WORDS OF INVITATION TO
      COMMUNION**
      which may be used after section 45

Either A:

President   Jesus is the Lamb of God
             who takes away the sins of the world.
             Happy are those who are called to his supper.
All   **Lord, I am not worthy to receive you,
             but only say the word, and I shall be healed.**

or B:

President   The gifts of God for the people of God.
All   **Jesus Christ is holy,
             Jesus Christ is Lord,
             to the glory of God the Father.**

or C: Easter Day to Pentecost

| President: | Alleluia! Christ our Passover is sacrificed for us. |
| **All** | **Alleluia! Let us keep the feast.** |

86   **ALTERNATIVE FINAL PRAYER**
Especially suitable for a service without Communion

All	**Almighty God,**
	we offer you our souls and bodies,
	to be a living sacrifice,
	through Jesus Christ our Lord.
	Send us out into the world
	in the power of your Spirit,
	to live and work
	to your praise and glory. Amen.

The Order for
Holy Communion

Rite B

NOTES

1 **Seasonal Material** The seasonal sentences (sections 1, 43) and blessings (section 54) are optional. Any other appropriate scriptural sentences may be read at sections 1 and 43 at the discretion of the priest and 'Alleluia' may be added to any sentence from Easter Day until Pentecost (Whit Sunday).

2 **1662 Material** It is permitted to use the 1662 text of the Gloria (sections 5, 48), the Creed (section 14), the Intercession (sections 17-18), the Confession (section 21), the Absolution (section 22), and the Lord's Prayer (sections 33, 36, 44) instead of the texts printed here.

3 **Gloria in excelsis** (section 5) This canticle is also appropriate at sections 1, 11, and 48.

4 **Collects and Readings** The collects and readings are either those set out in this book or those in the Book of Common Prayer, together with any others approved by the General Synod.

5 **The Sermon** The sermon (section 13) is an integral part of the Ministry of the Word. A sermon should normally be preached at all celebrations on Sundays and other Holy Days.

6 **The Peace** The priest may accompany the words of the Peace (sections 24-25) with a handclasp or similar action; and both the words and the action may be passed through the congregation.

7 **The Prayers of Intercession and The Thanksgiving** (sections 17-18, 30-31) The use of the first Intercession does not presume the use of the first Thanksgiving. Either Prayer of Intercession may be used with either Thanksgiving.

8   **Proper Prefaces** The Proper Prefaces set out for use in the first Thanksgiving and those for Christmas, Passiontide, Easter and Ascension in the second Thanksgiving are obligatory.

9   **The First Thanksgiving** (section 30) The Prayer of Humble Access may, if desired, be said after the Sanctus; and the Thanksgiving may end after the words, 'Do this, as oft as ye shall drink it, in remembrance of me'; in which case the people then say **Amen.**

10   **The Blessing** (section 49) In addition to the blessings provided here and at section 54 the priest may at his discretion use others.

11   **Notices** Banns of marriage and other notices may be published after section 1, section 12, or section 42, if they are not published at section 15.

12   **Hymns, Canticles, The Peace, The Collection and Presentation of the Offerings of the People, and The Preparation of the Gifts of Bread and Wine.** Points are indicated for these, but if occasion requires they may occur elsewhere.

13   **Silence** After sections 8, 10, 12, 13, 20, 43 and after the biddings in sections 17-18 silence may be kept.

14   **A Service without Communion** When there is no communion the minister reads the service as far as the Absolution (section 22) and then adds the Lord's Prayer (section 36), the General Thanksgiving, and/or other prayers at his discretion, ending with the Grace. When such a service is led by a deacon or lay person, 'us' is said instead of 'you' in the Absolution.

The Order for
Holy Communion
Rite B

THE WORD AND THE PRAYERS

THE PREPARATION

1   At the entry of the ministers A SENTENCE may be used; and
    A HYMN, A CANTICLE, or A PSALM may be sung.

2   The minister may say

	The Lord be with you
All	**and with thy spirit.**

3   This prayer may be said.

All	**Almighty God,**
	unto whom all hearts be open,
	all desires known,
	and from whom no secrets are hid:
	cleanse the thoughts of our hearts
	by the inspiration of thy Holy Spirit,
	that we may perfectly love thee,
	and worthily magnify thy holy name;
	through Christ our Lord. Amen.

4   One of the following may be used.

Either THE COMMANDMENTS (section 55);
or THE SUMMARY OF THE LAW (section 56);
or KYRIE ELEISON in English or Greek (section 57),
each petition being said once, twice, or three times.

5   GLORIA IN EXCELSIS may be said.

All   Glory be to God on high,
             and in earth peace, good will towards men.

             We praise thee, we bless thee,
             we worship thee, we glorify thee,
             we give thanks to thee for thy great glory,
             O Lord God, heavenly King,
             God the Father almighty.
             O Lord, the only-begotten Son, Jesus Christ:
             O Lord God, Lamb of God, Son of the Father,
             that takest away the sins of the world,
             have mercy upon us.
             Thou that takest away the sins of the world,
             receive our prayer.
             Thou that sittest at the right hand of God
                the Father,
             have mercy upon us.

             For thou only art holy;
             thou only art the Lord;
             thou only, O Christ,
             with the Holy Ghost,
             art the Most High,
             in the glory of God the Father. Amen.

6   THE COLLECT

THE MINISTRY OF THE WORD

7   Either two or three readings from scripture follow, the last of
    which is always the Gospel.

8   **Sit**
    OLD TESTAMENT READING

    At the end the reader may say

             This is the word of the Lord.
All   Thanks be to God.

9   A PSALM may be used.

10   **Sit**
    NEW TESTAMENT READING (EPISTLE)

    At the end the reader may say

            This is the word of the Lord.
All   **Thanks be to God.**

11   A CANTICLE, A HYMN, or A PSALM may be used.

12   **Stand**
    THE GOSPEL. When it is announced

All   **Glory be to thee, O Lord.**

    At the end the reader says

            This is the Gospel of Christ.
All   **Praise be to thee, O Christ.**

13   **Sit**
    THE SERMON

14   **Stand**
    THE NICENE CREED is said on Sundays and other Holy
    Days, and may be said on other days.

All   **I believe in one God**
                the Father almighty,
                maker of heaven and earth,
                and of all things visible and invisible:

                And in one Lord Jesus Christ,
                the only-begotten Son of God,
                begotten of his Father before all worlds,
                God of God, Light of Light,
                very God of very God,
                begotten, not made,
                being of one substance with the Father,
                by whom all things were made;

who for us men and for our salvation
came down from heaven,
and was incarnate by the Holy Ghost
     of the Virgin Mary,
and was made man,
and was crucified also for us
     under Pontius Pilate.
He suffered and was buried,
and the third day he rose again
according to the scriptures,
and ascended into heaven,
and sitteth on the right hand of the Father.
And he shall come again with glory
to judge both the quick and the dead:
whose kingdom shall have no end.

And I believe in the Holy Ghost,
the Lord, the Giver of life,
who proceedeth from the Father
     and the Son,
who with the Father and the Son together
     is worshipped and glorified,
who spake by the prophets.
And I believe one holy catholic and
     apostolic Church.
I acknowledge one baptism for the
     remission of sins.
And I look for the resurrection
     of the dead,
and the life of the world to come. Amen.

PRAYERS OF INTERCESSION

15   Banns of marriage and other notices may be published;
      the offerings of the people may be collected and presented;
      a hymn may be sung; and verses of scripture may be read.

16   INTERCESSIONS are led by the priest, or by others. These
      may be introduced by biddings.

      It is not necessary to include specific subjects in any section
      of the following prayers.

The set passages may follow one another as a continuous whole, or this versicle and response may be used after each paragraph.

Minister	Lord, in thy mercy
All	**hear our prayer.**

Either section 17 or section 18 is used.

17   FIRST INTERCESSION

Minister   Let us pray for the whole Church of God
                in Christ Jesus,
            and for all men according to their needs.

Almighty and everliving God, who by thy holy
apostle hast taught us to make prayers and
supplications, and to give thanks, for all men:
we humbly beseech thee most mercifully *(to
accept our alms and oblations, and) to receive
these our prayers, which we offer unto thy
divine majesty; beseeching thee to inspire
continually the universal Church with the spirit
of truth, unity, and concord; and grant that all
they that do confess thy holy name may agree in
the truth of thy holy word, and live in unity and
godly love.

We beseech thee also to lead all nations in the
way of righteousness and peace; and so to direct
all kings and rulers, that under them thy people
may be godly and quietly governed. And grant
unto thy servant Elizabeth our Queen and to all
that are put in authority under her, that they
may truly and impartially administer justice, to
the punishment of wickedness and vice, and to
the maintenance of thy true religion and virtue.
Give grace, O heavenly Father, to all bishops,
priests, and deacons, especially to thy servant N
our bishop, that they may both by their life and

*If the offerings of the people have not been presented these
words in brackets are omitted.

doctrine set forth thy true and lively word and rightly and duly administer thy holy sacraments.

Guide and prosper, we pray thee, those who are labouring for the spread of thy gospel among the nations, and enlighten with thy Spirit all places of education and learning; that the whole world may be filled with the knowledge of thy truth.

And to all thy people give thy heavenly grace; and specially to this congregation here present, that with meek heart and due reverence, they may hear and receive thy holy word; truly serving thee in holiness and righteousness all the days of their life.

And we most humbly beseech thee of thy goodness, O Lord, to comfort and succour all them who in this transitory life are in trouble, sorrow, need, sickness, or any other adversity.

And we commend to thy gracious keeping, O Lord, all thy servants departed this life in thy faith and fear, beseeching thee, according to thy promises, to grant them refreshment, light, and peace.

And here we give thee most high praise and hearty thanks for all thy saints, who have been the chosen vessels of thy grace, and lights of the world in their several generations; and we pray that, rejoicing in their fellowship and following their good examples, we may be partakers with them of thy heavenly kingdom.

Grant this, O Father, for Jesus Christ's sake, our only mediator and advocate, who liveth and reigneth with thee in the unity of the Holy Spirit, one God, world without end. **Amen.**

The service continues at either section 19 or section 20.

Minister   Let us pray for the whole Church of God
                in Christ Jesus,
             and for all men according to their needs.

             Almighty God, who hast promised to hear the
             prayers of those who ask in faith:

             Here he may pray for the Church throughout
             the world, especially for the diocese and its
             bishop; and for any particular needs of the
             Church.

             Grant that we and all who confess thy name may
             be united in thy truth, live together in thy love,
             and show forth thy glory in the world.

             Here he may pray for the nations of the world,
             for this kingdom, and for all men in their various
             callings.

             Give wisdom to all in authority, bless Elizabeth
             our Queen, and direct this nation and all nations
             in the ways of justice and of peace; that men may
             honour one another, and seek the common
             good.

             Here he may pray for the local community; for
             families, friends, and particular persons.

             Give grace to us, our families and friends, and to
             all our neighbours in Christ, that we may serve
             him in one another, and love as he loves us.

             Here he may pray for the sick, the poor, and
             those in trouble, and for the needs of particular
             persons.

             Save and comfort those who suffer, that they
             may hold to thee through good and ill, and trust
             in thy unfailing love.

*Here he may commemorate the departed; he
may commend them by name.*

Hear us as we remember those who have died in
faith, and grant us with them a share in thy
eternal kingdom.

Merciful Father,
All   **accept these prayers,
for the sake of thy Son,
our Saviour Jesus Christ. Amen.**

PRAYERS OF PENITENCE

19   The minister may say one or more of
THE COMFORTABLE WORDS.

Hear what comfortable words our Saviour
Christ says to all who truly turn to him:
Come unto me, all that travail, and are heavy
laden, and I will refresh you. *Matthew 11.28*

So God loved the world, that he gave his
only-begotten Son, to the end that all that
believe in him should not perish, but have
everlasting life. *John 3.16*

Hear what Saint Paul says:
This is a true saying and worthy of all men to be
received, that Christ Jesus came into the world
to save sinners. *1 Timothy 1.15*

Hear what Saint John says:
If any man sin, we have an advocate with the
Father, Jesus Christ the righteous; and he is the
propitiation for our sins. *1 John 2.1*

| 20 | Minister | *(Ye that do truly and earnestly repent you of your sins, and are in love and charity with your neighbours, and intend to lead a new life, following the commandments of God, and walking from henceforth in his holy ways;) draw near with faith, and take this holy sacrament to your comfort; and make your humble confession to almighty God (meekly kneeling upon your knees). |
| | or | Seeing we have a great high priest who has passed into the heavens, Jesus the Son of God, let us draw near with a true heart, in full assurance of faith, and make our confession to our heavenly Father. |

21 **Kneel**
All

Almighty God, our heavenly Father,
we have sinned against thee,
through our own fault,
in thought, and word, and deed,
and in what we have left undone.
We are heartily sorry,
and repent of all our sins,
For thy Son our Lord Jesus Christ's sake,
forgive us all that is past;
and grant that we may serve thee in newness
of life,
to the glory of thy name. Amen.

22 Priest

Almighty God,
who forgives all who truly repent,
have mercy upon *you*,
pardon and deliver *you* from all *your* sins,
confirm and strengthen *you* in all goodness,
and keep *you* in life eternal;
through Jesus Christ our Lord. **Amen.**

*The words in brackets may be omitted.

We do not presume
to come to this thy table, O merciful Lord,
trusting in our own righteousness,
but in thy manifold and great mercies.
We are not worthy
so much as to gather up the crumbs under
    thy table.
But thou art the same Lord
whose nature is always to have mercy.
Grant us therefore, gracious Lord,
so to eat the flesh of thy dear Son
    Jesus Christ
and to drink his blood,
(that our sinful bodies may be made clean
    by his body
and our souls washed through his most
    precious blood, and)
that we may evermore dwell in him
and he in us. Amen.

THE MINISTRY OF THE SACRAMENT

THE PEACE

24 **Stand**

Priest   We are the Body of Christ.
By one Spirit we were all baptized into
     one body.
Endeavour to keep the unity of the Spirit
in the bond of peace.

He then says

     The peace of the Lord be always with you

All   **and with thy spirit.**

25   All may exchange a sign of peace.

THE PREPARATION OF THE BREAD AND WINE

26   The priest begins THE OFFERTORY.

The bread and the wine are placed on the holy table.

27   The offerings of the people may be collected and presented if
this has not already been done.
These words may be used.

     Thine, O Lord, is the greatness and
       the power
     and the glory and the victory and
       the majesty.
     All that is in heaven and earth is thine.
     All things come of thee, O Lord,
     and of thine own do we give thee.

28   At the preparation of the gifts A HYMN may be sung.

THE THANKSGIVING

29   The priest says THE PRAYER OF CONSECRATION using either section 30 or section 31.

30   FIRST THANKSGIVING

Priest	The Lord be with you
All	**and with thy spirit.**

Priest	Lift up your hearts.
All	**We lift them up unto the Lord.**

Priest	Let us give thanks unto the Lord our God.
All	**It is meet and right so to do.**

Priest   It is very meet, right, and our bounden duty,
that we should at all times and in all places
      give thanks unto thee,
O Lord, holy Father,
almighty, everlasting God,
Creator of heaven and earth,

PROPER PREFACE, when appropriate (section 52)

The following is used when no Proper Preface is provided.

through Jesus Christ our Lord; for he is the true
High Priest, who has washed us from our sins,
and has made us to be a kingdom and priests
unto thee, our God and Father.

Therefore with angels and archangels,
and with all the company of heaven,
we laud and magnify thy glorious name,
evermore praising thee and saying:

**Holy, holy, holy, Lord God of Hosts,
heaven and earth are full of thy glory.
Glory be to thee, O Lord most high. (Amen.)**

**(Blessed is he that cometh in the name of
    the Lord.
Hosanna in the highest.)**

All glory be to thee,
almighty God, our heavenly Father,
who of thy tender mercy
didst give thine only Son Jesus Christ
to suffer death upon the cross
    for our redemption;
who made there,
by his one oblation of himself once offered,
a full, perfect, and sufficient sacrifice,
    oblation, and satisfaction
for the sins of the whole world;
and did institute,
and in his holy gospel command us to continue,
a perpetual memory of that his precious death,
until his coming again.

Hear us, O merciful Father,
we most humbly beseech thee;
and grant that by the power of thy Holy Spirit,
we receiving these thy creatures
    of bread and wine,
according to thy Son our Saviour
    Jesus Christ's holy institution,
in remembrance of his death and passion,
may be partakers
    of his most blessed body and blood.
Who, in the same night that he was betrayed,
took bread;
Here the priest is to take the paten into his hands.
and when he had given thanks,
he brake it, *Here he may break the bread.*
and gave it to his disciples, saying, Take, eat;
Here he is to lay his hand upon the bread.
this is my body which is given for you:
do this in remembrance of me.
Likewise after supper he took the cup;
Here he is to take the cup into his hand.
and when he had given thanks,
he gave it to them, saying, Drink ye all of this;
for this is my blood of the New Testament,
Here to lay his hand upon the cup.
which is shed for you and for many

for the remission of sins:
do this, as oft as ye shall drink it,
in remembrance of me.

Wherefore, O Lord and heavenly Father,
we thy humble servants,
having in remembrance
the precious death and passion of thy dear Son,
his mighty resurrection and glorious ascension
entirely desire thy fatherly goodness
mercifully to accept this our sacrifice
   of praise and thanksgiving;
most humbly beseeching thee to grant that
by the merits and death of thy Son Jesus Christ,
and through faith in his blood,
we and all thy whole Church
may obtain remission of our sins,
and all other benefits of his passion.
And although we be unworthy
   through our manifold sins
to offer unto thee any sacrifice,
yet we beseech thee to accept
   this our bounden duty and service,
not weighing our merits
   but pardoning our offences.
We pray that all we who are partakers
   of this holy communion
may be fulfilled with thy grace
   and heavenly benediction:
through Jesus Christ our Lord,
by whom, and with whom, and in whom,
in the unity of the Holy Spirit,
all honour and glory be unto thee,
O Father almighty,
world without end. **Amen.**

Silence may be kept.

The service continues at either section 32 or section 33 or
section 34.

Priest	The Lord be with you
All	**and with thy spirit.**

Priest	Lift up your hearts.
All	**We lift them up unto the Lord.**

Priest	Let us give thanks unto the Lord our God.
All	**It is meet and right so to do.**

Priest   It is very meet, right, and our bounden duty,
that we should at all times and in all places
    give thanks unto thee,
O Lord, holy Father,
almighty, everlasting God,
through Jesus Christ
thine only Son our Lord:

Because through him thou hast created
    all things from the beginning,
and fashioned us men in thine own image;

through him thou didst redeem us
    from the slavery of sin,
giving him to be born as man,
    to die upon the cross,
and to rise again for us:

through him thou hast made us a people
    for thine own possession,
exalting him to thy right hand on high,
and sending forth through him
    thy holy and life-giving Spirit.

PROPER PREFACE, when appropriate (section 53)

Therefore with angels and archangels,
and with all the company of heaven,
we laud and magnify thy glorious name,
evermore praising thee and saying,

Holy, holy, holy, Lord God of hosts,
heaven and earth are full of thy glory.
Glory be to thee, O Lord most high.

(Blessed is he that cometh in the name of
   the Lord.
Hosanna in the highest.)

Hear us, O Father,
through Christ thy Son our Lord;
through him accept our sacrifice of praise;
and grant that by the power of thy Holy Spirit
these gifts of bread and wine
may be unto us his body and blood:

Who, in the same night that he was betrayed,
took bread;
Here the priest is to take the bread into his hands.
and when he had given thanks to thee,
he broke it,
and gave it to his disciples, saying, Take, eat;
this is my body which is given for you:
do this in remembrance of me.

Likewise after supper he took the cup;
Here he is to take the cup into his hands.
and when he had given thanks to thee,
he gave it to them saying, Drink ye all of this;
for this is my blood of the new covenant,
which is shed for you and for many
for the remission of sins:
do this, as oft as ye shall drink it,
   in remembrance of me.

Wherefore, O Lord and heavenly Father,
with this bread and this cup
we make the memorial of his saving passion,
his resurrection from the dead,
and his glorious ascension into heaven,
and we look for the coming of his kingdom.
We pray thee to accept this
   our duty and service,

and grant that we may so eat and drink
these holy things
in the presence of thy divine majesty,
that we may be filled with thy grace
and heavenly blessing.

Through Jesus Christ our Lord,
by whom, and with whom, and in whom,
in the unity of the Holy Spirit,
all honour and glory be unto thee,
O Father almighty,
world without end. **Amen.**

Silence may be kept.

32   THE BENEDICTUS may follow, if it has not already
been said.

Blessed is he that cometh in the name of
the Lord.
Hosanna in the highest.

33   The priest and people together say THE LORD'S PRAYER
either here or at section 36, or at section 44. (The text is
printed at section 36.)

THE COMMUNION

THE BREAKING OF THE BREAD AND
THE GIVING OF THE BREAD AND CUP

34   The priest breaks the consecrated bread, if he has not already
done so, saying

We break this bread
to share in the body of Christ.
All   **Though we are many, we are one body,**
because we all share in one bread.

35   Either here or during the distribution this anthem may be said

> O Lamb of God,
> that takest away the sins of the world,
> have mercy upon us.
>
> O Lamb of God,
> that takest away the sins of the world,
> have mercy upon us.
>
> O Lamb of God,
> that takest away the sins of the world,
> grant us thy peace.

36   The priest and people may say THE LORD'S PRAYER, if it
has not already been said.

Priest   As our Saviour has taught us, so we pray.
All   **Our Father, who art in heaven,**
          hallowed be thy name;
          thy kingdom come;
          thy will be done;
          on earth as it is in heaven.
          Give us this day our daily bread.
          And forgive us our trespasses,
          as we forgive those who trespass
          against us.
          And lead us not into temptation;
          but deliver us from evil.

          For thine is the kingdom, the power,
          and the glory,
          for ever and ever. Amen.

37   The priest and people receive the communion.

The communion may be administered in one of the
following ways:

38   The minister says to each communicant

> The body of our Lord Jesus Christ, which was
> given for you, preserve your body and soul unto
> everlasting life. Take and eat this in
> remembrance that Christ died for you, and feed
> on him in your hearts by faith with thanksgiving.

> The blood of our Lord Jesus Christ, which was
> shed for you, preserve your body and soul unto
> everlasting life. Drink this in remembrance that
> Christ's blood was shed for you, and be thankful.

39   or

The priest first says to all the communicants

> Draw near and receive the body of our Lord
> Jesus Christ, which was given for you, and his
> blood, which was shed for you. Take this in
> remembrance that Christ died for you, and feed
> on him in your hearts by faith with thanksgiving.

One of the ministers then delivers the bread to each
communicant, saying

> The body of Christ.

or

> The body of Christ preserve your body and soul
> unto everlasting life.

or

> The body of our Lord Jesus Christ, which was
> given for you, preserve your body and soul unto
> everlasting life.

One of the ministers then delivers the cup to each
communicant, saying

> The blood of Christ.

or   The blood of Christ preserve your body and sou[l]
              unto everlasting life.

or   The blood of our Lord Jesus Christ, which was
              shed for you, preserve your body and soul unto
              everlasting life.

The communicant may reply each time **Amen,** and then
receives.

40   During the distribution HYMNS and ANTHEMS may
     be sung.

41   If either or both of the consecrated elements are likely to
     prove insufficient, the priest returns to the holy table and
     adds more, with these words.

              Having given thanks to thee, O Father, over the
              bread and the cup according to the institution of
              thy Son Jesus Christ, who said, Take, eat; this is
              my body (and/or Drink this; this is my blood) we
              pray that this bread/wine also may be to us
              his body/blood, and be received in remembranc[e]
              of him.

42   Any consecrated bread and wine which is not required for
     purposes of communion is consumed at the end of the
     distribution, or after the service.

AFTER COMMUNION

43   AN APPROPRIATE SENTENCE may be said (pp. 42, 43)
     and A HYMN may be sung.

44   The priest and people say THE LORD'S PRAYER, if it has
     not already been said. (The text is printed at section 36.)

45 Either or both of the following PRAYERS or either of those in the Appendices (section 58) are said.

46 Priest   Almighty and everliving God, we most heartily thank thee, for that thou dost vouchsafe to feed us, who have duly received these holy mysteries, with the spiritual food of the most precious body and blood of thy Son our Saviour Jesus Christ; and dost assure us thereby of thy favour and goodness towards us; and that we are very members incorporate in the mystical body of thy Son, which is the blessed company of all faithful people, and are also heirs through hope of thy everlasting kingdom, by the merits of the most precious death and passion of thy dear Son. And we most humbly beseech thee, O heavenly Father, so to assist us with thy grace, that we may continue in that holy fellowship, and do all such good works as thou hast prepared for us to walk in; through Jesus Christ our Lord, to whom, with thee and the Holy Spirit, be all honour and glory, world without end. **Amen.**

47 **All**   **Almighty God,**
we thank thee for feeding us
with the body and blood of thy Son
    Jesus Christ our Lord.
Through him we offer thee our souls
    and bodies
to be a living sacrifice.
Send us out
in the power of thy Spirit,
to live and work
to thy praise and glory. Amen.

48 GLORIA IN EXCELSIS may be used, if it has not been used already (the text is printed at section 5); or some other suitable canticle or hymn may be sung.

THE DISMISSAL

49　The priest may say this or an alternative BLESSING
　　(section 54).

> The peace of God, which passes all
> understanding, keep your hearts and minds in
> the knowledge and love of God, and of his Son
> Jesus Christ our Lord; and the blessing of God
> almighty, the Father, the Son, and the Holy
> Spirit, be among you and remain with you
> always. **Amen.**

50　Priest　　Go in peace and serve the Lord.
　　All　　**In the name of Christ. Amen.**

　　or

　　Priest　　Go in the peace of Christ.
　　All　　**Thanks be to God.**

51　The ministers and people depart.

Appendices

PROPER PREFACES FOR THE FIRST THANKSGIVING

Christmas, Presentation, and Annunciation
because thou didst give Jesus Christ thine only Son to be
born for our salvation: who, by the operation of the Holy
Spirit, was made true man of the substance of the Virgin
Mary his mother: and that without spot of sin, to make us
clean from all sin.

Epiphany
through Jesus Christ our Lord: who in substance of our
mortal flesh manifested forth his glory: that he might bring
all men out of darkness into his own marvellous light.

Thursday before Easter
through Jesus Christ our Lord: who having loved his own
that were in the world loved them unto the end; and on the
night he suffered, sitting at meat with his disciples, did
institute these holy mysteries; that we, redeemed by his
death and quickened by his resurrection, might be partakers
of his divine nature.

Easter
but chiefly we are bound to praise thee for the glorious
resurrection of thy Son Jesus Christ our Lord: for he is the
true Paschal Lamb which was offered for us, and has taken
away the sin of the world; who by his death has destroyed
death, and by his rising to life again has restored us to
everlasting life.

Ascension
through thy most dearly beloved Son Jesus Christ our Lord:
who after his most glorious resurrection manifestly
appeared to all his apostles; and in their sight ascended up
into heaven to prepare a place for us; that where he is,
thither we might also ascend, and reign with him in glory.

Pentecost

through Jesus Christ our Lord: who after he had ascended
up far above all the heavens, and was set down at the right
hand of thy majesty, did as at this time send forth upon the
universal Church thy holy and life-giving Spirit: that
through his glorious power the joy of the everlasting gospel
might go forth into all the world; whereby we have been
brought out of darkness and error into the clear light and
true knowledge of thee, and of thy Son our Saviour
Jesus Christ.

Trinity Sunday

who with thine only-begotten Son and the Holy Spirit art
one God, one Lord in trinity of Persons and in unity of
substance: for that which we believe of thy glory, O Father,
the same we believe of thy Son and of the Holy Spirit,
without any difference or inequality.

Transfiguration

because the divine glory of the incarnate Word shone forth
upon the holy mount before the chosen witnesses of his
majesty; and thine own voice from heaven proclaimed thy
beloved Son.

Saints' Days

who in the righteousness of thy saints hast given us an
example of godly living, and in their blessedness a glorious
pledge of the hope of our calling, that, being encompassed
about with so great a cloud of witnesses, we may run with
patience the race that is set before us, and with them receive
the crown of glory that fadeth not away.

Consecration or Dedication of a Church

who, though the heaven of heavens cannot contain thee,
and thy glory is in all the world, dost deign to hallow places
for thy worship, and in them dost pour forth gifts of grace
upon thy faithful people.

Funerals

because through thy Son Jesus Christ our Lord, thou hast
given us eternal life, and delivered us from the bondage of
sin and the fear of death into the glorious liberty of the
children of God

or

because through thy Son Jesus Christ our Lord, thou hast
given us the hope of a glorious resurrection, so that although
death comes to us all, yet we rejoice in the promise of eternal
life; for to thy faithful people life is changed, not taken away,
and when our mortal flesh is laid aside, an everlasting
dwelling place is made ready for us in heaven.

53   **PROPER PREFACES FOR THE SECOND
THANKSGIVING**

Advent

And now we give thee thanks, because the day of our
deliverance has dawned; and through him thou wilt make all
things new, as he comes in power and triumph to judge
the world.

Christmas, Presentation, and Annunciation

And now we give thee thanks, for by the operation of the
Holy Spirit, he was made man of the Virgin Mary his
mother; and that without spot of sin, to make us clean from
all sin.

Epiphany

And now we give thee thanks, because in coming to dwell
among us as man, he revealed the radiance of his glory, and
brought us out of darkness into his own marvellous light.

Lent

And now we give thee thanks, because through him thou
hast given us the spirit of discipline, that we may triumph
over evil and grow in grace.

Passiontide

And now we give thee thanks, because for our salvation he was obedient even to death on the cross. The tree of defeat became the tree of glory: and where life was lost, there life has been restored.

Thursday before Easter

And now we give thee thanks, because having loved his own that were in the world he loved them unto the end; and on the night before he suffered, sitting at meat with his disciples, did institute these holy mysteries; that we, redeemed by his death and quickened by his resurrection, might be partakers of his divine nature.

Easter

And now we give thee thanks, for his glorious resurrection from the dead. For he is the true Paschal Lamb which was offered for us, and has taken away the sin of the world; who by his death has destroyed death, and by his rising to life again has restored to us everlasting life.

Ascension

And now we give thee thanks, because in his risen body he appeared to his disciples and in their sight was taken into heaven, to reign with thee in glory.

Pentecost

And now we give thee thanks, because by the same Spirit we are led into all truth and are given power to proclaim thy gospel to the nations and to serve thee as a royal priesthood.

Trinity Sunday

And now we give thee thanks, because thou hast revealed thy glory as the glory of thy Son and of the Holy Spirit: three persons equal in majesty, undivided in splendour, yet one Lord, one God, ever to be worshipped and adored.

Transfiguration
And now we give thee thanks, because the divine glory of
the incarnate Word shone forth upon the holy mount before
the chosen witnesses of his majesty; and thine own voice
from heaven proclaimed thy beloved Son.

Saints' Days
And now we give thee thanks, for the glorious pledge of the
hope of our calling which thou hast given us in thy saints;
that following their example and strengthened by their
fellowship, we may run with perseverance the race that is set
before us, and with them receive the unfading crown of
glory.

Dedication
And now we give thee thanks, for thy blessings on this
house of prayer, where we are stirred to faithful witness,
and are built up by thy Spirit into a temple made without
hands, even the body of thy Son Jesus Christ.

Funerals
And now we give thee thanks, because through him thou
hast given us eternal life, and delivered us from the bondage
of sin and the fear of death into the glorious liberty of the
children of God.

or

And now we give thee thanks, because through him thou
hast given us the hope of a glorious resurrection, so that
although death comes to us all, yet we rejoice in the promise
of eternal life; for to thy faithful people life is changed, not
taken away, and when our mortal flesh is laid aside, an
everlasting dwelling place is made ready for us in heaven.

54   ALTERNATIVE BLESSINGS

Advent
Christ the Sun of righteousness shine upon you and scatter
the darkness from before your path: and the blessing . . .

Christmas

Christ the Son of God gladden your hearts with the good news of his kingdom: and the blessing . . .

Lent

Christ give you grace to grow in holiness, to deny yourselves, and to take up your cross, and follow him: and the blessing . . .

Passiontide

Christ crucified draw you to himself, so that you find in him a sure ground for faith, a firm support for hope, and the assurance of sins forgiven: and the blessing . . .

Easter

The God of peace, who brought again from the dead our Lord Jesus, that great shepherd of the sheep, make you perfect in every good work to do his will: and the blessing . . .

Ascension

Christ our king make you faithful and strong to do his will, that you may reign with him in glory: and the blessing . . .

Pentecost

The Spirit of truth lead you into all truth, give you grace to confess that Jesus Christ is Lord, and to proclaim the word and works of God: and the blessing . . .

Trinity Sunday

God the Holy Trinity make you strong in faith and love, defend you on every side, and guide you in truth and peace: and the blessing . . .

Saints' Days

God give you grace to follow his saints in faith and hope and love: and the blessing . . .

Unity

Christ the Good Shepherd, who laid down his life for his sheep, draw you and all who hear his voice to be one within one fold: and the blessing . . .

Minister	God spake these words and said: I am the Lord thy God, thou shalt have none other gods but me.
All	**Lord, have mercy upon us, and incline our hearts to keep this law.**

Minister	Thou shalt not make to thyself any graven image, nor the likeness of anything that is in heaven above, or in the earth beneath, or in the water under the earth. Thou shalt not bow down to them, nor worship them.
All	**Lord, have mercy upon us, and incline our hearts to keep this law.**

Minister	Thou shalt not take the name of the Lord thy God in vain.
All	**Lord, have mercy upon us, and incline our hearts to keep this law.**

Minister	Remember that thou keep holy the Sabbath day. Six days shalt thou labour, and do all that thou hast to do; but the seventh day is the Sabbath of the Lord thy God.
All	**Lord, have mercy upon us, and incline our hearts to keep this law.**

Minister	Honour thy father and thy mother.
All	**Lord, have mercy upon us, and incline our hearts to keep this law.**

Minister	Thou shalt do no murder.
All	**Lord, have mercy upon us, and incline our hearts to keep this law.**

Minister	Thou shalt not commit adultery.
All	**Lord, have mercy upon us, and incline our hearts to keep this law.**

Minister	Thou shalt not steal.
All	**Lord, have mercy upon us,**
	and incline our hearts to keep this law.

Minister	Thou shalt not bear false witness.
All	**Lord, have mercy upon us,**
	and incline our hearts to keep this law.

Minister	Thou shalt not covet.
All	**Lord, have mercy upon us,**
	and write all these thy laws in our hearts,
	we beseech thee.

56 THE SUMMARY OF THE LAW

Minister	Our Lord Jesus Christ said: Hear O Israel, the Lord our God is one Lord; and thou shalt love the Lord thy God with all thy heart, and with all thy soul, and with all thy mind, and with all thy strength. This is the first commandment. And the second is like, namely this: Thou shalt love thy neighbour as thyself. There is none other commandment greater than these. On these two commandments hang all the law and the prophets
All	**Lord, have mercy upon us,**
	and write all these thy laws in our hearts,
	we beseech thee.

57 KYRIE ELEISON

Lord, have mercy (upon us.)	Kyrie eleison.
Lord, have mercy (upon us.)	**Kyrie eleison.**
Lord, have mercy (upon us.)	Kyrie eleison.

Christ, have mercy (upon us.)	**Christe eleison.**
Christ, have mercy (upon us.)	Christe eleison.
Christ, have mercy (upon us.)	**Christe eleison.**

Lord, have mercy (upon us.)	Kyrie eleison.
Lord, have mercy (upon us.)	**Kyrie eleison.**
Lord, have mercy (upon us.)	Kyrie eleison.

Either of the following prayers may be used instead of those in sections 46 and 47.

Priest	O Lord and heavenly Father, we thy humble servants entirely desire thy fatherly goodness mercifully to accept this our sacrifice of praise and thanksgiving; most humbly beseeching thee to grant by the merits and death of thy Son Jesus Christ, and through faith in his blood, we and all thy whole Church may obtain remission of our sins, and all other benefits of his passion. And here we offer and present unto thee, O Lord, ourselves, our souls and bodies, to be a reasonable, holy, and lively sacrifice unto thee; humbly beseeching thee, that all we, who are partakers of this Holy Communion, may be fulfilled with thy grace and heavenly benediction. And although we be unworthy, through our manifold sins, to offer unto thee any sacrifice, yet we beseech thee to accept this our bounden duty and service, not weighing our merits, but pardoning our offences; through Jesus Christ our Lord, by whom, and with whom, in the unity of the Holy Ghost, all honour and glory be unto thee, O Father almighty, world without end. **Amen.**

All	**Almighty Lord, and everlasting God,**
	we offer and present unto thee ourselves,
	    our souls and bodies,
	to be a reasonable, holy, and living
	    sacrifice unto thee:
	humbly beseeching thee,
	that all we, who are partakers of this Holy
	    Communion,
	may be fulfilled with thy grace and heavenly
	    benediction.
	And although we be unworthy, through our
	    manifold sins,

to offer unto thee any sacrifice,
yet we beseech thee to accept this our bounden
    duty and service,
not weighing our merits, but pardoning our
    offences;
through Jesus Christ our Lord,
to whom, with thee and the Holy Ghost,
be all honour and glory, world without end.
Amen.

Initiation Services

Thanksgiving for the Birth of a Child
Thanksgiving after Adoption

NOTES

1   **Explanation** Unless Baptism is to follow immediately, the minister shall explain to the parents or adoptive parents on some occasion before the service or after sections 4 or 20, that the service of thanksgiving is not baptism, which is the sacrament instituted by Christ for those who wish to become members of his Church.

2   **The Place** These services should normally be used in church. Use in the home or in hospital is permitted at the discretion of the priest.

3   **The Presence of the Family** Whenever possible, in addition to both parents or adoptive parents and the child, any other children of the family should be present.

4   **Holy Communion, or Morning and Evening Prayer** These services may be used at Holy Communion or at Morning or Evening Prayer.
At Holy Communion they may be used either at the beginning of the service or after the Sermon; and the Prayers of Intercession may be omitted.
At Morning or Evening Prayer they may be used either at the beginning of the service or after the Second Reading or after the Sermon.

5   **Additional Material** If these services are used on their own, the minister may add suitable hymns and scripture readings (see section 29) and a sermon.

6   **Baptism** If these services are to be followed immediately by Baptism, it is sufficient to use, after a birth, sections 1-3; after an adoption, sections 17-19, 23, and 24.

Thanksgiving for the Birth of a Child

1   Minister   Let us thank God that in his goodness
            he has given you *this son/daughter*.

            God our Father,
            maker of all that is living,
            we praise you for the wonder and joy
                of creation.
            We thank you from our hearts
            for the life of *this child,*
            for a safe delivery,
            and for the privilege of parenthood.
            Accept our thanks and praise
            through Jesus Christ our Lord. **Amen.**

2   The parents of the *child* may say together

            God our Father,
            in giving us *this child*
            you have shown us your love.
            Help us to be trustworthy parents.
            Make us patient and understanding,
            that our *child* may always be sure of
                our love
            and grow up to be happy and responsible;
            through Jesus Christ our Lord. **Amen.**

3   The following VERSICLES AND RESPONSES are said,
    or PSALM 100.

    Minister   My soul proclaims the greatness of the Lord,
    All   **my spirit rejoices in God my saviour.**

    Minister   Glory and honour and power
            are yours by right, O Lord our God;
    All   **for you created all things,**
            and by your will they have their being.

Minister	Holy, holy, holy is God
	the sovereign Lord of all,
All	**who is, and who was, and who is to come.**

Minister	Great and marvellous are your deeds,
	O Lord God,
All	**just and true are your ways,**
	O King of the ages.

| Minister | Praise our God, all you his servants, |
| **All** | **you that fear him, both great and small.** |

| Minister | His mercy rests on those who fear him, |
| **All** | **now and for countless ages. Amen.** |

PSALM 100

1 **O shout to the Lord in triumph ᴵ all the ᴵ earth:**
   serve the Lord with gladness
   and come before his ᴵ face with ᴵ songs of ᴵ joy.

2 **Know that the Lord ᴵ he is ᴵ God:**
   it is he who has made us and we are his
   we are his ᴵ people · and the ᴵ sheep of · his ᴵ pasture.

3 **Come into his gates with thanksgiving**
   and into his ᴵ courts with ᴵ praise:
   give thanks to him and ᴵ bless his ᴵ holy ᴵ name.

4 **For the Lord is good * his loving mercy ᴵ is for ᴵ ever:**
   his faithfulness through ᴵ out all ᴵ gener ᴵ ations.

   Glory to the Father and ᴵ to the ᴵ Son:
   and ᴵ to the ᴵ Holy ᴵ Spirit;
   as it was in the be ᴵ ginning is ᴵ now:
   and shall be for ᴵ ever. ᴵ A ᴵ men.

   or a hymn may be sung.

4   Minister

Hear these words from the Gospel according to St Mark:
They brought children for Jesus to touch. The disciples
rebuked them, but when Jesus saw this he was indignant
and said to them, 'Let the children come to me; do not try to
stop them; for the kingdom of God belongs to such as these.
I tell you, whoever does not accept the kingdom of God like a
child will never enter it.' And he put his arms round them,
laid his hands upon them, and blessed them.
Mark 10.13-16 NEB

5   The minister may give a copy of one of the gospels to the
parents, saying

> This book contains the Good News of God's
> love. Read it, for it tells how you and your family
> can share in eternal life, through repentance and
> faith in Jesus Christ.

6   Minister   Jesus taught us to call God our Father,
                     and so in faith and trust we say
      All   **Our Father in heaven,**
                     hallowed be your name,
                     your kingdom come,
                     your will be done,
                     on earth as in heaven.
                     Give us today our daily bread.
                     Forgive us our sins
                     as we forgive those who sin against us.
                     Lead us not into temptation
                     but deliver us from evil.
                     For the kingdom, the power, and the glory
                        are yours
                     now and for ever. Amen.

7   Minister   Almighty God, look with favour on *this child*;
                     grant that, being nourished with all goodness,
                     he may grow in discipline and grace until *he*
                     comes to the fullness of faith; through Jesus
                     Christ our Lord. **Amen.**

8   The minister then says one or more of these prayers.

9   Heavenly Father, whose blessed Son shared at
             Nazareth the life of an earthly home: bless the
             home of this child, and help all *the family* to live
             together in your love. Teach them to serve you
             and each other, and make them always ready to
             show your love to those in need; for the sake of
             Jesus Christ our Lord. **Amen.**

10   Father in heaven, bless these parents, that they
             may cherish their *child;* make them wise and
             understanding, to help *him* as *he grows,* and
             surround *this family* with the light of your truth
             and the warmth of your love; through Jesus
             Christ our Lord. **Amen.**

11   Almighty Father, we thank you that you have
             made the love of Christ for his bride the Church
             to be a pattern for the marriage of husband and
             wife. We pray that these your servants may
             grow in love and self-giving to each other all the
             days of their life; through Jesus Christ our
             Lord. **Amen.**

12   God our Father, we pray to you for all who have
             the care of *this child.* Guide them with your Holy
             Spirit, that they may bring *him* up in the ways of
             truth and love. Through their care enable *him* to
             grow in grace and become daily more like your
             Son, our Saviour Jesus Christ. **Amen.**

13   Almighty God, the fountain of all wisdom, you
             know our needs before we ask, and our
             ignorance in asking. Have compassion on our
             weakness, and give us those things which for
             our unworthiness we dare not and for our
             blindness we cannot ask, for the sake of your
             Son, Jesus Christ our Lord. **Amen.**

14   This prayer may be said by all.

> **God our Father,**
> **we pray for** *this child*,
> **that in due time**
> *he* **may be received by baptism**
> **into the family of your Church,**
> **and become** *an inheritor* **of your kingdom;**
> **through Jesus Christ our Lord. Amen.**

15   The minister ends the service with one of these BLESSINGS.

> The Lord bless you and watch over you,
> the Lord make his face shine upon you
> and be gracious to you,
> the Lord look kindly on you and give you peace;
> and the blessing of God almighty,
> the Father, the Son, and the Holy Spirit,
> be among you and remain with you always.
> **Amen.**

or

> The love of the Lord Jesus
> draw you to himself,
> the power of the Lord Jesus
> strengthen you in his service,
> the joy of the Lord Jesus fill your hearts;
> and the blessing of God almighty,
> the Father, the Son, and the Holy Spirit,
> be among you and remain with you always.
> **Amen.**

16   When this service is used on its own (see note 5), readings
may be chosen from the following.

Genesis 1.26-28, 31a   1 Samuel 1.20-end
Tobit 8.5-6

Romans 8.28-30   Romans 12.1, 2
Ephesians 3.14-21

Matthew 7.24-27   Luke 2.22, 28a (28b-35)
John 15.9-12

Thanksgiving after Adoption

17   Minister   Let us thank God that in his goodness
he has given you *this son/daughter*.

God our Father,
maker of all that is living,
we praise you for the wonder and joy
   of creation.
We thank you from our hearts
for the life of *this child*,
and for the privilege of parenthood.
Accept our thanks and praise
through Jesus Christ our Lord. **Amen.**

18   The parents of the *child* may say together

God our Father,
in giving us *this child*
you have shown us your love.
Help us to be trustworthy parents.
Make us patient and understanding,
that our *child* may always be sure of
   our love,
and grow up to be happy and responsible;
through Jesus Christ our Lord. **Amen.**

19   The following VERSICLES AND RESPONSES are said,
or PSALM 100.

Minister   My soul proclaims the greatness of the Lord,
All   **my spirit rejoices in God my Saviour.**

Minister   Glory and honour and power
are yours by right, O Lord our God;
All   **for you created all things,**
and by your will they have their being.

Minister	Holy, holy, holy is God
	the sovereign Lord of all,
All	**who is, and who was, and who is to come.**

Minister	Great and marvellous are your deeds,
	O Lord God,
All	**just and true are your ways,**
	O King of the ages.

| Minister | Praise our God, all you his servants, |
| **All** | **you that fear him, both great and small.** |

| Minister | His mercy rests on those who fear him, |
| **All** | **now and for countless ages. Amen.** |

PSALM 100

1 **O shout to the Lord in triumph ǀ all the ǀ earth:**
   serve the Lord with gladness
   and come before his ǀ face with ǀ songs of ǀ joy.

2 **Know that the Lord ǀ he is ǀ God:**
   it is he who has made us and we are his
   we are his ǀ people · and the ǀ sheep of · his ǀ pasture.

3 **Come into his gates with thanksgiving**
   and into his ǀ courts with ǀ praise:
   give thanks to him and ǀ bless his ǀ holy ǀ name.

4 **For the Lord is good * his loving mercy ǀ is for ǀ ever:**
   his faithfulness through ǀout all ǀ generǀations.

   Glory to the Father and ǀ to the ǀ Son:
   and ǀ to the ǀ Holy ǀ Spirit;
   as it was in the beǀginning is ǀ now:
   and shall be for ǀ ever. ǀ Aǀmen.

or a hymn may be sung.

20   Minister

Hear these words from the Gospel according to St Mark:
They brought children for Jesus to touch. The disciples
rebuked them, but when Jesus saw this he was indignant
and said to them, 'Let the children come to me; do not try to
stop them; for the kingdom of God belongs to such as these.
I tell you, whoever does not accept the kingdom of God like a
child will never enter it.' And he put his arms round them,
laid his hands upon them, and blessed them.
Mark 10.13-16 NEB

21   The minister may give a copy of one of the gospels to the
parents, saying

> This book contains the Good News of God's
> love. Read it, for it tells how you and your family
> can share in eternal life, through repentance and
> faith in Jesus Christ.

22   Minister   Jesus taught us to call God our Father,
and so in faith and trust we say

       All   **Our Father in heaven,**
hallowed be your name,
your kingdom come,
your will be done,
on earth as in heaven.
Give us today our daily bread.
Forgive us our sins
as we forgive those who sin against us.
Lead us not into temptation
but deliver us from evil.
For the kingdom, the power, and the glory
     are yours
now and for ever. Amen.

23   Minister   Almighty God, look with favour on *this child*;
grant that, being nourished with all goodness,
he may grow in discipline and grace until *he*
comes to the fullness of faith; through Jesus
Christ our Lord. **Amen.**

24   God, whose nature is always to have mercy,
     look down with love on the natural father and
     mother of *this child*; keep them in your good
     providence, and give them your peace in their
     hearts; through Jesus Christ our Lord. **Amen.**

25   The members of the family then say together

     We receive *this child* into our family with
     thanksgiving and joy.
     Through the love of God we receive *him*;
     with the love of God we will care for *him*;
     by the love of God we will guide *him*;
     and in the love of God may we all abide for
     ever. **Amen.**

26   Minister   Heavenly Father, whose blessed Son shared at
     Nazareth the life of an earthly home: bless the
     home of *this child*, and help all *the family* to live
     together in your love. Teach them to serve you
     and each other, and make them always ready to
     show your love to those in need; for the sake of
     Jesus Christ our Lord. **Amen.**

27   This prayer may be said by all.

     **God our Father,
     we pray for** *this child*,
     that in due time
     he **may be received by baptism
     into the family of your Church,
     and become** *an inheritor* **of your kingdom;
     through Jesus Christ our Lord. Amen.**

28   The minister ends the service with one of these BLESSINGS.

     The Lord bless you and watch over you,
     the Lord make his face shine upon you
     and be gracious to you,
     the Lord look kindly on you and give you peace;

and the blessing of God almighty,
the Father, the Son, and the Holy Spirit,
be among you and remain with you always.
Amen.

or   The love of the Lord Jesus
draw you to himself,
the power of the Lord Jesus
strengthen you in his service,
the joy of the Lord Jesus fill your hearts;
and the blessing of God almighty,
the Father, the Son, and the Holy Spirit,
be among you and remain with you always.
Amen.

29   When this service is used on its own (see note 5), readings
may be chosen from the following.

Genesis 1.26-28, 31a	1 Samuel 1.20-end
Tobit 8.5-6	
Romans 8.28-30	Romans 12.1, 2
Ephesians 3.14-21	
Matthew 7.24-27	Luke 2.22, 28a (28b-35)
John 15.9-12	

Baptism, Confirmation, and Holy Communion

An order of service for:
The baptism and confirmation of adults
The baptism of families and confirmation of adults
The baptism of adults
The baptism of families
The baptism of children
The confirmation of those already baptized

If either the baptism of children or the confirmation of those already baptized is to be administered on its own, then the separate services at sections 42 and 64 respectively should be used.

NOTES

1 **Baptism without Confirmation** Adults who are to be baptized should normally be confirmed at the same service; but when they are to be baptized without confirmation, sections 23-26 are omitted.

2 **Family Baptism** When children who are not old enough to answer for themselves are to be baptized at the same time as their parents, the parents answer the questions for themselves and for their children, saying
We turn to Christ.
We repent of our sins.
We renounce evil.
We believe and trust in him.
When children who are old enough to respond are baptized, the parents and godparents answer the questions, and, at the discretion of the priest, the children also may answer them. When children and their parents are baptized on the same occasion, it is fitting that the children are baptized immediately after their own parents.

3 **The Signing with the Cross** The signing with the cross may take place either at section 14 or at section 21. The sign of the cross may be made in oil blessed for this purpose.

4 **The Giving of a Candle** A lighted candle, which may be the paschal candle, may be made ready so that other candles may be lighted from it.

5 **The Use of the Candidate's Name** At the signing with the cross and the giving of a candle, the Bishop or other minister may address the candidate by name.

6 **The People's Responses** At the signing with the cross it is sufficient if the people join in and say their part (sections 14 and 21) once only, when all have been signed; and if a candle is given to those who have been baptized, it is sufficient if the people join in and say their part (section 22) once only, when all have received a candle.

7   **Anointing with Oil** At section 25 the Bishop may anoint
     candidates with oil which he has previously blessed for this
     purpose.

8   **Delegation by the Bishop** Where it is prescribed that
     anything is to be said or done by the Bishop, he may delegate
     it to other ministers; but only the Bishop is to confirm
     (sections 23-25).

9   **Readings** The Bishop may direct readings to be used other
     than those appointed in this order, subject to the provisions
     of Rule 1b in the *Rules to Order the Service*.

10   **The Ordering of the Service** When candidates for
     confirmation are presented at the same service as candidates
     for both baptism and confirmation, the precise ordering of
     the service and the place of baptism should be determined
     by consultation between the Bishop and the parish priest.

11   **The Administration of Baptism** A threefold administration
     of water (whether by dipping or pouring) is a very ancient
     practice of the Church and is commended as testifying to the
     faith of the Trinity in which candidates are baptized.
     Nevertheless, a single administration is also lawful
     and valid.

12   **The Renewal of Baptismal Vows** At the discretion of the
     Bishop, the renewal of baptismal vows by members of the
     congregation may take place after section 10 instead of at
     section 28.

Baptism, Confirmation, and Holy Communion

THE PREPARATION

1   At the entry of the ministers this, or another APPROPRIATE
SENTENCE, may be used:

> The Lord is my strength and my song,
> and has become my salvation. *Psalm 118.14*

and A HYMN or A CANTICLE may be sung.

2   Bishop   The Lord be with you
All   **and also with you.**

3   If THE PRAYERS OF PENITENCE (Holy Communion Rite A,
sections 5-8) are to be used, they follow here.

4   Bishop   Heavenly Father,
by the power of your Holy Spirit
you give to your faithful people
new life in the water of baptism.
Guide and strengthen us by that same Spirit,
that we who are born again
may serve you in faith and love,
and grow into the full stature of your Son
   Jesus Christ,
who is alive and reigns with you and the
   Holy Spirit,
one God now and for ever. **Amen.**

THE MINISTRY OF THE WORD

5   **Sit**
If AN OLD TESTAMENT READING is to be read, one of the
following may be chosen (see pp. 262-268).

Genesis 7.17-23 (or 7.17–8.5) Exodus 14.19-31
Deuteronomy 30.15-20   2 Kings 5.1-15a
Isaiah 43.1-3a, 6b-7   Isaiah 44.1-5
Jeremiah 31.31-34   Ezekiel 36.25a, 26-28

At the end the reader may say

> This is the word of the Lord.
> **All**　**Thanks be to God.**

Silence may be kept.

6　PSALM 107.1-9 may be sung (p. 261).

7　If A NEW TESTAMENT READING is to be read, one of the
　following may be chosen (see pp. 268-271).

Acts 16.25-34   Romans 6.3-11
Romans 8.11-17   1 Corinthians 12.12-13
Galatians 5.16-25   1 Peter 2.4-10

At the end the reader may say

> This is the word of the Lord.
> **All**　**Thanks be to God.**

Silence may be kept.

8　A CANTICLE or A HYMN may be sung.

9　**Stand**
　THE GOSPEL. When it is announced

All　**Glory to Christ our Saviour.**

One of the following may be chosen (see pp. 271-274).

Matthew 16.24-27   Matthew 28.16-20
Mark 1.1-11   Mark 1.14-20
John 3.1-8   John 15.1-11

At the end the reader may say

> This is the Gospel of Christ.

All　　　　　**Praise to Christ our Lord.**

Silence may be kept.

10　**Sit**
　　THE SERMON

At the end, silence may be kept.

THE DECISION

11　If children are to be baptized, sections 42 and 43 may be used
　　here.

12　Those who are to be baptized, the parents and godparents of
　　children to be baptized, and those who are to be confirmed
　　stand before the Bishop. He says

Our Lord Jesus Christ suffered death on the cross and rose
again from the dead for the salvation of mankind. Baptism is
the outward sign by which we receive for ourselves what he
has done for us: we are united with him in his death; we are
granted the forgiveness of sins; we are raised with Christ to
new life in the Spirit.

Those of you who have come for baptism must affirm your
allegiance to Christ and your rejection of all that is evil.

(Those parents and godparents who present children for
baptism must bring them up to fight against evil and to
follow Christ.)*

Those of you who come to be confirmed must with your own
mouth and from your own heart declare your allegiance to
Christ and your rejection of all that is evil.

*When no children are to be baptized, the words in brackets
are omitted.

13   Therefore I ask these questions:
     (Parents and godparents must answer both for themselves
     and for *these children*.)*

              Do you turn to Christ?
     Answer   **I turn to Christ.**

              Do you repent of your sins?
     Answer   **I repent of my sins.**

              Do you renounce evil?
     Answer   **I renounce evil.**

14   Either here or at section 21 the Bishop makes THE SIGN OF
     THE CROSS on the forehead of each one who is to be
     baptized and says to each

              I sign you with the cross, the sign of Christ.

     After the signing of each or all, he says

              Do not be ashamed to confess the faith of
              Christ crucified.
     All   **Fight valiantly under the banner of Christ
              against sin, the world, and the devil,
              and continue his faithful** *soldiers* **and** *servants*
              to the end of your *lives*.

15   Bishop   May almighty God deliver you from the powers
              of darkness, and lead you in the light and
              obedience of Christ. **Amen.**

16   PSALM 121 (p. 262) or some other suitable psalm or hymn
     may be sung.

*When no children are to be baptized, the words in brackets
are omitted.

THE BAPTISM

17   The Bishop stands before the water of baptism and says

Praise God who made heaven and earth,

All   **who keeps his promise for ever.**

Bishop   Almighty God, whose Son Jesus Christ
was baptized in the river Jordan:
we thank you for the gift of water
to cleanse us and revive us;
we thank you that through the waters of the
Red Sea, you led your people out of slavery
to freedom in the promised land;
we thank you that through the deep waters
of death you brought your Son, and raised
him to life in triumph.
Bless this water, that your *servants* who *are*
washed in it may be made one with Christ
in his death and in his resurrection,
to be cleansed and delivered from all sin.
Send your Holy Spirit upon *them* to bring
them to new birth in the family of your
Church, and raise *them* with Christ to full
and eternal life.
For all might, majesty, authority, and power
are yours, now and for ever. **Amen.**

18   The Bishop says to adults who are to be baptized

You must now declare before God and his
Church the Christian faith into which you are to
be baptized and in which you will live and grow.

(To parents and godparents of children who are to be
baptized he says

You must now declare before God and his
Church the Christian faith into which *these
children are* to be baptized, and in which you will
help *them* to live and grow. You must answer for

yourselves and for *these children*.)

(To those who have already been baptized and are now to be confirmed, he says

> You must now declare before God and his Church that you accept the Christian faith into which you were baptized, and in which you will live and grow.)

Then he says

> Do you believe and trust in God the Father, who made the world?

Answer **I believe and trust in him.**

> Do you believe and trust in his Son Jesus Christ, who redeemed mankind?

Answer **I believe and trust in him.**

> Do you believe and trust in his Holy Spirit, who gives life to the people of God?

Answer **I believe and trust in him.**

19 The Bishop turns to the congregation and says

> This is the faith of the Church.

All **This is our faith.**
We believe and trust in one God,
Father, Son, and Holy Spirit.

20 The Bishop then baptizes the candidates. He dips each one in the water or pours water on him, addressing him by name.

> *N*, I baptize you in the name of the Father, and of the Son, and of the Holy Spirit.

And each one of his sponsors answers

> **Amen.**

21 The Bishop makes THE SIGN OF THE CROSS on the
    forehead of each one, if he has not already done so. The
    appropriate words are printed at section 14.

22 The priest or other person may give A LIGHTED CANDLE
    to each adult who has been baptized, and to a parent or
    godparent for each child, saying to each

                    Receive this light.

    And when a candle has been given to each one, he says

                    This is to show that you have passed
                    from darkness to light.
    All   **Shine as a light in the world**
                    to the glory of God the Father.

THE CONFIRMATION

23 The Bishop stands before those to be confirmed and says

                    Our help is in the name of the Lord
    All   **who has made heaven and earth.**

                    Blessed be the name of the Lord
    All   **now and for ever. Amen.**

24 The Bishop stretches out his hands towards them and says

                    Almighty and everliving God,
                    you have given your *servants* new birth
                    in baptism by water and the Spirit,
                    and have forgiven *them* all *their* sins.
                    Let your Holy Spirit rest upon *them*:
                    the Spirit of wisdom and understanding;
                    the Spirit of counsel and inward strength;
                    the Spirit of knowledge and true godliness;
                    and let *their* delight be in the fear of the Lord.
                    Amen.

25   The Bishop lays his hand on the head of each candidate,
      saying

              Confirm, O Lord, your servant *N* with your
              Holy Spirit.

      and each one answers

              Amen.

26   After confirmation, the Bishop invites the people to join with
      him and say

              Defend, O Lord, your *servants* **with your
                  heavenly grace,**
              that *they* **may continue yours for ever,**
              **and daily increase in your Holy Spirit
                  more and more,**
              until *they come* **to your everlasting
                  kingdom. Amen.**

THE WELCOME

27   The Bishop and the congregation, representing the whole
      Church, welcome the candidates.

      Bishop   God has received you by baptism into
                  his Church.
      All   **We welcome you into the Lord's Family.**
                  **We are members together of the body
                      of Christ;**
                  we are children of the same heavenly Father;
                  **we are inheritors together of the kingdom
                      of God.**
                  We welcome you.

28   If some members of the congregation are now to make a
      renewal of their baptismal vows, sections 94-98 may be used
      here.

THE COMMUNION

29 The Bishop resumes the Communion Service at THE PEACE
(Holy Communion Rite A, sections 30-31; Rite B, sections
24-25).

30 These special forms are used.

PROPER PREFACE
And now we give you thanks because by the Holy Spirit you
lead us into all truth and give us power to preach your gospel
to the nations, and to serve you as a royal priesthood.

POSTCOMMUNION SENTENCE
God who raised Christ Jesus from the dead will also give life
to your mortal bodies through his Spirit who dwells in you.
Romans 8.11

31 The Bishop says both THE BLESSING and THE DISMISSAL
(Holy Communion Rite A, sections 54-56; Rite B, sections
49-50).

Baptism and Confirmation without Holy Communion

The service follows the order to be used at Holy Communion (sections 1-28 above). One, two, or three readings may be used as the Bishop directs.

After section 28 the Bishop says one or more of these prayers.

32 For adults who have now been baptized

> We thank you, heavenly Father, that by your Holy Spirit you have given your *servants* new birth, adopted *them* to be your *children*, and made *them members* of your Church. We pray that, in the power of the Spirit, *they* may live and grow in your service, and attain your promises; through Jesus Christ our Lord. **Amen.**

33 For those who have now been confirmed

> Heavenly Father, we pray for your *servants* upon whom we have now laid our hands, after the example of the apostles, to assure *them* by this sign of your favour towards *them*. May your fatherly hand ever be over *them*, your Holy Spirit ever be with *them*. Strengthen *them* continually with the body and blood of your Son, and so lead *them* in the knowledge and obedience of your word, that in the end *they* may obtain everlasting life; through Jesus Christ our Lord. **Amen.**

34 For children who have been baptized and their parents

> Lord God our Father, maker of heaven and earth, we thank you that by your Holy Spirit *these children* have been born again into new life,

adopted for your own, and received into the
fellowship of your Church: we pray that *they*
may grow in the faith into which *they have* been
baptized; that *they* may profess it for *themselves*
when *they come* to be confirmed; and that all
things belonging to the Spirit may live and grow
in *them*. We pray also for *their* parents; give them
the spirit of wisdom and love, that their *homes*
may reflect the joy of your eternal kingdom;
through Jesus Christ our Lord. **Amen.**

35   For all Christian people

Almighty God, we thank you for our fellowship
in the household of faith with all those who have
been baptized in your name. Keep us faithful to
our baptism, and so make us ready for that day
when the whole creation shall be made perfect
in your Son, our Saviour Jesus Christ. **Amen.**

36   For the Church's witness

Almighty God, whose Holy Spirit equips the
Church with a rich variety of gifts; grant that we
may use them to bear witness to Christ by lives
built on faith and love. Make us ready to live his
gospel and eager to do his will, that we may
share with all your Church in the joys of eternal
life; through Jesus Christ our Lord. **Amen.**

37   **Lord, make us instruments of your peace.**
Where there is hatred, let us sow love;
where there is injury, let there be pardon;
where there is discord, union;
where there is doubt, faith;
where there is despair, hope;
where there is darkness, light;
where there is sadness, joy;
for your mercy and for your truth's sake. Amen.

38   **Lord Jesus Christ, we thank you**
for all the benefits you have won for us,
for all the pains and insults you have borne
**   for us.**
Most merciful redeemer,
friend and brother,
may we know you more clearly,
love you more dearly,
and follow you more nearly,
day by day. Amen.

39   **Eternal God,**
you have declared in Christ
the completion of your purpose of love.
May we live by faith, walk in hope,
and be renewed in love,
until the world reflects your glory,
and you are all in all.
Even so; come, Lord Jesus. Amen.

40   Then all say the Lord's Prayer.

                        Our Father in heaven,
hallowed be your name,
your kingdom come,
your will be done,
on earth as in heaven.
Give us today our daily bread.
Forgive us our sins
as we forgive those who sin against us.
Lead us not into temptation
but deliver us from evil.

                        For the kingdom, the power, and the glory
**   are yours**
now and for ever. Amen.

41   The Bishop ends the service with A BLESSING.

Baptism and Confirmation at Morning or Evening Prayer

When the service is used at Morning or Evening Prayer, proper psalms and readings may be chosen from those printed above (sections 5-9); and the sentence (section 1) and collect (section 4) may also be used instead of those of the day.

The service follows this order:

1 Morning or Evening Prayer, to the end of the second reading.

2 A sermon may be preached.

3 Baptism and Confirmation sections 11-28 (or those parts which are required).

4 Morning or Evening Prayer, from the canticle after the second reading to the end of the service.

5 At the end of the service, prayers from sections 32-39 above may be used.

The Baptism of Children

NOTES

1   **The Administration of Baptism** Holy Baptism is normally
    administered by the parish priest in the course of public
    worship on Sunday; but it may be administered at other
    times, and he may delegate its administration to other lawful
    ministers. Where rubrics indicate that a passage is to be said
    by 'the priest', this must be understood to include any other
    minister authorized to administer Holy Baptism.

2   **The Answering of the Questions** When children who are old
    enough to respond are baptized, the parents and godparents
    answer the questions (sections 48 and 53), and at the
    discretion of the priest the children may also answer them.

3   **The Signing with the Cross** The signing with the cross may
    take place either at section 49 or at section 56. The sign of the
    cross may be made in oil blessed for this purpose.

4   **The Giving of a Candle** A lighted candle, which may be the
    paschal candle, may be made ready so that other candles
    may be lighted from it.

5   **The Use of the Candidate's Name** At the signing with the
    cross and the giving of a candle, the priest or other minister
    may address the candidate by name.

6   **The People's Responses** At the signing with the cross it is
    sufficient if the people join in and say their part (sections 49
    and 56) once only, when all have been signed; and if a candle
    is given to those who have been baptized, it is sufficient if the
    people join in and say their part (section 57) once only, when
    all have received a candle.

7   **The Attendance of the People** This order of service should
    normally be used at Holy Communion or Morning or
    Evening Prayer. At other times representatives of the

regular congregation should attend the service, so that they may welcome the newly baptized (section 58) and be put in mind of their own baptism.

8   **Hymns** If occasion requires, hymns may be sung at points other than those which are indicated in this order.

9   **The Administration of the Water** A threefold administration of water (whether by dipping or pouring) is a very ancient practice of the Church, and is commended as testifying to the faith of the Trinity in which candidates are baptized. Nevertheless, a single administration is also lawful and valid.

10   **Alternative Readings** Section 45 may be omitted and either Matthew 28.16-20 or John 3.1-8 read in its place.

The Baptism of Children

THE DUTIES OF PARENTS AND GODPARENTS

42 The priest says

> Children who are too young to profess the
> Christian faith are baptized on the
> understanding that they are brought up as
> Christians within the family of the Church.
>
> As they grow up, they need the help and
> encouragement of that family, so that they learn
> to be faithful in public worship and private
> prayer, to live by trust in God, and come to
> confirmation.
>
> Parents and godparents, the *children* whom you
> have brought for baptism *depend* chiefly on you
> for the help and encouragement *they need*. Are
> you willing to give it to *them* by your prayers, by
> your example, and by your teaching?

Parents and godparents

I am willing.

43 And if the *child is* old enough to understand, the priest
speaks to *him* in these or similar words.

> *N*, when you are baptized, you become *a member*
> of a new family. God takes you for his own *child*,
> and all Christian people will be your brothers
> and sisters.

THE MINISTRY OF THE WORD

Sections 44, 45, and 46 may be omitted when Baptism is administered at Holy Communion or at Morning or Evening Prayer.

44 Priest   The Lord is loving to everyone;
      All   **and his mercy is over all his works.**

45 Priest

God is the creator of all things, and by the birth of children he gives to parents a share in the work and joy of creation. But we who are born of earthly parents need to be born again. For in the Gospel Jesus tells us that unless a man has been born again, he cannot see the Kingdom of God. And so God gives us the way to a second birth, a new creation and life in union with him.

Baptism is the sign and seal of this new birth. In St Matthew's Gospel we read of the risen Christ commanding his followers to make disciples of all nations and to baptize men everywhere; and in the Acts of the Apostles we read of St Peter preaching in these words: 'Repent and be baptized in the name of Jesus Christ for the forgiveness of sins; and you shall receive the gift of the Holy Spirit. For the promise is to you and your children and to all that are afar off, everyone whom the Lord calls to him.'

In obedience to this same command we ourselves were baptized and now bring *these children* to baptism.

46 Priest   We thank God therefore for our baptism to life in Christ, and we pray for *these children (N)* and say together
      All   **Heavenly Father, in your love**
            you have called us to know you,
            led us to trust you,
            and bound our life with yours.
            Surround *these children* **with your love;**
            protect *them* **from evil;**
            fill *them* **with your Holy Spirit;**

and receive *them* **into the family of your Church;
that** *they* **may walk with us in the way of Christ
and grow in the knowledge of your love. Amen.**

THE DECISION

47   The parents and godparents stand, and the priest says
to them

Those who bring children to be baptized must
affirm their allegiance to Christ and their
rejection of all that is evil.

It is your duty to bring up *these children* to fight
against evil and to follow Christ.

48   Therefore I ask these questions which you must
answer for yourselves and for *these* children.

Do you turn to Christ?
Answer   **I turn to Christ.**

Do you repent of your sins?
Answer   **I repent of my sins.**

Do you renounce evil?
Answer   **I renounce evil.**

49   Either here or at section 56 the priest makes THE SIGN OF
THE CROSS on the forehead of each child, saying to each

I sign you with the cross, the sign of Christ.

After the signing of each or all, he says

Do not be ashamed to confess the faith of Christ
crucified.
All   **Fight valiantly under the banner of Christ
against sin, the world, and the devil, and
continue his faithful** *soldiers* **and** *servants* **to the
end of your** *lives.*

| 50 | Priest | May almighty God deliver you from the powers of darkness, and lead you in the light and obedience of Christ. **Amen.** |

51   A HYMN or PSALM may be sung.

THE BAPTISM

52   The priest stands before the water of baptism and says

| | Praise God who made heaven and earth, |
| **All** | **who keeps his promise for ever.** |

| Priest⋅ | Almighty God, whose Son Jesus Christ was baptized in the river Jordan; we thank you for the gift of water to cleanse us and revive us; ⋅ we thank you that through the waters of the Red Sea, you led your people out of slavery to freedom in the promised land; we thank you that through the deep waters of death you brought your Son, and raised him to live in triumph. Bless this water, that your *servants* who *are* washed in it may be made one with Christ in his death and in his resurrection, to be cleansed and delivered from all sin. Send your Holy Spirit upon *them* to bring *them* to new birth in the family of your Church, and raise *them* with Christ to full and eternal life. For all might, majesty, authority, and power are yours, now and for ever. **Amen.** |

53   The priest says to the parents and godparents

| | You have brought *these children* to baptism. You must now declare before God and his Church |

the Christian faith into which *they are* to be
baptized, and in which you will help *them* to
grow. You must answer for yourselves and for
these children.

Do you believe and trust in God the Father,
who made the world?

Answer **I believe and trust in him.**

Do you believe and trust in his Son Jesus Christ,
who redeemed mankind?

Answer **I believe and trust in him.**

Do you believe and trust in his Holy Spirit,
who gives life to the people of God?

Answer **I believe and trust in him.**

54 The priest turns to the congregation and says

This is the faith of the Church.

All **This is our faith.**
We believe and trust in one God,
Father, Son, and Holy Spirit.

55 The parents and godparents being present with each child,
the priest baptizes *him*. He dips *him* in the water or pours
water on *him*, addressing *him* by name.

N, I baptize you in the name of the Father,
and of the Son, and of the Holy Spirit.

And each one of his sponsors answers

Amen.

56 The priest makes THE SIGN OF THE CROSS on the
forehead of each child if he has not already done so. The
appropriate words are printed at section 49.

57   The priest or other person may give to a parent or godparent
     for each child A LIGHTED CANDLE, saying to each

                   Receive this light.

And when a candle has been given to each one, he says

                   This is to show that you have passed
                   from darkness to light.
All   **Shine as a light in the world**
                   to the glory of God the Father.

THE WELCOME

58   The priest and the congregation, representing the whole
     Church, welcome the newly baptized.

     Priest   God has received you by baptism into
                   his Church.
     All   **We welcome you into the Lord's Family.**
                   We are members together of the body of Christ;
                   we are children of the same heavenly Father;
                   we are inheritors together of the kingdom
                   of God.
                   We welcome you.

THE PRAYERS

59   The prayers that follow are omitted when Baptism
     is administered at Holy Communion; and may be
     omitted when Baptism is administered at Morning or
     Evening Prayer.

     Priest   Lord God our Father, maker of heaven and
                   earth, we thank you that by your Holy Spirit
                   these children have been born again into new life,
                   adopted for your own, and received into the
                   fellowship of your Church:
                   grant that *they* may grow in the faith
                   into which *they have* been baptized,
                   that *they* may profess it for *themselves*

when *they come* to be confirmed,
and that all things belonging to the Spirit
may live and grow in *them*. **Amen.**

60   Priest   Heavenly Father, we pray for the parents of *these children*; give them the spirit of wisdom and love, that their *homes* may reflect the joy of your eternal kingdom. **Amen.**

61   Priest   Almighty God, we thank you for our fellowship in the household of faith with all those who have been baptized in your name. Keep us faithful to our baptism, and so make us ready for that day when the whole creation shall be made perfect in your Son, our Saviour Jesus Christ. **Amen.**

62   Priest   Jesus taught us to call God our Father, and so in faith and trust we say

       All   **Our Father in heaven,**
hallowed be your name,
your kingdom come,
your will be done,
on earth as in heaven.
Give us today our daily bread.
Forgive us our sins
as we forgive those who sin against us.
Lead us not into temptation
but deliver us from evil.

For the kingdom, the power, and the glory
are yours
now and for ever. Amen.

63   Priest   The grace of our Lord Jesus Christ, and the love of God, and the fellowship of the Holy Spirit be with us all evermore. **Amen.**

The Baptism of Children at Holy Communion

Section numbers refer to Holy Communion Rite A, but the corresponding sections of Holy Communion Rite B may be used in place of these.

Order	Service	Section
Seasonal Sentence	Holy Communion	1
Preparation	Holy Communion	2-11
Ministry of the Word	Holy Communion	12-18
Duties of Parents and Godparents	Baptism	42, 43
(Ministry of the Word	Baptism	44-46 optional)
Decision	Baptism	47-51
Baptism	Baptism	52-57
The Welcome	Baptism	58

The service then follows the Holy Communion service from the Peace (section 30).

These special forms are used.

SENTENCE

For anyone who is in Christ, there is a new creation; the old order has gone, and a new order has already begun.
2 Corinthians 5.17

PROPER PREFACE

And now we give you thanks because through baptism we have been buried with Christ so that we may rise with him to the new life.

POSTCOMMUNION SENTENCE

Through faith you are all the children of God in union with Christ Jesus. Baptized into union with him, you have all put on Christ as a garment. *Galatians 3.26, 27*

The Baptism of Children at Morning or Evening Prayer

The service follows this order.

1   Morning or Evening Prayer, to the end of the second reading.

2   The Baptism of Children:
The Duties of Parents and Godparents, sections 42, 43.
The Ministry of the Word, sections 44-46 (optional).
The Decision, sections 47-51.
The Baptism, sections 52-57.
The Welcome, section 58.
The Prayers, sections 59-61 (optional).

3   Morning or Evening Prayer, from the canticle after the second reading to the end of the service.

4   At the end of the service the prayers in The Baptism of Children, sections 59-61, may be said.

When it is appropriate, the service of Morning Prayer or Evening Prayer may be abbreviated.

The Confirmation
of those already baptized

NOTES

1 **Sermon** A sermon may be preached after the last reading in the Ministry of the Word, or at some other point in the service at the Bishop's discretion.

2 **Anointing with Oil** At section 80 the Bishop may anoint candidates with oil which he has previously blessed for this purpose.

3 **Delegation by the Bishop** Where it is prescribed that anything is to be said or done by the Bishop, he may delegate it to other ministers; but only the Bishop is to confirm (sections 78-80).

4 **Readings** The Bishop may direct readings to be used other than those appointed in this order, subject to the provisions of Rule 1b in the *Rules to Order the Service*.

5 **The Renewal of Baptismal Vows** At the discretion of the Bishop, the renewal of baptismal vows by members of the congregation may take place after section 74 instead of after section 82.

6 **Hymns** If occasion requires, hymns may be sung at points other than those which are indicated in this order.

Confirmation with Holy Communion

THE PREPARATION

64 At the entry of the ministers this, or another APPROPRIATE
SENTENCE, may be used:

> The Lord is my strength and my song,
> and has become my salvation. *Psalm 118.14*

and A HYMN, A CANTICLE, or A PSALM may be sung.

65 **Bishop**   The Lord be with you
All   **and also with you.**

66 If THE PRAYERS OF PENITENCE (Holy Communion Rite A
sections 5-8) are to be used, they follow here.

67 **Bishop**   Heavenly Father,
by the power of your Holy Spirit
you give to your faithful people
new life in the water of baptism.
Guide and strengthen us by that same Spirit,
that we who are born again
may serve you in faith and love,
and grow into the full stature of your Son
  Jesus Christ,
who is alive and reigns with you and the
  Holy Spirit,
one God now and for ever. **Amen.**

THE MINISTRY OF THE WORD

68 **Sit**
If AN OLD TESTAMENT READING is to be read, one of the
following may be chosen (see pp. 265-268).

Joshua 24.14-24   Jeremiah 31.31-34
Ezekiel 36.25a, 26-28

At the end the reader may say

This is the word of the Lord.
All **Thanks be to God.**

Silence may be kept.

69 A PSALM or A HYMN may be sung.

70 If A NEW TESTAMENT READING is to be read, one of the
following may be chosen (see pp. 269-271).

1 Corinthians 12.12, 13 Galatians 5.16-25
1 Peter 2.4-10

At the end the reader may say

This is the word of the Lord.
All **Thanks be to God.**

Silence may be kept.

71 A CANTICLE or A HYMN may be sung.

72 **Stand**
THE GOSPEL. When it is announced

All **Glory to Christ our Saviour.**

One of the following may be chosen (see pp. 271-273).

Matthew 16.24-27 Mark 1.14-20
Luke 24.45-end John 14.15-18

At the end the reader may say

This is the Gospel of Christ.
All **Praise to Christ our Lord.**

Silence may be kept.

73 **Sit**
THE SERMON

At the end, silence may be kept.

74 A HYMN may be sung.

THE RENEWAL OF BAPTISMAL VOWS

75 The candidates stand before the Bishop; he says

> You have come here to be confirmed. You stand in the presence of God and his Church. With your own mouth and from your own heart you must declare your allegiance to Christ and your rejection of all that is evil. Therefore I ask these questions:

> Do you turn to Christ?

Answer **I turn to Christ.**

> Do you repent of your sins?

Answer **I repent of my sins.**

> Do you renounce evil?

Answer **I renounce evil.**

76 Then the Bishop says

> You must now declare before God and his Church that you accept the Christian faith into which you were baptized, and in which you will live and grow.

> Do you believe and trust in God the Father, who made the world?

Answer **I believe and trust in him.**

> Do you believe and trust in his Son Jesus Christ, who redeemed mankind?

Answer **I believe and trust in him.**

Do you believe and trust in his Holy Spirit,
who gives life to the people of God?
Answer **I believe and trust in him.**

The Bishop turns to the congregation and says

All
This is the faith of the Church.
This is our faith.
We believe and trust in one God,
Father, Son, and Holy Spirit.

THE CONFIRMATION

78 The Bishop stands before those to be confirmed and says

All
Our help is in the name of the Lord
who has made heaven and earth.

All
Blessed be the name of the Lord
now and for ever. Amen.

79 The Bishop stretches out his hands towards them and says

Almighty and everliving God,
you have given your *servants* new birth
in baptism by water and the Spirit,
and have forgiven *them* all *their* sins.
Let your Holy Spirit rest upon *them*:
the Spirit of wisdom and understanding;
the Spirit of counsel and inward strength;
the Spirit of knowledge and true godliness;
and let *their* delight be in the fear of the Lord.
Amen.

80 The Bishop lays his hand on the head of each candidate,
saying

Confirm, O Lord, your servant *N* with your
Holy Spirit.

and each one answers

Amen.

81 After confirmation, the Bishop invites the people to join with him and say

> **Defend, O Lord, your servants with your**
> **heavenly grace,**
> **that they may continue yours for ever,**
> **and daily increase in your Holy Spirit**
> **more and more,**
> **until they come to your everlasting**
> **kingdom. Amen.**

82 If some members of the congregation are now to make a renewal of their baptismal vows, sections 94-98 may be used here.

THE COMMUNION

83 The Bishop resumes the Communion Service at THE PEACE (Holy Communion Rite A, sections 30, 31; Rite B, sections 24, 25).

84 These special forms are used.

PROPER PREFACE
And now we give you thanks because by the Holy Spirit you lead us into all truth and give us power to preach your gospel to the nations, and to serve you as a royal priesthood.

POSTCOMMUNION SENTENCE
God who raised Christ Jesus from the dead will also give life to your mortal bodies through his Spirit who dwells in you. *Romans 8.11*

85 The Bishop says both THE BLESSING and THE DISMISSAL (Holy Communion Rite A, sections 54-56; Rite B, sections 49, 50).

Confirmation without Holy Communion

The service follows the order to be used at Holy Communion (sections 64-81 above). One, two, or three readings may be used as the Bishop directs. After section 81, the Bishop says one or more of these prayers.

86 For those who have now been confirmed

> Heavenly Father, we pray for your *servants* upon whom we have now laid our hands, after the example of the apostles, to assure *them* by this sign of your favour towards *them*. May your fatherly hand ever be over *them*, your Holy Spirit ever be with *them*. Strengthen *them* continually with the Body and Blood of your Son, and so lead *them* in the knowledge and obedience of your word that in the end *they* may obtain everlasting life; through Jesus Christ our Lord. **Amen.**

87 For all Christian people

> Almighty Father, we thank you for our fellowship in the household of faith with all those who have been baptized in your name. Keep us faithful to our baptism, and so make us ready for that day when the whole creation shall be made perfect in your Son, our Saviour Jesus Christ. **Amen.**

88 For the Church's witness

> Almighty God, whose Holy Spirit equips the Church with a rich variety of gifts; grant that we may use them to bear witness to Christ by lives built on faith and love. Make us ready to live his

Gospel and eager to do his will, that we may
share with all your Church in the joys of eternal
life; through Jesus Christ our Lord. **Amen.**

89   **Lord, make us instruments of your peace.**
Where there is hatred, let us sow love;
where there is injury, let there be pardon;
where there is discord, union;
where there is doubt, faith;
where there is despair, hope;
where there is darkness, light;
where there is sadness, joy;
for your mercy and for your truth's sake. Amen.

90   **Lord Jesus Christ, we thank you**
for all the benefits you have won for us,
for all the pains and insults you have borne
    for us.
Most merciful redeemer,
friend and brother,
may we know you more clearly,
love you more dearly,
and follow you more nearly,
day by day. Amen.

91   **Eternal God,**
you have declared in Christ
the completion of your purpose of love.
May we live by faith, walk in hope,
and be renewed in love,
until the world reflects your glory,
and you are all in all.
Even so; come, Lord Jesus. Amen.

92   Then all say THE LORD'S PRAYER.

93   The Bishop ends the service with A BLESSING.

Confirmation at
Morning or Evening Prayer

When the service is used at Morning or Evening Prayer, proper readings may be chosen from those printed on pp. 262-274; and the sentence (section 64) and collect (section 67) may also be used instead of those of the day.

The service follows this order.

1   Morning or Evening Prayer, to the end of the second reading.

2   A sermon may be preached.

3   Confirmation, sections 75-81.

4   Morning or Evening Prayer, from the canticle after the second reading to the end of the service.

5   At the end of the service, prayers from sections 86-91 above may be used.

Psalms and Readings
for Baptism and Confirmation

The following psalms and readings may be used at Holy Communion or at Morning or Evening Prayer.

PSALMS

PSALM 107.1-9

1 **O give thanks to the Lord for** | **he is** | **good:**
  for his loving | **mercy** | **is for** | **ever.**

2 **Let the Lord's re** | **deemed** | **say so:**
  whom he has redeemed from the | **hand** | **of the** | **enemy,**

†3 **and gathered in from every land**
  from the east and | **from the** | **west:**
  from the | **north and** | **from the** | **south.**

4 **Some went astray in the wilderness and** | **in the** | **desert:**
  and found no | **path to · an in** | **habit·ed** | **city;**

5 **they were** | **hungry · and** | **thirsty:**
  and their | **heart** | **fainted · with** | **in them.**

6 **Then they cried to the Lord in** | **their dis** | **tress:**
  and he | **took them** | **out of · their** | **trouble.**

7 **He led them by the** | **right** | **path:**
  till they | **came to · an in** | **habit·ed** | **city.**

8 **Let them thank the** | **Lord · for his** | **goodness:**
  and for the wonders that he | **does · for the** |
  children · of | **men;**

9 **for he** | **satisfies · the** | **thirsty:**
  and fills the | **hungry · with** | **good** | **things.**

Glory to the Father and | **to the** | **Son:**
  and | **to the** | **Holy** | **Spirit;**
as it was in the be | **ginning is** | **now:**
  and shall be for | **ever.** | **A** | **men.**

PSALM 121

1 I lift up my ˈ eyes · to the ˈ hills:
   but ˈ where · shall I ˈ find ˈ help?

2 My help ˈ comes · from the ˈ Lord:
   who has ˈ made ˈ heaven · and ˈ earth.

3 He will not suffer your ˈ foot to ˈ stumble:
   and he who watches ˈ over · you ˈ will not ˈ sleep.

4 Be sure he who has ˈ charge of ˈ Israel:
   will ˈ neither ˈ slumber · nor ˈ sleep.

5 The Lord himˈself is · your ˈ keeper:
   the Lord is your defence upˈon your ˈ right ˈ hand;

6 the sun shall not ˈ strike you · by ˈ day:
   nor ˈ shall the ˈ moon by ˈ night.

7 The Lord will defend you from ˈ all ˈ evil:
   it is ˈ he · who will ˈ guard your ˈ life.

8 The Lord will defend your going out and your ˈ
   coming ˈ in:
   from this time ˈ forward · for ˈ everˈmore.

   Glory to the Father and ˈ to the ˈ Son:
   and ˈ to the ˈ Holy ˈ Spirit;
   as it was in the beˈginning is ˈ now:
   and shall be for ˈ ever. ˈ Aˈmen.

OTHER PSALMS which may be used:

18.32-39; 25.1-10; 27.1-8; 34.1-8; 97.9-end.

OLD TESTAMENT READINGS

Genesis 7.17-23 (or 7.17—8.5) RSV
The flood continued forty days upon the earth; and the
waters increased, and bore up the ark, and it rose high above
the earth. The waters prevailed and increased greatly upon
the earth; and the ark floated on the face of the waters. And
the waters prevailed so mightily upon the earth that all the
high mountains under the whole heaven were covered; the
waters prevailed above the mountains, covering them

fifteen cubits deep. And all flesh died that moved upon the earth, birds, cattle, beasts, all swarming creatures that swarm upon the earth, and every man; everything on the dry land in whose nostrils was the breath of life died. He blotted out every living thing that was upon the face of the ground, man and animals and creeping things and birds of the air; they were blotted out from the earth. Only Noah was left, and those that were with him in the ark.

(And the waters prevailed upon the earth a hundred and fifty days. But God remembered Noah and all the beasts and all the cattle that were with him in the ark. And God made a wind blow over the earth, and the waters subsided; the fountains of the deep and the windows of the heavens were closed, the rain from the heavens was restrained, and the waters receded from the earth continually. At the end of a hundred and fifty days the waters had abated; and in the seventh month, on the seventeenth day of the month, the ark came to rest upon the mountains of Ararat. And the waters continued to abate until the tenth month; in the tenth month, on the first day of the month, the tops of the mountains were seen.)

Exodus 14.19-31 RSV
The angel of God who went before the host of Israel moved and went behind them; and the pillar of cloud moved from before them and stood behind them, coming between the host of Egypt and the host of Israel. And there was the cloud and the darkness; and the night passed without one coming near the other all night.

Then Moses stretched out his hand over the sea; and the Lord drove the sea back by a strong east wind all night, and made the sea dry land, and the waters were divided. And the people of Israel went into the midst of the sea on dry ground, the waters being a wall to them on their right hand and on their left. The Egyptians pursued, and went in after them into the midst of the sea, all Pharaoh's horses, his chariots, and his horsemen. And in the morning watch the Lord in the pillar of fire and of cloud looked down upon the host of the Egyptians, and discomfited the host of the Egyptians, clogging their chariot wheels so that they drove heavily; and the Egyptians said, 'Let us flee from before Israel; for the Lord fights for them against the Egyptians.'

Then the Lord said to Moses, 'Stretch out your hand over the sea, that the water may come back upon the Egyptians, upon their chariots, and upon their horsemen.' So Moses stretched forth his hand over the sea, and the sea returned to its wonted flow when the morning appeared; and the Egyptians fled into it, and the Lord routed the Egyptians in the midst of the sea. The waters returned and covered the chariots and the horsemen and all the host of Pharaoh that had followed them into the sea; not so much as one of them remained. But the people of Israel walked on dry ground through the sea, the waters being a wall to them on their right hand and on their left.

Thus the Lord saved Israel that day from the hand of the Egyptians; and Israel saw the Egyptians dead upon the seashore. And Israel saw the great work which the Lord did against the Egyptians, and the people feared the Lord; and they believed in the Lord and in his servant Moses.

Deuteronomy 30.15-20 RSV
Moses said to the people, 'See, I have set before you this day life and good, death and evil. If you obey the commandments of the Lord your God which I command you this day, by loving the Lord your God, by walking in his ways, and by keeping his commandments and his statutes and his ordinances, then you shall live and multiply, and the Lord your God will bless you in the land which you are entering to take possession of it. But if your heart turns away, and you will not hear, but are drawn away to worship other gods and serve them, I declare to you this day, that you shall perish; you shall not live long in the land which you are going over the Jordan to enter and possess. I call heaven and earth to witness against you this day, that I have set before you life and death, blessing and curse; therefore choose life, that you and your descendants may live, loving the Lord your God, obeying his voice and cleaving to him; for that means life to you and length of days, that you may dwell in the land which the Lord swore to your fathers, to Abraham, to Isaac, and to Jacob, to give them.'

Joshua 24.14-24 NEB

Joshua said to the people, 'Hold the Lord in awe then, and worship him in loyalty and truth. Banish the gods whom your fathers worshipped beside the Euphrates and in Egypt, and worship the Lord. But if it does not please you to worship the Lord, choose here and now whom you will worship: the gods whom your forefathers worshipped beside the Euphrates, or the gods of the Amorites in whose land you are living. But I and my family, we will worship the Lord.' The people answered, 'God forbid that we should forsake the Lord to worship other gods, for it was the Lord our God who brought us and our fathers up from Egypt, that land of slavery; it was he who displayed those great signs before our eyes and guarded us on all our wanderings among the many peoples through whose lands we passed. The Lord drove out before us the Amorites and all the peoples who lived in that country. We too will worship the Lord; he is our God.' Joshua answered the people, 'You cannot worship the Lord. He is a holy God, a jealous God, and he will not forgive your rebellion and your sins. If you forsake the Lord and worship foreign gods, he will turn and bring adversity upon you and, although he once brought you prosperity, he will make an end of you.' The people said to Joshua, 'No; we will worship the Lord.' He said to them, 'You are witnesses against yourselves that you have chosen the Lord and will worship him.' 'Yes,' they answered, 'we are witnesses.' He said to them, 'Then here and now banish the foreign gods that are among you, and turn your hearts to the Lord the God of Israel.' The people said to Joshua, 'The Lord our God we will worship and his voice we will obey.'

2 Kings 5.1-15a NEB

Naaman, commander of the king of Aram's army, was a great man highly esteemed by his master, because by his means the Lord had given victory to Aram; but he was a leper. On one of their raids the Aramaeans brought back as a captive from the land of Israel a little girl, who became a servant to Naaman's wife. She said to her mistress, 'If only my master could meet the prophet who lives in Samaria, he would get rid of the disease for him.' Naaman went in and reported to his master word for word what the girl from the land of Israel had said. 'Very well, you may go,' said the king of Aram, 'and I will send a letter to the king of Israel.' So Naaman went, taking with him ten talents of silver, six thousand shekels of gold, and ten changes of clothing. He delivered the letter to the king of Israel, which read thus: 'This letter is to inform you that I am sending to you my servant Naaman, and I beg you to rid him of his disease.' When the king of Israel read the letter, he rent his clothes and said, 'Am I a god to kill and to make alive, that this fellow sends to me to cure a man of his disease? Surely you must see that he is picking a quarrel with me.' When Elisha, the man of God, heard how the king of Israel had rent his clothes, he sent to him saying, 'Why did you rend your clothes? Let the man come to me, and he will know that there is a prophet in Israel.' So Naaman came with his horses and chariots and stood at the entrance to Elisha's house. Elisha sent out a messenger to say to him, 'If you will go and wash seven times in the Jordan, your flesh will be restored and you will be clean.' Naaman was furious and went away, saying, 'I thought he would at least have come out and stood, and invoked the Lord his God by name, waved his hand over the place and so rid me of the disease. Are not Abana and Pharpar, rivers of Damascus, better than all the waters of Israel? Can I not wash in them and be clean?' So he turned and went off in a rage. But his servants came up to him and said, 'If the prophet had bidden you do something difficult, would you not do it? How much more then, if he tells you to wash and be clean?' So he went down and dipped himself in the Jordan seven times as the man of God had told him, and his flesh was restored as a little child's, and he was clean.

Then he and his retinue went back to the man of God and stood before him; and he said, 'Now I know that there is no god anywhere on earth except in Israel.'

Isaiah 43.1-3a, 6b-7 NEB
But now this is the word of the Lord,
the word of your creator, O Jacob,
of him who fashioned you, Israel:

Have no fear; for I have paid your ransom;
I have called you by name and you are my own.
When you pass through deep waters, I am with you,
when you pass through rivers,
they will not sweep you away;
walk through fire and you will not be scorched,
through flames and they will not burn you.
For I am the Lord your God,
the Holy One of Israel, your deliverer.

Bring my sons and daughters from afar,
bring them from the ends of the earth;
bring every one who is called by my name,
all of whom I have created, whom I have formed,
all whom I have made for my glory.

Isaiah 44.1-5 NEB
Hear me now, Jacob my servant,
hear me, my chosen Israel.
Thus says the Lord your maker,
your helper, who fashioned you from birth:
have no fear, Jacob my servant,
Jeshurun whom I have chosen,
for I will pour down rain on a thirsty land,
showers on the dry ground.
I will pour out my spirit on your offspring
and my blessing on your children.
They shall spring up like a green tamarisk,
like poplars by a flowing stream.
This man shall say, 'I am the Lord's man',
that one shall call himself a son of Jacob,
another shall write the Lord's name on his hand
and shall add the name of Israel to his own.

Jeremiah 31.31-34 NEB
The time is coming, says the Lord, when I will make a new
covenant with Israel and Judah. It will not be like the
covenant I made with their forefathers when I took them by
the hand and led them out of Egypt. Although they broke
my covenant, I was patient with them, says the Lord. But
this is the covenant which I will make with Israel after those

days, says the Lord; I will set my law within them and write it on their hearts; I will become their God and they shall become my people. No longer need they teach one another to know the Lord; all of them, high and low alike, shall know me, says the Lord, for I will forgive their wrongdoing and remember their sin no more.

Ezekiel 36.25a, 26-28 NEB
The Lord God says, I will sprinkle clean water over you, and you shall be cleansed from all that defiles you. I will give you a new heart and put a new spirit within you; I will take the heart of stone from your body and give you a heart of flesh. I will put my spirit into you and make you conform to my statutes, keep my laws and live by them. You shall live in the land which I gave to your ancestors; you shall become my people, and I will become your God.

NEW TESTAMENT READINGS

Acts 16.25-34 NEB
About midnight Paul and Silas, at their prayers, were singing praises to God, and the other prisoners were listening, when suddenly there was such a violent earthquake that the foundations of the jail were shaken; all the doors burst open and all the prisoners found their fetters unfastened. The jailer woke up to see the prison doors wide open, and assuming that the prisoners had escaped, drew his sword intending to kill himself. But Paul shouted, 'Do yourself no harm; we are all here.' The jailer called for lights, rushed in and threw himself down before Paul and Silas, trembling with fear. He then escorted them out and said, 'Masters, what must I do to be saved?' They said, 'Put your trust in the Lord Jesus, and you will be saved, you and your household.' Then they spoke the word of the Lord to him and to everyone in his house. At that late hour of the night he took them and washed their wounds; and immediately afterwards he and his whole family were baptized. He brought them into his house, set out a meal, and rejoiced with his whole household in his new-found faith in God.

Romans 6.3-11 NEB

Have you forgotten that when we were baptized into union with Christ Jesus we were baptized into his death? By baptism we were buried with him, and lay dead, in order that, as Christ was raised from the dead in the splendour of the Father, so also we might set our feet upon the new path of life.

For if we have become incorporate with him in a death like his, we shall also be one with him in a resurrection like his. We know that the man we once were has been crucified with Christ, for the destruction of the sinful self, so that we may no longer be the slaves of sin, since a dead man is no longer answerable for his sin. But if we thus died with Christ, we believe that we shall also come to life with him. We know that Christ, once raised from the dead, is never to die again: he is no longer under the dominion of death. For in dying as he died, he died to sin, once for all, and in living as he lives, he lives to God. In the same way you must regard yourselves as dead to sin and alive to God, in union with Christ Jesus.

Romans 8.11-17 RSV

If the Spirit of him who raised Jesus from the dead dwells in you, he who raised Christ Jesus from the dead will give life to your mortal bodies also through his Spirit which dwells in you.

So then, brethren, we are debtors, not to the flesh, to live according to the flesh—for if you live according to the flesh you will die, but if by the Spirit, you put to death the deeds of the body you will live. For all who are led by the Spirit of God are sons of God. For you did not receive the spirit of slavery to fall back into fear, but you have received the spirit of sonship. When we cry 'Abba! Father!' it is the Spirit himself bearing witness with our spirit that we are children of God, and if children, then heirs, heirs of God and fellow heirs with Christ, provided we suffer with him in order that we may also be glorified with him.

1 Corinthians 12.12, 13 NEB

Christ is like a single body with its many limbs and organs, which, many as they are, together make up one body. For indeed we were all brought into one body by baptism, in the one Spirit, whether we are Jews or Greeks, whether slaves or free men, and that one Holy Spirit was poured out for all of us to drink.

Galatians 5.16-25 RSV
Walk by the Spirit, and do not gratify the desires of the flesh. For the desires of the flesh are against the Spirit, and the desires of the Spirit are against the flesh; for these are opposed to each other, to prevent you from doing what you would. But if you are led by the Spirit you are not under the law. Now the works of the flesh are plain: immorality, impurity, licentiousness, idolatry, sorcery, enmity, strife, jealousy, anger, selfishness, dissension, party spirit, envy, drunkenness, carousing, and the like. I warn you, as I warned you before, that those who do such things shall not inherit the kingdom of God. But the fruit of the Spirit is love, joy, peace, patience, kindness, goodness, faithfulness, gentleness, self-control; against such there is no law. And those who belong to Christ Jesus have crucified the flesh with its passions and desires. If we live by the Spirit, let us also walk by the Spirit.

1 Peter 2.4-10 NEB
Come to Christ, our living Stone—the stone rejected by men but choice and precious in the sight of God. Come, and let yourselves be built, as living stones, into a spiritual temple; become a holy priesthood, to offer spiritual sacrifices acceptable to God through Jesus Christ. For it stands written:

'I lay in Zion a choice corner-stone of great worth.
The man who has faith in it will not be put to shame.'

The great worth of which it speaks is for you who have faith. For those who have no faith, the stone which the builders rejected has become not only the corner-stone, but also 'a stone to trip over, a rock to stumble against'. They fall when they disbelieve the Word. Such was their appointed lot!

But you are a chosen race, a royal priesthood, a dedicated nation, and a people claimed by God for his own, to proclaim the triumphs of him who has called you out of darkness into his marvellous light. You are now the people of God, who once were not his people; outside his mercy once, you have now received his mercy.

GOSPELS

Matthew 16.24-27 JB
Jesus said to his disciples, 'If anyone wants to be a follower of mine, let him renounce himself and take up his cross and follow me. For anyone who wants to save his life will lose it; but anyone who loses his life for my sake will find it. What, then, will a man gain if he wins the whole world and ruins his life? Or what has a man to offer in exchange for his life?

For the Son of Man is going to come in the glory of his Father with his angels, and, when he does, he will reward each one according to his behaviour.'

Matthew 28.16-20 JB
The eleven disciples set out for Galilee, to the mountain where Jesus had arranged to meet them. When they saw him they fell down before him, though some hesitated. Jesus came up and spoke to them. He said, 'All authority in heaven and on earth has been given to me. Go, therefore, make disciples of all the nations; baptize them in the name of the Father and of the Son and of the Holy Spirit, and teach them to observe all the commands I gave you. And know that I am with you always; yes, to the end of time.'

Mark 1.1-11 NEB
Here begins the Gospel of Jesus Christ the Son of God. In the prophet Isaiah it stands written: 'Here is my herald whom I send on ahead of you, and he will prepare your way. A voice crying aloud in the wilderness, "Prepare a way for the Lord; clear a straight path for him."' And so it was that John the Baptist appeared in the wilderness proclaiming a baptism in token of repentance, for the forgiveness of sins; and they flocked to him from the whole Judaean country-side and the city of Jerusalem, and were baptized by him in the River Jordan, confessing their sins.

John was dressed in a rough coat of camel's hair, with a leather belt round his waist, and he fed on locusts and wild honey. His proclamation ran: 'After me comes one who is mightier than I. I am not fit to unfasten his shoes. I have baptized you with water; he will baptize you with the Holy Spirit.'

It happened at this time that Jesus came from Nazareth in Galilee and was baptized in the Jordan by John. At the moment when he came up out of the water, he saw the heavens torn open and the Spirit, like a dove, descending upon him. And a voice spoke from heaven: 'Thou art my Son, my Beloved; on thee my favour rests.'

Mark 1.14-20 NEB
After John had been arrested, Jesus came into Galilee proclaiming the Gospel of God: 'The time has come; the kingdom of God is upon you; repent, and believe the Gospel.'

Jesus was walking by the Sea of Galilee when he saw Simon and his brother Andrew on the lake at work with a casting-net; for they were fishermen. Jesus said to them, 'Come with me, and I will make you fishers of men.' And at once they left their nets and followed him.

When he had gone a little further he saw James son of Zebedee and his brother John, who were in the boat overhauling their nets. He called them; and, leaving their father Zebedee in the boat with the hired men, they went off to follow him.

Luke 24.45-end JB
Jesus opened the disciples' minds to understand the scriptures, and he said to them, 'So you see how it is written that the Christ would suffer and on the third day rise from the dead, and that, in his name, repentance for the forgiveness of sins would be preached to all the nations, beginning from Jerusalem. You are witnesses to this. And now I am sending down to you what the Father has promised. Stay in the city then, until you are clothed with the power from on high.'

Then he took them out as far as the outskirts of Bethany, and lifting up his hands he blessed them. Now as he blessed them, he withdrew from them and was carried up to heaven. They worshipped him and then went back to Jerusalem full of joy; and they were continually in the Temple praising God.

John 3.1-8 NEB
There was one of the Pharisees named Nicodemus, a member of the Jewish Council, who came to Jesus by night. 'Rabbi,' he said, 'we know that you are a teacher sent by God; no one could perform these signs of yours unless God were with him.' Jesus answered, 'In truth, in very truth I tell you, unless a man has been born over again he cannot see the kingdom of God.' 'But how is it possible', said Nicodemus, 'for a man to be born when he is old? Can he enter his mother's womb a second time and be born?' Jesus answered, 'In truth I tell you, no one can enter the kingdom of God without being born from water and spirit. Flesh can give birth only to flesh; it is spirit that gives birth to spirit. You ought not to be astonished, then, when I tell you that you must be born over again. The wind blows where it wills; you hear the sound of it, but you do not know where it comes from, or where it is going. So with everyone who is born from spirit.'

John 14.15-18 JB
Jesus said to his disciples,
'If you love me you will keep my commandments.
I shall ask the Father,
and he will give you another Advocate
to be with you for ever,
that Spirit of truth
whom the world can never receive
since it neither sees nor knows him;
but you know him,
because he is with you, he is in you.
I will not leave you orphans;
I will come back to you.'

John 15.1-11 JB

Jesus said,
'I am the true vine,
and my Father is the vinedresser.
Every branch in me that bears no fruit
he cuts away,
and every branch that does bear fruit he prunes
to make it bear even more.
You are pruned already,
by means of the word that I have spoken to you.
Make your home in me, as I make mine in you.
As a branch cannot bear fruit all by itself,
but must remain part of the vine,
neither can you unless you remain in me.
I am the vine,
you are the branches.
Whoever remains in me, with me in him,
bears fruit in plenty;
for cut off from me you can do nothing.
Anyone who does not remain in me
is like a branch that has been thrown away
—he withers;
these branches are collected and thrown on the fire,
and they are burnt.
If you remain in me
and my words remain in you,
you may ask what you will
and you shall get it.
It is to the glory of my Father that you should bear
much fruit,
and then you will be my disciples.
As the Father has loved me,
so I have loved you.
Remain in my love.
If you keep my commandments
you will remain in my love,
just as I have kept my Father's commandments
and remain in his love.
I have told you this
so that my own joy may be in you
and your joy be complete.'

The Renewal of Baptismal Vows on Various Occasions

NOTES

1   This order of service may be used at Easter, at New Year, and on other suitable occasions, and sections 94-98 may be used in conjunction with Baptism, Confirmation, and Holy Communion after section 10 or at section 28, or with Confirmation and Holy Communion after section 74 or at section 82.

2   When this order is used at Holy Communion, it may be used after the Sermon, and the Creed may be omitted. The Prayers of Intercession and of Penitence may be omitted.

3   When this order is used at Morning or Evening Prayer, it may be used after a Sermon, either after the Second Reading or at the end of the service.

4   The collect, psalms, and readings of the service of Baptism and Confirmation may be used instead of those appointed for the day, subject to the provisions of Rule 1b in the *Rules to Order the Service*.

The Renewal of Baptismal Vows on Various Occasions

94   At Easter the minister says

As we celebrate again the resurrection of our Lord Jesus Christ from the dead, we remember that through the paschal mystery we have died and been buried with him in baptism, so that we may rise with him to a new life within the family of his Church. Now that we have completed our observance of Lent, we renew the promises made at our baptism, affirming our allegiance to Christ, and our rejection of all that is evil.

95   On other occasions the minister says

In our baptism we died with Christ and were buried with him, so that we might rise with him to a new life within the family of his Church. Today we renew the promises made at our baptism, affirming our allegiance to Christ, and our rejection of all that is evil.

96   Therefore I ask these questions

Do you turn to Christ?
Answer   **I turn to Christ.**

Do you repent of your sins?
Answer   **I repent of my sins.**

Do you renounce evil?
Answer   **I renounce evil.**

97   The minister says

And now I ask you to make the profession of Christian faith into which you were baptized, and in which you live and grow.

Do you believe and trust in God the Father,
who made the world?

Answer   **I believe and trust in him.**

Do you believe and trust in his Son Jesus Christ,
who redeemed mankind?

Answer   **I believe and trust in him.**

Do you believe and trust in his Holy Spirit,
who gives life to the people of God?

Answer   **I believe and trust in him.**

98   The minister says

This is the faith of the Church.

All   **This is our faith.
We believe and trust in one God,
Father, Son and Holy Spirit.**

99   The minister says one or more of these prayers.

100   Almighty God, we thank you for our fellowship
in the household of faith with all those who have
been baptized in your name. Keep us faithful to
our baptism, and so make us ready for that day
when the whole creation shall be made perfect
in your Son, our Saviour Jesus Christ. **Amen.**

101   Almighty God, whose Holy Spirit equips the
Church with a rich variety of gifts; grant that we
may use them to bear witness to Christ by lives
built on faith and love. Make us ready to live his
Gospel and eager to do his will, that we may
share with all your Church in the joys of eternal
life; through Jesus Christ our Lord. **Amen.**

102   **Lord, make us instruments of your peace.
Where there is hatred, let us sow love;
where there is injury, let there be pardon;
where there is discord, union;**

where there is doubt, faith;
where there is despair, hope;
where there is darkness, light;
where there is sadness, joy;
for your mercy and for your truth's sake. Amen.

103   Lord Jesus, we thank you
for all the benefits you have won for us,
for all the pains and insults you have borne
    for us.
Most merciful redeemer,
friend and brother,
may we know you more clearly,
love you more dearly,
and follow you more nearly,
day by day. Amen.

104   Eternal God,
you have declared in Christ
the completion of your purpose of love.
May we live by faith, walk in hope,
and be renewed in love,
until the world reflects your glory,
and you are all in all.
Even so; come, Lord Jesus. Amen.

Conditional Baptism

105   If it is not certain that a person was baptized with water in the name of the Father, and of the Son, and of the Holy Spirit, then the usual service of baptism is used, but the form of words at the baptism (sections 20, 55) shall be

N, if you have not already been baptized, I baptize you in the name of the Father, and of the Son, and of the Holy Spirit. **Amen.**

Emergency Baptism

106   The parents are responsible for requesting emergency baptism for an infant. They should be assured that questions of ultimate salvation or of the provision of a Christian funeral for an infant who dies do not depend upon whether or not *he* had been baptized.

107   In an emergency a lay person may be the minister of baptism, and should subsequently inform those who have the pastoral responsibility for the person so baptized.

108   The minister, having asked the name of the person to be baptized, pours water on *him*, saying

> I baptize you in the name of the Father, and of the Son, and of the Holy Spirit. **Amen.**

He then says at least the Lord's Prayer and ends with this blessing.

> God the Father, God the Son, God the Holy Spirit, bless, preserve, and keep you, this day and evermore.

109   When through the absence of parents, or for some other reason, there is uncertainty as to the name of the person, the baptism can be properly administered without the use of the name (so long as the identity of the person baptized can be duly recorded).

110   If *he* lives, a person so baptized shall afterwards come to church, or be brought to church, and the baptism service is said except that sections 17 and 20 (52 and 55) are omitted and at section 18 (53) the priest says

> You must now declare before God and his Church the Christian faith into which you have been baptized, and in which you will live and grow.

111   In the case of *a child* he says to the parents and godparents

> You must now declare before God and his
> Church the Christian faith into which *this child*
> has been baptized, and in which you will help
> *him* to grow. You must answer for yourselves
> and for *this child*.

The Marriage Service

NOTES

1   **The Banns** The banns are to be published in the church on three Sundays at the time of Divine Service by the officiant in the form set out in the Book of Common Prayer or in the following form: I publish the banns of marriage between *N* of . . . and *N* of . . . This is the first (second) (third) time of asking. If any of you know any reason in law why these persons may not marry each other you are to declare it now.

2   **Hymns and Canticles** These may be used at suitable points during the service. Sections 1, 20, and 23 may be sung if so desired.

3   **Seating** It is recommended that chairs should be provided for the bride and bridegroom during the readings and sermon.

4   **The Readings** At least one reading must be used, either at the beginning of the service (section 4) or after the Marriage (section 22); but readings must not be used at both places. At Holy Communion there are two readings, of which the Gospel must be one. Suggested readings are printed in section 40.

5   **The Giving Away** This ceremony is optional. If the bride is not given away by her father, this may be done by another member of her family, or by a friend representing the family.

6   **The Vows** In sections 11 and 12 the vows A and the vows B are not interchangeable. Either the vows A or the vows B must be used throughout. Before the day of the marriage the priest shall inquire of the couple which form of the vows they have agreed to use.
The couple may read the vows (sections 9-16) or repeat them after the priest.

7 **Prayers** Instead of the additional prayers (sections 31-38), prayers which the couple have written or selected in co-operation with the priest may be used. Silence may be kept; or free prayer may be offered.

8 **Congregational Prayers** Sections 32, 33, 36, and 38 may be said by the congregation if so desired.

The Marriage Service

THE INTRODUCTION

1 **Stand**
The bride and bridegroom stand before the priest.
THIS SENTENCE may be used.

> God is love, and those who live in love live in
> God: and God lives in them. *1 John 4.16*

2 The priest may say

> The Lord be with you
All **and also with you.**

3 Priest   God our Father,
you have taught us through your Son
that love is the fulfilling of the law.
Grant to your servants
that, loving one another,
they may continue in your love
    until their lives' end:
through Jesus Christ our Lord. **Amen.**

4 **Sit**
One or more READINGS may be used (see section 22).
If there are two or three readings, A PSALM (see section 23)
or A HYMN may be sung between them.

5 A SERMON may be preached.

THE MARRIAGE

6   The bride and bridegroom stand before the priest, and the priest says

We have come together in the presence of God, to witness the marriage of N and N, to ask his blessing on them, and to share in their joy. Our Lord Jesus Christ was himself a guest at a wedding in Cana of Galilee, and through his Spirit he is with us now.

The Scriptures teach us that marriage is a gift of God in creation and a means of his grace, a holy mystery in which man and woman become one flesh. It is God's purpose that, as husband and wife give themselves to each other in love throughout their lives, they shall be united in that love as Christ is united with his Church.

Marriage is given, that husband and wife may comfort and help each other, living faithfully together in need and in plenty, in sorrow and in joy. It is given, that with delight and tenderness they may know each other in love, and, through the joy of their bodily union, may strengthen the union of their hearts and lives. It is given, that they may have children and be blessed in caring for them and bringing them up in accordance with God's will, to his praise and glory.

In marriage husband and wife belong to one another, and they begin a new life together in the community. It is a way of life that all should honour; and it must not be undertaken carelessly, lightly, or selfishly, but reverently, responsibly, and after serious thought.

This is the way of life, created and hallowed by God, that N and N are now to begin. They will each give their consent to the other; they will join hands and exchange solemn vows, and in token of this they will give and receive a ring.

Therefore, on this their wedding day we pray with them, that, strengthened and guided by God, they may fulfil his purpose for the whole of their earthly life together.

7   The priest says to the congregation

> But first I am required to ask anyone present
> who knows a reason why these persons may not
> lawfully marry, to declare it now.

8   The priest says to the couple

> The vows you are about to take are to be made in
> the name of God, who is judge of all and who
> knows all the secrets of our hearts: therefore if
> either of you knows a reason why you may not
> lawfully marry, you must declare it now.

9   **Stand**
The priest says to the bridegroom

> N, will you take N to be your wife? Will you love
> her, comfort her, honour and protect her, and,
> forsaking all others, be faithful to her as long as
> you both shall live?

He answers

> I will.

10   The priest says to the bride

> N, will you take N to be your husband? Will you
> love him, comfort him, honour and protect him,
> and, forsaking all others, be faithful to him as
> long as you both shall live?

She answers

> I will.

11   Either A

The priest may receive the bride from the hands of
her father.
The bride and bridegroom face each other.
The bridegroom takes the bride's right hand in his, and says

> I, N, take you, N,
> to be my wife,
> to have and to hold
> from this day forward;
> for better, for worse,
> for richer, for poorer,
> in sickness and in health,
> to love and to cherish,
> till death us do part,
> according to God's holy law;
> and this is my solemn vow.

They loose hands.
The bride takes the bridegroom's right hand in hers,
and says

> I, N, take you, N,
> to be my husband,
> to have and to hold
> from this day forward;
> for better, for worse,
> for richer, for poorer,
> in sickness and in health,
> to love and to cherish,
> till death us do part,
> according to God's holy law;
> and this is my solemn vow.

They loose hands.

The service continues at section 13 on p. 292.

_____

The priest may receive the bride from the hands of her father.
The bride and bridegroom face each other.
The bridegroom takes the bride's right hand in his, and says

> I, *N*, take you, *N*,
> to be my wife,
> to have and to hold
> from this day forward;
> for better, for worse,
> for richer, for poorer,
> in sickness and in health,
> to love, cherish, and worship,
> till death us do part,
> according to God's holy law;
> and this is my solemn vow.

They loose hands.
The bride takes the bridegroom's right hand in hers, and says

> I, *N*, take you, *N*,
> to be my husband,
> to have and to hold
> from this day forward;
> for better, for worse,
> for richer, for poorer,
> in sickness and in health,
> to love, cherish, and obey,
> till death us do part,
> according to God's holy law;
> and this is my solemn vow.

They loose hands.

13   The priest receives the ring(s). He says

> Heavenly Father, by your blessing, let this ring
> be to *N* and *N* a symbol of unending love and
> faithfulness, to remind them of the vow and
> covenant which they have made this day;
> through Jesus Christ our Lord. **Amen.**

14   The bridegroom places the ring on the fourth finger of the
bride's left hand, and holding it there, says

> I give you this ring
> as a sign of our marriage.
> With my body I honour you,
> all that I am I give to you,
> and all that I have I share with you,
> within the love of God,
> Father, Son, and Holy Spirit.

15   If only one ring is used, before they loose hands the
bride says

> I receive this ring
> as a sign of our marriage.
> With my body I honour you,
> all that I am I give to you,
> and all that I have I share with you,
> within the love of God,
> Father, Son, and Holy Spirit.

16   If rings are exchanged, they loose hands and the bride places
a ring on the fourth finger of the bridegroom's left hand, and
holding it there, says

> I give you this ring
> as a sign of our marriage.
> With my body I honour you,
> all that I am I give to you,
> and all that I have I share with you,
> within the love of God,
> Father, Son, and Holy Spirit.

17   The priest addresses the people.

> In the presence of God, and before this
> congregation, N and N have given their consent
> and made their marriage vows to each other.
> They have declared their marriage by the joining
> of hands and by the giving and receiving of a
> ring. I therefore proclaim that they are husband
> and wife.

18   The priest joins their right hands together and says

> That which God has joined together,
> let not man divide.

19   The congregation remain standing.
      The husband and wife kneel, and the priest blesses them.

> God the Father,
> God the Son,
> God the Holy Spirit,
> bless, preserve, and keep you;
> the Lord mercifully grant you the
>   riches of his grace,
> that you may please him both in body and soul,
> and, living together in faith and love,
> may receive the blessings of eternal life. **Amen.**

20   These acclamations may be used.

Priest	Blessed are you, heavenly Father:
All	**You give joy to bridegroom and bride.**
Priest	Blessed are you, Lord Jesus Christ:
All	**You have brought new life to mankind.**
Priest	Blessed are you, Holy Spirit of God:
All	**You bring us together in love.**
Priest	Blessed be Father, Son, and Holy Spirit:
All	**One God, to be praised for ever. Amen.**

21 **Sit**

THE REGISTRATION of the marriage takes place now or at the end of the service.

22 If sections 4 and 5 have been omitted, at least ONE READING is used here, and A SERMON may be preached.

23 **Stand**

One or more of the following PSALMS are used, or A HYMN may be sung.

PSALM 67

1 Let God be gracious to ˈ us and ˈ bless us:
   and make his ˈ face ˈ shine up ˈon us,

2 that your ways may be ˈ known on ˈ earth:
   your liberating ˈ power · a ˈmong all ˈ nations.

3 Let the peoples ˈ praise you · O ˈ God:
   let ˈ all the ˈ peoples ˈ praise you.

4 Let the nations be ˈ glad and ˈ sing:
   for you judge the peoples with integrity
   and govern the ˈ nations · up ˈon ˈ earth.

5 Let the peoples ˈ praise you · O ˈ God:
   let ˈ all the ˈ peoples ˈ praise you.

6 Then the earth will ˈ yield its ˈ fruitfulness:
   and ˈ God our ˈ God will ˈ bless us.

†7 God ˈ shall ˈ bless us:
   and all the ˈ ends · of the ˈ earth will ˈ fear him.

Glory to the Father and ˈ to the ˈ Son:
   and ˈ to the ˈ Holy ˈ Spirit;
as it was in the be ˈginning is ˈ now:
   and shall be for ˈ ever. ˈ A ˈmen.

PSALM 121

1 I lift up my | eyes · to the | hills:
  but | where · shall I | find | help?

2 My help | comes · from the | Lord:
  who has | made | heaven · and | earth.

3 He will not suffer your | foot to | stumble:
  and he who watches | over · you | will not | sleep.

4 Be sure he who has | charge of | Israel:
  will | neither | slumber · nor | sleep.

5 The Lord him | self · is your | keeper:
  the Lord is your defence up | on your | right | hand;

6 the sun shall not | strike you · by | day:
  nor | shall the | moon by | night.

7 The Lord will defend you from | all | evil:
  it is | he · who will | guard your | life.

8 The Lord will defend your going out and your |
  coming | in:
  from this time | forward · for | ever | more.

  Glory to the Father and | to the | Son:
  and | to the | Holy | Spirit;
  as it was in the be | ginning is | now:
  and shall be for | ever. | A | men.

PSALM 128

1 Blessèd is everyone who | fears the | Lord:
  and walks in the | confine | of his | ways.

2 You will eat the | fruit of · your | labours:
  happy shall you | be and | all · shall go | well with you.

3 Your wife with | in your | house:
  shall | be · as a | fruitful | vine;

4 your children a | round your | table:
  like the fresh | shoots | of the | olive.

5   **Behold thus shall the | man be | blessed:**
          who | lives · in the | fear · of the | Lord.

6   **May the Lord so | bless you · from | Zion:**
          that you see Jerusalem in prosperity | ‿
          all the | days of · your | life.

†7   **May you see your | children's | children:**
          and in | Israel | let there · be | peace.

     Glory to the Father and | to the | Son:
          and | to the | Holy | Spirit;
   as it was in the be|ginning is | now:
          and shall be for | ever. | A |men.

THE PRAYERS

24   **Kneel**
The husband and wife kneel before the holy table.

     Priest   Almighty God,
                 you send your Holy Spirit
                 to be the life and light of all your people.
                 Open the hearts of these your children
                     to the riches of his grace,
                 that they may bring forth the fruit of the Spirit
                 in love and joy and peace;
                 through Jesus Christ our Lord. **Amen.**

25   Either or both of these prayers are said.

26   Priest   Heavenly Father,
                 maker of all things,
                 you enable us to share in your work of creation.
                 Bless this couple in the gift and care of children,
                 that their home may be a place of love,
                     security, and truth,
                 and their children grow up
                     to know and love you in your Son
                 Jesus Christ our Lord. **Amen.**

27	Priest	Lord and Saviour Jesus Christ,

27   Priest   Lord and Saviour Jesus Christ,
who shared at Nazareth the life of an
    earthly home:
reign in the home of these your servants
    as Lord and King;
give them grace to minister to others
    as you have ministered to men,
and grant that by deed and word
they may be witnesses of your
    saving love
to those among whom they live;
for the sake of your holy name. **Amen.**

28   Other prayers may be said here (see sections 31-38).

29   Priest   As our Saviour taught us, so we pray.
      All   **Our Father in heaven,**
hallowed be your name,
your kingdom come,
your will be done,
on earth as in heaven.
Give us today our daily bread.
Forgive us our sins
as we forgive those who sin against us.
Lead us not into temptation
but deliver us from evil.

For the kingdom, the power, and the glory
**   are yours**
now and for ever. Amen.

30   The priest blesses the couple and the congregation, saying

           God the Holy Trinity make you strong in faith
and love, defend you on every side, and guide
you in truth and peace; and the blessing of God
almighty, the Father, the Son, and the Holy
Spirit, be among you and remain with you
always. **Amen.**

ADDITIONAL PRAYERS

31   Almighty God, giver of life and love, bless N and
N, whom you have now joined in Christian
marriage. Grant them wisdom and devotion in
their life together, that each may be to the other a
strength in need, a comfort in sorrow, and a
companion in joy. So unite their wills in your
will, and their spirits in your Spirit, that they live
and grow together in love and peace all the days
of their life; through Jesus Christ our Lord.
Amen.

32   Almighty and most merciful Father,
the strength of all who put their trust
     in you:
we pray that, as you have brought N
     and N together by your providence,
so you will enrich them by your grace;
that those vows which they have made
     to one another in your sight,
they may truly and faithfully perform;
through Jesus Christ our Lord. **Amen.**

33   Almighty Father,
you have created all mankind
to glorify you in body and in spirit.
Give these your children joy in
     one another,
as living temples of the Holy Spirit,
and bring them by this joy to know
     and share
in your creative and redeeming love;
through Jesus Christ our Lord. **Amen.**

34   Eternal God, true and loving Father, in holy
marriage you make your servants one. May their
life together witness to your love in this troubled
world; may unity overcome division,
forgiveness heal injury, and joy triumph over
sorrow; through Jesus Christ our Lord. **Amen.**

35   We praise you, Father, that you have made all
things, and hold all things in being. In the
beginning you created the universe, and made
mankind in your own likeness: because it was
not good for them to be alone, you created them
male and female; and in marriage you join man
and woman as one flesh, teaching us that what
you have united may never be divided.

We praise you that you have made this holy
mystery a symbol of the marriage of Christ with
his Church, and an image of your eternal
covenant with your people.

And we pray for your blessing on this man and
this woman, who come before you as partners
and heirs together of your promises. Grant that
this man may love his wife as Christ loves his
bride the Church, giving himself for it and
cherishing it as his own flesh; and grant that this
woman may love her husband and follow the
example of those holy women whose praises are
sung in the Scriptures. Strengthen them with
your grace that they may be witnesses of Christ
to others; let them live to see their children's
children, and bring them at the last to fullness of
life with your saints in the kingdom of heaven;
through Jesus Christ our Lord. **Amen.**

36   Heavenly Father,
we thank you that in our earthly lives
you speak to us of your eternal life:
we pray that through their marriage
N and N
may know you more clearly,
love you more dearly,
and follow you more nearly,
day by day;
through Jesus Christ our Lord. **Amen.**

37   O God of love, look mercifully upon *N* and *N* in
the new life which they begin together this day.
Unite them evermore in your love. Keep them
faithful to the vows they have made one to the
other. Strengthen them with every good gift.
And let your peace be with them, now and
always; for the sake of Jesus Christ our Lord.
Amen.

38   Almighty God, our heavenly Father,
             who gave marriage to be a source of
               blessing to mankind,
           we thank you for the joys of family life.
           May we know your presence and peace
             in our homes;
           fill them with your love,
           and use them for your glory;
           through Jesus Christ our Lord. **Amen.**

The Marriage Service
with Holy Communion

39 When the Marriage Service is combined with the Holy
Communion Service either of the following orders may be
used. Optional parts of the services may be omitted in
accordance with the normal instructions. The readings must
include
(i) either an Old Testament or a New Testament Reading
(ii) a Gospel.
The Eucharistic Prayer should include the Proper Preface
(see section 40).
Section numbers refer to Holy Communion Rite A, but the
corresponding sections of Holy Communion Rite B may be
used in place of these.

First Order	Service	Section
Sentence	Marriage	1
Collect	Marriage	2, 3
Psalm	Marriage	23
Readings	Marriage	4, 40
Sermon	Marriage	5
Marriage	Marriage	6-21
Peace	Holy Communion	30, 31 optional
Taking of the Bread and Wine	Holy Communion	32-35
Eucharistic Prayer	Holy Communion	36-41, 63-65
Proper Preface	Marriage	40
Breaking of the Bread	Holy Communion	42-44
Giving of the Bread and Cup	Holy Communion	45-47, 49, 66
Postcommunion Sentence	Marriage	40
Postcommunion Prayers	Marriage and/or	31-38 optional
	Holy Communion	52, 53
Blessing	Marriage	30
Dismissal	Holy Communion	55 optional

Second Order	Service	Section
Marriage	Marriage	6-21
Sentence	Marriage	1
Collect and Readings	Marriage	2-4
Sermon	Marriage	5

The service then follows the First Order continuing from THE PEACE.

PROPERS

40   INTRODUCTORY SENTENCE

God is love, and those who live in love live in God: and God lives in them. *1 John 4.16*

OLD TESTAMENT READING

Genesis 1.26-28, 31a NEB

God said, 'Let us make man in our image and likeness to rule the fish in the sea, the birds of heaven, the cattle, all wild animals on earth, and all reptiles that crawl upon the earth.' So God created man in his own image; in the image of God he created him; male and female he created them. God blessed them and said to them, 'Be fruitful and increase, fill the earth and subdue it, rule over the fish in the sea, the birds of heaven, and every living thing that moves upon the earth.' So it was; and God saw all that he had made, and it was very good.

NEW TESTAMENT READING

Ephesians 3.14-end RSV

I bow my knees before the Father, from whom every family in heaven and on earth is named, that according to the riches of his glory he may grant you to be strengthened with might through his Spirit in the inner man, and that Christ may dwell in your hearts through faith; that you, being rooted and grounded in love, may have power to comprehend with all the saints what is the breadth and length and height and depth, and to know the love of Christ which surpasses knowledge, that you may be filled with all the fullness of God. Now to him who by the power at work within us is able to do far more abundantly than all that we ask or think, to him be glory in the church and in Christ Jesus to all generations, for ever and ever. Amen.

or *Ephesians 5.21-33 JB*

Give way to one another in obedience to Christ. Wives should regard their husbands as they regard the Lord, since as Christ is head of the Church and saves the whole body, so is a husband the head of his wife; and as the Church submits to Christ, so should wives to their husbands, in everything. Husbands should love their wives just as Christ loved the Church and sacrificed himself for her to make her holy. He made her clean by washing her in water with a form of words, so that when he took her to himself she would be glorious, with no speck or wrinkle or anything like that, but holy and faultless. In the same way, husbands must love their wives as they love their own bodies; for a man to love his wife is for him to love himself. A man never hates his own body, but he feeds it and looks after it; and that is the way Christ treats the Church, because it is his body—and we are its living parts. For this reason, a man must leave his father and mother and be joined to his wife, and the two will become one body. This mystery has many implications; but I am saying it applies to Christ and the Church. To sum up; you too, each one of you, must love his wife as he loves himself; and let every wife respect her husband.

Alternative READINGS: *Romans 12.1, 2, 9-13; 1 Corinthians 13; Colossians 3.12-17; 1 John 4.7-12*

THE GOSPEL

Matthew 7.21, 24-27 RSV

Jesus said, 'Not every one who says to me, "Lord, Lord," shall enter the kingdom of heaven, but he who does the will of my Father who is in heaven. Every one then who hears these words of mine and does them will be like a wise man who built his house upon the rock; and the rain fell, and the floods came, and the winds blew and beat upon that house, but it did not fall, because it had been founded on the rock. And every one who hears these words of mine and does not do them will be like a foolish man who built his house upon the sand; and the rain fell, and the floods came, and the winds blew and beat against that house, and it fell; and great was the fall of it.'

or *John 15.9-12 JB*

Jesus said to his disciples,
'As the Father has loved me,
so I have loved you.
Remain in my love.
If you keep my commandments
you will remain in my love,
just as I have kept my Father's commandments
and remain in his love.
I have told you this
so that my own joy may be in you
and your joy be complete.
This is my commandment:
love one another,
as I have loved you.'

Alternative READINGS: *Mark 10.6-9; John 2.1-11*

PROPER PREFACE

And now we give you thanks because you have made the
union between Christ and his Church a pattern for the
marriage between husband and wife. Therefore with
angels . . .

POSTCOMMUNION SENTENCE

Jesus said, As the Father has loved me, so have I loved you;
dwell in my love. *John 15.9*

Funeral Services

NOTES

1 **Bold Type** If desired, sections in bold type may be said by the congregation and minister, or by the minister alone.

2 **The Service in Church** The phrase 'in Church' does not preclude the possibility of the service being held elsewhere than in the parish church.

3 **A Sermon** A sermon may be preached elsewhere than at section 6.

4 **Service at a Crematorium** When the whole service is said at the crematorium, sections 13-16 or 28-30 are omitted.

5 **At Sea** When the service is said at sea, sections 13-16 or 28-30 are omitted; and in sections 17, 31, and 43 'the deep' is substituted for 'the ground', and the words 'earth to earth, ashes to ashes, dust to dust' are omitted.

6 **The Committal** If it is desired to take the Committal before the Prayers, the following order may be observed: sections 1-7, 12, 17, 18, 8, 9, 10, 11, 19. In the case of a cremation, the Committal may precede the Service in Church.

7 **The Committal and Interment of the Ashes** If pastoral needs require, additional material (see sections 46 and 50-60) may be used at the Committal and the Interment of the Ashes.

Funeral Service

THE SERVICE IN CHURCH

1 **Stand**
Minister   Jesus said, I am the resurrection, and I am the
life; he who believes in me, though he die, yet
shall he live, and whoever lives and believes in
me shall never die. *John 11.25, 26*

2 He may add one or more of these or other SENTENCES
OF SCRIPTURE.

We brought nothing into the world, and we take nothing
out. The Lord gives, and the Lord takes away: blessed be the
name of the Lord. *1 Timothy 6.7; Job 1.21*

The eternal God is your refuge, and underneath are the
everlasting arms. *Deuteronomy 33.27*

The steadfast love of the Lord never ceases, his compassion
never fails: every morning they are renewed.
Lamentations 3.22, 23

Blessed are those who mourn, for they shall be comforted.
Matthew 5.4

God so loved the world that he gave his only Son, that
whoever believes in him should not perish, but have eternal
life. *John 3.16*

I am sure that neither death, nor life, nor angels, nor
principalities, nor powers, nor things present, nor things to
come, nor height, nor depth, nor anything else in all
creation, will be able to separate us from the love of God in
Christ Jesus our Lord. *Romans 8.38, 39*

Eye has not seen, nor ear heard, nor the heart of man conceived, what God has prepared for those who love him. *1 Corinthians 2.9*

We believe that Jesus died and rose again; and so it will be for those who died as Christians; God will bring them to life with Jesus. Thus we shall always be with the Lord. Comfort one another with these words. *1 Thessalonians 4.14, 18*

3 **All**   **Heavenly Father,**
in your Son Jesus Christ
you have given us a true faith and
a sure hope.
Strengthen this faith and hope in us
all our days,
that we may live as those who believe in
the communion of saints,
the forgiveness of sins,
and the resurrection to eternal life;
through your Son Jesus Christ our Lord.
Amen.

4   One or more of the following PSALMS

PSALM 23

1 **The Lord ˈ is my ˈ shepherd:**
therefore ˈ can I ˈ lack ˈ nothing.

2 **He will make me lie down in ˈ green ˈ pastures:**
and ˈ lead me · beˈside still ˈ waters.

3 **He will reˈfresh my ˈ soul:**
and guide me in right pathways ˈ for his ˈ name's ˈ sake.

4 **Though I walk through the valley of the shadow of death**
I will ˈ fear no ˈ evil:
for you are with me
your ˈ rod · and your ˈ staff ˈ comfort me.

5 **You spread a table before me**
in the face of ˈ those who ˈ trouble me:
you have anointed my head with oil ˈ and my ˈ
cup · will be ˈ full.

6   Surely your goodness and loving-kindness
       will follow me * all the ⏐ days · of my ⏐ life:
          and I shall dwell in the ⏐ house · of the ⏐ Lord
       for ⏐ ever.

       Glory to the Father and ⏐ to the ⏐ Son:
          and ⏐ to the ⏐ Holy ⏐ Spirit;
       as it was in the be ⏐ ginning is ⏐ now:
          and shall be for ⏐ ever. ⏐ A ⏐ men.

Verses from PSALM 90

1   Lord you have ⏐ been our ⏐ refuge:
          from one gener ⏐ ation ⏐ to an ⏐ other.

2   Before the mountains were born
       or the earth and the world were ⏐ brought to ⏐ be:
          from eternity to e ⏐ tern·ity ⏐ you are ⏐ God.

3   You turn man ⏐ back · into ⏐ dust:
          saying 'Return to ⏐ dust you ⏐ sons of ⏐ Adam.'

4   For a thousand years in your sight
       are like ⏐ yester·day ⏐ passing:
          or ⏐ like one ⏐ watch · of the ⏐ night.

5   You cut them ⏐ short · like a ⏐ dream:
          like the fresh ⏐ grass ⏐ of the ⏐ morning;

6   in the morning it is ⏐ green and ⏐ flourishes:
          at evening it is ⏐ withered · and ⏐ dried ⏐ up.

10   The days of our life are three score years and ten
       or if we have ⏐ strength four ⏐ score:
          the pride of our labours is but toil and sorrow
          for it passes quickly a ⏐ way and ⏐ we are ⏐ gone.

12   Teach us so to ⏐ number · our ⏐ days:
          that we may ap ⏐ ply our ⏐ hearts to ⏐ wisdom.

14   O satisfy us early ⏐ with your ⏐ mercy:
          that all our days we ⏐ may re ⏐ joice and ⏐ sing.

16   Show your I servants · your I work:
        and let their I children I see your I glory.

† 17   May the gracious favour of the Lord our I
        God · be up I on us:
        prosper the work of our hands
        O I prosper · the I work · of our I hands!

        Glory to the Father and I to the I Son:
        and I to the I Holy I Spirit;
        as it was in the be I ginning is I now:
        and shall be for I ever. I A I men.

PSALM 121

1   I lift up my I eyes · to the I hills:
        but I where · shall I I find I help?

2   My help I comes · from the I Lord:
        who has I made I heaven · and I earth.

3   He will not suffer your I foot to I stumble:
        and he who watches I over · you I will not I sleep.

4   Be sure he who has I charge of I Israel:
        will I neither I slumber · nor I sleep.

5   The Lord him I self is · your I keeper:
        the Lord is your defence up I on your I right I hand.

6   The sun shall not I strike you · by I day:
        nor I shall the I moon by I night.

7   The Lord will defend you from I all I evil:
        it is I he · who will I guard your I life.

8   The Lord will defend your going out and your I
        coming I in:
        from this time I forward · for I ever I more.

        Glory to the Father and I to the I Son:
        and I to the I Holy I Spirit;
        as it was in the be I ginning is now:
        and shall be for I ever. I A I men.

PSALM 130

1 **Out of the depths have I called to | you O | Lord:**
  Lord | hear | my | voice;

2 **O let your ears con | sider | well:**
  the | voice · of my | suppli | cation.

3 **If you Lord should note what | we do | wrong:**
  who | then O | Lord could | stand?

4 **But there is for | giveness · with | you:**
  so that | you | shall be | feared.

5 **I wait for the Lord * my | soul | waits for him:**
  and | in his | word · is my | hope.

6 **My soul | looks · for the | Lord:**
  more than watchmen for the morning
  more I say than | watchmen | for the | morning.

7 **O Israel trust in the Lord * for with the |**
  Lord · there is | mercy:
  and with | him is | ample · re | demption.

8 **He will re | deem | Israel:**
  from the | multi·tude | of his | sins.

  Glory to the Father and | to the | Son:
  and | to the | Holy | Spirit;
  as it was in the be | ginning is | now:
  and shall be for | ever. | A | men.

Alternative PSALMS:
27; 42.1-7; 118.14-21, 28-29; 139.1-11, 17-18

5 **Sit**
  One or more of the following READINGS

John 14.1-6 JB
Jesus said to his disciples,
'Do not let your hearts be troubled.
Trust in God still, and trust in me.
There are many rooms in my Father's house;
if there were not, I should have told you.

I am going now to prepare a place for you,
and after I have gone and prepared you a place,
I shall return to take you with me;
so that where I am
you may be too.
You know the way to the place where I am going.'

Thomas said, 'Lord, we do not know where you are going,
so how can we know the way?' Jesus said,

'I am the Way, the Truth and the Life.
No one can come to the Father except through me.'

1 Corinthians 15.20-26, 35-38, 42-44a, 53-end RSV
Christ has been raised from the dead, the first fruits of those
who have fallen asleep. For as by a man came death, by a
man has come also the resurrection of the dead. For as in
Adam all die, so also in Christ shall all be made alive. But
each in his own order: Christ the first fruits, then at his
coming those who belong to Christ. Then comes the end,
when he delivers the kingdom to God the Father after
destroying every rule and every authority and power. For he
must reign until he has put all his enemies under his feet.
The last enemy to be destroyed is death.

But someone will ask, 'How are the dead raised? With what
kind of body do they come?' You foolish man! What you sow
does not come to life unless it dies. And what you sow is not
the body which is to be, but a bare kernel, perhaps of wheat
or of some other grain. But God gives it a body as he has
chosen, and to each kind of seed its own body.

So it is with the resurrection of the dead. What is sown is
perishable, what is raised is imperishable. It is sown in
dishonour, it is raised in glory. It is sown in weakness, it is
raised in power. It is sown a physical body, it is raised a
spiritual body.

For this perishable nature must put on the imperishable, and
this mortal nature must put on immortality. When the
perishable puts on the imperishable, and the mortal puts on
immortality, then shall come to pass the saying that is
written: 'Death is swallowed up in victory.' 'O death, where

is thy victory? O death, where is thy sting?' The sting of
death is sin, and the power of sin is the law. But thanks be to
God, who gives us the victory through our Lord Jesus
Christ.

Therefore, my beloved brethren, be steadfast, immoveable,
always abounding in the work of the Lord, knowing that in
the Lord your labour is not in vain.

1 Thessalonians 4.13-18 RSV
We would not have you ignorant, brethren, concerning
those who are asleep, that you may not grieve as others do
who have no hope. For since we believe that Jesus died and
rose again, even so, through Jesus, God will bring with him
those who have fallen asleep. For this we declare to you by
the word of the Lord, that we who are alive, who are left
until the coming of the Lord, shall not precede those who
have fallen asleep. For the Lord himself will descend from
heaven with a cry of command, with the archangel's call,
and with the sound of the trumpet of God. And the dead in
Christ will rise first; then we who are alive, who are left, shall
be caught up together with them in the clouds to meet the
Lord in the air; and so we shall always be with the Lord.
Therefore comfort one another with these words.

Alternative READINGS:
Wisdom 4.8, 10, 11, 13-15; John 5.19-25; John 6.35-40;
John 11.17-27; Romans 8.31b-39; Romans 14.7-9;
2 Corinthians 1.3-5; 2 Corinthians 4.7-18;
Philippians 3.10-end; Revelation 21.1-7

6   A SERMON may be preached.

7   **Stand**
    Verses from TE DEUM, or A HYMN

    You Christ are the | King of | glory:
    the e|ternal | Son · of the | Father.

    When you became man to | set us | free:
    you did not ab|hor the | Virgin's | womb.

You overcame the | sting of | death:
and opened the kingdom of | heaven · to | all be|lievers.

You are seated at God's right | hand in | glory:
we believe that you will | come and | be our | judge.

Come then Lord and | help your | people:
bought with the | price of | your own | blood;

and bring us | with your | saints:
to | glory | ever|lasting.

8   Minister   Let us pray.

                      Lord, have mercy upon us.
All   **Christ, have mercy upon us.**
Minister   Lord, have mercy upon us.

All   **Our Father in heaven,
hallowed be your name,
your kingdom come,
your will be done,
on earth as in heaven.
Give us today our daily bread.
Forgive us our sins
as we forgive those who sin against us.
Lead us not into temptation
but deliver us from evil.**

                    **For the kingdom, the power, and the glory
are yours
now and for ever. Amen.**

9   PRAYERS may be said here (see also sections 50-60).

10   Minister   Grant us, Lord, the wisdom and the grace to use
aright the time that is left to us here on earth.
Lead us to repent of our sins, the evil we have
done and the good we have not done; and
strengthen us to follow the steps of your Son, in
the way that leads to the fullness of eternal life;
through Jesus Christ our Lord. **Amen.**

11   A HYMN may be sung.

| 12 | Minister | Let us commend our *brother N* to the mercy of God our Maker and Redeemer. |

Heavenly Father, by your mighty power you gave us life, and in your love you have given us new life in Christ Jesus. We entrust *N* to your merciful keeping: in the faith of Jesus Christ your Son our Lord, who died and rose again to save us, and is now alive and reigns with you and the Holy Spirit in glory for ever. **Amen.**

| 13 | Minister | May God in his infinite love and mercy bring the whole Church, living and departed in the Lord Jesus, to a joyful resurrection and the fulfilment of his eternal kingdom. **Amen.** |

THE COMMITTAL

14 Before the Committal the minister may say

I heard a voice from heaven, saying, 'Write this: "Happy are the dead who die in the faith of Christ! Henceforth," says the Spirit, "they may rest from their labours; for they take with them the record of their deeds."' *Revelation 14.13*

15 The minister says verses from PSALM 103, or the following sentences.

16 Verses from PSALM 103

The Lord is full of compassion and mercy:
slow to anger and of great goodness.
As a father is tender towards his children:
so is the Lord tender to those that fear him.
For he knows of what we are made:
he remembers that we are but dust.
The days of man are but as grass:
he flourishes like a flower of the field;
when the wind goes over it, it is gone:
and its place will know it no more.

But the merciful goodness of the Lord
endures for ever and ever
toward those that fear him:
and his righteousness upon their
children's children.

or

Man born of a woman has but a short time to
live. Like a flower he blossoms and then withers;
like a shadow he flees and never stays.

In the midst of life we are in death; to whom can
we turn for help, but to you, Lord, who are
justly angered by our sins?

Lord God, holy and mighty, holy and immortal,
holy and most merciful Saviour, deliver us from
the bitter pains of eternal death. You know the
secrets of our hearts: in your mercy hear our
prayer, forgive us our sins, and at our last hour
let us not fall away from you.

17   We have entrusted our *brother N* to God's
merciful keeping, and we now commit *his* body
to the ground (*or* to be cremated): *[earth to
earth, ashes to ashes, dust to dust:] in sure and
certain hope of the resurrection to eternal life
through our Lord Jesus Christ, who died, was
buried, and rose again for us. To him be glory for
ever and ever.

18   God will show us the path of life;
in his presence is the fullness of joy:
and at his right hand
there is pleasure for evermore. *Psalm 16.11*

*The words in square brackets may be omitted (see note 5
p. 306).

19

Unto him that is able to keep us from falling, and to present us faultless before the presence of his glory with exceeding joy, to the only wise God our Saviour, be glory and majesty, dominion and power, both now and ever. **Amen.**
Jude 24, 25

or section 13 may be used.

The Funeral of a Child

20 **Stand**

Minister   The Lamb who is at the throne will be their
             shepherd and will lead them to springs of living
             water; and God will wipe away all tears from
             their eyes. *Revelation 7.17*

He may add one or more other SENTENCES OF
SCRIPTURE (see sections 1 and 2).

21 PSALM 23

1   **The Lord | is my | shepherd:**
    therefore | can I | lack | nothing.

2   **He will make me lie down in | green | pastures:**
    and | lead me · be|side still | waters.

3   **He will re|fresh my | soul:**
    and guide me in right pathways | for his | name's | sake.

4   **Though I walk through the valley of the shadow of death**
    I will | fear no | evil:
    for you are with me
    your | rod · and your | staff | comfort me.

5   **You spread a table before me**
    in the face of | those who | trouble me:
    you have anointed my head with oil | and my |
    cup · will be | full.

6   **Surely your goodness and loving-kindness‿**
    will follow me * all the | days · of my | life:
    and I shall dwell in the | house · of the | Lord
    for | ever.

    Glory to the Father and | to the | Son:
    and | to the | Holy | Spirit;
    as it was in the be|ginning is | now:
    and shall be for | ever. | A|men.

22   **Sit**
     Either or both of the following READINGS

Mark 10.13-16 NEB
They brought children for Jesus to touch. The disciples
rebuked them, but when Jesus saw this he was indignant,
and said to them, 'Let the children come to me; do not try to
stop them; for the kingdom of God belongs to such as these.
I tell you, whoever does not accept the kingdom of God like a
child will never enter it.' And he put his arms round them,
laid his hands upon them, and blessed them.

Ephesians 3.14-19 RSV
I bow my knees before the Father, from whom every family
in heaven and on earth is named, that according to the riches
of his glory he may grant you to be strengthened with might
through his Spirit in the inner man, and that Christ may
dwell in your hearts through faith; that you, being rooted
and grounded in love, may have power to comprehend with
all the saints what is the breadth and length and height and
depth, and to know the love of Christ which surpasses
knowledge, that you may be filled with all the fullness
of God.

23   Minister   Let us pray.
                  Lord, have mercy upon us.
     All   **Christ, have mercy upon us.**
     Minister   Lord, have mercy upon us.

     All   **Our Father in heaven,**
                  hallowed be your name,
                  your kingdom come,
                  your will be done,
                  on earth as in heaven.
                  Give us today our daily bread.
                  Forgive us our sins
                  as we forgive those who sin against us.
                  Lead us not into temptation
                  but deliver us from evil.

> **For the kingdom, the power, and the glory
> are yours
> now and for ever. Amen.**

24 Minister   Father in heaven, you gave your Son Jesus
Christ to suffering and to death on the cross, and
raised him to life in glory. Grant us a patient
faith in time of darkness, and strengthen our
hearts with the knowledge of your love; through
Jesus Christ our Lord. **Amen.**

25 PRAYERS may be said here.

26 Minister   Grant us, Lord, the wisdom and the grace to use
aright the time that is left to us here on earth.
Lead us to repent of our sins, the evil we have
done and the good we have not done; and
strengthen us to follow the steps of your Son, in
the way that leads to the fullness of eternal life;
through Jesus Christ our Lord. **Amen.**

27 Minister   Let us commend this child N to the love of God
our Father.

              Heavenly Father, by your mighty power you
gave us life, and in your love you have given us
new life in Christ Jesus. We entrust N to your
merciful keeping, in the faith of Jesus Christ
your Son our Lord, who died and rose again to
save us, and is now alive and reigns with you
and the Holy Spirit in glory for ever. **Amen.**

28 Minister   May God in his infinite love and mercy bring the
whole Church, living and departed in the Lord
Jesus, to a joyful resurrection and the fulfilment
of his eternal kingdom. **Amen.**

THE COMMITTAL

29   Before the Committal, SENTENCES may be said (see section 2).

30   Verses from PSALM 103 may be said.

> The Lord is full of compassion and mercy:
> slow to anger and of great goodness.
> As a father is tender towards his children:
> so is the Lord tender to those that fear him.
> For he knows of what we are made:
> he remembers that we are but dust.
> The days of man are but as grass:
> he flourishes like a flower of the field;
> when the wind goes over it, it is gone:
> and its place will know it no more.
> But the merciful goodness of the Lord
> endures for ever and ever
> toward those that fear him:
> and his righteousness upon their
> children's children.

31   Minister   We have entrusted N to God's merciful keeping,
and we now commit *his* body to the ground (*or* to
be cremated): *[earth to earth, ashes to ashes,
dust to dust;] in sure and certain hope of the
resurrection to eternal life through our Lord
Jesus Christ, who died, was buried, and rose
again for us. To him be glory for ever and ever.

32   Unto him that is able to keep us from falling, and
to present us faultless before the presence of his
glory with exceeding joy, to the only wise God
our Saviour, be glory and majesty, dominion
and power, both now and ever. **Amen.** *Jude* 24, 25

or section 28 may be used.

*The words in square brackets may be omitted (see note 5
p. 306).

Prayers after
the Birth of a still-born Child or
the Death of a newly-born Child

33   These prayers may be used in church, in hospital, or in the
home; and where appropriate they may be used at the burial
or cremation of a still-born or newly-born child.

34   Gracious Father,
in darkness and in light,
in trouble and in joy,
help us to trust your love,
to serve your purpose,
and to praise your name;
through Jesus Christ our Lord. **Amen.**

35   Loving Father, in your mercy you have brought
your daughter N through childbirth in safety.
We pray that she will know your support in this
time of trouble and enjoy your protection
always; through Jesus Christ our Lord. **Amen.**

36   Almighty God, you make nothing in vain, and
love all that you have made. Comfort this
woman (and her husband) in *their* sorrow, and
console *them* by the knowledge of your unfailing
love; through Jesus Christ our Lord. **Amen.**

37   God of loving kindness, comfort N *(and N)* in
their distress that *they* may hold to you through
good and ill, and always trust in your unfailing
love; through Jesus Christ our Lord. **Amen.**

38   Father in heaven, you gave your Son Jesus
Christ to suffering and to death on the cross, and
raised him to life in glory. Grant us a patient
faith in time of darkness, and strengthen our

hearts with the knowledge of your love; through
Jesus Christ our Lord. **Amen.**

39   Let us commend this child to the love of God
our Father.

Heavenly Father, by your mighty power you
gave us life, and in your love you have given us
new life in Christ Jesus. We entrust this child to
your merciful keeping, in the faith of Jesus
Christ your Son our Lord, who died and rose
again to save us, and is now alive and reigns
with you and the Holy Spirit in glory for ever.
Amen.

40   God is our refuge and strength:
a very present help in trouble.
Though my flesh and my heart fail me:
you, O God, are my portion for ever.
Forsake me not, O Lord,
go not far from me, my God:
hasten to my help, O Lord my salvation.
Why are you so full of heaviness, my soul:
and why so unquiet within me?
O put your trust in God:
for I will praise him yet,
who is my deliverer and my God.

Glory to the Father, and to the Son,
and to the Holy Spirit:
as it was in the beginning, is now,
and shall be for ever. **Amen.**

41   The following Psalms may be used as alternatives to
section 40:
23; 31.1-6; 103.8, 13-17; 130; 139.1-9; 142.1-6

A Form which may be used at the Interment of the Ashes

42 At the graveside A SENTENCE may be said (see section 2).

43 Minister   We have entrusted our *brother N* to God's merciful keeping and we now commit *his* ashes to the ground; *[earth to earth, ashes to ashes, dust to dust;] in sure and certain hope of the resurrection to eternal life through our Lord Jesus Christ, who died, was buried, and rose again for us. To him be glory for ever and ever.

44   Almighty God, grant that we, with all those who have believed in you, may be united in the full knowledge of your love and the unclouded vision of your glory; through Jesus Christ our Lord. **Amen.**

45   The grace of our Lord Jesus Christ, and the love of God, and the fellowship of the Holy Spirit be with us all evermore. **Amen.**

*The words in square brackets may be omitted (see note 5 p. 306).

A Service which may be used before a Funeral

46 If the body is brought to church the day before the funeral, the following service may be used.

SENTENCE (see section 2)

THE READING *Romans 8.31b-39 RSV*
If God is for us, who is against us? He who did not spare his own Son but gave him up for us all, will he not also give us all things with him? Who shall bring any charge against God's elect? It is God who justifies; who is to condemn? Is it Christ Jesus, who died, yes, who was raised from the dead, who is at the right hand of God, who indeed intercedes for us? Who shall separate us from the love of Christ? Shall tribulation, or distress, or persecution, or famine, or nakedness, or peril, or sword? As it is written,

'For thy sake we are being killed all the day long;
we are regarded as sheep to be slaughtered'.

No, in all these things we are more than conquerors through him who loved us. For I am sure that neither death, nor life, nor angels, nor principalities, nor things present, nor things to come, nor powers, nor height, nor depth, nor anything else in all creation, will be able to separate us from the love of God in Christ Jesus our Lord.

Verses from PSALM 27

1 **The Lord is my light and my salvation**
   whom then ˈ **shall I** ˈ **fear?**
       the Lord is the stronghold of my life
       of whom ˈ **shall I** ˈ **be a** ˈ**fraid?**

2 **When the wicked   even my enemies and my foes**
   come upon me ˈ **to de**ˈ**vour me:**
       they shall ˈ **stumble** ˈ **and** ˈ **fall.**

3   If an army encamp against me
     my heart shall | not · be a |fraid:
       and if war should rise a |gainst me | yet · will I | trust.

4   One thing I have asked from the Lord which I |
     will re |quire:
       that I may dwell in the house of the Lord | ⌣
       all the | days · of my | life,

†5   to see the fair | beauty · of the | Lord:
       and to | seek his | will · in his | temple.

6   For he will hide me under his shelter in the |
     day of | trouble:
       and conceal me in the shadow of his tent
       and set me | high up |on a | rock.

7   And now he will lift | up my | head:
       above my | ene·mies | round a |bout me.

†8   And I will offer sacrifices in his sanctuary with |
     exul |tation:
       I will sing   I will sing | praises | to the | Lord.

     Glory to the Father and | to the | Son:
       and | to the | Holy | Spirit;
     as it was in the be |ginning is | now:
       and shall be for | ever. | A |men.

Verses from PSALM 139

1   O Lord you have searched me | out and | known me:
     you know when I sit or when I stand
     you comprehend my | thoughts | long be |fore.

2   You discern my path and the places | where I | rest:
     you are ac |quainted · with | all my | ways.

3   For there is not a | word · on my | tongue:
     but you Lord | know it | alto |gether.

4   You have encompassed me be |hind · and be |fore:
     and have | laid your | hand up |on me.

†5   Such knowledge is too | wonder·ful | for me:
     so | high · that I | cannot · en |dure it.

6   Where shall I ˈ go · from your ˈ spirit:
      or where shall I ˈ flee ˈ from your ˈ presence?

7   If I ascend into heaven ˈ you are ˈ there:
      if I make my bed in the grave ˈ you are ˈ there ˈ also.

8   If I spread out my wings to ˈwards the ˈ morning:
      or dwell in the ˈ utter·most ˈ parts · of the ˈ sea,

9   even there your ˈ hand shall ˈ lead me:
      and ˈ your right ˈ hand shall ˈ hold me.

10   If I say 'Surely the ˈ darkness · will ˈ cover me:
      and the ˈ night ˈ will en ˈclose me',

11   the darkness is no darkness with you
     but the night is as ˈ clear · as the ˈ day:
      the darkness and the ˈ light are ˈ both a ˈlike.

17   How deep are your thoughts to ˈ me O ˈ God:
      and how ˈ great ˈ is the ˈ sum of them!

18   Were I to count them
     they are more in number ˈ than the ˈ sand:
      were I to come to the ˈ end · I would ˈ still be ˈ
     with you.

    Glory to the Father and ˈ to the ˈ Son:
      and ˈ to the ˈ Holy ˈ Spirit;
   as it was in the be ˈginning is ˈ now:
      and shall be for ˈ ever. ˈ A ˈmen.

THE LORD'S PRAYER

ADDITIONAL PRAYERS (see sections 50-60)

THE GRACE

Alternatively, this service may be said in the home before the
body is taken to church.

The Funeral Service
with Holy Communion

47 When the Funeral Service is combined with the Holy
    Communion Service, the following order may be used.
    Optional parts of the service may be omitted in accordance
    with the normal instructions. The readings must include
    (i) either an Old Testament or a New Testament Reading
    (ii) a Gospel.
    The Eucharistic Prayer should include the Proper Preface
    (see section 49).
    Section numbers refer to Holy Communion Rite A, but the
    corresponding sections of Holy Communion Rite B may be
    used in place of these.

Order	Service	Section
Sentence	Funeral	1, 2
Collect	Funeral	3, 49, 51-53
Psalm	Funeral	4
Reading	Funeral	5, 48
Gospel	Funeral	5, 48
Sermon	Funeral	6
Prayers	Holy Communion or Funeral	20, 21 50-60
Penitence	Holy Communion	25-29 optional
Peace	Holy Communion	30, 31 optional
Preparation of the Gifts	Holy Communion	32-34
Eucharistic Prayer	Holy Communion	36-41, 63-65
Proper Preface	Funeral	49
Breaking of the Bread	Holy Communion	42-44
Giving of the Bread and Cup	Holy Communion	45-47, 66
Prayers	Funeral	9, 10, 12, 13
After Communion	Holy Communion	50-55, 69-74
Committal	Funeral	14-19

PROPERS

48   When the Funeral of a Child is combined with the Holy
Communion Service, the following are used.

PSALM 23 (see section 4)

THE COLLECT
> Heavenly Father,
> whose Son our Saviour
> took little children into his arms
>   and blessed them:
> receive, we pray, your child *N*
> in your never-failing care and love,
> comfort all who have loved *him* on earth,
> and bring us all to your everlasting kingdom;
> through Jesus Christ our Lord. **Amen.**

OLD TESTAMENT READING

Lamentations 3.22-26, 31-33 NEB
The Lord's true love is surely not spent,
  nor has his compassion failed;
they are new every morning,
  so great is his constancy.
The Lord, I say, is all that I have;
  therefore I will wait for him patiently.
The Lord is good to those who look for him,
  to all who seek him;
it is good to wait in patience and sigh
  for deliverance by the Lord.
For the Lord will not cast off
  his servants for ever.
He may punish cruelly, yet he will have compassion
  in the fullness of his love;
he does not willingly afflict
  or punish any mortal man.

NEW TESTAMENT READING *Ephesians 3.14-19 RSV*
(see section 22)

THE GOSPEL *Mark 10.13-16 NEB* (see section 22)

49 At a service of Holy Communion not combined with the
    Funeral Service, the following may be used.

Verses from PSALM 42

1 **As a deer longs for the | running | brooks:**
   so longs my | soul for | you O | God.

2 **My soul is thirsty for God * thirsty for the |**
   living | God:
   when shall I | come and | see his | face?

3 **My tears have been my food | day and | night:**
   while they ask me all day long | 'Where now |
   is your | God?'

4 **As I pour out my soul by myself I re | member | this:**
   how I went to the house of the Mighty One | ⌣
   into · the | temple · of | God,

†5 **to the shouts and | songs of · thanks | giving:**
   a multitude | keeping | high | festival.

6 **Why are you so full of | heaviness · my | soul:**
   and | why · so un | quiet · with | in me?

7 **O put your | trust in | God:**
   for I will praise him yet
   who is my de | liver · er | and my | God.

   Glory to the Father and | to the | Son:
   and | to the | Holy | Spirit;
   as it was in the be | ginning is | now:
   and shall be for | ever. | A | men.

Verses from PSALM 118

14 **The Lord is my | strength · and my | song:**
   and has be | come | my sal | vation.

15 **The sounds of | joy · and de | liverance:**
   are | in the | tents · of the | righteous.

16 **The right hand of the Lord does | mighty | things:**
   the right hand of the | Lord | raises | up.

17   I shall not ˈ die but ˈ live:
        and proˈclaim the ˈ works · of the ˈ Lord.

18   The Lord has ˈ disciplined · me ˈ hard:
        but he has not ˈ given · me ˈ over · to ˈ death.

19   Open me the ˈ gates of ˈ righteousness:
        and I will enter and give ˈ thanks ˈ to the ˈ Lord.

20   This is the ˈ gate · of the ˈ Lord:
        the ˈ righteous ˈ shall ˈ enter it.

21   I will praise you ˈ for you ˈ answered me:
        and have beˈcome ˈ my salˈvation.

28   You are my God and ˈ I will ˈ praise you:
        you are my ˈ God I ˈ will exˈalt you.

29   O give thanks to the Lord for ˈ he is ˈ good:
        and his ˈ mercy · enˈdures for ˈ ever.

      Glory to the Father and ˈ to the ˈ Son:
        and ˈ to the ˈ Holy ˈ Spirit;
      as it was in the beˈginning is ˈ now:
        and shall be for ˈ ever. ˈ Aˈmen.

THE COLLECT

Merciful God,
whose Son Jesus Christ is the resurrection
    and the life of all the faithful:
raise us from the death of sin
to the life of righteousness,
that at the last we, with our *brother N*,
may come to your eternal joy;
through Jesus Christ our Lord. **Amen.**

OLD TESTAMENT READING

Isaiah 25.8-9 NEB
The Lord God will swallow up death for ever.
He will wipe away the tears
from every face
and remove the reproach of his people from the whole earth.
The Lord has spoken.

On that day men will say,
See, this is our God
for whom we have waited to deliver us;
this is the Lord for whom we have waited;
let us rejoice and exult in his deliverance.

NEW TESTAMENT READING

1 Peter 1.3-9 NEB

Praise be to the God and Father of our Lord Jesus Christ,
who in his great mercy gave us new birth into a living hope
by the resurrection of Jesus Christ from the dead! The
inheritance to which we are born is one that nothing can
destroy or spoil or wither. It is kept for you in heaven, and
you, because you put your faith in God, are under the
protection of his power until salvation comes—the salvation
which is even now in readiness and will be revealed at the
end of time.

This is cause for great joy, even though now you smart for a
little while, if need be, under trials of many kinds. Even gold
passes through the assayer's fire, and more precious than
perishable gold is faith which has stood the test. These trials
come so that your faith may prove itself worthy of all praise,
glory, and honour when Jesus Christ is revealed.

You have not seen him, yet you love him; and trusting in him
now without seeing him, you are transported with a joy too
great for words, while you reap the harvest of your faith,
that is, salvation for your souls.

THE GOSPEL

John 20.1-9 RSV

On the first day of the week Mary Magdalen came to the
tomb early, while it was still dark, and saw that the stone had
been taken away from the tomb. So she ran, and went to
Simon Peter and the other disciple, the one whom Jesus
loved, and said to them, 'They have taken the Lord out of the
tomb, and we do not know where they have laid him.' Peter
then came out with the other disciple, and they went toward

the tomb. They both ran, but the other disciple outran Peter and reached the tomb first; and stooping to look in, he saw the linen cloths lying there, but he did not go in. Then Simon Peter came, following him, and he went into the tomb; he saw the linen cloths lying, and the napkin, which had been on his head, not lying with the linen cloths but rolled up in a place by itself. Then the other disciple, who reached the tomb first, also went in, and he saw and believed; for as yet they did not know the scripture, that he must rise from the dead.

Or *John 14.1-6* may be read (see section 5).

The seasonal material for Easter and other suitable SENTENCES may be used.

PROPER PREFACE

And now we give you thanks because through him you have given us eternal life, and delivered us from the bondage of sin and the fear of death into the glorious liberty of the children of God. Therefore . . .

or

And now we give you thanks, because through him you have given us the hope of a glorious resurrection, so that although death comes to us all, yet we rejoice in the promise of eternal life; for to your faithful people life is changed, not taken away, and when our mortal flesh is laid aside, an everlasting dwelling place is made ready for us in heaven. Therefore . . .

or a Preface of the Resurrection (15) or (16) is said.

A Selection of Additional Prayers which may be used

50   Merciful Father and Lord of all life, we praise you that men are made in your image and reflect your truth and light. We thank you for the life of your *son N*, for the love and mercy *he* received from you and showed among us. Above all we rejoice at your gracious promise to all your servants, living and departed: that we shall rise again at the coming of Christ. And we ask that in due time we may share with our *brother* that clearer vision, when we shall see your face in the same Christ our Lord. **Amen.**

51   O God, the maker and redeemer of all mankind: grant us, with your servant *N* and all the faithful departed, the sure benefits of your Son's saving passion and glorious resurrection; that in the last day, when you gather up all things in Christ, we may with them enjoy the fullness of your promises; through Jesus Christ our Lord. **Amen.**

52   Hear, Lord, the prayers of your people, as we remember before you *N* our *brother*: and grant that we who confess your name on earth may with *him* be made perfect in the kingdom of your glory; through Jesus Christ our Lord. **Amen.**

53   Remember, O Lord, this your servant, who has gone before us with the sign of faith, and now rests in the sleep of peace. According to your promises, grant to *him* and to all who rest in Christ, refreshment, light, and peace; through the same Christ our Lord. **Amen.**

54　Eternal Lord God, you hold all souls in life: shed forth, we pray, upon your whole Church in paradise and on earth the bright beams of your light and heavenly comfort; and grant that we, following the good example of those who have loved and served you here and are now at rest, may at the last enter with them into the fullness of your eternal joy; through Jesus Christ our Lord. **Amen.**

55　Father in heaven, you gave your Son Jesus Christ to suffering and to death on the cross, and raised him to life in glory. Grant us a patient faith in time of darkness, and strengthen our hearts with the knowledge of your love; through Jesus Christ our Lord. **Amen.**

56　Father of all, by whose mercy and grace your saints remain in everlasting light and peace: we remember with thanksgiving those whom we love but see no longer; and we pray that in them your perfect will may be fulfilled; through Jesus Christ our Lord. **Amen.**

57　Almighty God, Father of all mercies and giver of all comfort: deal graciously, we pray, with those who mourn, that casting all their care on you, they may know the consolation of your love; through Jesus Christ our Lord. **Amen.**

58　O Lord, support us all the day long of this troublous life, until the shades lengthen, and the evening comes, and the busy world is hushed, the fever of life is over, and our work is done. Then, Lord, in your mercy grant us safe lodging, a holy rest, and peace at the last; through Jesus Christ our Lord. **Amen.**

59   We pray for those who mourn . . .
                We commemorate the departed . . .

                We commend all men to your unfailing love,
that in them your will may be fulfilled; and we
rejoice at the faithful witness of your saints in
every age, praying that we may share with them
in your eternal kingdom; through Jesus Christ
our Lord. **Amen.**

60   Let us pray with confidence to God our Father,
who raised Christ his Son from the dead for the
salvation of all. Grant, Lord, that your servant
may know the fullness of life which you have
promised to those who love you.
Lord, in your mercy
hear our prayer

Be close to those who mourn: increase their faith
in your undying love.
Lord, in your mercy
hear our prayer

May we be strengthened in our faith, live the
rest of our lives in following your Son, and be
ready when you shall call us to eternal life.
Lord, in your mercy
hear our prayer

Show your mercy to the dying; strengthen them
with hope, and fill them with the peace and joy
of your presence.
Lord, in your mercy
hear our prayer

Lord, we commend all those who have died to
your unfailing love, that in them your will may
be fulfilled; and we pray that we may share with
them in your eternal kingdom; through Jesus
Christ our Lord. **Amen.**

The Ordinal

NOTES

1   **The threefold Ministry** The Church of England maintains
the historic threefold ministry of bishops, priests, and
deacons. Its ministers are ordained by bishops according to
authorized forms of service, with prayer and the laying on of
hands (see Canons C 1-4).

2   **Ordination of Bishops** Bishops must be ordained by at least
three other bishops, joining together in the act of ordination,
of whom one shall be the archbishop of the province or
his deputy.

3   **Ordination of Priests and Deacons** Priests share with the
bishop in laying hands on the heads of those ordained to the
order of priesthood. The bishop alone lays his hands on the
heads of those ordained to the order of deacon.

4   **Form of Service** Questions concerning the form of service to
be used, and other matters concerning the conduct of the
service, are to be determined by the bishop who presides at
it, in accordance with the rubrics of the service and having
regard to tradition and local custom. It is appropriate that the
newly ordained should be invited by the bishop to exercise
their new ministry in the course of the service.

5   **Holy Communion** Any form of service of Holy Communion
which is authorized by Canon B 1 may be used at these
Ordination Services (see Canon C 3. 4A).

6   **Readings** The presiding bishop may choose alternative
Old Testament or New Testament readings suitable to
the occasion.

7   **Vesture** Where it is agreed that those to be ordained are to be
clothed in their customary vesture, it is appropriate that this
should take place after the Declaration.

8   **Symbols** Where it is so agreed, symbols of the priest's office
(chalice and paten) or the bishop's office (pastoral staff) may
be presented after the Giving of the Bible.

The Ordination of Deacons

THE PREPARATION

1   At the entry of the ministers, A HYMN, A CANTICLE, or
A PSALM may be sung.

2   Bishop   The Lord be with you
      All   **and also with you.**

3   Bishop   God our Father, Lord of all the world,
                     we thank you that through your Son
                     you have called us into the fellowship of
                         your universal Church.
                     Hear our prayer for your faithful people
                     that each in his vocation and ministry
                     may be an instrument of your love,
                     and give your servants now to be ordained
                     the needful gifts of grace;
                     through our Lord and Saviour Jesus Christ.
                     Amen.

THE MINISTRY OF THE WORD

4   **Sit**
OLD TESTAMENT READING

Isaiah 6.1-8 RSV
In the year that King Uzziah died I saw the Lord sitting upon
a throne, high and lifted up; and his train filled the temple.
Above him stood the seraphim; each had six wings: with two
he covered his face, and with two he covered his feet, and
with two he flew. And one called to another and said: 'Holy,
holy, holy is the Lord of hosts; the whole earth is full of his
glory.' And the foundations of the thresholds shook at the
voice of him who called, and the house was filled with
smoke. And I said: 'Woe is me! For I am lost; for I am a man of
unclean lips, and I dwell in the midst of a people of unclean
lips; for my eyes have seen the King, the Lord of hosts!'

Then flew one of the seraphim to me, having in his hand a burning coal which he had taken with tongs from the altar. And he touched my mouth, and said: 'Behold, this has touched your lips; your guilt is taken away, and your sin forgiven.' And I heard the voice of the Lord saying, 'Whom shall I send, and who will go for us?' Then I said, 'Here I am! Send me.'

At the end the reader may say

This is the word of the Lord.
All   **Thanks be to God.**

5   **Stand**
Verses from PSALM 119

33   **Teach me O Lord the | way of · your | statutes:**
     and I will | honour · it | to the | end.

34   **Give me understanding that I may | keep your | law:**
     that I may keep it | with my | whole | heart.

35   **Guide me in the path of | your com | mandments:**
     for there | in is | my de | light.

36   **Incline my heart to | your com | mands:**
     and | not to | selfish | gain.

37   **Turn away my eyes from | looking · on | vanities:**
     as I walk in your | way | give me | life.

38   **Make good your promise | to your | servant:**
     the promise that en | dures for | all who |
     fear you.

Glory to the Father and | to the | Son:
     and | to the | Holy | Spirit;
as it was in the be | ginning is | now:
     and shall be for | ever. | A | men.

6   **Sit**
    NEW TESTAMENT READING

    Romans 12.1-12 RSV
    I appeal to you, brethren, by the mercies of God, to present
    your bodies as a living sacrifice, holy and acceptable to God,
    which is your spiritual worship. Do not be conformed to this
    world but be transformed by the renewal of your mind, that
    you may prove what is the will of God, what is good and
    acceptable and perfect.

    For by the grace given to me I bid every one among you not
    to think of himself more highly than he ought to think, but to
    think with sober judgement, each according to the measure
    of faith which God has assigned him. For as in one body we
    have many members, and all the members do not have the
    same function, so we, though many, are one body in Christ,
    and individually members one of another. Having gifts that
    differ according to the grace given to us, let us use them: if
    prophecy, in proportion to our faith; if service, in our
    serving; he who teaches, in his teaching; he who exhorts, in
    his exhortation; he who contributes, in liberality; he who
    gives aid, with zeal; he who does acts of mercy, with
    cheerfulness.

    Let love be genuine; hate what is evil, hold fast to what is
    good; love one another with brotherly affection; outdo one
    another in showing honour. Never flag in zeal, be aglow
    with the Spirit, serve the Lord. Rejoice in your hope, be
    patient in tribulation, be constant in prayer.

    At the end the reader may say

            This is the word of the Lord.
    All   **Thanks be to God.**

7   **Stand**
    A CANTICLE or A HYMN may be sung.

8 THE GOSPEL *Mark 10.35-45 NEB*

When it is announced

All   **Glory to Christ our Saviour.**

James and John, the sons of Zebedee, approached Jesus and said, 'Master, we should like you to do us a favour.' 'What is it you want me to do?' he asked. They answered, 'Grant us the right to sit in state with you, one at your right and the other at your left.' Jesus said to them, 'You do not understand what you are asking. Can you drink the cup that I drink, or be baptized with the baptism I am baptized with?' 'We can', they answered. Jesus said, 'The cup that I drink you shall drink, and the baptism I am baptized with shall be your baptism; but to sit at my right or left is not for me to grant; it is for those to whom it has already been assigned.'

When the other ten heard this, they were indignant with James and John. Jesus called them to him and said, 'You know that in the world the recognized rulers lord it over their subjects, and their great men make them feel the weight of authority. That is not the way with you; among you, whoever wants to be great must be your servant, and whoever wants to be first must be the willing slave of all. For even the Son of Man did not come to be served but to serve, and to give up his life as a ransom for many.'

At the end the reader says

         This is the Gospel of Christ.
All   **Praise to Christ our Lord.**

9   **Sit**
    THE SERMON

10 **Stand**
    THE NICENE CREED may be said.

    All   **We believe in one God,
              the Father, the almighty,**

maker of heaven and earth,
of all that is,
seen and unseen.

We believe in one Lord, Jesus Christ,
the only Son of God,
eternally begotten of the Father,
God from God, Light from Light,
true God from true God,
begotten, not made,
of one Being with the Father.
Through him all things were made.
For us men and for our salvation
he came down from heaven;
by the power of the Holy Spirit
he became incarnate of the Virgin Mary,
    and was made man.
For our sake he was crucified under
    Pontius Pilate;
he suffered death and was buried.
On the third day he rose again
in accordance with the Scriptures;
he ascended into heaven
and is seated at the right hand of the Father.
He will come again in glory
to judge the living and the dead,
and his kingdom will have no end.

We believe in the Holy Spirit,
the Lord, the giver of life,
who proceeds from the Father and the Son.
With the Father and the Son he is worshipped
    and glorified.
He has spoken through the Prophets.

We believe in one holy catholic
    and apostolic Church.
We acknowledge one baptism for the
    forgiveness of sins.
We look for the resurrection of the dead,
and the life of the world to come. Amen.

THE PRESENTATION

11 The Archdeacon or other person appointed reads the name of each person to be ordained deacon, and that of the place where he is to serve, first saying

> Reverend Father, I present these persons to be ordained to the office of deacon in the Church of God.

12 The Bishop presents the candidates to the people, and says

> Those whose duty it is to inquire about these persons and examine them have found them to be of godly life and sound learning, and believe them to be duly called to serve God in this ministry. Is it therefore your will that they should be ordained?

People   **It is.**

Bishop   Will you uphold them in their ministry?
People   **We will.**

THE DECLARATION

13 **Sit**
The candidates stand before the Bishop, and the people sit.

Bishop   A deacon is called to serve the Church of God, and to work with its members in caring for the poor, the needy, the sick, and all who are in trouble. He is to strengthen the faithful, search out the careless and the indifferent, and to preach the word of God in the place to which he is licensed. A deacon assists the priest under whom he serves, in leading the worship of the people, especially in the administration of the Holy Communion. He may baptize when required to do so. It is his general duty to do such pastoral work as is entrusted to him.

In order that we may know your mind and purpose, and that you may be strengthened in your resolve to fulfil your ministry, you must make the declarations we now put to you.

Do you believe, so far as you know your own heart, that God has called you to the office and work of a deacon in his Church?

Answer   I believe that God has called me.

Bishop   Do you accept the holy Scriptures as revealing all things necessary for eternal salvation through faith in Jesus Christ?

Answer   I do so accept them.

Bishop   Do you believe the doctrine of the Christian faith as the Church of England has received it, and in your ministry will you expound and teach it?

Answer   I believe it, and will so do.

Bishop   Will you accept the discipline of this Church, and give due respect to those in authority?

Answer   By the help of God, I will.

Bishop   Will you be diligent in prayer, in reading holy Scripture, and in all studies that will deepen your faith and fit you to uphold the truth of the Gospel against error?

Answer   By the help of God, I will.

Bishop   Will you strive to fashion your own life and that of your household according to the way of Christ?

Answer   By the help of God, I will.

Bishop   Will you promote unity, peace, and love among all Christian people, and especially among those whom you serve?

Answer   By the help of God, I will.

Bishop	Will you then, in the strength of the Holy Spirit, continually stir up the gift of God that is in you, to make Christ known to all men?
Answer	By the help of God, I will.
Bishop	Almighty God, who has given you the will to undertake all these things, give you also the strength to perform them; that he may complete that work which he has begun in you; through Jesus Christ our Lord. **Amen.**

THE PRAYERS

15 **Kneel**

The Bishop commends those who are to be ordained to THE PRAYERS OF THE PEOPLE and silence is kept.

16 Bishop   Let us pray.

The Bishop or some other minister leads THE PRAYERS for the candidates and for the ministry of the whole Church.

God the Father,
have mercy on us.

God the Son,
have mercy on us.

God the Holy Spirit,
have mercy on us.

Holy, blessed, and glorious Trinity,
have mercy on us.

From all evil and mischief;
from pride, vanity, and hypocrisy;
from envy, hatred, and malice;
and from all evil intent,
Good Lord, deliver us.

From sloth, worldliness, and love of money;
from hardness of heart
and contempt for your word and your laws,
Good Lord, deliver us.

From sins of body and mind;
from the deceits of the world, the flesh,
    and the devil,
from error and false doctrine,
Good Lord, deliver us.

In all times of sorrow,
in all times of joy;
in the hour of death,
and at the day of judgement,
Good Lord, deliver us.

Govern and direct your holy Church; fill it with
love and truth; and grant it that unity which is
your will.
Hear us, good Lord.

Give us boldness to preach the gospel in all the
world, and to make disciples of all the nations.
Hear us, good Lord.

Enlighten your ministers with knowledge and
understanding, that by their teaching and their
lives they may proclaim your word.
Hear us, good Lord.

Bless your servants now to be made deacons,
that they may serve your Church and reveal
your glory in the world.
Hear us, good Lord.

Give your people grace to hear and receive your
word, and to bring forth the fruit of the Spirit.
Hear us, good Lord.

Bring into the way of truth all who have erred
and are deceived.
Hear us, good Lord.

Strengthen those who stand; comfort and help
the fainthearted; raise up the fallen; and finally
beat down Satan under our feet.
Hear us, good Lord.

Give us true repentance;
forgive us our sins of negligence and ignorance,
and our deliberate sins;
and grant us the grace of your Holy Spirit
to amend our lives according to your holy word.
**Holy God,
holy and strong,
holy and immortal,
have mercy on us.**

17   Bishop   Lord, you are merciful and forgive our sins. You
hear those who pray in the name of your Son.
Grant that what we have asked in faith we may
obtain according to your will; through Jesus
Christ our Lord. **Amen.**

THE ORDINATION

18   The candidates kneel before the Bishop; he stretches out his
hands towards them, and says

19   We praise and glorify you, most merciful Father,
because in your great love of mankind you sent
your only Son Jesus Christ to take the form of a
servant; he came to serve and not to be served;
and taught us that he who would be great
among us must be the servant of all; he humbled
himself for our sake, and in obedience accepted
death, even death on a cross; therefore you
highly exalted him and gave him the name
which is above every name.

And now we give you thanks that you have
called these your servants, whom we ordain in
your name, to share this ministry entrusted to
your Church.

Here the Bishop lays his hands on the head of each candidate, and says

> Send down the Holy Spirit upon your servant *N* for the office and work of a deacon in your Church.

When the Bishop has laid hands on all of them, he continues

> Almighty Father, give to these your servants grace and power to fulfil their ministry. Make them faithful to serve, ready to teach, constant in advancing your gospel; and grant that, always having full assurance of faith, abounding in hope, and being rooted and grounded in love, they may continue strong and steadfast in your Son Jesus Christ our Lord; to whom, with you and your Holy Spirit, belong glory and honour, worship and praise, now and for ever. **Amen.**

THE GIVING OF THE NEW TESTAMENT

20 Sit

The newly-ordained deacons stand, and the Bishop gives THE NEW TESTAMENT to each one, saying

> Receive this Book, as a sign of the authority given you this day to speak God's word to his people. Build them up in his truth and serve them in his name.

THE COMMUNION

21 Stand

The Bishop resumes the Communion Service at THE PEACE (Holy Communion Rite A, sections 30, 31; Rite B, sections 24, 25).

22

These special forms are used.

PROPER PREFACE
And now we give you thanks because within the royal priesthood of your Church you ordain ministers to proclaim the word of God, to care for your people, and to celebrate the sacraments of the new covenant.

POSTCOMMUNION SENTENCE
The Son of Man came not to be served but to serve, and to give his life as a ransom for many. *Mark 10.45*

POSTCOMMUNION COLLECT which may be said after the Sentence
Father,
you have taught the ministers of your Church
to be the willing servants of others.
Give to these your deacons
skill and gentleness in the practice of
their ministry,
and perseverance always in prayer;
through Jesus Christ our Lord. **Amen.**

BLESSING
Almighty God, who for the salvation of mankind gives to his people many gifts and ministries to the advancement of his glory, stir up in you the gifts of his grace, sustain each one of you in your own ministry; and the blessing . . .

The Ordination of Priests
(also called Presbyters)

THE PREPARATION

1   At the entry of the ministers, A HYMN, A CANTICLE, or A PSALM may be sung.

2   Bishop   The Lord be with you
      All   **and also with you.**

3   Bishop   God our Father, Lord of all the world,
                 we thank you that through your Son
                 you have called us into the fellowship of
                    your universal Church.
                 Hear our prayer for your faithful people
                 that each in his vocation and ministry
                 may be an instrument of your love,
                 and give your servants now to be ordained
                 the needful gifts of grace;
                 through our Lord and Saviour Jesus Christ.
                 Amen.

THE MINISTRY OF THE WORD

4   **Sit**
    OLD TESTAMENT READING

Isaiah 61.1-3a NEB
The spirit of the Lord God is upon me
because the Lord has anointed me;
he has sent me to bring good news to the humble,
to bind up the broken-hearted,
to proclaim liberty to captives
and release to those in prison;
to proclaim a year of the Lord's favour
and a day of the vengeance of our God;
to comfort all who mourn,
to give them garlands instead of ashes,

oil of gladness instead of mourners' tears,
a garment of splendour for the heavy heart.

or *Malachi 2.5-7 RSV*

My covenant with him was a covenant of life and peace, and
I gave them to him, that he might fear; and he feared me, he
stood in awe of my name. True instruction was in his mouth,
and no wrong was found on his lips. He walked with me in
peace and uprightness, and he turned many from iniquity.
For the lips of a priest should guard knowledge, and men
should seek instruction from his mouth, for he is the
messenger of the Lord of hosts.

At the end the reader may say

This is the word of the Lord.
All **Thanks be to God.**

5 **Stand**
Verses from PSALM 145

1 **I will exalt you O ˈ God my ˈ king:**
I will bless your ˈ name for ˈ ever · and ˈ ever.

2 **Every ˈ day · will I ˈ bless you:**
and praise your ˈ name for ˈ ever · and ˈ ever.

3 **Great is the Lord * and wonderfully ˈ worthy ·**
to be ˈ praised:
his greatness is ˈ past ˈ searching ˈ out.

4 **One generation shall praise your ˈ works · to an ˈother:**
and deˈclare your ˈ mighty ˈ acts.

5 **As for me * I will be talking of the glorious splendour ˈ**
of your ˈ majesty:
I will tell the ˈstory · of your ˈ marvel·lous ˈ works.

6 **Men shall recount the power of your ˈ terri·ble ˈ deeds:**
and ˈ I will · proˈclaim your ˈ greatness.

7 **Their lips shall flow‿**
with the remembrance of your aˈbundant ˈ goodness:
they shall ˈ shout for ˈ joy at · your ˈ righteousness.

21 **My mouth shall speak the ∣ praises · of the ∣ Lord:**
   and let all flesh bless his holy ∣ name
   for ∣ ever · and ∣ ever.

   Glory to the Father and ∣ to the ∣ Son:
   and ∣ to the ∣ Holy ∣ Spirit;
   as it was in the be∣ginning is ∣ now:
   and shall be for ∣ ever. ∣ A ∣men.

6 **Sit**
NEW TESTAMENT READING

2 Corinthians 5.14-19 NEB
The love of Christ leaves us no choice, when once we have
reached the conclusion that one man died for all and
therefore all mankind has died. His purpose in dying for all
was that men, while still in life, should cease to live for
themselves, and should live for him who for their sake died
and was raised to life. With us therefore worldly standards
have ceased to count in our estimate of any man; even if once
they counted in our understanding of Christ, they do so now
no longer. When anyone is united to Christ, there is a new
world; the old order has gone, and a new order has already
begun.

From first to last this has been the work of God. He has
reconciled us men to himself through Christ, and he has
enlisted us in this service of reconciliation. What I mean is,
that God was in Christ reconciling the world to himself, no
longer holding men's misdeeds against them, and that he
has entrusted us with the message of reconciliation.

At the end the reader may say

        This is the word of the Lord.
All   **Thanks be to God.**

7 **Stand**
A CANTICLE or A HYMN may be sung.

8   THE GOSPEL *John 20.19-23 RSV*

When it is announced

All   **Glory to Christ our Saviour.**

On the evening of that day, the first day of the week, the
doors being shut where the disciples were, for fear of the
Jews, Jesus came and stood among them and said to them,
'Peace be with you.' When he had said this, he showed them
his hands and his side. Then the disciples were glad when
they saw the Lord. Jesus said to them again, 'Peace be with
you. As the Father has sent me, even so I send you.' And
when he had said this, he breathed on them, and said to
them, 'Receive the Holy Spirit. If you forgive the sins of any,
they are forgiven; if you retain the sins of any, they
are retained.'

At the end the reader says

            This is the Gospel of Christ.
All   **Praise to Christ our Lord.**

9   **Sit**
     THE SERMON

10   **Stand**
     THE NICENE CREED may be said.

All   **We believe in one God,**
            the Father, the almighty,
            maker of heaven and earth,
            of all that is,
            seen and unseen.

            We believe in one Lord, Jesus Christ,
            the only Son of God,
            eternally begotten of the Father,
            God from God, Light from Light,
            true God from true God,
            begotten, not made,

of one Being with the Father.
Through him all things were made.
For us men and for our salvation
he came down from heaven;
by the power of the Holy Spirit
he became incarnate of the Virgin Mary,
   and was made man.
For our sake he was crucified under
   Pontius Pilate;
he suffered death and was buried.
On the third day he rose again
in accordance with the Scriptures;
he ascended into heaven
and is seated at the right hand of the Father.
He will come again in glory
to judge the living and the dead,
and his kingdom will have no end.

We believe in the Holy Spirit,
the Lord, the giver of life,
who proceeds from the Father and the Son.
With the Father and the Son he is worshipped
   and glorified.
He has spoken through the Prophets.

We believe in one holy catholic
   and apostolic Church.
We acknowledge one baptism for the
   forgiveness of sins.
We look for the resurrection of the dead,
and the life of the world to come. Amen.

THE PRESENTATION

11   The Archdeacon or other person appointed reads the name
      of each person to be ordained priest, and that of the place
      where he is to serve, first saying

         Reverend Father, I present these persons to be
         ordained to the office of priesthood in the
         Church of God.

12   The Bishop presents the candidates to the people, and says

Those whose duty it is to inquire about these
persons and examine them have found them to
be of godly life and sound learning, and believe
them to be duly called to serve God in this
ministry. Is it therefore your will that they
should be ordained?

People   **It is.**

Bishop   Will you uphold them in their ministry?
People   **We will.**

THE DECLARATION

13   **Sit**
Bishop   A priest is called by God to work with the bishop
and with his fellow-priests, as servant and
shepherd among the people to whom he is sent.
He is to proclaim the word of the Lord, to call his
hearers to repentance, and in Christ's name to
absolve, and to declare the forgiveness of sins.
He is to baptize, and prepare the baptized for
Confirmation. He is to preside at the celebration
of the Holy Communion. He is to lead his people
in prayer and worship, to intercede for them, to
bless them in the name of the Lord, and to teach
and encourage by word and example. He is to
minister to the sick, and prepare the dying for
their death. He must set the Good Shepherd
always before him as the pattern of his calling,
caring for the people committed to his charge,
and joining with them in a common witness to
the world.

In the name of our Lord we bid you remember
the greatness of the trust now to be committed to
your charge, about which you have been taught
in your preparation for this ministry. You are to
be messengers, watchmen, and stewards of the
Lord; you are to teach and to admonish, to feed

and to provide for the Lord's family, to search for his children in the wilderness of this world's temptations and to guide them through its confusions, so that they may be saved through Christ for ever.

Remember always with thanksgiving that the treasure now to be entrusted to you is Christ's own flock, bought through the shedding of his blood on the cross. The Church and congregation among whom you will serve are one with him: they are his body. Serve them with joy, build them up in faith, and do all in your power to bring them to loving obedience to Christ.

Because you cannot bear the weight of this ministry in your own strength but only by the grace and power of God, pray earnestly for his Holy Spirit. Pray that he will each day enlarge and enlighten your understanding of the Scriptures, so that you may grow stronger and more mature in your ministry, as you fashion your life and the lives of your people on the word of God.

We trust that long ago you began to weigh and ponder all this, and that you are fully determined, by the grace of God, to give yourselves wholly to his service and devote to him your best powers of mind and spirit, so that, as you daily follow the rule and teaching of our Lord, with the heavenly assistance of his Holy Spirit, you may grow up into his likeness, and sanctify the lives of all with whom you have to do.

14   The Bishop says to those who are to be ordained

In order that we may know your mind and purpose, and that you may be strengthened in your resolve to fulfil your ministry, you must make the declarations we now put to you.

Do you believe, so far as you know your own heart, that God has called you to the office and work of a priest in his Church?

Answer   I believe that God has called me.

Bishop   Do you accept the holy Scriptures as revealing all things necessary for eternal salvation through faith in Jesus Christ?

Answer   I do so accept them.

Bishop   Do you believe the doctrine of the Christian faith as the Church of England has received it, and in your ministry will you expound and teach it?

Answer   I believe it, and will so do.

Bishop   Will you accept the discipline of this Church, and give due respect to those in authority?

Answer   By the help of God, I will.

Bishop   Will you be diligent in prayer, in reading holy Scripture, and in all studies that will deepen your faith and fit you to uphold the truth of the Gospel against error?

Answer   By the help of God, I will.

Bishop   Will you strive to fashion your own life and that of your household according to the way of Christ?

Answer   By the help of God, I will.

Bishop   Will you promote unity, peace, and love among all Christian people, and especially among those whom you serve?

Answer   By the help of God, I will.

Bishop	Will you then, in the strength of the Holy Spirit, continually stir up the gift of God that is in you, to make Christ known to all men?
Answer	By the help of God, I will.
Bishop	Almighty God, who has given you the will to undertake all these things, give you also the strength to perform them; that he may complete that work which he has begun in you; through Jesus Christ our Lord. **Amen.**

THE PRAYERS

15 **Kneel**

The Bishop commends those who are to be ordained to THE PRAYERS OF THE PEOPLE and silence is kept.

16 VENI CREATOR is sung.

**Come, Holy Ghost, our souls inspire,
And lighten with celestial fire;
Thou the anointing Spirit art,
Who dost thy sevenfold gifts impart;**

**Thy blessèd unction from above
Is comfort, life, and fire of love;
Enable with perpetual light
The dullness of our blinded sight.**

**Anoint and cheer our soilèd face
With the abundance of thy grace;
Keep far our foes, give peace at home;
Where thou art guide no ill can come.**

**Teach us to know the Father, Son,
And thee, of both, to be but One;
That through the ages all along
This may be our endless song,**

**Praise to thy eternal merit,
Father, Son, and Holy Spirit. Amen.**

17 Bishop   Let us pray.

The Bishop or some other minister leads THE PRAYERS for the candidates and for the ministry of the whole Church.

God the Father,
have mercy on us.

God the Son,
have mercy on us.

God the Holy Spirit,
have mercy on us.

Holy, blessed, and glorious Trinity,
have mercy on us.

From all evil and mischief;
from pride, vanity, and hypocrisy;
from envy, hatred, and malice;
and from all evil intent,
Good Lord, deliver us.

From sloth, worldliness, and love of money;
from hardness of heart
and contempt for your word and your laws,
Good Lord, deliver us.

From sins of body and mind;
from the deceits of the world, the flesh,
    and the devil,
from error and false doctrine,
Good Lord, deliver us.

In all times of sorrow,
in all times of joy;
in the hour of death,
and at the day of judgement,
Good Lord, deliver us.

Govern and direct your holy Church; fill it with love and truth; and grant it that unity which is your will.
Hear us, good Lord.

Give us boldness to preach the gospel in all the world, and to make disciples of all the nations.
Hear us, good Lord.

Enlighten your ministers with knowledge and understanding, that by their teaching and their lives they may proclaim your word.
Hear us, good Lord.

Bless your servants now to be made priests, that they may serve your Church and reveal your glory in the world.
Hear us, good Lord.

Give your people grace to hear and receive your word, and to bring forth the fruit of the Spirit.
Hear us, good Lord.

Bring into the way of truth all who have erred and are deceived.
Hear us, good Lord.

Strengthen those who stand; comfort and help the fainthearted; raise up the fallen; and finally beat down Satan under our feet.
Hear us, good Lord.

Give us true repentance;
forgive us our sins of negligence and ignorance, and our deliberate sins;
and grant us the grace of your Holy Spirit
to amend our lives according to your holy word.
Holy God,
holy and strong,
holy and immortal,
have mercy on us.

Bishop   Lord, you are merciful and forgive our sins. You hear those who pray in the name of your Son. Grant that what we have asked in faith we may obtain according to your will; through Jesus Christ our Lord. **Amen.**

18 The Bishop stands with the priests who assist him; the
candidates kneel before him; he stretches out his hands
towards them, and says

19 We praise and glorify you, almighty Father,
because you have formed throughout the world
a holy people for your own possession, a royal
priesthood, a universal Church.

We praise and glorify you because you have
given us your only Son Jesus Christ to be the
Apostle and High Priest of our faith, and the
Shepherd of our souls.

We praise and glorify you that by his death he
has overcome death; and that, having ascended
into heaven, he has given his gifts abundantly,
making some, apostles; some, prophets; some,
evangelists; some, pastors and teachers; to
equip your people for the work of ministry and
to build up his body.

And now we give you thanks that you have
called these your servants, whom we ordain in
your name, to share this ministry entrusted to
your Church.

Here the Bishop and priests lay their hands on the head of
each candidate, and the Bishop says

Send down the Holy Spirit upon your servant *N*
for the office and work of a priest in your
Church.

When the Bishop has laid hands on all of them, he continues

Almighty Father, give to these your servants
grace and power to fulfil their ministry among
those committed to their charge; to watch over
them and care for them; to absolve and bless
them in your name, and to proclaim the gospel

of your salvation. Set them among your people
to offer with them spiritual sacrifices acceptable
in your sight and to minister the sacraments of
the new covenant. As you have called them to
your service, make them worthy of their calling.
Give them wisdom and discipline to work
faithfully with all their fellow-servants in Christ,
that the world may come to know your glory and
your love.

Accept our prayers, most merciful Father,
through your Son Jesus Christ our Lord, to
whom, with you and your Holy Spirit, belong
glory and honour, worship and praise, now and
for ever. **Amen.**

THE GIVING OF THE BIBLE

20   **Sit**
The newly-ordained priests stand, and the Bishop gives
THE BIBLE to each one, saying

> Receive this Book, as a sign of the authority
> which God has given you this day to preach the
> gospel of Christ and to minister his
> Holy Sacraments.

THE COMMUNION

21   **Stand**
The Bishop resumes the Communion Service at THE PEACE
(Holy Communion Rite A, sections 30, 31; Rite B, sections
24, 25).

22   These special forms are used.

PROPER PREFACE
And now we give you thanks because within the royal
priesthood of your Church you ordain ministers to proclaim
the word of God, to care for your people, and to celebrate the
sacraments of the new covenant.

POSTCOMMUNION SENTENCE

The Son of Man came not to be served but to serve, and to give his life as a ransom for many. *Mark 10.45*

POSTCOMMUNION COLLECT which may be said after the Sentence

Father,
you have appointed your Son
to be our high priest for ever.
Fulfil now your purpose in choosing these men
to be ministers and stewards
    of your word and sacraments;
and grant that they may be found faithful
in the ministry they have received;
through Jesus Christ our Lord. **Amen.**

BLESSING

Almighty God, who for the salvation of mankind gives to his people many gifts and ministries to the advancement of his glory, stir up in you the gifts of his grace, sustain each one of you in your own ministry; and the blessing . . .

The Ordination of Deacons and Priests
(also called Presbyters)

THE PREPARATION

1 At the entry of the ministers, A HYMN, A CANTICLE, or
   A PSALM may be sung.

2 Bishop   The Lord be with you
   All   **and also with you.**

3 Bishop   God our Father, Lord of all the world,
           we thank you that through your Son
           you have called us into the fellowship of
               your universal Church.
           Hear our prayer for your faithful people
           that each in his vocation and ministry
           may be an instrument of your love,
           and give your servants now to be ordained
           the needful gifts of grace;
           through our Lord and Saviour Jesus Christ.
           Amen.

THE MINISTRY OF THE WORD

4 **Sit**
   OLD TESTAMENT READING

   Isaiah 6.1-8 RSV
   In the year that King Uzziah died I saw the Lord sitting upon
   a throne, high and lifted up; and his train filled the temple.
   Above him stood the seraphim; each had six wings: with two
   he covered his face, and with two he covered his feet, and
   with two he flew. And one called to another and said: 'Holy,
   holy, holy is the Lord of hosts; the whole earth is full of his
   glory.' And the foundations of the thresholds shook at the
   voice of him who called, and the house was filled with
   smoke. And I said: 'Woe is me! For I am lost; for I am a man of

unclean lips, and I dwell in the midst of a people of unclean lips; for my eyes have seen the King, the Lord of hosts!' Then flew one of the seraphim to me, having in his hand a burning coal which he had taken with tongs from the altar. And he touched my mouth, and said: 'Behold, this has touched your lips; your guilt is taken away, and your sin forgiven.' And I heard the voice of the Lord saying, 'Whom shall I send, and who will go for us?' Then I said, 'Here I am! Send me.'

At the end the reader may say

This is the word of the Lord.

All   **Thanks be to God.**

5 **Stand**
Verses from PSALM 145

1 **I will exalt you O ǀ God my ǀ king:**
    I will bless your ǀ name for ǀ ever · and ǀ ever.

2 **Every ǀ day · will I ǀ bless you:**
    and praise your ǀ name for ǀ ever · and ǀ ever.

3 **Great is the Lord * and wonderfully ǀ worthy ·**
to be ǀ praised:
    his greatness is ǀ past ǀ searching ǀ out.

4 **One generation shall praise your ǀ works · to an ǀother:**
    and de ǀclare your ǀ mighty ǀ acts.

5 **As for me * I will be talking of the glorious splendour ǀ**
of your ǀ majesty:
    I will tell the ǀ story · of your ǀ marvel ǀlous ǀ works.

6 **Men shall recount the power of your ǀ terri · ble ǀ deeds:**
    and ǀ I will · pro ǀclaim your ǀ greatness.

7 **Their lips shall flow‿**
with the remembrance of your a ǀbundant ǀ goodness:
    they shall ǀ shout for ǀ joy at · your ǀ righteousness.

21 **My mouth shall speak the ǀ praises · of the ǀ Lord:**
    and let all flesh bless his holy ǀ name
    for ǀ ever · and ǀ ever.

Glory to the Father and │ to the │ Son:
   and │ to the │ Holy │ Spirit;
as it was in the be│ginning is │ now:
   and shall be for │ ever. │ A│men.

6   **Sit**
   NEW TESTAMENT READING

Romans 12.1-12 RSV
I appeal to you, brethren, by the mercies of God, to present
your bodies as a living sacrifice, holy and acceptable to God,
which is your spiritual worship. Do not be conformed to this
world but be transformed by the renewal of your mind, that
you may prove what is the will of God, what is good and
acceptable and perfect.

For by the grace given to me I bid every one among you not
to think of himself more highly than he ought to think, but to
think with sober judgement, each according to the measure
of faith which God has assigned him. For as in one body we
have many members, and all the members do not have the
same function, so we, though many, are one body in Christ,
and individually members one of another. Having gifts that
differ according to the grace given to us, let us use them: if
prophecy, in proportion to our faith; if service, in our
serving; he who teaches, in his teaching; he who exhorts, in
his exhortation; he who contributes, in liberality; he who
gives aid, with zeal; he who does acts of mercy, with
cheerfulness.

Let love be genuine; hate what is evil, hold fast to what is
good; love one another with brotherly affection; outdo one
another in showing honour. Never flag in zeal, be aglow
with the Spirit, serve the Lord. Rejoice in your hope, be
patient in tribulation, be constant in prayer.

At the end the reader may say

               This is the word of the Lord.
All   **Thanks be to God.**

7   A CANTICLE or A HYMN may be sung.

8   THE GOSPEL *John 20.19-23 RSV*

When it is announced

All   **Glory to Christ our Saviour.**

On the evening of that day, the first day of the week, the
doors being shut where the disciples were, for fear of the
Jews, Jesus came and stood among them and said to them,
'Peace be with you.' When he had said this, he showed them
his hands and his side. Then the disciples were glad when
they saw the Lord. Jesus said to them again, 'Peace be with
you. As the Father has sent me, even so I send you.' And
when he had said this, he breathed on them, and said to
them, 'Receive the Holy Spirit. If you forgive the sins of any,
they are forgiven; if you retain the sins of any, they
are retained.'

At the end the reader says

            This is the Gospel of Christ.
All   **Praise to Christ our Lord.**

9   **Sit**
     THE SERMON

10   **Stand**
     THE NICENE CREED may be said.

     All   **We believe in one God,**
                      the Father, the almighty,
                      maker of heaven and earth,
                      of all that is,
                      seen and unseen.

We believe in one Lord, Jesus Christ,
the only Son of God,
eternally begotten of the Father,
God from God, Light from Light,
true God from true God,
begotten, not made,
of one Being with the Father.
Through him all things were made.
For us men and for our salvation
he came down from heaven;
by the power of the Holy Spirit
he became incarnate of the Virgin Mary,
    and was made man.
For our sake he was crucified under
    Pontius Pilate;
he suffered death and was buried.
On the third day he rose again
in accordance with the Scriptures;
he ascended into heaven
and is seated at the right hand of the Father.
He will come again in glory
to judge the living and the dead,
and his kingdom will have no end.

We believe in the Holy Spirit,
the Lord, the giver of life,
who proceeds from the Father and the Son.
With the Father and the Son he is worshipped
    and glorified.
He has spoken through the Prophets.

We believe in one holy catholic
    and apostolic Church.
We acknowledge one baptism for the
    forgiveness of sins.
We look for the resurrection of the dead,
and the life of the world to come. Amen.

THE PRESENTATION OF DEACONS

11   The Archdeacon or other person appointed reads the name
     of each person to be ordained deacon, and that of the place
     where he is to serve, first saying

> Reverend Father, I present these persons to be
> ordained to the office of deacon in the Church
> of God.

12   The Bishop presents the candidates to the people, and says

> Those whose duty it is to inquire about these
> persons and examine them have found them to
> be of godly life and sound learning, and believe
> them to be duly called to serve God in this
> ministry. Is it therefore your will that they
> should be ordained?

People   **It is.**

Bishop   Will you uphold them in their ministry?
People   **We will.**

13   **Sit**
     The candidates stand before the Bishop, and the people sit.

Bishop   A deacon is called to serve the Church of God,
             and to work with its members in caring for the
             poor, the needy, the sick, and all who are in
             trouble. He is to strengthen the faithful, search
             out the careless and the indifferent, and to
             preach the word of God in the place to which he
             is licensed. A deacon assists the priest under
             whom he serves, in leading the worship of the
             people, especially in the administration of the
             Holy Communion. He may baptize when
             required to do so. It is his general duty to do
             such pastoral work as is entrusted to him.

THE PRESENTATION OF PRIESTS

14 **Stand**

The Archdeacon or other person appointed reads the name of each person to be ordained priest, and that of the place where he is to serve, first saying

> Reverend Father, I present these persons to be ordained to the office of priesthood in the Church of God.

15 The Bishop presents the candidates to the people, and says

> Those whose duty it is to inquire about these persons and examine them have found them to be of godly life and sound learning, and believe them to be duly called to serve God in this ministry. Is it therefore your will that they should be ordained?

People **It is.**

Bishop Will you uphold them in their ministry?
People **We will.**

16 **Sit**

The candidates stand before the Bishop, and the people sit.

Bishop A priest is called by God to work with the bishop and with his fellow-priests, as servant and shepherd among the people to whom he is sent. He is to proclaim the word of the Lord, to call his hearers to repentance, and in Christ's name to absolve, and declare the forgiveness of sins. He is to baptize, and to prepare the baptized for Confirmation. He is to preside at the celebration of the Holy Communion. He is to lead his people in prayer and worship, to intercede for them, to bless them in the name of the Lord, and to teach and encourage by word and example. He is to minister to the sick, and prepare the dying for their death. He must set the Good Shepherd always before him as the pattern of his calling, caring for the people committed to his charge, and joining with them in a common witness to the world.

In the name of our Lord we bid you remember the greatness of the trust now to be committed to your charge, about which you have been taught in your preparation for this ministry. You are to be messengers, watchmen, and stewards of the Lord; you are to teach and to admonish, to feed and to provide for the Lord's family, to search for his children in the wilderness of this world's temptations and to guide them through its confusions, so that they may be saved through Christ for ever.

Remember always with thanksgiving that the treasure now to be entrusted to you is Christ's own flock, bought through the shedding of his blood on the cross. The Church and congregation among whom you will serve are one with him: they are his body. Serve them with joy, build them up in faith, and do all in your power to bring them to loving obedience to Christ.

Because you cannot bear the weight of this ministry in your own strength but only by the grace and power of God, pray earnestly for his Holy Spirit. Pray that he will each day enlarge and enlighten your understanding of the Scriptures, so that you may grow stronger and more mature in your ministry, as you fashion your life and the lives of your people on the word of God.

We trust that long ago you began to weigh and ponder all this, and that you are fully determined, by the grace of God, to give yourselves wholly to his service and devote to him your best powers of mind and spirit, so that, as you daily follow the rule and teaching of our Lord, with the heavenly assistance of his Holy Spirit, you may grow up into his likeness, and sanctify the lives of all with whom you have to do.

THE DECLARATION

17   The Bishop says to those who are to be ordained

In order that we may know your mind and purpose, and that you may be strengthened in your resolve to fulfil your ministry, you must make the declarations we now put to you.

Do you believe, so far as you know your own heart, that God has called you to the office and work of a deacon or of a priest in his Church?

Answer   I believe that God has called me.

Bishop   Do you accept the holy Scriptures as revealing all things necessary for eternal salvation through faith in Jesus Christ?

Answer   I do so accept them.

Bishop   Do you believe the doctrine of the Christian faith as the Church of England has received it, and in your ministry will you expound and teach it?

Answer   I believe it, and will so do.

Bishop   Will you accept the discipline of this Church, and give due respect to those in authority?

Answer   By the help of God, I will.

Bishop   Will you be diligent in prayer, in reading holy Scripture, and in all studies that will deepen your faith and fit you to uphold the truth of the Gospel against error?

Answer   By the help of God, I will.

Bishop	Will you strive to fashion your own life and that of your household according to the way of Christ?
Answer	By the help of God, I will.
Bishop	Will you promote unity, peace, and love among all Christian people, and especially among those whom you serve?
Answer	By the help of God, I will.
Bishop	Will you then, in the strength of the Holy Spirit, continually stir up the gift of God that is in you to make Christ known to all men?
Answer	By the help of God, I will.
Bishop	Almighty God, who has given you the will to undertake all these things, give you also the strength to perform them, that he may complete that work which he has begun in you; through Jesus Christ our Lord. **Amen.**

THE PRAYERS

15 **Kneel**

The Bishop commends those who are to be ordained to THE PRAYERS OF THE PEOPLE and silence is kept.

16 VENI CREATOR is sung.

> Come, Holy Ghost, our souls inspire,
> And lighten with celestial fire;
> Thou the anointing Spirit art,
> Who dost thy sevenfold gifts impart;
>
> Thy blessèd unction from above
> Is comfort, life, and fire of love;
> Enable with perpetual light
> The dullness of our blinded sight.

Anoint and cheer our soilèd face
With the abundance of thy grace;
Keep far our foes, give peace at home;
Where thou art guide no ill can come.

Teach us to know the Father, Son,
And thee, of both, to be but One;
That through the ages all along
This may be our endless song,

Praise to thy eternal merit,
Father, Son, and Holy Spirit. Amen.

20 Bishop   Let us pray.

The Bishop or some other minister leads THE PRAYERS for
the candidates and the ministry of the whole Church.

God the Father,
have mercy on us.

God the Son,
have mercy on us.

God the Holy Spirit,
have mercy on us.

Holy, blessed, and glorious Trinity,
have mercy on us.

From all evil and mischief;
from pride, vanity, and hypocrisy;
from envy, hatred, and malice;
and from all evil intent,
Good Lord, deliver us.

From sloth, worldliness, and love of money;
from hardness of heart
and contempt for your word and your laws,
Good Lord, deliver us.

From sins of body and mind;
from the deceits of the world, the flesh,
    and the devil,
from error and false doctrine,
Good Lord, deliver us.

In all times of sorrow,
in all times of joy;
in the hour of death,
and at the day of judgement,
Good Lord, deliver us.

Govern and direct your holy Church; fill it with
love and truth; and grant it that unity which is
your will.
Hear us, good Lord.

Give us boldness to preach the gospel in all the
world, and to make disciples of all the nations.
Hear us, good Lord.

Enlighten your ministers with knowledge and
understanding, that by their teaching and their
lives they may proclaim your word.
Hear us, good Lord.

Bless your servants now to be made deacons
and priests, that they may serve your Church
and reveal your glory in the world.
Hear us, good Lord.

Give your people grace to hear and receive your
word, and to bring forth the fruit of the Spirit.
Hear us, good Lord.

Bring into the way of truth all who have erred
and are deceived.
Hear us, good Lord.

Strengthen those who stand; comfort and help
the fainthearted; raise up the fallen; and finally
beat down Satan under our feet.
Hear us, good Lord.

Give us true repentance;
forgive us our sins of negligence and ignorance,
and our deliberate sins;
and grant us the grace of your Holy Spirit
to amend our lives according to your holy word.

Holy God,
holy and strong,
holy and immortal,
have mercy on us.

Bishop Lord, you are merciful and forgive our sins. You
hear those who pray in the name of your Son.
Grant that what we have asked in faith we may
obtain according to your will; through Jesus
Christ our Lord. **Amen.**

THE ORDINATION OF DEACONS

21 The candidates kneel before the Bishop; he stretches out his
hands towards them, and says

22 We praise and glorify you, most merciful Father,
because in your great love of mankind you sent
your only Son Jesus Christ to take the form of a
servant; he came to serve and not to be served;
and taught us that he who would be great
among us must be the servant of all; he humbled
himself for our sake, and in obedience accepted
death, even death on a cross; therefore you
highly exalted him and gave him the name
which is above every name.

And now we give you thanks that you have
called these your servants, whom we ordain in
your name, to share this ministry entrusted to
your Church.

Here the Bishop lays his hands on the head of each
candidate, and says

Send down the Holy Spirit upon your servant N
for the office and work of a deacon in your
Church.

When the Bishop has laid hands on all of them, he continues

Almighty Father, give to these your servants grace and power to fulfil their ministry. Make them faithful to serve, ready to teach, constant in advancing your gospel; and grant that, always having full assurance of faith, abounding in hope, and being rooted and grounded in love, they may continue strong and steadfast in your Son Jesus Christ our Lord; to whom, with you and your Holy Spirit, belong glory and honour, worship and praise, now and for ever. **Amen.**

THE GIVING OF THE NEW TESTAMENT

23 **Sit**

The newly-ordained deacons stand, and the Bishop gives THE NEW TESTAMENT to each one, saying

Receive this Book, as a sign of the authority given you this day to speak God's word to his people. Build them up in his truth, and serve them in his name.

THE ORDINATION OF PRIESTS

24 The Bishop stands with the priests who assist him; the candidates for the priesthood kneel before him; he stretches out his hands towards them, and says

25 We praise and glorify you, almighty Father, because you have formed throughout the world a holy people for your own possession, a royal priesthood, a universal Church.

We praise and glorify you because you have given us your only Son Jesus Christ to be the Apostle and High Priest of our faith, and the Shepherd of our souls.

We praise and glorify you that by his death he
has overcome death; and that, having ascended
into heaven, he has given his gifts abundantly,
making some, apostles; some, prophets; some,
evangelists; some, pastors and teachers; to
equip your people for the work of ministry and
to build up his body.

And now we give you thanks that you have
called these your servants, whom we ordain in
your name, to share this ministry entrusted to
your Church.

Here the Bishop and priests lay their hands on the head of
each candidate, and the Bishop says

Send down the Holy Spirit upon your servant *N*
for the office and work of a priest in your
Church.

When the Bishop has laid hands on all of them, he continues

Almighty Father, give to these your servants
grace and power to fulfil their ministry among
those committed to their charge; to watch over
them and care for them; to absolve and bless
them in your name, and to proclaim the gospel
of your salvation. Set them among your people
to offer with them spiritual sacrifices acceptable
in your sight and to minister the sacraments of
the new covenant. As you have called them to
your service, make them worthy of their calling.
Give them wisdom and discipline to work
faithfully with all their fellow-servants in Christ,
that the world may come to know your glory and
your love.

Accept our prayers, most merciful Father,
through your Son Jesus Christ our Lord, to
whom, with you and your Holy Spirit, belong
glory and honour, worship and praise, now and
for ever. **Amen.**

THE GIVING OF THE BIBLE

26 Sit

The newly-ordained priests stand, and the Bishop gives
THE BIBLE to each one, saying

> Receive this Book, as a sign of the authority
> which God has given you this day to preach the
> gospel of Christ and to minister his Holy
> Sacraments.

THE COMMUNION

27 Stand

The Bishop resumes the Communion Service at THE PEACE
(Holy Communion Rite A, sections 30, 31; Rite B, sections
24, 25).

28 These special forms are used.

PROPER PREFACE
And now we give you thanks because within the royal
priesthood of your Church you ordain ministers to proclaim
the word of God, to care for your people, and to celebrate the
sacraments of the new covenant.

POSTCOMMUNION SENTENCE
The Son of Man came not to be served but to serve, and to
give his life as a ransom for many. *Mark 10.45*

POSTCOMMUNION COLLECTS which may be said after
the Sentence

> Father,
> you have taught the ministers of your Church
> to be the willing servants of others.
> Give to these your deacons
> skill and gentleness in the practice of
>   their ministry,
> and perseverance always in prayer;
> through Jesus Christ our Lord. **Amen.**

Father,
you have appointed your Son
to be our high priest for ever.
Fulfil now your purpose in choosing these men
to be ministers and stewards
    of your word and sacraments;
and grant that they may be found faithful
in the ministry they have received;
through Jesus Christ our Lord. **Amen.**

BLESSING

Almighty God, who for the salvation of mankind gives to his people many gifts and ministries to the advancement of his glory, stir up in you the gifts of his grace, sustain each one of you in your own ministry; and the blessing . . .

The Ordination or Consecration of a Bishop

THE PREPARATION

1   At the entry of the ministers, A HYMN, A CANTICLE, or A PSALM may be sung.

2   Archbishop The Lord be with you
     All   **and also with you.**

3   Archbishop God our Father, Lord of all the world,
                  we thank you that through your Son
                  you have called us into the fellowship of
                     your universal Church.
                  Hear our prayer for your faithful people
                  that each in his vocation and ministry
                  may be an instrument of your love,
                  and give your servant now to be ordained
                     bishop,
                  the needful gifts of grace;
                  through our Lord and Saviour Jesus Christ.
                  Amen.

THE MINISTRY OF THE WORD

4   **Sit**
     OLD TESTAMENT READING

Numbers 27.15-20, 22, 23 RSV
Moses said to the Lord, 'Let the Lord, the God of the spirits of all flesh, appoint a man over the congregation, who shall go out before them and come in before them, who shall lead them out and bring them in; that the congregation of the Lord may not be as sheep which have no shepherd.' And the Lord said to Moses, 'Take Joshua the son of Nun, a man in whom is the spirit, and lay your hand upon him; cause him to stand before Eleazar the priest and all the congregation, and you shall commission him in their sight. You shall invest

him with some of your authority, that all the congregation of the people of Israel may obey.' And Moses did as the Lord commanded him; he took Joshua and caused him to stand before Eleazar the priest and the whole congregation, and he laid his hands upon him, and commissioned him as the Lord directed through Moses.

At the end the reader may say

	This is the word of the Lord.
All	**Thanks be to God.**

5 **Stand**
Verses from PSALM 119

165 **Great is the peace of those who ˈ love your ˈ law:**
    and ˈ nothing · shall ˈ make them ˈ stumble.

166 **Lord I have waited for ˈ your salˈvation:**
    and I have ˈ done ˈ your comˈmandments.

167 **My soul has heeded ˈ your comˈmands:**
    and I ˈ love them · beˈyond ˈ measure.

168 **I have kept your precepts ˈ and comˈmands:**
    for all my ˈ ways are ˈ open · beˈfore you.

169 **Let my cry ˈ come to you · O ˈ Lord:**
    O give me understanding acˈcording ˈ to your ˈ word.

170 **Let my supplication ˈ come beˈfore you:**
    and deliver me acˈcording ˈ to your ˈ promise.

171 **My lips shall pour ˈ forth your ˈ praise:**
    beˈcause you ˈ teach me · your ˈ statutes;

172 **my tongue shall ˈ sing of · your ˈ word:**
    for ˈ all · your comˈmandments · are ˈ righteousness.

173 **Let your hand be ˈ swift to ˈ help me:**
    for ˈ I have ˈ chosen · your ˈ precepts.

174 **Lord I have longed for ˈ your salˈvation:**
    and your ˈ law is ˈ my deˈlight.

Glory to the Father and | to the | Son:
** and | to the | Holy | Spirit;**
as it was in the be|ginning is | now:
** and shall be for | ever. | A|men.**

6   **Sit**
NEW TESTAMENT READING

2 Corinthians 4.1-10 NEB
Seeing that we have been entrusted with this commission,
which we owe entirely to God's mercy, we never lose heart.
We have renounced the deeds that men hide for very shame;
we neither practise cunning nor distort the word of God;
only by declaring the truth openly do we recommend
ourselves, and then it is to the common conscience of our
fellow-men and in the sight of God. And if indeed our
gospel be found veiled, the only people who find it so are
those on the way to perdition. Their unbelieving minds are
so blinded by the god of this passing age, that the gospel of
the glory of Christ, who is the very image of God, cannot
dawn upon them and bring them light. It is not ourselves
that we proclaim; we proclaim Christ Jesus as Lord, and
ourselves as your servants, for Jesus' sake. For the same God
who said, 'Out of darkness let light shine', has caused his
light to shine within us, to give the light of revelation—the
revelation of the glory of God in the face of Jesus Christ.

We are no better than pots of earthenware to contain this
treasure, and this proves that such transcendent power does
not come from us, but is God's alone. Hard-pressed on
every side, we are never hemmed in; bewildered, we are
never at our wits' end; hunted, we are never abandoned to
our fate; struck down, we are not left to die. Wherever we go
we carry death with us in our body, the death that Jesus
died, that in this body also life may reveal itself, the life that
Jesus lives.

At the end the reader may say

           This is the word of the Lord.
All   **Thanks be to God.**

7   **Stand**
     A CANTICLE or A HYMN may be sung.

8   THE GOSPEL *John 21.15-17 RSV*

     When it is announced

     All   **Glory to Christ our Saviour.**

     When they had finished breakfast, Jesus said to Simon
     Peter, 'Simon, son of John, do you love me more than these?'
     He said to him, 'Yes, Lord; you know that I love you.' He
     said to him, 'Feed my lambs.' A second time he said to him,
     'Simon, son of John, do you love me?' He said to him, 'Yes,
     Lord; you know that I love you.' He said to him, 'Tend my
     sheep.' He said to him the third time, 'Simon, son of John,
     do you love me?' Peter was grieved because he said to him
     the third time, 'Do you love me?' And he said to him, 'Lord,
     you know everything; you know that I love you.' Jesus said
     to him, 'Feed my sheep.'

     At the end the reader says

                     This is the Gospel of Christ.
     All   **Praise to Christ our Lord.**

9   **Sit**
     THE SERMON

10   **Stand**
     THE NICENE CREED may be said.

     All   **We believe in one God,**
                     the Father, the almighty,
                     maker of heaven and earth,
                     of all that is,
                     seen and unseen.

                     We believe in one Lord, Jesus Christ,
                     the only Son of God,
                     eternally begotten of the Father,

God from God, Light from Light,
true God from true God,
begotten, not made,
of one Being with the Father.
Through him all things were made.
For us men and for our salvation
he came down from heaven;
by the power of the Holy Spirit
he became incarnate of the Virgin Mary,
    and was made man.
For our sake he was crucified under
    Pontius Pilate;
he suffered death and was buried.
On the third day he rose again
in accordance with the Scriptures;
he ascended into heaven
and is seated at the right hand of the Father.
He will come again in glory
to judge the living and the dead,
and his kingdom will have no end.

We believe in the Holy Spirit,
the Lord, the giver of life,
who proceeds from the Father and the Son.
With the Father and the Son he is worshipped
    and glorified.
He has spoken through the Prophets.

We believe in one holy catholic
    and apostolic Church.
We acknowledge one baptism for the
    forgiveness of sins.
We look for the resurrection of the dead,
and the life of the world to come. Amen.

THE PRESENTATION

11   Two bishops present the Bishop-elect, saying

> Reverend Father, we present *N* to be ordained and consecrated to the office of bishop in the Church of God.

Archbishop Let the authority for the ordination be read.

The Provincial Registrar reads the Royal Mandate.

12   When the Mandate has been read, the Archbishop presents the Bishop-elect to the people, saying

> Those who have authority to do so have chosen *N*, as a man of godly life and sound learning, to be a bishop in the Church of God. Is it therefore your will that he should be ordained?

People   **It is.**

Archbishop Will you uphold him in his ministry?
People   **We will.**

The Archbishop then reads THE PREFACE TO THE DECLARATION OF ASSENT.

> The Church of England is part of the one, holy, catholic, and apostolic Church, worshipping the one true God, Father, Son, and Holy Spirit. It professes the faith uniquely revealed in the holy Scriptures and set forth in the catholic creeds, which faith the Church is called upon to proclaim afresh in each generation. Led by the Holy Spirit, it has borne witness to Christian truth in its historic formularies, the Thirty-nine Articles of Religion, the Book of Common Prayer, and the Ordering of Bishops, Priests, and Deacons. In the declaration you are about to make, will you affirm your loyalty to this inheritance of faith as your inspiration and

guidance under God in bringing the grace and truth of Christ to this generation and making him known to those in your care?

The Bishop-elect

I, *N*, do so affirm, and accordingly declare my belief in the faith which is revealed in the holy Scriptures and set forth in the catholic creeds and to which the historic formularies of the Church of England bear witness; and in public prayer and administration of the sacraments, I will use only the forms of service which are authorized or allowed by Canon.

THE DECLARATION

13 **Sit**

The Bishop-elect stands before the Archbishop, and the people sit.

Archbishop A bishop is called to lead in serving and caring for the people of God and to work with them in the oversight of the Church. As a chief pastor he shares with his fellow bishops a special responsibility to maintain and further the unity of the Church, to uphold its discipline, and to guard its faith. He is to promote its mission throughout the world. It is his duty to watch over and pray for all those committed to his charge, and to teach and govern them after the example of the Apostles, speaking in the name of God and interpreting the gospel of Christ. He is to know his people and be known by them. He is to ordain and to send new ministers, guiding those who serve with him and enabling them to fulfil their ministry.

He is to baptize and confirm, to preside at the Holy Communion, and to lead the offering of prayer and praise. He is to be merciful, but with firmness, and to minister discipline, but with mercy. He is to have a special care for the outcast and needy; and to those who turn to God he is to declare the forgiveness of sins.

14   The Archbishop says to the Bishop-elect

In order that we may know your mind and purpose, and that you may be strengthened in your resolve to fulfil your ministry, you must make the declarations we now put to you.

Do you believe, so far as you know your own heart, that God has called you to the office and work of a bishop in his Church?

Answer   I believe that God has called me.

Archbishop   Do you accept the holy Scriptures as revealing all things necessary for eternal salvation through faith in Jesus Christ?

Answer   I do so accept them.

Archbishop   Do you believe the doctrine of the Christian faith as the Church of England has received it, and in your ministry will you expound and teach it?

Answer   I believe it, and will so do.

Archbishop   Will you accept the discipline of this Church, and faithfully exercise authority within it?

Answer   By the help of God, I will.

Archbishop   Will you be diligent in prayer, in reading holy Scripture, and in all studies that will deepen your faith and fit you to uphold the truth of the Gospel against error?

Answer   By the help of God, I will.

Archbishop   Will you strive to fashion your own life and that of your household according to the way of Christ?

Answer   By the help of God, I will.

| Archbishop | Will you promote unity, peace, and love among all Christian people, and especially among those whom you serve? |
| Answer | By the help of God, I will. |

| Archbishop | Will you then be a faithful witness to Christ to those among whom you live, and lead your people to obey our Saviour's command to make disciples of all nations? |
| Answer | By the help of God, I will. |

| Archbishop | Almighty God, who has given you the will to undertake all these things, give you also the strength to perform them; that he may complete that work which he has begun in you; through Jesus Christ our Lord. **Amen.** |

THE PRAYERS

15   The Archbishop commends the Bishop-elect to THE PRAYERS OF THE PEOPLE and silence is kept.

16   VENI CREATOR is sung.

> Come, Holy Ghost, our souls inspire,
> And lighten with celestial fire;
> Thou the anointing Spirit art,
> Who dost thy sevenfold gifts impart;
>
> Thy blessèd unction from above
> Is comfort, life, and fire of love;
> Enable with perpetual light
> The dullness of our blinded sight.
>
> Anoint and cheer our soilèd face
> With the abundance of thy grace;
> Keep far our foes, give peace at home;
> Where thou art guide no ill can come.

Teach us to know the Father, Son,
And thee, of both, to be but One;
That through the ages all along
This may be our endless song,

Praise to thy eternal merit,
Father, Son, and Holy Spirit. Amen.

17   Archbishop Let us pray.

The Archbishop or some other minister leads THE
PRAYERS for the Bishop-elect and for the ministry of the
whole Church.

God the Father,
have mercy on us.

God the Son,
have mercy on us.

God the Holy Spirit,
have mercy on us.

Holy, blessed, and glorious Trinity,
have mercy on us.

From all evil and mischief;
from pride, vanity, and hypocrisy;
from envy, hatred, and malice;
and from all evil intent,
Good Lord, deliver us.

From sloth, worldliness, and love of money;
from hardness of heart
and contempt for your word and your laws,
Good Lord, deliver us.

From sins of body and mind;
from the deceits of the world, the flesh,
    and the devil,
from error and false doctrine,
Good Lord, deliver us.

In all times of sorrow,
in all times of joy;
in the hour of death,
and at the day of judgement,
Good Lord, deliver us.

Govern and direct your holy Church; fill it with
love and truth; and grant it that unity which is
your will.
Hear us, good Lord.

Give us boldness to preach the gospel in all the
world, and to make disciples of all the nations.
Hear us, good Lord.

Enlighten your ministers with knowledge and
understanding, that by their teaching and their
lives they may proclaim your word.
Hear us, good Lord.

Bless your servant now to be made bishop
that he may serve your Church and reveal
your glory in the world.
Hear us, good Lord.

Give your people grace to hear and receive your
word, and to bring forth the fruit of the Spirit.
Hear us, good Lord.

Bring into the way of truth all who have erred
and are deceived.
Hear us, good Lord.

Strengthen those who stand; comfort and help
the fainthearted; raise up the fallen; and finally
beat down Satan under our feet.
Hear us, good Lord.

Give us true repentance;
forgive us our sins of negligence and ignorance,
and our deliberate sins;
and grant us the grace of your Holy Spirit
to amend our lives according to your holy word.

Holy God,
holy and strong,
holy and immortal,
have mercy on us.

Archbishop Lord, you are merciful and forgive our sins. You
hear those who pray in the name of your Son.
Grant that what we have asked in faith we may
obtain according to your will: through Jesus
Christ our Lord. **Amen.**

THE ORDINATION

18 The Archbishop stands with the bishops who assist him; the
Bishop-elect kneels before him; he stretches out his hands
towards him, and says

19 We praise and glorify you, almighty Father,
because you have formed throughout the world
a holy people for your own possession, a royal
priesthood, a universal Church.

We praise and glorify you because you have
given us your only Son Jesus Christ to be the
Apostle and High Priest of our faith, and the
Shepherd of our souls.

We praise and glorify you that by his death he
has overcome death; and that, having ascended
into heaven, he has given his gifts abundantly to
your people, making some, apostles; some,
prophets; some, evangelists; some, pastors and
teachers; to equip them for the work of ministry
and to build up his body.

And now we give you thanks that you have
called this your servant, whom we consecrate in
your name, to share this ministry entrusted to
your Church.

Here the Archbishop and other bishops lay their hands on the head of the Bishop-elect, and the Archbishop says

Send down the Holy Spirit upon your servant *N* for the office and work of a bishop in your Church.

The Archbishop then continues

Almighty Father, fill this your servant with the grace and power which you gave to your apostles, that he may lead those committed to his charge in proclaiming the gospel of salvation. Through him increase your Church, renew its ministry, and unite its members in a holy fellowship of truth and love. Enable him as a true shepherd to feed and govern your flock; make him wise as a teacher, and steadfast as a guardian of its faith and sacraments. Guide and direct him in presiding at the worship of your people. Give him humility, that he may use his authority to heal, not to hurt; to build up, not to destroy. Defend him from all evil, that as a ruler over your household and an ambassador for Christ he may stand before you blameless, and finally, with all your servants, enter your eternal joy.

Accept our prayers, most merciful Father, through your Son Jesus Christ our Lord, to whom, with you and your Holy Spirit, belong glory and honour, worship and praise, now and for ever. **Amen.**

THE GIVING OF THE BIBLE

20 **Sit**

The newly-ordained Bishop stands, and the Archbishop gives THE BIBLE to him, saying

Receive this Book; here are words of eternal life. Take them for your guide, and declare them to the world. Keep watch over the whole flock in which the Holy Spirit has appointed you shepherd. Encourage the faithful, restore the lost, build up the body of Christ; that when the Chief Shepherd shall appear, you may receive the unfading crown of glory.

THE COMMUNION

21 **Stand**
The Archbishop resumes the Communion Service at THE PEACE (Holy Communion Rite A, sections 30, 31; Rite B, sections 24, 25)

22 These special forms are used.

PROPER PREFACE
And now we give you thanks because within the royal priesthood of your Church you ordain ministers to proclaim the word of God, to care for your people, and to celebrate the sacraments of the new covenant.

POSTCOMMUNION SENTENCE
The Son of Man came not to be served but to serve, and to give his life as a ransom for many. *Mark 10.45*

POSTCOMMUNION COLLECT which may be said after the Sentence
God our Father,
shepherd and guide of all
    your faithful people:
look with favour on *N* your servant
whom you have chosen to be a pastor over
    your Church;
and grant that by word and example
he may lead the people committed to his
    charge,
and with them come to your eternal kingdom;
through Jesus Christ our Lord. **Amen.**

BLESSING

Almighty God, who for the salvation of mankind gives to his people many gifts and ministries to the advancement of his glory, stir up in you the gifts of his grace, sustain each one of you in your own ministry; and the blessing . . .

Sentences, Collects, and Readings
(a) Sundays and Seasons

NINTH SUNDAY BEFORE CHRISTMAS
(Fifth Sunday before Advent)   Green

INTRODUCTORY SENTENCE

The earth belongs to the Lord, and all that it contains: the whole earth, and all who live in it. *Psalm 24.1*

COLLECT

Almighty God,
you have created the heavens and the earth
and made man in your own image.
Teach us to discern your hand in all your works,
and to serve you
    with reverence and thanksgiving;
through Jesus Christ our Lord,
who with you and the Holy Spirit
    reigns supreme over all things
now and for ever.

PSALMS 104, 1-10; 29

READINGS YEAR 1

Old Testament *Genesis 1.1-3, 24-31a NEB*

In the beginning of creation, when God made heaven and earth, the earth was without form and void, with darkness over the face of the abyss, and a mighty wind that swept over the surface of the waters. God said, 'Let there be light', and there was light.

God said, 'Let the earth bring forth living creatures, according to their kind: cattle, reptiles, and wild animals, all according to their kind.' So it was; God made wild animals, cattle, and all reptiles, each according to its kind; and he saw that it was good. Then God said, 'Let us make man in our image and likeness to rule the fish in the sea, the birds of heaven, the cattle, all wild animals on earth, and all reptiles that crawl upon the earth.' So God created man in his own image; in the image of God he created him; male and female he created them. God blessed them and said to them, 'Be fruitful and increase, fill the earth and subdue it, rule over the fish in the sea, the birds of heaven, and every living thing that moves upon the earth.' God also said, 'I give you all plants that bear seed everywhere on earth, and every tree bearing fruit which yields seed: they shall be yours for food. All green plants I give for food to the wild animals, to all the birds of heaven, and to all reptiles on earth, every living creature.' So it was; and God saw all that he had made, and it was very good.

New Testament *Colossians 1.15-20 JB*

Christ is the image of the unseen God
and the first-born of all creation,
for in him were created
all things in heaven and on earth:
everything visible and everything invisible,
Thrones, Dominations, Sovereignties, Powers—
all things were created through him and for him.
Before anything was created, he existed,
and he holds all things in unity.
Now the Church is his body,
he is its head.

As he is the Beginning,
he was first to be born from the dead,
so that he should be first in every way;
because God wanted all perfection
to be found in him
and all things to be reconciled through him and for him,
everything in heaven and everything on earth,
when he made peace
by his death on the cross.

Gospel *John 1.1-14 RSV*

In the beginning was the Word, and the Word was with God, and the Word was God. He was in the beginning with God; all things were made through him, and without him was not anything made that was made. In him was life, and the life was the light of men. The light shines in the darkness, and the darkness has not overcome it.

There was a man sent from God, whose name was John. He came for testimony, to bear witness to the light, that all might believe through him. He was not the light, but came to bear witness to the light.

The true light that enlightens every man was coming into the world. He was in the world, and the world was made through him, yet the world knew him not. He came to his own home, and his own people received him not. But to all who received him, who believed in his name, he gave power to become children of God; who were born, not of blood nor of the will of the flesh nor of the will of man, but of God.

And the Word became flesh and dwelt among us, full of grace and truth; we have beheld his glory, glory as of the only Son from the Father.

READINGS YEAR 2

Old Testament *Genesis 2.4-9, 15-end NEB*

This is the story of the making of heaven and earth when they were created.

When the Lord God made earth and heaven, there was neither shrub nor plant growing wild upon the earth, because the Lord God had sent no rain on the earth; nor was there any man to till the ground. A flood used to rise out of the earth and water all the surface of the ground. Then the Lord God formed a man from the dust of the ground and breathed into his nostrils the breath of life. Thus the man became a living creature. Then the Lord God planted a garden in Eden away to the east, and there he put the man whom he had formed. The Lord God made trees spring from the ground, all trees pleasant to look at and good for food; and in the middle of the garden he set the tree of life and the tree of the knowledge of good and evil.

The Lord God took the man and put him in the garden of Eden to till it and care for it. He told the man, 'You may eat from every tree in the garden, but not from the tree of the knowledge of good and evil; for on the day that you eat from it, you will certainly die.' Then the Lord God said, 'It is not good for the man to be alone. I will provide a partner for him.' So God formed out of the ground all the wild animals and all the birds of heaven. He brought them to the man to see what he would call them, and whatever the man called each living creature, that was its name. Thus the man gave names to all cattle, to the birds of heaven, and to every wild animal; but for the man himself no partner had yet been found. And so the Lord God put the man into a trance, and while he slept, he took one of his ribs and closed the flesh over the place. The Lord God then built up the rib, which he had taken out of the man, into a woman. He brought her to the man, and the man said:

'Now this, at last—
bone from my bones,
flesh from my flesh!—
this shall be called woman,
for from man was this taken.'

That is why a man leaves his father and mother and is united to his wife, and the two become one flesh. Now they were both naked, the man and his wife, but they had no feeling of shame towards one another.

New Testament *Revelation 4 NEB*

I looked, and there before my eyes was a door opened in heaven; and the voice that I had first heard speaking to me like a trumpet said, 'Come up here, and I will show you what must happen hereafter.' At once I was caught up by the Spirit. There in heaven stood a throne, and on the throne sat one whose appearance was like the gleam of jasper and cornelian; and round the throne was a rainbow, bright as an emerald. In a circle about this throne were twenty-four other thrones, and on them sat twenty-four elders, robed in white and wearing crowns of gold. From the throne went out flashes of lightning and peals of thunder. Burning before the throne were seven flaming torches, the seven spirits of God, and in front of it stretched what seemed a sea of glass, like a sheet of ice.

In the centre, round the throne itself, were four living creatures, covered with eyes, in front and behind. The first creature was like a lion, the second like an ox, the third had a human face, the fourth was like an eagle in flight. The four living creatures, each of them with six wings, had eyes all over, inside and out; and by day and by night without a pause they sang:

'Holy, holy, holy is God the sovereign Lord of all, who was, and is, and is to come!'

As often as the living creatures give glory and honour and thanks to the One who sits on the throne, who lives for ever and ever, the twenty-four elders fall down before the One who sits on the throne and worship him who lives for ever and ever; and as they lay their crowns before the throne they cry:

'Thou art worthy, O Lord our God, to receive glory and honour and power, because thou didst create all things; by thy will they were created, and have their being!'

Gospel *John 3.1-8 NEB*

There was one of the Pharisees named Nicodemus, a member of the Jewish Council, who came to Jesus by night. 'Rabbi,' he said, 'we know that you are a teacher sent by God; no one could perform these signs of yours unless God were with him.' Jesus answered, 'In truth, in very truth I tell you, unless a man has been born over again he cannot see the kingdom of God.' 'But how is it possible', said Nicodemus, 'for a man to be born when he is old? Can he enter his mother's womb a second time and be born?' Jesus answered, 'In truth I tell you, no one can enter the kingdom of God without being born from water and spirit. Flesh can give birth only to flesh; it is spirit that gives birth to spirit. You ought not to be astonished, then, when I tell you that you must be born over again. The wind blows where it wills; you hear the sound of it, but you do not know where it comes from, or where it is going. So with everyone who is born from spirit.'

POSTCOMMUNION SENTENCE

All creatures depend on you, O Lord, to feed them through the year; with a generous hand you satisfy their hunger.
Psalm 104.27

EIGHTH SUNDAY BEFORE CHRISTMAS
(Fourth Sunday before Advent)   Green

INTRODUCTORY SENTENCE

As by one man's disobedience many were made sinners, so by one man's obedience many will be made righteous.
Romans 5.19

COLLECT

Heavenly Father,
whose blessed Son was revealed
    that he might destroy the works of the devil
and make us the sons of God
and heirs of eternal life:
grant that we, having this hope,
may purify ourselves even as he is pure;
that when he shall appear in power and great glory
we may be made like him
    in his eternal and glorious kingdom;
where he is alive and reigns with you and the Holy Spirit,
one God, now and for ever.

PSALMS 130; 10.13-end

READINGS YEAR 1

Old Testament *Genesis 4.1-10 NEB*

Adam lay with his wife Eve, and she conceived and gave birth to Cain. She said, 'With the help of the Lord I have brought a man into being.' Afterwards she had another child, his brother Abel. Abel was a shepherd and Cain a tiller of the soil. The day came when Cain brought some of the produce of the soil as a gift to the Lord; and Abel brought some of the first-born of his flock, the fat portions of them. The Lord received Abel and his gift with favour; but Cain and his gift he did not receive. Cain was very angry and his face fell. Then the Lord said to Cain, 'Why are you so angry and cast down?

If you do well, you are accepted;
if not, sin is a demon crouching at the door.
It shall be eager for you, and you will be mastered by it.'

Cain said to his brother Abel, 'Let us go into the open country.' While they were there, Cain attacked his brother Abel and murdered him. Then the Lord said to Cain, 'Where is your brother Abel?' Cain answered, 'I do not know. Am I my brother's keeper?' The Lord said, 'What have you done? Hark! your brother's blood that has been shed is crying out to me from the ground.'

New Testament 1 *John* 3.9-18 *TEV*

Whoever is a child of God does not continue to sin, for God's very nature is in him; and because God is his Father, he cannot continue to sin. This is the clear difference between God's children and the Devil's children: anyone who does not do what is right or does not love his brother is not God's child.

The message you heard from the very beginning is this: we must love one another. We must not be like Cain; he belonged to the Evil One and murdered his own brother Abel. Why did Cain murder him? Because the things he himself did were wrong, but the things his brother did were right.

So do not be surprised, my brothers, if the people of the world hate you. We know that we have left death and come over into life; we know it because we love our brothers. Whoever does not love is still under the power of death. Whoever hates his brother is a murderer, and you know that a murderer has not got eternal life in him. This is how we know what love is: Christ gave his life for us. We too, then, ought to give our lives for our brothers! If a rich person sees his brother in need, yet closes his heart against his brother, how can he claim that he loves God? My children, our love should not be just words and talk; it must be true love, which shows itself in action.

Gospel *Mark 7.14-23 NEB*

On another occasion Jesus called the people and said to them, 'Listen to me, all of you, and understand this: nothing that goes into a man from outside can defile him; no, it is the things that come out of him that defile a man.'

When he had left the people and gone indoors, his disciples questioned him about the parable. He said to them, 'Are you as dull as the rest? Do you not see that nothing that goes from outside into a man can defile him, because it does not enter into his heart but into his stomach, and so passes out into the drain?' Thus he declared all goods clean. He went on, 'It is what comes out of a man that defiles him. For from inside, out of a man's heart, come evil thoughts, acts of fornication, of theft, murder, adultery, ruthless greed, and malice; fraud, indecency, envy, slander, arrogance, and folly; these evil things all come from inside, and they defile the man.'

READINGS YEAR 2

Old Testament *Genesis 3.1-15 NEB*

The serpent was more crafty than any wild creature that the Lord God had made. He said to the woman, 'Is it true that God has forbidden you to eat from any tree in the garden?' The woman answered the serpent, 'We may eat the fruit of any tree in the garden, except for the tree in the middle of the garden; God has forbidden us either to eat or to touch the fruit of that; if we do, we shall die.' The serpent said, 'Of course you will not die. God knows that as soon as you eat it, your eyes will be opened and you will be like God knowing both good and evil.' When the woman saw that the fruit of the tree was good to eat, and that it was pleasing to the eye and tempting to contemplate, she took some and ate it. She also gave her husband some and he ate it. Then the eyes of both of them were opened and they discovered that they were naked; so they stitched fig-leaves together and made themselves loincloths.

The man and his wife heard the sound of the Lord God walking in the garden at the time of the evening breeze and hid from the Lord God among the trees of the garden. But the Lord God called to the man and said to him, 'Where are you?' He replied, 'I heard the sound as you were walking in the garden, and I was afraid because I was naked, and I hid myself.' God answered, 'Who told you that you were naked? Have you eaten from the tree which I forbade you?' The man said, 'The woman you gave me for a companion, she gave me fruit from the tree and I ate it.' Then the Lord God said to the woman, 'What is this that you have done?' The woman said, 'The serpent tricked me, and I ate.' Then the Lord God said to the serpent:

'Because you have done this you are accursed
more than all cattle and all wild creatures.
On your belly you shall crawl, and dust you shall eat
all the days of your life.
I will put enmity between you and the woman,
between your brood and hers.
They shall strike at your head,
and you shall strike at their heel.'

New Testament *Romans 7.7-13 TEV*

Shall we say that the Law itself is sinful? Of course not! But it was the Law that made me know what sin is. If the Law had not said, 'Do not desire what belongs to someone else,' I would not have known such a desire. But by means of that commandment sin found its chance to stir up all kinds of selfish desires in me. Apart from law, sin is a dead thing. I myself was once alive apart from law; but when the commandment came, sin sprang to life, and I died. And the commandment which was meant to bring life, in my case brought death. Sin found its chance, and by means of the commandment it deceived me and killed me.

So then, the Law itself is holy, and the commandment is holy, right, and good. But does this mean that what is good caused my death? By no means! It was sin that did it; by using what is good, sin brought death to me, in order that its true nature as sin might be revealed. And so, by means of the commandment sin is shown to be even more terribly sinful.

Gospel *John 3.13-21 RSV*

Jesus said, 'No one has ascended into heaven but he who descended from heaven, the Son of Man. And as Moses lifted up the serpent in the wilderness, so must the Son of Man be lifted up, that whoever believes in him may have eternal life.'

For God so loved the world that he gave his only Son, that whoever believes in him should not perish but have eternal life. For God sent the Son into the world, not to condemn the world, but that the world might be saved through him. He who believes in him is not condemned; he who does not believe is condemned already, because he has not believed in the name of the only Son of God. And this is the judgement, that the light has come into the world, and men loved darkness rather than light, because their deeds were evil. For every one who does evil hates the light, and does not come to the light, lest his deeds should be exposed. But he who does what is true comes to the light, that it may be clearly seen that his deeds have been wrought in God.

POSTCOMMUNION SENTENCE

As in Adam all die, so also in Christ shall all be made alive.
1 Corinthians 15.22

SEVENTH SUNDAY BEFORE CHRISTMAS
(Third Sunday before Advent)   Green

INTRODUCTORY SENTENCE

Abraham is the father of all: as Scripture says, I have made you the father of many nations. *Romans 4.16*

COLLECT

Almighty God,
whose chosen servant Abraham
faithfully obeyed your call
and rejoiced in your promise
that, in him, all the families of the earth should be blessed:
give us a faith like his,
that, in us, your promises may be fulfilled;
through Jesus Christ our Lord.

PSALMS 1; 105.1-11

READINGS YEAR 1

Old Testament *Genesis 12.1-9 TEV*

The Lord said to Abram, 'Leave your native land, your
relatives, and your father's home, and go to a country that I
am going to show you. I will give you many descendants,
and they will become a great nation. I will bless you and
make your name famous, so that you will be a blessing.
I will bless those who bless you,
But I will curse those who curse you.
And through you I will bless all the nations.'

When Abram was seventy-five years old, he started out
from Haran, as the Lord had told him to do; and Lot went
with him. Abram took his wife Sarai, his nephew Lot, and all
the wealth and all the slaves they had acquired in Haran, and
they started out for the land of Canaan.

When they arrived in Canaan, Abram travelled through the
land until he came to the sacred tree of Moreh, the holy place
at Shechem. (At that time the Canaanites were still living in
the land.) The Lord appeared to Abram and said to him,
'This is the country that I am going to give to your
descendants.' Then Abram built an altar there to the Lord,
who had appeared to him. After that, he moved on south to
the hill-country east of the city of Bethel and set up his camp
between Bethel on the west and Ai on the east. There also he
built an altar and worshipped the Lord. Then he moved on
from place to place, going towards the southern part
of Canaan.

New Testament *Romans 4.13-end JB*

The promise of inheriting the world was not made to
Abraham and his descendants on account of any law but on
account of the righteousness which consists in faith. If the
world is only to be inherited by those who submit to the
Law, then faith is pointless and the promise worth nothing.
Law involves the possibility of punishment for breaking the
law—only where there is no law can that be avoided. That is
why what fulfils the promise depends on faith, so that it may
be a free gift and be available to all of Abraham's
descendants, not only those who belong to the Law but also
those who belong to the faith of Abraham who is the father
of all of us. As scripture says: 'I have made you the ancestor
of many nations'—Abraham is our father in the eyes of God,
in whom he put his faith, and who brings the dead to life and
calls into being what does not exist.

Though it seemed Abraham's hope could not be fulfilled, he
hoped and he believed, and through doing so he did become
the father of many nations exactly as he had been promised:
'Your descendants will be as many as the stars.' Even the
thought that his body was past fatherhood—he was about a
hundred years old—and Sarah too old to become a mother,
did not shake his belief. Since God had promised it,
Abraham refused either to deny it or even to doubt it, but
drew strength from faith and gave glory to God, convinced
that God had power to do what he had promised. This is the
faith that was 'considered as justifying him'. Scripture
however does not refer only to him but to us as well when it
says that his faith was thus 'considered'; our faith too will be
'considered' if we believe in him who raised Jesus our Lord
from the dead, Jesus who was put to death for our sins and
raised to life to justify us.

Gospel *John 8.51-end NEB*

Jesus said, 'In very truth I tell you, if anyone obeys my
teaching he shall never know what it is to die.'

The Jews said, 'Now we are certain that you are possessed.
Abraham is dead; the prophets are dead; and yet you say, "If
anyone obeys my teaching he shall not know what it is to

die." Are you greater than our father Abraham, who is dead? The prophets are dead too. What do you claim to be?'

Jesus replied, 'If I glorify myself, that glory of mine is worthless. It is the Father who glorifies me, he of whom you say, "He is our God", though you do not know him. But I know him; if I said that I did not know him I should be a liar like you. But in truth I know him and obey his word.

'Your father Abraham was overjoyed to see my day; he saw it and was glad.' The Jews protested, 'You are not yet fifty years old. How can you have seen Abraham?' Jesus said, 'In very truth I tell you, before Abraham was born, I am.'

They picked up stones to throw at him, but Jesus was not to be seen; and he left the temple.

READINGS YEAR 2

Old Testament *Genesis 22.1-18 NEB*

The time came when God put Abraham to the test. 'Abraham', he called, and Abraham replied, 'Here I am.' God said, 'Take your son Isaac, your only son, whom you love, and go to the land of Moriah. There you shall offer him as a sacrifice on one of the hills which I will show you.' So Abraham rose early in the morning and saddled his ass, and he took with him two of his men and his son Isaac; and he split the firewood for the sacrifice, and set out for the place of which God had spoken. On the third day Abraham looked up and saw the place in the distance. He said to his men, 'Stay here with the ass while I and the boy go over there; and when we have worshipped we will come back to you.' So Abraham took the wood for the sacrifice and laid it on his son Isaac's shoulder; he himself carried the fire and the knife, and the two of them went on together. Isaac said to Abraham, 'Father', and he answered, 'What is it, my son?' Isaac said, 'Here are the fire and the wood, but where is the young beast for the sacrifice?' Abraham answered, 'God will provide himself with a young beast for a sacrifice, my son.' And the two of them went on together and came to the place of which God had spoken. There Abraham built an altar and arranged the wood. He bound his son Isaac and laid him on the altar on top of the wood. Then he stretched out his hand and took the knife to kill his son; but the angel of the Lord called to him from heaven, 'Abraham, Abraham.' He answered, 'Here I am.' The angel of the Lord said, 'Do not raise your hand against the boy; do not touch him. Now I know that you are a God-fearing man. You have not withheld from me your son, your only son.' Abraham looked up, and there he saw a ram caught by its horns in a thicket. So he went and took the ram and offered it as a sacrifice instead of his son. Abraham named that place Jehovah-jireh; and to this day the saying is: 'In the mountain of the Lord it was provided.' Then the angel of the Lord called from heaven a second time to Abraham, 'This is the word of the Lord: By my own self I swear: inasmuch as you have done this and have not withheld your son, your only son, I will bless you abundantly and greatly multiply your descendants until they are as numerous as the stars in the sky and the grains of sand on the sea-shore. Your descendants shall possess the cities of their enemies. All nations on earth shall pray to be blessed as your descendants are blessed, and this because you have obeyed me.'

New Testament *James 2.14-24 (25, 26) NEB*

My brothers, what use is it for a man to say he has faith when he does nothing to show it? Can that faith save him? Suppose a brother or a sister is in rags with not enough food for the day, and one of you says, 'Good luck to you, keep yourselves warm, and have plenty to eat', but does nothing to supply their bodily needs, what is the good of that? So with faith; if it does not lead to action, it is in itself a lifeless thing.

But someone may object: 'Here is one who claims to have faith and another who points to his deeds.' To which I reply: 'Prove to me that this faith you speak of is real though not accompanied by deeds, and by my deeds I will prove to you my faith.' You have faith enough to believe that there is one God. Excellent! The devils have faith like that, and it makes them tremble. But can you not see, you quibbler, that faith divorced from deeds is barren? Was it not by his action, in offering his son Isaac upon the altar, that our father

Abraham was justified? Surely you can see that faith was at work in his actions, and that by these actions the integrity of his faith was fully proved. Here was fulfilment of the words of Scripture: 'Abraham put his faith in God, and that faith was counted to him as righteousness'; and elsewhere he is called 'God's friend'. You see then that a man is justified by deeds and not by faith in itself. (The same is true of the prostitute Rahab also. Was not she justified by her action in welcoming the messengers into her house and sending them away by a different route? As the body is dead when there is no breath left in it, so faith divorced from deeds is lifeless as a corpse.)

Gospel *Luke 20.9-17 JB*

Jesus went on to tell the people this parable: 'A man planted a vineyard and leased it to tenants, and went abroad for a long while. When the time came, he sent a servant to the tenants to get his share of the produce of the vineyard from them. But the tenants thrashed him, and sent him away empty-handed. But he persevered and sent a second servant; they thrashed him too and treated him shamefully and sent him away empty-handed. He still persevered and sent a third; they wounded this one also, and threw him out. Then the owner of the vineyard said, "What am I to do? I will send them my dear son. Perhaps they will respect him." But when the tenants saw him they put their heads together. "This is the heir," they said, "let us kill him so that the inheritance will be ours." So they threw him out of the vineyard and killed him.

'Now what will the owner of the vineyard do to them? He will come and make an end of these tenants and give the vineyard to others.' Hearing this they said, 'God forbid!' But he looked hard at them and said, 'Then what does this text in the scriptures mean:

It was the stone rejected by the builders
that became the keystone?'

POSTCOMMUNION SENTENCE

By faith Abraham obeyed the call of God, and set out not knowing where he was going, and came to the promised land. *Hebrews 11.8*

SIXTH SUNDAY BEFORE CHRISTMAS
(Second Sunday before Advent)   Green

INTRODUCTORY SENTENCE

The law was given by Moses: grace and truth came through Jesus Christ. *John 1.17*

COLLECT

Lord God our redeemer,
who heard the cry of your people
and sent your servant Moses to lead them out of slavery:
free us from the tyranny of sin and death
and, by the leading of your Spirit,
bring us to our promised land;
through Jesus Christ our Lord.

PSALMS 135.1-6; 77.11-end

READINGS YEAR 1

Old Testament *Exodus 3.7-15 RSV*

The Lord said, 'I have seen the affliction of my people who are in Egypt, and have heard their cry because of their taskmasters; I know their sufferings, and I have come down to deliver them out of the hand of the Egyptians, and to bring them up out of that land to a good and broad land, a land flowing with milk and honey, to the place of the Canaanites, the Hittites, the Amorites, the Perizzites, the Hivites, and the Jebusites. And now, behold, the cry of the people of Israel has come to me, and I have seen the oppression with which the Egyptians oppress them. Come, I will send you to Pharaoh that you may bring forth my people, the sons of Israel, out of Egypt.' But Moses said to God, 'Who am I that I should go to Pharaoh, and bring the sons of Israel out of Egypt?' He said, 'But I will be with you; and this shall be the sign for you, that I have sent you: when you have brought forth the people out of Egypt, you shall serve God upon this mountain.'

Then Moses said to God, 'If I come to the people of Israel and say to them, "The God of your fathers has sent me to you," and they ask me, "What is his name?" what shall I say to them?' God said to Moses, 'I AM WHO I AM.' And he said, 'Say this to the people of Israel, "I AM has sent me to you."' God also said to Moses, 'Say this to the people of Israel, "The Lord, the God of your fathers, the God of Abraham, the God of Isaac, and the God of Jacob, has sent me to you": this is my name for ever, and thus I am to be remembered throughout all generations.'

New Testament *Hebrews 3.1-6 TEV*

My Christian brothers, who also have been called by God! Think of Jesus, whom God sent to be the High Priest of the faith we profess. He was faithful to God, who chose him to do this work, just as Moses was faithful in his work in God's house. A man who builds a house receives more honour than the house itself. In the same way Jesus is worthy of much greater honour than Moses. Every house, of course, is built by someone—and God is the one who has built all things. Moses was faithful in God's house as a servant, and he spoke of the things that God would say in the future. But Christ is faithful as the Son in charge of God's house. We are his house if we keep up our courage and our confidence in what we hope for.

Gospel *John 6.25-35 RSV*

When they found Jesus on the other side of the sea, they said to him, 'Rabbi, when did you come here?' Jesus answered them, 'Truly, truly, I say to you, you seek me, not because you saw signs, but because you ate your fill of the loaves. Do not labour for the food which perishes, but for the food which endures to eternal life, which the Son of man will give to you: for on him has God the Father set his seal.' Then they said to him, 'What must we do, to be doing the work of God?' Jesus answered them, 'This is the work of God, that you believe in him whom he has sent.' So they said to him, 'Then what sign do you do, that we may see, and believe you? What work do you perform? Our fathers ate the manna in the wilderness; as it is written, "He gave them bread from heaven to eat."' Jesus then said to them, 'Truly, truly, I say to you, it was not Moses who gave you the bread from heaven; my Father gives you the true bread from heaven. For the bread of God is that which comes down from heaven, and gives life to the world.' They said to him, 'Lord, give us this bread always.'

Jesus said to them, 'I am the bread of life; he who comes to me shall not hunger, and he who believes in me shall never thirst.'

READINGS YEAR 2

Old Testament *Exodus 6.2-8 NEB*

God spoke to Moses and said, 'I am the Lord. I appeared to Abraham, Isaac, and Jacob as God Almighty. But I did not let myself be known to them by my name JEHOVAH. Moreover, I made a covenant with them to give them Canaan, the land where they settled for a time as foreigners. And now I have heard the groaning of the Israelites, enslaved by the Egyptians, and I have called my covenant to mind. Say therefore to the Israelites, "I am the Lord. I will release you from your labours in Egypt. I will rescue you from slavery there. I will redeem you with arm outstretched and with mighty acts of judgement. I will adopt you as my people, and I will become your God. You shall know that I, the Lord, am your God, the God who releases you from your labours in Egypt. I will lead you to the land which I swore with uplifted hand to give to Abraham, to Isaac and to Jacob. I will give it you for your possession. I am the Lord."'

New Testament *Hebrews 11.17-31 RSV*

By faith Abraham, when he was tested, offered up Isaac, and he who had received the promises was ready to offer up his only son, of whom it was said, 'Through Isaac shall your descendants be named.' He considered that God was able to raise men even from the dead; hence, figuratively speaking, he did receive him back. By faith Isaac invoked future blessings on Jacob and Esau. By faith Jacob, when dying, blessed each of the sons of Joseph, bowing in worship over the head of his staff. By faith Joseph, at the end of his life, made mention of the exodus of the Israelites and gave directions concerning his burial.

By faith Moses, when he was born, was hid for three months by his parents, because they saw that the child was beautiful; and they were not afraid of the king's edict. By faith Moses, when he was grown up, refused to be called the son of Pharaoh's daughter, choosing rather to share ill-treatment with the people of God than to enjoy the fleeting pleasures of sin. He considered abuse suffered for the Christ greater wealth than the treasures of Egypt, for he looked to the reward. By faith he left Egypt, not being afraid of the anger of the king; for he endured as seeing him who is invisible. By faith he kept the Passover and sprinkled the blood, so that the Destroyer of the first-born might not touch them.

By faith the people crossed the Red Sea as if on dry land; but the Egyptians, when they attempted to do the same, were drowned. By faith the walls of Jericho fell down after they had been encircled for seven days. By faith Rahab the harlot did not perish with those who were disobedient, because she had given friendly welcome to the spies.

Gospel *Mark 13.5-13 NEB*

Jesus said to his disciples, 'Take care that no one misleads you. Many will come claiming my name, and saying, "I am he", and many will be misled by them.

'When you hear the noise of battle near at hand and the news of battles far away, do not be alarmed. Such things are bound to happen; but the end is still to come. For nation will make war upon nation, kingdom upon kingdom; there will be earthquakes in many places; there will be famines. With these things the birth-pangs of the new age begin.

'As for you, be on your guard. You will be handed over to the courts. You will be flogged in synagogues. You will be summoned to appear before governors and kings on my account to testify in their presence. But before the end the Gospel must be proclaimed to all nations. So when you are arrested and taken away, do not worry beforehand about what you will say, but when the time comes say whatever is given you to say; for it is not you who will be speaking, but the Holy Spirit. Brother will betray brother to death, and the father his child; children will turn against their parents and send them to their death. All will hate you for your allegiance to me; but the man who holds out to the end will be saved.'

POSTCOMMUNION SENTENCE

This is the bread come down from heaven: anyone who eats this bread will live for ever. *John 6.58*

FIFTH SUNDAY BEFORE CHRISTMAS
(The Sunday next before Advent)   Green

INTRODUCTORY SENTENCE

The root of Jesse shall stand as an ensign to the peoples: the nations shall seek him, and his dwellings shall be glorious. *Isaiah 11.10*

COLLECTS

Almighty God,
who spoke to the prophets
that they might make your will and purpose known:
inspire the guardians of your truth,
that through the faithful witness of the few
the children of earth may be made one
    with the saints in glory;
by the power of Jesus Christ our Lord,
who alone redeemed mankind
and reigns with you and the Holy Spirit,
one God, now and for ever.

Stir up, O Lord,
the wills of your faithful people;
that richly bearing the fruit of good works,
they may by you be richly rewarded;
through Jesus Christ our Lord.

PSALMS 80.1-7; 80.8-end

READINGS YEAR 1

Old Testament *1 Kings 19.9-18 RSV*

Elijah came to a cave, and lodged there; and behold, the word of the Lord came to him, and he said to him, 'What are you doing here, Elijah?' He said, 'I have been very jealous for the Lord, the God of hosts; for the people of Israel have forsaken your covenant, thrown down your altars, and slain your prophets with the sword; and I, even I only, am left; and they seek my life, to take it away.' And he said, 'Go forth, and stand upon the mount before the Lord.' And behold, the Lord passed by, and a great and strong wind rent the mountains, and broke in pieces the rocks before the Lord, but the Lord was not in the wind; and after the wind an earthquake, but the Lord was not in the earthquake; and after the earthquake a fire, but the Lord was not in the fire; and after the fire a still small voice. And when Elijah heard it, he wrapped his face in his mantle and went out and stood at the entrance of the cave. And behold, there came a voice to him, and said, 'What are you doing here, Elijah?' He said, 'I have been very jealous for the Lord, the God of hosts; for the people of Israel have forsaken your covenant, thrown down your altars, and slain your prophets with the sword; and I, even I only, am left; and they seek my life, to take it away.' And the Lord said to him, 'Go, return on your way to the wilderness of Damascus; and when you arrive, you shall anoint Hazael to be king over Syria; and Jehu the son of Nimshi you shall anoint to be king over Israel; and Elisha the son of Shaphat of Abelmeholah you shall anoint to be prophet in your place. And him who escapes from the sword of Hazael shall Jehu slay; and him who escapes from the sword of Jehu shall Elisha slay. Yet I will leave seven thousand in Israel, all the knees that have not bowed to Baal, and every mouth that has not kissed him.'

New Testament *Romans 11.13-24 NEB*

I have something to say to you Gentiles. I am a missionary to the Gentiles, and as such I give all honour to that ministry when I try to stir emulation in the men of my own race, and so to save some of them. For if their rejection has meant the reconciliation of the world, what will their acceptance mean? Nothing less than life from the dead! If the first portion of dough is consecrated, so is the whole lump. If the root is consecrated, so are the branches. But if some of the branches have been lopped off, and you, a wild olive, have been grafted in among them, and have come to share the same root and sap as the olive, do not make yourself superior to the branches. If you do so, remember that it is not you who sustain the root: the root sustains you.

You will say, 'Branches were lopped off so that I might be grafted in.' Very well: they were lopped off for lack of faith, and by faith you hold your place. Put away your pride, and be on your guard; for if God did not spare the native branches, no more will he spare you. Observe the kindness and the severity of God—severity to those who fell away, divine kindness to you, if only you remain within its scope; otherwise you too will be cut off, whereas they, if they do not continue faithless, will be grafted in; for it is in God's power to graft them in again. For if you were cut from your native wild olive and against all nature grafted into the cultivated olive, how much more readily will they, the natural olive-branches, be grafted into their native stock!

Gospel *Matthew 24.37-44 NEB*

Jesus said, 'As things were in Noah's days, so will they be when the Son of Man comes. In the days before the flood they ate and drank and married, until the day that Noah went into the ark, and they knew nothing until the flood came and swept them all away. That is how it will be when the Son of Man comes. Then there will be two men in the field; one will be taken, the other left; two women grinding at the mill; one will be taken, the other left.

'Keep awake, then; for you do not know on what day your Lord is to come. Remember, if the householder had known at what time of night the burglar was coming, he would have kept awake and not have let his house be broken into. Hold yourselves ready, therefore, because the Son of Man will come at the time you least expect him.'

READINGS YEAR 2

Old Testament *Isaiah 10.20-23 RSV*

On the day of the Lord the remnant of Israel and the survivors of the house of Jacob will no more lean upon him that smote them, but will lean upon the Lord, the Holy One of Israel, in truth. A remnant will return, the remnant of Jacob, to the mighty God. For though your people Israel be as the sand of the sea, only a remnant of them will return. Destruction is decreed, overflowing with righteousness. For the Lord, the Lord of hosts, will make a full end, as decreed, in the midst of all the earth.

New Testament *Romans 9.19-28 JB*

You will ask, 'How can God ever blame anyone, since no one can oppose his will?' But what right have you, a human being, to cross-examine God? The pot has no right to say to the potter: 'Why did you make me this shape?' Surely a potter can do what he likes with the clay? It is surely for him to decide whether he will use a particular lump of clay to make a special pot or an ordinary one?

Or else imagine that although God is ready to show his anger and display his power, yet he patiently puts up with the people who make him angry, however much they deserve to be destroyed. He puts up with them for the sake of those other people, to whom he wants to be merciful, to whom he wants to reveal the richness of his glory, people he had prepared for this glory long ago. Well, we are those people; whether we are Jews or pagans we are the ones he has called.

That is exactly what God says in Hosea: 'I shall say to a people that was not mine, "You are my people", and to a nation I never loved, "I love you". Instead of being told, "You are no people of mine", they will now be called the sons of the living God.' Referring to Israel Isaiah had this to say: 'Though Israel should have as many descendants as there are grains of sand on the seashore, only a remnant will be saved, for without hesitation or delay the Lord will execute his sentence on the earth.'

Gospel Mark 13.14-23 NEB

Jesus said, 'But when you see "the abomination of desolation" usurping a place which is not his (let the reader understand), then those who are in Judaea must take to the hills. If a man is on the roof, he must not come down into the house to fetch anything out; if in the field, he must not turn back for his coat. Alas for women with child in those days, and for those who have children at the breast! Pray that it may not come in winter. For those days will bring distress such as never has been until now since the beginning of the world which God created—and will never be again. If the Lord had not cut short that time of troubles, no living thing could survive. However, for the sake of his own, whom he has chosen, he has cut short the time.

'Then, if anyone says to you, "Look, here is the Messiah", or, "Look, there he is", do not believe it. Imposters will come claiming to be messiahs or prophets, and they will produce signs and wonders to mislead God's chosen, if such a thing were possible. But you be on your guard; I have forewarned you of it all.'

POSTCOMMUNION SENTENCE

The Lord is my strength and my song, and he has become my salvation: sing to the Lord, for he has done marvellous things; make them known to the whole world. *Isaiah 12.2, 5*

ADVENT SUNDAY
(Fourth Sunday before Christmas)   Violet

INTRODUCTORY SENTENCE

Now is the time to wake out of sleep: for now our salvation is nearer than when we first believed. *Romans 13.11*

COLLECT

Almighty God,
give us grace to cast away the works of darkness
and to put on the armour of light,
now in the time of this mortal life,
in which your Son Jesus Christ
    came to us in great humility:
so that on the last day,
when he shall come again in his glorious majesty
    to judge the living and the dead,
we may rise to the life immortal;
through him who is alive and reigns
    with you and the Holy Spirit,
one God, now and for ever.

PSALMS 50.1-6; 82

READINGS YEAR 1

Old Testament *Isaiah 52.7-10 NEB*

How lovely on the mountains are the feet of the herald
who comes to proclaim prosperity and bring good news,
the news of deliverance,
calling to Zion, 'Your God is king.'
Hark, your watchmen raise their voices
and shout together in triumph;
for with their own eyes they shall see
the Lord returning in pity to Zion.
Break forth together in shouts of triumph,
you ruins of Jerusalem;
for the Lord has taken pity on his people
and has ransomed Jerusalem.

The Lord has bared his holy arm
in the sight of all nations,
and the whole world from end to end
shall see the deliverance of our God.

New Testament *1 Thessalonians 5.1-11 NEB*

About dates and times, my friends, we need not write to
you, for you know perfectly well that the Day of the Lord
comes like a thief in the night. While they are talking of peace
and security, all at once calamity is upon them, sudden as
the pangs that come upon a woman with child; and there
will be no escape. But you, my friends, are not in the dark,
that the day should overtake you like a thief. You are all
children of light, children of day. We do not belong to night
or darkness, and we must not sleep like the rest, but keep
awake and sober. Sleepers sleep at night, and drunkards are
drunk at night, but we, who belong to daylight, must keep
sober, armed with faith and love for coat of mail, and the
hope of salvation for helmet. For God has not destined us to
the terrors of judgement, but to the full attainment of
salvation through our Lord Jesus Christ. He died for us so
that we, awake or asleep, might live in company with him.
Therefore hearten one another, fortify one another—as
indeed you do.

Gospel *Luke 21.25-33 NEB*

Jesus said to the people, 'Portents will appear in sun, moon,
and stars. On earth nations will stand helpless, not knowing
which way to turn from the roar and surge of the sea; men
will faint with terror at the thought of all that is coming upon
the world; for the celestial powers will be shaken. And then
they will see the Son of Man coming on a cloud with great
power and glory. When all this begins to happen, stand
upright and hold your heads high, because your liberation
is near.'

He told them this parable: 'Look at the fig-tree, or any other
tree. As soon as it buds, you can see for yourselves that
summer is near. In the same way, when you see all this
happening, you may know that the kingdom of God is near.

'I tell you this: the present generation will live to see it all.
Heaven and earth will pass away; my words will never
pass away.'

READINGS YEAR 2

Old Testament *Isaiah 51.4-11 NEB*

Pay heed to me, my people,
and hear me, O my nation;
for my law shall shine forth
and I will flash the light of my judgement over the nations.
My victory is near, my deliverance has gone forth
and my arm shall rule the nations;
for me coasts and islands shall wait
and they shall look to me for protection.

Lift your eyes to the heavens,
look at the earth beneath:
the heavens grow murky as smoke;
the earth wears into tatters like a garment,
and those who live on it die like maggots;
but my deliverance is everlasting
and my saving power shall never wane.

Listen to me, my people who know what is right,
you who lay my law to heart:
do not fear the taunts of men,
let no reproaches dismay you;
for the grub will devour them like a garment
and the moth as if they were wool,
but my saving power shall last for ever
and my deliverance to all generations.

Awake, awake, put on your strength, O arm of the Lord,
awake as you did long ago, in days gone by.
Was it not you
who hacked the Rahab in pieces and ran the dragon
    through?
Was it not you
who dried up the sea, the waters of the great abyss,
and made the ocean depths a path for the ransomed?
So the Lord's people shall come back, set free,

and enter Zion with shouts of triumph,
crowned with everlasting joy;
joy and gladness shall overtake them as they come,
and sorrow and sighing shall flee away.

New Testament *Romans 13.8-end NEB*

Leave no claim outstanding against you, except that of
mutual love. He who loves his neighbour has satisfied every
claim of the law. For the commandments, 'Thou shalt not
commit adultery, thou shalt not kill, thou shalt not steal,
thou shalt not covet', and any other commandment there
may be, are all summed up in the one rule, 'Love your
neighbour as yourself.' Love cannot wrong a neighbour;
therefore the whole law is summed up in love.

In all this, remember how critical the moment is. It is time for
you to wake out of sleep, for deliverance is nearer to us now
than it was when first we believed. It is far on in the night;
day is near. Let us therefore throw off the deeds of darkness
and put on our armour as soldiers of the light. Let us behave
with decency as befits the day: no revelling or drunkenness,
no debauchery or vice, no quarrels or jealousies! Let Christ
Jesus himself be the armour that you wear; give no more
thought to satisfying the bodily appetites.

Gospel *Matthew 25.31-end NEB*

Jesus said to his disciples, 'When the Son of Man comes in
his glory and all the angels with him, he will sit in state on his
throne, with all the nations gathered before him. He will
separate men into two groups, as a shepherd separates the
sheep from the goats, and he will place the sheep on his right
hand and the goats on his left. Then the king will say to those
on his right hand, ''You have my Father's blessing; come,
enter and possess the kingdom that has been ready for you
since the world was made. For when I was hungry, you gave
me food; when thirsty, you gave me drink; when I was a
stranger you took me into your home, when naked you
clothed me; when I was ill you came to my help, when in
prison you visited me.'' Then the righteous will reply,
''Lord, when was it that we saw you hungry and fed you, or

thirsty and gave you drink, a stranger and took you home, or naked and clothed you? When did we see you ill or in prison, and come to visit you?" And the king will answer, "I tell you this: anything you did for one of my brothers here, however humble, you did for me." Then he will say to those on his left hand, "The curse is upon you; go from my sight to the eternal fire that is ready for the devil and his angels. For when I was hungry you gave me nothing to eat, when thirsty nothing to drink; when I was a stranger you gave me no home, when naked you did not clothe me; when I was ill and in prison you did not come to my help." And they too will reply, "Lord, when was it that we saw you hungry or thirsty or a stranger or naked or ill or in prison, and did nothing for you?" And he will answer, "I tell you this: anything you did not do for one of these, however humble, you did not do for me." And they will go away to eternal punishment, but the righteous will enter eternal life.'

PROPER PREFACE

Rite A. A Preface of Advent (1) is said throughout the week.
Rite B. Second Thanksgiving. The Preface of Advent is said throughout the week.

POSTCOMMUNION SENTENCE

Watch at all times, praying for the strength to stand with confidence before the Son of Man. *Luke 21.36*

ADVENT 2
(Third Sunday before Christmas)   Violet

INTRODUCTORY SENTENCE

The kingdom of God is close at hand. Repent, and believe the gospel. *Mark 1.15*

COLLECT

Blessed Lord,
who caused all holy Scriptures
   to be written for our learning:

help us so to hear them,
to read, mark, learn, and inwardly digest them
that, through patience, and the comfort
   of your holy word,
we may embrace and for ever hold fast
   the hope of everlasting life,
which you have given us in our Saviour Jesus Christ.

PSALMS 19.7-end; 119.129-136

READINGS YEAR 1

Old Testament *Isaiah 55.1-11 NEB*

Come, all who are thirsty, come, fetch water;
come, you who have no food, buy corn and eat;
come and buy, not for money, not for a price.
Why spend money and get what is not bread,
why give the price of your labour and go unsatisfied?
Only listen to me and you will have good food to eat,
and you will enjoy the fat of the land.
Come to me and listen to my words,
hear me, and you shall have life:
I will make a covenant with you, this time for ever,
to love you faithfully as I loved David.
I made him a witness to all races,
a prince and instructor of peoples;
and you in turn shall summon nations you do not know,
and nations that do not know you shall come running
   to you,
because the Lord your God,
the Holy One of Israel, has glorified you.

Inquire of the Lord while he is present,
call upon him when he is close at hand.
Let the wicked abandon their ways
and evil men their thoughts:
let them return to the Lord, who will have pity on them,
return to our God, for he will freely forgive.
For my thoughts are not your thoughts,
and your ways are not my ways.
This is the very word of the Lord.

For as the heavens are higher than the earth,
so are my ways higher than your ways
and my thoughts than your thoughts;
and as the rain and the snow come down from heaven
and do not return until they have watered the earth,
making it blossom and bear fruit,
and give seed for sowing and bread to eat,
so shall the word which comes from my mouth prevail;
it shall not return to me fruitless
without accomplishing my purpose
or succeeding in the task I gave it.

New Testament *2 Timothy 3.14—4.5 TEV*

Continue in the truths that you were taught and firmly
believe. You know who your teachers were, and you
remember that ever since you were a child, you have known
the Holy Scriptures, which are able to give you the wisdom
that leads to salvation through faith in Christ Jesus. All
Scripture is inspired by God and is useful for teaching the
truth, rebuking error, correcting faults, and giving
instruction for right living, so that the person who serves
God may be fully qualified and equipped to do every kind of
good deed.

In the presence of God and of Christ Jesus, who will judge
the living and the dead, and because he is coming to rule as
King, I solemnly urge you to preach the message, to insist
upon proclaiming it (whether the time is right or not), to
convince, reproach, and encourage, as you teach with all
patience. The time will come when people will not listen to
sound doctrine, but will follow their own desires and will
collect for themselves more and more teachers who will tell
them what they are itching to hear. They will turn away from
listening to the truth and give their attention to legends. But
you must keep control of yourself in all circumstances;
endure suffering, do the work of a preacher of the Good
News, and perform your whole duty as a servant of God.

Gospel *John 5.36b-end* JB

Jesus said to the Jews,
'The works my Father has given me to carry out,
these same works of mine
testify that the Father has sent me.
Besides, the Father who sent me
bears witness to me himself.
You have never heard his voice,
you have never seen his shape,
and his words find no home in you
because you do not believe
in the one he has sent.

'You study the scriptures,
believing that in them you have eternal life;
now these same scriptures testify to me,
and yet you refuse to come to me for life!
As for human approval, this means nothing to me.
Besides, I know you too well:
you have no love of God in you.
I have come in the name of my Father
and you refuse to accept me;
if someone else comes in his own name
you will accept him.

'How can you believe,
since you look to one another for approval
and are not concerned
with the approval that comes from the one God?
Do not imagine that I am going to accuse you before
    the Father:
you place your hopes on Moses,
and Moses will be your accuser.
If you really believed him
you would believe me too,
since it was I that he was writing about;
but if you refuse to believe what he wrote,
how can you believe what I say?'

READINGS YEAR 2

Old Testament *Isaiah 64.1-7 JB*

Oh, that you would tear the heavens open and come down
—at your Presence the mountains would melt,
as fire sets brushwood alight,
as fire causes water to boil—
to make known your name to your enemies,
and make the nations tremble at your Presence,
working unexpected miracles
such as no one has ever heard of before.

No ear has heard,
no eye has seen
any god but you act like this
for those who trust him.
You guide those who act with integrity
and keep your ways in mind.
You were angry when we were sinners;
we had long been rebels against you.
We were all like men unclean,
all that integrity of ours like filthy clothing.
We have all withered like leaves
and our sins blew us away like the wind.
No one invoked your name
or roused himself to catch hold of you.
For you hid your face from us
and gave us up to the power of our sins.
And yet, Lord, you are our Father.

New Testament *Romans 15.4-13 NEB*

All the ancient scriptures were written for our own
instruction, in order that through the encouragement they
give us we may maintain our hope with fortitude. And may
God, the source of all fortitude and all encouragement, grant
that you may agree with one another after the manner of
Christ Jesus, so that with one mind and one voice you may
praise the God and Father of our Lord Jesus Christ.

In a word, accept one another as Christ accepted us, to the
glory of God. I mean that Christ became a servant of the

Jewish people to maintain the truth of God by making good his promises to the patriarchs, and at the same time to give the Gentiles cause to glorify God for his mercy. As Scripture says, 'Therefore I will praise thee among the Gentiles and sing hymns to thy name'; and again, 'Gentiles, make merry together with his own people'; and yet again, 'All Gentiles, praise the Lord; let all peoples praise him.' Once again, Isaiah says, 'There shall be the Scion of Jesse, the one raised up to govern the Gentiles; on him the Gentiles shall set their hope.' And may the God of hope fill you with all joy and peace by your faith in him, until, by the power of the Holy Spirit, you overflow with hope.

Gospel *Luke 4.14-21 NEB*

Jesus, armed with the power of the Spirit, returned to Galilee; and reports about him spread through the whole country-side. He taught in their synagogues and all men sang his praises.

So he came to Nazareth, where he had been brought up, and went to synagogue on the Sabbath day as he regularly did. He stood up to read the lesson and was handed the scroll of the prophet Isaiah. He opened the scroll and found the passage which says,

'The spirit of the Lord is upon me because he has
    anointed me;
he has sent me to announce good news to the poor,
to proclaim release for prisoners and recovery of sight
    for the blind;
to let the broken victims go free,
to proclaim the year of the Lord's favour.'

He rolled up the scroll, gave it back to the attendant, and sat down; and all eyes in the synagogue were fixed on him.

He began to speak: 'Today', he said, 'in your very hearing this text has come true.'

PROPER PREFACE

Rite A. A Preface of Advent (1) is said throughout the week.
Rite B. Second Thanksgiving. The Preface of Advent is said
throughout the week.

POSTCOMMUNION SENTENCE

How sweet are the words of the Lord to the taste, sweeter
than honey to the mouth. Through his precepts we get
understanding. *Psalm 119.103*

ADVENT 3
(Second Sunday before Christmas)   Violet

INTRODUCTORY SENTENCE

When the Lord comes, he will bring to light things now
hidden in darkness, and will disclose the purposes of the
heart. *1 Corinthians 4.5*

COLLECT

Almighty God,
who sent your servant John the Baptist
to prepare your people for the coming of your Son:
inspire the ministers and stewards of your truth
to turn our disobedient hearts to the law of love;
that when he comes again in glory,
we may stand with confidence before him as our judge;
who is alive and reigns with you and the Holy Spirit,
one God, now and for ever.

PSALMS 126; Benedictus

READINGS YEAR 1

Old Testament *Isaiah 40.1-11 RSV*

Comfort, comfort my people,
says your God.
Speak tenderly to Jerusalem,
and cry to her

that her warfare is ended,
that her iniquity is pardoned,
that she has received from the Lord's hand
double for all her sins.

A voice cries:
'In the wilderness prepare the way of the Lord,
make straight in the desert a highway for our God.
Every valley shall be lifted up,
and every mountain and hill be made low;
the uneven ground shall become level,
and the rough places a plain.
And the glory of the Lord shall be revealed,
and all flesh shall see it together,
for the mouth of the Lord has spoken.'

A voice says, 'Cry!'
And I said, 'What shall I cry?'
All flesh is grass,
and all its beauty is like the flower of the field.
The grass withers, the flower fades,
when the breath of the Lord blows upon it;
surely the people is grass.
The grass withers, the flower fades;
but the word of our God will stand for ever.

Get you up to a high mountain,
O herald of good tidings to Zion;
lift up your voice with strength,
O herald of good tidings to Jerusalem,
lift it up, fear not;
say to the cities of Judah,
'Behold your God!'
Behold, the Lord God comes with might,
and his arm rules for him;
behold, his reward is with him,
and his recompense before him.
He will feed his flock like a shepherd,
he will gather the lambs in his arms,
he will carry them in his bosom,
and gently lead those that are with young.

New Testament *1 Corinthians 4.1-5 RSV*

This is how one should regard us, as servants of Christ and stewards of the mysteries of God. Moreover it is required of stewards that they be found trustworthy. But with me it is a very small thing that I should be judged by you or by any human court. I do not even judge myself. I am not aware of anything against myself, but I am not thereby acquitted. It is the Lord who judges me. Therefore do not pronounce judgement before the time, before the Lord comes, who will bring to light the things now hidden in darkness and will disclose the purposes of the heart. Then every man will receive his commendation from God.

Gospel *John 1.19-28 JB*

This is how John appeared as a witness. When the Jews sent priests and Levites from Jerusalem to ask him, 'Who are you?' he not only declared, but he declared quite openly, 'I am not the Christ.' 'Well then,' they asked, 'are you Elijah?' 'I am not' he said. 'Are you the Prophet?' He answered, 'No'. So they said to him, 'Who are you? We must take back an answer to those who sent us. What have you to say about yourself?' So John said, 'I am, as Isaiah prophesied:

a voice that cries in the wilderness:
"Make a straight way for the Lord."'

Now these men had been sent by the Pharisees, and they put this further question to him, 'Why are you baptizing if you are not the Christ, and not Elijah, and not the prophet?' John replied, 'I baptize with water; but there stands among you—unknown to you—the one who is coming after me; and I am not fit to undo his sandal-strap.' This happened at Bethany, on the far side of the Jordan, where John was baptizing.

READINGS YEAR 2

Old Testament *Malachi 3.1-5 NEB*

Look, I am sending my messenger who will clear a path before me. Suddenly the Lord whom you seek will come to his temple; the messenger of the covenant in whom you delight is here, here already, says the Lord of Hosts. Who can endure the day of his coming? Who can stand firm when he appears? He is like a refiner's fire, like fuller's soap; he will take his seat, refining and purifying; he will purify the Levites and cleanse them like gold and silver, and so they shall be fit to bring offerings to the Lord. Thus the offerings of Judah and Jerusalem shall be pleasing to the Lord as they were in days of old, in years long past. I will appear before you in court, prompt to testify against sorcerers, adulterers, and perjurers, against those who wrong the hired labourer, the widow, and the orphan, who thrust the alien aside and have no fear of me, says the Lord of Hosts.

New Testament *Philippians 4.4-9 RSV*

Rejoice in the Lord always; again I will say, Rejoice. Let all men know your forbearance. The Lord is at hand. Have no anxiety about anything, but in everything by prayer and supplication with thanksgiving let your requests be made known to God. And the peace of God, which passes all understanding, will keep your hearts and your minds in Christ Jesus.

Finally, brethren, whatever is true, whatever is honourable, whatever is just, whatever is pure, whatever is lovely, whatever is gracious, if there is any excellence, if there is anything worthy of praise, think about these things. What you have learned and received and heard and seen in me, do; and the God of peace will be with you.

Gospel *Matthew 11.2-15 NEB*

John, who was in prison, heard what Christ was doing, and sent his own disciples to him with this message: 'Are you the one who is to come, or are we to expect some other?' Jesus answered, 'Go and tell John what you hear and see: the blind recover their sight, the lame walk, the lepers are made clean, the deaf hear, the dead are raised to life, the poor are hearing the good news—and happy is the man who does not find me a stumbling-block.'

When the messengers were on their way back, Jesus began to speak to the people about John: 'What was the spectacle that drew you to the wilderness? A reed-bed swept by the wind? No? Then what did you go out to see? A man dressed in silks and satins? Surely you must look in palaces for that. But why did you go out? To see a prophet? Yes indeed, and far more than a prophet. He is the man of whom Scripture says,

"Here is my herald, whom I send on ahead of you, and he will prepare your way before you."

'I tell you this: never has there appeared on earth a mother's son greater than John the Baptist, and yet the least in the kingdom of Heaven is greater than he.

'Ever since the coming of John the Baptist the kingdom of Heaven has been subjected to violence and violent men are seizing it. For all the prophets and the Law foretold things to come until John appeared, and John is the destined Elijah, if you will but accept it. If you have ears, then hear.'

PROPER PREFACE

Rite A. A Preface of Advent (1) or (2) is said throughout the week.
Rite B. Second Thanksgiving. The Preface of Advent is said throughout the week.

POSTCOMMUNION SENTENCE

Our Lord says, Surely I come quickly. Even so: come, Lord Jesus! *Revelation 22.20*

ADVENT 4
(The Sunday next before Christmas)   Violet

INTRODUCTORY SENTENCE

The glory of the Lord shall be revealed: and all mankind shall see it. *Isaiah 40.5*

COLLECT

Heavenly Father,
who chose the Virgin Mary, full of grace,
to be the mother of our Lord and Saviour:
fill us with your grace,
that in all things we may accept your holy will
and with her rejoice in your salvation;
through Jesus Christ our Lord.

PSALMS 45.10-end; Magnificat

READINGS YEAR 1

Old Testament *Isaiah 11.1-9 NEB*

A shoot shall grow from the stock of Jesse,
and a branch shall spring from his roots.
The spirit of the Lord shall rest upon him,
a spirit of wisdom and understanding,
a spirit of counsel and power,
a spirit of knowledge and the fear of the Lord.
He shall not judge by what he sees
nor decide by what he hears;
he shall judge the poor with justice
and defend the humble in the land with equity;
his mouth shall be a rod to strike down the ruthless,
and with a word he shall slay the wicked.
Round his waist he shall wear the belt of justice,
and good faith shall be the girdle round his body.
Then the wolf shall live with the sheep,
and the leopard lie down with the kid;
the calf and the young lion shall grow up together,
and a little child shall lead them;
the cow and the bear shall be friends,
and their young shall lie down together.
The lion shall eat straw like cattle;
the infant shall play over the hole of the cobra,
and the young child dance over the viper's nest.
They shall not hurt or destroy in all my holy mountain;
for as the waters fill the sea,
so shall the land be filled with the knowledge of the Lord.

New Testament *1 Corinthians 1.26-end TEV*

Now remember what you were, my brothers, when God
called you. From the human point of view few of you were
wise or powerful or of high social standing. God purposely
chose what the world considers nonsense in order to shame
the wise, and he chose what the world considers weak in
order to shame the powerful. He chose what the world looks
down on and despises, and thinks is nothing, in order to
destroy what the world thinks is important. This means that
no one can boast in God's presence. But God has brought
you into union with Christ Jesus, and God has made Christ
to be our wisdom. By him we are put right with God; we
become God's holy people and are set free. So then, as the
scripture says, 'Whoever wants to boast must boast of what
the Lord has done.'

Gospel *Luke 1.26-38a RSV*

In the sixth month the angel Gabriel was sent from God to a
city of Galilee named Nazareth, to a virgin betrothed to a
man whose name was Joseph, of the house of David; and the
virgin's name was Mary. And he came to her and said, 'Hail,
O favoured one, the Lord is with you!' But she was greatly
troubled at the saying, and considered in her mind what sort
of greeting this might be. And the angel said to her, 'Do not
be afraid, Mary, for you have found favour with God. And
behold, you will conceive in your womb and bear a son, and
you shall call his name Jesus.
He will be great, and will be called the Son of the Most High;
and the Lord God will give to him the throne
    of his father David,
and he will reign over the house of Jacob for ever;
and of his kingdom there will be no end.'

And Mary said to the angel, 'How can this be, since I have no
husband?' And the angel said to her,
'The Holy Spirit will come upon you,
and the power of the Most High will overshadow you;
therefore the child to be born will be called holy,
the Son of God.
And behold, your kinswoman Elizabeth in her old age has

also conceived a son; and this is the sixth month with her who was called barren. For with God nothing will be impossible.' And Mary said, 'Behold I am the handmaid of the Lord; let it be to me according to your word.'

READINGS YEAR 2

Old Testament *Zechariah 2.10-end NEB*

Shout aloud and rejoice, daughter of Zion; I am coming, I will make my dwelling among you, says the Lord. Many nations shall come over to the Lord on that day and become his people, and he will make his dwelling with you. Then you shall know that the Lord of Hosts has sent me to you. The Lord will once again claim Judah as his own possession in the holy land, and make Jerusalem the city of his choice.

Silence, all mankind, in the presence of the Lord! For he has bestirred himself out of his holy dwelling-place.

New Testament *Revelation 21.1-7 RSV*

I saw a new heaven and a new earth; for the first heaven and the first earth had passed away, and the sea was no more. And I saw the holy city, new Jerusalem, coming down out of heaven from God, prepared as a bride adorned for her husband; and I heard a great voice from the throne saying, 'Behold, the dwelling of God is with men. He will dwell with them, and they shall be his people, and God himself will be with them; he will wipe away every tear from their eyes, and death shall be no more, neither shall there be mourning nor crying nor pain any more, for the former things have passed away.'

And he who sat upon the throne said, 'Behold, I make all things new.' Also he said, 'Write this, for these words are trustworthy and true.' And he said to me, 'It is done! I am the Alpha and the Omega, the beginning and the end. To the thirsty I will give water from the fountain of the water of life without payment. He who conquers shall have this heritage, and I will be his God and he shall be my son.'

Gospel *Matthew 1.18-23 RSV*

Now the birth of Jesus Christ took place in this way. When his mother Mary had been betrothed to Joseph, before they came together she was found to be with child of the Holy Spirit; and her husband Joseph, being a just man and unwilling to put her to shame, resolved to divorce her quietly. But as he considered this, behold, an angel of the Lord appeared to him in a dream, saying, 'Joseph, son of David, do not fear to take Mary your wife, for that which is conceived in her is of the Holy Spirit; she will bear a son, and you shall call his name Jesus, for he will save his people from their sins.' All this took place to fulfil what the Lord had spoken by the prophet:
'Behold, a virgin shall conceive and bear a son,
and his name shall be called Emmanuel'
(which means, God with us).

PROPER PREFACE

Rite A. A Preface of Advent (1) or the Incarnation (2) is said until Christmas Day.
Rite B. The Preface of Advent is said until Christmas Day.

POSTCOMMUNION SENTENCE

The virgin is with child and will soon give birth to a son: and she will call him Emmanuel, God-is-with-us. *Isaiah 7.14*

CHRISTMAS EVE   Violet

INTRODUCTORY SENTENCE

In the morning you shall see the glory of the Lord.
Exodus 16.7

COLLECT

Almighty God,
you make us glad with the yearly remembrance
of the birth of your Son Jesus Christ.
Grant that, as we joyfully receive him for our redeemer,

we may with sure confidence behold him
when he shall come to be our judge;
who is alive and reigns with you and the Holy Spirit,
one God, now and for ever.

PSALMS 89.1-7 (8-18); 89.19-30

READINGS YEARS 1 and 2

Old Testament *Isaiah 62.1-5 RSV*

For Zion's sake I will not keep silent,
and for Jerusalem's sake I will not rest,
until her vindication goes forth as brightness,
and her salvation as a burning torch.
The nations shall see your vindication,
and all the kings your glory;
and you shall be called by a new name
which the mouth of the Lord will give.
You shall be a crown of beauty in the hand of the Lord,
and a royal diadem in the hand of your God.
You shall no more be termed Forsaken,
and your land shall no more be termed Desolate;
but you shall be called My delight is in her,
and your land Married;
for the Lord delights in you,
and your land shall be married.
For as a young man marries a virgin,
so shall your sons marry you,
and as the bridegroom rejoices over the bride,
so shall your God rejoice over you.

New Testament *Acts 13.16-26 JB*

Paul stood up, held up a hand for silence and began to speak:

'Men of Israel, and fearers of God, listen! The God of our
nation Israel chose our ancestors, and made our people great
when they were living as foreigners in Egypt; then by divine
power he led them out, and for about forty years took care of
them in the wilderness. When he had destroyed seven
nations in Canaan, he put them in possession of their land
for about four hundred and fifty years. After this he gave

them judges, down to the prophet Samuel. Then they demanded a king, and God gave them Saul son of Kish, a man of the tribe of Benjamin. After forty years, he deposed him and made David their king, of whom he approved in these words, "I have selected David son of Jesse, a man after my own heart, who will carry out my whole purpose." To keep his promise, God has raised up for Israel one of David's descendants, Jesus, as Saviour, whose coming was heralded by John when he proclaimed a baptism of repentance for the whole people of Israel. Before John ended his career he said, "I am not the one you imagine me to be; that one is coming after me and I am not fit to undo his sandal."

'My brothers, sons of Abraham's race, and all you who fear God, this message of salvation is meant for you.'

Gospel *Luke 1.67-79 RSV*

Zechariah was filled with the Holy Spirit,
    and prophesied, saying,
'Blessed be the Lord God of Israel,
for he has visited and redeemed his people,
and has raised up a horn of salvation for us
in the house of his servant David,
as he spoke by the mouth of his holy prophets from of old,
that we should be saved from our enemies,
and from the hand of all who hate us;
to perform the mercy promised to our fathers,
and to remember his holy covenant,
the oath which he swore to our father Abraham,
    to grant us
that we, being delivered from the hand of our enemies,
might serve him without fear,
in holiness and righteousness before him
    all the days of our life.
And you, child, will be called the prophet of the Most High;
for you will go before the Lord to prepare his ways,
to give knowledge of salvation to his people
in the forgiveness of their sins,
through the tender mercy of our God,
when the day shall dawn upon us from on high

to give light to those who sit in darkness
     and in the shadow of death,
to guide our feet into the way of peace.'

POSTCOMMUNION SENTENCE

The glory of the Lord shall be revealed: and all mankind shall
see it. *Isaiah 40.5*

CHRISTMAS DAY   White or Gold

INTRODUCTORY SENTENCES

The people who walked in darkness have seen a great light:
those who dwell in the land of deep darkness, on them has
the light shone. *Isaiah 9.2 (For use during the night)*

or

I bring you news of great joy, a joy to be shared by the whole
people: today in the town of David a Saviour has been born
to you; he is Christ the Lord. *Luke 2.10 (For use in the early
morning)*

or

To us a child is born, to us a son is given: and his name will be
called the Prince of Peace. *Isaiah 9.6 (For use during the day)*

COLLECTS

All praise to you,
Almighty God and heavenly king,
who sent your Son into the world
to take our nature upon him
and to be born of a pure virgin.
Grant that, as we are born again in him,
so he may continually dwell in us
and reign on earth as he reigns in heaven
with you and the Holy Spirit,
now and for ever.

or this may be used at midnight or in the early morning
Eternal God,
who made this most holy night
to shine with the brightness of your one true light:
bring us, who have known the revelation
    of that light on earth,
to see the radiance of your heavenly glory;
through Jesus Christ our Lord.

PSALMS 85; 96; 98

READINGS YEARS 1 and 2

Old Testament *Isaiah 9.2, 6-7 RSV*

The people who walked in darkness
have seen a great light;
those who dwelt in a land of deep darkness,
on them has light shined.
For to us a child is born,
to us a son is given;
and the government will be upon his shoulder,
and his name will be called
'Wonderful Counsellor, Mighty God,
Everlasting Father, Prince of Peace.'
Of the increase of his government and of peace
there will be no end,
upon the throne of David, and over his kingdom,
to establish it, and to uphold it
with justice and with righteousness
from this time forth and for evermore.
The zeal of the Lord of hosts will do this.

or *Isaiah 62.10-12 NEB*

Go out of the gates, go out,
prepare a road for my people;
build a highway, build it up,
clear away the boulders;
raise a signal to the peoples.
This is the Lord's proclamation
to earth's farthest bounds:

Tell the daughter of Zion,
Behold, your deliverance has come.
His recompense comes with him;
he carries his reward before him;
and they shall be called a Holy People,
the Ransomed of the Lord,
a People long-sought, a City not forsaken.

or *Micah 5.2-4 RSV*

You, O Bethlehem Ephrathah,
who are little to be among the clans of Judah,
from you shall come forth for me
one who is to be ruler in Israel,
whose origin is from of old,
from ancient days.
Therefore he shall give them up until the time
when she who is in travail has brought forth;
then the rest of his brethren shall return
to the people of Israel.
And he shall stand and feed his flock
in the strength of the Lord,
in the majesty of the name of the Lord his God.
And they shall dwell secure, for now he shall be great
to the ends of the earth.

New Testament *Titus 2.11-14; 3.3-7 NEB*

The grace of God has dawned upon the world with healing
for all mankind; and by it we are disciplined to renounce
godless ways and worldly desires, and to live a life of
temperance, honesty, and godliness in the present age,
looking forward to the happy fulfilment of our hope when
the splendour of our great God and Saviour Christ Jesus will
appear. He it is who sacrificed himself for us, to set us free
from all wickedness and to make us a pure people marked
out for his own, eager to do good.

For at one time we ourselves in our folly and obstinacy were
all astray. We were slaves to passions and pleasures of every
kind. Our days were passed in malice and envy; we were
odious ourselves and we hated one another. But when the

kindness and generosity of God our Saviour dawned upon the world, then, not for any good deeds of our own, but because he was merciful, he saved us through the water of rebirth and the renewing power of the Holy Spirit. For he sent down the Spirit upon us plentifully through Jesus Christ our Saviour, so that, justified by his grace, we might in hope become heirs to eternal life.

or *Hebrews 1.1-5 (6-12) JB*

At various times in the past and in various different ways, God spoke to our ancestors through the prophets; but in our own time, the last days, he has spoken to us through his Son, the Son that he has appointed to inherit everything and through whom he made everything there is. He is the radiant light of God's glory and the perfect copy of his nature, sustaining the universe by his powerful command; and now that he has destroyed the defilement of sin, he has gone to take his place in heaven at the right hand of divine Majesty. So he is now as far above the angels as the title which he has inherited is higher than their own name. God has never said to any angel: 'You are my Son, today I have become your father'; or: 'I will be a father to him and he a son to me.'

(Again, when he brings the First-born into the world, he says: 'Let all the angels of God worship him.' About the angels, he says: 'He makes his angels winds and his servants flames of fire', but to his Son he says: 'God, your throne shall last for ever and ever', and: 'his royal sceptre is the sceptre of virtue; virtue you love as much as you hate wickedness. This is why God, your God, has anointed you with the oil of gladness, above all your rivals.' And again: 'It is you, Lord, who laid earth's foundations in the beginning, the heavens are the work of your hands; all will vanish, though you remain, all wear out like a garment; you will roll them up like a cloak, and like a garment they will be changed. But yourself, you never change and your years are unending.')

or *1 John 4.7-14 JB*

My dear people,
let us love one another

since love comes from God
and everyone who loves is begotten by God and knows God.
Anyone who fails to love can never have known God,
because God is love.
God's love for us was revealed
when God sent into the world his only Son
so that we could have life through him;
this is the love I mean:
not our love for God,
but God's love for us when he sent his Son
to be the sacrifice that takes our sins away.
My dear people,
since God has loved us so much,
we too should love one another.
No one has ever seen God;
but as long as we love one another
God will live in us
and his love will be complete in us.
We can know that we are living in him
and he is living in us
because he lets us share his Spirit.
We ourselves saw and we testify
that the Father sent his Son
as saviour of the world.

Gospel *Luke 2.1-14 (15-20) RSV*

In those days a decree went out from Caesar Augustus that
all the world should be enrolled. This was the first
enrolment, when Quirinius was governor of Syria. And all
went to be enrolled, each to his own city. And Joseph also
went up from Galilee, from the city of Nazareth, to Judaea,
to the city of David, which is called Bethlehem, because he
was of the house and lineage of David, to be enrolled with
Mary, his betrothed, who was with child. And while they
were there, the time came for her to be delivered. And she
gave birth to her first-born son and wrapped him in
swaddling cloths, and laid him in a manger, because there
was no place for them in the inn.

And in that region there were shepherds out in the field,
keeping watch over their flock by night. And an angel of the

Lord appeared to them, and the glory of the Lord shone around them, and they were filled with fear. And the angel said to them, 'Be not afraid; for behold, I bring you good news of a great joy which will come to all the people; for to you is born this day in the city of David a Saviour, who is Christ the Lord. And this will be a sign for you: you will find a babe wrapped in swaddling cloths and lying in a manger.' And suddenly there was with the angel a multitude of the heavenly host praising God and saying,
'Glory to God in the highest,
and on earth peace among men with whom he is pleased!'

(When the angels went away from them into heaven, the shepherds said to one another, 'Let us go over to Bethlehem and see this thing that has happened, which the Lord has made known to us.' And they went with haste, and found Mary and Joseph, and the babe lying in a manger. And when they saw it they made known the saying which had been told them concerning this child; and all who heard it wondered at what the shepherds told them. But Mary kept all these things, pondering them in her heart. And the shepherds returned, glorifying and praising God for all they had heard and seen, as it had been told them.)

or *Luke 2.8-20 RSV*

There were shepherds out in the field, keeping watch over their flock by night. And an angel of the Lord appeared to them, and the glory of the Lord shone around them, and they were filled with fear. And the angel said to them, 'Be not afraid; for behold, I bring you good news of a great joy which will come to all the people; for to you is born this day in the city of David a Saviour, who is Christ the Lord. And this will be a sign for you: you will find a babe wrapped in swaddling cloths and lying in a manger.' And suddenly there was with the angel a multitude of the heavenly host praising God and saying,
'Glory to God in the highest,
and on earth peace among men with whom he is pleased!'

When the angels went away from them into heaven, the shepherds said to one another, 'Let us go over to Bethlehem and see this thing that has happened, which the Lord has made known to us.' And they went with haste, and found Mary and Joseph, and the babe lying in a manger. And when they saw it they made known the saying which had been told them concerning this child; and all who heard it wondered at what the shepherds told them. But Mary kept all these things, pondering them in her heart. And the shepherds returned, glorifying and praising God for all they had heard and seen, as it had been told them.

or *John 1.1-14 RSV*

In the beginning was the Word, and the Word was with God, and the Word was God. He was in the beginning with God; all things were made through him, and without him was not anything made that was made. In him was life, and the life was the light of men. The light shines in the darkness, and the darkness has not overcome it.

There was a man sent from God, whose name was John. He came for testimony, to bear witness to the light, that all might believe through him. He was not the light, but came to bear witness to the light.

The true light that englightens every man was coming into the world. He was in the world, and the world was made through him, yet the world knew him not. He came to his own home, and his own people received him not. But to all who received him, who believed in his name, he gave power to become children of God; who were born, not of blood nor of the will of the flesh nor of the will of man, but of God.

And the Word became flesh and dwelt among us, full of grace and truth; we have beheld his glory, glory as of the only Son from the Father.

PROPER PREFACE

Rite A. A Preface of the Incarnation (3) or (4) is said. Preface (3) is not suitable for use with the Third Eucharistic Prayer. A Preface of the Incarnation (3), (4), or (6) is said on weekdays until the Epiphany.
Rite B. The Preface of Christmas is said daily until the Epiphany.

POSTCOMMUNION SENTENCES

The shepherds said, 'Let us go to Bethlehem, and see the thing that the Lord has made known to us.' *Luke 2.15 (For use during the night)*

or

The Word was made flesh, and lived among us: and we saw his glory. *John 1.14 (For use in the early morning)*

or

The bread of God is he who comes down from heaven and gives life to the world. *John 6.33 (For use during the day)*

SUNDAY AFTER CHRISTMAS DAY   White or Gold

INTRODUCTORY SENTENCE

God's love for us was revealed when God sent his only Son into the world so that we could have life through him. *1 John 4.9*

COLLECT YEAR 1

Almighty God,
who wonderfully created us in your own image
and yet more wonderfully restored us
through your Son Jesus Christ:
grant that, as he came to share in our humanity,
so we may share the life of his divinity;
who is alive and reigns with you and the Holy Spirit
one God, now and for ever.

COLLECT YEAR 2

Almighty Father,
whose Son Jesus Christ was presented in the Temple
and acclaimed the glory of Israel
    and the light of the nations:
grant that in him we may be presented to you
and in the world may reflect his glory;
through Jesus Christ our Lord.

PSALMS 2; 116.11-18

READINGS YEAR 1

Old Testament *Isaiah 7.10-14 NEB*

The Lord spoke to Ahaz and said, 'Ask the Lord your God
for a sign, from lowest Sheol or from highest heaven.' But
Ahaz said, 'No, I will not put the Lord to the test by asking
for a sign.' Then the answer came: 'Listen, house of David.
Are you not content to wear out men's patience? Must you
also wear out the patience of my God? Therefore the Lord
himself shall give you a sign: A young woman is with child,
and she will bear a son, and will call him Emmanuel.'

New Testament *Galatians 4.1-7 NEB*

So long as the heir is a minor, he is no better off than a slave,
even though the whole estate is his; he is under guardians
and trustees until the date fixed by his father. And so it was
with us. During our minority we were slaves to the
elemental spirits of the universe, but when the term was
completed, God sent his own Son, born of a woman, born
under the law, to purchase freedom for the subjects of the
law, in order that we might attain the status of sons.

To prove that you are sons, God has sent into our hearts the
Spirit of his Son, crying 'Abba! Father!' You are therefore no
longer a slave but a son, and if a son, then also by God's own
act an heir.

Gospel *John 1.14-18 RSV*

The Word became flesh and dwelt among us, full of grace
and truth; we have beheld his glory, glory as of the only Son
from the Father. John bore witness to him, and cried, 'This
was he of whom I said, "He who comes after me ranks before
me, for he was before me"'. And from his fullness have we
all received, grace upon grace. For the law was given
through Moses; grace and truth came through Jesus Christ.
No one has ever seen God; the only Son, who is in the bosom
of the Father, he has made him known.

READINGS YEAR 2

Old Testament *1 Samuel 1.20-end NEB*

Elkanah had intercourse with his wife Hannah, and the Lord remembered her. She conceived, and in due time bore a son, whom she named Samuel, 'because', she said, 'I asked the Lord for him.'

Elkanah, with his whole household, went up to make the annual sacrifice to the Lord and to redeem his vow. Hannah did not go with them, but said to her husband, 'When the child is weaned I will come up with him to enter the presence of the Lord, and he shall stay there always.' Her husband Elkanah said to her, 'Do what you think best; stay at home until you have weaned him. Only, may the Lord indeed see your vow fulfilled.' So the woman stayed and nursed her son until she had weaned him; and when she had weaned him, she took him up with her. She took also a bull three years old, an ephah of meal, and a flagon of wine, and she brought him, child as he was, into the house of the Lord at Shiloh. They slaughtered the bull, and brought the boy to Eli. Hannah said to him, 'Sir, as sure as you live, I am the woman who stood near you here praying to the Lord. It was this boy that I prayed for and the Lord has given me what I asked. What I asked I have received; and now I lend him to the Lord; for his whole life he is lent to the Lord.' And they prostrated themselves there before the Lord.

New Testament *Romans 12.1-8 NEB*

My brothers, I implore you by God's mercy to offer your very selves to him: a living sacrifice, dedicated and fit for his acceptance, the worship offered by mind and heart. Adapt yourselves no longer to the pattern of this present world, but let your minds be remade and your whole nature thus transformed. Then you will be able to discern the will of God, and to know what is good, acceptable, and perfect.

In virtue of the gift that God in his grace has given me I say to everyone among you: do not be conceited or think too highly of yourself; but think your way to a sober estimate based on the measure of faith that God has dealt to each of you. For just as in a single human body there are many limbs and organs, all with different functions, so all of us, united with Christ, form one body, serving individually as limbs and organs to one another.

The gifts we possess differ as they are allotted to us by God's grace, and must be exercised accordingly: the gift of inspired utterance, for example, in proportion to a man's faith; or the gift of administration, in administration. A teacher should employ his gift in teaching, and one who has the gift of stirring speech should use it to stir his hearers. If you give to charity, give with all your heart; if you are a leader, exert yourself to lead; if you are helping others in distress, do it cheerfully.

Gospel *Luke 2.22-40 JB*

When the day came for them to be purified as laid down by the Law of Moses, the parents of Jesus took him up to Jerusalem to present him to the Lord—observing what stands written in the Law of the Lord: Every first-born male must be consecrated to the Lord—and also to offer in sacrifice, in accordance with what is said in the Law of the Lord, a pair of turtledoves or two young pigeons. Now in Jerusalem there was a man named Simeon. He was an upright and devout man; he looked forward to Israel's comforting and the Holy Spirit rested on him. It had been revealed to him by the Holy Spirit that he would not see death until he had set eyes on the Christ of the Lord. Prompted by the Spirit he came to the Temple: and when the parents brought in the child Jesus to do for him what the Law required, he took him into his arms and blessed God; and he said:

'Now, Master, you can let your servant go in peace,
just as you promised;
because my eyes have seen the salvation
which you have prepared for all the nations to see,
a light to enlighten the pagans
and the glory of your people Israel.'

As the child's father and mother stood there wondering at the things that were being said about him, Simeon blessed them and said to Mary his mother, 'You see this child: he is destined for the fall and for the rising of many in Israel, destined to be a sign that is rejected—and a sword will pierce your own soul too—so that the secret thoughts of many may be laid bare.'

There was a prophetess also, Anna the daughter of Phanuel, of the tribe of Asher. She was well on in years. Her days of girlhood over, she had been married for seven years before becoming a widow. She was now eighty-four years old and never left the Temple, serving God night and day with fasting and prayer. She came by just at that moment and began to praise God; and she spoke of the child to all who looked forward to the deliverance of Jerusalem.

When they had done everything the Law of the Lord required, they went back to Galilee, to their own town of Nazareth. Meanwhile the child grew to maturity, and he was filled with wisdom; and God's favour was with him.

PROPER PREFACE

Rite A. A Preface of the Incarnation (3), (4), or (7) is said. Preface (3) is not suitable for use with the Third Eucharistic Prayer.
Rite B. The Preface of Christmas is said.

POSTCOMMUNION SENTENCE

Mary treasured all things concerning Jesus, and pondered them in her heart; and Jesus increased in wisdom and in stature, and in favour with God and man. *Luke 2.19, 52*

CHRISTMAS 2 White or Gold

INTRODUCTORY SENTENCES

The grace of God has dawned on the world with healing for all mankind. *Titus 2.11*

or

Stand up, Jerusalem, and look towards the east; see your

children, gathered from west to east at the word of the Holy
One, rejoicing that God has remembered them. *Baruch 5.5*

COLLECT YEAR 1

Heavenly Father,
whose blessed Son shared at Nazareth
    the life of an earthly home:
help us to live as the holy family,
united in love and obedience,
and bring us at last to our home in heaven;
through Jesus Christ our Lord.

COLLECT YEAR 2

Eternal God,
who by the shining of a star
led the wise men to the worship of your Son:
guide by his light the nations of the earth,
that the whole world may behold your glory;
through Jesus Christ our Lord.

PSALMS Nunc Dimittis; 27.1-8

READINGS YEAR 1

Old Testament *Ecclesiasticus 3.2-7 JB*

Do what I tell you, and so be safe;
for the Lord honours the father in his children,
and upholds the rights of a mother over her sons.
Whoever respects his father is atoning for his sins,
he who honours his mother is like someone amassing
    a fortune.
Whoever respects his father will be happy with children
    of his own,
he shall be heard on the day when he prays.
Long life comes to him who honours his father,
he who sets his mother at ease is showing obedience
    to the Lord.
He serves his parents as he does his Lord.

or *Exodus 12.21-27 NEB*

Moses summoned all the elders of Israel and said to them, 'Go at once and get sheep for your families and slaughter the Passover. Then take a bunch of marjoram, dip it in the blood in the basin and smear some blood from the basin on the lintel and the two door-posts. Nobody may go out through the door of his house till morning. The Lord will go through Egypt and strike it, but when he sees the blood on the lintel and the two door-posts, he will pass over that door and will not let the destroyer enter your houses to strike you. You shall keep this as a rule for you and your children for all time. When you enter the land which the Lord will give you as he promised, you shall observe this rite. Then, when your children ask you, "What is the meaning of this rite?" you shall say, "It is the Lord's Passover, for he passed over the houses of the Israelites in Egypt when he struck the Egyptians but spared our houses."' The people bowed down and prostrated themselves.

New Testament *Romans 8.11-17 RSV*

If the Spirit of him who raised Jesus from the dead dwells in you, he who raised Christ Jesus from the dead will give life to your mortal bodies also through his Spirit which dwells in you.

So then, brethren, we are debtors, not to the flesh, to live according to the flesh—for if you live according to the flesh you will die, but if by the Spirit you put to death the deeds of the body you will live. For all who are led by the Spirit of God are sons of God. For you did not receive the spirit of slavery to fall back into fear, but you have received the spirit of sonship. When we cry, 'Abba! Father!' it is the Spirit himself bearing witness with our spirit that we are children of God, and if children, then heirs, heirs of God and fellow heirs with Christ, provided we suffer with him in order that we may also be glorified with him.

Gospel *Luke 2.41-end NEB*

Now it was the practice of Joseph and Mary to go to Jerusalem every year for the Passover festival; and when

Jesus was twelve, they made the pilgrimage as usual. When the festive season was over and they started for home, the boy Jesus stayed behind in Jerusalem. His parents did not know of this; but thinking that he was with the party they journeyed on for a whole day, and only then did they begin looking for him among their friends and relations. As they could not find him they returned to Jerusalem to look for him; and after three days they found him sitting in the temple surrounded by the teachers, listening to them and putting questions; and all who heard him were amazed at his intelligence and the answers he gave. His parents were astonished to see him there, and his mother said to him, 'My son, why have you treated us like this? Your father and I have been searching for you in great anxiety.' 'What made you search?' he said. 'Did you not know that I was bound to be in my Father's house?' But they did not understand what he meant. Then he went back with them to Nazareth, and continued to be under their authority; his mother treasured up all these things in her heart. As Jesus grew up he advanced in wisdom and in favour with God and men.

READINGS YEAR 2

Old Testament *Isaiah 60.1-6 NEB*

Arise, Jerusalem,
rise clothed in light; your light has come
and the glory of the Lord shines over you.
For, though darkness covers the earth
and dark night the nations,
the Lord shall shine upon you
and over you shall his glory appear;
and the nations shall march towards your light
and their kings to your sunrise.

Lift up your eyes and look all around:
they flock together, all of them, and come to you;
your sons also shall come from afar,
your daughters walking beside them leading the way.
Then shall you see, and shine with joy,
then your heart shall thrill with pride:
the riches of the sea shall be lavished upon you
and you shall possess the wealth of nations.

Camels in droves shall cover the land,
dromedaries of Midian and Ephah,
all coming from Sheba
laden with golden spice and frankincense,
heralds of the Lord's praise.

New Testament *Revelation 21.22—22.5 NEB*

I saw no temple in the city; for its temple was the sovereign
Lord God and the Lamb. And the city had no need of sun or
moon to shine upon it; for the glory of God gave it light, and
its lamp was the Lamb. By its light shall the nations walk,
and the kings of the earth shall bring into it all their
splendour. The gates of the city shall never be shut by day—
and there will be no night. The wealth and splendour of the
nations shall be brought into it; but nothing unclean shall
enter, nor anyone whose ways are false or foul, but only
those who are inscribed in the Lamb's roll of the living.

Then the angel showed me the river of the water of life,
sparkling like crystal, flowing from the throne of God and of
the Lamb down the middle of the city's street. On either side
of the river stood a tree of life, which yields twelve crops of
fruit, one for each month of the year; the leaves of the trees
serve for the healing of the nations. Every accursed thing
shall disappear. The throne of God and of the Lamb will be
there, and his servants shall worship him; they shall see him
face to face, and bear his name on their foreheads. There
shall be no more night, nor will they need the light of lamp or
sun, for the Lord God will give them light; and they shall
reign for evermore.

Gospel *Matthew 2.1-12, 19-23 RSV*

When Jesus was born in Bethlehem of Judaea in the days of
Herod the king, behold, wise men from the East came to
Jerusalem, saying, 'Where is he who has been born king of
the Jews? For we have seen his star in the East, and have
come to worship him.' When Herod the king heard this, he
was troubled, and all Jerusalem with him; and assembling all
the chief priests and scribes of the people, he inquired of
them where the Christ was to be born. They told him, 'In

Bethlehem of Judaea; for so it is written by the prophet:
"And you, O Bethlehem, in the land of Judah,
are by no means least among the rulers of Judah;
for from you shall come a ruler
who will govern my people Israel."'

Then Herod summoned the wise men secretly and
ascertained from them what time the star appeared; and he
sent them to Bethlehem, saying, 'Go and search diligently
for the child, and when you have found him bring me word,
that I too may come and worship him.' When they had heard
the king they went their way; and lo, the star which they had
seen in the East went before them, till it came to rest over the
place where the child was. When they saw the star, they
rejoiced exceedingly with great joy; and going into the house
they saw the child with Mary his mother, and they fell down
and worshipped him. Then, opening their treasures, they
offered him gifts, gold and frankincense and myrrh. And
being warned in a dream not to return to Herod, they
departed to their own country by another way.

But when Herod died, behold, an angel of the Lord
appeared in a dream to Joseph in Egypt, saying, 'Rise, take
the child and his mother, and go to the land of Israel, for
those who sought the child's life are dead.' And he rose and
took the child and his mother, and went to the land of Israel.
But when he heard that Archelaus reigned over Judaea in
place of his father Herod, he was afraid to go there, and
being warned in a dream he withdrew to the district of
Galilee. And he went and dwelt in a city called Nazareth,
that what was spoken by the prophets might be fulfilled, 'He
shall be called a Nazarene.'

PROPER PREFACE

Rite A. A Preface of the Incarnation (4) or (7) is said.
Rite B. The Preface of Christmas is said.

POSTCOMMUNION SENTENCE

The child Jesus grew and became strong, filled with wisdom;
and the favour of God was upon him. *Luke 2.40*

EPIPHANY OF OUR LORD   White or Gold

INTRODUCTORY SENTENCES

Arise, shine, Jerusalem, for your light has come, and the
glory of the Lord has risen upon you. *Isaiah 60.1*

or

From the rising of the sun to its setting, my name is great
among the nations, says the Lord. *Malachi 1.11*

COLLECT

Eternal God,
who by the shining of a star
led the wise men to the worship of your Son:
guide by his light the nations of the earth,
that the whole world may behold your glory;
through Jesus Christ our Lord.

PSALMS 72.1-8; 72.10-end

READINGS YEARS 1 and 2

Old Testament *Isaiah 49.1-6 NEB*

Listen to me, you coasts and islands,
pay heed, you peoples far away:
from birth the Lord called me,
he named me from my mother's womb.
He made my tongue his sharp sword
and concealed me under cover of his hand;
he made me a polished arrow
and hid me out of sight in his quiver.
He said to me, 'You are my servant,
Israel through whom I shall win glory';
so I rose to honour in the Lord's sight
and my God became my strength.
Once I said, 'I have laboured in vain;
I have spent my strength for nothing, to no purpose';
yet in truth my cause is with the Lord
and my reward is in God's hands.

And now the Lord who formed me in the womb to be
    his servant,
to bring Jacob back to him
that Israel should be gathered to him,
now the Lord calls me again:
it is too slight a task for you, as my servant,
to restore the tribes of Jacob,
to bring back the descendants of Israel:
I will make you a light to the nations,
to be my salvation to earth's farthest bounds.

New Testament *Ephesians 3.1-12 TEV*

For this reason I, Paul, the prisoner of Christ Jesus for the
sake of you Gentiles, pray to God. Surely you have heard
that God in his grace has given me this work to do for your
good. God revealed his secret plan and made it known to
me. (I have written briefly about this, and if you will read
what I have written, you can learn about my understanding
of the secret of Christ.) In past times mankind was not told
this secret, but God has revealed it now by the Spirit to his
holy apostles and prophets. The secret is that by means of
the gospel the Gentiles have a part with the Jews in God's
blessings; they are members of the same body and share in
the promise that God made through Christ Jesus.

I was made a servant of the gospel by God's special gift,
which he gave me through the working of his power. I am
less than the least of all God's people; yet God gave me this
privilege of taking to the Gentiles the Good News about the
infinite riches of Christ, and of making all people see how
God's secret plan is to be put into effect. God, who is the
Creator of all things, kept his secret hidden through all the
past ages, in order that at the present time, by means of the
church, the angelic rulers and powers in the heavenly world
might learn of his wisdom in all its different forms. God did
this according to his eternal purpose, which he achieved
through Christ Jesus our Lord. In union with Christ and
through our faith in him we have the boldness to go into
God's presence with all confidence.

Gospel *Matthew 2.1-12 RSV*

When Jesus was born in Bethlehem of Judaea in the days of Herod the king, behold, wise men from the East came to Jerusalem, saying, 'Where is he who has been born king of the Jews? For we have seen his star in the East, and have come to worship him.' When Herod the king heard this, he was troubled, and all Jerusalem with him; and assembling all the chief priests and scribes of the people, he inquired of them where the Christ was to be born. They told him, 'In Bethlehem of Judaea; for so it is written by the prophet:
"And you, O Bethlehem, in the land of Judah,
are by no means least among the rulers of Judah;
for from you shall come a ruler
who will govern my people Israel."'

Then Herod summoned the wise men secretly and ascertained from them what time the star appeared; and he sent them to Bethlehem, saying, 'Go and search diligently for the child, and when you have found him bring me word, that I too may come and worship him.' When they had heard the king they went their way; and lo, the star which they had seen in the East went before them, till it came to rest over the place were the child was. When they saw the star, they rejoiced exceedingly with great joy; and going into the house they saw the child with Mary his mother, and they fell down and worshipped him. Then, opening their treasures, they offered him gifts, gold and frankincense and myrrh. And being warned in a dream not to return to Herod, they departed to their own country by another way.

PROPER PREFACE

Rite A. A Preface of the Incarnation (5) is said.
Rite B. First Thanksgiving. The Preface of the Epiphany is said.

POSTCOMMUNION SENTENCE

We have seen his star in the east and have come with gifts to worship the Lord. *Matthew 2.2*

EPIPHANY 1
White or Gold for Sunday   Green from Monday

INTRODUCTORY SENTENCE

There came a voice from heaven: This is my Son, the
Beloved, in whom I am well pleased. *Matthew 3.17*

COLLECT

Almighty God,
who anointed Jesus at his baptism with the Holy Spirit
and revealed him as your beloved Son:
inspire us, your children,
who are born of water and the Spirit,
to surrender our lives to your service,
that we may rejoice to be called the sons of God;
through Jesus Christ our Lord.

PSALMS 36.5-10; 89.19-30

READINGS YEAR 1

Old Testament *1 Samuel 16.1-13a NEB*

The Lord said to Samuel, 'How long will you mourn for Saul
because I have rejected him as king over Israel? Fill your
horn with oil and take it with you; I am sending you to Jesse
of Bethlehem; for I have chosen myself a king among his
sons.' Samuel answered, 'How can I go? Saul will hear of it
and kill me.' 'Take a heifer with you,' said the Lord; 'say you
have come to offer a sacrifice to the Lord, and invite Jesse to
the sacrifice; then I will let you know what you must do. You
shall anoint for me the man whom I show you.' Samuel did
as the Lord had told him, and went to Bethlehem. The elders
of the city came in haste to meet him, saying, 'Why have you
come? Is all well?' 'All is well,' said Samuel; 'I have come to
sacrifice to the Lord. Hallow yourselves and come with me to
the sacrifice.' He himself hallowed Jesse and his sons and
invited them to the sacrifice also. They came, and when
Samuel saw Eliab he thought, 'Here, before the Lord, is his
anointed king.' But the Lord said to him, 'Take no account of
it if he is handsome and tall; I reject him. The Lord does not

see as man sees; men judge by appearances but the Lord judges by the heart.' Then Jesse called Abinadab and made him pass before Samuel, but he said, 'No, the Lord has not chosen this one.' Then he presented Shammah, and Samuel said, 'Nor has the Lord chosen him.' Seven of his sons Jesse presented to Samuel, but he said, 'The Lord has not chosen any of these.' Then Samuel asked, 'Are these all?' Jesse answered, 'There is still the youngest, but he is looking after the sheep.' Samuel said to Jesse, 'Send and fetch him; we will not sit down until he comes.' So he sent and fetched him. He was handsome, with ruddy cheeks and bright eyes. The Lord said, 'Rise and anoint him: this is the man.' Samuel took the horn of oil and anointed him in the presence of his brothers. Then the spirit of the Lord came upon David and was with him from that day onwards.

New Testament *Acts 10.34-38a NEB*

Peter said, 'I now see how true it is that God has no favourites, but that in every nation the man who is godfearing and does what is right is acceptable to him. He sent his word to the Israelites and gave the good news of peace through Jesus Christ, who is Lord of all. I need not tell you what happened lately all over the land of the Jews, starting from Galilee after the baptism proclaimed by John. You know about Jesus of Nazareth, how God anointed him with the Holy Spirit and with power.'

Gospel *Matthew 3.13-end NEB*

Jesus arrived at the Jordan from Galilee, and came to John to be baptized by him. John tried to dissuade him. 'Do you come to me?' he said; 'I need rather to be baptized by you.' Jesus replied, 'Let it be so for the present; we do well to conform in this way with all that God requires.' John then allowed him to come. After baptism Jesus came up out of the water at once, and at that moment heaven opened; he saw the Spirit of God descending like a dove to alight upon him; and a voice from heaven was heard saying, 'This is my Son, my Beloved, on whom my favour rests.'

READINGS YEAR 2

Old Testament *Isaiah 42.1-7 NEB*

Here is my servant, whom I uphold,
my chosen one in whom I delight,
I have bestowed my spirit upon him,
and he will make justice shine on the nations.
He will not call out or lift his voice high,
or make himself heard in the open street.
He will not break a bruised reed,
or snuff out a smouldering wick;
he will make justice shine on every race,
never faltering, never breaking down,
he will plant justice on earth,
while coasts and islands wait for his teaching.

Thus speaks the Lord who is God,
he who created the skies and stretched them out,
who fashioned the earth and all that grows in it,
who gave breath to its people,
the breath of life to all who walk upon it:
I, the Lord, have called you with righteous purpose
and taken you by the hand;
I have formed you, and appointed you
to be a light to all peoples,
a beacon for the nations,
to open eyes that are blind,
to bring captives out of prison,
out of the dungeons where they lie in darkness.

New Testament *Ephesians 2.1-10 JB*

You were dead, through the crimes and the sins in which
you used to live when you were following the way of this
world, obeying the ruler who governs the air, the spirit who
is at work in the rebellious. We all were among them too in
the past, living sensual lives, ruled entirely by our own
physical desires and our own ideas; so that by nature we
were as much under God's anger as the rest of the world. But
God loved us with so much love that he was generous with
his mercy: when we were dead through our sins, he brought
us to life with Christ—it is through grace that you have been

saved—and raised us up with him and gave us a place with him in heaven, in Christ Jesus.

This was to show for all ages to come, through his goodness towards us in Christ Jesus, how infinitely rich he is in grace. Because it is by grace that you have been saved, through faith; not by anything of your own, but by a gift from God; not by anything that you have done, so that nobody can claim the credit. We are God's work of art, created in Christ Jesus to live the good life as from the beginning he had meant us to live it.

Gospel *John 1.29-34 JB*

Seeing Jesus coming towards him, John said, 'Look, there is the lamb of God that takes away the sin of the world. This is the one I spoke of when I said: "A man is coming after me who ranks before me because he existed before me." I did not know him myself, and yet it was to reveal him to Israel that I came baptizing with water.' John also declared, 'I saw the Spirit coming down on him from heaven like a dove and resting on him. I did not know him myself, but he who sent me to baptize with water had said to me, "The man on whom you see the Spirit come down and rest is the one who is going to baptize with the Holy Spirit." Yes, I have seen and I am the witness that he is the Chosen One of God.'

PROPER PREFACE

Rite A. A Preface of the Incarnation (5) is said.
Rite B. The Preface of the Epiphany is said.

POSTCOMMUNION SENTENCE

I have seen it myself, and bear witness, that this is the Chosen One of God. *John 1.34*

EPIPHANY 2   Green

INTRODUCTORY SENTENCE

Jesus said to the fishermen, Follow me, and I will make you
fishers of men. *Mark 1.17*

COLLECT

Almighty God,
by whose grace alone we are accepted
   and called to your service:
strengthen us by your Holy Spirit
and make us worthy of our calling;
through Jesus Christ our Lord.

PSALMS 100; 145.1-12

READINGS YEAR 1

Old Testament *Jeremiah 1.4-10 NEB*

The word of the Lord came to me: 'Before I formed you in the
womb I knew you for my own; before you were born I
consecrated you, I appointed you a prophet to the nations.'
'Ah! Lord God,' I answered, 'I do not know how to speak; I
am only a child.' But the Lord said, 'Do not call yourself a
child; for you shall go to whatever people I send you and say
whatever I tell you to say. Fear none of them, for I am with
you and will keep you safe.' This was the very word of the
Lord. Then the Lord stretched out his hand and touched my
mouth, and said to me, 'I put my words into your mouth.
This day I give you authority over nations and over
kingdoms, to pull down and to uproot, to destroy and to
demolish, to build and to plant.'

New Testament *Acts 26.1, 9-20 NEB*

Agrippa said to Paul, 'You have our permission to speak for
yourself.' Then Paul stretched out his hand and began his
defence:

'I myself once thought it my duty to work actively against the
name of Jesus of Nazareth; and I did so in Jerusalem. It was I

who imprisoned many of God's people by authority obtained from the chief priests; and when they were condemned to death, my vote was cast against them. In all the synagogues I tried by repeated punishment to make them renounce their faith; indeed my fury rose to such a pitch that I extended my persecution to foreign cities.

'On one such occasion I was travelling to Damascus with authority and commission from the chief priests; and as I was on my way, Your Majesty, in the middle of the day I saw a light from the sky, more brilliant than the sun, shining all around me and my travelling-companions. We all fell to the ground, and then I heard a voice saying to me in the Jewish language, "Saul, Saul, why do you persecute me? It is hard for you, this kicking against the goad." I said, "Tell me, Lord, who you are"; and the Lord replied, "I am Jesus, whom you are persecuting. But now, rise to your feet and stand upright. I have appeared to you for a purpose: to appoint you my servant and witness, to testify both to what you have seen and to what you shall yet see of me. I will rescue you from this people and from the Gentiles to whom I am sending you. I send you to open their eyes and turn them from darkness to light, from the dominion of Satan to God, so that, by trust in me, they may obtain forgiveness of sins, and a place with those whom God has made his own."

'And so, King Agrippa, I did not disobey the heavenly vision. I turned first to the inhabitants of Damascus, and then to Jerusalem and all the country of Judaea, and to the Gentiles, and sounded the call to repent and turn to God, and to prove their repentance by deeds.'

Gospel *Mark 1.14-20 NEB*

After John had been arrested, Jesus came into Galilee proclaiming the Gospel of God: 'The time has come; the kingdom of God is upon you; repent, and believe the Gospel.'

Jesus was walking by the Sea of Galilee when he saw Simon and his brother Andrew on the lake at work with a casting-net; for they were fishermen. Jesus said to them,

'Come with me, and I will make you fishers of men.' And at once they left their nets and followed him.

When he had gone a little further he saw James son of Zebedee and his brother John, who were in the boat overhauling their nets. He called them; and, leaving their father Zebedee in the boat with the hired men, they went off to follow him.

READINGS YEAR 2

Old Testament *1 Samuel 3.1-10 RSV*

Now the boy Samuel was ministering to the Lord under Eli. And the word of the Lord was rare in those days; there was no frequent vision.

At that time Eli, whose eyesight had begun to grow dim, so that he could not see, was lying down in his own place; the lamp of God had not yet gone out, and Samuel was lying down within the temple of the Lord, where the ark of God was. Then the Lord called, 'Samuel! Samuel!' and he said, 'Here I am!' and ran to Eli, and said, 'Here I am, for you called me.' But he said, 'I did not call; lie down again.' So he went and lay down. And the Lord called again, 'Samuel!' And Samuel arose and went to Eli, and said, 'Here I am, for you called me.' But he said, 'I did not call, my son; lie down again.' Now Samuel did not yet know the Lord, and the word of the Lord had not yet been revealed to him. And the Lord called Samuel again the third time. And he arose and went to Eli, and said, 'Here I am, for you called me.' Then Eli perceived that the Lord was calling the boy. Therefore Eli said to Samuel, 'Go, lie down; and if he calls you, you shall say, "Speak, Lord, for your servant hears."' So Samuel went and lay down in his place.

And the Lord came and stood forth, calling as at other times, 'Samuel! Samuel!' And Samuel said, 'Speak, for your servant hears.'

New Testament *Galatians 1.11-end NEB*

I must make it clear to you, my friends, that the gospel you heard me preach is no human invention. I did not take it over from any man; no man taught it me; I received it through a revelation of Jesus Christ.

You have heard what my manner of life was when I was still a practising Jew: how savagely I persecuted the church of God, and tried to destroy it; and how in the practice of our national religion I was outstripping many of my Jewish contemporaries in my boundless devotion to the traditions of my ancestors. But then in his good pleasure God, who had set me apart from birth and called me through his grace, chose to reveal his Son to me and through me, in order that I might proclaim him among the Gentiles. When that happened, without consulting any human being, without going up to Jerusalem to see those who were apostles before me, I went off at once to Arabia, and afterwards returned to Damascus.

Three years later I did go up to Jerusalem to get to know Cephas. I stayed with him for a fortnight, without seeing any other of the apostles, except James the Lord's brother. What I write is plain truth; before God I am not lying.

Next I went to the regions of Syria and Cilicia, and remained unknown by sight to Christ's congregations in Judaea. They only heard it said, 'Our former persecutor is preaching the good news of the faith which once he tried to destroy'; and they praised God for me.

Gospel *John 1.35-end NEB*

John was standing with two of his disciples when Jesus passed by. John looked towards him and said, 'There is the Lamb of God.' The two disciples heard him say this, and followed Jesus. When he turned and saw them following him, he asked, 'What are you looking for?' They said, 'Rabbi' (which means a teacher), 'where are you staying?' 'Come and see', he replied. So they went and saw where he was staying, and spent the rest of the day with him. It was then about four in the afternoon.

One of the two who followed Jesus after hearing what John said was Andrew, Simon Peter's brother. The first thing he did was to find his brother Simon. He said to him, 'We have found the Messiah' (which is the Hebrew for 'Christ'). He brought Simon to Jesus, who looked at him and said, 'You are Simon son of John. You shall be called Cephas' (that is, Peter, the Rock).

The next day Jesus decided to leave for Galilee. He met Philip, who, like Andrew and Peter, came from Bethsaida, and said to him, 'Follow me.' Philip went to find Nathanael, and told him, 'We have met the man spoken of by Moses in the Law, and by the prophets: it is Jesus son of Joseph, from Nazareth.' 'Nazareth!' Nathanael exclaimed; 'can anything good come from Nazareth?' Philip said, 'Come and see.' When Jesus saw Nathanael coming, he said, 'Here is an Israelite worthy of the name; there is nothing false in him.' Nathanael asked him, 'How do you come to know me?' Jesus replied, 'I saw you under the fig-tree before Philip spoke to you.' 'Rabbi,' said Nathanael, 'you are the son of God; you are king of Israel.' Jesus answered, 'Is this the ground of your faith, that I told you I saw you under the fig-tree? You shall see greater things than that.' Then he added, 'In truth, in very truth I tell you all, you shall see heaven wide open, and God's angels ascending and descending upon the Son of Man.'

PROPER PREFACE

Rite A. A Preface of the Incarnation (5) is said.
Rite B. The Preface of the Epiphany is said.

POSTCOMMUNION SENTENCE

Lord, to whom else can we go? You have the words of life. *John 6.68*

EPIPHANY 3   Green

INTRODUCTORY SENTENCE

Jesus was attested to us by God with mighty works and wonders and signs which God did through him. *Acts 2.22*

COLLECT

Almighty God,
whose Son revealed in signs and miracles
the wonder of your saving love:
renew your people with your heavenly grace,
and in all our weakness
sustain us by your mighty power;
through Jesus Christ our Lord.

PSALMS 46; 107.1-9

READINGS YEAR 1

Old Testament *Exodus 33.12-end JB*

Moses said to the Lord, 'See, you yourself say to me, ''Make the people go on'', but you do not let me know who it is you will send with me. Yet you yourself have said, ''I know you by name and you have won my favour.'' If indeed I have won your favour, please show me your ways, so that I can understand you and win your favour. Remember, too, that this nation is your own people.' The Lord replied, 'I myself will go with you, and I will give you rest.' Moses said, 'If you are not going with us yourself, do not make us leave this place. By what means can it be known that I, I and my people, have won your favour, if not by your going with us? By this we shall be marked out, I and my people, from all the peoples on the face of the earth.' The Lord said to Moses, 'Again I will do what you have asked, because you have won my favour and because I know you by name.'

Moses said, 'Show me your glory, I beg you.' And he said, 'I will let all my splendour pass in front of you, and I will pronounce before you the name Jehovah. I have compassion on whom I will, and I show pity to whom I please. You cannot see my face,' he said, 'for man cannot see me and live.' And the Lord said, 'Here is a place beside me. You must stand on the rock, and when my glory passes by, I will put you in a cleft of the rock and shield you with my hand while I pass by. Then I will take my hand away and you shall see the back of me; but my face is not to be seen.'

New Testament *1 John 1.1-7 TEV*

We write to you about the Word of life, which has existed from the very beginning. We have heard it, and we have seen it with our eyes; yes, we have seen it, and our hands have touched it. When this life became visible, we saw it; so we speak of it and tell you about the eternal life which was with the Father and was made known to us. What we have seen and heard we announce to you also, so that you will join with us in the fellowship that we have with the Father and with his Son Jesus Christ. We write this in order that our joy may be complete.

Now the message that we have heard from his Son and announce is this: God is light, and there is no darkness at all in him. If, then, we say that we have fellowship with him, yet at the same time live in the darkness, we are lying both in our words and in our actions. But if we live in the light—just as he is in the light—then we have fellowship with one another, and the blood of Jesus, his Son, purifies us from every sin.

Gospel *John 2.1-11 NEB*

On the third day there was a wedding at Cana-in-Galilee. The mother of Jesus was there, and Jesus and his disciples were guests also. The wine gave out, so Jesus' mother said to him, 'They have no wine left.' He answered, 'Your concern, mother, is not mine. My hour has not yet come.' His mother said to the servants, 'Do whatever he tells you.' There were six stone water-jars standing near, of the kind used for Jewish rites of purification; each held from twenty to thirty gallons. Jesus said to the servants, 'Fill the jars with water', and they filled them to the brim. 'Now draw some off', he ordered, 'and take it to the steward of the feast'; and they did so. The steward tasted the water now turned into wine, not knowing its source; though the servants who had drawn the water knew. He hailed the bridegroom and said, 'Everyone serves the best wine first, and waits until the guests have drunk freely before serving the poorer sort; but you have kept the best wine till now.'

This deed at Cana-in-Galilee is the first of the signs by which Jesus revealed his glory and led his disciples to believe in him.

READINGS YEAR 2

Old Testament *Deuteronomy 8.1-6 NEB*

Moses said to Israel, 'You must carefully observe everything that I command you this day so that you may live and increase and may enter and occupy the land which the Lord promised to your forefathers upon oath. You must remember all that road by which the Lord your God has led you these forty years in the wilderness to humble you, to test you and to discover whether or no it was in your heart to keep his commandments. He humbled you and made you hungry; then he fed you on manna which neither you nor your fathers had known before, to teach you that man cannot live on bread alone but lives by every word that comes from the mouth of the Lord. The clothes on your backs did not wear out nor did your feet swell all these forty years. Take this lesson to heart: that the Lord your God was disciplining you as a father disciplines his son; and keep the commandments of the Lord your God, conforming to his ways and fearing him.'

New Testament *Philippians 4.10-20 JB*

It is a great joy to me, in the Lord, that at last you have shown some concern for me again; though of course you were concerned before, and only lacked an opportunity. I am not talking about shortage of money: I have learnt to manage on whatever I have, I know how to be poor and I know how to be rich too. I have been through my initiation and now I am ready for anything anywhere: full stomach or empty stomach, poverty or plenty. There is nothing I cannot master with the help of the One who gives me strength. All the same, it was good of you to share with me in my hardships. In the early days of the Good News, as you people of Philippi well know, when I left Macedonia, no other church helped me with gifts of money. You were the only ones; and twice since my stay in Thessalonica you have sent me what I needed. It is not your gift that I value; what is valuable to me is the interest that is mounting up in your account. Now for the time being I have everything that I need and more: I am fully provided now that I have received from Epaphroditus the offering that you sent, a sweet fragrance—the sacrifice that God accepts and finds pleasing. In return my God will fulfil all your needs, in Christ Jesus, as lavishly as only God can. Glory to God, our Father, for ever and ever. Amen.

Gospel *John 6.1-14 NEB*

Jesus withdrew to the farther shore of the Sea of Galilee (or Tiberias), and a large crowd of people followed who had seen the signs he performed in healing the sick. Then Jesus went up the hill-side and sat down with his disciples. It was near the time of Passover, the great Jewish festival. Raising his eyes and seeing a large crowd coming towards him, Jesus said to Philip, 'Where are we to buy bread to feed these people?' This he said to test him; Jesus himself knew what he meant to do. Philip replied, 'Twenty pounds would not buy enough bread for every one of them to have a little.' One of his disciples, Andrew, the brother of Simon Peter, said to him, 'There is a boy here who has five barley loaves and two fishes; but what is that among so many?' Jesus said, 'Make the people sit down.' There was plenty of grass there, so the men sat down, about five thousand of them. Then Jesus took the loaves, gave thanks, and distributed them to the people as they sat there. He did the same with the fishes, and they had as much as they wanted. When everyone had had enough, he said to his disciples, 'Collect the pieces left over, so that nothing may be lost.' This they did, and filled twelve baskets with the pieces left uneaten of the five barley loaves.

When the people saw the sign Jesus had performed, the word went round, 'Surely this must be the prophet that was to come into the world.'

PROPER PREFACE

Rite A. A Preface of the Incarnation (5) is said.
Rite B. The Preface of the Epiphany is said.

POSTCOMMUNION SENTENCE

We have beheld his glory, glory as of the only Son from the Father. *John 1.14*

EPIPHANY 4   Green

INTRODUCTORY SENTENCE

Do you not know that you are God's temple and that God's Spirit dwells in you? *1 Corinthians 3.16*

COLLECT

Almighty God,
in Christ you make all things new.
Transform the poverty of our nature
    by the riches of your grace,
and in the renewal of our lives
make known your heavenly glory;
through Jesus Christ our Lord.

PSALMS 48.9-end; 84.1-7

READINGS YEAR 1

Old Testament *1 Kings 8.22-30 JB*

In the presence of the whole assembly of Israel Solomon stood before the altar of the Lord and, stretching out his hands towards heaven, said, 'O Lord, God of Israel, not in heaven above nor on earth beneath is there such a God as you, true to your covenant and your kindness towards your servants when they walk wholeheartedly in your way. You have kept the promise you made to your servant David my father; what you promised with your mouth, today you have carried out by your hand. And now, O Lord, God of Israel, keep the promise you made to your servant David when you said, "You shall never lack for a man to sit before me on the throne of Israel, if only your sons are careful how they behave, walking before me as you yourself have done." So now, God of Israel, let the words come true which you spoke to your servant David my father. Yet will God really live with men on the earth? Why, the heavens and their own heavens cannot contain you. How much less this house that I have built! Listen to the prayer and entreaty of your servant, O Lord my God; listen to the cry and to the prayer your servant makes to you today. Day and night let your eyes watch over this house, over this place of which you have said, "My name shall be there". Listen to the prayer that your servant will offer in this place.'

New Testament *1 Corinthians 3.10-17 NEB*

You are God's building. I am like a skilled master-builder who by God's grace laid the foundation, and someone else is putting up the building. Let each take care how he builds. There can be no other foundation beyond that which is already laid; I mean Jesus Christ himself. If anyone builds on that foundation with gold, silver, and fine stone, or with wood, hay, and straw, the work that each man does will at last be brought to light; the day of judgement will expose it. For that day dawns in fire, and the fire will test the worth of each man's work. If a man's building stands, he will be rewarded; if it burns, he will have to bear the loss; and yet he will escape with his life, as one might from a fire. Surely you know that you are God's temple, where the Spirit of God dwells. Anyone who destroys God's temple will himself be destroyed by God, because the temple of God is holy; and that temple you are.

Gospel *John 2.13-22 NEB*

As it was near the time of the Jewish Passover, Jesus went up to Jerusalem. There he found in the temple the dealers in cattle, sheep, and pigeons, and the money-changers seated at their tables. Jesus made a whip of cords and drove them out of the temple, sheep, cattle, and all. He upset the tables of the money-changers, scattering their coins. Then he turned on the dealers in pigeons: 'Take them out,' he said; 'you must not turn my Father's house into a market.' His disciples recalled the words of Scripture, 'Zeal for thy house will destroy me.' The Jews challenged Jesus: 'What sign', they asked, 'can you show as authority for your action?'

'Destroy this temple', Jesus replied, 'and in three days I will raise it again.' They said, 'It has taken forty-six years to build this temple. Are you going to raise it again in three days?' But the temple he was speaking of was his body. After his resurrection his disciples recalled what he had said, and they believed the Scripture and the words that Jesus had spoken.

READINGS YEAR 2

Old Testament *Jeremiah 7.1-11 NEB*

This word came from the Lord to Jeremiah. Stand at the gate of the Lord's house and there make your proclamation: Listen to the words of the Lord, all you men of Judah who come in through these gates to worship him. These are the words of the Lord of Hosts the God of Israel: Mend your ways and your doings, that I may let you live in this place. You keep saying, 'This place is the temple of the Lord, the temple of the Lord, the temple of the Lord!' This catchword of yours is a lie; put no trust in it. Mend your ways and your doings, deal fairly with one another, do not oppress the alien, the orphan, and the widow, shed no innocent blood in this place, do not run after other gods to your own ruin. Then will I let you live in this place, in the land which I gave long ago to your forefathers for all time. You gain nothing by putting your trust in this lie. You steal, you murder, you commit adultery and perjury, you burn sacrifices to Baal, you run after other gods whom you have not known; then you come and stand before me in this house, which bears my name, and say, 'We are safe'; safe, you think, to indulge in all these abominations. Do you think that this house, this house which bears my name, is a robbers' cave?

New Testament *Hebrews 12.18-end JB*

What you have come to is nothing known to the senses: not a blazing fire, or a gloom turning to total darkness, or a storm; or trumpeting thunder or the great voice speaking which made everyone that heard it beg that no more should be said to them. They were appalled at the order that was given: If even an animal touches the mountain, it must be stoned. The whole scene was so terrible that Moses said: I am afraid, and was trembling with fright. But what you have come to is Mount Zion and the city of the living God, the heavenly Jerusalem where the millions of angels have gathered for the festival, with the whole Church in which everyone is a 'first-born son' and a citizen of heaven. You have come to God himself, the supreme Judge, and been placed with spirits of the saints who have been made perfect; and to Jesus, the mediator who brings a new covenant and a blood for purification which pleads more insistently than Abel's. Make sure that you never refuse to listen when he speaks. The people who refused to listen to the warning from a voice on earth could not escape their punishment, and how shall we escape if we turn away from a voice that warns us from heaven? That time his voice made the earth shake, but now he has given us this promise: I shall make the earth shake once more and not only the earth but heaven as well. The words 'once more' show that since the things being shaken are created things, they are going to be changed, so that the unshakeable things will be left. We have been given possession of an unshakeable kingdom. Let us therefore hold on to the grace that we have been given and use it to worship God in the way that he finds acceptable, in reverence and fear. For our God is a consuming fire.

Gospel *John 4.19-26 JB*

The woman said to Jesus, 'Sir, I see you are a prophet. Our fathers worshipped on this mountain, while you say that Jerusalem is the place where one ought to worship.'
Jesus said:

'Believe me, woman, the hour is coming
when you will worship the Father
neither on this mountain nor in Jerusalem.
You worship what you do not know;
we worship what we do know:
for salvation comes from the Jews.
But the hour will come—in fact it is here already—
when true worshippers will worship the Father in
     spirit and truth:
that is the kind of worshipper
the Father wants.

God is spirit,
and those who worship
must worship in spirit and truth.'

The woman said to him, 'I know that Messiah—that is,
Christ—is coming; and when he comes he will tell us
everything.' 'I who am speaking to you,' said Jesus, 'I
am he.'

PROPER PREFACE

Rite A. A Preface of the Incarnation (5) is said.
Rite B. The Preface of the Epiphany is said.

POSTCOMMUNION SENTENCE

Come to him, that living stone, and like living stones be
yourselves built into a spiritual house. *1 Peter 2.4, 5*

EPIPHANY 5   Green

INTRODUCTORY SENTENCE

To those who are called, Christ is the power of God and the
wisdom of God. *1 Corinthians 1.24*

COLLECT

Give us, Lord, we pray,
the spirit to think and to do always
   those things that are right:
that we who can do no good thing without you
may have power to live according to your holy will;
through Jesus Christ our Lord.

PSALMS 36; 49.1-12

READINGS YEARS 1 and 2

Old Testament *Proverbs 2.1-9 NEB*

My son, if you take my words to heart
and lay up my commands in your mind,

giving attention to wisdom
and your mind to understanding,
if you summon discernment to your aid
and invoke understanding,
if you seek her out like silver
and dig for her like buried treasure,
then you will understand the fear of the Lord
and attain to the knowledge of God;
for the Lord bestows wisdom
and teaches knowledge and understanding.
Out of his store he endows the upright with ability
as a shield for those who live blameless lives;
for he guards the course of justice
and keeps watch over the way of his loyal servants.
Then you will understand what is right and just
and keep only to the good man's path.

or *Ecclesiasticus 42.15-end JB*

I will remind you of the works of the Lord,
and tell of what I have seen.
By the words of the Lord his works come into being
and all creation obeys his will.
As the sun in shining looks on all things,
so the work of the Lord is full of his glory.
The Lord has not granted to the holy ones
to tell of all his marvels
which the Almighty Lord has solidly constructed
for the universe to stand firm in his glory.
He has fathomed the deep and the heart,
and seen into their devious ways;
for the Most High knows all the knowledge there is,
and has observed the signs of the times.
He declares what is past and what will be,
and uncovers the traces of hidden things.
Not a thought escapes him,
not a single word is hidden from him.
He has imposed an order on the magnificent works of
     his wisdom,
he is from everlasting to everlasting,
nothing can be added to him, nothing taken away,

he needs no one's advice.
How desirable are all his works,
how dazzling to the eye!
They all live and last for ever,
whatever the circumstances all obey him.
All things go in pairs, by opposites,
and he has made nothing defective;
the one consolidates the excellence of the other,
who could ever be sated with gazing at his glory?

New Testament *1 Corinthians 3.18-end NEB*

Make no mistake about this: if there is anyone among you
who fancies himself wise—wise, I mean, by the standards of
this passing age—he must become a fool to gain true
wisdom. For the wisdom of this world is folly in God's sight.
Scripture says, 'He traps the wise in their cunning', and
again, 'The Lord knows that the arguments of the wise are
futile.' So never make mere men a cause for pride. For
though everything belongs to you—Paul, Apollos, and
Cephas, the world, life, and death, the present and the
future, all of them belong to you—yet you belong to Christ,
and Christ to God.

Gospel *Matthew 12.38-42 NEB*

Some of the doctors of the law and the Pharisees said,
'Master, we should like you to show us a sign.' Jesus
answered: 'It is a wicked, godless generation that asks for a
sign; and the only sign that will be given it is the sign of the
prophet Jonah. Jonah was in the sea-monster's belly for
three days and three nights, and in the same way the Son of
Man will be three days and three nights in the bowels of the
earth. At the Judgement, when this generation is on trial, the
men of Nineveh will appear against it and ensure its
condemnation, for they repented at the preaching of Jonah;
and what is here is greater than Jonah. The Queen of the
South will appear at the Judgement when this generation is
on trial, and ensure its condemnation, for she came from the
ends of the earth to hear the wisdom of Solomon; and what
is here is greater than Solomon.'

PROPER PREFACE

Rite A. A Preface of the Incarnation (5) is said.
Rite B. The Preface of the Epiphany is said.

POSTCOMMUNION SENTENCE

We impart the secret and hidden wisdom of God, which
none of the rulers of this age understood; for if they had,
they would not have crucified the Lord of glory.
1 Corinthians 2.7

EPIPHANY 6 Green

INTRODUCTORY SENTENCE

With many parables Jesus spoke the word to the crowds, as
they were able to hear it, but privately to his own disciples he
explained everything. *Mark 4.33, 34*

COLLECT

Heavenly Father,
whose blessed Son was revealed
    that he might destroy the works of the devil
and make us the sons of God
and heirs of eternal life:
grant that we, having this hope,
may purify ourselves even as he is pure;
that when he shall appear in power and great glory
we may be made like him
    in his eternal and glorious kingdom;
where he is alive and reigns with you and the Holy Spirit,
one God, now and for ever.

PSALMS 43; 25.1-10

READINGS YEARS 1 and 2

Old Testament *2 Samuel 12.1-10 NEB*

The Lord sent Nathan the prophet to David, and when he
entered his presence, he said to him, 'There were once two

men in the same city, one rich and the other poor. The rich man had large flocks and herds, but the poor man had nothing of his own except one little ewe lamb. He reared it himself, and it grew up in his home with his own sons. It ate from his dish, drank from his cup and nestled in his arms; it was like a daughter to him. One day a traveller came to the rich man's house, and he, too mean to take something from his own flocks and herds to serve to his guest, took the poor man's lamb and served up that.' David was very angry, and burst out, 'As the Lord lives, the man who did this deserves to die! He shall pay for the lamb four times over, because he has done this and shown no pity.' Then Nathan said to David, 'You are the man. This is the word of the Lord the God of Israel to you: "I anointed you king over Israel, I rescued you from the power of Saul, I gave you your master's daughter and his wives to be your own, I gave you the daughters of Israel and Judah; and, had this not been enough, I would have added other favours as great. Why then have you flouted the word of the Lord by doing what is wrong in my eyes? You have struck down Uriah the Hittite with the sword; the man himself you murdered by the sword of the Ammonites, and you have stolen his wife. Now, therefore, since you have despised me and taken the wife of Uriah the Hittite to be your own wife, your family shall never again have rest from the sword."'

New Testament *Romans 1.18-25 NEB*

We see divine retribution revealed from heaven and falling upon all the godless wickedness of men. In their wickedness they are stifling the truth. For all that may be known of God by men lies plain before their eyes; indeed God himself has disclosed it to them. His invisible attributes, that is to say his everlasting power and deity, have been visible, ever since the world began, to the eye of reason, in the things he has made. There is therefore no possible defence for their conduct; knowing God, they have refused to honour him as God, or to render him thanks. Hence all their thinking has ended in futility, and their misguided minds are plunged in darkness. They boast of their wisdom, but they have made fools of themselves, exchanging the splendour of immortal

God for an image shaped like mortal man, even for images like birds, beasts, and creeping things.

For this reason God has given them up to the vileness of their own desires, and the consequent degradation of their bodies, because they have bartered away the true God for a false one, and have offered reverence and worship to created things instead of to the Creator, who is blessed for ever; amen.

Gospel *Matthew 13.24-30 RSV*

Jesus said, 'The kingdom of heaven may be compared to a man who sowed good seed in his field; but while men were sleeping, his enemy came and sowed weeds among the wheat, and went away. So when the plants came up and bore grain, then the weeds appeared also. And the servants of the householder came and said to him, "Sir, did you not sow good seed in your field? How then has it weeds?" He said to them, "An enemy has done this." The servants said to him, "Then do you want us to go and gather them?" But he said, "No; lest in gathering the weeds you root up the wheat along with them. Let both grow together until the harvest; and at harvest time I will tell the reapers, Gather the weeds first and bind them in bundles to be burned, but gather the wheat into my barn!"'

PROPER PREFACE

Rite A. A Preface of the Incarnation (5) is said.
Rite B. The Preface of the Epiphany is said.

POSTCOMMUNION SENTENCE

To you it has been given to know the secrets of the kingdom of heaven. *Matthew 13.11*

NINTH SUNDAY BEFORE EASTER
(Third Sunday before Lent)   Green

INTRODUCTORY SENTENCE

The law of the Lord is perfect, and revives the soul: the
testimony of the Lord is sure, making wise the simple.
Psalm 19.7

COLLECT

Eternal God,
whose Son Jesus Christ is for all mankind
   the way, the truth, and the life:
grant us to walk in his way,
to rejoice in his truth,
and to share his risen life;
who is alive and reigns with you and the Holy Spirit,
one God, now and for ever.

PSALMS 103.1-13; 34.11-18

READINGS YEAR 1

Old Testament *Isaiah 30.18-21 NEB*

Yet the Lord is waiting to show you his favour,
yet he yearns to have pity on you;
for the Lord is a God of justice.
Happy are all who wait for him!

O people of Zion who dwell in Jerusalem, you shall weep no
more. The Lord will show you favour and answer you when
he hears your cry for help. The Lord may give you bread of
adversity and water of affliction, but he who teaches you
shall no longer be hidden out of sight, but with your own
eyes you shall see him always. If you stray from the road to
right or left you shall hear with your own ears a voice behind
you saying, This is the way; follow it.

New Testament *1 Corinthians 4.8-13 JB*

Is it that you have everything you want—that you are rich
already, in possession of your kingdom, with us left outside?

Indeed I wish you were really kings, and we could be kings with you! But instead, it seems to me, God has put us apostles at the end of his parade, with the men sentenced to death; it is true—we have been put on show in front of the whole universe, angels as well as men. Here we are, fools for the sake of Christ, while you are the learned men in Christ; we have no power, but you are influential; you are celebrities, we are nobodies. To this day, we go without food and drink and clothes; we are beaten and have no homes; we work for our living with our own hands. When we are cursed, we answer with a blessing; when we are hounded, we put up with it; we are insulted and we answer politely. We are treated as the offal of the world, still to this day, the scum of the earth.

Gospel *Matthew 5.1-12 NEB*

When Jesus saw the crowds he went up the hill. There he took his seat, and when his disciples had gathered round him he began to address them. And this is the teaching he gave:

How blest are those who know their need of God;
the kingdom of Heaven is theirs.
How blest are the sorrowful;
they shall find consolation.
How blest are those of a gentle spirit;
they shall have the earth for their possession.
How blest are those who hunger and thirst to see
    right prevail;
they shall be satisfied.
How blest are those who show mercy;
mercy shall be shown to them.
How blest are those whose hearts are pure;
they shall see God.
How blest are the peacemakers;
God shall call them his sons.
How blest are those who have suffered persecution
    for the cause of right;
the kingdom of Heaven is theirs.

'How blest you are, when you suffer insults and persecution

and every kind of calumny for my sake. Accept it with gladness and exultation, for you have a rich reward in heaven; in the same way they persecuted the prophets before you.'

READINGS YEAR 2

Old Testament *Proverbs 3.1-8 RSV*

My son, do not forget my teaching,
but let your heart keep my commandments;
for length of days and years of life
and abundant welfare will they give you.
Let not loyalty and faithfulness forsake you;
bind them about your neck,
write them on the tablet of your heart.
So you will find favour and good repute
in the sight of God and man.
Trust in the Lord with all your heart,
and do not rely on your own insight.
In all your ways acknowledge him,
and he will make straight your paths.
Be not wise in your own eyes;
fear the Lord, and turn away from evil.
It will be healing to your flesh
and refreshment to your bones.

New Testament *1 Corinthians 2.1-10 NEB*

Brothers, when I came to you, I declared the attested truth of God without display of fine words or wisdom. I resolved that while I was with you I would think of nothing but Jesus Christ—Christ nailed to the cross. I came before you weak, nervous, and shaking with fear. The word I spoke, the gospel I proclaimed, did not sway you with subtle arguments; it carried conviction by spiritual power, so that your faith might be built not upon human wisdom but upon the power of God.

And yet I do speak words of wisdom to those who are ripe for it, not a wisdom belonging to this passing age, nor to any of its governing powers, which are declining to their end; I speak God's hidden wisdom, his secret purpose framed from the very beginning to bring us to our full glory. The powers that rule the world have never known it; if they had, they would not have crucified the Lord of glory. But, in the words of Scripture, 'Things beyond our seeing, things beyond our hearing, things beyond our imagining, all prepared by God for those who love him', these it is that God has revealed to us through the Spirit. For the Spirit explores everything, even the depths of God's own nature.

Gospel *Luke 8.4b-15 RSV*

Jesus said in a parable, 'A sower went out to sow his seed; and as he sowed, some fell along the path, and was trodden under foot, and the birds of the air devoured it. And some fell on the rock; and as it grew up, it withered away, because it had no moisture. And some fell among thorns; and the thorns grew with it and choked it. And some fell into good soil and grew, and yielded a hundredfold.' As he said this, he called out, 'He who has ears to hear, let him hear.'

And when his disciples asked him what this parable meant, he said, 'To you it has been given to know the secrets of the kingdom of God; but for others they are in parables, so that seeing they may not see, and hearing they may not understand. Now the parable is this: The seed is the word of God. The ones along the path are those who have heard; then the devil comes and takes away the word from their hearts, that they may not believe and be saved. And the ones on the rock are those who, when they hear the word, receive it with joy; but these have no root, they believe for a while and in time of temptation fall away. And as for what fell among the thorns, they are those who hear, but as they go on their way they are choked by the cares and riches and pleasures of life, and their fruit does not mature. And as for that in the good soil, they are those who, hearing the word, hold it fast in an honest and good heart, and bring forth fruit with patience.'

POSTCOMMUNION SENTENCE

The people were astounded at the teachings of Jesus: for he taught them with authority. *Matthew 7.28, 29*

EIGHTH SUNDAY BEFORE EASTER

(Second Sunday before Lent)   Green

INTRODUCTORY SENTENCE

The Spirit of the Lord is upon me: he has anointed me to
bring the good news to the poor, and to heal the
broken-hearted. *Isaiah 61.1*

COLLECT

Almighty and everliving God,
whose Son Jesus Christ healed the sick
and restored them to wholeness of life:
look with compassion on the anguish of the world,
and by your healing power
make whole both men and nations;
through our Lord and Saviour Jesus Christ,
who is alive and reigns with you and the Holy Spirit,
one God, now and for ever.

PSALMS 147.1-11; 131

READINGS YEAR 1

Old Testament *Zephaniah 3.14-end RSV*

Sing aloud, O daughter of Sion;
shout, O Israel!
Rejoice and exult with all your heart,
O daughter of Jerusalem!
The Lord has taken away the judgements against you,
he has cast out your enemies.
The King of Israel, the Lord, is in your midst;
you shall fear evil no more.
On that day it shall be said to Jerusalem:
'Do not fear, O Zion;
let not your hands grow weak.
The Lord, your God, is in your midst,
a warrior who gives victory;
he will rejoice over you with gladness,
he will renew you in his love;
he will exult over you with loud singing

as on a day of festival.
I will remove disaster from you,
so that you will not bear reproach for it.
Behold, at that time I will deal
with all your oppressors.
And I will save the lame
and gather the outcast,
and I will change their shame into praise
and renown in all the earth.
At that time I will bring you home,
at the time when I gather you together;
yea, I will make you renowned and praised
among all the peoples of the earth,
when I restore your fortunes
before your eyes,' says the Lord.

New Testament *James 5.13-16a RSV*

Is anyone among you suffering? Let him pray. Is any
cheerful? Let him sing praise. Is any among you sick? Let
him call for the elders of the church, and let them pray over
him, anointing him with oil in the name of the Lord; and the
prayer of faith will save the sick man, and the Lord will raise
him up; and if he has committed sins, he will be forgiven.
Therefore confess your sins to one another, and pray for one
another, that you may be healed.

Gospel *Mark 2.1-12 NEB*

When Jesus returned to Capernaum, the news went round
that he was at home; and such a crowd collected that the
space in front of the door was not big enough to hold them.
And while he was proclaiming the message to them, a man
was brought who was paralysed. Four men were carrying
him, but because of the crowd they could not get him near.
So they opened up the roof over the place where Jesus was,
and when they had broken through they lowered the
stretcher on which the paralysed man was lying. When Jesus
saw their faith, he said to the paralysed man, 'My son, your
sins are forgiven.'

Now there were some lawyers sitting there and they thought

to themselves, 'Why does the fellow talk like that? This is blasphemy! Who but God alone can forgive sins?' Jesus knew in his own mind that this was what they were thinking, and said to them: 'Why do you harbour thoughts like these? Is it easier to say to this paralysed man, "Your sins are forgiven", or to say, "Stand up, take your bed, and walk"? But to convince you that the Son of Man has the right on earth to forgive sins'—he turned to the paralysed man—'I say to you, stand up, take your bed, and go home.' And he got up, and at once took his stretcher and went out in full view of them all, so that they were astounded and praised God. 'Never before', they said, 'have we seen the like.'

READINGS YEAR 2

Old Testament 2 Kings 5.1-14 NEB

Naaman, commander of the king of Aram's army, was a great man highly esteemed by his master, because by his means the Lord had given victory to Aram; but he was a leper. On one of their raids the Aramaeans brought back as a captive from the land of Israel a little girl, who became a servant to Naaman's wife. She said to her mistress, 'If only my master could meet the prophet who lives in Samaria, he would get rid of the disease for him.' Naaman went in and reported to his master word for word what the girl from the land of Israel had said. 'Very well, you may go,' said the king of Aram, 'and I will send a letter to the king of Israel.' So Naaman went, taking with him ten talents of silver, six thousand shekels of gold, and ten changes of clothing. He delivered the letter to the king of Israel, which read thus: 'This letter is to inform you that I am sending to you my servant Naaman, and I beg you to rid him of his disease.' When the king of Israel read the letter, he rent his clothes and said, 'Am I a god to kill and to make alive, that this fellow sends to me to cure a man of his disease? Surely you must see that he is picking a quarrel with me.' When Elisha, the man of God, heard how the king of Israel had rent his clothes, he sent to him saying, 'Why did you rend your clothes? Let the man come to me, and he will know that there is a prophet in Israel.' So Naaman came with his horses and chariots and stood at the entrance to Elisha's house. Elisha sent out a messenger to say to him, 'If you will go and wash seven times in the Jordan, your flesh will be restored and you will be clean.' Naaman was furious and went away, saying, 'I thought he would at least have come out and stood, and invoked the Lord his God by name, waved his hand over the place and so rid me of the disease. Are not Abana and Pharpar, rivers of Damascus, better than all the waters of Israel? Can I not wash in them and be clean?' So he turned and went off in a rage. But his servants came up to him and said, 'If the prophet had bidden you do something difficult, would you not do it? How much more then, if he tells you to wash and be clean?' So he went down and dipped himself in the Jordan seven times as the man of God had told him, and his flesh was restored as a little child's, and he was clean.

New Testament *2 Corinthians 12.1-10 JB*

Must I go on boasting, though there is nothing to be gained by it? But I will move on to the visions and revelations I have had from the Lord. I know a man in Christ who, fourteen years ago, was caught up—whether still in the body or out of the body, I do not know; God knows—right into the third heaven. I do know, however, that this same person— whether in the body or out of the body, I do not know; God knows—was caught up into paradise and heard things which must not and cannot be put into human language. I will boast about a man like that, but not about anything of my own except my weaknesses. If I should decide to boast, I should not be made to look foolish, because I should only be speaking the truth; but I am not going to, in case anyone should begin to think I am better than he can actually see and hear me to be.

In view of the extraordinary nature of these revelations, to stop me from getting too proud I was given a thorn in the flesh, an angel of Satan to beat me and stop me from getting too proud! About this thing, I have pleaded with the Lord three times for it to leave me, but he has said, 'My grace is enough for you: my power is at its best in weakness.' So I shall be very happy to make my weaknesses my special boast so that the power of Christ may stay over me, and that is why I am quite content with my weaknesses, and with insults, hardships, persecutions, and the agonies I go through for Christ's sake. For it is when I am weak that I am strong.

Gospel *Mark 7.24-end NEB*

Jesus left that place and went away into the territory of Tyre. He found a house to stay in, and he would have liked to remain unrecognized, but this was impossible. Almost at once a woman whose young daughter was possessed by an unclean spirit heard of him, came in, and fell at his feet. (She was a Gentile, a Phoenician of Syria by nationality.) She begged him to drive the spirit out of her daughter. He said to her, 'Let the children be satisfied first; it is not fair to take the children's bread and throw it to the dogs.' 'Sir,' she answered, 'even the dogs under the table eat the children's scraps.' He said to her, 'For saying that, you may go home content; the unclean spirit has gone out of your daughter.' And when she returned home, she found the child lying in bed; the spirit had left her.

On his return journey from Tyrian territory he went by way of Sidon to the Sea of Galilee through the territory of the Ten Towns. They brought to him a man who was deaf and had an impediment in his speech, with the request that he would lay his hand on him. He took the man aside, away from the crowd, put his fingers into his ears, spat, and touched his tongue. Then, looking up to heaven, he sighed, and said to him, 'Ephphatha', which means 'Be opened.' With that his ears were opened, and at the same time the impediment was removed and he spoke plainly. Jesus forbade them to tell anyone; but the more he forbade them, the more they published it. Their astonishment knew no bounds: 'All that he does, he does well,' they said; 'he even makes the deaf hear and the dumb speak.'

POSTCOMMUNION SENTENCE

The Lord has done all things well: he makes the deaf hear and the dumb speak. *Mark 7.37*

SEVENTH SUNDAY BEFORE EASTER

(The Sunday next before Lent)   Green

INTRODUCTORY SENTENCE

The Lord is gracious and merciful: and his compassion is over all that he has made. *Psalm 145.8, 9*

COLLECT

Merciful Lord,
grant to your faithful people pardon and peace:
that we may be cleansed from all our sins
and serve you with a quiet mind;
through Jesus Christ our Lord.

PSALMS 32; 119.65-72

READINGS YEAR 1

Old Testament *Hosea 14.1-7 JB*

Israel, come back to the Lord your God;
your iniquity was the cause of your downfall.
Provide yourself with words
and come back to the Lord.
Say to him, 'Take all iniquity away
so that we may have happiness again
and offer you our words of praise.
Assyria cannot save us,
we will not ride horses any more,
or say, "Our God!" to what our own hands have made,
for you are the one in whom orphans find compassion.'
—I will heal their disloyalty,
I will love them with all my heart,
for my anger has turned from them.
I will fall like dew on Israel.
He shall bloom like the lily,
and thrust out roots like the poplar,
his shoots will spread far;
he will have the beauty of the olive
and the fragrance of Lebanon.

New Testament *Philemon 1-16 TEV*

From Paul, a prisoner for the sake of Christ Jesus, and from our brother Timothy—

To our friend and fellow worker Philemon, and the church that meets in your house, and our sister Apphia, and our fellow-soldier Archippus:

May God our Father and the Lord Jesus Christ give you grace and peace.

Brother Philemon, every time I pray, I mention you and give thanks to my God. For I hear of your love for all God's people and the faith you have in the Lord Jesus. My prayer is that our fellowship with you as believers will bring about a deeper understanding of every blessing which we have in our life in union with Christ. Your love, dear brother, has brought me great joy and much encouragement! You have cheered the hearts of all God's people.

For this reason I could be bold enough, as your brother in Christ, to order you to do what should be done. But because I love you, I make a request instead. I do this even though I am Paul, the ambassador of Christ Jesus and at present also a prisoner for his sake. So I make a request to you on behalf of Onesimus, who is my own son in Christ; for while in prison I have become his spiritual father. At one time he was of no use to you, but now he is useful both to you and to me.

I am sending him back to you now, and with him goes my heart. I would like to keep him here with me, while I am in prison for the gospel's sake, so that he could help me in your place. However, I do not want to force you to help me; rather, I would like you to do it of your own free will. So I will not do anything unless you agree.

It may be that Onesimus was away from you for a short time so that you might have him back for all time. And now he is not just a slave, but much more than a slave: he is a dear brother in Christ. How much he means to me! And how much more he will mean to you, both as a slave and as a brother in the Lord!

Gospel *Mark 2.13-17 NEB*

Jesus went away to the lake-side. All the crowd came to him, and he taught them there. As he went along, he saw Levi son of Alphaeus at his seat in the custom-house, and said to him, 'Follow me'; and Levi rose and followed him.

When Jesus was at table in his house, many bad characters—tax gatherers and others—were seated with him and his disciples; for there were many who followed him. Some doctors of the law who were Pharisees noticed him eating in this bad company, and said to his disciples, 'He eats with tax gatherers and sinners!' Jesus heard it and said to them, 'It is not the healthy that need a doctor, but the sick; I did not come to invite virtuous people, but sinners.'

READINGS YEAR 2

Old Testament *Numbers 15.32-36 NEB*

During the time that the Israelites were in the wilderness, a man was found gathering sticks on the sabbath day. Those who had caught him in the act brought him to Moses and Aaron and all the community, and they kept him in custody, because it was not clearly known what was to be done with him. The Lord said to Moses, 'The man must be put to death; he must be stoned by all the community outside the camp.' So they took him outside the camp and all stoned him to death, as the Lord had commanded Moses.

New Testament *Colossians 1.18-23 NEB*

Christ is the head of the body, the church. He is its origin, the first to return from the dead, to be in all things alone supreme. For in him the complete being of God, by God's own choice, came to dwell. Through him God chose to reconcile the whole universe to himself, making peace through the shedding of his blood upon the cross—to reconcile all things, whether on earth or in heaven, through him alone.

Formerly you were yourselves estranged from God; you were his enemies in heart and mind, and your deeds were evil. But now by Christ's death in his body of flesh and blood

God has reconciled you to himself, so that he may present you before himself as dedicated men, without blemish and innocent in his sight. Only you must continue in your faith, firm on your foundations, never to be dislodged from the hope offered in the gospel which you heard. This is the gospel which has been proclaimed in the whole creation under heaven; and I, Paul, have become its minister.

Gospel *John 8.2-11 NEB*

At daybreak Jesus appeared in the temple, and all the people gathered round him. He had taken his seat and was engaged in teaching them when the doctors of the law and the Pharisees brought in a woman caught committing adultery. Making her stand out in the middle they said to him, 'Master, this woman was caught in the very act of adultery. In the Law Moses has laid down that such women are to be stoned. What do you say about it?' They put the question as a test, hoping to frame a charge against him. Jesus bent down and wrote with his finger on the ground. When they continued to press their question he sat up straight and said, 'That one of you who is faultless shall throw the first stone.' Then once again he bent down and wrote on the ground. When they heard what he said, one by one they went away, the eldest first; and Jesus was left alone, with the woman still standing there. Jesus again sat up and said to the woman, 'Where are they? Has no one condemned you?' She answered, 'No one, sir.' Jesus said, 'Nor do I condemn you. You may go; do not sin again.'

POSTCOMMUNION SENTENCE

I take no pleasure in anyone's death, says the Lord: Repent and live. *Ezekiel 18.32*

ASH WEDNESDAY   Violet (or Lent array)

INTRODUCTORY SENTENCE

The sacrifice of God is a broken spirit: a broken and contrite heart he will not despise. *Psalm 51.17*

COLLECT

Almighty and everlasting God,
you hate nothing that you have made
and forgive the sins of all those who are penitent.
Create and make in us new and contrite hearts,
that, lamenting our sins
    and acknowledging our wretchedness,
we may receive from you, the God of all mercy,
perfect forgiveness and peace;
through Jesus Christ our Lord.

PSALMS 6; 51.1-17; 90.1-12

READINGS YEARS 1 and 2

Old Testament *Isaiah 58.1-8 TEV*

The Lord says, 'Shout as loud as you can! Tell my people
Israel about their sins! They worship me every day, claiming
that they are eager to know my ways and obey my laws.
They say they want me to give them just laws and that they
take pleasure in worshipping me.'

The people ask, 'Why should we fast if the Lord never
notices? Why should we go without food if he pays
no attention?'

The Lord says to them, 'The truth is that at the same time as
you fast, you pursue your own interests and oppress your
workers. Your fasting makes you violent, and you quarrel
and fight. Do you think this kind of fasting will make me
listen to your prayers? When you fast, you make yourselves
suffer; you bow your heads low like a blade of grass, and
spread out sackcloth and ashes to lie on. Is that what you call
fasting? Do you think I will be pleased with that?

'The kind of fasting I want is this: Remove the chains of
oppression and the yoke of injustice, and let the oppressed
go free. Share your food with the hungry and open your
homes to the homeless poor. Give clothes to those who have
nothing to wear, and do not refuse to help your
own relatives.

'Then my favour will shine on you like the morning sun, and
your wounds will be quickly healed. I will always be with
you to save you; my presence will protect you on every side.'

or *Joel 2.12-17 RSV*

'Yet even now,' says the Lord,
'return to me with all your heart,
with fasting, with weeping, and with mourning;
and rend your hearts and not your garments.'
Return to the Lord, your God,
for he is gracious and merciful,
slow to anger, and abounding in steadfast love,
and repents of evil.
Who knows whether he will not turn and repent,
and leave a blessing behind him,
a cereal offering and a drink offering
for the Lord, your God?

Blow the trumpet in Zion;
sanctify a fast;
call a solemn assembly;
gather the people.
Sanctify the congregation;
assemble the elders;
gather the children,
even nursing infants.
Let the bridegroom leave his room
and the bride her chamber.

Between the vestibule and the altar
let the priests, the ministers of the Lord, weep
and say, 'Spare your people, O Lord,
and make not your heritage a reproach,
a byword among the nations.
Why should they say among the peoples,
"Where is their God?"'

or *Amos 5.6-15 NEB*

If you would live, resort to the Lord,
or he will break out against Joseph like fire,
fire which will devour Israel with no one to quench it;

he who made the Pleiades and Orion,
who turned darkness into morning
and darkened day into night,
who summoned the waters of the sea
and poured them over the earth,
who makes Taurus rise after Capella
and Taurus set hard on the rising of the Vintager—
he who does this, his name is the Lord.
You that turn justice upside down
and bring righteousness to the ground,
you that hate a man who brings the wrongdoer to court
and loathe him who speaks the whole truth:
for all this, because you levy taxes on the poor
and exhort a tribute of grain from them,
though you have built houses of hewn stone,
you shall not live in them,
though you have planted pleasant vineyards,
you shall not drink wine from them.
For I know how many your crimes are
and how countless your sins,
you who persecute the guiltless, hold men to ransom
and thrust the destitute out of court.
At that time, therefore, a prudent man will stay quiet,
for it will be an evil time.

Seek good and not evil,
that you may live,
that the Lord the God of Hosts may be firmly on your side,
as you say he is.
Hate evil and love good;
enthrone justice in the courts;
it may be that the Lord the God of Hosts
will be gracious to the survivors of Joseph.

New Testament *1 Corinthians 9.24-end NEB*

You know (do you not?) that at the sports all the runners run
the race, though only one wins the prize. Like them, run to
win! But every athlete goes into strict training. They do it to
win a fading wreath; we, a wreath that never fades. For my
part, I run with a clear goal before me; I am like a boxer who
does not beat the air; I bruise my own body and make it

know its master, for fear that after preaching to others I should find myself rejected.

or *James 4.1-10 JB*

Where do these wars and battles between yourselves first start? Isn't it precisely in the desires fighting inside your own selves? You want something and you haven't got it; so you are prepared to kill. You have an ambition that you cannot satisfy; so you fight to get your way by force. Why you don't have what you want is because you don't pray for it; when you do pray and don't get it, it is because you have not prayed properly, you have prayed for something to indulge your own desires.

You are as unfaithful as adulterous wives; don't you realize that making the world your friend is making God your enemy? Anyone who chooses the world for his friend turns himself into God's enemy. Surely you don't think scripture is wrong when it says: the spirit which he sent to live in us wants us for himself alone? But he has been even more generous to us, as scripture says: 'God opposes the proud but he gives generously to the humble.' Give in to God, then; resist the devil, and he will run away from you. The nearer you go to God, the nearer he will come to you. Clean your hands, you sinners, and clear your minds, you waverers. Look at your wretched condition, and weep for it in misery; be miserable instead of laughing, gloomy instead of happy. Humble yourselves before the Lord and he will lift you up.

Gospel *Matthew 6.16-21 NEB*

Jesus said, 'When you fast, do not look gloomy like the hypocrites: they make their faces unsightly so that other people may see that they are fasting. I tell you this: they have their reward already. But when you fast, anoint your head and wash your face, so that men may not see that you are fasting, but only your Father who is in the secret place; and your Father who sees what is secret will give you your reward.

'Do not store up for yourselves treasure on earth, where it grows rusty and moth-eaten, and thieves break in to steal it. Store up treasure in heaven, where there is no moth and no rust to spoil it, no thieves to break in and steal. For where your treasure is, there will your heart be also.'

or *Luke 18.9-14 NEB*

Jesus told a parable, which was aimed at those who were sure of their own goodness and looked down on everyone else. 'Two men went up to the temple to pray, one a Pharisee and the other a tax gatherer. The Pharisee stood up and prayed thus: "I thank thee, O God, that I am not like the rest of men, greedy, dishonest, adulterous; or, for that matter, like this tax gatherer. I fast twice a week; I pay tithes on all that I get." But the other kept his distance and would not even raise his eyes to heaven, but beat upon his breast, saying, "O God, have mercy on me, sinner that I am." It was this man, I tell you, and not the other, who went home acquitted of his sins. For everyone who exalts himself will be humbled; and whoever humbles himself will be exalted.'

PROPER PREFACE

Rite A. The Preface of Lent (8) is said on weekdays until Lent 3.
Rite B. Second Thanksgiving. The Preface of Lent is said.

POSTCOMMUNION SENTENCE

Blessed is the man who meditates day and night on the law of the Lord: he will yield fruit in due season. *Psalm 1.3*

LENT 1
(Sixth Sunday before Easter)   Violet (or Lent array)

INTRODUCTORY SENTENCE

Jesus was in the wilderness forty days, tempted by Satan: and he was with the wild beasts; and the angels ministered to him. *Mark 1.13*

or

Jesus is able to sympathize with our weaknesses, for he was
in every respect tempted as we are, yet without
sinning. *Hebrews 4.15-16*

COLLECT

Almighty God,
whose Son Jesus Christ fasted forty days in the wilderness,
and was tempted as we are, yet without sin:
give us grace to discipline ourselves
   in obedience to your Spirit;
and, as you know our weakness,
so may we know your power to save;
through Jesus Christ our Lord.

PSALMS 119.1-8; 91.1-12

READINGS YEAR 1

Old Testament *Genesis 2.7-9; 3.1-7 NEB*

The Lord God formed a man from the dust of the ground and
breathed into his nostrils the breath of life. Thus the man
became a living creature. Then the Lord God planted a
garden in Eden away to the east, and there he put the man
whom he had formed. The Lord God made trees spring from
the ground, all trees pleasant to look at and good for food;
and in the middle of the garden he set the tree of life and the
tree of the knowledge of good and evil.

The serpent was more crafty than any wild creature that the
Lord God had made. He said to the woman, 'Is it true that
God has forbidden you to eat from any tree in the garden?'
The woman answered the serpent, 'We may eat the fruit of
any tree in the garden, except for the tree in the middle of the
garden; God has forbidden us either to eat or to touch the
fruit of that; if we do, we shall die.' The serpent said, 'Of
course you will not die. God knows that as soon as you eat it,
your eyes will be opened and you will be like gods knowing
both good and evil.' When the woman saw that the fruit of
the tree was good to eat, and that it was pleasing to the eye

and tempting to contemplate, she took some and ate it. She also gave her husband some and he ate it. Then the eyes of both of them were opened and they discovered that they were naked; so they stitched fig-leaves together and made themselves loincloths.

New Testament *Hebrews 2.14-end NEB*

The children of a family share the same flesh and blood; and so Jesus too shared ours, so that through death he might break the power of him who had death at his command, that is, the devil; and might liberate those who, through fear of death, had all their lifetime been in servitude. It is not angels, mark you, that he takes to himself, but the sons of Abraham. And therefore he had to be made like these brothers of his in every way, so that he might be merciful and faithful as their high priest before God, to expiate the sins of the people. For since he himself has passed through the test of suffering, he is able to help those who are meeting their test now.

Gospel *Matthew 4.1-11 RSV*

Jesus was led up by the Spirit into the wilderness to be tempted by the devil. And he fasted forty days and forty nights, and afterward he was hungry. And the tempter came and said to him, 'If you are the Son of God, command these stones to become loaves of bread.' But he answered, 'It is written,
"Man shall not live by bread alone,
but by every word that proceeds from the mouth of God."'
Then the devil took him to the holy city, and set him on the pinnacle of the temple, and said to him, 'If you are the Son of God, throw yourself down; for it is written,
"He will give his angels charge of you,"
and
"On their hands they will bear you up,
lest you strike your foot against a stone."'
Jesus said to him, 'Again it is written, "You shall not tempt the Lord your God."' Again, the devil took him to a very high mountain, and showed him all the kingdoms of the world and the glory of them; and he said to him, 'All these I

will give you, if you will fall down and worship me.' Then
Jesus said to him, 'Begone, Satan! for it is written,
"You shall worship the Lord your God
and him only shall you serve."'
Then the devil left him, and behold, angels came and
ministered to him.

READINGS YEAR 2

Old Testament *Genesis 4.1-10 NEB*

Adam lay with his wife Eve, and she conceived and gave
birth to Cain. She said, 'With the help of the Lord I have
brought a man into being.' Afterwards she had another
child, his brother Abel. Abel was a shepherd and Cain a tiller
of the soil. The day came when Cain brought some of the
produce of the soil as a gift to the Lord; and Abel brought
some of the first-born of his flock, the fat portions of them.
The Lord received Abel and his gift with favour; but Cain
and his gift he did not receive. Cain was very angry and his
face fell. Then the Lord said to Cain, 'Why are you so angry
and cast down?

If you do well, you are accepted;
if not, sin is a demon crouching at the door.
It shall be eager for you, and you will be mastered by it.'

Cain said to his brother Abel, 'Let us go into the open
country.' While they were there, Cain attacked his brother
Abel and murdered him. Then the Lord said to Cain, 'Where
is your brother Abel?' Cain answered, 'I do not know. Am I
my brother's keeper?' The Lord said, 'What have you done?
Hark! your brother's blood that has been shed is crying out
to me from the ground.'

New Testament *Hebrews 4.12-end RSV*

The word of God is living and active, sharper than any
two-edged sword, piercing to the division of soul and spirit,
of joints and marrow, and discerning the thoughts and
intentions of the heart. And before him no creature is
hidden, but all are open and laid bare to the eyes of him with
whom we have to do.

Since then we have a great high priest who has passed through the heavens, Jesus, the Son of God, let us hold fast our confession. For we have not a high priest who is unable to sympathize with our weaknesses, but one who in every respect has been tempted as we are, yet without sinning. Let us then with confidence draw near to the throne of grace, that we may receive mercy and find grace to help in time of need.

Gospel *Luke 4.1-13 RSV*

Jesus, full of the Holy Spirit, returned from the Jordan, and was led by the Spirit for forty days in the wilderness, tempted by the devil. And he ate nothing in those days; and when they were ended, he was hungry. The devil said to him, 'If you are the Son of God, command this stone to become bread.' And Jesus answered him, 'It is written, "Man shall not live by bread alone."' And the devil took him up, and showed him all the kingdoms of the world in a moment of time, and said to him, 'To you I will give all this authority and their glory; for it has been delivered to me, and I give it to whom I will. If you, then, will worship me, it shall all be yours.' And Jesus answered him, 'It is written,
"You shall worship the Lord your God,
and him only shall you serve."'
And he took him to Jerusalem, and set him on the pinnacle of the temple, and said to him, 'If you are the Son of God, throw yourself down from here; for it is written,
"He will give his angels charge of you, to guard you," and
"On their hands they will bear you up,
lest you strike your foot against a stone."'
And Jesus answered him, 'It is said, "You shall not tempt the Lord your God."' And when the devil had ended every temptation, he departed from him until an opportune time.

PROPER PREFACE

Rite A. The Preface of Lent (8) is said.
Rite B. Second Thanksgiving. The Preface of Lent is said.

POSTCOMMUNION SENTENCE

Man does not live on bread alone, but on every word that comes from the mouth of God. *Matthew 4.4*

LENT 2
(Fifth Sunday before Easter)   Violet (or Lent array)

INTRODUCTORY SENTENCE

Compassion and forgiveness belong to the Lord our God, though we have rebelled against him. *Daniel 9.9*

COLLECT

Lord God Almighty,
grant your people grace
to withstand the temptations
    of the world, the flesh, and the devil,
and with pure hearts and minds
to follow you, the only God;
through Jesus Christ our Lord.

PSALMS 119.33-40; 18.18-26

READINGS YEAR 1

Old Testament *Genesis 6.11-end NEB*

God saw that the whole world was corrupt and full of violence. In his sight the world had become corrupted, for all men had lived corrupt lives on earth. God said to Noah, 'The loathsomeness of all mankind has become plain to me, for through them the earth is full of violence. I intend to destroy them, and the earth with them. Make yourself an ark with ribs of cypress; cover it with reeds and coat it inside and out with pitch. This is to be its plan: the length of the ark shall be three hundred cubits, its breadth fifty cubits, and its height thirty cubits. You shall make a roof for the ark, giving it a fall of one cubit when complete; and put a door in the side of the ark, and build three decks, upper, middle, and lower. I intend to bring the waters of the flood over the earth to destroy every human being under heaven that has the spirit of life; everything on earth shall perish. But with you I will make a covenant, and you shall go into the ark, you and your sons, your wife and your sons' wives with you. And you shall bring living creatures of every kind into the ark to keep them alive with you, two of each kind, a male and a female; two of every kind of bird, beast, and reptile, shall come to you to be kept alive. See that you take and store every kind of food that can be eaten; this shall be food for you and for them.' Exactly as God had commanded him, so Noah did.

New Testament *1 John 4.1-6 JB*

It is not every spirit, my dear people, that you can trust;
test them, to see if they come from God,
there are many false prophets, now, in the world.
You can tell the spirits that come from God by this:
every spirit which acknowledges that Jesus the Christ
    has come in the flesh
is from God;
but any spirit which will not say this of Jesus
is not from God,
but is the spirit of Antichrist,
whose coming you were warned about.
Well, now he is here, in the world.
Children,
you have already overcome these false prophets,
because you are from God and you have in you
one who is greater than anyone in this world;
as for them, they are of the world,
and so they speak the language of the world
and the world listens to them.
But we are children of God,
and those who know God listen to us;
those who are not of God refuse to listen to us.
This is how we can tell
the spirit of truth from the spirit of falsehood.

Gospel *Luke 19.41-end NEB*

When Jesus came in sight of the city, he wept over it and said, 'If only you had known, on this great day, the way that leads to peace! But no; it is hidden from your sight. For a time will come upon you, when your enemies will set up siege-works against you; they will encircle you and hem you in at every point; they will bring you to the ground, you and your children within your walls, and not leave you one stone standing on another, because you did not recognize God's moment when it came.'

Then he went into the temple and began driving out the traders, with these words: 'Scripture says, "My house shall be a house of prayer"; but you have made it a robber's cave.'

Day by day he taught in the temple. And the chief priests and lawyers were bent on making an end of him, with the support of the leading citizens, but found they were helpless, because the people all hung upon his words.

READINGS YEAR 2

Old Testament *Genesis 7.17-end RSV*

The flood continued forty days upon the earth; and the waters increased, and bore up the ark, and it rose high above the earth. The waters prevailed and increased greatly upon the earth; and the ark floated on the face of the waters. And the waters prevailed so mightily upon the earth that all the high mountains under the whole heaven were covered; the waters prevailed above the mountains, covering them fifteen cubits deep. And all flesh died that moved upon the earth, birds, cattle, beasts, all swarming creatures that swarm upon the earth, and every man; everything on the dry land in whose nostrils was the breath of life died. He blotted out every living thing that was upon the face of the ground, man and animals and creeping things and birds of the air; they were blotted out from the earth. Only Noah was left, and those that were with him in the ark. And the waters prevailed upon the earth a hundred and fifty days.

New Testament *1 John 3.1-10 NEB*

How great is the love that the Father has shown to us! We were called God's children, and such we are; and the reason why the godless world does not recognize us is that it has not known him. Here and now, dear friends, we are God's children; what we shall be has not yet been disclosed, but we know that when it is disclosed we shall be like him, because we shall see him as he is. Everyone who has this hope before him purifies himself, as Christ is pure.

To commit sin is to break God's law: sin, in fact, is lawlessness. Christ appeared, as you know, to do away with sins, and there is no sin in him. No man therefore who dwells in him is a sinner; the sinner has not seen him and does not know him.

My children, do not be misled: it is the man who does right who is righteous, as God is righteous; the man who sins is a child of the devil, for the devil has been a sinner from the first; and the Son of God appeared for the very purpose of undoing the devil's work.

A child of God does not commit sin, because the divine seed remains in him; he cannot be a sinner, because he is God's child. That is the distinction between the children of God and the children of the devil: no one who does not do right is God's child, nor is anyone who does not love his brother.

Gospel *Matthew 12.22-32 NEB*

They brought to Jesus a man who was possessed; he was blind and dumb; and Jesus cured him, restoring both speech and sight. The bystanders were all amazed, and the word went round: 'Can this be the Son of David?' But when the Pharisees heard it they said, 'It is only by Beelzebub prince of devils that this man drives the devils out.'

He knew what was in their minds; so he said to them, 'Every kingdom divided against itself goes to ruin; and no town, no household, that is divided against itself can stand. And if it is Satan who casts out Satan, Satan is divided against himself; how then can his kingdom stand? And if it is by Beelzebub that I cast out devils, by whom do your own people drive them out? If this is your argument, they themselves will refute you. But if it is by the Spirit of God that I drive out the devils, then be sure the kingdom of God has already come upon you.

'Or again, how can anyone break into a strong man's house and make off with his goods, unless he has first tied the strong man up before ransacking the house?

'He who is not with me is against me, and he who does not gather with me scatters.

'And so I tell you this: no sin, no slander, is beyond forgiveness for men, except slander spoken against the Spirit, and that will not be forgiven. Any man who speaks a word against the Son of Man will be forgiven; but if anyone speaks against the Holy Spirit, for him there is no forgiveness, either in this age or in the age to come.'

PROPER PREFACE

Rite A. The Preface of Lent (8) is said.
Rite B. Second Thanksgiving. The Preface of Lent is said.

POSTCOMMUNION SENTENCE

My heart has prompted me to seek your face: I seek it Lord; do not hide from me. *Psalm 27.8*

LENT 3
(Fourth Sunday before Easter)   Violet (or Lent array)

INTRODUCTORY SENTENCE

The sacrifice of God is a broken spirit: a broken and contrite heart he will not despise. *Psalm 51.17*

COLLECT

Almighty God,
whose most dear Son went not up to joy
   but first he suffered pain,
and entered not into glory before he was crucified:

mercifully grant that we, walking in the way of the cross,
may find it none other than the way of life and peace;
through Jesus Christ our Lord.

PSALMS 119.97-104; 115.1-7

READINGS YEAR 1

Old Testament *Genesis 22.1-13 NEB*

The time came when God put Abraham to the test.
'Abraham', he called, and Abraham replied, 'Here I am.'
God said, 'Take your son Isaac, your only son, whom you
love, and go to the land of Moriah. There you shall offer him
as a sacrifice on one of the hills which I will show you.' So
Abraham rose early in the morning and saddled his ass, and
he took with him two of his men and his son Isaac; and he
split the firewood for the sacrifice, and set out for the place of
which God had spoken. On the third day Abraham looked
up and saw the place in the distance. He said to his men,
'Stay here with the ass while I and the boy go over there; and
when we have worshipped we will come back to you.' So
Abraham took the wood for the sacrifice and laid it on his son
Isaac's shoulder; he himself carried the fire and the knife,
and the two of them went on together. Isaac said to
Abraham, 'Father', and he answered, 'What is it, my son?'
Isaac said, 'Here are the fire and the wood, but where is the
young beast for the sacrifice?' Abraham answered, 'God will
provide himself with a young beast for a sacrifice, my son.'
And the two of them went on together and came to the place
of which God had spoken. There Abraham built an altar and
arranged the wood. He bound his son Isaac and laid him on
the altar on top of the wood. Then he stretched out his hand
and took the knife to kill his son; but the angel of the Lord
called to him from heaven, 'Abraham, Abraham.' He
answered, 'Here I am.' The angel of the Lord said, 'Do not
raise your hand against the boy; do not touch him. Now I
know that you are a God-fearing man. You have not
withheld from me your son, your only son.' Abraham
looked up, and there he saw a ram caught by its horns in a
thicket. So he went and took the ram and offered it as a
sacrifice instead of his son.

New Testament *Colossians 1.24-end NEB*

It is now my happiness to suffer for you. This is my way of helping to complete, in my poor human flesh, the full tale of Christ's afflictions still to be endured, for the sake of his body which is the church. I became its servant by virtue of the task assigned to me by God for your benefit: to deliver his message in full; to announce the secret hidden for long ages and through many generations, but now disclosed to God's people, to whom it was his will to make it known—to make known how rich and glorious it is among all nations. The secret is this: Christ in you, the hope of a glory to come.

He it is whom we proclaim. We admonish everyone without distinction, we instruct everyone in all the ways of wisdom, so as to present each one of you as a mature member of Christ's body. To this end I am toiling strenuously with all the energy and power of Christ at work in me.

Gospel *Luke 9.18-27 JB*

One day when Jesus was praying alone in the presence of his disciples he put this question to them, 'Who do the crowds say I am?' And they answered, 'John the Baptist; others Elijah; and others say one of the ancient prophets come back to life'. 'But you,' he said, 'who do you say I am?' It was Peter who spoke up. 'The Christ of God', he said. But he gave them strict orders not to tell anyone anything about this.

'The Son of Man', he said, 'is destined to suffer grievously, to be rejected by the elders and chief priests and scribes and to be put to death, and to be raised up on the third day.'

Then to all he said, 'If anyone wants to be a follower of mine, let him renounce himself and take up his cross every day and follow me. For anyone who wants to save his life will lose it; but anyone who loses his life for my sake, that man will save it. What gain, then, is it for a man to have won the whole world and to have lost or ruined his very self? For if anyone is ashamed of me and of my words, of him the Son of Man will be ashamed when he comes in his own glory and in the glory of the Father and the holy angels.

'I tell you truly, there are some standing here who will not taste death before they see the kingdom of God.'

READINGS YEAR 2

Old Testament *Genesis 12.1-9 TEV*

The Lord said to Abram, 'Leave your native land, your relatives, and your father's home, and go to a country that I am going to show you. I will give you many descendants, and they will become a great nation. I will bless you and make your name famous, so that you will be a blessing.
I will bless those who bless you,
But I will curse those who curse you.
And through you I will bless all the nations.'

When Abram was seventy-five years old, he started out from Haran, as the Lord had told him to do; and Lot went with him. Abram took his wife Sarai, his nephew Lot, and all the wealth and all the slaves they had acquired in Haran, and they started out for the land of Canaan.

When they arrived in Canaan, Abram travelled through the land until he came to the sacred tree of Moreh, the holy place at Shechem. (At that time the Canaanites were still living in the land.) The Lord appeared to Abram and said to him, 'This is the country that I am going to give to your descendants.' Then Abram built an altar there to the Lord, who had appeared to him. After that, he moved on south to the hill-country east of the city of Bethel and set up his camp between Bethel on the west and Ai on the east. There also he built an altar and worshipped the Lord. Then he moved on from place to place, going towards the southern part of Canaan.

New Testament *1 Peter 2.19-end TEV*

God will bless you for this, if you endure the pain of undeserved suffering because you are conscious of his will. For what credit is there if you endure the beatings you deserve for having done wrong? But if you endure suffering even when you have done right, God will bless you for it. It was to this that God called you, for Christ himself suffered for you and left you an example, so that you would follow in his steps. He committed no sin, and no one ever heard a lie come from his lips. When he was insulted, he did not answer back with an insult; when he suffered, he did not threaten, but placed his hopes in God, the righteous Judge. Christ himself carried our sins in his body to the cross, so that we might die to sin and live for righteousness. It is by his wounds that you have been healed. You were like sheep that had lost their way, but now you have been brought back to follow the Shepherd and Keeper of your souls.

Gospel *Matthew 16.13-end JB*

When Jesus came to the region of Caesarea Philippi he put this question to his disciples, 'Who do people say the Son of Man is?' And they said, 'Some say he is John the Baptist, some Elijah, and others Jeremiah or one of the prophets.' 'But you,' he said, 'who do you say I am?' Then Simon Peter spoke up, 'You are the Christ,' he said, 'the Son of the living God.' Jesus replied, 'Simon son of Jonah, you are a happy man! Because it was not flesh and blood that revealed this to you but my Father in heaven. So I now say to you: You are Peter and on this rock I will build my Church. And the gates of the underworld can never hold out against it. I will give you the keys of the kingdom of heaven: whatever you bind on earth shall be considered bound in heaven; whatever you loose on earth shall be considered loosed in heaven.' Then he gave the disciples strict orders not to tell anyone that he was the Christ.

From that time Jesus began to make it clear to his disciples that he was destined to go to Jerusalem and suffer grievously at the hands of the elders and chief priests and scribes, to be put to death and to be raised up on the third day. Then, taking him aside, Peter started to remonstrate with him. 'Heaven preserve you, Lord;' he said, 'this must not happen to you.' But he turned and said to Peter, 'Get behind me, Satan! You are an obstacle in my path, because the way you think is not God's way but man's.'

Then Jesus said to his disciples, 'If anyone wants to be a follower of mine, let him renounce himself and take up his cross and follow me. For anyone who wants to save his life will lose it; but anyone who loses his life for my sake will find it. What, then, will a man gain if he wins the whole world and ruins his life? Or what has a man to offer in exchange for his life?

'For the Son of Man is going to come in the glory of his Father with his angels, and, when he does, he will reward each one according to his behaviour. I tell you solemnly, there are some of these standing here who will not taste death before they see the Son of Man coming with his kingdom.'

PROPER PREFACE

Rite A. The Preface of Lent (8) or of the Cross (9) is said on weekdays until Lent 5.
Rite B. Second Thanksgiving. The Preface of Lent is said.

POSTCOMMUNION SENTENCE

Jesus said, You are those who have continued with me in my trials; you shall eat and drink at my table in my kingdom.
Luke 22.28, 30

LENT 4
(Third Sunday before Easter)   Violet (or Lent array)

INTRODUCTORY SENTENCE

When Christ is revealed, we shall be like him: for we shall see him as he is. *1 John 3.2*

COLLECT

Almighty Father,
whose Son was revealed in majesty
    before he suffered death upon the cross:
give us faith to perceive his glory,
that we may be strengthened to suffer with him
and be changed into his likeness, from glory to glory;
who is alive and reigns with you and the Holy Spirit,
one God, now and for ever.

READINGS YEAR 1

Old Testament *Exodus 34.29-end NEB*

Moses came down from Mount Sinai with the two stone
tablets of the Tokens in his hands, and when he descended,
he did not know that the skin of his face shone because he
had been speaking with the Lord. When Aaron and the
Israelites saw how the skin of Moses' face shone, they were
afraid to approach him. He called out to them, and Aaron
and all the chiefs in the congregation turned towards him.
Moses spoke to them, and afterwards all the Israelites drew
near. He gave them all the commands with which the Lord
had charged him on Mount Sinai, and finished what he had
to say.

Then Moses put a veil over his face, and whenever he went
in before the Lord to speak with him, he removed the veil
until he came out. Then he would go out and tell the
Israelites all the commands he had received. Whenever the
skin of Moses' face shone in the sight of the Israelites, he
would put the veil back over his face until he went in again to
speak with the Lord.

New Testament *2 Corinthians 3.4-end TEV*

We say this because we have confidence in God through
Christ. There is nothing in us that allows us to claim that we
are capable of doing this work. The capacity we have comes
from God; it is he who made us capable of serving the new
covenant, which consists not of a written law but of the
Spirit. The written law brings death, but the Spirit gives life.

The Law was carved in letters on stone tablets, and God's
glory appeared when it was given. Even though the
brightness on Moses' face was fading, it was so strong that
the people of Israel could not keep their eyes fixed on him. If
the Law, which brings death when it is in force, came with
such glory, how much greater is the glory that belongs to the
activity of the Spirit! The system which brings

condemnation was glorious; how much more glorious is the activity which brings salvation! We may say that because of the far brighter glory now the glory that was so bright in the past is gone. For if there was glory in that which lasted for a while, how much more glory is there in that which lasts for ever!

Because we have this hope, we are very bold. We are not like Moses, who had to put a veil over his face so that the people of Israel would not see the brightness fade and disappear. Their minds, indeed, were closed; and to this very day their minds are covered with the same veil as they read the books of the old covenant. The veil is removed only when a person is joined to Christ. Even today, whenever they read the Law of Moses, the veil still covers their minds. But it can be removed, as the scripture says about Moses: 'His veil was removed when he turned to the Lord.' Now, 'the Lord' in this passage is the Spirit; and where the Spirit of the Lord is present, there is freedom. All of us, then, reflect the glory of the Lord with uncovered faces; and that same glory, coming from the Lord, who is the Spirit, transforms us into his likeness in an ever greater degree of glory.

Gospel *Luke 9.28-36 NEB*

Jesus took Peter, John, and James with him and went up into the hills to pray. And while he was praying the appearance of his face changed and his clothes became dazzling white. Suddenly there were two men talking with him; these were Moses and Elijah, who appeared in glory and spoke of his departure, the destiny he was to fulfil in Jerusalem. Meanwhile Peter and his companions had been in a deep sleep; but when they awoke, they saw his glory and the two men who stood beside him. And as these were moving away from Jesus, Peter said to him, 'Master, how good it is that we are here! Shall we make three shelters, one for you, one for Moses, and one for Elijah?'; but he spoke without knowing what he was saying. The words were still on his lips, when there came a cloud which cast a shadow over them; they were afraid as they entered the cloud, and from it came a voice: 'This is my Son, my Chosen; listen to him.' When the voice had spoken, Jesus was seen to be alone. The disciples kept silence and at that time told nobody anything of what they had seen.

READINGS YEAR 2

Old Testament *Exodus 3.1-6 JB*

Moses was looking after the flock of Jethro, his father-in-law, priest of Midian. He led his flock to the far side of the wilderness and came to Horeb, the mountain of God. There the angel of the Lord appeared to him in the shape of a flame of fire, coming from the middle of a bush. Moses looked; there was the bush blazing but it was not being burnt up. 'I must go and look at this strange sight,' Moses said, 'and see why the bush is not burnt.' Now the Lord saw him go forward to look, and God called to him from the middle of the bush. 'Moses, Moses!', he said. 'Here I am', he answered. 'Come no nearer', he said. 'Take off your shoes, for the place on which you stand is holy ground. I am the God of your father,' he said, 'the God of Abraham, the God of Isaac, and the God of Jacob.' At this Moses covered his face, afraid to look at God.

New Testament *2 Peter 1.16-19 NEB*

It was not on tales artfully spun that we relied when we told you of the power of our Lord Jesus Christ and his coming; we saw him with our own eyes in majesty, when at the hands of God the Father he was invested with honour and glory, and there came to him from the sublime Presence a voice which said: 'This is my Son, my Beloved, on whom my favour rests.' This voice from heaven we ourselves heard; when it came, we were with him on the sacred mountain.

All this only confirms for us the message of the prophets, to which you will do well to attend, because it is like a lamp shining in a murky place, until the day breaks and the morning star rises to illuminate your minds.

Gospel *Matthew 17.1-13 NEB*

Jesus took Peter, James, and John the brother of James, and led them up a high mountain where they were alone; and in their presence he was transfigured; his face shone like the sun, and his clothes became white as the light. And they saw Moses and Elijah appear, conversing with him. Then Peter spoke: 'Lord,' he said, 'how good it is that we are here! If you wish it, I will make three shelters here, one for you, one for Moses, and one for Elijah.' While he was still speaking, a bright cloud suddenly overshadowed them, and a voice called from the cloud: 'This is my Son, my Beloved, on whom my favour rests; listen to him.' At the sound of the voice the disciples fell on their faces in terror. Jesus then came up to them, touched them, and said, 'Stand up; do not be afraid.' And when they raised their eyes they saw no one, but only Jesus.

On their way down from the mountain, Jesus enjoined them not to tell anyone of the vision until the Son of Man had been raised from the dead. The disciples put a question to him: 'Why then do our teachers say that Elijah must come first?' He replied, 'Yes, Elijah will come and set everything right. But I tell you that Elijah has already come, and they failed to recognize him, and worked their will upon him; and in the same way the Son of Man is to suffer at their hands.' Then the disciples understood that he meant John the Baptist.

PROPER PREFACE

Rite A. The Preface of the Transfiguration (20) is said.
Rite B. The Preface of the Transfiguration is said.

POSTCOMMUNION SENTENCE

This is my Son, my Beloved, in whom is all my delight: listen to him. *Matthew 17.5*

LENT 5
(Second Sunday before Easter)   Violet (or Lent array)

INTRODUCTORY SENTENCE

Jesus died for all: so that living men should live no longer for themselves, but for him who died and was raised to life for them. *2 Corinthians 5.15*

COLLECT

Most merciful God,
who by the death and resurrection of your Son Jesus Christ
delivered and saved mankind:
grant that by faith in him who suffered on the cross,
we may triumph in the power of his victory;
through Jesus Christ our Lord.

PSALMS 76.1-9; 22.23-29

READINGS YEAR 1

Old Testament *Exodus 6.2-13 NEB*

God spoke to Moses and said, 'I am the Lord. I appeared to
Abraham, Isaac, and Jacob as God Almighty. But I did not let
myself be known to them by my name JEHOVAH.
Moreover, I made a covenant with them to give them
Canaan, the land where they settled for a time as foreigners.
And now I have heard the groaning of the Israelites,
enslaved by the Egyptians, and I have called my covenant to
mind. Say therefore to the Israelites, "I am the Lord. I will
release you from your labours in Egypt. I will rescue you
from slavery there. I will redeem you with arm outstretched
and with mighty acts of judgement. I will adopt you as my
people, and I will become your God. You shall know that I,
the Lord, am your God, the God who releases you from your
labours in Egypt. I will lead you to the land which I swore
with uplifted hand to give to Abraham, to Isaac and to Jacob.
I will give it you for your possession. I am the Lord."'

Moses repeated these words to the Israelites, but they did
not listen to him; they had become impatient because of their
cruel slavery.

Then the Lord spoke to Moses and said, 'Go and tell Pharoah
king of Egypt to set the Israelites free to leave his country.'
Moses made answer in the presence of the Lord, 'If the
Israelites do not listen to me, how will Pharoah listen to such
a halting speaker as I am?'

Thus the Lord spoke to Moses and Aaron and gave them

their commission to the Israelites and to Pharoah, namely that they should bring the Israelites out of Egypt.

New Testament *Colossians 2.8-15 NEB*

Be on your guard; do not let your minds be captured by hollow and delusive speculations, based on traditions of man-made teaching and centred on the elemental spirits of the universe and not on Christ.

For it is in Christ that the complete being of the Godhead dwells embodied, and in him you have been brought to completion. Every power and authority in the universe is subject to him as Head. In him also you were circumcised, not in a physical sense, but by being divested of the lower nature; this is Christ's way of circumcision. For in baptism you were buried with him, in baptism also you were raised to life with him through your faith in the active power of God who raised him from the dead. And although you were dead because of your sins and because you were morally uncircumcised, he has made you alive with Christ. For he has forgiven us all our sins; he has cancelled the bond which pledged us to the decrees of the law. It stood against us, but he has set it aside, nailing it to the cross. On that cross he discarded the cosmic powers and authorities like a garment; he made a public spectacle of them and led them as captives in his triumphal procession.

Gospel *John 12.20-32 JB*

Among those who went up to worship at the festival were some Greeks. These approached Philip, who came from Bethsaida in Galilee, and put this request to him, 'Sir, we should like to see Jesus.' Philip went to tell Andrew, and Andrew and Philip together went to tell Jesus.

Jesus replied to them,
'Now the hour has come
for the Son of Man to be glorified.
I tell you, most solemnly,
unless a wheat grain falls on the ground and dies,
it remains only a single grain;

but if it dies,
it yields a rich harvest.
Anyone who loves his life loses it;
anyone who hates his life in this world
will keep it for the eternal life.
If a man serves me, he must follow me,
wherever I am, my servant will be there too.
If anyone serves me, my Father will honour him.
Now my soul is troubled.
What shall I say:
Father, save me from this hour?
But it was for this very reason that I have come to this hour.
Father, glorify your name!'

A voice came from heaven, 'I have glorified it, and I will
glorify it again.' People standing by, who heard this, said it
was a clap of thunder; others said, 'It was an angel speaking
to him.' Jesus answered, 'It was not for my sake that this
voice came, but for yours.

'Now sentence is being passed on this world;
now the prince of this world is to be overthrown.
And when I am lifted up from the earth,
I shall draw all men to myself.'

READINGS YEAR 2

Old Testament *Jeremiah 31.31-34 NEB*

The time is coming, says the Lord, when I will make a new
covenant with Israel and Judah. It will not be like the
covenant I made with their forefathers when I took them by
the hand and led them out of Egypt. Although they broke
my covenant, I was patient with them, says the Lord. But
this is the covenant which I will make with Israel after those
days, says the Lord; I will set my law within them and write
it on their hearts; I will become their God and they shall
become my people. No longer need they teach one another
to know the Lord; all of them, high and low alike, shall know
me, says the Lord, for I will forgive their wrongdoing and
remember their sin no more.

New Testament *Hebrews 9.11-14 JB*

Now Christ has come, as the high priest of all the blessings
which were to come. He has passed through the greater, the
more perfect tent, which is better than the one made by
men's hands because it is not of this created order; and he
has entered the sanctuary once and for all, taking with him
not the blood of goats and bull calves, but his own blood,
having won an eternal redemption for us. The blood of goats
and bulls and the ashes of a heifer are sprinkled on those
who have incurred defilement and they restore the holiness
of their outward lives; how much more effectively the blood
of Christ, who offered himself as the perfect sacrifice to God
through the eternal Spirit, can purify our inner self from
dead actions so that we do our service to the living God.

Gospel *Mark 10.32-45 NEB*

Jesus and his disciples were on the road, going up to
Jerusalem, Jesus leading the way; and the disciples were
filled with awe, while those who followed behind were
afraid. He took the Twelve aside and began to tell them what
was to happen to him. 'We are now going to Jerusalem,' he
said; 'and the Son of Man will be given up to the chief priests
and the doctors of the law; they will condemn him to death
and hand him over to the foreign power. He will be mocked
and spat upon, flogged and killed; and three days
afterwards, he will rise again.'

James and John, the sons of Zebedee, approached him and
said, 'Master, we should like you to do us a favour.' 'What is
it you want me to do?' he asked. They answered, 'Grant us
the right to sit in state with you, one at your right and the
other at your left.' Jesus said to them, 'You do not
understand what you are asking. Can you drink the cup that
I drink, or be baptized with the baptism I am baptized with?'
'We can', they answered. Jesus said, 'The cup that I drink
you shall drink, and the baptism I am baptized with shall be
your baptism; but to sit at my right or left is not for me to
grant; it is for those to whom it has already been assigned.'

When the other ten heard this, they were indignant with
James and John. Jesus called them to him and said, 'You

know that in the world the recognized rulers lord it over their subjects, and their great men make them feel the weight of authority. That is not the way with you; among you, whoever wants to be great must be your servant, and whoever wants to be first must be the willing slave of all. For even the Son of Man did not come to be served but to serve, and to give up his life as a ransom for many.'

PROPER PREFACE

Rite A. The Preface of the Cross (10) is said throughout the week.
Rite B. Second Thanksgiving. The Preface of Passiontide is said.

POSTCOMMUNION SENTENCE

Unless a grain of wheat falls on the ground and dies, it remains a single grain: but, if it dies, it yields a rich harvest. *John 12.24*

PALM SUNDAY
(The Sunday next before Easter)   Red

INTRODUCTORY SENTENCE

Hosanna to the Son of David! Blessed is he who comes in the name of the Lord! Hosanna in the highest! *Matthew 21.9*

COLLECT

Almighty and everlasting God,
who in your tender love towards mankind
    sent your Son our Saviour Jesus Christ
to take upon him our flesh
and to suffer death upon the cross:
grant that we may follow the example
    of his patience and humility,
and also be made partakers of his resurrection;
through Jesus Christ our Lord.

PSALMS 22.1-11; 69.1-9 or 24; 45.1-7

READINGS YEARS 1 and 2

Old Testament *Isaiah 50.4-9a NEB*

The Lord God has given me
the tongue of a teacher
and skill to console the weary
with a word in the morning;
he sharpened my hearing
that I might listen like one who is taught.
The Lord God opened my ears
and I did not disobey or turn back in defiance.
I offered my back to the lash,
and let my beard be plucked from my chin,
I did not hide my face from spitting and insult;
but the Lord God stands by to help me;
therefore no insult can wound me.
I have set my face like flint,
for I know that I shall not be put to shame,
because one who will clear my name is at my side.
Who dare argue against me? Let us confront one another.
Who will dispute my cause? Let him come forward.
The Lord God will help me;
who then can prove me guilty?

New Testament *Philippians 2.5-11 NEB*

Let your bearing towards one another arise out of your life in
Christ Jesus. For the divine nature was his from the first; yet
he did not think to snatch at equality with God, but made
himself nothing, assuming the nature of a slave. Bearing the
human likeness, revealed in human shape, he humbled
himself, and in obedience accepted even death—death on a
cross. Therefore God raised him to the heights and
bestowed on him the name above all names, that at the name
of Jesus every knee should bow—in heaven, on earth, and in
the depths—and every tongue confess, 'Jesus Christ is
Lord', to the glory of God the Father.

Jesus and his disciples went to a place which was called Gethsemane; and he said to them, 'Sit here, while I pray.' And he took with him Peter and James and John, and began to be greatly distressed and troubled. And he said to them, 'My soul is very sorrowful, even to death; remain here, and watch.' And going a little farther, he fell on the ground and prayed that, if it were possible, the hour might pass from him. And he said, 'Abba, Father, all things are possible to you; remove this cup from me; yet not what I will, but what you will.' And he came and found them sleeping, and he said to Peter, 'Simon, are you asleep? Could you not watch one hour? Watch and pray that you may not enter into temptation; the spirit indeed is willing, but the flesh is weak.' And again he went away and prayed, saying the same words. And again he came and found them sleeping, for their eyes were very heavy; and they did not know what to answer him. And he came the third time, and said to them, 'Are you still sleeping and taking your rest? It is enough; the hour has come; the Son of man is betrayed into the hands of sinners. Rise, let us be going; see, my betrayer is at hand.'

And immediately, while he was still speaking, Judas came, one of the twelve, and with him a crowd with swords and clubs, from the chief priests and the scribes and the elders. Now the betrayer had given them a sign, saying, 'The one I shall kiss is the man; seize him and lead him away safely.' And when he came, he went up to him at once, and said, 'Master!' And he kissed him. And they laid hands on him and seized him. But one of those who stood by drew his sword, and struck the slave of the high priest and cut off his ear. And Jesus said to them, 'Have you come out as against a robber, with swords and clubs to capture me? Day after day I was with you in the temple teaching, and you did not seize me. But let the scriptures be fulfilled.' And they all forsook him, and fled.

And a young man followed him, with nothing but a linen cloth about his body; and they seized him, but he left the linen cloth and ran away naked.

And they led Jesus to the high priest; and all the chief priests and the elders and the scribes were assembled. And Peter had followed him at a distance, right into the courtyard of the high priest; and he was sitting with the guards, and warming himself at the fire. Now the chief priests and the whole council sought testimony against Jesus to put him to death; but they found none. For many bore false witness against him, and their witness did not agree. And some stood up and bore false witness against him, saying, 'We heard him say, "I will destroy this temple that is made with hands, and in three days I will build another, not made with hands."' Yet not even so did their testimony agree. And the high priest stood up in the midst, and asked Jesus, 'Have you no answer to make? What is it that these men testify against you?' But he was silent and made no answer. Again the high priest asked him, 'Are you the Christ, the Son of the Blessed?' And Jesus said, 'I am; and you will see the Son of Man sitting at the right hand of Power, and coming with the clouds of heaven.' And the high priest tore his mantle, and said, 'Why do we still need witnesses? You have heard his blasphemy. What is your decision?' And they all condemned him as deserving death. And some began to spit on him, and to cover his face, and to strike him, saying to him, 'Prophesy!' And the guards received him with blows.

And as Peter was below in the courtyard, one of the maids of the high priest came; and seeing Peter warming himself, she looked at him, and said, 'You also were with the Nazarene, Jesus.' But he denied it, saying, 'I neither know nor understand what you mean.' And he went out into the gateway. And the maid saw him, and began again to say to the bystanders, 'This man is one of them.' But again he denied it. And after a little while again the bystanders said to Peter, 'Certainly you are one of them; for you are a Galilean.' But he began to invoke a curse on himself and to swear, 'I do not know this man of whom you speak.' And immediately the cock crowed a second time. And Peter remembered how Jesus had said to him, 'Before the cock crows twice, you will deny me three times.' And he broke down and wept.

And as soon as it was morning the chief priests, with the elders and scribes, and the whole council held a consultation; and they bound Jesus and led him away and delivered him to Pilate. And Pilate asked him, 'Are you the King of the Jews?' And he answered him, 'You have said so.' And the chief priests accused him of many things. And Pilate again asked him, 'Have you no answer to make? See how many charges they bring against you.' But Jesus made no further answer, so that Pilate wondered.

Now at the feast he used to release for them any one prisoner whom they asked. And among the rebels in prison, who had committed murder in the insurrection, there was a man called Barabbas. And the crowd came up and began to ask Pilate to do as he was wont to do for them. And he answered them, 'Do you want me to release for you the King of the Jews?' For he perceived that it was out of envy that the chief priests had delivered him up. But the chief priests stirred up the crowd to have him release for them Barabbas instead. And Pilate again said to them, 'Then what shall I do with the man whom you call the King of the Jews?' And they cried out again, 'Crucify him.' And Pilate said to them, 'Why, what evil has he done?' But they shouted all the more, 'Crucify him.' So Pilate, wishing to satisfy the crowd, released for them Barabbas; and having scourged Jesus, he delivered him to be crucified.

And the soldiers led him away inside the palace (that is, the Praetorium); and they called together the whole battalion. And they clothed him in a purple cloak, and plaiting a crown of thorns they put it on him. And they began to salute him, 'Hail, King of the Jews!' And they struck his head with a reed, and spat upon him, and they knelt down in homage to him. And when they had mocked him, they stripped him of the purple cloak, and put his own clothes on him. And they led him out to crucify him.

And they compelled a passer-by, Simon of Cyrene, who was coming in from the country, the father of Alexander and Rufus, to carry his cross. And they brought him to the place called Golgotha (which means the place of a skull). And they offered him wine mingled with myrrh; but he did not take it. And they crucified him, and divided his garments among them, casting lots for them, to decide what each should take.

And it was the third hour, when they crucified him. And the inscription of the charge against him read, 'The King of the Jews.' And with him they crucified two robbers, one on his right and one on his left. And those who passed by derided him, wagging their heads, and saying, 'Aha! You who would destroy the temple and build it in three days, save yourself, and come down from the cross!' So also the chief priests mocked him to one another with the scribes, saying, 'He saved others; he cannot save himself. Let the Christ, the King of Israel, come down now from the cross, that we may see and believe.' Those who were crucified with him also reviled him.

And when the sixth hour had come, there was darkness over the whole land until the ninth hour. And at the ninth hour Jesus cried with a loud voice, 'Eloi, Eloi, lama sabach-thani?' which means, 'My God, my God, why have you forsaken me?' And some of the bystanders hearing it said, 'Behold, he is calling Elijah.' And one ran and, filling a sponge full of vinegar, put it on a reed and gave it to him to drink, saying, 'Wait, let us see whether Elijah will come to take him down.' And Jesus uttered a loud cry, and breathed his last. And the curtain of the temple was torn in two, from top to bottom. And when the centurion, who stood facing him, saw that he thus breathed his last, he said, 'Truly this man was a son of God!'

There were also women looking on from afar, among whom were Mary Magdalen, and Mary the mother of James the younger and of Joses, and Salome, who, when he was in Galilee, followed him, and ministered to him; and also many other women who came up with him to Jerusalem.

or

Old Testament *Zechariah 9.9-12 RSV*

Rejoice greatly, O daughter of Zion!
Shout aloud, O daughter of Jerusalem!
Lo, your king comes to you;
triumphant and victorious is he,
humble and riding on an ass,
on a colt the foal of an ass.

I will cut off the chariot from Ephraim
and the war horse from Jerusalem;
and the battle bow shall be cut off,
and he shall command peace to the nations;
his dominion shall be from sea to sea,
and from the River to the ends of the earth.

As for you also, because of the blood of my covenant
    with you,
I will set your captives free from the waterless pit.
Return to your stronghold, O prisoners of hope;
today I declare that I will restore to you double.

New Testament *1 Corinthians 1.18-25 RSV*

The word of the cross is folly to those who are perishing, but
to us who are being saved it is the power of God. For it
is written,
'I will destroy the wisdom of the wise,
and the cleverness of the clever I will thwart.'
Where is the wise man? Where is the scribe? Where is the
debater of this age? Has not God made foolish the wisdom of
the world? For since, in the wisdom of God, the world did
not know God through wisdom, it pleased God through the
folly of what we preach to save those who believe. For Jews
demand signs and Greeks seek wisdom, but we preach
Christ crucified, a stumbling-block to Jews and folly to
Gentiles, but to those who are called, both Jews and Greeks,
Christ the power of God and the wisdom of God. For the
foolishness of God is wiser than men, and the weakness of
God is stronger than men.

Gospel *Matthew 21.1-13 NEB*

Jesus and his disciples were nearing Jerusalem; and when
they reached Bethphage at the Mount of Olives, Jesus sent
two of them with these instructions: 'Go to the village
opposite, where you will at once find a donkey tethered with
her foal beside her; untie them, and bring them to me. If
anyone speaks to you, say, "Our Master needs them"; and
he will let you take them at once.' This was to fulfil the
prophecy which says, 'Tell the daughter of Zion, "Here is

your king, who comes to you in gentleness, riding on an ass, riding on the foal of a beast of burden."'

The disciples went and did as Jesus had directed, and brought the donkey and her foal; they laid their cloaks on them and Jesus mounted. Crowds of people carpeted the road with their cloaks, and some cut branches from the trees to spread in his path. Then the crowd that went ahead and the others that came behind raised the shout: 'Hosanna to the Son of David! Blessings on him who comes in the name of the Lord! Hosanna in the heavens!'

When he entered Jerusalem the whole city went wild with excitement. 'Who is this?' people asked, and the crowd replied, 'This is the prophet Jesus, from Nazareth in Galilee.'

Jesus then went into the temple and drove out all who were buying and selling in the temple precincts; he upset the tables of the money-changers and the seats of the dealers in pigeons; and said to them, 'Scripture says, "My house shall be called a house of prayer"; but you are making it a robbers' cave.'

PROPER PREFACE

Rite A. The Preface of the Cross (10) is said.
Rite B. Second Thanksgiving. The Preface of Passiontide is said.

POSTCOMMUNION SENTENCE

Jesus said, Father, if this cup may not pass from me, but I must drink it, your will be done. *Matthew 26.42*

MONDAY IN HOLY WEEK   Red, or as in Lent

INTRODUCTORY SENTENCE

Deliver me, O Lord, from evil men: preserve me from wicked men. *Psalm 140.1*

COLLECT

Almighty and everlasting God,
who in your tender love towards mankind
    sent your Son our Saviour Jesus Christ
to take upon him our flesh
and to suffer death upon the cross:
grant that we may follow the example
    of his patience and humility,
and also be made partakers of his resurrection;
through Jesus Christ our Lord.

PSALMS 55.1-9; 55.9-15

READINGS YEARS 1 and 2

Old Testament *Isaiah 42.1-7 RSV*

Behold my servant, whom I uphold,
my chosen, in whom my soul delights;
I have put my spirit upon him,
he will bring forth justice to the nations.
He will not cry or lift up his voice,
or make it heard in the street;
a bruised reed he will not break,
and a dimly burning wick he will not quench;
he will faithfully bring forth justice.
He will not fail or be discouraged
till he has established justice in the earth;
and the coastlands wait for his law.

Thus says God, the Lord,
who created the heavens and stretched them out,
who spread forth the earth and what comes from it,
who gives breath to the people upon it
and spirit to those who walk in it:
'I am the Lord, I have called you in righteousness,
I have taken you by the hand and kept you;
I have given you as a covenant to the people,
a light to the nations,
to open the eyes that are blind,
to bring out the prisoners from the dungeon,
from the prison those who sit in darkness.

New Testament *Hebrews 2.9-18 NEB*

In Jesus we see one who for a short while was made lower than the angels, crowned now with glory and honour because he suffered death, so that, by God's gracious will, in tasting death he should stand for us all.

It was clearly fitting that God for whom and through whom all things exist should, in bringing many sons to glory, make the leader who delivers them perfect through sufferings. For a consecrating priest and those whom he consecrates are all of one stock; and that is why the Son does not shrink from calling men his brothers, when he says, 'I will proclaim thy name to my brothers; in full assembly I will sing thy praise'; and again, 'I will keep my trust fixed on him'; and again, 'Here am I, and the children whom God has given me.' The children of a family share the same flesh and blood; and so he too shared ours, so that through death he might break the power of him who had death at his command, that is, the devil; and might liberate those who, through fear of death, had all their lifetime been in servitude. It is not angels, mark you, that he takes to himself, but the sons of Abraham. And therefore he had to be made like these brothers of his in every way, so that he might be merciful and faithful as their high priest before God, to expiate the sins of the people. For since he himself has passed through the test of suffering, he is able to help those who are meeting their test now.

Gospel Year 1 *Matthew 26.1-30 JB*

Jesus had finished all he wanted to say, and he told his disciples, 'It will be Passover, as you know, in two days' time, and the Son of Man will be handed over to be crucified.'

Then the chief priests and the elders of the people assembled in the palace of the high priest, whose name was Caiaphas, and made plans to arrest Jesus by some trick and have him put to death. They said, however, 'It must not be during the festivities; there must be no disturbance among the people.'

Jesus was at Bethany in the house of Simon the leper, when a woman came to him with an alabaster jar of the most expensive ointment, and poured it on his head as he was at table. When they saw this, the disciples were indignant; 'Why this waste?' they said. 'This could have been sold at a high price and the money given to the poor.' Jesus noticed this. 'Why are you upsetting the woman?' he said to them. 'What she has done for me is one of the good works indeed! You have the poor with you always, but you will not always have me. When she poured this ointment on my body, she did it to prepare me for burial. I tell you solemnly, wherever in all the world this Good News is proclaimed, what she has done will be told also, in remembrance of her.'

Then one of the Twelve, the man called Judas Iscariot, went to the chief priests and said, 'What are you prepared to give me if I hand him over to you?' They paid him thirty silver pieces, and from that moment he looked for an opportunity to betray him.

Now on the first day of Unleavened Bread the disciples came to Jesus to say, 'Where do you want us to make the preparations for you to eat the Passover?' 'Go to so-and-so in the city', he replied, 'and say to him, "The Master says: My time is near. It is at your house that I am keeping Passover with my disciples."' The disciples did what Jesus told them and prepared the Passover.

When evening came he was at table with the twelve disciples. And while they were eating he said, 'I tell you solemnly, one of you is about to betray me.' They were greatly distressed and started asking him in turn, 'Not I, Lord, surely?' He answered, 'Someone who has dipped his hand into the dish with me, will betray me. The Son of Man is going to his fate, as the scriptures say he will, but alas for that man by whom the Son of Man is betrayed! Better for that man if he had never been born!' Judas, who was to betray him, asked in his turn, 'Not I, Rabbi, surely?' 'They are your own words', answered Jesus.

Now as they were eating, Jesus took some bread, and when he had said the blessing he broke it and gave it to the disciples. 'Take it and eat;' he said, 'this is my body.' Then he took a cup, and when he had returned thanks he gave it to them. 'Drink all of you from this,' he said, 'for this is my blood, the blood of the covenant, which is to be poured out for many for the forgiveness of sins. From now on, I tell you, I shall not drink wine until the day I drink the new wine with you in the kingdom of my Father.'

After psalms had been sung they left for the Mount of Olives.

Gospel Year 2 *Luke 22.1-38 RSV*

Now the feast of Unleavened Bread drew near, which is called the Passover. And the chief priests and the scribes were seeking how to put Jesus to death; for they feared the people.

Then Satan entered into Judas called Iscariot, who was of the number of the twelve; he went away and conferred with the chief priests and captains how he might betray him to them. And they were glad, and engaged to give him money. So he agreed, and sought an opportunity to betray him to them in the absence of the multitude.

Then came the day of Unleavened Bread, on which the Passover lamb had to be sacrificed. So Jesus sent Peter and John, saying, 'Go and prepare the Passover for us, that we may eat it.' They said to him, 'Where will you have us prepare it?' He said to them, 'Behold, when you have entered the city, a man carrying a jar of water will meet you; follow him into the house which he enters, and tell the householder, "The teacher says to you, Where is the guest room, where I am to eat the Passover with my disciples?" And he will show you a large upper room furnished; there make ready.' And they went, and found it as he had told them; and they prepared the Passover.

And when the hour came, he sat at table, and the apostles with him. And he said to them, 'I have earnestly desired to eat this Passover with you before I suffer; for I tell you I shall not eat it until it is fulfilled in the kingdom of God.' And he took a cup, and when he had given thanks he said, 'Take this, and divide it among yourselves; for I tell you that from now on I shall not drink of the fruit of the vine until the kingdom of God comes.' And he took bread, and when he had given thanks he broke it and gave it to them, saying, 'This is my body. But behold the hand of him who betrays me is with me on the table. For the Son of man goes as it has been determined; but woe to that man by whom he is betrayed!' And they began to question one another, which of them it was that would do this.

A dispute also arose among them, which of them was to be regarded as the greatest. And he said to them, 'The kings of the Gentiles exercise lordship over them; and those in authority over them are called benefactors. But not so with you; rather let the greatest among you become as the youngest, and the leader as one who serves. For which is the greater, one who sits at table, or one who serves? Is it not the one who sits at table? But I am among you as one who serves.

'You are those who have continued with me in my trials; as my Father appointed a kingdom for me, so do I appoint for you that you may eat and drink at my table in my kingdom, and sit on thrones judging the twelve tribes of Israel.

'Simon, Simon, behold, Satan demanded to have you, that he might sift you like wheat, but I have prayed for you that your faith may not fail; and when you have turned again, strengthen your brethren.' And he said to him, 'Lord, I am ready to go with you to prison and to death.' He said, 'I tell you, Peter, the cock will not crow this day, until you three times deny that you know me.'

And he said to them, 'When I sent you out with no purse or bag or sandals, did you lack anything?' They said, 'Nothing.' He said to them, 'But now, let him who has a purse take it, and likewise a bag. And let him who has no sword sell his mantle and buy one. For I tell you that this scripture must be fulfilled in me, "And he was reckoned with transgressors"; for what is written about me has its fulfilment.' And they said, 'Look, Lord, here are two swords.' And he said to them, 'It is enough.'

PROPER PREFACE

Rite A. The Preface of the Cross (10) is said.
Rite B. Second Thanksgiving. The Preface of Passiontide is said.

POSTCOMMUNION SENTENCE

Lord, when I am in trouble, do not hide your face from me:
hear me when I call, and answer quickly. *Psalm 102.2*

TUESDAY IN HOLY WEEK   Red, or as in Lent

INTRODUCTORY SENTENCE

False witnesses have risen against me: and they breathe out
violence. *Psalm 27.12*

COLLECT

Almighty and everlasting God,
who in your tender love towards mankind
    sent your Son our Saviour Jesus Christ
to take upon him our flesh
and to suffer death upon the cross:
grant that we may follow the example
    of his patience and humility,
and also be made partakers of his resurrection;
through Jesus Christ our Lord.

PSALMS 55.18-26; 13

READINGS YEARS 1 and 2

Old Testament *Isaiah 49.1-6 NEB*

Listen to me, you coasts and islands,
pay heed, you peoples far away:
from birth the Lord called me,
he named me from my mother's womb.
He made my tongue his sharp sword
and concealed me under cover of his hand;
he made me a polished arrow
and hid me out of sight in his quiver.
He said to me, 'You are my servant,
Israel through whom I shall win glory';
so I rose to honour in the Lord's sight
and my God became my strength.

Once I said, 'I have laboured in vain;
I have spent my strength for nothing, to no purpose';
yet in truth my cause is with the Lord
and my reward is in God's hands.
And now the Lord who formed me in the womb to be
    his servant,
to bring Jacob back to him
that Israel should be gathered to him,
now the Lord calls me again:
it is too slight a task for you, as my servant,
to restore the tribes of Jacob,
to bring back the descendants of Israel:
I will make you a light to the nations,
to be my salvation to earth's farthest bounds.

New Testament *Hebrews 8.1-6 RSV*

The point in what we are saying is this: we have such a high priest, one who is seated at the right hand of the throne of the Majesty in heaven, a minister in the sanctuary and the true tent which is set up not by man but by the Lord. For every high priest is appointed to offer gifts and sacrifices; hence it is necessary for this priest also to have something to offer. Now if he were on earth, he would not be a priest at all, since there are priests who offer gifts according to the law. They serve a copy and shadow of the heavenly sanctuary; for when Moses was about to erect the tent, he was instructed by God, saying, 'See that you make everything according to the pattern which was shown you on the mountain.' But as it is, Christ has obtained a ministry which is as much more excellent than the old as the covenant he mediates is better, since it is enacted on better promises.

Gospel Year 1 *Matthew 26.31-end JB*

Jesus said to his disciples, 'You will all lose faith in me this night, for the scripture says: "I shall strike the shepherd and the sheep of the flock will be scattered", but after my resurrection I shall go before you to Galilee.' At this, Peter said, 'Though all lose faith in you, I will never lose faith.' Jesus answered him, 'I tell you solemnly, this very night, before the cock crows, you will have disowned me three times.' Peter said to him, 'Even if I have to die with you, I will never disown you.' And all the disciples said the same.

Then Jesus came with them to a small estate called Gethsemane; and he said to his disciples, 'Stay here while I go over there to pray.' He took Peter and the two sons of Zebedee with him. And sadness came over him, and great distress. Then he said to them, 'My soul is sorrowful to the point of death. Wait here and keep awake with me.' And going on a little further he fell on his face and prayed. 'My Father,' he said, 'if it is possible, let this cup pass me by. Nevertheless, let it be as you, not I, would have it.' He came back to the disciples and found them sleeping, and he said to Peter, 'So you had not the strength to keep awake with me one hour? You should be awake, and praying not to be put to the test. The spirit is willing, but the flesh is weak.' Again, a second time, he went away and prayed: 'My Father,' he said, 'if this cup cannot pass by without my drinking it, your will be done!' And he came again back and found them sleeping, their eyes were so heavy. Leaving them there, he went away again and prayed for the third time, repeating the same words. Then he came back to the disciples and said to them, 'You can sleep on now and take your rest. Now the hour has come when the Son of Man is to be betrayed into the hands of sinners. Get up! Let us go! My betrayer is already close at hand.'

He was still speaking when Judas, one of the Twelve, appeared, and with him a large number of men armed with swords and clubs, sent by the chief priests and elders of the people. Now the traitor had arranged a sign with them. 'The one I kiss,' he had said, 'he is the man. Take him in charge.' So he went straight up to Jesus and said, 'Greetings, Rabbi', and kissed him. Jesus said to him, 'My friend, do what you are here for.' Then they came forward, seized Jesus and took him in charge. At that, one of the followers of Jesus grasped his sword and drew it; he struck out at the high priest's servant, and cut off his ear. Jesus then said, 'Put your sword back, for all who draw the sword will die by the sword. Or do you think that I cannot appeal to my Father who would promptly send more than twelve legions of angels to my defence? But then, how would the scriptures be fulfilled that say this is the way it must be?' It was at this time that Jesus said to the crowds, 'Am I a brigand, that you had to set out to capture me with swords and clubs? I sat teaching in the Temple day after day and you never laid hands on me.' Now all this happened to fulfil the prophecies in scripture. Then all the disciples deserted him and ran away.

The men who had arrested Jesus led him off to Caiaphas the high priest, where the scribes and the elders were assembled. Peter followed him at a distance, and when he reached the high priest's palace, he went in and sat down with the attendants to see what the end would be.

The chief priests and the whole Sanhedrin were looking for evidence against Jesus, however false, on which they might pass the death-sentence. But they could not find any, though several lying witnesses came forward. Eventually two stepped forward and made a statement, 'This man said, "I have power to destroy the Temple of God and in three days build it up."' The high priest then stood up and said to him, 'Have you no answer to that? What is this evidence these men are bringing against you?' But Jesus was silent. And the high priest said to him, 'I put you on oath by the living God to tell us if you are the Christ, the Son of God.' 'The words are your own', answered Jesus. 'Moreover, I tell you that from this time onward you will see the Son of Man seated at the right hand of the Power and coming on the clouds of heaven.' At this, the high priest tore his clothes and said, 'He has blasphemed. What need of witnesses have we now? There! You have just heard the blasphemy. What is your opinion?' They answered, 'He deserves to die.'

Then they spat in his face and hit him with their fists; others said as they struck him, 'Play the prophet, Christ! Who hit you then?'

Meanwhile Peter was sitting outside in the courtyard, and a servant-girl came up to him and said, 'You too were with Jesus the Galilean.' But he denied it in front of them all. 'I do not know what you are talking about', he said. When he went out to the gateway another servant-girl saw him and said to the people there, 'This man was with Jesus the Nazarene.' And again, with an oath, he denied it, 'I do not know the man.' A little later the bystanders came up and said to Peter, 'You are one of them for sure! Why, your accent gives you away.' Then he started calling down curses on himself and swearing, 'I do not know the man.' At that moment the cock crew, and Peter remembered what Jesus had said, 'Before the cock crows you will have disowned me three times.' And he went outside and wept bitterly.

Gospel Year 2 *Luke 22.39-end RSV*

Jesus came out, and went, as was his custom, to the Mount of Olives; and the disciples followed him. And when he came to the place he said to them, 'Pray that you may not enter into temptation.' And he withdrew from them about a stone's throw, and knelt down and prayed, 'Father, if you are willing, remove this cup from me; nevertheless not my will, but yours, be done.' And there appeared to him an angel from heaven, strengthening him. And being in an agony he prayed more earnestly; and his sweat became like great drops of blood falling down upon the ground. And when he rose from prayer, he came to the disciples and found them sleeping for sorrow, and he said to them, 'Why do you sleep? Rise and pray that you may not enter into temptation.'

While he was still speaking, there came a crowd, and the man called Judas, one of the twelve, was leading them. He drew near to Jesus to kiss him; but Jesus said to him, 'Judas, would you betray the Son of Man with a kiss?' And when those who were about him saw what would follow, they said, 'Lord, shall we strike with the sword?' And one of them struck the slave of the high priest and cut off his right ear. But Jesus said, 'No more of this!' And he touched his ear and healed him. Then Jesus said to the chief priests and captains of the temple and elders, who had come out against him, 'Have you come out as against a robber, with swords and clubs? When I was with you day after day in the temple, you did not lay hands on me. But this is your hour, and the power of darkness.'

Then they seized him and led him away, bringing him into the high priest's house. Peter followed at a distance; and

when they had kindled a fire in the middle of the courtyard
and sat down together, Peter sat among them. Then a maid,
seeing him as he sat in the light and gazing at him, said, 'This
man also was with him.' But he denied it, saying, 'Woman, I
do not know him.' And a little later some one else saw him
and said, 'You also are one of them.' But Peter said, 'Man, I
am not.' And after an interval of about an hour still another
insisted, saying, 'Certainly this man also was with him; for
he is a Galilean.' But Peter said, 'Man, I do not know what
you are saying.' And immediately, while he was still
speaking, the cock crowed. And the Lord turned and looked
at Peter. And Peter remembered the word of the Lord, how
he had said to him, 'Before the cock crows today, you will
deny me three times.' And he went out and wept bitterly.

Now the men who were holding Jesus mocked him and beat
him; they also blindfolded him and asked him, 'Prophesy!
Who is it that struck you?' And they spoke many other
words against him, reviling him.

When day came, the assembly of the elders of the people
gathered together, both chief priests and scribes; and they
led him away to their council, and they said, 'If you are the
Christ, tell us.' But he said to them, 'If I tell you, you will not
believe; and if I ask you, you will not answer. But from now
on the Son of Man shall be seated at the right hand of the
power of God.' And they all said, 'Are you the Son of God,
then?' And he said to them, 'You say that I am.' And they
said, 'What further testimony do we need? We have heard it
ourselves from his own lips.'

PROPER PREFACE

Rite A. The Preface of the Cross (10) is said.
Rite B. Second Thanksgiving. The Preface of Passiontide
is said.

POSTCOMMUNION SENTENCE

God did not spare his own Son: but gave him up for us all.
Will he not also with him freely give us all things?
Romans 8.32

WEDNESDAY IN HOLY WEEK   Red, or as in Lent

INTRODUCTORY SENTENCE

Christ Jesus, being found in human form, humbled himself:
and became obedient even to death, death on a cross.
Philippians 2.8

COLLECT

Almighty and everlasting God,
who in your tender love towards mankind
    sent your Son our Saviour Jesus Christ
to take upon him our flesh
and to suffer death upon the cross:
grant that we may follow the example
    of his patience and humility,
and also be made partakers of his resurrection;
through Jesus Christ our Lord.

PSALMS 54; 102.1-11

READINGS YEARS 1 and 2

Old Testament *Isaiah 50.4-9a NEB*

The Lord God has given me
the tongue of a teacher
and skill to console the weary
with a word in the morning;
he sharpened my hearing
that I might listen like one who is taught.
The Lord God opened my ears
and I did not disobey or turn back in defiance.
I offered my back to the lash,
and let my beard be plucked from my chin,
I did not hide my face from spitting and insult;
but the Lord God stands by to help me;
therefore no insult can wound me.
I have set my face like flint,
for I know that I shall not be put to shame,
because one who will clear my name is at my side.
Who dare argue against me? Let us confront one another.

Who will dispute my cause? Let him come forward.
The Lord God will help me;
who then can prove me guilty?

New Testament *1 Peter 2.19-end TEV*

God will bless you for this, if you endure the pain of
undeserved suffering because you are conscious of his will.
For what credit is there if you endure the beatings you
deserve for having done wrong? But if you endure suffering
even when you have done right, God will bless you for it. It
was to this that God called you, for Christ himself suffered
for you and left you an example, so that you would follow in
his steps. He committed no sin, and no one ever heard a lie
come from his lips. When he was insulted, he did not answer
back with an insult; when he suffered, he did not threaten,
but placed his hopes in God, the righteous Judge. Christ
himself carried our sins in his body to the cross, so that we
might die to sin and live for righteousness. It is by his
wounds that you have been healed. You were like sheep that
had lost their way, but now you have been brought back to
follow the Shepherd and Keeper of your souls.

Gospel Year 1 *Matthew 27.1-56 JB*

When morning came, all the chief priests and the elders of
the people met in council to bring about the death of Jesus.
They had him bound, and led him away to hand him over to
Pilate, the governor.

When he found that Jesus had been condemned, Judas his
betrayer was filled with remorse and took the thirty silver
pieces back to the chief priests and elders. 'I have sinned;' he
said, 'I have betrayed innocent blood.' 'What is that to us?'
they replied, 'That is your concern.' And flinging down the
silver pieces in the sanctuary he made off, and went and
hanged himself. The chief priests picked up the silver pieces
and said, 'It is against the Law to put this into the treasury; it
is blood-money.' So they discussed the matter and bought
the potter's field with it as a graveyard for foreigners, and
this is why the field is called the Field of Blood today. The
words of the prophet Jeremiah were then fulfilled: 'And they

took the thirty silver pieces, the sum at which the precious One was priced by children of Israel, and they gave them for the potter's field, just as the Lord directed me.'

Jesus, then, was brought before the governor, and the governor put to him this question, 'Are you the king of the Jews?' Jesus replied, 'It is you who say it.' But when he was accused by the chief priests and the elders he refused to answer at all. Pilate then said to him, 'Do you not hear how many charges they have brought against you?' But to the governor's complete amazement, he offered no reply to any of the charges.

At festival time it was the governor's practice to release a prisoner for the people, anyone they chose. Now there was at that time a notorious prisoner whose name was Barabbas. So when the crowd gathered, Pilate said to them, 'Which do you want me to release for you: Barabbas, or Jesus who is called Christ?' For Pilate knew it was out of jealousy that they had handed him over.

Now as he was seated in the chair of judgement, his wife sent him a message, 'Have nothing to do with that man; I have been upset all day by a dream I had about him.'

The chief priests and the elders, however, had persuaded the crowd to demand the release of Barabbas and the execution of Jesus. So when the governor spoke and asked them, 'Which of the two do you want me to release for you?', they said, 'Barabbas.' 'But in that case,' Pilate said to them, 'what am I to do with Jesus who is called Christ?' They all said, 'Let him be crucified!' 'Why?' he asked, 'What harm has he done?' But they shouted all the louder, 'Let him be crucified!' Then Pilate saw that he was making no impression, that in fact a riot was imminent. So he took some water, washed his hands in front of the crowd and said, 'I am innocent of this man's blood. It is your concern.' And the people, to a man, shouted back, 'His blood be on us and on our children!' Then he released Barabbas for them. He ordered Jesus to be first scourged and then handed over to be crucified.

The governor's soldiers took Jesus with them into the Praetorium and collected the whole cohort round him. Then they stripped him and made him wear a scarlet cloak, and having twisted some thorns into a crown they put this on his head and placed a reed in his right hand. To make fun of him they knelt to him saying, 'Hail, king of the Jews!' And they spat on him and took the reed and struck him on the head with it. And when they had finished making fun of him, they took off the cloak and dressed him in his own clothes and led him away to crucify him.

On their way out, they came across a man from Cyrene, Simon by name, and enlisted him to carry his cross. When they had reached a place called Golgotha, that is, the place of the skull, they gave him wine to drink mixed with gall, which he tasted but refused to drink. When they had finished crucifying him they shared out his clothing by casting lots, and then sat down and stayed there keeping guard over him.

Above his head was placed the charge against him; it read: 'This is Jesus, the King of the Jews'. At the same time two robbers were crucified with him, one on the right and one on the left.

The passers-by jeered at him; they shook their heads and said, 'So you would destroy the Temple and rebuild it in three days! Then save yourself! If you are God's son, come down from the cross!' The chief priests with the scribes and elders mocked him in the same way. 'He saved others;' they said, 'he cannot save himself. He is the king of Israel; let him come down from the cross now, and we will believe in him. He puts his trust in God; now let God rescue him if he wants him. For he did say, "I am the son of God."' Even the robbers who were crucified with him taunted him in the same way.

From the sixth hour there was darkness over all the land until the ninth hour. And about the ninth hour, Jesus cried out in a loud voice, 'Eli, Eli, lama sabach-thani?' that is, 'My God, my God, why have you deserted me?' When some of those who stood there heard this, they said, 'The man is calling on Elijah', and one of them quickly ran to get a sponge which he dipped in vinegar and, putting it on a reed, gave it him to drink. 'Wait!' said the rest of them, 'and see if Elijah will come to save him.' But Jesus, again crying out in a loud voice, yielded up his spirit.

At that, the veil of the Temple was torn in two from top to bottom; the earth quaked; the rocks were split; the tombs opened and the bodies of many holy men rose from the dead, and these, after his resurrection, came out of the tombs, entered the Holy City and appeared to a number of people. Meanwhile the centurion, together with the others guarding Jesus, had seen the earthquake and all that was taking place, and they were terrified and said, 'In truth this was a son of God.'

And many women were there, watching from a distance, the same women who had followed Jesus from Galilee and looked after him. Among them were Mary of Magdala, Mary the mother of James and Joseph, and the mother of Zebedee's sons.

Gospel Year 2 *Luke 23.1-49 RSV*

The whole company of the chief priests and scribes arose, and brought Jesus before Pilate. And they began to accuse him, saying, 'We found this man perverting our nation, and forbidding us to give tribute to Caesar, and saying that he himself is Christ a king.' And Pilate asked him, 'Are you the King of the Jews?' And he answered him, 'You have said so.' And Pilate said to the chief priests and the multitudes, 'I find no crime in this man.' But they were urgent, saying, 'He stirs up the people, teaching throughout all Judaea, from Galilee even to this place.'

When Pilate heard this, he asked whether the man was a Galilean. And when he learned that he belonged to Herod's jurisdiction, he sent him over to Herod, who was himself in Jerusalem at that time. When Herod saw Jesus, he was very glad, for he had long desired to see him, because he had heard about him, and he was hoping to see some sign done by him. So he questioned him at some length; but he made no answer. The chief priests and the scribes stood by, vehemently accusing him. And Herod with his soldiers treated him with contempt and mocked him; then, arraying him in gorgeous apparel, he sent him back to Pilate. And Herod and Pilate became friends with each other that very day, for before this they had been at enmity with each other.

Pilate then called together the chief priests and the rulers and the people, and said to them, 'You brought me this man as one who was perverting the people; and after examining him before you, behold, I did not find this man guilty of any of your charges against him; neither did Herod, for he sent him back to us. Behold, nothing deserving death has been done by him; I will therefore chastise him and release him.'

But they all cried out together, 'Away with this man, and release to us Barabbas'—a man who had been thrown into prison for an insurrection started in the city, and for murder. Pilate addressed them once more, desiring to release Jesus; but they shouted out, 'Crucify, crucify him!' A third time he said to them, 'Why, what evil has he done? I have found in him no crime deserving death; I will therefore chastise him and release him.' But they were urgent, demanding with loud cries that he should be crucified. And their voices prevailed. So, Pilate gave sentence that their demand should be granted. He released the man who had been thrown into prison for insurrection and murder, whom they asked for; but Jesus he delivered up to their will.

And as they led him away, they seized one Simon of Cyrene, who was coming in from the country, and laid on him the cross, to carry it behind Jesus. And there followed him a great multitude of the people, and of women who bewailed and lamented him. But Jesus turning to them said, 'Daughters of Jerusalem, do not weep for me, but weep for yourselves and for your children. For behold, the days are coming when they will say, "Blessed are the barren, and the wombs that never bore, and the breasts that never gave suck!" Then they will begin to say to the mountains, "Fall on us"; and to the hills, "Cover us." For if they do this when the wood is green, what will happen when it is dry?'

Two others also, who were criminals, were led away to be put to death with him. And when they came to the place which is called The Skull, there they crucified him, and the criminals, one on the right and one on the left. And Jesus said, 'Father, forgive them; for they know not what they do.' And they cast lots to divide his garments. And the people stood by, watching; but the rulers scoffed at him, saying, 'He saved others; let him save himself, if he is the Christ of God, his Chosen One!' The soldiers also mocked him, coming up and offering him vinegar, and saying, 'If you are the King of the Jews, save yourself!' There was also an inscription over him, 'This is the King of the Jews.'

One of the criminals who were hanged railed at him, saying, 'Are you not the Christ? Save yourself and us!' But the other rebuked him, saying, 'Do you not fear God, since you are under the same sentence of condemnation? And we indeed justly; for we are receiving the due reward for our deeds; but this man has done nothing wrong.' And he said, 'Jesus, remember me when you come in your kingly power.' And he said to him, 'Truly, I say to you, today you will be with me in Paradise.'

It was now about the sixth hour, and there was darkness over the whole land until the ninth hour, while the sun's light failed; and the curtain of the temple was torn in two. Then Jesus, crying with a loud voice, said, 'Father, into your hands I commit my spirit!' And having said this he breathed his last. Now when the centurion saw what had taken place, he praised God, and said, 'Certainly this man was innocent!' And all the multitudes who assembled to see the sight, when they saw what had taken place, returned home beating their breasts. And all his acquaintances and the women who had followed him from Galilee stood at a distance and saw these things.

PROPER PREFACE

Rite A. The Preface of the Cross (10) is said.
Rite B. Second Thanksgiving. The Preface of Passiontide is said.

POSTCOMMUNION SENTENCE

The Son of Man did not come to be served, but to serve: and to give his life as a ransom for many. *Matthew 20.28*

MAUNDY THURSDAY
Red, or as in Lent; White at Holy Communion

INTRODUCTORY SENTENCE

Jesus said, A new commandment I give to you, that you love one another, as I have loved you. *John 13.34*

COLLECTS

Almighty and heavenly Father,
we thank you that in this wonderful sacrament
you have given us the memorial
   of the passion of your Son Jesus Christ.
Grant us so to reverence
the sacred mysteries of his body and blood,
that we may know within ourselves
and show forth in our lives the fruits of his redemption;
who is alive and reigns with you and the Holy Spirit,
one God, now and for ever.

Almighty Father,
whose Son Jesus Christ has taught us
that what we do for the least of our brethren
   we do also for him:
give us the will to be the servant of others
   as he was the servant of all,
who gave up his life and died for us,
yet is alive and reigns with you and the Holy Spirit,
one God, now and for ever.

PSALMS 116.11-end; 26

READINGS YEARS 1 and 2

Old Testament *Exodus 12.1-14 NEB*

The Lord said to Moses and Aaron in Egypt: This month is for you the first of months; you shall make it the first month of the year. Speak to the whole community of Israel and say to them: On the tenth day of this month let each man take a lamb or a kid for his family, one for each household, but if a household is too small for one lamb or one kid, then the man

and his nearest neighbour may take one between them.
They shall share the cost, taking into account both the
number of persons and the amount each of them eats. Your
lamb or kid must be without blemish, a yearling male. You
may take equally a sheep or a goat. You must have it in safe
keeping until the fourteenth day of this month, and then all
the assembled community of Israel shall slaughter the victim
between dusk and dark. They must take some of the blood
and smear it on the two door-posts and on the lintel of every
house in which they eat the lamb. On that night they shall
eat the flesh roast on the fire; they shall eat it with
unleavened cakes and bitter herbs. You are not to eat any of
it raw or even boiled in water, but roasted, head, shins, and
entrails. You shall not leave any of it till morning; if anything
is left over until morning, it must be destroyed by fire.

This is the way in which you must eat it: you shall have your
belt fastened, your sandals on your feet and your staff in
your hand, and you must eat in urgent haste. It is the Lord's
Passover. On that night I shall pass through the land of
Egypt and kill every first-born of man and beast. Thus will I
execute judgement, I the Lord, against all the gods of Egypt.
And as for you, the blood will be a sign on the houses in
which you are: when I see the blood I will pass over you; the
mortal blow shall not touch you, when I strike the land
of Egypt.

You shall keep this day as a day of remembrance, and make
it a pilgrim-feast, a festival of the Lord; you shall keep it
generation after generation as a rule for all time.

New Testament *1 Corinthians 11.23-29 NEB*

The tradition which I handed on to you came to me from the
Lord himself: that the Lord Jesus, on the night of his arrest,
took bread and, after giving thanks to God, broke it and said:
'This is my body, which is for you; do this as a memorial of
me.' In the same way, he took the cup after supper, and said:
'This cup is the new covenant sealed by my blood.
Whenever you drink it, do this as a memorial of me.' For
every time you eat this bread and drink the cup, you
proclaim the death of the Lord, until he comes.

It follows that anyone who eats the bread or drinks the cup of the Lord unworthily will be guilty of desecrating the body and blood of the Lord. A man must test himself before eating his share of the bread and drinking from the cup. For he who eats and drinks eats and drinks judgement on himself if he does not discern the Body.

Gospel *John 13.1-15 NEB*

It was before the Passover festival. Jesus knew that his hour had come and he must leave this world and go to the Father. He had always loved his own who were in the world, and now he was to show the full extent of his love.

The devil had already put it into the mind of Judas son of Simon Iscariot to betray him. During supper, Jesus, well aware that the Father had entrusted everything to him, and that he had come from God and was going back to God, rose from table, laid aside his garments, and taking a towel, tied it round him. Then he poured water into a basin, and began to wash his disciples' feet and to wipe them with the towel.

When it was Simon Peter's turn, Peter said to him, 'You, Lord, washing my feet?' Jesus replied, 'You do not understand now what I am doing, but one day you will.' Peter said, 'I will never let you wash my feet.' 'If I do not wash you,' Jesus replied, 'you are not in fellowship with me.' 'Then Lord,' said Simon Peter, 'not my feet only; wash my hands and head as well!'

Jesus said, 'A man who has bathed needs no further washing; he is altogether clean; and you are clean, though not every one of you.' He added the words, 'not every one of you' because he knew who was going to betray him.

After washing their feet and taking his garments again, he sat down. 'Do you understand what I have done for you?' he asked. 'You call me "Master" and "Lord", and rightly so, for that is what I am. Then if I, your Lord and Master, have washed your feet, you also ought to wash one another's feet. I have set you an example: you are to do as I have done for you.'

PROPER PREFACE

Rite A. The Preface of Maundy Thursday (11) is said.
Rite B. The Preface of Maundy Thursday is said.

POSTCOMMUNION SENTENCE

My eyes are ever fixed on the Lord, for he releases my feet
from the snare: turn to me and take pity on me, for I am
wretched and alone. *Psalm 25.15*

THE BLESSING OF THE OILS   White

INTRODUCTORY SENTENCE

Jesus Christ has made us a kingdom of priests to serve his
God and Father; glory and kingship be his for ever and ever.
Amen. *Revelation 1.6*

COLLECT

Heavenly Father,
you anointed your Son Jesus Christ
with the Holy Spirit and with power
to bring to man the blessings of your kingdom.
Anoint your Church with the same Holy Spirit,
that we who share in his suffering and his victory
may bear witness to the gospel of salvation;
through Jesus Christ our Lord.

PSALMS 89.19-30; 133

READINGS

Old Testament *Isaiah 61.1-9 NEB*

The spirit of the Lord God is upon me
because the Lord has anointed me;
he has sent me to bring good news to the humble,
to bind up the broken-hearted,
to proclaim liberty to captives
and release to those in prison;
to proclaim a year of the Lord's favour

and a day of the vengeance of our God;
to comfort all who mourn,
to give them garlands instead of ashes,
oil of gladness instead of mourners' tears,
a garment of splendour for the heavy heart.
They shall be called Trees of Righteousness,
planted by the Lord for his glory.
Ancient ruins shall be rebuilt
and sites long desolate restored;
they shall repair the ruined cities
and restore what has long lain desolate.
Foreigners shall serve as shepherds of your flocks,
and aliens shall till your land and tend your vines;
but you shall be called priests of the Lord
and be named ministers of our God;
you shall enjoy the wealth of other nations
and be furnished with their riches.
And so, because shame in double measure
and jeers and insults have been my people's lot,
they shall receive in their own land a double measure
    of wealth,
and everlasting joy shall be theirs.
For I, the Lord, love justice
and hate robbery and wrong-doing;
I will grant them a sure reward
and make an everlasting covenant with them;
their posterity will be renowned among the nations
and their offspring among the peoples;
all who see them will acknowledge in them
a race whom the Lord has blessed.

New Testament *James 5.13-16a RSV*

Is any one among you suffering? Let him pray. Is any
cheerful? Let him sing praise. Is any among you sick? Let
him call for the elders of the church, and let them pray over
him, anointing him with oil in the name of the Lord; and the
prayer of faith will save the sick man, and the Lord will raise
him up; and if he has committed sins, he will be forgiven.
Therefore confess your sins to one another, and pray for one
another, that you may be healed.

or *Revelation 1.5b-8 NEB*

To him who loves us and freed us from our sins with his life's blood, who made of us a royal house, to serve as the priests of his God and Father—to him be glory and dominion for ever and ever! Amen.

Behold, he is coming with the clouds! Every eye shall see him, and among them those who pierced him; and all the peoples of the world shall lament in remorse. So it shall be. Amen.

'I am the Alpha and the Omega', says the Lord God, who is and who was and who is to come, the sovereign Lord of all.

Gospel *Luke 4.16-21 NEB*

Jesus came to Nazareth, where he had been brought up, and went to synagogue on the Sabbath day as he regularly did. He stood up to read the lesson and was handed the scroll of the prophet Isaiah. He opened the scroll and found the passage which says,

'The spirit of the Lord is upon me because he has
    anointed me;
he has sent me to announce good news to the poor,
to proclaim release for prisoners and recovery of
    sight for the blind;
to let the broken victims go free,
to proclaim the year of the Lord's favour.'

He rolled up the scroll, gave it back to the attendant, and sat down; and all eyes in the synagogue were fixed on him.

He began to speak: 'Today', he said, 'in your very hearing this text has come true.'

PROPER PREFACE

Rite A. The Preface for the Blessing of the Oils (12) is said.

POSTCOMMUNION SENTENCE

God has set his seal upon us, and as a pledge of what is to come has given the Spirit to dwell in our hearts.
2 Corinthians 1.22

GOOD FRIDAY   Red, hangings removed

INTRODUCTORY SENTENCE

God showed his love for us in that while we were still
sinners Christ died for us. *Romans 5.8*

COLLECTS

Almighty Father,
look with mercy on this your family
for which our Lord Jesus Christ
   was content to be betrayed
   and given up into the hands of wicked men
   and to suffer death upon the cross;
who is alive and glorified
   with you and the Holy Spirit,
one God, now and for ever.

Almighty and everlasting God,
by whose Spirit the whole body of the Church
   is governed and sanctified:
hear our prayer which we offer
   for all your faithful people;
that each in his vocation and ministry
may serve you in holiness and truth
to the glory of your Name;
through our Lord and Saviour Jesus Christ.

Merciful God,
who made all men and hate nothing
   that you have made:
you desire not the death of a sinner
but rather that he should be converted and live.
Have mercy upon your ancient people the Jews,
and upon all who have not known you,
or who deny the faith of Christ crucified;
take from them all ignorance, hardness of heart,
   and contempt for your word,
and so fetch them home to your fold
that they may be made one flock under one shepherd;
through Jesus Christ our Lord.

PSALMS 22.14-22; 69.17-23

READINGS YEARS 1 and 2

Old Testament *Isaiah 52.13—53 end TEV*

The Lord says,
'My servant will suceed in his task;
he will be highly honoured.
Many people were shocked when they saw him;
he was so disfigured that he hardly looked human.
But now many nations will marvel at him,
and kings will be speechless with amazement.
They will see and understand
something they had never known.'

The people reply,
'Who would have believed what we now report?
Who could have seen the Lord's hand in this?
It was the will of the Lord that his servant
should grow like a plant taking root in dry ground.
He had no dignity or beauty
to make us take notice of him.
There was nothing attractive about him,
nothing that would draw us to him.
We despised him and rejected him;
he endured suffering and pain.
No one would even look at him—
we ignored him as if he were nothing.

But he endured the suffering that
should have been ours,
the pain that we should have borne.
All the while we thought that his suffering
was punishment sent by God.
But because of our sins he was wounded,
beaten because of the evil we did.
We are healed by the punishment he suffered,
made whole by the blows he received.
All of us were like sheep that were lost,
each of us going his own way.
But the Lord made the punishment fall on him,
the punishment all of us deserved.

He was treated harshly, but endured it humbly;
he never said a word.
Like a lamb about to be slaughtered,
like a sheep about to be sheared,
he never said a word.
He was arrested and sentenced and led off to die,
and no one cared about his fate.
He was put to death for the sins of our people.
He was placed in a grave with evil men,
he was buried with the rich,
even though he had never committed a crime
or ever told a lie.'

The Lord says,
'It was my will that he should suffer;
his death was a sacrifice to bring forgiveness.
And so he will see his descendants;
he will live a long life,
and through him my purpose will succeed.
After a life of suffering, he will again have joy;
he will know that he did not suffer in vain.
My devoted servant, with whom I am pleased,
will bear the punishment of many
and for his sake I will forgive them.
And so I will give him a place of honour,
a place among great and powerful men.
He willingly gave his life
and shared the fate of evil men.
He took the place of many sinners
and prayed that they might be forgiven.'

New Testament *Hebrews 10.1-25 TEV*

The Jewish Law is not a full and faithful model of the real
things; it is only a faint outline of the good things to come.
The same sacrifices are offered for ever, year after year. How
can the Law, then, by means of these sacrifices make perfect
the people who come to God? If the people worshipping
God had really been purified from their sins, they would not
feel guilty of sin any more, and all sacrifices would stop. As it
is, however, the sacrifices serve year after year to remind

people of their sins. For the blood of bulls and goats can never take away sins.

For this reason, when Christ was about to come into the world, he said to God:
'You do not want sacrifices and offerings,
but you have prepared a body for me.
You are not pleased with animals burnt whole on the altar
or with sacrifices to take away sins.
Then I said, "Here I am, to do your will, O God,
just as it is written of me in the book of the Law."'
First he said, 'You neither want nor are you pleased with sacrifices and offerings or with animals burnt on the altar and the sacrifices to take away sins.' He said this even though all these sacrifices are offered according to the Law. Then he said, 'Here I am, O God, to do your will.' So God does away with all the old sacrifices and puts the sacrifice of Christ in their place. Because Jesus Christ did what God wanted him to do, we are all purified from sin by the offering that he made of his own body once and for all.

Every Jewish priest performs his services every day and offers the same sacrifices many times; but these sacrifices can never take away sins. Christ, however, offered one sacrifice for sins, an offering that is effective for ever, and then he sat down at the right-hand side of God. There he now waits until God puts his enemies as a footstool under his feet. With one sacrifice, then, he has made perfect for ever those who are purified from sin.

And the Holy Spirit also gives us his witness. First he says,
'This is the covenant that I will make with them
in the days to come, says the Lord:
I will put my laws in their hearts
and write them on their minds.'
And then he says, 'I will not remember their sins and evil deeds any longer.' So when these have been forgiven, an offering to take away sins is no longer needed.

We have, then, my brothers, complete freedom to go into the Most Holy Place by means of the death of Jesus. He opened for us a new way, a living way, through the curtain—that is, through his own body. We have a great

priest in charge of the house of God. So let us come near to
God with a sincere heart and a sure faith, with hearts that
have been purified from a guilty conscience and with bodies
washed with clean water. Let us hold on firmly to the hope
we profess, because we can trust God to keep his promise.
Let us be concerned for one another, to help one another to
show love and to do good. Let us not give up the habit of
meeting together, as some are doing. Instead, let us
encourage one another all the more, since you see that the
Day of the Lord is coming nearer.

or *Hebrews 10.12-22 TEV*

Christ offered one sacrifice for sins, an offering that is
effective for ever, and then he sat down at the right-hand
side of God. There he now waits until God puts his enemies
as a footstool under his feet. With one sacrifice, then, he has
made perfect for ever those who are purified from sin.

And the Holy Spirit also gives us his witness.
First he says,
'This is the covenant that I will make with them
in the days to come, says the Lord:
I will put my laws in their hearts
and write them on their minds.'
And then he says, 'I will not remember their sins and evil
deeds any longer.' So when these have been forgiven, an
offering to take away sins is no longer needed.

We have, then, my brothers, complete freedom to go into
the Most Holy Place by means of the death of Jesus. He
opened for us a new way, a living way, through the
curtain—that is, through his own body. We have a great
priest in charge of the house of God. So let us come near to
God with a sincere heart and a sure faith, with hearts that
have been purified from a guilty conscience and with bodies
washed with clean water.

or *Hebrews 4.14-16; 5.7-9 NEB*

Since we have a great high priest who has passed through
the heavens, Jesus the Son of God, let us hold fast to the
religion we profess. For ours is not a high priest unable to

sympathize with our weaknesses, but one who, because of his likeness to us, has been tested every way, only without sin. Let us therefore boldly approach the throne of our gracious God, where we may receive mercy and in his grace find timely help.

In the days of his earthly life Jesus offered up prayers and petitions, with loud cries and tears, to God who was able to deliver him from the grave. Because of his humble submission his prayer was heard: son though he was, he learned obedience in the school of suffering, and, once perfected, became the source of eternal salvation for all who obey him.

Gospel John 18.1—19.37 JB

Jesus left the city with his disciples and crossed the Kedron valley. There was a garden there, and he went into it with his disciples. Judas the traitor knew the place well, since Jesus had often met his disciples there, and he brought the cohort to this place together with a detachment of guards sent by the chief priests and the Pharisees, all with lanterns and torches and weapons. Knowing everything that was going to happen to him, Jesus then came forward and said, 'Who are you looking for?' They answered, 'Jesus the Nazarene.' He said, 'I am he.' Now Judas the traitor was standing among them. When Jesus said, 'I am he', they moved back and fell to the ground. He asked them a second time, 'Who are you looking for?' They said, 'Jesus the Nazarene.' 'I have told you that I am he', replied Jesus. 'If I am the one you are looking for, let these others go.' This was to fulfil the words he had spoken, 'Not one of those you gave me have I lost.'

Simon Peter, who carried a sword, drew it and wounded the high priest's servant, cutting off his right ear. The servant's name was Malchus. Jesus said to Peter, 'Put your sword back in its scabbard; am I not to drink the cup that the Father has given me?'

The cohort and its captain and the Jewish guards seized Jesus and bound him. They took him first to Annas, because Annas was the father-in-law of Caiaphas, who was high priest that year. It was Caiaphas who had suggested to the

Jews, 'It is better for one man to die for the people.'

Simon Peter, with another disciple, followed Jesus. This disciple, who was known to the high priest, went with Jesus into the high priest's palace, but Peter stayed outside the door. So the other disciple, the one known to the high priest, went out, spoke to the woman who was keeping the door and brought Peter in. The maid on duty at the door said to Peter, 'Aren't you another of that man's disciples?' He answered, 'I am not.' Now it was cold, and the servants and guards had lit a charcoal fire and were standing there warming themselves; so Peter stood there too, warming himself with the others.

The high priest questioned Jesus about his disciples and his teaching. Jesus answered, 'I have spoken openly for all the world to hear; I have always taught in the synagogue and in the Temple where all the Jews meet together: I have said nothing in secret. But why ask me? Ask my hearers what I taught: they know what I said.' At these words, one of the guards standing by gave Jesus a slap in the face, saying, 'Is that the way to answer the high priest?' Jesus replied, 'If there is something wrong in what I said, point it out; but if there is no offence in it, why do you strike me?' Then Annas sent him, still bound, to Caiaphas the high priest.

As Simon Peter stood there warming himself, someone said to him, 'Aren't you another of his disciples?' He denied it saying, 'I am not.' One of the high priest's servants, a relation of the man whose ear Peter had cut off, said, 'Didn't I see you in the garden with him?' Again Peter denied it; and at once a cock crew.

They then led Jesus from the house of Caiaphas to the Praetorium. It was now morning. They did not go into the Praetorium themselves or they would be defiled and unable to eat the Passover. So Pilate came outside to them and said, 'What charge do you bring against this man?' They replied, 'If he were not a criminal, we should not be handing him over to you.' Pilate said, 'Take him yourselves, and try him by your own Law.' The Jews answered, 'We are not allowed to put a man to death.' This was to fulfil the words Jesus had spoken indicating the way he was going to die.

So Pilate went back into the Praetorium and called Jesus to him. 'Are you the king of the Jews?' he asked. Jesus replied, 'Do you ask this of your own accord, or have others spoken to you about me?' Pilate answered, 'Am I a Jew? It is your own people and the chief priests who have handed you over to me: what have you done?' Jesus replied, 'Mine is not a kingdom of this world; if my kingdom were of this world, my men would have fought to prevent my being surrendered to the Jews. But my kingdom is not of this kind.' 'So you are a king then?', said Pilate. 'It is you who say it', answered Jesus. 'Yes, I am a king. I was born for this, I came into the world for this: to bear witness to the truth; and all who are on the side of truth listen to my voice.' 'Truth?', said Pilate, 'What is that?'; and with that he went out again to the Jews and said, 'I find no case against him. But according to a custom of yours I should release one prisoner at the Passover; would you like me, then, to release the king of the Jews?' At this they shouted: 'Not this man,' they said, 'but Barabbas.' Barabbas was a brigand.

Pilate then had Jesus taken away and scourged; and after this, the soldiers twisted some thorns into a crown and put it on his head, and dressed him in a purple robe. They kept coming up to him and saying, 'Hail, king of the Jews!'; and they slapped him in the face.

Pilate came outside again and said to them, 'Look, I am going to bring him out to you to let you see that I find no case.' Jesus then came out wearing the crown of thorns and the purple robe. Pilate said, 'Here is the man.' When they saw him the chief priests and the guards shouted, 'Crucify him! Crucify him!' Pilate said, 'Take him yourselves and crucify him: I can find no case against him.' 'We have a Law', the Jews replied, 'and according to that Law he ought to die, because he has claimed to be the Son of God.'

When Pilate heard them say this his fears increased. Re-entering the Praetorium, he said to Jesus, 'Where do you come from?' But Jesus made no answer. Pilate then said to him, 'Are you refusing to speak to me? Surely you know I have power to release you and I have power to crucify you?' 'You would have no power over me', replied Jesus, 'if it had not been given you from above; that is why the one who handed me over to you has the greater guilt.'

From that moment Pilate was anxious to set him free, but the Jews shouted, 'If you set him free you are no friend of Caesar's; anyone who makes himself king is defying Caesar.' Hearing these words, Pilate had Jesus brought out, and seated himself on the chair of judgement at a place called the Pavement, in Hebrew Gabbatha. It was Passover Preparation Day, about the sixth hour. 'Here is your king', said Pilate to the Jews. 'Take him away, take him away!' they said. 'Crucify him!' 'Do you want me to crucify your king?' said Pilate. The chief priests answered, 'We have no king except Caesar.' So in the end Pilate handed him over to them to be crucified.

They then took charge of Jesus, and carrying his own cross he went out of the city to the place of the skull or, as it was called in Hebrew, Golgotha, where they crucified him with two others, one on either side with Jesus in the middle. Pilate wrote out a notice and had it fixed to the cross; it ran: 'Jesus the Nazarene, King of the Jews.' This notice was read by many of the Jews, because the place were Jesus was crucified was not far from the city, and the writing was in Hebrew, Latin and Greek. So the Jewish chief priests said to Pilate, 'You should not write "King of the Jews", but "This man said: I am King of the Jews."' Pilate answered, 'What I have written, I have written.'

When the soldiers had finished crucifying Jesus they took his clothing and divided it into four shares, one for each soldier. His undergarment was seamless, woven in one piece from neck to hem; so they said to one another, 'Instead of tearing it, let's throw dice to decide who is to have it.' In this way the words of scripture were fulfilled:

'They shared out my clothing among them.
They cast lots for my clothes.'

This is exactly what the soldiers did.

Near the cross of Jesus stood his mother and his mother's sister, Mary the wife of Clopas, and Mary of Magdala. Seeing his mother and the disciple he loved standing near

her, Jesus said to his mother, 'Woman, this is your son.'
Then to the disciple he said, 'This is your mother.' And from
that moment the disciple made a place for her in his home.

After this, Jesus knew that everything had now been
completed, and to fulfil the scripture perfectly he said:

'I am thirsty.'

A jar full of vinegar stood there, so putting a sponge soaked
in the vinegar on a hyssop stick they held it up to his mouth.
After Jesus had taken the vinegar he said, 'It is accomplished';
and bowing his head he gave up his spirit.

It was Preparation Day, and to prevent the bodies remaining
on the cross during the sabbath—since that sabbath was a
day of special solemnity—the Jews asked Pilate to have the
legs broken and the bodies taken away. Consequently the
soldiers came and broke the legs of the first man who had
been crucified with him and then of the other. When they
came to Jesus, they found he was already dead, and so
instead of breaking his legs one of the soldiers pierced his
side with a lance; and immediately there came out blood and
water. This is the evidence of one who saw it—trustworthy
evidence, and he knows he speaks the truth—and he gives it
so that you may believe as well. Because all this happened to
fulfil the words of scripture:

'Not one bone of his will be broken;'

and again, in another place scripture says:

'They will look on the one whom they have pierced.'

or *John 19.1-37 JB*

Pilate had Jesus taken away and scourged; and after this, the
soldiers twisted some thorns into a crown and put it on his
head, and dressed him in a purple robe. They kept coming
up to him and saying, 'Hail, king of the Jews!'; and they
slapped him in the face.

Pilate came outside again and said to them, 'Look, I am
going to bring him out to you to let you see that I find no
case.' Jesus then came out wearing the crown of thorns and

the purple robe. Pilate said, 'Here is the man.' When they saw him the chief priests and the guards shouted, 'Crucify him! Crucify him!' Pilate said, 'Take him yourselves and crucify him: I can find no case against him.' 'We have a Law', the Jews replied, 'and according to that Law he ought to die, because he has claimed to be the Son of God.'

When Pilate heard them say this his fears increased. Re-entering the Praetorium, he said to Jesus, 'Where do you come from?' But Jesus made no answer. Pilate then said to him, 'Are you refusing to speak to me? Surely you know I have power to release you and I have power to crucify you?' 'You would have no power over me', replied Jesus, 'if it had not been given you from above; that is why the one who handed me over to you has the greater guilt.'

From that moment Pilate was anxious to set him free, but the Jews shouted, 'If you set him free you are no friend of Caesar's; anyone who makes himself king is defying Caesar.' Hearing these words, Pilate had Jesus brought out, and seated himself on the chair of judgement at a place called the Pavement, in Hebrew Gabbatha. It was Passover Preparation Day, about the sixth hour. 'Here is your king', said Pilate to the Jews. 'Take him away, take him away!', they said, 'Crucify him!' 'Do you want me to crucify your king?', said Pilate. The chief priests answered, 'We have no king except Caesar.' So in the end Pilate handed him over to them to be crucified.

They then took charge of Jesus, and carrying his own cross he went out of the city to the place of the skull or, as it was called in Hebrew, Golgotha, where they crucified him with two others, one on either side with Jesus in the middle. Pilate wrote out a notice and had it fixed to the cross; it ran: 'Jesus the Nazarene, King of the Jews.' This notice was read by many of the Jews, because the place where Jesus was crucified was not far from the city, and the writing was in Hebrew, Latin and Greek. So the Jewish chief priests said to Pilate, 'You should not write "King of the Jews", but "This man said: I am King of the Jews."' Pilate answered, 'What I have written, I have written.'

When the soldiers had finished crucifying Jesus they took his clothing and divided it into four shares, one for each soldier. His undergarment was seamless, woven in one piece from neck to hem; so they said to one another, 'Instead of tearing it, let's throw dice to decide who is to have it.' In this way the words of scripture were fulfilled:

'They shared out my clothing among them.
They cast lots for my clothes.'

This is exactly what the soldiers did.

Near the cross of Jesus stood his mother and his mother's sister, Mary the wife of Clopas, and Mary of Magdala. Seeing his mother and the disciple he loved standing near her, Jesus said to his mother, 'Woman, this is your son.' Then to the disciple he said, 'This is your mother.' And from that moment the disciple made a place for her in his home.

After this, Jesus knew that everything had now been completed, and to fulfil the scripture perfectly he said:

'I am thirsty.'

A jar full of vinegar stood there, so putting a sponge soaked in the vinegar on a hyssop stick they held it up to his mouth. After Jesus had taken the vinegar he said, 'It is accomplished'; and bowing his head he gave up his spirit.

It was Preparation Day, and to prevent the bodies remaining on the cross during the sabbath—since that sabbath was a day of special solemnity—the Jews asked Pilate to have the legs broken and the bodies taken away. Consequently the soldiers came and broke the legs of the first man who had been crucified with him and then of the other. When they came to Jesus, they found he was already dead, and so instead of breaking his legs one of the soldiers pierced his side with a lance; and immediately there came out blood and water. This is the evidence of one who saw it—trustworthy evidence, and he knows he speaks the truth—and he gives it so that you may believe as well. Because all this happened to fulfil the words of scripture:

'Not one bone of his will be broken;'

and again, in another place scripture says:

'They will look on the one whom they have pierced.'

POSTCOMMUNION SENTENCE

As we eat this bread and drink this cup we proclaim the
death of the Lord until he comes. *1 Corinthians 11.26*

EASTER EVE   Hangings removed

INTRODUCTORY SENTENCE

When we were baptized into Christ Jesus, we were baptized
into his death; so that, as Christ was raised from the dead by
the Father's glory, we also might walk in newness of life.
Romans 6.3, 4

COLLECT

Grant, Lord,
that we who are baptized into the death
    of your Son our Saviour Jesus Christ
may continually put to death our evil desires
    and be buried with him;
that through the grave and gate of death
we may pass to our joyful resurrection;
through his merits, who died and was buried
    and rose again for us,
your Son Jesus Christ our Lord.

PSALMS 16.8-end; 23

READINGS YEARS 1 and 2

Old Testament *Job 14.1-14 JB*

Man, born of woman,
has a short life yet has his fill of sorrow.
He blossoms, and he withers, like a flower;
fleeting as a shadow, transient.
And is this what you deign to turn your gaze on,
him that you would bring before you to be judged?

Who can bring the clean out of the unclean?
No man alive!
Since man's days are measured out,
since his tale of months depends on you,
since you assign him bounds he cannot pass,
turn your eyes from him, leave him alone,
like a hired drudge, to finish his day.
There is always hope for a tree:
when felled, it can start its life again;
its shoots continue to sprout.
Its roots may be decayed in the earth,
its stump withering in the soil,
but let it scent the water, and it buds,
and puts out branches like a plant new set.
But man? He dies, and lifeless he remains;
man breathes his last, and then where is he?
The waters of the seas may disappear,
all the rivers may run dry or drain away;
but man, once in his resting place, will never rise again.
The heavens will wear away before he wakes,
before he rises from his sleep.

If only you would hide me in Sheol,
and shelter me there until your anger is past,
fixing a certain day for calling me to mind—
for once a man is dead can he come back to life?—
day after day of my service I would wait
for my relief to come.

New Testament *1 Peter 3.17-end NEB*

It is better to suffer for well-doing, if such should be the will
of God, than for doing wrong. For Christ also died for our
sins once and for all. He, the just, suffered for the unjust, to
bring us to God.

In the body he was put to death; in the spirit he was brought
to life. And in the spirit he went and made his proclamation
to the imprisoned spirits. They had refused obedience long
ago, while God waited patiently in the days of Noah and the
building of the ark, and in the ark a few persons, eight in all,
were brought to safety through the water. This water

prefigured the water of baptism through which you are now brought to safety. Baptism is not the washing away of bodily pollution, but the appeal made to God by a good conscience; and it brings salvation through the resurrection of Jesus Christ, who entered heaven after receiving the submission of angelic authorities and powers, and is now at the right hand of God.

Gospel *Matthew 27.57-end NEB*

When evening fell, there came a man of Arimathaea, Joseph by name, who was a man of means, and had himself become a disciple of Jesus. He approached Pilate, and asked for the body of Jesus; and Pilate gave orders that he should have it. Joseph took the body, wrapped it in a clean linen sheet, and laid it in his own unused tomb, which he had cut out of the rock; he then rolled a large stone against the entrance, and went away. Mary of Magdala was there, and the other Mary, sitting opposite the grave.

Next day, the morning after that Friday, the chief priests and the Pharisees came in a body to Pilate. 'Your Excellency,' they said, 'we recall how that imposter said while he was still alive, "I am to be raised again after three days." So will you give orders for the grave to be made secure until the third day? Otherwise his disciples may come, steal the body, and then tell the people that he has been raised from the dead; and the final deception will be worse than the first.' 'You may have your guard,' said Pilate; 'go and make it secure as best you can.' So they went and made the grave secure; they sealed the stone, and left the guard in charge.

or *John 2.18-22 NEB*

The Jews challenged Jesus: 'What sign', they asked, 'can you show as authority for your action?' 'Destroy this temple,' Jesus replied, 'and in three days I will raise it again.' They said, 'It has taken forty-six years to build this temple. Are you going to raise it again in three days?' But the temple he was speaking of was his body. After his resurrection his disciples recalled what he had said, and they believed the Scripture and the words that Jesus had spoken.

PROPER PREFACE

Rite A. A Preface of the Resurrection (13) or of Baptism (20) may be said.

POSTCOMMUNION SENTENCE

Jesus said, Destroy this temple and in three days I will raise it up. *John 2.19*

EASTER DAY White or Gold

INTRODUCTORY SENTENCES

Very early in the morning on the first day of the week they came to the tomb, just as the sun was rising. Alleluia!
Mark 16.2 (For use in the early morning)

or

On the first day of the week the disciples went to the tomb, and they found the stone rolled away from the tomb.
Alleluia! *Luke 24.1 (For use during the day)*

or

In the evening of that same day, the first day of the week, Jesus came and stood among the disciples, and said to them: 'Peace be with you!' Alleluia! *John 20.19 (For use in the evening)*

COLLECTS

Lord of all life and power,
who through the mighty resurrection of your Son
overcame the old order of sin and death
to make all things new in him:
grant that we, being dead to sin
and alive to you in Jesus Christ,
may reign with him in glory;
to whom with you and the Holy Spirit
be praise and honour, glory and might,
now and in all eternity.

Almighty God,
who through your only-begotten Son Jesus Christ
overcame death and opened to us
    the gate of everlasting life:
we humbly beseech you that,
as by your special grace going before us
you put into our minds good desires,
so by your continued help
we may bring them to good effect;
through Jesus Christ our Lord,
who is alive and reigns with you and the Holy Spirit,
one God, now and for ever.

PSALMS 118.14-24; 114; Easter Anthems; Te Deum.

READINGS YEARS 1 and 2

Old Testament *Isaiah 12 RSV*

You will say in that day:
'I will give thanks to you, O Lord,
for though you were angry with me,
your anger turned away,
and you comforted me.

'Behold, God is my salvation;
I will trust, and will not be afraid;
for the Lord God is my strength and my song,
and he has become my salvation.'

With joy you will draw water from the wells of salvation.
And you will say in that day:
'Give thanks to the Lord,
call upon his name;
make known his deeds among the nations,
proclaim that his name is exalted.

'Sing praises to the Lord, for he has done gloriously;
let this be known in all the earth.
Shout, and sing for joy, O inhabitant of Zion,
for great in your midst is the Holy One of Israel.'

or *Exodus 14.15-22 NEB*

The Lord said to Moses, 'What is the meaning of this clamour? Tell the Israelites to strike camp. And you shall raise high your staff, stretch out your hand over the sea and cleave it in two, so that the Israelites can pass through the sea on dry ground. For my part I will make the Egyptians obstinate and they will come after you; thus will I win glory for myself at the expense of Pharaoh and his army, chariots and cavalry all together. The Egyptians will know that I am the Lord when I win glory for myself at the expense of their Pharaoh, his chariots and cavalry.'

The angel of God, who had kept in front of the Israelites, moved away to the rear. The pillar of cloud moved from the front and took its place behind them and so came between the Egyptians and the Israelites. And the cloud brought on darkness and early nightfall, so that contact was lost throughout the night.

Then Moses stretched out his hand over the sea, and the Lord drove the sea away all night with a strong east wind and turned the sea-bed into dry land. The waters were torn apart, and the Israelites went through the sea on the dry ground, while the waters made a wall for them to right and to left.

or *Isaiah 43.16-21 NEB*

Thus says the Lord,
who opened a way in the sea
and a path through mighty waters,
who drew on chariot and horse to their destruction,
a whole army, men of valour;
there they lay, never to rise again;
they were crushed, snuffed out like a wick:
Cease to dwell on days gone by
and to brood over past history.
Here and now I will do a new thing;
this moment it will break from the bud.
Can you not perceive it?
I will make a way even through the wilderness
and paths in the barren desert;

the wild beasts shall do me honour,
the wolf and the ostrich;
for I will provide water in the wilderness
and rivers in the barren desert,
where my chosen people may drink.
I have formed this people for myself
and they shall proclaim my praises.

New Testament *Revelation 1.10-18 RSV*

I was in the Spirit on the Lord's day, and I heard behind me a loud voice like a trumpet saying, 'Write what you see in a book and send it to the seven churches, to Ephesus and to Smyrna and to Pergamum and to Thyatira and to Sardis and to Philadelphia and to Laodicea.'

Then I turned to see the voice that was speaking to me, and on turning I saw seven golden lampstands, and in the midst of the lampstands one like a son of man, clothed with a long robe and with a golden girdle round his breast; his head and his hair were white as white wool, white as snow; his eyes were like a flame of fire, his feet were like burnished bronze, refined as in a furnace, and his voice was like the sound of many waters; in his right hand he held seven stars, from his mouth issued a sharp two-edged sword, and his face was like the sun shining in full strength.

When I saw him, I fell at his feet as though dead. But he laid his right hand upon me, saying, 'Fear not, I am the first and the last, and the living one; I died, and behold I am alive for evermore, and I have the keys of Death and Hades.'

or *1 Corinthians 15.12-20 NEB*

If this is what we proclaim, that Christ was raised from the dead, how can some of you say there is no resurrection of the dead? If there be no resurrection, then Christ was not raised; and if Christ was not raised, then our gospel is null and void, and so is your faith; and we turn out to be lying witnesses for God, because we bore witness that he raised Christ to life, whereas, if the dead are not raised, he did not raise him. For if the dead are not raised, it follows that Christ was not raised; and if Christ was not raised, your faith has nothing in it and you are still in your old state of sin. It follows also that those who have died within Christ's fellowship are utterly lost. If it is for this life only that Christ has given us hope, we of all men are most to be pitied.

But the truth is, Christ was raised to life—the firstfruits of the harvest of the dead.

or *Colossians 3.1-11 RSV*

If you have been raised with Christ, seek the things that are above, where Christ is, seated at the right hand of God. Set your minds on things that are above, not on things that are on earth. For you have died, and your life is hid with Christ in God. When Christ who is our life appears, then you also will appear with him in glory.

Put to death therefore what is earthly in you: immorality, impurity, passion, evil desire, and covetousness, which is idolatry. On account of these the wrath of God is coming. In these you once walked, when you lived in them. But now put them all away: anger, wrath, malice, slander, and foul talk from your mouth. Do not lie to one another, seeing that you have put off the old nature with its practices and have put on the new nature, which is being renewed in knowledge after the image of its creator. Here there cannot be Greek and Jew, circumcised and uncircumcised, barbarian, Scythian, slave, free man, but Christ is all, and in all.

Gospel *Matthew 28.1-10 NEB*

The Sabbath was over, and it was about daybreak on Sunday, when Mary of Magdala and the other Mary came to look at the grave. Suddenly there was a violent earthquake; an angel of the Lord descended from heaven; he came to the stone and rolled it away, and sat himself down on it. His face shone like lightning; his garments were white as snow. At the sight of him the guards shook with fear and lay like the dead.

The angel then addressed the women: 'You', he said, 'have nothing to fear. I know you are looking for Jesus who was

crucified. He is not here; he has been raised again, as he said
he would be. Come and see the place where he was laid, and
then go quickly and tell his disciples: ''He has been raised
from the dead and is going on before you into Galilee; there
you will see him.'' That is what I had to tell you.'

They hurried away from the tomb in awe and great joy, and
ran to tell the disciples. Suddenly Jesus was there in their
path. He gave them his greeting, and they came up and
clasped his feet, falling prostrate before him. Then Jesus said
to them, 'Do not be afraid. Go and take word to my brothers
that they are to leave for Galilee. They will see me there.'

or *John 20.1-10 (or -18) RSV*

On the first day of the week Mary Magdalen came to the
tomb early, while it was still dark, and saw that the stone had
been taken away from the tomb. So she ran, and went to
Simon Peter and the other disciple, the one whom Jesus
loved, and said to them, 'They have taken the Lord out of the
tomb, and we do not know where they have laid him.' Peter
then came out with the other disciple, and they went toward
the tomb. They both ran, but the other disciple outran Peter
and reached the tomb first; and stooping to look in, he saw
the linen cloths lying there, but he did not go in. Then Simon
Peter came, following him, and he went into the tomb; he
saw the linen cloths lying, and the napkin, which had been
on his head, not lying with the linen cloths but rolled up in a
place by itself. Then the other disciple, who reached the
tomb first, also went in, and he saw and believed; for as yet
they did not know the scripture, that he must rise from the
dead. Then the disciples went back to their homes.

(But Mary stood weeping outside the tomb, and as she wept
she stooped to look into the tomb; and she saw two angels in
white, sitting where the body of Jesus had lain, one at the
head and one at the feet. They said to her, 'Woman, why are
you weeping?' She said to them, 'Because they have taken
away my Lord, and I do not know where they have laid him.'
Saying this, she turned round and saw Jesus standing, but
she did not know that it was Jesus. Jesus said to her,
'Woman, why are you weeping? Whom do you seek?'

Supposing him to be the gardener, she said to him, 'Sir, if you have carried him away, tell me where you have laid him, and I will take him away.' Jesus said to her, 'Mary.' She turned and said to him in Hebrew, 'Rabboni!' (which means Teacher). Jesus said to her, 'Do not hold me, for I have not yet ascended to the Father; but go to my brethren and say to them, I am ascending to my Father and your Father, to my God and your God.' Mary Magdalen went and said to the disciples, 'I have seen the Lord'; and she told them that he had said these things to her.)

or *Mark 16.1-8 NEB*

When the Sabbath was over, Mary of Magdala, Mary the mother of James, and Salome bought aromatic oils intending to go and anoint Jesus; and very early on the Sunday morning, just after sunrise, they came to the tomb. They were wondering among themselves who would roll away the stone for them from the entrance to the tomb, when they looked up and saw that the stone, huge as it was, had been rolled back already. They went into the tomb, where they saw a youth sitting on the right-hand side, wearing a white robe; and they were dumbfounded. But he said to them, 'Fear nothing; you are looking for Jesus of Nazareth, who was crucified. He has been raised again; he is not here; look, there is the place where they laid him. But go and give this message to his disciples and Peter: "He is going on before you into Galilee; there you will see him, as he told you."' Then they went out and ran away from the tomb, beside themselves with terror. They said nothing to anybody, for they were afraid.

PROPER PREFACE

Rite A. A Preface of the Resurrection (13) is said.
Rite B. The Preface of Easter is said.

POSTCOMMUNION SENTENCES

Christ our Passover has been sacrificed for us: therefore let us keep the feast with the unleavened bread of sincerity and truth. Alleluia! *1 Corinthians 5.7, 8*

or

The disciples were filled with joy when they knew the Lord;
and he said to them again: Peace be with you! Alleluia!
John 20.20, 21

MONDAY IN EASTER WEEK   White or Gold

INTRODUCTORY SENTENCE

It was necessary that Christ should suffer these things, and
so enter into his glory. Alleluia! *Luke 24.26*

COLLECTS

Lord of all life and power,
who through the mighty resurrection of your Son
overcame the old order of sin and death
to make all things new in him:
grant that we, being dead to sin
and alive to you in Jesus Christ,
may reign with him in glory;
to whom with you and the Holy Spirit
be praise and honour, glory and might,
now and in all eternity.

Almighty God,
who through your only-begotten Son Jesus Christ
overcame death and opened to us
    the gate of everlasting life:
we humbly beseech you that,
as by your special grace going before us
you put into our minds good desires,
so by your continued help
we may bring them to good effect;
through Jesus Christ our Lord,
who is alive and reigns with you and the Holy Spirit,
one God, now and for ever.

PSALMS Easter Anthems; Te Deum (part 2).

READINGS YEARS 1 and 2

Old Testament *Isaiah 42.10-16 RSV*

Sing to the Lord a new song,
his praise from the end of the earth!
Let the sea roar and all that fills it,
the coastlands and their inhabitants.
Let the desert and its cities lift up their voice,
the villages that Kedar inhabits;
let the inhabitants of Sela sing for joy,
let them shout from the top of the mountains.
Let them give glory to the Lord,
and declare his praise in the coastlands.
The Lord goes forth like a mighty man,
like a man of war he stirs up his fury;
he cries out, he shouts aloud,
he shows himself mighty against his foes.

For a long time I have held my peace,
I have kept still and restrained myself;
now I will cry out like a woman in travail,
I will gasp and pant.
I will lay waste mountains and hills,
and dry up all their herbage;
I will turn the rivers into islands,
and dry up the pools.
And I will lead the blind
in a way that they know not,
in paths that they have not known
I will guide them.
I will turn the darkness before them into light,
the rough places into level ground.
These are the things I will do,
and I will not forsake them.

New Testament *1 Peter 1.1-12 NEB*

From Peter, apostle of Jesus Christ, to those of God's
scattered people who lodge for a while in Pontus, Galatia,
Cappadocia, Asia, and Bithynia—chosen of old in the
purpose of God the Father, hallowed to his service by the

Spirit, and consecrated with the sprinkled blood of Jesus Christ.

Grace and peace to you in fullest measure.

Praise be to the God and Father of our Lord Jesus Christ, who in his great mercy gave us new birth into a living hope by the resurrection of Jesus Christ from the dead! The inheritance to which we are born is one that nothing can destroy or spoil or wither. It is kept for you in heaven, and you, because you put your faith in God, are under the protection of his power until salvation comes—the salvation which is even now in readiness and will be revealed at the end of time.

This is cause for great joy, even though now you smart for a little while, if need be, under trials of many kinds. Even gold passes through the assayer's fire, and more precious than perishable gold is faith which has stood the test. These trials come so that your faith may prove itself worthy of all praise, glory, and honour when Jesus Christ is revealed.

You have not seen him, yet you love him; and trusting in him now without seeing him, you are transported with a joy too great for words, while you reap the harvest of your faith, that is, salvation for your souls. This salvation was the theme which the prophets pondered and explored, those who prophesied about the grace of God awaiting you. They tried to find out what was the time, and what the circumstances, to which the spirit of Christ in them pointed, foretelling the sufferings in store for Christ and the splendours to follow; and it was disclosed to them that the matter they treated of was not for their time but for yours. And now it has been openly announced to you through preachers who brought you the Gospel in the power of the Holy Spirit sent from heaven. These are things that angels long to see into.

Gospel *Luke 24.13-35 JB*

That very same day, two of the disciples were on their way to a village called Emmaus, seven miles from Jerusalem, and they were talking together about all that had happened. Now as they talked this over, Jesus himself came up and walked by their side; but something prevented them from recognizing him. He said to them, 'What matters are you discussing as you walk along?' They stopped short, their faces downcast.

Then one of them, called Cleopas, answered him, 'You must be the only person staying in Jerusalem who does not know the things that have been happening there these last few days.' 'What things?' he asked. 'All about Jesus of Nazareth', they answered, 'who proved he was a great prophet by the things he said and did in the sight of God and of the whole people; and how our chief priests and our leaders handed him over to be sentenced to death, and had him crucified. Our own hope had been that he would be the one to set Israel free. And this is not all: two whole days have gone by since it all happened; and some women from our group have astounded us: they went to the tomb in the early morning, and when they did not find the body, they came back to tell us they had seen a vision of angels who declared he was alive. Some of our friends went to the tomb and found everything exactly as the women had reported, but of him they saw nothing.'

Then he said to them, 'You foolish men! So slow to believe the full message of the prophets! Was it not ordained that the Christ should suffer and so enter into his glory?' Then, starting with Moses and going through all the prophets, he explained to them the passages throughout the scriptures that were about himself.

When they drew near to the village to which they were going, he made as if to go on; but they pressed him to stay with them. 'It is nearly evening', they said, 'and the day is almost over.' So he went in to stay with them. Now while he was with them at table, he took the bread and said the blessing; then he broke it and handed it to them. And their eyes were opened and they recognized him; but he had vanished from their sight. Then they said to each other, 'Did not our hearts burn within us as he talked to us on the road and explained the scriptures to us?'

They set out that instant and returned to Jerusalem. There they found the Eleven assembled together with their companions, who said to them, Yes, it is true. The Lord has risen and has appeared to Simon.' Then they told their story of what had happened on the road and how they had recognized him at the breaking of bread.

PROPER PREFACE

Rite A. A Preface of the Resurrection (13) is said.
Rite B. The Preface of Easter is said.

POSTCOMMUNION SENTENCE

Christ being raised from the dead will never die again: death no longer has power over him. Alleluia! *Romans 6.9*

TUESDAY IN EASTER WEEK   White or Gold

INTRODUCTORY SENTENCE

Thus it is written, that the Christ should suffer: and on the third day rise from the dead. Alleluia! *Luke 24.46*

COLLECTS

Lord of all life and power,
who through the mighty resurrection of your Son
overcame the old order of sin and death
to make all things new in him:
grant that we, being dead to sin
and alive to you in Jesus Christ,
may reign with him in glory;
to whom with you and the Holy Spirit
be praise and honour, glory and might,
now and in all eternity.

Almighty God,
who through your only-begotten Son Jesus Christ
overcame death and opened to us
    the gate of everlasting life:
we humbly beseech you that,
as by your special grace going before us
you put into our minds good desires,

so by your continued help
we may bring them to good effect;
through Jesus Christ our Lord,
who is alive and reigns with you and the Holy Spirit,
one God, now and for ever.

PSALMS 16.8-end; 30

READINGS YEARS 1 and 2

Old Testament *Micah 7.7-end TEV*

I will watch for the Lord; I will wait confidently for God, who
will save me. My God will hear me.

Our enemies have no reason to gloat over us. We have
fallen, but we will rise again. We are in darkness now, but
the Lord will give us light. We have sinned against the Lord,
so now we must endure his anger for a while. But in the end
he will defend us and right the wrongs that have been done
to us. He will bring us out to the light; we will live to see him
save us. Then our enemies will see this and be disgraced—
the same enemies who taunted us by asking, 'Where is the
Lord your God?' We will see them defeated, trampled down
like mud in the streets.

People of Jerusalem, the time to rebuild the city walls is
coming. At that time your territory will be enlarged. Your
people will return to you from everywhere—from Assyria in
the east, from Egypt in the south, from the region of the
Euphrates, from distant seas and far-off mountains. But the
earth will become a desert because of the wickedness of
those who live on it.

Be a shepherd to your people, Lord, the people you have
chosen. Although they live apart in the wilderness, there is
fertile land around them. Let them go and feed in the rich
pastures of Bashan and Gilead, as they did long ago.

Work miracles for us, Lord, as you did in the days when you
brought us out of Egypt. The nations will see this and be
frustrated in spite of all their strength. In dismay they will

close their mouths and cover their ears. They will crawl in the dust like snakes; they will come from their fortresses, trembling and afraid. They will turn in fear to the Lord our God.

There is no other god like you, O Lord; you forgive the sins of your people who have survived. You do not stay angry for ever, but you take pleasure in showing us your constant love. You will be merciful to us once again. You will trample our sins underfoot and send them to the bottom of the sea! You will show your faithfulness and constant love to your people, the descendants of Abraham and of Jacob, as you promised our ancestors long ago.

New Testament *1 Peter 1.13-end NEB*

You must be mentally stripped for action, perfectly self-controlled. Fix your hopes on the gift of grace which is to be yours when Jesus Christ is revealed. As obedient children, do not let your characters be shaped any longer by the desires you cherished in your days of ignorance. The One who called you is holy; like him, be holy in all your behaviour, because Scripture says, 'You shall be holy, for I am holy.'

If you say 'our Father' to the One who judges every man impartially on the record of his deeds, you must stand in awe of him while you live out your time on earth. Well you know that it was no perishable stuff, like gold or silver, that bought your freedom from the empty folly of your traditional ways. The price was paid in precious blood, as it were of a lamb without mark or blemish—the blood of Christ. Predestined before the foundation of the world, he was made manifest in this last period of time for your sake. Through him you have come to trust in God who raised him from the dead and gave him glory, and so your faith and hope are fixed on God.

Now that by obedience to the truth you have purified your souls until you feel sincere affection towards your brother Christians, love one another whole-heartedly with all your strength. You have been born anew, not of mortal parentage

but of immortal, through the living and enduring word of
God. For (as Scripture says)

'All mortals are like grass;
all their splendour like the flower of the field;
the grass withers, the flower falls;
but the word of the Lord endures for evermore.'

And this 'word' is the word of the Gospel preached to you.

Gospel *Luke 24.36-49 JB*

Jesus himself stood among the disciples and said to them,
'Peace be with you!' In a state of alarm and fright, they
thought they were seeing a ghost. But he said, 'Why are you
so agitated, and why are these doubts rising in your hearts?
Look at my hands and feet; yes, it is I indeed. Touch me and
see for yourselves; a ghost has no flesh and bones as you can
see I have.' And as he said this he showed them his hands
and feet. Their joy was so great that they still could not
believe it, and they stood there dumbfounded; so he said to
them, 'Have you anything here to eat?' And they offered
him a piece of grilled fish, which he took and ate before
their eyes.

Then he told them, 'That is what I meant when I said, while I
was still with you, that everything written about me in the
law of Moses, in the Prophets and in the Psalms, has to be
fulfilled.' He then opened their minds to understand the
scriptures, and he said to them, 'So you see how it is written
that the Christ would suffer and on the third day rise from
the dead, and that, in his name, repentance for the
forgiveness of sins would be preached to all the nations,
beginning from Jerusalem. You are witnesses to this.

'And now I am sending down to you what the Father has
promised. Stay in the city then, until you are clothed with
the power from on high.'

PROPER PREFACE

Rite A. A Preface of the Resurrection (13) is said.
Rite B. The Preface of Easter is said.

POSTCOMMUNION SENTENCE

The disciples knew the Lord Jesus in the breaking of the bread. Alleluia! *Luke 24.35*

WEDNESDAY IN EASTER WEEK   White or Gold

INTRODUCTORY SENTENCE

These things are written, that you may believe that Jesus is the Christ, the Son of God. Alleluia! *John 20.31*

COLLECTS

Lord of all life and power,
who through the mighty resurrection of your Son
overcame the old order of sin and death
to make all things new in him:
grant that we, being dead to sin
and alive to you in Jesus Christ,
may reign with him in glory;
to whom with you and the Holy Spirit
be praise and honour, glory and might,
now and in all eternity.

Almighty God,
who through your only-begotten Son Jesus Christ
overcame death and opened to us
    the gate of everlasting life:
we humbly beseech you that,
as by your special grace going before us
you put into our minds good desires,
so by your continued help
we may bring them to good effect;
through Jesus Christ our Lord,
who is alive and reigns with you and the Holy Spirit,
one God, now and for ever.

PSALMS 111; 112

READINGS YEARS 1 and 2

Old Testament *1 Kings 17.17-end TEV*

The son of the widow in Zarephath fell ill; he got worse and worse, and finally he died. She said to Elijah, 'Man of God, why did you do this to me? Did you come here to remind God of my sins and so cause my son's death?'

'Give the boy to me,' Elijah said. He took the boy from her arms, carried him upstairs to the room where he was staying, and laid him on the bed. Then he prayed aloud, 'O Lord my God, why have you done such a terrible thing to this widow? She has been kind enough to take care of me, and now you kill her son!' Then Elijah stretched himself out on the boy three times and prayed, 'O Lord my God, restore this child to life!' The Lord answered Elijah's prayer; the child started breathing again and revived.

Elijah took the boy back downstairs to his mother and said to her, 'Look, your son is alive!'

She answered, 'Now I know that you are a man of God and that the Lord really speaks through you!'

New Testament *1 Peter 2.1-10 NEB*

Away with all malice and deceit, away with all pretence and jealousy and recrimination of every kind! Like the new-born infants you are, you must crave for pure milk (spiritual milk, I mean), so that you may thrive upon it to your soul's health. Surely you have tasted that the Lord is good.

So come to him, our living Stone—the stone rejected by men but choice and precious in the sight of God. Come, and let yourselves be built, as living stones, into a spiritual temple; become a holy priesthood, to offer spiritual sacrifices acceptable to God through Jesus Christ. For it stands written:

'I lay in Zion a choice corner-stone of great worth.
The man who has faith in it will not be put to shame.'

The great worth of which it speaks is for you who have faith. For those who have no faith, the stone which the builders rejected has become not only the corner-stone, but also 'a stone to trip over, a rock to stumble against'. They fall when they disbelieve the Word. Such was their appointed lot!

But you are a chosen race, a royal priesthood, a dedicated nation, and a people claimed by God for his own, to proclaim the triumphs of him who has called you out of darkness into his marvellous light. You are now the people of God, who once were not his people; outside his mercy once, you have now received his mercy.

Gospel *John 20.24-end RSV*

Now Thomas, one of the twelve, called the Twin, was not with them when Jesus came. So the other disciples told him, 'We have seen the Lord.' But he said to them, 'Unless I see in his hands the print of the nails, and place my finger in the mark of the nails, and place my hand in his side, I will not believe.'

Eight days later, his disciples were again in the house, and Thomas was with them. The doors were shut, but Jesus came and stood among them, and said, 'Peace be with you.' Then he said to Thomas, 'Put your finger here, and see my hands; and put out your hand, and place it in my side; do not be faithless, but believing.' Thomas answered him, 'My Lord and my God!' Jesus said to him, 'Have you believed because you have seen me? Blessed are those who have not seen and yet believe.'

Now Jesus did many other signs in the presence of the disciples, which are not written in this book; but these are written that you may believe that Jesus is the Christ, the Son of God, and that believing you may have life in his name.

PROPER PREFACE

Rite A. A Preface of the Resurrection (13) is said.
Rite B. The Preface of Easter is said.

POSTCOMMUNION SENTENCE

You are a people God claims as his own: to praise him who called you out of darkness into his marvellous light. Alleluia!
1 Peter 2.9

THURSDAY IN EASTER WEEK   White or Gold

INTRODUCTORY SENTENCE

Jesus revealed himself to the disciples by the Sea of Tiberias.
Alleluia! *John 21.1*

COLLECTS

Lord of all life and power,
who through the mighty resurrection of your Son
overcame the old order of sin and death
to make all things new in him:
grant that we, being dead to sin
and alive to you in Jesus Christ,
may reign with him in glory;
to whom with you and the Holy Spirit
be praise and honour, glory and might,
now and in all eternity.

Almighty God,
who through your only-begotten Son Jesus Christ
overcame death and opened to us
    the gate of everlasting life:
we humbly beseech you that,
as by your special grace going before us
you put into our minds good desires,
so by your continued help
we may bring them to good effect;
through Jesus Christ our Lord,
who is alive and reigns with you and the Holy Spirit,
one God, now and for ever.

PSALMS 113; 114

READINGS YEARS 1 and 2

Old Testament *Jeremiah 31.1-14 RSV*

'At that time, says the Lord, I will be the God of all the
families of Israel, and they shall be my people.'

Thus says the Lord,
'The people who survived the sword
found grace in the wilderness;
when Israel sought for rest,
the Lord appeared to him from afar.
I have loved you with an everlasting love;
therefore I have continued my faithfulness to you.
Again I will build you, and you shall be built,
O virgin Israel!
Again you shall adorn yourself with timbrels,
and shall go forth in the dance of the merrymakers.
Again you shall plant vineyards
upon the mountains of Samaria;
the planters shall plant,
and shall enjoy the fruit.
For there shall be a day when watchmen will call
in the hill country of Ephraim:
"Arise, and let us go up to Zion,
to the Lord our God."'

For thus says the Lord,
'Sing aloud with gladness for Jacob,
and raise shouts for the chief of the nations;
proclaim, give praise, and say,
"The Lord has saved his people,
the remnant of Israel."
Behold, I will bring them from the north country,
and gather them from the farthest parts of the earth,
among them the blind and the lame,
the woman with child and her who is in travail, together;
a great company, they shall return here.
With weeping they shall come,
and with consolations I will lead them back,
I will make them walk by brooks of water,
in a straight path in which they shall not stumble;
for I am a father to Israel,
and Ephraim is my first born.

'Hear the word of the Lord, O nations,
and declare it in the coastlands afar off;

say, "He who scattered Israel will gather him,
and will keep him as a shepherd keeps his flock."
For the Lord has ransomed Jacob,
and has redeemed him from hands too strong for him.
They shall come and sing aloud on the height of Zion,
and they shall be radiant over the goodness of the Lord,
over the grain, the wine, and the oil,
and over the young of the flock and the herd;
their life shall be like a watered garden,
and they shall languish no more.
Then shall the maidens rejoice in the dance,
and the young men and the old shall be merry.
I will turn their mourning into joy,
I will comfort them, and give them gladness for sorrow.
I will feast the soul of the priests with abundance,
and my people shall be satisfied with my goodness,
says the Lord.'

New Testament *1 Peter 2.11-end NEB*

Dear friends, I beg you, as aliens in a foreign land, to abstain
from the lusts of the flesh which are at war with the soul. Let
all your behaviour be such as even pagans can recognize as
good, and then, whereas they malign you as criminals now,
they will come to see for themselves that you live good lives,
and will give glory to God on the day when he comes to
hold assize.

Submit yourselves to every human institution for the sake of
the Lord, whether to the sovereign as supreme, or to the
governor as his deputy for the punishment of criminals and
the commendation of those who do right. For it is the will of
God that by your good conduct you should put ignorance
and stupidity to silence.

Live as free men; not however as though your freedom were
there to provide a screen for wrongdoing, but as slaves in
God's service. Give due honour to everyone: love to the
brotherhood, reverence to God, honour to the sovereign.
Servants, accept the authority of your masters with all due
submission, not only when they are kind and considerate,

but even when they are perverse. For it is a fine thing if a man endure the pain of undeserved suffering because God is in his thoughts. What credit is there in fortitude when you have done wrong and are beaten for it? But when you have behaved well and suffer for it, your fortitude is a fine thing in the sight of God. To that you were called, because Christ suffered on your behalf, and thereby left you an example; it is for you to follow in his steps. He committed no sin, he was convicted of no falsehood; when he was abused he did not retort with abuse, when he suffered he uttered no threats, but committed his cause to the One who judges justly. In his own person he carried our sins to the gibbet, so that we might cease to live for sin and begin to live for righteousness. By his wounds you have been healed. You were straying like sheep, but now you have turned towards the Shepherd and Guardian of your souls.

Gospel *John 21.1-14 RSV*

Jesus revealed himself again to the disciples by the Sea of Tiberias; and he revealed himself in this way. Simon Peter, Thomas called the Twin, Nathanael of Cana in Galilee, the sons of Zebedee, and two others of his disciples were together. Simon Peter said to them, 'I am going fishing.' They said to him, 'We will go with you.' They went out and got into the boat; but that night they caught nothing.

Just as day was breaking, Jesus stood on the beach; yet the disciples did not know that it was Jesus. Jesus said to them, 'Children, have you any fish?' They answered him, 'No.' He said to them, 'Cast the net on the right side of the boat, and you will find some.' So they cast it, and now they were not able to haul it in, for the quantity of fish. That disciple whom Jesus loved said to Peter, 'It is the Lord!' When Simon Peter heard that it was the Lord, he put on his clothes, for he was stripped for work, and sprang into the sea. But the other disciples came in the boat, dragging the net full of fish, for they were not far from the land, but about a hundred yards off.

When they got out on land, they saw a charcoal fire there,

with fish lying on it, and bread. Jesus said to them, 'Bring some of the fish that you have just caught.' So Simon Peter went aboard and hauled the net ashore, full of large fish, a hundred and fifty-three of them; and although there were so many, the net was not torn. Jesus said to them, 'Come and have breakfast.' Now none of the disciples dared to ask him, 'Who are you?' They knew it was the Lord. Jesus came and took the bread and gave it to them, and so with the fish. This was now the third time that Jesus was revealed to the disciples after he was raised from the dead.

PROPER PREFACE

Rite A. A Preface of the Resurrection (13) is said.
Rite B. The Preface of Easter is said.

POSTCOMMUNION SENTENCE

Jesus said to his disciples, 'Come and eat'; and he took bread, and gave it to them. Alleluia! *John 21.12*

FRIDAY IN EASTER WEEK   White or Gold

INTRODUCTORY SENTENCE

Jesus said, I am the good shepherd, and I know my sheep, and am known by mine. Alleluia! *John 10.14*

COLLECTS

Lord of all life and power,
who through the mighty resurrection of your Son
overcame the old order of sin and death
to make all things new in him:
grant that we, being dead to sin
and alive to you in Jesus Christ,
may reign with him in glory;
to whom with you and the Holy Spirit
be praise and honour, glory and might,
now and in all eternity.

Almighty God,
who through your only-begotten Son Jesus Christ
overcame death and opened to us
    the gate of everlasting life:
we humbly beseech you that,
as by your special grace going before us
you put into our minds good desires,
so by your continued help
we may bring them to good effect;
through Jesus Christ our Lord,
who is alive and reigns with you and the Holy Spirit,
one God, now and for ever.

PSALMS 115; 116.1-9

READINGS YEARS 1 and 2

Old Testament *Ezekiel 37.1-14 JB*

The hand of the Lord was laid on me, and he carried me
away by the spirit of the Lord and set me down in the middle
of a valley, a valley full of bones. He made me walk up and
down among them. There were vast quantities of these
bones on the ground the whole length of the valley; and they
were quite dried up. He said to me, 'Son of man, can these
bones live?' I said, 'You know, Lord God.' He said,
'Prophesy over these bones. Say, "Dry bones, hear the word
of the Lord. The Lord God says this to these bones: I am now
going to make the breath enter you, and you will live. I shall
put sinews on you, I shall make flesh grow on you, I shall
cover you with skin and give you breath, and you will live;
and you will learn that I am the Lord."' I prophesied as I had
been ordered. While I was prophesying, there was a noise, a
sound of clattering; and the bones joined together. I looked,
and saw that they were covered with sinews; flesh was
growing on them and skin was covering them, but there was
no breath in them. He said to me, 'Prophesy to the breath;
prophesy, son of man. Say to the breath, "The Lord God
says this: Come from the four winds, breath; breathe on
these dead; let them live!"' I prophesied as he had ordered
me, and the breath entered them; they came to life again and
stood up on their feet, a great, an immense army.

Then he said, 'Son of man, these bones are the whole House of Israel. They keep saying, "Our bones are dried up, our hope has gone; we are as good as dead." So prophesy. Say to them "The Lord God says this: I am now going to open your graves; I mean to raise you from your graves, my people, and lead you back to the soil of Israel. And you will know that I am the Lord, when I open your graves and raise you from your graves, my people. And I shall put my spirit in you; and you will live, and I shall resettle you on your own soil; and you will know that I, the Lord, have said and done this—it is the Lord God who speaks."'

New Testament *1 Peter 3.1-12 NEB*

You women must accept the authority of your husbands, so that if there are any of them who disbelieve the Gospel they may be won over, without a word being said, by observing the chaste and reverent behaviour of their wives. Your beauty should reside, not in outward adornment—the braiding of the hair, or jewellery, or dress—but in the inmost centre of your being, with its imperishable ornament, a gentle, quiet spirit, which is of high value in the sight of God. Thus it was among God's people in days of old: the women who fixed their hopes on him adorned themselves by submission to their husbands. Such was Sarah, who obeyed Abraham and called him 'my master'. Her children you have now become, if you do good and show no fear.

In the same way, you husbands must conduct your married life with understanding: pay honour to the woman's body, not only because it is weaker, but also because you share together in the grace of God which gives you life. Then your prayers will not be hindered.

To sum up: be one in thought and feeling, all of you; be full of brotherly affection, kindly and humble-minded. Do not repay wrong with wrong, or abuse with abuse; on the contrary, retaliate with blessing, for a blessing is the inheritance to which you yourselves have been called.

'Whoever loves life and would see good days
must restrain his tongue from evil
and his lips from deceit;

must turn from wrong and do good,
seek peace and pursue it.
For the Lord's eyes are turned towards the righteous,
his ears are open to their prayers;
but the Lord's face is set against wrong-doers.'

Gospel *John 21.15-17 RSV*

When they had finished breakfast, Jesus said to Simon
Peter, 'Simon, son of John, do you love me more than these?'
He said to him, 'Yes, Lord; you know that I love you.' He
said to him, 'Feed my lambs.' A second time he said to him,
'Simon, son of John, do you love me?' He said to him, 'Yes,
Lord; you know that I love you.' He said to him, 'Tend my
sheep.' He said to him the third time, 'Simon, son of John,
do you love me?' Peter was grieved because he said to him
the third time, 'Do you love me?' And he said to him, 'Lord,
you know everything; you know that I love you.' Jesus said
to him, 'Feed my sheep.'

PROPER PREFACE

Rite A. A Preface of the Resurrection (13) is said.
Rite B. The Preface of Easter is said.

POSTCOMMUNION SENTENCE

Christ being raised from the dead will never die again: death
no longer has power over him. Alleluia! *Romans 6.9*

SATURDAY IN EASTER WEEK   White or Gold

INTRODUCTORY SENTENCE

Jesus presented himself alive after his passion by many
proofs, appearing to his disciples. Alleluia! *Acts 1.3*

COLLECTS

Lord of all life and power,
who through the mighty resurrection of your Son
overcame the old order of sin and death

to make all things new in him:
grant that we, being dead to sin
and alive to you in Jesus Christ,
may reign with him in glory;
to whom with you and the Holy Spirit
be praise and honour, glory and might,
now and in all eternity.

Almighty God,
who through your only-begotten Son Jesus Christ
overcame death and opened to us
    the gate of everlasting life:
we humbly beseech you that,
as by your special grace going before us
you put into our minds good desires,
so by your continued help
we may bring them to good effect;
through Jesus Christ our Lord,
who is alive and reigns with you and the Holy Spirit,
one God, now and for ever.

PSALMS 118.1-4, 22-27a; 118.14-21

READINGS YEARS 1 and 2

Old Testament *Job 14.1-14 JB*

Man, born of woman,
has a short life yet has his fill of sorrow.
He blossoms, and he withers, like a flower;
fleeting as a shadow, transient.
And is this what you deign to turn your gaze on,
him that you would bring before you to be judged?
Who can bring the clean out of the unclean?
No man alive!
Since man's days are measured out,
since his tale of months depends on you,
since you assign him bounds he cannot pass,
turn your eyes from him, leave him alone,
like a hired drudge, to finish his day.
There is always hope for a tree:

when felled, it can start its life again;
its shoots continue to sprout.
Its roots may be decayed in the earth,
its stump withering in the soil,
but let it scent the water, and it buds,
and puts out branches like a plant new set.
But man? He dies, and lifeless he remains;
man breathes his last, and then where is he?
The waters of the seas may disappear,
all the rivers may run dry or drain away;
but man, once in his resting place, will never rise again.
The heavens will wear away before he wakes,
before he rises from his sleep.

If only you would hide me in Sheol,
and shelter me there until your anger is past,
fixing a certain day for calling me to mind—
for once a man is dead can he come back to life?—
day after day of my service I would wait
for my relief to come.

New Testament *1 Peter 4.1-11 NEB*

Remembering that Christ endured bodily suffering, you
must arm yourselves with a temper of mind like his. When a
man has thus endured bodily suffering he has finished with
sin, and for the rest of his days on earth he may live, not for
the things that men desire, but for what God wills. You had
time enough in the past to do all the things that men want to
do in the pagan world. Then you lived in licence and
debauchery, drunkenness, revelry, and tippling, and the
forbidden worship of idols. Now, when you no longer
plunge with them into all this reckless dissipation, they
cannot understand it, and they vilify you accordingly; but
they shall answer for it to him who stands ready to pass
judgement on the living and the dead. Why was the Gospel
preached to those who are dead? In order that, although in
the body they received the sentence common to men, they
might in the spirit be alive with the life of God.

The end of all things is upon us, so you must lead an ordered and sober life, given to prayer. Above all, keep your love for one another at full strength, because love cancels innumerable sins. Be hospitable to one another without complaining. Whatever gift each of you may have received, use it in service to one another, like good stewards dispensing the grace of God in its varied forms. Are you a speaker? Speak as if you uttered oracles of God. Do you give service? Give it as in the strength which God supplies. In all things so act that the glory may be God's through Jesus Christ; to him belong glory and power for ever and ever. Amen.

Gospel *John* 21.20-end RSV

Peter turned and saw following them the disciple whom Jesus loved, who had lain close to his breast at the supper and had said, 'Lord, who is it that is going to betray you?' When Peter saw him, he said to Jesus, 'Lord, what about this man?' Jesus said to him, 'If it is my will that he remain until I come, what is that to you? Follow me!' The saying spread abroad among the brethren that this disciple was not to die; yet Jesus did not say to him that he was not to die, but, 'If it is my will that he remains until I come, what is that to you?'

This is the disciple who is bearing witness to these things, and who has written these things; and we know that his testimony is true.

But there are also many other things which Jesus did; were every one of them to be written, I suppose that the world itself could not contain the books that would be written.

PROPER PREFACE

Rite A. A Preface of the Resurrection (13) is said.
Rite B. The Preface of Easter is said.

POSTCOMMUNION SENTENCE

All you who have been baptized have been clothed with Christ. Alleluia! *Galatians* 3.27

EASTER 1   White or Gold

INTRODUCTORY SENTENCE YEAR 1

Jesus came and stood among his disciples, and said to them,
'Peace be with you!' Alleluia! *John 20.19*

INTRODUCTORY SENTENCE YEAR 2

Jesus said to his disciples, This is the will of my Father, that
whoever sees the Son and believes in him should have
eternal life, and that I shall raise him up on the last day.
Alleluia! *John 6.40*

COLLECT

Almighty Father,
who in your great mercy made glad the disciples
    with the sight of the risen Lord:
give us such knowledge of his presence with us,
that we may be strengthened and sustained
    by his risen life
and serve you continually in righteousness and truth;
through Jesus Christ our Lord.

PSALMS 145.1-12; 34.1-10

READINGS YEAR 1

Old Testament *Exodus 15.1-11 RSV*

Moses and the people of Israel sang this song to the
Lord, saying,
'I will sing to the Lord, for he has triumphed gloriously;
the horse and his rider he has thrown into the sea.
The Lord is my strength and my song,
and he has become my salvation;
this is my God, and I will praise him,
my father's God, and I will exalt him.
The Lord is a man of war;
the Lord is his name.

'Pharaoh's chariots and his host he cast into the sea;
and his picked officers are sunk in the Red Sea.

The floods cover them;
they went down into the depths like a stone.
Your right hand, O Lord, glorious in power,
your right hand, O Lord, shatters the enemy.
In the greatness of your majesty you overthrow your
    adversaries;
you send forth your fury, it consumes them like stubble.
At the blast of your nostrils the waters piled up,
the floods stood up in a heap;
the deeps congealed in the heart of the sea.
The enemy said, "I will pursue, I will overtake,
I will divide the spoil, my desire shall have its fill of them.
I will draw my sword, my hand shall destroy them."
You did blow with your wind, the sea covered them;
they sank as lead in the mighty waters.

'Who is like you, O Lord, among the gods?
Who is like you, majestic in holiness,
terrible in glorious deeds, doing wonders?'

New Testament *1 Peter 1.3-9 NEB*

Praise be to the God and Father of our Lord Jesus Christ,
who in his great mercy gave us new birth into a living hope
by the resurrection of Jesus Christ from the dead! The
inheritance to which we are born is one that nothing can
destroy or spoil or wither. It is kept for you in heaven, and
you, because you put your faith in God, are under the
protection of his power until salvation comes—the salvation
which is even now in readiness and will be revealed at the
end of time.

This is cause for great joy, even though now you smart for a
little while, if need be, under trials of many kinds. Even gold
passes through the assayer's fire, and more precious than
perishable gold is faith which has stood the test. These trials
come so that your faith may prove itself worthy of all praise,
glory, and honour when Jesus Christ is revealed.

You have not seen him, yet you love him; and trusting in him
now without seeing him, you are transported with a joy too
great for words, while you reap the harvest of your faith,
that is, salvation for your souls.

Gospel *John 20.19-29 RSV*

On the evening of the first day of the week, the doors being shut where the disciples were, for fear of the Jews, Jesus came and stood among them and said to them, 'Peace be with you.' When he had said this, he showed them his hands and his side. Then the disciples were glad when they saw the Lord. Jesus said to them again, 'Peace be with you. As the Father has sent me, even so I send you.' And when he had said this, he breathed on them, and said to them, 'Receive the Holy Spirit. If you forgive the sins of any, they are forgiven; if you retain the sins of any, they are retained.'

Now Thomas, one of the twelve, called the Twin, was not with them when Jesus came. So the other disciples told him, 'We have seen the Lord.' But he said to them, 'Unless I see in his hands the print of the nails, and place my finger in the mark of the nails, and place my hand in his side, I will not believe.'

Eight days later, his disciples were again in the house, and Thomas was with them. The doors were shut, but Jesus came and stood among them, and said, 'Peace be with you.' Then he said to Thomas, 'Put your finger here, and see my hands; and put out your hand, and place it in my side; do not be faithless, but believing.' Thomas answered him, 'My Lord and my God!' Jesus said to him 'Have you believed because you have seen me? Blessed are those who have not seen and yet believe.'

READINGS YEAR 2

Old Testament *Exodus 16.2-15 NEB*

The Israelites complained to Moses and Aaron in the wilderness and said, 'If only we had died at the Lord's hand in Egypt, where we sat round the fleshpots and had plenty of bread to eat! But you have brought us out into this wilderness to let this whole assembly starve to death.' The Lord said to Moses, 'I will rain down bread from heaven for you. Each day the people shall go out and gather a day's supply, so that I can put them to the test and see whether they will follow my instructions or not. But on the sixth day, when they prepare what they bring in, it shall be twice as much as they have gathered on other days.' Moses and Aaron then said to all the Israelites, 'In the evening you will know that it was the Lord who brought you out of Egypt, and in the morning you will see the glory of the Lord, because he has heeded your complaints against him; it is not against us that you bring your complaints; we are nothing.' 'You shall know this', Moses said, 'when the Lord, in answer to your complaints, gives you flesh to eat in the evening, and in the morning bread in plenty. What are we? It is against the Lord that you bring your complaints, and not against us.'

Moses told Aaron to say to the whole community of Israel, 'Come into the presence of the Lord, for he has heeded your complaints.' While Aaron was speaking to the community of the Israelites, they looked towards the wilderness, and there was the glory of the Lord appearing in the cloud. The Lord spoke to Moses and said, 'I have heard the complaints of the Israelites. Say to them, "Between dusk and dark you will have flesh to eat and in the morning bread in plenty. You shall know that I the Lord am your God."'

That evening a flock of quails flew in and settled all over the camp, and in the morning a fall of dew lay all around it. When the dew had gone, there in the wilderness, fine flakes appeared, fine as hoar-frost on the ground. When the Israelites saw it, they said to one another, 'What is that?', because they did not know what it was. Moses said to them, 'That is the bread which the Lord has given you to eat.'

New Testament *1 Corinthians 15.53-end NEB*

This perishable being must be clothed with the imperishable, and what is mortal must be clothed with immortality. And when our mortality has been clothed with immortality, then the saying of Scripture will come true: 'Death is swallowed up; victory is won!' 'O Death, where is your victory? O Death, where is your sting?' The sting of death is sin, and sin gains its power from the law; but, God be praised, he gives us the victory through our Lord Jesus Christ.

Therefore, my beloved brothers, stand firm and
immoveable, and work for the Lord always, work without
limit, since you know that in the Lord your labour cannot be lost.

Gospel *John 6.32-40 JB*

Jesus said,
'I tell you most solemnly,
it was not Moses who gave you bread from heaven,
it is my Father who gives you the bread from heaven,
the true bread;
for the bread of God
is that which comes down from heaven
and gives life to the world.'

'Sir,' the people said, 'give us that bread always.'

Jesus answered,
'I am the bread of life.
He who comes to me will never be hungry;
he who believes in me will never thirst.
But, as I have told you,
you can see me and still you do not believe.
All that the Father gives me will come to me,
and whoever comes to me
I shall not turn him away;
because I have come from heaven,
not to do my own will,
but to do the will of the one who sent me.
Now the will of him who sent me
is that I should lose nothing
of all that he has given to me,
and that I should raise it up on the last day.
Yes, it is my Father's will
that whoever sees the Son and believes in him
shall have eternal life,
and that I shall raise him up on the last day.'

PROPER PREFACE

Rite A. A Preface of the Resurrection (13) is said.
A Preface of the Resurrection (13), (14), (15), or (16) is said on
weekdays until Ascension Day.

Rite B. The Preface of Easter is said daily until Ascension Day.

POSTCOMMUNION SENTENCE YEAR 1

Like new-born babes, you should thirst for milk, on which your spirit can grow to strength. Alleluia! *1 Peter 2.2*

POSTCOMMUNION SENTENCE YEAR 2

I am the bread of life. He who comes to me will never be hungry, he who believes in me will never thirst. Alleluia! *John 6.35*

EASTER 2   White

INTRODUCTORY SENTENCE YEAR 1

Beginning with Moses and all the prophets, Jesus expounded to the disciples all that was written about him in the scriptures. (Alleluia!) *Luke 24.27*

INTRODUCTORY SENTENCE YEAR 2

Jesus said, I am the good shepherd, and I know my sheep, and am known by mine. (Alleluia!) *John 10.14*

COLLECT

God of peace,
who brought again from the dead
    our Lord Jesus Christ,
that great shepherd of the sheep,
by the blood of the eternal covenant:
make us perfect in every good work to do your will,
and work in us that which is well-pleasing
    in your sight;
through Jesus Christ our Lord.

PSALMS 111; 23

READINGS YEAR 1

Old Testament *Isaiah 25.6-9 NEB*

On this mountain the Lord of Hosts will prepare
a banquet of rich fare for all the peoples,
a banquet of wines well matured and richest fare,
well-matured wines strained clear.
On this mountain the Lord will swallow up
that veil that shrouds all the peoples,
the pall thrown over all the nations;
he will swallow up death for ever.
Then the Lord God will wipe away the tears from every face
and remove the reproach of his people from the whole earth.
The Lord has spoken.

On that day men will say,
See, this is our God
for whom we have waited to deliver us;
this is the Lord for whom we have waited;
let us rejoice and exult in his deliverance.

New Testament *Revelation 19.6-9 NEB*

I heard what sounded like a vast crowd, like the noise of
rushing water and deep roars of thunder, and they cried:

'Alleluia! The Lord our God, sovereign over all, has entered
on his reign! Exult and shout for joy and do him homage, for
the wedding-day of the Lamb has come! His bride has made
herself ready, and for her dress she has been given fine
linen, clean and shining.'

(Now the fine linen signifies the righteous deeds of God's
people.)

Then the angel said to me, 'Write this: "Happy are those
who are invited to the wedding-supper of the Lamb!"' And
he added, 'These are the very words of God.'

Gospel *Luke 24.13-35 JB*

That very same day, two of the disciples were on their way to
a village called Emmaus, seven miles from Jerusalem, and
they were talking together about all that had happened.

Now as they talked this over, Jesus himself came up and walked by their side; but something prevented them from recognizing him. He said to them, 'What matters are you discussing as you walk along?' They stopped short, their faces downcast.

Then one of them, called Cleopas, answered him, 'You must be the only person staying in Jerusalem who does not know the things that have been happening there these last few days.' 'What things?' he asked. 'All about Jesus of Nazareth', they answered, 'who proved he was a great prophet by the things he said and did in the sight of God and of the whole people; and how our chief priests and our leaders handed him over to be sentenced to death, and had him crucified. Our own hope had been that he would be the one to set Israel free. And this is not all: two whole days have gone by since it all happened; and some women from our group have astounded us: they went to the tomb in the early morning, and when they did not find the body, they came back to tell us they had seen a vision of angels who declared he was alive. Some of our friends went to the tomb and found everything exactly as the women had reported, but of him they saw nothing.'

Then he said to them, 'You foolish men! So slow to believe the full message of the prophets! Was it not ordained that the Christ should suffer and so enter into his glory?' Then, starting with Moses and going through all the prophets, he explained to them the passages throughout the scriptures that were about himself.

When they drew near to the village to which they were going, he made as if to go on; but they pressed him to stay with them. 'It is nearly evening', they said, 'and the day is almost over.' So he went in to stay with them. Now while he was with them at table, he took the bread and said the blessing; then he broke it and handed it to them. And their eyes were opened and they recognized him; but he had vanished from their sight. Then they said to each other, 'Did not our hearts burn within us as he talked to us on the road and explained the scriptures to us?'

They set out that instant and returned to Jerusalem. There they found the Eleven assembled together with their companions, who said to them, 'Yes, it is true. The Lord has risen and has appeared to Simon.' Then they told their story of what had happened on the road and how they had recognized him at the breaking of bread.

READINGS YEAR 2

Old Testament *Ezekiel 34.7-16 NEB*

You shepherds, hear the words of the Lord. As surely as I live, says the Lord God, because my sheep are ravaged by wild beasts and have become their prey for lack of a shepherd, because my shepherds have not asked after the sheep but have cared only for themselves and not for the sheep—therefore, you shepherds, hear the words of the Lord. These are the words of the Lord God: I am against the shepherds and will demand my sheep from them. I will dismiss those shepherds: they shall care only for themselves no longer; I will rescue my sheep from their jaws, and they shall feed on them no more.

For these are the words of the Lord God: Now I myself will ask after my sheep and go in search of them. As a shepherd goes in search of his sheep when his flock is dispersed all around him, so I will go in search of my sheep and rescue them, no matter where they were scattered in dark and cloudy days. I will bring them out from every nation, gather them in from other lands, and lead them home to their own soil. I will graze them on the mountains of Israel, by her streams and in all her green fields. I will feed them on good grazing-ground, and their pasture shall be the high mountains of Israel. There they will rest, there in good pasture, and find rich grazing on the mountains of Israel. I myself will tend my flock, I myself pen them in their fold, says the Lord God. I will search for the lost, recover the straggler, bandage the hurt, strengthen the sick, leave the healthy and strong to play, and give them their proper food.

New Testament *1 Peter 5.1-11 NEB*

I appeal to the elders of your community, as a fellow-elder and a witness of Christ's sufferings, and also a partaker in the splendour that is to be revealed. Tend that flock of God whose shepherds you are, and do it, not under compulsion, but of your own free will, as God would have it; not for gain but out of sheer devotion; not tyrannizing over those who are allotted to your care, but setting an example to the flock. And then, when the Head Shepherd appears, you will receive for your own the unfading garland of glory.

In the same way you younger men must be subordinate to your elders. Indeed, all of you should wrap yourselves in the garment of humility towards each other, because God sets his face against the arrogant but favours the humble. Humble yourselves then under God's mighty hand, and he will lift you up in due time. Cast all your cares on him, for you are his charge.

Awake! be on the alert! Your enemy the devil, like a roaring lion, prowls round looking for someone to devour. Stand up to him, firm in faith, and remember that your brother Christians are going through the same kinds of suffering while they are in the world. And the God of all grace, who called you into his eternal glory in Christ, will himself, after your brief suffering, restore, establish, and strengthen you on a firm foundation. He holds dominion for ever and ever. Amen.

Gospel *John 10.7-16 NEB*

Jesus said, 'In truth, in very truth I tell you, I am the door of the sheepfold. The sheep paid no heed to any who came before me, for these were all thieves and robbers. I am the door; anyone who comes into the fold through me shall be safe. He shall go in and out and shall find pasturage.

'The thief comes only to steal, to kill, to destroy; I have come that men may have life, and may have it in all its fullness. I am the good shepherd; the good shepherd lays down his life for the sheep. The hireling, when he sees the wolf coming, abandons the sheep and runs away, because he is no shepherd and the sheep are not his. Then the wolf harries the flock and scatters the sheep. The man runs away because he is a hireling and cares nothing for the sheep.

'I am the good shepherd; I know my own sheep and my sheep know me—as the Father knows me and I know the Father—and I lay down my life for the sheep. But there are other sheep of mine, not belonging to this fold, whom I must bring in; and they too will listen to my voice. There will then be one flock, one shepherd.'

PROPER PREFACE

Rite A. A Preface of the Resurrection (13) or (14) is said.
Rite B. The Preface of Easter is said.

POSTCOMMUNION SENTENCE YEAR 1

The disciples knew the Lord Jesus in the breaking of the bread. (Alleluia!) *Luke 24.35*

POSTCOMMUNION SENTENCE YEAR 2

Jesus said, I have come so that they may have life and have it more abundantly. (Alleluia!) *John 10.10*

EASTER 3   White

INTRODUCTORY SENTENCE YEAR 1

Jesus appeared to his disciples at the sea of Tiberias, after he had risen from the dead. (Alleluia!) *John 21.1, 14*

INTRODUCTORY SENTENCE YEAR 2

Jesus said, I am the resurrection and the life. (Alleluia!) *John 11.25*

COLLECT

Almighty God,
whose Son Jesus Christ is the resurrection
    and the life of all who put their trust in him:

raise us, we pray, from the death of sin
    to the life of righteousness;
that we may seek the things which are above,
where he reigns with you and the Holy Spirit,
one God, now and for ever.

PSALMS 16; 30

READINGS YEAR 1

Old Testament *Isaiah 61.1-7 NEB*

The spirit of the Lord God is upon me
because the Lord has anointed me;
he has sent me to bring good news to the humble,
to bind up the broken-hearted,
to proclaim liberty to captives
and release to those in prison;
to proclaim a year of the Lord's favour
and a day of the vengeance of our God;
to comfort all who mourn,
to give them garlands instead of ashes,
oil of gladness instead of mourners' tears,
a garment of splendour for the heavy heart.
They shall be called Trees of Righteousness,
planted by the Lord for his glory.
Ancient ruins shall be rebuilt
and sites long desolate restored;
they shall repair the ruined cities
and restore what has long lain desolate.
Foreigners shall serve as shepherds of your flocks,
and aliens shall till your land and tend your vines;
but you shall be called priests of the Lord
and be named ministers of our God;
you shall enjoy the wealth of other nations
and be furnished with their riches.
And so, because shame in double measure
and jeers and insults have been my people's lot,
they shall receive in their own land a double measure
    of wealth,
and everlasting joy shall be theirs.

New Testament *1 Corinthians 15.1-11 NEB*

My brothers, I must remind you of the gospel that I preached to you; the gospel which you received, on which you have taken your stand, and which is now bringing you salvation. Do you still hold fast the Gospel as I preached it to you? If not, your conversion was in vain.

First and foremost, I handed on to you the facts which had been imparted to me: that Christ died for our sins, in accordance with the scriptures; that he was buried; that he was raised to life on the third day, according to the scriptures; and that he appeared to Cephas, and afterwards to the Twelve. Then he appeared to over five hundred of our brothers at once, most of whom are still alive, though some have died. Then he appeared to James, and afterwards to all the apostles.

In the end he appeared even to me. It was like an abnormal birth; I had persecuted the church of God and am therefore inferior to all other apostles—indeed not fit to be called an apostle. However, by God's grace I am what I am, nor has his grace been given to me in vain; on the contrary, in my labours I have outdone them all—not I, indeed, but the grace of God working with me. But what matter, I or they? This is what we all proclaim, and this is what you believed.

Gospel *John 21.1-14 RSV*

Jesus revealed himself again to the disciples by the Sea of Tiberias; and he revealed himself in this way. Simon Peter, Thomas called the Twin, Nathanael of Cana in Galilee, the sons of Zebedee, and two others of his disciples were together. Simon Peter said to them, 'I am going fishing.' They said to him, 'We will go with you.' They went out and got into the boat; but that night they caught nothing.

Just as day was breaking, Jesus stood on the beach; yet the disciples did not know that it was Jesus. Jesus said to them, 'Children, have you any fish?' They answered him, 'No.' He said to them, 'Cast the net on the right side of the boat, and you will find some.' So they cast it, and now they were not able to haul it in, for the quantity of fish. That disciple whom

Jesus loved said to Peter, 'It is the Lord!' When Simon Peter heard that it was the Lord, he put on his clothes, for he was stripped for work, and sprang into the sea. But the other disciples came in the boat, dragging the net full of fish, for they were not far from the land, but about a hundred yards off.

When they got out on land, they saw a charcoal fire there, with fish lying on it, and bread. Jesus said to them, 'Bring some of the fish that you have just caught.' So Simon Peter went aboard and hauled the net ashore, full of large fish, a hundred and fifty-three of them; and although there were so many, the net was not torn. Jesus said to them, 'Come and have breakfast.' Now none of the disciples dared to ask him, 'Who are you?' They knew it was the Lord. Jesus came and took the bread and gave it to them, and so with the fish. This was now the third time that Jesus was revealed to the disciples after he was raised from the dead.

READINGS YEAR 2

Old Testament 1 Kings 17.17-end TEV

The son of the widow in Zarephath fell ill; he got worse and worse, and finally he died. She said to Elijah, 'Man of God, why did you do this to me? Did you come here to remind God of my sins and so cause my son's death?'

'Give the boy to me,' Elijah said. He took the boy from her arms, carried him upstairs to the room where he was staying, and laid him on the bed. Then he prayed aloud, 'O Lord my God, why have you done such a terrible thing to this widow? She has been kind enough to take care of me, and now you kill her son!' Then Elijah stretched himself out on the boy three times and prayed, 'O Lord my God, restore this child to life!' The Lord answered Elijah's prayer; the child started breathing again and revived.

Elijah took the boy back downstairs to his mother and said to her, 'Look, your son is alive!'

She answered, 'Now I know that you are a man of God and that the Lord really speaks through you!'

New Testament *Colossians 3.1-11 NEB*

Were you not raised to life with Christ? Then aspire to the realm above, where Christ is, seated at the right hand of God, and let your thoughts dwell on that higher realm, not on this earthly life. I repeat, you died; and now your life lies hidden with Christ in God. When Christ, who is our life, is manifested, then you too will be manifested with him in glory.

Then put to death those parts of you which belong to the earth—fornication, indecency, lust, foul cravings, and the ruthless greed which is nothing less than idolatry. Because of these, God's dreadful judgement is impending; and in the life you once lived these are the ways you yourselves followed. But now you must yourselves lay aside all anger, passion, malice, cursing, filthy talk—have done with them! Stop lying to one another, now that you have discarded the old nature with its deeds and have put on the new nature, which is being constantly renewed in the image of its Creator and brought to know God. There is no question here of Greek and Jew, circumcised and uncircumcised, barbarian, Scythian, slave and freeman; but Christ is all, and is in all.

Gospel *John 11.17-27 NEB*

On his arrival Jesus found that Lazarus had already been four days in the tomb. Bethany was just under two miles from Jerusalem, and many of the people had come from the city to Martha and Mary to condole with them on their brother's death. As soon as she heard that Jesus was on his way, Martha went to meet him, while Mary stayed at home.

Martha said to Jesus, 'If you had been here, sir, my brother would not have died. Even now I know that whatever you ask of God, God will grant you.' Jesus said, 'Your brother will rise again.' 'I know that he will rise again,' said Martha, 'at the resurrection on the last day.' Jesus said, 'I am the resurrection and I am life. If a man has faith in me, even though he die, he shall come to life; and no one who is alive and has faith shall ever die. Do you believe this?' 'Lord, I do,' she answered; 'I now believe that you are the Messiah, the Son of God who was to come into the world.'

PROPER PREFACE

Rite A. A Preface of the Resurrection (13), (15), or (16) is said.
Rite B. The Preface of Easter is said.

POSTCOMMUNION SENTENCE YEAR 1

Jesus said to his disciples, 'Come and eat'; and he took bread and gave it to them. (Alleluia!) *John 21.12, 13*

POSTCOMMUNION SENTENCE YEAR 2

Set your mind on things that are above, and not on things that are on the earth. For you have died, and your life is hidden with Christ in God. (Alleluia!) *Colossians 3.2, 3*

EASTER 4   White

INTRODUCTORY SENTENCE YEAR 1

Without having seen Christ you love him; though you do not now see him, you believe in him and rejoice with unutterable and exalted joy. (Alleluia!) *1 Peter 1.8*

INTRODUCTORY SENTENCE YEAR 2

Jesus said, I am the way, and the truth, and the life. (Alleluia!) *John 14.6*

COLLECT

Almighty God,
who alone can bring order
to the unruly wills and passions of sinful men:
give us grace,
    to love what you command
    and to desire what you promise,
that in all the changes and chances of this world,
our hearts may surely there be fixed
where lasting joys are to be found;
through Jesus Christ our Lord.

PSALMS 33.1-12; 37.23-32

READINGS YEAR 1

Old Testament *Isaiah 62.1-5 RSV*

For Zion's sake I will not keep silent,
and for Jerusalem's sake I will not rest,
until her vindication goes forth as brightness,
and her salvation as a burning torch.
The nations shall see your vindication,
and all the kings your glory;
and you shall be called by a new name
which the mouth of the Lord will give.
You shall be a crown of beauty in the hand of the Lord,
and a royal diadem in the hand of your God.
You shall no more be termed Forsaken,
and your land shall no more be termed Desolate;
but you shall be called My delight is in her,
and your land Married;
for the Lord delights in you,
and your land shall be married.
For as a young man marries a virgin,
so shall your sons marry you,
and as the bridegroom rejoices over the bride,
so shall your God rejoice over you.

New Testament *Revelation 3.14-end RSV*

'To the angel of the church in Laodicea write: ''The words of
the Amen, the faithful and true witness, the beginning of
God's creation.

'''I know your works: you are neither cold nor hot. Would
that you were cold or hot! So, because you are lukewarm,
and neither cold nor hot, I will spew you out of my mouth.
For you say, I am rich, I have prospered, and I need nothing;
not knowing that you are wretched, pitiable, poor, blind,
and naked. Therefore I counsel you to buy from me gold
refined by fire, that you may be rich, and white garments to
clothe you and to keep the shame of your nakedness from
being seen, and salve to anoint your eyes, that you may see.
Those whom I love, I reprove and chasten; so be zealous and

repent. Behold, I stand at the door and knock; if any one hears my voice and opens the door, I will come in to him and eat with him, and he with me. He who conquers, I will grant him to sit with me on my throne, as I myself conquered and sat down with my Father on his throne. He who has an ear, let him hear what the Spirit says to the churches.'''

Gospel *John 21.15-22 RSV*

When they had finished breakfast, Jesus said to Simon Peter, 'Simon, son of John, do you love me more than these?' He said to him, 'Yes, Lord; you know that I love you.' He said to him, 'Feed my lambs.' A second time he said to him, 'Simon, son of John, do you love me?' He said to him, 'Yes, Lord; you know that I love you.' He said to him, 'Tend my sheep.' He said to him the third time, 'Simon, son of John, do you love me?' Peter was grieved because he said to him the third time, 'Do you love me?' And he said to him, 'Lord, you know everything; you know that I love you.' Jesus said to him, 'Feed my sheep. Truly, truly, I say to you, when you were young, you girded yourself and walked where you would; but when you are old, you will stretch out your hands, and another will gird you and carry you where you do not wish to go.' (This he said to show by what death he was to glorify God.) And after this he said to him, 'Follow me.'

Peter turned and saw following them the disciple whom Jesus loved, who had lain close to his breast at the supper and had said, 'Lord, who is it that is going to betray you?' When Peter saw him, he said to Jesus, 'Lord, what about this man?' Jesus said to him, 'If it is my will that he remain until I come, what is that to you? Follow me!'

READINGS YEAR 2

Old Testament *Proverbs 4.10-19 RSV*

Hear, my son, and accept my words,
that the years of your life may be many.
I have taught you the way of wisdom;
I have led you in the paths of uprightness.
When you walk, your step will not be hampered;

and if you run, you will not stumble.
Keep hold of instruction, do not let go;
guard her, for she is your life.
Do not enter the path of the wicked,
and do not walk in the way of evil men.
Avoid it; do not go on it;
turn away from it and pass on.
For they cannot sleep unless they have done wrong;
they are robbed of sleep unless they have made
    someone stumble.
For they eat the bread of wickedness
and drink the wine of violence.
But the path of the righteous is like the light of dawn,
which shines brighter and brighter until full day.
The way of the wicked is like deep darkness;
they do not know over what they stumble.

New Testament *2 Corinthians 4.13—5.5 NEB*

Scripture says, 'I believed, and therefore I spoke out', and
we too, in the same spirit of faith, believe and therefore
speak out; for we know that he who raised the Lord Jesus to
life will with Jesus raise us too, and bring us to his presence,
and you with us. Indeed, it is for your sake that all things are
ordered, so that, as the abounding grace of God is shared by
more and more, the greater may be the chorus of
thanksgiving that ascends to the glory of God.

No wonder we do not lose heart! Though our outward
humanity is in decay, yet day by day we are inwardly
renewed. Our troubles are slight and short-lived; and their
outcome an eternal glory which outweighs them far.
Meanwhile our eyes are fixed, not on the things that are
seen, but on the things that are unseen: for what is seen
passes away; what is unseen is eternal. For we know that if
the earthly frame that houses us today should be
demolished, we possess a building which God has
provided—a house not made by human hands, eternal, and
in heaven. In this present body we do indeed groan; we
yearn to have our heavenly habitation put on over this
one—in the hope that, being thus clothed, we shall not find
ourselves naked. We groan indeed, we who are enclosed

within this earthly frame; we are oppressed because we do not want to have the old body stripped off. Rather our desire is to have the new body put on over it, so that our mortal part may be absorbed into life immortal. God himself has shaped us for this very end; and as a pledge of it he has given us the Spirit.

Gospel *John 14.1-11 NEB*

Jesus said, 'Set your troubled hearts at rest. Trust in God always; trust also in me. There are many dwelling-places in my Father's house; if it were not so I should have told you; for I am going there on purpose to prepare a place for you. And if I go and prepare a place for you, I shall come again and receive you to myself, so that where I am you may be also; and my way there is known to you.' Thomas said, 'Lord, we do not know where you are going, so how can we know the way?' Jesus replied, 'I am the way; I am the truth and I am life; no one comes to the Father except by me.

'If you knew me you would know my Father too. From now on you do know him; you have seen him.' Philip said to him, 'Lord, show us the Father and we ask no more.' Jesus answered, 'Have I been all this time with you, Philip, and you still do not know me? Anyone who has seen me has seen the Father. Then how can you say, "Show us the Father"? Do you not believe that I am in the Father, and the Father in me? I am not myself the source of the words I speak to you: it is the Father who dwells in me doing his own work. Believe me when I say that I am in the Father and the Father in me; or else accept the evidence of the deeds themselves.'

PROPER PREFACE

Rite A. A Preface of the Resurrection (13) or (14) is said.
Rite B. The Preface of Easter is said.

POSTCOMMUNION SENTENCE YEAR 1

Jesus said, I stand at the door and knock; if anyone hears my voice and opens the door, I will come and have supper with him, and he with me. (Alleluia!) *Revelation 3.20*

POSTCOMMUNION SENTENCE YEAR 2

Jesus said, If you had known me you would have known the Father also; henceforth you know him and have seen him. (Alleluia!) *John 14.7*

EASTER 5   White

INTRODUCTORY SENTENCE

With a voice of singing, tell it to the ends of the earth; the Lord has set his people free. (Alleluia!) *Isaiah 48.20*

COLLECT

Almighty and everlasting God,
you are always more ready to hear than we to pray
and give more than either we desire or deserve.
Pour down upon us the abundance of your mercy,
forgiving us those things
   of which our conscience is afraid
and giving us those good things
   which we are not worthy to ask
save through the merits and mediation
of Jesus Christ your Son our Lord.

PSALMS 84; 15

READINGS YEAR 1

Old Testament *Hosea 6.1-6 NEB*

Come, let us return to the Lord;
for he has torn us and will heal us,
he has struck us and he will bind up our wounds;
after two days he will revive us,
on the third day he will restore us,
that in his presence we may live.
Let us humble ourselves, let us strive to know the Lord,
whose justice dawns like morning light,
and its dawning is as sure as the sunrise.

It will come to us like a shower,
like spring rains that water the earth.

O Ephraim, how shall I deal with you?
How shall I deal with you, Judah?
Your loyalty to me is like the morning mist,
like dew that vanishes early.
Therefore have I lashed you through the prophets
and torn you to shreds with my words;
loyalty is my desire, not sacrifice,
not whole-offerings but the knowledge of God.

New Testament *1 Corinthians 15.21-28 RSV*

As by a man came death, by a man has come also the
resurrection of the dead. For as in Adam all die, so also in
Christ shall all be made alive. But each in his own order:
Christ the first fruits, then at his coming those who belong to
Christ. Then comes the end, when he delivers the kingdom
to God the Father after destroying every rule and every
authority and power. For he must reign until he has put all
his enemies under his feet. The last enemy to be destroyed is
death. 'For God has put all things in subjection under his
feet.' But when it says, 'All things are put in subjection
under him,' it is plain that he is excepted who put all things
under him. When all things are subjected to him, then the
Son himself will also be subjected to him who put all things
under him, that God may be everything to every one.

Gospel *John 16.25-end NEB*

Jesus said, 'Till now I have been using figures of speech; a
time is coming when I shall no longer use figures, but tell
you of the Father in plain words. When that day comes you
will make your request in my name, and I do not say that I
shall pray to the Father for you, for the Father loves you
himself, because you have loved me and believed that I came
from God. I came from the Father and have come into the
world. Now I am leaving the world again and going to the
Father.' His disciples said, 'Why, this is plain speaking; this

is no figure of speech. We are certain now that you know everything, and do not need to be questioned; because of this we believe that you have come from God.'

Jesus answered, 'Do you now believe? Look, the hour is coming, has indeed already come, when you are all to be scattered, each to his home, leaving me alone. Yet I am not alone, because the Father is with me. I have told you all this so that in me you may find peace. In the world you will have trouble. But courage! The victory is mine; I have conquered the world.'

READINGS YEAR 2

Old Testament *Deuteronomy 34 RSV*

Moses went up from the plains of Moab to Mount Nebo, to the top of Pisgah, which is opposite Jericho. And the Lord showed him all the land, Gilead as far as Dan, all Naphtali, the land of Ephraim and Manasseh, all the land of Judah as far as the Western Sea, the Negeb, and the Plain, that is, the valley of Jericho the city of palm trees, as far as Zoar. And the Lord said to him, 'This is the land of which I swore to Abraham, to Isaac, and to Jacob, "I will give it to your descendants." I have let you see it with your eyes, but you shall not go over there.' So Moses the servant of the Lord died there in the land of Moab, according to the word of the Lord, and he buried him in the valley in the land of Moab opposite Beth-peor; but no man knows the place of his burial to this day. Moses was a hundred and twenty years old when he died; his eye was not dim, nor his natural force abated. And the people of Israel wept for Moses in the plains of Moab thirty days; then the days of weeping and mourning for Moses were ended.

And Joshua the son of Nun was full of the spirit of wisdom, for Moses had laid his hands upon him; so the people of Israel obeyed him, and did as the Lord commanded Moses. And there has not arisen a prophet since in Israel like Moses, whom the Lord knew face to face, none like him for all the signs and the wonders which the Lord sent him to do in the land of Egypt, to Pharaoh and to all his servants and to all his land, and for all the mighty power and all the great and terrible deeds which Moses wrought in the sight of all Israel.

New Testament *Romans 8.28-end RSV*

We know that in everything God works for good with those who love him, who are called according to his purpose. For those whom he foreknew he also predestined to be conformed to the image of his Son, in order that he might be the first-born among many brethren. And those whom he predestined he also called; and those whom he called he also justified; and those whom he justified he also glorified.

What then shall we say to this? If God is for us, who is against us? He who did not spare his own Son but gave him up for us all, will he not also give us all things with him? Who shall bring any charge against God's elect? It is God who justifies; who is to condemn? Is it Christ Jesus, who died, yes, who was raised from the dead, who is at the right hand of God, who indeed intercedes for us? Who shall separate us from the love of Christ? Shall tribulation, or distress, or persecution, or famine, or nakedness, or peril, or sword? As it is written,

'For your sake we are being killed all the day long;
we are regarded as sheep to be slaughtered.'

No, in all these things we are more than conquerors through him who loved us. For I am sure that neither death, nor life, nor angels, nor principalities, nor things present, nor things to come, nor powers, nor height, nor depth, nor anything else in all creation, will be able to separate us from the love of God in Christ Jesus our Lord.

Gospel *John 16.12-24 NEB*

Jesus said, 'There is still much that I could say to you, but the burden would be too great for you now. However, when he comes who is the Spirit of truth, he will guide you into all the truth; for he will not speak on his own authority, but will tell only what he hears; and he will make known to you the things that are coming. He will glorify me, for everything that he makes known to you he will draw from what is mine. All that the Father has is mine, and that is why I said, "Everything that he makes known to you he will draw from what is mine."

'A little while, and you see me no more; again a little while, and you will see me.' Some of his disciples said to one another, 'What does he mean by this: "A little while, and you will not see me, and again a little while, and you will see me", and by this: "Because I am going to my Father"?' So they asked, 'What is this "little while" that he speaks of? We do not know what he means.'

Jesus knew that they were wanting to question him, and said, 'Are you discussing what I said: "A little while, and you will not see me, and again a little while and you will see me"? In very truth I tell you, you will weep and mourn, but the world will be glad. But though you will be plunged in grief, your grief will be turned to joy. A woman in labour is in pain because her time has come; but when the child is born she forgets the anguish in her joy that a man has been born into the world. So it is with you: for the moment you are sad at heart; but I shall see you again, and then you will be joyful, and no one shall rob you of your joy. When that day comes you will ask nothing of me. In very truth I tell you, if you ask the Father for anything in my name, he will give it you. So far you have asked nothing in my name. Ask and you will receive, that your joy may be complete.'

PROPER PREFACE

Rite A. A Preface of the Resurrection (13), (14), or (16) is said.
Rite B. The Preface of Easter is said.

POSTCOMMUNION SENTENCE

Jesus said, I came from the Father and have come into the world; again, I am leaving the world and going to the Father. (Alleluia!) *John 16.28*

ASCENSION DAY   White or Gold

INTRODUCTORY SENTENCES

We have a great high priest who has passed through the
heavens, Jesus the Son of God. (Alleluia!) *Hebrews 4.14*

or

Jesus lifted up his hands: and, while he blessed his disciples,
he parted from them. (Alleluia!) *Luke 24.50, 51*

COLLECT

Almighty God,
as we believe your only-begotten Son our Lord Jesus Christ
to have ascended into the heavens,
so may we also in heart and mind thither ascend
and with him continually dwell;
who is alive and reigns with you and the Holy Spirit,
one God, now and for ever.

PSALMS 8; 21.1-7

READINGS YEARS 1 and 2

Old Testament *Daniel 7.9-14 RSV*

As I looked,
thrones were placed
and one that was ancient of days took his seat;
his raiment was white as snow,
and the hair of his head like pure wool;
his throne was fiery flames,
its wheels were burning fire.
A stream of fire issued
and came forth from before him;
a thousand thousands served him,
and ten thousand times ten thousand stood before him;
the court sat in judgement,
and the books were opened.

I looked then because of the sound of the great words which
the horn was speaking. And as I looked, the beast was slain,

and its body destroyed and given over to be burned with
fire. As for the rest of the beasts, their dominion was taken
away, but their lives were prolonged for a season and a time.
I saw in the night visions,
and behold, with the clouds of heaven
there came one like a son of man,
and he came to the Ancient of Days
and was presented before him.
And to him was given dominion and glory and kingdom,
that all peoples, nations, and languages should serve him;
his dominion is an everlasting dominion
    which shall not pass away,
and his kingdom one that shall not be destroyed.

New Testament *Acts 1.1-11 TEV*

Dear Theophilus:
In my first book I wrote about all the things that Jesus did
and taught from the time he began his work until the day he
was taken up to heaven. Before he was taken up, he gave
instructions by the power of the Holy Spirit to the men he
had chosen as his apostles. For forty days after his death he
appeared to them many times in ways that proved beyond
doubt that he was alive. They saw him, and he talked with
them about the Kingdom of God. And when they came
together, he gave them this order: 'Do not leave Jerusalem,
but wait for the gift I told you about, the gift my Father
promised. John baptized with water, but in a few days you
will be baptized with the Holy Spirit.'

When the apostles met together with Jesus, they asked him,
'Lord, will you at this time give the Kingdom back to Israel?'

Jesus said to them, 'The times and occasions are set by my
Father's own authority, and it is not for you to know when
they will be. But when the Holy Spirit comes upon you, you
will be filled with power, and you will be witnesses for me in
Jerusalem, in all Judaea and Samaria, and to the ends of the
earth.' After saying this, he was taken up to heaven as they
watched him, and a cloud hid him from their sight.

They still had their eyes fixed on the sky as he went away,
when two men dressed in white suddenly stood beside them

and said, 'Galileans, why are you standing there looking up at the sky? This Jesus, who was taken from you into heaven, will come back in the same way that you saw him go to heaven.'

Gospel *Matthew 28.16-end JB*

The eleven disciples set out for Galilee, to the mountain where Jesus had arranged to meet them. When they saw him they fell down before him, though some hesitated. Jesus came up and spoke to them. He said, 'All authority in heaven and on earth has been given to me. Go, therefore, make disciples of all the nations; baptize them in the name of the Father and of the Son and of the Holy Spirit, and teach them to observe all the commands I gave you. And know that I am with you always; yes, to the end of time.'

PROPER PREFACE

Rite A. The Preface of the Ascension (17) is said until Pentecost.
Rite B. The Preface of the Ascension is said until Pentecost.

POSTCOMMUNION SENTENCES

Jesus said, I am with you always: to the end of the world. (Alleluia!) *Matthew 28.20*

or

Why stand looking up into heaven? This Jesus will come in the same way as you saw him go into heaven. (Alleluia!) *Acts 1.11*

THE SUNDAY AFTER ASCENSION DAY
(Easter 6)   White

INTRODUCTORY SENTENCES

Why stand looking up into heaven? This Jesus will come in the same way as you saw him go into heaven. (Alleluia!) *Acts 1.11*

or

We have a great high priest who has passed through the
heavens, Jesus the Son of God. (Alleluia!) *Hebrews 4.14*

COLLECT

Eternal God, the King of Glory,
you have exalted your only Son
with great triumph to your kingdom in heaven.
Leave us not comfortless,
but send your Holy Spirit to strengthen us
and exalt us to the place
where Christ is gone before,
and where with you and the Holy Spirit
he is worshipped and glorified,
now and for ever.

PSALMS 24; 47

READINGS YEAR 1

Old Testament *Daniel 7.9-14 RSV*

As I looked,
thrones were placed
and one that was ancient of days took his seat;
his raiment was white as snow,
and the hair of his head like pure wool;
his throne was fiery flames,
its wheels were burning fire.
A stream of fire issued
and came forth from before him;
a thousand thousands served him,
and ten thousand times ten thousand stood before him;
the court sat in judgement,
and the books were opened.

I looked then because of the sound of the great words which
the horn was speaking. And as I looked, the beast was slain,
and its body destroyed and given over to be burned with
fire. As for the rest of the beasts, their dominion was taken
away, but their lives were prolonged for a season and a time.

I saw in the night visions,
and behold, with the clouds of heaven
there came one like a son of man,
and he came to the Ancient of Days
and was presented before him.
And to him was given dominion and glory and kingdom,
that all peoples, nations, and languages should serve him;
his dominion is an everlasting dominion
    which shall not pass away,
and his kingdom one that shall not be destroyed.

New Testament *Ephesians 1.15-end TEV*

Ever since I heard of your faith in the Lord Jesus and your
love for all God's people, I have not stopped giving thanks to
God for you. I remember you in my prayers and ask the God
of our Lord Jesus Christ, the glorious Father, to give you the
Spirit, who will make you wise and reveal God to you, so
that you will know him. I ask that your minds may be
opened to see his light, so that you will know what is the
hope to which he has called you, how rich are the wonderful
blessings he promises his people, and how very great is his
power at work in us who believe. This power working in us
is the same as the mighty strength which he used when he
raised Christ from death and seated him at his right side in
the heavenly world. Christ rules there above all heavenly
rulers, authorities, powers, and lords; he has a title superior
to all titles of authority in this world and in the next. God put
all things under Christ's feet and gave him to the church as
supreme Lord over all things. The church is Christ's body,
the completion of him who himself completes all things
everywhere.

Gospel *Luke 24.45-end JB*

Jesus opened the disciples' minds to understand the
scriptures, and he said to them, 'So you see how it is written
that the Christ would suffer and on the third day rise from
the dead, and that, in his name, repentance for the
forgiveness of sins would be preached to all the nations,
beginning from Jerusalem. You are witnesses to this.

'And now I am sending down to you what the Father has promised. Stay in the city then, until you are clothed with the power from on high.'

Then he took them out as far as the outskirts of Bethany, and lifting up his hands he blessed them. Now as he blessed them, he withdrew from them and was carried up to heaven. They worshipped him and then went back to Jerusalem full of joy; and they were continually in the Temple praising God.

READINGS YEAR 2

Old Testament 2 Kings 2.1-15 NEB

The time came when the Lord would take Elijah up to heaven in a whirlwind. Elijah and Elisha left Gilgal, and Elijah said to Elisha, 'Stay here; for the Lord has sent me to Bethel.' But Elisha said, 'As the Lord lives, your life upon it, I will not leave you.' So they went down country to Bethel. There a company of prophets came out to Elisha and said to him, 'Do you know that the Lord is going to take your lord and master from you today?' 'I do know', he replied; 'say no more.' Then Elijah said to him, 'Stay here, Elisha; for the Lord has sent me to Jericho.' But he replied, 'As the Lord lives, your life upon it, I will not leave you.' So they went to Jericho. There a company of prophets came up to Elisha and said to him, 'Do you know that the Lord is going to take your lord and master from you today?' 'I do know,' he said; 'say no more.' Then Elijah said to him, 'Stay here; for the Lord has sent me to the Jordan.' The other replied, 'As the Lord lives, your life upon it, I will not leave you.' So the two of them went on.

Fifty of the prophets followed them, and stood watching from a distance as the two of them stopped by the Jordan. Elijah took his cloak, rolled it up and struck the water with it. The water divided to right and left, and they both crossed over on dry ground. While they were crossing, Elijah said to Elisha, 'Tell me what I can do for you before I am taken from you.' Elisha said, 'Let me inherit a double share of your spirit.' 'You have asked a hard thing', said Elijah. 'If you see me taken from you, may your wish be granted; if you do not, it shall not be granted.' They went on, talking as they went, and suddenly there appeared chariots of fire and horses of fire, which separated them one from the other, and Elijah was carried up in the whirlwind to heaven. When Elisha saw it, he cried, 'My father, my father, the chariots and the horsemen of Israel!', and he saw him no more. Then he took hold of his mantle and rent it in two, and he picked up the cloak which had fallen from Elijah, and came back and stood on the bank of the Jordan. There he too struck the water with Elijah's cloak and said, 'Where is the Lord the God of Elijah?' When he struck the water, it was again divided to right and left, and he crossed over. The prophets from Jericho, who were watching, saw him and said, 'The spirit of Elijah has settled on Elisha.'

New Testament *Ephesians 4.1-13 NEB*

I entreat you,—I, a prisoner for the Lord's sake: as God has called you, live up to your calling. Be humble always and gentle, and patient too. Be forbearing with one another and charitable. Spare no effort to make fast with bonds of peace the unity which the Spirit gives. There is one body and one Spirit, as there is also one hope held out in God's call to you; one Lord, one faith, one baptism; one God and Father of all, who is over all and through all and in all.

But each of us has been given his gift, his due portion of Christ's bounty. Therefore Scripture says:

'He ascended into the heights
with captives in his train;
he gave gifts to men.'

Now, the word 'ascended' implies that he also descended to the lowest level, down to the very earth. He who descended is no other than he who ascended far above all heavens, so that he might fill the universe. And these were his gifts: some to be apostles, some prophets, some evangelists, some pastors and teachers, to equip God's people for work in his service, to the building up of the body of Christ. So shall we all at last attain to the unity inherent in our faith and our knowledge of the Son of God—to mature manhood, measured by nothing less than the full stature of Christ.

Gospel *Luke 24.45-end JB*

Jesus opened the disciples' minds to understand the scriptures, and he said to them, 'So you see how it is written that the Christ would suffer and on the third day rise from the dead, and that, in his name, repentance for the forgiveness of sins would be preached to all the nations, beginning from Jerusalem. You are witnesses to this.

'And now I am sending down to you what the Father has promised. Stay in the city then, until you are clothed with the power from on high.'

Then he took them out as far as the outskirts of Bethany, and lifting up his hands he blessed them. Now as he blessed them, he withdrew from them and was carried up to heaven. They worshipped him and then went back to Jerusalem full of joy; and they were continually in the Temple praising God.

PROPER PREFACE

Rite A. The Preface of the Ascension (17) is said.
Rite B. The Preface of the Ascension is said.

POSTCOMMUNION SENTENCE

The disciples worshipped Jesus and went back to Jerusalem full of joy; and were continually in the Temple, praising God. (Alleluia!) *Luke 24.52, 53*

PENTECOST
(Whit Sunday)   Red

INTRODUCTORY SENTENCES

The love of God has been poured into our hearts through the Holy Spirit who has been given to us. (Alleluia!) *Romans 5.5*

or

You shall receive power when the Holy Spirit has come upon you; and you shall be my witnesses. (Alleluia!) *Acts 1.8*

COLLECTS

Almighty God,
who at this time
taught the hearts of your faithful people
by sending to them the light of your Holy Spirit:
grant us by the same Spirit
   to have a right judgement in all things,
and evermore to rejoice in his holy comfort;
through the merits of Christ Jesus our Saviour,
who is alive and reigns with you in the unity of the Spirit,
one God, now and for ever.

Almighty God,
who on the day of Pentecost
sent your Holy Spirit to the disciples
with the wind from heaven and in tongues of flame,
filling them with joy
   and boldness to preach the Gospel:
send us out in the power of the same Spirit
to witness to your truth
and to draw all men to the fire of your love;
through Jesus Christ our Lord.

PSALMS 122; 36.5-10

READINGS YEARS 1 and 2

Old Testament *Genesis 11.1-9 NEB*

Once upon a time all the world spoke a single language and
used the same words. As men journeyed in the east, they
came upon a plain in the land of Shinar and settled there.
They said to one another, 'Come, let us make bricks and
bake them hard'; they used bricks for stone and bitumen for
mortar. 'Come,' they said, 'let us build ourselves a city and a
tower with its top in the heavens, and make a name for
ourselves; or we shall be dispersed all over the earth.' Then
the Lord came down to see the city and tower which mortal
men had built, and he said, 'Here they are, one people with a
single language, and now they have started to do this; and
henceforward nothing they have a mind to do will be

beyond their reach. Come, let us go down there and confuse their speech, so that they will not understand what they say to one another.' So the Lord dispersed them from there all over the earth, and they left off building the city. That is why it is called Babel, because the Lord there made a babble of language of all the world; from that place the Lord scattered men all over the face of the earth.

or *Exodus 19.16-25 TEV*

On the morning of the third day there was thunder and lightning, a thick cloud appeared on the mountain, and a very loud trumpet blast was heard. All the people in the camp trembled with fear. Moses led them out of the camp to meet God, and they stood at the foot of the mountain. The whole of Mount Sinai was covered with smoke, because the Lord had come down on it in fire. The smoke went up like the smoke of a furnace, and all the people trembled violently. The sound of the trumpet became louder and louder. Moses spoke, and God answered him with thunder. The Lord came down on the top of Mount Sinai and called Moses to the top of the mountain. Moses went up and the Lord said to him, 'Go down and warn the people not to cross the boundary to come and look at me; if they do, many of them will die. Even the priests who come near me must purify themselves, or I will punish them.'

Moses said to the Lord, 'The people cannot come up, because you commanded us to consider the mountain sacred and to mark a boundary round it.'

The Lord replied, 'Go down and bring Aaron back with you. But the priests and the people must not cross the boundary to come up to me, or I will punish them.' Moses then went down to the people and told them what the Lord had said.

New Testament *Acts 2.1-11 RSV*

When the day of Pentecost had come, the disciples were all together in one place. And suddenly a sound came from heaven like the rush of a mighty wind, and it filled all the house where they were sitting. And there appeared to them tongues as of fire, distributed and resting on each one of them. And they were all filled with the Holy Spirit and began to speak in other tongues, as the Spirit gave them utterance.

Now there were dwelling in Jerusalem Jews, devout men from every nation under heaven. And at this sound the multitude came together, and they were bewildered, because each one heard them speaking in his own language. And they were amazed and wondered, saying, 'Are not all these who are speaking Galileans? And how is it that we hear, each of us in his own native language? Parthians and Medes and Elamites and residents of Mesopotamia, Judaea and Cappadocia, Pontus and Asia, Phrygia and Pamphylia, Egypt and the parts of Libya belonging to Cyrene, and visitors from Rome, both Jews and proselytes, Cretans and Arabians, we hear them telling in our own tongues the mighty works of God.'

or *Acts 2.1-21 RSV*

When the day of Pentecost had come, the disciples were all together in one place. And suddenly a sound came from heaven like the rush of a mighty wind, and it filled all the house where they were sitting. And there appeared to them tongues as of fire, distributed and resting on each one of them. And they were all filled with the Holy Spirit and began to speak in other tongues, as the Spirit gave them utterance.

Now there were dwelling in Jerusalem Jews, devout men from every nation under heaven. And at this sound the multitude came together, and they were bewildered, because each one heard them speaking in his own language. And they were amazed and wondered, saying, 'Are not all these who are speaking Galileans? And how is it that we hear, each of us in his own native language? Parthians and Medes and Elamites and residents of Mesopotamia, Judaea and Cappadocia, Pontus and Asia, Phrygia and Pamphylia, Egypt and the parts of Libya belonging to Cyrene, and visitors from Rome, both Jews and proselytes, Cretans and Arabians, we hear them telling in our own tongues the mighty works of God.' And all were amazed and perplexed, saying to one another, 'What does this mean?' But others mocking said, 'They are filled with new wine.'

But Peter, standing with the eleven, lifted up his voice and addressed them, 'Men of Judaea and all who dwell in Jerusalem, let this be known to you, and give ear to my words. For these men are not drunk, as you suppose, since it is only the third hour of the day; but this is what was spoken by the prophet Joel:

''And in the last days it shall be, God declares,
that I will pour out my Spirit upon all flesh,
and your sons and your daughters shall prophesy,
and your young men shall see visions,
and your old men shall dream dreams;
yea, and on my menservants and my maidservants in
    those days
I will pour out my Spirit; and they shall prophesy.
And I will show wonders in the heaven above
and signs on the earth beneath,
blood, and fire, and vapour of smoke;
the sun shall be turned into darkness
and the moon into blood,
before the day of the Lord comes,
the great and manifest day.
And it shall be that whoever calls on the name of the Lord
    shall be saved.''

Gospel *John 14.15-26 JB*

Jesus said,
'If you love me you will keep my commandments.
I shall ask the Father,
and he will give you another Advocate
to be with you for ever,
that Spirit of truth
whom the world can never receive
since it neither sees nor knows him;
but you know him,
because he is with you, he is in you.
I will not leave you orphans;
I will come back to you.
In a short time the world will no longer see me;

but you will see me,
because I live and you will live.
On that day
you will understand that I am in my Father
and you in me and I in you.
Anybody who receives my commandments and keeps them
will be one who loves me;
and anybody who loves me will be loved by my Father,
and I shall love him and show myself to him.'

Judas—this was not Judas Iscariot—said to him, 'Lord, what is all this about? Do you intend to show yourself to us and not to the world?' Jesus replied:

'If anyone loves me he will keep my word,
and my Father will love him,
and we shall come to him
and make our home with him.
Those who do not love me do not keep my words.
And my word is not my own:
it is the word of the one who sent me.
I have said these things to you
while still with you;
but the Advocate, the Holy Spirit,
whom the Father will send in my name,
will teach you everything
and remind you of all I have said to you.'

or *John 20.19-23 RSV*

On the evening of the first day of the week, the doors being shut where the disciples were, for fear of the Jews, Jesus came and stood among them and said to them, 'Peace be with you.' When he had said this, he showed them his hands and his side. Then the disciples were glad when they saw the Lord. Jesus said to them again, 'Peace be with you. As the Father has sent me, even so I send you.' And when he had said this, he breathed on them, and said to them, 'Receive the Holy Spirit. If you forgive the sins of any, they are forgiven; if you retain the sins of any, they are retained.'

PROPER PREFACE

Rite A. The Preface of Pentecost (18) is said until Trinity Sunday.
Rite B. The Preface of Pentecost is said until Trinity Sunday.

POSTCOMMUNION SENTENCE

The disciples were all filled with the Holy Spirit, and spoke of the great things God had done. (Alleluia!) *Acts 2.4, 11*

TRINITY SUNDAY

(Pentecost 1)   White or Gold on Sunday; Green from Monday

INTRODUCTORY SENTENCE

Holy, holy, holy is the Lord God almighty: who was, and is, and is to come. *Revelation 4.8*

COLLECTS

Almighty and everlasting God,
you have given us your servants grace,
by the confession of a true faith
to acknowledge the glory of the eternal Trinity,
and in the power of the divine Majesty to worship the Unity.
Keep us steadfast in this faith,
that we may evermore be defended
   from all adversities;
through Jesus Christ our Lord,
who is alive and reigns with you and the Holy Spirit,
one God, now and for ever.

Almighty and eternal God,
you have revealed yourself
   as Father, Son, and Holy Spirit,
and live and reign in the perfect unity of love.
Hold us firm in this faith,
that we may know you in all your ways
and evermore rejoice in your eternal glory,
who are three Persons in one God,
now and for ever.

PSALMS 93; 97

READINGS YEARS 1 and 2

Old Testament *Isaiah 6.1-8 RSV*

In the year that King Uzziah died I saw the Lord sitting upon a throne, high and lifted up; and his train filled the temple. Above him stood the seraphim; each had six wings: with two he covered his face, and with two he covered his feet, and with two he flew. And one called to another and said:

'Holy, holy, holy is the Lord of hosts;
the whole earth is full of his glory.'

And the foundations of the thresholds shook at the voice of him who called, and the house was filled with smoke. And I said: 'Woe is me! For I am lost; for I am a man of unclean lips, and I dwell in the midst of a people of unclean lips; for my eyes have seen the King, the Lord of hosts!'

Then flew one of the seraphim to me, having in his hand a burning coal which he had taken with tongs from the altar. And he touched my mouth, and said: 'Behold, this has touched your lips; your guilt is taken away, and your sin forgiven.' And I heard the voice of the Lord saying, 'Whom shall I send, and who will go for us?' Then I said, 'Here I am! Send me.'

New Testament *Ephesians 1.3-14 NEB*

Praise be to the God and Father of our Lord Jesus Christ, who has bestowed on us in Christ every spiritual blessing in the heavenly realms. In Christ he chose us before the world was founded, to be dedicated, to be without blemish in his sight, to be full of love; and he destined us—such was his will and pleasure—to be accepted as his sons through Jesus Christ, in order that the glory of his gracious gift, so graciously bestowed on us in his Beloved, might redound to his praise. For in Christ our release is secured and our sins are forgiven through the shedding of his blood. Therein lies the richness of God's free grace lavished upon us, imparting full wisdom and insight. He has made known to us his hidden purpose—such was his will and pleasure determined beforehand in Christ—to be put into effect when the time was ripe; namely, that the universe, all in heaven and on earth, might be brought into a unity in Christ.

In Christ indeed we have been given our share in the heritage, as was decreed in his design whose purpose is everywhere at work. For it was his will that we, who were the first to set our hope on Christ, should cause his glory to be praised. And you too, when you had heard the message of the truth, the good news of your salvation, and had believed it, became incorporate in Christ and received the seal of the promised Holy Spirit; and that Spirit is in the pledge that we shall enter upon our heritage, when God has redeemed what is his own, to his praise and glory.

Gospel *John 14.8-17 JB*

Philip said to Jesus, 'Lord, let us see the Father and then we shall be satisfied.' 'Have I been with you all this time, Philip,' said Jesus to him, 'and you still do not know me?

'To have seen me is to have seen the Father,
so how can you say, "Let us see the Father"?
Do you not believe
that I am in the Father and the Father is in me?
The words I say to you I do not speak as from myself:
it is the Father, living in me, who is doing this work.
You must believe me when I say
that I am in the Father and the Father is in me;
believe it on the evidence of this work, if for no other reason.
I tell you most solemnly,
whoever believes in me
will perform the same works as I do myself,
he will perform even greater works,
because I am going to the Father.
Whatever you ask for in my name I will do,
so that the Father may be glorified in the Son.
If you ask for anything in my name,
I will do it.
If you love me you will keep my commandments.
I shall ask the Father,
and he will give you another Advocate

to be with you for ever,
that Spirit of truth
whom the world can never receive
since it neither sees nor knows him;
but you know him,
because he is with you, he is in you.'

PROPER PREFACE

Rite A. The Preface of Trinity Sunday (19) is said.
Rite B. The Preface of Trinity Sunday is said.

POSTCOMMUNION SENTENCE

You are the children of God; so God has sent the Spirit of his
Son into your hearts, to make you cry out, Abba, Father!
Galatians 4.6

PENTECOST 2
(Trinity 1)   Green

INTRODUCTORY SENTENCE YEAR 1

By one Spirit we have all been baptized into one body and
have all been made to drink of the Spirit. *1 Corinthians 12.13*

INTRODUCTORY SENTENCE YEAR 2

That which we have seen and heard we proclaim to you, so
that you may have fellowship with us; and our fellowship is
with the Father and with his Son Jesus Christ. *1 John 1.3*

COLLECT

Almighty and everlasting God,
by whose Spirit the whole body of the Church
    is governed and sanctified:
hear our prayer which we offer for all your faithful people;
that each in his vocation and ministry
may serve you in holiness and truth
to the glory of your name;
through our Lord and Saviour Jesus Christ.

PSALMS 95.1-7; 135.1-6

READINGS YEAR 1

Old Testament *Exodus 19.1-6 RSV*

On the third new moon after the people of Israel had gone
forth out of the land of Egypt, on that day they came into the
wilderness of Sinai. And when they set out from Rephidim
and came into the wilderness of Sinai, they encamped in the
wilderness; and there Israel encamped before the mountain.
And Moses went up to God, and the Lord called him out of
the mountain, saying, 'Thus you shall say to the house of
Jacob, and tell the people of Israel: You have seen what I did
to the Egyptians, and how I bore you on eagles' wings and
brought you to myself. Now therefore, if you will obey my
voice and keep my covenant, you shall be my own
possession among all peoples; for all the earth is mine, and
you shall be to me a kingdom of priests and a holy nation.
These are the words which you shall speak to the children
of Israel.'

New Testament *1 Peter 2.1-10 NEB*

Away with all malice and deceit, away with all pretence and
jealousy and recrimination of every kind! Like the new-born
infants you are, you must crave for pure milk (spiritual milk,
I mean), so that you may thrive upon it to your soul's health.
Surely you have tasted that the Lord is good.

So come to him, our living Stone—the stone rejected by men
but choice and precious in the sight of God. Come, and let
yourselves be built, as living stones, into a spiritual temple;
become a holy priesthood, to offer spiritual sacrifices
acceptable to God through Jesus Christ. For it stands written:

'I lay in Zion a choice corner-stone of great worth.
The man who has faith in it will not be put to shame.'

The great worth of which it speaks is for you who have faith.
For those who have no faith, the stone which the builders
rejected has become not only the corner-stone, but also 'a
stone to trip over, a rock to stumble against'. They fall when
they disbelieve the Word. Such was their appointed lot!

But you are a chosen race, a royal priesthood, a dedicated nation, and a people claimed by God for his own, to proclaim the triumphs of him who has called you out of darkness into his marvellous light. You are now the people of God, who once were not his people; outside his mercy once, you have now received his mercy.

Gospel *John 15.1-5 JB*

Jesus said,
'I am the true vine,
and my Father is the vinedresser.
Every branch in me that bears no fruit
he cuts away,
and every branch that does bear fruit he prunes
to make it bear even more.
You are pruned already,
by means of the word that I have spoken to you.
Make your home in me, as I make mine in you.
As a branch cannot bear fruit all by itself,
but must remain part of the vine,
neither can you unless you remain in me.
I am the vine,
you are the branches.
Whoever remains in me, with me in him,
bears fruit in plenty;
for cut off from me you can do nothing.'

READINGS YEAR 2

Old Testament *2 Samuel 7.4-16 NEB*

The word of the Lord came to Nathan: 'Go and say to David my servant, "This is the word of the Lord: Are you the man to build me a house to dwell in? Down to this day I have never dwelt in a house since I brought Israel up from Egypt; I made my journey in a tent and a tabernacle. Wherever I journeyed with Israel, did I ever ask any of the judges whom I appointed shepherds of my people Israel why they had not built me a house of cedar?" Then say this to my servant David: "This is the word of the Lord of Hosts: I took you from the pastures, and from following the sheep, to be a prince over my people Israel. I have been with you wherever you have gone, and have destroyed all the enemies in your path. I will make you a great name among the great ones of the earth. I will assign a place for my people Israel; there I will plant them, and they shall dwell in their own land. They shall be disturbed no more, never again shall wicked men oppress them as they did in the past, ever since the time when I appointed judges over Israel my people; and I will give you peace from all your enemies. The Lord has told you that he would build up your royal house. When your life ends and you rest with your forefathers, I will set up one of your family, one of your own children, to succeed you and I will establish his kingdom. It is he who shall build a house in honour of my name, and I will establish his royal throne for ever. I will be his father, and he shall be my son. When he does wrong, I will punish him as any father might, and not spare the rod. My love will never be withdrawn from him as I withdrew it from Saul, whom I removed from your path. Your family shall be established and your kingdom shall stand for all time in my sight, and your throne shall be established for ever.'"

New Testament *Acts 2.37-end NEB*

When the crowd heard this they were cut to the heart, and said to Peter and the apostles, 'Friends, what are we to do?' 'Repent,' said Peter, 'repent and be baptized, every one of you, in the name of Jesus the Messiah for the forgiveness of your sins; and you will receive the gift of the Holy Spirit. For the promise is to you, and to your children, and to all who are far away, everyone whom the Lord our God may call.'

In these and many other words he pressed his case and pleaded with them: 'Save yourselves', he said, 'from this crooked age.' Then those who accepted his word were baptized, and some three thousand were added to their number that day.

They met constantly to hear the apostles teach, and to share the common life, to break bread, and to pray. A sense of awe was everywhere, and many marvels and signs were brought about through the apostles. All whose faith had drawn them together held everything in common; they would sell their property and possessions and make a general distribution as the need of each required. With one mind they kept up their daily attendance at the temple, and, breaking bread in private houses, shared their meals with unaffected joy, as they praised God and enjoyed the favour of the whole people. And day by day the Lord added to their number those whom he was saving.

Gospel *Luke 14.15-24 NEB*

One of the company said to Jesus, 'Happy the man who shall sit at the feast in the kingdom of God!' Jesus answered, 'A man was giving a big dinner party and had sent out many invitations. At dinner-time he sent his servant with a message for his guests, "Please come, everything is now ready." They began one and all to excuse themselves. The first said, "I have bought a piece of land, and I must go and look over it; please accept my apologies." The second said, "I have bought five yoke of oxen, and I am on my way to try them out; please accept my apologies." The next said, "I have just got married and for that reason I cannot come." When the servant came back he reported this to his master. The master of the house was angry and said to him, "Go out quickly into the streets and alleys of the town, and bring me in the poor, the crippled, the blind, and the lame." The servant said, "Sir, your orders have been carried out and there is still room." The master replied, "Go out on to the highways and along the hedgerows and make them come in; I want my house to be full. I tell you that not one of those who were invited shall taste my banquet."'

PROPER PREFACE

Rite A. The Preface of Unity (29) may be said.

POSTCOMMUNION SENTENCE YEAR 1

You are no longer strangers and sojourners, but you are fellow-citizens with the saints and members of the household of God, Christ Jesus himself being the chief corner-stone. *Ephesians 2.19, 20*

POSTCOMMUNION SENTENCE YEAR 2

Jesus said, By this will all men know that you are my disciples, if you have love one for another. *John 13.35*

PENTECOST 3
(Trinity 2)   Green

INTRODUCTORY SENTENCE YEAR 1

You have been buried with Christ in baptism, in which you have also been raised with him through faith in the working of God, who raised him from the dead. *Colossians 2.12*

INTRODUCTORY SENTENCE YEAR 2

Abide in Christ, so that when he appears we may have confidence in him and not shrink from him at his coming. *1 John 2.28*

COLLECT

Lord God our Father,
through our Saviour Jesus Christ
you have assured mankind of eternal life
and in baptism have made us one with him.
Deliver us from the death of sin
and raise us to new life in your love,
in the fellowship of the Holy Spirit,
by the grace of our Lord Jesus Christ.

PSALMS 44.1-9; 150

READINGS YEAR 1

Old Testament *Deuteronomy 6.17-end NEB*

You must diligently keep the commandments of the Lord your God as well as the precepts and statutes which he gave you. You must do what is right and good in the Lord's eyes so that all may go well with you, and you may enter and occupy the rich land which the Lord promised by oath to your forefathers; then you shall drive out all your enemies before you, as the Lord promised.

When your son asks you in time to come, 'What is the
meaning of the precepts, statutes, and laws which the Lord
our God gave you?', you shall say to him, 'We were
Pharaoh's slaves in Egypt, and the Lord brought us out of
Egypt with his strong hand, sending great disasters, signs,
and portents against the Egyptians and against Pharaoh and
all his family, as we saw for ourselves. But he led us out from
there to bring us into the land and give it to us as he had
promised to our forefathers. The Lord commanded us to
observe all these statutes and to fear the Lord our God; it will
be for our own good at all times, and he will continue to
preserve our lives. It will be counted to our credit if we keep
all these commandments in the sight of the Lord our God, as
he has bidden us.'

New Testament *Romans 6.3-11 NEB*

Have you forgotten that when we were baptized into union
with Christ Jesus we were baptized into his death? By
baptism we were buried with him, and lay dead, in order
that, as Christ was raised from the dead in the splendour of
the Father, so also we might set our feet upon the new path
of life.

For if we have become incorporate with him in a death like
his, we shall also be one with him in a resurrection like his.
We know that the man we once were has been crucified with
Christ, for the destruction of the sinful self, so that we may
no longer be the slaves of sin, since a dead man is no longer
answerable for his sin. But if we thus died with Christ, we
believe that we shall also come to life with him. We know
that Christ, once raised from the dead, is never to die again:
he is no longer under the dominion of death. For in dying as
he died, he died to sin, once for all, and in living as he lives,
he lives to God. In the same way you must regard yourselves
as dead to sin and alive to God, in union with Christ Jesus.

Gospel *John 15.5-11 JB*

Jesus said,
'I am the vine,

you are the branches.
Whoever remains in me, with me in him,
bears fruit in plenty;
for cut off from me you can do nothing.
Anyone who does not remain in me
is like a branch that has been thrown away
—he withers;
these branches are collected and thrown on the fire,
and they are burnt.
If you remain in me
and my words remain in you,
you may ask what you will
and you shall get it.
It is to the glory of my Father that you should bear
    much fruit,
and then you will be my disciples.
As the Father has loved me,
so I have loved you.
Remain in my love.
If you keep my commandments
you will remain in my love,
just as I have kept my Father's commandments
and remain in his love.
I have told you this
so that my own joy may be in you
and your joy be complete.'

READINGS YEAR 2

Old Testament *Deuteronomy 8.11-end NEB*

Take care not to forget the Lord your God and do not fail to
keep his commandments, laws, and statutes which I give
you this day. When you have plenty to eat and live in fine
houses of your own building, when your herds and flocks
increase, and your silver and gold and all your possessions
increase too, do not become proud and forget the Lord your
God who brought you out of Egypt, out of the land of
slavery; he led you through the vast and terrible wilderness
infested with poisonous snakes and scorpions, a thirsty,
waterless land, where he caused water to flow from the hard
rock; he fed you in the wilderness on manna which your

fathers did not know, to humble you and test you, and in the end to make you prosper. Nor must you say to yourselves, 'My own strength and energy have gained me this wealth', but remember the Lord your God; it is he that gives you strength to become prosperous, so fulfilling the convenant guaranteed by oath with your forefathers, as he is doing now.

If you forget the Lord your God and adhere to other gods, worshipping them and bowing down to them, I give you a solemn warning this day that you will certainly be destroyed. You will be destroyed because of your disobedience to the Lord your God, as surely as were the nations whom the Lord destroyed at your coming.

New Testament *Acts 4.8-12 NEB*

Peter, filled with the Holy Spirit, said, 'Rulers of the people and elders, if the question put to us today is about help given to a sick man, and we are asked by what means he was cured, here is the answer, for all of you and for all the people of Israel: it was by the name of Jesus Christ of Nazareth, whom you crucified, whom God raised from the dead; it is by his name that this man stands here before you fit and well. This Jesus is the stone rejected by the builders which has become the keystone—and you are the builders. There is no salvation in anyone else at all, for there is no other name under heaven granted to men, by which we may receive salvation.'

Gospel *Luke 8.41-end NEB*

A man appeared—Jairus was his name and he was president of the synagogue. Throwing himself down at Jesus' feet he begged him to come to his house, because he had an only daughter, about twelve years old, who was dying. And while Jesus was on his way he could hardly breathe for the crowds.

Among them was a woman who had suffered from haemorrhages for twelve years; and nobody had been able to cure her. She came up from behind and touched the edge of his cloak, and at once her haemorrhage stopped. Jesus said,

'Who was it that touched me?' All disclaimed it, and Peter and his companions said, 'Master, the crowds are hemming you in and pressing upon you!' But Jesus said, 'Someone did touch me, for I felt that power had gone out from me.' Then the woman, seeing that she was detected, came trembling and fell at his feet. Before all the people she explained why she had touched him and how she had been instantly cured. He said to her, 'My daughter, your faith has cured you. Go in peace.'

While he was still speaking, a man came from the president's house with the message, 'Your daughter is dead; trouble the Rabbi no further.' But Jesus heard, and interposed. 'Do not be afraid,' he said; 'only show faith and she will be well again.' On arrival at the house he allowed no one to go in with him except Peter, John, and James, and the child's father and mother. And all were weeping and lamenting for her. He said, 'Weep no more; she is not dead: she is asleep'; and they only laughed at him, well knowing that she was dead. But Jesus took hold of her hand and called her: 'Get up, my child.' Her spirit returned, she stood up immediately, and he told them to give her something to eat. Her parents were astounded; but he forbade them to tell anyone what had happened.

PROPER PREFACE

Rite A. In Year 1 the Preface of Baptism (30) may be said.

POSTCOMMUNION SENTENCE YEAR 1

God saved us, not because of deeds done by us in righteousness, but in virtue of his own mercy, by the washing of regeneration and renewal in the Holy Spirit. *Titus 3.5*

POSTCOMMUNION SENTENCE YEAR 2

God has said, 'I will never fail you nor forsake you.' Hence we can confidently say, 'The Lord is my helper, I will not be afraid; what can man do to me?' *Hebrews 13.5, 6*

PENTECOST 4
(Trinity 3)   Green

INTRODUCTORY SENTENCE YEAR 1

Live as free men, yet without using your freedom as a
pretext for evil; but live as servants of God. *1 Peter 2.16*

INTRODUCTORY SENTENCE YEAR 2

Whoever does not renounce all that he has cannot be
Christ's disciple. *Luke 14.33*

COLLECT

Almighty God,
you have broken the tyranny of sin
and have sent the Spirit of your Son into our hearts
whereby we call you Father.
Give us grace to dedicate our freedom to your service,
that all mankind may be brought
   to the glorious liberty of the sons of God;
through Jesus Christ our Lord.

PSALMS 63.1-9; 67

READINGS YEAR 1

Old Testament *Deuteronomy 7.6-11 NEB*

You are a people holy to the Lord your God; the Lord your
God chose you out of all nations on earth to be his
special possession.

It was not because you were more numerous than any other
nation that the Lord cared for you and chose you, for you
were the smallest of all nations; it was because the Lord
loved you and stood by his oath to your forefathers, that he
brought you out with his strong hand and redeemed you
from the land of slavery, from the power of Pharaoh king of
Egypt. Know then that the Lord your God is God, the
faithful God; with those who love him and keep his
commandments he keeps covenant and faith for a thousand
generations, but those who defy him and show their hatred

for him he repays with destruction: he will not be slow to requite any who so hate him.

You are to observe these commandments, statutes, and laws which I give you this day, and keep them.

New Testament *Galatians 3.23—4.7 TEV*

Before the time for faith came, the Law kept us all locked up as prisoners until this coming faith should be revealed. And so the Law was in charge of us until Christ came, in order that we might then be put right with God through faith. Now that the time for faith is here, the Law is no longer in charge of us.

It is through faith that all of you are God's sons in union with Christ Jesus. You were baptized into union with Christ, and now you are clothed, so to speak, with the life of Christ himself. So there is no difference between Jews and Gentiles, between slaves and free men, between men and women; you are all one in union with Christ Jesus. If you belong to Christ, then you are the descendants of Abraham and will receive what God has promised.

But now to continue—the son who will receive his father's property is treated just like a slave while he is young, even though he really owns everything. While he is young, there are men who take care of him and manage his affairs until the time set by his father. In the same way, we too were slaves of the ruling spirits of the universe before we reached spiritual maturity. But when the right time finally came, God sent his own Son. He came as the son of a human mother and lived under the Jewish Law, to redeem those who were under the Law, so that we might become God's sons.

To show that you are his sons, God sent the Spirit of his Son into our hearts, the Spirit who cries out, 'Father, my Father.' So then, you are no longer a slave but a son. And since you are his son, God will give you all that he has for his sons.

Gospel *John 15.12-17 JB*

Jesus said,
'This is my commandment:

love one another,
as I have loved you.
A man can have no greater love
than to lay down his life for his friends.
You are my friends,
if you do what I command you.
I shall not call you servants any more,
because a servant does not know
his master's business;
I call you friends,
because I have made known to you
everything I have learnt from my Father.
You did not choose me,
no, I chose you;
and I commissioned you
to go out and to bear fruit,
fruit that will last;
and then the Father will give you
anything you ask him in my name.
What I command you
is to love one another.'

READINGS YEAR 2

Old Testament *Isaiah 63.7-14 RSV*

I will recount the steadfast love of the Lord,
the praises of the Lord,
according to all that the Lord has granted us,
and the great goodness to the house of Israel
which he has granted them according to his mercy,
according to the abundance of his steadfast love.
For he said, Surely they are my people,
sons who will not deal falsely;
and he became their Saviour.
In all their affliction he was afflicted,
and the angel of his presence saved them;
in his love and in his pity he redeemed them;
he lifted them up and carried them all the days of old.

But they rebelled
and grieved his holy Spirit;

therefore he turned to be their enemy,
and himself fought against them.
Then he remembered the days of old,
of Moses his servant.
Where is he who brought up out of the sea
the shepherds of his flock?
Where is he who put in the midst of them
his holy Spirit,
who caused his glorious arm
to go at the right hand of Moses,
who divided the waters before them
to make for himself an everlasting name,
who led them through the depths?
Like a horse in the desert,
they did not stumble.
Like cattle that go down into the valley,
the Spirit of the Lord gave them rest.
So you lead your people,
to make for yourself a glorious name.

New Testament *Acts 8.26-38 JB*

The angel of the Lord spoke to Philip saying, 'Be ready to set
out at noon along the road that goes from Jerusalem down to
Gaza, the desert road.' So he set off on his journey. Now it
happened that an Ethiopian had been on pilgrimage to
Jerusalem; he was a eunuch and an officer at the court of the
kandake, or queen, of Ethiopia, and was in fact her chief
treasurer. He was now on his way home; and as he sat in his
chariot he was reading the prophet Isaiah. The Spirit said to
Philip, 'Go up and meet that chariot.' When Philip ran up,
he heard him reading Isaiah the prophet and asked, 'Do you
understand what you are reading?' 'How can I', he replied,
'unless I have someone to guide me?' So he invited Philip to
get in and sit by his side. Now the passage of scripture he
was reading was this:

'Like a sheep that is led to the slaughter-house,
like a lamb that is dumb in front of its shearers,
like these he never opens his mouth.
He has been humiliated and has no one to defend him.
Who will ever talk about his descendants,

since his life on earth has been cut short!'

The eunuch turned to Philip and said, 'Tell me, is the prophet referring to himself or someone else?' Starting, therefore, with this text of scripture Philip proceeded to explain the Good News of Jesus to him.

Further along the road they came to some water, and the eunuch said, 'Look, there is some water here; is there anything to stop me being baptized?' He ordered the chariot to stop, then Philip and the eunuch both went down into the water and Philip baptized him.

Gospel *Luke 15.1-10 RSV*

Now the tax collectors and sinners were all drawing near to hear Jesus. And the Pharisees and the scribes murmured, saying, 'This man receives sinners and eats with them.'

So he told them this parable: 'What man of you, having a hundred sheep, if he has lost one of them, does not leave the ninety-nine in the wilderness, and go after the one which is lost, until he finds it? And when he has found it, he lays it on his shoulders, rejoicing. And when he comes home, he calls together his friends and his neighbours, saying to them, "Rejoice with me, for I have found my sheep which was lost." Even so, I tell you, there will be more joy in heaven over one sinner who repents than over ninety-nine righteous persons who need no repentance.

'Or what woman, having ten silver coins, if she loses one coin, does not light a lamp and sweep the house and seek diligently until she finds it? And when she has found it, she calls together her friends and neighbours, saying, "Rejoice with me, for I have found the coin which I had lost." Even so, I tell you, there is joy before the angels of God over one sinner who repents.'

PROPER PREFACE

Rite A. In Year 1 a Preface of the Resurrection may be said.
Rite B. In Year 1 the Preface of Easter may be said.

POSTCOMMUNION SENTENCE YEAR 1

If the Son makes you free, you will be free indeed. *John 8.36*

POSTCOMMUNION SENTENCE YEAR 2

The king said to his servants, Go into the streets, and invite to the marriage feast as many as you find. *Matthew 22.8, 9*

PENTECOST 5
(Trinity 4)   Green

INTRODUCTORY SENTENCE YEAR 1

Owe no one anything, except to love one another; for he who loves his neighbour has fulfilled the law. *Romans 13.8*

INTRODUCTORY.SENTENCE YEAR 2

Lift up your eyes and see how the fields are already white for harvest. *John 4.35*

COLLECT

Almighty God,
you show to those who are in error the light of your truth,
that they may return to the way of righteousness.
May we and all who have been admitted
    to the fellowship of Christ's religion
reject those things which are contrary to our profession
and follow all such things as are agreeable to the same;
through Jesus Christ our Lord.

PSALMS 119.57-64; 119.89-96

READINGS YEAR 1

Old Testament *Exodus 20.1-17 NEB*

God spoke, and these were his words:
I am the Lord your God who brought you out of Egypt, out of the land of slavery.

You shall have no other god to set against me.

You shall not make a carved image for yourself nor the likeness of anything in the heavens above, or on the earth below, or in the waters under the earth.

You shall not bow down to them or worship them; for I, the Lord your God, am a jealous god. I punish the children for the sins of the fathers to the third and fourth generations of those who hate me. But I keep faith with thousands, with those who love me and keep my commandments.

You shall not make wrong use of the name of the Lord your God; the Lord will not leave unpunished the man who misuses his name.

Remember to keep the sabbath day holy. You have six days to labour and do all your work. But the seventh day is a sabbath of the Lord your God; that day you shall not do any work, you, your son or your daughter, your slave or your slave-girl, your cattle or the alien within your gates; for in six days the Lord made heaven and earth, the sea, and all that is in them, and on the seventh day he rested. Therefore the Lord blessed the sabbath day and declared it holy.

Honour your father and your mother, that you may live long in the land which the Lord your God is giving you.

You shall not commit murder.

You shall not commit adultery.

You shall not steal.

You shall not give false evidence against your neighbour.

You shall not covet your neighbour's house; you shall not covet your neighbour's wife, his slave, his slave-girl, his ox, his ass, or anything that belongs to him.

New Testament *Ephesians 5.1-10 NEB*

As God's dear children, try to be like Christ, and live in love as he loved you, and gave himself up on your behalf as an offering and sacrifice whose fragrance is pleasing to God.

Fornication and indecency of any kind, or ruthless greed, must not be so much as mentioned among you, as befits the people of God. No coarse, stupid, or flippant talk; these things are out of place; you should rather be thanking God. For be very sure of this: no one given to fornication or indecency, or the greed which makes an idol of gain, has any share in the kingdom of Christ and of God.

Let no one deceive you with shallow arguments; it is for all these things that God's dreadful judgement is coming upon his rebel subjects. Have no part or lot with them. For though you were once all darkness, now as Christians you are light.

Live like men who are at home in daylight, for where light is, there all goodness springs up, all justice and truth. Try to find out what would please the Lord.

Gospel *Matthew 19.16-26 NEB*

A man came up and asked Jesus, 'Master, what good must I do to gain eternal life?' 'Good?' said Jesus. 'Why do you ask me about that? One alone is good. But if you wish to enter into life, keep the commandments.' 'Which commandments?' he asked. Jesus answered, 'Do not murder; do not commit adultery; do not steal; do not give false evidence; honour your father and mother; and love your neighbour as yourself.' The young man answered, 'I have kept all these. Where do I still fall short?' Jesus said to him, 'If you wish to go the whole way, go, sell your possessions, and give to the poor, and then you will have riches in heaven; and come, follow me.' When the young man heard this, he went away with a heavy heart; for he was a man of great wealth.

Jesus said to his disciples, 'I tell you this: a rich man will find it hard to enter the kingdom of Heaven. I repeat, it is easier for a camel to pass through the eye of a needle than for a rich man to enter the kingdom of God.' The disciples were amazed to hear this. 'Then who can be saved?' they asked. Jesus looked at them, and said, 'For men this is impossible; but everything is possible for God.'

READINGS YEAR 2

Old Testament *Ruth 1.8-17, 22 NEB*

Naomi said to her two daughters-in-law, 'Go back, both of you, to your mothers' homes. May the Lord keep faith with you, as you have kept faith with the dead and with me; and may he grant each of you security in the home of a new husband.' She kissed them and they wept aloud. Then they said to her, 'We will return with you to your own people.' But Naomi said, 'Go back, my daughters. Why should you go with me? Am I likely to bear any more sons to be husbands for you? Go back, my daughters, go. I am too old to marry again. But even if I could say that I had hope of a child, if I were to marry this night and if I were to bear sons, would you then wait until they grew up? Would you then refrain from marrying? No, no, my daughters, my lot is more bitter than yours, because the Lord has been against me.' At this they wept again. Then Orpah kissed her mother-in-law and returned to her people, but Ruth clung to her.

'You see,' said Naomi, 'your sister-in-law has gone back to her people and her gods; go back with her.' 'Do not urge me to go back and desert you,' Ruth answered. 'Where you go, I will go, and where you stay, I will stay. Your people shall be my people, and your God my God. Where you die, I will die, and there I will be buried. I swear a solemn oath before the Lord your God: nothing but death shall divide us.'

This is how Naomi's daughter-in-law, Ruth the Moabitess, returned with her from the Moabite country. The barley harvest was beginning when they arrived in Bethlehem.

New Testament *Acts 11.4-18 NEB*

Peter began by laying before those who were of Jewish birth the facts as they had happened.

'I was in the city of Joppa', he said, 'at prayer; and while in a trance I had a vision: a thing was coming down that looked like a great sheet of sail-cloth, slung by the four corners and lowered from the sky till it reached me. I looked intently to make out what was in it and I saw four-footed creatures of the earth, wild beasts, and things that crawl or fly. Then I heard a voice saying to me, "Up, Peter, kill and eat." But I said, "No, Lord, no: nothing profane or unclean has ever entered my mouth." A voice from heaven answered a second time, "It is not for you to call profane what God counts clean." This happened three times, and then they were all drawn up again into the sky. At that moment three men, who had been sent to me from Caesarea, arrived at the house where I was staying; and the Spirit told me to go with them. My six companions here came with me and we went into the man's house. He told us how he had seen an angel standing in his house who said, "Send to Joppa for Simon also called Peter. He will speak words that will bring salvation to you and all your household." Hardly had I begun speaking, when the Holy Spirit came upon them, just as upon us at the beginning. Then I recalled what the Lord had said: "John baptized with water, but you will be baptized with the Holy Spirit." God gave them no less a gift than he gave us when we put our trust in the Lord Jesus Christ; then how could I possibly stand in God's way?'

When they heard this their doubts were silenced. They gave praise to God and said, 'This means that God has granted life-giving repentance to the Gentiles also.'

Gospel *Luke 10.1-12 NEB*

The Lord appointed a further seventy-two and sent them on ahead in pairs to every town and place he was going to visit himself. He said to them: 'The crop is heavy, but labourers are scarce; you must therefore beg the owner to send labourers to harvest his crop. Be on your way. And look, I am sending you like lambs among wolves. Carry no purse or pack, and travel barefoot. Exchange no greetings on the road. When you go into a house, let your first words be, "Peace to this house." If there is a man of peace there, your peace will rest upon him; if not, it will return and rest upon you. Stay in that one house, sharing their food and drink; for the worker earns his pay. Do not move from house to house. When you come into a town and they make you welcome, eat the food provided for you; heal the sick there, and say, "The kingdom of God has come close to you." When you enter a town and they do not make you welcome, go out into its streets and say, "The very dust of your town that clings to our feet we wipe off to your shame. Only take note of this: the kingdom of God has come close." I tell you, it will be more bearable for Sodom on the great Day than for that town.'

PROPER PREFACE

Rite A. In Year 2 the Preface of Pentecost (18) may be said.
Rite B. In Year 2 the Preface of Pentecost may be said.

POSTCOMMUNION SENTENCE YEAR 1

After those days, says the Lord, I will put my laws into their minds, and write them on their hearts, and I will be their God, and they shall be my people. *Hebrews 8.10*

POSTCOMMUNION SENTENCE YEAR 2

Jesus said, All authority in heaven and on earth has been given to me. Go therefore and make disciples of all nations. *Matthew 28.18, 19*

PENTECOST 6
(Trinity 5)   Green

INTRODUCTORY SENTENCE

Put on the Lord Jesus Christ, and make no provision for the flesh. *Romans 13.14*

COLLECT

Almighty God,
without you we are not able to please you.
Mercifully grant that your Holy Spirit
may in all things direct and rule our hearts;
through Jesus Christ our Lord.

PSALMS 112; 1

READINGS YEAR 1

Old Testament *Exodus 24.3-11 RSV*

Moses came and told the people all the words of the Lord and all the ordinances; and all the people answered with one voice, and said, 'All the words which the Lord has spoken we will do.' And Moses wrote all the words of the Lord. And he rose early in the morning, and built an altar at the foot of the mountain, and twelve pillars, according to the twelve tribes of Israel. And he sent young men of the people of Israel, who offered burnt offerings and sacrificed peace offerings of oxen to the Lord. And Moses took half of the blood and put it in basins, and half of the blood he threw against the altar. Then he took the book of the covenant, and read it in the hearing of the people; and they said, 'All that the Lord has spoken we will do, and we will be obedient.' And Moses took the blood and threw it upon the people, and said, 'Behold the blood of the covenant which the Lord has made with you in accordance with all these words.'

Then Moses and Aaron, Nadab, and Abihu, and seventy of the elders of Israel went up, and they saw the God of Israel; and there was under his feet as it were a pavement of sapphire stone, like the very heaven for clearness. And he did not lay his hand on the chief men of the people of Israel; they beheld God, and ate and drank.

New Testament *Colossians 3.12-17 RSV*

Put on, as God's chosen ones, holy and beloved, compassion, kindness, lowliness, meekness, and patience, forbearing one another and, if one has a complaint against another, forgiving each other; as the Lord has forgiven you, so you also must forgive. And above all these put on love, which binds everything together in perfect harmony. And let the peace of Christ rule in your hearts, to which indeed you were called in the one body. And be thankful. Let the word of Christ dwell in you richly, as you teach and admonish one another in all wisdom, and as you sing psalms and hymns and spiritual songs with thankfulness in your hearts to God. And whatever you do, in word or deed, do everything in the name of the Lord Jesus, giving thanks to God the Father through him.

Gospel *Luke 15.11-end RSV*

Jesus said, 'There was a man who had two sons; and the younger of them said to his father, "Father, give me the share of property that falls to me." And he divided his living between them. Not many days later, the younger son gathered all he had and took his journey into a far country, and there he squandered his property in loose living. And when he had spent everything, a great famine arose in that country, and he began to be in want. So he went and joined himself to one of the citizens of that country, who sent him into his fields to feed swine. And he would gladly have fed on the pods that the swine ate; and no one gave him anything. But when he came to himself he said, "How many of my father's hired servants have bread enough and to spare, but I perish here with hunger! I will arise and go to my father, and I will say to him, "Father, I have sinned against heaven and before you; I am no longer worthy to be called your son; treat me as one of your hired servants." And he arose and came to his father. But while he was yet at a distance, his father saw him and had compassion, and ran and embraced him and kissed him. And the son said to him, "Father, I have sinned against heaven and before you; I am no longer worthy to be called your son." But the father said to his servants, "Bring quickly the best robe, and put it on him; and put a ring on his hand, and shoes on his feet; and bring the fatted calf and kill it, and let us eat and make merry; for this my son was dead, and is alive again; he was lost, and is found." And they began to make merry.

'Now his elder son was in the field; and as he came and drew near to the house, he heard music and dancing. And he called one of the servants and asked what this meant. And he said to him, "Your brother has come, and your father has killed the fatted calf, because he has received him safe and sound." But he was angry and refused to go in. His father came out and entreated him, but he answered his father, "Lo, these many years I have served you, and I never disobeyed your command; yet you never gave me a kid, that

I might make merry with my friends. But when this son of yours came, who has devoured your living with harlots, you killed for him the fatted calf!" And he said to him, "Son, you are always with me, and all that is mine is yours. It was fitting to make merry and be glad, for this your brother was dead, and is alive; he was lost, and is found.""

READINGS YEAR 2

Old Testament *Micah 6.1-8 RSV*

Hear what the Lord says;
Arise, plead your case before the mountains,
and let the hills hear your voice.
Hear, you mountains, the controversy of the Lord,
and you enduring foundations of the earth;
for the Lord has a controversy with his people,
and he will contend with Israel.

'O my people, what have I done to you?
In what have I wearied you? Answer me!
For I brought you up from the land of Egypt,
and redeemed you from the house of bondage;
and I sent before you Moses, Aaron, and Miriam.
O my people, remember what Balak king of Moab devised,
and what Balaam the son of Beor answered him,
and what happened from Shittim to Gilgal,
that you may know the saving acts of the Lord.'

'With what shall I come before the Lord,
and bow myself before God on high?
Shall I come before him with burnt offerings,
with calves a year old?
Will the Lord be pleased with thousands of rams,
with ten thousands of rivers of oil?
Shall I give my first-born for my transgression,
the fruit of my body for the sin of my soul?
He has showed you, O man, what is good;
and what does the Lord require of you
but to do justice, and to love kindness,
and to walk humbly with your God?'

New Testament *Ephesians 4.17-end RSV*

Now this I affirm and testify in the Lord, that you must no longer live as the Gentiles do, in the futility of their minds; they are darkened in their understanding, alienated from the life of God because of the ignorance that is in them, due to their hardness of heart; they have become callous and have given themselves up to licentiousness, greedy to practise every kind of uncleanness. You did not so learn Christ!—assuming that you have heard about him and were taught in him, as the truth is in Jesus. Put off your old nature which belongs to your former manner of life and is corrupt through deceitful lusts, and be renewed in the spirit of your minds, and put on the new nature, created after the likeness of God in true righteousness and holiness.

Therefore, putting away falsehood, let every one speak the truth with his neighbour, for we are members one of another. Be angry but do not sin; do not let the sun go down on your anger, and give no opportunity to the devil. Let the thief no longer steal, but rather let him labour, doing honest work with his hands, so that he may be able to give to those in need. Let no evil talk come out of your mouths, but only such as is good for edifying, as fits the occasion, that it may impart grace to those who hear. And do not grieve the Holy Spirit of God, in whom you were sealed for the day of redemption. Let all bitterness and wrath and anger and clamour and slander be put away from you, with all malice, and be kind to one another, tenderhearted, forgiving one another, as God in Christ forgave you.

Gospel *Mark 10.46-end NEB*

Jesus and his disciples came to Jericho; and as he was leaving the town, with his disciples and a large crowd, Bartimaeus son of Timaeus, a blind beggar, was seated at the roadside. Hearing that it was Jesus of Nazareth, he began to shout, 'Son of David, Jesus, have pity on me!' Many of the people told him to hold his tongue; but he shouted all the more, 'Son of David, have pity on me.' Jesus stopped and said, 'Call him'; so they called the blind man and said, 'Take heart; stand up; he is calling you.' At that he threw off his cloak, sprang up, and came to Jesus. Jesus said to him, 'What do you want me to do for you?' 'Master,' the blind man answered, 'I want my sight back.' Jesus said to him, 'Go; your faith has cured you.' And at once he recovered his sight and followed him on the road.

POSTCOMMUNION SENTENCE

Therefore if any one is in Christ, he is a new creation; the old has passed away, behold, the new has come.
2 Corinthians 5.17

PENTECOST 7
(Trinity 6)   Green

INTRODUCTORY SENTENCE

It is my prayer that your love may abound more and more, so that you may approve what is excellent, and may be pure and blameless for the day of Christ. *Philippians 1.9, 10*

COLLECT

Lord, you have taught us
that all our doings without love are nothing worth.
Send your Holy Spirit
and pour into our hearts that most excellent gift of love,
the true bond of peace and of all virtues,
without which whoever lives is counted dead before you.
Grant this for the sake of your only Son,
Jesus Christ our Lord.

PSALMS 62; 103.8-18

READINGS YEAR 1

Old Testament *Hosea 11.1-9 NEB*

When Israel was a boy, I loved him;
I called my son out of Egypt;
but the more I called, the further they went from me;
they must needs sacrifice to the Baalim

and burn offerings before carved images.
It was I who taught Ephraim to walk,
I who had taken them in my arms;
but they did not know that I harnessed them in
    leading-strings
and led them with bonds of love—
that I had lifted them like a little child to my cheek,
that I had bent down to feed them.
Back they shall go to Egypt,
the Assyrian shall be their king;
for they have refused to return to me.
The sword shall be swung over their blood-spattered altars
and put an end to their prattling priests
and devour my people in return for all their schemings,
bent on rebellion as they are.
Though they call on their high god,
even then he will not reinstate them.
How can I give you up, Ephraim,
how surrender you, Israel?
How can I make you like Admah
or treat you as Zeboyim?
My heart is changed within me,
my remorse kindles already.
I will not let loose my fury,
I will not turn round and destroy Ephraim;
for I am God and not a man,
the Holy One in your midst.

New Testament *1Corinthians 12.27—13 end NEB*

You are Christ's body, and each of you a limb or organ of it.
Within our community God has appointed, in the first place
apostles, in the second place prophets, thirdly teachers; then
miracle-workers, then those who have gifts of healing, or
ability to help others or power to guide them, or the gift of
ecstatic utterance of various kinds. Are all apostles? all
prophets? all teachers? Do all work miracles? Have all gifts of
healing? Do all speak in tongues of ecstasy? Can all interpret
them? The higher gifts are those you should aim at.

And now I will show you the best way of all.

I may speak in tongues of men or of angels, but if I am without love, I am a sounding gong or a clanging cymbal. I may have the gift of prophecy, and know every hidden truth; I may have faith strong enough to move mountains; but if I have no love, I am nothing. I may dole out all I possess, or even give my body to be burnt, but if I have no love, I am none the better.

Love is patient; love is kind and envies no one. Love is never boastful, nor conceited, nor rude; never selfish, not quick to take offence. Love keeps no score of wrongs; does not gloat over other men's sins, but delights in the truth. There is nothing love cannot face; there is no limit to its faith, its hope, and its endurance.

Love will never come to an end. Are there prophets? their work will be over. Are there tongues of ecstasy? they will cease. Is there knowledge? it will vanish away; for our knowledge and our prophecy alike are partial, and the partial vanishes when wholeness comes. When I was a child, my speech, my outlook, and my thoughts were all childish. When I grew up, I had finished with childish things. Now we see only puzzling reflections in a mirror, but then we shall see face to face. My knowledge now is partial; then it will be whole, like God's knowledge of me. In a word, there are three things that last for ever: faith, hope, and love; but the greatest of them all is love.

Gospel *Matthew 18.21-end JB*

Peter went up to Jesus and said, 'Lord, how often must I forgive my brother if he wrongs me? As often as seven times?' Jesus answered, 'Not seven, I tell you, but seventy-seven times.

'And so the kingdom of heaven may be compared to a king who decided to settle his accounts with his servants. When the reckoning began, they brought him a man who owed ten thousand talents; but he had no means of paying, so his master gave orders that he should be sold, together with his wife and children and all his possessions, to meet the debt. At this, the servant threw himself down at his master's feet. "Give me time," he said, "and I will pay the whole sum."

And the servant's master felt so sorry for him that he let him go and cancelled the debt. Now as this servant went out, he happened to meet a fellow servant who owed him one hundred denarii; and he seized him by the throat and began to throttle him. "Pay what you owe me", he said. His fellow servant fell at his feet and implored him, saying, "Give me time and I will pay you." But the other would not agree; on the contrary, he had him thrown into prison till he should pay the debt. His fellow servants were deeply distressed when they saw what had happened, and they went to their master and reported the whole affair to him. Then the master sent for him. "You wicked servant," he said, "I cancelled all that debt of yours when you appealed to me. Were you not bound, then, to have pity on your fellow servant just as I had pity on you?" And in his anger the master handed him over to the torturers till he should pay all his debt. And that is how my heavenly Father will deal with you unless you each forgive your brother from your heart.'

READINGS YEAR 2

Old Testament Deuteronomy 10.12—11.1 NEB

What, O Israel, does the Lord your God ask of you? Only to fear the Lord your God, to conform to all his ways, to love him and to serve him with all your heart and soul. This you will do by keeping the commandments of the Lord and his statutes which I give you this day for your good. To the Lord your God belong heaven itself, the highest heaven, the earth and everything in it; yet the Lord cared for your forefathers in his love for them and chose their descendants after them. Out of all nations you were his chosen people as you are this day. So now you must circumcise the foreskin of your hearts and not be stubborn any more, for the Lord your God is God of gods and Lord of lords, the great, mighty, and terrible God. He is no respecter of persons and is not to be bribed; he secures justice for widows and orphans, and loves the alien who lives among you, giving him food and clothing. You too must love the alien, for you once lived as aliens in Egypt. You must fear the Lord your God, serve him, hold fast to him and take your oaths in his name. He is your praise, your God who has done for you these great and terrible things

which you have seen with your own eyes. When your
forefathers went down into Egypt they were only seventy
strong, but now the Lord your God has made you countless
as the stars in the sky.

You shall love the Lord your God and keep for all time the
charge he laid upon you, the statutes, the laws, and
the commandments.

New Testament *Romans 8.1-11 JB*

The reason why those who are in Christ Jesus are not
condemned, is that the law of the spirit of life in Christ Jesus
has set you free from the law of sin and death. God has done
what the Law, because of our unspiritual nature, was unable
to do. God dealt with sin by sending his own Son in a body
as physical as any sinful body, and in that body God
condemned sin. He did this in order that the Law's just
demands might be satisfied in us, who behave not as our
unspiritual nature but as the spirit dictates.

The unspiritual are interested only in what is unspiritual,
but the spiritual are interested in spiritual things. It is death
to limit oneself to what is unspiritual; life and peace can only
come with concern for the spiritual. That is because to limit
oneself to what is unspiritual is to be at enmity with God:
such a limitation never could and never does submit to
God's law. People who are interested only in unspiritual
things can never be pleasing to God. Your interests,
however, are not in the unspiritual, but in the spiritual, since
the Spirit of God has made his home in you. In fact, unless
you possessed the Spirit of Christ you would not belong to
him. Though your body may be dead it is because of sin, but
if Christ is in you then your spirit is life itself because you
have been justified; and if the Spirit of him who raised Jesus
from the dead is living in you, then he who raised Jesus from
the dead will give life to your own mortal bodies through his
Spirit living in you.

Gospel *Mark 12.28-34 NEB*

One of the lawyers, who had been listening to the
discussions and had noted how well Jesus answered, came

forward and asked him, 'Which commandment is first of all?' Jesus answered, 'The first is, "Hear, O Israel: the Lord our God is the only Lord; love the Lord your God with all your heart, with all your soul, with all your mind, and with all your strength." The second is this: "Love your neighbour as yourself." There is no other commandment greater than these.' The lawyer said to him, 'Well said, Master. You are right in saying that God is one and beside him there is no other. And to love him with all your heart, all your understanding, and all your strength, and to love your neighbour as yourself—that is far more than any burnt offerings or sacrifices.' When Jesus saw how sensibly he answered, he said to him, 'You are not far from the kingdom of God.'

POSTCOMMUNION SENTENCE

In this is love, not that we loved God, but that he loved us and sent his Son to be the propitiation for our sins.
1 John 4.10

PENTECOST 8
(Trinity 7)   Green

INTRODUCTORY SENTENCE

A sound tree cannot bear evil fruit, nor can a bad tree bear good fruit. Thus you will be known by your fruits.
Matthew 7.18, 20

COLLECT

Almighty God,
who sent your Holy Spirit
to be the life and light of your Church:
open our hearts to the riches of his grace,
that we may bring forth the fruit of the Spirit
in love and joy and peace;
through Jesus Christ our Lord.

PSALMS 25.1-10; 27.1-8

READINGS YEAR 1

Old Testament *Ezekiel 36.24-28 NEB*

I will take you out of the nations and gather you from every
land and bring you to your own soil. I will sprinkle clean
water over you, and you shall be cleansed from all that
defiles you; I will cleanse you from the taint of all your idols. I
will give you a new heart and put a new spirit within you; I
will take the heart of stone from your body and give you a
heart of flesh. I will put my spirit into you and make you
conform to my statutes, keep my laws and live by them. You
shall live in the land which I gave to your ancestors; you shall
become my people, and I will become your God.

New Testament *Galatians 5.16-25 JB*

If you are guided by the Spirit you will be in no danger of
yielding to self-indulgence, since self-indulgence is the
opposite of the Spirit, the Spirit is totally against such a
thing, and it is precisely because the two are so opposed that
you do not always carry out your good intentions. If you are
led by the Spirit, no law can touch you. When
self-indulgence is at work the results are obvious:
fornication, gross indecency and sexual irresponsibility;
idolatry and sorcery; feuds and wrangling, jealousy, bad
temper and quarrels; disagreements, factions, envy;
drunkenness, orgies and similar things. I warn you now, as I
warned you before: those who behave like this will not
inherit the kingdom of God. What the Spirit brings is very
different: love, joy, peace, patience, kindness, goodness,
trustfulness, gentleness, and self-control. There can be no
law against things like that, of course. You cannot belong to
Christ Jesus unless you crucify all self-indulgent passions
and desires.

Gospel *John 15.16-end JB*

Jesus said,
'You did not choose me,
no, I chose you;
and I commissioned you

to go out and to bear fruit,
fruit that will last;
and then the Father will give you
anything you ask him in my name.
What I command you
is to love one another.

'If the world hates you,
remember that it hated me before you.
If you belonged to the world,
the world would love you as its own;
but because you do not belong to the world,
because my choice withdrew you from the world,
therefore the world hates you.
Remember the words I said to you:
A servant is not greater than his master.
If they persecuted me,
they will persecute you too;
if they kept my word,
they will keep yours as well.
But it will be on my account that they will do all this,
because they do not know the one who sent me.
If I had not come,
if I had not spoken to them,
they would have been blameless;
but as it is they have no excuse for their sin.
Anyone who hates me hates my Father.
If I had not performed such works among them
as no one else has ever done,
they would be blameless;
but as it is, they have seen all this,
and still they hate both me and my Father.
But all this was only to fulfil the words written in their Law:
''They hated me for no reason.''
When the Advocate comes,
whom I shall send to you from the Father,
the Spirit of truth who issues from the Father,
he will be my witness.
And you too will be witnesses,
because you have been with me from the outset.'

READINGS YEAR 2

Old Testament *Ezekiel 37.1-14 JB*

The hand of the Lord was laid on me, and he carried me away by the spirit of the Lord and set me down in the middle of a valley, a valley full of bones. He made me walk up and down among them. There were vast quantities of these bones on the ground the whole length of the valley; and they were quite dried up. He said to me, 'Son of man, can these bones live?' I said, 'You know, Lord God.' He said, 'Prophesy over these bones. Say, "Dry bones, hear the word of the Lord. The Lord God says this to these bones: I am now going to make the breath enter you, and you will live. I shall put sinews on you, I shall make flesh grow on you, I shall cover you with skin and give you breath, and you will live; and you will learn that I am the Lord."' I prophesied as I had been ordered. While I was prophesying, there was a noise, a sound of clattering; and the bones joined together. I looked, and saw that they were covered with sinews; flesh was growing on them and skin was covering them, but there was no breath in them. He said to me, 'Prophesy to the breath; prophesy, son of man. Say to the breath, "The Lord God says this: Come from the four winds, breath; breathe on these dead; let them live!"' I prophesied as he had ordered me, and the breath entered them; they came to life again and stood up on their feet, a great, an immense army.

Then he said, 'Son of man, these bones are the whole House of Israel. They keep saying, "Our bones are dried up, our hope has gone; we are as good as dead." So prophesy. Say to them, "The Lord God says this: I am now going to open your graves; I mean to raise you from your graves, my people, and lead you back to the soil of Israel. And you will know that I am the Lord, when I open your graves and raise you from your graves, my people. And I shall put my spirit in you, and you will live, and I shall resettle you on your own soil; and you will know that I, the Lord, have said and done this—it is the Lord God who speaks."'

New Testament *1 Corinthians 12.4-13 NEB*

There are varieties of gifts, but the same Spirit. There are varieties of service, but the same Lord. There are many forms of work, but all of them, in all men, are the work of the same God. In each of us the Spirit is manifested in one particular way, for some useful purpose. One man, through the Spirit, has the gift of wise speech, while another, by the power of the same Spirit, can put the deepest knowledge into words. Another, by the same Spirit, is granted faith; another, by the one Spirit, gifts of healing, and another miraculous powers; another has the gift of prophecy, and another ability to distinguish true spirits from false; yet another has the gift of ecstatic utterance of different kinds, and another the ability to interpret it. But all these gifts are the work of one and the same Spirit, distributing them separately to each individual at will.

For Christ is like a single body with its many limbs and organs, which, many as they are, together make up one body. For indeed we were all brought into one body by baptism, in the one Spirit, whether we are Jews or Greeks, whether slaves or free men, and that one Holy Spirit was poured out for all of us to drink.

Gospel *Luke 6.27-38 NEB*

Jesus said: 'To you who hear me I say:
Love your enemies; do good to those who hate you; bless those who curse you; pray for those who treat you spitefully. When a man hits you on the cheek, offer him the other cheek too; when a man takes your coat, let him have your shirt as well. Give to everyone who asks you; when a man takes what is yours, do not demand it back. Treat others as you would like them to treat you.

'If you love only those who love you, what credit is that to you? Even sinners love those who love them. Again, if you do good only to those who do good to you, what credit is that to you? Even sinners do as much. And if you lend only where you expect to be repaid, what credit is that to you? Even sinners lend to each other to be repaid in full. But you must love your enemies and do good; and lend without expecting any return; and you will have a rich reward: you will be sons of the Most High, because he himself is kind to the ungrateful and wicked. Be compassionate as your Father is compassionate.

'Pass no judgement, and you will not be judged; do not condemn, and you will not be condemned; acquit, and you will be acquitted; give, and gifts will be given you. Good measure, pressed down, shaken together, and running over, will be poured into your lap; for whatever measure you deal out to others will be dealt to you in return.'

POSTCOMMUNION SENTENCE

Once you were darkness, but now you are light in the Lord; walk as children of light (for the fruit of light is found in all that is good and right and true). *Ephesians 5.8, 9*

PENTECOST 9
(Trinity 8)   Green

INTRODUCTORY SENTENCE

The Lord put on righteousness as a breastplate, and a helmet of salvation upon his head. *Isaiah 59.17*

COLLECT

Almighty God,
you see that we have no power of ourselves
    to help ourselves.
Keep us both outwardly in our bodies
    and inwardly in our souls,
that we may be defended from all adversities
    which may happen to the body,
and from all evil thoughts
    which may assault and hurt the soul;
through Jesus Christ our Lord.

PSALMS 18.1-7; 18.32-38

READINGS YEAR 1

Old Testament *Joshua 1.1-9 RSV*

After the death of Moses the servant of the Lord, the Lord said to Joshua the son of Nun, Moses' minister, 'Moses my servant is dead; now therefore arise, go over this Jordan, you and all this people, into the land which I am giving to them, to the people of Israel. Every place that the sole of your foot will tread upon I have given to you, as I promised to Moses. From the wilderness and this Lebanon as far as the great river, the river Euphrates, all the land of the Hittites to the Great Sea toward the going down of the sun shall be your territory. No man shall be able to stand before you all the days of your life; as I was with Moses, so I will be with you; I will not fail you or forsake you. Be strong and of good courage; for you shall cause this people to inherit the land which I swore to their fathers to give them. Only be strong and very courageous, being careful to do according to all the law which Moses my servant commanded you; turn not from it to the right hand or to the left, that you may have good success wherever you go. This book of the law shall not depart out of your mouth, but you shall meditate on it day and night, that you may be careful to do according to all that is written in it; for then you shall make your way prosperous, and then you shall have good success. Have I not commanded you? Be strong and of good courage; be not frightened, neither be dismayed; for the Lord your God is with you wherever you go.'

New Testament *Ephesians 6.10-20 RSV*

Be strong in the Lord and in the strength of his might. Put on the whole armour of God, that you may be able to stand against the wiles of the devil. For we are not contending against flesh and blood, but against principalities, against the powers, against the world rulers of this present darkness, against the spiritual hosts of wickedness in the heavenly places. Therefore take the whole armour of God, that you may be able to withstand in the evil day, and having done all, to stand. Stand therefore, having girded your loins with truth, and having put on the breastplate of righteousness, and having shod your feet with the equipment of the gospel of peace; above all taking the shield of faith, with which you can quench all the flaming darts of the evil one. And take the helmet of salvation, and the sword of the Spirit, which is the word of God. Pray at all times in the Spirit, with all prayer and supplication. To that end keep alert with all perseverance, making supplication for all the saints, and also for me, that utterance may be given me in opening my mouth boldly to proclaim the mystery of the gospel, for which I am an ambassador in chains; that I may declare it boldly, as I ought to speak.

Gospel *John 17.11b-19 JB*

Jesus raised his eyes to heaven and said,
'Holy Father,
keep those you have given me true to your name,
so that they may be one like us.
While I was with them,
I kept those you had given me true to your name.
I have watched over them and not one is lost
except for one who chose to be lost,
and this was to fulfil the scriptures.
But now I am coming to you
and while still in the world I say these things
to share my joy with them to the full.
I passed your word on to them,
and the world hated them,
because they belong to the world
no more than I belong to the world.
I am not asking you to remove them from the world,
but to protect them from the evil one.
They do not belong to the world
any more than I belong to the world.
Consecrate them in the truth;
your word is truth.
As you sent me into the world,
I have sent them into the world,
and for their sake I consecrate myself
so that they too may be consecrated in truth.

READINGS YEAR 2

Old Testament *1 Samuel 17.37-50 NEB*

David said to Saul, 'The Lord who saved me from the lion and the bear will save me from this Philistine.' 'Go then,' said Saul; 'and the Lord will be with you.' He put his own tunic on David, placed a bronze helmet on his head and gave him a coat of mail to wear; he then fastened his sword on David over his tunic. But David hesitated, because he had not tried them, and said to Saul, 'I cannot go with these, because I have not tried them.' So he took them off. Then he picked up his sling, chose five smooth stones from the brook and put them in a shepherd's bag which served as his pouch. He walked out to meet the Philistine with his sling in his hand.

The Philistine came on towards David, with his shield-bearer marching ahead; and he looked David up and down and had nothing but contempt for this handsome lad with his ruddy cheeks and bright eyes. He said to David, 'Am I a dog that you come out against me with sticks?' And he swore at him in the name of his god. 'Come on,' he said, 'and I will give your flesh to the birds and the beasts.' David answered, 'You have come against me with sword and spear and dagger, but I have come against you in the name of the Lord of Hosts, the God of the army of Israel which you have defied. The Lord will put you into my power this day; I will kill you and cut your head off and leave your carcass and the carcasses of the Philistines to the birds and the wild beasts; all the world shall know that there is a God in Israel. All those who are gathered here shall see that the Lord saves neither by sword nor spear; the battle is the Lord's, and he will put you all into our power.'

When the Philistine began moving towards him again, David ran quickly to engage him. He put his hand into his bag, took out a stone, slung it, and struck the Philistine in the forehead. The stone sank into his forehead, and he fell flat on his face on the ground. So David proved the victor with his sling and stone; he struck Goliath down and gave him a mortal wound, although he had no sword.

New Testament *2 Corinthians 6.3-10 NEB*

In order that our service may not be brought into discredit, we avoid giving offence in anything. As God's servants, we try to recommend ourselves in all circumstances by our steadfast endurance: in distress, hardships, and dire straits; flogged, imprisoned, mobbed; overworked, sleepless, starving. We recommend ourselves by the innocence of our behaviour, our grasp of truth, our patience and kindliness; by gifts of the Holy Spirit, by sincere love, by declaring the truth, by the power of God. We wield the weapons of righteousness in right hand and left. Honour and dishonour, praise and blame, are alike our lot: we are the impostors who speak the truth, the unknown men whom all men know; dying we still live on; disciplined by suffering, we are not done to death; in our sorrows we have always cause for joy; poor ourselves, we bring wealth to many; penniless, we own the world.

Gospel *Mark 9.14-29 NEB*

When Jesus, with Peter, James, and John came back to the disciples they saw a large crowd surrounding them and lawyers arguing with them. As soon as they saw Jesus the whole crowd were overcome with awe, and they ran forward to welcome him. He asked them, 'What is this argument about?' A man in the crowd spoke up: 'Master, I brought my son to you. He is possessed by a spirit which makes him speechless. Whenever it attacks him, it dashes him to the ground, and he foams at the mouth, grinds his teeth, and goes rigid. I asked your disciples to cast it out, but they failed.' Jesus answered: 'What an unbelieving and perverse generation! How long shall I be with you? How long must I endure you? Bring him to me.' So they brought the boy to him; and as soon as the spirit saw him it threw the boy into convulsions, and he fell on the ground and rolled about foaming at the mouth. Jesus asked his father, 'How long has he been like this?' 'From childhood,' he replied; 'often it has tried to make an end of him by throwing him into the fire or into water. But if it is at all possible for you, take pity upon us and help us.' 'If it is possible!' said Jesus. 'Everything is possible to one who has faith.' 'I have faith,' cried the boy's father; 'help me where faith falls short.' Jesus saw then that the crowd was closing in upon them, so he rebuked the unclean spirit. 'Deaf and dumb spirit,' he said, 'I command you, come out of him and never go back!' After crying aloud and racking him fiercely, it came out; and the boy looked like a corpse; in fact, many said, 'He is dead.' But Jesus took his hand and raised him to his feet, and he stood up.

Then Jesus went indoors, and his disciples asked him privately, 'Why could not we cast it out?' He said, 'There is no means of casting out this sort but prayer.'

POSTCOMMUNION SENTENCE

Let us be sober, and put on the breast-plate of faith and love, and for a helmet the hope of salvation. *1 Thessalonians 5.8*

PENTECOST 10
(Trinity 9)   Green

INTRODUCTORY SENTENCE

Who has known the mind of the Lord so as to instruct him? But we have the mind of Christ. *1 Corinthians 2.16*

COLLECT

Father of mankind,
who gave your only-begotten Son
to take upon himself the form of a servant
and to be obedient even to death on a cross:
give us the same mind that was in Christ Jesus
that, sharing his humility,
we may come to be with him in his glory;
who is alive and reigns with you and the Holy Spirit,
one God, now and for ever.

PSALMS 71.1-8; 73.23-end

READINGS YEAR 1

Old Testament *Job 42.1-6 TEV*

Job answered the Lord,
'I know, Lord, that you are all-powerful;
that you can do everything you want.
You ask how I dare question your wisdom
when I am so very ignorant.
I talked about things I did not understand,
about marvels too great for me to know.
You told me to listen while you spoke
and to try to answer your questions.
Then I knew only what others had told me,
but now I have seen you with my own eyes.
So I am ashamed of all I have said
and repent in dust and ashes.'

New Testament *Philippians 2.1-11 NEB*

If our common life in Christ yields anything to stir the heart,
any loving consolation, any sharing of the Spirit, any
warmth of affection or compassion, fill up my cup of
happiness by thinking and feeling alike, with the same love
for one another, the same turn of mind, and a common care
for unity. There must be no room for rivalry and personal
vanity among you, but you must humbly reckon others
better than yourselves. Look to each other's interest and not
merely to your own.

Let your bearing towards one another arise out of your life in
Christ Jesus. For the divine nature was his from the first; yet
he did not think to snatch at equality with God, but made
himself nothing, assuming the nature of a slave. Bearing the
human likeness, revealed in human shape, he humbled
himself, and in obedience accepted even death—death on a
cross. Therefore God raised him to the heights and
bestowed on him the name above all names, that at the name
of Jesus every knee should bow—in heaven, on earth, and in
the depths—and every tongue confess, 'Jesus Christ is
Lord', to the glory of God the Father.

Gospel *John 13.1-15 NEB*

It was before the Passover festival. Jesus knew that his hour had come and he must leave this world and go to the Father. He had always loved his own who were in the world, and now he was to show the full extent of his love.

The devil had already put it into the mind of Judas son of Simon Iscariot to betray him. During supper, Jesus, well aware that the Father had entrusted everything to him, and that he had come from God and was going back to God, rose from table, laid aside his garments, and taking a towel, tied it round him. Then he poured water into a basin, and began to wash his disciples' feet and wipe them with the towel.

When it was Simon Peter's turn, Peter said to him, 'You, Lord, washing my feet?' Jesus replied, 'You do not understand now what I am doing, but one day you will.' Peter said, 'I will never let you wash my feet.' 'If I do not wash you,' Jesus replied, 'you are not in fellowship with me.' 'Then, Lord,' said Simon Peter, 'not my feet only; wash my hands and head as well!'

Jesus said, 'A man who has bathed needs no further washing; he is altogether clean; and you are clean, though not every one of you.' He added the words 'not every one of you' because he knew who was going to betray him.

After washing their feet and taking his garments again, he sat down. 'Do you understand what I have done for you?' he asked. 'You call me "Master" and "Lord", and rightly so, for that is what I am. Then if I, your Lord and Master, have washed your feet, you also ought to wash one another's feet. I have set you an example: you are to do as I have done for you.'

READINGS YEAR 2

Old Testament *1 Samuel 24.9-17 (or 1-17) NEB*

(When Saul returned from the pursuit of the Philistines, he learnt that David was in the wilderness of En-gedi. So he took three thousand men picked from the whole of Israel and went in search of David and his men to the east of the

Rocks of the Wild Goats. There beside the road were some sheepfolds, and near by was a cave, at the far end of which David and his men were sitting concealed. Saul came to the cave and went in to relieve himself. His men said to David, 'The day has come: the Lord has put your enemy into your hands, as he promised he would, and you may do what you please with him.' David said to his men, 'God forbid that I should harm my master, the Lord's anointed, or lift a finger against him; he is the Lord's anointed.' So David reproved his men severely and would not let them attack Saul. He himself got up stealthily and cut off a piece of Saul's cloak; but when he had cut it off, his conscience smote him. Saul rose, left the cave and went on his way; whereupon David also came out of the cave and called after Saul, 'My lord the king!').

When Saul looked round, David prostrated himself in obeisance and said to him, 'Why do you listen when they say that David is out to do you harm? Today you can see for yourself that the Lord put you into my power in the cave; I had a mind to kill you, but no, I spared your life and said, "I cannot lift a finger against my master, for he is the Lord's anointed." Look, my dear lord, look at this piece of your cloak in my hand. I cut it off, but I did not kill you; this will show you that I have no thought of violence or treachery against you, and that I have done you no wrong; yet you are resolved to take my life. May the Lord judge between us! but though he may take vengeance on you for my sake, I will never lift my hand against you; "One wrong begets another", as the old saying goes, yet I will never lift my hand against you. Who has the king of Israel come out against? What are you pursuing? A dead dog, a mere flea. The Lord will be judge and decide between us; let him look into my cause, he will plead for me and will acquit me.'

When David had finished speaking, Saul said, 'Is that you, David my son?', and he wept. Then he said, 'The right is on your side, not mine; you have treated me so well, I have treated you so badly.'

New Testament *Galatians 6.1-10 NEB*

We must not be conceited, challenging one another to
rivalry, jealous of one another. If a man should do
something wrong, my brothers, on a sudden impulse, you
who are endowed with the Spirit must set him right again
very gently. Look to yourself, each one of you: you may be
tempted too. Help one another to carry these heavy loads,
and in this way you will fulfil the law of Christ.

For if a man imagines himself to be somebody, when he is
nothing, he is deluding himself. Each man should examine
his own conduct for himself; then he can measure his
achievement by comparing himself with himself and not
with anyone else. For everyone has his own proper burden
to bear.

When anyone is under instruction in the faith, he should
give his teacher a share of all good things he has.

Make no mistake about this: God is not to be fooled; a man
reaps what he sows. If he sows seed in the field of his lower
nature, he will reap from it a harvest of corruption, but if he
sows in the field of the Spirit, the Spirit will bring him a
harvest of eternal life. So let us never tire of doing good, for if
we do not slacken our efforts we shall in due time reap our
harvest. Therefore, as opportunity offers, let us work for the
good of all, especially members of the household of the faith.

Gospel *Luke 7.36-end JB*

One of the Pharisees invited Jesus to a meal. When he
arrived at the Pharisee's house and took his place at table, a
woman came in, who had a bad name in the town. She had
heard he was dining with the Pharisee and had brought with
her an alabaster jar of ointment. She waited behind him at
his feet, weeping, and her tears fell on his feet, and she
wiped them away with her hair; then she covered his feet
with kisses and anointed them with the ointment.

When the Pharisee who had invited him saw this, he said to
himself, 'If this man were a prophet, he would know who
this woman is that is touching him and what a bad name she
has.' Then Jesus took him up and said, 'Simon, I have

something to say to you.' 'Speak, Master', was the reply.
'There was once a creditor who had two men in his debt; one
owed him five hundred denarii, the other fifty. They were
unable to pay, so he pardoned them both. Which of them
will love him more?' 'The one who was pardoned more, I
suppose', answered Simon. Jesus said, 'You are right.'

Then he turned to the woman. 'Simon,' he said, 'you see this
woman? I came into your house, and you poured no water
over my feet, but she has poured out her tears over my feet
and wiped them away with her hair. You gave me no kiss,
but she has been covering my feet with kisses ever since I
came in. You did not anoint my head with oil, but she has
anointed my feet with ointment. For this reason I tell you
that her sins, her many sins, must have been forgiven her, or
she would not have shown such great love. It is the man who
is forgiven little who shows little love.' Then he said to her,
'Your sins are forgiven.' Those who were with him at table
began to say to themselves, 'Who is this man, that he even
forgives sins?' But he said to the woman, 'Your faith has
saved you; go in peace.'

POSTCOMMUNION SENTENCE

To set the mind on the flesh is death, but to set the mind on
the Spirit is life and peace. *Romans 8.6*

PENTECOST 11
(Trinity 10)   Green

INTRODUCTORY SENTENCE

God has not given us a spirit of timidity, but a spirit of power
and love and self-control. *2 Timothy 1.7*

COLLECT

Almighty Father,
whose Son Jesus Christ has taught us
that what we do for the least of our brethren
    we do also for him;

give us the will to be the servant of others
    as he was the servant of all,
who gave up his life and died for us,
but is alive and reigns with you and the Holy Spirit,
one God, now and for ever.

PSALMS 31.21-end; 40.1-7

READINGS YEAR 1

Old Testament *Isaiah 42.1-7 RSV*

Behold my servant, whom I uphold,
my chosen, in whom my soul delights;
I have put my spirit upon him,
he will bring forth justice to the nations.
He will not cry or lift up his voice,
or make it heard in the street;
a bruised reed he will not break,
and a dimly burning wick he will not quench;
he will faithfully bring forth justice.
He will not fail or be discouraged
till he has established justice in the earth;
and the coastlands wait for his law.

Thus says God, the Lord,
who created the heavens and stretched them out,
who spread forth the earth and what comes from it,
who gives breath to the people upon it
and spirit to those who walk in it:
'I am the Lord, I have called you in righteousness,
I have taken you by the hand and kept you;
I have given you as a convenant to the people,
a light to the nations,
to open the eyes that are blind,
to bring out the prisoners from the dungeon,
from the prison those who sit in darkness.'

New Testament *2 Corinthians 4.1-10 NEB*

Seeing that we have been entrusted with this commission,
which we owe entirely to God's mercy, we never lose heart.
We have renounced the deeds that men hide for very shame;

we neither practise cunning nor distort the word of God; only by declaring the truth openly do we recommend ourselves, and then it is to the common conscience of our fellow-men and in the sight of God. And if indeed our gospel be found veiled, the only people who find it so are those on the way to perdition. Their unbelieving minds are so blinded by the god of this passing age, that the gospel of the glory of Christ, who is the very image of God, cannot dawn upon them and bring them light. It is not ourselves that we proclaim; we proclaim Christ Jesus as Lord, and ourselves as your servants, for Jesus' sake. For the same God who said, 'Out of darkness let light shine', has caused his light to shine within us, to give the light of revelation—the revelation of the glory of God in the face of Jesus Christ.

We are no better than pots of earthenware to contain this treasure, and this proves that such transcendent power does not come from us, but is God's alone. Hard-pressed on every side, we are never hemmed in; bewildered, we are never at our wits' end; hunted, we are never abandoned to our fate; struck down, we are not left to die. Wherever we go we carry death with us in our body, the death that Jesus died, that in this body also life may reveal itself, the life that Jesus lives.

Gospel *John 13.31-35 JB*

Jesus said,
'Now has the Son of Man been glorified,
and in him God has been glorified.
If God has been glorified in him,
God will in turn glorify him in himself,
and will glorify him very soon.

'My little children,
I shall not be with you much longer.
You will look for me,
and, as I told the Jews,
where I am going,
you cannot come.
I give you a new commandment:
love one another;

just as I have loved you,
you also must love one another.
By this love you have for one another,
everyone will know that you are my disciples.'

READINGS YEAR 2

Old Testament *1 Chronicles 29.1-9 NEB*

King David said to the whole assembly, 'My son Solomon is the one chosen by God, Solomon alone, a boy of tender years; and this is a great work, for it is a palace not for man but for the Lord God. Now to the best of my strength I have made ready for the house of my God gold for the gold work, silver for the silver, bronze for the bronze, iron for the iron, and wood for the woodwork, together with cornelian and other gems for setting, stones for mosaic work, precious stones of every sort, and marble in plenty. Further, because I delight in the house of my God, I give my own private store of gold and silver for the house of my God—over and above all the store which I have collected for the sanctuary— namely three thousand talents of gold, gold from Ophir, and seven thousand talents of fine silver for overlaying the walls of the buildings, for providing gold for the gold work, silver for the silver, and for any work to be done by skilled craftsmen. Now who is willing to give with open hand to the Lord today?'

Then the heads of families, the officers administering the tribes of Israel, the officers over units of a thousand and a hundred, and the officers in charge of the king's service, responded willingly and gave for the work of the house of God five thousand talents of gold, ten thousand darics, ten thousand talents of silver, eighteen thousand talents of bronze, and a hundred thousand talents of iron. Further, those who possessed precious stones gave them to the treasury of the house of the Lord, into the charge of Jehiel the Gershonite. The people rejoiced at this willing response, because in the loyalty of their hearts they had given willingly to the Lord.

New Testament *Philippians 1.1-11 NEB*

From Paul and Timothy, servants of Christ Jesus, to all those of God's people, incorporate in Christ Jesus, who live at Philippi, including their bishops and deacons.

Grace to you and peace from God our Father and the Lord Jesus Christ.

I thank my God whenever I think of you; and when I pray for you all, my prayers are always joyful, because of the part you have taken in the work of the Gospel from the first day until now. Of one thing I am certain: the One who started the good work in you will bring it to completion by the Day of Christ Jesus. It is indeed only right that I should feel like this about you all, because you hold me in such affection, and because, when I lie in prison or appear in the dock to vouch for the truth of the Gospel, you all share in the privilege that is mine. God knows how I long for you all, with the deep yearning of Christ Jesus himself. And this is my prayer, that your love may grow ever richer and richer in knowledge and insight of every kind, and may thus bring you the gift of true discrimination. Then on the Day of Christ you will be flawless and without blame, reaping the full harvest of righteousness that comes through Jesus Christ, to the glory and praise of God.

Gospel *Matthew 20.1-16 NEB*

Jesus said to his disciples, 'The kingdom of Heaven is like this. There was once a landowner who went out early one morning to hire labourers for his vineyard; and after agreeing to pay them the usual day's wage he sent them off to work. Going out three hours later he saw some more men standing idle in the market-place. "Go and join the others in the vineyard," he said, "and I will pay you a fair wage"; so off they went. At midday he went out again, and at three in the afternoon, and made the same arrangement as before. An hour before sunset he went out and found another group standing there; so he said to them, "Why are you standing about like this all day with nothing to do?" "Because no one has hired us", they replied; so he told them, "Go and join the others in the vineyard." When evening fell, the owner of the vineyard said to his steward, "Call the labourers and give them their pay, beginning with those who came last and ending with the first." Those who had started work an hour before sunset came forward, and were paid the full day's wage. When it was the turn of the men who had come first, they expected something extra, but were paid the same amount as the others. As they took it, they grumbled at their employer: "These late-comers have done only one hour's work, yet you have put them on a level with us, who have sweated the whole day long in the blazing sun!" The owner turned to one of them and said, "My friend, I am not being unfair to you. You agreed on the usual wage for the day, did you not? Take your pay and go home. I choose to pay the last man the same as you. Surely I am free to do what I like with my own money. Why be jealous because I am kind?" Thus will the last be first, and the first last.'

POSTCOMMUNION SENTENCE

Jesus said, You call me Teacher and Lord; and you are right, for so I am. If I then, your Lord and Teacher, have washed your feet, you also ought to wash one another's feet. *John 13.13, 14*

PENTECOST 12
(Trinity 11)   Green

INTRODUCTORY SENTENCE

With great power the apostles gave their testimony to the resurrection of the Lord Jesus, and great grace was upon them. *Acts 4.33*

COLLECT

Almighty God,
who called your Church to witness
that you were in Christ reconciling men to yourself:
help us so to proclaim the good news of your love,
that all who hear it may be reconciled to you;

through him who died for us and rose again
and reigns with you and the Holy Spirit,
one God, now and for ever.

PSALMS 96.1-6; 96.7-end

READINGS YEAR 1

Old Testament *Isaiah 49.1-6 NEB*

Listen to me, you coasts and islands,
pay heed, you peoples far away:
from birth the Lord called me,
he named me from my mother's womb.
He made my tongue his sharp sword
and concealed me under cover of his hand;
he made me a polished arrow
and hid me out of sight in his quiver.
He said to me, 'You are my servant,
Israel through whom I shall win glory';
so I rose to honour in the Lord's sight
and my God became my strength.
Once I said, 'I have laboured in vain;
I have spent my strength for nothing, to no purpose';
yet in truth my cause is with the Lord
and my reward is in God's hands.
And now the Lord who formed me in the womb
    to be his servant,
to bring Jacob back to him
that Israel should be gathered to him,
now the Lord calls me again:
it is too slight a task for you, as my servant,
to restore the tribes of Jacob,
to bring back the descendants of Israel:
I will make you a light to the nations,
to be my salvation to earth's farthest bounds.

New Testament *2 Corinthians 5.14—6.2 NEB*

The love of Christ leaves us no choice, when once we have
reached the conclusion that one man died for all and
therefore all mankind has died. His purpose in dying for all

was that men, while still in life, should cease to live for themselves, and should live for him who for their sake died and was raised to life. With us therefore worldly standards have ceased to count in our estimate of any man; even if once they counted in our understanding of Christ, they do so now no longer. When anyone is united to Christ, there is a new world; the old order has gone, and a new order has already begun.

From first to last this has been the work of God. He has reconciled us men to himself through Christ, and he has enlisted us in this service of reconciliation. What I mean is, that God was in Christ reconciling the world to himself, no longer holding men's misdeeds against them, and that he has entrusted us with the message of reconciliation. We come therefore as Christ's ambassadors. It is as if God were appealing to you through us: in Christ's name, we implore you, be reconciled to God! Christ was innocent of sin, and yet for our sake God made him one with the sinfulness of men, so that in him we might be made one with the goodness of God himself. Sharing in God's work, we urge this appeal upon you: you have received the grace of God; do not let it go for nothing. God's own words are:

'In the hour of my favour I gave heed to you; on the day of deliverance I came to your aid.'

The hour of favour has now come; now, I say, has the day of deliverance dawned.

Gospel *John* 17.20-end JB

Jesus raised his eyes to heaven and said,
'I pray not only for these,
but for those also
who through their words will believe in me.
May they all be one.
Father, may they be one in us,
as you are in me and I am in you,
so that the world may believe it was you who sent me.
I have given them the glory you gave to me,
that they may be one as we are one.
With me in them and you in me,

may they be so completely one
that the world will realise that it was you who sent me
and that I have loved them as much as you loved me.
Father,
I want those you have given me
to be with me where I am,
so that they may always see the glory
you have given me
because you loved me
before the foundation of the world.
Father, Righteous One,
the world has not known you,
but I have known you,
and these have known
that you have sent me.
I have made your name known to them
and will continue to make it known,
so that the love with which you loved me may be in them,
and so that I may be in them.'

READINGS YEAR 2

Old Testament *Micah 4.1-5 RSV*

It shall come to pass in the latter days
that the mountain of the house of the Lord
shall be established as the highest of the mountains,
and shall be raised up above the hills;
and peoples shall flow to it,
and many nations shall come, and say:
'Come, let us go up to the mountain of the Lord,
to the house of the God of Jacob;
that he may teach us his ways
and we may walk in his paths.'
For out of Zion shall go forth the law,
and the word of the Lord from Jerusalem.
He shall judge between many peoples,
and shall decide for strong nations afar off;
and they shall beat their swords into ploughshares,
and their spears into pruning hooks;
nation shall not lift up sword against nation,
neither shall they learn war any more;

but they shall sit every man under his vine
　　and under his fig tree,
and none shall make them afraid;
for the mouth of the Lord of hosts has spoken.

For all the peoples walk each in the name of its god,
but we will walk in the name of the Lord our God
for ever and ever.

New Testament *Acts 17.22-end NEB*

Paul stood up before the Court of Areopagus and said: 'Men
of Athens, I see that in everything that concerns religion you
are uncommonly scrupulous. For as I was going round
looking at the objects of your worship, I noticed among other
things an altar bearing the inscription "To an Unknown
God". What you worship but do not know—this is what I
now proclaim.

'The God who created the world and everything in it, and
who is Lord of heaven and earth, does not live in shrines
made by men. It is not because he lacks anything that he
accepts service at men's hands, for he is himself the
universal giver of life and breath and all else. He created
every race of men of one stock, to inhabit the whole earth's
surface. He fixed the epochs of their history and the limits of
their territory. They were to seek God, and, it might be,
touch and find him; though indeed he is not far from each
one of us, for in him we live and move, in him we exist; as
some of your own poets have said, "We are also his
offspring." As God's offspring, then, we ought not to
suppose that the deity is like an image in gold or silver or
stone, shaped by human craftsmanship and design. As for
the times of ignorance, God has overlooked them; but now
he commands mankind, all men everywhere, to repent,
because he has fixed the day on which he will have the world
judged, and justly judged, by a man of his choosing; of this
he has given assurance to all by raising him from the dead.'

When they heard about the raising of the dead, some
scoffed; and others said, 'We will hear you on this subject
some other time.' And so Paul left the assembly. However,
some men joined him and became believers, including

Dionysius, a member of the Court of Areopagus; also a woman named Damaris, and others besides.

Gospel *Matthew 5.13-16 JB*

Jesus said, 'You are the salt of the earth. But if salt becomes tasteless, what can make it salty again? It is good for nothing, and can only be thrown out to be trampled underfoot by men.

'You are the light of the world. A city built on a hill-top cannot be hidden. No one lights a lamp to put it under a tub; they put it on the lamp-stand where it shines for everyone in the house. In the same way your light must shine in the sight of men, so that, seeing your good works, they may give the praise to your Father in heaven.'

POSTCOMMUNION SENTENCE

You are the light of the world. A city set on a hill cannot be hid. *Matthew 5.14*

PENTECOST 13
(Trinity 12)   Green

INTRODUCTORY SENTENCE

It has been granted to us that for the sake of Christ we should not only believe in him, but also suffer for his sake. *Philippians 1.29*

COLLECT

Lord God,
whose blessed Son our Saviour
gave his back to the smiters
and did not hide his face from shame:
give us grace to endure the sufferings of this present time
with sure confidence in the glory that shall be revealed;
through Jesus Christ our Lord.

PSALMS 31.1-5; 43

READINGS YEAR 1

Old Testament *Isaiah 50.4-9a RSV*

The Lord God has given me
the tongue of those who are taught,
that I may know how to sustain with a word
him that is weary.
Morning by morning he wakens,
he wakens my ear
to hear as those who are taught.
The Lord God has opened my ear,
and I was not rebellious,
I turned not backward.
I gave my back to the smiters,
and my cheeks to those who pulled out the beard;
I hid not my face
from shame and spitting.

For the Lord God helps me;
therefore I have not been confounded;
therefore I have set my face like a flint,
and I know that I shall not be put to shame;
he who vindicates me is near.
Who will contend with me?
Let us stand up together.
Who is my adversary?
Let him come near to me.
Behold, the Lord God helps me;
who will declare me guilty?

New Testament *Acts 7.54—8.1 RSV*

When the Council heard these things they were enraged,
and they ground their teeth against Stephen. But he, full of
the Holy Spirit, gazed into heaven and saw the glory of God,
and Jesus standing at the right hand of God; and he said,
'Behold, I see the heavens opened, and the Son of man
standing at the right hand of God.' But they cried out with a
loud voice and stopped their ears and rushed together upon
him. Then they cast him out of the city and stoned him; and
the witnesses laid down their garments at the feet of a young
man named Saul. And as they were stoning Stephen, he

prayed, 'Lord Jesus, receive my spirit.' And he knelt down and cried with a loud voice, 'Lord, do not hold this sin against them.' And when he had said this, he fell asleep. And Saul was consenting to his death.

And on that day a great persecution arose against the church in Jerusalem; and they were all scattered throughout the region of Judaea and Samaria, except the apostles.

Gospel *John 16.1-11 TEV*

Jesus said, 'I have told you this, so that you will not give up your faith. You will be expelled from the synagogues, and the time will come when anyone who kills you will think that by doing this he is serving God. People will do these things to you because they have not known either the Father or me. But I have told you this, so that when the time comes for them to do these things, you will remember that I told you.

'I did not tell you these things at the beginning, for I was with you. But now I am going to him who sent me, yet none of you asks me where I am going. And now that I have told you, your hearts are full of sadness. But I am telling you the truth: it is better for you that I go away, because if I do not go, the Helper will not come to you. But if I do go away, then I will send him to you. And when he comes, he will prove to the people of the world that they are wrong about sin and about what is right and about God's judgement. They are wrong about sin, because they do not believe in me; they are wrong about what is right, because I am going to the Father and you will not see me any more; and they are wrong about judgement, because the ruler of this world has already been judged.'

READINGS YEAR 2

Old Testament *Jeremiah 20.7-11a RSV*

O Lord, you have deceived me,
and I was deceived;
you are stronger than I,
and you have prevailed.
I have become a laughingstock all the day;

everyone mocks me.
For whenever I speak, I cry out,
I shout, 'Violence and destruction!'
For the word of the Lord has become for me
a reproach and derision all day long.
If I say, 'I will not mention him,
or speak any more in his name,'
there is in my heart as it were a burning fire
shut up in my bones,
and I am weary with holding it in,
and I cannot.
For I hear many whispering.
Terror is on every side!
'Denounce him! Let us denounce him!'
say all my familiar friends,
watching for my fall.
'Perhaps he will be deceived,
then we can overcome him,
and take our revenge on him.'
But the Lord is with me as a dread warrior;
therefore my persecutors will stumble,
and they will not overcome me.

New Testament *Acts 20.17-35 TEV*

From Miletus Paul sent a message to Ephesus, asking the
elders of the church to meet him. When they arrived, he said
to them, 'You know how I spent the whole time I was with
you, from the first day I arrived in the province of Asia. With
all humility and many tears I did my work as the Lord's
servant during the hard times that came to me because of the
plots of the Jews. You know that I did not hold back anything
that would be of help to you as I preached and taught in
public and in your homes. To Jews and Gentiles alike I gave
solemn warning that they should turn from their sins to God
and believe in our Lord Jesus. And now, in obedience to the
Holy Spirit I am going to Jerusalem, not knowing what will
happen to me there. I only know that in every city the Holy
Spirit has warned me that prison and troubles wait for me.
But I reckon my own life to be worth nothing to me; I only
want to complete my mission and finish the work that the

Lord Jesus gave me to do, which is to declare the Good News about the grace of God.

'I have gone about among all of you, preaching the Kingdom of God. And now I know that none of you will ever see me again. So I solemnly declare to you this very day: if any of you should be lost, I am not responsible. For I have not held back from announcing to you the whole purpose of God. So keep watch over yourselves and over all the flock which the Holy Spirit has placed in your care. Be shepherds of the church of God, which he made his own through the death of his Son. I know that after I leave, fierce wolves will come among you, and they will not spare the flock. The time will come when some men from your own group will tell lies to lead the believers away after them. Watch, then, and remember that with many tears, day and night, I taught every one of you for three years.

'And now I commend you to the care of God and to the message of his grace, which is able to build you up and give you the blessings God has for all his people. I have not wanted anyone's silver or gold or clothing. You yourselves know that I have worked with these hands of mine to provide everything that my companions and I have needed. I have shown you in all things that by working hard in this way we must help the weak, remembering the words that the Lord Jesus himself said, "There is more happiness in giving than in receiving."'

Gospel *Matthew 10.16-22 JB*

Jesus said, 'Remember, I am sending you out like sheep among wolves; so be cunning as serpents and yet as harmless as doves.

'Beware of men: they will hand you over to sanhedrins and scourge you in their synagogues. You will be dragged before governors and kings for my sake, to bear witness before them and the pagans. But when they hand you over, do not worry about how to speak or what to say; what you are to say will be given to you when the time comes; because it is not you who will be speaking; the Spirit of your Father will be speaking in you.

'Brother will betray brother to death, and the father his child; children will rise against their parents and have them put to death. You will be hated by all men on account of my name; but the man who stands firm to the end will be saved.'

POSTCOMMUNION SENTENCE

Rejoice in so far as you share Christ's sufferings, that you also may rejoice and be glad when his glory is revealed. *1 Peter 4.13*

PENTECOST 14
(Trinity 13)   Green

INTRODUCTORY SENTENCE

As a father pities his children, so the Lord pities those who fear him. *Psalm 103.13*

COLLECT

Lord God,
the protector of all who trust in you,
without whom nothing is strong, nothing is holy:
increase and multiply upon us your mercy,
that you being our ruler and guide,
we may so pass through things temporal
that you finally lose not the things eternal.
Grant this, heavenly Father,
for the sake of Jesus Christ our Lord.

PSALMS 127; 128

READINGS YEAR 1

Old Testament *Proverbs 31.10-end RSV*

A good wife who can find?
She is far more precious than jewels.
The heart of her husband trusts in her,
and he will have no lack of gain.
She does him good, and not harm,

all the days of her life.
She seeks wool and flax,
and works with willing hands.
She is like the ships of the merchant,
she brings her food from afar.
She rises while it is yet night
and provides food for her household
and tasks for her maidens.
She considers a field and buys it;
with the fruit of her hands she plants a vineyard.
She girds her loins with strength
and makes her arms strong.
She perceives that her merchandise is profitable.
Her lamp does not go out at night.
She put her hands to the distaff,
and her hands hold the spindle.
She opens her hand to the poor,
and reaches out her hands to the needy.
She is not afraid of snow for her household,
for all her household are clothed in scarlet.
She makes herself coverings;
her clothing is fine linen and purple.
Her husband is known in the gates,
when he sits among the elders of the land.
She makes linen garments and sells them;
she delivers girdles to the merchant.
Strength and dignity are her clothing,
and she laughs at the time to come.
She opens her mouth with wisdom,
and the teaching of kindness is on her tongue.
She looks well to the ways of her household,
and does not eat the bread of idleness.
Her children rise up and call her blessed;
her husband also, and he praises her:
'Many women have done excellently,
but you surpass them all.'
Charm is deceitful, and beauty is vain,
but a woman who fears the Lord is to be praised.
Give her of the fruit of her hands,
and let her works praise her in the gates.

New Testament *Ephesians 5.25—6.4 JB*

Husbands should love their wives just as Christ loved the Church and sacrificed himself for her to make her holy. He made her clean by washing her in water with a form of words, so that when he took her to himself she would be glorious, with no speck or wrinkle or anything like that, but holy and faultless. In the same way, husbands must love their wives as they love their own bodies; for a man to love his wife is for him to love himself. A man never hates his own body, but he feeds it and looks after it; and that is the way Christ treats the Church, because it is his body—and we are its living parts. For this reason, a man must leave his father and mother and be joined to his wife, and the two will become one body. This mystery has many implications; but I am saying it applies to Christ and the Church. To sum up; you too, each of you, must love his wife as he loves himself; and let every wife respect her husband.

Children, be obedient to your parents in the Lord—that is your duty. The first commandment that has a promise attached to it is: Honour your father and mother, and the promise is: and you will prosper and have a long life in the land. And parents, never drive your children to resentment but in bringing them up correct them and guide them as the Lord does.

Gospel *Mark 10.2-16 NEB*

The question was put to Jesus from the crowd: 'Is it lawful for a man to divorce his wife?' This was to test him. He asked in return, 'What did Moses command you?' They answered, 'Moses permitted a man to divorce his wife by note of dismissal.' Jesus said to them, 'It was because your minds were closed that he made this rule for you; but in the beginning, at the creation, God made them male and female. For this reason a man shall leave his father and mother, and be made one with his wife; and the two shall become one flesh. It follows that they are no longer two individuals: they are one flesh. What God has joined together, man must not separate.'

When they were indoors again the disciples questioned him

about this matter; he said to them, 'Whoever divorces his wife and marries another commits adultery against her: so too, if she divorces her husband and marries another, she commits adultery.'

They brought children for him to touch. The disciples rebuked them, but when Jesus saw this he was indignant, and said to them, 'Let the children come to me; do not try to stop them; for the kingdom of God belongs to such as these. I tell you, whoever does not accept the kingdom of God like a child will never enter it.' And he put his arms round them, laid his hands upon them, and blessed them.

READINGS YEAR 2

Old Testament *Genesis 45.1-15 NEB*

Joseph could no longer control his feelings in front of his attendants, and he called out, 'Let everyone leave my presence.' So there was nobody present when Joseph made himself known to his brothers, but so loudly did he weep that the Egyptians and Pharaoh's household heard him. Joseph said to his brothers, 'I am Joseph; can my father be still alive?' His brothers were so dumbfounded at finding themselves face to face with Joseph that they could not answer. Then Joseph said to his brothers, 'Come closer', and so they came close. He said, 'I am your brother Joseph whom you sold into Egypt. Now do not be distressed or take it amiss that you sold me into slavery here; it was God who sent me ahead of you to save men's lives. For there have now been two years of famine in the country, and there will be another five years with neither ploughing nor harvest. God sent me ahead of you to ensure that you will have descendants on earth, and to preserve you all, a great band of survivors. So it was not you who sent me here, but God, and he has made me a father to Pharaoh, and lord over all his household and ruler of all Egypt. Make haste and go back to my father and give him this message from his son Joseph: "God has made me lord of all Egypt. Come down to me; do not delay. You shall live in the land of Goshen and be near me, you, your sons and your grandsons, your flocks and herds and all that you have. I will take care of you there, you and your household and all that you have, and see that you are not reduced to poverty; there are still five years of famine to come.'' You can see for yourselves, and so can my brother Benjamin, that it is Joseph himself who is speaking to you. Tell my father of all the honour which I enjoy in Egypt, tell him all you have seen, and make haste to bring him down here.' Then he threw his arms round his brother Benjamin and wept, and Benjamin too embraced him weeping. He kissed all his brothers and wept over them, and afterwards his brothers talked with him.

New Testament *Ephesians 3.14-end RSV*

I bow my knees before the Father, from whom every family in heaven and on earth is named, that according to the riches of his glory he may grant you to be strengthened with might through his Spirit in the inner man, and that Christ may dwell in your hearts through faith; that you, being rooted and grounded in love, may have power to comprehend with all the saints what is the breadth and length and height and depth, and to know the love of Christ which surpasses knowledge, that you may be filled with all the fullness of God.

Now to him who by the power at work within us is able to do far more abundantly than all that we ask or think, to him be glory in the church and in Christ Jesus to all generations, for ever and ever. Amen.

Gospel *Luke 11.1-13 JB*

Jesus was in a certain place praying, and when he had finished one of his disciples said, 'Lord, teach us to pray, just as John taught his disciples.' He said to them, 'Say this when you pray:

''Father, may your name be held holy,
your kingdom come;
give us each day our daily bread,
and forgive us our sins,
for we ourselves forgive each one who is in debt to us.
And do not put us to the test.'''

He also said to them, 'Suppose one of you has a friend and goes to him in the middle of the night to say, "My friend, lend me three loaves, because a friend of mine on his travels has just arrived at my house and I have nothing to offer him"; and the man answers from inside the house, "Do not bother me. The door is bolted now, and my children and I are in bed; I cannot get up to give it you." I tell you, if the man does not get up and give it him for friendship's sake, persistence will be enough to make him get up and give his friend all he wants.

'So I say to you: Ask, and it will be given to you; search, and you will find; knock, and the door will be opened to you. For the one who asks always receives; the one who searches always finds; the one who knocks will always have the door opened to him. What father among you would hand his son a stone when he asked for bread? Or hand him a snake instead of a fish? Or hand him a scorpion if he asked for an egg? If you then, who are evil, know how to give your children what is good, how much more will the heavenly Father give the Holy Spirit to those who ask him!'

PROPER PREFACE

Rite A. A Preface for the Incarnation (7) or of Marriage (27) may be said.

POSTCOMMUNION SENTENCE

The steadfast love of the Lord is from everlasting to everlasting upon those who fear him, and his righteousness to children's children. *Psalm 103.17*

PENTECOST 15
(Trinity 14)   Green

INTRODUCTORY SENTENCE

Be subject for the Lord's sake to every human institution. *1 Peter 2.13*

COLLECT

Almighty Father,
whose will is to restore all things
    in your beloved Son, the king of all:
govern the hearts and minds of those in authority,
and bring the families of the nations,
divided and torn apart by the ravages of sin,
to be subject to his just and gentle rule;
who is alive and reigns with you and the Holy Spirit,
one God, now and for ever.

PSALMS 82; 20

READINGS YEAR 1

Old Testament *Isaiah 45.1-7 NEB*

Thus says the Lord to Cyrus his anointed,
Cyrus whom he has taken by the hand
to subdue nations before him
and undo the might of kings;
before whom gates shall be opened
and no doors be shut:
I will go before you
and level the swelling hills;
I will break down gates of bronze
and hack through iron bars.
I will give you treasures from dark vaults,
hoarded in secret places,
that you may know that I am the Lord,
Israel's God who calls you by name.
For the sake of Jacob my servant and Israel my chosen
I have called you by name
and given you your title, though you have not known me.
I am the Lord, there is no other;
there is no god beside me.
I will strengthen you though you have not known me,
so that men from the rising and the setting sun
may know that there is none but I:
I am the Lord, there is no other;
I make the light, I create darkness,

author alike of prosperity and trouble.
I, the Lord, do all these things.

New Testament *Romans 13.1-7 JB*

You must all obey the governing authorities. Since all government comes from God, the civil authorities were appointed by God, and so anyone who resists authority is rebelling against God's decision, and such an act is bound to be punished. Good behaviour is not afraid of magistrates; only criminals have anything to fear. If you want to live without being afraid of authority, you must live honestly and authority may even honour you. The state is there to serve God for your benefit. If you break the law, however, you may well have fear: the bearing of the sword has its significance. The authorities are there to serve God: they carry out God's revenge by punishing wrongdoers. You must obey, therefore, not only because you are afraid of being punished, but also for conscience' sake. This is also the reason why you must pay taxes, since all government officials are God's officers. They serve God by collecting taxes. Pay every government official what he has a right to ask—whether it be direct tax or indirect, fear or honour.

Gospel *Matthew 22.15-22 JB*

The Pharisees went away to work out between them how to trap Jesus in what he said. And they sent their disciples to him, together with the Herodians, to say, 'Master, we know that you are an honest man and teach the way of God in an honest way, and that you are not afraid of anyone, because a man's rank means nothing to you. Tell us your opinion, then. Is it permissible to pay taxes to Caesar or not?' But Jesus was aware of their malice and replied, 'You hypocrites! Why do you set this trap for me? Let me see the money you pay the tax with.' They handed him a denarius, and he said, 'Whose head is this? Whose name?' 'Caesar's', they replied. He then said to them, 'Very well, give back to Caesar what belongs to Caesar— and to God what belongs to God.' This reply took them by surprise, and they left him alone and went away.

READINGS YEAR 2

Old Testament *1 Kings 3.4-15 RSV*

King Solomon went to Gibeon to sacrifice there, for that was the great high place; Solomon used to offer a thousand burnt offerings upon that altar. At Gibeon the Lord appeared to Solomon in a dream by night; and God said, 'Ask what I shall give you.' And Solomon said, 'You have shown great and steadfast love to your servant David my father, because he walked before you in faithfulness, in righteousness, and in uprightness of heart towards you; and you have kept for him this great and steadfast love, and have given him a son to sit on his throne this day. And now, O Lord my God, you have made your servant king in place of David my father, although I am but a little child; I do not know how to go out or come in. And your servant is in the midst of your people whom you have chosen, a great people, that cannot be numbered or counted for multitude. Give your servant therefore an understanding mind to govern your people, that I may discern between good and evil; for who is able to govern this your great people?'

It pleased the Lord that Solomon had asked this. And God said to him, 'Because you have asked this, and have not asked for yourself long life or riches or the life of your enemies, but have asked for yourself understanding to discern what is right, behold, I now do according to your word. Behold, I give you a wise and discerning mind, so that none like you has been before you and none like you shall arise after you. I give you also what you have not asked, both riches and honour, so that no other king shall compare with you, all your days. And if you will walk in my ways, keeping my statutes and my commandments, as your father David walked, then I will lengthen your days.'

And Solomon awoke, and behold, it was a dream. Then he came to Jerusalem, and stood before the ark of the covenant of the Lord, and offered up burnt offerings and peace offerings, and made a feast for all his servants.

New Testament *1 Timothy 2.1-7 NEB*

First of all I urge that petitions, prayers, intercessions, and thanksgivings be offered for all men; for sovereigns and all in high office, that we may lead a tranquil and quiet life in full observance of religion and high standards of morality. Such prayer is right, and approved by God our Saviour, whose will it is that all men should find salvation and come to know the truth. For there is one God, and also one mediator between God and men, Christ Jesus, himself man, who sacrificed himself to win freedom for all mankind, so providing, at the fitting time, proof of the divine purpose; of this I was appointed herald and apostle (this is no lie, but the truth), to instruct the nations in the true faith.

Gospel *Matthew 14.1-12 NEB*

Reports about Jesus reached the ears of Prince Herod. 'This is John the Baptist,' he said to his attendants; 'John has been raised to life, and that is why these miraculous powers are at work in him.' Now Herod had arrested John, put him in chains, and thrown him into prison, on account of Herodias, his brother Philip's wife; for John had told him: 'You have no right to her.' Herod would have liked to put him to death, but he was afraid of the people, in whose eyes John was a prophet. But at his birthday celebrations the daughter of Herodias danced before the guests, and Herod was so delighted that he took an oath to give her anything she cared to ask. Prompted by her mother, she said, 'Give me here on a dish the head of John the Baptist.' The king was distressed when he heard it; but out of regard for his oath and for his guests, he ordered the request to be granted, and had John beheaded in prison. The head was brought in on a dish and given to the girl; and she carried it to her mother. Then John's disciples came and took away the body, and buried it; and they went and told Jesus.

POSTCOMMUNION SENTENCE

The kingdom of the world is to become the kingdom of our Lord and of his Christ, and he shall reign for ever.
Revelation 11.15

PENTECOST 16
(Trinity 15)   Green

INTRODUCTORY SENTENCE

The king will say, As you did it to one of the least of these my brethren, you will do it to me. *Matthew 25.40*

COLLECT

Almighty God,
you have taught us through your Son
that love is the fulfilling of the law.
Grant that we may love you with our whole heart
and our neighbours as ourselves;
through Jesus Christ our Lord.

PSALMS 34.1-10; 34.11-18

READINGS YEAR 1

Old Testament *Leviticus 19.9-18 NEB*

When you reap the harvest of your land, you shall not reap right into the edges of your field; neither shall you glean the loose ears of your crop; you shall not completely strip your vineyard nor glean the fallen grapes. You shall leave them for the poor and the alien. I am the Lord your God.

You shall not steal; you shall not cheat or deceive a fellow-countryman. You shall not swear in my name with intent to deceive and thus profane the name of your God. I am the Lord. You shall not oppress your neighbour, nor rob him. You shall not keep back a hired man's wages till next morning. You shall not treat the deaf with contempt, nor put an obstruction in the way of the blind. You shall fear your God. I am the Lord.

You shall not pervert justice, either by favouring the poor or by subservience to the great. You shall judge your fellow-countryman with strict justice. You shall not go about spreading slander among your father's kin, nor take sides against your neighbour on a capital charge. I am the Lord. You shall not nurse hatred against your brother. You shall reprove your fellow-countryman frankly and so you will have no share in his guilt. You shall not seek revenge, or cherish anger towards your kinsfolk; you shall love your neighbour as a man like yourself. I am the Lord.

New Testament *Romans 12.9-end RSV*

Let love be genuine; hate what is evil, hold fast to what is good; love one another with brotherly affection; outdo one another in showing honour. Never flag in zeal, be aglow with the Spirit, serve the Lord. Rejoice in your hope, be patient in tribulation, be constant in prayer. Contribute to the needs of the saints, practise hospitality.

Bless those who persecute you; bless and do not curse them. Rejoice with those who rejoice, weep with those who weep. Live in harmony with one another; do not be haughty, but associate with the lowly; never be conceited. Repay no one evil for evil, but take thought for what is noble in the sight of all. If possible, so far as it depends upon you, live peaceably with all. Beloved, never avenge yourselves, but leave it to the wrath of God; for it is written, 'Vengeance is mine, I will repay, says the Lord.' No, 'if your enemy is hungry, feed him; if he is thirsty, give him drink; for by so doing you will heap burning coals upon his head.' Do not be overcome by evil, but overcome evil with good.

Gospel *Luke 10.25-37 RSV*

A lawyer stood up to put Jesus to the test, saying, 'Teacher, what shall I do to inherit eternal life?' He said to him, 'What is written in the law? How do you read?' And he answered, 'You shall love the Lord your God with all your heart, and with all your soul, and with all your strength, and with all your mind; and your neighbour as yourself.' And he said to him, 'You have answered right; do this, and you will live.'

But he, desiring to justify himself, said to Jesus, 'And who is my neighbour?' Jesus replied, 'A man was going down from Jerusalem to Jericho, and he fell among robbers, who stripped him and beat him, and departed, leaving him half-dead. Now by chance a priest was going down that road; and when he saw him he passed by on the other side.

So likewise a Levite, when he came to the place and saw him, passed by on the other side. But a Samaritan, as he journeyed, came to where he was; and when he saw him, he had compassion, and went to him and bound up his wounds, pouring on oil and wine; then he set him on his own beast and brought him to an inn, and took care of him. And the next day he took out two denarii and gave them to the innkeeper, saying, "Take care of him; and whatever more you spend, I will repay you when I come back." Which of these three, do you think, proved neighbour to the man who fell among the robbers?' He said, 'The one who showed mercy on him.' And Jesus said to him, 'Go and do likewise.'

READINGS YEAR 2

Old Testament *Deuteronomy 15.7-11 NEB*

Moses said to all Israel, 'When one of your fellow-countrymen in any of your settlements in the land which the Lord your God is giving you becomes poor, do not be hard-hearted or close-fisted with your countryman in his need. Be open-handed towards him and lend him on pledge as much as he needs. See that you do not harbour iniquitous thoughts when you find that the seventh year, the year of remission, is near, and look askance at your needy countryman and give him nothing. If you do, he will appeal to the Lord against you, and you will be found guilty of sin. Give freely to him and do not begrudge him your bounty, because it is for this very bounty that the Lord your God will bless you in everything that you do or undertake. The poor will always be with you in the land, and for that reason I command you to be open-handed with your countrymen, both poor and distressed, in your own land.'

New Testament *1 John 4.15-end JB*

If anyone acknowledges that Jesus is the son of God,
God lives in him, and he in God.
We ourselves have known and put our faith in
God's love towards ourselves.
God is love
and anyone who lives in love lives in God,

and God lives in him.
Love will come to its perfection in us
when we can face the day of Judgement without fear;
because even in this world
we have become as he is.
In love there can be no fear,
but fear is driven out by perfect love:
because to fear is to expect punishment,
and anyone who is afraid is still imperfect in love.
We are to love, then,
because he loved us first.
Anyone who says, 'I love God',
and hates his brother,
is a liar,
since a man who does not love the brother that he can see
cannot love God, whom he has never seen.
So this is the commandment that he has given us,
that anyone who loves God must also love his brother.

Gospel *Luke 16.19-end JB*

Jesus said, 'There was a rich man who used to dress in
purple and fine linen and feast magnificently every day.
And at his gate there lay a poor man called Lazarus, covered
with sores, who longed to fill himself with the scraps that fell
from the rich man's table. Dogs even came and licked his
sores. Now the poor man died and was carried away by
angels to the bosom of Abraham. The rich man also died and
was buried.

'In his torment in Hades he looked up and saw Abraham a
long way off with Lazarus in his bosom. So he cried out,
"Father Abraham, pity me and send Lazarus to dip the tip of
his finger in water and cool my tongue, for I am in agony in
these flames." "My son," Abraham replied, "remember that
during your life good things came your way, just as bad
things came the way of Lazarus. Now he is being comforted
here while you are in agony. But that is not all: between us
and you a great gulf has been fixed, to stop anyone, if he
wanted to , crossing from our side to yours, and to stop any
crossing from your side to ours."

'The rich man replied, "Father, I beg you then to send Lazarus to my father's house, since I have five brothers, to give them warning so that they do not come to this place of torment too." "They have Moses and the prophets," said Abraham, "let them listen to them." "Ah no, father Abraham," said the rich man, "but if someone comes to them from the dead, they will repent." Then Abraham said to him, "If they will not listen either to Moses or to the prophets, they will not be convinced even if someone should rise from the dead."'

POSTCOMMUNION SENTENCE

One must help the weak, remembering the words of the Lord Jesus, It is more blessed to give than to receive. *Acts 20.35*

PENTECOST 17
(Trinity 16)   Green

INTRODUCTORY SENTENCE

As the body apart from the spirit is dead, so faith apart from works is dead. *James 2.26*

COLLECT

Lord of all power and might,
the author and giver of all good things:
graft in our hearts the love of your name,
increase in us true religion,
nourish in us all goodness,
and of your great mercy keep us in the same;
through Jesus Christ our Lord.

PSALMS 56; 57

READINGS YEAR 1

Old Testament *Jeremiah 7.1-11 NEB*

This word came from the Lord to Jeremiah. Stand at the gate of the Lord's house and there make your proclamation:

Listen to the words of the Lord, all you men of Judah who come in through these gates to worship him. These are the words of the Lord of Hosts the God of Israel: Mend your ways and your doings, that I may let you live in this place. You keep saying, 'This place is the temple of the Lord, the temple of the Lord, the temple of the Lord!' This catchword of yours is a lie; put no trust in it. Mend your ways and your doings, deal fairly with one another, do not oppress the alien, the orphan, and the widow, shed no innocent blood in this place, do not run after other gods to your own ruin. Then will I let you live in this place, in the land which I gave long ago to your forefathers for all time. You gain nothing by putting your trust in this lie. You steal, you murder, you commit adultery and perjury, you burn sacrifices to Baal, you run after other gods whom you have not known; then you come and stand before me in this house, which bears my name, and say, 'We are safe'; safe, you think, to indulge in all these abominations. Do you think that this house, this house which bears my name, is a robbers' cave? I myself have seen all this, says the Lord.

New Testament *James 1.16-end NEB*

Make no mistake, my friends. All good giving, every perfect gift, comes from above, from the Father of the lights of heaven. With him there is no variation, no play of passing shadows. Of his set purpose, by declaring the truth, he gave us birth to be a kind of firstfruit of his creatures.

Of that you may be certain, my friends. But each of you must be quick to listen, slow to speak, and slow to be angry. For a man's anger cannot promote the justice of God. Away then with all that is sordid, and the malice that hurries to excess, and quietly accept the message planted in your hearts, which can bring you salvation.

Only be sure that you act on the message and do not merely listen; for that would be to mislead yourselves. A man who listens to the message but never acts upon it is like one who looks in a mirror at the face nature gave him. He glances at himself and goes away, and at once forgets what he looked like. But the man who looks closely into the perfect law, the law that makes us free, and who lives in its company, does not forget what he hears, but acts upon it; and that is the man who by acting will find happiness.

A man may think he is religious, but if he has no control over his tongue, he is deceiving himself; that man's religion is futile. The kind of religion which is without stain or fault in the sight of God our Father is this: to go to the help of orphans and widows in their distress and keep oneself untarnished by the world.

Gospel *Luke 17.11-19 JB*

Now on the way to Jerusalem Jesus travelled along the border between Samaria and Galilee. As he entered one of the villages, ten lepers came to meet him. They stood some way off and called to him, 'Jesus! Master! Take pity on us.' When he saw them he said, 'Go and show yourselves to the priests.' Now as they were going away they were cleansed. Finding himself cured, one of them turned back praising God at the top of his voice and threw himself at the feet of Jesus and thanked him. The man was a Samaritan. This made Jesus say, 'Were not all ten made clean? The other nine, where are they? It seems that no one has come back to give praise to God, except this foreigner.' And he said to the man, 'Stand up and go on your way. Your faith has saved you.'

READINGS YEAR 2

Old Testament *Jeremiah 32.6-15 NEB*

Jeremiah said, The word of the Lord came to me: Hanamel son of your uncle Shallum is coming to see you and will say, 'Buy my field at Anathoth; you have the right of redemption, as next of kin, to buy it.' As the Lord had foretold, my cousin Hanamel came to the court of the guard-house and said, 'Buy my field at Anathoth in Benjamin. You have the right of redemption and possession as next of kin; buy it.' I knew that this was the Lord's message; so I bought the field at Anathoth from my cousin Hanamel and weighed out the price, seventeen shekels of silver. I signed and sealed the deed and had it witnessed; then I weighed out the money on the scales. I took my copies of the deed of purchase, both the sealed and the unsealed, and gave them to Baruch son of Neriah, son of Mahseiah, in the presence of Hanamel my cousin, of the witnesses whose names were on the deed of purchase, and of the Judaeans sitting in the court of the guard-house. In the presence of them all I gave my instructions to Baruch: These are the words of the Lord of Hosts the God of Israel: Take these copies of the deed of purchase, the sealed and the unsealed, and deposit them in an earthenware jar so that they may be preserved for a long time. For these are the words of the Lord of Hosts the God of Israel: The time will come when houses, fields, and vineyards will again be bought and sold in this land.

New Testament *Galatians 2.15—3.9 RSV*

We ourselves, who are Jews by birth and not Gentile sinners, yet who know that a man is not justified by works of the law but through faith in Jesus Christ, even we have believed in Christ Jesus, in order to be justified by faith in Christ, and not by works of the law, because by works of the law shall no one be justified. But if, in our endeavour to be justified in Christ, we ourselves were found to be sinners, is Christ then an agent of sin? Certainly not! But if I build up again those things which I tore down, then I prove myself a transgressor. For I through the law died to the law, that I might live to God. I have been crucified with Christ; it is no longer I who live, but Christ who lives in me; and the life I now live in the flesh I live by faith in the Son of God, who loved me and gave himself for me. I do not nullify the grace of God; for if justification were through the law, then Christ died to no purpose.

O foolish Galatians! Who has bewitched you, before whose eyes Jesus Christ was publicly portrayed as crucified? Let me ask you only this: Did you receive the Spirit by works of the law, or by hearing with faith? Are you so foolish? Having begun with the Spirit, are you now ending with the flesh? Did you experience so many things in vain?—if it really is in vain. Does he who supplies the Spirit to you and works miracles among you do so by works of the law, or by hearing with faith?

Thus Abraham 'believed God, and it was reckoned to him as righteousness.' So you see that it is men of faith who are the sons of Abraham. And the scripture, foreseeing that God would justify the Gentiles by faith, preached the gospel beforehand to Abraham, saying, 'In thee shall all the nations be blessed.' So then, those who are men of faith are blessed with Abraham who had faith.

Gospel *Luke 7.1-10 JB*

When Jesus had come to the end of all he wanted the people to hear, he went into Capernaum. A centurion there had a servant, a favourite of his, who was sick and near death. Having heard about Jesus he sent some Jewish elders to him to ask him to come and heal his servant. When they came to Jesus they pleaded earnestly with him. 'He deserves this of you', they said, 'because he is friendly towards our people; in fact, he is the one who built the synagogue.' So Jesus went with them, and was not very far from the house when the centurion sent word to him by some friends: 'Sir,' he said, 'do not put yourself to trouble; because I am not worthy to have you under my roof; and for this same reason I did not presume to come to you myself; but give the word and let my servant be cured. For I am under authority myself, and have soldiers under me; and I say to one man: Go, and he goes; to another: Come here, and he comes; to my servant: Do this, and he does it.' When Jesus heard these words he was astonished at him and, turning round, said to the crowd following him, 'I tell you, not even in Israel have I found faith like this.' And when the messengers got back to the house they found the servant in perfect health.

POSTCOMMUNION SENTENCE

We know that we have passed from death to life because we love the brethren. *1 John 3.14*

PENTECOST 18

(Trinity 17)   Green

INTRODUCTORY SENTENCE

Whatever you do, in word or deed, do everything in the name of the Lord Jesus. *Colossians 3.17*

COLLECT

Almighty God,
you have made us for yourself,
and our hearts are restless
till they find their rest in you.
Teach us to offer ourselves to your service,
that here we may have your peace,
and in the world to come may see you face to face;
through Jesus Christ our Lord.

PSALMS 145.14-end; 90.13-end

READINGS YEAR 1

Old Testament *Deuteronomy 26.1-11 TEV*

Moses said to all Israel, 'After you have occupied the land that the Lord your God is giving you and have settled there, each of you must place in a basket the first part of each crop that you harvest and you must take it with you to the one place of worship. Go to the priest in charge at that time and say to him, "I now acknowledge to the Lord my God that I have entered the land that he promised our ancestors to give us."

'The priest will take the basket from you and place it before the altar of the Lord your God. Then, in the Lord's presence you will recite these words: "My ancestor was a wandering Aramaean, a homeless refugee, who took his family to Egypt to live. They were few in number when they went there, but they became a large and powerful nation. The Egyptians treated us harshly and forced us to work as slaves. Then we cried out for help to the Lord, the God of our ancestors. He heard us and saw our suffering, hardship, and misery. By his great power and strength he rescued us from Egypt. He worked miracles and wonders, and caused terrifying things to happen. He brought us here and gave us this rich and fertile land. So now I bring to the Lord the first part of the harvest that he has given me."

'Then set the basket down in the Lord's presence and worship there. Be grateful for the good things that the Lord your God has given you and your family; and let the Levites and the foreigners who live among you join in the celebration.'

New Testament *2 Corinthians 8.1-9 NEB*

We must tell you, friends, about the grace of generosity which God has imparted to our congregations in Macedonia. The troubles they have been through have tried them hard, yet in all this they have been so exuberantly happy that from the depths of their poverty they have shown themselves lavishly open-handed. Going to the limit of their resources, as I can testify, and even beyond that limit, they begged us most insistently, and on their own initiative, to be allowed to share in this generous service to their fellow-Christians. And their giving surpassed our expectations; for they gave their very selves, offering them in the first instance to the Lord, but also, under God, to us. The upshot is that we have asked Titus, who began it all, to visit you and bring this work of generosity also to completion. You are so rich in everything—in faith, speech, knowledge, and zeal of every kind, as well as in the loving regard you have for us—surely you should show yourselves equally lavish in this generous service! This is not meant as an order; by telling you how keen others are I am putting your love to the test. For you know how generous our Lord Jesus Christ has been: he was rich, yet for your sake he became poor, so that through his poverty you might become rich.

Gospel *Matthew 5.17-26 NEB*

Jesus said, 'Do not suppose that I have come to abolish the Law and the prophets; I did not come to abolish, but to complete. I tell you this: so long as heaven and earth endure, not a letter, not a stroke, will disappear from the Law until all that must happen has happened. If any man therefore sets aside even the least of the Law's demands, and teaches others to do the same, he will have the lowest place in the kingdom of Heaven, whereas anyone who keeps the Law, and teaches others so, will stand high in the kingdom of Heaven. I tell you, unless you show yourselves far better men than the Pharisees and the doctors of the law, you can never enter the kingdom of Heaven.

'You have learned that our forefathers were told, "Do not commit murder; anyone who commits murder must be brought to judgement." But what I tell you is this: Anyone who nurses anger against his brother must be brought to judgement. If he abuses his brother he must answer for it to the court; if he sneers at him he will have to answer for it in the fires of hell.

'If, when you are bringing your gift to the altar, you suddenly remember that your brother has a grievance against you, leave your gift where it is before the altar. First go and make your peace with your brother, and only then come back and offer your gift.

'If someone sues you, come to terms with him promptly while you are both on your way to court; otherwise he may hand you over to the judge, and the judge to the constable, and you will be put in jail. I tell you, once you are there you will not be let out till you have paid the last farthing.'

READINGS YEAR 2

Old Testament *Nehemiah 6.1-16 NEB*

When the news came to Sanballat, Tobiah, Geshem the Arab, and the rest of our enemies, that I had rebuilt the wall and that not a single breach remained in it, although I had not yet set up the doors in the gates, Sanballat and Geshem sent me an invitation to come and confer with them at Hakkephirim in the plain of Ono; this was a ruse on their part to do me harm. So I sent messengers to them with this reply: 'I have important work on my hands at the moment; I cannot come down. Why should the work be brought to a standstill while I leave it and come down to you?' They sent me a similar invitation four times, and each time I gave them the same answer. On a fifth occasion Sanballat made a similar approach, but this time his messenger came with an open letter. It ran as follows: 'It is reported among the nations—and Gashmu confirms it—that you and the Jews are plotting rebellion, and it is for this reason that you are rebuilding the wall, and—so the report goes—that you yourself want to be king. You are also said to have put up prophets to proclaim in Jerusalem that Judah has a king, meaning yourself. The king will certainly hear of this. So come at once and let us talk the matter over.' Here is the reply I sent: 'No such thing as you allege has taken place; you have made up the whole story.' They were all trying to intimidate us, in the hope that we should then relax our efforts and that the work would never be finished. So I applied myself to it with greater energy.

One day I went to the house of Shemaiah son of Delaiah, son of Mehetabel, for he was confined to his house. He said, 'Let us meet in the house of God, within the sanctuary, and let us shut the doors, for they are coming to kill you—they are coming to kill you by night.' But I said, 'Should a man like me run away? And can a man like me go into the sanctuary and survive? I will not go in.' Then it dawned on me: God had not sent him. His prophecy aimed at harming me, and Tobiah and Sanballat had bribed him to utter it. He had been bribed to frighten me into compliance and into committing sin; then they could give me a bad name and discredit me. Remember Tobiah and Sanballat, O God, for what they have done, and also the prophetess Noadiah and all the other prophets who have tried to intimidate me.

On the twenty-fifth day of the month Elul the wall was finished; it had taken fifty-two days. When our enemies heard of it, and all the surrounding nations saw it, they thought it a very wonderful achievement, and they recognized that this work had been accomplished by the help of our God.

or *Ecclesiasticus 38.24-end NEB*

A scholar's wisdom comes of ample leisure;
if a man is to be wise he must be relieved of other tasks.
How can a man become wise who guides the plough,
whose pride is in wielding his goad,
who is absorbed in the task of driving oxen,
and talks only about cattle?
He concentrates on ploughing his furrows,
and works late to give the heifers their fodder.
So it is with every craftsman or designer
who works by night as well as by day,
such as those who make engravings on signets,
and patiently vary the design;
they concentrate on making an exact representation,
and sit up late to finish their task.
So it is with the smith, sitting by his anvil,
intent on his iron-work.
The smoke of the fire shrivels his flesh,
as he wrestles in the heat of the furnace.
The hammer rings again and again in his ears,
and his eyes are on the pattern he is copying.
He concentrates on completing the task,
and stays up late to give it a perfect finish.
So it is with the potter, sitting at his work,
turning the wheel with his feet,
always engrossed in the task
of making up his tally;
he moulds the clay with his arm,
crouching forward to apply his strength.
He concentrates on finishing the glazing,
and stays awake to clean out the furnace.

All these rely on their hands,
and each is skilful at his own craft.
Without them a city would have no inhabitants;
no settlers or travellers would come to it.
Yet they are not in demand at public discussions
or prominent in the assembly.
They do not sit on the judge's bench
or understand the decisions of the courts.
They cannot expound moral or legal principles

and are not ready with maxims.
But they maintain the fabric of this world,
and their prayers are about their daily work.

New Testament *1 Peter 4.7-11 NEB*

The end of all things is upon us, so you must lead an ordered
and sober life, given to prayer. Above all, keep your love for
one another at full strength, because love cancels
innumerable sins. Be hospitable to one another without
complaining. Whatever gift each of you may have received,
use it in service to one another, like good stewards
dispensing the grace of God in its varied forms. Are you a
speaker? Speak as if you uttered oracles of God. Do you give
service? Give it as in the strength which God supplies. In all
things so act that the glory may be God's through Jesus
Christ; to him belong glory and power for ever and
ever. Amen.

Gospel *Matthew 25.14-30 JB*

Jesus said, 'The kingdom of Heaven is like a man on his way
abroad who summoned his servants and entrusted his
property to them. To one he gave five talents, to another
two, to a third one; each in proportion to his ability. Then he
set out. The man who had received the five talents promptly
went and traded with them and made five more. The man
who had received two made two more in the same way. But
the man who had received one went off and dug a hole in the
ground and hid his master's money. Now a long time after,
the master of those servants came back and went through his
accounts with them. The man who had received the five
talents came forward bringing five more. "Sir," he said,
"you entrusted me with five talents; here are five more that I
have made." His master said to him, "Well done, good and
faithful servant; you have shown you can be faithful in small
things, I will trust you with greater; come and join in your
master's happiness." Next the man with the two talents
came forward. "Sir," he said, "you entrusted me with two
talents; here are two more that I have made." His master said
to him, "Well done, good and faithful servant; you have
shown you can be faithful in small things, I will trust you

with greater; come and join in your master's happiness."
Last came forward the man who had the one talent. "Sir,"
said he, "I had heard you were a hard man, reaping where
you have not sown and gathering where you have not
scattered; so I was afraid, and I went off and hid your talent
in the ground. Here it is; it was yours, you have it back." But
his master answered him, "You wicked and lazy servant! So
you knew that I reap where I have not sown and gather
where I have not scattered? Well then, you should have
deposited my money with the bankers, and on my return I
would have recovered my capital with interest. So now, take
the talent from him and give it to the man who has the five
talents. For to everyone who has will be given more, and he
will have more than enough; but from the man who has not,
even what he has will be taken away. As for this
good-for-nothing servant, throw him out into the dark,
where there will be weeping and grinding of teeth."'

POSTCOMMUNION SENTENCE

I appeal to you, brethren, to present your bodies as a living
sacrifice, holy and acceptable to God. *Romans 12.1*

PENTECOST 19
(Trinity 18)   Green

INTRODUCTORY SENTENCE

We walk by faith, not by sight. *2 Corinthians 5.7*

COLLECT

Almighty and everlasting God,
increase in us your gift of faith;
that, forsaking what lies behind
and reaching out to that which is before,
we may run the way of your commandments
and win the crown of everlasting joy;
through Jesus Christ our Lord.

PSALMS 139.1-11; 65.1-7

READINGS YEAR 1

Old Testament *Genesis 28.10-end JB*

Jacob left Beersheba and set out for Haran. When he had
reached a certain place he passed the night there, since the
sun had set. Taking one of the stones to be found at that
place, he made it his pillow and lay down where he was. He
had a dream: a ladder was there, standing on the ground
with its top reaching into heaven; and there were angels of
God going up it and coming down. And the Lord was there,
standing over him, saying, 'I am the Lord, the God of
Abraham your father, and the God of Isaac. I will give to you
and your descendants the land on which you are lying. Your
descendants shall be like the specks of dust on the ground;
you shall spread to the west and the east, to the north and
the south, and all the tribes of the earth shall bless
themselves by you and your descendants. Be sure that I am
with you; I will keep you safe wherever you go, and bring
you back to this land, for I will not desert you before I have
done all that I have promised you.' Then Jacob awoke from
his sleep and said, 'Truly, the Lord is in this place and I never
knew it!' He was afraid and said, 'How awe-inspiring this
place is! This is nothing less than a house of God; this is the
gate of heaven!' Rising early in the morning, Jacob took the
stone he had used for his pillow, and set it up as a
monument, pouring oil over the top of it. He named the
place Bethel, but before that the town was called Luz.

Jacob made this vow, 'If God goes with me and keeps me
safe on this journey I am making, if he gives me bread to eat
and clothes to wear, and if I return home safely to my father,
then the Lord shall be my God. This stone I have set up as a
monument shall be a house of God, and I will surely pay you
a tenth part of all you give me.'

New Testament *Hebrews 11.1-2, 8-16 NEB*

What is faith? Faith gives substance to our hopes, and makes
us certain of realities we do not see.

It is for their faith that the men of old stand on record.

By faith Abraham obeyed the call to go out to a land destined for himself and his heirs, and left home without knowing where he was to go. By faith he settled as an alien in the land promised him, living in tents, as did Isaac and Jacob, who were heirs to the same promise. For he was looking forward to the city with firm foundations, whose architect and builder is God.

By faith even Sarah herself received strength to conceive, though she was past the age, because she judged that he who had promised would keep faith; and therefore from one man, and one as good as dead, there sprang descendants numerous as the stars or as the countless grains of sand on the sea-shore.

All these persons died in faith. They were not yet in possession of the things promised, but had seen them far ahead and hailed them, and confessed themselves no more than strangers or passing travellers on earth. Those who use such language show plainly that they are looking for a country of their own. If their hearts had been in the country they had left, they could have found opportunity to return. Instead, we find them longing for a better country—I mean, the heavenly one. That is why God is not ashamed to be called their God; for he has a city ready for them.

Gospel *Matthew 6.24-end NEB*

Jesus said, 'No servant can be the slave of two masters; for either he will hate the first and love the second, or he will be devoted to the first and think nothing of the second. You cannot serve God and Money.

'Therefore I bid you put away anxious thoughts about food and drink to keep you alive, and clothes to cover your body. Surely life is more than food, the body more than clothes. Look at the birds of the air; they do not sow and reap and store in barns, yet your heavenly Father feeds them. You are worth more than the birds! Is there a man of you who by anxious thought can add a foot to his height? And why be anxious about clothes? Consider how the lilies grow in the fields; they do not work, they do not spin; and yet, I tell you, even Solomon in all his splendour was not attired like one of these. But if that is how God clothes the grass in the fields, which is there today, and tomorrow is thrown on the stove, will he not all the more clothe you? How little faith you have! No, do not ask anxiously, "What are we to eat? What are we to drink? What shall we wear?" All these are things for the heathen to run after, not for you, because your heavenly Father knows that you need them all. Set your mind on God's kingdom and his justice before everything else, and all the rest will come to you as well. So do not be anxious about tomorrow; tomorrow will look after itself. Each day has troubles enough of its own.'

READINGS YEAR 2

Old Testament *Daniel 6.10-23 RSV*

When Daniel knew that the document had been signed, he went to his house where he had windows in his upper chamber open toward Jerusalem; and he got down upon his knees three times a day and prayed and gave thanks before his God, as he had done previously. Then these men came by agreement and found Daniel making petition and supplication before his God. Then they came near and said before the king, concerning the interdict, 'O king! Did you not sign an interdict, that any man who makes petition to any god or man within thirty days except to you, O king, shall be cast into the den of lions?' The king answered, 'The thing stands fast, according to the law of the Medes and Persians, which cannot be revoked.' Then they answered before the king, 'That Daniel, who is one of the exiles from Judah, pays no heed to you, O king, or the interdict you have signed, but makes his petition three times a day.'

Then the king, when he heard these words, was much distressed, and set his mind to deliver Daniel; and he laboured till the sun went down to rescue him. Then these men came by agreement to the king, and said to the king, 'Know, O king, that it is a law of the Medes and Persians that no interdict or ordinance which the king establishes can be changed.'

Then the king commanded, and Daniel was brought and cast into the den of lions. The king said to Daniel, 'May your God, whom you serve continually, deliver you!' And a stone was brought and laid upon the mouth of the den, and the king sealed it with his own signet and with the signet of his lords, that nothing might be changed concerning Daniel. Then the king went to his palace, and spent the night fasting; no diversions were brought to him, and sleep fled from him.

Then at break of day, the king arose and went in haste to the den of lions. When he came near to the den where Daniel was, he cried out in a tone of anguish and said to Daniel, 'O Daniel, servant of the living God, has your God, whom you serve continually, been able to deliver you from the lions?' Then Daniel said to the king, 'O king, live for ever! My God sent his angel and shut the lions' mouths, and they have not hurt me, because I was found blameless before him; and also before you, O king, I have done no wrong.' Then the king was exceedingly glad, and commanded that Daniel be taken up out of the den. So Daniel was taken up out of the den, and no kind of hurt was found upon him, because he had trusted in his God.

New Testament *Romans 5.1-11 RSV*

Since we are justified by faith, we have peace with God through our Lord Jesus Christ. Through him we have obtained access to this grace in which we stand, and we rejoice in our hope of sharing the glory of God. More than that, we rejoice in our sufferings, knowing that suffering produces endurance, and endurance produces character, and character produces hope, and hope does not disappoint us, because God's love has been poured into our hearts through the Holy Spirit which has been given to us.

While we were yet helpless, at the right time Christ died for the ungodly. Why, one will hardly die for a righteous man—though perhaps for a good man one will dare even to die. But God shows his love for us in that while we were yet sinners Christ died for us. Since, therefore, we are now justified by his blood, much more shall we be saved by him from the wrath of God. For if while we were enemies we were reconciled to God by the death of his Son, much more, now that we are reconciled, shall we be saved by his life. Not only so, but we also rejoice in God through our Lord Jesus

Christ, through whom we have now received
our reconciliation.

Gospel *Luke 19.1-10 NEB*

Entering Jericho Jesus made his way through the city. There
was a man there named Zacchaeus; he was superintendent
of taxes and very rich. He was eager to see what Jesus looked
like; but, being a little man, he could not see him for the
crowd. So he ran on ahead and climbed a sycomore-tree in
order to see him, for he was to pass that way. When Jesus
came to the place, he looked up and said, 'Zacchaeus, be
quick and come down; I must come and stay with you
today.' He climbed down as fast as he could and welcomed
him gladly. At this there was a general murmur of
disapproval. 'He has gone in', they said, 'to be the guest of a
sinner.' But Zacchaeus stood there and said to the Lord,
'Here and now, sir, I give half my possessions to charity; and
if I have cheated anyone, I am ready to repay him four times
over.' Jesus said to him, 'Salvation has come to this house
today!—for this man too is a son of Abraham, and the Son of
Man has come to seek and save what is lost.'

POSTCOMMUNION SENTENCE

Though you do not now see Christ, yet you have faith in him
and rejoice with unutterable and exalted joy. *1 Peter 1.8*

PENTECOST 20
(Trinity 19)   Green

INTRODUCTORY SENTENCE

Be steadfast, immoveable, always abounding in the work of
the Lord. *1 Corinthians 15.58*

COLLECT

Almighty God,
your Son has opened for us
a new and living way into your presence.

Give us pure hearts and steadfast wills
to worship you in spirit and in truth;
through the same Jesus Christ our Lord.

PSALMS 37.35-end; 121

READINGS YEAR 1

Old Testament *Daniel 3.13-26 NEB*

In rage and fury Nebuchadnezzar ordered Shadrach,
Meshach and Abed-nego to be fetched, and they were
brought into the king's presence. Nebuchadnezzar said to
them, 'Is it true, Shadrach, Meshach and Abed-nego, that
you do not serve my god or worship the golden image which
I have set up? If you are ready at once to prostrate yourselves
when you hear the sound of horn, pipe, zither, triangle,
dulcimer, music, and singing of every kind, and to worship
the image that I have set up, well and good. But if you do not
worship it, you shall forthwith be thrown into the blazing
furnace; and what god is there that can save you from my
power?' Shadrach, Meshach and Abed-nego said to King
Nebuchadnezzar, 'We have no need to answer you on this
matter. If there is a god who is able to save us from the
blazing furnace, it is our God whom we serve, and he will
save us from your power, O king; but if not, be it known to
your majesty that we will neither serve your god nor
worship the golden image that you have set up.'

Then Nebuchadnezzar flew into a rage with Shadrach,
Meshach and Abed-nego, and his face was distorted with
anger. He gave orders that the furnace should be heated up
to seven times its usual heat, and commanded some of the
strongest men in his army to bind Shadrach, Meshach and
Abed-nego and throw them into the blazing furnace. Then
those men in their trousers, their shirts, and their hats and
all their other clothes, were bound and thrown into the
blazing furnace. Because the king's order was urgent and the
furnace exceedingly hot, the men who were carrying
Shadrach, Meshach and Abed-nego were killed by the
flames that leapt out; and those three men, Shadrach,
Meshach and Abed-nego, fell bound into the

blazing furnace.

Then King Nebuchadnezzar was amazed and sprang to his feet in great trepidation. He said to his courtiers, 'Was it not three men whom we threw bound into the fire?' They answered the king, 'Assuredly, your majesty.' He answered, 'Yet I see four men walking about in the fire free and unharmed; and the fourth looks like a god.' Nebuchadnezzar approached the door of the blazing furnace and said to the men, 'Shadrach, Meshach and Abed-nego, servants of the Most High God, come out, come here.' Then Shadrach, Meshach and Abed-nego came out from the fire.

New Testament *Romans 8.18-25 RSV*

I consider that the sufferings of this present time are not worth comparing with the glory that is to be revealed to us. For the creation waits with eager longing for the revealing of the sons of God; for the creation was subjected to futility, not of its own will but by the will of him who subjected it in hope; because the creation itself will be set free from its bondage to decay and obtain the glorious liberty of the children of God. We know that the whole creation has been groaning in travail together until now; and not only the creation, but we ourselves, who have the firstfruits of the Spirit, groan inwardly as we wait for adoption as sons, the redemption of our bodies. For in this hope we were saved. Now hope that is seen is not hope. For who hopes for what he sees? But if we hope for what we do not see, we wait for it with patience.

Gospel *Luke 9.51-end NEB*

As the time approached when Jesus was to be taken up to heaven, he set his face resolutely towards Jerusalem, and sent messengers ahead. They set out and went into a Samaritan village to make arrangements for him; but the villagers would not have him because he was making for Jerusalem. When the disciples James and John saw this they said, 'Lord, may we call down fire from heaven to burn them up?' But he turned and rebuked them, and they went on to another village.

As they were going along the road a man said to him, 'I will follow you wherever you go.' Jesus answered, 'Foxes have their holes, the birds their roosts; but the Son of Man has nowhere to lay his head.' To another he said, 'Follow me', but the man replied, 'Let me go and bury my father first.' Jesus said, 'Leave the dead to bury their dead; you must go and announce the kingdom of God.'

Yet another said, 'I will follow you, sir; but let me first say good-bye to my people at home.' To him Jesus said, 'No one who sets his hand to the plough and then keeps looking back is fit for the kingdom of God.'

READINGS YEAR 2

Old Testament *Genesis 32.22-30 RSV*

Jacob arose and took his two wives, his two maids, and his eleven children, and crossed the ford of the Jabbok. He took them and sent them across the stream, and likewise everything that he had. And Jacob was left alone; and a man wrestled with him until the breaking of the day. When the man saw that he did not prevail against Jacob, he touched the hollow of his thigh; and Jacob's thigh was put out of joint as he wrestled with him. Then he said, 'Let me go, for the day is breaking.' But Jacob said, 'I will not let you go, unless you bless me.' And he said to him, 'What is your name?' And he said, 'Jacob.' Then he said, 'Your name shall no more be called Jacob, but Israel, for you have striven with God and with men, and have prevailed.' Then Jacob asked him, 'Tell me, I pray, your name.' But he said, 'Why is it that you ask my name?' And there he blessed him. So Jacob called the name of the place Peniel, saying, 'For I have seen God face to face, and yet my life is preserved.'

New Testament *1 Corinthians 9.19-end TEV*

I am a free man, nobody's slave; but I make myself everybody's slave in order to win as many people as possible. While working with the Jews, I live like a Jew in order to win them; and even though I myself am not subject to the law of Moses, I live as though I were when working with those who are, in order to win them. In the same way, when working with Gentiles, I live like a Gentile, outside the Jewish Law, in order to win Gentiles. This does not mean that I don't obey God's law; I am really under Christ's law. Among the weak in faith I become weak like one of them, in order to win them. So I become all things to all men, that I may save some of them by whatever means are possible.

All this I do for the gospel's sake, in order to share in its blessings. Surely you know that many runners take part in a race, but only one of them wins the prize. Run, then, in such a way as to win the prize. Every athlete in training submits to strict discipline, in order to be crowned with a wreath that will not last; but we do it for one that will last for ever. That is why I run straight for the finishing-line; that is why I am like a boxer who does not waste his punches. I harden my body with blows and bring it under complete control, to keep myself from being disqualified after having called others to the contest.

Gospel *Matthew 7.13-27 NEB*

Jesus said, 'Enter by the narrow gate. The gate is wide that leads to perdition, there is plenty of room on the road, and many go that way; but the gate that leads to life is small and the road is narrow, and those who find it are few.

'Beware of false prophets, men who come to you dressed up as sheep while underneath they are savage wolves. You will recognize them by the fruits they bear. Can grapes be picked from briars, or figs from thistles? In the same way, a good tree always yields good fruit, and a poor tree bad fruit. A good tree cannot bear bad fruit, or a poor tree good fruit. And when a tree does not yield good fruit it is cut down and burnt. That is why I say you will recognize them by their fruits.

'Not everyone who calls me "Lord, Lord" will enter the kingdom of Heaven, but only those who do the will of my heavenly Father. When that day comes, many will say to me, "Lord, Lord, did we not prophesy in your name, cast out devils in your name, and in your name perform many miracles?" Then I will tell them to their face, "I never knew you; out of my sight, you and your wicked ways!"

'What then of the man who hears these words of mine and acts upon them? He is like a man who had the sense to build his house on rock. The rain came down, the floods rose, the wind blew, and beat upon that house; but it did not fall, because its foundations were on rock. But what of the man who hears these words of mine and does not act upon them? He is like a man who was foolish enough to build his house on sand. The rain came down, the floods rose, the wind blew, and beat upon that house; down it fell with a great crash.'

POSTCOMMUNION SENTENCE

Jesus says, Be faithful unto death, and I will give you the crown of life. *Revelation 2.10*

PENTECOST 21
(Trinity 20)   Green

INTRODUCTORY SENTENCE

Here we have no lasting city, but we seek the city that is to come. *Hebrews 13.14*

COLLECT

Eternal Father,
whose Son Jesus Christ ascended to the throne of heaven
that he might rule over all things as Lord:
keep the Church in the unity of the Spirit
and in the bond of his peace,
and bring the whole created order to worship at his feet;
who is alive and reigns with you and the Holy Spirit,
one God, now and for ever.

PSALMS 126; 11

READINGS YEAR 1

Old Testament *Habakkuk 2.1-4 TEV*

I will climb my watch-tower and wait to see what the Lord will tell me to say and what answer he will give to my complaint.

The Lord gave me this answer: 'Write down clearly on clay tablets what I reveal to you, so that it can be read at a glance. Put it in writing, because it is not yet time for it to come true. But the time is coming quickly, and what I show you will come true. It may seem slow in coming, but wait for it; it will certainly take place, and it will not be delayed. And this is the message: "Those who are evil will not survive, but those who are righteous will live because they are faithful to God."'

New Testament *Acts 26.1-8 NEB*

Agrippa said to Paul, 'You have our permission to speak for yourself.' Then Paul stretched out his hand and began his defence:

'I consider myself fortunate, King Agrippa, that it is before you that I am to make my defence today upon all the charges brought against me by the Jews, particularly as you are expert in all Jewish matters, both our customs and our disputes. And therefore I beg you to give me a patient hearing.

'My life from my youth up, the life I led from the beginning among my people and in Jerusalem, is familiar to all Jews. Indeed they have known me long enough and could testify, if they only would, that I belonged to the strictest group in our religion: I lived as a Pharisee. And it is for a hope kindled by God's promise to our forefathers that I stand in the dock today. Our twelve tribes hope to see the fulfilment of that promise, worshipping with intense devotion day and night; and for this very hope I am impeached, and impeached by Jews, Your Majesty. Why is it considered incredible among you that God should raise men to life?'

Gospel *Luke 18.1-8 JB*

Jesus told the disciples a parable about the need to pray continually and never lose heart. 'There was a judge in a certain town', he said, 'who had neither fear of God nor respect for man. In the same town there was a widow who kept on coming to him and saying, "I want justice from you against my enemy!" For a long time he refused, but at last he said to himself, "Maybe I have neither fear of God nor respect for man, but since she keeps pestering me I must give this widow her just rights, or she will persist in coming and worry me to death."'

And the Lord said, 'You notice what the unjust judge has to say? Now will not God see justice done to his chosen who cry to him day and night even when he delays to help them? I promise you, he will see justice done to them, and done speedily. But when the Son of Man comes, will he find any faith on earth?'

READINGS YEAR 2

Old Testament *Ezekiel 12.21-end NEB*

The word of the Lord came to me: Man, he said, what is this proverb current in the land of Israel: 'Time runs on, visions die away'? Say to them, These are the words of the Lord God: I have put an end to this proverb; it shall never be heard in Israel again. Say rather to them, The time, with all the vision means, is near. There will be no more false visions, no specious divination among the Israelites, for I, the Lord, will say what I will, and it shall be done. It shall be put off no longer: in your lifetime, you rebellious people, I will speak, I will act. This is the very word of the Lord God.

The word of the Lord came to me: Man, he said, the Israelites say that the vision you now see is not to be fulfilled for many years: you are prophesying of a time far off. Say to them, These are the words of the Lord God: No word of mine shall be delayed; even as I speak it shall be done. This is the very word of the Lord God.

New Testament *1 Peter 1.13-21 NEB*

You must be mentally stripped for action, perfectly self-controlled. Fix your hopes on the gift of grace which is to be yours when Jesus Christ is revealed. As obedient children, do not let your characters be shaped any longer by the desires you cherished in your days of ignorance. The One who called you is holy; like him, be holy in all your behaviour, because Scripture says, 'You shall be holy, for I am holy.'

If you say 'our Father' to the One who judges every man impartially on the record of his deeds, you must stand in awe of him while you live out your time on earth. Well you know that it was no perishable stuff, like gold or silver, that brought your freedom from the empty folly of your traditional ways. The price was paid in precious blood, as it were of a lamb without mark or blemish—the blood of Christ. Predestined before the foundation of the world, he was made manifest in this last period of time for your sake. Through him you have come to trust in God who raised him from the dead and gave him glory, and so your faith and hope are fixed on God.

Gospel *John 11.17-27 NEB*

On his arrival Jesus found that Lazarus had already been four days in the tomb. Bethany was just under two miles from Jerusalem, and many of the people had come from the city to Martha and Mary to condole with them on their brother's death. As soon as she heard that Jesus was on his way, Martha went to meet him, while Mary stayed at home.

Martha said so Jesus, 'If you had been here, sir, my brother would not have died. Even now I know that whatever you ask of God, God will grant you.' Jesus said, 'Your brother will rise again.' 'I know that he will rise again', said Martha, 'at the resurrection on the last day.' Jesus said, 'I am the resurrection and I am life. If a man has faith in me, even though he die, he shall come to life; and no one who is alive and has faith shall ever die. Do you believe this?' 'Lord, I do,' she answered; 'I now believe that you are the Messiah, the Son of God who was to come into the world.'

POSTCOMMUNION SENTENCE

We rejoice in our hope of sharing the glory of God, and hope does not disappoint us, because God's love has been poured into our hearts through the Holy Spirit. *Romans 5.2, 5*

PENTECOST 22
(Trinity 21)   Green

INTRODUCTORY SENTENCE

No man can serve two masters; you cannot serve God and mammon. *Luke 16.13*

COLLECT

Stir up, O Lord,
the wills of your faithful people;
that richly bearing the fruit of good works,
they may by you be richly rewarded;
through Jesus Christ our Lord.

PSALMS 119.1-8; 112

READINGS YEARS 1 and 2

Old Testament *Deuteronomy 11.18-28 NEB*

Moses said to all Israel, 'You shall take these words of mine to heart and keep them in mind; you shall bind them as a sign on the hand and wear them as a phylactery on the forehead. Teach them to your children, and speak of them indoors and out of doors, when you lie down and when you rise. Write them up on the door-posts of your houses and on your gates. Then you will live long, you and your children, in the land which the Lord swore to your forefathers to give them, for as long as the heavens are above the earth.

'If you diligently keep all these commandments that I now charge you to observe, by loving the Lord your God, by conforming to his ways and by holding fast to him, the Lord will drive out all these nations before you and you shall occupy the territory of nations greater and more powerful than you. Every place where you set the soles of your feet shall be yours. Your borders shall run from the wilderness to the Lebanon and from the River, the river Euphrates, to the western sea. No man will be able to withstand you; the Lord your God will put the fear and dread of you upon the whole land on which you set foot, as he promised you. Understand that this day I offer you the choice of a blessing and a curse. The blessing will come if you listen to the commandments of the Lord your God which I give you this day, and the curse if you do not listen to the commandments of the Lord your God but turn aside from the way that I command you this day and follow other gods whom you do not know.'

New Testament *1 John 2.22-end JB*

The man who denies that Jesus is the Christ—
he is the liar,
he is Antichrist;
and he is denying the Father as well as the Son,
because no one who has the Father can deny the Son,
and to acknowledge the Son is to have the Father as well.
Keep alive in yourselves what you were taught in
    the beginning:
as long as what you were taught in the beginning
    is alive in you,
you will live in the Son
and in the Father;
and what is promised to you by his own promise
is eternal life.
This is all that I am writing to you about the people
    who are trying to lead you astray.
But you have not lost the anointing that he gave you,
and you do not need anyone to teach you;
the anointing he gave teaches you everything;
you are anointed with truth, not with a lie,
and as it has taught you, so you must stay in him.
Live in Christ, then, my children,
so that if he appears, we may have full confidence,
and not turn from him in shame
at his coming.
You know that God is righteous—

then you must recognize that everyone
  whose life is righteous
has been begotten by him.

Gospel *Luke 16.1-9 NEB*

Jesus said to his disciples, 'There was a rich man who had a
steward, and he received complaints that this man was
squandering the property. So he sent for him, and said,
"What is this that I hear? Produce your accounts, for you
cannot be manager here any longer." The steward said to
himself, "What am I to do now that my employer is
dismissing me? I am not strong enough to dig, and too proud
to beg. I know what I must do, to make sure that, when I
have to leave, there will be people to give me house and
home." He summoned his master's debtors one by one. To
the first he said, "How much do you owe my master?" He
replied, "A thousand gallons of olive oil." He said, "Here is
your account. Sit down and make it five hundred; and be
quick about it." Then he said to another, "And you, how
much do you owe?" He said, "A thousand bushels of
wheat", and was told, "Take your account and make it eight
hundred." And the master applauded the dishonest
steward for acting so astutely. For the worldly are more
astute than the other-worldly in dealing with their
own kind.

'So I say to you, use your worldly wealth to win friends for
yourselves, so that when money is a thing of the past you
may be received into an eternal home.'

POSTCOMMUNION SENTENCE

Enter by the narrow gate. For the gate is narrow and the way
is hard that leads to life, and those who find it are few.
Matthew 7.13, 14

LAST SUNDAY AFTER PENTECOST   Green

INTRODUCTORY SENTENCE

According to God's promise, we wait for new heavens and a new earth in which righteousness dwells. *2 Peter 3.13*

COLLECT

Merciful God,
you have prepared for those who love you
such good things as pass man's understanding.
Pour into our hearts such love towards you
that we, loving you above all things,
may obtain your promises,
which exceed all that we can desire;
through Jesus Christ our Lord.

PSALMS 15; 146

READINGS YEAR 1

Old Testament *Jeremiah 29.1, 4-14 RSV*

These are the words of the letter which Jeremiah the prophet sent from Jerusalem to the elders of the exiles, and to the priests, the prophets, and all the people, whom Nebuchadnezzar had taken into exile from Jerusalem to Babylon.

'Thus says the Lord of hosts, the God of Israel, to all the exiles whom I have sent into exile from Jerusalem to Babylon: Build houses and live in them; plant gardens and eat their produce. Take wives and have sons and daughters; take wives for your sons, and give your daughters in marriage, that they may bear sons and daughters; multiply there, and do not decrease. But seek the welfare of the city where I have sent you into exile, and pray to the Lord on its behalf, for in its welfare you will find your welfare. For thus says the Lord of hosts, the God of Israel: Do not let your prophets and your diviners who are among you deceive you, and do not listen to the dreams which they dream, for it is a lie which they are prophesying to you in my name; I did not send them, says the Lord.

'For thus says the Lord: When seventy years are completed for Babylon, I will visit you, and I will fulfil to you my promise and bring you back to this place. For I know the plans I have for you, says the Lord, plans for welfare and not for evil, to give you a future and a hope. Then you will call upon me and come and pray to me, and I will hear you. You will seek me and find me; when you seek me with all your heart, I will be found by you, says the Lord, and I will restore your fortunes and gather you from all the nations and all the places where I have driven you, says the Lord, and I will bring you back to the place from which I sent you into exile.'

New Testament *Philippians 3.7-end JB*

Because of Christ, I have come to consider all these advantages that I had as disadvantages. Not only that, but I believe nothing can happen that will outweigh the supreme advantage of knowing Christ Jesus my Lord. For him I have accepted the loss of everything, and I look on everything as so much rubbish if only I can have Christ and be given a place in him. I am no longer trying for perfection by my own efforts, the perfection that comes from the Law, but I want only the perfection that comes through faith in Christ, and is from God and based on faith. All I want is to know Christ and the power of his resurrection and to share his sufferings by reproducing the pattern of his death. That is the way I can hope to take my place in the resurrection of the dead. Not that I have become perfect yet: I have not yet won, but I am still running, trying to capture the prize for which Christ Jesus captured me. I can assure you my brothers, I am far from thinking that I have already won. All I can say is that I forget the past and I strain ahead for what is still to come; I am racing for the finish, for the prize to which God calls us upwards to receive in Christ Jesus. We who are called 'perfect' must all think in this way. If there is some point on which you see things differently, God will make it clear to you; meanwhile, let us go forward on the road that has brought us to where we are.

My brothers, be united in following my rule of life. Take as your models everybody who is already doing this and study them as you used to study us. I have told you often, and I repeat it today with tears, there are many who are behaving as the enemies of the cross of Christ. They are destined to be lost. They make foods into their god and they are proudest of something they ought to think shameful; the things they think important are earthly things. For us, our homeland is in heaven, and from heaven comes the saviour we are waiting for, the Lord Jesus Christ, and he will transfigure these wretched bodies of ours into copies of his glorious body. He will do that by the same power with which he can subdue the whole universe.

Gospel John 17.1-10 JB

Jesus raised his eyes to heaven and said,
'Father, the hour has come:
glorify your Son
so that your Son may glorify you;
and, through the power over all mankind
that you have given him,
let him give eternal life
to all those you have entrusted to him.
And eternal life is this:
to know you,
the only true God,
and Jesus Christ whom you have sent.
I have glorified you on earth
and finished the work
that you gave me to do.
Now, Father, it is time for you to glorify me
with that glory I had with you
before ever the world was.
I have made your name known
to the men you took from the world to give me.
They were yours and you gave them to me,
and they have kept your word.
Now at last they know
that all you have given me comes indeed from you;
for I have given them
the teaching you gave to me,

and they have truly accepted this, that I came from you,
and have believed that it was you who sent me.
I pray for them;
I am not praying for the world
but for those you have given me,
because they belong to you:
all I have is yours
and all you have is mine,
and in them I am glorified.'

READINGS YEAR 2

Old Testament *Isaiah 33.17-22 RSV*

Your eyes will see the king in his beauty;
they will behold a land that stretches afar.
Your mind will muse on the terror:
'Where is he who counted,
where is he who weighed the tribute?
Where is he who counted the towers?'
You will see no more the insolent people,
the people of an obscure speech
which you cannot comprehend,
stammering in a tongue which you cannot understand.
Look upon Zion, the city of our appointed feasts!
Your eyes will see Jerusalem,
a quiet habitation, an immoveable tent,
whose stakes will never be plucked up,
nor will any of its cords be broken.
But there the Lord in majesty will be for us
a place of broad rivers and streams,
where no galley with oars can go,
nor stately ship can pass.
For the Lord is our judge, the Lord is our ruler,
the Lord is our king; he will save us.

New Testament *Revelation 7.2-4, 9-end RSV*

I saw another angel ascend from the rising of the sun, with
the seal of the living God, and he called with a loud voice to
the four angels who had been given power to harm earth and
sea, saying, 'Do not harm the earth or the sea or the trees, till

we have sealed the servants of our God upon their foreheads.' And I heard the number of the sealed, a hundred and forty-four thousand sealed, out of every tribe of the sons of Israel.

After this I looked, and behold, a great multitude which no man could number, from every nation, from all tribes and peoples and tongues, standing before the throne and before the Lamb, clothed in white robes, with palm branches in their hands, and crying out with a loud voice, 'Salvation belongs to our God who sits upon the throne, and to the Lamb!' And all the angels stood round the throne and round the elders and the four living creatures, and they fell on their faces before the throne and worshipped God, saying, 'Amen! Blessing and glory and wisdom and thanksgiving and honour and power and might be to our God for ever and ever! Amen.'

Then one of the elders addressed me, saying, 'Who are these, clothed in white robes, and whence have they come?' I said to him, 'Sir, you know.' And he said to me, 'These are they who have come out of the great tribulation; they have washed their robes and made them white in the blood of the Lamb.

'Therefore are they before the throne of God,
and serve him day and night within his temple;
and he who sits upon the throne
    will shelter them with his presence.
They shall hunger no more, neither thirst any more;
the sun shall not strike them, nor any scorching heat.
For the Lamb in the midst of the throne
    will be their shepherd,
and he will guide them to springs of living water;
and God will wipe away every tear from their eyes.'

Gospel *Matthew 25.1-13 NEB*

Jesus said, 'When that day comes, the kingdom of Heaven will be like this. There were ten girls, who took their lamps and went out to meet the bridegroom. Five of them were foolish, and five prudent; when the foolish ones took their lamps, they took no oil with them, but the others took flasks of oil with their lamps. As the bridegroom was late in coming they all dozed off to sleep. But at midnight a cry was heard: "Here is the bridegroom! Come out to meet him." With that the girls all got up and trimmed their lamps. The foolish said to the prudent, "Our lamps are going out; give us some of your oil." "No," they said; "there will never be enough for all of us. You had better go to the shop and buy some for yourselves." While they were away the bridegroom arrived; those who were ready went in with him to the wedding; and the door was shut. And then the other five came back. "Sir, sir," they cried, "open the door for us." But he answered, "I declare, I do not know you." Keep awake then; for you never know the day or the hour.'

POSTCOMMUNION SENTENCE

Jesus said, My disciples are not of this world, even as I am not of this world. *John 17.16*

Sentences, Collects, and Readings
(b) Festivals and Holy Days

THE NAMING OF JESUS, OR
THE CIRCUMCISION OF CHRIST (1 January)   White

INTRODUCTORY SENTENCE

From the rising of the sun to its going down, let the name of
the Lord be praised. *Psalm 113.3*

COLLECT

Almighty God,
whose blessed Son was circumcised
in obedience to the law for man's sake
and given the Name that is above every name:
give us grace faithfully to bear his Name,
to worship him in the freedom of the Spirit,
and to proclaim him as the Saviour of mankind,
who is alive and reigns with you and the Holy Spirit,
one God, now and for ever.

PSALMS 8; 62.1-8

READINGS

Old Testament *Isaiah 9.2, 6-7 RSV*

The people who walked in darkness
have seen a great light;
those who dwelt in a land of deep darkness,
on them has light shined.
For to us a child is born,
to us a son is given;
and the government will be upon his shoulder,
and his name will be called
'Wonderful Counsellor, Mighty God,
Everlasting Father, Prince of Peace.'
Of the increase of his government and of peace
there will be no end,
upon the throne of David, and over his kingdom,
to establish it, and to uphold it
with justice and with righteousness
from this time forth and for evermore.
The zeal of the Lord of hosts will do this.

New Testament *Acts 4.8-12 NEB*

Peter, filled with the Holy Spirit, said, 'Rulers of the people and elders, if the question put to us today is about help given to a sick man, and we are asked by what means he was cured, here is the answer, for all of you and for all the people of Israel: it was by the name of Jesus Christ of Nazareth, whom you crucified, whom God raised from the dead; it is by his name that this man stands here before you fit and well. This Jesus is the stone rejected by the builders which has become the keystone—and you are the builders. There is no salvation in anyone else at all, for there is no other name under heaven granted to men, by which we may receive salvation.'

Gospel *Luke 2.15-21 RSV*

When the angels went away from them into heaven, the shepherds said to one another, 'Let us go over to Bethlehem and see this thing that has happened, which the Lord has made known to us.' And they went with haste, and found Mary and Joseph, and the babe lying in a manger. And when they saw it they made known the saying which had been told them concerning this child; and all who heard it wondered at what the shepherds told them. But Mary kept all these things, pondering them in her heart. And the shepherds returned, glorifying and praising God for all they had heard and seen, as it had been told them.

And at the end of eight days, when he was circumcised, he was called Jesus, the name given by the angel before he was conceived in the womb.

PROPER PREFACE

Rite A. A Preface of the Incarnation (3) or (4) is said. Preface (3) is not suitable for use with the Third Eucharistic Prayer. Rite B. The Preface of Christmas is said.

POSTCOMMUNION SENTENCE

Whatever you do, in word or deed, do everything in the name of the Lord Jesus. *Colossians 3.17*

THE CONVERSION OF ST PAUL (25 January)   White

INTRODUCTORY SENTENCE

The Lord said to Saul, I am Jesus whom you are persecuting; but rise, for I am sending you to open the eyes of the Gentiles, that they may turn from darkness to light. *Acts 26.15-18*

or

Paul writes, As to righteousness under the law, I was blameless. But whatever gain I had of that sort, I counted as loss for the sake of Christ. *Philippians 3.6, 7*

COLLECT

Almighty God,
who caused the light of the gospel
    to shine throughout the world
through the preaching of your servant Saint Paul:
grant that we who celebrate his wonderful conversion
may follow him in bearing witness to your truth;
through Jesus Christ our Lord.

PSALMS 126; 67

READINGS

Old Testament *1 Kings 19.15-end RSV*

The Lord said to Elijah, 'Go, return on your way to the wilderness of Damascus; and when you arrive, you shall anoint Hazael to be king over Syria; and Jehu the son of Nimshi you shall anoint to be king over Israel; and Elisha the son of Shaphat of Abel-meholah you shall anoint to be prophet in your place. And him who escapes from the sword of Hazael shall Jehu slay; and him who escapes from the sword of Jehu shall Elisha slay. Yet I will leave seven thousand in Israel, all the knees that have not bowed to Baal, and every mouth that has not kissed him.'

So he departed from there, and found Elisha the son of Shaphat, who was ploughing, with twelve yoke of oxen before him, and he was with the twelfth. Elijah passed by him and cast his mantle upon him. And he left the oxen, and ran after Elijah, and said, 'Let me kiss my father and my mother, and then I will follow you.' And he said to him, 'Go back again; for what have I done to you?' And he returned from following him, and took the yoke of oxen, and slew them, and boiled their flesh with the yokes of the oxen, and gave it to the people, and they ate. Then he arose and went after Elijah, and ministered to him.

New Testament *Acts 9.1-22 JB*

Saul was still breathing threats to slaughter the Lord's disciples. He had gone to the high priest and asked for letters addressed to the synagogues in Damascus, that would authorize him to arrest and take to Jerusalem any followers of the Way, men or women, that he could find.

Suddenly, while he was travelling to Damascus and just before he reached the city, there came a light from heaven all round him. He fell to the ground, and then he heard a voice saying, 'Saul, Saul, why are you persecuting me?' 'Who are you, Lord?', he asked, and the voice answered, 'I am Jesus, and you are persecuting me. Get up now and go into the city, and you will be told what you have to do.' The men travelling with Saul stood there speechless, for though they heard the voice they could see no one. Saul got up from the ground, but even with his eyes wide open he could see nothing at all, and they had to lead him into Damascus by the hand. For three days he was without his sight, and took neither food nor drink.

A disciple called Ananias who lived in Damascus had a vision in which he heard the Lord say to him, 'Ananias!' When he replied, 'Here I am, Lord', the Lord said, 'You must go to Straight Street and ask at the house of Judas for someone called Saul, who comes from Tarsus. At this moment he is praying, having had a vision of a man called Ananias coming in and laying hands on him to give him back his sight.'

When he heard that, Ananias said, 'Lord, several people have told me about this man and all the harm he has been doing to your saints in Jerusalem. He has only come here because he holds a warrant from the chief priests to arrest everybody who invokes your name.' The Lord replied, 'You must go all the same, because this man is my chosen instrument to bring my name before pagans and pagan kings and before the people of Israel; I myself will show him how much he himself must suffer for my name.' Then Ananias went. He entered the house, and at once laid his hands on Saul and said, 'Brother Saul, I have been sent by the Lord Jesus who appeared to you on your way here so that you may recover your sight and be filled with the Holy Spirit.' Immediately it was as though scales fell away from Saul's eyes and he could see again. So he was baptized there and then, and after taking some food he regained his strength.

After he had spent only a few days with the disciples in Damascus, he began preaching in the synagogues, 'Jesus is the Son of God.' All his hearers were amazed. 'Surely', they said, 'this is the man who organized the attack in Jerusalem against the people who invoke this name, and who came here for the sole purpose of arresting them to have them tried by the chief priests?' Saul's power increased steadily, and he was able to throw the Jewish colony at Damascus into complete confusion by the way he demonstrated that Jesus was the Christ.

Gospel *Matthew 19.27-end NEB*

Peter said to Jesus, 'We here have left everything to become your followers. What will there be for us?' Jesus replied, 'I tell you this: in the world that is to be, when the Son of Man is seated on his throne in heavenly splendour, you my followers will have thrones of your own, where you will sit as judges of the twelve tribes of Israel. And anyone who has left brothers or sisters, father, mother, or children, land or houses for the sake of my name will be repaid many times over, and gain eternal life. But many who are first will be last, and the last first.'

PROPER PREFACE

Rite A. The Preface of Apostles and Evangelists (23) is said.
Rite B. The Preface of Saints' Days is said.

POSTCOMMUNION SENTENCE

I live by faith in the Son of God, who loved me and sacrificed himself for me. *Galatians 2.20*

THE PRESENTATION OF CHRIST
IN THE TEMPLE (2 February)   White

INTRODUCTORY SENTENCE

Open me the gates of righteousness: and I will enter and give thanks to the Lord. *Psalm 118.19*

COLLECT

Almighty Father,
whose Son Jesus Christ was presented in the Temple
and acclaimed the glory of Israel and the light of the nations:
grant that in him we may be presented to you
and in the world may reflect his glory;
through Jesus Christ our Lord.

PSALMS 48.1-8; 48.9-end

READINGS

Old Testament *Malachi 3.1-5 NEB*

Look, I am sending my messenger who will clear a path before me. Suddenly the Lord whom you seek will come to his temple; the messenger of the covenant in whom you delight is here, here already, says the Lord of Hosts. Who can endure the day of his coming? Who can stand firm when he appears? He is like a refiner's fire, like fuller's soap; he will take his seat, refining and purifying; he will purify the Levites and cleanse them like gold and silver, and so they shall be fit to bring offerings to the Lord. Thus the offerings of Judah and Jerusalem shall be pleasing to the Lord as they were in days of old, in years long past. I will appear before you in court, prompt to testify against sorcerers, adulterers, and perjurers, against those who wrong the hired labourer, the widow, and the orphan, who thrust the alien aside and have no fear of me, says the Lord of Hosts.

New Testament *1 Peter 2.1-10 NEB*

Away with all malice and deceit, away with all pretence and jealousy and recrimination of every kind! Like the new-born infants you are, you must crave for pure milk (spiritual milk, I mean), so that you may thrive upon it to your souls' health. Surely you have tasted that the Lord is good.

So come to him, our living Stone—the stone rejected by men but choice and precious in the sight of God. Come, and let yourselves be built as living stones into a spiritual temple; become a holy priesthood, to offer spiritual sacrifices acceptable to God through Jesus Christ. For it stands written:

'I lay in Zion a choice corner-stone of great worth. The man who has faith in it will not be put to shame.' The great worth of which it speaks is for you who have faith. For those who have no faith, the stone which the builders rejected has become not only the corner-stone, but also 'a stone to trip over, a rock to stumble against'. They fall when they disbelieve the Word. Such was their appointed lot!

But you are a chosen race, a royal priesthood, a dedicated nation, and a people claimed by God for his own, to proclaim the triumphs of him who has called you out of darkness into his marvellous light. You are now the people of God, who once were not his people; outside his mercy once, you have now received his mercy.

Gospel *Luke 2.22-35 JB*

When the day came for them to be purified as laid down by the Law of Moses, the parents of Jesus took him up to Jerusalem to present him to the Lord—observing what stands written in the Law of the Lord: Every first-born male must be consecrated to the Lord—and also to offer in sacrifice, in accordance with what is said in the Law of the Lord, a pair of turtledoves or two young pigeons. Now in Jerusalem there was a man named Simeon. He was an upright and devout man; he looked forward to Israel's comforting and the Holy Spirit rested on him. It had been revealed to him by the Holy Spirit that he would not see death until he had set eyes on the Christ of the Lord. Prompted by the Spirit he came to the Temple: and when the parents brought in the child Jesus to do for him what the Law required, he took him into his arms and blessed God; and he said:

'Now, Master, you can let your servant go in peace,
just as you promised;
because my eyes have seen the salvation
which you have prepared for all the nations to see,
a light to enlighten the pagans
and the glory of your people Israel.'

As the child's father and mother stood there wondering at the things that were being said about him, Simeon blessed them and said to Mary his mother, 'You see this child: he is destined for the fall and for the rising of many in Israel, destined to be a sign that is rejected—and a sword will pierce your own soul too—so that the secret thoughts of many may be laid bare.'

PROPER PREFACE

Rite A. A Preface of the Incarnation (3), (4), or (7) is said.
Preface (3) is not suitable for use with the Third
Eucharistic Prayer.
Rite B. The Preface of Christmas is said.

POSTCOMMUNION SENTENCE

Present your bodies as a living sacrifice, holy and acceptable to God. *Romans 12.1*

ST JOSEPH OF NAZARETH, HUSBAND OF THE BLESSED VIRGIN MARY

(19 March)   White

INTRODUCTORY SENTENCE

Joseph was the husband of Mary, of whom Jesus was born, who is called Christ. *Matthew 1.16*

COLLECT

Almighty God,
who called Joseph to be the husband of the Virgin Mary,
and the guardian of your only Son:
open our eyes and our ears
to the messages of your holy will,
and give us the courage to act upon them;
through Jesus Christ our Lord.

PSALMS 89.1-8; 89.19-30   or   15; 112

READINGS

Old Testament *Isaiah 7.10-14 NEB*

The Lord spoke to Ahaz and said, 'Ask the Lord your God for a sign, from lowest Sheol or from highest heaven.' But Ahaz said, 'No, I will not put the Lord to the test by asking for a sign.' Then the answer came: 'Listen, house of David. Are you not content to wear out men's patience? Must you also wear out the patience of my God? Therefore the Lord himself shall give you a sign: A young woman is with child, and she will bear a son, and will call him Emmanuel.'

or *Genesis 1.26—2.3 NEB*

God said, 'Let us make man in our image and likeness to rule the fish in the sea, the birds of heaven, the cattle, all wild animals on earth, and all reptiles that crawl upon the earth.' So God created man in his own image; in the image of God he created him; male and female he created them. God blessed them and said to them, 'Be fruitful and increase, fill the earth and subdue it, rule over the fish in the sea, the birds of heaven, and every living thing that moves upon the earth.' God also said, 'I give you all plants that bear seed everywhere on earth, and every tree bearing fruit which yields seed: they shall be yours for food. All green plants I give for food to the wild animals, to all the birds of heaven, and to all reptiles on earth, every living creature.' So it was; and God saw all that he had made, and it was very good. Evening came, and morning came, a sixth day.

Thus heaven and earth were completed with all their mighty throng. On the sixth day God completed all the work he had been doing, and on the seventh day he ceased from all his work. God blessed the seventh day and made it holy, because on that day he ceased from all the work he had set himself to do.

New Testament *1 Peter 3.1-7 JB*

Wives should be obedient to their husbands. Then, if there are some husbands who have not yet obeyed the word, they may find themselves won over, without a word spoken, by the way their wives behave, when they see how faithful and conscientious they are. Do not dress up for show: doing up your hair, wearing gold bracelets and fine clothes; all this should be inside, in a person's heart, imperishable: the ornament of a sweet and gentle disposition—this is what is precious in the sight of God. That was how the holy women of the past dressed themselves attractively—they hoped in God and were tender and obedient to their husbands; like Sarah, who was obedient to Abraham, and called him her lord. You are now her children, as long as you live good lives and do not give way to fear or worry.

In the same way, husbands must always treat their wives with consideration in their life together, respecting a woman as one who, though she may be the weaker partner, is equally an heir to the life of grace. This will stop anything from coming in the way of your prayers.

or *Colossians 3.12-15, 17, 23, 24 RSV*

Put on as God's chosen ones, holy and beloved, compassion, kindness, lowliness, meekness, and patience, forbearing one another and, if one has a complaint against another, forgiving each other; as the Lord has forgiven you, so you also must forgive. And above all these put on love, which binds everything together in perfect harmony. And let the peace of Christ rule in your hearts, to which indeed you were called in the one body. And be thankful.

And whatever you do, in word or deed, do everything in the name of the Lord Jesus, giving thanks to God the Father through him. Whatever your task, work heartily, as serving the Lord and not men, knowing that from the Lord you will receive the inheritance as your reward; you are serving the Lord Christ.

Gospel *Matthew 1.18-end RSV*

Now the birth of Jesus Christ took place in this way. When his mother Mary had been betrothed to Joseph, before they came together she was found to be with child of the Holy Spirit; and her husband Joseph, being a just man and unwilling to put her to shame, resolved to divorce her quietly. But as he considered this, behold, an angel of the Lord appeared to him in a dream, saying 'Joseph, son of David, do not fear to take Mary your wife, for that which is conceived in her is of the Holy Spirit; she will bear a son, and you shall call his name Jesus, for he will save his people from their sins.' All this took place to fulfil what the Lord had spoken by the prophet:

'Behold, a virgin shall conceive and bear a son, and his name shall be called Emmanuel' (which means, God with us). When Joseph woke from sleep, he did as the angel of the Lord commanded him; he took his wife, but knew her not until she had borne a son; and he called his name Jesus.

or *Matthew 13.54-end NEB*

Jesus came to his home town, where he taught the people in their synagogue. In amazement they asked, 'Where does he get this wisdom from, and these miraculous powers? Is he not the carpenter's son? Is not his mother called Mary, his brothers James, Joseph, Simon, and Judas? And are not all

his sisters here with us? Where then has he got all this from?'
So they fell foul of him, and this led him to say, 'A prophet
will always be held in honour, except in his home town, and
in his own family.' And he did not work many miracles
there: such was their want of faith.

PROPER PREFACE

Rite A. A Preface of the Incarnation (7) is said.
Rite B. The Preface of Christmas is said.

POSTCOMMUNION SENTENCE

The Jews said, Where did this man Jesus get this wisdom,
and these miraculous powers? Is not this the carpenter's
son? *Matthew 13.55*

THE ANNUNCIATION OF OUR LORD
TO THE BLESSED VIRGIN MARY (25 March) White

INTRODUCTORY SENTENCE

A virgin shall conceive and bear a Son: and his name shall be
called Emmanuel, God-is-with-us. *Matthew 1.23; Isaiah 7.14*

COLLECT

We beseech you, O Lord,
to pour your grace into our hearts;
that as we have known the incarnation
   of your Son Jesus Christ
by the message of an angel,
so by his cross and passion
we may be brought to the glory of his resurrection;
through Jesus Christ our Lord.

PSALMS 113; 131

READINGS

Old Testament *Isaiah 52.7-10 NEB*

How lovely on the mountains are the feet of the herald
who comes to proclaim prosperity and bring good news,
the news of deliverance,
calling to Zion, 'Your God is king.'
Hark, your watchmen raise their voices
and shout together in triumph;
for with their own eyes they shall see
the Lord returning in pity to Zion.
Break forth together in shouts of triumph,
you ruins of Jerusalem;
for the Lord has taken pity on his people
and has ransomed Jerusalem.
The Lord has bared his holy arm
in the sight of all nations,
and the whole world from end to end
shall see the deliverance of our God.

New Testament *Galatians 4.1-5 RSV*

The heir, as long as he is a child, is no better than a slave,
though he is the owner of all the estate; but he is under
guardians and trustees until the date set by the father. So
with us; when we were children, we were slaves to the
elemental spirits of the universe. But when the time had
fully come, God sent forth his Son, born of woman, born
under the law, to redeem those who were under the law, so
that we might receive adoption as sons.

Gospel *Luke 1.26-38a RSV*

In the sixth month the angel Gabriel was sent from God to a
city of Galilee named Nazareth, to a virgin betrothed to a
man whose name was Joseph, of the house of David; and the
virgin's name was Mary. And he came to her and said, 'Hail,
O favoured one, the Lord is with you!' But she was greatly
troubled at the saying, and considered in her mind what sort
of greeting this might be. And the angel said to her, 'Do not
be afraid, Mary, for you have found favour with God. And

behold, you will conceive in your womb and bear a son, and
you shall call his name Jesus.
He will be great, and will be called the Son
    of the Most High;
and the Lord God will give to him the throne
    of his father David,
and he will reign over the house of Jacob for ever;
and of his kingdom there will be no end.'

And Mary said to the angel, 'How can this be, since I have no
husband?' And the angel said to her,
'The Holy Spirit will come upon you,
and the power of the Most High will overshadow you;
therefore the child to be born will be called holy,
the Son of God.
And behold, your kinswoman Elizabeth in her old age has
also conceived a son; and this is the sixth month with her
who was called barren. For with God nothing will be
impossible.' And Mary said, 'Behold I am the handmaid of
the Lord; let it be to me according to your word.'

PROPER PREFACE

Rite A. A Preface of the Incarnation (3) or (6) is said. Preface
(3) is not suitable for use with the Third Eucharistic Prayer.
Rite B. The Preface of Christmas is said.

POSTCOMMUNION SENTENCE

The Word was made flesh, and lived among us. *John 1.14*

ST MARK THE EVANGELIST (25 April)   Red

INTRODUCTORY SENTENCE

Go out to the whole world, and preach the gospel to all
creatures. *Mark 16.15*

or

Fear nothing; you are looking for Jesus of Nazareth who was
crucified; he has risen, and you will see him, as he told you.
Mark 16.6, 7

COLLECT

Almighty God,
you have enlightened your holy Church
    through the inspired witness
    of your evangelist Saint Mark.
Grant that we, being firmly grounded
    in the truth of the gospel,
may be faithful to its teaching
both in word and deed;
through Jesus Christ our Lord.

PSALMS 45.1-5; 119.9-16

READINGS

Old Testament *Proverbs 15.28-end NEB*

The righteous think before they answer;
a bad man's ready tongue is full of mischief.
The Lord stands aloof from the wicked,
he listens to the righteous man's prayer.
A bright look brings joy to the heart,
and good news warms a man's marrow.
Whoever listens to wholesome reproof
shall enjoy the society of the wise.
He who refuses correction is his own worst enemy,
but he who listens to reproof learns sense.
The fear of the Lord is a training in wisdom,
and the way to honour is humility.

New Testament *Ephesians 4.7-16 NEB*

Each of us has been given his gift, his due portion of Christ's
bounty. Therefore Scripture says:

'He ascended into the heights
with captives in his train;
he gave gifts to men.'

Now, the word 'ascended' implies that he also descended to
the lowest level, down to the very earth. He who descended
is no other than he who ascended far above all heavens, so

that he might fill the universe. And these were his gifts: some to be apostles, some prophets, some evangelists, some pastors and teachers, to equip God's people for work in his service, to the building up of the body of Christ. So shall we all at last attain to the unity inherent in our faith and our knowledge of the Son of God—to mature manhood, measured by nothing less than the full stature of Christ. We are no longer to be children, tossed by the waves and whirled about by every fresh gust of teaching, dupes of crafty rogues and their deceitful schemes. No, let us speak the truth in love; so shall we fully grow up into Christ. He is the head, and on him the whole body depends. Bonded and knit together by every constituent joint, the whole frame grows through the due activity of each part, and builds itself up in love.

Gospel *Mark 13.5-13 NEB*

Jesus said to his disciples, 'Take care that no one misleads you. Many will come claiming my name, and saying, "I am he"; and many will be misled by them.

'When you hear the noise of battle near at hand and the news of battles far away, do not be alarmed. Such things are bound to happen; but the end is still to come. For nation will make war upon nation, kingdom upon kingdom; there will be earthquakes in many places; there will be famines. With these things the birth-pangs of the new age begin.

'As for you, be on your guard. You will be handed over to the courts. You will be flogged in synagogues. You will be summoned to appear before governors and kings on my account to testify in their presence. But before the end the Gospel must be proclaimed to all nations. So when you are arrested and taken away, do not worry beforehand about what you will say, but when the time comes say whatever is given you to say; for it is not you who will be speaking, but the Holy Spirit. Brother will betray brother to death, and the father his child; children will turn against their parents and send them to their death. All will hate you for your allegiance to me; but the man who holds out to the end will be saved.'

PROPER PREFACE

Rite A. The Preface of Apostles and Evangelists (23) or of the Resurrection (14) is said.
Rite B. The Preface of Saints' Days or of Easter is said.

POSTCOMMUNION SENTENCE

Jesus said, I am with you always: to the end of the world. *Matthew 28.20*

ST PHILIP AND ST JAMES, APOSTLES (1 May)   Red

INTRODUCTORY SENTENCE

Jesus said, Whatever you ask in my name, I will do it, that the Father may be glorified in the Son. *John 14.13*

COLLECT

Almighty Father,
whom truly to know is eternal life:
teach us to know your Son Jesus Christ
as the way, the truth, and the life;
that we may follow the steps
    of your holy apostles Philip and James,
and walk steadfastly in the way that leads to your glory;
through Jesus Christ our Lord.

PSALMS 33.1-5; 25.1-10

READINGS

Old Testament *Proverbs 4.10-18 RSV*

Hear, my son, and accept my words,
that the years of your life may be many.
I have taught you the way of wisdom;
I have led you in the paths of uprightness.
When you walk, your step will not be hampered;
and if you run, you will not stumble.
Keep hold of instruction, do not let go;
guard her, for she is your life.

Do not enter the path of the wicked,
and do not walk in the way of evil men.
Avoid it; do not go on it;
turn away from it and pass on.
For they cannot sleep unless they have done wrong;
they are robbed of sleep unless
they have made some one stumble.
For they eat the bread of wickedness
and drink the wine of violence.
But the path of the righteous is like the light of dawn,
which shines brighter and brighter until full day.

New Testament *Ephesians 1.3-14 NEB*

Praise be to the God and Father of our Lord Jesus Christ,
who has bestowed on us in Christ every spiritual blessing in
the heavenly realms. In Christ he chose us before the world
was founded, to be dedicated, to be without blemish in his
sight, to be full of love; and he destined us—such was his
will and pleasure—to be accepted as his sons through Jesus
Christ, in order that the glory of his gracious gift, so
graciously bestowed on us in his Beloved, might redound to
his praise. For in Christ our release is secured and our sins
are forgiven through the shedding of his blood. Therein lies
the richness of God's free grace lavished upon us, imparting
full wisdom and insight. He has made known to us his
hidden purpose—such was his will and pleasure
determined beforehand in Christ—to be put into effect when
the time was ripe: namely, that the universe, all in heaven
and on earth, might be brought into a unity in Christ.

In Christ indeed we have been given our share in the
heritage, as was decreed in his design whose purpose is
everywhere at work. For it was his will that we, who were
the first to set our hope on Christ, should cause his glory to
be praised. And you too, when you had heard the message
of the truth, the good news of your salvation, and had
believed it, became incorporate in Christ and received the
seal of the promised Holy Spirit; and that Spirit is in the
pledge that we shall enter upon our heritage, when God has
redeemed what is his own, to his praise and glory.

Gospel *John 14.1-14 JB*

Jesus said,
'Do not let your hearts be troubled.
Trust in God still, and trust in me.
There are many rooms in my Father's house;
if there were not, I should have told you.
I am going now to prepare a place for you,
and after I have gone and prepared you a place,
I shall return to take you with me;
so that where I am
you may be too.
You know the way to the place were I am going.'

Thomas said, 'Lord we do not know where you are going,
so how can we know the way?' Jesus said,

'I am the Way, the Truth and the Life.
No one can come to the Father except through me.
If you know me, you know my Father too.
From this moment you know him and have seen him.'

Philip said, 'Lord, let us see the Father and then we shall be
satisfied'. 'Have I been with you all this time, Philip,' said
Jesus to him, 'and you still do not know me?

'To have seen me is to have seen the Father,
so how can you say, "Let us see the Father"?
Do you not believe
that I am in the Father and the Father is in me?
The words I say to you I do not speak as from myself:
it is the Father, living in me, who is doing this work.
You must believe me when I say
that I am in the Father and the Father is in me;
believe it on the evidence of this work, if for no other reason.
I tell you most solemnly,
whoever believes in me
will perform the same works as I do myself,
he will perform even greater works,
because I am going to the Father.
Whatever you ask for in my name I will do,
so that the Father may be glorified in the Son.

If you ask for anything in my name,
I will do it.'

PROPER PREFACE

Rite A. The Preface of Apostles and Evangelists (23) or of the
Resurrection (14) is said.
Rite B. The Preface of Saints' Days or of Easter is said.

POSTCOMMUNION SENTENCE

Philip said, Lord, let us see the Father, and we shall be
content. Jesus said, He who sees me sees the Father.
John 14.8

ST MATTHIAS THE APOSTLE (14 May)   Red

INTRODUCTORY SENTENCE

You have not chosen me, I have chosen you, says the Lord.
Go and bear fruit that will last. *John 15.16*

COLLECT

Almighty God,
who in the place of the traitor Judas
chose your faithful servant Matthias
to be of the number of the Twelve:
preserve your Church from false apostles,
and by the ministry of faithful pastors and teachers,
keep us steadfast in your truth;
through Jesus Christ our Lord.

PSALMS 16.1-6; 80.8-15

READINGS

Old Testament *1 Samuel 2.27-35 NEB*

A man of God came to Eli and said, 'This is the word of the
Lord: You know that I revealed myself to your forefather
when he and his family were in Egypt in slavery in the house

of Pharaoh. You know that I chose him from all the tribes of Israel to be my priest, to mount the steps of my altar, to burn sacrifices and to carry the ephod before me; and that I assigned all the food-offerings of the Israelites to your family. Why then do you show disrespect for my sacrifices and the offerings which I have ordained? What makes you resent them? Why do you honour your sons more than me by letting them batten on the choicest offerings of my people Israel? The Lord's word was, "I promised that your house and your father's house shall serve before me for all time"; but now his word is, "I will have no such thing: I will honour those who honour me, and those who despise me shall meet with contempt. The time is coming when I will lop off every limb of your own and of your father's family, so that no man in your house shall come to old age. You will even resent the prosperity I give to Israel; never again shall there be an old man in your house. If I allow any to survive to serve my altar, his eyes will grow dim and his appetite fail, his issue will be weaklings and die off. The fate of your two sons shall be a sign to you: Hophni and Phinehas shall both die on the same day. I will appoint for myself a priest who will be faithful, who will do what I have in my mind and in my heart. I will establish his family to serve in perpetual succession before my anointed king."'

New Testament *Acts 1.15-17, 20-end TEV*

There was a meeting of the believers, about a hundred and twenty in all, and Peter stood up to speak. 'My brothers,' he said, 'the scripture had to come true in which the Holy Spirit, speaking through David, made a prediction about Judas, who was the guide for those who arrested Jesus. Judas was a member of our group, for he had been chosen to have a part in our work.

'For it is written in the book of Psalms,
"May his house become empty;
may no one live in it."
It is also written,
"May someone else take his place of service."

'So then, someone must join us as a witness to the resurrection of the Lord Jesus. He must be one of the men who were in our group during the whole time that the Lord Jesus travelled about with us, beginning from the time John preached his message of baptism until the day Jesus was taken up from us to heaven.'

So they proposed two men: Joseph, who was called Barsabbas (also known as Justus), and Matthias. Then they prayed, 'Lord, you know the thoughts of everyone, so show us which of these two you have chosen to serve as an apostle in the place of Judas, who left to go to the place where he belongs.' Then they drew lots to choose between the two men, and the one chosen was Matthias, who was added to the group of eleven apostles.

Gospel *John 15.1-11 JB*

Jesus said,
'I am the true vine,
and my Father is the vinedresser.
Every branch in me that bears no fruit
he cuts away,
and every branch that does bear fruit he prunes
to make it bear even more.
You are pruned already,
by means of the word that I have spoken to you.
Make your home in me, so I make mine in you.
As a branch cannot bear fruit all by itself,
but must remain part of the vine,
neither can you unless you remain in me.
I am the vine,
you are the branches.
Whoever remains in me, with me in him,
bears fruit in plenty;
for cut off from me you can do nothing.
Anyone who does not remain in me
is like a branch that has been thrown away
—he withers;
these branches are collected and thrown on the fire,

and they are burnt.
If you remain in me
and my words remain in you,
you may ask what you will
and you shall get it.
It is to the glory of my Father that you should bear
    much fruit,
and then you will be my disciples.
As the Father has loved me,
so I have loved you.
Remain in my love.
If you keep my commandments
you will remain in my love,
just as I have kept my Father's commandments
and remain in his love.
I have told you this
so that my own joy may be in you
and your joy be complete.'

PROPER PREFACE

Rite A. The Preface of Apostles and Evangelists (23) or of the Resurrection (14) is said. After Ascension Day the Preface of the Ascension (17) may be said.
Rite B. The Preface of Saints' Days or of Easter is said. After Ascension Day the Preface of the Ascension may be said.

POSTCOMMUNION SENTENCE

This is my commandment, says the Lord: Love one another as I have loved you. *John 15.12*

ST BARNABAS THE APOSTLE (11 June)   Red

INTRODUCTORY SENTENCE

Barnabas was a good man, full of the Holy Spirit and of faith. *Acts 11.24*

COLLECT

Lord God Almighty,
whose Son Jesus Christ has taught us
that it is more blessed to give than to receive:
help us by the example of your apostle Barnabas
to be generous in our judgements
and unselfish in our service;
through Jesus Christ our Lord.

PSALMS 145.8-15; 112

READINGS

Old Testament *Job 29.11-16 NEB*

Job said,
'Whoever heard of me spoke in my favour,
and those who saw me bore witness to my merit,
how I saved the poor man when he called for help
and the orphan who had no protector.
The man threatened with ruin blessed me,
and I made the widow's heart sing for joy.
I put on righteousness as a garment and it clothed me;
justice, like a cloak or a turban, wrapped me round.
I was eyes to the blind
and feet to the lame;
I was a father to the needy,
and I took up the stranger's cause.'

New Testament *Acts 11.19-end RSV*

Now those who were scattered because of the persecution
that arose over Stephen travelled as far as Phoenicia and
Cyprus and Antioch, speaking the word to none except
Jews. But there were some of them, men of Cyprus and
Cyrene, who on coming to Antioch spoke to the Greeks also,
preaching the Lord Jesus. And the hand of the Lord was
with them, and a great number that believed turned to the
Lord. News of this came to the ears of the church in
Jerusalem, and they sent Barnabas to Antioch. When he
came and saw the grace of God, he was glad; and he
exhorted them all to remain faithful to the Lord with

steadfast purpose; for he was a good man, full of the Holy Spirit and of faith. And a large company was added to the Lord. So Barnabas went to Tarsus to look for Saul; and when he had found him, he brought him to Antioch. For a whole year they met with the church, and taught a large company of people; and in Antioch the disciples were for the first time called Christians.

Now in these days prophets came down from Jerusalem to Antioch. And one of them named Agabus stood up and foretold by the Spirit that there would be a great famine over all the world; and this took place in the days of Claudius. And the disciples determined, every one according to his ability, to send relief to the brethren who lived in Judaea; and they did so, sending it to the elders by the hand of Barnabas and Saul.

Gospel *John 15.12-17 JB*

Jesus said,
'This is my commandment:
love one another,
as I have loved you.
A man can have no greater love
than to lay down his life for his friends.
You are my friends,
if you do what I command you.
I shall not call you servants any more,
because a servant does not know
his master's business;
I call you friends,
because I have made known to you
everything I have learnt from my Father.
You did not choose me,
no, I chose you;
and I commissioned you
to go out and to bear fruit,
fruit that will last;
and then the Father will give you
anything you ask him in my name.
What I command you
is to love one another.'

PROPER PREFACE

Rite A. The Preface of Apostles and Evangelists (23) is said.
Rite B. The Preface of Saints' Days is said.

POSTCOMMUNION SENTENCE

Jesus said, No longer shall I call you servants, but friends; for
I have revealed to you all that I have heard from my Father.
John 15.15

THE BIRTH OF ST JOHN THE BAPTIST (24 June)   White

INTRODUCTORY SENTENCE

There was a man sent from God, whose name was John. He
came to bear witness to the light. *John 1.6, 7*

COLLECT

Almighty God,
whose servant John the Baptist
was wonderfully born to fulfil your purpose
by preparing the way for the advent of your Son:
lead us to repent according to his preaching
and after his example
constantly to speak the truth, boldly rebuke vice,
and patiently suffer for the truth's sake;
through Jesus Christ our Lord.

PSALMS 119.161-168; 80.1-7

READINGS

Old Testament *Isaiah 40.1-11 RSV*

Comfort, comfort my people,
says your God.
Speak tenderly to Jerusalem,
and cry to her
that her warfare is ended,
that her iniquity is pardoned,

that she has received from the Lord's hand
double for all her sins.

A voice cries:
'In the wilderness prepare the way of the Lord,
make straight in the desert a highway for our God.
Every valley shall be lifted up,
and every mountain and hill be made low;
the uneven ground shall become level,
and the rough places a plain.
And the glory of the Lord shall be revealed,
and all flesh shall see it together,
for the mouth of the Lord has spoken.'

A voice says, 'Cry!'
And I said, 'What shall I cry?'
All flesh is grass,
and all its beauty is like the flower of the field.
The grass withers, the flower fades,
when the breath of the Lord blows upon it;
surely the people is grass.
The grass withers, the flower fades;
but the word of our God will stand for ever.

Get you up to a high mountain,
O herald of good tidings to Zion;
lift up your voice with strength,
O herald of good tidings to Jerusalem,
lift it up, fear not;
say to the cities of Judah,
'Behold your God!'
Behold, the Lord God comes with might,
and his arm rules for him;
behold, his reward is with him,
and his recompense before him.
He will feed his flock like a shepherd,
he will gather the lambs in his arms,
he will carry them in his bosom,
and gently lead those that are with young.

New Testament *Acts 13.16-26 JB*

Paul stood up, held up a hand for silence and began to speak:

'Men of Israel, and fearers of God, listen! The God of our nation Israel chose our ancestors, and made our people great when they were living as foreigners in Egypt; then by divine power he led them out, and for about forty years took care of them in the wilderness. When he had destroyed seven nations in Canaan, he put them in possession of their land for about four hundred and fifty years. After this he gave them judges, down to the prophet Samuel. Then they demanded a king, and God gave them Saul son of Kish, a man of the tribe of Benjamin. After forty years, he deposed him and made David their king, of whom he approved in these words, "I have selected David son of Jesse, a man after my own heart, who will carry out my whole purpose." To keep his promise, God has raised up for Israel one of David's descendants, Jesus, as Saviour, whose coming was heralded by John when he proclaimed a baptism of repentance for the whole people of Israel. Before John ended his career he said, "I am not the one you imagine me to be; that one is coming after me and I am not fit to undo his sandal."

'My brothers, sons of Abraham's race, and all you who fear God, this message of salvation is meant for you.'

Gospel *Luke 1.57-66, 80 RSV*

The time came for Elizabeth to be delivered, and she gave birth to a son. And her neighbours and kinsfolk heard that the Lord had shown great mercy to her, and they rejoiced with her. And on the eighth day they came to circumcise the child; and they would have named him Zechariah after his father, but his mother said, 'Not so; he shall be called John.' And they said to her, 'None of your kindred is called by this name.' And they made signs to his father, inquiring what he would have him called. And he asked for a writing tablet, and wrote, 'His name is John.' And they all marvelled. And immediately his mouth was opened and his tongue loosed, and he spoke, blessing God. And fear came on all their neighbours. And all these things were talked about through

all the hill country of Judaea; and all who heard them laid
them up in their hearts, saying, 'What then will this child
be?' For the hand of the Lord was with him.

And the child grew and became strong in spirit, and he was
in the wilderness till the day of his manifestation to Israel.

PROPER PREFACE

Rite A. The Preface of Advent (2) is said.
Rite B. First Thanksgiving—the Preface of Saints' Days
is said.
          Second Thanksgiving—the Preface of Advent or of
Saints' Days is said.

POSTCOMMUNION SENTENCE

Through the tender mercy of our God the Dayspring from
on high has broken upon us. *Luke 1.78*

ST PETER THE APOSTLE (29 June)   Red

INTRODUCTORY SENTENCE

Jesus said to Peter, I have prayed for you, that your faith
may not fail: strengthen your brothers. *Luke 22.31, 32*

or

Jesus said to his disciples, Who do you say that I am?; and
Peter answered, You are the Christ of God. *Luke 9.20*

COLLECT

Almighty God,
who inspired your apostle Saint Peter
to confess Jesus as Christ and Son of the living God:
build up your Church upon this rock,
that in unity and peace
it may proclaim one truth and follow one Lord,
your Son our Saviour Jesus Christ,
who is alive and reigns with you and the Holy Spirit,
one God, now and for ever.

READINGS

Old Testament *Ezekiel 3.4-11 RSV*

The Lord God said to me, 'Son of man, go, get you to the house of Israel, and speak with my words to them. For you are not sent to a people of foreign speech and a hard language, but to the house of Israel—not to many peoples of foreign speech and a hard language, whose words you cannot understand. Surely, if I sent you to such, they would listen to you. But the house of Israel will not listen to you; for they are not willing to listen to me; because all the house of Israel are of a hard forehead and of a stubborn heart. Behold, I have made your face hard against their faces, and your forehead hard against their foreheads. Like adamant harder than flint have I made your forehead; fear them not, nor be dismayed at their looks, for they are a rebellious house.' Moreover he said to me, 'Son of man, all my words that I shall speak to you receive in your heart, and hear with your ears. And go, get you to the exiles, to your people, and say to them, "Thus says the Lord God"; whether they hear or refuse to hear.'

New Testament *1 Peter 2.19-end TEV*

God will bless you for this, if you endure the pain of undeserved suffering because you are conscious of his will. For what credit is there if you endure the beatings you deserve for having done wrong? But if you endure suffering even when you have done right, God will bless you for it. It was to this that God called you, for Christ himself suffered for you and left you an example, so that you would follow in his steps. He committed no sin, and no one ever heard a lie come from his lips. When he was insulted, he did not answer back with an insult; when he suffered, he did not threaten, but placed his hopes in God, the righteous Judge. Christ himself carried our sins in his body to the cross, so that we might die to sin and live for righteousness. It is by his wounds that you have been healed. You were like sheep that had lost their way, but now you have been brought back to follow the Shepherd and Keeper of your souls.

Gospel *Matthew 16.13-20 JB*

When Jesus came to the region of Caesarea Philippi he put this question to his disciples, 'Who do people say the Son of Man is?' And they said, 'Some say he is John the Baptist, some Elijah, and others Jeremiah or one of the prophets.' 'But you,' he said, 'who do you say I am?' Then Simon Peter spoke up, 'You are the Christ,' he said, 'the Son of the living God.' Jesus replied, 'Simon son of Jonah, you are a happy man! Because it was not flesh and blood that revealed this to you but my Father in heaven. So I now say to you: You are Peter and on this rock I will build my Church. And the gates of the underworld can never hold out against it. I will give you the keys of the kingdom of heaven: whatever you bind on earth shall be considered bound in heaven; whatever you loose on earth shall be considered loosed in heaven.' Then he gave the disciples strict orders not to tell anyone that he was the Christ.

PROPER PREFACE

Rite A. The Preface of Apostles and Evangelists (23) is said.
Rite B. The Preface of Saints' Days is said.

POSTCOMMUNION SENTENCE

Jesus said, Simon, son of John, do you love me? Peter said, Lord, you know all things; you know that I love you. *John 21.15, 17*

ST PETER AND ST PAUL, APOSTLES   Red

If St Paul is commemorated with St Peter the following may be used:

INTRODUCTORY SENTENCE

God who made Peter an apostle to the Jews, also made Paul an apostle to the Gentiles. *Galatians 2.8*

COLLECT

Almighty God,
your apostles Peter and Paul glorified you
in their death as in their life.
Grant that your Church,
inspired by their teaching and example,
may ever stand firm on the one foundation
which is your Son, Jesus Christ our Lord.

PSALMS 125; 126

READINGS

Old Testament *Zechariah 4.1-6a, 10b-14 JB*

The angel who was talking to me came back and roused me
as a man is roused from his sleep. And he asked me, 'What
can you see?' I answered, 'As I look, this is what I see: there
is a lamp-stand entirely of gold with a bowl at the top of it;
seven lamps are on the lamp-stand, and seven lips for the
lamps on it. By it are two olive trees, one to the right of it and
one to the left.' Speaking again, I said to the angel who was
talking to me, 'What do those things mean, my lord?' The
angel who was talking to me replied, 'Do you not know what
these things mean?' I said, 'No, my lord.' He then gave me
this answer, 'These seven are the eyes of the Lord; they
cover the whole world.' In reply to this I asked him, 'What is
the meaning of these two olive trees, to the right and to the
left of the lamp-stand?' (Speaking again, I asked him, 'What
is the meaning of the two olive branches pouring the oil
through the two golden pipes?') He replied, 'Do you not
know what these things mean?' I said, 'No, my lord.' He
said, 'These are the two anointed ones who stand before the
Lord of the whole world.'

or *Wisdom 3.1-9 NEB*

The souls of the just are in God's hand, and torment shall not
touch them. In the eyes of foolish men they seemed to be
dead; their departure was reckoned as defeat, and their
going from us as disaster. But they are at peace, for though in

the sight of men they may be punished, they have a sure hope of immortality; and after a little chastisement they will receive great blessings, because God has tested them and found them worthy to be his. Like gold in a crucible he put them to the proof, and found them acceptable like an offering burnt whole upon the altar. In the moment of God's coming to them they will kindle into flame, like sparks that sweep through stubble; they will be judges and rulers over the nations of the world, and the Lord shall be their king for ever and ever. Those who have put their trust in him shall understand that he is true, and the faithful shall attend upon him in love; they are his chosen, and grace and mercy shall be theirs.

New Testament *2 Timothy 4.6-8, 16-18 TEV*

The hour has come for me to be sacrificed; the time is here for me to leave this life. I have done my best in the race, I have run the full distance, and I have kept the faith. And now there is waiting for me the prize of victory awarded for a righteous life, the prize which the Lord, the righteous Judge, will give me on that Day—and not only to me, but to all those who wait with love for him to appear.

No one stood by me the first time I defended myself; all deserted me. May God not count it against them! But the Lord stayed with me and gave me strength, so that I was able to proclaim the full message for all the Gentiles to hear; and I was rescued from being sentenced to death. And the Lord will rescue me from all evil and take me safely into his heavenly Kingdom. To him be the glory for ever and ever! Amen.

Gospel *Matthew 16.13-20 JB*

When Jesus came to the region of Caesarea Philippi he put this question to his disciples, 'Who do people say the Son of Man is?' And they said, 'Some say he is John the Baptist, some Elijah, and others Jeremiah or one of the prophets.' 'But you,' he said, 'who do you say I am?' Then Simon Peter spoke up, 'You are the Christ,' he said, 'the Son of the living God.' Jesus replied, 'Simon son of Jonah, you are a happy man! Because it was not flesh and blood that revealed this to you but my Father in heaven. So I now say to you: You are Peter and on this rock I will build my Church. And the gates of the underworld can never hold out against it. I will give you the keys of the kingdom of heaven: whatever you bind on earth shall be considered bound in heaven; whatever you loose on earth shall be considered loosed in heaven.' Then he gave the disciples strict orders not to tell anyone that he was the Christ.

PROPER PREFACE

Rite A. The Preface of Apostles and Evangelists (23) is said.
Rite B. The Preface of Saints' Days is said.

POSTCOMMUNION SENTENCE

Paul and Peter both are your servants: but you belong to Christ, and Christ belongs to God. *1 Corinthians 3.22*

ST THOMAS THE APOSTLE (3 July)   Red

INTRODUCTORY SENTENCE

Jesus said, Thomas, because you have seen me, you have believed; blessed are those who have not seen, and yet believe. *John 20.29*

COLLECT

Almighty and eternal God,
who, for the firmer foundation of our faith,
allowed the apostle Saint Thomas
    to doubt the resurrection of your Son
till word and sight convinced him:
grant to us, who have not seen,
that we also may believe
and so receive the fullness of Christ's blessing;
who is alive and reigns with you and the Holy Spirit,
one God, now and for ever.

PSALMS 139.1-11; 31.1-5

READINGS

Old Testament *Genesis 12.1-4 RSV*

The Lord said to Abram, 'Go from your country and your
kindred and your father's house to the land that I will show
you. And I will make of you a great nation, and I will bless
you, and make your name great, so that you will be a
blessing. I will bless those who bless you, and him who
curses you I will curse; and by you all the families of the earth
shall bless themselves.'

So Abram went, as the Lord had told him; and Lot went with
him. Abram was seventy-five years old when he departed
from Haran.

New Testament *Hebrews 10.35—11.1 NEB*

Do not throw away your confidence, for it carries a great
reward. You need endurance, if you are to do God's will and
win what he has promised. For 'soon, very soon' (in the
words of Scripture), 'he who is to come will come; he will not
delay; and by faith my righteous servant shall find life; but if
a man shrinks back, I take no pleasure in him.' But we are not
among those who shrink back and are lost; we have the faith
to make life our own.

And what is faith? Faith gives substance to our hopes, and
makes us certain of realities we do not see.

Gospel *John 20.24-29 RSV*

Now Thomas, one of the twelve, called the Twin, was not
with them when Jesus came. So the other disciples told him,
'We have seen the Lord.' But he said to them, 'Unless I see in
his hands the print of the nails, and place my finger in the
mark of the nails, and place my hand in his side, I will
not believe.'

Eight days later, his disciples were again in the house, and
Thomas was with them. The doors were shut, but Jesus
came and stood among them, and said, 'Peace be with you.'

Then he said to Thomas, 'Put your finger here, and see my hands; and put out your hand, and place it in my side; do not be faithless, but believing.' Thomas answered him, 'My Lord and my God!' Jesus said to him, 'Have you believed because you have seen me? Blessed are those who have not seen and yet believe.'

PROPER PREFACE

Rite A. The Preface of Apostles and Evangelists (23) is said.
Rite B. The Preface of Saints' Days is said.

POSTCOMMUNION SENTENCE

Thomas said to Jesus, My Lord and my God. *John 20.28*

ST MARY MAGDALEN (22 July)   White

INTRODUCTORY SENTENCE

On the first day of the week, Mary Magdalen came to the tomb early, while it was yet dark. *John 20.1*

COLLECT

Almighty God,
whose Son restored Mary Magdalen
    to health of mind and body
and called her to be a witness to his resurrection:
forgive us and heal us by your grace,
that we may serve you in the power of his risen life;
who is alive and reigns with you and the Holy Spirit,
one God, now and for ever.

PSALMS 139.1-11; 30.1-5

READINGS

Old Testament *Zephaniah 3.14-end RSV*

Sing aloud, O daughter of Zion;
shout, O Israel!

Rejoice and exult with all your heart,
O daughter of Jerusalem!
The Lord has taken away the judgements against you,
he has cast out your enemies.
The King of Israel, the Lord, is in your midst;
you shall fear evil no more.
On that day it shall be said to Jerusalem:
'Do not fear, O Zion;
let not your hands grow weak.
The Lord, your God, is in your midst,
a warrior who gives victory;
he will rejoice over you with gladness,
he will renew you in his love;
he will exult over you with loud singing
as on a day of festival.
I will remove disaster from you,
so that you will not bear reproach for it.
Behold, at that time I will deal
with all your oppressors.
And I will save the lame
and gather the outcast,
and I will change their shame into praise
and renown in all the earth.
At that time I will bring you home,
at the time when I gather you together;
yea, I will make you renowned and praised
among all the peoples of the earth,
when I restore your fortunes
before your eyes,' says the Lord.

New Testament *2 Corinthians 5.14-17 NEB*

The love of Christ leaves us no choice, when once we have
reached the conclusion that one man died for all and
therefore all mankind has died. His purpose in dying for all
was that men, while still in life, should cease to live for
themselves, and should live for him who for their sake died
and was raised to life. With us therefore worldly standards
have ceased to count in our estimate of any man; even if once
they counted in our understanding of Christ, they do so now
no longer. When anyone is united to Christ, there is a new

world; the old order has gone, and a new order has already begun.

Gospel *John 20.11-18 RSV*

Mary stood weeping outside the tomb, and as she wept she stooped to look into the tomb; and she saw two angels in white, sitting where the body of Jesus had lain, one at the head and one at the feet. They said to her, 'Woman, why are you weeping?' She said to them, 'Because they have taken away my Lord, and I do not know where they have laid him.' Saying this, she turned round and saw Jesus standing, but she did not know that it was Jesus. Jesus said to her, 'Woman, why are you weeping? Whom do you seek?' Supposing him to be the gardener, she said to him, 'Sir, if you have carried him away, tell me where you have laid him, and I will take him away.' Jesus said to her, 'Mary.' She turned and said to him in Hebrew, 'Rabboni!' (which means Teacher). Jesus said to her, 'Do not hold me, for I have not yet ascended to the Father; but go to my brethren and say to them, I am ascending to my Father and your Father, to my God and your God.' Mary Magdalen went and said to the disciples, 'I have seen the Lord'; and she told them that he had said these things to her.

PROPER PREFACE

Rite A. The Preface of Saints (25) is said.
Rite B. The Preface of Saints' Days is said.

POSTCOMMUNION SENTENCE

Jesus said to her, Mary; she said to him, Rabboni—that is to say, Master. *John 20.16*

ST JAMES THE APOSTLE (25 July)   Red

INTRODUCTORY SENTENCE

As Jesus walked by the Sea of Galilee he saw James and John, and he called them; and immediately they followed him. *Matthew 4.18, 21*

COLLECT

Merciful God,
we pray that as your holy apostle Saint James
left his father and all that he had
and obeyed the calling
    of your Son Jesus Christ even to death:
so may we forsake every selfish desire
and be ready at all times to answer your call;
through Jesus Christ our Lord.

PSALMS 15; 75.6-end

READINGS

Old Testament *Jeremiah 45. RSV*

The word that Jeremiah the prophet spoke to Baruch the son
of Neriah, when he wrote these words in a book at the
dictation of Jeremiah, in the fourth year of Jehoiakim the son
of Josiah, king of Judah: 'Thus says the Lord, the God of
Israel, to you, O Baruch: You said, "Woe is me! for the Lord
has added sorrow to my pain; I am weary with my groaning,
and I find no rest." Thus shall you say to him, Thus says the
Lord: Behold, what I have built I am breaking down, and
what I have planted I am plucking up—that is, the whole
land. And do you seek great things for yourself? Seek them
not; for, behold, I am bringing evil upon all flesh, says the
Lord; but I will give you your life as a prize of war in all places
to which you may go.'

New Testament *Acts 11.27—12.2 NEB*

Some prophets came down from Jerusalem to Antioch. One
of them, Agabus by name, was inspired to stand up and
predict a severe and world-wide famine, which in fact
occurred in the reign of Claudius. So the disciples agreed to
make a contribution, each according to his means, for the
relief of their fellow-Christians in Judaea. This they did, and
sent it off to the elders, in the charge of Barnabas and Saul.
It was about this time that King Herod attacked certain
members of the church. He beheaded James, the brother
of John.

Gospel *Mark 10.35-45 NEB*

James and John, the sons of Zebedee, approached Jesus and said, 'Master, we should like you to do us a favour.' 'What is it you want me to do?' he asked. They answered, 'Grant us the right to sit in state with you, one at your right and the other at your left.' Jesus said to them, 'You do not understand what you are asking. Can you drink the cup that I drink, or be baptized with the baptism I am baptized with?' 'We can', they answered. Jesus said, 'The cup that I drink you shall drink, and the baptism I am baptized with shall be your baptism; but to sit at my right or left is not for me to grant; it is for those to whom it has already been assigned.'

When the other ten heard this, they were indignant with James and John. Jesus called them to him and said, 'You know that in the world the recognized rulers lord it over their subjects, and their great men make them feel the weight of authority. That is not the way with you; among you, whoever wants to be great must be your servant, and whoever wants to be first must be the willing slave of all. For even the Son of Man did not come to be served but to serve, and to give up his life as a ransom for many.'

PROPER PREFACE

Rite A. The Preface of Apostles and Evangelists (23) is said.
Rite B. The Preface of Saints' Days is said.

POSTCOMMUNION SENTENCE

Jesus said, You shall drink of the cup that I am going to drink; but to sit at my right hand and my left is not mine to give. *Matthew 20.23*

THE TRANSFIGURATION OF OUR LORD
(6 August)   White

INTRODUCTORY SENTENCE

God has shone in our hearts to give the light of the knowledge of his glory in the face of Jesus Christ. *2 Corinthians 4.6*

COLLECT

Almighty Father,
whose Son was revealed in majesty
    before he suffered death upon the cross:
give us faith to perceive his glory,
that we may be strengthened to suffer with him
and be changed into his likeness, from glory to glory;
who is alive and reigns with you and the Holy Spirit,
one God, now and for ever.

PSALMS 84.1-7; 84.8-end

READINGS

Old Testament *Exodus 34.29-end NEB*

Moses came down from Mount Sinai with the two stone
tablets of the Tokens in his hands, and when he descended,
he did not know that the skin of his face shone because he
had been speaking with the Lord. When Aaron and the
Israelites saw how the skin of Moses' face shone, they were
afraid to approach him. He called out to them, and Aaron
and all the chiefs in the congregation turned towards him.
Moses spoke to them, and afterwards all the Israelites drew
near. He gave them all the commands with which the Lord
had charged him on Mount Sinai, and finished what he had
to say.

Then Moses put a veil over his face, and whenever he went
in before the Lord to speak with him, he removed the veil
until he came out. Then he would go out and tell the
Israelites all the commands he had received. Whenever the
skin of Moses' face shone in the sight of the Israelites, he
would put the veil back over his face until he went in again to
speak with the Lord.

New Testament *2 Corinthians 3.4-end TEV*

We say this because we have confidence in God through
Christ. There is nothing in us that allows us to claim that we
are capable of doing this work. The capacity we have comes
from God; it is he who made us capable of serving the new

covenant, which consists not of a written law but of the Spirit. The written law brings death, but the Spirit gives life.

The Law was carved in letters on stone tablets, and God's glory appeared when it was given. Even though the brightness of Moses' face was fading, it was so strong that the people of Israel could not keep their eyes fixed on him. If the Law, which brings death when it is in force, came with such glory, how much greater is the glory that belongs to the activity of the Spirit! The system which brings condemnation was glorious; how much more glorious is the activity which brings salvation! We may say that because of the far brighter glory now the glory that was so bright in the past is gone. For if there was glory in that which lasted for a while, how much more glory is there in that which lasts for ever!

Because we have this hope, we are very bold. We are not like Moses, who had to put a veil over his face so that the people of Israel would not see the brightness fade and disappear. Their minds, indeed, were closed; and to this very day their minds are covered with the same veil as they read the books of the old covenant. The veil is removed only when a person is joined to Christ. Even today, whenever they read the Law of Moses, the veil still covers their minds. But it can be removed, as the scripture says about Moses: 'His veil was removed when he turned to the Lord.' Now, 'the Lord' in this passage is the Spirit; and where the Spirit of the Lord is present, there is freedom. All of us, then, reflect the glory of the Lord with uncovered faces; and that same glory, coming from the Lord, who is the Spirit, transforms us into his likeness in an even greater degree of glory.

Gospel *Luke 9.28-36 NEB*

Jesus took Peter, John, and James with him and went up into the hills to pray. And while he was praying the appearance of his face changed and his clothes became dazzling white. Suddenly there were two men talking with him; these were Moses and Elijah, who appeared in glory and spoke of his departure, the destiny he was to fulfil in Jerusalem. Meanwhile Peter and his companions had been in a deep sleep; but when they awoke, they saw his glory and the two men who stood beside him. And as these were moving away from Jesus, Peter said to him, 'Master, how good it is that we are here! Shall we make three shelters, one for you, one for Moses, and one for Elijah?'; but he spoke without knowing what he was saying. The words were still on his lips, when there came a cloud which cast a shadow over them; they were afraid as they entered the cloud, and from it came a voice: 'This is my Son, my Chosen; listen to him.' When the voice had spoken, Jesus was seen to be alone. The disciples kept silence and at that time told nobody anything of what they had seen.

PROPER PREFACE

Rite A. The Preface of the Transfiguration (20) is said.
Rite B. The Preface of the Transfiguration is said.

POSTCOMMUNION SENTENCE

Master, it is good for us to be here. *Matthew 17.4*

ST BARTHOLOMEW THE APOSTLE (24 August)   Red

INTRODUCTORY SENTENCE

Day after day proclaim the salvation of the Lord: tell his glory to all nations. *Psalm 96.2, 3*

COLLECT

Almighty God,
who gave to your apostle Bartholomew
grace truly to believe and to preach your word:
grant that your Church
may love that word which he believed
and may faithfully preach and receive the same;
through Jesus Christ our Lord.

PSALMS 116.11-end; 97.10-end

READINGS

Old Testament *Isaiah 61.4-9 NEB*

Ancient ruins shall be rebuilt
and sites long desolate restored;
they shall repair the ruined cities
and restore what has long lain desolate.
Foreigners shall serve as shepherds of your flocks,
and aliens shall till your land and tend your vines;
but you shall be called priests of the Lord
and be named ministers of our God;
you shall enjoy the wealth of other nations
and be furnished with their riches.
And so, because shame in double measure
and jeers and insults have been my people's lot,
they shall receive in their own land a double measure
    of wealth,
and everlasting joy shall be theirs.
For I, the Lord, love justice
and hate robbery and wrong-doing;
I will grant them a sure reward
and make an everlasting covenant with them;
their posterity will be renowned among the nations
and their offspring among the peoples;
all who see them will acknowledge in them
a race whom the Lord has blessed.

New Testament *Acts 5.12b-16 NEB*

Many remarkable and wonderful things took place among
the people at the hands of the apostles.

They used to meet by common consent in Solomon's
Portico, no one from outside their number venturing to join
with them. But people in general spoke highly of them, and
more than that, numbers of men and women were added to
their ranks as believers in the Lord. In the end the sick were
actually carried out into the streets and laid there on beds
and stretchers, so that even the shadow of Peter might fall on
one or another as he passed by; and the people from the
towns round Jerusalem flocked in, bringing those who were
ill or harassed by unclean spirits, and all of them were cured.

Gospel *Luke 22.24-30 RSV*

A dispute arose among the apostles, which of them was to be
regarded as the greatest. And Jesus said to them, 'The kings
of the Gentiles exercise lordship over them; and those in
authority over them are called benefactors. But not so with
you; rather let the greatest among you become as the
youngest, and the leader as one who serves. For which is the
greater, one who sits at table, or one who serves? Is it not the
one who sits at table? But I am among you as one who serves.

'You are those who have continued with me in my trials; as
my Father appointed a kingdom for me, so do I appoint for
you that you may eat and drink at my table in my kingdom,
and sit on thrones judging the twelve tribes of Israel.'

PROPER PREFACE

Rite A. The Preface of Apostles and Evangelists (23) is said.
Rite B. The Preface of Saints' Days is said.

POSTCOMMUNION SENTENCE

Jesus said, I will give you the kingdom that my Father gave
to me; and in that kingdom you will eat and drink at my
table. *Luke 22.29*

THE BLESSED VIRGIN MARY (8 September)   White

INTRODUCTORY SENTENCE

Blessed is she who believed that there would be a fulfilment
of what was spoken to her from the Lord. *Luke 1.45*

or

Mary said, Behold the handmaid of the Lord; let it be done to
me according to your word. *Luke 1.38*

COLLECT

Almighty God,
who chose the blessed Virgin Mary
   to be the mother of your only Son:

grant that we who are redeemed by his blood
may share with her
in the glory of your eternal kingdom;
through Jesus Christ our Lord,
who is alive and reigns with you and the Holy Spirit,
one God, now and for ever.

PSALMS 45.10-end; Magnificat

READINGS

Old Testament *Micah 5.2-4 RSV*

You, O Bethlehem Ephrathah,
who are little to be among the clans of Judah,
from you shall come forth for me
one who is to be ruler in Israel,
whose origin is from of old,
from ancient days.
Therefore he shall give them up until the time
when she who is in travail has brought forth;
then the rest of his brethren shall return
to the people of Israel.
And he shall stand and feed his flock in
    the strength of the Lord,
in the majesty of the name of the Lord his God.
And they shall dwell secure, for now he shall be great
to the ends of the earth.

New Testament *Revelation 21.1-7 RSV*

I saw a new heaven and a new earth; for the first heaven and
the first earth had passed away, and the sea was no more.
And I saw the holy city, new Jerusalem, coming down out of
heaven from God, prepared as a bride adorned for her
husband; and I heard a great voice from the throne saying,
'Behold, the dwelling of God is with men. He will dwell with
them, and they shall be his people, and God himself will be
with them; he will wipe away every tear from their eyes, and
death shall be no more, neither shall there be mourning nor
crying nor pain any more, for the former things have
passed away.'

And he who sat upon the throne said, 'Behold, I make all things new.' Also he said, 'Write this, for these words are trustworthy and true.' And he said to me, 'It is done! I am the Alpha and the Omega, the beginning and the end. To the thirsty I will give water without price from the fountain of the water of life. He who conquers shall have this heritage, and I will be his God and he shall be my son.'

Gospel *Luke 1.39-49 RSV*

Mary arose and went with haste into the hill country, to a city of Judah, and she entered the house of Zechariah and greeted Elizabeth. And when Elizabeth heard the greeting of Mary, the babe leaped in her womb; and Elizabeth was filled with the Holy Spirit and she exclaimed with a loud cry, 'Blessed are you among women, and blessed is the fruit of your womb! And why is this granted me, that the mother of my Lord should come to me? For behold, when the voice of your greeting came to my ears, the babe in my womb leaped for joy. And blessed is she who believed that there would be a fulfilment of what was spoken to her from the Lord.' And Mary said,
'My soul magnifies the Lord,
and my spirit rejoices in God my Saviour,
for he has regarded the low estate of his handmaiden.
For behold, henceforth all generations will call me blessed;
for he who is mighty has done great things for me,
and holy is his name.'

or *Luke 2.1-19 RSV*

In those days a decree went out from Caesar Augustus that all the world should be enrolled. This was the first enrolment, when Quirinius was governor of Syria. And all went to be enrolled, each to his own city. And Joseph also went up from Galilee, from the city of Nazareth to Judaea, to the city of David, which is called Bethlehem, because he was of the house and lineage of David, to be enrolled with Mary, his betrothed, who was with child. And while they were there, the time came for her to be delivered. And she gave birth to her first-born son and wrapped him in swaddling cloths, and laid him in a manger, because there was no place for them in the inn.

And in that region there were shepherds out in the field, keeping watch over their flock by night. And an angel of the Lord appeared to them, and the glory of the Lord shone around them, and they were filled with fear. And the angel said to them, 'Be not afraid; for behold, I bring you good news of a great joy which will come to all the people; for to you is born this day in the city of David a Saviour, who is Christ the Lord. And this will be a sign for you: you will find a babe wrapped in swaddling cloths and lying in a manger.' And suddenly there was with the angel a multitude of the heavenly host praising God and saying,
'Glory to God in the highest,
and on earth peace among men with whom he is pleased!'

When the angels went away from them into heaven, the shepherds said to one another, 'Let us go over to Bethlehem and see this thing that has happened, which the Lord has made known to us.' And they went with haste, and found Mary and Joseph, and the babe lying in a manger. And when they saw it they made known the saying which had been told them concerning this child; and all who heard it wondered at what the shepherds told them. But Mary kept all these things, pondering them in her heart. And the shepherds returned, glorifying and praising God for all they had heard and seen, as it had been told them.

PROPER PREFACE

Rite A. A Preface of the Incarnation (6) is said.
Rite B. The Preface of Christmas is said.

POSTCOMMUNION SENTENCE

Blessed are those who hear the word of God and keep it. *Luke 11.28*

or

Mary kept all things concerning Jesus, and pondered them in her heart. *Luke 2.19*

ST MATTHEW THE APOSTLE (21 September)   Red

INTRODUCTORY SENTENCE

Jesus saw Matthew at his seat in the custom-house; and he said to him, Follow me. *Matthew 9.9*

COLLECT

Almighty God,
who through your Son Jesus Christ
called Matthew from the selfish pursuit of gain
to become an apostle and evangelist:
free us from all possessiveness and love of riches
that we may follow in the steps of Jesus Christ our Lord;
who is alive and reigns with you and the Holy Spirit,
one God, now and for ever.

PSALMS 119.65-72; 119.89-96

READINGS

Old Testament *Proverbs 3.9-18 RSV*

Honour the Lord with your substance
and with the first fruits of all your produce;
then your barns will be filled with plenty,
and your vats will be bursting with wine.

My son, do not despise the Lord's discipline
or be weary of his reproof,
for the Lord reproves him whom he loves,
as a father the son in whom he delights.

Happy is the man who finds wisdom,
and the man who gets understanding,
for the gain from it is better than gain from silver
and its profit better than gold.
She is more precious than jewels,
and nothing you desire can compare with her.
Long life is in her right hand;
in her left hand are riches and honour.
Her ways are ways of pleasantness,
and all her paths are peace.

She is a tree of life to those who lay hold of her;
those who hold her fast are called happy.

New Testament *2 Corinthians 4.1-6 NEB*

Seeing that we have been entrusted with this commission,
which we owe entirely to God's mercy, we never lose heart.
We have renounced the deeds that men hide for very shame;
we neither practise cunning nor distort the word of God;
only by declaring the truth openly do we recommend
ourselves, and then it is to the common conscience of our
fellow-men and in the sight of God. And if indeed our
gospel be found veiled, the only people who find it so are
those on the way to perdition. Their unbelieving minds are
so blinded by the god of this passing age, that the gospel of
the glory of Christ, who is the very image of God, cannot
dawn upon them and bring them light. It is not ourselves
that we proclaim; we proclaim Christ Jesus as Lord, and
ourselves as your servants, for Jesus' sake. For the same God
who said, 'Out of darkness let light shine', has caused his
light to shine within us, to give the light of revelation—the
revelation of the glory of God in the face of Jesus Christ.

Gospel *Matthew 9.9-13 RSV*

Jesus saw a man called Matthew sitting at the tax office; and
he said to him, 'Follow me.' And he rose and followed him.

And as he sat at table in the house, behold, many tax
collectors and sinners came and sat down with Jesus and his
disciples. And when the Pharisees saw this, they said to his
disciples, 'Why does your teacher eat with tax collectors and
sinners?' But when he heard it, he said, 'Those who are well
have no need of a physician, but those who are sick. Go and
learn what this means, "I desire mercy, and not sacrifice."
For I came not to call the righteous, but sinners.'

PROPER PREFACE

Rite A. The Preface of Apostles and Evangelists (23) is said.
Rite B. The Preface of Saints' Days is said.

POSTCOMMUNION SENTENCE

Jesus sat at table with the tax collectors and sinners; and he said, It is not the healthy who need the doctor, but the sick. I did not come to call virtuous people, but sinners. *Matthew 9.10, 12, 13*

ST MICHAEL AND ALL ANGELS (29 September)   White

INTRODUCTORY SENTENCE

Bless the Lord, all you his angels, you mighty ones who do his word. *Psalm 103.20*

COLLECT

Eternal Lord God,
who ordained and constituted the service
    of angels and men in a wonderful order:
grant that as your holy angels
    always serve you in heaven,
so by your appointment
they may help and defend us on earth;
through Jesus Christ our Lord.

PSALMS 103.17-end; 91.5-12

READINGS

Old Testament *2 Kings 6.8-17 NEB*

Once, when the king of Aram was making war on Israel, he held a conference with his staff at which he said, 'I mean to attack in such and such a direction.' But the man of God warned the king of Israel: 'Take care to avoid this place, for the Aramaeans are going down that way.' So the king of Israel sent to the place about which the man of God had given him this warning; and the king took special precautions every time he found himself near that place. The king of Aram was greatly perturbed at this and, summoning his staff, he said to them, 'Tell me, one of you, who has betrayed us to the king of Israel?' 'None of us, my lord king,' said one of his staff; 'but Elisha, the prophet in Israel, tells the king of Israel the very words you speak in your bedchamber.' 'Go and find out where he is,' said the king, 'and I will send and seize him.' He was told that the prophet was at Dothan, and he sent a strong force there with horses and chariots. They came by night and surrounded the city.

When the disciple of the man of God rose early in the morning and went out, he saw a force with horses and chariots surrounding the city. 'Oh, master,' he said, 'which way are we to turn?' He answered, 'Do not be afraid, for those who are on our side are more than those on theirs.' Then Elisha offered this prayer: 'O Lord, open his eyes and let him see.' And the Lord opened the young man's eyes, and he saw the hills covered with horses and chariots of fire all round Elisha.

New Testament *Revelation 12.7-12 RSV*

War arose in heaven, Michael and his angels fighting against the dragon; and the dragon and his angels fought, but they were defeated and there was no longer any place for them in heaven. And the great dragon was thrown down, that ancient serpent, who is called the Devil and Satan, the deceiver of the whole world—he was thrown down to the earth, and his angels were thrown down with him. And I heard a loud voice in heaven, saying, 'Now the salvation and the power and the kingdom of our God and the authority of his Christ have come, for the accuser of our brethren has been thrown down, who accuses them day and night before our God. And they have conquered him by the blood of the Lamb and by the word of their testimony, for they loved not their lives even unto death. Rejoice then, O heaven and you that dwell therein! But woe to you, O earth and sea, for the devil has come down to you in great wrath, because he knows that his time is short!'

Gospel *Matthew 18.1-6, 10 NEB*

The disciples came to Jesus and asked, 'Who is the greatest in the kingdom of Heaven?' He called a child, set him in front of them, and said, 'I tell you this: unless you turn round and become like children, you will never enter the kingdom of Heaven. Let a man humble himself till he is like this child, and he will be the greatest in the kingdom of Heaven. Whoever receives one such child in my name receives me. But if a man is a cause of stumbling to one of these little ones who have faith in me, it would be better for him to have a millstone hung round his neck and be drowned in the depths of the sea.

'Never despise one of these little ones; I tell you, they have their guardian angels in heaven, who look continually on the face of my heavenly Father.'

PROPER PREFACE

Rite A. The Preface of Michaelmas (21) is said.

POSTCOMMUNION SENTENCE

O God, I will sing your praises in the sight of the angels. *Psalm 138.1*

ST LUKE THE EVANGELIST (18 October)   Red

INTRODUCTORY SENTENCE

Luke has written of all that Jesus did and taught from the beginning. *Acts 1.1*

COLLECT

Almighty God,
who inspired Luke the physician
to proclaim the love and healing power of your Son:
give your Church, by the grace of the Spirit
    and through the medicine of the gospel,
the same love and power to heal;
through Jesus Christ our Lord.

PSALMS 147.1-6; 22.23-29

READINGS

Old Testament *Isaiah 35.3-6 RSV*

Strengthen the weak hands,
and make firm the feeble knees.
Say to those who are of a fearful heart,
'Be strong, fear not!
Behold, your God
will come with vengeance,
with the recompense of God.
He will come and save you.'

Then the eyes of the blind shall be opened,
and the ears of the deaf unstopped;
then shall the lame man leap like a hart,
and the tongue of the dumb sing for joy.
For waters shall break forth in the wilderness,
and streams in the desert.

New Testament *Acts 16.6-12a RSV*

Paul and Timothy went through the region of Phrygia and
Galatia, having been forbidden by the Holy Spirit to speak
the word in Asia. And when they had come opposite Mysia,
they attempted to go into Bithynia, but the Spirit of Jesus did
not allow them; so, passing by Mysia, they went down to
Troas. And a vision appeared to Paul in the night: a man of
Macedonia was standing beseeching him and saying, 'Come
over to Macedonia and help us.' And when he had seen the
vision, immediately we sought to go on into Macedonia,
concluding that God had called us to preach the gospel
to them.

Setting sail therefore from Troas, we made a direct voyage to
Samothrace, and the following day to Neapolis, and from
there to Philippi, which is the leading city of the district of
Macedonia, and a Roman colony.

or *2 Timothy 4.5-13 NEB*

You yourself must keep calm and sane at all times; face
hardship, work to spread the Gospel, and do all the duties of
your calling.

As for me, already my life is being poured out on the altar, and the hour for my departure is upon me. I have run the great race, I have finished the course, I have kept faith. And now the prize awaits me, the garland of righteousness which the Lord, the all-just Judge, will award me on that great Day; and it is not for me alone, but for all who have set their hearts on his coming appearance.

Do your best to join me soon; for Demas has deserted me because his heart was set on this world; he has gone to Thessalonica, Crescens to Galatia, Titus to Dalmatia; I have no one with me but Luke. Pick up Mark and bring him with you, for I find him a useful assistant. Tychicus I have sent to Ephesus. When you come, bring the cloak I left with Carpus at Troas, and the books, above all my notebooks.

Gospel *Luke 10.1-9 NEB*

The Lord appointed a further seventy-two and sent them on ahead in pairs to every town and place he was going to visit himself. He said to them: 'The crop is heavy, but labourers are scarce; you must therefore beg the owner to send labourers to harvest his crop. Be on your way. And look, I am sending you like lambs among wolves. Carry no purse or pack, and travel barefoot. Exchange no greetings on the road. When you go into a house, let your first words be, "Peace to this house." If there is a man of peace there, your peace will rest upon him; if not, it will return and rest with you. Stay in that one house, sharing their food and drink; for the worker earns his pay. Do not move from house to house. When you come into a town and they make you welcome, eat the food provided for you; heal the sick there, and say, "The kingdom of God has come close to you."'

PROPER PREFACE

Rite A. The Preface of Apostles and Evangelists (23) is said.
Rite B. The Preface of Saints' Days is said.

POSTCOMMUNION SENTENCE

How beautiful on the mountains are the feet of him who brings good tidings of salvation. *Isaiah 52.7*

ST SIMON AND ST JUDE, APOSTLES (28 October) Red

INTRODUCTORY SENTENCE

Beloved, build yourselves up on your most holy faith; pray in the Holy Spirit. *Jude 20*

COLLECT

Almighty God,
you have built your Church upon the foundation
    of the apostles and prophets
with Jesus Christ himself as the chief corner-stone.
So join us together in unity of spirit by their doctrine,
that we may be made a holy temple acceptable to you;
through Jesus Christ our Lord.

PSALMS 15; 116.11-end

READINGS

Old Testament *Isaiah 28.9-16 TEV*

The prophets and the priests complain about me. They say, 'Who does that man think he's teaching? Who needs his message? It's only good for babies that have just been weaned! He is trying to teach us letter by letter, line by line, lesson by lesson.'

If you won't listen to me, then God will use foreigners speaking some strange-sounding language to teach you a lesson. He offered rest and comfort to all of you, but you refused to listen to him. That is why the Lord is going to teach you letter by letter, line by line, lesson by lesson. Then you will stumble with every step you take. You will be wounded, trapped, and taken prisoner.

Now you arrogant men who rule here in Jerusalem over this people, listen to what the Lord is saying. You boast that you have made a treaty with death and reached an agreement with the world of the dead. You are certain that disaster will spare you when it comes, because you depend on lies and deceit to keep you safe. This, now, is what the Sovereign

Lord says: 'I am placing in Zion a foundation that is firm and strong. In it I am putting a solid corner-stone on which are written the words, "Faith that is firm is also patient."'

New Testament *Ephesians 2.13-end NEB*

Now, in union with Christ Jesus you who once were far off have been brought near through the shedding of Christ's blood. For he is himself our peace. Gentiles and Jews, he has made the two one, and in his own body of flesh and blood has broken down the enmity which stood like a dividing wall between them; for he annulled the law with its rules and regulations, so as to create out of the two a single new humanity in himself, thereby making peace. This was his purpose, to reconcile the two in a single body to God through the cross, on which he killed the enmity.

So he came and proclaimed the good news: peace to you who were far off, and peace to those who were near by; for through him we both alike have access to the Father in the one Spirit. Thus you are no longer aliens in a foreign land, but fellow-citizens with God's people, members of God's household. You are built upon the foundation laid by the apostles and prophets, and Christ Jesus himself is the foundation-stone. In him the whole building is bonded together and grows into a holy temple in the Lord. In him you too are being built with all the rest into a spiritual dwelling for God.

Gospel *John 14.15-26 JB*

Jesus said,
'If you love me you will keep my commandments.
I shall ask the Father,
and he will give you another Advocate
to be with you for ever,
that Spirit of truth
whom the world can never receive
since it neither sees nor knows him;
but you know him,
because he is with you, he is in you.
I will not leave you orphans;

I will come back to you.
In a short time the world will no longer see me;
but you will see me,
because I live and you will live.
On that day
you will understand that I am in my Father
and you in me and I in you.
Anybody who receives my commandments and keeps them
will be one who loves me;
and anybody who loves me will be loved by my Father,
and I shall love him and show myself to him.'

Judas—this was not Judas Iscariot—said to him, 'Lord, what
is all this about? Do you intend to show yourself to us and
not to the world?' Jesus replied:
'If anyone loves me he will keep my word,
and my Father will love him,
and we shall come to him,
and make our home with him.
Those who do not love me do not keep my words.
And my word is not my own:
it is the word of the one who sent me.
I have said these things to you
while still with you;
but the Advocate, the Holy Spirit,
whom the Father will send in my name,
will teach you everything
and remind you of all I have said to you.'

PROPER PREFACE

Rite A. The Preface of Apostles and Evangelists (23) is said.
Rite B. The Preface of Saints' Days is said.

POSTCOMMUNION SENTENCE

Jesus said, If anyone loves me, he will keep my words, and
my Father will love him, and we will come to him, and make
our home with him. *John 14.23*

ALL SAINTS' DAY (1 November)   White

INTRODUCTORY SENTENCE

Praise our God, all you his servants: you who fear him, both small and great. *Revelation 19.5*

COLLECT

Almighty God,
you have knit together your elect
into one communion and fellowship
   in the mystical body of your Son.
Give us grace so to follow your blessed saints
in all virtuous and godly living,
that we may come to those unspeakable joys
which you have prepared for those who truly love you;
through Jesus Christ our Lord.

PSALMS 1; 15; 33.1-5; 145.8-13

READINGS

Old Testament *Jeremiah 31.31-34 NEB*

The time is coming, says the Lord, when I will make a new covenant with Israel and Judah. It will not be like the covenant I made with their forefathers when I took them by the hand and led them out of Egypt. Although they broke my covenant, I was patient with them, says the Lord. But this is the covenant which I will make with Israel after those days, says the Lord; I will set my law within them and write it on their hearts; I will become their God and they shall become my people. No longer need they teach one another to know the Lord; all of them, high and low alike, shall know me, says the Lord, for I will forgive their wrongdoing and remember their sin no more.

or *2 Esdras 2.42-end RSV*

I, Ezra, saw on Mount Zion a great multitude, which I could not number, and they all were praising the Lord with songs. In their midst was a young man of great stature, taller than any of the others, and on the head of each of them he placed a crown, but he was more exalted than they. And I was held spellbound. Then I asked an angel, 'Who are these, my Lord?' He answered and said to me, 'These are they who have put off mortal clothing and have put on the immortal, and they have confessed the name of God; now they are being crowned, and receive palms.' Then I said to the angel, 'Who is that young man who places crowns on them and puts palms in their hands?' He answered and said to me, 'He is the Son of God, whom they confessed in the world.' So I began to praise those who had stood valiantly for the name of the Lord. Then the angel said to me, 'Go, tell my people how great and many are the wonders of the Lord God which you have seen.'

or *Genesis 3.1-15 NEB*

The serpent was more crafty than any wild creature that the Lord God had made. He said to the woman, 'Is it true that God has forbidden you to eat from any tree in the garden?' The woman answered the serpent, 'We may eat the fruit of any tree in the garden, except for the tree in the middle of the garden; God has forbidden us either to eat or to touch the fruit of that; if we do, we shall die.' The serpent said, 'Of course you will not die. God knows that as soon as you eat it, your eyes will be opened and you will be like gods knowing both good and evil.' When the woman saw that the fruit of the tree was good to eat, and that it was pleasing to the eye and tempting to contemplate, she took some and ate it. She also gave her husband some and he ate it. Then the eyes of both of them were opened and they discovered that they were naked; so they stitched fig-leaves together and made themselves loincloths.

The man and his wife heard the sound of the Lord God walking in the garden at the time of the evening breeze and hid from the Lord God among the trees of the garden. But the Lord God called to the man and said to him, 'Where are you?' He replied, 'I heard the sound as you were walking in the garden, and I was afraid because I was naked, and I hid myself.' God answered, 'Who told you that you were

naked? Have you eaten from the tree which I forbade you?'
The man said, 'The woman you gave me for a companion,
she gave me fruit from the tree and I ate it.' Then the Lord
God said to the woman, 'What is this that you have done?'
The woman said, 'The serpent tricked me, and I ate.' Then
the Lord God said to the serpent:
'Because you have done this you are accursed
more than all cattle and all wild creatures.
On your belly you shall crawl, and dust you shall eat
all the days of your life.
I will put enmity between you and the woman,
between your brood and hers.
They shall strike at your head,
and you shall strike at their heel.'

New Testament *Hebrews 12.18-24 NEB*

Remember where you stand: not before the palpable,
blazing fire of Sinai, with the darkness, gloom, and
whirlwind, the trumpet-blast and the oracular voice, which
they heard, and begged to hear no more; for they could not
bear the command, 'If even an animal touches the mountain,
it must be stoned.' So appalling was the sight, that Moses
said, 'I shudder with fear.'

No, you stand before Mount Zion and the city of the living
God, heavenly Jerusalem, before myriads of angels, the full
concourse and assembly of the first-born citizens of heaven,
and God the judge of all, and the spirits of good men made
perfect, and Jesus the mediator of a new covenant, whose
sprinkled blood has better things to tell than the blood
of Abel.

or *Revelation 7.2-4, 9-end RSV*

I saw another angel ascend from the rising of the sun, with
the seal of the living God, and he called with a loud voice to
the four angels who had been given power to harm earth and
sea, saying, 'Do not harm the earth or the sea or the trees, till
we have sealed the servants of our God upon their
foreheads.' And I heard the number of the sealed, a hundred

and forty-four thousand sealed, out of every tribe of the sons of Israel.

After this I looked, and behold, a great multitude which no man could number, from every nation, from all tribes and peoples and tongues, standing before the throne and before the Lamb, clothed in white robes, with palm branches in their hands, and crying out with a loud voice, 'Salvation belongs to our God who sits upon the throne, and to the Lamb!' And all the angels stood round the throne and round the elders and the four living creatures, and they fell on their faces before the throne and worshipped God, saying, 'Amen! Blessing and glory and wisdom and thanksgiving and honour and power and might be to our God for ever and ever! Amen.'

Then one of the elders addressed me, saying, 'Who are these, clothed in white robes, and whence have they come?' I said to him, 'Sir, you know.' And he said to me, 'These are they who have come out of the great tribulation; they have washed their robes and made them white in the blood of the Lamb.
Therefore are they before the throne of God,
and serve him day and night within his temple;
and he who sits upon the throne will
     shelter them with his presence.
They shall hunger no more, neither thirst any more;
the sun shall not strike them, nor any scorching heat.
For the Lamb in the midst of the throne
     will be their shepherd,
and he will guide them to springs of living water;
and God will wipe away every tear from their eyes.'

Gospel *Matthew 5.1-12 NEB*

When Jesus saw the crowds he went up the hill. There he took his seat, and when his disciples had gathered round him he began to address them. And this is the teaching he gave:

'How blest are those who know their need of God;
the kingdom of Heaven is theirs.

How blest are the sorrowful;
they shall find consolation.
How blest are those of a gentle spirit;
they shall have the earth for their possession.
How blest are those who hunger and thirst to see
right prevail;
they shall be satisfied.
How blest are those who show mercy;
mercy shall be shown to them.
How blest are those whose hearts are pure;
they shall see God.
How blest are the peacemakers;
God shall call them his sons.
How blest are those who have suffered persecution
for the cause of right;
the kingdom of Heaven is theirs.

'How blest you are, when you suffer insults and persecution
and every kind of calumny for my sake. Accept it with
gladness and exultation, for you have a rich reward in
heaven; in the same way they persecuted the prophets
before you.'

or *Luke 6.20-23 NEB*

Turning to his disciples Jesus began to speak:
'How blest are you who are in need; the kingdom of God
is yours.
'How blest are you who now go hungry; your hunger shall
be satisfied.
'How blest are you who weep now; you shall laugh.
'How blest you are when men hate you, when they outlaw
you and insult you, and ban your very name as infamous,
because of the Son of Man. On that day be glad and dance for
joy; for assuredly you have a rich reward in heaven; in just
the same way did their fathers treat the prophets.'

PROPER PREFACE

Rite A. The Preface of All Saints' Day (22) is said.
Rite B. The Preface of Saints' Days is said.

POSTCOMMUNION SENTENCE

I heard the noise of a great multitude, crying, Alleluia! The
Lord our God has entered into his kingdom. Happy are
those who are called to the supper of the Lamb.
Revelation 19.6, 9.

Psalms and readings for Evening Prayer on the previous day
may be chosen from this provision.

ST ANDREW THE APOSTLE (30 November)   Red

INTRODUCTORY SENTENCE

Jesus said, Come, follow me, and I will make you fishers of
men. *Matthew 4.19*

COLLECT

Almighty God,
who gave such grace to your apostle Saint Andrew
that he readily obeyed the call of your Son
    and brought his brother with him:
give us, who are called by your holy Word,
grace to follow without delay
and to tell the good news of your kingdom;
through Jesus Christ our Lord.

PSALMS 92.1-5; 87

READINGS

Old Testament *Zechariah 8.20-end JB*

The Lord of Hosts says this. There will be other peoples yet,
and citizens of great cities. And the inhabitants of one city
will go to the next and say, 'Come, let us go and entreat the
favour of the Lord, and seek the Lord of Hosts; I am going
myself.' And many peoples and great nations will come to
see the Lord of Hosts in Jerusalem and to entreat the favour
of the Lord.

The Lord of Hosts says this. In those days, ten men of nations of every language will take a Jew by the sleeve and say, 'We want to go with you, since we have learnt that God is with you.'

New Testament *Romans 10.12-18 RSV*

There is no distinction between Jew and Greek; the same Lord is Lord of all and bestows his riches upon all who call upon him. For, 'everyone who calls upon the name of the Lord will be saved.'

But how are men to call upon him in whom they have not believed? And how are they to believe in him of whom they have never heard? And how are they to hear without a preacher? And how can men preach unless they are sent? As it is written, 'How beautiful are the feet of those who preach good news!' But they have not all heeded the gospel; for Isaiah says, 'Lord, who has believed what he has heard from us?' So faith comes from what is heard, and what is heard comes by the preaching of Christ.

But I ask, have they not heard? Indeed they have; for
'Their voice has gone out to all the earth,
and their words to the ends of the world.'

Gospel *Matthew 4.12-20 JB*

Hearing that John had been arrested Jesus went back to Galilee, and leaving Nazareth he went and settled in Capernaum, a lakeside town on the borders of Zebulun and Naphtali. In this way the prophecy of Isaiah was to be fulfilled:

Land of Zebulun! Land of Naphtali!
Way of the sea on the far side of Jordan,
Galilee of the nations!
The people that lived in darkness
has seen a great light;
on those who dwell in the land and shadows of death
a light has dawned.

From that moment Jesus began his preaching with the message, 'Repent, for the kingdom of heaven is close at hand'.

As he was walking by the Sea of Galilee he saw two brothers, Simon, who was called Peter, and his brother Andrew; they were making a cast in the lake with their net, for they were fishermen. And he said to them, 'Follow me and I will make you fishers of men.' And they left their nets at once and followed him.

PROPER PREFACE

Rite A. The Preface of Apostles and Evangelists (23) is said.
Rite B. The Preface of Saints' Days is said.

POSTCOMMUNION SENTENCE

Andrew said to Simon, We have found the Messiah—
which means, the Christ. And he brought him to Jesus.
John 1.41, 42

ST STEPHEN THE FIRST MARTYR (26 December)   Red

INTRODUCTORY SENTENCE

Stephen, full of grace and power, did great signs and
wonders among the people. *Acts 6.8*

COLLECT

Heavenly Father,
give us grace in all our sufferings for the truth
to follow the example of your first martyr Saint Stephen:
that we also may look to him who was crucified
and pray for those who persecute us;
through Jesus Christ our Lord.

PSALMS 119.17-24; 119.161-168

READINGS

Old Testament 2 *Chronicles 24.20-22 NEB*

The spirit of God took possession of Zechariah son of
Jehoiada the priest, and he stood looking down on the
people and said to them, 'This is the word of God: "Why do
you disobey the commands of the Lord and court disaster?
Because you have forsaken the Lord, he has forsaken you."'
But they made common cause against him, and on orders
from the king they stoned him to death in the court of the
house of the Lord. King Joash did not remember the loyalty
of Zechariah's father Jehoiada but killed his son, who said as
he was dying, 'May the Lord see this and exact the penalty.'

New Testament *Acts 7.54-end RSV*

When the Council heard these things they were enraged,
and they ground their teeth against him. But he, full of the
Holy Spirit, gazed into heaven and saw the glory of God,
and Jesus standing at the right hand of God; and he said,
'Behold, I see the heavens opened, and the Son of man
standing at the right hand of God.' But they cried out with a
loud voice and stopped their ears and rushed together upon
him. Then they cast him out of the city and stoned him; and
the witnesses laid down their garments at the feet of a young
man named Saul. And as they were stoning Stephen, he
prayed, 'Lord Jesus, receive my spirit.' And he knelt down
and cried with a loud voice, 'Lord, do not hold this sin
against them.' And when he had said this, he fell asleep.

Gospel *Matthew 23.34-end NEB*

Jesus said, 'I send you prophets, sages, and teachers; some
of them you will kill and crucify, others you will flog in your
synagogues and hound from city to city. And so, on you will
fall the guilt of all the innocent blood spilt on the ground,
from innocent Abel to Zechariah son of Berachiah, whom
you murdered between the sanctuary and the altar. Believe
me, this generation will bear the guilt of it all.

'O Jerusalem, Jerusalem, the city that murders the prophets
and stones the messengers sent to her! How often have I

longed to gather your children, as a hen gathers her brood under her wings; but you would not let me. Look, look! there is your temple, forsaken by God. And I tell you, you shall never see me until the time when you say "Blessings on him who comes in the name of the Lord."'

PROPER PREFACE

Rite A. A Preface of the Incarnation (3), (4), or (6) is said.
Preface (3) is not suitable for use with the Third Eucharistic Prayer.
Rite B. The Preface of Christmas is said.

POSTCOMMUNION SENTENCE

I can see the Son of Man standing at God's right hand. Lord Jesus, receive my spirit. *Acts 7.56, 59*

ST JOHN THE EVANGELIST (27 December)   White

INTRODUCTORY SENTENCE

This is the disciple who is bearing witness to these things, and we know that his testimony is true. *John 21.24*

COLLECT

Merciful Father,
whose Son is the light of the world:
so guide your Church by the teaching
    of your apostle and evangelist Saint John,
that we may walk by the light that has come among us
and finally know him as the light of everlasting life;
who is alive and reigns with you and the Holy Spirit,
one God, now and for ever.

PSALMS 117; 92.12-end

READINGS

Old Testament *Exodus 33.12-end JB*

Moses said to the Lord, 'See, you yourself say to me, "Make the people go on", but you do not let me know who it is you will send with me. Yet you yourself have said, "I know you by name and you have won my favour." If indeed I have won your favour, please show me your ways, so that I can understand you and win your favour. Remember, too, that this nation is your own people.' The Lord replied, 'I myself will go with you, and I will give you rest.' Moses said, 'If you are not going with us yourself, do not make us leave this place. By what means can it be known that I, I and my people, have won your favour, if not by your going with us? By this we shall be marked out, I and my people, from all the peoples on the face of the earth.' The Lord said to Moses, 'Again I will do what you have asked, because you have won my favour and because I know you by name.'

Moses said, 'Show me your glory, I beg you.' And he said, 'I will let all my splendour pass in front of you, and I will pronounce before you the name Jehovah, I have compassion on whom I will, and I show pity to whom I please. You cannot see my face,' he said, 'for men cannot see me and live.' And the Lord said, 'Here is a place beside me. You must stand on the rock, and when my glory passes by, I will put you in a cleft of the rock and shield you with my hand while I pass by. Then I will take my hand away and you shall see the back of me; but my face is not to be seen.'

New Testament *1 John 2.1-11 RSV*

My little children, I am writing this to you so that you may not sin; but if any one does sin, we have an advocate with the Father, Jesus Christ the righteous; and he is the expiation for our sins, and not for ours only but also for the sins of the whole world. And by this we may be sure that we know him, if we keep his commandments. He who says 'I know him' but disobeys his commandments is a liar, and the truth is not in him; but whoever keeps his word, in him truly love for God is perfected. By this we may be sure that we are in him:

he who says he abides in him ought to walk in the same way in which he walked.

Beloved, I am writing you no new commandment, but an old commandment which you had from the beginning; the old commandment is the word which you have heard. Yet I am writing you a new commandment, which is true in him and in you, because the darkness is passing away and the true light is already shining. He who says he is in the light and hates his brother is in the darkness still. He who loves his brother abides in the light, and in it there is no cause for stumbling. But he who hates his brother is in the darkness and walks in the darkness, and does not know where he is going, because the darkness has blinded his eyes.

Gospel *John 21.20-end RSV*

Peter turned and saw following them the disciple whom Jesus loved, who had lain close to his breast at the supper and had said, 'Lord, who is it that is going to betray you?' When Peter saw him, he said to Jesus, 'Lord, what about this man?' Jesus said to him, 'If it is my will that he remain until I come, what is that to you? Follow me!' The saying spread abroad among the brethren that this disciple was not to die; yet Jesus did not say to him that he was not to die, but, 'If it is my will that he remain until I come, what is that to you?'

This is the disciple who is bearing witness to these things, and who has written these things; and we know that his testimony is true.

But there are also may other things which Jesus did; were every one of them to be written, I suppose that the world itself could not contain the books that would be written.

PROPER PREFACE

Rite A. A Preface of the Incarnation (3), (4), or (6) is said.
Preface (3) is not suitable for use with the Third Eucharistic Prayer.
Rite B. The Preface of Christmas is said.

POSTCOMMUNION SENTENCE

The Word was made flesh and lived among us; and we have all received of his fullness, grace upon grace. *John 1.14, 16*

THE HOLY INNOCENTS (28 December)   Red

INTRODUCTORY SENTENCE

I will turn their mourning into joy; I will comfort them and give them gladness for sorrow. *Jeremiah 31.13*

COLLECT

Heavenly Father,
whose children suffered at the hands of Herod,
though they had done no wrong:
give us grace neither to act cruelly
nor to stand indifferently by,
but to defend the weak from the tyranny of the strong;
in the name of Jesus Christ who suffered for us,
but is alive and reigns with you and the Holy Spirit,
one God, now and for ever.

PSALMS 123; 131

READINGS

Old Testament *Jeremiah 31.15-17 NEB*

These are the words of the Lord:
Hark, lamentation is heard in Ramah, and bitter weeping,
Rachel weeping for her sons.
She refuses to be comforted: they are no more.

These are the words of the Lord:
Cease your loud weeping,
shed no more tears;
for there shall be a reward for your toil,
they shall return from the land of the enemy.
You shall leave descendants after you;
your sons shall return to their own land.

New Testament *1 Corinthians 1.26-29 TEV*

Now remember what you were, my brothers, when God called you. From the human point of view few of you were wise or powerful or of high social standing. God purposely chose what the world considers nonsense in order to shame the wise, and he chose what the world considers weak in order to shame the powerful. He chose what the world looks down on and despises, and thinks is nothing, in order to destroy what the world thinks is important. This means that no one can boast in God's presence.

Gospel *Matthew 2.13-18 JB*

After the wise men had left, the angel of the Lord appeared to Joseph in a dream and said, 'Get up, take the child and his mother with you, and escape into Egypt, and stay there until I tell you, because Herod intends to search for the child and do away with him.' So Joseph got up and, taking the child and his mother with him, left that night for Egypt, where he stayed until Herod was dead. This was to fulfil what the Lord had spoken through the prophet:

'I called my son out of Egypt.'

Herod was furious when he realised that he had been outwitted by the wise men, and in Bethlehem and its surrounding district he had all the male children killed who were two years old or under, reckoning by the date he had been careful to ask the wise men. It was then that the words spoken through the prophet Jeremiah were fulfilled:

'A voice was heard in Ramah,
sobbing and loudly lamenting:
it was Rachel weeping for her children,
refusing to be comforted
because they were no more.'

PROPER PREFACE

Rite A. A Preface of the Incarnation (3), (4), or (6) is said. Preface (3) is not suitable for use with the Third Eucharistic Prayer.
Rite B. The Preface of Christmas is said.

POSTCOMMUNION SENTENCE

They have been ransomed as the first fruits of mankind, and they follow the Lamb wherever he goes. *Revelation 14.4*

FESTIVAL OF THE DEDICATION OR CONSECRATION OF A CHURCH White

INTRODUCTORY SENTENCE

How awesome is this place! This is none other than the house of God, and this is the gate of heaven. *Genesis 28.17*

COLLECT

Almighty God,
to whose glory we celebrate
    the *dedication* of this house of prayer:
we praise you for the many blessings
you have given to those who worship here;
and we pray that all who seek you in this place may find you,
and being filled with the Holy Spirit
may become a living temple acceptable to you;
through Jesus Christ our Lord.

PSALMS 84.1-7; 122   or   24; 132

READINGS

Old Testament *1 Kings 8.22-30 JB*

In the presence of the whole assembly of Israel Solomon stood before the altar of the Lord and, stretching out his hands towards heaven, said, 'O Lord, God of Israel, not in heaven above nor on earth beneath is there such a God as you, true to your covenant and your kindness towards your servants when they walk wholeheartedly in your way. You have kept the promise you made to your servant David my father; what you promised with your mouth, today you have carried out by your hand. And now, O Lord, God of Israel, keep the promise you made to your servant David when you said, "You shall never lack for a man to sit before me on the throne of Israel, if only your sons are careful how they behave, walking before me as you yourself have done.'' So now, God of Israel, let the words come true which you spoke to your servant David my father. Yet will God really live with men on the earth? Why, the heavens and their own heavens cannot contain you. How much less this house that I have built! Listen to the prayer and entreaty of your servant, O Lord my God; listen to the cry and to the prayer your servant makes to you today. Day and night let your eyes watch over this house, over this place of which you have said, ''My name shall be there.'' Listen to the prayer that your servant will offer in this place.'

New Testament *1 Peter 2.1-10 NEB*

Away with all malice and deceit, away with all pretence and jealousy and recrimination of every kind! Like the new-born infants you are, you must crave for pure milk (spiritual milk, I mean), so that you may thrive upon it to your soul's health. Surely you have tasted that the Lord is good.

So come to him, our living Stone—the stone rejected by men but choice and precious in the sight of God. Come, and let yourselves be built, as living stones, into a spiritual temple; become a holy priesthood, to offer spiritual sacrifices acceptable to God through Jesus Christ. For it stands written:

'I lay in Zion a choice corner-stone of great worth. The man who has faith in it will not be put to shame.'

The great worth of which it speaks is for you who have faith. For those who have no faith, the stone which the builders rejected has become not only the corner-stone, but also 'a stone to trip over, a rock to stumble against'. They fall when they disbelieve the Word. Such was their appointed lot!

But you are a chosen race, a royal priesthood, a dedicated nation, and a people claimed by God for his own, to proclaim the triumphs of him who has called you out of darkness into his marvellous light. You are now the people of God, who once were not his people; outside his mercy once, you have now received his mercy.

Gospel *Matthew 21.12-16 RSV*

Jesus entered the temple of God and drove out all who sold and bought in the temple, and he overturned the tables of the money-changers and the seats of those who sold pigeons. He said to them, 'It is written, "My house shall be called a house of prayer"; but you make it a den of robbers.'

And the blind and the lame came to him in the temple, and he healed them. But when the chief priests and the scribes saw the wonderful things that he did, and the children crying out in the temple, 'Hosanna to the Son of David!' they were indignant; and they said to him, 'Do you hear what these are saying?' And Jesus said to them, 'Yes, have you never read,
"Out of the mouth of babes and sucklings
thou hast brought perfect praise"?'

PROPER PREFACE

Rite A. The Preface of the Dedication (26) is said.
Rite B. The Preface of the Dedication is said.

POSTCOMMUNION SENTENCE

You are the temple of the living God, and the Spirit of God dwells in you. The temple of God is holy: you are that temple. *1 Corinthians 3.16*

FESTIVAL OF THE PATRON SAINT OR TITLE OF A CHURCH

If this day is provided with propers, these are used; but if not, the propers for All Saints' Day or other appropriate propers may be used.

Sentences, Collects, and Readings
(c) Lesser Festivals and Holy Days

TIMOTHY AND TITUS (26 January)   White

INTRODUCTORY SENTENCE

Follow after righteousness, godliness, faith, love, fortitude,
and gentleness: for to this you were called, and you
confessed your faith before many witnesses.
1 Timothy 6.11, 12

COLLECT

Heavenly Father,
who sent your apostle Paul to preach the Gospel,
and gave him Timothy and Titus
to be his companions in the faith:
grant that our fellowship in the Holy Spirit
may bear witness to the name of Jesus;
who is alive and reigns with you and the Holy Spirit,
one God, now and for ever.

PSALMS 97; 100

READINGS

Old Testament *Isaiah 61.1-3 NEB*

The spirit of the Lord God is upon me
because the Lord has anointed me;
he has sent me to bring good news to the humble,
to bind up the broken-hearted,
to proclaim liberty to captives
and release to those in prison;
to proclaim a year of the Lord's favour
and a day of the vengeance of our God;
to comfort all who mourn,
to give them garlands instead of ashes,
oil of gladness instead of mourners' tears,
a garment of splendour for the heavy heart.
They shall be called Trees of Righteousness,
planted by the Lord for his glory.

New Testament *2 Timothy 1.1-8 NEB*

From Paul, Apostle of Jesus Christ by the will of God, whose promise of life is fulfilled in Christ Jesus, to Timothy his dear son.

Grace, mercy, and peace to you from God the Father and our Lord Jesus Christ.

I thank God—whom I, like my forefathers, worship with a pure intention—when I mention you in my prayers; this I do constantly night and day. And when I remember the tears you shed, I long to see you again to make my happiness complete. I am reminded of the sincerity of your faith, a faith which was alive in Lois your grandmother and Eunice your mother before you, and which, I am confident, lives in you also.

That is why I now remind you to stir into flame the gift of God which is within you through the laying on of my hands. For the spirit that God gave us is no craven spirit, but one to inspire strength, love, and self-discipline. So never be ashamed of your testimony to our Lord, nor of me his prisoner, but take your share of suffering for the sake of the Gospel, in the strength that comes from God.

or *Titus 1.1-5 TEV*

From Paul, a servant of God and an apostle of Jesus Christ.

I was chosen and sent to help the faith of God's chosen people and to lead them to the truth taught by our religion, which is based on the hope for eternal life. God, who does not lie, promised us this life before the beginning of time, and at the right time he revealed it in his message. This was entrusted to me, and I proclaim it by order of God our Saviour.

I write to Titus, my true son in the faith that we have in common.

May God the Father and Christ Jesus our Saviour give you grace and peace.

I left you in Crete, so that you could put in order the things that still needed doing and appoint church elders in every town. Remember my instructions.

Gospel *Mark 16.14-end NEB*

While the Eleven were at table Jesus appeared to them and reproached them for their incredulity and dullness, because they had not believed those who had seen him after he was raised from the dead. Then he said to them: 'Go forth to every part of the world, and proclaim the Good News to the whole creation. Those who believe it and receive baptism will find salvation; those who do not believe will be condemned. Faith will bring with it these miracles: believers will cast out devils in my name and speak in strange tongues; if they handle snakes or drink any deadly poison, they will come to no harm; and the sick on whom they lay their hands will recover.'

So after talking with them the Lord Jesus was taken up into heaven, and he took his seat at the right hand of God; but they went out to make their proclamation everywhere, and the Lord worked with them and confirmed their words by the miracles that followed.

PROPER PREFACE

Rite A. The Preface of Ordination (28) may be said.
Rite B. The Preface of Saints' Days may be said.

POSTCOMMUNION SENTENCE

The grace of God has dawned on the world with healing for all mankind. *Titus 2.11*

THE VISIT OF THE BLESSED VIRGIN MARY TO ELIZABETH (31 May)   White

INTRODUCTORY SENTENCE

Blessed is she who believed that there would be a fulfilment of what was spoken to her from the Lord. *Luke 1.45*

COLLECT

Almighty God,
by whose grace Elizabeth rejoiced with Mary
and hailed her as the mother of the Lord:
fill us with your grace
that we may acclaim her Son as our Saviour
and rejoice to be called his brethren;
through Jesus Christ our Lord.

PSALMS 113; 131

READINGS

Old Testament *Zechariah 2.10-end NEB*

Shout aloud and rejoice, daughter of Zion; I am coming, I
will make my dwelling among you, says the Lord. Many
nations shall come over to the Lord on that day and become
his people, and he will make his dwelling with you. Then
you shall know that the Lord of Hosts has sent me to you.
The Lord will once again claim Judah as his own possession
in the holy land, and make Jerusalem the city of his choice.

Silence, all mankind, in the presence of the Lord! For he has
bestirred himself out of his holy dwelling-place.

New Testament *Galatians 4.1-5 RSV*

The heir, as long as he is a child, is no better than a slave,
though he is the owner of all the estate; but he is under
guardians and trustees until the date set by the father. So
with us; when we were children, we were slaves to the
elemental spirits of the universe. But when the time had
fully come, God sent forth his Son, born of woman, born
under the law, to redeem those who were under the law, so
that we might receive adoption as sons.

Gospel *Luke 1.39-49 RSV*

Mary arose and went with haste into the hill country, to a
city of Judah, and she entered the house of Zechariah and
greeted Elizabeth. And when Elizabeth heard the greeting of
Mary, the babe leaped in her womb; and Elizabeth was filled

with the Holy Spirit and she exclaimed with a loud cry,
'Blessed are you among women, and blessed is the fruit of
your womb! And why is this granted me, that the mother of
my Lord should come to me? For behold, when the voice of
your greeting came to my ears, the babe in my womb leaped
for joy. And blessed is she who believed that there would be
a fulfilment of what was spoken to her from the Lord.'

And Mary said,
'My soul magnifies the Lord,
and my spirit rejoices in God my Saviour,
for he has regarded the low estate of his handmaiden.
For behold, henceforth all generations will call me blessed;
for he who is mighty has done great things for me,
and holy is his name.'

PROPER PREFACE

Rite A. The Preface of the Incarnation (6) is said.
Rite B. The Preface of Christmas is said.

POSTCOMMUNION SENTENCE

The Lord has exalted the humble and meek and has filled the
hungry with good things. *Luke 1.52, 53*

HOLY CROSS DAY (14 September)   Red

INTRODUCTORY SENTENCE

We should glory in the cross of our Lord Jesus Christ:
through which the world is crucified to us and we to the
world. *Galatians 6.14*

COLLECT

Almighty God,
who in the passion of your blessed Son
made an instrument of shameful death
to be for us the means of life:

grant us so to glory in the cross of Christ
that we may gladly suffer for his sake;
who is alive and reigns with you and the Holy Spirit
one God, now and for ever.

PSALMS 2; 8

READINGS

Old Testament *Numbers 21.4-9 NEB*

The Israelites left Mount Hor by way of the Red Sea to march
round the flank of Edom. But on the way they grew
impatient and spoke against God and Moses. 'Why have
you brought us up from Egypt', they said, 'to die in the
desert where there is neither food nor water? We are heartily
sick of this miserable fare.' Then the Lord sent poisonous
snakes among the people, and they bit the Israelites so that
many of them died. The people came to Moses and said, 'We
sinned when we spoke against the Lord and you. Plead with
the Lord to rid us of the snakes.' Moses therefore pleaded
with the Lord for the people; and the Lord told Moses to
make a serpent of bronze and erect it as a standard, so that
anyone who had been bitten could look at it and recover. So
Moses made a bronze serpent and erected it as a standard, so
that when a snake had bitten a man, he could look at the
bronze serpent and recover.

New Testament *Philippians 2.5-11 NEB*

Let your bearing towards one another arise out of your life in
Christ Jesus. For the divine nature was his from the first; yet
he did not think to snatch at equality with God, but made
himself nothing, assuming the nature of a slave. Bearing the
human likeness, revealed in human shape, he humbled
himself, and in obedience accepted even death—death on a
cross. Therefore God raised him to the heights and
bestowed on him the name above all names, that at the name
of Jesus every knee should bow—in heaven, on earth, and in
the depths—and every tongue confess, 'Jesus Christ is
Lord', to the glory of God the Father.

Gospel *John 12.31-36a JB*

Jesus said,
'Now sentence is being passed on this world;
now the prince of this world is to be overthrown.
And when I am lifted up from the earth,
I shall draw all men to myself.'

By these words he indicated the kind of death he would die.
The crowd answered, 'The Law has taught us that the Christ
will remain for ever. How can you say, "The Son of Man
must be lifted up"? Who is this Son of Man?' Jesus then said,
'The light will be with you only a little longer now.
Walk while you have the light,
or the dark will overtake you;
he who walks in the dark does not know where he is going.
While you still have the light,
believe in the light
and you will become sons of light.'

PROPER PREFACE

Rite A. The Preface of the Cross (9) or (10) is said.
Rite B. Second Thanksgiving. The Preface of Passiontide
is said.

POSTCOMMUNION SENTENCE

Jesus said, When I am lifted up from the earth, I will draw all
men to myself. *John 12.32*

COMMEMORATION OF THE FAITHFUL DEPARTED
(2 November)   Violet, Black, or White

INTRODUCTORY SENTENCE

Since we believe that Jesus died and rose again, so will it be
for those who have died: God will bring them to life with
Jesus. *1 Thessalonians 4.14*

COLLECT

Merciful God,
whose Son Jesus Christ is the resurrection
   and the life of all the faithful:
raise us from the death of sin
to the life of righteousness,
that at the last we, with our *brother N*,
may come to your eternal joy;
through Jesus Christ our Lord.

PSALMS 42.1-7; 118.14-21, 28, 29

READINGS

Old Testament *Isaiah 25.6-9 NEB*

On this mountain the Lord of Hosts will prepare
a banquet of rich fare for all the peoples,
a banquet of wines well matured and richest fare,
well-matured wines strained clear.
On this mountain the Lord will swallow up
that veil that shrouds all the peoples,
the pall thrown over all the nations;
he will swallow up death for ever.
Then the Lord God will wipe away the tears from every face
and remove the reproach of his people from the whole earth.
The Lord has spoken.

On that day men will say,
See, this is our God
for whom we have waited to deliver us;
this is the Lord for whom we have waited;
let us rejoice and exult in his deliverance.

New Testament *1 Peter 1.3-9 NEB*

Praise be to the God and Father of our Lord Jesus Christ,
who in his great mercy gave us new birth into a living hope
by the resurrection of Jesus Christ from the dead! The
inheritance to which we are born is one that nothing can
destroy or spoil or wither. It is kept for you in heaven, and
you, because you put your faith in God, are under the

protection of his power until salvation comes—the salvation which is even now in readiness and will be revealed at the end of time.

This is cause for great joy, even though now you smart for a little while, if need be, under trials of many kinds. Even gold passes through the assayer's fire, and more precious than perishable gold is faith which has stood the test. These trials come so that your faith may prove itself worthy of all praise, glory, and honour when Jesus Christ is revealed.

You have not seen him, yet you love him; and trusting in him now without seeing him, you are transported with a joy too great for words, while you reap the harvest of your faith, that is, salvation for your souls.

Gospel *John 20.1-9 RSV*

On the first day of the week Mary Magdalen came to the tomb early, while it was still dark, and saw that the stone had been taken away from the tomb. So she ran, and went to Simon Peter and the other disciple, the one whom Jesus loved, and said to them, 'They have taken the Lord out of the tomb, and we do not know where they have laid him.' Peter then came out with the other disciple, and they went toward the tomb. They both ran, but the other disciple outran Peter and reached the tomb first; and stooping to look in, he saw the linen cloths lying there, but he did not go in. Then Simon Peter came, following him, and he went into the tomb; he saw the linen cloths lying, and the napkin, which had been on his head, not lying with the linen cloths but rolled up in a place by itself. Then the other disciple, who reached the tomb first, also went in, and he saw and believed; for as yet they did not know the scripture, that he must rise from the dead.

PROPER PREFACE

Rite A. A Preface of the Resurrection (13) or (14) is said.
Rite B. The Preface for Funerals is said.

POSTCOMMUNION SENTENCE

Jesus said, Whoever eats my flesh and drinks my blood has
eternal life, and I will raise him up on the last day. *John 6.54*

or

Jesus said, I am the resurrection and I am the life: whoever
lives and believes in me will never die. *John 11.25, 26*

GROUP COMMEMORATIONS White

Europe (3 February)
Africa (21 February)
The Americas (8 April)
Australia and the Pacific (20 September)
The Reformation Era (31 October)
England (8 November)
Asia (3 December)

INTRODUCTORY SENTENCE

Praise the Lord, all nations, praise him all peoples: for great
is his mercy towards us. *Psalm 117.1, 2*

or

Those whom God has called, he has justified: and those
whom he has justified, he has glorified. *Romans 8.30*

COLLECT

Almighty God,
you call your witnesses from every nation
and reveal your glory in their lives.
Make us thankful for their example
and strengthen us by their fellowship,
that we, like them, may be faithful
    in the service of your kingdom;
through Jesus Christ our Lord.

PSALMS 87; 67

READINGS

Old Testament *Isaiah 61.4-9 NEB*

Ancient ruins shall be rebuilt
and sites long desolate restored;
they shall repair the ruined cities
and restore what has long lain desolate.
Foreigners shall serve as shepherds of your flocks,
and aliens shall till your land and tend your vines;
but you shall be called priests of the Lord
and be named ministers of our God;
you shall enjoy the wealth of other nations
and be furnished with their riches.
And so, because shame in double measure
and jeers and insults have been my people's lot,
they shall receive in their own land a double measure
    of wealth,
and everlasting joy shall be theirs.
For I, the Lord, love justice
and hate robbery and wrong-doing;
I will grant them a sure reward
and make an everlasting covenant with them;
their posterity will be renowned among the nations
and their offspring among the peoples;
all who see them will acknowledge in them
a race whom the Lord has blessed.

or *Ecclesiasticus 2.10-18 RSV*

Consider the ancient generations and see:
whoever trusted in the Lord
and was put to shame?
Or who ever persevered in the fear of the Lord
and was forsaken?
Or who ever called upon him
and was overlooked?
For the Lord is compassionate and merciful;
he forgives sins and saves in time of affliction.

Woe to timid hearts and to slack hands,
and to the sinner who walks along two ways!
Woe to the faint heart, for it has no trust!

Therefore it will not be sheltered.
Woe to you who have lost your endurance!
What will you do when the Lord punishes you?
Those who fear the Lord will not disobey his words,
and those who love him will keep his ways.
Those who fear the Lord will seek his approval,
and those who love him will be filled with the law.
Those who fear the Lord will prepare their hearts,
and will humble themselves before him.
Let us fall into the hands of the Lord,
but not into the hands of men;
for as his majesty is,
so also is his mercy.

or *Ecclesiasticus 44.1-15 RSV*

Let us now praise famous men,
and our fathers in their generations.
The Lord apportioned to them great glory,
his majesty from the beginning.
There were those who ruled in their kingdoms,
and were men renowned for their power,
giving counsel by their understanding,
and proclaiming prophecies;
leaders of the people in their deliberations
and in understanding of learning for the people,
wise in their words of instruction;
those who composed musical tunes,
and set forth verses in writing;
rich men furnished with resources,
living peaceably in their habitations—
all these were honoured in their generations,
and were the glory of their times.
There are some of them who have left a name,
so that men declare their praise.
And there are some who have no memorial,
who have perished as though they had not lived;
they have become as though they had not been born,
and so have their children after them.
But these were men of mercy,
whose righteous deeds have not been forgotten;

their prosperity will remain with their descendants,
and their inheritance to their children's children.
Their descendants stand by the covenants;
their children also, for their sake.
Their posterity will continue for ever,
and their glory will not be blotted out.
Their bodies were buried in peace,
and their name lives to all generations.
Peoples will declare their wisdom,
and the congregation proclaims their praise.

New Testament *2 Corinthians 4.5-12 NEB*

It is not ourselves that we proclaim; we proclaim Christ Jesus as Lord, and ourselves as your servants, for Jesus' sake. For the same God who said, 'Out of darkness let light shine', has caused his light to shine within us, to give the light of revelation—the revelation of the glory of God in the face of Jesus Christ.

We are no better than pots of earthenware to contain this treasure, and this proves that such transcendent power does not come from us, but is God's alone. Hard-pressed on every side, we are never hemmed in; bewildered, we are never at our wits' end; hunted, we are never abandoned to our fate; struck down, we are not left to die. Wherever we go we carry death with us in our body, the death that Jesus died, that in this body also life may reveal itself, the life that Jesus lives. For continually, while still alive, we are being surrendered into the hands of death, for Jesus' sake, so that the life of Jesus also may be revealed in this mortal body of ours. Thus death is at work in us, and life in you.

or *Hebrews 11.32—12.2 RSV*

What more shall I say? For time would fail me to tell of Gideon, Barak, Samson, Jephthah, of David and Samuel and the prophets—who through faith conquered kingdoms, enforced justice, received promises, stopped the mouths of lions, quenched raging fire, escaped the edge of the sword, won strength out of weakness, became mighty in war, put foreign armies to flight. Women received their dead by resurrection. Some were tortured, refusing to accept release, that they might rise again to a better life. Others suffered mocking and scourging, and even chains and imprisonment. They were stoned, they were sawn in two, they were killed with the sword; they went about in skins of sheep and goats, destitute, afflicted, ill-treated—of whom the world was not worthy—wandering over deserts and mountains, and in dens and caves of the earth.

And all these, though well attested by their faith, did not receive what was promised, since God had foreseen something better for us, that apart from us they should not be made perfect.

Therefore, since we are surrounded by so great a cloud of witnesses, let us also lay aside every weight, and sin which clings so closely, and let us run with perseverance the race that is set before us, looking to Jesus the pioneer and perfecter of our faith, who for the joy that was set before him endured the cross, despising the shame, and is seated at the right hand of the throne of God.

or *Hebrews 13.7, 8, 15, 16 RSV*

Remember your leaders, those who spoke to you the word of God; consider the outcome of their life, and imitate their faith. Jesus Christ is the same yesterday and today and for ever. Through him then let us continually offer up a sacrifice of praise to God, that is, the fruit of lips that acknowledge his name. Do not neglect to do good and to share what you have, for such sacrifices are pleasing to God.

Gospel *John 12.20-26 JB*

Among those who went up to worship at the festival were some Greeks. These approached Philip, who came from Bethsaida in Galilee, and put this request to him, 'Sir, we should like to see Jesus.' Philip went to tell Andrew, and Andrew and Philip together went to tell Jesus.

Jesus replied to them,
'Now the hour has come
for the Son of Man to be glorified.

I tell you, most solemnly,
unless a wheat grain falls on the ground and dies,
it remains only a single grain;
but if it dies,
it yields a rich harvest.
Anyone who loves his life loses it;
anyone who hates his life in this world
will keep it for the eternal life.
If a man serves me, he must follow me,
wherever I am, my servant will be there too.
If anyone serves me, my Father will honour him.'

or *John 15.16-end JB*

Jesus said,
'You did not choose me,
no, I chose you;
and I commissioned you
to go out and to bear fruit,
fruit that will last;
and then the Father will give you
anything you ask him in my name.
What I command you
is to love one another.

'If the world hates you,
remember that it hated me before you.
If you belonged to the world,
the world would love you as its own;
but because you do not belong to the world,
because my choice withdrew you from the world,
therefore the world hates you.
Remember the words I said to you:
A servant is not greater than his master.
If they persecuted me,
they will persecute you too;
if they kept my word,
they will keep yours as well.
But it will be on my account that they will do all this,
because they do not know the one who sent me.
If I had not come,
if I had not spoken to them,

they would have been blameless;
but as it is they have no excuse for their sin.
Anyone who hates me hates my Father.
If I had not performed such works among them
as no one else has ever done,
they would be blameless;
but as it is, they have seen all this,
and still they hate both me and my Father.
But all this was only to fulfil the words written in their Law:
They hated me for no reason.
When the Advocate comes,
whom I shall send to you from the Father,
the Spirit of truth who issues from the Father,
he will be my witness.
And you too will be witnesses,
because you have been with me from the outset.'

or *John 17.18-23 JB*

Jesus raised his eyes to heaven and said,
'As you sent me into the world,
I have sent them into the world,
and for their sake I consecrate myself
so that they too may be consecrated in truth.
I pray not only for these,
but for those also
who through their words will believe in me.
May they all be one.
Father, may they be one in us,
as you are in me and I am in you,
so that the world may believe it was you who sent me.
I have given them the glory you gave to me,
that they may be one as we are one.
With me in them and you in me,
may they be so completely one
that the world will realise that it was you who sent me
and that I have loved them as much as you loved me.'

PROPER PREFACE

Rite A. The Preface of All Saints' Day (22) may be said.
Rite B. The Preface of Saints' Days may be said.

POSTCOMMUNION SENTENCE

All the ends of the earth have seen the salvation of our God.
Psalm 98.3

or

Neither death nor life nor anything in all creation can
separate us from the love of God in Christ Jesus our Lord.
Romans 8.38, 39

OF A MARTYR OR MARTYRS   Red

INTRODUCTORY SENTENCE

Anyone who wants to save his life will lose it: but anyone
who loses his life for the sake of Christ and the gospel will
save it. *Mark 8.35*

COLLECT

Almighty God,
by whose grace and power your holy *martyr N*
triumphed over suffering and *was* faithful unto death:
strengthen us with your grace,
that we may endure reproach and persecution,
and faithfully bear witness to the name
    of Jesus Christ our Lord;
who is alive and reigns with you and the Holy Spirit,
one God, now and for ever.

PSALMS 3; 11; 119.161-168

READINGS

Old Testament *2 Chronicles 24.17-21 NEB*

After the death of Jehoiada the leading men of Judah came
and made obeisance to King Joash. He listened to them, and
they forsook the house of the Lord the God of their fathers
and worshipped sacred poles and idols. And Judah and
Jerusalem suffered for this wickedness. But the Lord sent
prophets to bring them back to himself, prophets who

denounced them and were not heeded. Then the spirit of God took possession of Zechariah son of Jehoiada the priest, and he stood looking down on the people and said to them, 'This is the word of God: "Why do you disobey the commands of the Lord and court disaster? Because you have forsaken the Lord, he has forsaken you."' But they made common cause against him, and on orders from the king they stoned him to death in the court of the house of the Lord.

or *Jeremiah 11.18-20 JB*

The Lord revealed it to me; I was warned. O Lord, that was when you opened my eyes to their scheming. I for my part was like a trustful lamb being led to the slaughter-house, not knowing the schemes they were plotting against me, 'Let us destroy the tree in its strength, let us cut him off from the land of the living, so that his name may be quickly forgotten!'

But you, O Lord of hosts, who pronounce a just sentence, who probe the loins and the heart,
let me see the vengeance you will take on them,
for I have committed my cause to you.

or *Wisdom 4.10-15 RSV*

There was one who pleased God and was loved by him,
and while living among sinners he was taken up.
He was caught up lest evil change his understanding
or guile deceive his soul.
For the fascination of wickedness obscures what is good,
and roving desire perverts the innocent mind.
Being perfected in a short time, he fulfilled long years;
for his soul was pleasing to the Lord,
therefore he took him quickly from the midst of wickedness.
Yet the peoples saw and did not understand,
nor take such a thing to heart,
that God's grace and mercy are with his elect,
and he watches over his holy ones.

New Testament *Romans 8.35-end RSV*

Who shall separate us from the love of Christ? Shall tribulation, or distress, or persecution, or famine, or nakedness, or peril, or sword? As it is written,

'For thy sake we are being killed all the day long;
we are regarded as sheep to be slaughtered.'

No, in all these things we are more than conquerors through him who loved us. For I am sure that neither death, nor life, nor angels, nor principalities, nor things present, nor things to come, nor powers, nor height, nor depth, nor anything else in all creation, will be able to separate us from the love of God in Christ Jesus our Lord.

or *2 Timothy 2.3-7 NEB*

Take your share of hardship, like a good soldier of Christ Jesus. A soldier on active service will not let himself be involved in civilian affairs; he must be wholly at his commanding officer's disposal. Again, no athlete can win a prize unless he has kept the rules. The farmer who gives his labour has first claim on the crop. Reflect on what I say, for the Lord will help you to full understanding.

or *Hebrews 11.32-40 RSV*

What more shall I say? For time would fail me to tell of Gideon, Barak, Samson, Jephthah, of David and Samuel and the prophets—who through faith conquered kingdoms, enforced justice, received promises, stopped the mouths of lions, quenched raging fire, escaped the edge of the sword, won strength out of weakness, became mighty in war, put foreign armies to flight. Women received their dead by resurrection. Some were tortured, refusing to accept release, that they might rise again to a better life. Others suffered mocking and scourging, and even chains and imprisonment. They were stoned, they were sawn in two, they were killed with the sword; they went about in skins of sheep and goats, destitute, afflicted, ill-treated—of whom the world was not worthy—wandering over deserts and mountains, and in dens and caves of the earth.

And all these, though well attested by their faith, did not receive what was promised, since God had foreseen something better for us, that apart from us they should not be made perfect.

or *Revelation 7.13-end RSV*

One of the elders addressed me, saying, 'Who are these, clothed in white robes, and whence have they come?' I said to him, 'Sir, you know.' And he said to me, 'These are they who have come out of the great tribulation; they have washed their robes and made them white in the blood of the Lamb.
Therefore are they before the throne of God,
and serve him day and night within his temple;
and he who sits upon the throne
    will shelter them with his presence.
They shall hunger no more, neither thirst any more;
the sun shall not strike them, nor any scorching heat,
For the Lamb in the midst of the throne
    will be their shepherd,
and he will guide them to springs of living water;
and God will wipe away every tear from their eyes.'

Gospel *Matthew 10.16-22 JB*

Jesus said, 'Remember, I am sending you out like sheep among wolves; so be cunning as serpents and yet as harmless as doves.

'Beware of men: they will hand you over to sanhedrins and scourge you in their synagogues. You will be dragged before governors and kings for my sake, to bear witness before them and the pagans. But when they hand you over, do not worry about how to speak or what to say; what you are to say will be given to you when the time comes; because it is not you who will be speaking; the Spirit of your Father will be speaking in you.

'Brother will betray brother to death, and the father his child; children will rise against their parents and have them put to death. You will be hated by all men on account of my name; but the man who stands firm to the end will be saved.'

Of a Martyr/847

or *Matthew 14.1-12 NEB*

Reports about Jesus reached the ears of Prince Herod. 'This is John the Baptist,' he said to his attendants; 'John has been raised to life, and that is why these miraculous powers are at work in him.'

Now Herod had arrested John, put him in chains, and thrown him into prison, on account of Herodias, his brother Philip's wife; for John had told him: 'You have no right to her.' Herod would have liked to put him to death, but he was afraid of the people, in whose eyes John was a prophet. But at his birthday celebrations the daughter of Herodias danced before the guests, and Herod was so delighted that he took an oath to give her anything she cared to ask. Prompted by her mother, she said, 'Give me here on a dish the head of John the Baptist.' The king was distressed when he heard it; but out of regard for his oath and for his guests, he ordered the request to be granted, and had John beheaded in prison. The head was brought in on a dish and given to the girl; and she carried it to her mother. Then John's disciples came and took away the body, and buried it; and they went and told Jesus.

or *Matthew 16.24-26 RSV*

Jesus told his disciples, 'If any man would come after me, let him deny himself and take up his cross and follow me. For whoever would save his life will lose it, and whoever loses his life for my sake will find it. For what will it profit a man, if he gains the whole world and forfeits his life? Or what shall a man give in return for his life?'

or *John 15.18-21 JB*

Jesus said,
'If the world hates you,
remember that it hated me before you.
If you belonged to the world,
the world would love you as its own;
but because you do not belong to the world,
because my choice withdrew you from the world,
therefore the world hates you.

Remember the words I said to you:
A servant is not greater than his master.
If they persecuted me,
they will persecute you too;
if they kept my word,
they will keep yours as well.
But it will be on my account that they will do all this,
because they do not know the one who sent me.'

PROPER PREFACE

Rite A. The Preface of Martyrs (24) may be said.
Rite B. The Preface of Saints' Days may be said.

POSTCOMMUNION SENTENCE

Jesus said, Unless a grain of wheat falls on the ground and
dies, it remains a single grain: but, if it dies, it yields a rich
harvest. *John 12.24*

OF A TEACHER OF THE FAITH OR CONFESSOR White

INTRODUCTORY SENTENCE

Jesus said, Every scribe who has been trained for the
kingdom of heaven is like a householder who brings out of
his treasure what is new and what is old. *Matthew 13.52*

COLLECT

Almighty God,
you have enlightened your Church
    by the teaching of your servant *N*.
Enrich it evermore with your heavenly grace,
and raise up faithful witnesses,
who by their life and teaching
may proclaim to all men the truth of your salvation;
through Jesus Christ our Lord.

PSALMS 34.11-17; 37.30-35; 119.97-104

READINGS

Old Testament *Nehemiah 8.1-10 NEB*

When the seventh month came, and the Israelites were now settled in their towns, the people assembled as one man in the square in front of the Water Gate, and Ezra the scribe was asked to bring the book of the law of Moses, which the Lord had enjoined upon Israel . On the first day of the seventh month, Ezra the priest brought the law before the assembly, every man and woman, and all who were capable of understanding what they heard. He read from it, facing the square in front of the Water Gate, from early morning till noon, in the presence of the men and the women, and those who could understand; all the people listened attentively to the book of the law. Ezra the scribe stood on a wooden platform made for the purpose, and beside him stood Mattithiah, Shema, Anaiah, Uriah, Hilkiah, and Maaseiah on his right hand; and on his left Pedaiah, Mishael, Malchiah, Hashum, Hashbaddanah, Zechariah and Meshullam. Ezra opened the book in the sight of all the people, for he was standing above them; and when he opened it, they all stood. Ezra blessed the Lord, the great God, and all the people raised their hands and answered, 'Amen, Amen'; and they bowed their heads and prostrated themselves humbly before the Lord. Jeshua, Bani, Sherebiah, Jamin, Akkub, Shabbethai, Hodiah, Maaseiah, Kelita, Azariah, Jozabad, Hanan, Pelaiah, the Levites, expounded the law to the people while they remained in their places. They read from the book of the law of God clearly, made its sense plain and gave instruction in what was read.

Then Nehemiah the governor and Ezra the priest and scribe, and the Levites who instructed the people, said to them all, 'This day is holy to the Lord your God; do not mourn or weep.' For all the people had been weeping while they listened to the words of the law. Then he said to them, 'You may go now; refresh yourselves with rich food and sweet drinks, and send a share to all who cannot provide for themselves; for this day is holy to our Lord. Let there be no sadness, for joy in the Lord is your strength.'

or *Proverbs 4.1-9 RSV*

Hear, O sons, a father's instruction,
and be attentive, so that you may gain insight;
for I give you good precepts:
do not forsake my teaching.
When I was a son with my father,
tender, the only one in the sight of my mother,
he taught me, and said to me,
'Let your heart hold fast my words;
keep my commandments, and live;
do not forget, and do not turn away from the words of
my mouth.
Get wisdom; get insight.
Do not forsake her, and she will keep you;
love her , and she will guard you.
The beginning of wisdom is this: Get wisdom,
and whatever you get, get insight.
Prize her highly, and she will exalt you;
she will honour you if you embrace her.
She will place on your head a fair garland;
she will bestow on you a beautiful crown.'

or *Ecclesiasticus 39.1-10 RSV*

He who devotes himself
to the study of the law of the Most High
will seek out the wisdom of all the ancients,
and will be concerned with prophecies;
he will preserve the discourse of notable men
and penetrate the subtleties of parables;
he will seek out the hidden meanings of proverbs
and be at home with the obscurities of parables.
He will serve among great men
and appear before rulers;
he will travel through the lands of foreign nations,
for he tests the good and the evil among men.
He will set his heart to rise early
to seek the Lord who made him,
and he will make supplication before the Most High;
he will open his mouth in prayer
and make supplication for his sins.

If the great Lord is willing,
he will be filled with the spirit of understanding;
he will pour forth words of wisdom
and give thanks to the Lord in prayer.
He will direct his counsel and knowledge aright,
and meditate on his secrets.
He will reveal instruction in his teaching,
and will glory in the law of the Lord's covenant.
Many will praise his understanding,
and it will never be blotted out;
his memory will not disappear,
and his name will live through all generations.
Nations will declare his wisdom,
and the congregation will proclaim his praise.

New Testament *1 Corinthians 2.6-13 NEB*

I speak words of wisdom to those who are ripe for it, not a wisdom belonging to this passing age, nor to any of its governing powers, which are declining to their end; I speak of God's hidden wisdom, his secret purpose framed from the very beginning to bring us to our full glory. The powers that rule the world have never known it; if they had, they would not have crucified the Lord of glory. But, in the words of Scripture, 'Things beyond our seeing, things beyond our hearing, things beyond our imagining, all prepared by God for those who love him', these it is that God has revealed to us through the Spirit.

For the Spirit explores everything, even the depths of God's own nature. Among men, who knows what a man is but the man's own spirit within him? In the same way, only the Spirit of God knows what God is. This is the Spirit that we have received from God, and not the spirit of the world, so that we may know all that God of his own grace has given us; and, because we are interpreting spiritual truths to those who have the Spirit, we speak of these gifts of God in words found for us not by our human wisdom but by the Spirit.

or *2 Timothy 4.1-8 NEB*

Before God, and before Christ Jesus who is to judge men living and dead, I charge you solemnly by his coming appearance and his reign, proclaim the message, press it home on all occasions, convenient or inconvenient, use argument, reproof, and appeal, with all the patience that the work of teaching requires. For the time will come when they will not stand wholesome teaching, but will follow their own fancy and gather a crowd of teachers to tickle their ears. They will stop their ears to the truth and turn to mythology. But you yourself must keep calm and sane at all times; face hardship, work to spread the Gospel, and do all the duties of your calling.

As for me, already my life is being poured out on the altar, and the hour for my departure is upon me. I have run the great race, I have finished the course, I have kept faith. And now the prize awaits me, the garland of righteousness which the Lord, the all-just Judge, will award me on that great Day; and it is not for me alone, but for all who have set their hearts on his coming appearance.

or *Titus 2.1-8 NEB*

For your own part, what you say must be in keeping with wholesome doctrine. Let the older men know that they should be sober, high-principled, and temperate, sound in faith, in love, and in endurance. The older women, similarly, should be reverent in their bearing, not scandal-mongers or slaves to strong drink; they must set a high standard, and school the younger women to be loving wives and mothers, temperate, chaste, and kind, busy at home, respecting the authority of their own husbands. Thus the Gospel will not be brought into disrepute.

Urge the younger men, similarly, to be temperate in all things, and set them a good example yourself. In your teaching, you must show integrity and high principle, and use wholesome speech to which none can take exception. This will shame any opponent, when he finds not a word to say to our discredit.

Gospel *Matthew 5.13-19 JB*

Jesus said, 'You are the salt of the earth. But if salt becomes tasteless, what can make it salty again? It is good for nothing, and can only be thrown out to be trampled underfoot by men.

'You are the light of the world. A city built on a hill-top cannot be hidden. No one lights a lamp to put it under a tub; they put it on the lamp-stand where it shines for everyone in the house. In the same way your light must shine in the sight of men, so that, seeing your good works, they may give the praise to your Father in heaven.

'Do not imagine that I have come to abolish the Law or the Prophets. I have come not to abolish but to complete them. I tell you solemnly, till heaven and earth disappear, not one dot, not one little stroke, shall disappear from the Law until its purpose is achieved. Therefore, the man who infringes even one of the least of these commandments and teaches others to do the same will be considered the least in the kingdom of heaven; but the man who keeps them and teaches them will be considered great in the kingdom of heaven.'

or *Matthew 13.52-end NEB*

Jesus said to his disciples, 'When a teacher of the law has become a learner in the kingdom of Heaven, he is like a householder who can produce from his store both the new and the old.'

When he had finished these parables Jesus left that place, and came to his home town, where he taught the people in their synagogue. In amazement they asked, 'Where does he get this wisdom from, and these miraculous powers? Is he not the carpenter's son? Is not his mother called Mary, his brothers James, Joseph, Simon, and Judas? And are not all his sisters here with us? Where then has he got all this from?' So they fell foul of him, and this led him to say, 'A prophet will always be held in honour, except in his home town, and in his own family.' And he did not work many miracles there: such was their want of faith.

or *John 16.12-15 NEB*

Jesus said: 'There is still much that I could say to you, but the burden would be too great for you now. However, when he comes who is the Spirit of truth, he will guide you into all the truth; for he will not speak on his own authority, but will tell only what he hears; and he will make known to you the things that are coming. He will glorify me, for everything that he makes known to you he will draw from what is mine. All that the Father has is mine, and that is why I said, "Everything that he makes known to you he will draw from what is mine."'

PROPER PREFACE

Rite A. The Preface of Saints (25) may be said.
Rite B. The Preface of Saints' Days may be said.

POSTCOMMUNION SENTENCE

Jesus said, If anyone serves me, he must follow me: where I am, there my servant will be, and whoever serves me will be honoured by my Father. *John 12.26*

OF A BISHOP   White

INTRODUCTORY SENTENCE

The Spirit of the Lord is upon me, because he has anointed me; he has sent me to bring good news, to proclaim release, to set the downtrodden free, and to proclaim the year of the Lord's favour. *Luke 4.18, 19*

COLLECT

Almighty God,
the light of the faithful
and shepherd of souls,
who set your servant *N* to be a bishop in the Church,
to feed your sheep by his word
and guide them by his example:

give us grace to keep the faith which he taught
and to follow in his footsteps;
through Jesus Christ our Lord.

PSALMS 1; 15; 99

READINGS

Old Testament *Numbers 27.15-end NEB*

Moses said, 'Let the Lord, the God of the spirits of all
mankind, appoint a man over the community to go out and
come in at their head, to lead them out and bring them
home, so that the community of the Lord may not be like
sheep without a shepherd.' The Lord answered Moses,
'Take Joshua son of Nun, a man endowed with spirit; lay
your hand on him and set him before Eleazar the priest and
all the community. Give him his commission in their
presence, and delegate some of your authority to him, so
that all the community of the Israelites may obey him. He
must appear before Eleazar the priest, who will obtain a
decision for him by consulting the Urim before the Lord; at
his word they shall go out and shall come home, both Joshua
and the whole community of the Israelites.'

Moses did as the Lord had commanded him. He took
Joshua, presented him to Eleazar the priest and the whole
community, laid his hands on him and gave him his
commission, as the Lord had instructed him.

or *Jeremiah 1.4-10 NEB*

The word of the Lord came to me: 'Before I formed you in the
womb I knew you for my own; before you were born I
consecrated you, I appointed you a prophet to the nations.'
'Ah! Lord God,' I answered, 'I do not know how to speak; I
am only a child.' But the Lord said, 'Do not call yourself a
child; for you shall go to whatever people I send you and say
whatever I tell you to say. Fear none of them, for I am with
you and will keep you safe.' This was the very word of the
Lord. Then the Lord stretched out his hand and touched my
mouth, and said to me, 'I put my words into your mouth.
This day I give you authority over nations and over

kingdoms, to pull down and to uproot, to destroy and to demolish, to build and to plant.'

or *Ezekiel 34.11-16 NEB*

These are the words of the Lord God: Now I myself will ask after my sheep and go in search of them. As a shepherd goes in search of his sheep when his flock is dispersed all around him, so I will go in search of my sheep and rescue them, no matter where they were scattered in dark and cloudy days. I will bring them out from every nation, gather them in from other lands, and lead them home to their own soil. I will graze them on the mountains of Israel, by her streams and in all her green fields. I will feed them on good grazing ground, and their pasture shall be the high mountains of Israel. There they will rest, there in good pasture, and find rich grazing on the mountains of Israel. I myself will tend my flock, I myself pen them in their fold, says the Lord God. I will search for the lost, recover the straggler, bandage the hurt, strengthen the sick, leave the healthy and strong to play, and give them their proper food.

New Testament *Acts 20.28-35 TEV*

'Keep watch over yourselves and over all the flock which the Holy Spirit has placed in your care. Be shepherds of the church of God, which he made his own through the death of his Son. I know that after I leave, fierce wolves will come among you, and they will not spare the flock. The time will come when some men from your own group will tell lies to lead the believers away after them. Watch, then, and remember that with many tears, day and night, I taught every one of you for three years.

'And now I commend you to the care of God and to the message of his grace, which is able to build you up and give you the blessings God has for all his people. I have not wanted anyone's silver or gold or clothing. You yourselves know that I have worked with these hands of mine to provide everything that my companions and I have needed. I have shown you in all things that by working hard in this way we must help the weak, remembering the words that the Lord Jesus himself said, "There is more happiness in giving than in receiving."'

or *2 Corinthians 4.1-10 NEB*

Seeing that we have been entrusted with this commission, which we owe entirely to God's mercy, we never lose heart. We have renounced the deeds that men hide for very shame; we neither practise cunning nor distort the word of God; only by declaring the truth openly do we recommend ourselves, and then it is to the common conscience of our fellow-men and in the sight of God. And if indeed our gospel be found veiled, the only people who find it so are those on the way to perdition. Their unbelieving minds are so blinded by the god of this passing age, that the gospel of the glory of Christ, who is the very image of God, cannot dawn upon them and bring them light. It is not ourselves that we proclaim; we proclaim Christ Jesus as Lord, and ourselves as your servants, for Jesus' sake. For the same God who said, 'Out of darkness let light shine', has caused his light to shine within us, to give the light of revelation—the revelation of the glory of God in the face of Jesus Christ.

We are no better than pots of earthenware to contain this treasure, and this proves that such transcendent power does not come from us, but is God's alone. Hard-pressed on every side, we are never hemmed in; bewildered, we are never at our wits' end; hunted, we are never abandoned to our fate; struck down, we are not left to die. Wherever we go we carry death with us in our body, the death that Jesus died, that in this body also life may reveal itself, the life that Jesus lives.

or *Ephesians 4.7-16 NEB*

Each of us has been given his gift, his due portion of Christ's bounty. Therefore Scripture says:

'He ascended into the heights
with captives in his train;
he gave gifts to men.'

Now, the word 'ascended' implies that he also descended to the lowest level, down to the very earth. He who descended is no other than he who ascended far above all heavens, so that he might fill the universe. And these were his gifts: some to be apostles, some prophets, some evangelists, some pastors and teachers, to equip God's people for work in his service, to the building up of the body of Christ. So shall we all at last attain to the unity inherent in our faith and our knowledge of the Son of God—to mature manhood, measured by nothing less than the full stature of Christ. We are no longer to be children, tossed by the waves and whirled about by every fresh gust of teaching, dupes of crafty rogues and their deceitful schemes. No, let us speak the truth in love; so shall we fully grow up into Christ. He is the head, and on him the whole body depends. Bonded and knit together by every constituent joint, the whole frame grows through the due activity of each part, and builds itself up in love.

or *1 Peter 5.1-4 NEB*

I appeal to the elders of your community, as a fellow-elder and a witness of Christ's sufferings, and also a partaker in the splendour that is to be revealed. Tend that flock of God whose shepherds you are, and do it, not under compulsion, but of your own free will, as God would have it; not for gain but out of sheer devotion; not tyrannizing over those who are allotted to your care, but setting an example to the flock. And then, when the Head Shepherd appears, you will receive for your own the unfading garland of glory.

Gospel *Matthew 24.42-46 NEB*

Jesus said, 'Keep awake for you do not know on what day your Lord is to come. Remember, if the householder had known at what time of night the burglar was coming, he would have kept awake and not have let his house be broken into. Hold yourselves ready, therefore, because the Son of Man will come at the time you least expect him.

'Who is the trusty servant, the sensible man charged by his master to manage his household staff and issue their rations at the proper time? Happy that servant who is found at his task when his master comes!'

or *John 10.11-16 NEB*

Jesus said, 'I am the good shepherd; the good shepherd lays down his life for the sheep. The hireling, when he sees the wolf coming, abandons the sheep and runs away, because he is no shepherd and the sheep are not his. Then the wolf harries the flock and scatters the sheep. The man runs away because he is a hireling and cares nothing for the sheep.

'I am the good shepherd; I know my own sheep and my sheep know me—as the Father knows me and I know the Father—and I lay down my life for the sheep. But there are other sheep of mine, not belonging to this fold, whom I must bring in; and they too will listen to my voice. There will then be one flock, one shepherd.'

or *John 21.15-17 RSV*

When they had finished breakfast, Jesus said to Simon Peter, 'Simon, son of John, do you love me more than these?' He said to him, 'Yes, Lord; you know that I love you.' He said to him, 'Feed my lambs.' A second time he said to him, 'Simon, son of John, do you love me?' He said to him, 'Yes, Lord; you know that I love you.' He said to him, 'Tend my sheep.' He said to him the third time, 'Simon, son of John, do you love me?' Peter was grieved because he said to him the third time, 'Do you love me?' And he said to him, 'Lord, you know everything; you know that I love you.' Jesus said to him, 'Feed my sheep.'

PROPER PREFACE

Rite A. The Preface of Saints (25) may be said.
Rite B. The Preface of Saints' Days may be said.

POSTCOMMUNION SENTENCE

Jesus said, You have not chosen me; I have chosen you. Go and bear fruit that will last. *John 15.16*

OF AN ABBOT OR ABBESS   White

INTRODUCTORY SENTENCE

The Lord is my inheritance and my cup: he alone will give me my reward. *Psalm 16.5*

COLLECT

Almighty God,
by whose grace *N*,
kindled with the fire of your love,
became a burning and a shining light in the Church:
inflame us with the same spirit
of discipline and love,
that we may ever walk before you
as children of light;
through Jesus Christ our Lord.

PSALMS 119.57-64; 123; 131

READINGS

Old Testament *1 Kings 19.9-18 RSV*

Elijah came to a cave, and lodged there; and behold, the word of the Lord came to him, and he said to him, 'What are you doing here, Elijah?' He said, 'I have been very jealous for the Lord, the God of hosts; for the people of Israel have forsaken your covenant, thrown down your altars, and slain your prophets with the sword; and I, even I only, am left; and they seek my life, to take it away.' And he said, 'Go forth, and stand upon the mount before the Lord.' And behold, the Lord passed by, and a great and strong wind rent the mountains, and broke in pieces the rocks before the Lord, but the Lord was not in the wind; and after the wind an earthquake, but the Lord was not in the earthquake; and after the earthquake a fire, but the Lord was not in the fire; and after the fire a still small voice. And when Elijah heard it, he wrapped his face in his mantle and went out and stood at the entrance of the cave. And behold, there came a voice to him, and said, 'What are you doing here, Elijah?' He said, 'I have been very jealous for the Lord, the God of hosts; for the people of Israel have forsaken your covenant, thrown down your altars, and slain your prophets with the sword; and I, even I only, am left; and they seek my life, to take it away.' And the Lord said to him, 'Go, return on your way to the wilderness of Damascus; and when you arrive, you shall anoint Hazael to be king over Syria; and Jehu the son of Nimshi you shall anoint to be king over Israel; and Elisha the son of Shaphat of Abelmeholah you shall anoint to be prophet in your place. And him who escapes from the sword of Hazael shall Jehu slay; and him who escapes from the sword of Jehu shall Elisha slay. Yet I will leave seven thousand in Israel, all the knees that have not bowed to Baal, and every mouth that has not kissed him.'

or *Proverbs 10.27-32 RSV*

The fear of the Lord prolongs life,
but the years of the wicked will be short.
The hope of the righteous ends in gladness,
but the expectation of the wicked comes to nought.
The Lord is a stronghold to him whose way is upright,
but destruction to evildoers.
The righteous will never be removed,
but the wicked will not dwell in the land.
The mouth of the righteous brings forth wisdom,
but the perverse tongue will be cut off.
The lips of the righteous know what is acceptable,
but the mouth of the wicked, what is perverse.

or *Isaiah 61.10—62.5 RSV*

I will greatly rejoice in the Lord,
my soul shall exult in my God;
for he has clothed me with the garments of salvation,
he has covered me with the robe of righteousness,
as a bridegroom decks himself with a garland,
and as a bride adorns herself with her jewels.
For as the earth brings forth its shoots,
and as a garden causes what is sown in it to spring up,
so the Lord God will cause righteousness and praise
to spring forth before all the nations.

For Zion's sake I will not keep silent,
and for Jerusalem's sake I will not rest,
until her vindication goes forth as brightness,
and her salvation as a burning torch.
The nations shall see your vindication,
and all the kings your glory;
and you shall be called by a new name
which the mouth of the Lord will give.
You shall be a crown of beauty in the hand of the Lord,
and a royal diadem in the hand of your God.
You shall no more be termed Forsaken,
and your land shall no more be termed Desolate;
but you shall be called My delight is in her,
and your land Married;
for the Lord delights in you,
and your land shall be married.
For as a young man marries a virgin,
so shall your sons marry you,
and as the bridegroom rejoices over the bride,
so shall your God rejoice over you.

New Testament *Philippians 3.7-14 JB*

Because of Christ, I have come to consider all these
advantages that I had as disadvantages. Not only that, but I
believe nothing can happen that will outweigh the supreme
advantage of knowing Christ Jesus my Lord. For him I have
accepted the loss of everything, and I look on everything as
so much rubbish if only I can have Christ and be given a
place in him. I am no longer trying for perfection by my own
efforts, the perfection that comes from the Law, but I want
only the perfection that comes through faith in Christ, and is
from God and based on faith.

All I want is to know Christ and the power of his resurrection
and to share his sufferings by reproducing the pattern of his
death. That is the way I can hope to take my place in the
resurrection of the dead. Not that I have become perfect yet:
I have not yet won, but I am still running, trying to capture
the prize for which Christ Jesus captured me. I can assure
you my brothers, I am far from thinking that I have already
won. All I can say is that I forget the past and I strain ahead

for what is still to come; I am racing for the finish, for the prize to which God calls us upwards to receive in Christ Jesus.

or 1 John 2.15-17 NEB

Do not set your hearts on the godless world or anything in it. Anyone who loves the world is a stranger to the Father's love. Everything the world affords, all that panders to the appetites or entices the eyes, all the glamour of its life, springs not from the Father but from the godless world. And that world is passing away with all its allurements, but he who does God's will stands for evermore.

or 3 John 2-8 NEB

My dear Gaius, I pray that you may enjoy good health, and that all may go well with you, as I know it goes well with your soul. I was delighted when friends came and told me how true you have been; indeed you are true in your whole life. Nothing gives me greater joy than to hear that my children are living by the truth.

My dear friend, you show a fine loyalty in everything that you do for these our fellow-Christians, strangers though they are to you. They have spoken of your kindness before the congregation here. Please help them on their journey in a manner worthy of the God we serve. It was on Christ's work that they went out; and they would accept nothing from pagans. We are bound to support such men, and so play our part in spreading the truth.

Gospel *Matthew 11.25-30 JB*

Jesus said, 'I bless you, Father, Lord of heaven and of earth, for hiding these things from the learned and the clever and revealing them to mere children. Yes, Father, for that is what it pleased you to do. Everything has been entrusted to me by my Father; and no one knows the Son except the Father, just as no one knows the Father except the Son and those to whom the Son chooses to reveal him.

'Come to me, all you who labour and are overburdened, and I will give you rest. Shoulder my yoke and learn from me, for I am gentle and humble in heart, and you will find rest for your souls. Yes, my yoke is easy and my burden light.'

or *Matthew 19.23-end NEB*

Jesus said to his disciples, 'I tell you this: a rich man will find it hard to enter the kingdom of Heaven. I repeat, it is easier for a camel to pass through the eye of a needle than for a rich man to enter the kingdom of God.' The disciples were amazed to hear this. 'Then who can be saved?' they asked. Jesus looked at them, and said, 'For men this is impossible; but everything is possible for God.'

At this Peter said, 'We here have left everything to become your followers. What will there be for us?' Jesus replied, 'I tell you this: in the world that is to be, when the Son of Man is seated on his throne in heavenly splendour, you my followers will have thrones of your own, where you will sit as judges of the twelve tribes of Israel. And anyone who has left brothers or sisters, father, mother, or children, land or houses for the sake of my name will be repaid many times over, and gain eternal life. But many who are first will be last, and the last first.'

or *Luke 12.32-37 NEB*

Jesus said, 'Have no fear, little flock; for your Father has chosen to give you the Kingdom. Sell your possessions and give in charity. Provide for yourselves purses that do not wear out, and never-failing treasure in heaven, where no thief can get near it, no moth destroy it. For where your treasure is, there will your heart be also.

'Be ready for action, with belts fastened and lamps alight. Be like men who wait for their master's return from a wedding-party, ready to let him in the moment he arrives and knocks. Happy are those servants whom the master finds on the alert when he comes. I tell you this: he will fasten his belt, seat them at table, and come and wait on them.'

PROPER PREFACE

Rite A. The Preface of Saints (25) may be said.
Rite B. The Preface of Saints' Days may be said.

POSTCOMMUNION SENTENCE

Those who have left houses, brothers, sisters, father,
mother, children, or land, for the sake of Christ, will be
repaid a hundredfold and will inherit eternal life.
Matthew 19.29

OF MISSIONARIES   White

INTRODUCTORY SENTENCE

How beautiful on the mountains are the feet of those who
bring the good news of peace, joy, and salvation. *Isaiah 52.7*

COLLECT

Everlasting God,
whose *servant N* carried the good news of your Son
to the dark places of the world:
grant that we who commemorate *his* service
may know the hope of the gospel in our hearts
and manifest its light in all our ways;
through Jesus Christ our Lord.

PSALMS 67; 96.1-6; 96.7-end

READINGS

Old Testament *Isaiah 52.7-10 NEB*

How lovely on the mountains are the feet of the herald
who comes to proclaim prosperity and bring good news,
the news of deliverance,
calling to Zion, 'Your God is king.'
Hark, your watchmen raise their voices
and shout together in triumph;
for with their own eyes they shall see
the Lord returning in pity to Zion.

Break forth together in shouts of triumph,
you ruins of Jerusalem;
for the Lord has taken pity on his people
and has ransomed Jerusalem.
The Lord has bared his holy arm
in the sight of all nations,
and the whole world from end to end
shall see the deliverance of our God.

or *Isaiah 61.1-3a NEB*

The spirit of the Lord God is upon me
because the Lord has anointed me;
he has sent me to bring good news to the humble;
to bind up the broken-hearted,
to proclaim liberty to captives
and release to those in prison;
to proclaim a year of the Lord's favour
and a day of the vengeance of our God;
to comfort all who mourn,
to give them garlands instead of ashes,
oil of gladness instead of mourners' tears,
a garment of splendour for the heavy heart.

or *Jonah 3.1-5 TEV*

Once again the Lord spoke to Jonah. He said, 'Go to
Nineveh, that great city, and proclaim to the people the
message I have given you.' So Jonah obeyed the Lord and
went to Nineveh, a city so large that it took three days to
walk through it. Jonah started through the city, and after
walking a whole day, he proclaimed, 'In forty days Nineveh
will be destroyed!'

The people of Nineveh believed God's message. So they
decided that everyone should fast, and all the people, from
the greatest to the least, put on sackcloth to show that they
had repented.

New Testament *Acts 16.6-10 RSV*

Paul and Timothy went through the region of Phrygia and
Galatia, having been forbidden by the Holy Spirit to speak

the word in Asia. And when they had come opposite Mysia, they attempted to go into Bithynia, but the Spirit of Jesus did not allow them; so, passing by Mysia, they went down to Troas. And a vision appeared to Paul in the night: a man of Macedonia was standing beseeching him and saying, 'Come over to Macedonia and help us.' And when he had seen the vision, immediately we sought to go on into Macedonia, concluding that God had called us to preach the gospel to them.

or *Romans 15.17-21 NEB*

In the fellowship of Christ Jesus I have ground for pride in the service of God. I will venture to speak of those things alone in which I have been Christ's instrument to bring the Gentiles into his allegiance, by word and deed, by the force of miraculous signs and by the power of the Holy Spirit. As a result I have completed the preaching of the gospel of Christ from Jerusalem as far as Illyricum. It is my ambition to bring the Gospel to places where the very name of Christ has not been heard, for I do not want to build on another man's foundation; but, as Scripture says,

'They who had no news of him shall see,
and they who never heard of him shall understand.'

or *2 Corinthians 5.11—6.2 NEB*

With this fear of the Lord before our eyes we address our appeal to men. To God our lives lie open, as I hope they also lie open to you in your heart of hearts. This is not another attempt to recommend ourselves to you: we are rather giving you a chance to show yourselves proud of us; then you will have something to say to those whose pride is all in outward show and not in inward worth. It may be we are beside ourselves, but it is for God; if we are in our right mind, it is for you. For the love of Christ leaves us no choice, when once we have reached the conclusion that one man died for all and therefore all mankind has died. His purpose in dying for all was that men, while still in life, should cease to live for themselves, and should live for him who for their sake died and was raised to life. With us therefore worldly standards have ceased to count in our estimate of any man; even if once they counted in our understanding of Christ, they do so now no longer. When anyone is united to Christ, there is a new world; the old order has gone, and a new order has already begun.

From first to last this has been the work of God. He has reconciled us men to himself through Christ, and he has enlisted us in this service of reconciliation. What I mean is, that God was in Christ reconciling the world to himself, no longer holding men's misdeeds against them, and that he has entrusted us with the message of reconciliation. We come therefore as Christ's ambassadors. It is as if God were appealing to you through us: in Christ's name, we implore you, be reconciled to God! Christ was innocent of sin, and yet for our sake God made him one with the sinfulness of men, so that in him we might be made one with the goodness of God himself. Sharing in God's work, we urge this appeal upon you: you have received the grace of God; do not let it go for nothing. God's own words are:

'In the hour of my favour I gave heed to you;
on the day of deliverance I came to your aid.'

The hour of favour has now come; now, I say, has the day of deliverance dawned.

Gospel *Matthew 9.35-end NEB*

Jesus went round all the towns and villages teaching in their synagogues, announcing the good news of the Kingdom, and curing every kind of ailment and disease. The sight of the people moved him to pity: they were like sheep without a shepherd, harassed and helpless; and he said to his disciples, 'The crop is heavy, but labourers are scarce; you must therefore beg the owner to send labourers to harvest his crop.'

or *Matthew 28.16-end JB*

The eleven disciples set out for Galilee, to the mountain where Jesus had arranged to meet them. When they saw him they fell down before him, though some hesitated. Jesus came up and spoke to them. He said, 'All authority in heaven and on earth has been given to me. Go, therefore, make disciples of all the nations, baptize them in the name of the Father and of the Son and of the Holy Spirit, and teach them to observe all the commands I gave you. And know that I am with you always; yes, to the end of time.'

or *Luke 10.1-9 NEB*

The Lord appointed a further seventy-two and sent them on ahead in pairs to every town and place he was going to visit himself. He said to them: 'The crop is heavy, but labourers are scarce; you must therefore beg the owner to send labourers to harvest his crop. Be on your way. And look, I am sending you like lambs among wolves. Carry no purse or pack, and travel barefoot. Exchange no greetings on the road. When you go into a house, let your first words be, "Peace to this house." If there is a man of peace there, your peace will rest upon him; if not, it will return and rest upon you. Stay in that one house, sharing their food and drink; for the worker earns his pay. Do not move from house to house. When you come into a town and they make you welcome, eat the food provided for you; heal the sick there, and say, "The kingdom of God has come close to you."'

PROPER PREFACE

Rite A. The Preface of Pentecost (18) or of Saints (25) may be said.
Rite B. The Preface of Pentecost or of Saints' Days may be said.

POSTCOMMUNION SENTENCE

Go out to all the world and proclaim the good news to all creation. *Mark 16.15*

OF ANY SAINT White

INTRODUCTORY SENTENCE

a. For Women Saints

The woman that fears the Lord shall be praised: her children
stand up and proclaim her blessed, her husband praises her.
Proverbs 31.30, 28

or

I have betrothed you to Christ as a chaste virgin to her true
and only husband. *2 Corinthians 11.2*

b. General

The righteous shall receive blessing from the Lord,
vindication from God their Saviour: for these are the people
who long to see his face. *Psalm 24.5, 6*

COLLECT

Almighty God,
you have built up your Church
through the love and devotion of your saints.
We give thanks for your *servant N*,
whom we commemorate today.
Inspire us to follow *his* example,
that we in our generation may rejoice with *him*
in the vision of your glory;
through Jesus Christ our Lord.

PSALMS 32; 34.1-10; 34.11-18; 112; 119.1-8

READINGS

Old Testament *Proverbs 8.1-11 RSV*

Does not wisdom call,
does not understanding raise her voice?
On the heights beside the way,
in the paths she takes her stand;
beside the gates in front of the town,
at the entrance of the portals she cries aloud:

'To you, O men, I call,
and my cry is to the sons of men.
O simple ones, learn prudence;
O foolish men, pay attention.
Hear, for I will speak noble things,
and from my lips will come what is right;
for my mouth will utter truth;
wickedness is an abomination to my lips.
All the words of my mouth are righteous;
there is nothing twisted or crooked in them.
They are all straight to him who understands
and right to those who find knowledge.
Take my instruction instead of silver,
and knowledge rather than choice gold;
for wisdom is better than jewels,
and all that you may desire cannot compare with her.'

or *Proverbs 31.10-end RSV*

A good wife who can find?
She is far more precious than jewels.
The heart of her husband trusts in her,
and he will have no lack of gain.
She does him good, and not harm,
all the days of her life.
She seeks wool and flax,
and works with willing hands.
She is like the ships of the merchant,
she brings her food from afar.
She rises while it is yet night
and provides food for her household
and tasks for her maidens.
She considers a field and buys it;
with the fruit of her hands she plants a vineyard.
She girds her loins with strength
and makes her arms strong.
She perceives that her merchandise is profitable.
Her lamp does not go out at night.
She puts her hands to the distaff,
and her hands hold the spindle.
She opens her hand to the poor,

and reaches out her hands to the needy.
She is not afraid of snow for her household,
for all her household are clothed in scarlet.
She makes herself coverings;
her clothing is fine linen and purple.
Her husband is known in the gates,
when he sits among the elders of the land.
She makes linen garments and sells them;
she delivers girdles to the merchant.
Strength and dignity are her clothing,
and she laughs at the time to come.
She opens her mouth with wisdom,
and the teaching of kindness is on her tongue.
She looks well to the ways of her household,
and does not eat the bread of idleness.
Her children rise up and call her blessed;
her husband also, and he praises her:
'Many women have done excellently,
but you surpass them all.'
Charm is deceitful, and beauty is vain,
but a woman who fears the Lord is to be praised.
Give her of the fruit of her hands,
and let her works praise her in the gates.

or *Malachi 2.5-7 RSV*

My covenant with him was a covenant of life and peace, and
I gave them to him, that he might fear; and he feared me, he
stood in awe of my name. True instruction was in his mouth,
and no wrong was found on his lips. He walked with me in
peace and uprightness, and he turned many from iniquity.
For the lips of a priest should guard knowledge, and men
should seek instruction from his mouth, for he is the
messenger of the Lord of hosts.

or *Ecclesiasticus 2.1-6 RSV*

My son, if you come forward to serve the Lord,
prepare yourself for temptation.
Set your heart right and be steadfast,
and do not be hasty in time of calamity.
Cleave to him and do not depart,

that you may be honoured at the end of your life.
Accept whatever is brought upon you,
and in changes that humble you be patient.
For gold is tested in the fire,
and acceptable men in the furnace of humiliation.
Trust in him, and he will help you;
make your ways straight, and hope in him.

New Testament 2 *Corinthians 4.11-18 NEB*

Continually, while still alive, we are being surrendered into
the hands of death, for Jesus' sake, so that the life of Jesus
also may be revealed in this mortal body of ours. Thus death
is at work in us, and life in you.

But Scripture says, 'I believed, and therefore I spoke out',
and we too, in the same spirit of faith, believe and therefore
speak out; for we know that he who raised the Lord Jesus to
life will with Jesus raise us too, and bring us to his presence,
and you with us. Indeed, it is for your sake that all things are
ordered, so that, as the abounding grace of God is shared by
more and more, the greater may be the chorus of
thanksgiving that ascends to the glory of God.

No wonder we do not lose heart! Though our outward
humanity is in decay, yet day by day we are inwardly
renewed. Our troubles are slight and short-lived; and their
outcome an eternal glory which outweighs them far.
Meanwhile our eyes are fixed, not on the things that are
seen, but on the things that are unseen: for what is seen
passes away; what is unseen is eternal.

or *Ephesians 4.22-end RSV*

Put off your old nature which belongs to your former
manner of life and is corrupt through deceitful lusts, and be
renewed in the spirit of your minds, and put on the new
nature, created after the likeness of God in true
righteousness and holiness.

Therefore, putting away falsehood, let everyone speak the
truth with his neighbour, for we are members one of
another. Be angry but do not sin; do not let the sun go down

on your anger, and give no opportunity to the devil. Let the thief no longer steal, but rather let him labour doing honest work with his hands, so that he may be able to give to those in need. Let no evil talk come out of your mouths, but only such as is good for edifying, as fits the occasion, that it may impart grace to those who hear. And do not grieve the Holy Spirit of God, in whom you were sealed for the day of redemption. Let all bitterness and wrath and anger and clamour and slander be put away from you, with all malice, and be kind to one another, tender-hearted, forgiving one another, as God in Christ forgave you.

or *Ephesians 6.11-18 RSV*

Put on the whole armour of God, that you may be able to stand against the wiles of the devil. For we are not contending against flesh and blood, but against principalities, against the powers, against the world rulers of this present darkness, against the spiritual hosts of wickedness in the heavenly places. Therefore take the whole armour of God, that you may be able to withstand in the evil day, and having done all, to stand. Stand therefore, having girded your loins with truth, and having put on the breastplate of righteousness, and having shod your feet with the equipment of the gospel of peace; above all taking the shield of faith, with which you can quench all the flaming darts of the evil one. And take the helmet of salvation, and the sword of the Spirit, which is the word of God. Pray at all times in the Spirit, with all prayer and supplication. To that end keep alert with all perseverance, making supplication for all the saints.

or *Hebrews 13.1-3 NEB*

Never cease to love your fellow-Christians.

Remember to show hospitality. There are some who, by so doing, have entertained angels without knowing it.

Remember those in prison as if you were there with them; and those who are being maltreated, for you like them are still in the world.

Gospel *Matthew 19.16-21 NEB*

A man came up and asked Jesus, 'Master, what good must I do to gain eternal life?' 'Good?' said Jesus. 'Why do you ask me about that? One alone is good. But if you wish to enter into life, keep the commandments.' 'Which commandments?' he asked. Jesus answered, 'Do not murder; do not commit adultery; do not steal; do not give false evidence; honour your father and mother; and love your neighbour as yourself.' The young man answered, 'I have kept all these. Where do I still fall short?' Jesus said to him, 'If you wish to go the whole way, go, sell your possessions, and give to the poor, and then you will have riches in heaven; and come, follow me.'

or *Matthew 25.31-end NEB*

Jesus said, 'When the Son of Man comes in his glory and all the angels with him, he will sit in state on his throne, with all the nations gathered before him. He will separate men into two groups, as a shepherd separates the sheep from the goats, and he will place the sheep on his right hand and the goats on his left. Then the king will say to those on his right hand, "You have my Father's blessing; come, enter and possess the kingdom that has been ready for you since the world was made. For when I was hungry, you gave me food; when thirsty, you gave me drink; when I was a stranger you took me into your home, when naked you clothed me; when I was ill you came to my help, when in prison you visited me." Then the righteous will reply, "Lord, when was it that we saw you hungry and fed you, or thirsty and gave you drink, a stranger and took you home, or naked and clothed you? When did we see you ill or in prison, and come to visit you?" And the king will answer, "I tell you this: anything you did for one of my brothers here, however humble, you did for me." Then he will say to those on his left hand, "The curse is upon you; go from my sight to the eternal fire that is ready for the devil and his angels. For when I was hungry you gave me nothing to eat, when thirsty nothing to drink; when I was a stranger you gave me no home, when naked you did not clothe me; when I was ill and in prison you did not come to my help." And they too will reply, "Lord, when was it that we saw you hungry or thirsty or a stranger or naked or ill or in prison, and did nothing for you?" And he will answer, "I tell you this: anything you did not do for one of these, however humble, you did not do for me." And they will go away to eternal punishment, but the righteous will enter eternal life.'

or *Mark 10.42-45 NEB*

Jesus called his disciples to him and said, 'You know that in the world the recognized rulers lord it over their subjects, and their great men make them feel the weight of authority. That is not the way with you; among you, whoever wants to be great must be your servant, and whoever wants to be first must be the willing slave of all. For even the Son of Man did not come to be served, but to serve, and to give up his life as a ransom for many.'

or *Luke 10.38-end NEB*

Jesus came to a village where a woman named Martha made him welcome in her home. She had a sister, Mary, who seated herself at the Lord's feet and stayed there listening to his words. Now Martha was distracted by her many tasks, so she came to him and said, 'Lord, do you not care that my sister has left me to get on with the work by myself? Tell her to come and lend a hand.' But the Lord answered, 'Martha, Martha, you are fretting and fussing about so many things; but one thing is necessary. The part that Mary has chosen is best; and it shall not be taken away from her.'

PROPER PREFACE

Rite A. The Preface of Saints (25) may be said.
Rite B. The Preface of Saints' Days may be said.

POSTCOMMUNION SENTENCE

a. For Women Saints

Many women have done admirable things, but you have surpassed them all. *Proverbs 31.29*

or

Behold, the Bridegroom is here: let us go out to meet him.
Matthew 25.6

b. General

Jesus said, If anyone wishes to be a follower of mine, he must
renounce himself, take up his cross, and follow me.
Matthew 16.24

THE EMBER WEEKS Colour of the season

INTRODUCTORY SENTENCE

Pray the Lord of the harvest to send labourers to harvest his
crop. *Matthew 9.38*

or of the season

COLLECTS

For those to be Ordained

Almighty God,
the giver of all good gifts,
by your Holy Spirit you have appointed
    various orders of ministry in the Church.
Look with mercy and favour on your servants
    now called to be deacons and priests.
Maintain them in truth
and renew them in holiness,
that by word and good example
they may faithfully serve you
    to the glory of your name
    and the benefit of your Church;
through the merits of our Saviour Jesus Christ.

For Vocations

Almighty God,
you have entrusted to your Church
a share in the ministry of your Son, our great High Priest.

Inspire by your Holy Spirit the hearts and minds of many
to offer themselves for the sacred ministry,
that as deacons and priests
they may draw all men to your kingdom;
through Jesus Christ our Lord.

PSALMS 122; 84.8-end

READINGS

Advent

Old Testament *Jeremiah 1.4-10 NEB*

The word of the Lord came to me: 'Before I formed you in the
womb I knew you for my own; before you were born I
consecrated you, I appointed you a prophet to the nations.'
'Ah! Lord God,' I answered, 'I do not know how to speak;
I am only a child.' But the Lord said, 'Do not call yourself a
child; for you shall go to whatever people I send you and say
whatever I tell you to say. Fear none of them, for I am with
you and will keep you safe.'

This was the very word of the Lord. Then the Lord stretched
out his hand and touched my mouth, and said to me, 'I put
my words into your mouth. This day I give you authority
over nations and over kingdoms, to pull down and to
uproot, to destroy and to demolish, to build and to plant.'

New Testament *1 Peter 4.7-11 NEB*

The end of all things is upon us, so you must lead an ordered
and sober life, given to prayer. Above all, keep your love for
one another at full strength, because love cancels
innumerable sins. Be hospitable to one another without
complaining. Whatever gift each of you may have received,
use it in service to one another, like good stewards
dispensing the grace of God in its varied forms. Are you a
speaker? Speak as if you uttered oracles of God. Do you give
service? Give it as in the strength which God supplies. In all
things so act that the glory may be God's through Jesus
Christ; to him belong glory and power for ever and
ever. Amen.

Gospel *Luke 12.35-43 NEB*

Jesus said to his disciples, 'Be ready for action, with belts
fastened and lamps alight. Be like men who wait for their
master's return from a wedding-party, ready to let him in
the moment he arrives and knocks. Happy are those
servants whom the master finds on the alert when he comes.
I tell you this: he will fasten his belt, seat them at table, and
come and wait on them. Even if it is the middle of the night
or before dawn when he comes, happy they if he finds them
alert. And remember, if the householder had known what
time the burglar was coming he would not have let his house
be broken into. Hold yourselves ready, then, because the
Son of Man will come at the time you least expect him.'

Peter said, 'Lord, do you intend this parable specially for us
or is it for everyone?' The Lord said, 'Well, who is the trusty
and sensible man whom his master will appoint as his
steward, to manage his servants and issue their rations at the
proper time? Happy that servant who is found at his task
when his master comes!'

Lent and St Peterstide

Old Testament *Numbers 11.16-17, 24-29 RSV*

The Lord said to Moses, 'Gather for me seventy men of the
elders of Israel, whom you know to be the elders of the
people and officers over them; and bring them to the tent of
meeting, and let them take their stand there with you. And I
will come down and talk with you there; and I will take some
of the spirit which is upon you and put it upon them; and
they shall bear the burden of the people with you, that you
may not bear it yourself alone.'

So Moses went out and told the people the words of the
Lord; and he gathered seventy men of the elders of the
people, and placed them round about the tent. Then the
Lord came down in the cloud and spoke to him, and took
some of the spirit that was upon him and put it upon the
seventy elders; and when the spirit rested upon them, they
prophesied. But they did so no more.

Now two men remained in the camp, one named Eldad, and the other named Medad, and the spirit rested upon them; they were among those registered, but they had not gone out to the tent, and so they prophesied in the camp. And a young man ran and told Moses, 'Eldad and Medad are prophesying in the camp.' And Joshua the son of Nun, the minister of Moses, one of his chosen men, said, 'My lord Moses, forbid them.' But Moses said to him, 'Are you jealous for my sake? Would that all the Lord's people were prophets, that the Lord would put his spirit upon them!'

New Testament *Acts 20.28-35 TEV*

Keep watch over yourselves and over all the flock which the Holy Spirit has placed in your care. Be shepherds of the church of God, which he made his own through the death of his Son. I know that after I leave, fierce wolves will come among you, and they will not spare the flock. The time will come when some men from your own group will tell lies to lead the believers away after them. Watch, then, and remember that with many tears, day and night, I taught every one of you for three years.

And now I commend you to the care of God and to the message of his grace, which is able to build you up and give you the blessings God has for all his people. I have not wanted anyone's silver or gold or clothing. You yourselves know that I have worked with these hands of mine to provide everything that my companions and I have needed. I have shown you in all things that by working hard in this way we must help the weak, remembering the words that the Lord Jesus himself said, 'There is more happiness in giving than in receiving.'

Gospel *Luke 4.16-21 NEB*

Jesus came to Nazareth, where he had been brought up, and went to synagogue on the Sabbath day as he regularly did. He stood up to read the lesson and was handed the scroll of the prophet Isaiah. He opened the scroll and found the passage which says,

'The spirit of the Lord is upon me because he has
anointed me;
he has sent me to announce good news to the poor,
to proclaim release for prisoners and recovery of sight
    for the blind;
to let the broken victims go free,
to proclaim the year of the Lord's favour.'
He rolled up the scroll, gave it back to the attendant, and sat
down; and all eyes in the synagogue were fixed on him.

He began to speak: 'Today', he said, 'in your very hearing
this text has come true.'

Michaelmas

Old Testament *Numbers 27.15-end NEB*

Moses said, 'Let the Lord, the God of the spirits of all
mankind, appoint a man over the community to go out and
come in at their head, to lead them out and bring them
home, so that the community of the Lord may not be like
sheep without a shepherd.' The Lord answered Moses,
'Take Joshua son of Nun, a man endowed with spirit; lay
your hand on him and set him before Eleazar the priest and
all the community. Give him his commission in their
presence, and delegate some of your authority to him, so
that all the community of the Israelites may obey him. He
must appear before Eleazar the priest, who will obtain a
decision for him by consulting the Urim before the Lord; at
his word they shall go out and shall come home, both Joshua
and the whole community of the Israelites.'

Moses did as the Lord had commanded him. He took
Joshua, presented him to Eleazar the priest and the whole
community, laid his hands on him and gave him his
commission, as the Lord had instructed him.

New Testament *1 Corinthians 3.3-11 NEB*

Can you not see that while there is jealousy and strife among
you, you are living on the purely human level of your lower
nature? When one says, 'I am Paul's man', and another, 'I
am for Apollos', are you not all too human?

After all, what is Apollos? What is Paul? We are simply God's agents in bringing you to the faith. Each of us performed the task which the Lord allotted to him: I planted the seed, and Apollos watered it; but God made it grow. Thus it is not the gardeners with their planting and watering who count, but God, who makes it grow. Whether they plant or water, they work as a team, though each will get his own pay for his own labour. We are God's fellow-workers; and you are God's garden.

Or again, you are God's building. I am like a skilled master-builder who by God's grace laid the foundation, and someone else is putting up the building. Let each take care how he builds. There can be no other foundation beyond that which is already laid; I mean Jesus Christ himself.

Gospel *John 4.31-38 JB*

The disciples were urging Jesus, 'Rabbi, do have something to eat'; but he said, 'I have food to eat that you do not know about'. So the disciples asked one another, 'Has someone been bringing him food?' But Jesus said,
'My food
is to do the will of the one who sent me,
and to complete his work.
Have you not got a saying:
Four months and then the harvest?
Well, I tell you:
Look around you, look at the fields;
already they are white, ready for harvest!
Already the reaper is being paid his wages,
already he is bringing in the grain for eternal life,
and thus sower and reaper rejoice together.
For here the proverb holds good:
one sows, another reaps;
I sent you to reap
a harvest you had not worked for.
Others worked for it;
and you have come into the rewards of their trouble.'

Any of these readings may be used in the Ember weeks in addition to those which are appointed for the particular seasons.

PROPER PREFACE

Rite A. Advent. A Preface of Advent (1) is said.
       Lent. The Preface of Lent (8) is said.
       St Peterstide. The Preface of Ordination (28) is said.
       Michaelmas. The Preface of Ordination (28) is said.
Rite B. Second Thanksgiving
       Advent. The Preface of Advent is said.
       Lent. The Preface of Lent is said.

POSTCOMMUNION SENTENCE

Father, make them holy in the truth: your word is truth.
John 17.17

or of the season

THE ROGATION DAYS   White

INTRODUCTORY SENTENCE

May the goodness of the Lord be upon us; may he prosper
the work of our hands. *Psalm 90.17*

COLLECTS

Almighty and everlasting God,
you are always more ready to hear than we to pray
and give more than either we desire or deserve.
Pour down upon us the abundance of your mercy,
forgiving us those things
   of which our conscience is afraid
and giving us those good things
   which we are not worthy to ask
save through the merits and mediation
of Jesus Christ your Son our Lord.

Almighty God,
you have provided the resources of the world
to maintain the life of your children,
and have so ordered our life
that we are dependent upon each other.

Bless all men in their daily work,
and, as you have given us the knowledge
    to produce plenty,
so give us the will to bring it within reach of all;
through Jesus Christ our Lord.

Almighty God,
whose will it is that the earth
should bear its fruits in their seasons:
direct the labours of those who work on the land,
that they may employ the resources of nature
    to your glory,
        for our own well-being,
    and for the relief of those in need;
through Jesus Christ our Lord.

PSALMS 107.1-9; 121

READINGS

Monday

Old Testament *Job 28.1-11 NEB*

There are mines for silver
and places where men refine gold;
where iron is won from the earth
and copper smelted from the ore;
the end of the seam lies in darkness,
and it is followed to its farthest limit.
Strangers cut the galleries;
they are forgotten as they drive forward far from men.
While corn is springing from the earth above,
what lies beneath is raked over like a fire,
and out of its rocks comes lapis lazuli,
dusted with flecks of gold.
No bird of prey knows the way there,
and the falcon's keen eye cannot descry it;
proud beasts do not set foot on it,
and no serpent comes that way.
Man sets his hand to the granite rock
and lays bare the roots of the mountains;

he cuts galleries in the rocks,
and gems of every kind meet his eye;
he dams up the sources of the streams
and brings the hidden riches of the earth to light.

New Testament *2 Thessalonians 3.6-13 JB*

In the name of the Lord Jesus Christ, we urge you, brothers, to keep away from any of the brothers who refuses to work or to live according to the tradition we passed on to you.

You know how you are supposed to imitate us: now we were not idle when we were with you, nor did we ever have our meals at anyone's table without paying for them; no, we worked night and day, slaving and straining, so as not to be a burden on any of you. This was not because we had no right to be, but in order to make ourselves an example for you to follow.

We gave you a rule when we were with you: not to let anyone have any food if he refused to do any work. Now we hear that there are some of you who are living in idleness, doing no work themselves but interfering with everyone else's. In the Lord Jesus Christ, we order and call on people of this kind to go on quietly working and earning the food that they eat.

My brothers, never grow tired of doing what is right.

Gospel *Matthew 6.1-15 JB*

Jesus said, 'Be careful not to parade your good deeds before men to attract their notice; by doing this you will lose all reward from your Father in heaven. So when you give alms, do not have it trumpeted before you; this is what the hypocrites do in the synagogues and in the streets to win men's admiration. I tell you solemnly, they have had their reward. But when you give alms, your left hand must not know what your right is doing; your almsgiving must be secret, and your Father who sees all that is done in secret will reward you.

'And when you pray, do not imitate the hypocrites: they love to say their prayers standing up in the synagogues and

at the street corners for people to see them. I tell you
solemnly, they have had their reward. But when you pray,
go to your private room and, when you have shut your door,
pray to your Father who is in that secret place, and your
Father who sees all that is done in secret will reward you.

'In your prayers do not babble as the pagans do, for they
think that by using many words they will make themselves
heard. Do not be like them; your Father knows what you
need before you ask him. So you should pray like this:

"Our Father in heaven,
may your name be held holy,
your kingdom come,
your will be done,
on earth as in heaven.
Give us today our daily bread.
And forgive us our debts,
as we have forgiven those who are in debt to us.
And do not put us to the test,
but save us from the evil one."

'Yes, if you forgive others their failings, your heavenly
Father will forgive you yours; but if you do not forgive
others, your Father will not forgive your failings either.'

Tuesday

Old Testament *Deuteronomy 8.1-10 NEB*

Moses said to all Israel, 'You must carefully observe
everything that I command you this day so that you may live
and increase and may enter and occupy the land which the
Lord promised to your forefathers upon oath. You must
remember all that road by which the Lord your God has led
you these forty years in the wilderness to humble you, to test
you and to discover whether or no it was in your heart to
keep his commandments. He humbled you and made you
hungry; then he fed you on manna which neither you nor
your fathers had known before, to teach you that man
cannot live on bread alone but lives by every word that
comes from the mouth of the Lord. The clothes on your
backs did not wear out nor did your feet swell all these forty
years. Take this lesson to heart: that the Lord your God was

disciplining you as a father disciplines his son; and keep the commandments of the Lord your God, conforming to his ways and fearing him. For the Lord your God is bringing you to a rich land, a land of streams, of springs and underground waters gushing out in hill and valley, a land of wheat and barley, of vines, fig-trees, and pomegranates, a land of olives, oil, and honey. It is a land where you will never live in poverty nor want for anything, a land whose stones are iron-ore and from whose hills you will dig copper. You will have plenty to eat and will bless the Lord your God for the rich land that he has given you.'

New Testament *Philippians 4.4-7 RSV*

Rejoice in the Lord always; again I will say, Rejoice. Let all men know your forbearance. The Lord is at hand. Have no anxiety about anything, but in everything by prayer and supplication with thanksgiving let your requests be made known to God. And the peace of God, which passes all understanding, will keep your hearts and your minds in Christ Jesus.

Gospel *Luke 11.5-13 JB*

Jesus said, 'Suppose one of you has a friend and goes to him in the middle of the night to say, "My friend, lend me three loaves, because a friend of mine on his travels has just arrived at my house and I have nothing to offer him"; and the man answers from inside the house, "Do not bother me. The door is bolted now, and my children and I are in bed; I cannot get up to give it you". I tell you, if the man does not get up and give it him for friendship's sake, persistence will be enough to make him get up and give his friend all he wants.

'So I say to you: Ask, and it will be given to you; search, and you will find; knock, and the door will be opened to you. For the one who asks always receives; the one who searches always finds; the one who knocks will always have the door opened to him. What father among you would hand his son a stone when he asked for bread? Or hand him a snake instead of a fish? Or hand him a scorpion if he had asked for an egg? If you then, who are evil, know how to give your children what is good, how much more will the heavenly Father give the Holy Spirit to those who ask him?'

Wednesday

Old Testament *1 Kings 8.35-40 RSV*

Solomon said to the Lord, 'When heaven is shut up and there is no rain because they have sinned against you, if they pray toward this place, and acknowledge your name, and turn from their sin, when you afflict them, then hear in heaven, and forgive the sin of your servants, your people Israel, when you teach them the good way in which they should walk; and grant rain upon your land, which you have given to your people as an inheritance.

'If there is famine in the land, if there is pestilence or blight or mildew or locust or caterpillar; if their enemy besieges them in any of their cities; whatever plague, whatever sickness there is; whatever prayer, whatever supplication is made by any man or by all your people Israel, each knowing the affliction of his own heart and stretching out his hands toward this house; then hear in heaven your dwelling place, and forgive, and act, and render to each whose heart you know, according to all his ways (for you, you only, know the hearts of all the children of men); that they may fear you all the days that they live in the land which you gave to our fathers.'

New Testament *1 John 5.12-15 JB*

Anyone who has the Son has life,
anyone who does not have the Son does not have life.

I have written all this to you
so that you who believe in the name of the Son of God
may be sure that you have eternal life.

We are quite confident that if we ask him for anything,
and it is in accordance with his will, he will hear us;
and, knowing that whatever we may ask, he hears us,
we know that we have already been granted what we asked
of him.

Gospel *Mark 11.22-24 NEB*

Jesus said to his disciples, 'Have faith in God. I tell you this: if anyone says to this mountain, "Be lifted from your place and hurled into the sea", and has no inward doubts, but believes that what he says is happening, it will be done for him. I tell you, then, whatever you ask for in prayer, believe that you have received it and it will be yours.'

PROPER PREFACE

Rite A. A Preface of the Resurrection (14) is said.
Rite B. The Preface for Easter is said.

POSTCOMMUNION SENTENCE

God will give us his good gifts, and our land will yield its fruit. *Psalm 85.12*

HARVEST THANKSGIVING   Colour of the season

INTRODUCTORY SENTENCE

The land has yielded its harvest: God, our God has blessed us. *Psalm 67.6*

COLLECT

Almighty and everlasting God,
we offer you our hearty thanks
for your fatherly goodness and care
in giving us the fruits of the earth in their seasons.
Give us grace to use them rightly,
    to your glory,
    for our own well-being,
    and for the relief of those in need;
through Jesus Christ our Lord.

PSALMS 104.21-30; 65 or 67; 145; 147; 148; 150

READINGS

Old Testament *Deuteronomy 8.1-10 NEB*

Moses said to all Israel, 'You must carefully observe everything that I command you this day so that you may live and increase and may enter and occupy the land which the Lord promised to your forefathers upon oath. You must remember all that road by which the Lord your God has led you these forty years in the wilderness to humble you, to test you and to discover whether or no it was in your heart to keep his commandments. He humbled you and made you hungry; then he fed you on manna which neither you nor your fathers had known before, to teach you that man cannot live on bread alone but lives by every word that comes from the mouth of the Lord. The clothes on your backs did not wear out nor did your feet swell all these forty years. Take this lesson to heart: that the Lord your God was disciplining you as a father disciplines his son; and keep the commandments of the Lord your God, conforming to his ways and fearing him. For the Lord your God is bringing you to a rich land, a land of streams, of springs and underground waters gushing out in hill and valley, a land of wheat and barley, of vines, fig-trees, and pomegranates, a land of olives, oil, and honey. It is a land where you will never live in poverty nor want for anything, a land whose stones are iron-ore and from whose hills you will dig copper. You will have plenty to eat and will bless the Lord your God for the rich land that he has given you.'

or *Genesis 1.1-3, 24-31a NEB*

In the beginning of creation, when God made heaven and earth, the earth was without form and void, with darkness over the face of the abyss, and a mighty wind that swept over the surface of the waters. God said, 'Let there be light', and there was light.

God said, 'Let the earth bring forth living creatures, according to their kind: cattle, reptiles, and wild animals, all according to their kind.' So it was; God made wild animals, cattle, and all reptiles, each according to its kind; and he saw that it was good. Then God said, 'Let us make man in our image and likeness to rule the fish in the sea, the birds of heaven, the cattle, all wild animals on earth, and all reptiles that crawl upon the earth.' So God created man in his own image; in the image of God he created him; male and female he created them. God blessed them and said to them, 'Be fruitful and increase, fill the earth and subdue it, rule over the fish in the sea, the birds of heaven, and every living thing that moves upon the earth.' God also said, 'I give you all plants that bear seed everywhere on earth, and every tree bearing fruit which yields seed: they shall be yours for food. All green plants I give for food to the wild animals, to all the birds of heaven, and to all reptiles on earth, every living creature.' So it was; and God saw all that he had made, and it was very good.

New Testament *Acts 14.13-17 NEB*

The priest of Jupiter, whose temple was just outside the city, brought oxen and garlands to the gates, and he and all the people were about to offer sacrifice.

But when the apostles Barnabas and Paul heard of it, they tore their clothes and rushed into the crowd shouting, 'Men, what is this that you are doing? We are only human beings, no less mortal than you. The good news we bring tells you to turn from these follies to the living God, who made heaven and earth and sea and everything in them. In past ages he allowed all nations to go their own way; and yet he has not left you without some clue to his nature, in the kindness he shows: he sends you rain from heaven and crops in their seasons, and gives you food and good cheer in plenty.'

or *1 Timothy 6.6-10 JB*

Religion does bring large profits, but only to those who are content with what they have. We brought nothing into the world, and we can take nothing out of it; but as long as we have food and clothing, let us be content with that. People who long to be rich are a prey to temptation; they get trapped into all sorts of foolish and dangerous ambitions which eventually plunge them into ruin and destruction. 'The love of money is the root of all evils' and there are some who, pursuing it, have wandered away from the faith, and so given their souls any number of fatal wounds.

Gospel *Luke 12.16-31 JB*

Jesus told the people a parable: 'There was once a rich man who, having had a good harvest from his land, thought to himself, "What am I to do? I have not enough room to store my crops." Then he said, "This is what I will do: I will pull down my barns and build bigger ones, and store all my grain and my goods in them, and I will say to my soul: My soul, you have plenty of good things laid by for many years to come; take things easy, eat, drink, have a good time." But God said to him, "Fool! This very night the demand will be made for your soul; and this hoard of yours, whose will it be then?" So it is when a man stores up treasure for himself in place of making himself rich in the sight of God.'

Then he said to his disciples, 'That is why I am telling you not to worry about your life and what you are to eat, nor about your body and how you are to clothe it. For life means more than food, and the body more than clothing. Think of the ravens. They do not sow or reap; they have no storehouses and no barns; yet God feeds them. And how much more are you worth than the birds! Can any of you, for all his worrying, add a single cubit to his span of life? If the smallest things, therefore, are outside your control, why worry about the rest? Think of the flowers; they never have to spin or weave; yet, I assure you, not even Solomon in all his regalia was robed like one of these. Now if that is how God clothes the grass in the field which is there today and thrown into the furnace tomorrow, how much more will he look after you, you men of little faith! But you, you must not set your hearts on things to eat and things to drink; nor must you worry. It is the pagans of this world who set their hearts on all these things. Your Father well knows you need them. No; set your hearts on his kingdom, and these other things will be given you as well.'

or *John 6.27-35 RSV*

Jesus said, 'Do not labour for the food which perishes, but for the food which endures to eternal life, which the Son of Man will give to you; for on him has God the Father set his seal.' Then the people said to him, 'What must we do, to be doing the work of God?' Jesus answered them, 'This is the work of God, that you believe in him whom he has sent.' So they said to him, 'Then what sign do you do, that we may see, and believe you? What work do you perform? Our fathers ate the manna in the wilderness; as it is written, "He gave them bread from heaven to eat."' Jesus then said to them, 'Truly, truly, I say to you, it was not Moses who gave you the bread from heaven; my Father gives you the true bread from heaven. For the bread of God is that which comes down from heaven, and gives life to the world.' They said to him, 'Lord, give us this bread always.'

OTHER SUITABLE READINGS

Old Testament *Genesis 1.1—2.3 NEB*

In the beginning of creation, when God made heaven and earth, the earth was without form and void, with darkness over the face of the abyss, and a mighty wind that swept over the surface of the waters. God said, 'Let there be light', and there was light; and God saw that the light was good, and he separated light from darkness. He called the light day, and the darkness night. So evening came, and morning came, the first day.

God said, 'Let there be a vault between the waters, to separate water from water.' So God made the vault, and separated the water under the vault from the water above it, and so it was; and God called the vault heaven. Evening came, and morning came, a second day.

God said, 'Let the waters under heaven be gathered into one place, so that dry land may appear'; and so it was. God called the dry land earth, and the gathering of the waters he called seas; and God saw that it was good. Then God said, 'Let the earth produce fresh growth, let there be on the earth plants bearing seed, fruit-trees bearing fruit each with seed according to its kind.' So it was; the earth yielded fresh growth, plants bearing seed according to their kind and trees bearing fruit each with seed according to its kind; and God saw that it was good. Evening came, and morning came, a third day.

God said, 'Let there be lights in the vault of heaven to separate day from night, and let them serve as signs both for festivals and for seasons and years. Let them also shine in the vault of heaven to give light on earth.' So it was; God made the two great lights, the greater to govern the day and the lesser to govern the night; and with them he made the stars. God put these lights in the vault of heaven to give light on earth, to govern day and night, and to separate light from darkness; and God saw that it was good. Evening came, and morning came, a fourth day.

God said, 'Let the waters teem with countless living creatures, and let birds fly above the earth across the vault of heaven.' God then created the great sea-monsters and all living creatures that move and swarm in the waters, according to their kind, and every kind of bird; and God saw that it was good. So he blessed them and said, 'Be fruitful and increase, fill the waters of the seas; and let the birds increase on land.' Evening came, and morning came, a fifth day.

God said, 'Let the earth bring forth living creatures, according to their kind: cattle, reptiles, and wild animals, all according to their kind.' So it was; God made wild animals, cattle, and all reptiles, each according to its kind; and he saw that it was good. Then God said, 'Let us make man in our image and likeness to rule the fish in the sea, the birds of heaven, the cattle, all wild animals on earth, and all reptiles that crawl upon the earth.' So God created man in his own image; in the image of God he created him; male and female he created them. God blessed them and said to them, 'Be fruitful and increase, fill the earth and subdue it, rule over the fish in the sea, the birds of heaven, and every living thing that moves upon the earth.' God also said, 'I give you all plants that bear seed everywhere on earth, and every tree bearing fruit which yields seed: they shall be yours for food.

All green plants I give for food to the wild animals, to all the birds of heaven, and to all reptiles on earth, every living creature.' So it was; and God saw all that he had made, and it was very good. Evening came, and morning came, a sixth day.

Thus heaven and earth were completed with all their mighty throng. On the sixth day God completed all the work he had been doing, and on the seventh day he ceased from all his work. God blessed the seventh day and made it holy, because on that day he ceased from all the work he had set himself to do.

or Deuteronomy 26.1-11 TEV

Moses said to all Israel, 'After you have occupied the land that the Lord your God is giving you and have settled there, each of you must place in a basket the first part of each crop that you harvest and you must take it with you to the one place of worship. Go to the priest in charge at that time and say to him, "I now acknowledge to the Lord my God that I have entered the land that he promised our ancestors to give us."

'The priest will take the basket from you and place it before the altar of the Lord your God. Then, in the Lord's presence you will recite these words: "My ancestor was a wandering Aramaean, a homeless refugee, who took his family to Egypt to live. They were few in number when they went there, but they became a large and powerful nation. The Egyptians treated us harshly and forced us to work as slaves. Then we cried out for help to the Lord, the God of our ancestors. He heard us and saw our suffering, hardship, and misery. By his great power and strength he rescued us from Egypt. He worked miracles and wonders, and caused terrifying things to happen. He brought us here and gave us this rich and fertile land. So now I bring to the Lord the first part of the harvest that he has given me."

'Then set the basket down in the Lord's presence and worship there. Be grateful for the good things that the Lord your God has given you and your family; and let the Levites

and the foreigners who live among you join in
the celebration.'

or *Deuteronomy 28.1-14 NEB*

Moses said to all Israel, 'If you will obey the Lord your God
by diligently observing all his commandments which I lay
upon you this day, then the Lord your God will raise you
high above all nations of the earth, and all these blessings
shall come to you and light upon you, because you obey the
Lord your God:

'A blessing on you in the city; a blessing on you in the
country.

'A blessing on the fruit of your body, the fruit of your land
and of your cattle, the offspring of your herds and of your
lambing flocks.

'A blessing on your basket and your kneading-trough.

'A blessing on you as you come in; and a blessing on you as
you go out.

'May the Lord deliver up the enemies who attack you and let
them be put to rout before you. Though they come out
against you by one way, they shall flee before you by
seven ways.

'May the Lord grant you a blessing in your granaries and in
all your labours; may the Lord your God bless you in the
land which he is giving you.

'The Lord will set you up as his own holy people, as he swore
to you, if you keep the commandments of the Lord your God
and conform to his ways. Then all people on earth shall see
that the Lord has named you as his very own, and they shall
go in fear of you. The Lord will make you prosper greatly in
the fruit of your body and of your cattle, and in the fruit of
the ground in the land which he swore to your forefathers to
give you. May the Lord open the heavens for you, his rich
treasure house, to give rain upon your land at the proper
time and bless everything to which you turn your hand. You
shall lend to many nations, but you shall not borrow; the
Lord will make you the head and not the tail: you shall be

always at the top and never at the bottom, when you listen to the commandments of the Lord your God, which I give you this day to keep and to fulfil. You shall turn neither to the right nor to the left from all the things which I command you this day nor shall you follow after and worship other gods.'

New Testament *Acts 10.10-16 NEB*

Peter grew hungry and wanted something to eat. While they were getting it ready, he fell into a trance. He saw a rift in the sky, and a thing coming down that looked like a great sheet of sail-cloth. It was slung by the four corners, and was being lowered to the ground. In it he saw creatures of every kind, whatever walks or crawls or flies. Then there was a voice which said to him, 'Up, Peter, kill and eat.' But Peter said, 'No, Lord, no: I have never eaten anything profane or unclean.' The voice came again a second time: 'It is not for you to call profane what God counts clean.' This happened three times; and then the thing was taken up again into the sky.

or *2 Corinthians 9.6-end NEB*

Remember: sparse sowing, sparse reaping; sow bountifully, and you will reap bountifully. Each person should give as he has decided for himself; there should be no reluctance, no sense of compulsion; God loves a cheerful giver. And it is in God's power to provide you richly with every good gift; thus you will have ample means in yourselves to meet each and every situation, with enough and to spare for every good cause. Scripture says of such a man: 'He has lavished his gifts on the needy, his benevolence stands fast for ever.' Now he who provides seed for sowing and bread for food will provide the seed for you to sow; he will multiply it and swell the harvest of your benevolence, and you will always be rich enough to be generous. Through our action such generosity will issue in thanksgiving to God, for as a piece of willing service this is not only a contribution towards the needs of God's people; more than that, it overflows in a flood of thanksgiving to God. For through the proof which this affords, many will give honour to God when they see

how humbly you obey him and how faithfully you confess
the gospel of Christ; and will thank him for your liberal
contribution to their need and to the general good. And as
they join in prayer on your behalf, their hearts will go out to
you because of the richness of the grace which God has
imparted to you. Thanks be to God for his gift
beyond words!

or *Revelation 14.14-18 NEB*

As I looked there appeared a white cloud, and on the cloud
sat one like a son of man. He had on his head a crown of gold
and in his hand a sharp sickle. Another angel came out of the
temple and called in a loud voice to him who sat on the
cloud: 'Stretch out your sickle and reap; for harvest-time has
come, and earth's crop is over-ripe.' So he who sat on the
cloud put his sickle to the earth and its harvest was reaped.

Then another angel came out of the heavenly temple, and he
also had a sharp sickle. Then from the altar came yet
another, the angel who has authority over fire, and he
shouted to the one with the sharp sickle: 'Stretch out your
sickle, and gather in earth's grape-harvest, for its clusters
are ripe.'

Gospel *Matthew 6.24-end NEB*

Jesus said, 'No servant can be the slave of two masters; for
either he will hate the first and love the second, or he will be
devoted to the first and think nothing of the second. You
cannot serve God and Money.

'Therefore I bid you put away anxious thoughts about food
and drink to keep you alive, and clothes to cover your body.
Surely life is more than food, the body more than clothes.
Look at the birds of the air; they do not sow and reap and
store in barns, yet your heavenly Father feeds them. You are
worth more than the birds! Is there a man of you who by
anxious thought can add a foot to his height? And why be
anxious about clothes? Consider how the lilies grow in the
fields; they do not work, they do not spin; and yet, I tell you,
even Solomon in all his splendour was not attired like one of

these. But if that is how God clothes the grass in the fields, which is there today, and tomorrow is thrown on the stove, will he not all the more clothe you? How little faith you have! No, do not ask anxiously, "What are we to eat? What are we to drink? What shall we wear?" All these are things for the heathen to run after, not for you, because your heavenly Father knows that you need them all. Set your mind on God's kingdom and his justice before everything else, and all the rest will come to you as well. So do not be anxious about tomorrow; tomorrow will look after itself. Each day has troubles enough of its own.'

or *Matthew 13.18-30 NEB*

Jesus said to his disciples, 'You, then, may hear the parable of the sower. When a man hears the word that tells of the Kingdom but fails to understand it, the evil one comes and carries off what has been sown in his heart. There you have the seed sown along the footpath. The seed sown on rocky ground stands for the man who, on hearing the word, accepts it at once with joy; but as it strikes no root in him he has no staying-power, and when there is trouble or persecution on account of the word he falls away at once. The seed sown among thistles represents the man who hears the word, but worldly cares and the false glamour of wealth choke it, and it proves barren. But the seed that fell into good soil is the man who hears the word and understands it, who accordingly bears fruit, and yields a hundredfold or, it may be, sixtyfold or thirtyfold.'

Here is another parable that he put before them: 'The kingdom of Heaven is like this. A man sowed his field with good seed; but while everyone was asleep his enemy came, sowed darnel among the wheat, and made off. When the corn sprouted and began to fill out, the darnel could be seen among it. The farmer's men went to their master and said, "Sir, was it not good seed that you sowed in your field? Then where has the darnel come from?" "This is an enemy's doing", he replied. "Well, then," they said, "shall we go and gather the darnel?" "No," he answered; "in gathering it you might pull up the wheat at the same time. Let them both grow together till harvest; and at harvest-time I will tell the reapers, 'Gather the darnel first, and tie it in bundles for burning; then collect the wheat into my barn.'''

or *John 4.31-38 JB*

The disciples were urging Jesus, 'Rabbi, do have something to eat'; but he said, 'I have food to eat that you do not know about'. So the disciples asked one another, 'Has someone been bringing him food?' But Jesus said,
'My food
is to do the will of the one who sent me,
and to complete his work.
Have you not got a saying:
Four months and then the harvest?
Well, I tell you:
Look around you, look at the fields;
already they are white, ready for harvest!
Already the reaper is being paid his wages,
already he is bringing in the grain for eternal life,
and thus sower and reaper rejoice together.
For here the proverb holds good:
one sows, another reaps;
I sent you to reap
a harvest you had not worked for.
Others worked for it;
and you have come into the rewards of their trouble.'

POSTCOMMUNION SENTENCE

The earth is filled with the gifts of the Lord: wine and oil and bread, to strengthen us and cheer our hearts. *Psalm 104.13, 15*

Sentences, Collects, and Readings
(d) Various Occasions

FOR THE UNITY OF THE CHURCH

INTRODUCTORY SENTENCE

There is one body, and one Spirit, one hope held out in
God's call to us: one Lord, one faith, one baptism, one God
and Father of all, who is over all, and through all, and in all.
Ephesians 4.4-6

COLLECTS

Heavenly Father,
whose Son our Lord Jesus Christ said to his apostles,
Peace I leave with you, my peace I give to you:
regard not our sins but the faith of your Church,
and grant it that peace and unity
    which is agreeable to your will;
through Jesus Christ our Lord.

Father, Son, and Holy Spirit,
holy and undivided Trinity,
three persons in one God:
inspire your whole Church, founded upon this faith,
to witness to the perfect unity of your love,
one God, now and for ever.

Heavenly Father,
you have called us
in the Body of your Son Jesus Christ
to continue his work of reconciliation
and reveal you to mankind.
Forgive us the sins which tear us apart;
give us the courage to overcome our fears
and to seek that unity
which is your gift and your will;
through Jesus Christ our Lord.

PSALMS 133; 122

READINGS

Old Testament *Jeremiah 33.6-9a NEB*

The Lord said, 'I will heal and cure Judah and Israel, and will let my people see an age of peace and security. I will restore their fortunes and build them again as once they were. I will cleanse them of all the wickedness and sin that they have committed; I will forgive all the evil deeds they have done in rebellion against me. This city will win me a name and praise and glory before all the nations on earth, when they hear of all the blessings I bestow on her.'

New Testament *Ephesians 4.1-6 NEB*

I entreat you—I, a prisoner for the Lord's sake: as God has called you, live up to your calling. Be humble always and gentle, and patient too. Be forbearing with one another and charitable. Spare no effort to make fast with bonds of peace the unity which the Spirit gives. There is one body and one Spirit, as there is also one hope held out in God's call to you; one Lord, one faith, one baptism; one God and Father of all, who is over all and through all and in all.

Gospel *John 17.11b-23 JB*

Jesus raised his eyes to heaven and said,
'Holy Father,
keep those you have given me true to your name,
so that they may be one like us.
While I was with them,
I kept those you had given me true to your name.
I have watched over them and not one is lost
except the one who chose to be lost,
and this was to fulfil the scriptures.
But now I am coming to you
and while still in the world I say these things
to share my joy with them to the full.
I passed your word on to them,
and the world hated them,
because they belong to the world
no more than I belong to the world.
I am not asking you to remove them from the world,

but to protect them from the evil one.
They do not belong to the world
any more than I belong to the world.
Consecrate them in the truth;
your word is truth.
As you sent me into the world,
I have sent them into the world,
and for their sake I consecrate myself
so that they too may be consecrated in truth.
I pray not only for these,
but for those also
who through their words will believe in me.
May they all be one.
Father, may they be one in us,
as you are in me and I am in you,
so that the world may believe it was you who sent me.
I have given them the glory you gave to me,
that they may be one as we are one.
With me in them and you in me,
may they be so completely one
that the world will realise that it was you who sent me
and that I have loved them as much as you loved me.'

PROPER PREFACE

Rite A. The Preface of Unity (29) is said.
This Preface may be used with the proper readings between
18 and 24 January.

POSTCOMMUNION SENTENCE

Because there is one loaf, we, many as we are, are one body,
for we all share in one loaf. *1 Corinthians 10.17*

FOR THE MISSIONARY WORK OF THE CHURCH

INTRODUCTORY SENTENCE

Proclaim the glory of the Lord among the nations, his
marvellous deeds to all peoples: great is the Lord, worthy
of praise. *Psalm 96.3*

COLLECT

Almighty God,
who called your Church to witness
that you were in Christ reconciling men to yourself:
help us so to proclaim the good news of your love,
that all who hear it may be reconciled to you;
through him who died for us and rose again
and reigns with you and the Holy Spirit,
one God, now and for ever.

PSALMS 97; 100 (or 2; 46; 47; 67; 87; 96; 117)

READINGS

Old Testament *Isaiah 49.1-6 NEB*

Listen to me, you coasts and islands,
pay heed, you peoples far away:
from birth the Lord called me,
he named me from my mother's womb.
He made my tongue his sharp sword
and concealed me under cover of his hand;
he made me a polished arrow
and hid me out of sight in his quiver.
He said to me, 'You are my servant,
Israel through whom I shall win glory';
so I rose to honour in the Lord's sight
and my God became my strength.
Once I said, 'I have laboured in vain;
I have spent my strength for nothing, to no purpose';
yet in truth my cause is with the Lord
and my reward is in God's hands.
And now the Lord who formed me in the womb to be
    his servant,
to bring Jacob back to him
that Israel should be gathered to him,
now the Lord calls me again:
it is too slight a task for you, as my servant,
to restore the tribes of Jacob,
to bring back the descendants of Israel:
I will make you a light to the nations,

to be my salvation to earth's farthest bounds.

New Testament *Ephesians 2.13-end NEB*

Now in union with Christ Jesus you who once were far off
have been brought near through the shedding of Christ's
blood. For he is himself our peace. Gentiles and Jews, he has
made the two one, and in his own body of flesh and blood
has broken down the enmity which stood like a dividing wall
between them; for he annulled the law with its rules and
regulations, so as to create out of the two a single new
humanity in himself, thereby making peace. This was his
purpose, to reconcile the two in a single body to God
through the cross, on which he killed the enmity.

So he came and proclaimed the good news: peace to you
who were far off, and peace to those who were near by; for
through him we both alike have access to the Father in the
one Spirit. Thus you are no longer aliens in a foreign land,
but fellow-citizens with God's people, members of God's
household. You are built upon the foundation laid by the
apostles and prophets, and Christ Jesus himself is the
foundation-stone. In him the whole building is bonded
together and grows into a holy temple in the Lord. In him
you too are being built with all the rest into a spiritual
dwelling for God.

Gospel *Matthew 28.16-end JB*

The eleven disciples set out for Galilee, to the mountain
where Jesus had arranged to meet them. When they saw him
they fell down before him, though some hesitated. Jesus
came up and spoke to them. He said, 'All authority in
heaven and on earth has been given to me. Go, therefore,
make disciples of all the nations; baptize them in the name of
the Father and of the Son and of the Holy Spirit, and teach
them to observe all the commands I gave you. And know
that I am with you always; yes, to the end of time.'

PROPER PREFACE

Rite A. The Preface of Pentecost (18) may be said.
Rite B. The Preface of Pentecost may be said.

POSTCOMMUNION SENTENCE

Go out to all the world and proclaim the good news to all creation. *Mark 16.15*

FOR THE GUIDANCE OF THE HOLY SPIRIT

INTRODUCTORY SENTENCE

When the Spirit of truth comes, he will lead us into all truth. *John 16.13*

COLLECTS

Almighty God,
at all times
you teach the hearts of your faithful people
by sending to them the light of your Holy Spirit.
Grant us by the same Spirit
   to have a right judgement in all things,
and evermore to rejoice in his holy comfort;
through the merits of Christ Jesus our Saviour,
who is alive and reigns with you in the unity of the Spirit,
one God, now and for ever.

We beseech you, O Lord,
to hear the prayers of your people;
and grant that they may both perceive and know
what things they ought to do,
and also may have grace and power
faithfully to fulfil the same;
through Jesus Christ our Lord.

PSALMS 25.1-9; 143.8-10

READINGS

Old Testament *Wisdom 9.13-17 JB*

What man indeed can know the intentions of God?
Who can divine the will of the Lord?
The reasonings of mortals are unsure

and our intentions unstable;
for a perishable body presses down the soul,
and this tent of clay weighs down the teeming mind.
It is hard enough for us to work out what is on earth,
laborious to know what lies within our reach;
who, then, can discover what is in the heavens?
As for your intention, who could have learnt it, had you not
 granted Wisdom
and sent your holy spirit from above?

or *Isaiah 30.15-21 NEB*

These are the words of the Lord God the Holy One of Israel:

Come back, keep peace, and you will be safe;
in stillness and in staying quiet, there lies your strength.
But you would have none of it; you said, No,
we will take horse and flee;
therefore you shall be put to flight:
We will ride apace;
therefore swift shall be the pace of your pursuers.
When a thousand flee at the challenge of one,
you shall all flee at the challenge of five, until you are left
like a pole on a mountain-top, a signal post on a hill.
Yet the Lord is waiting to show you his favour,
yet he yearns to have pity on you;
for the Lord is a God of justice.
Happy are all who wait for him!

O people of Zion who dwell in Jerusalem, you shall weep no
more. The Lord will show you favour and answer you when
he hears your cry for help. The Lord may give you bread of
adversity and water of affliction, but he who teaches you
shall no longer be hidden out of sight, but with your own
eyes you shall see him always. If you stray from the road to
right or left you shall hear with your own ears a voice behind
you saying, This is the way; follow it.

New Testament *1 Corinthians 12.4-13 NEB*

There are varieties of gifts, but the same Spirit. There are
varieties of service, but the same Lord. There are many
forms of work, but all of them, in all men, are the work of the

same God. In each of us the Spirit is manifested in one particular way, for some useful purpose. One man, through the Spirit, has the gift of wise speech, while another, by the power of the same Spirit, can put the deepest knowledge into words. Another, by the same Spirit, is granted faith; another, by the one Spirit, gifts of healing, and another miraculous powers; another has the gift of prophecy, and another ability to distinguish true spirits from false; yet another has the gift of ecstatic utterance of different kinds, and another the ability to interpret it. But all these gifts are the work of one and the same Spirit, distributing them separately to each individual at will.

For Christ is like a single body with its many limbs and organs, which, many as they are, together make up one body. For indeed we were all brought into one body by baptism, in the one Spirit, whether we are Jews or Greeks, whether slaves or free men, and that one Holy Spirit was poured out for all of us to drink.

Gospel *John 14.23-26 JB*

Jesus said,
'If anyone loves me he will keep my word,
and my Father will love him,
and we shall come to him
and make our home with him.
Those who do not love me do not keep my words.
And my word is not my own:
it is the word of the one who sent me.
I have said these things to you
while still with you;
but the Advocate, the Holy Spirit,
whom the Father will send in my name,
will teach you everything
and remind you of all I have said to you.'

PROPER PREFACE

Rite A. The Preface of Pentecost (18) may be said.
Rite B. The Preface of Pentecost may be said.

POSTCOMMUNION SENTENCE

The love of God has been poured into our hearts through the Holy Spirit he has given us. *Romans 5.5*

FOR THE PEACE OF THE WORLD

INTRODUCTORY SENTENCE

Try to grow perfect; help one another; be united; live in peace, and the God of love and peace will be with you. *2 Corinthians 13.11*

COLLECTS

Almighty God,
from whom all thoughts of truth and peace proceed:
kindle, we pray, in the hearts of all men
   the true love of peace;
and guide with your pure and peaceable wisdom
those who take counsel for the nations of the earth;
that in tranquillity your kingdom may go forward,
till the earth is filled with the knowledge of your love;
through Jesus Christ our Lord.

Almighty God,
whose will is to restore all things
   in your beloved Son, the king of all:
govern the hearts and minds of those in authority,
and bring the families of the nations,
divided and torn apart by the ravages of sin,
to be subject to his just and gentle rule;
who is alive and reigns with you and the Holy Spirit,
one God, now and for ever.

PSALMS 72.1-7; 85.8-13

READINGS

Old Testament *Micah 4.1-5 RSV*

It shall come to pass in the latter days
that the mountain of the house of the Lord
shall be established as the highest of the mountains,
and shall be raised up above the hills;
and peoples shall flow to it,
and many nations shall come, and say:
'Come, let us go up to the mountain of the Lord,
to the house of the God of Jacob;
that he may teach us his ways
and we may walk in his paths.'
For out of Zion shall go forth the law,
and the word of the Lord from Jerusalem.
He shall judge between many peoples,
and shall decide for strong nations afar off;
and they shall beat their swords into ploughshares,
and their spears into pruning hooks;
nation shall not lift up sword against nation,
neither shall they learn war any more;
but they shall sit every man
under his vine and under his fig tree,
and none shall make them afraid;
for the mouth of the Lord of hosts has spoken.

For all the peoples walk each in the name of its god,
but we will walk in the name of the Lord our God
for ever and ever.

New Testament *1 Timothy 2.1-6 NEB*

First of all I urge that petitions, prayers, intercessions, and
thanksgivings be offered for all men; for sovereigns and all in
high office, that we may lead a tranquil and quiet life in full
observance of religion and high standards of morality. Such
prayer is right, and approved by God our Saviour, whose
will it is that all men should find salvation and come to know
the truth. For there is one God, and also one mediator
between God and men, Christ Jesus, himself man, who
sacrificed himself to win freedom for all mankind, so
providing, at the fitting time, proof of the divine purpose.

The Peace of the World / 913

Gospel *Matthew 5.43-end RSV*

Jesus said, 'You have heard that it was said, "You shall love your neighbour and hate your enemy." But I say to you, Love your enemies and pray for those who persecute you, so that you may be sons of your Father who is in heaven; for he makes his sun rise on the evil and on the good, and sends rain on the just and on the unjust. For if you love those who love you, what reward have you? Do not even the tax collectors do the same? And if you salute only your brethren, what more are you doing than others? Do not even the Gentiles do the same? You, therefore, must be perfect, as your heavenly Father is perfect.'

PROPER PREFACE

Rite A. A Preface of the Resurrection (14) may be said.
Rite B. The Preface of Easter may be said.

POSTCOMMUNION SENTENCE

Jesus said, Peace I leave with you, my own peace I give you; do not let your heart be troubled or afraid. *John 14.27*

IN TIME OF TROUBLE

INTRODUCTORY SENTENCE

The eternal God is your refuge: and underneath are the everlasting arms. *Deuteronomy 33.27*

COLLECTS

Almighty God,
you know us to be set in the midst
    of so many and great dangers,
that, because of the frailty of our nature,
    we cannot always stand upright.
Give us such strength and protection
as may support us in all dangers
and carry us through all temptations;
through Jesus Christ our Lord.

Lord God,
whose blessed Son our Saviour
gave his back to the smiters
and did not hide his face from shame:
give us grace to endure the sufferings of this present time
with sure confidence in the glory that shall be revealed;
through Jesus Christ our Lord.

PSALMS 86.1-7; 142.1-7

READINGS

Old Testament *Job 1.13-end RSV*

Now there was a day when Job's sons and daughters were
eating and drinking wine in their eldest brother's house; and
there came a messenger to Job, and said, 'The oxen were
ploughing and the asses feeding beside them; and the
Sabaeans fell upon them and took them, and slew the
servants with the edge of the sword; and I alone have
escaped to tell you.' While he was yet speaking, there came
another, and said, 'The fire of God fell from heaven and
burned up the sheep and the servants, and consumed them;
and I alone have escaped to tell you.' While he was yet
speaking, there came another, and said, 'The Chaldaeans
formed three companies, and made a raid upon the camels
and took them, and slew the servants with the edge of the
sword; and I alone have escaped to tell you.' While he was
yet speaking there came another, and said, 'Your sons and
daughters were eating and drinking wine in their eldest
brother's house; and behold, a great wind came across the
wilderness, and struck the four corners of the house, and it
fell upon the young people, and they are dead; and I alone
have escaped to tell you.'

Then Job arose, and rent his robe, and shaved his head, and
fell upon the ground, and worshipped. And he said, 'Naked
I came from my mother's womb, and naked shall I return;
the Lord gave, and the Lord has taken away; blessed be the
name of the Lord.'

In all this Job did not sin or charge God with wrong.

or *Genesis 9.8-17 NEB*

God spoke to Noah and to his sons with him: 'I now make my covenant with you and with your descendants after you, and with every living creature that is with you, all birds and cattle, all the wild animals with you on earth, all that have come out of the ark. I will make my covenant with you: never again shall all living creatures be destroyed by the waters of the flood, never again shall there be a flood to lay waste the earth.'

God said, 'This is the sign of the covenant which I establish between myself and you and every living creature with you, to endless generations:

My bow I set in the cloud,
sign of the covenant
between myself and earth.
When I cloud the sky over the earth,
the bow shall be seen in the cloud.

Then will I remember the covenant which I have made between myself and you and living things of every kind. Never again shall the waters become a flood to destroy all living creatures. The bow shall be in the cloud; when I see it, it will remind me of the everlasting covenant between God and living things on earth of every kind.' God said to Noah, 'This is the sign of the covenant which I make between myself and all that lives on earth.'

New Testament *Romans 3.21-26 RSV*

The righteousness of God has been manifested apart from law, although the law and the prophets bear witness to it, the righteousness of God through faith in Jesus Christ for all who believe. For there is no distinction; since all have sinned and fall short of the glory of God, they are justified by his grace as a gift, through the redemption which is in Christ Jesus, whom God put forward as an expiation by his blood, to be received by faith. This was to show God's righteousness, because in his divine forbearance he had passed over former sins; it was to prove at the present time that he himself is righteous and that he justifies him who has faith in Jesus.

or *Romans 8.18-25 RSV*

I consider that the sufferings of this present time are not worth comparing with the glory that is to be revealed to us. For the creation waits with eager longing for the revealing of the sons of God; for the creation was subjected to futility, not of its own will but by the will of him who subjected it in hope; because the creation itself will be set free from its bondage to decay and obtain the glorious liberty of the children of God. We know that the whole creation has been groaning in travail together until now; and not only the creation, but we ourselves, who have the first fruits of the Spirit, groan inwardly as we wait for adoption as sons, the redemption of our bodies. For in this hope we were saved. Now hope that is seen is not hope. For who hopes for what he sees? But if we hope for what we do not see, we wait for it with patience.

Gospel *Luke 12.1-7 NEB*

When a crowd of many thousands had gathered, packed so close that they were treading on one another, Jesus began to speak first to his disciples: 'Beware of the leaven of the Pharisees; I mean their hypocrisy. There is nothing covered up that will not be uncovered, nothing hidden that will not be made known. You may take it, then, that everything you have said in the dark will be heard in broad daylight, and what you have whispered behind closed doors will be shouted from the house-tops.

'To you who are my friends I say: Do not fear those who kill the body and after that have nothing more they can do. I will warn you whom to fear: fear him who, after he has killed, has authority to cast into hell. Believe me, he is the one to fear.

'Are not sparrows five for twopence? And yet not one of them is overlooked by God. More than that, even the hairs of your head have all been counted. Have no fear; you are worth more than any number of sparrows.'

or *Mark 11.22-26 NEB*

Jesus said to his disciples, 'Have faith in God. I tell you this: if anyone says to this mountain, "Be lifted from your place and hurled into the sea", and has no inward doubts, but believes that what he says is happening, it will be done for him. I tell you, then, whatever you ask for in prayer, believe that you have received it and it will be yours.

'And when you stand praying, if you have a grievance against anyone, forgive him, so that your Father in heaven may forgive you the wrongs you have done. But if you do not forgive others, then the wrongs you have done will not be forgiven by your Father in heaven.'

POSTCOMMUNION SENTENCE

Jesus said, If you ask the Father anything in my name, he will give it to you. Ask and you shall receive, that your joy may be full. *John 16.23, 24*

THANKSGIVING FOR THE INSTITUTION OF HOLY BAPTISM

INTRODUCTORY SENTENCE

For anyone who is in Christ, there is a new creation; the old order has gone, and a new order has already begun.
2 Corinthians 5.17

COLLECT

Almighty God,
who anointed Jesus at his baptism with the Holy Spirit
and revealed him as your beloved Son:
inspire us, your children,
who are born of water and the Spirit,
to surrender our lives to your service,
that we may rejoice to be called the sons of God;
through Jesus Christ our Lord.

PSALMS 42.1-7; 34.1-8

READINGS

Old Testament *Ezekiel 36.24-28 or 25a, 26-28 NEB*

(I will take you out of the nations and gather you from every land and bring you to your own soil.) I will sprinkle clean water over you, and you shall be cleansed from all that defiles you (; I will cleanse you from the taint of all your idols). I will give you a new heart and put a new spirit within you; I will take the heart of stone from your body and give you a heart of flesh. I will put my spirit into you and make you conform to my statutes, keep my laws and live by them. You shall live in the land which I gave to your ancestors; you shall become my people, and I will become your God.

New Testament *Romans 6.3-11 NEB*

Have you forgotten that when we were baptized into union with Christ Jesus we were baptized into his death? By baptism we were buried with him, and lay dead, in order that, as Christ was raised from the dead in the splendour of the Father, so also we might set our feet upon the new path of life.

For if we have become incorporate with him in a death like his, we shall also be one with him in a resurrection like his. We know that the man we once were has been crucified with Christ, for the destruction of the sinful self, so that we may no longer be the slaves of sin, since a dead man is no longer answerable for his sin. But if we thus died with Christ, we believe that we shall also come to life with him. We know that Christ, once raised from the dead, is never to die again: he is no longer under the dominion of death. For in dying as he died, he died to sin, once for all, and in living as he lives, he lives to God. In the same way you must regard yourselves as dead to sin and alive to God, in union with Christ Jesus.

Gospel *Matthew 28.16-end JB*

The eleven disciples set out for Galilee, to the mountain where Jesus had arranged to meet them. When they saw him they fell down before him, though some hesitated. Jesus came up and spoke to them. He said, 'All authority in heaven and on earth has been given to me. Go, therefore, make disciples of all the nations; baptize them in the name of the Father and of the Son and of the Holy Spirit, and teach them to observe all the commands I gave you. And know that I am with you always; yes, to the end of time.'

PROPER PREFACE

Rite A. The Preface of Baptism (30) is said.

POSTCOMMUNION SENTENCE

Through faith you are all the children of God in union with Christ Jesus. Baptized into union with him, you have all put on Christ as a garment. *Galatians 3.26, 27*

THANKSGIVING FOR THE INSTITUTION OF HOLY COMMUNION

INTRODUCTORY SENTENCE

Every time you eat this bread and drink this cup, you proclaim the death of the Lord, until he comes.
1 Corinthians 11.26

COLLECT

Almighty and heavenly Father,
we thank you that in this wonderful sacrament
you have given us the memorial
    of the passion of your Son Jesus Christ.
Grant us so to reverence
the sacred mysteries of his body and blood,
that we may know within ourselves
and show forth in our lives the fruits of his redemption;
who is alive and reigns with you and the Holy Spirit,
one God, now and for ever.

PSALMS 43; 116.11-16

READINGS

Old Testament *Exodus 16.2-15 NEB*

The Israelites complained to Moses and Aaron in the wilderness and said, 'If only we had died at the Lord's hand in Egypt, where we sat round the fleshpots and had plenty of bread to eat! But you have brought us out into this wilderness to let this whole assembly starve to death.' The Lord said to Moses, 'I will rain down bread from heaven for you. Each day the people shall go out and gather a day's supply, so that I can put them to the test and see whether they will follow my instructions or not. But on the sixth day, when they prepare what they bring in, it shall be twice as much as they have gathered on other days.' Moses and Aaron then said to all the Israelites, 'In the evening you will know that it was the Lord who brought you out of Egypt, and in the morning you will see the glory of the Lord, because he has heeded your complaints against him; it is not against us that you bring your complaints; we are nothing.' 'You shall know this', Moses said, 'when the Lord, in answer to your complaints, gives you flesh to eat in the evening, and in the morning bread in plenty. What are we? It is against the Lord that you bring your complaints, and not against us.'

Moses told Aaron to say to the whole community of Israel, 'Come into the presence of the Lord, for he has heeded your complaints.' While Aaron was speaking to the community of the Israelites, they looked towards the wilderness, and there was the glory of the Lord appearing in the cloud. The Lord spoke to Moses and said, 'I have heard the complaints of the Israelites. Say to them, "Between dusk and dark you will have flesh to eat and in the morning bread in plenty. You shall know that I the Lord am your God."'

That evening a flock of quails flew in and settled all over the camp, and in the morning a fall of dew lay all around it. When the dew was gone, there in the wilderness, fine flakes appeared, fine as hoar-frost on the ground. When the Israelites saw it, they said to one another, 'What is that?', because they did not know what it was. Moses said to them, 'That is the bread which the Lord has given you to eat.'

New Testament *1 Corinthians 11.23-29 NEB*

The tradition which I handed on to you came to me from the Lord himself: that the Lord Jesus, on the night of his arrest, took bread and, after giving thanks to God, broke it and said: 'This is my body, which is for you; do this as a memorial of me.' In the same way, he took the cup after supper, and said: 'This cup is the new covenant sealed by my blood. Whenever you drink it, do this as a memorial of me.' For every time you eat this bread and drink the cup, you proclaim the death of the Lord, until he comes.

It follows that anyone who eats the bread or drinks the cup of the Lord unworthily will be guilty of desecrating the body and blood of the Lord. A man must test himself before eating his share of the bread and drinking from the cup. For he who eats and drinks eats and drinks judgement on himself if he does not discern the Body.

Gospel *John 6.53-58 NEB*

Jesus said, 'In truth, in very truth I tell you, unless you eat the flesh of the Son of Man and drink his blood you can have no life in you. Whoever eats my flesh and drinks my blood possesses eternal life, and I will raise him up on the last day. My flesh is real food; my blood is real drink. Whoever eats my flesh and drinks my blood dwells continually in me and I dwell in him. As the living Father sent me, and I live because of the Father, so he who eats me shall live because of me. This is the bread which came down from heaven; and it is not like the bread which our fathers ate: they are dead, but whoever eats this bread shall live for ever.'

PROPER PREFACE

Rite A. The Preface of Maundy Thursday (11) is said.
Rite B. The Preface of Maundy Thursday is said.

POSTCOMMUNION SENTENCE

Jesus said, Whoever eats my flesh and drinks my blood will live in me, and I in him. *John 6.56*

AT A MARRIAGE

INTRODUCTORY SENTENCE

God is love, and those who live in love, live in God: and God lives in them. *1 John 4.16*

COLLECT

God our Father,
you have taught us through your Son
that love is the fulfilling of the law.
Grant to your servants
that, loving one another,
they may continue in your love until their lives' end;
through Jesus Christ our Lord.

PSALMS 67; 121; 128

READINGS

Old Testament *Genesis 1.26-28, 31a NEB*

God said, 'Let us make man in our image and likeness to rule the fish in the sea, the birds of heaven, the cattle, all wild animals on earth, and all reptiles that crawl upon the earth.' So God created man in his own image; in the image of God he created him; male and female he created them. God blessed them and said to them, 'Be fruitful and increase, fill the earth and subdue it, rule over the fish in the sea, the birds of heaven, and every living thing that moves upon the earth.' So it was; and God saw all that he had made, and it was very good.

New Testament *Romans 12.1, 2, 9-13 NEB*

My brothers, I implore you by God's mercy to offer your very selves to him: a living sacrifice, dedicated and fit for his acceptance, the worship offered by mind and heart. Adapt yourselves no longer to the pattern of this present world, but let your minds be remade and your whole nature thus transformed. Then you will be able to discern the will of God, and to know what is good, acceptable, and perfect.

Love in all sincerity, loathing evil and clinging to the good. Let love for our brotherhood breed warmth of mutual affection. Give pride of place to one another in esteem.

With unflagging energy, in ardour of spirit, serve the Lord.

Let hope keep you joyful; in trouble stand firm; persist in prayer.

Contribute to the needs of God's people, and practise hospitality.

or 1 Corinthians 13 NEB

I may speak in tongues of men or of angels, but if I am without love, I am a sounding gong or a clanging cymbal. I may have the gift of prophecy, and know every hidden truth; I may have faith strong enough to move mountains; but if I have no love, I am nothing. I may dole out all I possess, or even give my body to be burnt, but if I have no love, I am none the better.

Love is patient; love is kind and envies no one. Love is never boastful, nor conceited, nor rude; never selfish, not quick to take offence. Love keeps no score of wrongs; does not gloat over other men's sins, but delights in the truth. There is nothing love cannot face; there is no limit to its faith, its hope, and its endurance.

Love will never come to an end. Are there prophets? their work will be over. Are there tongues of ecstasy? they will cease. Is there knowledge? it will vanish away; for our knowledge and our prophecy alike are partial, and the partial vanishes when wholeness comes. When I was a child, my speech, my outlook and my thoughts were all childish. When I grew up, I had finished with childish things. Now we see only puzzling reflections in a mirror, but then we shall see face to face. My knowledge now is partial; then it will be whole, like God's knowledge of me. In a word, there are three things that last for ever: faith, hope and love; but the greatest of them all is love.

or *Ephesians 3.14-end RSV*

I bow my knees before the Father, from whom every family
in heaven and on earth is named, that according to the riches
of his glory he may grant you to be strengthened with might
through his Spirit in the inner man, and that Christ may
dwell in your hearts through faith; that you, being rooted
and grounded in love, may have power to comprehend with
all the saints what is the breadth and length and height and
depth, and to know the love of Christ which surpasses
knowledge, that you may be filled with all the fullness
of God.

Now to him who by the power at work within us is able to do
far more abundantly than all that we ask or think, to him be
glory in the church and in Christ Jesus to all generations, for
ever and ever. Amen.

or *Ephesians 5.21-33 JB*

Give way to one another in obedience to Christ. Wives
should regard their husbands as they regard the Lord, since
as Christ is head of the Church and saves the whole body, so
is a husband the head of his wife; and as the Church submits
to Christ, so should wives to their husbands, in everything.
Husbands should love their wives just as Christ loved the
Church and sacrificed himself for her to make her holy. He
made her clean by washing her in water with a form of
words, so that when he took her to himself she would be
glorious, with no speck or wrinkle or anything like that, but
holy and faultless. In the same way, husbands must love
their wives as they love their own bodies; for a man to love
his wife is for him to love himself. A man never hates his
own body, but he feeds it and looks after it; and that is the
way Christ treats the Church, because it is his body—and we
are its living parts. For this reason, a man must leave his
father and mother and be joined to his wife, and the two will
become one body. This mystery has many implications; but I
am saying it applies to Christ and the Church. To sum up;
you too, each one of you, must love his wife as he loves
himself; and let every wife respect her husband.

or *Colossians 3.12-17 RSV*

Put on then, as God's chosen ones, holy and beloved,
compassion, kindness, lowliness, meekness, and patience,
forbearing one another and, if one has a complaint against
another, forgiving each other; as the Lord has forgiven you,
so you also must forgive. And above all these put on love,
which binds everything together in perfect harmony. And
let the peace of Christ rule in your hearts, to which indeed
you were called in the one body. And be thankful. Let the
word of Christ dwell in you richly, as you teach and
admonish one another in all wisdom, and as you sing psalms
and hymns and spiritual songs with thankfulness in your
hearts to God. And whatever you do, in word or deed, do
everything in the name of the Lord Jesus, giving thanks to
God the Father through him.

or *1 John 4.7-12 JB*

My dear people,
let us love one another
since love comes from God
and everyone who loves is begotten by God and
    knows God.
Anyone who fails to love can never have known God,
because God is love.
God's love for us was revealed
when God sent into the world his only Son
so that we could have life through him;
this is the love I mean:
not our love for God,
but God's love for us when he sent his Son
to be the sacrifice that takes our sins away.
My dear people,
since God has loved us so much,
we too should love one another.
No one has ever seen God;
but as long as we love one another
God will live in us
and his love will be complete in us.

Gospel *Matthew 7.21, 24-27 RSV*

Jesus said, 'Not every one who says to me, "Lord, Lord," shall enter the kingdom of heaven, but he who does the will of my Father who is in heaven.

'Every one then who hears these words of mine and does them will be like a wise man who built his house upon the rock; and the rain fell, and the floods came, and the winds blew and beat upon that house, but it did not fall, because it had been founded on the rock. And everyone who hears these words of mine and does not do them will be like a foolish man who built his house upon the sand; and the rain fell, and the floods came, and the winds blew and beat against that house, and it fell; and great was the fall of it.'

or *Mark 10.6-9 NEB*

Jesus said, 'In the beginning, at the creation, God made them male and female. For this reason a man shall leave his father and mother, and be made one with his wife; and the two shall become one flesh. It follows that they are no longer two individuals: they are one flesh. What God has joined together, man must not separate.'

or *John 2.1-11 NEB*

On the third day there was a wedding at Cana-in-Galilee. The mother of Jesus was there, and Jesus and his disciples were guests also. The wine gave out, so Jesus' mother said to him, 'They have no wine left.' He answered, 'Your concern, mother, is not mine. My hour has not yet come.' His mother said to the servants, 'Do whatever he tells you.' There were six stone water-jars standing near, of the kind used for Jewish rites of purification; each held from twenty to thirty gallons. Jesus said to the servants, 'Fill the jars with water', and they filled them to the brim. 'Now draw some off', he ordered, 'and take it to the steward of the feast'; and they did so. The steward tasted the water now turned into wine, not knowing its source; though the servants who had drawn the water knew. He hailed the bridegroom and said, 'Everyone serves the best wine first, and waits until the guests have drunk freely before serving the poorer sort; but you have kept the best wine till now.'

This deed at Cana-in-Galilee is the first of the signs by which Jesus revealed his glory and led his disciples to believe in him.

or John 15.9-12 JB

Jesus said,
'As the Father has loved me,
so I have loved you.
Remain in my love.
If you keep my commandments
you will remain in my love,
just as I have kept my Father's commandments
and remain in his love.
I have told you this
so that my own joy may be in you
and your joy be complete.
This is my commandment:
love one another,
as I have loved you.'

PROPER PREFACE

Rite A. The Preface of Marriage (27) is said.

POSTCOMMUNION SENTENCE

Jesus said, As the Father has loved me, so have I loved you; dwell in my love. *John 15.9*

FOR THE SICK

INTRODUCTORY SENTENCE

Have mercy on me, O Lord, for I am sick, and my bones are racked with pain. *Psalm 6.2*

or

Truly the Lord has borne our sufferings and carried our sorrows. *Isaiah 53.4*

COLLECTS

Heavenly Father,
giver of life and health:
comfort and restore those who are sick,
that they may be strengthened in their weakness
and have confidence in your unfailing love;
through Jesus Christ our Lord.

Creator and Father of all,
we pray for those who are ill.
Bless them, and those who serve their needs,
that they may put their whole trust in you
and be filled with your peace;
through Jesus Christ our Lord.

PSALMS 20.1-5; 42.1-7

READINGS

Old Testament *1 Kings 17.17-end TEV*

The son of the widow in Zarephath fell ill; he got worse and worse, and finally he died. She said to Elijah, 'Man of God, why did you do this to me? Did you come here to remind God of my sins and so cause my son's death?'

'Give the boy to me,' Elijah said. He took the boy from her arms, carried him upstairs to the room where he was staying, and laid him on the bed. Then he prayed aloud, 'O Lord my God, why have you done such a terrible thing to this widow? She has been kind enough to take care of me, and now you kill her son!' Then Elijah stretched himself out on the boy three times and prayed, 'O Lord my God, restore this child to life!' The Lord answered Elijah's prayer; the child started breathing again and revived.

Elijah took the boy back downstairs to his mother and said to her, 'Look, your son is alive!'

She answered, 'Now I know that you are a man of God and that the Lord really speaks through you!'

or *Hosea 6.1-3 NEB*

Come, let us return to the Lord;
for he has torn us and will heal us,
he has struck us and he will bind up our wounds;
after two days he will revive us,
on the third day he will restore us,
that in his presence we may live.
Let us humble ourselves, let us strive to know the Lord,
whose justice dawns like morning light,
and its dawning is as sure as the sunrise.
It will come to us like a shower,
like spring rains that water the earth.

New Testament *2 Corinthians 12.7-10 JB*

In view of the extraordinary nature of these revelations, to
stop me from getting too proud I was given a thorn in the
flesh, an angel of Satan to beat me and stop me from getting
too proud! About this thing, I have pleaded with the Lord
three times for it to leave me, but he has said, 'My grace is
enough for you: my power is at its best in weakness.' So I
shall be very happy to make my weaknesses my special
boast so that the power of Christ may stay over me, and that
is why I am quite content with my weaknesses, and with
insults, hardships, persecutions, and the agonies I go
through for Christ's sake. For it is when I am weak that I
am strong.

or *James 5.13-16a RSV*

Is any one among you suffering? Let him pray. Is any
cheerful? Let him sing praise. Is any among you sick? Let
him call for the elders of the church, and let them pray over
him, anointing him with oil in the name of the Lord; and the
prayer of faith will save the sick man, and the Lord will raise
him up; and if he has committed sins, he will be forgiven.
Therefore confess your sins to one another, and pray for one
another, that you may be healed.

Gospel *Matthew 8.5-13 (or -17) JB*

When Jesus went into Capernaum a centurion came up and pleaded with him. 'Sir,' he said, 'my servant is lying at home paralysed, and in great pain.' 'I will come myself and cure him', said Jesus. The centurion replied, 'Sir, I am not worthy to have you under my roof; just give the word and my servant will be cured. For I am under authority myself, and have soldiers under me; and I say to one man: Go, and he goes; to another: Come here, and he comes; to my servant: Do this, and he does it.' When Jesus heard this he was astonished and said to those following him, 'I tell you solemnly, nowhere in Israel have I found faith like this. And I tell you that many will come from east and west to take their places with Abraham and Isaac and Jacob at the feast in the kingdom of heaven; but the subjects of the kingdom will be turned out into the dark, where there will be weeping and grinding of teeth.' And to the centurion Jesus said, 'Go back, then; you have believed, so let this be done for you.' And the servant was cured at that moment.

(And going into Peter's house Jesus found Peter's mother-in-law in bed with fever. He touched her hand and the fever left her, and she got up and began to wait on him.

That evening they brought him many who were possessed by devils. He cast out the spirits with a word and cured all who were sick. This was to fulfil the prophecy of Isaiah: He took our sicknesses away and carried our diseases for us.)

or *Matthew 8.14-17 JB*

Going into Peter's house Jesus found Peter's mother-in-law in bed with fever. He touched her hand and the fever left her, and she got up and began to wait on him.

That evening they brought him many who were possessed by devils. He cast out the spirits with a word and cured all who were sick. This was to fulfil the prophecy of Isaiah: He took our sicknesses away and carried our diseases for us.

or *Mark 2.1-12 NEB*

When Jesus returned to Capernaum, the news went round that he was at home; and such a crowd collected that the space in front of the door was not big enough to hold them. And while he was proclaiming the message to them, a man was brought who was paralysed. Four men were carrying him, but because of the crowd they could not get him near. So they opened up the roof over the place where Jesus was, and when they had broken through they lowered the stretcher on which the paralysed man was lying. When Jesus saw their faith, he said to the paralysed man, 'My son, your sins are forgiven.'

Now there were some lawyers sitting there and they thought to themselves, 'Why does the fellow talk like that? This is blasphemy! Who but God alone can forgive sins?' Jesus knew in his own mind that this was what they were thinking, and said to them: 'Why do you harbour thoughts like these? Is it easier to say to this paralysed man, "Your sins are forgiven", or to say, "Stand up, take your bed and walk"? But to convince you that the Son of Man has the right on earth to forgive sins'—he turned to the paralysed man—'I say to you, stand up, take your bed, and go home.' And he got up, and at once took his stretcher and went out in full view of them all, so that they were astounded and praised God. 'Never before', they said, 'have we seen the like.'

POSTCOMMUNION SENTENCE

My grace is sufficient for you, for my power is made perfect in weakness. *2 Corinthians 12.9*

or

If anyone is sick, he should send for the elders of the church to pray over him (and anoint him with oil in the name of the Lord); the prayer offered in faith will save the sick man. *James 5.14, 15*

FOR THE DYING

INTRODUCTORY SENTENCE

Have mercy on me, O Lord, for I am sick, and my bones are racked with pain. *Psalm 6.2*

or

Truly the Lord has borne our sufferings and carried our sorrows. *Isaiah 53.4*

COLLECT

Heavenly Father,
into whose hands your Son Jesus Christ
commended his spirit at his last hour:
into those same hands
we now commend your servant . . .,
that death may be for *him* the gate to life
and to eternal fellowship with you;
through Jesus Christ our Lord.

PSALMS 39.1-8; 90.1-12

READINGS

Old Testament *Joshua 23.1-8 NEB*

A long time had passed since the Lord had given Israel security from all the enemies who surrounded them, and Joshua was now a very old man. He summoned all Israel, their elders and heads of families, their judges and officers, and said to them, 'I have become a very old man. You have seen for yourselves all that the Lord our God has done to these peoples for your sake; it was the Lord God himself who fought for you. I have allotted you your patrimony tribe by tribe, the land of all the peoples that I have wiped out and of all these that remain between the Jordan and the Great Sea which lies towards the setting sun. The Lord your God himself drove them out for your sake; he drove them out to make room for you, and you occupied their land, as the Lord your God had promised you. Be resolute therefore: observe

and perform everything written in the book of the law of
Moses, without swerving to right or to left. You must not
associate with the peoples that are left among you; you must
not call upon their gods by name, nor swear by them nor
prostrate yourselves in worship before them. You must hold
fast to the Lord your God as you have done down to
this day.'

or *Isaiah 53.3-5 RSV*

He was despised and rejected by men;
a man of sorrows, and acquainted with grief;
and as one from whom men hide their faces
he was despised, and we esteemed him not.

Surely he has borne our griefs
and carried our sorrows;
yet we esteemed him stricken,
smitten by God, and afflicted.
But he was wounded for our transgressions,
he was bruised for our iniquities;
upon him was the chastisement that made us whole,
and with his stripes we are healed.

New Testament *Romans 8.31b-end RSV*

If God is for us, who is against us? He who did not spare his
own Son but gave him up for us all, will he not also give us all
things with him? Who shall bring any charge against God's
elect? It is God who justifies; who is to condemn? Is it Christ
Jesus, who died, yes, who was raised from the dead, who is
at the right hand of God, who indeed intercedes for us? Who
shall separate us from the love of Christ? Shall tribulation, or
distress, or persecution, or famine, or nakedness, or peril, or
sword? As it is written,

'For thy sake we are being killed all the day long;
we are regarded as sheep to be slaughtered.'

No, in all these things we are more than conquerors through
him who loved us. For I am sure that neither death, nor life,
nor angels, nor principalities, nor things present, nor things
to come, nor powers, nor height, nor depth, nor anything

else in all creation, will be able to separate us from the love of God in Christ Jesus our Lord.

or *Philippians 1.20-26 JB*

My one hope and trust is that I shall never have to admit defeat, but that now as always I shall have the courage for Christ to be glorified in my body, whether by my life or by my death. Life to me, of course, is Christ, but then death would bring me something more; but then again, if living in this body means doing work which is having good results—I do not know what I should choose. I am caught in this dilemma: I want to be gone and be with Christ, which would be very much the better, but for me to stay alive in this body is a more urgent need for your sake. This weighs with me so much that I feel sure I shall survive and stay with you all, and help you to progress in the faith and even increase your joy in it; and so you will have another reason to give praise to Christ Jesus on my account when I am with you again.

Gospel *Luke 23.39-46 RSV*

One of the criminals who were hanged railed at Jesus, saying, 'Are you not the Christ? Save yourself and us!' But the other rebuked him, saying, 'Do you not fear God, since you are under the same sentence of condemnation? And we indeed justly; for we are receiving the due reward for our deeds; but this man has done nothing wrong.' And he said, 'Jesus, remember me when you come in your kingly power.' And he said to him, 'Truly, I say to you, today you will be with me in Paradise.'

It was now about the sixth hour, and there was darkness over the whole land until the ninth hour, while the sun's light failed; and the curtain of the temple was torn in two. Then Jesus, crying with a loud voice, said, 'Father, into your hands I commit my spirit!' And having said this he breathed his last.

or *John 14.1-3 JB*

Jesus said,
'Do not let your hearts be troubled.

Trust in God still, and trust in me.
There are many rooms in my Father's house;
if there were not, I should have told you.
I am going now to prepare a place for you,
and after I have gone and prepared you a place,
I shall return to take you with me;
so that where I am
you may be too.'

POSTCOMMUNION SENTENCE

My grace is sufficient for you, for my power is made perfect
in weakness. *2 Corinthians 12.9*

or

If anyone is sick, he should send for the elders of the church
to pray over him (and anoint him with oil in the name of the
Lord); the prayer offered in faith will save the sick man.
James 5.14, 15

AT A FUNERAL

INTRODUCTORY SENTENCE

Since we believe that Jesus died and rose again, so will it be
for those who have died: God will bring them to life with
Jesus. *1 Thessalonians 4.14*

COLLECTS

Heavenly Father,
in your Son Jesus Christ
you have given us a true faith and a sure hope.
Strengthen this faith and hope in us all our days,
that we may live as those who believe in
    the communion of saints,
    the forgiveness of sins,
    and the resurrection to eternal life;
through your Son Jesus Christ our Lord.

Merciful God,
whose Son Jesus Christ is the resurrection
    and the life of all the faithful:
raise us from the death of sin
to the life of righteousness,
that at the last we, with our *brother N*,
may come to your eternal joy;
through Jesus Christ our Lord.

O God,
the maker and redeemer of all mankind:
grant us, with your servant *N*
    and all the faithful departed,
the sure benefits of your Son's
    saving passion and glorious resurrection;
that in the last day,
when you gather up all things in Christ,
we may with them enjoy the fullness of your promises;
through Jesus Christ our Lord.

Other suitable prayers may be found in the Funeral Services
(sections 52 and 53, p. 334).

PSALMS 23; 27; 42.1-7; 90.1-6, 10, 12, 14, 16, 17; 103.8, 13-17;
118.14-21, 28, 29; 121; 130; 139.1-11, 17, 18

READINGS

Old Testament *Isaiah 25.8, 9 NEB*

The Lord God will swallow up death for ever;
he will wipe away the tears
from every face,
and remove the reproach of his people from the whole earth.
The Lord has spoken.

On that day men will say,
'See, this is our God
for whom we have waited to deliver us;
this is the Lord for whom we have waited;
let us rejoice and exult in his deliverance.'

or *Lamentations 3.22-26, 31-33 NEB*

The Lord's true love is surely not spent,
nor has his compassion failed;
they are new every morning,
so great is his constancy.
The Lord, I say, is all that I have;
therefore I will wait for him patiently.
The Lord is good to those who look for him,
to all who seek him;
it is good to wait in patience and sigh
for deliverance by the Lord.
For the Lord will not cast off
his servants for ever.
He may punish cruelly, yet he will have compassion
in the fullness of his love;
he does not willingly afflict
or punish any mortal man.

or *Wisdom 3.1-5, 9 NEB*

The souls of the just are in God's hand, and torment shall not
touch them. In the eyes of foolish men they seemed to be
dead; their departure was reckoned as defeat, and their
going from us as disaster. But they are at peace, for though in
the sight of men they may be punished, they have a sure
hope of immortality; and after a little chastisement they will
receive great blessings, because God has tested them and
found them worthy to be his. Those who have put their trust
in him shall understand that he is true, and the faithful shall
attend upon him in love; they are his chosen, and grace and
mercy shall be theirs.

or *Wisdom 4.8-11, 13-15 RSV*

For old age is not honoured for length of time,
nor measured by number of years;
but understanding is grey hair for men,
and a blameless life is ripe old age.

There was one who pleased God and was loved by him,
and while living among sinners he was taken up.
He was caught up lest evil change his understanding

or guile deceive his soul.
Being perfected in a short time, he fulfilled long years;
for his soul was pleasing to the Lord,
therefore he took him quickly from the midst of wickedness.
Yet the peoples saw and did not understand,
nor take such a thing to heart,
that God's grace and mercy are with his elect,
and he watches over his holy ones.

New Testament *Romans 8.31b-39 RSV*

If God is for us, who is against us? He who did not spare his
own Son but gave him up for us all, will he not also give us all
things with him? Who shall bring any charge against God's
elect? It is God who justifies; who is to condemn? Is it Christ
Jesus, who died, yes, who was raised from the dead, who is
at the right hand of God, who indeed intercedes for us? Who
shall separate us from the love of Christ? Shall tribulation, or
distress, or persecution, or famine, or nakedness, or peril, or
sword? As it is written,
'For thy sake we are being killed all the day long;
we are regarded as sheep to be slaughtered.'

No, in all these things we are more than conquerors through
him who loved us. For I am sure that neither death, nor life,
nor angels, nor principalities, nor things present, nor things
to come, nor powers, nor height, nor depth, nor anything
else in all creation, will be able to separate us from the love of
God in Christ Jesus our Lord.

or *Romans 14.7-9 RSV*

None of us lives to himself, and none of us dies to himself. If
we live, we live to the Lord, and if we die, we die to the Lord;
so then, whether we live or whether we die, we are
the Lord's. For to this end Christ died and lived again, that he
might be Lord both of the dead and of the living.

or *1 Corinthians 15.20-26, 35-38, 42-44a, 53-end RSV*

Christ has been raised from the dead, the first fruits of those
who have fallen asleep. For as by a man came death, by a
man has come also the resurrection of the dead. For as in

Adam all die, so also in Christ shall all be made alive. But each in his own order: Christ the first fruits, then at his coming those who belong to Christ. Then comes the end, when he delivers the kingdom to God the Father after destroying every rule and every authority and power. For he must reign until he has put all his enemies under his feet. The last enemy to be destroyed is death.

But someone will ask, 'How are the dead raised? With what kind of body do they come?' You foolish man! What you sow does not come to life unless it dies. And what you sow is not the body which is to be, but a bare kernel, perhaps of wheat or of some other grain. But God gives it a body as he has chosen, and to each kind of seed its own body.

So it is with the resurrection of the dead. What is sown is perishable, what is raised is imperishable. It is sown in dishonour, it is raised in glory. It is sown in weakness, it is raised in power. It is sown a physical body, it is raised a spiritual body.

For this perishable nature must put on the imperishable, and this mortal nature must put on immortality. When the perishable puts on the imperishable, and the mortal puts on immortality, then shall come to pass the saying that is written: 'Death is swallowed up in victory.' 'O death, where is thy victory? O death, where is thy sting?' The sting of death is sin, and the power of sin is the law. But thanks be to God, who give us the victory through our Lord Jesus Christ.

Therefore, my beloved brethren, be steadfast, immoveable, always abounding in the work of the Lord, knowing that in the Lord your labour is not in vain.

or 2 Corinthians 1.3-5 NEB

Praise be to the God and Father of our Lord Jesus Christ, the all-merciful Father, the God whose consolation never fails us! He comforts us in all our troubles, so that we in turn may be able to comfort others in any trouble of theirs and to share with them the consolation we ourselves receive from God. As Christ's cup of suffering overflows, and we suffer with him, so also through Christ our consolation overflows.

or *2 Corinthians 4.7-end NEB*

We are no better than pots of earthenware to contain this treasure, and this proves that such transcendent power does not come from us, but is God's alone. Hard-pressed on every side, we are never hemmed in; bewildered, we are never at our wits' end; hunted, we are never abandoned to our fate; struck down, we are not left to die. Wherever we go we carry death with us in our body, the death that Jesus died, that in this body also life may reveal itself, the life that Jesus lives. For continually, while still alive, we are being surrendered into the hands of death, for Jesus' sake, so that the life of Jesus also may be revealed in this mortal body of ours. Thus death is at work in us, and life in you.

But Scripture says, 'I believed, and therefore I spoke out', and we too, in the same spirit of faith, believe and therefore speak out; for we know that he who raised the Lord Jesus to life will with Jesus raise us too, and bring us to his presence, and you with us. Indeed, it is for your sake that all things are ordered, so that, as the abounding grace of God is shared by more and more, the greater may be the chorus of thanksgiving that ascends to the glory of God.

No wonder we do not lose heart! Though our outward humanity is in decay, yet day by day we are inwardly renewed. Our troubles are slight and short-lived; and their outcome an eternal glory which outweighs them far. Meanwhile our eyes are fixed, not on the things that are seen, but on the things that are unseen: for what is seen passes away; what is unseen is eternal.

or *Ephesians 3.14-19 RSV*

I bow my knees before the Father, from whom every family in heaven and on earth is named, that according to the riches of his glory he may grant you to be strengthened with might through his Spirit in the inner man, and that Christ may dwell in your hearts through faith; that you, being rooted and grounded in love, may have power to comprehend with all the saints what is the breadth and length and height and depth, and to know the love of Christ which surpasses

knowledge, that you may be filled with all the fullness
of God.

or *1 Thessalonians 4.13-18 RSV*

We would not have you ignorant, brethren, concerning
those who are asleep, that you may not grieve as others do
who have no hope. For since we believe that Jesus died and
rose again, even so, through Jesus, God will bring with him
those who have fallen asleep. For this we declare to you by
the word of the Lord, that we who are alive, who are left
until the coming of the Lord, shall not precede those who
have fallen asleep. For the Lord himself will descend from
heaven with a cry of command, with the archangel's call,
and with the sound of the trumpet of God. And the dead in
Christ will rise first; then we who are alive, who are left, shall
be caught up together with them in the clouds to meet the
Lord in the air; and so we shall always be with the Lord.
Therefore comfort one another with these words.

or *Philippians 3.10-end JB*

All I want is to know Christ and the power of his resurrection
and to share his sufferings by reproducing the pattern of his
death. That is the way I can hope to take my place in the
resurrection of the dead. Not that I have become perfect yet:
I have not yet won, but I am still running, trying to capture
the prize for which Christ Jesus captured me. I can assure
you my brothers, I am far from thinking that I have already
won. All I can say is that I forget the past and I strain ahead
for what is still to come; I am racing for the finish, for the
prize to which God calls us upwards to receive in Christ
Jesus. We who are called 'perfect' must all think in this way.
If there is some point on which you see things differently,
God will make it clear to you; meanwhile, let us go forward
on the road that has brought us to where we are.

My brothers, be united in following my rule of life. Take as
your models everybody who is already doing this and study
them as you used to study us. I have told you often, and I
repeat it today with tears, there are many who are behaving
as the enemies of the cross of Christ. They are destined to be

lost. They make foods into their god and they are proudest of something they ought to think shameful; the things they think important are earthly things. For us, our homeland is in heaven, and from heaven comes the saviour we are waiting for, the Lord Jesus Christ, and he will transfigure these wretched bodies of ours into copies of his glorious body. He will do that by the same power with which he can subdue the whole universe.

or *1 Peter 1.3-9 NEB*

Praise be to the God and Father of our Lord Jesus Christ, who in his great mercy gave us new birth into a living hope by the resurrection of Jesus Christ from the dead! The inheritance to which we are born is one that nothing can destroy or spoil or wither. It is kept for you in heaven, and you, because you put your faith in God, are under the protection of his power until salvation comes—the salvation which is even now in readiness and will be revealed at the end of time.

This is cause for great joy, even though now you smart for a little while, if need be, under trials of many kinds. Even gold passes through the assayer's fire, and more precious than perishable gold is faith which has stood the test. These trials come so that your faith may prove itself worthy of all praise, glory, and honour when Jesus Christ is revealed.

You have not seen him, yet you love him; and trusting in him now without seeing him, you are transported with a joy too great for words, while you reap the harvest of your faith, that is, salvation for your souls.

or *Revelation 21.1-7 RSV*

I saw a new heaven and a new earth; for the first heaven and the first earth had passed away, and the sea was no more. And I saw the holy city, new Jerusalem, coming down out of heaven from God, prepared as a bride adorned for her husband; and I heard a great voice from the throne saying, 'Behold, the dwelling of God is with men. He will dwell with them, and they shall be his people, and God himself will be with them; he will wipe away every tear from their eyes, and death shall be no more, neither shall there be mourning nor crying nor pain any more, for the former things have passed away.'

And he who sat upon the throne said, 'Behold, I make all things new.' Also he said, 'Write this, for these words are trustworthy and true.' And he said to me, 'It is done! I am the Alpha and the Omega, the beginning and the end. To the thirsty I will give water without price from the fountain of the water of life. He who conquers shall have this heritage, and I will be his God and he shall be my son.'

Gospel *Mark 10.13-16 NEB*

They brought children for Jesus to touch. The disciples rebuked them, but when Jesus saw this he was indignant, and said to them, 'Let the children come to me; do not try to stop them; for the kingdom of God belongs to such as these. I tell you, whoever does not accept the kingdom of God like a child will never enter it.' And he put his arms round them, laid his hands upon them, and blessed them.

or *John 5.19-25 JB*

Jesus said to the Jews,
'I tell you most solemnly,
the Son can do nothing by himself;
he can do only what he sees the Father doing:
and whatever the Father does the Son does too.
For the Father loves the Son
and shows him everything he does himself,
and he will show him even greater things than these,
works that will astonish you.
Thus, as the Father raises the dead and gives them life,
so the Son gives life to anyone he chooses;
for the Father judges no one;
he has entrusted all judgement to the Son,
so that all may honour the Son
as they honour the Father.
Whoever refuses honour to the Son
refuses honour to the Father who sent him.

I tell you most solemnly,
whoever listens to my words,
and believes in the one who sent me,
has eternal life;
without being brought to judgement
he has passed from death to life.
I tell you most solemnly,
the hour will come—in fact it is here already—
when the dead will hear the voice of the Son of God,
and all who hear it will live.'

or *John 6.35-40 JB*

Jesus said,
'I am the bread of life.
He who comes to me will never be hungry;
he who believes in me will never thirst.
But, as I have told you,
you can see me and still you do not believe.
All that the Father gives me will come to me,
and whoever comes to me
I shall not turn him away;
because I have come from heaven,
not to do my own will,
but to do the will of the one who sent me.
Now the will of him who sent me
is that I should lose nothing
of all that he has given to me,
and that I should raise it up on the last day.
Yes, it is my Father's will
that whoever sees the Son and believes in him
shall have eternal life,
and that I shall raise him up on the last day.'

or *John 11.17-27 NEB*

On his arrival Jesus found that Lazarus had already been
four days in the tomb. Bethany was just under two miles
from Jerusalem, and many of the people had come from the
city to Martha and Mary to condole with them on their
brother's death. As soon as she heard that Jesus was on his
way, Martha went to meet him, while Mary stayed at home.

Martha said to Jesus, 'If you had been here, sir, my brother would not have died. Even now I know that whatever you ask of God, God will grant you.' Jesus said, 'Your brother will rise again.' 'I know that he will rise again', said Martha, 'at the resurrection on the last day.' Jesus said, 'I am the resurrection and I am life. If a man has faith in me, even though he die, he shall come to life; and no one who is alive and has faith shall ever die. Do you believe this?' 'Lord, I do,' she answered; 'I now believe that you are the Messiah, the Son of God who was to come into the world.'

or *John 14.1-6 JB*

Jesus said to his disciples,
'Do not let your hearts be troubled.
Trust in God still, and trust in me.
There are many rooms in my Father's house;
if there were not, I should have told you.
I am going now to prepare a place for you,
and after I have gone and prepared you a place,
I shall return to take you with me;
so that where I am
you may be too.
You know the way to the place where I am going.'

Thomas said, 'Lord, we do not know where you are going, so how can we know the way?' Jesus said,
'I am the Way, the Truth and the Life.
No one can come to the Father except through me.'

or *John 20.1-9 RSV*

On the first day of the week Mary Magdalen came to the tomb early, while it was still dark, and saw that the stone had been taken away from the tomb. So she ran, and went to Simon Peter and the other disciple, the one whom Jesus loved, and said to them, 'They have taken the Lord out of the tomb, and we do not know where they have laid him.' Peter then came out with the other disciple, and they went toward the tomb. They both ran, but the other disciple outran Peter and reached the tomb first; and stooping to look in, he saw the linen cloths lying there, but he did not go in. Then Simon

Peter came, following him, and he went into the tomb; he saw the linen cloths lying, and the napkin, which had been on his head, not lying with the linen cloths but rolled up in a place by itself. Then the other disciple, who reached the tomb first, also went in, and he saw and believed; for as yet they did not know the scripture, that he must rise from the dead.

PROPER PREFACE

Rite A. A Preface of the Resurrection (15) or (16) is said.
Rite B. The Preface of Easter is said.

POSTCOMMUNION SENTENCE

Jesus said, Whoever eats my flesh and drinks my blood has eternal life, and I will raise him up on the last day. *John 6.54*

or

Jesus said, I am the resurrection and I am the life: whoever lives and believes in me will never die. *John 11.25, 26*

AT A FUNERAL OF A CHILD

INTRODUCTORY SENTENCE

The Lamb who is at the throne will be their shepherd and will lead them to springs of living water; and God will wipe away all tears from their eyes. *Revelation 7.17*

COLLECT

Heavenly Father,
whose Son our Saviour
took little children into his arms and blessed them:
receive, we pray, your child *N*
in your never-failing care and love,
comfort all who have loved *him* on earth,
and bring us all to your everlasting kingdom;
through Jesus Christ our Lord.

PSALM 23

READINGS

Old Testament *Lamentations 3.22-26, 31-33 NEB*

The Lord's true love is surely not spent,
nor has his compassion failed;
they are new every morning,
so great is his constancy.
The Lord, I say, is all that I have;
therefore I will wait for him patiently.
The Lord is good to those who look for him,
to all who seek him;
it is good to wait in patience and sigh
for deliverance by the Lord.
For the Lord will not cast off
his servants for ever.
He may punish cruelly, yet he will have compassion
in the fullness of his love;
he does not willingly afflict
or punish any mortal man.

New Testament *Ephesians 3.14-19 RSV*

I bow my knees before the Father, from whom every family
in heaven and on earth is named, that according to the riches
of his glory he may grant you to be strengthened with might
through his Spirit in the inner man, and that Christ may
dwell in your hearts through faith; that you, being rooted
and grounded in love, may have power to comprehend with
all the saints what is the breadth and length and height and
depth, and to know the love of Christ which surpasses
knowledge, that you may be filled with all the fullness
of God.

Gospel *Mark 10.13-16 NEB*

They brought children for Jesus to touch. The disciples
rebuked them, but when Jesus saw this he was indignant,
and said to them, 'Let the children come to me; do not try to
stop them; for the kingdom of God belongs to such as these.
I tell you, whoever does not accept the kingdom of God like a

child will never enter it.' And he put his arms round them, laid his hands upon them, and blessed them.

PROPER PREFACE

Rite A. A Preface of the Resurrection (15) or (16) is said.
Rite B. The Preface of Easter is said.

POSTCOMMUNION SENTENCE

Christ being raised from the dead will never die again: death no longer has power over him. *Romans 6.9*

FOR THE APPOINTMENT OF A BISHOP OR AN INCUMBENT

INTRODUCTORY SENTENCE

Lord, let your priests be clothed with righteousness, that your faithful people may rejoice. *Psalm 132.9*

COLLECT

Almighty God,
the giver of all good gifts,
guide with your heavenly wisdom
those who are to choose a faithful pastor
    for this *diocese/parish*:
that we may receive
one who will speak your word and serve your people
    according to your will;
through Jesus Christ our Lord.

PSALMS 15; 25.1-5

READINGS

Old Testament *Numbers 11.16, 17, 24-29 RSV*

The Lord said to Moses, 'Gather for me seventy men of the elders of Israel, whom you know to be the elders of the people and officers over them; and bring them to the tent of meeting, and let them take their stand there with you. And I will come down and talk with you there; and I will take some of the spirit which is upon you and put it upon them; and they shall bear the burden of the people with you, that you may not bear it yourself alone.'

So Moses went out and told the people the words of the Lord; and he gathered seventy men of the elders of the people, and placed them round about the tent. Then the Lord came down in the cloud and spoke to him, and took some of the spirit that was upon him and put it upon the seventy elders; and when the spirit rested upon them, they prophesied. But they did so no more.

Now two men remained in the camp, one named Eldad, and the other named Medad, and the spirit rested upon them; they were among those registered, but they had not gone out to the tent, and so they prophesied in the camp. And a young man ran and told Moses, 'Eldad and Medad are prophesying in the camp.' And Joshua the son of Nun, the minister of Moses, one of his chosen men, said, 'My lord Moses, forbid them.' But Moses said to him, 'Are you jealous for my sake? Would that all the Lord's people were prophets, that the Lord would put his spirit upon them!'

or 1 Samuel 16.1-13a NEB

The Lord said to Samuel, 'How long will you mourn for Saul because I have rejected him as king over Israel? Fill your horn with oil and take it with you; I am sending you to Jesse of Bethlehem; for I have chosen myself a king among his sons.' Samuel answered, 'How can I go? Saul will hear of it and kill me.' 'Take a heifer with you,' said the Lord; 'say you have come to offer a sacrifice to the Lord, and invite Jesse to the sacrifice; then I will let you know what you must do. You shall anoint for me the man whom I show you.' Samuel did as the Lord had told him, and went to Bethlehem. The elders of the city came in haste to meet him, saying, 'Why have you come? Is all well?' 'All is well,' said Samuel; 'I have come to sacrifice to the Lord. Hallow yourselves and come with me to the sacrifice.' He himself hallowed Jesse and his sons and invited them to the sacrifice also. They came, and when

Samuel saw Eliab he thought, 'Here, before the Lord, is his anointed king.' But the Lord said to him, 'Take no account of it if he is handsome and tall; I reject him. The Lord does not see as man sees; men judge by appearances but the Lord judges by the heart.' Then Jesse called Abinadab and made him pass before Samuel, but he said, 'No, the Lord has not chosen this one.' Then he presented Shammah, and Samuel said, 'Nor has the Lord chosen him.' Seven of his sons Jesse presented to Samuel, but he said, 'The Lord has not chosen any of these.' Then Samuel asked, 'Are these all?' Jesse answered, 'There is still the youngest, but he is looking after the sheep.' Samuel said to Jesse, 'Send and fetch him; we will not sit down until he comes.' So he sent and fetched him. He was handsome, with ruddy cheeks and bright eyes. The Lord said, 'Rise and anoint him: this is the man.' Samuel took the horn of oil and anointed him in the presence of his brothers. Then the spirit of the Lord came down upon David and was with him from that day onwards.

New Testament *Acts 1.15-17, 20-end TEV*

There was a meeting of the believers, about a hundred and twenty in all, and Peter stood up to speak. 'My brothers,' he said, 'the scripture had to come true in which the Holy Spirit, speaking through David, made a prediction about Judas, who was the guide for those who arrested Jesus. Judas was a member of our group, for he had been chosen to have a part in our work.

'For it is written in the book of Psalms,
"May his house become empty;
may no one live in it."
It is also written,
"May someone else take his place of service."

'So then, someone must join us as a witness to the resurrection of the Lord Jesus. He must be one of the men who were in our group during the whole time that the Lord Jesus travelled about with us, beginning from the time John preached his message of baptism until the day Jesus was taken up from us to heaven.'

So they proposed two men: Joseph, who was called

Barsabbas (also known as Justus), and Matthias. Then they prayed, 'Lord, you know the thoughts of everyone, so show us which of these two you have chosen to serve as an apostle in the place of Judas, who left to go to the place where he belongs.' Then they drew lots to choose between the two men, and the one chosen was Matthias, who was added to the group of eleven apostles.

or *Ephesians 4.7-16 NEB*

Each of us has been given his gift, his due portion of Christ's bounty. Therefore Scripture says:

'He ascended into the heights
with captives in his train;
he gave gifts to men.'

Now, the word 'ascended' implies that he also descended to the lowest level, down to the very earth. He who descended is no other than he who ascended far above all heavens, so that he might fill the universe. And these were his gifts: some to be apostles, some prophets, some evangelists, some pastors and teachers, to equip God's people for work in his service, to the building up of the body of Christ. So shall we all at last attain to the unity inherent in our faith and our knowledge of the Son of God—to mature manhood, measured by nothing less than the full stature of Christ. We are no longer to be children, tossed by the waves and whirled about by every fresh gust of teaching, dupes of crafty rogues and their deceitful schemes. No, let us speak the truth in love; so shall we fully grow up into Christ. He is the head, and on him the whole body depends. Bonded and knit together by every constituent joint, the whole frame grows through the due activity of each part, and builds itself up in love.

Gospel *John 4.34-38 RSV*

Jesus said to the disciples, 'My food is to do the will of him who sent me, and to accomplish his work. Do you not say, "There are yet four months, then comes the harvest"? I tell you, lift up your eyes, and see how the fields are already white for harvest. He who reaps receives wages, and gathers fruit for eternal life, so that sower and reaper may rejoice together. For here the saying holds true, "One sows and another reaps." I sent you to reap that for which you did not labour; others have laboured, and you have entered into their labour.'

or *John 15.9-17 JB*

Jesus said,
'As the Father has loved me,
so I have loved you.
Remain in my love.
If you keep my commandments
you will remain in my love,
just as I have kept my Father's commandments
and remain in his love.
I have told you this
so that my own joy may be in you
and your joy be complete.
This is my commandment:
love one another,
as I have loved you.
A man can have no greater love
than to lay down his life for his friends.
You are my friends,
if you do what I command you.
I shall not call you servants any more,
because a servant does not know
his master's business;
I call you friends,
because I have made known to you
everything I have learnt from my Father.
You did not choose me,
no, I chose you;
and I commissioned you
to go out and to bear fruit,
fruit that will last;
and then the Father will give you
anything you ask him in my name.
What I command you
is to love one another.'

PROPER PREFACE

Rite A. The Preface of Ordination (28) may be said.

POSTCOMMUNION SENTENCE

Jesus said, You have not chosen me; I have chosen you. Go and bear fruit that will last. *John 15.16*

FOR AN ENTHRONEMENT OR AN INSTALLATION OR AN INDUCTION

INTRODUCTORY SENTENCE

The Spirit of the Lord is upon me, because he has anointed me; he has sent me to bring good news, to proclaim release, to set the downtrodden free, and to proclaim the year of the Lord's favour. *Luke 4.18*

COLLECT

God our Father, Lord of all the world,
we thank you that through your Son
you have called us into the fellowship
   of your universal Church:
hear our prayer for your faithful people
that each in his vocation and ministry
may be an instrument of your love,
and give to your servant now to be *enthroned*
the needful gifts of grace;
through our Lord and Saviour Jesus Christ.

PSALMS 95.1-7; 101

READINGS

Old Testament *Numbers 3.5-9 NEB*

The Lord spoke to Moses and said, 'Bring forward the tribe of Levi and appoint them to serve Aaron the priest and to minister to him. They shall be in attendance on him and on the whole community before the Tent of the Presence, undertaking the service of the Tabernacle. They shall be in charge of all the equipment in the Tent of the Presence, and be in attendance on the Israelites, undertaking the service of the Tabernacle. You shall assign the Levites to Aaron and his sons as especially dedicated to him out of all the Israelites.'

or *Isaiah 61.1-3 NEB*

The spirit of the Lord God is upon me
because the Lord has anointed me;
he has sent me to bring good news to the humble;
to bind up the broken-hearted,
to proclaim liberty to captives
and release to those in prison;
to proclaim a year of the Lord's favour
and a day of the vengeance of our God;
to comfort all who mourn,
to give them garlands instead of ashes,
oil of gladness instead of mourners' tears,
a garment of splendour for the heavy heart.
They shall be called Trees of Righteousness,
planted by the Lord for his glory.

New Testament *Ephesians 4.1-7 NEB*

I entreat you—I, a prisoner for the Lord's sake: as God has called you, live up to your calling. Be humble always and gentle, and patient too. Be forbearing with one another and charitable. Spare no effort to make fast with bonds of peace the unity which the Spirit gives. There is one body and one Spirit, as there is also one hope held out in God's call to you; one Lord, one faith, one baptism; one God and Father of all, who is over all and through all and in all.

But each of us has been given his gift, his due portion of Christ's bounty.

or *Colossians 3.12-17 RSV*

Put on then, as God's chosen ones, holy and beloved, compassion, kindness, lowliness, meekness, and patience, forbearing one another and, if one has a complaint against another, forgiving each other; as the Lord has forgiven you, so you also must forgive. And above all these put on love, which binds everything together in perfect harmony. And let the peace of Christ rule in your hearts, to which indeed you were called in the one body. And be thankful. Let the word of Christ dwell in you richly, as you teach and admonish one another in all wisdom, and as you sing psalms and hymns and spiritual songs with thankfulness in your hearts to God. And whatever you do, in word or deed, do everything in the name of the Lord Jesus, giving thanks to God the Father through him.

Gospel *Luke 12.35-44 NEB*

Jesus said to his disciples, 'Be ready for action, with belts fastened and lamps alight. Be like men who wait for their master's return from a wedding-party, ready to let him in the moment he arrives and knocks. Happy are those servants whom the master finds on the alert when he comes. I tell you this: he will fasten his belt, seat them at table, and come and wait on them. Even if it is the middle of the night or before dawn when he comes, happy they if he finds them alert. And remember, if the householder had known what time the burglar was coming he would not have let his house be broken into. Hold yourselves ready, then, because the Son of Man will come at the time you least expect him.'

Peter said, 'Lord, do you intend this parable specially for us or is it for everyone?' The Lord said, 'Well, who is the trusty and sensible man whom his master will appoint as his steward, to manage his servants and issue their rations at the proper time? Happy that servant who is found at his task when his master comes! I tell you this: he will be put in charge of all his master's property.'

or *Luke 22.24-27 RSV*

A dispute arose among the apostles, which of them was to be regarded as the greatest. And Jesus said to them, 'The kings of the Gentiles exercise lordship over them; and those in authority over them are called benefactors. But not so with you; rather let the greatest among you become as the youngest, and the leader as one who serves. For which is the greater, one who sits at table, or one who serves? Is it not the one who sits at table? But I am among you as one who serves.'

PROPER PREFACE

Rite A. The Preface of Ordination (28) may be said.

POSTCOMMUNION SENTENCE

Jesus said, You have not chosen me; I have chosen you. Go and bear fruit that will last. *John 15.16*

FOR THE BLESSING OF AN ABBOT OR ABBESS OR THE INSTALLATION OF THE HEAD OF A COMMUNITY

INTRODUCTORY SENTENCE

The Lord is my inheritance and my cup: he alone will give me my reward. *Psalm 16.5*

COLLECT

God our Father, Lord of all the world,
we thank you that through your Son
you have called us into the fellowship
    of your universal Church:
hear our prayer for your faithful people
that each in his vocation and ministry
may be an instrument of your love,
and give to your servant now to be *blessed/installed*
the needful gifts of grace;
through our Lord and Saviour Jesus Christ.

PSALM 133

READINGS

Old Testament *Proverbs 2.1-9 NEB*

My son, if you take my words to heart,
and lay up my commands in your mind,
giving your attention to wisdom

and your mind to understanding,
if you summon discernment to your aid
and invoke understanding,
if you seek her out like silver
and dig for her like buried treasure,
then you will understand the fear of the Lord
and attain to the knowledge of God;
for the Lord bestows wisdom
and teaches knowledge and understanding.
Out of his store he endows the upright with ability
as a shield for those who live blameless lives;
for he guards the course of justice
and keeps watch over the way of his loyal servants.
Then you will understand what is right and just
and keep only to the good man's path.

or *Proverbs 4.7-13 NEB*

The first thing is to acquire wisdom;
gain understanding though it cost you all you have.
Do not forsake her, and she will keep you safe;
love her, and she will guard you;
cherish her, and she will lift you high;
if only you embrace her, she will bring you to honour.
She will set a garland of grace on your head
and bestow on you a crown of glory.

Listen, my son, take my words to heart,
and the years of your life shall be multiplied.
I will guide you in the paths of wisdom
and lead you in honest ways.
As you walk you will not slip,
and, if you run, nothing will bring you down.
Cling to instruction and never let it go;
observe it well, for it is your life.

New Testament *Ephesians 4.1-7 NEB*

I entreat you—I, a prisoner for the Lord's sake: as God has
called you, live up to your calling. Be humble always and
gentle, and patient too. Be forbearing with one another and
charitable. Spare no effort to make fast with bonds of peace

the unity which the Spirit gives. There is one body and one Spirit, as there is also one hope held out in God's call to you; one Lord, one faith, one baptism; one God and Father of all, who is over all and through all and in all.

But each of us has been given his gift, his due portion of Christ's bounty.

or *Colossians 3.12-17 RSV*

Put on then, as God's chosen ones, holy and beloved, compassion, kindness, lowliness, meekness, and patience, forbearing one another and, if one has a complaint against another, forgiving each other; as the Lord has forgiven you, so you also must forgive. And above all these put on love, which binds everything together in perfect harmony. And let the peace of Christ rule in your hearts, to which indeed you were called in the one body. And be thankful. Let the word of Christ dwell in you richly, as you teach and admonish one another in all wisdom, and as you sing psalms and hymns and spiritual songs with thankfulness in your hearts to God. And whatever you do, in word or deed, do everything in the name of the Lord Jesus, giving thanks to God the Father through him.

Gospel *Luke 12.35-44 NEB*

Jesus said to his disciples, 'Be ready for action, with belts fastened and lamps alight. Be like men who wait for their master's return from a wedding-party, ready to let him in the moment he arrives and knocks. Happy are those servants whom the master finds on the alert when he comes. I tell you this: he will fasten his belt, seat them at table, and come and wait on them. Even if it is the middle of the night or before dawn when he comes, happy they if he finds them alert. And remember, if the householder had known what time the burglar was coming he would not have let his house be broken into. Hold yourselves ready, then, because the Son of Man will come at the time you least expect him.'

Peter said, 'Lord, do you intend this parable specially for us or is it for everyone?' The Lord said, 'Well, who is the trusty

and sensible man whom his master will appoint as his
steward, to manage his servants and issue their rations at the
proper time? Happy that servant who is found at his task
when his master comes! I tell you this: he will be put in
charge of all his master's property.'

or *Luke 22.24-27 RSV*

A dispute arose among the apostles, which of them was to be
regarded as the greatest. And Jesus said to them, 'The kings
of the Gentiles exercise lordship over them; and those in
authority over them are called benefactors. But not so with
you; rather let the greatest among you become as the
youngest, and the leader as one who serves. For which is the
greater, one who sits at table, or one who serves? Is it not the
one who sits at table? But I am among you as one
who serves.'

POSTCOMMUNION SENTENCE

Those who have left houses, brothers, sisters, father, mother,
children, or land, for the sake of Christ, will be repaid a
hundredfold and will inherit eternal life. *Matthew 19.29*

FOR A SYNOD

INTRODUCTORY SENTENCE

To crown all things there must be love, to bind all together
and complete the whole. Let the peace of Christ rule in your
hearts. *Colossians 3.14, 15*

or the Sentences for Unity (p. 904) and Peace (p. 912).

COLLECT

Almighty God,
you have given your Holy Spirit to the Church
that he may lead us into all truth.
Bless with his grace and presence
   the members of this Synod;
Keep *us/them* steadfast in faith and united in love,

that *we/they* may reveal your glory
and prepare the way of your kingdom;
through Jesus Christ our Lord.

PSALM 25.1-9

READINGS

Old Testament *Numbers 9.15-end NEB*

On the day when they set up the Tabernacle, that is the Tent
of the Tokens, cloud covered it, and in the evening a
brightness like fire appeared over it till morning. So it
continued: the cloud covered it by day and a brightness like
fire by night. Whenever the cloud lifted from the tent, the
Israelites struck camp, and at the place where the cloud
settled, there they pitched their camp. At the command of
the Lord they struck camp, and at the command of the Lord
they encamped again, and continued in camp as long as the
cloud rested over the Tabernacle. When the cloud stayed
long over the Tabernacle, the Israelites remained in
attendance on the Lord and did not move on; and it was the
same when the cloud continued over the Tabernacle only a
few days: at the command of the Lord they remained in
camp, and at the command of the Lord they struck camp.
There were also times when the cloud continued only from
evening till morning, and in the morning, when the cloud
lifted, they moved on. Whether by day or by night, they
moved as soon as the cloud lifted. Whether it was for a day or
two, for a month or a year, whenever the cloud stayed long
over the Tabernacle, the Israelites remained where they
were and did not move on; they did so only when the cloud
lifted. At the command of the Lord they encamped, and at
his command they struck camp. At the Lord's command,
given through Moses, they remained in attendance on
the Lord.

or *Proverbs 24.3-7 NEB*

Wisdom builds the house,
good judgement makes it secure,
knowledge furnishes the rooms

with all the precious and pleasant things that wealth can buy.

Wisdom prevails over strength,
knowledge over brute force;
for wars are won by skilful strategy,
and victory is the fruit of long planning.

Wisdom is too high for a fool;
he dare not open his mouth in court.

New Testament *Acts 15.22-29 NEB*

The apostles and elders, with the agreement of the whole
church, resolved to choose representatives and send them to
Antioch with Paul and Barnabas. They chose two leading
men in the community, Judas Barsabbas and Silas, and gave
them this letter to deliver:

'We, the apostles and elders, send greetings as brothers to
our brothers of gentile origin in Antioch, Syria, and Cilicia.
Forasmuch as we have heard that some of our number,
without any instructions from us, have disturbed you with
their talk and unsettled your minds, we have resolved
unanimously to send to you our chosen representatives with
our well-beloved Barnabas and Paul, who have devoted
themselves to the cause of our Lord Jesus Christ. We are
therefore sending Judas and Silas, who will themselves
confirm this by word of mouth. It is the decision of the Holy
Spirit, and our decision, to lay no further burden upon you
beyond these essentials: you are to abstain from meat that
has been offered to idols, from blood, from anything that has
been strangled, and from fornication. If you keep yourselves
free from these things you will be doing right. Farewell.'

or *Philippians 2.1-11 NEB*

If our common life in Christ yields anything to stir the heart,
any loving consolation, any sharing of the Spirit, any
warmth of affection or compassion, fill up my cup of
happiness by thinking and feeling alike, with the same love
for one another, the same turn of mind, and a common care
for unity. There must be no room for rivalry and personal
vanity among you, but you must humbly reckon others

better than yourselves. Look to each other's interest and not merely to your own.

Let your bearing towards one another arise out of your life in Christ Jesus. For the divine nature was his from the first; yet he did not think to snatch at equality with God, but made himself nothing, assuming the nature of a slave. Bearing the human likeness, revealed in human shape, he humbled himself, and in obedience accepted even death—death on a cross. Therefore God raised him to the heights and bestowed on him the name above all names, that at the name of Jesus every knee should bow—in heaven, on earth, and in the depths—and every tongue confess, 'Jesus Christ is Lord', to the glory of God the Father.

Gospel *Luke 14.27-33 NEB*

Jesus said, 'No one who does not carry his cross and come with me can be a disciple of mine. Would any of you think of building a tower without first sitting down and calculating the cost, to see whether he could afford to finish it? Otherwise, if he has laid its foundation and then is not able to complete it, all the onlookers will laugh at him. "There is the man", they will say, "who started to build and could not finish." Or what king will march to battle against another king, without first sitting down to consider whether with ten thousand men he can face an enemy coming to meet him with twenty thousand? If he cannot, then, long before the enemy approaches, he sends envoys, and asks for terms. So also none of you can be a disciple of mine without parting with all his possessions.'

or *John 16.13-15 NEB*

Jesus said, 'When he comes who is the Spirit of truth, he will guide you into all the truth; for he will not speak on his own authority, but will tell only what he hears; and he will make known to you the things that are coming. He will glorify me, for everything that he makes known to you he will draw from what is mine. All that the Father has is mine, and that is why I said, "Everything that he makes known to you he will draw from what is mine."'

POSTCOMMUNION SENTENCE

Jesus said, Where two or three are gathered together in my name, I am there among them. *Matthew 18.20*

or the Sentences for Unity (p. 906) and Peace (p. 914).

FOR THOSE TAKING VOWS

INTRODUCTORY SENTENCE

Blessed is the man who puts his trust in the Lord; he is like a tree planted by the waterside, and never ceases to bear fruit. *Jeremiah 17.7, 8*

COLLECT

Almighty God,
by whose grace alone we are accepted
    and called to your service:
strengthen us by your Holy Spirit
and make us worthy of our calling;
through Jesus Christ our Lord.

PSALMS 99; 101

READINGS

Old Testament *1 Samuel 1.20-end NEB*

Elkanah had intercourse with his wife Hannah, and the Lord remembered her. She conceived, and in due time bore a son, whom she named Samuel, 'because', she said, 'I asked the Lord for him.' Elkanah, with his whole household, went up to make the annual sacrifice to the Lord and to redeem his vow. Hannah did not go with them, but said to her husband, 'When the child is weaned I will come up with him to enter the presence of the Lord, and he shall stay there always.' Her Husband Elkanah said to her, 'Do what you think best; stay at home until you have weaned him. Only, may the Lord indeed see your vow fulfilled.' So the woman stayed and nursed her son until she had weaned him; and when she had weaned him, she took him up with her. She took also a bull three years old, an ephah of meal, and a flagon of wine, and she brought him, child as he was, into the house of the Lord at Shiloh. They slaughtered the bull, and brought the boy to Eli. Hannah said to him, 'Sir, as sure as you live, I am the woman who stood near you here praying to the Lord. It was this boy that I prayed for and the Lord has given me what I asked. What I asked I have received; and now I lend him to the Lord; for his whole life he is lent to the Lord.' And they prostrated themselves there before the Lord.

or *Hosea 2.19, 20 NEB*

The Lord said to Israel, 'I will betroth you to myself for ever, betroth you in lawful wedlock with unfailing devotion and love; I will betroth you to myself to have and to hold, and you shall know the Lord.'

New Testament *Ephesians 1.3-14 NEB*

Praise be to the God and Father of our Lord Jesus Christ, who has bestowed on us in Christ every spiritual blessing in the heavenly realms. In Christ he chose us before the world was founded, to be dedicated, to be without blemish in his sight, to be full of love; and he destined us—such was his will and pleasure—to be accepted as his sons through Jesus Christ, in order that the glory of his gracious gift, so graciously bestowed on us in his Beloved, might redound to his praise. For in Christ our release is secured and our sins are forgiven through the shedding of his blood. Therein lies the richness of God's free grace lavished upon us, imparting full wisdom and insight. He has made known to us his hidden purpose—such was his will and pleasure determined beforehand in Christ—to be put into effect when the time was ripe: namely, that the universe, all in heaven and on earth, might be brought into a unity in Christ.

In Christ indeed we have been given our share in the heritage, as was decreed in his design whose purpose is everywhere at work. For it was his will that we, who were the first to set our hope on Christ, should cause his glory to be praised. And you too, when you had heard the message of the truth, the good news of your salvation, and had believed it, became incorporate in Christ and received the seal of the promised Holy Spirit; and that Spirit is the pledge that we shall enter upon our heritage, when God has redeemed what is his own, to his praise and glory.

or *Philippians 3.7-14 JB*

Because of Christ, I have come to consider all these advantages that I had as disadvantages. Not only that, but I believe nothing can happen that will outweigh the supreme advantage of knowing Christ Jesus my Lord. For him I have accepted the loss of everything, and I look on everything as so much rubbish if only I can have Christ and be given a place in him. I am no longer trying for perfection by my own efforts, the perfection that comes from the Law, but I want only the perfection that comes through faith in Christ, and is from God and based on faith. All I want is to know Christ and the power of his resurrection and to share his sufferings by reproducing the pattern of his death. That is the way I can hope to take my place in the resurrection of the dead. Not that I have become perfect yet: I have not yet won, but I am still running, trying to capture the prize for which Christ Jesus captured me. I can assure you my brothers, I am far from thinking that I have already won. All I can say is that I forget the past and I strain ahead for what is still to come; I am racing for the finish, for the prize to which God calls us upwards to receive in Christ Jesus.

Gospel *Luke 10.38-42 NEB*

Jesus came to a village where a woman named Martha made him welcome in her home. She had a sister, Mary, who seated herself at the Lord's feet and stayed there listening to his words. Now Martha was distracted by her many tasks, so she came to him and said, 'Lord, do you not care that my sister has left me to get on with the work by myself? Tell her to come and lend a hand.' But the Lord answered, 'Martha, Martha, you are fretting and fussing about so many things; but one thing is necessary. The part that Mary has chosen is best; and it shall not be taken away from her.'

or *John 12.24-26 JB*

Jesus said,
'I tell you, most solemnly,
unless a wheat grain falls on the ground and dies,
it remains only a single grain;
but if it dies,
it yields a rich harvest.
Anyone who loves his life loses it;
anyone who hates his life in this world
will keep it for the eternal life.
If a man serves me, he must follow me,
wherever I am, my servant will be there too.
If anyone serves me, my Father will honour him.'

PROPER PREFACE

Rite A. The Preface of Lent (8) may be said.
Rite B. Second Thanksgiving. The Preface of Lent may
be said.

POSTCOMMUNION SENTENCE

Jesus said, If anyone serves me, he must follow me: where I
am, there my servant will be, and whoever serves me will be
honoured by my Father. *John 12.26*

FOR VOCATIONS TO RELIGIOUS COMMUNITIES

INTRODUCTORY SENTENCE

Blessed is the man who puts his trust in the Lord; he is like a
tree planted by the waterside, and never ceases to bear
fruit. *Jeremiah 17.7, 8*

COLLECT

Almighty and everlasting God,
by whose Spirit the whole body of the Church
    is governed and sanctified:
hear our prayer which we offer for all your faithful people;

that each in his vocation and ministry
may serve you in holiness and truth
to the glory of your name;
through our Lord and Saviour Jesus Christ.

PSALM 63.1-8

READINGS

Old Testament *Jeremiah 1.4-9 NEB*

The word of the Lord came to me: 'Before I formed you in the
womb I knew you for my own; before you were born I
consecrated you, I appointed you a prophet to the nations.'
'Ah! Lord God,' I answered, 'I do not know how to speak; I
am only a child.' But the Lord said, 'Do not call yourself a
child; for you shall go to whatever people I send you and say
whatever I tell you to say. Fear none of them, for I am with
you and will keep you safe.' This was the very word of the
Lord. Then the Lord stretched out his hand and touched my
mouth, and said to me, 'I put my words into your mouth.'

New Testament *Philippians 3.7-14 JB*

Because of Christ, I have come to consider all these
advantages that I had as disadvantages. Not only that, but I
believe nothing can happen that will outweigh the supreme
advantage of knowing Christ Jesus my Lord. For him I have
accepted the loss of everything, and I look on everything as
so much rubbish if only I can have Christ and be given a
place in him. I am no longer trying for perfection by my own
efforts, the perfection that comes from the Law, but I want
only the perfection that comes through faith in Christ, and is
from God and based on faith. All I want is to know Christ
and the power of his resurrection and to share his sufferings
by reproducing the pattern of his death. That is the way I can
hope to take my place in the resurrection of the dead. Not
that I have become perfect yet: I have not yet won, but I am
still running, trying to capture the prize for which Christ
Jesus captured me. I can assure you my brothers, I am far
from thinking that I have already won. All I can say is that I

forget the past and I strain ahead for what is still to come; I am racing for the finish, for the prize to which God calls us upwards to receive in Christ Jesus.

Gospel *Matthew 6.24-34 NEB*

Jesus said, 'No servant can be the slave of two masters; for either he will hate the first and love the second, or he will be devoted to the first and think nothing of the second. You cannot serve God and Money.

'Therefore I bid you put away anxious thoughts about food and drink to keep you alive, and clothes to cover your body. Surely life is more than food, the body more than clothes. Look at the birds of the air; they do not sow and reap and store in barns, yet your heavenly Father feeds them. You are worth more than the birds! Is there a man of you who by anxious thought can add a foot to his height? And why be anxious about clothes? Consider how the lilies grow in the fields; they do not work, they do not spin; and yet, I tell you, even Solomon in all his splendour was not attired like one of these. But if that is how God clothes the grass in the fields, which is there today, and tomorrow is thrown on the stove, will he not all the more clothe you? How little faith you have! No, do not ask anxiously, "What are we to eat? What are we to drink? What shall we wear?" All these are things for the heathen to run after, not for you, because your heavenly Father knows that you need them all. Set your mind on God's kingdom and his justice before everything else, and all the rest will come to you as well. So do not be anxious about tomorrow; tomorrow will look after itself. Each day has troubles enough of its own.'

POSTCOMMUNION SENTENCE

Jesus said, If anyone serves me, he must follow me: where I am, there my servant will be, and whoever serves me will be honoured by my Father. *John 12.26*

FOR SOCIAL RESPONSIBILITY

INTRODUCTORY SENTENCE

To crown all things there must be love, to bind all together and complete the whole. Let the peace of Christ rule in your hearts. *Colossians 3.14, 15*

or the Sentences for Unity (p. 904) and Peace (p. 912).

COLLECT

Almighty Father,
whose Son Jesus Christ has taught us
that what we do for the least of our brethren
   we do also for him:
give us the will to be the servant of others
   as he was the servant of all,
who gave up his life and died for us,
but is alive and reigns with you and the Holy Spirit,
one God, now and for ever.

PSALMS 72.1-7; 146.5-10

READINGS

Old Testament *Amos 5.21-24 RSV*

Thus says the Lord,
'I hate, I despise your feasts,
and I take no delight in your solemn assemblies.
Even though you offer me your burnt offerings
   and cereal offerings,
I will not accept them,
and the peace offerings of your fatted beasts
I will not look upon.
Take away from me the noise of your songs;
to the melody of your harps I will not listen.
But let justice roll down like waters,
and righteousness like an ever-flowing stream.'

or *Amos 8.4-7 TEV*

Listen to this, you that trample on the needy and try to destroy the poor of the country. You say to yourselves, 'We can hardly wait for the holy days to be over so that we can sell our corn. When will the Sabbath end, so that we can start selling again? Then we can overcharge, use false measures, and tamper with the scales to cheat our customers. We can sell worthless wheat at a high price. We'll find a poor man who can't pay his debts, not even the price of a pair of sandals, and we'll buy him as a slave.'

The Lord, the God of Israel, has sworn, 'I will never forget their evil deeds.'

New Testament *Acts 5.1-11 TEV*

There was a man named Ananias, who with his wife Sapphira sold some property that belonged to them. But with his wife's agreement he kept part of the money for himself and handed the rest over to the apostles. Peter said to him, 'Ananias, why did you let Satan take control of you and make you lie to the Holy Spirit by keeping part of the money you received for the property? Before you sold the property, it belonged to you; and after you sold it, the money was yours. Why, then, did you decide to do such a thing? You have not lied to men—you have lied to God!' As soon as Ananias heard this, he fell down dead; and all who heard about it were terrified. The young men came in, wrapped up his body, carried him out, and buried him.

About three hours later his wife, not knowing what had happened, came in. Peter asked her, 'Tell me, was this the full amount you and your husband received for your property?' 'Yes,' she answered, 'the full amount.'

So Peter said to her, 'Why did you and your husband decide to put the Lord's Spirit to the test? The men who buried your husband are now at the door, and they will carry you out too!' At once she fell down at his feet and died. The young men came in and saw that she was dead, so they carried her out and buried her beside her husband. The whole church and all the others who heard of this were terrified.

or *James 2.1-4 JB*

My brothers, do not try to combine faith in Jesus Christ, our glorified Lord, with the making of distinctions between classes of people. Now suppose a man comes into your synagogue, beautifully dressed and with a gold ring on, and at the same time a poor man comes in, in shabby clothes, and you take notice of the well-dressed man, and say, 'Come this way to the best seats'; then you tell the poor man, 'Stand over there' or 'You can sit on the floor by my foot-rest.' Can't you see that you have used two different standards in your mind, and turned yourselves into judges, and corrupt judges at that?

Gospel *Matthew 25.31-end NEB*

Jesus said, 'When the Son of Man comes in his glory and all the angels with him, he will sit in state on his throne, with all the nations gathered before him. He will separate men into two groups, as a shepherd separates the sheep from the goats, and he will place the sheep on his right hand and the goats on his left. Then the king will say to those on his right hand, "You have my Father's blessing; come, enter and possess the kingdom that has been ready for you since the world was made. For when I was hungry, you gave me food; when thirsty, you gave me drink; when I was a stranger you took me into your home, when naked you clothed me; when I was ill you came to my help, when in prison you visited me." Then the righteous will reply, "Lord, when was it that we saw you hungry and fed you, or thirsty and gave you drink, a stranger and took you home, or naked and clothed you? When did we see you ill or in prison, and come to visit you?" And the king will answer, "I tell you this: anything you did for one of my brothers here, however humble, you did for me." Then he will say to those on his left hand, "The curse is upon you; go from my sight to the eternal fire that is ready for the devil and his angels. For when I was hungry you gave me nothing to eat, when thirsty nothing to drink; when I was a stranger you gave me no home, when naked you did not clothe me; when I was ill and in prison you did not come to my help." And they too will reply, "Lord, when was it that we saw you hungry or thirsty or a stranger or naked or ill or in prison, and did nothing for you?'' And he will answer, ''I tell you this: anything you did not do for one of these, however humble, you did not do for me.'' And they will go away to eternal punishment, but the righteous will enter eternal life.'

or *Mark 2.1-5 (6-12) NEB*

When Jesus returned to Capernaum, the news went round that he was at home; and such a crowd collected that the space in front of the door was not big enough to hold them. And while he was proclaiming the message to them, a man was brought who was paralysed. Four men were carrying him, but because of the crowd they could not get him near. So they opened up the roof over the place where Jesus was, and when they had broken through they lowered the stretcher on which the paralysed man was lying. When Jesus saw their faith, he said to the paralysed man, 'My son, your sins are forgiven.'

(Now there were some lawyers sitting there and they thought to themselves, 'Why does the fellow talk like that? This is blasphemy! Who but God alone can forgive sins?' Jesus knew in his own mind that this was what they were thinking, and said to them: 'Why do you harbour thoughts like these? Is it easier to say to this paralysed man, ''Your sins are forgiven'', or to say, ''Stand up, take your bed, and walk''? But to convince you that the Son of Man has the right on earth to forgive sins'—he turned to the paralysed man—'I say to you, stand up, take your bed, and go home.' And he got up, and at once took his stretcher and went out in full view of them all, so that they were astounded and praised God. 'Never before', they said, 'have we seen the like.')

PROPER PREFACE

Rite A. A Preface of the Resurrection (14) may be said.
Rite B. The Preface of Easter may be said.

POSTCOMMUNION SENTENCE

Jesus said, Where two or three are gathered together in my name, I am there among them. *Matthew 18.20*

or the Sentences for Unity (p. 906) and Peace (p. 914).

FOR CIVIC OCCASIONS

INTRODUCTORY SENTENCE

Be subject for the Lord's sake to every human institution. *1 Peter 2.13*

COLLECT

Almighty and eternal God,
to whom we must all give account:
guide with your Spirit the . . . of *this city*,
that *they* may be faithful to the mind of Christ,
and seek in all *their* purposes
to enrich our common life;
through Jesus Christ our Lord.

PSALMS 82; 20   or   67; 100

READINGS

Old Testament *Deuteronomy 5.1-21 NEB*

Moses summoned all Israel and said to them: Listen, O Israel, to the statutes and the laws which I proclaim in your hearing today. Learn them and be careful to observe them. The Lord our God made a covenant with us at Horeb. It was not with our forefathers that the Lord made this covenant, but with us, all of us who are alive and are here this day. The Lord spoke with you face to face on the mountain out of the fire. I stood between the Lord and you at that time to report the words of the Lord; for you were afraid of the fire and did not go up the mountain. And the Lord said:

I am the Lord your God who brought you out of Egypt, out of the land of slavery.

You shall have no other god to set against me.

You shall not make a carved image for yourself nor the likeness of anything in the heavens above, or on the earth below, or in the waters under the earth.

You shall not bow down to them or worship them; for I, the Lord your God, am a jealous god. I punish the children for the sins of the fathers to the third and fourth generations of those who hate me. But I keep faith with thousands, with those who love me and keep my commandments.

You shall not make wrong use of the name of the Lord your God; the Lord will not leave unpunished the man who misuses his name.

Keep the sabbath day holy as the Lord your God commanded you. You have six days to labour and do all your work. But the seventh day is a sabbath of the Lord your God; that day you shall not do any work, neither you, your son or your daughter, your slave or your slave-girl, your ox, your ass, or any of your cattle, nor the alien within your gates, so that your slaves and slave-girls may rest as you do. Remember that you were slaves in Egypt and the Lord your God brought you out with a strong hand and an outstretched arm, and for that reason the Lord your God commanded you to keep the sabbath day.

Honour your father and your mother, as the Lord your God commanded you, so that you may live long, and that it may be well with you in the land which the Lord your God is giving you.

You shall not commit murder.

You shall not commit adultery.

You shall not steal.

You shall not give false evidence against your neighbour.

You shall not covet your neighbour's wife; you shall not set your heart on your neighbour's house, his land, his slave, his slave-girl, his ox, his ass, or on anything that belongs to him.

or *Deuteronomy 6.1-13 NEB*

These are the commandments, statutes, and laws which the Lord your God commanded me to teach you to observe in the land into which you are passing to occupy it, a land flowing with milk and honey, so that you may fear the Lord your God and keep all his statutes and commandments which I am giving you, both you, your sons, and your descendants all your lives, and so that you may live long. If you listen, O Israel, and are careful to observe them, you will prosper and increase greatly as the Lord the God of your fathers promised you.

Hear, O Israel, the Lord is our God, one Lord, and you must love the Lord your God with all your heart and soul and strength. These commandments which I give you this day are to be kept in your heart; you shall repeat them to your sons, and speak of them indoors and out of doors, when you lie down and when you rise. Bind them as a sign on the hand and wear them as a phylactery on the forehead; write them up on the door-posts of your houses and on your gates.

The Lord your God will bring you into the land which he swore to your forefathers Abraham, Isaac and Jacob that he would give you, a land of great and fine cities which you did not build, houses full of good things which you did not provide, rock-hewn cisterns which you did not hew, and vineyards and olive-groves which you did not plant. When you eat your fill there, be careful not to forget the Lord who brought you out of Egypt, out of the land of slavery. You shall fear the Lord your God, serve him alone and take your oaths in his name.

New Testament *Philippians 2.1-11 NEB*

If our common life in Christ yields anything to stir the heart, any loving consolation, any sharing of the Spirit, any warmth of affection or compassion, fill up my cup of happiness by thinking and feeling alike, with the same love for one another, the same turn of mind, and a common care for unity. There must be no room for rivalry and personal vanity among you, but you must humbly reckon others better than yourselves. Look to each other's interest and not merely to your own.

Let your bearing towards one another arise out of your life in Christ Jesus. For the divine nature was his from the first; yet he did not think to snatch at equality with God, but made himself nothing, assuming the nature of a slave. Bearing the human likeness, revealed in human shape, he humbled himself, and in obedience accepted even death—death on a cross. Therefore God raised him to the heights and bestowed on him the name above all names, that at the name of Jesus every knee should bow—in heaven, on earth, and in the depths—and every tongue confess, 'Jesus Christ is Lord', to the glory of God the Father.

or Philippians 4.8-13 RSV

Brethren, whatever is true, whatever is honourable, whatever is just, whatever is pure, whatever is lovely, whatever is gracious, if there is any excellence, if there is anything worthy of praise, think about these things. What you have learned and received and heard and seen in me, do; and the God of peace will be with you.

I rejoice in the Lord greatly that now at length you have revived your concern for me; you were indeed concerned for me, but you had no opportunity. Not that I complain of want; for I have learned, in whatever state I am, to be content. I know how to be abased, and I know how to abound; in any and all circumstances I have learned the secret of facing plenty and hunger, abundance and want. I can do all things in him who strengthens me.

Gospel *Mark 10.42-45 NEB*

Jesus called his disciples to him and said, 'You know that in the world the recognized rulers lord it over their subjects, and their great men make them feel the weight of authority. That is not the way with you; among you, whoever wants to be great must be your servant, and whoever wants to be first must be the willing slave of all. For even the Son of Man did not come to be served but to serve, and to give up his life as a ransom for many.'

or *Luke 3.7-14 NEB*

Crowds of people came out to be baptized by John, and he said to them: 'You vipers' brood! Who warned you to escape from the coming retribution? Then prove your repentance by the fruit it bears; and do not begin saying to yourselves, "We have Abraham for our father." I tell you that God can make children for Abraham out of these stones here. Already the axe is laid to the roots of the trees; and every tree that fails to produce good fruit is cut down and thrown on the fire.'

The people asked him, 'Then what are we to do?' He replied, 'The man with two shirts must share with him who has none, and anyone who has food must do the same.' Among those who came to be baptized were tax-gatherers, and they said to him, 'Master, what are we to do?' He told them, 'Exact no more than the assessment.' Soldiers on service also asked him, 'And what of us?' To them he said, 'No bullying; no blackmail; make do with your pay!'

or the readings for Pentecost 15.

POSTCOMMUNION SENTENCE

The kingdom of the world is to become the kingdom of our Lord and of his Christ, and he shall reign for ever.
Revelation 11.15

Tables

The Lectionary

NOTES (A) GENERAL

1   The references in the following tables are to the Revised
    Standard Version of the Bible and to the Liturgical Psalter.
    When other versions are used, such adaptations may be
    made as are necessary.

2   When a reading begins with a personal pronoun, the reader
    may substitute the appropriate noun.

3   In these tables, verses are stated inclusively. The letter a after
    the number of a verse signifies the first part of that verse, and
    the letter b the second part.

4   Verses printed within brackets are permitted additions to
    the appointed passages.

5   Appropriate liturgical colours are suggested: they are not
    mandatory, and traditional or local uses may be followed
    where established.

    White or gold refers to the church's festal vestments and
    hangings, which should be predominantly white in colour,
    or gold.

    White refers to simpler vestments and hangings; but in
    many churches one white or gold set will suffice for all
    occasions.

    Violet is the colour for Advent and Lent; but it may vary in
    colour from dark blue through true violet-colour to 'roman'
    purple. In some churches a Lent array of unbleached linen is
    used as an alternative to violet, during Lent; it is not
    appropriate for Advent or other occasions. Rose-colour is
    sometimes used as an alternative on the Third Sunday in
    Advent and the Fourth Sunday in Lent. Black is sometimes
    used as an alternative to violet for funerals and on All Souls'
    Day. White is sometimes used for these occasions.

(B) PSALMS AND READINGS
OF SUNDAYS AND WEEKDAYS

1   When the Ninth Sunday before Christmas occurs in a year
     with an even number, the psalms and readings appointed
     for year 1 are read, and when it occurs in a year with an odd
     number, the psalms and readings appointed for year 2 are
     read, for the whole of the ecclesiastical year.

2   When two readings only are used at Holy Communion, the
     gospel must always be read, and when one of the others is
     marked with an asterisk, it is to be preferred.

3   The psalms and readings appointed for Holy Communion
     may be used at Morning or Evening Prayer on their
     appointed days.

4   The psalms and readings appointed for Morning Prayer may
     be used at Evening Prayer, and vice versa, except where
     indicated by a double obelisk (‡).

5   If there is to be a celebration of Holy Communion on a day
     for which no full provision is made,
     either
     the psalms and readings appointed for Morning or Evening
     Prayer on that day may be used; if these do not include a
     gospel reading, this is chosen from those appointed for Holy
     Communion in either year on the previous Sunday; if they
     do not include a reading from the New Testament, this may
     be chosen from those appointed for Holy Communion in
     either year on the previous Sunday;
     or
     the psalms and readings of the previous Sunday may be
     used, whether of year 1 or year 2; or the psalms and readings
     of Christmas, Epiphany, Ash Wednesday or Ascension Day,
     on the weekdays which follow them;
     or
     the psalms and readings may be chosen from those provided
     in Table 3d.

6   The psalms and readings appointed for Pentecost 19 to
     Pentecost 22 and the weekdays which follow them are to be
     used when they are needed, according to the date of Easter,
     but the psalms and readings of the last Sunday after
     Pentecost and the weekdays following are to be used in
     every year.

7   At Morning and Evening Prayer, either the psalms
     appointed in these tables are read, or else the psalms
     appointed in the Book of Common Prayer for the days of the
     month and for certain Holy Days. Either order of reading
     shall begin on the Ninth Sunday before Christmas and shall
     be read throughout the year that follows, except that when
     the Book of Common Prayer makes no provision recourse
     may be had to the provision in Tables 1 and 3.

TABLE 1A / PSALMS AND READINGS
FOR MORNING AND EVENING PRAYER
SUNDAYS AND WEEKDAYS, YEAR 1

	Psalms	First Reading	Second Reading

NINTH SUNDAY BEFORE CHRISTMAS
(Fifth Sunday before Advent)   Green

		Psalms	First Reading	Second Reading
S	M	104 or 104.1-25	Prov 8.1, 22-31	Rev 21.1-7, 22-end
	E	148, 150	Gen 2.4b-end	John 3.1-12
M	M	1, 2	Dan 1	Matt 1.18-end
	E	3, 4	Prov 1.1-19 or	
			Ecclus 1.1-10	Rev 1
T	M	5, 6	Dan 2.1-24	Matt 2.1-12
	E	7	Prov 1.20-end or	
			Ecclus 1.11-end	Rev 2.1-11
W	M	8, 9	Dan 2.25-end	Matt 2.13-end
	E	10	Prov 2 or	
			Ecclus 2	Rev 2.12-end
Th	M	11, 12	Dan 3.1-18	Matt 3
	E	13, 14	Prov 3.1-26 or	
			Ecclus 4.11-28	Rev 3.1-13
F	M	15, 16	Dan 3.19-end	Matt 4.1-11
	E	17	Prov 3.27—4.19 or	
			Ecclus 6.14-31	Rev 3.14-end
S	M	18.1-32	Dan 4.1-18	Matt 4.12-22
	E	18.33-end	Prov 6.1-19 or	
			Ecclus 7.27-end	Rev 4

EIGHTH SUNDAY BEFORE CHRISTMAS
(Fourth Sunday before Advent)   Green

S	M	25	Isa 44.6-22	1 Cor 10.1-13 (or -24)
	E	139.1-18	Gen 3	Rom 7.7-end
M	M	19	Dan 4.19-end	Matt 4.23—5.12
	E	20, 21	Prov 8.1-21 or	
			Ecclus 10.6-8, 12-24	Rev 5
T	M	22	Dan 5.1-12	Matt 5.13-20
	E	23, 24	Prov 8.22-end or	
			Ecclus 14.20—15.10	Rev 6

		Psalms	First Reading	Second Reading
W	M	25	Dan 5.13-end	Matt 5.21-26
	E	26, 27	Prov 9 or	
			Ecclus 15.11-end	Rev 7
Th	M	28, 29	Dan 6	Matt 5.27-37
	E	30	Prov 10.1-13 or	
			Ecclus 17.1-24	Rev 8
F	M	31	Dan 7.1-14	Matt 5.38-end
	E	32	Prov 11.1-12 or	
			Ecclus 22.6-22	Rev 9.1-12
S	M	33	Dan 7.15-end	Matt 6.1-18
	E	34	Prov 12.10-end or	
			Ecclus 22.27—23.15	Rev 9.13-end

SEVENTH SUNDAY BEFORE CHRISTMAS
(Third Sunday before Advent)   Green

S	M	32, 36	Gen 18.1-19	Rom 9.1-13
	E	135 or 136	Isa 41.8-20	Matt 21.28-43

Services for Remembrance Sunday
The following psalms and readings are suitable:
Psalms 46, 47, 93, 126, 130; Isa 2.1-5; Isa 10.33—11.9; Ezek 37.1-14;
Rom 8.31-end; Rev 21.1-7; Matt 5.1-12; John 15.9-17

M	M	35	Dan 9.1-3, 20-end	Matt 6.19-end
	E	36	Prov 14.31—15.17 or	
			Ecclus 24.1-22	Rev 10
T	M	37.1-22	Dan 10.1—11.1	Matt 7.1-12
	E	37.23-end	Prov 15.18-end or	
			Ecclus 24.23-end	Rev 11.1-13
W	M	38	Dan 12	Matt 7.13-end
	E	39	Prov 18.10-end or	
			Ecclus 38.1-14	Rev 11.14-end
Th	M	40	Hosea 1.1—2.1	Matt 8.1-13
	E	41	Prov 20.1-22 or	
			Ecclus 38.24-end	Rev 12
F	M	42, 43	Hosea 2.2-17	Matt 8.14-22
	E	44	Prov 22.1-16 or	
			Ecclus 39.1-11	Rev 13.1-10
S	M	45, 46	Hosea 2.18—3 end	Matt 8.23-end
	E	47, 48	Prov 24.23-end or	
			Ecclus 39.13-end	Rev 13.11-end

		Psalms	First Reading	Second Reading

SIXTH SUNDAY BEFORE CHRISTMAS
(Second Sunday before Advent)   Green

		Psalms	First Reading	Second Reading
S	M	66	Deut 18.15-end	Acts 3
	E	106.1-15, 42-end	Exod 6.2-13	Mark 13.1-13
M	M	49	Hosea 4.1-14	Matt 9.1-13
	E	50	Prov 25.1-14 or	
			Ecclus 42.15-end	Rev 14.1-13
T	M	51	Hosea 4.15—5.7	Matt 9.14-26
	E	52, 53	Prov 25.15-end or	
			Ecclus 43.1-12	Rev 14.14-end
W	M	54, 55	Hosea 5.8—6.6	Matt 9.27-end
	E	56, 57	Prov 26.12-end or	
			Ecclus 43.13-end	Rev 15
Th	M	(58), 59	Hosea 8	Matt 10.1-15
	E	60, 61	Prov 27.1-22 or	
			Ecclus 50.1-24	Rev 16.1-11
F	M	62, 63	Hosea 9.1-9	Matt 10.16-33
	E	64, 65	Prov 30.1-9 or	
			Ecclus 51.1-12	Rev 16.12-end
S	M	66, 67	Hosea 9.10-end	Matt 10.34—11.1
	E	68	Prov 31.10-end or	
			Ecclus 51.13-end	Rev 17

FIFTH SUNDAY BEFORE CHRISTMAS
(The Sunday next before Advent)   Green

		Psalms	First Reading	Second Reading
S	M	147	Gen 18.20-end	Mark 13.14-end
	E	75, 76	Jer 18.1-17	Rom 9.19-28
M	M	69	Hosea 10.1-8	Matt 11.2-19
	E	70, 71	Isa 40.1-11	Rev 18
T	M	72	Hosea 10.9-end	Matt 11.20-end
	E	73	Isa 40.12-26	Rev 19
W	M	74	Hosea 11.1-11	Matt 12.1-21
	E	75, 76	Isa 40.27—41.7	Rev 20
Th	M	77	Hosea 11.12—12 end	Matt 12.22-37
	E	78.1-38	Isa 41.8-20	Rev 21.1-8
F	M	78.39-end	Hosea 13.1-14	Matt 12.38-end
	E	79	Isa 41.21-end	Rev 21.9-21
S	M	80	Hosea 14	Matt 13.1-17
	E	81	Isa 42.1-9	Rev 21.22—22.5

		Psalms	**First Reading**	**Second Reading**

ADVENT SUNDAY (Fourth Sunday before Christmas) Violet

S	M	18.1-32	Isa 1.1-20	Luke 12.35-48
	E	68.1-20	Josh 7	Matt 25.31-end
M	M	82, 83	Isa 1.21-end	Matt 13.18-33
	E	84, 85	Isa 42.10-17	Rev 22.6-end
T	M	86	Isa 2.1-11	Matt 13.34-43
	E	87, 88	Isa 42.18-end	1 Thess 1
W	M	89.1-38	Isa 3.1-15	Matt 13.44-end
	E	89.39-end	Isa 43.1-13	1 Thess 2.1-12
Th	M	90	Isa 4.2—5.7	Matt 14.1-12
	E	91	Isa 43.14-end	1 Thess 2.13-end
F	M	92, 93	Isa 5.8-24	Matt 14.13-end
	E	94	Isa 44.1-8	1 Thess 3
S	M	95 (or 100), 96	Isa 5.25-end	Matt 15.1-20
	E	97, 98	Isa 44.9-23	1 Thess 4.1-12

ADVENT 2 (Third Sunday before Christmas) Violet

S	M	119.137-152	1 Kings 22.1-28 (or 1-17)	
	E	119.89-104	Amos 8.4-12	Rom 10.5-17
				Luke 4.14-30
M	M	99, 100 (or 95), 101	Isa 6	Matt 15.21-28
	E	102	Isa 44.24-end	1 Thess 4.13—5.11
T	M	103	Isa 7.1-17	Matt 15.29-end
	E	104	Isa 45.1-13	1 Thess 5.12-end
W	M	105.1-22	Isa 8.16—9.7	Matt 16.1-12
	E	105.23-end	Isa 45.15-end	2 Thess 1
Th	M	106.1-24	Isa 9.8—10.4	Matt 16.13-end
	E	106.25-end	Isa 46	2 Thess 2
F	M	107.1-22	Isa 10.5-19	Matt 17.1-13
	E	107.23-end	Isa 47	2 Thess 3
S	M	108, (109), 110	Isa 10.20-32	Matt 17.14-21
	E	111, 112, 113	Isa 48.1-11	Jude

ADVENT 3 (Second Sunday before Christmas) Violet

S	M	80	Amos 7	Luke 1.1-25
	E	11, 14	Mal 3.1-5; 4	Matt 11.2-19 or Phil 4.4-end

		Psalms	First Reading	Second Reading
M	M	114, 115	Isa 10.33—11.9	Col 1.1-14
	E	116, 117	Isa 48.12-end	Luke 20.9-18
T	M	118	Isa 11.10—12 end	Col 1.15-end
	E	119.1-24	Isa 50.4-10	Luke 20.19-26
W	M	119.25-40	Isa 13.1-13	Col 2.1-15
	E	119.41-56	Isa 51.1-8	Luke 20.27-44
Th	M	119.57-72	Isa 14.3-20	Col 2.16—3.11
	E	119.73-88	Isa 51.9-16	Luke 21.5-19
F	M	119.89-104	Isa 21.1-12	Col 3.12—4.1
	E	119.105-128	Isa 51.17-end	Luke 21.20-28
S	M	119.129-152	Isa 22.1-14	Col 4.2-end
	E	119.153-end	Isa 52.1-12	Luke 21.29-36

ADVENT 4 (The Sunday next before Christmas) Violet

S	M	40	1 Sam 1.1-20	Luke 1.39-55
	E	113, 123, 131	Zech 2	Rev 20.11—21.7
M	M	120, 121	Isa 24	2 John
	E	122, 123	Isa 52.13—53 end	John 1.19-37
T	M	124, 125	Isa 25.1-9	3 John
	E	126, 127	Isa 54	John 3.22-36
W	M	128, 129	Isa 26.1-13	Phil 4.4-9
	E	130, 131	Isa 55	John 5.30-end
Th	M	132	Isa 28.1-13	Titus 3.4-7
	E	133, 134	Isa 56.1-8	John 7.37-44
F	M	135	Isa 28.14-end	Philemon
	E	136	Isa 57.15-end	John 16.29—17.5

CHRISTMAS EVE (24 December)   Violet

	M	‡137, 138	‡Isa 58	‡Rom 1.1-7
	E	‡85	‡Isa 32.1-8	‡John 13.1-17

CHRISTMAS DAY   White or Gold

	M	19	‡Isa 35	‡John 3.16-21
	E	8, 110	‡Isa 65.17-end	‡1 John 1.1-9

ST STEPHEN (26 December)   Red

M	M	13, 46	‡Exod 18.13-26	‡Acts 6
	E	57, 86	‡Gen 4.1-10	‡John 15.20—16.4a

	Psalms	First Reading	Second Reading

ST JOHN (27 December)   White

| M | 97 | ‡Exod 33.7-11a | ‡1 John 5.1-12 |
| E | 21 | ‡Isa 6.1-8 | ‡John 13.21-35 |

THE HOLY INNOCENTS (28 December)   Red

M	36	‡Gen 37.13-20 or	
		Baruch 4.21-27	‡1 Pet 4.12-end
E	124, 128	‡Isa 49.14-25	‡Matt 18.1-10

SUNDAY AFTER CHRISTMAS DAY   White or Gold

| M | 132 | Isa 40.18-end | Col 1.1-20 |
| E | 84, 122 | Isa 12 | Phil 2.1-11 |

When Christmas Day falls on a Wednesday and the Presentation of Christ falls on a Sunday the readings appointed for Year 1 are always read.

29 DECEMBER

| M | 139 | Isa 29.1-14 | 2 Cor 8.1-9 |
| E | 140, 141 | Isa 59.1-15a | John 12.20-33 |

30 DECEMBER

| M | 142, 143 | Isa 29.15-end | Eph 3.14-end |
| E | 144 | Isa 59.15b-end | John 12.34-end |

31 DECEMBER

| M | ‡145 | ‡Isa 38.1-20 | ‡1 John 5.13-end |
| E | ‡90 | ‡Deut 10.12—11.1 | ‡Luke 21.25-36 |

THE NAMING OF JESUS (1 January)   White

| M | 115 | Josh 1.1-9 | Acts 3.1-16 |
| E | 148 | Jer 23.1-6 | Rom 10.5-13 |

THE SECOND SUNDAY AFTER CHRISTMAS   White or Gold

| M | 89.19-38 | Isa 43.1-13 | Matt 2 |
| E | 85, 87 | 1 Sam 1 | John 4.19-26 |

2 JANUARY

| M | 146 | Isa 30.1-18 | Matt 17.22-end |
| E | 147 | Isa 61 | 1 Cor 1 |

	Psalms	First Reading	Second Reading
3 JANUARY			
M	149, 150	Isa 30.19-end	Matt 18.1-20
E	1, 2, 3	Isa 62	1 Cor 3
4 JANUARY			
M	4, 5, 6	Isa 31	Matt 18.21-end
E	7	Isa 63	1 Cor 4
5 JANUARY			
M	‡9	‡Isa 33.1-16	‡Matt 19.1-15
E	‡98, 113	‡Isa 41.8-20 or	
		Baruch 4.36-end; 5	‡Eph 1.3-14

THE EPIPHANY OF OUR LORD (6 January)   White or Gold

M	2, 8	Isa 42.1-9	John 1.29-34
E	96, 97	Isa 49.7-13	John 2.1-11

The following psalms and readings are read on weekdays between Epiphany and the First Sunday after Epiphany:

7 JANUARY			
M	10	Isa 15	Matt 19.16-end
E	11, 12	Isa 60.1-12	1 Cor 5
8 JANUARY			
M	13, 14	Isa 16	Matt 20.1-16
E	15, 16	Isa 60.13-end	1 Cor 6.1-11
9 JANUARY			
M	17	Isa 17	Matt 20.17-end
E	18.1-32	Isa 64	1 Cor 6.12-end
10 JANUARY			
M	18.33-end	Isa 18	Matt 21.1-17
E	19	Isa 65.1-16	1 Cor 7.1-24
11 JANUARY			
M	20, 21	Isa 19.1-15	Matt 21.18-32
E	22	Isa 66.1-9	1 Cor 7.25-end
12 JANUARY			
M	23, 24	Isa 19.16-end	Matt 21.33-end
E	25	Isa 66.10-end	1 Cor 8

		Psalms	First Reading	Second Reading

EPIPHANY 1   White or Gold for Sunday, Green from Monday

S	M	46, 47	Isa 61	Eph 2.1-10
	E	29, 30	Josh 3	Mark 1.1-13
M	M	26, 27	Ezek 1.1-14	Matt 22.1-14
	E	28, 29	Jonah 1	1 Cor 9.1-14
T	M	30	Ezek 1.15—2.2	Matt 22.15-33
	E	31	Jonah 2	1 Cor 9.15-end
W	M	32	Ezek 2.3—3.11	Matt 22.34-end
	E	33	Jonah 3 & 4	1 Cor 10.1-13
Th	M	34	Ezek 3.12-end	Matt 23.1-15
	E	35	Joel 1.1-14	1 Cor 10.14—11.1
F	M	36	Ezek 8.1-18	Matt 23.16-28
	E	37.1-22	Joel 1.15-end	1 Cor 11.2-22
S	M	37.23-end	Ezek 10.1-19	Matt 23.29-end
	E	38	Joel 2.1-17	1 Cor 11.23-end

EPIPHANY 2   Green

S	M	15, 16	Ezek 2.1-7; 3.4-11	Matt 10.1-22
	E	121, 126	1 Sam 3.1—4.1a	John 1.35-end
M	M	39	Ezek 11.14-end	Matt 24.1-14
	E	40	Joel 2.18-27	1 Cor 12.1-11
T	M	41	Ezek 12.17-end	Matt 24.15-28
	E	42, 43	Joel 2.28-end	1 Cor 12.12-end
W	M	44	Ezek 13.1-16	Matt 24.29-35
	E	45, 46	Joel 3.1-3, 9-end	1 Cor 13
Th	M	47, 48	Ezek 14.1-11	Matt 24.36-end
	E	49	Lev 1 or	
			1 Macc 1.1-19	1 Cor 14.1-12
F	M	50	Ezek 14.12-end	Matt 25.1-13
	E	51	Lev 2 or	
			1 Macc 1.20-40	1 Cor 14.13-25
S	M	52, 53	Ezek 18.1-20	Matt 25.14-30
	E	54, 55	Lev 3 or	
			1 Macc 1.41-end	1 Cor 14.26-end

EPIPHANY 3   Green

| S | M | 135 or 136 | Isa 26.1-9 | John 4.43-end |
| | E | 33 | Deut 8.1-10 | John 6.1-21 |

		Psalms	First Reading	Second Reading
M	M	56, 57	Ezek 20.1-20	Matt 25.31-end
	E	(58), 59	Lev 4.27-end or	
			1 Macc 2.1-28	1 Cor 15.1-11
T	M	60, 61	Ezek 24.15-end	Matt 26.1-13
	E	62, 63	Lev 5.1-13 or	
			1 Macc 2.29-48	1 Cor 15.12-19
W	M	64, 65	Ezek 28.1-10	Matt 26.14-29
	E	66, 67	Lev 8 or	
			1 Macc 2.49-end	1 Cor 15.20-34
Th	M	68	Ezek 28.11-19	Matt 26.30-46
	E	69	Lev 9 or	
			1 Macc 3.1-26	1 Cor 15.35-49
F	M	70, 71	Ezek 33.1-20	Matt 26.47-56
	E	72	Lev 17 or	
			1 Macc 3.27-41	1 Cor 15.50-end
S	M	73	Ezek 33.21-end	Matt 26.57-end
	E	74	Lev 18.1-6, 19-end or	
			1 Macc 3.42-end	1 Cor 16

EPIPHANY 4   Green

S	M	34	Zech 8.1-17	Acts 15.1-21
	E	50	Exod 19.10-end	Heb 12.14-end
M	M	75, 76	Ezek 34.1-16	Matt 27.1-10
	E	77	Lev 19.1-18 or	
			1 Macc 4.1-25	Phil 1.1-11
T	M	78.1-38	Ezek 34.17-end	Matt 27.11-26
	E	78.39-end	Lev 19.23-end or	
			1 Macc 4.26-35	Phil 1.12-end
W	M	79	Ezek 36.1-15	Matt 27.27-44
	E	80	Lev 23.1-22 or	
			1 Macc 4.36-end	Phil 2.1-18
Th	M	81	Ezek 36.16-36	Matt 27.45-56
	E	82, 83	Lev 23.23-end or	
			1 Macc 6.1-17	Phil 2.19-end
F	M	84, 85	Ezek 37.1-14	Matt 27.57-end
	E	86	Lev 24.1-9 or	
			1 Macc 6.18-47	Phil 3.1—4.1
S	M	87, 88	Ezek 37.15-end	Matt 28
	E	89.1-38	Lev 25.1-24 or	
			1 Macc 7.1-20	Phil 4.2-end

		Psalms	First Reading	Second Reading

EPIPHANY 5 Green

S	M	119.121-136	Jer 10.1-16 or Wisdom 7.28—8.9	1 Tim 3.14—4.10
	E	92	Job 12 or Ecclus 43.13-end	1 Cor 1.18—2.5
M	M	89.39-end	Ezek 38.14-end	Rev 1.12-end
	E	90	Esther 1 or 1 Macc 7.21-end	1 Pet 1.1-12
T	M	91	Ezek 39.21-end	Rev 2.1-11
	E	92, 93	Esther 2.5-11, 15-end or 1 Macc 9.1-22	1 Pet 1.13-end
W	M	94	Ezek 40.1-4	Rev 2.12-end
	E	95 (or 100), 96	Esther 3 or 1 Macc 13.41-end; 14.4-15	1 Pet 2.1-10
Th	M	97, 98	Ezek 43.1-9	Rev 3.1-6
	E	99, 100 (or 95), 101	Esther 4 or 2 Macc 6.12-end	1 Pet 2.11-end
F	M	102	Ezek 44.4-8	Rev 3.7-13
	E	103	Esther 5 or 2 Macc 7.1-19	1 Pet 3.1-12
S	M	104	Ezek 47.1-12	Rev 3.14-end
	E	105.1-22	Esther 6 & 7, or 2 Macc 7.20-41	1 Pet 3.13-end

EPIPHANY 6 Green

S	M	127, 128, 133	Isa 5.1-7 (or -16)	John 15.1-11
	E	75, 76	Proverbs 1.20-end	James 3
M	M	105.23-end	Exod 16.9-15	John 6.25-35
	E	106.1-24	Num 9.1-14 or Baruch 1.15—2.10	1 Pet 4
T	M	106.25-end	Isa 60.13-20	John 8.12-19
	E	107.1-22	Num 16.1-19 or Baruch 2.11-end	1 Pet 5
W	M	107.23-end	Ezek 34.1-16	John 10.7-16
	E	108, (109)	Num 16.20-35 or Baruch 3.1-8	2 Pet 1.1-15

	Psalms	First Reading	Second Reading
Th M	110, 111	Dan 12.1-4	John 11.17-27
E	112, 113	Num 16.36-end or	
		Baruch 3.9-end	2 Pet 1.16—2.3
F M	114	Prov 8.1-21	John 14.1-6
E	115	Num 17.1-11 or	
		Baruch 4.21-30	2 Pet 2.4-end
S M	116, 117	Isa 5.1-7	John 15.1-8
E	118	Num 33.50—34.15 or	
		Baruch 4.36—5 end	2 Pet 3

NINTH SUNDAY BEFORE EASTER
(Third Sunday before Lent)   Green

S M	71	Deut 5.1-21	Luke 13.22-end
E	73	Prov 3.1-18	Mark 4.1-20
M M	1, 2, 3	Gen 1.1—2.3	2 Cor 1.1-14
E	4, 5, 6	Jer 1	John 1.1-18
T M	7	Gen 2.4-end	2 Cor 1.15—2.4
E	8, 9	Jer 2.1-13	John 1.19-34
W M	10	Gen 3	2 Cor 2.5-end
E	11, 12	Jer 2.14-32	John 1.35-end
Th M	13, 14	Gen 4.1-16	2 Cor 3
E	15, 16	Jer 3.6-18	John 2.1-12
F M	17	Gen 6.11—7.10	2 Cor 4
E	18.1-32	Jer 4.1-14	John 2.13-end
S M	18.33-end	Gen 7.11—8.14	2 Cor 5
E	19	Jer 4.19-end	John 3.1-15

EIGHTH SUNDAY BEFORE EASTER
(Second Sunday before Lent)   Green

S M	139.1-18	2 Kings 4.8-37	Mark 1.21-end
E	137.1-6; 146	2 Kings 5 (or 1-14)	Mark 7.24-end; 8.22-26
M M	20, 21	Gen 8.15—9.17	2 Cor 6.1-13
E	22	Jer 5.1-19	John 3.16-21
T M	23, 24	Gen 11.1-9	2 Cor 6.14—7.1
E	25	Jer 5.20-end	John 3.22-end

		Psalms	First Reading	Second Reading
W	M	26, 27	Gen 11.27—12.9	2 Cor 7.2-end
	E	28, 29	Jer 6.9-21	John 4.1-26
Th	M	30	Gen 13.2-end	2 Cor 8.1-15
	E	31	Jer 6.22-end	John 4.27-42
F	M	32	Gen 14	2 Cor 8.16—9.5
	E	33	Jer 7.1-20	John 4.43-end
S	M	34	Gen 16	2 Cor 9.6-end
	E	35	Jer 7.21-end	John 5.1-18

SEVENTH SUNDAY BEFORE EASTER
(The Sunday next before Lent)   Green

		Psalms	First Reading	Second Reading
S	M	56, 57	Jer 33.1-11	Luke 7.36—8.3
	E	103	Num 15.27-36	John 8.1-11
M	M	36	Gen 17.1-22	2 Cor 10
	E	37.1-22	Jer 8.18—9.3	John 5.19-29
T	M	37.23-end	Gen 18	2 Cor 11.1-15
	E	39	Jer 9.12-24	John 5.30-end

ASH WEDNESDAY   Violet (or Lent array)

		Psalms	First Reading	Second Reading
	M	‡102	‡Dan 9.3-19	‡1 Tim 6.6-19
	E	‡38	‡Isa 1.11-20	‡Matt 16.21-end
Th	M	40	Gen 19.1-3, 12-29	2 Cor 11.16-end
	E	41	Jer 10.1-16	John 6.1-15
F	M	42, 43	Gen 21.1-21	2 Cor 12
	E	44	Jer 10.17-24	John 6.16-29
S	M	45, 46	Gen 22.1-19	2 Cor 13
	E	47, 48	Jer 11.1-17	John 6.30-40

LENT 1 (Sixth Sunday before Easter)   Violet (or Lent array)

		Psalms	First Reading	Second Reading
S	M	119.9-24	1 Sam 26	Luke 22.1-23
	E	51	Deut 6	Heb 4
M	M	49	Gen 23	Gal 1
	E	50	Jer 12.1-6	John 6.41-51
T	M	51	Gen 24.1-28	Gal 2.1-10
	E	52, 53	Jer 13.20-end	John 6.52-59
W	M	54, 55	Gen 24.29-end	Gal 2.11-end
	E	56, 57	Jer 15.10-end	John 6.60-end

		Psalms	First Reading	Second Reading
Th	M	(58), 59	Gen 25.7-11, 19-end	Gal 3.1-14
	E	60, 61	Jer 17.5-18	John 7.1-13
F	M	62, 63	Gen 27.1-40	Gal 3.15-end
	E	64, 65	Jer 18.1-12	John 7.14-24
S	M	66, 67	Gen 27.41—28 end	Gal 4.1-20
	E	68	Jer 18.13-end	John 7.25-36

LENT 2 (Fifth Sunday before Easter)   Violet (or Lent array)

		Psalms	First Reading	Second Reading
S	M	119.73-88	Gen 37.1-28	Luke 22.24-53 (or 39-53)
	E	74	Isa 35	Luke 11.14-26
M	M	69	Gen 29.1-30	Gal 4.21—5.1
	E	70, 71	Jer 19.1-13	John 7.37-52
T	M	72	Gen 31.1-9, 14-21	Gal 5.2-end
	E	73	Jer 19.14—20.6	John 7.53—8.11
W	M	74	Gen 32.3-30	Gal 6
	E	75, 76	Jer 20.7-end	John 8.12-20
Th	M	77	Gen 35	Heb 1
	E	78.1-38	Jer 21.1-10	John 8.21-30
F	M	78.39-end	Gen 37	Heb 2.1-9
	E	79	Jer 22.1-5, 13-19	John 8.31-47
S	M	80	Gen 39	Heb 2.10-end
	E	81	Jer 22.20-end	John 8.48-end

LENT 3 (Fourth Sunday before Easter)   Violet (or Lent array)

		Psalms	First Reading	Second Reading
S	M	119.105-120	Exod 5.1—6.1	Luke 22.54-end
	E	31	Isa 45.14-end	Acts 12.1-17a
M	M	82, 83	Gen 40	Heb 3
	E	84, 85	Jer 23.1-15	John 9.1-12
T	M	86	Gen 41.1-40	Heb 4.1-13
	E	87, 88	Jer 23.16-29	John 9.13-23
W	M	89.1-38	Gen 41.41-end	Heb 4.14—5 end
	E	89.39-end	Jer 24	John 9.24-end
Th	M	90	Gen 42	Heb 6
	E	91	Jer 25.1-14	John 10.1-10
F	M	92, 93	Gen 43	Heb 7.1-10
	E	94	Jer 26.1-9	John 10.11-21

		Psalms	First Reading	Second Reading
S	M	95 (or 100), 96	Gen 44	Heb 7.11-end
	E	97, 98	Jer 26.10-end	John 10.22-end

LENT 4 (Third Sunday before Easter) Violet (or Lent array)

		Psalms	First Reading	Second Reading
S	M	119.161-176	Exod 24	Luke 23.1-25
	E	23, 27	1 Kings 19.1-18	2 Pet 1.1-19

Services for Mothering Sunday: Psalms and readings for Pentecost 14 are suitable, or
Psalms 27.1-7; 34, 84, 87, 122, 139.1-18
1 Sam 1.20-end; Proverbs 4.1-9; Proverbs 31.10-end; Micah 4.1-5
Col 3.12-17; 2 Tim 1.3-10; 1 Peter 2.1-10
Mark 10.13-16; Luke 2.41-end; John 19.23-27

		Psalms	First Reading	Second Reading
M	M	99, 100 (or 95), 101	Gen 45	Heb 8
	E	102	Jer 28	John 11.1-16
T	M	103	Gen 46.1-7, 28-end	Heb 9.1-14
	E	104	Jer 29.1-14	John 11.17-27
W	M	105.1-22	Gen 47.1-27	Heb 9.15-end
	E	105.23-end	Jer 30.1-11	John 11.28-37
Th	M	106.1-24	Gen 47.28—48 end	Heb 10.1-18
	E	106.25-end	Jer 30.12-22	John 11.38-44
F	M	107.1-22	Gen 49.1-32	Heb 10.19-end
	E	107.23-end	Jer 31.1-14	John 11.45-end
S	M	108, (109), 110	Gen 49.33—50 end	Heb 11.1-12
	E	111, 112, 113	Jer 31.15-22	John 12.1-11

LENT 5 (Second Sunday before Easter) Violet (or Lent array)

		Psalms	First Reading	Second Reading
S	M	66	Lam 3.19-33	Luke 23.26-49
	E	130, 143.1-11	Jer 31.27-37	Mark 10.32-45
M	M	114, 115	Exod 1.1-14, 22—2.10	Heb 11.13-22
	E	116, 117	Jer 31.35-end	John 12.12-19
T	M	118	Exod 2.11—3.12	Heb 11.23-31
	E	119.1-24	Jer 32.1-15	John 12.36b-end
W	M	119.25-40	Exod 4.1-23	Heb 11.32-end
	E	119.41-56	Jer 33.1-13	John 13.1-11
Th	M	119.57-72	Exod 4.27—6.1	Heb 12.1-13
	E	119.73-88	Jer 33.14-end	John 13.12-20

		Psalms	**First Reading**	**Second Reading**
F	M	119.89-104	Exod 7.8-end	Heb 12.14-end
	E	119.105-128	Jer 36.1-18	John 13.21-30
S	M	119.129-152	Exod 10	Heb 13
	E	119.153-end	Jer 36.19-end	John 13.31-end

PALM SUNDAY (The Sunday next before Easter)   Red

M	61, 62	Jer 7.1-11 or Exod 11	Luke 19.29-end or Mark 14
E	22.1-22	Isa 5.1-7	Mark 12.1-12

MONDAY IN HOLY WEEK   Red, or as in Lent

M	‡41	‡Lam 1.1-12a	‡John 14.1-14 (or -end)
E	‡25	‡Lam 2.8-19	‡John 14.15-end or Gal 6.11-end

TUESDAY IN HOLY WEEK   Red, or as in Lent

M	‡27	‡Lam 3.1-18 or 3.1-30	‡John 15.1-17 (or -end)
E	‡69.1-16	‡Lam 3.40-51	‡John 15.18-end or Rom 5.6-11

WEDNESDAY IN HOLY WEEK   Red, or as in Lent

M	‡31	‡Jer 11.18-20	‡John 16.1-15 (or -end)
E	‡88	‡Isa 63.1-9	‡John 16.16-end or Rom 5.12-19

MAUNDY THURSDAY   Red, or as in Lent

M	‡39	‡Exod 24.1-11	‡John 17
E	‡42, 43	‡Lev 16.2-24	‡John 13.16-35 or Eph 2.11-18

GOOD FRIDAY   Red, hangings removed

M	‡40 or 40.1-14	‡Gen 22.1-18	‡John 18 or Mark 15.21-41
E	‡130, 143.1-11	‡Lam 5.15-end	‡John 19.38-end or Col 1.18-23

		Psalms	First Reading	Second Reading

EASTER EVE Hangings removed

		Psalms	First Reading	Second Reading
	M	‡142	‡Hosea 6.1-6	‡1 Pet 4.1-6
	E	‡116	‡Job 19.21-27	‡1 John 5.5-12

EASTER DAY White or Gold

		Psalms	First Reading	Second Reading
	M	113, 114, 117	Isa 12	Rom 6.3-14
	E	118	Exod 14.5-end	John 20.11-23
M	M	120, 121	Exod 12.14-36	Col 3.1-11
	E	122, 123	Isa 25.1-9	Luke 24.1-12
T	M	124, 125	Exod 12.37-end	Matt 28.1-15
	E	126, 127	Isa 26.1-19	Phil 1.19-26
W	M	128, 129	Exod 13.1-16	Matt 28.16-end
	E	130, 131	Isa 61	1 Thess 4.13-end
Th	M	132	Exod 13.17—14.14	Rev 7.9-end
	E	133, 134	Song of Solomon 2.8-end	Mark 16
F	M	135	Exod 14.15-end	Luke 8.41-56
	E	136	Zeph 3.14-end	Acts 17.16-31
S	M	137, 138	Exod 15.1-21	Luke 16.19-end
	E	139	Zech 8.1-8	Acts 26.1-23

EASTER 1 White or Gold for Sunday, White from Monday

		Psalms	First Reading	Second Reading
S	M	30, 48	Deut 11.1-15	2 Cor 4.5-end
	E	115	Exod 16.1-15	John 6.24-51
M	M	140	Exod 15.22-end	John 20.1-10
	E	141	Ruth 1	1 Tim 1.1-17
T	M	142, 143	Exod 16.22-end	John 20.11-23
	E	144	Ruth 2	1 Tim 1.18—2 end
W	M	145	Exod 17	John 20.24-end
	E	146, 147	Ruth 3	1 Tim 3
Th	M	148	Exod 18.1-12	John 21.1-14
	E	149, 150	Ruth 4	1 Tim 4
F	M	1, 2	Exod 18.13-end	John 21.15-19
	E	3, 4	Deut 1.3-18	1 Tim 5.1-16
S	M	5, 6	Exod 19	John 21.20-end
	E	7	Deut 2.1-25	1 Tim 5.17-end

		Psalms	First Reading	Second Reading

EASTER 2   White

		Psalms	First Reading	Second Reading
S	M	49.1-16	Exod 32.1-14, 30-end	Luke 7.11-17
	E	2, 8	Ezek 34.1-16	John 10.1-18 or 1 Pet 5
M	M	(8), 9	Exod 20.1-21	Luke 1.1-25
	E	10	Deut 2.26—3.5	1 Tim 6.1-10
T	M	11, 12	Exod 22.30—23.17	Luke 1.26-38
	E	13, 14	Deut 4.1-13	1 Tim 6.11-end
W	M	15, 16	Exod 24	Luke 1.39-56
	E	17	Deut 4.14-31	2 Tim 1.1-14
Th	M	18.1-32	Exod 25.1-22	Luke 1.57-66
	E	18.33-end	Deut 4.32-40	2 Tim 1.15—2.13
F	M	19	Exod 28.1-4; 29.1-9	Luke 1.67-end
	E	20, 21	Deut 6	2 Tim 2.14-end
S	M	22	Exod 29.38—30.16	Luke 2.1-20
	E	23, 24	Deut 8	2 Tim 3

EASTER 3   White

		Psalms	First Reading	Second Reading
S	M	121, 126	Num 22.1-35 (or 1-20)	Acts 17.16-end
	E	18.1-32	1 Kings 17.8-end	John 11.17-44
M	M	25	Exod 32.1-14	Luke 2.21-32
	E	26, 27	Deut 9.1-21	2 Tim 4
T	M	28, 29	Exod 32.15-end	Luke 2.33-40
	E	30	Deut 10.12-end	Titus 1
W	M	31	Exod 33	Luke 2.41-end
	E	32	Deut 11.18-end	Titus 2
Th	M	33	Exod 34.1-10, 27-end	Luke 3.1-14
	E	34	Deut 12.1-14	Titus 3
F	M	35	Exod 35.20—36.7	Luke 3.15-23
	E	36	Deut 15.1-18	1 Pet 1.1-12
S	M	37.1-22	Exod 40.17-end	Luke 4.1-13
	E	37.23-end	Deut 16.1-20	1 Pet 1.13-end

EASTER 4   White

		Psalms	First Reading	Second Reading
S	M	57, 63.1-9	Num 22.36—23.12	Luke 16.19-end
	E	77	Prov 4.1-18	2 Cor 4.13—5.15

		Psalms	First Reading	Second Reading
M	M	38	Lev 6.8-end	Luke 4.14-30
	E	39	Deut 17.8-end	1 Pet 2.1-10
T	M	40	Lev 19.1-18, 30-end	Luke 4.31-end
	E	41	Deut 18.9-end	1 Pet 2.11-end
W	M	42, 43	Lev 25.1-24	Luke 5.1-11
	E	44	Deut 19	1 Pet 3.1-12
Th	M	45, 46	Num 9.15-end	Luke 5.12-26
	E	47, 48	Deut 21.22—22.8	1 Pet 3.13-end
F	M	49	Num 12	Luke 5.27-end
	E	50	Deut 24.5-end	1 Pet 4
S	M	51	Num 13.1-3, 17-end	Luke 6.1-11
	E	52, 53	Deut 26	1 Pet 5

EASTER 5   White

S	M	65, 67	Deut 28.1-14	Luke 10.38—11.13
	E	107.1-32	Deut 34	John 16.12-24

ROGATION MONDAY

	M	54, 55	Joel 2.21-27	Acts 14.8-18
	E	56, 57	Deut 7.6-13	Matt 6.19-end

ROGATION TUESDAY

	M	(58), 59	Haggai 1.1-11	2 Cor 9
	E	60, 61	Deut 11.8-21	James 5.1-18

ROGATION WEDNESDAY

	M	‡62, 63	‡Jer 14.1-9	‡John 6.22-40
	E	‡93, 99	‡Ezek 1.4-5, 26-end or The Song of the Three Children 29-37	‡Col 2.20—3.4

ASCENSION DAY   White or Gold

	M	‡96, 97	‡2 Sam 23.1-5	‡Heb 1.1—2.4
	E	‡15, 24	‡Isa 52.7-12	‡Heb 2.5-end
F	M	64, 65	Num 14.1-25	Luke 6.12-26
	E	66, 67	Deut 28.58-end	2 Pet 1.1-15
S	M	68	Num 20.1-13	Luke 6.27-38
	E	69	Deut 30	2 Pet 1.16—2.3

		Psalms	First Reading	Second Reading

THE SUNDAY AFTER ASCENSION DAY (Easter 6)   White

		Psalms	First Reading	Second Reading
S	M	108, 110	Isa 65.17-end	Rev 5
	E	138, 150	2 Kings 2.1-15	John 17 (or 1-13)
M	M	70, 71	Num 21.4-9	Luke 6.39-end
	E	72	Deut 31.1-13	2 Pet 2.4-end
T	M	73	Num 22.2-35	Luke 7.1-10
	E	74	Deut 31.14-29	2 Pet 3
W	M	75, 76	Num 22.36—23.12	Luke 7.11-23
	E	77	Deut 31.30—32.14	1 John 1.1—2.6
Th	M	78.1-38	Num 23.13-end	Luke 7.24-35
	E	78.39-end	Deut 32.15-47	1 John 2.7-17
F	M	79	Num 24	Luke 7.36-end
	E	80	Deut 33	1 John 2.18-end
S	M	‡81	‡Deut 32.48-end; 34	‡Luke 8.1-15
	E	‡48, 145	‡Deut 16.9-15	‡John 7.37-39

PENTECOST (Whit Sunday)   Red

		Psalms	First Reading	Second Reading
S	M	68.1-20	Joel 2.21-end	Rom 8.1-17
	E	104, or 104.1-5, 26-end	Ezek 37.1-14	Rom 8.18-27
M	M	82, 83	Ezek 11.14-20	1 Cor 2
	E	84, 85	1 Sam 10.1-10	Matt 3.13-end
T	M	86	Ezek 36.22-28	1 Cor 3
	E	87, 88	1 Kings 19.1-18	Matt 9.35—10.20
W	M	89.1-38	Isa 55.6-11	1 Cor 12.1-13
	E	89.39-end	Micah 3.1-8	Matt 11.25-end
Th	M	90	Isa 32.9-end	1 Cor 12.27—13 end
	E	91	Exod 35.30—36.1	Matt 12.22-32
F	M	92, 93	Num 11.16, 17, 24-29	Gal 5.13-end
	E	94	Jer 31.31-34	Matt 18.15-20
S	M	95 (or 100), 96	Num 27.15-end	Eph 6.10-20
	E	97, 98	Isa 44.1-5	John 17.17-end

TRINITY SUNDAY
(Pentecost 1)   White or Gold for Sunday, Green from Monday

		Psalms	First Reading	Second Reading
S	M	29, 33	Exod 34.1-10	Acts 2.22-36
	E	145	Isa 40.12-end	Mark 1.1-13

		Psalms	**First Reading**	**Second Reading**
M	M	99, 100 (or 95), 101	Josh 1.1-11	Luke 8.16-25
	E	102	2 Chron 1.1-13 or	
			Wisdom 1	1 John 3
T	M	103	Josh 2	Luke 8.26-39
	E	104	2 Chron 2.1-16 or	
			Wisdom 2	1 John 4
W	M	105.1-22	Josh 3	Luke 8.40-end
	E	105.23-end	2 Chron 5 or	
			Wisdom 3.1-9	1 John 5.1-12
Th	M	106.1-24	Josh 4.1—5.1	Luke 9.1-9
	E	106.25-end	2 Chron 6.1-21 or	
			Wisdom 4.7-end	1 John 5.13-end
F	M	107.1-22	Josh 5.13—6.20	Luke 9.10-17
	E	107.23-end	2 Chron 6.22-end or	
			Wisdom 5.1-16	James 1.1-11
S	M	108, (109), 110	Josh 7.1-15	Luke 9.18-27
	E	111, 112, 113	2 Chron 7 or	
			Wisdom 6.1-21	James 1.12-end

2ND SUNDAY AFTER PENTECOST (Trinity 1)   Green

S	M	85, 133	Deut 30.1-10	Matt 18.10-22
	E	89.1-18	2 Sam 7.1-17	Luke 14.7-24
M	M	114, 115	Josh 7.16-end	Luke 9.28-36
	E	116, 117	2 Chron 12 or	
			Wisdom 7.15—8.4	James 2.1-13
T	M	118	Josh 8.10-29	Luke 9.37-50
	E	119.1-24	2 Chron 13.1—14.1 or	
			Wisdom 8.5-18	James 2.14-end
W	M	119.25-40	Josh 9.3-end	Luke 9.51-end
	E	119.41-56	2 Chron 14.12-end or	
			Wisdom 8.21—9 end	James 3
Th	M	119.57-72	Josh 24.1-28	Luke 10.1-16
	E	119.73-88	2 Chron 17.1-12 or	
			Wisdom 10.15—11.10	James 4.1-12
F	M	119.89-104	Judges 2.6-end	Luke 10.17-24
	E	119.105-128	2 Chron 34.1-18 or	
			Wisdom 11.21—12.2	James 4.13—5.6
S	M	119.129-152	Judges 4	Luke 10.25-37
	E	119.153-end	2 Chron 34.19-33 or	
			Wisdom 12.12-21	James 5.7-end

	Psalms	First Reading	Second Reading

3RD SUNDAY AFTER PENTECOST (Trinity 2)   Green

S	M	11, 20	Micah 3.5-end	Matt 5.27-end
	E	32, 36	Deut 5.1-21	Acts 4.1-22
M	M	120, 121	Judges 5	Luke 10.38-end
	E	122, 123	Jer 37	Rom 1.1-7
T	M	124, 125	Judges 6.1, 11-end	Luke 11.1-13
	E	126, 127	Jer 38.1-13	Rom 1.8-17
W	M	128, 129	Judges 7	Luke 11.14-28
	E	130, 131	Jer 38.14-end	Rom 1.18-end
Th	M	132	Judges 9.1-21	Luke 11.29-36
	E	133, 134	Jer 39	Rom 2.1-16
F	M	135	Judges 9.22-end	Luke 11.37-44
	E	136	Jer 40	Rom 2.17-end
S	M	137, 138	Judges 11.1-6, 29-end	Luke 11.45-end
	E	139	Jer 41	Rom 3.1-20

4TH SUNDAY AFTER PENTECOST (Trinity 3)   Green

S	M	42, 43	Ezek 18.1-4, 19-end	Rom 14.1—15.3
	E	147	Josh 24.1-5, 13-31	Acts 8.26-end
M	M	140	Judges 13	Luke 12.1-12
	E	141	Jer 42	Rom 3.21-end
T	M	142	Judges 14	Luke 12.13-21
	E	143	Jer 43	Rom 4.1-12
W	M	144	Judges 15	Luke 12.22-31
	E	145	Jer 44.1-14	Rom 4.13-end
Th	M	146, 147	Judges 16.1-22	Luke 12.32-40
	E	148	Jer 44.15-end	Rom 5.1-11
F	M	149, 150	Judges 16.23-end	Luke 12.41-48
	E	1, 2	2 Chron 36.11-21	Rom 5.12-end
S	M	3, 4	Judges 18.1-20, 27-end	Luke 12.49-end
	E	5, 6	Ezra 1	Rom 6.1-14

5TH SUNDAY AFTER PENTECOST (Trinity 4)   Green

| S | M | 119.41-56 | Neh 8.1-12 | Luke 11.37-end |
| | E | 67, 98 | 2 Kings 6.24, 25; 7.3-end | Acts 11.1-18 |

		Psalms	First Reading	Second Reading
M	M	7	1 Sam 1.1-20	Luke 13.1-9
	E	8, 9	Ezra 3	Rom 6.15-end
T	M	10	1 Sam 1.21—2.11	Luke 13.10-21
	E	11, 12	Ezra 4.1-5	Rom 7.1-6
W	M	13, 14	1 Sam 3.1-19	Luke 13.22-end
	E	15, 16	Ezra 4.7-end	Rom 7.7-end
Th	M	17	1 Sam 4.1-18	Luke 14.1-11
	E	18.1-32	Ezra 5	Rom 8.1-11
F	M	18.33-end	1 Sam 5	Luke 14.12-24
	E	19	Ezra 6	Rom 8.12-17
S	M	20, 21	1 Sam 6.1-16	Luke 14.25-end
	E	22	Ezra 7	Rom 8.18-30

6TH SUNDAY AFTER PENTECOST (Trinity 5) Green

		Psalms	First Reading	Second Reading
S	M	77	Isa 43.14—44.5	Mark 2.18—3.6
	E	102	Dan 1	Eph 4.17-end
M	M	23, 24	1 Sam 8	Luke 15.1-10
	E	25	Ezra 8.15-end	Rom 8.31-end
T	M	26, 27	1 Sam 9.1-14	Luke 16.1-18
	E	28, 29	Ezra 9	Rom 9.1-13
W	M	30	1 Sam 9.15—10.1	Luke 16.19-end
	E	31	Ezra 10.1-19	Rom 9.14-29
Th	M	32	1 Sam 10.1-16	Luke 17.1-10
	E	33	Neh 1	Rom 9.30—10.10
F	M	34	1 Sam 10.17-end	Luke 17.11-19
	E	35	Neh 2	Rom 10.11-end
S	M	36	1 Sam 11	Luke 17.20-end
	E	37.1-22	Neh 4	Rom 11.1-12

7TH SUNDAY AFTER PENTECOST (Trinity 6) Green

		Psalms	First Reading	Second Reading
S	M	81	Gen 50.15-end	1 John 2.1-17
	E	99, 100, 101	Deut 10.12—11.1	Mark 12.28-end
M	M	37.23-end	1 Sam 12	Luke 18.1-14
	E	38	Neh 5	Rom 11.13-24
T	M	39	1 Sam 13	Luke 18.15-30
	E	40	Neh 6.1-16	Rom 11.25-end

		Psalms	First Reading	Second Reading
W	M	41	1 Sam 14.1-15	Luke 18.31-end
	E	42, 43	Neh 8.1-12	Rom 12.1-8
Th	M	44	1 Sam 14.24-46	Luke 19.1-10
	E	45, 46	Neh 8.13-end	Rom 12.9-end
F	M	47, 48	1 Sam 15.1-23	Luke 19.11-27
	E	49	Neh 9.1-23	Rom 13
S	M	50	1 Sam 16	Luke 19.28-40
	E	51	Neh 9.24-end	Rom 14.1-12

8TH SUNDAY AFTER PENTECOST (Trinity 7)   Green

		Psalms	First Reading	Second Reading
S	M	73	Num 11.16-17, 24-29	Acts 8.4-25
	E	91	Isa 32.9-18	1 Cor 12.1-31a
M	M	52, 53	1 Sam 17.1-25	Luke 19.41—20.8
	E	54, 55	Neh 13.1-14	Rom 14.13-end
T	M	56, 57	1 Sam 17.26-50	Luke 20.9-26
	E	(58), 59	Neh 13.15-end	Rom 15.1-13
W	M	60, 61	1 Sam 17.55—18.16	Luke 20.27-40
	E	62, 63	Haggai 1.1—2.9	Rom 15.14-21
Th	M	64, 65	1 Sam 19.1-18	Luke 20.41—21.4
	E	66, 67	Haggai 2.10-end	Rom 15.22-end
F	M	68	1 Sam 20.1-17	Luke 21.5-19
	E	69	Zech 1.1-17	Rom 16.1-16
S	M	70, 71	1 Sam 20.18-end	Luke 21.20-end
	E	72	Zech 1.18—2 end	Rom 16.17-end

9TH SUNDAY AFTER PENTECOST (Trinity 8)   Green

		Psalms	First Reading	Second Reading
S	M	90	Neh 4.7-end	Matt 6.1-18
	E	24, 46	1 Sam 17.1-11, 32-51	2 Cor 6.1-10
M	M	73	1 Sam 21.1—22.5	Luke 22.1-13
	E	74	Zech 3 & 4	Eph 1.1-14
T	M	75, 76	1 Sam 22.6-end	Luke 22.14-23
	E	77	Zech 6.9-end	Eph 1.15-end
W	M	78.1-38	1 Sam 23	Luke 22.24-34
	E	78.39-end	Zech 7	Eph 2.1-10
Th	M	79	1 Sam 26	Luke 22.35-46
	E	80	Zech 8.1-8	Eph 2.11-end

		Psalms	First Reading	Second Reading
F	M	81	1 Sam 28.3-end	Luke 22.47-62
	E	82, 83	Zech 8.9-end	Eph 3.1-13
S	M	84, 85	1 Sam 31	Luke 22.63—23.5
	E	86	Job 1	Eph 3.14-end

10TH SUNDAY AFTER PENTECOST (Trinity 9)   Green

S	M	19	1 Sam 18.1-16	Mark 9.30-end
	E	1, 4	1 Sam 24.1-17	Gal 6
M	M	87, 88	2 Sam 1	Luke 23.6-25
	E	89.1-38	Job 2	Eph 4.1-16
T	M	89.39-end	2 Sam 2	Luke 23.26-43
	E	90	Job 3	Eph 4.17-end
W	M	91	2 Sam 5.1-10, 17-end	Luke 23.44-56a
	E	92, 93	Job 4	Eph 5.1-14
Th	M	94	2 Sam 6.1-19	Luke 23.56b—24.12
	E	95 (or 100), 96	Job 5	Eph 5.15-end
F	M	97, 98	2 Sam 7.1-17	Luke 24.13-35
	E	99, 100 (or 95), 101	Job 6	Eph 6.1-9
S	M	102	2 Sam 7.18-end	Luke 24.36-end
	E	103	Job 7	Eph 6.10-end

11TH SUNDAY AFTER PENTECOST (Trinity 10)   Green

S	M	123, 124, 125	Exod 18.13-26	Acts 6
	E	82, 112	1 Chron 29.1-16	Luke 17.5-10
M	M	104	2 Sam 9	Acts 1.1-14
	E	105.1-22	Job 8	Mark 1.1-13
T	M	105.23-end	2 Sam 11	Acts 1.15-end
	E	106.1-24	Job 9	Mark 1.14-28
W	M	106.25-end	2 Sam 12.1-25	Acts 2.1-13
	E	107.1-22	Job 10	Mark 1.29-end
Th	M	107.23-end	2 Sam 15.1-12	Acts 2.14-36
	E	108, (109)	Job 11	Mark 2.1-12
F	M	110, 111	2 Sam 15.13-end	Acts 2.37-end
	E	112, 113	Job 12	Mark 2.13-22
S	M	114	2 Sam 16.1-14	Acts 3.1-10
	E	115	Job 13	Mark 2.23—3.6

		Psalms	First Reading	Second Reading

12TH SUNDAY AFTER PENTECOST (Trinity 11) Green

S	M	145, 150	Ezek 33.1-9, 30-end	Acts 16.1-15
	E	34	Jonah 1 & 2	Acts 28 (or 11-end)
M	M	116, 117	2 Sam 17.1-23	Acts 3.11—4.4
	E	118	Job 14	Mark 3.7-19a
T	M	119.1-24	2 Sam 18.1-18	Acts 4.5-22
	E	119.25-40	Job 15.1-16	Mark 3.19b-end
W	M	119.41-56	2 Sam 18.19—19.8a	Acts 4.23-31
	E	119.57-72	Job 16.1—17.2	Mark 4.1-20
Th	M	119.73-88	2 Sam 19.8b-23	Acts 4.32—5.11
	E	119.89-104	Job 17.3-end	Mark 4.21-34
F	M	119.105-128	2 Sam 19.24-end	Acts 5.12-26
	E	119.129-152	Job 18	Mark 4.35-end
S	M	119.153-end	2 Sam 23.1-7	Acts 5.27-end
	E	120, 121	Job 19	Mark 5.1-20

13TH SUNDAY AFTER PENTECOST (Trinity 12) Green

S	M	130, 137.1-6	2 Kings 19.8-19	Acts 16.16-end
	E	22.1-22	Jer 20.1-11a	Acts 20.17-end
M	M	122, 123	2 Sam 23.8-end	Acts 6
	E	124, 125	Job 21	Mark 5.21-34
T	M	126, 127	2 Sam 24	Acts 7.1-16
	E	128, 129	Job 22	Mark 5.35-end
W	M	130, 131	1 Kings 1.1-31	Acts 7.17-36
	E	132	Job 23	Mark 6.1-13
Th	M	133, 134	1 Kings 1.32-end	Acts 7.37-53
	E	135	Job 24	Mark 6.14-29
F	M	136	1 Kings 2.1-12	Acts 7.54—8.3
	E	137, 138	Job 25 & 26	Mark 6.30-44
S	M	139	1 Kings 3	Acts 8.4-25
	E	140, 141	Job 27	Mark 6.45-end

14TH SUNDAY AFTER PENTECOST (Trinity 13) Green

S	M	103	Gen 29.1-20	2 Tim 1.1-14
	E	45	Gen 45 (or 1-15)	Luke 2.41-end
M	M	142, 143	1 Kings 4.29—5.12	Acts 8.26-end
	E	144	Job 28	Mark 7.1-13

		Psalms	First Reading	Second Reading
T	M	145	1 Kings 6.1-22	Acts 9.1-19a
	E	146, 147	Job 29.1—30.1	Mark 7.14-23
W	M	148	1 Kings 8.1-30	Acts 9.19b-31
	E	149, 150	Job 31.13-end	Mark 7.24-end
Th	M	1, 2, 3	1 Kings 10.1-25	Acts 9.32-end
	E	4, 5, 6	Job 32	Mark 8.1-10
F	M	7	1 Kings 11.1-13	Acts 10.1-16
	E	8, 9	Job 33	Mark 8.11-21
S	M	10	1 Kings 11.26-end	Acts 10.17-33
	E	11, 12	Job 38.1-21	Mark 8.22-26

15TH SUNDAY AFTER PENTECOST (Trinity 14)   Green

		Psalms	First Reading	Second Reading
S	M	50	Dan 5	Acts 25.1-12
	E	72	1 Kings 3.4-15	
			(or 5-end)	1 Tim 1.12—2.8
M	M	13, 14	1 Kings 12.1-24	Acts 10.34-end
	E	15, 16	Job 38.22-end	Mark 8.27—9.1
T	M	17	1 Kings 12.25-end	Acts 11.1-18
	E	18.1-32	Job 39	Mark 9.2-13
W	M	18.33-end	1 Kings 13.1-10	Acts 11.19-end
	E	19	Job 40	Mark 9.14-29
Th	M	20, 21	1 Kings 13.11-end	Acts 12.1-11
	E	22	Job 41	Mark 9.30-37
F	M	23, 24	1 Kings 17	Acts 12.12-end
	E	25	Job 42	Mark 9.38-end
S	M	26, 27	1 Kings 18.1-20	Acts 13.1-12
	E	28, 29	Amos 1	Mark 10.1-16

16TH SUNDAY AFTER PENTECOST (Trinity 15)   Green

		Psalms	First Reading	Second Reading
S	M	107.1-32	1 Kings 21 (or 1-23)	Matt 7.1-12
	E	41, 133	Deut 15.1-18	1 John 4.7-end
M	M	30	1 Kings 18.21-end	Acts 13.13-41
	E	31	Amos 2	Mark 10.17-31
T	M	32	1 Kings 19	Acts 13.42—14.7
	E	33	Amos 3	Mark 10.32-34
W	M	34	1 Kings 20.1-22	Acts 14.8-end
	E	35	Amos 4	Mark 10.35-45

		Psalms	**First Reading**	**Second Reading**
Th	M	36	1 Kings 20.23-end	Acts 15.1-21
	E	37.1-22	Amos 5.1-17	Mark 10.46-end
F	M	37.23-end	1 Kings 21	Acts 15.22-35
	E	38	Amos 5.18-end	Mark 11.1-11
S	M	39	1 Kings 22.1-28	Acts 15.36—16.5
	E	40	Amos 6	Mark 11.12-26

17TH SUNDAY AFTER PENTECOST (Trinity 16)   Green

		Psalms	**First Reading**	**Second Reading**
S	M	91, 93	Judges 7.1-8, 19-23 (or 1-23)	John 7.1-24
	E	19, 20	Jer 32.1-15	Luke 14.25-end
M	M	41	1 Kings 22.29-40	Acts 16.6-24
	E	42, 43	Amos 7	Mark 11.27-end
T	M	44	2 Kings 2.1-15	Acts 16.25-end
	E	45, 46	Amos 8	Mark 12.1-12
W	M	47, 48	2 Kings 3.4-24	Acts 17.1-15
	E	49	Amos 9	Mark 12.13-27
Th	M	50	2 Kings 4.1-37	Acts 17.16-end
	E	51	Micah 1	Mark 12.28-34
F	M	52, 53	2 Kings 5	Acts 18.1-21
	E	54, 55	Micah 2	Mark 12.35-end
S	M	56, 57	2 Kings 6.8-23	Acts 18.22—19.7
	E	(58), 59	Micah 3	Mark 13.1-13

18TH SUNDAY AFTER PENTECOST (Trinity 17)   Green

		Psalms	**First Reading**	**Second Reading**
S	M	118	Eccles 11 & 12	Luke 12.1-21
	E	116	Neh 6.1-16 or Ecclus 38.24-end	Rom 12
M	M	60, 61	2 Kings 6.24—7.2	Acts 19.8-20
	E	62, 63	Micah 4.1—5.1	Mark 13.14-27
T	M	64, 65	2 Kings 7.3-end	Acts 19.21-end
	E	66, 67	Micah 5.2-end	Mark 13.28-end
W	M	68	2 Kings 9.1-13	Acts 20.1-16
	E	69	Micah 6	Mark 14.1-11
Th	M	70, 71	2 Kings 9.14-end	Acts 20.17-end
	E	72	Micah 7.1-7	Mark 14.12-25

		Psalms	First Reading	Second Reading
F	M	73	2 Kings 10.18-28	Acts 21.1-16
	E	74	Micah 7.8-end	Mark 14.26-42
S	M	75, 76	2 Kings 11.21—12 end	Acts 21.17-36
	E	77	Nahum 1	Mark 14.43-52

19TH SUNDAY AFTER PENTECOST (Trinity 18) Green

		Psalms	First Reading	Second Reading
S	M	37.1-22	Job 23.1-12	2 Cor 1.1-22
	E	85, 111	Dan 6.1-23	Luke 18.35—19.10
M	M	78.1-38	2 Kings 17.1-23	Acts 21.37—22.21
	E	78.39-end	Nahum 2	Mark 14.53-65
T	M	79	2 Kings 17.24-end	Acts 22.22—23.11
	E	80	Nahum 3	Mark 14.66-end
W	M	81	2 Kings 18.1-12	Acts 23.12-end
	E	82, 83	Hab 1	Mark 15.1-15
Th	M	84, 85	2 Kings 18.13-end	Acts 24.1-23
	E	86	Hab 2	Mark 15.16-32
F	M	87, 88	2 Kings 19.1-19	Acts 24.24—25.12
	E	89.1-38	Hab 3.2-end	Mark 15.33-end
S	M	89.39-end	2 Kings 19.20-end	Acts 25.13-end
	E	90	Zeph 1	Mark 16

20TH SUNDAY AFTER PENTECOST (Trinity 19) Green

		Psalms	First Reading	Second Reading
S	M	51	Job 1	2 Tim 2.1-19
	E	39	Gen 32.3-30	Acts 27.1-25 (or 13-25)
M	M	91	2 Kings 20	Acts 26.1-23
	E	92, 93	Zeph 2	Luke 10.25-37
T	M	94	2 Kings 22	Acts 26.24-end
	E	95 (or 100), 96	Zeph 3	Luke 12.13-21
W	M	97	2 Kings 23.1-20	Acts 27.1-26
	E	98	Mal 1	Luke 14.16-24
Th	M	99, 100 (or 95), 101	2 Kings 23.21—24.7	Acts 27.27-end
	E	102	Mal 2.1-16	Luke 15.11-32
F	M	103	2 Kings 24.8—25.12	Acts 28.1-16
	E	104	Mal 2.17—3.12	Luke 16.19-31
S	M	105.1-22	2 Kings 25.22-end	Acts 28.17-end
	E	105.23-end	Mal 3.13—4 end	Luke 18.9-14

		Psalms	First Reading	Second Reading

21ST SUNDAY AFTER PENTECOST (Trinity 20) Green

		Psalms	First Reading	Second Reading
S	M	23, 24 or 78.1-24	Ezek 34.11-24	2 Pet 3
	E	15, 16	Ezek 12.21-end	1 Pet 1.3-21
M	M	106.1-24	Song of Solomon 1.9—2.7	1 Tim 1.1-17
	E	106.25-end	Exod 30.1-10	Luke 1.5-23
T	M	107.1-22	Song of Solomon 2.8-end	1 Tim 1.18—2 end
	E	107.23-end	Lev 11.1-8, 44-end	Acts 10.9-16
W	M	108, (109)	Song of Solomon 3	1 Tim 3
	E	110, 111	Lev 12.6-7a, 8	Luke 2.21-32
Th	M	112, 113	Song of Solomon 5.2—6.3	1 Tim 4
	E	114	Lev 13.1-3, 45-46	Luke 5.12-14
F	M	115	Song of Solomon 7.10—8.4	1 Tim 5
	E	116, 117	Lev 14.1-9	Luke 17.11-19
S	M	118	Song of Solomon 8.5-7	1 Tim 6
	E	119.1-24	Num 6.1-5, 21-end	Acts 21.17-30

22ND SUNDAY AFTER PENTECOST (Trinity 21) Green

		Psalms	First Reading	Second Reading
S	M	42, 43	Prov 14.31—15.17	James 4.13—5.11
	E	40	Jer 6.16-21	Mark 3.7-end
M	M	119.25-40	Num 9.1-14 or Baruch 1.15—2.10	2 Tim 1.1-14
	E	119.41-56	Exod 16.9-15 or Wisdom 1	John 6.25-35
T	M	119.57-72	Num 16.1-19 or Baruch 2.11-end	2 Tim 1.15—2.13
	E	119.73-88	Isa 60.13-20 or Wisdom 2	John 8.12-19
W	M	119.89-104	Num 16.20-35 or Baruch 3.1-8	2 Tim 2.14-end
	E	119.105-128	Ezek 34.1-16 or Wisdom 5.1-16	John 10.7-16
Th	M	119.129-152	Num 16.36-end or Baruch 3.9-end	2 Tim 3
	E	119.153-end	Dan 12.1-4 or Wisdom 6.1-21	John 11.17-27

		Psalms	First Reading	Second Reading
F	M	120, 121	Num 17.1-11 or	
			Baruch 4.21-30	2 Tim 4.1-8
	E	122, 123	Prov 8.1-21 or	
			Wisdom 7.15—8.4	John 14.1-6
S	M	124, 125	Num 33.50—34.15 or	
			Baruch 4.36—5 end	2 Tim 4.9-end
	E	126, 127	Isa 5.1-7 or	
			Wisdom 8.21—9 end	John 15.1-8

LAST SUNDAY AFTER PENTECOST   Green

		Psalms	First Reading	Second Reading
S	M	89.1-18	Dan 10.2-19	Rev 1.1-18
	E	84, 122	Isa 33.13-22	Matt 24.45—25.13
M	M	128, 129	‡Eccles 1	Phil 1.1-11
	E	130, 131	‡Eccles 2.1-23	Luke 17.20-end
T	M	132	‡Eccles 3.1-15	Phil 1.12-end
	E	133, 134	‡Eccles 3.16—4 end	Luke 18.1-17
W	M	135	‡Eccles 5	Phil 2.1-18
	E	136	‡Eccles 6	Luke 18.18-30
Th	M	137, 138	‡Eccles 7	Phil 2.19-end
	E	139	‡Eccles 8	Luke 18.35-end
F	M	140, 141	‡Eccles 9	Phil 3.1—4.1
	E	142, 143	‡Eccles 11.1-8	Luke 19.1-10
S	M	144	‡Eccles 11.9—12 end	Phil 4.2-end
	E	145	‡Obadiah	Luke 19.11-27

TABLE 1B/PSALMS AND READINGS
FOR MORNING AND EVENING PRAYER
SUNDAYS AND WEEKDAYS, YEAR 2

	Psalms	First Reading	Second Reading

NINTH SUNDAY BEFORE CHRISTMAS
(Fifth Sunday before Advent)   Green

		Psalms	First Reading	Second Reading
S	M	104 or 104.1-25	Job 38.1-21; 42.1-6	Acts 14.8-17
	E	148, 150	Gen 1.1—2.3	John 1.1-14 (or -18)
M	M	1, 2	Prov 1.1-19 or Ecclus 1.1-10	Rev 1
	E	3, 4	Dan 1	Matt 1.18-end
T	M	5, 6	Prov 1.20-end or Ecclus 1.11-end	Rev 2.1-11
	E	7	Dan 2.1-24	Matt 2.1-12
W	M	8, 9	Prov 2 or Ecclus 2	Rev 2.12-end
	E	10	Dan 2.25-end	Matt 2.13-end
Th	M	11, 12	Prov 3.1-26 or Ecclus 4.11-28	Rev 3.1-13
	E	13, 14	Dan 3.1-18	Matt 3
F	M	15, 16	Prov 3.27—4.19 or Ecclus 6.14-31	Rev 3.14-end
	E	17	Dan 3.19-end	Matt 4.1-11
S	M	18.1-32	Prov 6.1-19 or Ecclus 7.27-end	Rev 4
	E	18.33-end	Dan 4.1-18	Matt 4.12-22

EIGHTH SUNDAY BEFORE CHRISTMAS
(Fourth Sunday before Advent)   Green

		Psalms	First Reading	Second Reading
S	M	25	Jer 17.5-14	Rom 5.12-end
	E	139.1-18	Exod 20.1-20	Mark 7.1-23
M	M	19	Prov 8.1-21 or Ecclus 10.6-8, 12-24	Rev 5
	E	20, 21	Dan 4.19-end	Matt 4.23—5.12
T	M	22	Prov 8.22-end or Ecclus 14.20—15.10	Rev 6
	E	23, 24	Dan 5.1-12	Matt 5.13-20

		Psalms	First Reading	Second Reading
W	M	25	Prov 9 or	
			Ecclus 15.11-end	Rev 7
	E	26, 27	Dan 5.13-end	Matt 5.21-26
Th	M	28, 29	Prov 10.1-13 or	
			Ecclus 17.1-24	Rev 8
	E	30	Dan 6	Matt 5.27-37
F	M	31	Prov 11.1-12 or	
			Ecclus 22.6-22	Rev 9.1-12
	E	32	Dan 7.1-14	Matt 5.38-end
S	M	33	Prov 12.10-end or	
			Ecclus 22.27—23.15	Rev 9.13-end
	E	34	Dan 7.15-end	Matt 6.1-18

SEVENTH SUNDAY BEFORE CHRISTMAS
(Third Sunday before Advent)   Green

		Psalms	First Reading	Second Reading
S	M	32, 36	Isa 55	Gal 3.1-14
	E	135 or 136	Gen 13	John 8.31-end

Services for Remembrance Sunday
The following psalms and readings are suitable:
Psalms 46, 47, 93, 126, 130; Isa 2.1-5; Isa 10.33—11.9; Ezek 37.1-14;
Rom 8.31-end; Rev 21.1-7; Matt 5.1-12; John 15.9-17

		Psalms	First Reading	Second Reading
M	M	35	Prov 14.31—15.17 or	
			Ecclus 24.1-22	Rev 10
	E	36	Dan 9.1-3, 20-end	Matt 6.19-end
T	M	37.1-22	Prov 15.18-end or	
			Ecclus 24.23-end	Rev 11.1-13
	E	37.23-end	Dan 10.1—11.1	Matt 7.1-12
W	M	38	Prov 18.10-end or	
			Ecclus 38.1-14	Rev 11.14-end
	E	39	Dan 12	Matt 7.13-end
Th	M	40	Prov 20.1-22 or	
			Ecclus 38.24-end	Rev 12
	E	41	Hosea 1.1—2.1	Matt 8.1-13
F	M	42, 43	Prov 22.1-16 or	
			Ecclus 39.1-11	Rev 13.1-10
	E	44	Hosea 2.2-17	Matt 8.14-22
S	M	45, 46	Prov 24.23-end or	
			Ecclus 39.13-end	Rev 13.11-end
	E	47, 48	Hosea 2.18—3 end	Matt 8.23-end

		Psalms	**First Reading**	**Second Reading**

SIXTH SUNDAY BEFORE CHRISTMAS
(Second Sunday before Advent)   Green

		Psalms	First Reading	Second Reading
S	M	66	Exod 1.8-14, 22—2.10	Heb 3
	E	106.1-15, 42-end	Exod 2.23—3.20	John 6.24-40
M	M	49	Prov 25.1-14 or Ecclus 42.15-end	Rev 14.1-13
	E	50	Hosea 4.1-14	Matt 9.1-13
T	M	51	Prov 25.15-end or Ecclus 43.1-12	Rev 14.14-end
	E	52, 53	Hosea 4.15—5.7	Matt 9.14-26
W	M	54, 55	Prov 26.12-end or Ecclus 43.13-end	Rev 15
	E	56, 57	Hosea 5.8—6.6	Matt 9.27-end
Th	M	(58), 59	Prov 27.1-22 or Ecclus 50.1-24	Rev 16.1-11
	E	60, 61	Hosea 8	Matt 10.1-15
F	M	62, 63	Prov 30.1-9 or Ecclus 51.1-12	Rev 16.12-end
	E	64, 65	Hosea 9.1-9	Matt 10.16-33
S	M	66, 67	Prov 31.10-end or Ecclus 51.13-end	Rev 17
	E	68	Hosea 9.10-end	Matt 10.34—11.1

FIFTH SUNDAY BEFORE CHRISTMAS
(The Sunday next before Advent)   Green

		Psalms	First Reading	Second Reading
S	M	147	Gen 6.5-end	1 Pet 3.8-end
	E	75, 76	Jer 5.1-19	Rom 11.1-24
M	M	69	Isa 40.1-11	Rev 18
	E	70, 71	Hosea 10.1-8	Matt 11.2-19
T	M	72	Isa 40.12-26	Rev 19
	E	73	Hosea 10.9-end	Matt 11.20-end
W	M	74	Isa 40.27—41.7	Rev 20
	E	75, 76	Hosea 11.1-11	Matt 12.1-21
Th	M	77	Isa 41.8-20	Rev 21.1-8
	E	78.1-38	Hosea 11.12—12 end	Matt 12.22-37
F	M	78.39-end	Isa 41.21-end	Rev 21.9-21
	E	79	Hosea 13.1-14	Matt 12.38-end
S	M	80	Isa 42.1-9	Rev 21.22—22.5
	E	81	Hosea 14	Matt 13.1-17

	Psalms	First Reading	Second Reading

ADVENT SUNDAY (Fourth Sunday before Christmas) Violet

		Psalms	First Reading	Second Reading
S	M	18.1-32	Isa 2.10-end	Matt 24.1-28
	E	68.1-20	Isa 52.1-12	1 Thess 5
M	M	82, 83	Isa 42.10-17	Rev 22.6-end
	E	84, 85	Isa 1.21-end	Matt 13.18-33
T	M	86	Isa 42.18-end	1 Thess 1
	E	87, 88	Isa 2.1-11	Matt 13.34-43
W	M	89.1-38	Isa 43.1-13	1 Thess 2.1-12
	E	89.39-end	Isa 3.1-15	Matt 13.44-end
Th	M	90	Isa 43.14-end	1 Thess 2.13-end
	E	91	Isa 4.2—5.7	Matt 14.1-12
F	M	92, 93	Isa 44.1-8	1 Thess 3
	E	94	Isa 5.8-24	Matt 14.13-end
S	M	95 (or 100), 96	Isa 44.9-23	1 Thess 4.1-12
	E	97, 98	Isa 5.25-end	Matt 15.1-20

ADVENT 2 (Third Sunday before Christmas) Violet

		Psalms	First Reading	Second Reading
S	M	119.137-152	Jer 36.9-end (or -26)	Matt 25.14-30
	E	119.89-104	1 Sam 28.3-20	2 Tim 3.14—4.8
M	M	99, 100 (or 95), 101	Isa 44.24-end	1 Thess 4.13—5.11
	E	102	Isa 6	Matt 15.21-28
T	M	103	Isa 45.1-13	1 Thess 5.12-end
	E	104	Isa 7.1-17	Matt 15.29-end
W	M	105.1-22	Isa 45.15-end	2 Thess 1
	E	105.23-end	Isa 8.16—9.7	Matt 16.1-12
Th	M	106.1-24	Isa 46	2 Thess 2
	E	106.25-end	Isa 9.8—10.4	Matt 16.13-end
F	M	107.1-22	Isa 47	2 Thess 3
	E	107.23-end	Isa 10.5-19	Matt 17.1-13
S	M	108, (109), 110	Isa 48.1-11	Jude
	E	111, 112, 113	Isa 10.20-32	Matt 17.14-21

ADVENT 3 (Second Sunday before Christmas) Violet

		Psalms	First Reading	Second Reading
S	M	80	1 Kings 18.17-39	Luke 3.1-20
	E	11, 14	Isa 40.1-11	1 Cor 3
M	M	114, 115	Isa 48.12-end	Luke 20.9-18
	E	116, 117	Isa 10.33—11.9	Col 1.1-14

		Psalms	First Reading	Second Reading
T	M	118	Isa 50.4-10	Luke 20.19-26
	E	119.1-24	Isa 11.10—12 end	Col 1.15-end
W	M	119.25-40	Isa 51.1-8	Luke 20.27-44
	E	119.41-56	Isa 13.1-13	Col 2.1-15
Th	M	119.57-72	Isa 51.9-16	Luke 21.5-19
	E	119.73-88	Isa 14.3-20	Col 2.16—3.11
F	M	119.89-104	Isa 51.17-end	Luke 21.20-28
	E	119.105-128	Isa 21.1-12	Col 3.12—4.1
S	M	119.129-152	Isa 52.1-12	Luke 21.29-36
	E	119.153-end	Isa 22.1-14	Col 4.2-end

ADVENT 4 (The Sunday next before Christmas)   Violet

S	M	40	Jer 33.10-16	Rev 22.6-end
	E	113, 123, 131	Isa 10.33—11.10	Luke 1.26-38a
M	M	120, 121	Isa 52.13—53 end	John 1.19-37
	E	122, 123	Isa 24	2 John
T	M	124, 125	Isa 54	John 3.22-36
	E	126, 127	Isa 25.1-9	3 John
W	M	128, 129	Isa 55	John 5.30-end
	E	130, 131	Isa 26.1-13	Phil 4.4-9
Th	M	132	Isa 56.1-8	John 7.37-44
	E	133, 134	Isa 28.1-13	Titus 3.4-7
F	M	135	Isa 57.15-end	John 16.29—17.5
	E	136	Isa 28.14-end	Philemon

CHRISTMAS EVE (24 December)   Violet

M	‡137, 138	‡Isa 58	‡Rom 1.1-7
E	‡85	‡Isa 32.1-8	‡John 13.1-17

CHRISTMAS DAY   White or Gold

M	19	‡Isa 35	‡John 3.16-21
E	8, 110	‡Isa 65.17-end	‡1 John 1.1-9

ST STEPHEN (26 December)   Red

M	13, 46	‡Exod 18.13-26	‡Acts 6
E	57, 86	‡Gen 4.1-10	‡John 15.20—16.4a

	Psalms	First Reading	Second Reading

ST JOHN (27 December)   White

| M | 97 | ‡Exod 33.7-11a | ‡1 John 5.1-12 |
| E | 21 | ‡Isa 6.1-8 | ‡John 13.21-35 |

THE HOLY INNOCENTS (28 December)   Red

M	36	‡Gen 37.13-20 or	
		Baruch 4.21-27	‡1 Pet 4.12-end
E	124, 128	‡Isa 49.14-25	‡Matt 18.1-10

SUNDAY AFTER CHRISTMAS DAY   White or Gold

M	132	Haggai 2.1-9	1 Pet 2.1-10 or
			Luke 2.41-end
E	84, 122	Ruth 2.1-20a;	
		4.13-17	Rom 1.1-17

When Christmas Day falls on a Wednesday and the Presentation of Christ falls on a Sunday the readings appointed for Year 1 are always used.

29 DECEMBER

| M | 139 | Isa 59.1-15a | John 12.20-33 |
| E | 140, 141 | Isa 29.1-14 | 2 Cor 8.1-9 |

30 DECEMBER

| M | 142, 143 | Isa 59.15b-end | John 12.34-end |
| E | 144 | Isa 29.15-end | Eph 3.14-end |

31 DECEMBER

| M | ‡145 | ‡Isa 38.1.20 | ‡1 John 5.13-end |
| E | ‡90 | ‡Deut 10.12—11.1 | ‡Luke 21.25-36 |

THE NAMING OF JESUS (1 January)   White

| M | 115 | Josh 1.1-9 | Acts 3.1-16 |
| E | 148 | Jer 23.1-6 | Rom 10.5-13 |

THE SECOND SUNDAY AFTER CHRISTMAS   White or Gold

| M | 89.19-38 | Isa 46.3-end | Rom 15.8-21 |
| E | 85, 87 | Isa 60.13-end | 1 Cor 2 |

2 JANUARY

| M | 146 | Isa 61 | 1 Cor 1 |
| E | 147 | Isa 30.1-18 | Matt 17.22-end |

	Psalms	First Reading	Second Reading

3 JANUARY

	Psalms	First Reading	Second Reading
M	149, 150	Isa 62	1 Cor 3
E	1, 2, 3	Isa 30.19-end	Matt 18.1-20

4 JANUARY

M	4, 5, 6	Isa 63	1 Cor 4
E	7	Isa 31	Matt 18.21-end

5 JANUARY

M	‡9	‡Isa 33.1-16	‡Matt 19.1-15
E	‡98, 113	‡Isa 41.8-20 or	
		Baruch 4.36-end; 5	‡Eph 1.3-14

THE EPIPHANY OF OUR LORD (6 January)   White or Gold

M	2, 8	Isa 42.1-9	John 1.29-34
E	96, 97	Isa 49.7-13	John 2.1-11

The following psalms and readings are used on weekdays between Epiphany and the First Sunday after Epiphany:

7 JANUARY

M	10	Isa 60.1-12	1 Cor 5
E	11, 12	Isa 15	Matt 19.16-end

8 JANUARY

M	13, 14	Isa 60.13-end	1 Cor 6.1-11
E	15, 16	Isa 16	Matt 20.1-16

9 JANUARY

M	17	Isa 64	1 Cor 6.12-end
E	18.1-32	Isa 17	Matt 20.17-end

10 JANUARY

M	18.33-end	Isa 65.1-16	1 Cor 7.1-24
E	19	Isa 18	Matt 21.1-17

11 JANUARY

M	20, 21	Isa 66.1-9	1 Cor 7.25-end
E	22	Isa 19.1-15	Matt 21.18-32

12 JANUARY

M	23, 24	Isa 66.10-end	1 Cor 8
E	25	Isa 19.16-end	Matt 21.33-end

		Psalms	First Reading	Second Reading

EPIPHANY 1 White or Gold for Sunday, Green from Monday

S	M	46, 47	Gen 8.15—9.17	Acts 18.24—19.6
	E	29, 30	1 Sam 16.1-13a	Matt 3
M	M	26, 27	Jonah 1	1 Cor 9.1-14
	E	28, 29	Ezek 1.1-14	Matt 22.1-14
T	M	30	Jonah 2	1 Cor 9.15-end
	E	31	Ezek 1.15—2.2	Matt 22.15-33
W	M	32	Jonah 3 & 4	1 Cor 10.1-13
	E	33	Ezek 2.3—3.11	Matt 22.34-end
Th	M	34	Joel 1.1-14	1 Cor 10.14—11.1
	E	35	Ezek 3.12-end	Matt 23.1-15
F	M	36	Joel 1.15-end	1 Cor 11.2-22
	E	37.1-22	Ezek 8.1-18	Matt 23.16-28
S	M	37.23-end	Joel 2.1-17	1 Cor 11.23-end
	E	38	Ezek 10.1-19	Matt 23.29-end

EPIPHANY 2 Green

S	M	15, 16	1 Kings 20.1-29	Matt 13.44-end
	E	121, 126	Jer 1.4-end	Luke 5.1-11
M	M	39	Joel 2.18-27	1 Cor 12.1-11
	E	40	Ezek 11.14-end	Matt 24.1-14
T	M	41	Joel 2.28-end	1 Cor 12.12-end
	E	42, 43	Ezek 12.17-end	Matt 24.15-28
W	M	44	Joel 3.1-3, 9-end	1 Cor 13
	E	45, 46	Ezek 13.1-16	Matt 24.29-35
Th	M	47, 48	Lev 1 or 1 Macc 1.1-19	1 Cor 14.1-12
	E	49	Ezek 14.1-11	Matt 24.36-end
F	M	50	Lev 2 or 1 Macc 1.20-40	1 Cor 14.13-25
	E	51	Ezek 14.12-end	Matt 25.1-13
S	M	52, 53	Lev 3 or 1 Macc 1.41-end	1 Cor 14.26-end
	E	54, 55	Ezek 18.1-20	Matt 25.14-30

		Psalms	First Reading	Second Reading

EPIPHANY 3 Green

		Psalms	First Reading	Second Reading
S	M	135 or 136	Nehemiah 13.15-22	John 5.1-21
	E	33	Exod 33.7-end	John 2.1-11
M	M	56, 57	Lev 4.27-end or	
			1 Macc 2.1-28	1 Cor 15.1-11
	E	(58), 59	Ezek 20.1-20	Matt 25.31-end
T	M	60, 61	Lev 5.1-13 or	
			1 Macc 2.29-48	1 Cor 15.12-19
	E	62, 63	Ezek 24.15-end	Matt 26.1-13
W	M	64, 65	Lev 8 or	
			1 Macc 2.49-end	1 Cor 15.20-34
	E	66, 67	Ezek 28.1-10	Matt 26.14-29
Th	M	68	Lev 9 or	
			1 Macc 3.1-26	1 Cor 15.35-49
	E	69	Ezek 28.11-19	Matt 26.30-46
F	M	70, 71	Lev 17 or	
			1 Macc 3.27-41	1 Cor 15.50-end
	E	72	Ezek 33.1-20	Matt 26.47-56
S	M	73	Lev 18.1-6, 19-end or	
			1 Macc 3.42-end	1 Cor 16
	E	74	Ezek 33.21-end	Matt 26.57-end

EPIPHANY 4 Green

		Psalms	First Reading	Second Reading
S	M	34	1 Sam 21.1-6	Matt 12.1-21
	E	50	1 Kings 8.22-34;	
			9.1-3	John 2.13-end
M	M	75, 76	Lev 19.1-18 or	
			1 Macc 4.1-25	Phil 1.1-11
	E	77	Ezek 34.1-16	Matt 27.1-10
T	M	78.1-38	Lev 19.23-end or	
			1 Macc 4.26-35	Phil 1.12-end
	E	78.39-end	Ezek 34.17-end	Matt 27.11-26
W	M	79	Lev 23.1-22 or	
			1 Macc 4.36-end	Phil 2.1-18
	E	80	Ezek 36.1-15	Matt 27.27-44
Th	M	81	Lev 23.23-end or	
			1 Macc 6.1-17	Phil 2.19-end
	E	82, 83	Ezek 36.16-36	Matt 27.45-56

		Psalms	**First Reading**	**Second Reading**
F	M	84, 85	Lev 24.1-9 or 1 Macc 6.18-47	
	E	86	Ezek 37.1-14	Phil 3.1—4.1 Matt 27.57-end
S	M	87, 88	Lev 25.1-24 or 1 Macc 7.1-20	Phil 4.2-end
	E	89.1-38	Ezek 37.15-end	Matt 28

EPIPHANY 5   Green

S	M	119.121-136	Jer 10.1-16 or Wisdom 7.28—8.9	1 Tim 3.14—4.10
	E	92	Job 12 or Ecclus 43.13-end	1 Cor 1.18—2.5
M	M	89.39-end	Esther 1 or 1 Macc 7.21-end	1 Pet 1.1-12
	E	90	Ezek 38.14-end	Rev 1.12-end
T	M	91	Esther 2.5-11, 15-end or 1 Macc 9.1-22	1 Pet 1.13-end
	E	92, 93	Ezek 39.21-end	Rev 2.1-11
W	M	94	Esther 3 or 1 Macc 13.41-end; 14.4-15	1 Pet 2.1-10
	E	95 (or 100), 96	Ezek 40.1-4	Rev 2.12-end
Th	M	97, 98	Esther 4 or 2 Macc 6.12-end	1 Pet 2.11-end
	E	99, 100 (or 95), 101	Ezek 43.1-9	Rev 3.1-6
F	M	102	Esther 5 or 2 Macc 7.1-19	1 Pet 3.1-12
	E	103	Ezek 44.4-8	Rev 3.7-13
S	M	104	Esther 6 & 7, or 2 Macc 7.20-41	1 Pet 3.13-end
	E	105.1-22	Ezek 47.1-12	Rev 3.14-end

EPIPHANY 6   Green

S	M	127, 128, 133	Isa 5.1-7 (or -16)	John 15.1-11
	E	75, 76	Proverbs 1.20-end	James 3
M	M	105.23-end	Num 9.1-14 or Baruch 1.15—2.10	1 Pet 4
	E	106.1-24	Exod 16.9-15	John 6.25-35
T	M	106.25-end	Num 16.1-19 or Baruch 2.11-end	1 Pet 5
	E	107.1-22	Isa 60.13-20	John 8.12-19

		Psalms	First Reading	Second Reading
W	M	107.23-end	Num 16.20-35 or	
			Baruch 3.1-8	2 Pet 1.1-15
	E	108, (109)	Ezek 34.1-16	John 10.7-16
Th	M	110, 111	Num 16.36-end or	
			Baruch 3.9-end	2 Pet 1.16—2.3
	E	112, 113	Dan 12.1-4	John 11.17-27
F	M	114	Num 17.1-11 or	
			Baruch 4.21-30	2 Pet 2.4-end
	E	115	Prov 8.1-21	John 14.1-6
S	M	116, 117	Num 33.50—34.15 or	
			Baruch 4.36—5 end	2 Pet 3
	E	118	Isa 5.1-7	John 15.1-8

NINTH SUNDAY BEFORE EASTER
(Third Sunday before Lent)   Green

S	M	71	Job 28 (or 9-end)	Luke 6.20-38
	E	73	Isa 30.8-21	Matt 4.23—5.12
M	M	1, 2, 3	Jer 1	John 1.1-18
	E	4, 5, 6	Gen 1.1—2.3	2 Cor 1.1-14
T	M	7	Jer 2.1-13	John 1.19-34
	E	8, 9	Gen 2.4-end	2 Cor 1.15—2.4
W	M	10	Jer 2.14-32	John 1.35-end
	E	11, 12	Gen 3	2 Cor 2.5-end
Th	M	13, 14	Jer 3.6-18	John 2.1-12
	E	15, 16	Gen 4.1-16	2 Cor 3
F	M	17	Jer 4.1-14	John 2.13-end
	E	18.1-32	Gen 6.11—7.10	2 Cor 4
S	M	18.33-end	Jer 4.19-end	John 3.1-15
	E	19	Gen 7.11—8.14	2 Cor 5

EIGHTH SUNDAY BEFORE EASTER
(Second Sunday before Lent)   Green

S	M	139.1-18	Num 21.4-9	John 9 (or 9.1-25)
	E	137.1-6; 146	2 Kings 20	Mark 5.1-20
M	M	20, 21	Jer 5.1-19	John 3.16-21
	E	22	Gen 8.15—9.17	2 Cor 6.1-13
T	M	23, 24	Jer 5.20-end	John 3.22-end
	E	25	Gen 11.1-9	2 Cor 6.14—7.1

		Psalms	First Reading	Second Reading
W	M	26, 27	Jer 6.9-21	John 4.1-26
	E	28, 29	Gen 11.27—12.9	2 Cor 7.2-end
Th	M	30	Jer 6.22-end	John 4.27-42
	E	31	Gen 13.2-end	2 Cor 18.1-15
F	M	32	Jer 7.1-20	John 4.43-end
	E	33	Gen 14	2 Cor 8.16—9.5
S	M	34	Jer 7.21-end	John 5.1-18
	E	35	Gen 16	2 Cor 9.6-end

SEVENTH SUNDAY BEFORE EASTER
(The Sunday next before Lent)   Green

		Psalms	First Reading	Second Reading
S	M	56, 57	Jer 30.1-3, 10-22	Luke 13.1-17
	E	103	Hosea 14	Philemon
M	M	36	Jer 8.18—9.3	John 5.19-29
	E	37.1-22	Gen 17.1-22	2 Cor 10
T	M	37.23-end	Jer 9.12-24	John 5.30-end
	E	39	Gen 18	2 Cor 11.1-15

ASH WEDNESDAY   Violet (or Lent array)

		Psalms	First Reading	Second Reading
	M	‡102	‡Dan 9.3-19	‡1 Tim 6.6-19
	E	‡38	‡Isa 1.11-20	‡Matt 16.21-end
Th	M	40	Jer 10.1-16	John 6.1-15
	E	41	Gen 19.1-3, 12-29	2 Cor 11.16-end
F	M	42, 43	Jer 10.17-24	John 6.16-29
	E	44	Gen 21.1-21	2 Cor 12
S	M	45, 46	Jer 11.1-17	John 6.30-40
	E	47, 48	Gen 22.1-19	2 Cor 13

LENT 1 (Sixth Sunday before Easter)   Violet (or Lent array)

		Psalms	First Reading	Second Reading
S	M	119.9-24	Exod 17.1-13	Matt 26.1-30
	E	51	Deut 30.11-end	Heb 2.5-end
M	M	49	Jer 12.1-6	John 6.41-51
	E	50	Gen 23	Gal 1
T	M	51	Jer 13.20-end	John 6.52-59
	E	52, 53	Gen 24.1-28	Gal 2.1-10
W	M	54, 55	Jer 15.10-end	John 6.60-end
	E	56, 57	Gen 24.29-end	Gal 2.11-end

		Psalms	First Reading	Second Reading
Th	M	(58), 59	Jer 17.5-18	John 7.1-13
	E	60, 61	Gen 25.7-11, 19-end	Gal 3.1-14
F	M	62, 63	Jer 18.1-12	John 7.14-24
	E	64, 65	Gen 27.1-40	Gal 3.15-end
S	M	66, 67	Jer 18.13-end	John 7.25-36
	E	68	Gen 27.41—28 end	Gal 4.1-20

LENT 2 (Fifth Sunday before Easter)   Violet (or Lent array)

		Psalms	First Reading	Second Reading
S	M	119.73-88	Amos 3	Matt 26.31-56
	E	74	2 Kings 6.8-23	Luke 19.41—20.8
M	M	69	Jer 19.1-13	John 7.37-52
	E	70, 71	Gen 29.1-30	Gal 4.21—5.1
T	M	72	Jer 19.14—20.6	John 7.53—8.11
	E	73	Gen 31.1-9, 14-21	Gal 5.2-end
W	M	74	Jer 20.7-end	John 8.12-20
	E	75, 76	Gen 32.3-30	Gal 6
Th	M	77	Jer 21.1-10	John 8.21-30
	E	78.1-38	Gen 35	Heb 1
F	M	78.39-end	Jer 22.1-5, 13-19	John 8.31-47
	E	79	Gen 37	Heb 2.1-9
S	M	80	Jer 22.20-end	John 8.48-end
	E	81	Gen 39	Heb 2.10-end

LENT 3 (Fourth Sunday before Easter)   Violet (or Lent array)

		Psalms	First Reading	Second Reading
S	M	119.105-120	Job 2	Matt 26.57-end
	E	31	Isa 59.9-20	Col 1.24—2.7
M	M	82, 83	Jer 23.1-15	John 9.1-12
	E	84, 85	Gen 40	Heb 3
T	M	86	Jer 23.16-29	John 9.13-23
	E	87, 88	Gen 41.1-40	Heb 4.1-13
W	M	89.1-38	Jer 24	John 9.24-end
	E	89.39-end	Gen 41.41-end	Heb 4.14—5 end
Th	M	90	Jer 25.1-14	John 10.1-10
	E	91	Gen 42	Heb 6
F	M	92, 93	Jer 26.1-9	John 10.11-21
	E	94	Gen 43	Heb 7.1-10

		Psalms	First Reading	Second Reading
S	M	95 (or 100), 96	Jer 26.10-end	John 10.22-end
	E	97, 98	Gen 44	Heb 7.11-end

LENT 4 (Third Sunday before Easter)   Violet (or Lent array)

		Psalms	First Reading	Second Reading
S	M	119.161-176	Isa 52.13—53.6	Matt 27.1-32
	E	23, 27	Exod 34.1-5, 29-end	2 Cor 3

Services for Mothering Sunday: Psalms and readings for Pentecost 14 are suitable, or
Psalms 27.1-6; 34, 84, 87, 122, 139.1-18
1 Sam 1.20-end; Proverbs 4.1-9; Proverbs 31.10-end; Micah 4.1-5
Col 3.12-17; 2 Tim 1.3-10; 1 Peter 2.1-10
Mark 10.13-16; Luke 2.41-end; John 19.23-27

		Psalms	First Reading	Second Reading
M	M	99, 100 (or 95), 101	Jer 28	John 11.1-16
	E	102	Gen 45	Heb 8
T	M	103	Jer 29.1-14	John 11.17-27
	E	104	Gen 46.1-7, 28-end	Heb 9.1-14
W	M	105.1-22	Jer 30.1-11	John 11.28-37
	E	105.23-end	Gen 47.1-27	Heb 9.15-end
Th	M	106.1-24	Jer 30.12-22	John 11.38-44
	E	106.25-end	Gen 47.28—48 end	Heb 10.1-18
F	M	107.1-22	Jer 31.1-14	John 11.45-end
	E	107.23-end	Gen 49.1-32	Heb 10.19-end
S	M	108, (109), 110	Jer 31.15-22	John 12.1-11
	E	111, 112, 113	Gen 49.33—50 end	Heb 11.1-12

LENT 5 (Second Sunday before Easter)   Violet (or Lent array)

		Psalms	First Reading	Second Reading
S	M	66	Isa 53.7-end	Matt 27.33-54
	E	130, 143.1-11	Isa 63.1-16	John 12.20-36a
M	M	114, 115	Jer 31.35-end	John 12.12-19
	E	116, 117	Exod 1.1-14, 22—2.10	Heb 11.13-22
T	M	118	Jer 32.1-15	John 12.36b-end
	E	119.1-24	Exod 2.11—3.12	Heb 11.23-31
W	M	119.25-40	Jer 33.1-13	John 13.1-11
	E	119.41-56	Exod 4.1-23	Heb 11.32-end
Th	M	119.57-72	Jer 33.14-end	John 13.12-20
	E	119.73-88	Exod 4.27—6.1	Heb 12.1-13

		Psalms	First Reading	Second Reading
F	M	119.89-104	Jer 36.1-18	John 13.21-30
	E	119.105-128	Exod 7.8-end	Heb 12.14-end
S	M	119.129-152	Jer 36.19-end	John 13.31-end
	E	119.153-end	Exod 10	Heb 13

PALM SUNDAY (The Sunday next before Easter)   Red

	M	61, 62	Jer 7.1-11 or	Luke 19.29-end or
			Exod 11	Mark 14
	E	22.1-22	Isa 5.1-7	Mark 12.1-12

MONDAY IN HOLY WEEK   Red, or as in Lent

	M	‡41	‡Lam 1.1-12a	‡John 14.1-14 (or -end)
	E	‡25	‡Lam 2.8-19	‡John 14.15-end or Gal 6.11-end

TUESDAY IN HOLY WEEK   Red, or as in Lent

	M	‡27	‡Lam 3.1-18 or 3.1-30	‡John 15.1-17 (or -end)
	E	‡69.1-16	‡Lam 3.40-51	‡John 15.18-end or Rom 5.6-11

WEDNESDAY IN HOLY WEEK   Red, or as in Lent

	M	‡31	‡Jer 11.18-20	‡John 16.1-15 (or -end)
	E	‡88	‡Isa 63.1-9	‡John 16.16-end or Rom 5.12-19

MAUNDY THURSDAY   Red, or as in Lent

	M	‡39	‡Exod 24.1-11	‡John 17
	E	‡42, 43	‡Lev 16.2-24	‡John 13.16-35 or Eph 2.11-18

GOOD FRIDAY   Red, hangings removed

	M	‡40 or 40.1-14	‡Gen 22.1-18	‡John 18 or ‡Mark 15.21-41
	E	‡130, 143.1-11	‡Lam 5.15-end	‡John 19.38-end or Col 1.18-23

		Psalms	First Reading	Second Reading

EASTER EVE   Hangings removed

		Psalms	First Reading	Second Reading
	M	‡142	‡Hosea 6.1-6	‡1 Pet 4.1-6
	E	‡116	‡Job 19.21-27	‡1 John 5.5-12

EASTER DAY   White or Gold

		Psalms	First Reading	Second Reading
	M	113, 114, 117	Isa 12	Rom 6.3-14
	E	118	Exod 14.5-end	John 20.11-23
M	M	120, 121	Isa 25.1-9	Luke 24.1-12
	E	122, 123	Exod 12.14-36	Col 3.1-11
T	M	124, 125	Isa 26.1-19	Phil 1.19-26
	E	126, 127	Exod 12.37-end	Matt 28.1-15
W	M	128, 129	Isa 61	1 Thess 4.13-end
	E	130, 131	Exod 13.1-16	Matt 28.16-end
Th	M	132	Song of Solomon 2.8-end	Mark 16
	E	133, 134	Exod 13.17—14.14	Rev 7.9-end
F	M	135	Zeph 3.14-end	Acts 17.16-31
	E	136	Exod 14.15-end	Luke 8.41-end
S	M	137, 138	Zech 8.1-8	Acts 26.1-23
	E	139	Exod 15.1-21	Luke 16.19-end

EASTER 1   White or Gold for Sunday, White from Monday

		Psalms	First Reading	Second Reading
S	M	30, 48	Deut 4.25-40	Rev 2.1-11
	E	115	Isa 51.1-16	John 20.24-end
M	M	140	Ruth 1	1 Tim 1.1-17
	E	141	Exod 15.22-end	John 20.1-10
T	M	142, 143	Ruth 2	1 Tim 1.18—2 end
	E	144	Exod 16.22-end	John 20.11-23
W	M	145	Ruth 3	1 Tim 3
	E	146, 147	Exod 17	John 20.24-end
Th	M	148	Ruth 4	1 Tim 4
	E	149, 150	Exod 18.1-12	John 21.1-14
F	M	1, 2	Deut 1.3-18	1 Tim 5.1-16
	E	3, 4	Exod 18.13-end	John 21.15-19
S	M	5, 6	Deut 2.1-25	1 Tim 5.17-end
	E	7	Exod 19	John 21.20-end

		Psalms	First Reading	Second Reading

EASTER 2 White

S	M	49.1-16	Ezra 1.1-8	Rev 2.12-end
	E	2, 8	Isa 25.1-9	Luke 24.13-35
M	M	(8), 9	Deut 2.26—3.5	1 Tim 6.1-10
	E	10	Exod 20.1-21	Luke 1.1-25
T	M	11, 12	Deut 4.1-13	1 Tim 6.11-end
	E	13, 14	Exod 22.30—23.17	Luke 1.26-38
W	M	15, 16	Deut 4.14-31	2 Tim 1.1-14
	E	17	Exod 24	Luke 1.39-56
Th	M	18.1-32	Deut 4.32-40	2 Tim 1.15—2.13
	E	18.33-end	Exod 25.1-22	Luke 1.57-66
F	M	19	Deut 6	2 Tim 2.14-end
	E	20, 21	Exod 28.1-4; 29.1-9	Luke 1.67-end
S	M	22	Deut 8	2 Tim 3
	E	23, 24	Exod 29.38—30.16	Luke 2.1-20

EASTER 3 White

S	M	121, 126	Ezra 3	Rev 3.1-13
	E	18.1-32	Num 13.1-2, 17-end	John 21.1-14
M	M	25	Deut 9.1-21	2 Tim 4
	E	26, 27	Exod 32.1-14	Luke 2.21-32
T	M	28, 29	Deut 10.12-end	Titus 1
	E	30	Exod 32.15-end	Luke 2.33-40
W	M	31	Deut 11.18-end	Titus 2
	E	32	Exod 33	Luke 2.41-end
Th	M	33	Deut 12.1-14	Titus 3
	E	34	Exod 34.1-10, 27-end	Luke 3.1-14
F	M	35	Deut 15.1-18	1 Pet 1.1-12
	E	36	Exod 35.20—36.7	Luke 3.15-23
S	M	37.1-22	Deut 16.1-20	1 Pet 1.13-end
	E	37.23-end	Exod 40.17-end	Luke 4.1-13

EASTER 4 White

S	M	57, 63.1-9	Nehemiah 1	1 Cor 15.1-28
	E	77	Isa 62	John 21.15-end
M	M	38	Deut 17.8-end	1 Pet 2.1-10
	E	39	Lev 6.8-end	Luke 4.14-30

		Psalms	First Reading	Second Reading
T	M	40	Deut 18.9-end	1 Pet 2.11-end
	E	41	Lev 19.1-18, 30-end	Luke 4.31-end
W	M	42, 43	Deut 19	1 Pet 3.1-12
	E	44	Lev 25.1-24	Luke 5.1-11
Th	M	45, 46	Deut 21.22—22.8	1 Pet 3.13-end
	E	47, 48	Num 9.15-end	Luke 5.12-26
F	M	49	Deut 24.5-end	1 Pet 4
	E	50	Num 12	Luke 5.27-end
S	M	51	Deut 26	1 Pet 5
	E	52, 53	Num 13.1-3, 17-end	Luke 6.1-11

EASTER 5 White

S	M	65, 67	Nehemiah 2	Matt 13.24-43
	E	107.1-32	Hosea 6.1-6	1 Cor 15.35-end

ROGATION MONDAY

	M	54, 55	Deut 7.6-13	Matt 6.19-end
	E	56, 57	Joel 2.21-27	Acts 14.8-18

ROGATION TUESDAY

	M	(58), 59	Deut 11.8-21	James 5.1-18
	E	60, 61	Haggai 1.1-11	2 Cor 9

ROGATION WEDNESDAY

	M	‡62, 63	‡Jer 14.1-9	‡John 6.22-40
	E	‡93, 99	‡Ezek 1.4-5, 26-end or The Song of the Three Children 29-37	‡Col 2.20—3.4

ASCENSION DAY White or Gold

	M	‡96, 97	‡2 Sam 23.1-5	‡Heb 1.1—2.4
	E	‡15, 24	‡Isa 52.7-12	‡Heb 2.5-end
F	M	64, 65	Deut 28.58-end	2 Pet 1.1-15
	E	66, 67	Num 14.1-25	Luke 6.12-26
S	M	68	Deut 30	2 Pet 1.16—2.3
	E	69	Num 20.1-13	Luke 6.27-38

		Psalms	First Reading	Second Reading

THE SUNDAY AFTER ASCENSION DAY (Easter 6)   White

		Psalms	First Reading	Second Reading
S	M	108, 110	Jer 31.1-13	Phil 2.1-18
	E	138, 150	Dan 7.9-14	Eph 1.15-end
M	M	70, 71	Deut 31.1-13	2 Pet 2.4-end
	E	72	Num 21.4-9	Luke 6.39-end
T	M	73	Deut 31.14-29	2 Pet 3
	E	74	Num 22.2-35	Luke 7.1-10
W	M	75, 76	Deut 31.30—32.14	1 John 1.1—2.6
	E	77	Num 22.36—23.12	Luke 7.11-23
Th	M	78.1-38	Deut 32.15-47	1 John 2.7-17
	E	78.39-end	Num 23.13-end	Luke 7.24-35
F	M	79	Deut 33	1 John 2.18-end
	E	80	Num 24	Luke 7.36-end
S	M	‡81	‡Deut 32.48-end; 34	‡Luke 8.1-15
	E	‡48, 145	‡Deut 16.9-15	‡John 7.37-39

PENTECOST (Whit Sunday)   Red

		Psalms	First Reading	Second Reading
S	M	68.1-20	Joel 2.21-end	Rom 8.1-17
	E	104, or 104.1-5, 26-end	Ezek 37.1-14	Rom 8.18-27
M	M	82, 83	1 Sam 10.1-10	Matt 3.13-end
	E	84, 85	Ezek 11.14-20	1 Cor 2
T	M	86	1 Kings 19.1-18	Matt 9.35—10.20
	E	87, 88	Ezek 36.22-28	1 Cor 3
W	M	89.1-38	Micah 3.1-8	Matt 11.25-end
	E	89.39-end	Isa 55.6-11	1 Cor 12.1-13
Th	M	90	Exod 35.30—36.1	Matt 12.22-32
	E	91	Isa 32.9-end	1 Cor 12.27—13 end
F	M	92, 93	Jer 31.31-34	Matt 18.15-20
	E	94	Num 11.16, 17, 24-29	Gal 5.13-end
S	M	95 (or 100), 96	Isa 44.1-5	John 17.17-end
	E	97, 98	Num 27.15-end	Eph 6.10-20

TRINITY SUNDAY
(Pentecost 1)   White or Gold for Sunday, Green from Monday

		Psalms	First Reading	Second Reading
S	M	29, 33	Exod 34.1-10	Acts 2.22-36
	E	145	Isa 40.12-end	Mark 1.1-13

		Psalms	First Reading	Second Reading
M	M	99, 100 (or 95), 101	2 Chron 1.1-13 or Wisdom 1	1 John 3
	E	102	Josh 1.1-11	Luke 8.16-25
T	M	103	2 Chron 2.1-16 or Wisdom 2	1 John 4
	E	104	Josh 2	Luke 8.26-39
W	M	105.1-22	2 Chron 5 or Wisdom 3.1-9	1 John 5.1-12
	E	105.23-end	Josh 3	Luke 8.40-end
Th	M	106.1-24	2 Chron 6.1-21 or Wisdom 4.7-end	1 John 5.13-end
	E	106.25-end	Josh 4.1—5.1	Luke 9.1-9
F	M	107.1-22	2 Chron 6.22-end or Wisdom 5.1-16	James 1.1-11
	E	107.23-end	Josh 5.13—6.20	Luke 9.10-17
S	M	108, (109), 110	2 Chron 7 or Wisdom 6.1-21	James 1.12-end
	E	111, 112, 113	Josh 7.1-15	Luke 9.18-27

2ND SUNDAY AFTER PENTECOST (Trinity 1)   Green

		Psalms	First Reading	Second Reading
S	M	85, 133	Ezek 37.15-end	Eph 2.11-end
	E	89.1-18	Exod 19.1-11	1 Pet 2.1-10
M	M	114, 115	2 Chron 12 or Wisdom 7.15—8.4	James 2.1-13
	E	116, 117	Josh 7.16-end	Luke 9.28-36
T	M	118	2 Chron 13.1—14.1 or Wisdom 8.5-18	James 2.14-end
	E	119.1-24	Josh 8.10-29	Luke 9.37-50
W	M	119.25-40	2 Chron 14.12-end or Wisdom 8.21—9 end	James 3
	E	119.41-56	Josh 9.3-end	Luke 9.51-end
Th	M	119.57-72	2 Chron 17.1-12 or Wisdom 10.15—11.10	James 4.1-12
	E	119.73-88	Josh 24.1-28	Luke 10.1-16
F	M	119.89-104	2 Chron 34.1-18 or Wisdom 11.21—12.2	James 4.13—5.6
	E	119.105-128	Judges 2.6-end	Luke 10.17-24
S	M	119.129-152	2 Chron 34.19-33 or Wisdom 12.12-21	James 5.7-end
	E	119.153-end	Judges 4	Luke 10.25-37

		Psalms	First Reading	Second Reading

3RD SUNDAY AFTER PENTECOST (Trinity 2) Green

S	M	11, 20	Isa 32.1-8	Mark 4.21-end
	E	32, 36	Deut 6.10-end	Acts 23.11-24
M	M	120, 121	Jer 37	Rom 1.1-7
	E	122, 123	Judges 5	Luke 10.38-end
T	M	124, 125	Jer 38.1-13	Rom 1.8-17
	E	126, 127	Judges 6.1, 11-end	Luke 11.1-13
W	M	128, 129	Jer 38.14-end	Rom 1.18-end
	E	130, 131	Judges 7	Luke 11.14-28
Th	M	132	Jer 39	Rom 2.1-16
	E	133, 134	Judges 9.1-21	Luke 11.29-36
F	M	135	Jer 40	Rom 2.17-end
	E	136	Judges 9.22-end	Luke 11.37-44
S	M	137, 138	Jer 41	Rom 3.1-20
	E	139	Judges 11.1-6, 29-end	Luke 11.45-end

4TH SUNDAY AFTER PENTECOST (Trinity 3) Green

S	M	42, 43	1 Kings 10.1-13	John 4.1-26 or 1-42
	E	147	Deut 7.1-11	John 15.12-end
M	M	140	Jer 42	Rom 3.21-end
	E	141	Judges 13	Luke 12.1-12
T	M	142	Jer 43	Rom 4.1-12
	E	143	Judges 14	Luke 12.13-21
W	M	144	Jer 44.1-14	Rom 4.13-end
	E	145	Judges 15	Luke 12.22-31
Th	M	146, 147	Jer 44.15-end	Rom 5.1-11
	E	148	Judges 16.1-22	Luke 12.32-40
F	M	149, 150	2 Chron 36.11-21	Rom 5.12-end
	E	1, 2	Judges 16.23-end	Luke 12.41-48
S	M	3, 4	Ezra 1	Rom 6.1-14
	E	5, 6	Judges 18.1-20, 27-end	Luke 12.49-end

5TH SUNDAY AFTER PENTECOST (Trinity 4) Green

| S | M | 119.41-56 | Jonah 3 & 4 | Acts 13.1-13 |
| | E | 67, 98 | Exod 20.1-20 | Matt 19.16-end |

		Psalms	First Reading	Second Reading
M	M	7	Ezra 3	Rom 6.15-end
	E	8, 9	1 Sam 1.1-20	Luke 13.1-9
T	M	10	Ezra 4.1-5	Rom 7.1-6
	E	11, 12	1 Sam 1.21—2.11	Luke 13.10-21
W	M	13, 14	Ezra 4.7-end	Rom 7.7-end
	E	15, 16	1 Sam 3.1-19	Luke 13.22-end
Th	M	17	Ezra 5	Rom 8.1-11
	E	18.1-32	1 Sam 4.1-18	Luke 14.1-11
F	M	18.33-end	Ezra 6	Rom 8.12-17
	E	19	1 Sam 5	Luke 14.12-24
S	M	20, 21	Ezra 7	Rom 8.18-30
	E	22	1 Sam 6.1-16	Luke 14.25-end

6TH SUNDAY AFTER PENTECOST (Trinity 5) Green

		Psalms	First Reading	Second Reading
S	M	77	2 Sam 12.1-18a (or -23)	Acts 9.1-22
	E	102	2 Kings 22	Luke 15.11-end
M	M	23, 24	Ezra 8.15-end	Rom 8.31-end
	E	25	1 Sam 8	Luke 15.1-10
T	M	26, 27	Ezra 9	Rom 9.1-13
	E	28, 29	1 Sam 9.1-14	Luke 16.1-18
W	M	30	Ezra 10.1-19	Rom 9.14-29
	E	31	1 Sam 9.15—10.1	Luke 16.19-end
Th	M	32	Neh 1	Rom 9.30—10.10
	E	33	1 Sam 10.1-16	Luke 17.1-10
F	M	34	Neh 2	Rom 10.11-end
	E	35	1 Sam 10.17-end	Luke 17.11-19
S	M	36	Neh 4	Rom 11.1-12
	E	37.1-22	1 Sam 11	Luke 17.20-end

7TH SUNDAY AFTER PENTECOST (Trinity 6) Green

		Psalms	First Reading	Second Reading
S	M	81	Deut 24.10-end	1 John 3.13-end
	E	99, 100, 101	Hosea 11.1-9	1 Cor 12.27—13 end
M	M	37.23-end	Neh 5	Rom 11.13-24
	E	38	1 Sam 12	Luke 18.1-14
T	M	39	Neh 6.1-16	Rom 11.25-end
	E	40	1 Sam 13	Luke 18.15-30

		Psalms	First Reading	Second Reading
W	M	41	Neh 8.1-12	Rom 12.1-8
	E	42, 43	1 Sam 14.1-15	Luke 18.31-end
Th	M	44	Neh 8.13-end	Rom 12.9-end
	E	45, 46	1 Sam 14.24-46	Luke 19.1-10
F	M	47, 48	Neh 9.1-23	Rom 13
	E	49	1 Sam 15.1-23	Luke 19.11-27
S	M	50	Neh 9.24-end	Rom 14.1-12
	E	51	1 Sam 16	Luke 19.28-40

8TH SUNDAY AFTER PENTECOST (Trinity 7)   Green

		Psalms	First Reading	Second Reading
S	M	73	Prov 8.1-17	Luke 6.39-end
	E	91	Exod 35.20—36.7	1 Cor 14.1-19
M	M	52, 53	Neh 13.1-14	Rom 14.13-end
	E	54, 55	1 Sam 17.1-25	Luke 19.41—20.8
T	M	56, 57	Neh 13.15-end	Rom 15.1-13
	E	(58), 59	1 Sam 17.26-50	Luke 20.9-26
W	M	60, 61	Haggai 1.1—2.9	Rom 15.14-21
	E	62, 63	1 Sam 17.55—18.16	Luke 20.27-40
Th	M	64, 65	Haggai 2.10-end	Rom 15.22-end
	E	66, 67	1 Sam 19.1-18	Luke 20.41—21.4
F	M	68	Zech 1.1-17	Rom 16.1-16
	E	69	1 Sam 20.1-17	Luke 21.5-19
S	M	70, 71	Zech 1.18—2 end	Rom 16.17-end
	E	72	1 Sam 20.18-end	Luke 21.20-end

9TH SUNDAY AFTER PENTECOST (Trinity 8)   Green

		Psalms	First Reading	Second Reading
S	M	90	2 Sam 1.1-12, 17-end	1 Tim 6.6-end
	E	24, 46	Num 6.1-5, 22-end	Eph 6.10-end
M	M	73	Zech 3 & 4	Eph 1.1-14
	E	74	1 Sam 21.1—22.5	Luke 22.1-13
T	M	75, 76	Zech 6.9-end	Eph 1.15-end
	E	77	1 Sam 22.6-end	Luke 22.14-23
W	M	78.1-38	Zech 7	Eph 2.1-10
	E	78.39-end	1 Sam 23	Luke 22.24-34
Th	M	79	Zech 8.1-8	Eph 2.11-end
	E	80	1 Sam 26	Luke 22.35-46

		Psalms	First Reading	Second Reading
F	M	81	Zech 8.9-end	Eph 3.1-13
	E	82, 83	1 Sam 28.3-end	Luke 22.47-62
S	M	84, 85	Job 1	Eph 3.14-end
	E	86	1 Sam 31	Luke 22.63—23.5

10TH SUNDAY AFTER PENTECOST (Trinity 9)   Green

		Psalms	First Reading	Second Reading
S	M	19	2 Sam 9	Matt 6.19-end
	E	1, 4	Job 38; 42.1-6 or	
			Job 38.1-11; 42.1-6	John 13.1-20
M	M	87, 88	Job 2	Eph 4.1-16
	E	89.1-38	2 Sam 1	Luke 23.6-25
T	M	89.39-end	Job 3	Eph 4.17-end
	E	90	2 Sam 2	Luke 23.26-43
W	M	91	Job 4	Eph 5.1-14
	E	92, 93	2 Sam 5.1-10, 17-end	Luke 23.44-56a
Th	M	94	Job 5	Eph 5.15-end
	E	95 (or 100), 96	2 Sam 6.1-19	Luke 23.56b—24.12
F	M	97, 98	Job 6	Eph 6.1-9
	E	99, 100 (or 95), 101	2 Sam 7.1-17	Luke 24.13-35
S	M	102	Job 7	Eph 6.10-end
	E	103	2 Sam 7.18-end	Luke 24.36-end

11TH SUNDAY AFTER PENTECOST (Trinity 10)   Green

		Psalms	First Reading	Second Reading
S	M	123, 124, 125	1 Kings 12.1-20	2 Cor 9
	E	82, 112	Isa 42.1-12	John 13.21-end
M	M	104	Job 8	Mark 1.1-13
	E	105.1-22	2 Sam 9	Acts 1.1-14
T	M	105.23-end	Job 9	Mark 1.14-28
	E	106.1-24	2 Sam 11	Acts 1.15-end
W	M	106.25-end	Job 10	Mark 1.29-end
	E	107.1-22	2 Sam 12.1-25	Acts 2.1-13
Th	M	107.23-end	Job 11	Mark 2.1-12
	E	108, (109)	2 Sam 15.1-12	Acts 2.14-36
F	M	110, 111	Job 12	Mark 2.13-22
	E	112, 113	2 Sam 15.13-end	Acts 2.37-end
S	M	114	Job 13	Mark 2.23—3.6
	E	115	2 Sam 16.1-14	Acts 3.1-10

		Psalms	First Reading	Second Reading

12TH SUNDAY AFTER PENTECOST (Trinity 11)   Green

S	M	145, 150	Amos 5.14-24 (or 6-24)	Rom 15.14-29
	E	34	Isa 49.1-13	2 Cor 5.11—6.2
M	M	116, 117	Job 14	Mark 3.7-19a
	E	118	2 Sam 17.1-23	Acts 3.11—4.4
T	M	119.1-24	Job 15.1-16	Mark 3.19b-end
	E	119.25-40	2 Sam 18.1-18	Acts 4.5-22
W	M	119.41-56	Job 16.1—17.2	Mark 4.1-20
	E	119.57-72	2 Sam 18.19—19.8a	Acts 4.23-31
Th	M	119.73-88	Job 17.3-end	Mark 4.21-34
	E	119.89-104	2 Sam 19.8b-23	Acts 4.32—5.11
F	M	119.105-128	Job 18	Mark 4.35-end
	E	119.129-152	2 Sam 19.24-end	Acts 5.12-26
S	M	119.153-end	Job 19	Mark 5.1-20
	E	120, 121	2 Sam 23.1-7	Acts 5.27-end

13TH SUNDAY AFTER PENTECOST (Trinity 12)   Green

S	M	130, 137.1-6	Isa 49.13-23	Matt 11.20-end
	E	22.1-22	Isa 50.4-9a	1 Pet 4
M	M	122, 123	Job 21	Mark 5.21-34
	E	124, 125	2 Sam 23.8-end	Acts 6
T	M	126, 127	Job 22	Mark 5.35-end
	E	128, 129	2 Sam 24	Acts 7.1-16
W	M	130, 131	Job 23	Mark 6.1-13
	E	132	1 Kings 1.1-31	Acts 7.17-36
Th	M	133, 134	Job 24	Mark 6.14-29
	E	135	1 Kings 1.32-end	Acts 7.37-53
F	M	136	Job 25 & 26	Mark 6.30-44
	E	137, 138	1 Kings 2.1-12	Acts 7.54—8.3
S	M	139	Job 27	Mark 6.45-end
	E	140, 141	1 Kings 3	Acts 8.4-25

14TH SUNDAY AFTER PENTECOST (Trinity 13)   Green

S	M	103	Gen 47.1-12	Col 3.12-21
	E	45	Proverbs 31.10-end	1 Cor 1.1-18
M	M	142, 143	Job 28	Mark 7.1-13
	E	144	1 Kings 4.29—5.12	Acts 8.26-end

		Psalms	First Reading	Second Reading
T	M	145	Job 29.1—30.1	Mark 7.14-23
	E	146, 147	1 Kings 6.1-22	Acts 9.1-19a
W	M	148	Job 31.13-end	Mark 7.24-end
	E	149, 150	1 Kings 8.1-30	Acts 9.19b-31
Th	M	1, 2, 3	Job 32	Mark 8.1-10
	E	4, 5, 6	1 Kings 10.1-25	Acts 9.32-end
F	M	7	Job 33	Mark 8.11-21
	E	8, 9	1 Kings 11.1-13	Acts 10.1-16
S	M	10	Job 38.1-21	Mark 8.22-26
	E	11, 12	1 Kings 11.26-end	Acts 10.17-33

15TH SUNDAY AFTER PENTECOST (Trinity 14) Green

		Psalms	First Reading	Second Reading
S	M	50	1 Sam 8.4-22a	1 Pet 2.11-end
	E	72	Isa 45.1-13	Matt 22.1-33
M	M	13, 14	Job 38.22-end	Mark 8.27—9.1
	E	15, 16	1 Kings 12.1-24	Acts 10.34-end
T	M	17	Job 39	Mark 9.2-13
	E	18.1-32	1 Kings 12.25-end	Acts 11.1-18
W	M	18.33-end	Job 40	Mark 9.14-29
	E	19	1 Kings 13.1-10	Acts 11.19-end
Th	M	20, 21	Job 41	Mark 9.30-37
	E	22	1 Kings 13.11-end	Acts 12.1-11
F	M	23, 24	Job 42	Mark 9.38-end
	E	25	1 Kings 17	Acts 12.12-end
S	M	26, 27	Amos 1	Mark 10.1-16
	E	28, 29	1 Kings 18.1-20	Acts 13.1-12

16TH SUNDAY AFTER PENTECOST (Trinity 15) Green

		Psalms	First Reading	Second Reading
S	M	107.1-32	Prov 25.6-22	James 2.1-13
	E	41, 133	Lev 19.1-4, 9-18	Luke 10.25-37
M	M	30	Amos 2	Mark 10.17-31
	E	31	1 Kings 18.21-end	Acts 13.13-41
T	M	32	Amos 3	Mark 10.32-34
	E	33	1 Kings 19	Acts 13.42—14.7
W	M	34	Amos 4	Mark 10.35-45
	E	35	1 Kings 20.1-22	Acts 14.8-end

		Psalms	First Reading	Second Reading
Th	M	36	Amos 5.1-17	Mark 10.46-end
	E	37.1-22	1 Kings 20.23-end	Acts 15.1-21
F	M	37.23-end	Amos 5.18-end	Mark 11.1-11
	E	38	1 Kings 21	Acts 15.22-35
S	M	39	Amos 6	Mark 11.12-26
	E	40	1 Kings 22.1-28	Acts 15.36—16.5

17TH SUNDAY AFTER PENTECOST (Trinity 16) Green

		Psalms	First Reading	Second Reading
S	M	91, 93	Josh 5.13—6.20	John 6.51-69
	E	19, 20	Josh 14.6-14	Acts 19.21-end
M	M	41	Amos 7	Mark 11.27-end
	E	42, 43	1 Kings 22.29-40	Acts 16.6-24
T	M	44	Amos 8	Mark 12.1-12
	E	45, 46	2 Kings 2.1-15	Acts 16.25-end
W	M	47, 48	Amos 9	Mark 12.13-27
	E	49	2 Kings 3.4-24	Acts 17.1-15
Th	M	50	Micah 1	Mark 12.28-34
	E	51	2 Kings 4.1-37	Acts 17.16-end
F	M	52, 53	Micah 2	Mark 12.35-end
	E	54, 55	2 Kings 5	Acts 18.1-21
S	M	56, 57	Micah 3	Mark 13.1-13
	E	(58), 59	2 Kings 6.8-23	Acts 18.22—19.7

18TH SUNDAY AFTER PENTECOST (Trinity 17) Green

		Psalms	First Reading	Second Reading
S	M	118	Jer 26.1-16	Phil 1.12-26
	E	116	Haggai 1	Matt 5.13-26
M	M	60, 61	Micah 4.1—5.1	Mark 13.14-27
	E	62, 63	2 Kings 6.24—7.2	Acts 19.8-20
T	M	64, 65	Micah 5.2-end	Mark 13.28-end
	E	66, 67	2 Kings 7.3-end	Acts 19.21-end
W	M	68	Micah 6	Mark 14.1-11
	E	69	2 Kings 9.1-13	Acts 20.1-16
Th	M	70, 71	Micah 7.1-7	Mark 14.12-25
	E	72	2 Kings 9.14-end	Acts 20.17-end
F	M	73	Micah 7.8-end	Mark 14.26-42
	E	74	2 Kings 10.18-28	Acts 21.1-16
S	M	75, 76	Nahum 1	Mark 14.43-52
	E	77	2 Kings 11.21—12 end	Acts 21.17-36

		Psalms	First Reading	Second Reading

19TH SUNDAY AFTER PENTECOST (Trinity 18) Green

S	M	37.1-22	Josh 23	2 Cor 11.16-31
	E	85, 111	Gen 28.10-end	Heb 11.1-16
M	M	78.1-38	Nahum 2	Mark 14.53-65
	E	78.39-end	2 Kings 17.1-23	Acts 21.37—22.21
T	M	79	Nahum 3	Mark 14.66-end
	E	80	2 Kings 17.24-end	Acts 22.22—23.11
W	M	81	Hab 1	Mark 15.1-15
	E	82, 83	2 Kings 18.1-12	Acts 23.12-end
Th	M	84, 85	Hab 2	Mark 15.16-32
	E	86	2 Kings 18.13-end	Acts 24.1-23
F	M	87, 88	Hab 3.2-end	Mark 15.33-end
	E	89.1-38	2 Kings 19.1-19	Acts 24.24—25.12
S	M	89.39-end	Zeph 1	Mark 16
	E	90	2 Kings 19.20-end	Acts 25.13-end

20TH SUNDAY AFTER PENTECOST (Trinity 19) Green

S	M	51	Jer 38.1-13	James 1.1-15
	E	39	Dan 3	Heb 11.32—12.2
M	M	91	Zeph 2	Luke 10.25-37
	E	92, 93	2 Kings 20	Acts 26.1-23
T	M	94	Zeph 3	Luke 12.13-21
	E	95 (or 100), 96	2 Kings 22	Acts 26.24-end
W	M	97	Mal 1	Luke 14.16-24
	E	98	2 Kings 23.1-20	Acts 27.1-26
Th	M	99, 100 (or 95), 101	Mal 2.1-16	Luke 15.11-32
	E	102	2 Kings 23.21—24.7	Acts 27.27-end
F	M	103	Mal 2.17—3.12	Luke 16.19-31
	E	104	2 Kings 24.8—25.12	Acts 28.1-16
S	M	105.1-22	Mal 3.13—4 end	Luke 18.9-14
	E	105.23-end	2 Kings 25.22-end	Acts 28.17-end

21ST SUNDAY AFTER PENTECOST (Trinity 20) Green

S	M	23, 24 or 78.1-24	Job 4.1 & 5.1-16	Heb 10.19-end
	E	15, 16	Hab 2.1-14	Luke 18.1-14

		Psalms	First Reading	Second Reading
M	M	106.1-24	Exod 30.1-10	Luke 1.5-23
	E	106.25-end	Song of Solomon 1.9—2.7	1 Tim 1.1-17
T	M	107.1-22	Lev 11.1-8, 44-end	Acts 10.9-16
	E	107.23-end	Song of Solomon 2.8-end	1 Tim 1.18—2 end
W	M	108, (109)	Lev 12.6-7a, 8	Luke 2.21-32
	E	110, 111	Song of Solomon 3	1 Tim 3
Th	M	112, 113	Lev 13.1-3, 45-46	Luke 5.12-14
	E	114	Song of Solomon 5.2—6.3	1 Tim 4
F	M	115	Lev 14.1-9	Luke 17.11-19
	E	116, 117	Song of Solomon 7.10—8.4	1 Tim 5
S	M	118	Num 6.1-5, 21-end	Acts 21.17-30
	E	119.1-24	Song of Solomon 8.5-7	1 Tim 6

22ND SUNDAY AFTER PENTECOST (Trinity 21) Green

		Psalms	First Reading	Second Reading
S	M	42, 43	Prov 14.31—15.17	James 4.13—5.11
	E	40	Jer 6.16-21	Mark 3.7-end
M	M	119.25-40	Exod 16.9-15 or Wisdom 1	John 6.25-35
	E	119.41-56	Num 9.1-14 or Baruch 1.15—2.10	2 Tim 1.1-14
T	M	119.57-72	Isa 60.13-20 or Wisdom 2	John 8.12-19
	E	119.73-88	Num 16.1-19 or Baruch 2.11-end	2 Tim 1.15—2.13
W	M	119.89-104	Ezek 34.1-16 or Wisdom 5.1-16	John 10.7-16
	E	119.105-128	Num 16.20-35 or Baruch 3.1-8	2 Tim 2.14-end
Th	M	119.129-152	Dan 12.1-4 or Wisdom 6.1-21	John 11.17-27
	E	119.153-end	Num 16.36-end or Baruch 3.9-end	2 Tim 3
F	M	120, 121	Prov 8.1-21 or Wisdom 7.15—8.4	John 14.1-6
	E	122, 123	Num 17.1-11 or Baruch 4.21-30	2 Tim 4.1-8

		Psalms	First Reading	Second Reading
S	M	124, 125	Isa 5.1-7 or	
			Wisdom 8.21—9 end	John 15.1-8
	E	126, 127	Num 33.50—34.15 or	
			Baruch 4.36—5 end	2 Tim 4.9-end

LAST SUNDAY AFTER PENTECOST Green

		Psalms	First Reading	Second Reading
S	M	89.1-18	Ezek 11.14-21	Heb 13.1-21
	E	84, 122	Jer 29.1-14	Phil 3.7-end
M	M	128, 129	‡Eccles 1	Luke 17.20-end
	E	130, 131	‡Eccles 2.1-23	Phil 1.1-11
T	M	132	‡Eccles 3.1-15	Luke 18.1-17
	E	133, 134	‡Eccles 3.16—4 end	Phil 1.12-end
W	M	135	‡Eccles 5	Luke 18.18-30
	E	136	‡Eccles 6	Phil 2.1-18
Th	M	137, 138	‡Eccles 7	Luke 18.35-end
	E	139	‡Eccles 8	Phil 2.19-end
F	M	140, 141	‡Eccles 9	Luke 19.1-10
	E	142, 143	‡Eccles 11.1-8	Phil 3.1—4.1
S	M	144	‡Eccles 11.9—12 end	Luke 19.11-27
	E	145	‡Obadiah	Phil 4.2-end

TABLE 1C / PSALMS AND READINGS
FOR MORNING AND EVENING PRAYER
THE FESTIVALS

Psalms	First Reading	Second Reading

1. When the orders of Morning Prayer and Holy Communion, or of Evening Prayer and Holy Communion, are combined, the readings are those appointed for Holy Communion.

2. The readings appointed for Holy Communion may be used at Morning or Evening Prayer instead of the readings in this table.

THE NAMING OF JESUS, OR THE CIRCUMCISION OF CHRIST
(1 January)   White

M	115	Joshua 1.1-9	Acts 3.1-16
E	148	Jer 23.1-6	Rom 10.5-13

THE CONVERSION OF ST PAUL (25 January)   White

M	18.22-35	Ezek 3.22-end or Ecclus 39.1-10	Col 1.24—2.7
E	119.41-56	Isa 56.1-8	Phil 3.1-14

THE PRESENTATION OF CHRIST IN THE TEMPLE (2 February)   White

M	122, 123	Haggai 2.1-9	Heb 10.1-10
E	42, 43	1 Sam 1.20-end	Rom 12.1-8

If 2 February falls on a Sunday the psalms and readings appointed for the Presentation take precedence.

ST JOSEPH OF NAZARETH, HUSBAND OF THE BLESSED VIRGIN MARY (19 March)   White

M	1	1 Chron 17.3-15	Rom 4.13-22
E	34	Hosea 11	Matt 2.13-end

THE ANNUNCIATION OF OUR LORD TO THE BLESSED VIRGIN MARY
(25 March)   White

M	85	1 Sam 2.1-10	Heb 2.5-end
E	111	Gen 3.8-15	Rom 5.12-end

	Psalms	First Reading	Second Reading

ST MARK THE EVANGELIST (25 April)   Red

M	19	Isa 62.6-end or	
		Ecclus 51.13-end	2 Tim 4.1-11
E	96	Ezek 1.4-14	Acts 15.35-end

ST PHILIP AND ST JAMES, APOSTLES (1 May)   Red

| M | 27 | Job 23.1-12 | Acts 2.37-end |
| E | 119.137-152 | Isa 30.15-21 | John 1.43-end |

ST MATTHIAS THE APOSTLE (14 May)   Red

| M | 33 | Isa 22.15-22 | Matt 7.15-27 |
| E | 92 | 1 Sam 16.1-13a | 1 Cor 4.1-7 |

ST BARNABAS THE APOSTLE (11 June)   Red

M	100, 101	Eccles 12.9-end or	
		Tobit 4.5-11	Acts 4.32-end
E	15	Isa 42.5-12	Acts 9.26-31

THE BIRTH OF ST JOHN THE BAPTIST (24 June)   White

| M | 50 | Judges 13.2-7, 24-end | Matt 11.2-19 |
| E | 116 | Mal 4 | Luke 3.1-20 |

ST PETER THE APOSTLE (29 June)   Red

| M | 71 | Ezek 2.1-7 | Acts 9.32-end |
| E | 145 | Ezek 34.11-16 | John 21.15-22 |

If St Paul is commemorated with St Peter the following may be used:

| M | 19 | Jer 1.4-10 | Acts 12.1-11 |
| E | 139 | Ezek 3.22-end | John 21.15-22 |

ST THOMAS THE APOSTLE (3 July)   Red

| M | 34 | Job 42.1-6 | 1 Pet 1.3-9 |
| E | 92 | 2 Sam 15.17-21 | John 11.1-16 |

ST MARY MAGDALEN (22 July)   White

| M | 32 | 1 Sam 16.14-end | Luke 8.1-3 |
| E | 63 | Hosea 14 | Mark 15.40—16.8 |

Psalms	First Reading	Second Reading

ST JAMES THE GREAT, APOSTLE (25 July)   Red

M	29	2 Kings 1.9-15	Luke 9.46-56
E	94	Jer 26.1-16	Mark 1.14-20

THE TRANSFIGURATION OF OUR LORD (6 August)   White

M	27	1 Kings 19.1-16 or	
		Ecclus 48.1-10	2 Pet 1.12-19
E	72	Exod 24.12-end	1 John 3.1-3

ST BARTHOLOMEW THE APOSTLE (24 August)   Red

M	86	Isa 43.8-13	Matt 10.1-15
E	15	Deut 18.15-19	Matt 10.16-22

THE BLESSED VIRGIN MARY (8 September)   White

M	72	Isa 61.10—62.3	John 2.1-12
E	98, 138	Prov 8.22-31	John 19.23-27

ST MATTHEW THE APOSTLE (21 September)   Red

M	25	Eccles 5.4-12	Matt 19.16-end
E	34	1 Chron 29.9-18	1 Tim 6.6-19

ST MICHAEL AND ALL ANGELS (29 September)   White

M	148	Dan 10.4-end	Rev 5
E	91	Gen 28.10-17	John 1.43-end

ST LUKE THE EVANGELIST (18 October)   Red

M	103	Isa 55	2 Tim 3.10-end
E	19	Isa 61.1-6 or	
		Ecclus 38.1-14	Col 4.7-end

ST SIMON AND ST JUDE, APOSTLES (28 October)   Red

M	124, 125, 126	Isa 45.18-end or	
		Wisdom 5.1-16	Rev 21.9-14
E	119.1-16	Jer 3.11-18 or	
		1 Macc 2.42-66	Luke 6.12-23

	Psalms	First Reading	Second Reading

ALL SAINTS' DAY (1 November)   White

M	97, 149.1-5	Isa 65.17-end or Ecclus 44.1-15	Luke 9.18-27
E	111, 112	Isa 40.27-end or Wisdom 3.1-9	Heb 11.32—12.2

Psalms and readings for the previous evening may be chosen from this provision or from that provided for Holy Communion (p. 1064).

ST ANDREW THE APOSTLE (30 November)   Red

M	47, 48	Isa 49.1-9a	1 Cor 1.18-end
E	67, 96	Ezek 47.1-12	John 1.35-42

ST STEPHEN (26 December)   Red

M	13, 46	Exod 18.13-26	Acts 6
E	57, 86	Gen 4.1-10	John 15.20—16.4a

ST JOHN THE EVANGELIST (27 December)   White

M	97	Exod 33.7-11a	1 John 5.1-12
E	21	Isa 6.1-8	John 13.21-35

THE HOLY INNOCENTS (28 December)   Red

M	36	Gen 37.13-20 or Baruch 4.21-27	1 Pet 4.12-end
E	124, 128	Isa 49.14-25	Matt 18.1-10

FESTIVAL OF THE DEDICATION OR CONSECRATION OF A CHURCH
White

M	103	Gen 28.10-end	Rev 21.9-14, 22-end
E	48	1 Chron 29.6-19	1 Cor 3.9-17

FESTIVAL OF THE PATRON SAINT OR TITLE OF A CHURCH

If the day is provided with proper readings in these tables, these are used: if not, the readings for All Saints' Day or other appropriate readings may be used.

TABLE 2 / PSALMS FOR MORNING AND EVENING PRAYER
(Book of Common Prayer)

Day	Morning	Evening
1	1, 2, 3, 4, 5	6, 7, 8
2	9, 10, 11	12, 13, 14
3	15, 16, 17	18
4	19, 20, 21	22, 23
5	24, 25, 26	27, 28, 29
6	30, 31	32, 33, 34
7	35, 36	37
8	38, 39, 40	41, 42, 43
9	44, 45, 46	47, 48, 49
10	50, 51, 52	53, 54, 55
11	56, 57, 58	59, 60, 61
12	62, 63, 64	65, 66, 67
13	68	69, 70
14	71, 72	73, 74
15	75, 76, 77	78
16	79, 80, 81	82, 83, 84, 85
17	86, 87, 88	89
18	90, 91, 92	93, 94
19	95, 96, 97	98, 99, 100, 101
20	102, 103	104
21	105	106
22	107	108, 109
23	110, 111, 112, 113	114, 115
24	116, 117, 118	119 vv. 1-32
25	119 vv. 33-72	119 vv. 73-104
26	119 vv. 105-144	119 vv. 145-176
27	120, 121, 122, 123, 124, 125	126, 127, 128, 129, 130, 131
28	132, 133, 134, 135	136, 137, 138
29	139, 140, 141	142, 143
30	144, 145, 146	147, 148, 149, 150

1   In February the Psalms are read only to the 28th or 29th day of the month.

2   In January, March, May, July, August, October and December, all of which have 31 days, the same psalms are said on the last day of the month (being an ordinary weekday) which were read the day before, or else the psalms of the monthly course omitted on one of the Sundays in that month.

Proper Psalms on Certain Days (BCP)

Day	Morning	Evening
Christmas Day	19, 45, 85	89, 110, 132
Ash Wednesday	6, 32, 38	102, 130, 143
Good Friday	22, 40, 54	69, 88
Easter Day	2, 57, 111	113, 114, 118
Ascension Day	8, 15, 21	24, 47, 108
Whit Sunday	48, 68	104, 145

TABLE 3A / PSALMS AND READINGS FOR HOLY COMMUNION SUNDAYS AND SEASONS

Psalms	Year 1	Year 2

NINTH SUNDAY BEFORE CHRISTMAS
(Fifth Sunday before Advent)   Green

104.1-10; 29	*Gen 1.1-3, 24-31a	*Gen 2.4b-9, 15-end
	Col 1.15-20	Rev 4
	John 1.1-14	John 3.1-8

EIGHTH SUNDAY BEFORE CHRISTMAS
(Fourth Sunday before Advent)   Green

130; 10.13-end	*Gen 4.1-10	*Gen 3.1-15
	1 John 3.9-18	Rom 7.7-13
	Mark 7.14-23	John 3.13-21

SEVENTH SUNDAY BEFORE CHRISTMAS
(Third Sunday before Advent)   Green

1; 105.1-11	*Gen 12.1-9	*Gen 22.1-18
	Rom 4.13-end	Jas 2.14-24 (25, 26)
	John 8.51-end	Luke 20.9-17

Services for Remembrance Sunday
The following psalms and readings are suitable:
Psalms 46, 47, 93, 126, 130; Isa 2.1-5; Isa 10.33—11.9; Ezek 37.1-14;
Rom 8.31-end; Rev 21.1-7; Matt 5.1-12; John 15.9-17

SIXTH SUNDAY BEFORE CHRISTMAS
(Second sunday before Advent)   Green

135.1-6;	*Exod 3.7-15	*Exod 6.2-8
77.11-end	Heb 3.1-6	Heb 11.17-31
	John 6.25-35	Mark 13.5-13

FIFTH SUNDAY BEFORE CHRISTMAS
(The Sunday next before Advent)   Green

80.1-7;	*1 Kings 19.9-18	*Isa 10.20-23
80.8-end	Rom 11.13-24	Rom 9.19-28
	Matt 24.37-44	Mark 13.14-23

Psalms	Year 1	Year 2

ADVENT SUNDAY (Fourth Sunday before Christmas)   Violet

50.1-6; 82	*Isa 52.7-10	*Isa 51.4-11
	1 Thess 5.1-11	Rom 13.8-end
	Luke 21.25-33	Matt 25.31-end

ADVENT 2 (Third Sunday before Christmas)   Violet

19.7-end;	*Isa 55.1-11	*Isa 64.1-7
119.129-136	2 Tim 3.14—4.5	Rom 15.4-13
	John 5.36b-end	Luke 4.14-21

ADVENT 3 (Second Sunday before Christmas)   Violet

126;	*Isa 40.1-11	*Mal 3.1-5
Benedictus	1 Cor 4.1-5	Phil 4.4-9
	John 1.19-28	Matt 11.2-15

ADVENT 4 (The Sunday next before Christmas)   Violet

45.10-end;	*Isa 11.1-9	*Zech 2.10-end
Magnificat	1 Cor 1.26-end	Rev 21.1-7
	Luke 1.26-38a	Matt 1.18-23

Years 1 and 2

CHRISTMAS EVE (24 December)   Violet

89.1-7 (8-18);	Isa 62.1-5
89.19-30	Acts 13.16-26
	Luke 1.67-79

CHRISTMAS DAY   White or Gold

85; 96; 98	Isa 9.2, 6-7 or Isa 62.10-12 or Micah 5.2-4
	Titus 2.11-14; 3.3-7 or Heb 1.1-5 (6-12) or 1 John 4.7-14
	Luke 2.1-14 (15-20) or Luke 2.8-20 or John 1.1-14

	Year 1	Year 2

SUNDAY AFTER CHRISTMAS DAY   White or Gold

2; 116.11-end	Isa 7.10-14	1 Sam 1.20-end
	Gal 4.1-7	Rom 12.1-8
	John 1.14-18	Luke 2.22-40

Psalms	Year 1	Year 2

THE SECOND SUNDAY AFTER CHRISTMAS   White or Gold

Nunc	Ecclus 3.2-7 or	
Dimittis;	Exod 12.21-27	Isa 60.1-6
27.1-8	Rom 8.11-17	Rev 21.22—22.5
	Luke 2.41-end	Matt 2.1-12, 19-end

Years 1 and 2

THE EPIPHANY OF OUR LORD (6 January)   White or Gold

72.1-8;	Isa 49.1-6	
72.10-end	Eph 3.1-12	
	Matt 2.1-12	

	Year 1	Year 2

EPIPHANY 1   White or Gold for Sunday, Green from Monday

36.5-10	1 Sam 16.1-13a	Isa 42.1-7
89.19-30	Acts 10.34-48a	Eph 2.1-10
	Matt 3.13-end	John 1.29-34

EPIPHANY 2   Green

100; 145.1-12	Jer 1.4-10	1 Sam 3.1-10
	Acts 26.1, 9-20	Gal 1.11-end
	Mark 1.14-20	John 1.35-end

EPIPHANY 3   Green

46; 107.1-9	Exod 33.12-end	Deut 8.1-6
	1 John 1.1-7	Phil 4.10-20
	John 2.1-11	John 6.1-14

EPIPHANY 4   Green

48.9-end;	1 Kings 8.22-30	Jer 7.1-11
84.1-7	1 Cor 3.10-17	Heb 12.18-end
	John 2.13-22	John 4.19-26

Psalms	Years 1 and 2

EPIPHANY 5   Green

36; 49.1-12	Prov 2.1-9 or
	Ecclus 42.15-end
	1 Cor 3.18-end
	Matt 12.38-42

EPIPHANY 6   Green

43; 25.1-11	2 Sam 12.1-10
	Rom 1.18-25
	Matt 13.24-30

	Year 1	Year 2

NINTH SUNDAY BEFORE EASTER
(Third Sunday before Lent)   Green

103.1-13;	Isa 30.18-21	Prov 3.1-8
34.11-18	1 Cor 4.8-13	1 Cor 2.1-10
	Matt 5.1-12	Luke 8.4-15

EIGHTH SUNDAY BEFORE EASTER
(Second Sunday before Lent)   Green

147.1-11; 131	Zeph 3.14-end	2 Kings 5.1-14
	Jas 5.13-16a	2 Cor 12.1-10
	Mark 2.1-12	Mark 7.24-end

SEVENTH SUNDAY BEFORE EASTER
(The Sunday next before Lent)   Green

32; 119.65-72	Hosea 14.1-7	Num 15.32-36
	Philemon 1-16	Col 1.18-23
	Mark 2.13-17	John 8.2-11

	Years 1 and 2

ASH WEDNESDAY   Violet (or Lent array)

6; 51.1-17;	Isa 58.1-8 or Joel 2.12-17 or Amos 5.6-15
90.1-12	1 Cor 9.24-end or Jas 4.1-10
	Matt 6.16-21 or Luke 18.9-14

Psalms	Year 1	Year 2

LENT 1 (Sixth Sunday before Easter)   Violet (or Lent array)

119.1-8;	Gen 2.7-9; 3.1-7	Gen 4.1-10
91.1-12	Heb 2.14-end	Heb 4.12-end
	Matt 4.1-11	Luke 4.1-13

LENT 2 (Fifth Sunday before Easter)   Violet (or Lent array)

119.33-40;	Gen 6.11-end	Gen 7.17-end
18.18-26	1 John 4.1-6	1 John 3.1-10
	Luke 19.41-end	Matt 12.22-32

LENT 3 (Fourth Sunday before Easter)   Violet (or Lent array)

119.97-104;	Gen 22.1-13	Gen 12.1-9
115.1-7	Col 1.24-end	1 Pet 2.19-end
	Luke 9.18-27	Matt 16.13-end

LENT 4 (Third Sunday before Easter)   Violet (or Lent array)

119.153-160;	Exod 34.29-end	Exod 3.1-6
18.27-38	2 Cor 3.4-end	2 Pet 1.16-19
	Luke 9.28-36	Matt 17.1-13

[Services for Mothering Sunday—see p. 996]

LENT 5 (Second Sunday before Easter)   Violet (or Lent array)

76.1-9;	Exod 6.2-13	Jer 31.31-34
22.23-29	Col 2.8-15	Heb 9.11-14
	John 12.20-32	Mark 10.32-45

Years 1 and 2

PALM SUNDAY (The Sunday next before Easter)   Red

22.1-11;	Isa 50.4-9a	
69.1-9	Phil 2.5-11	
or	Mark 14.32—15.41	
24; 45.1-7	or	
	Zech 9.9-12	
	1 Cor 1.18-25	
	Matt 21.1-13	

Psalms   **Years 1 and 2**

MONDAY IN HOLY WEEK   Red, or as in Lent

55.1-9; 55.9-15   Isa 42.1-7
                 Heb 2.9-18
                 Matt 26.1-30 (Year 1)
                 Luke 22.1-38 (Year 2)

TUESDAY IN HOLY WEEK   Red, or as in Lent

55.18-26; 13   Isa 49.1-6
                 Heb 8.1-6
                 Matt 26.31-end (Year 1)
                 Luke 22.39-end (Year 2)

WEDNESDAY IN HOLY WEEK   Red, or as in Lent

54; 102.1-11   Isa 50.4-9a
                 1 Pet 2.19-end
                 Matt 27.1-56 (Year 1)
                 Luke 23.1-49 (Year 2)

MAUNDY THURSDAY   White

116.11-end; 26   Exod 12.1-14
                 1 Cor 11.23-29
                 John 13.1-15

THE BLESSING OF THE OILS

89.19-30; 133   Isa 61.1-9
                 Jas 5.13-16a or Rev 1.5b-8
                 Luke 4.16-21

GOOD FRIDAY   Red, hangings removed

22.14-22;   Isa 52.13—53 end
69.17-23   Heb 10.1-25 or 12-22 or Heb 4.14-16; 5.7-9
                 John 18.1—19.37 (or 19.1-37)

EASTER EVE   Hangings removed

16.8-11; 23   Job 14.1-14
                 1 Pet 3.17-end
                 Matt 27.57-end or John 2.18-22

Psalms	Years 1 and 2

EASTER DAY White or Gold

118.14-24; 114;	Isa 12
Easter	Rev 1.10-18
Anthems;	Matt 28.1-10
Te Deum	or
	Exod 14.15-22
	1 Cor 15.12-20
	John 20.1-10 (or -18)
	or
	Isa 43.16-21
	Col 3.1-11
	Mark 16.1-8

MONDAY IN EASTER WEEK White or Gold

Easter	Isa 42.10-16
Anthems;	1 Pet 1.1-12
Te Deum	Luke 24.13-35
(Part 2)	

TUESDAY IN EASTER WEEK White or Gold

16.8-11; 30	Micah 7.7-end
	1 Pet 1.13-end
	Luke 24.36-49

WEDNESDAY IN EASTER WEEK White or Gold

111; 112	1 Kings 17.17-24
	1 Pet 2.1-10
	John 20.24-end

THURSDAY IN EASTER WEEK White or Gold

113; 114	Jer 31.1-14
	1 Pet 2.11-end
	John 21.1-14

FRIDAY IN EASTER WEEK White or Gold

115; 116.1-9	Ezek 37.1-14
	1 Pet 3.1-12
	John 21.15-17

Psalms	Years 1 and 2

SATURDAY IN EASTER WEEK   White or Gold

118.1-4, 22-27a; 118.14-21	Job 14.1-14 1 Pet 4.1-11 John 21.20-end

	Year 1	Year 2

EASTER 1   White or Gold

145.1-12; 34.1-10	Exod 15.1-11 1 Pet 1.3-9 John 20.19-29	Exod 16.2-15 1 Cor 15.53-end John 6.32-40

EASTER 2   White

111; 23	Isa 25.6-9 Rev 19.6-9 Luke 24.13-35	Ezek 34.7-16 1 Pet 5.1-11 John 10.7-16

EASTER 3   White

16; 30	Isa 61.1-7 1 Cor 15.1-11 John 21.1-14	1 Kings 17.17-end Col 3.1-11 John 11.17-27

EASTER 4   White

33.1-12; 37.23-32	Isa 62.1-5 Rev 3.14-end John 21.15-22	Prov 4.10-19 2 Cor 4.13—5.5 John 14.1-11

EASTER 5   White

84; 15	Hosea 6.1-6 1 Cor 15.21-28 John 16.25-end	Deut 34 Rom 8.28-end John 16.12-24

Years 1 and 2

ASCENSION DAY   White or Gold

8; 21.1-7	Dan 7.9-14 Acts 1.1-11 Matt 28.16-end

Psalms	Year 1	Year 2

THE SUNDAY AFTER ASCENSION DAY (Easter 6)   White

Psalms	Year 1	Year 2
24; 47	Dan 7.9-14	2 Kings 2.1-15
	Eph 1.15-end	Eph 4.1-13
	Luke 24.45-end	Luke 24.45-end

Years 1 and 2

PENTECOST (Whit Sunday)   Red

122; 36.5-10	Gen 11.1-9
	*Acts 2.1-11
	John 14.15-26
	or
	Exod 19.16-end
	*Acts 2.1-21
	John 20.19-23

TRINITY SUNDAY (Pentecost 1)   White or Gold

93; 97	Isa 6.1-8
	*Eph 1.3-14
	John 14.8-17

	Year 1	Year 2

2ND SUNDAY AFTER PENTECOST (Trinity 1)   Green

95.1-7;	Exod 19.1-6	2 Sam 7.4-16
135.1-6	*1 Pet 2.1-10	*Acts 2.37-end
	John 15.1-5	Luke 14.15-24

3RD SUNDAY AFTER PENTECOST (Trinity 2)   Green

44.1-9; 150	Deut 6.17-end	Deut 8.11-end
	*Rom 6.3-11	*Acts 4.8-12
	John 15.5-11	Luke 8.41-end

4TH SUNDAY AFTER PENTECOST (Trinity 3)   Green

63.1-9; 67	Deut 7.6-11	Isa 63.7-14
	*Gal 3.23—4.7	*Acts 8.26-38
	John 15.12-17	Luke 15.1-10

Psalms	Year 1	Year 2

5TH SUNDAY AFTER PENTECOST (Trinity 4)   Green

119.57-64;	Exod 20.1-17	Ruth 1.8-17, 22
119.89-96	*Eph 5.1-10	*Acts 11.4-18
	Matt 19.16-26	Luke 10.1-12

6TH SUNDAY AFTER PENTECOST (Trinity 5)   Green

112; 1	Exod 24.3-11	Micah 6.1-8
	*Col 3.12-17	*Eph 4.17-end
	Luke 15.11-end	Mark 10.46-end

7TH SUNDAY AFTER PENTECOST (Trinity 6)   Green

62; 103.8-18	Hosea 11.1-9	Deut 10.12—11.1
	*1 Cor 12.27—13 end	*Rom 8.1-11
	Matt 18.21-end	Mark 12.28-34

8TH SUNDAY AFTER PENTECOST (Trinity 7)   Green

25.1-10;	Ezek 36.24-28	Ezek 37.1-14
27.1-8	*Gal 5.16-25	*1 Cor 12.4-13
	John 15.16-end	Luke 6.27-38

9TH SUNDAY AFTER PENTECOST (Trinity 8)   Green

18.1-7;	Josh 1.1-9	1 Sam 17.37-50
18.32-38	*Eph 6.10-20	*2 Cor 6.3-10
	John 17.11b-19	Mark 9.14-29

10TH SUNDAY AFTER PENTECOST (Trinity 9)   Green

71.1-8;	Job 42.1-6	1 Sam 24.9-17 (or 1-17)
73.23-end	*Phil 2.1-11	*Gal 6.1-10
	John 13.1-15	Luke 7.36-end

11TH SUNDAY AFTER PENTECOST (Trinity 10)   Green

31.21-end;	Isa 42.1-7	1 Chron 29.1-9
40.1-7	*2 Cor 4.1-10	*Phil 1.1-11
	John 13.31-35	Matt 20.1-16

Psalms	Year 1	Year 2

12TH SUNDAY AFTER PENTECOST (Trinity 11)   Green

96.1-6;	Isa 49.1-6	Micah 4.1-5
96.7-end	*2 Cor 5.14—6.2	*Acts 17.22-end
	John 17.20-end	Matt 5.13-16

13TH SUNDAY AFTER PENTECOST (Trinity 12)   Green

31.1-5; 43	Isa 50.4-9a	Jer 20.7-11a
	*Acts 7.54—8.1	*Acts 20.17-35
	John 16.1-11	Matt 10.16-22

14TH SUNDAY AFTER PENTECOST (Trinity 13)   Green

127; 128	Proverbs 31.10-end	Gen 45.1-15
	*Eph 5.25—6.4	*Eph 3.14-end
	Mark 10.2-16	Luke 11.1-13

15TH SUNDAY AFTER PENTECOST (Trinity 14)   Green

82; 20	Isa 45.1-7	1 Kings 3.4-15
	*Rom 13.1-7	*1 Tim 2.1-7
	Matt 22.15-22	Matt 14.1-12

16TH SUNDAY AFTER PENTECOST (Trinity 15)   Green

34.1-10;	Lev 19.9-18	Deut 15.7-11
34.11-18	*Rom 12.9-end	*1 John 4.15-end
	Luke 10.25-37	Luke 16.19-end

17TH SUNDAY AFTER PENTECOST (Trinity 16)   Green

56; 57	Jer 7.1-11	Jer 32.6-15
	*James 1.16-end	*Gal 2.15—3.9
	Luke 17.11-19	Luke 7.1-10

18TH SUNDAY AFTER PENTECOST (Trinity 17)   Green

145.14-end;	Deut 26.1-11	Nehemiah 6.1-16 or
90.13-end		Ecclus 38.24-end
	*2 Cor 8.1-9	*1 Pet 4.7-11
	Matt 5.17-26	Matt 25.14-30

Psalms	Year 1	Year 2

19TH SUNDAY AFTER PENTECOST (Trinity 18)   Green

139.1-11;	Gen 28.10-end	Dan 6.10-23
65.1-7	*Heb 11.1-2, 8-16	*Rom 5.1-11
	Matt 6.24-end	Luke 19.1-10

20TH SUNDAY AFTER PENTECOST (Trinity 19)   Green

37.35-end;	Dan 3.13-26	Gen 32.22-30
121	*Rom 8.18-25	*1 Cor 9.19-end
	Luke 9.51-end	Matt 7.13-27

21ST SUNDAY AFTER PENTECOST (Trinity 20)   Green

126; 11	Hab 2.1-4	Ezek 12.21-end
	*Acts 26.1-8	1 Pet 1.13-21
	Luke 18.1-8	John 11.17-27

Years 1 and 2

22ND SUNDAY AFTER PENTECOST (Trinity 21)   Green

119.1-8; 112	Deut 11.18-28
	*1 John 2.22-end
	Luke 16.1-9

Year 1	Year 2

LAST SUNDAY AFTER PENTECOST   Green

15; 146	Jer 29.1, 4-14	Isa 33.17-22
	*Phil 3.7-end	*Rev 7.2-4, 9-end
	John 17.1-10	Matt 25.1-13

TABLE 3B/PSALMS AND READINGS FOR HOLY COMMUNION FESTIVALS AND HOLY DAYS

Psalms	Readings

THE NAMING OF JESUS, OR THE CIRCUMCISION OF CHRIST
(1 January)   White

8; 62.1-8	Isa 9.2, 6-7
	Acts 4.8-12
	Luke 2.15-21

THE CONVERSION OF ST PAUL (25 January)   White

126; 67	1 Kings 19.15-end
	Acts 9.1-22
	Matt 19.27-end

THE PRESENTATION OF CHRIST IN THE TEMPLE (2 February)   White

48.1-8;	Mal 3.1-5
48.9-end	1 Pet 2.1-10
	Luke 2.22-35

If 2 February falls on a Sunday the psalms and readings appointed for the Presentation take precedence.

ST JOSEPH OF NAZARETH, HUSBAND OF THE BLESSED VIRGIN MARY (19 March)   White

89.1-8;	Isa 7.10-14
89.19-30	1 Pet 3.1-7
	Matt 1.18-end

or the following may be used:

15; 112	Gen 1.26—2.3
	Col 3.12-15, 17, 23-24
	Matt 13.54-end

THE ANNUNCIATION OF OUR LORD TO THE BLESSED VIRGIN MARY
(25 March)   White

113; 131	Isa 52.7-10
	Gal 4.1-5
	Luke 1.26-38a

Psalms	Readings

ST MARK THE EVANGELIST (25 April)   Red

45.1-5;	Prov 15.28-end
119.9-16	Eph 4.7-16
	Mark 13.5-13

ST PHILIP AND ST JAMES, APOSTLES (1 May)   Red

33.1-5;	Prov 4.10-18
25.1-10	Eph 1.3-14
	John 14.1-14

ST MATTHIAS THE APOSTLE (14 May)   Red

16.1-6;	1 Sam 2.27-35
80.8-15	Acts 1.15-17, 20-end
	John 15.1-11

ST BARNABAS THE APOSTLE (11 June)   Red

145.8-15; 112	Job 29.11-16
	Acts 11.19-end
	John 15.12-17

THE BIRTH OF ST JOHN THE BAPTIST (24 June)   White

119.161-168;	Isa 40.1-11
80.1-7	Acts 13.16-26
	Luke 1.57-66, 80

ST PETER THE APOSTLE (29 June)   Red

125; 18.33-37	Ezek 3.4-11
	1 Pet 2.19-end
	Matt 16.13-20

If St Paul is commemorated with St Peter the following may be used:

125; 126	Zech 4.1-6a, 10b-14 or
	Wisdom 3.1-9
	2 Tim 4.6-8, 16-18
	Matt 16.13-20

ST THOMAS THE APOSTLE (3 July)   Red

139.1-11;	Gen 12.1-4
31.1-5	Heb 10.35—11.1
	John 20.24-29

Psalms	Readings

ST MARY MAGDALEN (22 July)   White

139.1-11;	Zeph 3.14-end
30.1-5	2 Cor 5.14-17
	John 20.11-18

ST JAMES THE GREAT, APOSTLE (25 July)   Red

15; 75.6-end	Jer 45
	Acts 11.27—12.2
	Mark 10.35-45

THE TRANSFIGURATION OF OUR LORD (6 August)   White

84.1-7;	Exod 34.29-end
84.8-end	2 Cor 3.4-end
	Luke 9.28-36

ST BARTHOLOMEW THE APOSTLE (24 August)   Red

116.11-end;	Isa 61.4-9
97.10-end	Acts 5.12b-16
	Luke 22.24-30

THE BLESSED VIRGIN MARY (8 September)   White

45.10-end;	Micah 5.2-4
Magnificat	Rev 21.1-7
	Luke 1.39-49 or 2.1-19

ST MATTHEW THE APOSTLE (21 September)   Red

119.65-72;	Prov 3.9-18
119.89-96	2 Cor 4.1-6
	Matt 9.9-13

ST MICHAEL AND ALL ANGELS (29 September)   White

103.17-end;	2 Kings 6.8-17
91.5-12	Rev 12.7-12
	Matt 18.1-6, 10

ST LUKE THE EVANGELIST (18 October)   Red

147.1-6;	Isa 35.3-6
22.23-29	Acts 16.6-12a or 2 Tim 4.5-15
	Luke 10.1-9

Psalms	Readings

ST SIMON AND ST JUDE, APOSTLES (28 October)   Red

15; 116.11-end   Isa 28.9-16
                 Eph 2.13-end
                 John 14.15-26

ALL SAINTS' DAY (1 November)   White

1; 15; 33.1-5;   Jer 31.31-34 or 2 Esdras 2.42-end or Gen 3.1-15
145.8-13   Heb 12.18-24 or Rev 7.2-4, 9-end
                 Matt 5.1-12 or Luke 6.20-23

ST ANDREW THE APOSTLE (30 November)   Red

92.1-5; 87   Zech 8.20-end
             Rom 10.12-18
             Matt 4.12-20

ST STEPHEN (26 December)   Red

119.17-24;   2 Chron 24.20-22
119.161-168   Acts 7.54-end
              Matt 23.34-end

ST JOHN THE EVANGELIST (27 December)   White

117; 92.12-end   Exod 33.12-end
                 1 John 2.1-11
                 John 21.20-end

THE HOLY INNOCENTS (28 December)   Red

123; 131   Jer 31.15-17
           1 Cor 1.26-29
           Matt 2.13-18

FESTIVAL OF THE DEDICATION OR CONSECRATION OF A CHURCH   White

84.1-7; 122   1 Kings 8.22-30
(or 24, 132)   1 Pet 2.1-10
               Matt 21.12-16

FESTIVAL OF THE PATRON SAINT OR TITLE OF A CHURCH

If the day is provided with proper readings in these tables, these are used: if not, the readings for All Saints' Day or other appropriate readings may be used.

TABLE 3C/PSALMS AND READINGS FOR HOLY COMMUNION LESSER FESTIVALS AND HOLY DAYS

Psalms	Readings

TIMOTHY AND TITUS (26 January)   White

97; 100	Isa 61.1-3
	2 Tim 1.1-8 or Titus 1.1-5
	Mark 16.14-end

THE VISIT OF THE BLESSED VIRGIN MARY TO ELIZABETH
(31 May)   White

113; 131	Zech 2.10-end
	Gal 4.1-5
	Luke 1.39-49

HOLY CROSS DAY (14 September)   Red

2; 8	Num 21.4-9
	Phil 2.5-11
	John 12.31-36a

COMMEMORATION OF THE FAITHFUL DEPARTED
(2 November)   Violet, Black, or White

42.1-7	Isa 25.6-9
118.14-21,	1 Pet 1.3-9
28, 29	John 20.1-9

GROUP COMMEMORATIONS

(Europe, 3 February; Africa, 21 February; The Americas, 8 April;
Australia and the Pacific, 20 September; The Reformation Era, 31 October;
England, 8 November; Asia, 3 December)

87; 67	Isa 61.4-9 or Ecclus 2.10-18 or Ecclus 44.1-15
	2 Cor 4.5-12 or Heb 11.32—12.2 or Heb 13.7-8, 15-16
	John 12.20-26 or John 15.16-end or John 17.18-23

COMMON OF SAINTS

Psalms	Readings

OF A MARTYR OR MARTYRS   Red

3; 11;	2 Chron 24.17-21 or Jer 11.18-20 or Wisdom 4.10-15
119.161-168	Rom 8.35-end or 2 Tim 2.3-7 or Heb 11.32-40 or Rev 7.13-end
	Matt 10.16-22 or Matt 14.1-12 or Matt 16.24-26 or John 15.18-21

OF A TEACHER OF THE FAITH OR CONFESSOR   White

34.11-17;	Neh 8.1-10 or Prov 4.1-9 or Ecclus 39.1-10
37.30-35;	1 Cor 2.6-13 or 2 Tim 4.1-8 or Titus 2.1-8
119.97-104	Matt 5.13-19 or Matt 13.52-end or John 16.12-15

OF A BISHOP   White

1; 15; 99	Num 27.15-23 or Jer 1.4-10 or Ezek 34.11-16
	Acts 20.28-35 or 2 Cor 4.1-10 or Eph 4.7-16 or 1 Pet 5.1-4
	Matt 24.42-46 or John 10.11-16 or John 21.15-17

OF AN ABBOT OR ABBESS   White

119.57-64;	1 Kings 19.9-18 or Prov 10.27-end or Isa 61.10—62.5
123; 131	Phil 3.7-14 or 1 John 2.15-17 or 3 John 2-8
	Matt 11.25-end or Matt 19.23-end or Luke 12.32-37

OF MISSIONARIES   White

67; 96.1-6;	Isa 52.7-10 or Isa 61.1-3a or Jonah 3.1-5
96.7-end	Acts 16.6-10 or Rom 15.17-21 or 2 Cor 5.11—6.2
	Matt 9.35-end or Matt 28.16-end or Luke 10.1-9

OF ANY SAINT   White

32; 34.1-10;	Prov 8.1-11 or Prov 31.10-end or Mal 2.5-7 or Ecclus 2.1-6
34.11-18;	2 Cor 4.11-18 or Eph 4.22-end or Eph 6.11-18 or Heb 13.1-3
112; 119.1-8	Matt 19.16-21 or Matt 25.31-end or Mark 10.42-45 or
	Luke 10.38-end

Psalms	Readings

THE EMBER WEEKS   Colour of the season

ADVENT
122; 84.8-end   Jer 1.4-10
1 Pet 4.7-11
Luke 12.35-43

LENT AND ST PETERSTIDE
122; 84.8-end   Num 11.16-17, 24-29
Acts 20.28-35
Luke 4.16-21

MICHAELMAS
122; 84.8-end   Num 27.15-end
1 Cor 3.3-11
John 4.31-38

Any of these readings may be used in the Ember weeks in addition to those
which are appointed for the season.

THE ROGATION DAYS   White

MONDAY
107.1-9; 121   Job 28.1-11
2 Thess 3.6-13
Matt 6.1-15

TUESDAY
107.1-9; 121   Deut 8.1-10
Phil 4.4-7
Luke 11.5-13

WEDNESDAY
107. 1-9; 121   1 Kings 8.35-40
1 John 5.12-15
Mark 11.22-24

HARVEST THANKSGIVING   Colour of the season

104.21-30; 65   Deut 8.1-10 or Gen 1.1-3, 24-31a
(other psalms: Acts 14.13-17 or 1 Tim 6.6-10
67, 145, 147,   Luke 12.16-31 or John 6.27-35
148, 150)   (other lessons:
Gen 1.1—2.3; Deut 26.1-11; Deut 28.1-14;
Acts 10.10-16; 2 Cor 9.6-end; Rev 14.14-18;
Matt 6.24-end; Matt 13.18-30; John 4.31-38)

TABLE 3D / PSALMS AND READINGS
FOR HOLY COMMUNION
VARIOUS OCCASIONS

Psalms   **Readings**

FOR THE UNITY OF THE CHURCH

133; 122   Jer 33.6-9a
                Eph 4.1-6
                John 17.11b-23

FOR THE MISSIONARY WORK OF THE CHURCH

97; 100   Isa 49.1-6
(other psalms: Eph 2.13-end
2, 46, 47, 67, Matt 28.16-end
87, 96, 117)

FOR THE GUIDANCE OF THE HOLY SPIRIT

25.1-10;   Wisdom 9.13-17 or Isa 30.15-21
143.8-10   1 Cor 12.4-13
                John 14.23-26

FOR THE PEACE OF THE WORLD

72.1-7;   Micah 4.1-5
85.8-end   1 Tim 2.1-6
                Matt 5.43-end

IN TIME OF TROUBLE

86.1-7;   Job 1.13-end or Gen 9.8-17
142.1-7   Rom 3.21-26 or Rom 8.18-25
                Luke 12.1-7 or Mark 11.22-26

THANKSGIVING FOR THE INSTITUTION OF HOLY BAPTISM

42.1-7;   Ezek 36.24-28 or 25a, 26-28
34.1-8   Rom 6.3-11
                Matt 28.16-end

THANKSGIVING FOR THE INSTITUTION OF HOLY COMMUNION

43; 116.11-end Exod 16.2-15
                1 Cor 11.23-29
                John 6.53-58

Psalms	Readings

AT A MARRIAGE

67; 121; 128
Gen 1.26-28, 31a
Rom 12.1-2, 9-13 or 1 Cor 13 or Eph 3.14-end or Eph 5.21-33
or Col 3.12-17 or 1 John 4.7-12
Matt 7.21, 24-27 or Mark 10.6-9 or John 2.1-11 or John 15.9-12

FOR THE SICK

20.1-5;
42.1-7
1 Kings 17.17-end or Hosea 6.1-3
2 Cor 12.7-10 or James 5.13-16a
Matt 8.5-13 (or -17) or Matt 8.14-17 or Mark 2.1-12

FOR THE DYING

39.1-8;
90.1-12
Josh 23.1-8 or Isa 53.3-5
Rom 8.31b-end or Phil 1.20-26
Luke 23.39-46 or John 14.1-3

AT A FUNERAL

23; 27; 42.1-7;
90.1-6, 10, 12,
14, 16, 17;
103.8, 13-17;
118.14-21,
28, 29; 121;
130; 139.1-11,
17, 18
Isa 25.8, 9 or Lam 3.22-26, 31-33 or Wisdom 3.1-5, 9
or Wisdom 4.8, 10, 11, 13-15
Rom 8.31b-end or Rom 14.7-9 or
1 Cor 15.20-26, 35-38, 42-44a, 53-end or
2 Cor 1.3-5 or 2 Cor 4.7-end or Eph 3.14-19 or
1 Thess 4.13-end or Phil 3.10-end or 1 Pet 1.3-9 or
Rev 21.1-7
Mark 10.13-16 or John 5.19-25 or John 6.35-40 or
John 11.17-27 or John 14.1-6 or John 20.1-9

AT THE FUNERAL OF A CHILD

23
Lam 3.22-26, 31-33
Eph 3.14-19
Mark 10.13-16

FOR THE APPOINTMENT OF A BISHOP OR AN INCUMBENT

15; 25.1-6
Num 11.16-17, 24-29 or 1 Sam 16.1-13a
Acts 1.15-17, 20-26 or Eph 4.7-16
John 4.34-38 or John 15.9-17

Psalms	Readings

FOR AN ENTHRONEMENT OR AN INSTALLATION OR AN INDUCTION

95.1-7; 101   Num 3.5-9 or Isa 61.1-3
               Eph 4.1-7 or 1 Pet 5.1-11
               Luke 10.1-9 or John 10.11-16

FOR THE BLESSING OF AN ABBOT OR AN ABBESS (OR THE INSTALLATION OF THE HEAD OF A COMMUNITY)

133   Prov 2.1-9 or Prov 4.7-13
               Eph 4.1-7 or Col 3.12-17
               Luke 12.35-44 or Luke 22.24-27

FOR A SYNOD

25.1-10   Num 9.15-end or Prov 24.3-7
               Acts 15.22-29 or Phil 2.1-11
               Luke 14.27-33 or John 16.13-15

FOR THOSE TAKING VOWS

99; 101   1 Sam 1.20-end or Hosea 2.19-20
               Eph 1.3-14 or Phil 3.7-14
               Luke 10.38-end or John 12.24-26

FOR VOCATIONS TO RELIGIOUS COMMUNITIES

63.1-9   Jer 1.4-9
               Phil 3.7-14
               Matt 6.24-end

FOR SOCIAL RESPONSIBILITY

72.1-7;   Amos 5.21-24 or Amos 8.4-7
146.6-end   Acts 5.1-11 or James 2.1-4
               Matt 25.31-end or Mark 2.1-5 (6-12)

FOR CIVIC OCCASIONS

67; 100   Deut 5.1-21 or Deut 6.1-13
               Phil 2.1-11 or Phil 4.8-13
               Mark 10.42-45 or Luke 3.7-14
or the psalms and readings for Pentecost 15.

TABLE 4/A DAILY EUCHARISTIC LECTIONARY

NOTES

1   The following table may be used at Holy Communion only on any weekday for which no provision is made in Table 1 and Tables 3a and 3b; except that the psalms and readings provided for Christmas Eve and Easter Week may be read instead of, and the psalms and readings for Holy Week may be read in addition to, those appointed in Table 1.

2   The psalms and readings for 'weeks of the year' are begun on the Monday after the First Sunday after Epiphany and continue until Shrove Tuesday inclusive. They are resumed on the Monday after Pentecost, except that it is permissible to use the proper readings for the week after Pentecost and omit those of the appropriate week of the year.

3   In a year with an odd number, the psalms and readings appointed for year 1 are read, and in a year with an even number, the psalms and readings appointed for year 2 are read, for the whole of the calendar year.

4   The readings for Week 34 are always read in the week before Advent Sunday.

5   The psalms may be omitted, or replaced by other suitable psalms and canticles.

6   When a reading from the Apocrypha occurs, it may be replaced by one of the Old Testament readings for Morning or Evening Prayer.

7   When the course of readings is interrupted by a festival, the readings for that day may be added either to the day preceding or the day following.

	First Reading	Psalm	Gospel

ADVENT SUNDAY

M	Isa 2.1-5 or 4.2-6	122	Matt 8.5-11
T	Isa 11.1-10	72.1-4, 20, 21	Luke 10.21-24
W	Isa 25.6-10a	23	Matt 15.29-37
Th	Isa 26.1-6	118.18-27a	Matt 7.21, 24-27
F	Isa 29.17-end	27.1-4, 16, 17	Matt 9.27-31
S	Isa 30.19-21, 23-26	146.4-11	Matt 9.35—10.1, 6-8

ADVENT 2

M	Isa 35	85.7-end	Luke 5.17-26
T	Isa 40.1-11	96.1, 10-end	Matt 18.12-14
W	Isa 40.25-end	103.8-13	Matt 11.28-end
Th	Isa 41.13-20	145.1, 8-13	Matt 11.11-15
F	Isa 48.17-19	1	Matt 11.16-19
S	Ecclus 48.1-4, 9-11	80.1-3, 17, 18	Matt 17.10-13

ADVENT 3

M	Num 24.2-7, 15-17	25.3-9	Matt 21.23-27
T	Zeph 3.1, 2, 9-13	34.1-6, 21, 22	Matt 21.28-32
W	Isa 45.5-8, 19, 21-end	85.7-13	Luke 7.19-23
Th	Isa 54.1-10	30.1-5, 11, 12	Luke 7.24-30
F	Isa 56.1-3, 6-8	67	John 5.33-36

From December 17 to the Saturday after Epiphany inclusive, readings (except on ADVENT 4) are according to date.

DECEMBER

17	Gen 49.2, 8-10	72.1-5, 20, 21	Matt 1.1-17
18	Jer 23.5-8	72.1, 6-8, 20, 21	Matt 1.18-24
19	Judges 13.2-7, 24, 25	71.3-8	Luke 1.5-25
20	Isa 7.10-14	24.1-6	Luke 1.26-38
21	Song of Songs 2.8-14 or Zeph 3.14-18	33.1-4, 11, 12, 19-end	Luke 1.39-45
22	1 Sam 1.24-28	1 Sam 2.1, 4-8 or Ps 113	Luke 1.46-56
23	Mal 3.1-4; 4.5-6	25.3-10	Luke 1.57-66
24	2 Sam 7.1-5, 8-11, 16	89.2, 21-27	Luke 1.67-79
29	1 John 2.3-11	96.1-4	Luke 2.22-35
30	1 John 2.12-17	96.7-10	Luke 2.36-40
31	1 John 2.18-21	96.1, 11-end	John 1.1-18

	First Reading	Psalm	Gospel

JANUARY

2	1 John 2.22-28	98.1-4	John 1.19-28
3	1 John 2.29—3.6	98.2-7	John 1.29-34
4	1 John 3.7-10	97.1, 8-end	John 1.35-42
5	1 John 3.11-21	100	John 1.43-end
7	1 John 3.22—4.6	149.1-5	Matt 4.12-17, 23-end
8	1 John 4.7-10	72.1-8	Mark 6.34-44
9	1 John 4.11-18	72.1, 10-13	Mark 6.45-52
10	1 John 4.19—5.4	72.1, 18-end	Luke 4.14-22
11	1 John 5.5-13	147.12-end	Luke 5.12-16
12	1 John 5.14-end	149.1-5	John 3.22-30

ASH WEDNESDAY

Th	Deut 30.15-end	1	Luke 9.22-25
F	Isa 58.1-9a	51.1-4, 16, 17	Matt 9.14, 15
S	Isa 58.9b-end	86.1-7	Luke 5.27-32

LENT 1

M	Lev 19.1, 2, 11-18	19.7-end	Matt 25.31-end
T	Isa 55.10, 11	34.4-6, 21, 22	Matt 6.7-15
W	Jonah 3	51.1-4, 16, 17	Luke 11.29-32
Th	Esther 14.1-5, 12-14	138	Matt 7.7-12
F	Ezek 18.21-28	130	Matt 5.20-26
S	Deut 26.16-end	119.1-8	Matt 5.43-end

LENT 2

M	Dan 9.4-10	79.8, 9, 11, 13	Luke 6.36-38
T	Isa 1.10, 16-20	50.8, 16-end	Matt 23.1-12
W	Jer 18.18-20	31.4, 5, 14-18	Matt 20.17-28
Th	Jer 17.5-10	1	Luke 16.19-end
F	Gen 37.3, 4, 12, 13, 17-28	105.16-22	Matt 21.33-43, 45, 46
S	Micah 7.14, 15, 18-20	103.1-4, 9-12	Luke 15.1-3, 11-end

LENT 3

M	2 Kings 5.1-15	42.1, 2; 43.1-4	Luke 4.24-30
T	Dan 3.28, 35-44 (Apocrypha)	25.3-10	Matt 18.21-end
W	Deut 4.1, 5-9	147.12-end	Matt 5.17-19

	First Reading	Psalm	Gospel
Th	Jer 7.23-28	95.1-2, 6-end	Luke 11.14-23
F	Hosea 14.2-10	81.6-10, 13, 16	Mark 12.28-34
S	Hosea 5.15—6.6	51.1, 2, 16-end	Luke 18.9-14

ON ANY DAY

	Exod 17.1-7	95.1, 2, 6-end	John 4.5-42

LENT 4

	First Reading	Psalm	Gospel
M	Isa 65.17-21	30.1-5, 8, 11, 12	John 4.43-end
T	Ezek 47.1-9, 12	46.1-8	John 5.1-3, 5-16
W	Isa 49.8-15	145.8-17	John 5.17-30
Th	Exod 32.7-14	106.20-24	John 5.31-47
F	Wis 2.1, 12-22	34.15-end	John 7.1, 2, 10, 25-30
S	Jer 11.18-20	7.1, 2, 9-11	John 7.40-52

ON ANY DAY

	Micah 7.7-9	27.1, 9, 10, 16, 17	John 9.1-41

LENT 5

	First Reading	Psalm	Gospel
M	Susanna 1-9, 15-17, 19-30, 33-62 or 41-62	23	John 8.1-11 or 8.12-20
T	Num 21.4-9	102.1, 2, 15-22	John 8.21-30
W	Dan 3.14-20, 24, 25, 28	Benedicite (short form)	John 8.31-42
Th	Gen 17.3-9	105.4-9	John 8.51-end
F	Jer 20.10-13	18.1-6	John 10.31-end
S	Ezek 37.21-end	Jer 31.10-13 or Ps. 121	John 11.45-end

ON ANY DAY

	2 Kings 4.18-21, 32-37	17.1-8, 16	John 11.1-45

HOLY WEEK

	First Reading	Psalm	Gospel
M	Isa 42.1-7	27.1-3, 16, 17	John 12.1-11
T	Isa 49.1-6	71.1-6, 15, 16	John 13.21-33, 36-38
W	Isa 50.4-9	69.7-9, 32-35	Matt 26.14-25

	First Reading	**Psalm**	**Gospel**

EASTER WEEK

M	Acts 2.14, 22-32	16.1, 2, 6-end	Matt 28.8-15
T	Acts 2.36-41	33.4, 5, 17-end	John 20.11-18
W	Acts 3.1-10	105.1-9	Luke 24.13-35
Th	Acts 3.11-end	8	Luke 24.35-48
F	Acts 4.1-12	118.1-4, 22-26	John 21.1-14
S	Acts 4.13-21	118.1-4, 14-21	Mark 16.9-15

EASTER 1

M	Acts 4.23-31	2.1-8	John 3.1-8
T	Acts 4.32-end	93	John 3.7-15
W	Acts 5.17-26	34.1-8	John 3.16-21
Th	Acts 5.27-33	34.1, 15-end	John 3.31-end
F	Acts 5.34-end	27.1-5, 16, 17	John 6.1-15
S	Acts 6.1-7	33.1-5, 17, 18	John 6.16-21

EASTER 2

M	Acts 6.8-end	119.17-24	John 6.22-29
T	Acts 7.51—8.1	31.1-5, 18	John 6.30-35
W	Acts 8.1-8	66.1-6	John 6.35-40
Th	Acts 8.26-end	66.7, 8, 15-end	John 6.44-51
F	Acts 9.1-20	117	John 6.52-59
S	Acts 9.31-42	116.11-16	John 6.60-69

EASTER 3

M	Acts 11.1-18	42.1, 2; 43.1-4	John 10.1-10 or 11-18
T	Acts 11.19-26	87	John 10.22-30
W	Acts 12.24—13.5	67	John 12.44-end
Th	Acts 13.13-25	89.1, 2, 21-27	John 13.16-20
F	Acts 13.26-33	2	John 14.1-6
S	Acts 13.44-end	98.1-5	John 14.7-12

EASTER 4

M	Acts 14.5-18	118.1-3, 14, 15	John 14.21-26
T	Acts 14.19-end	145.10-end	John 14.27-end
W	Acts 15.1-6	122.1-5	John 15.1-8
Th	Acts 15.7-21	96.1-3, 7-10	John 15.9-11
F	Acts 15.22-31	57.8-end	John 15.12-17
S	Acts 16.1-10	100	John 15.18-21

	First Reading	Psalm	Gospel

EASTER 5

M	Acts 16.11-15	149.1-5	John 15.26—16.4
T	Acts 16.22-34	138	John 16.5-11
W	Acts 17.15, 22—18.8	148.1, 2, 11-end	John 16.12-19
F	Acts 18.9-18	47.1-6	John 16.20-23
S	Acts 18.23-end	47.1, 2, 7-end	John 16.23-28

THE SUNDAY AFTER ASCENSION DAY

M	Acts 19.1-8	68.1-6	John 16.29-end
T	Acts 20.17-27	68.9, 10, 19, 20	John 17.1-11
W	Acts 20.28-end	68.28, 29, 32-end	John 17.11-19
Th	Acts 22.30; 23.6-11	16.1, 2, 6-end	John 17.20-end
F	Acts 25.13-21	103.1, 2, 11, 12, 19, 20	John 21.15-19
S	Acts 28.16-20, 30, 31	11.4-end	John 21.20-25

PENTECOST

M	Acts 10.42-48a	18.10-14	John 3.16-21
T	Acts 8.14-17	18.22-25	John 10.1-10
W	Acts 5.12-16	33.1-6	John 6.44-51
Th	Acts 8.5-8	104.31-36	Luke 9.1-6
F	Joel 2.23-24, 26-27	146.1-5, 12	Luke 5.17-26
S	Rom 5.1-5	117	Luke 4.38-end

YEAR 1

	First Reading	**Psalm**	**Gospel**

WEEK 1 OF YEAR 1

	First Reading	Psalm	Gospel
M	Heb 1.1-6	97.1, 2, 6-10	Mark 1.14-20
T	Heb 2.5-12	8	Mark 1.21-28
W	Heb 2.14-end	105.1-9	Mark 1.29-39
Th	Heb 3.7-14	95.1, 8-end	Mark 1.40-end
F	Heb 4.1-5, 11	78.3-8	Mark 2.1-12
S	Heb 4.12-16	19.7-end	Mark 2.13-17

WEEK 2 OF YEAR 1

M	Heb 5.1-10	110.1-4	Mark 2.18-22
T	Heb 6.10-end	111	Mark 2.23-end
W	Heb 7.1-3, 15-17	110.1-4	Mark 3.1-6
Th	Heb 7.25—8.6	40.8-11, 20-end	Mark 3.7-12
F	Heb 8.6-end	85.7-end	Mark 3.13-19
S	Heb 9.2, 3, 11-14	47.1-8	Mark 3.20, 21

WEEK 3 OF YEAR 1

M	Heb 9.15, 24-end	98.1-7	Mark 3.22-30
T	Heb 10.1-10	40.1-5, 8-11	Mark 3.31-end
W	Heb 10.11-18	110.1-4	Mark 4.1-20
Th	Heb 10.19-25	24.1-6	Mark 4.21-25
F	Heb 10.32-end	37.3-6, 40, 41	Mark 4.26-34
S	Heb 11.1, 2, 8-19	Benedictus 1-6	Mark 4.35-end

WEEK 4 OF YEAR 1

M	Heb 11.32-end	31.21-end	Mark 5.1-20
T	Heb 12.1-4	22.27-end	Mark 5.21-end
W	Heb 12.4-7, 11-15	103.1, 2, 13-18	Mark 6.1-6
Th	Heb 12.18, 19, 21-24	48.1-3, 8-10	Mark 6.7-13
F	Heb 13.1-8	27.1-6, 9-12	Mark 6.14-29
S	Heb 13.15-17, 20, 21	23	Mark 6.30-34

WEEK 5 OF YEAR 1

M	Gen 1.1-19	104.1, 2, 6-13, 26	Mark 6.53-end
T	Gen 1.20—2.4a	8	Mark 7.1-13
W	Gen 2.4b-9, 15-17	104.12, 29-32	Mark 7.14-23
Th	Gen 2.18-end	128	Mark 7.24-30
F	Gen 3.1-8	32.1-8	Mark 7.31-end
S	Gen 3.9-end	90.1-12	Mark 8.1-10

	First Reading	Psalm	Gospel

WEEK 6 OF YEAR 1

M	Gen 4.1-15, 25	50.1, 8, 16-end	Mark 8.11-13
T	Gen 6.5-8; 7.1-5, 10	29	Mark 8.14-21
W	Gen 8.6-13, 20-end	116.11-end	Mark 8.22-26
Th	Gen 9.1-13	102.15-22	Mark 8.27-33
F	Gen 11.1-9	33.10-14	Mark 8.34—9.1
S	Heb 11.1-7	145.1-10	Mark 9.2-13

WEEK 7 OF YEAR 1

M	Ecclus 1.1-10	93	Mark 9.14-29
T	Ecclus 2.1-11	37.3-6, 27, 28	Mark 9.30-37
W	Ecclus 4.11-19	119.161-168	Mark 9.38-40
Th	Ecclus 5.1-8	1	Mark 9.41-end
F	Ecclus 6.5-17	119.19-24	Mark 10.1-12
S	Ecclus 17.1-15	103.13-18	Mark 10.13-16

WEEK 8 OF YEAR 1

M	Ecclus 17.24-29	32.1-8	Mark 10.17-27
T	Ecclus 35.1-12	50.1-6	Mark 10.28-31
W	Ecclus 36.1, 4, 5, 10-17	29.8, 9, 11, 13	Mark 10.32-45
Th	Ecclus 42.15-end	33.1-9	Mark 10.46-end
F	Ecclus 44.1, 9-13	149.1-5	Mark 11.11-26
S	Ecclus 51.12-20	19.7-end	Mark 11.27-end

WEEK 9 OF YEAR 1

M	Tobit 1.1-2; 2.1-8	15	Mark 12.1-12
T	Tobit 2.9-14	112	Mark 12.13-17
W	Tobit 3.1-11, 16, 17	25.1-8	Mark 12.18-27
Th	Tobit 6.9-11; 7.1-15; 8.4-8	128	Mark 12.28-34
F	Tobit 11.5-15	146	Mark 12.35-37
S	Tobit 12.1, 5-15, 20a	103.1, 8-13	Mark 12.38-end

WEEK 10 OF YEAR 1

M	2 Cor 1.1-7	34.1-8	Matt 5.1-12
T	2 Cor 1.18-22	119.129-136	Matt 5.13-16
W	2 Cor 3.4-11	78.1-4	Matt 5.17-19
Th	2 Cor 3.15—4.1, 3-6	78.35-39	Matt 5.20-26
F	2 Cor 4.7-15	99	Matt 5.27-32
S	2 Cor 5.14-end	103.1-12	Matt 5.33-37

	First Reading	Psalm	Gospel

WEEK 11 OF YEAR 1

	First Reading	Psalm	Gospel
M	2 Cor 6.1-10	98	Matt 5.38-42
T	2 Cor 8.1-9	146	Matt 5.43-end
W	2 Cor 9.6-11	112	Matt 6.1-6, 16-18
Th	2 Cor 11.1-11	111	Matt 6.7-15
F	2 Cor 11.18, 21a-30	34.1-6	Matt 6.19-23
S	2 Cor 12.1-10	89.21-34	Matt 6.24-end

WEEK 12 OF YEAR 1

	First Reading	Psalm	Gospel
M	Gen 12.1-9	33.12-21	Matt 7.1-5
T	Gen 13.2, 5-end	15	Matt 7.6, 12-14
W	Gen 15.1-12, 17, 18	105.1-9	Matt 7.15-20
Th	Gen 16.1-12, 15, 16	106.1-5	Matt 7.21-end
F	Gen 17.1, 9, 10, 15-22	128	Matt 8.1-4
S	Gen 18.1-15	Magnificat	Matt 8.5-17

WEEK 13 OF YEAR 1

	First Reading	Psalm	Gospel
M	Gen 18.16-end	103.6-17	Matt 8.18-22
T	Gen 19.15-29	26	Matt 8.23-27
W	Gen 21.5, 8-20	34.1-12	Matt 8.28-end
Th	Gen 22.1-19	116.1-7	Matt 9.1-8
F	Gen 23.1-4, 19; 24.1-8, 62-end	106.1-5	Matt 9.9-13
S	Gen 27.1-5a, 15-29	135.1-6	Matt 9.14-17

WEEK 14 OF YEAR 1

	First Reading	Psalm	Gospel
M	Gen 28.10-end	91.1-10	Matt 9.18-26
T	Gen 32.22-end	17.1-8	Matt 9.32-end
W	Gen 41.55-end; 42.5-7, 17-end	33.1-4, 17-21	Matt 10.1-7
Th	Gen 44.18-21, 23-29; 45.1-5	105.11-17	Matt 10.7-15
F	Gen 46.1-7, 28-30	37.3-6, 27-28	Matt 10.16-23
S	Gen 49.29-end; 50.15-25	105.1-7	Matt 10.24-33

WEEK 15 OF YEAR 1

	First Reading	Psalm	Gospel
M	Exod 1.8-14, 22	124	Matt 10.34—11.1
T	Exod 2.1-15	69.1, 2, 31-end	Matt 11.20-24
W	Exod 3.1-6, 9-12	103.1-7	Matt 11.25-27
Th	Exod 3.13-20	105.1, 2, 23	Matt 11.28-end

	First Reading	Psalm	Gospel
F	Exod 11.10—12.14	116.11-end	Matt 12.1-8
S	Exod 12.37-42	136.1-4, 10-15	Matt 12.14-21

WEEK 16 OF YEAR 1

	First Reading	Psalm	Gospel
M	Exod 14.5-18	136.1-4, 10-15	Matt 12.38-42
T	Exod 14.21—15.1	105.37-44 or Exod 15.1-10	Matt 12.46-end
W	Exod 16.1-5, 9-15	78.16-30	Matt 13.1-9
Th	Exod 19.1, 2, 9-11, 16-20	Bless the Lord	Matt 13.10-17
F	Exod 20.1-17	19.7-11	Matt 13.18-23
S	Exod 24.3-8	50.1-6, 14, 15	Matt 13.24-30

WEEK 17 OF YEAR 1

	First Reading	Psalm	Gospel
M	Exod 32.15-24, 30-34	106.19-23	Matt 13.31-35
T	Exod 33.7-11; 34.5-9, 28	103.8-12	Matt 13.36-43
W	Exod 34.29-end	99	Matt 13.44-46
Th	Exod 40.16-21, 34-end	84.1-7	Matt 13.47-53
F	Lev 23.1, 4-11, 15, 16, 27, 34-37	81.1-8	Matt 13.54-end
S	Lev 25.1, 8-17	67	Matt 14.1-12

WEEK 18 OF YEAR 1

	First Reading	Psalm	Gospel
M	Num 11.4-15	81.11-end	Matt 14.13-21 or 14.22-end
T	Num 12.1-13	51.1-7	Matt 14.22-end or 15.1-2, 10-14
W	Num 13.1, 2, 25—14.1, 26-35	106.14-24	Matt 15.21-28
Th	Num 20.1-13	95.1, 8-end	Matt 16.13-23
F	Deut 4.32-40	77.11-end	Matt 16.24-end
S	Deut 6.4-13	18.1, 2, 48-end	Matt 17.14-20

WEEK 19 OF YEAR 1

	First Reading	Psalm	Gospel
M	Deut 10.12-end	147.12-end	Matt 17.22-end
T	Deut 31.1-8	107.1-3, 42, 43	Matt 18.1-5, 10, 12-14
W	Deut 34	66.15-end	Matt 18.15-20
Th	Josh 3.7-11, 13-17	114	Matt 18.21—19.1
F	Josh 24.1-13	136.1-3, 16-22	Matt 19.3-12
S	Josh 24.14-29	16.1, 6-end	Matt 19.13-15

	First Reading	Psalm	Gospel

WEEK 20 OF YEAR 1

M	Judges 2.11-19	106.35-43	Matt 19.16-22
T	Judges 6.11-24	85.8-end	Matt 19.23-end
W	Judges 9.6-15	21.1-6	Matt 20.1-16
Th	Judges 11.29-end	40.5-13	Matt 22.1-14
F	Ruth 1.1, 3-6, 14-16, 22	146	Matt 22.34-40
S	Ruth 2.1-3, 8-11; 4.13-17	128	Matt 23.1-12

WEEK 21 OF YEAR 1

M	1 Thess 1.2-5, 8-10	149.1-5	Matt 23.13-22
T	1 Thess 2.1-8	139.1-9	Matt 23.23-26
W	1 Thess 2.9-13	126	Matt 23.27-32
Th	1 Thess 3.7-end	90.13-end	Matt 24.42-end
F	1 Thess 4.1-8	97	Matt 25.1-13
S	1 Thess 4.9-12	98.1, 2, 8-end	Matt 25.14-30

WEEK 22 OF YEAR 1

M	1 Thess 4.13-end	96	Luke 4.16-30
T	1 Thess 5.1-6, 9-11	27.1-8	Luke 4.31-37
W	Col 1.1-8	34.11-18	Luke 4.38-end
Th	Col 1.9-14	98.1-5	Luke 5.1-11
F	Col 1.15-20	89.20-29	Luke 5.33-end
S	Col 1.21-23	117	Luke 6.1-5

WEEK 23 OF YEAR 1

M	Col 1.24—2.3	62.1-7	Luke 6.6-11
T	Col 2.6-15	8	Luke 6.12-19
W	Col 3.1-11	15	Luke 6.20-26
Th	Col 3.12-17	149.1-5	Luke 6.27-38
F	1 Tim 1.1, 2, 12-14	16	Luke 6.39-42
S	1 Tim 1.15-17	113	Luke 6.43-end

WEEK 24 OF YEAR 1

M	1 Tim 2.1-8	28	Luke 7.1-10
T	1 Tim 3.1-13	101	Luke 7.11-17
W	1 Tim 3.14-end	111.1-5	Luke 7.31-35
Th	1 Tim 4.12-end	111.6-end	Luke 7.36-end
F	1 Tim 6.2-12	49.1-9	Luke 8.1-3
S	1 Tim 6.13-16	100	Luke 8.4-15

	First Reading	Psalm	Gospel

WEEK 25 OF YEAR 1

	First Reading	Psalm	Gospel
M	Ezra 1.1-6	126	Luke 8.16-18
T	Ezra 6.7, 8, 12, 14-20	124	Luke 8.19-21
W	Ezra 9.5-9	Tob 13.2, 4, 6-8 or	
		Ps 103.1-6	Luke 9.1-6
Th	Hag 1.1-8	149.1-5	Luke 9.7-9
F	Hag 1.15b—2.9	43	Luke 9.18-22
S	Zech 2.1-5, 10, 11	125	Luke 9.43-45

WEEK 26 OF YEAR 1

	First Reading	Psalm	Gospel
M	Zech 8.1-8	102.12-22	Luke 9.46-50
T	Zech 8.20-end	87	Luke 9.51-56
W	Neh 2.1-8	137.1-6	Luke 9.57-end
Th	Neh 8.1-12	19.7-11	Luke 10.1-12
F	Baruch 1.15-end	79.1-9	Luke 10.13-16
S	Baruch 4.5-12, 27-29	69.33-37	Luke 10.17-24

WEEK 27 OF YEAR 1

	First Reading	Psalm	Gospel
M	Jonah 1.1—2.1, 2, 10	Jonah 2.3-5, 8, or	
		Ps 69.1-6	Luke 10.25-37
T	Jonah 3	130	Luke 10.38-end
W	Jonah 4	86.1-9	Luke 11.1-4
Th	Mal 3.13—4.2a	1	Luke 11.5-13
F	Joel 1.13-15; 2.1, 2	9.1-7	Luke 11.15-26
S	Joel 3.12-21	97.1, 8-end	Luke 11.27, 28

WEEK 28 OF YEAR 1

	First Reading	Psalm	Gospel
M	Rom 1.1-7	98	Luke 11.29-32
T	Rom 1.16-25	19.1-4	Luke 11.37-41
W	Rom 2.1-11	62.1-8	Luke 11.42-46
Th	Rom 3.21-30	130	Luke 11.47-end
F	Rom 4.1-8	32	Luke 12.1-7
S	Rom 4.13, 16-18	105.6-10, 41-44	Luke 12.8-12

WEEK 29 OF YEAR 1

	First Reading	Psalm	Gospel
M	Rom 4.20-end	Benedictus 1-6	Luke 12.13-21
T	Rom 5.12, 15, 17-end	40.8-14	Luke 12.35-38
W	Rom 6.12-18	124	Luke 12.39-48
Th	Rom 6.19-end	1	Luke 12.49-53
F	Rom 7.18-end	119.33-40	Luke 12.54-end
S	Rom 8.1-11	24.1-6	Luke 13.1-9

	First Reading	Psalm	Gospel

WEEK 30 OF YEAR 1

	First Reading	Psalm	Gospel
M	Rom 8.12-17	68.1-6, 20	Luke 13.10-17
T	Rom 8.18-25	126	Luke 13.18-21
W	Rom 8.26-30	13	Luke 13.22-30
Th	Rom 8.31-end	109.20, 21	Luke 13.31-end
F	Rom 9.1-5	147.12-end	Luke 14.1-6
S	Rom 11.1, 2, 11, 12, 25-29	94.14-19	Luke 14.1, 7-11

WEEK 31 OF YEAR 1

	First Reading	Psalm	Gospel
M	Rom 11.29-end	69.31-37	Luke 14.12-14
T	Rom 12.5-16	131	Luke 14.15-24
W	Rom 13.8-10	112	Luke 14.25-33
Th	Rom 14.7-12	27.13-16	Luke 15.1-10
F	Rom 15.14-21	98	Luke 16.1-8
S	Rom 16.3-9, 16, 22-end	145.1-7	Luke 16.9-15

WEEK 32 OF YEAR 1

	First Reading	Psalm	Gospel
M	Wisdom 1.1-7	139.1-9	Luke 17.1-6
T	Wisdom 2.23—3.9	34.1-6	Luke 17.7-10
W	Wisdom 6.1-11	82	Luke 17.11-19
Th	Wisdom 7.22—8.1	119.89-96	Luke 17.20-25
F	Wisdom 13.1-9	19.1-4	Luke 17.26-end
S	Wisdom 18.14-16; 19.6-9	105.1-5, 35-42	Luke 18.1-8

WEEK 33 OF YEAR 1

	First Reading	Psalm	Gospel
M	1 Macc 1.10-15, 41-43, 54-57, 62-64	79.1-5	Luke 18.35-end
T	2 Macc 6.18-end	11	Luke 19.1-10
W	2 Macc 7.1, 20-31	116.11-end	Luke 19.11-28
Th	1 Macc 2.15-29	129	Luke 19.41-44
F	1 Macc 4.36, 37, 52-59	122	Luke 19.45-end
S	1 Macc 6.1-13	124	Luke 20.27-40

WEEK 34 OF YEAR 1

	First Reading	Psalm	Gospel
M	Dan 1.1-6, 8-20	Bless the Lord	Luke 21.1-4
T	Dan 2.31-45	Benedicite 1-4	Luke 21.5-11
W	Dan 5.1-6, 13, 14, 16, 17, 23-28	Benedicite 5-11	Luke 21.12-19
Th	Dan 6.12-end	Benedicite 9-13	Luke 21.20-28
F	Dan 7.2-14	Benedicite 13-17	Luke 21.29-33
S	Dan 7.15-27	Benedicite 18-end	Luke 21.34-36

YEAR 2

	First Reading	Psalm	Gospel
WEEK 1 OF YEAR 2			
M	1 Sam 1.1-8	116.11-16	Mark 1.14-20
T	1 Sam 1.9-20	1 Sam 2.1, 4-8 or Magnificat	Mark 1.21-28
W	1 Sam 3.1-10, 19-20	40.1-5, 8-11	Mark 1.29-39
Th	1 Sam 4.1-11	44.10-15, 24, 25	Mark 1.40-end
F	1 Sam 8.4-7, 10-end	89.15-18	Mark 2.1-12
S	1 Sam 9.1-4, 17-19; 10.1	21.1-6	Mark 2.13-17
WEEK 2 OF YEAR 2			
M	1 Sam 15.16-23	50.8-10, 16, 17, 24	Mark 2.18-22
T	1 Sam 16.1-13	89.19-27	Mark 2.23-end
W	1 Sam 17.32, 33, 37, 40-51	144.1, 2, 9, 10	Mark 3.1-6
Th	1 Sam 18.6-9; 19.1-7	56.1, 2, 8-end	Mark 3.7-12
F	1 Sam 24.3-22a	57.1, 2, 8-end	Mark 3.13-19
S	2 Sam 1.1-4, 11, 12, 17-19, 23-end	80.1-6	Mark 3.20, 21
WEEK 3 OF YEAR 2			
M	2 Sam 5.1-7, 10	89.19-27	Mark 3.22-30
T	2 Sam 6.12-15, 17-19	24.7-end	Mark 3.31-end
W	2 Sam 7.4-17	89.19-27	Mark 4.1-20
Th	2 Sam 7.18, 19, 24-end	132.1-4, 10-14	Mark 4.21-25
F	2 Sam 11.1-10, 13-17	51.1-5, 8	Mark 4.26-34
S	2 Sam 12.1-7, 10-17	51.10-15	Mark 4.35-end
WEEK 4 OF YEAR 2			
M	2 Sam 15.13, 14, 30; 16.5-13	3	Mark 5.1-20
T	2 Sam 18.9, 10, 14, 24, 25, 30—19.3	86.1-6	Mark 5.21-end
W	2 Sam 24.2, 9-17	32.1-8	Mark 6.1-6
Th	1 Kings 2.1-4, 10-12	1 Chron 29.10-12 or Ps 145.1-5	Mark 6.7-13
F	Ecclus 47.2-11	18.32-37, 52	Mark 6.14-29
S	1 Kings 3.4-13	119.9-16	Mark 6.30-34

	First Reading	Psalm	Gospel

WEEK 5 OF YEAR 2

	First Reading	Psalm	Gospel
M	1 Kings 8.1-7, 9-13	132.1-9	Mark 6.53-end
T	1 Kings 8.22, 23, 27-30	84.1-10	Mark 7.1-13
W	1 Kings 10.1-10	37.3-6, 30-32	Mark 7.14-23
Th	1 Kings 11.4-13	106.3, 36-42	Mark 7.24-30
F	1 Kings 11.29-32; 12.19	81.8-14	Mark 7.31-end
S	1 Kings 12.26-32; 13.33, 34	106.6, 7, 20-23	Mark 8.1-10

WEEK 6 OF YEAR 2

	First Reading	Psalm	Gospel
M	James 1.1-11	119.65-72	Mark 8.11-13
T	James 1.12-18	94.12-18	Mark 8.14-21
W	James 1.19-end	15	Mark 8.22-26
Th	James 2.1-9	34.1-7	Mark 8.27-33
F	James 2.14-24, 26	112	Mark 8.34—9.1
S	James 3.1-10	12.1-7	Mark 9.2-13

WEEK 7 OF YEAR 2

	First Reading	Psalm	Gospel
M	James 3.13-end	19.7-end	Mark 9.14-29
T	James 4.1-10	55.6-8, 25	Mark 9.30-37
W	James 4.13-end	49.1-6, 16-18	Mark 9.38-40
Th	James 5.1-6	49.12-19	Mark 9.41-end
F	James 5.9-12	103.1-4, 8-13	Mark 10.1-12
S	James 5.13-end	141.1-4	Mark 10.13-16

WEEK 8 OF YEAR 2

	First Reading	Psalm	Gospel
M	1 Peter 1.3-9	111	Mark 10.17-27
T	1 Peter 1.10-16	98.1-5	Mark 10.28-31
W	1 Peter 1.18-end	147.12-end	Mark 10.32-45
Th	1 Peter 2.2-5, 9-12	100	Mark 10.46-end
F	1 Peter 4.7-13	96.10-end	Mark 11.11-26
S	Jude 17, 20-end	63.1-6	Mark 11.27-end

WEEK 9 OF YEAR 2

	First Reading	Psalm	Gospel
M	2 Peter 1.2-7	91.1, 2, 14-16	Mark 12.1-12
T	2 Peter 3.11-15, 17, 18	90.12-17	Mark 12.13-17
W	2 Tim 1.1-3, 6-12	123	Mark 12.18-27
Th	2 Tim 2.8-15	25.4-12	Mark 12.28-34
F	2 Tim 3.10-end	119.161-168	Mark 12.35-37
S	2 Tim 4.1-8	71.7-16	Mark 12.38-end

	First Reading	Psalm	Gospel

WEEK 10 OF YEAR 2

	First Reading	Psalm	Gospel
M	1 Kings 17.1-6	121	Matt 5.1-12
T	1 Kings 17.7-16	4	Matt 5.13-16
W	1 Kings 18.20-39	16.1, 6-end	Matt 5.17-19
Th	1 Kings 18.41-end	65.8-end	Matt 5.20-26
F	1 Kings 19.9, 11-16	27.8-16	Matt 5.27-32
S	1 Kings 19.19-end	16.1-7	Matt 5.33-37

WEEK 11 OF YEAR 2

M	1 Kings 21.1-16	5.1-5	Matt 5.38-42
T	1 Kings 21.17-end	51.1-9	Matt 5.43-end
W	2 Kings 2.1, 6-14	31.21-end	Matt 6.1-6, 16-18
Th	Ecclus 48.1-14	97.1-8	Matt 6.7-15
F	2 Kings 11.1-4, 9-18, 20	132.1-4,10-12	Matt 6.19-23
S	2 Chron 24.17-25	89.25-33	Matt 6.24-end

WEEK 12 OF YEAR 2

M	2 Kings 17.5-8, 13-15, 18	60.1-5, 11, 12	Matt 7.1-5
T	2 Kings 19.9-11, 14-21a, 31-36	48.1, 2, 8-13	Matt 7.6, 12-14
W	2 Kings 22.8-13; 23.1-3	119.33-40	Matt 7.15-20
Th	2 Kings 24.8-17	79.1-9, 11	Matt 7.21-end
F	2 Kings 25.1-12	137.1-6	Matt 8.1-4
S	Lam 2.2, 10-14, 18, 19	74.1-3, 22, 23	Matt 8.5-17

WEEK 13 OF YEAR 2

M	Amos 2.6-10, 13-end	50.16-23	Matt 8.18-22
T	Amos 3.1-8; 4.11, 12	5.7-end	Matt 8.23-27
W	Amos 5.14, 15, 21-24	50.7-14	Matt 8.28-end
Th	Amos 7.10-end	19.7-10	Matt 9.1-8
F	Amos 8.4-6, 9-12	119.1-8	Matt 9.9-13
S	Amos 9.11-end	85.8-13	Matt 9.14-17

WEEK 14 OF YEAR 2

M	Hosea 2.16-18, 21, 22	145.2-9	Matt 9.18-26
T	Hosea 8.4-7, 11-13	103.8-12	Matt 9.32-end
W	Hosea 10.1-3, 7, 8, 12	115.3-10	Matt 10.1-7
Th	Hosea 11.1, 3, 4, 8, 9	105.1-7	Matt 10.7-15
F	Hosea 14.2-end	80.1-7	Matt 10.16-23
S	Isa 6.1-8	51.1-7	Matt 10.24-33

	First Reading	Psalm	Gospel
WEEK 15 OF YEAR 2			
M	Isa 1.11-17	50.7-15	Matt 10.34—11.1
T	Isa 7.1-9	48.1-7	Matt 11.20-24
W	Isa 10.5-7, 13-16	94.5-11	Matt 11.25-27
Th	Isa 26.7-9, 16-19	102.13-20	Matt 11.28-end
F	Isa 38.1-6, 21, 22, 7, 8	Isa 38.10-16 or Ps 32.1-8	Matt 12.1-8
S	Micah 2.1-5	10.1-5, 13	Matt 12.14-21
WEEK 16 OF YEAR 2			
M	Micah 6.1-4, 6-8	50.3-7, 14	Matt 12.38-42
T	Micah 7.14, 15, 18-end	85.1-7	Matt 12.46-end
W	Jer 1.1, 4-10	70	Matt 13.1-9
Th	Jer 2.1-3, 7, 8, 12, 13	36.5-10	Matt 13.10-17
F	Jer 3.14-17	23 or Jer 31.10-13	Matt 13.18-23
S	Jer 7.1-11	84.1-7	Matt 13.24-30
WEEK 17 OF YEAR 2			
M	Jer 13.1-11	82 or Deut 31.18-21	Matt 13.31-35
T	Jer 14.17-end	79.8-end	Matt 13.36-43
W	Jer 15.10, 16-end	59.1-4, 18-end	Matt 13.44-46
Th	Jer 18.1-6	146.1-5	Matt 13.47-53
F	Jer 26.1-9	69.4-9	Matt 13.54-end
S	Jer 26.11-16, 24	69.13-19	Matt 14.1-12
WEEK 18 OF YEAR 2			
M	Jer 28	119.89-96	Matt 14.13-21 or 14.22-end
T	Jer 30.1, 2, 12-15, 18-22	102.16-21	Matt 14.22-end or 15.1-2, 10-14
W	Jer 31.1-7	121	Matt 15.21-28
Th	Jer 31.31-34	51.10-17	Matt 16.13-23
F	Nah 2.1, 3; 3.1-3, 6, 7	137.1-6 or Deut 32.35-36, 39, 41	Matt 16.24-end
S	Hab 1.12—2.4	9.7-11	Matt 17.14-20

	First Reading	Psalm	Gospel

WEEK 19 OF YEAR 2

	First Reading	Psalm	Gospel
M	Ezek 1.2-5, 24-end	148.1-4, 12, 13	Matt 17.22-end
T	Ezek 2.8—3.4	119.65-72	Matt 18.1-5, 10, 12-14
W	Ezek 9.1-7; 10.18-22	113	Matt 18.15-20
Th	Ezek 12.1-12	78.57-62	Matt 18.21—19.1
F	Ezek 16.1-15, 60-end	118.14-18	Matt 19.3-12
S	Ezek 18.1-10, 13, 30, 32	51.1-3, 15-17	Matt 19.13-15

WEEK 20 OF YEAR 2

	First Reading	Psalm	Gospel
M	Ezek 24.15-24	78.1-8	Matt 19.16-22
T	Ezek 28.1-10	107.1-3, 40, 43	Matt 19.23-end
W	Ezek 34.1-11	23	Matt 20.1-16
Th	Ezek 36.23-28	51.7-12	Matt 22.1-14
F	Ezek 37.1-14	107.1-8	Matt 22.34-40
S	Ezek 43.1-7	85.7-13	Matt 23.1-12

WEEK 21 OF YEAR 2

	First Reading	Psalm	Gospel
M	2 Thess 1.1-5, 11, 12	39.1-9	Matt 23.13-22
T	2 Thess 2.1-3a, 14-17	98	Matt 23.23-26
W	2 Thess 3.6-10, 16-end	128	Matt 23.27-32
Th	1 Cor 1.1-9	145.1-7	Matt 24.42-end
F	1 Cor 1.17-25	33.6-12	Matt 25.1-13
S	1 Cor 1.26-end	33.12-14, 19-end	Matt 25.14-30

WEEK 22 OF YEAR 2

	First Reading	Psalm	Gospel
M	1 Cor 2.1-5	33.12-21	Luke 4.16-30
T	1 Cor 2.10-end	145.10-17	Luke 4.31-37
W	1 Cor 3.1-9	62	Luke 4.38-end
Th	1 Cor 3.18-end	24.1-6	Luke 5.1-11
F	1 Cor 4.1-5	37.3-8	Luke 5.33-end
S	1 Cor 4.6-15	145.17-end	Luke 6.1-5

WEEK 23 OF YEAR 2

	First Reading	Psalm	Gospel
M	1 Cor 5.1-8	5.4-8	Luke 6.6-11
T	1 Cor 6.1-11	149.1-5	Luke 6.12-19
W	1 Cor 7.25-31	45.11-end	Luke 6.20-26
Th	1 Cor 8.1-7, 11-end	139.1-9	Luke 6.27-38
F	1 Cor 9.16-19, 22-end	84.1-7	Luke 6.39-42
S	1 Cor 10.14-22	116.11-end	Luke 6.43-end

	First Reading	Psalm	Gospel

WEEK 24 OF YEAR 2

	First Reading	Psalm	Gospel
M	1 Cor 11.17-26, 33	40.8-13	Luke 7.1-10
T	1 Cor 12.12-14, 27-end	100	Luke 7.11-17
W	1 Cor 12.31b—13 end	33.1-12	Luke 7.31-35
Th	1 Cor 15.1-11	118.1, 2, 17-20	Luke 7.36-end
F	1 Cor 15.12-20	17.1-8	Luke 8.1-3
S	1 Cor 15.35-37, 42-49	30.1-5	Luke 8.4-15

WEEK 25 OF YEAR 2

	First Reading	Psalm	Gospel
M	Prov 3.27-34	15	Luke 8.16-18
T	Prov 21.1-6, 10-13	119.1-8	Luke 8.19-21
W	Prov 30.5-9	119.105-112	Luke 9.1-6
Th	Eccles 1.2-11	90.1-6	Luke 9.7-9
F	Eccles 3.1-11	144.1-4	Luke 9.18-22
S	Eccles 11.9—12.8	90.1, 2, 12-17	Luke 9.43-45

WEEK 26 OF YEAR 2

	First Reading	Psalm	Gospel
M	Job 1.6-end	17.1-11	Luke 9.46-50
T	Job 3.1-3, 11-17, 20-23	88.13-18	Luke 9.51-56
W	Job 9.1-12, 14-16	88.1-5, 10	Luke 9.57-end
Th	Job 19.21-27a	27.13-16	Luke 10.1-12
F	Job 38.1, 12-21; 40.3-5	139.6-11	Luke 10.13-16
S	Job 42.1-3, 6, 12-end	119.169-176	Luke 10.17-24

WEEK 27 OF YEAR 2

	First Reading	Psalm	Gospel
M	Gal 1.6-12	111.1-6	Luke 10.25-37
T	Gal 1.13-end	139.1-9	Luke 10.38-end
W	Gal 2.1, 2, 7-14	117	Luke 11.1-4
Th	Gal 3.1-5	Benedictus	Luke 11.5-13
F	Gal 3.7-14	111.4-10	Luke 11.15-26
S	Gal 3.22-end	105.1-7	Luke 11.27, 28

WEEK 28 OF YEAR 2

	First Reading	Psalm	Gospel
M	Gal 4.21-24, 26, 27, 31; 5.1	113	Luke 11.29-32
T	Gal 5.1-6	119.41-48	Luke 11.37-41
W	Gal 5.18-end	1	Luke 11.42-46
Th	Eph 1.1, 3-10	98.1-4	Luke 11.47-end
F	Eph 1.11-14	33.1-6, 12	Luke 12.1-7
S	Eph 1.15-end	8	Luke 12.8-12

	First Reading	**Psalm**	**Gospel**

WEEK 29 OF YEAR 2

M	Eph 2.1-10	100	Luke 12.13-21
T	Eph 2.12-end	85.7-end	Luke 12.35-38
W	Eph 3.2-12	98	Luke 12.39-48
Th	Eph 3.14-end	33.1-6	Luke 12.49-53
F	Eph 4.1-6	24.1-6	Luke 12.54-end
S	Eph 4.7-16	122	Luke 13.1-9

WEEK 30 OF YEAR 2

M	Eph 4.32—5.8	1	Luke 13.10-17
T	Eph 5.21-end	128	Luke 13.18-21
W	Eph 6.1-9	145.10-19	Luke 13.22-30
Th	Eph 6.10-20	144.1, 2, 9-11	Luke 13.31-end
F	Phil 1.1-11	111	Luke 14.1-6
S	Phil 1.18-26	42.1-7	Luke 14.1, 7-11

WEEK 31 OF YEAR 2

M	Phil 2.1-4	131	Luke 14.12-14
T	Phil 2.5-11	22.23-28	Luke 14.15-24
W	Phil 2.12-18	27.1-5	Luke 14.25-33
Th	Phil 3.3-8	105.1-7	Luke 15.1-10
F	Phil 3.17—4.1	122	Luke 16.1-8
S	Phil 4.10-19	112	Luke 16.9-15

WEEK 32 OF YEAR 2

M	Titus 1.1-9	24.1-6	Luke 17.1-6
T	Titus 2.1-8, 11-14	37.3-5, 30-32	Luke 17.7-10
W	Titus 3.1-7	23	Luke 17.11-19
Th	Philemon 7-20	146.5-end	Luke 17.20-25
F	2 John 4-9	119.1-8	Luke 17.26-end
S	3 John 5-8	112	Luke 18.1-8

WEEK 33 OF YEAR 2

M	Rev 1.1-4; 2.1-5	1	Luke 18.35-end
T	Rev 3.1-6, 14-end	15	Luke 19.1-10
W	Rev 4	150	Luke 19.11-28
Th	Rev 5.1-10	149.1-5	Luke 19.41-44
F	Rev 10.8-11	119.65-72	Luke 19.45-end
S	Rev 11.4-12	144.1-9	Luke 20.27-40

	First Reading	Psalm	Gospel

WEEK 34 OF YEAR 2

	First Reading	Psalm	Gospel
M	Rev 14.1-5	24.1-6	Luke 21.1-4
T	Rev 14.14-19	96	Luke 21.5-11
W	Rev 15.1-4	98	Luke 21.12-19
Th	Rev 18.1, 2, 21-23;		
	19.1-3, 9	100	Luke 21.20-28
F	Rev 20.1-4, 11—21.2	84.1-7	Luke 21.29-33
S	Rev 22.1-7	95.1-7	Luke 21.34-36

TABLE 5 / SUNDAY THEMES

These Sunday themes are to be understood as guides for those who wish to follow them.

9th Sunday before Christmas	*The Creation*
8th Sunday before Christmas	*The Fall*
7th Sunday before Christmas	*The Election of God's People: Abraham*
6th Sunday before Christmas	*The Promise of Redemption: Moses*
5th Sunday before Christmas	*The Remnant of Israel*

1st Sunday in Advent	*The Advent Hope*
2nd Sunday in Advent	*The Word of God in the Old Testament*
3rd Sunday in Advent	*The Forerunner*
4th Sunday in Advent	*The Annunciation*

1st Sunday after Christmas	*The Incarnation*
2nd Sunday after Christmas	*The Holy Family*

1st Sunday after the Epiphany	*Revelation: The Baptism of Jesus*
2nd Sunday after the Epiphany	*Revelation: The First Disciples*
3rd Sunday after the Epiphany	*Revelation: Signs of Glory*
4th Sunday after the Epiphany	*Revelation: The New Temple*
5th Sunday after the Epiphany	*Revelation: The Wisdom of God*
6th Sunday after the Epiphany	*Revelation: Parables*

9th Sunday before Easter	*Christ the Teacher*
8th Sunday before Easter	*Christ the Healer*
7th Sunday before Easter	*Christ the Friend of Sinners*

1st Sunday in Lent	*The King and the Kingdom: Temptation*
2nd Sunday in Lent	*The King and the Kingdom: Conflict*
3rd Sunday in Lent	*The King and the Kingdom: Suffering*
4th Sunday in Lent	*The King and the Kingdom: Transfiguration*
5th Sunday in Lent	*The King and the Kingdom: The Victory of the Cross*
Palm Sunday	*The Way of the Cross*

Easter Day	
1st Sunday after Easter	*The Upper Room/The Bread of Life*
2nd Sunday after Easter	*The Emmaus Road/The Good Shepherd*
3rd Sunday after Easter	*The Lakeside/The Resurrection and the Life*
4th Sunday after Easter	*The Charge to Peter/The Way, the Truth, and the Life*
5th Sunday after Easter	*Going to the Father*
Sunday after Ascension Day	*The Ascension of Christ*

Pentecost

Trinity Sunday

2nd Sunday after Pentecost (Trinity 1)   *The People of God/The Church's Unity and Fellowship*

3rd Sunday after Pentecost (Trinity 2)   *The Life of the Baptized/The Church's Confidence in Christ*

4th Sunday after Pentecost (Trinity 3)   *The Freedom of the Sons of God/The Church's Mission to the Individual*

5th Sunday after Pentecost (Trinity 4)   *The New Law/The Church's Mission to All Men*

6th Sunday after Pentecost (Trinity 5)   *The New Man*

7th Sunday after Pentecost (Trinity 6)   *The More Excellent Way*

8th Sunday after Pentecost (Trinity 7)   *The Fruit of the Spirit*

9th Sunday after Pentecost (Trinity 8)   *The Whole Armour of God*

10th Sunday after Pentecost (Trinity 9)   *The Mind of Christ*

11th Sunday after Pentecost (Trinity 10)   *The Serving Community*

12th Sunday after Pentecost (Trinity 11)   *The Witnessing Community*

13th Sunday after Pentecost (Trinity 12)   *The Suffering Community*

14th Sunday after Pentecost (Trinity 13)   *The Family*

15th Sunday after Pentecost (Trinity 14)   *Those in Authority*

16th Sunday after Pentecost (Trinity 15)   *The Neighbour*

17th Sunday after Pentecost (Trinity 16)   *The Proof of Faith*

18th Sunday after Pentecost (Trinity 17)   *The Offering of Life*

19th Sunday after Pentecost (Trinity 18)   *The Life of Faith*

20th Sunday after Pentecost (Trinity 19)   *Endurance*

21st Sunday after Pentecost (Trinity 20)   *The Christian Hope*

22nd Sunday after Pentecost (Trinity 21)   *The Two Ways*

Last Sunday after Pentecost   *Citizens of Heaven*

The Liturgical Psalter

PSALM 1

1 Blessèd is the man who has not walked ⌣
in the counsel ❘ of the · un❘godly:
  nor followed the way of sinners
  nor taken his ❘ seat a❘mongst the ❘ scornful.

2 But his delight is in the ❘ law · of the ❘ Lord:
  and on that law will he ❘ ponder ❘ day and ❘ night.

3 He is like a tree planted beside ❘ streams of ❘ water:
  that yields its ❘ fruit in ❘ due ❘ season.

4 Its leaves also ❘ shall not ❘ wither:
  and look what❘ever · he ❘ does · it shall ❘ prosper.

5 As for the ungodly * it is not ❘ so with ❘ them:
  they are like the ❘ chaff · which the ❘ wind ❘ scatters.

6 Therefore the ungodly shall not stand ❘ up · at the ❘
judgement:
  nor sinners in the congre❘gation ❘ of the ❘ righteous.

†7 For the Lord cares for the ❘ way · of the ❘ righteous:
  but the ❘ way of · the un❘godly · shall ❘ perish.

PSALM 2

1 Why are the ❘ nations · in ❘ tumult:
  and why do the peoples ❘ cherish · a ❘ vain ❘ dream?

2 The kings of the earth rise up
and the rulers con❘spire to❘gether:
  against the Lord and a❘gainst · his an❘ointed ❘ saying,

†3 'Let us break their ❘ bonds a❘sunder:
  let us throw ❘ off their ❘ chains ❘ from us.'

4 He that dwells in heaven shall ❘ laugh them · to ❘ scorn:
  the Lord will ❘ hold them ❘ in de❘rision.

5 Then will he speak to them in his wrath
and terrify them ❘ in his ❘ fury:
  'I the Lord have set up my king on ❘ Zion · my ❘
holy ❘ hill.'

6   I will announce the Lord's decree
     that which | he has | spoken:
       'You are my son   this | day have | I be|gotten you.

7   'Ask of me
     and I will give you the nations for ˙ your in|heritance:
       the uttermost parts of the | earth for | your pos|session.

†8   'You shall break them with a | rod of | iron:
     and shatter them in | pieces · like a | potter's | vessel.'

9   Now therefore be | wise O | kings:
     be advised   you that are | judges | of the | earth.

10   Serve the Lord with awe
     and govern yourselves in | fear and | trembling:
       lest he be angry and you | perish | in your | course.

†11   For his wrath is | quickly | kindled:
     blessèd are those that | turn to | him for | refuge.

PSALM 3

1   Lord how numerous | are my | enemies:
     many they | are that | rise a|gainst me.

2   Many there are that | talk of me · and | say:
     'There is no | help for · him | in his | God.'

3   But you Lord are about me | as a | shield:
     you are my glory   and the | lifter | up · of my | head.

4   I cry to the Lord with a | loud | voice:
     and he answers me | from his | holy | hill.

5   I lay myself | down and | sleep:
     I wake again be|cause the | Lord sus|tains me.

6   Therefore I will not be afraid ‿
     of the multitudes | of the | nations:
       who have set themselves a|gainst me · on | every | side.

7   Arise Lord   and deliver me | O my | God:
     for you will strike all my enemies upon the cheek
     you will | break the | teeth of · the un|godly.

8   Deliverance be|longs · to the | Lord:
       O let your | blessing · be up|on your | people.

PSALM 4

1   Answer me when I call O | God of · my | righteousness:
       when I was hard-pressed you set me free
       be gracious to me | now and | hear my | prayer.

2   Sons of men   how long will you turn my | glory ·
to my | shame:
       how long will you love what is worthless
       and | seek | after | lies?

3   Know that the Lord has shown me
       his | wonder·ful | kindness:
       when I call to the | Lord | he will | hear me.

4   Tremble and | do no | sin:
       commune with your own heart
       up|on your | bed · and be | still.

5   Offer the sacrifices | that are | right:
       and | put your | trust · in the | Lord.

6   There are many who say   'Who will |
show us · any | good?
       the light of your countenance O | Lord has | gone |
       from us.'

7   Yet you have given my | heart more | gladness:
       than they have when their corn | wine and |
       oil in|crease.

8   In peace I will lie | down and | sleep:
       for you alone Lord | make me | dwell in | safety.

PSALM 5

1   Hear my words O Lord   give | heed · to my | groaning:
       listen to my cry   you that are my | king |
       and my | God.

2   In the morning when I pray to you
surely you will **|** hear my **|** voice:
    at daybreak I lay my prayers be **|** fore you ·
    and **⌈** look **|** up.

3   For you are not a God who takes **|** pleasure ·
in **|** wickedness:
    nor can any **|** evil **|** dwell with **|** you.

4   The boastful cannot **|** stand in · your **|** sight:
    you hate all **|** those that **|** work **|** mischief.

5   Those who speak **|** lies · you des **|** troy:
    you abhor the treacherous O Lord
    and **|** those · that are **|** stained with **|** blood.

6   But because of your great goodness
I will **|** come into · your **|** house:
    I will bow down toward your holy **|**
    temple · in **|** awe and **|** fear of you.

7   Lead me O Lord in your righteousness
for my enemies **|** lie in **|** wait:
    make **|** straight your **|** way be **|** fore me.

8   For there is no **|** truth · in their **|** mouth:
    and within they are **|** eaten **|** up by **|** malice.

9   Their throat is an **|** open **|** sepulchre:
    and their tongue speaks **|** smooth and **|**
    flatter·ing **|** words.

10   Destroy them O God * let them fall by their **|**
own con **|** triving:
    cast them out for their many offences
    for **|** they have · re **|** belled a **|** gainst you.

11   But let all who put their trust in **|** you re **|** joice:
    let them **|** shout with **|** joy for **|** ever.

12   Be the defender of those who **|** love your **|** name:
    let them ex **|** ult be **|** cause of **|** you.

✝13 For you will bless O Lord the **|** man · that is **|** righteous:
    you will cover him with your **|** favour **|**
    as · with a **|** shield.

PSALM 6

1 O Lord rebuke me not in your ˈ indigˈnation:
   nor chasten me ˈ in your ˈ fierce disˈpleasure.

2 Have mercy upon me O Lord for ˈ I am ˈ weak:
   O Lord heal me for my ˈ very ˈ bones · are aˈfraid.

3 My soul also is ˈ greatly ˈ troubled:
   and you Lord how ˈ long will ˈ you deˈlay?

4 Turn again O Lord and deˈliver · my ˈ soul:
   O save me ˈ for your ˈ mercy's ˈ sake.

5 For in death ˈ no man · reˈmembers you:
   and who can ˈ give you ˈ thanks · from the ˈ grave?

6 I am wearied ˈ with my ˈ groaning:
   every night I drown my bed with weeping
   and ˈ water · my ˈ couch · with my ˈ tears.

†7 My eyes waste aˈway for ˈ sorrow:
   they grow dim beˈcause of ˈ all my ˈ enemies.

8 Away from me all ˈ you that · do ˈ evil:
   for the Lord has ˈ heard the ˈ voice · of my ˈ weeping.

9 The Lord has heard my ˈ suppliˈcation:
   the ˈ Lord · will reˈceive my ˈ prayer.

†10 All my enemies shall be put to shame and ˈ
   greatly · disˈmayed:
     they shall turn back and be conˈfounded ˈ
     in a ˈ moment.

PSALM 7

1 O Lord my God   to you have I ˈ come for ˈ shelter:
   save me from all who pursue me
   O ˈ save ˈ and deˈliver me,

2 lest like lions they ˈ tear my ˈ throat:
   lest they carry me ˈ off and ˈ none can ˈ save me.

3   O Lord my God   if I have **|** done · such a **|** thing:
    if there is any **|** wicked·ness **|** on my **|** hands,

4   if I have repaid with evil him that **|** was my **|** friend:
    or plundered my **|** enemy · with **|** out just **|** cause,

† 5 then let the enemy pursue me and **|** over **|** take me:
    let him trample my life to the ground
    and lay my **|** honour **|** in the **|** dust.

6   Arise O **|** Lord · in your **|** anger:
    rise up in **|** wrath a **|** gainst my **|** adversaries.

7   Awake my God * you that or **|** dain **|** justice:
    and let the assembly of the **|** peoples **|**
    gather · a **|** bout you;

8   take your seat **|** high a **|** bove them:
    and sit in judgement O **|** Lord **|** over · the **|** nations.

9   Judge for me O Lord   according **|** to my **|**
    righteousness:
    and **|** as · my in **|** tegrity · re **|** quires.

10 Let the wickedness of the ungodly cease
    but es **|** tablish · the **|** righteous:
    for you try the very hearts and minds of **|**
    men O **|** righteous **|** God.

11 God is my **|** shield **|** over me:
    he pre **|** serves the **|** true of **|** heart.

12 God is a **|** righteous **|** judge:
    and God condemns **|** evil **|** every **|** day.

13 If a man does not turn he **|** whets his **|** sword:
    he bends his **|** bow and **|** makes it **|** ready;

† 14 he prepares the **|** instruments · of **|** death:
    and makes his **|** arrows **|** darts of **|** fire.

15 See how the ungodly con **|** ceives **|** mischief:
    how he swells with wickedness **|** and gives **|**
    birth to **|** lies.

16 He digs a pit and **|** hollows · it **|** out:
    but falls himself into the **|** trap · he had **|**
    made for **|** others.

17   His mischief rebounds upon his ˈ own ˈ head:
        and his violence comes ˈ down · on his ˈ own ˈ pate.

18   I will thank the ˈ Lord · for his ˈ justice:
        I will sing ˈ praises · to the ˈ Lord Most ˈ High.

PSALM 8

1   O ˈ Lord our ˈ Governor:
        how glorious is your ˈ name in ˈ all the ˈ earth!

2   Your majesty above the heavens is ˈ yet reˈcounted:
        by the ˈ mouths of ˈ babes and ˈ sucklings.

†3   You have founded a strong defence‿
        a ˈgainst your ˈ adversaries:
        to quell the ˈ ene·my ˈ and · the a ˈvenger.

4   When I consider your heavens the ˈ work of ·
        your ˈ fingers:
        the moon and the stars which ˈ you have ˈ
        set in ˈ order,

5   what is man   that you should be ˈ mindful ˈ of him:
        or the son of ˈ man that ˈ you should ˈ care for him?

6   Yet you have made him little ˈ less · than a ˈ god:
        and have ˈ crowned him · with ˈ glory · and ˈ honour.

7   You have made him the ˈ master · of your ˈ handiwork:
        and have put all things in sub ˈjection · be ˈneath
        his ˈ feet,

8   all ˈ sheep and ˈ oxen:
        and all the ˈ creatures ˈ of the ˈ field,

9   the birds of the air and the ˈ fish · of the ˈ sea:
        and everything that moves‿
        in the pathways ˈ of the ˈ great ˈ waters.

†10   O ˈ Lord our ˈ Governor:
        how glorious is your ˈ name in ˈ all the ˈ earth!

PSALM 9

1   I will give you thanks O Lord with my | whole | heart:
      I will tell of all the | wonders | you have | done.

2   I will re |joice · and be | glad in you:
      I will make my songs to your | name | O Most | High.

3   For my enemies are | driven | back:
      they stumble and | perish | at your | presence.

4   You have maintained my | cause · and my | right:
      you sat en |throned · as a | righteous | judge.

5   You rebuked the heathen nations
      you brought the | wicked · to de |struction:
      you blotted out their | name for | ever · and | ever.

6   The strongholds of the enemy are made a perpetual |
      deso |lation:
      you plucked up their cities‿
      and | even · their | memory · has | perished.

7   The Lord confounds them * but the Lord en |dures
      for | ever:
      he has | set up · his | throne for | judgement.

8   He shall judge the | world with | righteousness:
      and deal true | justice | to the | peoples.

9   The Lord is a strong tower to | him that · is op |pressed:
      he is a tower of | strength in | time of | need.

10   All who heed your name will | trust in | you:
      for you have never for |saken | those that | seek you.

11   O sing praises to the Lord who | dwells in | Zion:
      tell among the peoples what | great things |
      he has | done.

12   For he that avenges blood has re |membered · the | poor:
      he has | not for |gotten · their | cry.

13 The Lord has been merciful toward me
 he saw what I **|** suffered · from my **|** foes:
  he raised me up a **|** gain · from the **|** gates of **|** death,

14 that I might tell all your praises in the **|** gates of **|** Zion:
  that I might re **|** joice in **|** your de **|** liverance.

15 The nations have sunk into the pit they **|**
 dug for **|** others:
  in the very snare they **|** laid · is their **|** foot **|** taken;

16 the Lord has declared himself and up **|** held the **|** right:
  the wicked are trapped in the **|** work · of their **|**
 own **|** hands.

17 The wicked shall be given **|** over · to **|** death:
  and all the nations **|** that for **|** get **|** God.

18 For the needy shall not always **|** be for **|** gotten:
  nor shall the hope of the **|** poor **|** perish · for **|** ever.

19 Arise Lord   let not **|** man pre **|** vail:
  let the **|** nations · be **|** judged be **|** fore you.

20 Put them in **|** fear O **|** Lord:
  and let the nations **|** know · that they **|** are but **|** men.

PSALM 10

1 Why do you stand far **|** off O **|** Lord:
  why do you hide your **|** face in **|** time of **|** need?

2 The ungodly in their pride **|** persecute · the **|** poor:
  let them be caught in the **|** schemes they **|**
 have de **|** vised.

3 For the ungodly man boasts of his **|** heart's de **|** sire:
  he grasps at profit   he **|** spurns · and blas **|** phemes
 the **|** Lord.

4 He says in his arrogance **|** 'God will · not a **|** venge':
  'There is no **|** God' is **|** all his **|** thought.

5 He is settled in **|** all his **|** ways:
  your statutes O Lord are far above him **|** ⌣
 and he **|** does not **|** see.

6   He snorts defiance at his enemies
    he says in his heart 'I shall | never · be | shaken:
        I shall walk se|cure from | any · man's | curse.'

7   His mouth is full of op|pression · and de|ceit:
        mischief and | wickedness · lie | under · his | tongue.

8   He skulks | about · in the | villages:
        and | secret·ly | murders · the | innocent.

9   His eyes watch | out · for the | helpless:
        he lurks con|cealed · like a | lion · in a | thicket.

10 He lies in wait to | seize up·on the | poor:
        he lays hold on the poor man and | drags him | off ·
        in his | net.

11 The upright are crushed and | humbled · be|fore him:
        and the helpless | fall in|to his | power.

12 He says in his heart | 'God · has for|gotten:
        he has covered his | face and | sees | nothing.'

13 Arise O Lord God   lift | up your | hand:
        for|get · not the | poor for | ever.

14 Why should the wicked man | spurn | God:
        why should he say in his heart | 'He will | not a|venge'?

15 Surely you see the | trouble · and the | sorrow:
        you look on   and will take it | into · your | own | hands.

16 The helpless commits him|self to | you:
        for you are the | helper | of the | fatherless.

†17 Break the | power of · the un|godly:
        search out his wickedness | till · it is | found no | more.

18 The Lord is king for | ever · and | ever:
        the heathen have | perished | from his | land.

19 You have heard the longing of the | meek O | Lord:
        you turned your | ear · to their | hearts' de|sire,

†20 to help the poor and fatherless | to their | right:
        that men may no more be | terri·fied | from
        their | land.

PSALM 11

1 In the Lord I have | found my | refuge:
  how then can you say to me |
  'Flee · like a | bird · to the | mountains;

2 'look how the wicked bend their bows
  and notch the arrow up | on the | string:
  to shoot from the | darkness · at the | true of | heart;

3 'if the foundations | are des | troyed:
  what | can the | just man | do?'

4 The Lord is in his holy place
  the Lord is en | throned in | heaven:
  his eyes search out
  his glance | tries the | children · of | men.

5 He tries the | righteous · and the | wicked:
  and him that delights in | violence · his | soul ab | hors.

6 He will rain down coals of fire and brimstone⏝
  up | on the | wicked:
  a scorching wind shall | be their | cup to | drink.

†7 For the Lord is righteous and loves | righteous | acts:
  the | upright · shall | see his | face.

PSALM 12

1 Help Lord   for there is not one | godly · man | left:
  the faithful have vanished from a | mong the |
  children · of | men.

2 Everyone tells | lies · to his | neighbour:
  they flatter with their lips⏝
  but | speak · from a | double | heart.

3 If only the Lord would cut off all | flatter · ing | lips:
  and the | tongue that | speaks so | proudly!

4 They say   'By our tongues we | shall pre | vail:
  our lips are our servants   who is | lord | over | us?'

5   Because of the oppression of the poor
    because of the ꞁ groaning · of the ꞁ needy:
        'I will arise' says the Lord
        'and set them in safety from ꞁ those that ꞁ
        snarl ꞁ after them.'

6   The words of the Lord are pure
    as silver re ꞁfined · in a ꞁ crucible:
        as gold that is seven times ꞁ puri·fied ꞁ in the ꞁ fire.

7   You will surely ꞁ guard us · O ꞁ Lord:
        and shield us for ever from this ꞁ evil ꞁ gener ꞁation,

8   though the ungodly strut on ꞁ every ꞁ side:
        though the vilest of men have ꞁ master·y ꞁ
        of man ꞁkind.

PSALM 13

1   How long O Lord will you so ꞁ utterly · for ꞁget me:
        how long will you ꞁ hide your ꞁ face ꞁ from me?

2   How long must I suffer anguish in my soul
    and be so grieved in my heart ꞁ day and ꞁ night:
        how long shall my ꞁ ene·my ꞁ triumph ꞁ over me?

3   Look upon me O Lord my ꞁ God and ꞁ answer me:
        lighten my ꞁ eyes · lest I ꞁ sleep in ꞁ death;

4   lest my enemy say   'I have pre ꞁvailed a ꞁgainst him':
        lest my foes ex ꞁult ꞁ at my ꞁ overthrow.

5   Yet I put my trust in your un ꞁfailing ꞁ love:
        O let my heart re ꞁjoice in ꞁ your sal ꞁvation.

6   And I will make my ꞁ song · to the ꞁ Lord:
        because he ꞁ deals so ꞁ bounti·fully ꞁ with me.

PSALM 14

1   The fool has said in his heart 'There ꞁ is no ꞁ God':
        they have all become vile and abominable in their
        doings   there ꞁ is not ꞁ one that · does ꞁ good.

2   The Lord looked down from heaven upon the ^I
children · of ^I men:
>> to see if there were any who would act ^I wisely ·
>> and ^I seek · after ^I God.

† 3   But they have all turned out of the way
they have all alike be ^I come cor ^I rupt:
>> there is none that does ^I good ^I no not ^I one.

4   Are all the evildoers devoid of ^I under ^I standing:
>> who eat up my people as men eat bread ⏝
>> and ^I do not ^I pray · to the ^I Lord?

5   They shall be ^I struck with ^I terror:
>> for God is with the ^I compa·ny ^I of the ^I righteous.

6   Though they frustrate the poor man ^I in his ^I hopes:
>> surely the ^I Lord ^I is his ^I refuge.

7   O that deliverance for Israel might come ^I forth
from ^I Zion:
>> when the Lord turns again the fortunes of his people
>> then shall Jacob re ^I joice and ^I Israel · be ^I glad.

PSALM 15

1   Lord who may a ^I bide in · your ^I tabernacle:
>> or who may dwell up ^I on your ^I holy ^I hill?

2   He that leads an uncorrupt life
and does the ^I thing · which is ^I right:
>> who speaks the truth from his heart
>> and has not ^I slandered ^I with his ^I tongue;

3   he that has done no evil ^I to his ^I fellow:
>> nor vented a ^I buse a ^I gainst his ^I neighbour;

4   in whose eyes the worthless ^I have no ^I honour:
>> but he makes much of ^I those that ^I fear the ^I Lord;

5   he that has ^I sworn · to his ^I neighbour:
>> and will ^I not go ^I back · on his ^I oath;

6   he that has not put his ^I money · to ^I usury:
>> nor taken a ^I bribe a ^I gainst the ^I innocent.

† 7   He that l does these l things:
       shall l never · be l over l thrown.

PSALM 16

1   Preserve l me O l God:
      for in l you · have I l taken l refuge.

2   I have said to the Lord l You are l my lord:
      and all my l good de l pends on l you.

3   As for those who are held l holy · on the l earth:
      the other l gods · in whom l men de l light,

4   though the idols are many that l men run l after:
      their offerings of blood I will not offer
      nor take their l name up l on my l lips.

5   The Lord is my appointed portion l and my l cup:
      you l hold my l lot · in your l hands.

6   The share that has fallen to me is in l pleasant l places:
      and a fair l land is l my pos l session.

7   I will bless the Lord who has l given · me l counsel:
      at night also l he · has in l structed · my l heart.

8   I have set the Lord l always · be l fore me:
      he is at my right l hand · and I l shall not l fall.

† 9   Therefore my heart is glad and my l spirit · re l joices:
      my flesh l also · shall l rest se l cure.

10   For you will not give me over to the l power of l death:
      nor suffer your l faithful one · to l see the l Pit.

11   You will show me the l path of l life:
      in your presence is the fulness of joy
      and from your right hand flow de l lights for l
      ever l more.

PSALM 17

1   Hear my just cause O Lord give l heed to · my l cry:
      listen to my prayer that l comes from · no ⌈
      lying l lips.

2 Let judgement for me come | forth from
your | presence:
    and let your | eyes dis |cern the | right.

3 Though you search my heart   and visit me | in the |
night-time:
    though you try me by fire   you will | find no |
    wicked·ness ⌐ in me.

4 My mouth does not transgress like the | mouth
of | others:
    for I have | kept the | word of · your | lips.

†5 My steps have held firm in the way of | your
com |mands:
    and my feet have not | stumbled | from your | paths.

6 I call upon you O God for you will | surely | answer:
    incline your ear to | me and | hear my ⌐ words.

7 Show me the wonders of your steadfast love
O saviour of those who come to | you for | refuge:
    who by your right hand deliver them⌣
    from | those that · rise | up a |gainst them.

8 Keep me as the | apple · of your | eye:
    hide me under the | shadow | of your | wings,

9 from the onslaught | of the | wicked:
    from my enemies that en |circle me · to |
    take my | life.

10 They have closed their | hearts to | pity:
    and their | mouths speak | proud | things.

11 They advance upon me * they surround me on |
every | side:
    watching how they may | bring me | to the | ground,

†12 like a lion that is | greedy · for its | prey:
    like a lion's whelp | lurking · in ⌐ hidden | places.

13 Arise O Lord * stand in their way and | cast
them | down:
    deliver me from the | wicked | by your | sword.

[14 Slay them by your hand O Lord
　　slay them so that they **|** perish · from the **|** earth:
　　　de **|** stroy them · from a **|** mong the **|** living.]

15 But as for your cherished ones
　　let their bellies be filled and let their **|** sons
　　be **|** satisfied:
　　　let them pass on their **|** wealth **|** to their **|** children.

(†) 16 And I also shall see your face　because my **|**
　　cause is **|** just:
　　　when I awake and see you as you **|** are I **|**
　　　shall be **|** satisfied.

PSALM 18

1 I love you O **|** Lord my **|** strength:
　　O Lord my crag my **|** fortress · and **|** my de **|** liverer,

2 my God　the rock to which I **|** come for **|** refuge:
　　my shield my mighty saviour **|** and my **|** high de **|** fence.

† 3 I called to the Lord with **|** loud · lamen **|** tation:
　　and I was **|** rescued **|** from my **|** enemies.

4 The waves of **|** death en **|** compassed me:
　　and the floods of **|** chaos **|** over **|** whelmed me;

5 the cords of the grave **|** tightened · a **|** bout me:
　　and the snares of **|** death lay **|** in my **|** path.

6 In my anguish I **|** called · to the **|** Lord:
　　I cried for **|** help **|** to my **|** God.

7 From his temple he **|** heard my **|** voice:
　　and my cry came **|** even **|** to his **|** ears.

8 The earth heaved and quaked
　　the foundations of the **|** hills were **|** shaken:
　　　they **|** trembled · be **|** cause · he was **|** angry.

9 Smoke went **|** out · from his **|** nostrils:
　　and a consuming **|** fire **|** from his **|** mouth.

10 He parted the heavens and **|** came **|** down:
　　and there was **|** darkness **|** under · his **|** feet.

11 He rode upon the | cherubim · and | flew:
    he came swooping up |on the | wings · of the | wind.

12 He made the | darkness · his | covering:
    and his canopy was thick | cloud and |
    water·y | darkness.

13 Out of his clouds   from the | brightness · be|fore him:
    broke | hailstones · and | coals of | fire.

14 The Lord | thundered · in the | heavens:
    the Most | High | uttered · his | voice.

15 He let loose his arrows   he scattered them on |
    every | side:
    he hurled down | lightnings · with the | roar ·
    of the | thunderbolt.

16 The springs of the | sea · were un|covered:
    and the found|ations · of the | world laid | bare,

17 at your re|buke O | Lord:
    at the blast of the | breath of | your dis|pleasure.

18 He reached down from on | high and | took me:
    he drew me | out of · the | great | waters.

19 He delivered me from my | strongest | enemy:
    from my | foes · that were | mightier · than | I.

20 They confronted me in the | day of · my cal|amity:
    but the | Lord was | my up|holder.

21 He brought me into a | place of | liberty:
    and rescued me be|cause · I de|lighted · his | heart.

22 The Lord rewarded me for my | righteous | dealing:
    he recompensed me according to the | cleanness |
    of my | hands,

23 because I had kept to the | ways · of the | Lord:
    and had not turned from my | God to | do | evil.

24 For I had an eye to | all his | laws:
    and did not | put · his com|mandments | from me.

25   I was also | blameless · be | fore him:
         and I kept my | self from | wrong | doing.

† 26   Therefore the Lord re | warded · my | innocence:
         because my hands were | unde | filed · in his | sight.

27   With the faithful you | show your · self | faithful:
         with the | blameless · you | show your · self | blameless;

28   with the | pure · you are | pure:
         but with the | crooked · you | show yourself · per | verse.

29   For you will save a | humble | people:
         but you bring down the | high looks | of the | proud.

30   You light my lamp O | Lord my | God:
         you make my | darkness | to be | bright.

† 31   For with your help I can charge a | troop of | men:
         with the help of my God I can | leap a | city | wall.

32   The way of our God is perfect
         the word of the Lord has been | tried · in the | fire:
         he is a shield to | all that | trust in | him.

33   For who is | God · but the | Lord:
         or who is our | rock | but our | God?

34   It is God that | girded me · with | strength:
         that | made my | way | perfect.

35   He made my feet like the | feet · of a | hind:
         and set me sure | footed · up | on the | mountains.

36   He taught my | hands to | fight:
         and my arms to | aim an | arrow · of | bronze.

37   You gave me the shield of | your sal | vation:
         your right hand upheld me
         and your swift re | sponse has | made me | great.

38   You lengthened my | stride be | neath me:
         and my | ankles | did not | slip.

39   I pursued my enemies and ˈ overˈtook them:
      nor did I turn again ˈ till · I had ˈ made an ˈ
      end of them.

40   I smote them till they could ˈ rise no ˈ more:
      and they ˈ fell beˈneath my ˈ feet.

41   You girded me with ˈ strength · for the ˈ battle:
      you threw ˈ down my ˈ adver·saries ˈ under me.

42   You caused my enemies to ˈ show their ˈ backs:
      and I deˈstroyed ˈ those that ˈ hated me.

43   They cried for help   but there was ˈ none to ˈ
    save them:
      they cried to the ˈ Lord · but he ˈ would not ˈ answer.

44   I pounded them fine as dust beˈfore the ˈ wind:
      I trod them under ˈ like the ˈ mire · of the ˈ streets.

45   You delivered me from the strife of the peoples
    you made me the ˈ head · of the ˈ nations:
      a people that I had not ˈ known beˈcame my ˈ servants.

46   As soon as they heard me ˈ they oˈbeyed me:
      and aliens ˈ humbled · themˈselves beˈfore me.

47   The strength of the aliens ˈ withered · aˈway:
      they came ˈ falter·ing ˈ from their ˈ strongholds.

48   The Lord lives   and blessèd ˈ be my ˈ rock:
      exalted be the ˈ God of ˈ my salˈvation,

49   the God who sees to it that ˈ I am · aˈvenged:
      who subˈdues the ˈ peoples ˈ under me.

50   You set me free from my enemies
    you put me out of ˈ reach of · my atˈtackers:
      you deˈlivered me · from ˈ vio·lent ˈ men.

51   For this will I give you thanks among the ˈ
    nations · O ˈ Lord:
      and sing ˈ praises ˈ to your ˈ name,

†52   to him that gives great triumphs ˈ to his ˈ king:
      that deals so faithfully with his anointed
      with David and ˈ with his ˈ seed for ˈ ever.

PSALM 19

1 The heavens declare the | glory · of | God:
   and the | firmament · pro|claims his | handiwork;

2 one day | tells it · to an|other:
   and night to | night com|muni·cates | knowledge.

3 There is no | speech or | language:
   nor | are their | voices | heard;

4 yet their sound has gone out through | all the | world:
   and their | words · to the | ends · of the | earth.

5 There he has pitched a | tent · for the | sun:
   which comes out as a bridegroom from his chamber
   and rejoices like a | strong · man to |
   run his | course.

6 Its rising is at one end of the heavens
   and its circuit to their | farthest | bound:
   and nothing is | hidden | from its | heat.

7 The law of the Lord is perfect re|viving · the | soul:
   the command of the Lord is true |
   and makes | wise the | simple.

8 The precepts of the Lord are right
   and re|joice the | heart:
   the commandment of the Lord is pure |
   and gives | light · to the | eyes.

9 The fear of the Lord is clean and en|dures for | ever:
   the judgements of the Lord are unchanging
   and | righteous | every | one.

10 More to be desired are they than gold
   even | much fine | gold:
   sweeter also than honey
   than the | honey · that | drips · from the | comb.

11 Moreover by them is your | servant | taught:
   and in keeping them | there is | great re|ward.

12 Who can know his own un|witting | sins?
   O cleanse me | from my | secret | faults.

13 Keep your servant also from presumptuous sins
lest they get the ˡ master·y ˡ over me:
   so I shall be clean and ˡ innocent · of ˡ great ofˡfence.

14 May the words of my mouth and the meditation⌣
of my heart
be acceptable ˡ in your ˡ sight:
   O Lord my ˡ strength and ˡ my reˡdeemer.

PSALM 20

1 May the Lord hear you in the ˡ day of ˡ trouble:
   the God of Jacob ˡ lift you ˡ up to ˡ safety.

2 May he send you his ˡ help · from the ˡ sanctuary:
   and be your ˡ strong supˡport from ˡ Zion.

3 May he remember ˡ all your ˡ offerings:
   and accept with ˡ favour · your ˡ burnt ˡ sacrifices,

4 grant you your ˡ heart's deˡsire:
   and fulˡfil ˡ all your ˡ purposes.

†5 May we also rejoice in your victory
and triumph in the ˡ name of · our ˡ God:
   the Lord perˡform all ˡ your peˡtitions.

6 Now I know that the Lord will ˡ save · his aˡnointed: .
   that he will answer him from his holy heaven
   with the victorious ˡ strength · of his ˡ right ˡ hand.

7 Some put their trust in chariots and ˡ some in ˡ horses:
   but we will trust in the ˡ name · of the ˡ Lord
   our ˡ God.

8 They are brought ˡ down and ˡ fallen:
   but we are made ˡ strong and ˡ stand ˡ upright.

9 O Lord ˡ save the ˡ king:
   and hear us ˡ when we ˡ call upˡon you.

PSALM 21

1 The king shall rejoice in your | strength O | Lord:
   he shall ex|ult in | your sal|vation.

2 You have given him his | heart's de|sire:
   you have not de|nied him · the re|quest · of his | lips.

3 For you came to meet him with the | blessings ·
   of suc|cess:
   and placed a crown of | gold up|on his | head.

4 He asked you for | life · and you | gave it him:
   length of | days for | ever · and | ever.

5 Great is his glory because of | your sal|vation:
   you have | clothed him · with | honour · and | majesty.

6 You have given him ever|lasting · fe|licity:
   and made him | glad · with the | joy of ·
   your | presence.

†7 For the king puts his | trust · in the | Lord:
   and through the tender mercy of the Most High | ⌣
   he shall | never · be | moved.

8 Your hand shall light up|on your | enemies:
   and your right hand shall | find out | all who | hate you.

9 You will make them like a blazing furnace ⌣
   in the | day of · your | coming:
   the Lord will overwhelm them in his wrath ⌣
   and | fire | shall con|sume them.

10 You will root out their offspring | from the | earth:
   and their seed from a|mong the | children · of | men;

11 because they have stirred up | evil · a|gainst you:
   and plotted mischief | which they | cannot ·
   per|form.

12 Therefore will you set your | shoulder · to|ward them:
   and draw the string of the | bow to | strike at ·
   their | faces.

13 Arise O Lord in your | great | strength:
   and we will | sing and | praise your | power.

PSALM 22

1   My God my God   why have ⏐ you for⏐saken me:
     why are you so far from helping me
     and from the ⏐ words ⏐ of my ⏐ groaning?

2   My God I cry to you by day   but you ⏐ do not ⏐ answer:
     and by night ⎡ also · I ⏐ take no ⎡ rest.

3   But you con⏐tinue ⏐ holy:
     you that ⏐ are the ⏐ praise of ⏐ Israel.

4   In you our ⏐ fathers ⏐ trusted:
     they ⏐ trusted · and ⏐ you de⏐livered them;

5   to you they cried and ⏐ they were ⏐ saved:
     they put their trust in you ⏐ and were ⏐
     not con⏐founded.

6   But as for me   I am a worm and ⏐ no ⏐ man:
     the scorn of ⏐ men · and de⏐spised · by the ⏐ people.

7   All those that see me ⏐ laugh me · to ⏐ scorn:
     they shoot out their lips at me and ⏐ wag their ⏐
     heads ⏐ saying,

8   'He trusted in the Lord   ⏐ let him · de⏐liver him:
     let him de⏐liver him · if ⏐ he de⏐lights in him.'

9   But you are he that took me ⏐ out of · the ⏐ womb:
     that brought me to lie at ⏐ peace · on my ⏐
     mother's ⎡ breast.

10   On you have I been cast ⏐ since my ⏐ birth:
     you are my God ⏐ even · from my ⏐ mother's ⏐ womb.

11   O go not from me   for trouble is ⏐ hard at ⏐ hand:
     and ⏐ there is ⏐ none to ⏐ help.

12   Many ⏐ oxen · sur⏐round me:
     fat bulls of Bashan close me ⏐ in on ⏐ every ⏐ side.

13   They gape ⏐ wide their ⏐ mouths at me:
     like ⏐ lions · that ⏐ roar and ⏐ rend.

14   I am poured out like water
     and all my bones are ⏐ out of ⏐ joint:
     my heart within my ⏐ breast · is like ⏐ melting ⏐ wax.

15 My mouth is dried | up · like a | potsherd:
    and my | tongue | clings · to my | gums.

16 My hands and my | feet are | withered:
    and you | lay me · in the | dust of | death.

17 For many dogs are | come a|bout me:
    and a band of evil |doers | hem me | in.

18 I can count | all my | bones:
    they stand | staring · and | gazing · up|on me.

19 They part my | garments · a|mong them:
    and cast | lots | for my | clothing.

20 O Lord do not | stand far | off:
    you are my helper | hasten | to my | aid.

21 Deliver my | body · from the | sword:
    my | life · from the | power · of the | dogs;

22 O save me from the | lion's | mouth:
    and my afflicted soul from the | horns · of the |
    wild | oxen.

23 I will tell of your | name · to my | brethren:
    in the midst of the congre|gation | will I | praise you.

24 O praise the Lord all | you that | fear him:
    hold him in honour O seed of Jacob
    and let the seed of | Israel | stand in | awe of him.

†25 For he has not despised nor abhorred ⌣
    the poor man | in his | misery:
    nor did he hide his face from him
    but | heard him | when he | cried.

26 From you springs my praise in the | great ·
    congre|gation:
    I will pay my vows in the | sight of | all that | fear you;

27 the meek shall eat of the sacrifice | and be | satisfied:
    and those who seek the Lord shall praise him
    may their | hearts re|joice for | ever!

28 Let all the ends of the earth remember⌣
and ˡ turn · to the ˡ Lord:
   and let all the families of the ˡ nations ˡ worship ·
   be ˡfore him.

29 For the kingdom ˡ is the ˡ Lord's:
   and he shall be ˡ ruler ˡ over · the ˡ nations.

30 How can those who sleep in the earth ˡ do him ˡ homage:
   or those that descend to the ˡ dust bow ˡ down
   be ˡfore him?

31 But he has saved my ˡ life · for him ˡself:
   and ˡ my pos ˡterity · shall ˡ serve him.

† 32 This shall be told of my Lord to a future ˡ gener ˡation:
   and his righteousness declared ⌣
   to a people yet un ˡborn   that ˡ he has ˡ done it.

PSALM 23

1 The Lord ˡ is my ˡ shepherd:
   therefore ˡ can I ˡ lack ˡ nothing.

2 He will make me lie down in ˡ green ˡ pastures:
   and ˡ lead me · be ˡside still ˡ waters.

3 He will re ˡfresh my ˡ soul:
   and guide me in right pathways ˡ for his ˡ
   name's ˡ sake.

4 Though I walk through the valley of the
   shadow of death   I will ˡ fear no ˡ evil:
   for you are with me
   your ˡ rod · and your ˡ staff ˡ comfort me.

5 You spread a table before me
   in the face of ˡ those who ˡ trouble me:
   you have anointed my head with oil ˡ and my ˡ cup ·
   will be ˡ full.

6 Surely your goodness and loving-kindness⌣
   will follow me * all the ˡ days · of my ˡ life:
   and I shall dwell in the ˡ house · of the ˡ Lord
   for ˡ ever.

PSALM 24

1 The earth is the Lord's and | all · that is | in it:
   the compass of the | world and | those who |
   dwell therein.

2 For he has founded it up|on the | seas:
   and es|tablished it · up|on the | waters.

3 Who shall ascend the | hill · of the | Lord:
   or who shall | stand · in his | holy | place?

4 He that has clean hands and a | pure | heart:
   who has not set his soul upon idols
   nor | sworn his | oath · to a | lie.

5 He shall receive | blessing · from the | Lord:
   and recompense from the | God of | his sal|vation.

6 Of such a kind as this are | those who | seek him:
   those who seek your | face O | God of | Jacob.

7 Lift up your heads O you gates
   and be lifted up you ever|lasting | doors:
   and the King of | glory | shall come | in.

8 Who is the | King of | glory?
   the Lord strong and mighty * the | Lord |
   mighty · in | battle.

9 Lift up your heads O you gates
   and be lifted up you ever|lasting | doors:
   and the King of | glory | shall come | in.

10 Who is the | King of | glory?
   the Lord of hosts | he · is the | King of | glory.

PSALM 25

1 In you O Lord my God have I | put my | hope:
   in you have I trusted   let me not be ashamed
   nor let my | ene·mies | triumph | over me.

2 Let none who wait for you be | put to | shame:
   but let those that break faith
   be con|founded · and | gain | nothing.

3   Show me your ꞁ ways O ꞁ Lord:
       and ꞁ teach me ꞁ your ꞁ paths.

4   Lead me in the ways of your ꞁ truth and ꞁ teach me:
       for you are the ꞁ God of ꞁ my sal ꞁ vation.

5   In you have I hoped ꞁ all the · day ꞁ long:
       be ꞁ cause of · your ꞁ goodness · O ꞁ Lord.

6   Call to mind your compassion and your ꞁ
       loving ꞁ kindness:
       for ꞁ they are ꞁ from of ꞁ old.

7   Remember not the sins of my youth nor ꞁ
       my trans ꞁ gressions:
       but according ꞁ to your ꞁ mercy ꞁ think on me.

8   Good and upright ꞁ is the ꞁ Lord:
       therefore will he direct ꞁ sinners ꞁ in the ꞁ way.

†9   The meek he will guide in the ꞁ path of ꞁ justice:
       and ꞁ teach the ꞁ humble · his ꞁ ways.

10   All the paths of the Lord are ꞁ faithful · and ꞁ true:
       for those who keep his ꞁ covenant · and ꞁ
       his com ꞁ mandments.

11   For your name's ꞁ sake O ꞁ Lord:
       be merciful to my ꞁ sin though ꞁ it is ꞁ great.

12   Who is he that ꞁ fears the ꞁ Lord?
       him will the Lord direct in the ꞁ way that ꞁ
       he should ꞁ choose.

13   His soul shall ꞁ dwell at ꞁ ease:
       and his ꞁ children · shall in ꞁ herit · the ꞁ land.

14   The confidences of God belong to ꞁ those that ꞁ
       fear him:
       and his covenant shall ꞁ give them ꞁ under ꞁ standing.

15   My eyes are ever ꞁ looking · to the ꞁ Lord:
       for he will bring my ꞁ feet ꞁ out of · the ꞁ net.

16   Turn your face toward me ꞁ and be ꞁ gracious:
       for ꞁ I am · a ꞁ lone · and in ꞁ misery.

17 O free my ˈ heart from ˈ pain:
    and bring me ˈ out of ˈ my disˈtress.

18 Give heed to my afˈfliction · and adˈversity:
    and forˈgive me ˈ all my ˈ sins.

19 Consider my enemies how ˈ many · they ˈ are:
    and they bear a ˈ vio·lent ˈ hate aˈgainst me.

20 O keep my ˈ life · and deˈliver me:
    put me not to shame   for I ˈ come to ˈ
    you for ˈ refuge.

21 Let innocence and integrity ˈ be my ˈ guard:
    for in ˈ you ˈ have I ˈ hoped.

†22 O God deˈliver ˈ Israel:
    out of ˈ all his ˈ tribuˈlation.

PSALM 26

1 Give judgement for me O Lord
    for I have walked in ˈ my inˈtegrity:
    I have trusted in the ˈ Lord and ˈ not ˈ wavered.

2 Put me to the test O ˈ Lord and ˈ prove me:
    try my ˈ mind ˈ and my ˈ heart.

3 For your steadfast love has been ever beˈfore my ˈ eyes:
    and ˈ I have ˈ walked in · your ˈ truth.

4 I have not ˈ sat · with deˈceivers:
    nor conˈsorted ˈ with the ˈ hypocrites;

5 I hate the asˈsembly · of the ˈ wicked:
    I will not ˈ sit ˈ with the · unˈgodly.

6 I wash my hands in ˈ innocence · O ˈ Lord:
    that I may ˈ go aˈbout your ˈ altar,

†7 and lift up the ˈ voice of ˈ thanksgiving:
    to tell of ˈ all your ˈ marvel·lous ˈ works.

8 Lord I love the house of your ˈ habitˈation:
    and the ˈ place · where your ˈ glory ˈ dwells.

9 Do not sweep me aˈway with ˈ sinners:
    nor my ˈ life with ˈ men of ˈ blood,

10   in whose hand is a⎪bomin⎪ation:
      and their right ⎪ hand is ⎪ full of ⎪ bribes.

11   As for me   I walk in ⎪ my in⎪tegrity:
      O ransom me ⎪ and be ⎪ favourable · to⎪ward me.

†12   My foot stands on an ⎪ even ⎪ path:
      I will bless the ⎪ Lord · in the ⎪ great · congre⎪gation.

PSALM 27

1   The Lord is my light and my salvation
    whom then ⎪ shall I ⎪ fear?
      the Lord is the stronghold of my life
      of whom ⎪ shall I ⎪ be a⎪fraid?

2   When the wicked   even my enemies and my foes
    come upon me ⎪ to de⎪vour me:
      they shall ⎪ stumble ⎪ and ⎪ fall.

3   If an army encamp against me
    my heart shall ⎪ not · be a⎪fraid:
      and if war should rise a⎪gainst me ⎪ yet · will I ⎪ trust.

4   One thing I have asked from the Lord which I ⎪
    will re⎪quire:
      that I may dwell in the house of the Lord ⎪ ‿
      all the ⎪ days · of my ⎪ life,

†5   to see the fair ⎪ beauty · of the ⎪ Lord:
      and to ⎪ seek his ⎪ will · in his ⎪ temple.

6   For he will hide me under his shelter in the ⎪
    day of ⎪ trouble:
      and conceal me in the shadow of his tent
      and set me ⎪ high up⎪on a ⎪ rock.

7   And now he will lift ⎪ up my ⎪ head:
      above my ⎪ ene·mies ⎪ round a⎪bout me.

†8   And I will offer sacrifices in his sanctuary‿
    with ⎪ exul⎪tation:
      I will sing   I will sing ⎪ praises ⎪ to the ⎪ Lord.

9   O Lord hear my ⎪ voice · when I ⎪ cry:
      have ⎪ mercy · up⎪on me · and ⎪ answer me.

10 My heart has said of you ❘ 'Seek his ❘ face':
    your ❘ face Lord ❘ I will ❘ seek.

11 Do not ❘ hide your ❘ face from me:
    or thrust your ❘ servant · a ❘ side · in dis ❘ pleasure;

12 for you have ❘ been my ❘ helper:
    do not cast me away or forsake me O ❘ God of ❘
    my sal ❘ vation.

† 13 Though my father and my ❘ mother · for ❘ sake me:
    the ❘ Lord will ❘ take me ❘ up.

14 Teach me your ❘ way O ❘ Lord:
    and lead me in an even path ❘ for they ❘ lie in ❘
    wait for me.

15 Do not give me over to the ❘ will of · my ❘ enemies:
    for false witnesses have risen against me
    and ❘ those who ❘ breathe out ❘ violence.

16 But I believe that I shall surely see the ❘ goodness ·
    of the ❘ Lord:
    in the ❘ land ❘ of the ❘ living.

17 O wait for the Lord
    stand firm and he will ❘ strengthen · your ❘ heart:
    and ❘ wait I ❘ say · for the ❘ Lord.

PSALM 28

1 To you will I cry O Lord my Rock
   be not ❘ deaf · to my ❘ prayer:
   lest if you turn away silent
   I become like those that go ❘ down ❘ to the ❘ grave.

2 Hear the voice of my supplication
   when I cry to ❘ you for ❘ help:
   when I lift up my hands
   towards the ❘ holi·est ❘ place of · your ❘ sanctuary.

3 Do not snatch me away with the ungodly
   with the ❘ evil ❘ doers:
   who speak peace to their neighbours
   but nourish ❘ malice ❘ in their ❘ hearts.

4   Repay them ac | cording · to their | deeds:
        and according to the | wickedness · of |
        their en | deavours;

5   requite them for the | work · of their | hands:
        and | give them | their de | serts.

6   For they pay no heed to the Lord's acts
        nor to the operation | of his | hands:
        therefore shall he break them | down · and not |
        build them | up.

7   Let the Lord's | name be | praised:
        for he has heard the | voice · of my | suppli | cation.

8   The Lord is my strength and my shield
        in him my heart trusts and | I am | helped:
        therefore my heart dances for joy
        and in my | song | will I | praise him.

9   The Lord is the | strength · of his | people:
        and a sure refuge for | his an | ointed | king.

10   O save your people * and give your | blessing ·
        to your | own:
        be their shepherd and | bear them | up for | ever.

PSALM 29

1   Ascribe to the Lord you | sons of | heaven:
        ascribe to the | Lord | glory · and | might.

2   Ascribe to the Lord the honour | due · to his | name:
        O worship the Lord in the | beauty | of his | holiness.

3   The voice of the Lord is up | on the | waters:
        the God of glory thunders   the Lord up | on the |
        great | waters.

4   The voice of the Lord is mighty in | oper | ation:
        the voice of the | Lord · is a | glori · ous | voice.

5   The voice of the Lord | breaks the | cedar-trees:
        the Lord breaks in | pieces · the | cedars · of | Lebanon.

6   He makes them | skip · like a | calf:
      Lebanon and Sirion | like a | young wild | ox.

7   The voice of the Lord di|vides the | lightning-flash:
      the voice of the Lord whirls the sands of the desert
      the Lord | whirls the | desert · of | Kadesh.

8   The voice of the Lord rends the terebinth trees
      and strips | bare the | forests:
      in his | temple | all cry | 'Glory'.

9   The Lord sits enthroned a|bove the | water-flood:
      the Lord sits en|throned · as a | king for | ever.

10 The Lord will give | strength · to his | people:
      the Lord will give to his | people · the | blessing ·
      of | peace.

PSALM 30

1   I will exalt you O Lord
      for you have drawn me | up · from the | depths:
      and have not suffered my | foes to | triumph | over me.

2   O Lord my | God I | cried to you:
      · and | you have | made me | whole.

†3 You brought me back O Lord from the | land of | silence:
      you saved my life‿
      from among | those that · go | down · to the | Pit.

4   Sing praises to the Lord all | you his | faithful ones:
      and give | thanks · to his | holy | name.

5   For if in his anger is havoc
      in his good | favour · is | life:
      heaviness may endure for a night
      but | joy comes | in the | morning.

6   In my prosperity I said   'I shall | never · be | moved:
      your goodness O Lord has | set me · on so |
      firm a | hill.'

7   Then you | hid your | face from me:
      and | I was | greatly · dis|mayed.

8   I cried to ˈ you O ˈ God:
      and made my petition ˈ humbly ˈ to my ˈ Lord.

9   'What profit is there in my blood
      if I go ˈ down · to the ˈ Pit:
        can the dust give you thanks ˈ ‿
        or deˈclare your ˈ faithfulness?

†10 'Hear O ˈ Lord · and be ˈ merciful:
        O ˈ Lord ˈ be my ˈ helper.'

11 You have turned my lamentation ˈ into ˈ dancing:
      you have put off my sackcloth and ˈ girded ˈ me
      with ˈ joy,

12 that my heart may sing your praise and ˈ never ·
      be ˈ silent:
        O Lord my God   I will ˈ give you ˈ thanks for ˈ ever.

PSALM 31

1   To you Lord have I ˈ come for ˈ shelter:
      let me ˈ never · be ˈ put to ˈ shame.

2   O deliver me ˈ in your ˈ righteousness:
      incline your ear to me ˈ and be ˈ swift to ˈ save me.

3   Be for me a rock of refuge   a fortress ˈ to deˈfend me:
      for you are my ˈ high rock ˈ and my ˈ stronghold.

4   Lead me and guide me for your ˈ name's ˈ sake:
      bring me out of the net that they have secretly
      laid for me * for ˈ you ˈ are my ˈ strength.

5   Into your hands I comˈmit my ˈ spirit:
      you will redeem me ˈ O Lord ˈ God of ˈ truth.

6   I hate those that ˈ clutch vain ˈ idols:
      but my ˈ trust is ˈ in the ˈ Lord.

7   I will rejoice and be glad in your ˈ lovingˈkindness:
      for you have looked on my distress
      and ˈ known me ˈ in adˈversity.

8 You have not given me over to the ˈ power ·
of the ˈ enemy:
    you have set my feet where ˈ I may ˈ walk at ˈ liberty.

9 Have mercy upon me O Lord   for ˈ I am · in ˈ trouble:
    my eye wastes away for grief
    my throat also ˈ and my ˈ inward ˈ parts.

10 For my life wears out in sorrow
and my ˈ years with ˈ sighing:
    my strength fails me in my affliction
    and my ˈ bones ˈ are con ˈ sumed.

11 I am become the scorn of ˈ all my ˈ enemies:
    and my neighbours ˈ wag their ˈ heads · in de ˈ rision.

12 I am a thing of ˈ horror · to my ˈ friends:
    and those that see me in the ˈ street ˈ shrink ˈ from me.

13 I am forgotten like a dead man ˈ out of ˈ mind:
    I have be ˈ come · like a ˈ broken ˈ vessel.

14 For I hear the ˈ whispering · of ˈ many:
    and ˈ fear · is on ˈ every ˈ side;

15 while they plot to ˈ gether · a ˈ gainst me:
    and scheme to ˈ take a ˈ way my ˈ life.

16 But in you Lord have I ˈ put my ˈ trust:
    I have said ˈ 'You ˈ are my ˈ God.'

17 All my days are ˈ in your ˈ hand:
    O deliver me from the power of my ˈ enemies ·
    and ˈ from my ˈ persecutors.

18 Make your face to shine up ˈ on your ˈ servant:
    and save me ˈ for your ˈ mercy's ˈ sake.

19 O Lord let me not be confounded
for I have ˈ called up ˈ on you:
    but let the wicked be put to shame
    and brought to ˈ silence ˈ in the ˈ grave.

20 Let the lying ˈ lips be ˈ dumb:
    that in pride and contempt
    speak such ˈ insolence · a ˈ gainst the ˈ just.

21 O how plentiful is your goodness
stored up for **|** those that **|** fear you:
    and prepared in the sight of men
    for all who **|** come to **|** you for **|** refuge.

22 You will hide them in the cover of your presence⌣
from the **|** plots of **|** men:
    you will shelter them in your refuge **|** ⌣
    from the **|** strife of **|** tongues.

23 Blessèd be the **|** Lord our **|** God:
    for he has wonderfully shown me his steadfast love
    when I was **|** as a **|** city · be **|** sieged.

24 When I was afraid I **|** said in · my **|** haste:
    'I am **|** cut off **|** from your **|** sight.'

25 But you heard the voice of my **|** suppli **|** cation:
    when I **|** cried to **|** you for **|** help.

26 Love the Lord all **|** you his **|** faithful ones:
    for the Lord guards the true
    but **|** fully · re **|** quites the **|** proud.

†27 Be strong   and let your **|** heart take **|** courage:
    all **|** you that **|** hope · in the **|** Lord.

PSALM 32

1 Blessèd is he whose **|** sin · is for **|** given:
    whose in **|** iquity · is **|** put a **|** way.

2 Blessèd is the man to whom the Lord im **|** putes
no **|** blame:
    and in whose **|** spirit · there **|** is no **|** guile.

3 For whilst I **|** held my **|** tongue:
    my bones wasted a **|** way · with my **|** daily ·
    com **|** plaining.

4 Your hand was heavy upon me **|** day and **|** night:
    and my moisture was dried **|** up · like a **|** drought
in **|** summer.

5 Then I ack **|** nowledged · my **|** sin to you:
    and my in **|** iquity · I **|** did not **|** hide;

6　I said ‘I will confess my trans|gressions · to the | Lord’:
　　and so you forgave the | wicked·ness | of my | sin.

7　For this cause shall everyone that is faithful ⏑
　　make his prayer to you * in the | day of | trouble:
　　　and in the time of the great water-floods ⏑
　　　they shall | not come | near him.

8　You are a place to hide me in
　　you will pre|serve me · from | trouble:
　　　you will surround me with de|liverance · on |
　　　every | side.

9　‘I will instruct you
　　and direct you in the way that | you should | go:
　　　I will fasten my eye up|on you · and |
　　　give you | counsel.

10　‘Be not like horse or mule that have no | under|standing:
　　whose forward course must be | curbed with | bit
　　and | bridle.’

11　Great tribulations remain | for the · un|godly:
　　but whoever puts his trust in the Lord
　　mercy em|braces him · on | every | side.

12　Rejoice in the Lord you righteous | and be | glad:
　　and shout for joy all | you · that are | true of | heart.

PSALM 33

1　Rejoice in the | Lord you | righteous:
　　for it be|fits the | just to | praise him.

2　Give the Lord thanks up|on the | harp:
　　and sing his praise to the | lute of | ten | strings.

3　O sing him a | new | song:
　　make sweetest | melody · with | shouts of | praise.

4　For the word of the | Lord is | true:
　　and | all his | works are | faithful.

5　He loves | righteousness · and | justice:
　　the earth is filled with the loving|kindness |
　　of the | Lord.

6   By the word of the Lord were the | heavens | made:
     and their numberless | stars · by the | breath of ·
     his | mouth.

7   He gathered the waters of the sea as | in a | water-skin:
     and laid up the | deep | in his | treasuries.

8   Let the whole earth | fear the | Lord:
     and let all the inhabitants of the | world |
     stand in | awe of him.

9   For he spoke and | it was | done:
     he commanded | and it | stood | fast.

10   The Lord frustrates the | counsels · of the | nations:
     he brings to nothing the de|vices | of the | peoples.

11   But the counsels of the Lord shall en|dure for | ever:
     the purposes of his heart from gener|ation ·
     to | gener|ation.

12   Blessèd is the nation whose | God · is the | Lord:
     the people he chose to | be his | own pos|session.

13   The Lord looks down from heaven
     and surveys all the | children · of | men:
     he considers from his dwelling-place
     all the in|habit·ants | of the | earth;

14   he who fashioned the | hearts of · them | all:
     and compre|hends all | that they | do.

15   A king is not saved by a | mighty | army:
     nor is a warrior de|livered · by | much | strength;

16   a horse is a vain hope to | save a | man:
     nor can he rescue | any · by his | great | power.

17   But the eye of the Lord is on | those that | fear him:
     on those that trust in | his un|failing | love,

18   to de|liver them · from | death:
     and to | feed them · in the | time of | dearth.

19   We have waited eagerly | for the | Lord:
     for | he is · our | help · and our | shield.

20 Surely our hearts shall re |joice in | him:
    for we have | trusted · in his | holy | name.

† 21 Let your merciful kindness be up |on us · O | Lord:
      even as our | hope | is in | you.

PSALM 34

1 I will bless the | Lord con |tinually:
   his praise shall be | always | in my | mouth.

2 Let my soul | boast · of the | Lord:
   the humble shall | hear it | and re |joice.

3 O praise the | Lord with | me:
   let us ex |alt his | name to |gether.

4 For I sought the Lord's | help · and he | answered:
   and he | freed me · from | all my | fears.

5 Look towards him and be | bright with | joy:
   your | faces · shall | not · be a |shamed.

6 Here is a wretch who cried and the | Lord | heard him:
   and | saved him · from | all his | troubles.

7 The angel of the Lord encamps round | those who | fear him:
   and de |livers · them | in their | need.

8 O taste and see that the | Lord is | good:
   happy the | man who | hides in | him!

9 Fear the Lord all | you his | holy ones:
   for those who | fear him | never | lack.

10 Lions may suffer | want · and go | hungry:
    but those who seek the | Lord lack | nothing | good.

11 Come my children | listen · to | me:
    and I will | teach you · the | fear · of the | Lord.

12 Which of you | relish·es | life:
    wants [time · to en |joy good | things?

13 Keep your | tongue from | evil:
    and your | lips from | telling | lies.

14 Turn from evil and | do | good:
    seek | peace | and pur|sue it.

15 The eyes of God are | on the | righteous:
    and his | ears to |wards their | cry.

16 The Lord sets his face against | wrong|doers:
    to root out their | memo·ry | from the | earth.

17 The righteous cry   the | Lord | hears it:
    and | frees them · from | all · their af|flictions.

18 The Lord is close to those who are | broken |hearted:
    and the | crushed in | spirit · he | saves.

19 The trials of the | righteous · are | many:
    but our God de|livers · him | from them | all.

20 He guards | all his | bones:
    so | that not | one is | broken.

21 Evil will | slay the | wicked:
    and those who hate the | righteous · will |
    be de|stroyed.

22 The Lord ransoms the | lives · of his | servants:
    and none who hide in | him will | be de|stroyed.

PSALM 35

1 Contend O Lord with those who con|tend with | me:
    fight against | those that | fight a|gainst me.

2 Take up | shield and | buckler:
    and a|rise a|rise to | help me.

3 Draw the spear
    and bar the way against | those · that pur|sue me:
    say to me | 'I am | your de|liverer.'

4 Let those that seek my life
    be put to | shame · and dis|graced:
    let those that plot my destruction
    be | turned | back · and con|founded.

5 Let them be like chaff be|fore the | wind:
    with the | angel · of the | Lord | driving them;

6   let their way be ⏐ dark and ⏐ slippery:
       with the ⏐ angel · of the ⏐ Lord pur⏐suing.

7   For without cause‿
    they have secretly ⎰ spread a ⏐ net for me:
       without cause they have ⏐ dug a ⏐ pit · to en⏐trap me.

8   Let sudden dis⏐aster ⏐ strike them:
       let the net that they have hidden catch them
       let them ⏐ fall to ⏐ their de⏐struction.

9   Then shall my soul be ⏐ joyful · in the ⏐ Lord:
       and I will re⏐joice in ⏐ his de⏐liverance.

10   All my bones shall say ⏐ 'Lord · who is ⏐ like you?
       for you deliver the poor man‿
       from him that is too strong for him
       the poor and needy‿
       from ⏐ him that ⏐ would de⏐spoil them.'

11   Malicious witnesses rise ⏐ up a⏐gainst me:
       I am questioned about things of ⏐ which I ⏐
       know ⏐ nothing.

12   They repay me ⏐ evil · for ⏐ good:
       I am as ⎰ one be⏐reaved of · his ⏐ children.

13   Yet when they were sick I ⏐ put on ⏐ sackcloth:
       I af⏐flicted · my⏐self with ⏐ fasting.

14   And if my prayer returned unanswered ⏐ to my ⏐ bosom:
       I went about mourning
       as though for a ⏐ brother ⏐ or a · com⏐panion;

15   I was bowed ⏐ down with ⏐ grief:
       as ⏐ though · for my ⏐ own ⏐ mother.

16   But when I stumbled   they rejoiced and gathered ‿
    together * they gathered to⏐gether · a⏐gainst me:
       as though they were strangers I never knew
       they ⏐ tore at · me ⏐ without ⏐ ceasing.

†17 When I ⏐ slipped they ⏐ mocked me:
       and ⏐ gnashed · at me ⏐ with their ⏐ teeth.

18   Lord how long will ǀ you look ǀ on?
         take me from the evil they intend
         take me ǀ from a ǀ midst the ǀ lions.

19   And I will give you thanks in the ǀ great · congre ǀ gation:
         I will ǀ praise you · in the ǀ throng · of the ǀ people.

20   Let not those that wrongfully are my enemies ǀ ⌣
         triumph ǀ over me:
            let not those that hate me without cause ǀ ⌣
            mock me ǀ with their ǀ eyes.

21   For they speak words that do not ǀ make for ǀ peace:
         they invent lies against those that are ǀ quiet ǀ
         in the ǀ land.

22   They stretch their mouths to ǀ jeer at me · and ǀ say:
         'Aha aha!   We have ǀ seen ǀ all that · we ǀ wish!'

23   And you also have seen O Lord   ǀ do not · be ǀ silent:
         O God ǀ go not ǀ far ǀ from me.

24   Bestir yourself   awake to ǀ do me ǀ right:
         to plead my ǀ cause O ǀ Lord my ǀ God.

25   Judge me O Lord my God   according ǀ
      to your ǀ righteousness:
         and let them ǀ not re ǀ joice ǀ over me.

26   Let them not say in their hearts   'We ǀ have our ǀ wish':
         let them not ǀ say 'We ǀ have de ǀ stroyed him.'

27   Let those that rejoice at my hurt
      be disgraced and confounded ǀ alto ǀ gether:
         let those that lord it over me ⌣
         be ǀ clothed in ǀ shame · and dis ǀ honour.

28   But let those that long for my vindication
      shout for ǀ joy · and re ǀ joice:
         let them say always that the Lord is great
         who takes such de ǀ light · in his ǀ servant's ǀ good.

29   And my tongue shall ǀ speak of · your ǀ righteousness:
         and of your ǀ praise ǀ all the · day ǀ long.

PSALM 36

1 The transgressor speaks⌣
   from the wickedness in his | own | heart:
      there is no fear of | God be | fore his | eyes.

2 For he flatters himself in his | own | sight:
      he hates his in | iquity · to be | found | out.

3 The words of his mouth are wickedness | and de | ceit:
      he has ceased to act | wisely · and | do | good.

4 He plots mischief as he lies up | on his | bed:
      he has set himself on a path that is not good
      he | does not | spurn | evil.

5 Your unfailing kindness O Lord is | in the | heavens:
      and your faithfulness | reaches | to the | clouds.

6 Your righteousness is like the | strong | mountains:
      and your justice as the great deep
      you O Lord | save both | man and | beast.

7 How precious O God is your en | during | kindness:
      the children of men shall take refuge⌣
      under the | shadow | of your | wings.

8 They shall be satisfied⌣
   with the good things | of your | house:
      and you will give them drink⌣
      from the | river · of | your de | lights.

9 For with you is the | well of | life:
      and in your | light shall | we see | light.

10 O continue your merciful kindness⌣
   toward | those who | know you:
      and your righteous dealing⌣
      to | those · that are | true of | heart.

11 Let not the foot of the | proud · come a | gainst me:
      nor the hand of the un | godly | drive · me a | way.

12 There are they fallen | those who · do | evil:
      they are thrust down and | shall not | rise a | gain.

PSALM 37

1   Do not ˈ vie · with the ˈ wicked:
    or ˈ envy ˈ those that · do ˈ wrong;

2   for they will soon ˈ wither · like the ˈ grass:
    and fade aˈway · like the ˈ green ˈ leaf.

3   Trust in the ˈ Lord and · do ˈ good:
    and you shall dwell in the land ⌣
    and ˈ feed in ˈ safe ˈ pastures.

4   Let the Lord be ˈ your deˈlight:
    and he will ˈ grant you · your ˈ heart's deˈsire.

5   Commit your ˈ way · to the ˈ Lord:
    trust ˈ him and ˈ he will ˈ act.

6   He will make your righteousness ⌣
    shine as ˈ clear · as the ˈ light:
    and your ˈ inno·cence ˈ as the ˈ noonday.

7   Be still before the Lord * and wait ˈ patient·ly ˈ for him:
    do not be vexed when a man prospers
    when he puts his ˈ evil ˈ purposes · to ˈ work.

8   Let go of anger and aˈbandon ˈ wrath:
    let not envy ˈ move you · to ˈ do ˈ evil.

9   For the wicked shall be ˈ cut ˈ down:
    but those who wait for the ˈ Lord · shall posˈsess
    the ˈ land.

10 In a little while the ungodly shall ˈ be no ˈ more:
    you will look for him in his place ⌣
    but ˈ he will ˈ not be ˈ found.

†11 But the meek shall posˈsess the ˈ land:
    and enˈjoy · the aˈbundance · of ˈ peace.

12 The ungodly man plots aˈgainst the ˈ righteous:
    and ˈ gnashes · at him ˈ with his ˈ teeth.

13 But the Lord shall ˈ laugh him · to ˈ scorn:
    for he sees that the ˈ day · for his ˈ overthrow ·
    is ˈ near.

14 The ungodly have drawn the sword and ' strung
the ' bow:
   to strike down the poor and needy
   to slaughter ' those that ' walk in ' innocence.

15 Their swords shall pierce their ' own ' hearts:
   and their ' bows ' shall be ' broken.

16 Though the righteous man ' has · but a ' little:
   it is better than the great ' wealth of ' the un'godly.

17 For the strong arm of the ungodly ' shall be ' broken:
   but the ' Lord up'holds the ' righteous.

18 The Lord cares for the ' lives · of the ' innocent:
   and their heritage ' shall be ' theirs for ' ever.

19 They shall not be put to shame in the ' evil ' days:
   but in time of famine ' they shall ' eat their ' fill.

† 20 As for the ungodly they shall perish
they are the enemies ' of the ' Lord:
   like fuel in a furnace they shall ' vanish ·
   a'way in ' smoke.

21 The ungodly man borrows but does ' not re'pay:
   but the ' righteous · is ' gracious · and ' gives.

22 Those who are blessed by God shall pos'sess the 'land:
   but those whom he has ' cursed · shall be ' cut ' down.

23 If a man's steps are ' guided · by the ' Lord:
   and ' he de'lights in · his ' way,

24 though he stumble he shall ' not fall ' headlong:
   for the Lord ' holds him ' by the ' hand.

25 I have been young and ' now am ' old:
   but I never saw the righteous man forsaken
   or his ' children ' begging · their ' bread.

26 He is ever ' gracious · and ' lends:
   and his ' children ' shall be ' blessed.

27 Turn from evil and ' do ' good:
   and you shall ' dwell · in the ' land for ' ever.

28 For the | Lord loves | justice:
    he will | not for | sake his | faithful ones.

29 But the unjust shall be de | stroyed for | ever:
    and the children of the un | godly · shall be |
    cut | down.

30 The just shall pos | sess the | land:
    and they shall | dwell in | it for | ever.

31 The mouth of the righteous man | utters | wisdom:
    and his | tongue speaks | what is | right.

32 The law of his God is | in his | heart:
    and his | footsteps | will not | slip.

33 The ungodly man watches | out · for the | righteous:
    and | seeks oc | casion · to | slay him.

34 But the Lord will not abandon him | to his | power:
    nor let him be con | demned when | he is | judged.

†35 Wait for the Lord and | hold to · his | way:
    and he will raise you up to possess the land
    to see the un | godly · when | they are · de | stroyed.

36 I have seen the ungodly in | terri·fying | power:
    spreading himself | like a · lux | uri·ant | tree;

37 I passed by again and | he was | gone:
    I searched for him | but · he could | not be | found.

38 Observe the blameless man and con | sider · the | upright:
    for the man of | peace shall | have pos | terity.

39 But transgressors shall be de | stroyed · alto | gether:
    and the posterity of the | wicked · shall be | cut | down.

40 Deliverance for the righteous shall | come ·
from the | Lord:
    he is their | strength in | time of | trouble.

41 The Lord will help them | and de | liver them:
    he will save them from the ungodly and deliver them
    because they | come to | him for | refuge.

PSALM 38

1 O Lord rebuke me not ǀ in your ǀ anger:
   nor chasten me ǀ in your ǀ fierce disǀpleasure.

2 For your arrows have been ǀ aimed aǀgainst me:
   and your hand has come ǀ down ǀ heavy · upǀon me.

3 There is no health in my flesh
   because of your ǀ indigǀnation:
   nor soundness in my bones by ǀ reason ǀ of my ǀ sin.

4 The tide of my iniquities has gone ǀ over · my ǀ head:
   their weight is a burden too ǀ heavy ·
   for ǀ me to ǀ bear.

5 My wounds ǀ stink and ǀ fester:
   beǀcause ǀ of my ǀ foolishness.

6 I am bowed down and ǀ brought so ǀ low:
   that I go ǀ mourning ǀ all the · day ǀ long.

7 For my loins are filled with a ǀ burning ǀ pain:
   and there is no sound ǀ part in ǀ all my ǀ body.

8 I am numbed and ǀ stricken · to the ǀ ground:
   I cry aloud in the ǀ yearning ǀ of my ǀ heart.

9 O Lord   all I long for ǀ is beǀfore you:
   and my deep sighing ǀ is not ǀ hidden ǀ from you.

10 My heart is in tumult   my ǀ strength ǀ fails me:
    and even the ǀ light of · my ǀ eyes has ǀ gone from me.

11 My friends and my companions hold aloof ⌣
    from ǀ my afǀfliction:
    and my ǀ kinsmen ǀ stand far ǀ off.

12 Those who seek my ǀ life ǀ strike at me:
    and those that desire my hurt spread evil tales
    and murmur ǀ slanders ǀ all the ǀ day.

13 But I am like a deaf man and ǀ hear ǀ nothing:
    like one that is dumb who ǀ does not ǀ open ·
    his ǀ mouth.

14 So I have become as one who | cannot | hear:
    in whose | mouth · there is | no re | tort.

15 For in you Lord have I | put my | trust:
    and you will | answer me · O | Lord my | God.

16 For I prayed   'Let them never ex | ult | over me:
    those who turn arrogant | when my | foot | slips.'

17 Truly I am | ready · to | fall:
    and my | pain is | with me · con | tinually.

18 But I ac | knowledge · my | wickedness:
    and I am filled with | sorrow | at my | sin.

19 Those that are my enemies without cause are |
    great in | number:
    and those who hate me | wrongful | ly are | many.

20 Those also who repay evil for good | are a | gainst me:
    because I | seek | after | good.

† 21 Forsake me not O Lord
    go not far | from me · my | God:
    hasten to my | help O | Lord · my sal | vation.

PSALM 39

1 I said 'I will keep watch over my ways
    lest I | sin · with my | tongue:
    I will keep a guard on my mouth
    while the | wicked · are | in my | sight.'

2 I held my tongue and | said | nothing:
    I kept | silent · but | found no | comfort.

3 My pain was increased   my heart grew | hot
    with | in me:
    while I mused the fire blazed and I | spoke |
    with my | tongue;

4 'Lord let me | know my | end:
    and the | number | of my | days,

† 5 'that I may know how | short my | time is:
    for you have made my days but a handsbreadth
    and my whole | span · is as | nothing · be | fore you.'

6 Surely every man though he stand secure |
    is but | breath:
        and | lives · as a | passing | shadow.

7 The riches he heaps are but a | puff of | wind:
        and he cannot ⌐ tell | who will | gather them.

8 And now Lord | what is · my | hope?
        truly my | hope | is in | you.

9 O deliver me from | all · my trans|gressions:
        do not | make me · the | butt of | fools.

10 I was dumb   I did not | open · my | mouth:
        for surely | it was | your | doing.

11 Take away your | plague | from me:
        I am brought to an ⌐ end · by the | blows ·
        of your | hand.

12 When with rebukes you chastise a | man for | sin:
        you cause his fair looks to dissolve in putrefaction
        surely | every · man | is but | breath.

13 Hear my prayer O Lord   and give | ear to · my | cry:
        be not ⌐ silent | at my | tears.

14 For I am but a | stranger · with | you:
        a passing guest as ⌐ all my | fathers | were.

15 Turn your eye from me   that I may | smile a|gain:
        before I go | hence and | am no | more.

PSALM 40

1 I waited patiently | for the | Lord:
        and he in|clined to me · and | heard my | cry.

2 He brought me up from the pit of roaring waters
    out of the | mire and | clay:
        and set my feet upon a | rock · and made | firm
        my | foothold.

3 And he has put a new | song · in my | mouth:
        even a song of | thanks·giving | to our | God.

4   Many shall ^l see it · and ^l fear:
       and shall ^l put their ^l trust · in the ^l Lord.

5   Blessèd is the man who has made the ^l Lord his ^l hope:
       who has not turned to the proud
       or to those who ^l wander ^l in de^lceit.

6   O Lord my God
       great are the wonderful things which you have done
       and your thoughts which ^l are to ^lwards us:
       there is none to ^l be com^lpared with ^l you;

†7   were I to de^lclare them · and ^l speak of them:
       they are more than I am ^l able ^l to ex^lpress.

8   Sacrifice and offering you do ^l not de^lsire:
       but my ^l ears · you have ^l marked · for o^lbedience;

9   Burnt-offering and sin-offering you have ^l
       not re^lquired:
       then ^l said I ^l Lo I ^l come.

10   In the scroll of the book it is written of me
       that I should ^l do your ^l will:
       O my God I long to do it* your ^l law de^llights
       my ^l heart.

11   I have declared your righteousness‿
       in the ^l great · congre^lgation:
       I have not restrained my lips O ^l Lord ‿
       and ^l that you ^l know.

12   I have not hidden your righteousness ^l in my ^l heart:
       I have spoken of your faithfulness ^l and of ^l
       your sal^lvation.

13   I have not kept back your loving-kindness ^l ‿
       and your ^l truth:
       from the ^l great ^l congre^lgation.

14   O Lord do not withhold your ^l mercy ^l from me:
       let your loving-kindness and your ^l truth ^l ever ·
       pre^lserve me.

15 For innumerable troubles have | come up | on me:
    my sins have overtaken me | and I | cannot | see.

16 They are more in number than the | hairs ·
    of my | head:
        there | fore my | heart | fails me.

17 Be pleased O | Lord · to de | liver me:
    O | Lord make | haste to | help me.

18 Let those who seek my life to | take it · a | way:
    be put to shame and con | founded | alto | gether.

19 Let them be turned back and disgraced who |
    wish me | evil:
        let them be aghast for shame who | say to me ·
        'A | ha a | ha!'

20 Let all who seek you be joyful and | glad ⏝
    be | cause of you:
        let those who love your salvation say | always ·
        'The | Lord is | great.'

21 As for me I am | poor and | needy:
    but the | Lord will | care | for me.

† 22 You are my helper and | my de | liverer:
    make no long de | lay O | Lord my | God.

PSALM 41

1 Blessèd is he that considers the | poor and | helpless:
    the Lord will deliver him | in the | day of | trouble.

2 The Lord will guard him and preserve his life
    he shall be counted | happy · in the | land:
        you will not give him | over · to the | will ·
        of his | enemies.

† 3 And if he lies sick on his bed the | Lord ·
    will sus | tain him:
        if illness lays him | low · you will | over | throw it.

4 I said 'O Lord be | merciful · to | ward me:
    heal me for | I have | sinned a | gainst you.'

5   My enemies speak evil ᛱ of me ᛱ saying:
      'When will he die and his ᛱ name ᛱ perish · for ᛱ ever?'

6   And if one should come to see me   he mouths ᛱ
      empty ᛱ words:
        while his heart gathers mischief
        and ᛱ when he · goes ᛱ out he ᛱ vents it.

7   All those that hate me whisper to ᛱgether · a ᛱgainst me:
      they de ᛱvise ᛱ plots a ᛱgainst me.

8   They say   'A deadly ᛱ thing has · got ᛱ hold of him:
      he will not get up a ᛱgain from ᛱ where he ᛱ lies.'

9   Even my bosom friend in ᛱ whom I ᛱ trusted:
      who shared my bread   has ᛱ lifted · his ᛱ heel
      a ᛱgainst me.

10   But you O Lord be gracious and ᛱ raise me ᛱ up:
      and I will repay them ᛱ what they ᛱ have de ᛱserved.

11   By this will I ᛱ know that · you ᛱ favour me:
      that my enemy ᛱ shall not ᛱ triumph ᛱ over me.

(†) 12   Because of my innocence you ᛱ hold me ᛱ fast:
      you have set me be ᛱfore your ᛱ face for ᛱ ever.

(13   Blessèd be the Lord the ᛱ God of ᛱ Israel:
      from everlasting to everlasting* ᛱ Amen ᛱ A ᛱmen.)

PSALM 42

1   As a deer longs for the ᛱ running ᛱ brooks:
      so longs my ᛱ soul for ᛱ you O ᛱ God.

2   My soul is thirsty for God* thirsty for the ᛱ
      living ᛱ God:
        when shall I ᛱ come and ᛱ see his ᛱ face?

3   My tears have been my food ᛱ day and ᛱ night:
      while they ask me all day long   ᛱ 'Where now ᛱ
      is your ᛱ God?'

4   As I pour out my soul by myself I re ᛱmember ᛱ this:
      how I went to the house of the Mighty One ᛱ ‿
      into · the ᛱ temple · of ᛱ God,

† 5   to the shouts and | songs of · thanks | giving:
        a multitude | keeping | high | festival.

6   *Why are you so full of* | *heaviness · my* | *soul:*
        and | *why · so un* | *quiet · with* | *in me?*

7   *O put your* | *trust in* | *God:*
        for I will praise him yet
        who is my de | *liver ·er* | *and my* | *God.*

8   My soul is | heavy · with | in me:
        therefore I will remember you from the⌣
        land of Jordan
        from Mizar a | mong the | hills of | Hermon.

9   Deep calls to deep in the | roar of · your | waters:
        all your waves and | breakers | have gone | over me.

10   Surely the Lord will grant his loving mercy |
    in the | day-time:
        and in the night his song will be with me
        a | prayer · to the | God · of my | life.

11   I will say to God my rock   'Why have | you
    for | gotten me:
        why must I go like a mourner be | cause the | enemy ·
        op | presses me?'

† 12   Like a sword through my bones my | enemies · have |
    mocked me:
        while they ask me all day long | 'Where now |
        is your | God?'

13   *Why are you so full of* | *heaviness · my* | *soul:*
        and | *why · so un* | *quiet · with* | *in me?*

14   *O put your* | *trust in* | *God:*
        for I will praise him yet
        who is my de | *liver ·er* | *and my* | *God.*

PSALM 43

1   Give judgement for me O God
    take up my cause against an un | godly | people:
        deliver me from de | ceitful · and | wicked | men.

2 For you are God my refuge   why have you ǀ turned ·
me a ǀ way:
   why must I go like a mourner‿
   be ǀ cause the ǀ enemy · op ǀ presses me?

3 O send out your light and your truth and ǀ let them ǀ
lead me:
   let them guide me to your holy ǀ hill and ǀ to your ǀ
   dwelling.

4 Then I shall go to the altar of God
to God my joy and ǀ my de ǀ light:
   and to the harp I shall sing your ǀ praises ·
   O ǀ God my ǀ God.

5 *Why are you so full of ǀ heaviness · my ǀ soul:*
and ǀ why · so un ǀ quiet · with ǀin me?

6 *O put your ǀ trust in ǀ God:*
for I will praise him yet
who is my de ǀ liver ·er ǀ and my ǀ God.

PSALM 44

1 We have heard with our ears O God ‿
our ǀ fathers · have ǀ told us:
   what things you did in their ǀ time · in the ǀ
   days of ǀ old;

2 how by your own hand you drove out the nations‿
and ǀ planted · us ǀ in:
   how you crushed the peoples
   but caused ǀ us to ǀ root and ǀ grow.

3 For it was not by their swords‿
that our fathers took pos ǀ session · of the ǀ land:
   nor did their own ǀ arm ǀ get them · the ǀ victory,

4 but your right hand   your arm‿
and the ǀ light of · your ǀ countenance:
   be ǀ cause · you de ǀ lighted · in ǀ them.

5 You are my ǀ king · and my ǀ God:
   who or ǀ dained ǀ victory · for ǀ Jacob.

6   By your power we struck our | ene·mies | through:
       in your name we trod down | those that | rose
       a | gainst us.

7   For I did not | trust · in my | bow:
       nor | could my | sword | save me;

8   but it was you that delivered us | from our | enemies:
       and put our | adver·saries | to con | fusion.

†9   In God we made our boast | all the · day | long:
       we gave | thanks to · your | name with·out | ceasing.

10   But now you have cast us off and | brought us ·
       to | shame:
       you | go not | out · with our | armies.

11   You have caused us to show our | backs · to the | enemy:
       so that our foes | plunder | us at | will.

12   You have given us like | sheep · to be | butchered:
       you have | scattered us · a | mong the | nations.

13   You have sold your | people · for | nothing:
       and | made a | profit·less | bargain.

14   You have made us a laughing-stock | to our |
       neighbours:
       mocked and held in de | rision · by | those a | bout us.

15   You have made us a byword a | mong the | nations:
       so that the peoples | toss their | heads in | scorn.

16   My disgrace is before me | all the | day:
       and | shame has | covered · my | face,

17   at the voice of the slanderer | and re | viler:
       at the sight of the | ene·my | and a | venger.

18   All this has come upon us   though we have |
       not for | gotten you:
       we have | not be | trayed your | covenant.

19   Our hearts have | not turned | back:
       nor have our steps | strayed | from your | paths.

20   And yet you have crushed us in the | haunt of | jackals:
       and covered us | with the | shadow · of | death.

21 If we had forgotten the | name of · our | God:
    or stretched out our hands in | prayer to · some |
    strange | god,

22 would not God | search it | out?
    for he knows the very | secrets | of the | heart.

23 But for your sake are we killed | all the · day | long:
    we are | counted · as | sheep · for the | slaughter.

24 Rouse yourself O Lord | why · do you | sleep?
    awake do not | cast us | off for | ever.

25 Why do you | hide your | face:
    and forget our | misery · and | our af|fliction?

26 Our souls are | bowed · to the | dust:
    our | bellies | cleave · to the | ground.

27 Arise O | Lord to | help us:
    and redeem us | for your | mercy's | sake.

PSALM 45

1 My heart is astir with fine phrases
    I make my | song · for a | king:
    my tongue is the | pen · of a | ready | writer.

2 You are the fairest of the sons of men
    grace | flows · from your | lips:
    therefore has God | blessed you · for | ever · and | ever.

3 Gird your sword upon your thigh O | mighty | warrior:
    in glory and majesty tread | down your | foes
    and | triumph!

4 Ride on in the | cause of | truth:
    and | for the | sake of | justice.

5 Your right hand shall teach a | terrible · in|struction:
    peoples shall fall beneath you * your arrows shall be⌣
    sharp in the | hearts · of the | king's | enemies.

6   Your throne is the throne of God   it en⎸dures for ⎸ever:
         and the sceptre of your ⎸kingdom · is a ⎸
         righteous ⎸sceptre.

7   You have loved righteousness and ⎸hated ⎸evil:
         therefore God your God * has anointed you
         with the oil of ⎸gladness · a⎸bove your ⎸fellows.

8   All your garments are fragrant
         with myrrh ⎸aloes · and ⎸cassia:
         music from ivory ⎸pala·ces ⎸makes you ⎸glad.

†9   Kings' daughters are among your ⎸noble ⎸women:
         the queen is at your right ⎸hand in ⎸gold of ⎸Ophir.

10   Hear O daughter   consider and in⎸cline your ⎸ear:
         forget your own ⎸people · and your ⎸father's ⎸house.

11   The king de⎸sires your ⎸beauty:
         he is your lord   ⎸therefore · bow ⎸down be⎸fore him.

†12   The richest among the people O ⎸daughter · of ⎸Tyre:
         shall en⎸treat your ⎸favour · with ⎸gifts.

13   The king's daughter is all ⎸glorious · with⎸in:
         her clothing is em⎸broidered ⎸cloth of ⎸gold.

14   In robes of many colours she is led to ⎸you O ⎸king:
         and after her the ⎸virgins ⎸that are ⎸with her.

†15   They are led with ⎸gladness · and re⎸joicing:
         they enter the ⎸palace ⎸of the ⎸king.

16   In place of your fathers ⎸you shall · have ⎸sons:
         and make them princes ⎸over ⎸all the ⎸land.

17   And I will make known your name to every ⎸
         gener⎸ation:
         therefore the peoples shall ⎸give you ⎸praise
         for ⎸ever.

PSALM 46

1   God is our ⎸refuge · and ⎸strength:
         a very ⎸present ⎸help in ⎸trouble.

2   Therefore we will not fear though the | earth
be | moved:
      and though the mountains are | shaken · in the |
      midst · of the | sea;

†3   though the waters | rage and | foam:
      and though the mountains quake at the | rising |
      of the | sea.

4   There is a river whose streams make glad the | city ·
of | God:
      the holy dwelling-place | of the | Most | High.

5   God is in the midst of her
therefore she shall | not be | moved:
      God will | help her · and at | break of | day.

6   The nations make uproar and the | kingdoms ·
are | shaken:
      but God has lifted his | voice · and the | earth
      shall | tremble.

7   *The Lord of | hosts is | with us:*
      the God of | Jacob | is our | stronghold.

8   Come then and see what the | Lord has | done:
      what destruction he has | brought up | on the | earth.

9   He makes wars to cease in | all the | world:
      he breaks the bow and shatters the spear
      and burns the | chari·ots | in the | fire.

10   'Be still and know that | I am | God:
      I will be exalted among the nations
      I will be ex | alted · up | on the | earth.'

11   *The Lord of | hosts is | with us:*
      the God of | Jacob | is our | stronghold.

PSALM 47

1   O clap your hands | all you | peoples:
      and cry aloud to | God with | shouts of | joy.

2 For the Lord Most High | is to · be | feared:
   he is a great | King · over | all the | earth.

3 He cast down | peoples | under us:
   and the | nations · be | neath our | feet.

4 He chose us a land for | our pos | session:
   that was the pride of | Jacob | whom he | loved.

5 God has gone up with the | sound · of re | joicing:
   and the | Lord · to the | blast · of the | horn.

6 O sing praises sing | praises · to | God:
   O sing praises sing | praises | to our | King.

7 For God is the King of | all the | earth:
   O | praise him · in a | well-wrought | psalm.

8 God has become the | King · of the | nations:
   he has taken his seat up | on his | holy | throne.

9 The princes of the peoples are | gathered · to | gether:
   with the | people · of the | God of | Abraham.

10 For the mighty ones of the earth
   are become the | servants · of | God:
   and | he is | greatly · ex | alted.

PSALM 48

1 Great is the Lord and | greatly · to be | praised:
   in the | city | of our | God.

2 High and beautiful is his | holy | hill:
   it is the | joy of | all the | earth.

†3 On Mount Zion where godhead truly dwells
   stands the city of the | Great | King:
   God is well known in her palaces | as a | sure de | fence.

4 For the kings of the | earth as | sembled:
   they gathered to | gether · and | came | on;

5 they saw   they were | struck | dumb:
   they were a | stonished · and | fled in | terror.

6   Trembling took | hold on them · and | anguish:
       as on a | woman | in her | travail;

7   like the breath of the | east | wind:
       that | shatters · the | ships of | Tarshish.

8   As we have heard   so have we seen⌣
     in the city of the | Lord of | hosts:
       in the city of our God ⌣
       which | God · has es|tablished · for|ever.

9   We have called to mind your loving|kindness · O | God:
       in the | midst of | your | temple.

10   As your name is great O God   so also | is your | praise:
       even to the | ends | of the | earth.

11   Your right hand is full of victory
     let Zion's | hill re|joice:
       let the daughters of Judah be | glad ⌣
       be|cause of · your | judgements.

12   Walk about Zion   go round about her⌣
     and | count · all her | towers:
       consider well her ramparts | pass |
       through her | palaces;

13   that you may tell those who come after that |
     such is | God:
       our God for ever and ever * and | he will |
       guide us · e|ternally.

PSALM 49

1   O hear this | all you | peoples:
       give ear all you in|habit·ants | of the | world,

2   all children of men and | sons of | Adam:
       both | rich and | poor a|like.

3   For my mouth shall | speak | wisdom:
       and the thoughts of my heart⌣
       shall be | full of | under|standing.

4   I will incline my ˈ ear · to a ˈ riddle:
        and unfold the mystery to the ˈ sounds ˈ of the ˈ harp.

5   Why should I fear in the ˈ evil ˈ days:
        when the wickedness of ˈ my deˈceivers ·
        surˈrounds me,

6   though they trust to their ˈ great ˈ wealth:
        and boast of the aˈbundance ˈ of their ˈ riches?

7   No man may ˈ ransom · his ˈ brother:
        or give ˈ God a ˈ price ˈ for him,

8   so that he may ˈ live for ˈ ever:
        and ˈ never ˈ see the ˈ grave;

9   for to ransom men's ˈ lives · is so ˈ costly:
        that he must aˈbandon ˈ it for ˈ ever.

10   For we see that ˈ wise men ˈ die:
        and perish with the foolish and the ignorant ˈ
        leaving · their ˈ wealth to ˈ others.

†11   The tomb is their home for ever
        their dwelling-place throughout ˈ all · generˈations:
        though they called estates ˈ after · their ˈ own ˈ names.

12   A rich man without ˈ underˈstanding:
        is ˈ like the ˈ beasts that ˈ perish.

13   This is the ˈ lot · of the ˈ foolish:
        the end of those who are ˈ pleased · with their ˈ
        own ˈ words.

14   They are driven like sheep into the grave‿
        and ˈ death · is their ˈ shepherd:
        they slip down ˈ easi·ly ˈ into · the ˈ tomb.

15   Their bright forms shall wear aˈway · in the ˈ grave:
        and ˈ lose their ˈ former ˈ glory.

†16   But God will ˈ ransom · my ˈ life:
        he will take me ˈ from the ˈ power · of the ˈ grave.

17   Do not fear when a ˈ man grows ˈ rich:
        when the ˈ wealth · of his ˈ household · inˈcreases,

18   for he will take nothing a ˈway : when he ˈ dies:
        nor will his ˈ wealth go ˈ down ˈ after him.

19   Though he counts himself happy ˈ while he ˈ lives:
        and praises you ˈ also ˈ when you ˈ prosper,

20   he will go to the company ˈ of his ˈ fathers:
        who will ˈ never ˈ see the ˈ light.

†21   A rich man without ˈ under ˈstanding:
        is ˈ like the ˈ beasts that ˈ perish.

PSALM 50

1   The Lord our God the ˈ Mighty One · has ˈ spoken:
        and summoned the earth
        from the rising of the sun to its ˈ setting ˈ ⌣
        in the ˈ west.

2   From Zion ˈ perfect · in ˈ beauty:
        God has ˈ shone ˈ out in ˈ glory.

3   Our God is coming   he will ˈ not keep ˈ silent:
        before him is devouring fire
        and ˈ tempest ˈ whirls a ˈbout him.

4   He calls to the ˈ heavens · a ˈbove:
        and to the earth so ˈ he may ˈ judge his ˈ people.

5   'Gather to ˈ me my ˈ faithful ones:
        those who by sacrifice ˈ made a ˈ coven·ant ˈ with me.'

6   The heavens shall pro ˈclaim his ˈ righteousness:
        for ˈ God him ˈself is ˈ judge.

7   'Listen my people and ˈ I will ˈ speak:
        O Israel I am God your God   and ˈ I will ˈ
        give my ˈ testimony.

8   'It is not for your sacrifices that ˈ I re ˈprove you:
        for your burnt ˈofferings · are ˈ always · be ˈfore me.

9   'I will take no ˈ bull · from your ˈ farms:
        or ˈ he-goat ˈ from your ˈ pens.

10   'For all the beasts of the forest be ˈlong to ˈ me:
        and so do the ˈ cattle · up ˈon the ˈ mountains.

11   'I know all the | birds · of the | air:
     and the grasshoppers of the | field are | in my | sight.

12   'If I were hungry I | would not | tell you:
     for the whole world is | mine and | all · that is | in it.

13   'Do I eat the | flesh of | bulls:
     or | drink the | blood of | goats?

14   'Offer to God a sacrifice of | thanks|giving:
     and pay your | vows · to the | Most | High.

† 15 'Call upon me in the | day of | trouble:
     I will bring you out   and | you shall | glori·fy | me.'

16   But God | says · to the | wicked:
     'What have you to do with reciting my laws
     or taking my | coven·ant | on your | lips,

17   'seeing you | loathe | discipline:
     and have | tossed my | words be|hind you?

18   'When you saw a thief you | went a |long with him:
     and you | threw in · your | lot · with ad|ulterers.

19   'You have loosed your | mouth in | evil:
     and your | tongue strings | lies to|gether.

20   'You sit and speak a|gainst your | brother:
     and slander your | own | mother's | son.

21   'These things you have done   and I | held my | tongue:
     and you thought I was just such an|other |
     as your|self.

22   'But I | will con|vict you:
     and set before your | eyes what | you have | done.

23   'O consider this   you who for|get | God:
     lest I tear you in pieces   and | there be | no one·
     to | save you.

† 24 'He honours me who brings sacrifice of | thanks|giving:
     and to him who keeps to my way
     I will | show the · sal|vation · of | God.'

PSALM 51

1   Have mercy on me O God in your en ˈduring ˈ goodness:
      according to the fulness of your compassion ˈ ⌣
      blot out ˈ my of ˈfences.

2   Wash me thoroughly ˈ from my ˈ wickedness:
      and ˈ cleanse me ˈ from my ˈ sin.

3   For I acknowledge ˈ my re ˈbellion:
      and my ˈ sin is ˈ ever · be ˈfore me.

4   Against you only have I sinned
   and done what is evil ˈ in your ˈ eyes:
      so you will be just in your sentence
      and ˈ blameless ˈ in your ˈ judging.

5   Surely in wickedness I was ˈ brought to ˈ birth:
      and in ˈ sin my ˈ mother · con ˈceived me.

6   You that desire truth in the ˈ inward ˈ parts:
      O teach me wisdom in the secret ˈ places ˈ
      of the ˈ heart.

7   Purge me with hyssop and I ˈ shall be ˈ clean:
      wash me and I ˈ shall be ˈ whiter · than ˈ snow.

8   Make me hear of ˈ joy and ˈ gladness:
      let the bones which ˈ you have ˈ broken · re ˈjoice.

9   Hide your ˈ face · from my ˈ sins:
      and ˈ blot out ˈ all · my in ˈiquities.

10   Create in me a clean ˈ heart O ˈ God:
      and re ˈnew a · right ˈ spirit · with ˈin me.

11   Do not cast me ˈ out · from your ˈ presence:
      do not take your ˈ holy ˈ spirit ˈ from me.

12   O give me the gladness of your ˈ help a ˈgain:
      and sup ˈport me · with a ˈ willing ˈ spirit.

†13   Then will I teach trans ˈgressors · your ˈ ways:
      and sinners shall ˈ turn to ˈ you a ˈgain.

14   O Lord God of my salvation   de ˈliver me ·
   from ˈ bloodshed:
      and my ˈ tongue shall ˈ sing of · your ˈ righteousness.

15 O Lord | open · my | lips:
    and my | mouth · shall pro|claim your | praise.

16 You take no pleasure in sacrifice or | I would | give it:
    burnt|offerings · you | do not | want.

17 The sacrifice of God is a | broken | spirit:
    a broken and contrite heart O God |
    you will | not de|spise.

18 In your graciousness do | good to | Zion:
    re|build the | walls · of Je|rusalem.

19 Then will you delight in right sacrifices
    in burnt-offerings | and ob|lations:
    then will they offer young | bulls up|on your | altar.

PSALM 52

1 Why O man of power do you boast | all the · day | long:
   of mischief done to | him · that is | faithful · to | God?

2 You contrive de|stroying | slanders:
   your tongue is like a sharpened | razor ·
   it | cuts de|ceitfully.

3 You have loved evil | and not | good:
   to tell lies | rather · than to | speak the | truth.

4 You love all words that | may do | hurt:
   and | every · de|ceit · of the | tongue.

5 But God will de|stroy you | utterly:
   he will snatch you away
   and pluck you out of your dwelling
   he will up|root you · from the | land · of the | living.

6 The righteous shall | see it · and | fear:
   they shall | laugh you · to | scorn and | say,

†7 'Behold   this is the man
   who did not take | God · for his | strength:
   but trusted in the abundance of his riches
   and | found his | strength in | slander.'

8 As for me   I am like a green olive tree in the |
house of | God:
   I will trust in the goodness of | God for |
   ever · and | ever.

9 I will always give you thanks * for this was |
your | doing:
   I will glorify your name before the faithful
   for | it is | good to | praise you.

PSALM 53

1 The fool has said in his heart   'There | is no | God':
   they have all become vile and abominable⌣
   in their wickedness
   there | is not | one that · does | good.

2 God looked down from heaven upon the |
children · of | men:
   to see if there were any who would act | wisely · ⌣
   and | seek · after | God.

3 But they have all turned aside
they have all alike be |come cor |rupt:
   there is none that does | good | no not | one.

4 Are all the evildoers devoid of | under |standing:
   who eat up my people as men eat bread
   and | do not | pray to | God?

5 They shall be | struck with | terror:
   for God will scatter the | bones | of the · un |godly.

6 They shall be | put to · con |fusion:
   because | God | has re |jected them.

†7 O that deliverance for Israel might come | forth
from | Zion:
   when the Lord turns again the fortunes of his people
   then shall Jacob re |joice and | Israel · be | glad.

PSALM 54

1 Save me O God by the | power of · your | name:
   and | vindicate · me | by your | might.

2   Hear my ǀ prayer O ǀ God:
       and ǀ listen · to the ǀ words of · my ǀ mouth.

3   For the insolent have ǀ risen · a ǀgainst me:
       ruthless men who have not set God be ǀfore them ǀ ⌣
       seek my ǀ life.

4   But surely ǀ God is · my ǀ helper:
       the Lord is the up ǀholder ǀ of my ǀ life.

[5   Let evil recoil on those that ǀ would way ǀlay me:
       O de ǀstroy them ǀ in your ǀ faithfulness!]

6   Then will I offer you sacrifice with a ǀ willing ǀ heart:
       I will praise your name O ǀ Lord for ǀ it is ǀ good.

[†] 7   For you will deliver me from ǀ every ǀ trouble:
       my eyes shall see the ǀ downfall ǀ of my ǀ enemies.

PSALM 55

1   Hear my ǀ prayer O ǀ God:
       and do not hide your ǀself from ǀ my pe ǀtition.

2   Give heed to ǀ me and ǀ answer me:
       I am ǀ restless · in ǀ my com ǀplaining.

3   I am in turmoil at the ǀ voice · of the ǀ enemy:
       at the ǀ onslaught ǀ of the ǀ wicked.

4   For they bring down dis ǀaster · up ǀon me:
       they persecute ǀ me with ǀ bitter ǀ fury.

5   My heart ǀ writhes with ǀin me:
       and the terrors of ǀ death have ǀ fallen · up ǀon me.

6   Fear and trembling ǀ come up ǀon me:
       and ǀ horror ǀ over ǀwhelms me.

7   And I said   'O for the ǀ wings · of a ǀ dove:
       that I might fly a ǀway and ǀ find ǀ rest.

8   'Then I would ǀ flee far ǀ off:
       and make my ǀ lodging ǀ in the ǀ wilderness.

9   'I would hasten to ǀ find me · a ǀ refuge:
       out ǀ of the ǀ blast of ǀ slander,

10 'out of the tempest of their | calumny · O | Lord:
      and | far · from their | double | tongues.'

11 For I have seen violence and | strife · in the | city:
      day and night they go | round it · up | on its | walls.

12 Evil and wickedness | are with | in it:
      iniquity is within it
      oppression and fraud do | not de | part ·
      from its | streets.

13 It was not an enemy that reviled me
   or I | might have | borne it:
      it was not my foe that dealt so insolently with me
      or I might have | hidden · my | self | from him;

14 but it was you a | man · like my | self:
      my companion | and · my fam | iliar | friend.

† 15 Together we en | joyed sweet | fellowship:
      in the | house | of our | God.

[16 Let them pass a | way · in con | fusion:
      let death | carry · them | to des | truction;

17 let them go down a | live to | Sheol:
      for evil is a | mong them | in their | dwellings.]

18 But I will | call to | God:
      and the | Lord my | God will | save me.

19 At evening at morning | and at | noon-day:
      I com | plain and | groan a | loud.

20 And he will | hear my | voice:
      and | ransom · my | soul in | peace,

21 from those that bear | down up | on me:
      for | there are | many · a | gainst me.

22 God will hear and | bring them | low:
      he that | is en | throned for | ever.

23 For they do not | keep their | word:
      and they | have no | fear of | God.

24   They lay violent hands⌣
      on those that ˺ are at ˺ peace with them:
          they ˺ break ˺ solemn ˺ covenants.

25   Their mouths are smooth as butter
      but war is ˺ in their ˺ hearts:
          their words are softer than oil
          yet ˺ they are ˺ drawn ˺ swords.

26   Cast your burden on the Lord and ˺ he ·
      will sus ˺ tain you:
          he will never suffer the ˺ righteous ˺ man to ˺ stumble.

27   But as for them   you will bring them ˺ down O ˺ God:
          even ˺ to the ˺ depths · of the ˺ Pit.

† 28 Bloodthirsty and deceitful men⌣
      shall not live out ˺ half their ˺ days:
          but ˺ I will ˺ trust in ˺ you.

PSALM 56

1   Be merciful to me O God   for men are ˺ treading ·
     me ˺ down:
         all day long my ˺ adver·sary ˺ presses · up ˺ on me.

2   My enemies tread me down ˺ all the ˺ day:
         for there are many that ˺ arrogant·ly ˺
         fight a ˺ gainst me.

3   In the ˺ hour of ˺ fear:
         I will ˺ put my ˺ trust in ˺ you.

4   In God whose word I praise * in God I ˺ trust
     and ˺ fear not:
         what can ˺ flesh ˺ do to ˺ me?

5   All day long they afflict me ˺ with their ˺ words:
         and every thought is ˺ how to ˺ do me ˺ evil.

6   They stir up hatred ˺ and con ˺ ceal themselves:
         they watch my steps   while they ˺ lie in ˺ wait for ·
         my ˺ life.

7   Let there be ˺ no es ˺ cape for them:
         bring down the ˺ peoples · in your ˺ wrath O ˺ God.

8 You have counted my anxious tossings
   put my ⎮ tears · in your ⎮ bottle:
       are not these things ⎮ noted ⎮ in your ⎮ book?

9 In the day that I call to you   my enemies
   shall ⎮ turn ⎮ back:
       this I ⎮ know for ⎮ God is ⎮ with me.

10 In God whose word I praise * in God I ⎮ trust
   and ⎮ fear not:
       what can ⎮ man ⎮ do to ⎮ me?

11 To you O God must I per⎮form my ⎮ vows:
       I will pay the thank⎤offer·ing ⎮ that is ⎮ due.

12 For you will deliver my soul from death‿
   and my ⎮ feet from ⎮ falling:
       that I may walk before ⎮ God · in the ⎮ light ·
       of the ⎮ living.

PSALM 57

1 Be merciful to me O ⎮ God be ⎮ merciful:
       for I ⎮ come to ⎮ you for ⎮ shelter;

2 and in the shadow of your wings will ⎮ I take ⎮ refuge:
       until these ⎮ troubles · are ⎮ over⎮past.

3 I will call to ⎮ God Most ⎮ High:
       to the God who will ful⎮fil his ⎮ purpose ⎮ for me.

4 He will send from ⎮ heaven · and ⎮ save me:
       he will send forth his faithfulness and his‿
       loving-kindness
       and rebuke ⎮ those · that would ⎮ trample ·
       me ⎮ down.

5 For I lie amidst ⎮ raven·ing ⎮ lions:
       men whose teeth are spears and arrows
       and their ⎮ tongue a ⎮ sharpened ⎮ sword.

6 *Be exalted O God a ⎮bove the ⎮ heavens:*
       and let your glory be ⎮ over ⎮ all the ⎮ earth.

7 They have set a net for my feet ┃ and I am ┃
brought ┃ low:
 they have dug a pit before me
 but shall ┃ fall · into ┃ it them ┃ selves.

8 My heart is fixed O God my ┃ heart is ┃ fixed:
 I will ┃ sing and ┃ make ┃ melody.

9 Awake my soul awake ┃ lute and ┃ harp:
 for ┃ I · will a ┃ waken · the ┃ morning.

10 I will give you thanks O Lord a ┃ mong the ┃ peoples:
 I will sing your ┃ praise a ┃ mong the ┃ nations.

11 For the greatness of your mercy ┃ reaches ·
to the ┃ heavens:
 and your ┃ faithful · ness ┃ to the ┃ clouds.

12 *Be exalted O God a ┃ bove the ┃ heavens:*
 and let your glory be ┃ over ┃ all the ┃ earth.

PSALM 58

[1 Do you indeed decree what is ┃ just O ┃ rulers:
 do you with uprightness ┃ judge the ┃ children ·
of ┌ men?

2 No you work in the land with ┃ evil ┃ heart:
 you look on the violence ┃ that your ┃ hands
have ┃ wrought.

3 The wicked are estranged ┃ even · from the ┃ womb:
 they are liars that go a ┃ stray ┃ from their ┃ birth.

4 They are venomous with the ┃ venom · of ┃ serpents:
 like the deaf ┃ asp that ┃ stops its ┃ ears,

†5 and will not heed the ┃ voice · of the ┃ charmers:
 though the ┃ binder · of ┃ spells be ┃ skilful.

6 Break their teeth O ┃ God · in their ┃ mouths:
 shatter the jaws of the ┃ young ┃ lions · O ┃ Lord.

7 Let them dissolve and drain a ┃ way like ┃ water:
 let them be trodden down ┃ let them ┃ wither ·
like ┃ grass,

8   Like a woman's miscarriage that melts and | passes ·
a | way:
    like an abortive birth that | has not | seen the | sun.

9   Before they know it   let them be cut | down like |
thorns:
    like brambles which a | man sweeps | angrily · a | side.

10   The righteous shall rejoice when he | sees
the | vengeance:
    he will wash his feet in the | blood of | the un | godly.

11   And men will say   'There is re | ward · for the |
righteous:
    there is indeed a | God who | judges · on | earth.']

PSALM 59

1   Deliver me from my | enemies · O | God:
    lift me to safety from | those that | rise a | gainst me;

2   O deliver me from the | evil | doers:
    and | save me · from | blood · thirsty | men.

3   For they lie in | wait · for my | life:
    savage men | stir up | violence · a | gainst me.

4   Not for my sin or my transgression O Lord
not for any | evil · I have | done:
    do they run and take | up po | sition · a | gainst me.

(†) 5   Arise to | meet me · and | see:
    you that are Lord of | hosts and | God of | Israel.

[6   Awake to punish | all the | nations:
    have no mercy on those that so |
treacherous · ly | do | wrong.]

7   They return every evening   they | howl like | dogs:
    they | prowl a | round the | city.

8   Look how their | mouths | slaver:
    swords strike from their lips
for they | say | 'Who will | hear it?'

9   But you O Lord will | laugh them · to | scorn:
    you will de | ride | all the | nations.

10   I will look to ᐧ you · O my ᐧ strength:
          for ᐧ God is · my ᐧ strong ᐧ tower.

11   My God in his steadfastness will ᐧ come to ᐧ meet me:
          God will show me the ᐧ downfall ᐧ of my ᐧ enemies.

12   Slay them not O Lord   lest my ᐧ people · for ᐧ get:
          but make them stagger by your ᐧ power and ᐧ
          bring them ᐧ down.

13   Give them over to punishment * for the sin of their
          mouths for the ᐧ words of · their ᐧ lips:
          let them be ᐧ taken ᐧ in their ᐧ pride.

[14   For the curses and lies that they have uttered
          O consume them ᐧ in your ᐧ wrath:
          consume them ᐧ till they ᐧ are no ᐧ more;]

[†] 15   that men may know that God ᐧ rules · over ᐧ Jacob:
          even to the ᐧ ends ᐧ of the ᐧ earth.

16   They return every evening   they ᐧ howl like ᐧ dogs:
          they ᐧ prowl aᐧround the ᐧ city.

17   They roam here and there ᐧ looking · for ᐧ food:
          and ᐧ growl · if they ᐧ are not ᐧ filled.

18   But I will ᐧ sing of · your ᐧ might:
          I will sing aloud each ᐧ morning ᐧ
          of your ᐧ goodness. ᐧ

19   For you have been my ᐧ strong ᐧ tower:
          and a sure refuge in the ᐧ day of ᐧ my disᐧtress.

†20   I will sing your praises ᐧ O my ᐧ strength:
          for ᐧ God is · my ᐧ strong ᐧ tower.

PSALM 60

1   O God you have cast us ᐧ off and ᐧ broken us:
          you were enraged against us   ᐧ O reᐧstore us · aᐧgain!

2   You have caused the land to quake   you have ᐧ
          rent it ᐧ open:
          heal the rifts for the ᐧ earth ᐧ quivers · and ᐧ breaks.

3   You have steeped your people in a | bitter | draught:
       you have given them a | wine to | make them | stagger.

4   You have caused those that fear you to | take | flight:
       so that they | run | from the | bow.

†5   O save us by your right | hand and | answer us:
       that those whom you | love may | be de|livered.

6   God has said in his | holy | place:
       'I will exult and divide Shechem
       I will parcel | out the | valley · of | Succoth.

7   'Gilead is mine and Ma|nasseh · is | mine:
       Ephraim is my helmet and | Judah · my |
       rod · of com|mand.

†8   'Moab is my wash-bowl   over Edom will I |
       cast my | shoe:
       against Philistia | will I | shout in | triumph.'

9   Who will lead me into the | forti · fied | city:
       who will | bring me | into | Edom?

10   Have you not cast us | off O | God?
       you | go not | out · with our | armies.

11   Give us your help a|gainst the | enemy:
       for | vain · is the | help of | man.

12   By the power of our God we | shall do | valiantly:
       for it is he that will | tread | down our | enemies.

PSALM 61

1   Hear my loud | crying · O | God:
       and give | heed | to my | prayer.

2   From the ends of the earth I call to you
       when my | heart | faints:
       O set me on the | rock · that is | higher · than | I.

3   For you have | been my | refuge:
       and my strong | tower a|gainst the | enemy.

4   I will dwell in your | tent for | ever:
        and find shelter in the | cover·ing | of your | wings.

5   For you have heard my | vows O | God:
        you have granted the desire of | those that |
        fear your | name.

6   You will give the | king long | life:
        and his years shall endure through |
        many | gener | ations.

7   He shall dwell before | God for | ever:
        loving-kindness and | truth shall | be his | guard.

8   So will I ever sing praises | to your | name:
        while I | daily · per | form my | vows.

PSALM 62

1   My soul waits in | silence · for | God:
        for from | him comes | my sal | vation.

2   He only is my rock and | my sal | vation:
        my strong tower   so that | I shall | never · be | moved.

3   How long will you all plot against a | man ·
    to de | stroy him:
        as though he were a leaning | fence ·
        or a | buckling | wall?

4   Their design is to thrust him from his height
    and their de | light · is in | lies:
        they bless with their | lips but | inwardly ·
        they | curse.

5   Nevertheless my soul   wait in | silence · for | God:
        for from | him | comes my | hope.

6   He only is my rock and | my sal | vation:
        my strong tower   so that | I shall | not be | moved.

7   In God is my deliverance | and my | glory:
        God is my strong | rock | and my | shelter.

8   Trust in him at all times | O my | people:
        pour out your hearts before him   for | God |
        is our | refuge.

9 The children of men are but breath
the children of | men · are a | lie:
place them in the scales and they fly upward
they | are as | light as | air.

10 Put no trust in extortion
do not grow | worthless · by | robbery:
if riches increase | set not · your | heart up |on them.

11 God has spoken once   twice have I | heard him | say:
that | power be |longs to | God,

12 that to the Lord belongs a | constant | goodness:
for you reward a man ac |cording | to his | works.

PSALM 63

1 O God | you are · my | God:
eagerly | will I | seek | you.

2 My soul thirsts for you   my | flesh | longs for you:
as a dry and thirsty | land · where no | water | is.

3 So it was when I beheld you | in the | sanctuary:
and | saw your | power · and your | glory.

4 For your unchanging goodness is | better · than | life:
there |fore my | lips shall | praise you.

5 And so I will bless you as | long as · I | live:
and in your name will I | lift my | hands on | high.

6 My longing shall be satisfied ⌣
as with | marrow · and | fatness:
my mouth shall | praise you · with ex |ultant | lips.

7 When I remember you up |on my | bed:
when I meditate up |on you · in the | night | watches,

8 how you have | been my | helper:
then I sing for joy in the | shadow | of your | wings,

†9 then my | soul | clings to you:
and | your right | hand up |holds me.

10 Those that seek my life are | marked · for de |struction:
they shall go down to the deep | places | of the | earth.

11   They shall be de˥livered · to the ˥ sword:
      they shall ˥ be a ˥ portion · for ˥ jackals.

† 12 The king will rejoice in God
    and all who take oaths on his ˥ name shall ˥ glory:
      but the mouths of ˥ liars ˥ shall be ˥ stopped.

PSALM 64

1   Hear my voice O God in ˥ my com˥plaining:
      preserve my ˥ life from ˥ fear · of the ˥ enemy.

2   Hide me from the conspiracy ˥ of the ˥ wicked:
      from the ˥ throng of ˥ evil˥doers,

3   who sharpen their ˥ tongues like ˥ swords:
      who string the bow   who take ˥ arrows ·
      of ˥ bitter ˥ words,

4   to shoot from hiding at the ˥ blameless ˥ man:
      to strike at him ˥ sudden·ly ˥ and un˥seen.

5   They are confirmed in an ˥ evil ˥ purpose:
      they confide it to one another while they lay⌣
      the snares   ˥ saying ˥ 'Who will ˥ see them?'

6   They hatch mischief   they hide a well-con˥sidered ˥
    plan:
      for the mind and heart of ˥ man is ˥ very ˥ deep.

7   But God will shoot at them with his ˥ swift ˥ arrows:
      they shall be ˥ sudden·ly ˥ struck ˥ through.

8   The Lord will bring them down⌣
    for what their ˥ tongues have ˥ spoken:
      and all that see it shall ˥ toss their ˥ heads in ˥ scorn.

9   Then ˥ all men · shall ˥ fear:
    and tell what the Lord has ˥ done and ˥
    ponder · his ˥ works.

10 The righteous man shall rejoice in the Lord
    and find in ˥ him his ˥ refuge:
      and all the ˥ upright · in ˥ heart · shall ex˥ult.

PSALM 65

1 You are to be praised O | God in | Zion:
    to you shall vows be paid | you that | answer | prayer.

2 To you shall all flesh come to con | fess their | sins:
    when our misdeeds prevail against us | ⌣
    you will | purge · them a | way.

† 3 Blessèd is the man whom you choose
    and take to yourself to dwell with | in your | courts:
    we shall be filled with the good things ⌣
    of your house | of your | holy | temple.

4 You will answer us in your righteousness ⌣
    with terrible deeds O | God our | saviour:
    you that are the hope of all the ends of the earth ⌣
    and | of the | distant | seas;

5 who by your strength made | fast the | mountains:
    you | that are | girded · with | power;

6 who stilled the raging of the seas ⌣
    the | roaring · of the | waves:
    and the | tumult | of the | peoples.

7 Those who dwell at the ends of the earth ⌣
    are a | fraid at · your | wonders:
    the dawn and the | even·ing | sing your | praises.

8 You tend the | earth and | water it:
    you | make it | rich and | fertile.

9 The river of God is | full of | water:
    and so providing for the earth ⌣
    you pro | vide | grain for | men.

10 You drench its furrows   you level the |
    ridges · be | tween:
    you soften it with showers and | bless
    its | early | growth.

11   You crown the ' year · with your ' goodness:
     and the tracks where you have ' passed '
     drip with ' fatness.

12   The pastures of the ' wilderness · run ' over:
     and the ' hills are ' girded · with ' joy.

13   The meadows are ' clothed with ' sheep:
     and the valleys stand so thick with corn‿
     they ' shout for ' joy and ' sing.

PSALM 66

1   O shout with joy to God ' all the ' earth:
     sing to the honour of his name
     and give him ' glory ' as his ' praise.

2   Say to God   'How fearful ' are your ' works:
     because of your great might‿
     your ' enemies · shall ' cower · be'fore you.'

3   All the ' earth shall ' worship you:
     and sing to you   and sing ' praises ' to your ' name.

4   Come then and see what ' God has ' done:
     how terrible are his ' dealings · with the '
     children · of ' men.

5   He turned the sea into dry land
     they crossed the ' river · on ' foot:
     then ' were we ' joyful · be'cause of him.

6   By his power he rules for ever
     his eyes keep ' watch · on the ' nations:
     and rebels shall ' never ' rise a'gainst him.

7   O bless our ' God you ' peoples:
     and cause his ' praises ' to re'sound,

8   who has held our ' souls in ' life:
     who has not ' suffered · our ' feet to ' slip.

9   For you have ' proved us · O ' God:
     you have ' tried us · as ' silver · is ' tried.

10   You brought us ' into · the ' net:
     you laid sharp ' torment ' on our ' loins.

† 11   You let men ride over our heads
       we went through ˡ fire and ˡ water:
          but you brought us out ˡ into · a ˡ place of ˡ liberty.

12   I will come into your house with ˡ burnt ˡoffering:
       and ˡ I will ˡ pay you · my ˡ vows,

13   the vows that ˡ opened · my ˡ lips:
       that my mouth uttered ˡ when I ˡ was in ˡ trouble.

14   I will offer you burnt-offerings of fattened beasts
       with the sweet ˡ smoke of ˡ rams:
          I will sacrifice a ˡ bull · and the ˡ flesh of ˡ goats.

15   Come then and hear   all ˡ you that · fear ˡ God:
       and I will ˡ tell what ˡ he has ˡ done for me.

16   I called to him ˡ with my ˡ mouth:
       and his ˡ praise was ˡ on my ˡ tongue.

17   If I had cherished wickedness ˡ in my ˡ heart:
       the ˡ Lord would ˡ not have ˡ heard me.

18   But ˡ God has ˡ heard me:
       he has ˡ heeded · the ˡ voice of · my ˡ prayer.

19   Praise ˡ be to ˡ God:
       who has not turned back my prayer
       or his ˡ steadfast ˡ love ˡ from me.

PSALM 67

1   Let God be gracious to ˡ us and ˡ bless us:
       and make his ˡ face ˡ shine up ˡon us,

2   that your ways may be ˡ known on ˡ earth:
       your liberating ˡ power · a ˡmong all ˡ nations.

3   Let the peoples ˡ praise you · O ˡ God:
       let ˡ all the ˡ peoples ˡpraise you.

4   Let the nations be ˡ glad and ˡ sing:
       for you judge the peoples with integrity
       and govern the ˡ nations · up ˡon ˡ earth.

5 Let the peoples **|** praise you · O **|** God:
  let **|** all the **|** peoples **|** praise you.

6 Then the earth will **|** yield its **|** fruitfulness:
  and **|** God our **|** God will **|** bless us.

†7 God **|** shall **|** bless us:
  and all the **|** ends · of the **|** earth will **|** fear him.

PSALM 68

1 God shall arise and his enemies **|** shall be **|** scattered:
  those that hate him shall **|** flee be **|** fore his **|** face.

2 As smoke is dispersed so shall **|** they · be dis **|** persed:
  as wax melts before a fire
  so shall the wicked **|** perish · at the **|**
  presence · of **|** God.

3 But the righteous shall be glad and ex **|** ult be · fore **|** God:
  they **|** shall re **|** joice with **|** gladness.

4 O sing to God sing praises **|** to his **|** name:
  glorify him that rode through the deserts
  him whose name is the Lord **|** and ex **|** ult be **|** fore him.

5 He is the father of the fatherless
  he upholds the **|** cause · of the **|** widow:
  God **|** in his **|** holy **|** dwelling place.

6 He gives the desolate a home to dwell in
  and brings the prisoners out **|** into · pros **|** perity:
  but rebels must **|** dwell · in a **|** barren **|** land.

7 O God when you went out be **|** fore your **|** people:
  when you **|** marched **|** through the **|** wilderness,

8 the earth shook the heavens **|** poured down **|** water:
  before the God of Sinai before **|** God the **|**
  God of **|** Israel.

9 You showered down a generous **|** rain O **|** God:
  you prepared the land of your pos **|** session ·
  when **|** it was **|** weary.

10   And there your ' people ' settled:
       in the place that your goodness O God ⌣
       had made ' ready ' for the ' poor.

11   The Lord spoke the word * and great was the
    company of those that ' carried · the ' tidings:
       'Kings with their armies are ' fleeing · are '
       fleeing · a 'way.

12   'Even the women at home may ' share · in the ' spoil:
       and will you sit ' idly · a 'mong the sheepfolds?

13   'There are images of doves ⌣
    whose wings are ' covered · with ' silver:
       and their ' pinions · with ' shining ' gold.'

14   When the Almighty ' scattered ' kings:
       they were like snow ' falling · up 'on Mount ' Zalmon.

15   The mountain of Bashan is a ' mighty ' mountain:
       the mountain of Bashan is a ' mountain · of '
       many ' peaks.

16   O mountains of many peaks   why ' look so ' enviously:
       at the mountain where God is pleased to dwell
       where the ' Lord · will re 'main for ' ever?

17   The chariots of God are twice ten thousand ⌣
    and ' thousands up · on ' thousands:
       the Lord came from Sinai ' into · his ' holy ' place.

18   When you ascended the heights ⌣
    you led the enemy captive
    you received ' tribute · from ' men:
       but rebels shall not ' dwell · in the ' presence ·
       of ' God.

19   Blessed be the Lord day by day
    who bears us ' as his ' burden:
       he is the ' God of ' our de 'liverance.

20   God is to us a ' God who ' saves:
       by God the Lord do ' we es 'cape ' death.

[21   But God shall smite the | heads · of his | enemies:
         the hairy scalp of | those that | walk · in their | sins.

22   The Lord said   'I will bring them | back from | Bashan:
         I will bring them a | gain · from the | deep | sea';

[†] 23   that you may dip your | feet in | blood:
         and the tongues of your | dogs ·
         in the | blood of · your | enemies.]

24   Your procession is | seen O | God:
         the procession of my | God and | King ·
         in the | sanctuary.

25   The singers go before   the mu|sicians · come | after:
         and around them the maidens | beating |
         on the | timbrels.

26   In their choirs they | bless | God:
         those that are sprung from the fount of | Israel |
         bless the | Lord.

27   There is the little tribe of | Benja·min | leading them:
         the throng of the princes of Judah
         the princes of | Zebulun · and the |
         princes · of | Naphtali.

28   Give the command my God * in accordance |
         with your | power:
         that godlike | power where|by you | act for us.

29   Give command from your temple | at Je | rusalem:
         and | kings shall | bring you | tribute.

30   Rebuke the beast of the reeds
         the herd of bulls amidst the | brutish | peoples:
         tread down those that are greedy for silver
         scatter the | peoples · that | relish | war.

31   Let them bring | bronze from | Egypt:
         let the hands of the Nubians | carry · it |
         swiftly · to | God.

32   Sing to God you I kingdoms · of the I earth:
      O sing I praises I to the I Lord,

33   to him that rides upon the highest heavens
      that were I from · the be I ginning:
      who utters his voice which I is a I mighty I voice.

34   Ascribe power to God   whose majesty is I over I Israel:
      and his I might is I in the I clouds.

35   Terrible is God who comes from his I holy I place:
      the God of Israel who gives⏝
      power and strength to his people I
      Blessèd I be I God.

PSALM 69

1   Save I me O I God:
      for the waters have come up I even I to my I throat.

2   I sink in the deep mire I where no I footing is:
      I have come into deep waters I and the ⌐flood
      sweeps I over me.

3   I am weary with crying out   my I throat is I parched:
      my eyes fail with I watching · so I long ·
      for my I God.

4   Those that hate me without cause
      are more in number than the I hairs · of my I head:
      those that would destroy me are many
      they oppose me wrongfully
      for I must restore I things · that I I never I took.

5   O God you I know my I foolishness:
      and my I sins · are not I hidden I from you.

6   Let not those who wait for you⏝
      be shamed because of me
      O Lord I God of I hosts:
      let not those who seek you⏝
      be disgraced on I my account · ⏝
      O I God of I Israel.

7   For your sake have I ˈ suffered · reˈproach:
       and ˈ shame has ˈ covered · my ˈ face.

8   I have become a stranger ˈ to my ˈ brothers:
       an alien ˈ to my · own ˈ mother's ˈ sons.

9   Zeal for your house has ˈ eaten · me ˈ up:
       and the taunts of those who taunt ˈ you have ˈ
       fallen · on ˈ me.

10   I afflicted my ˈself with ˈ fasting:
       and that was ˈ turned to ˈ my reˈproach.

11   I made ˈ sackcloth · my ˈ clothing:
       and I beˈcame a ˈ byword ˈ to them.

12   Those who sit in the gate ˈ talk of ˈ me:
       and the ˈ drunkards · make ˈ songs aˈbout me.

13   But to you Lord I ˈ make my ˈ prayer:
       at ˈ an acˈcepta·ble ˈ time.

14   Answer me O God in your aˈbundant ˈ goodness:
       and ˈ with your ˈ sure deˈliverance.

15   Bring me out of the mire   so that I ˈ may not ˈ sink:
       let me be delivered from my enemies
       and ˈ from the ˈ deep ˈ waters.

16   Let not the flood overwhelm me
       or the depths ˈ swallow · me ˈ up:
       let not the ˈ Pit · shut its ˈ mouth upˈon me.

17   Hear me O Lord   as your lovingˈkindness · is ˈ good:
       turn to me   as ˈ your comˈpassion · is ˈ great.

18   Do not hide your ˈ face · from your ˈ servant:
       for I am in trouble   ˈ O be ˈ swift to ˈ answer me!

19   Draw near to me ˈ and reˈdeem me:
       O ˈ ransom me · beˈcause of · my ˈ enemies!

20   You know ˈ all their ˈ taunts:
       my adversaries are ˈ all ˈ in your ˈ sight.

21   Insults have ˈ broken · my ˈ heart:
       my shame and disˈgrace are ˈ past ˈ healing.

22 I looked for someone to have pity on me
  but I there was I no man:
    for some to I comfort me · but I found I none.

† 23 They gave me I poison · for I food:
  and when I was thirsty they I gave me I
    vinegar · to I drink.

[24 Let their table be I come a I snare:
  and their sacri I fici·al I feasts a I trap.

25 Let their eyes be darkened   so that they I cannot I see:
  and make their I loins I shake con I tinually.

26 Pour out your I wrath up I on them:
  and let your fierce I anger I over I take them.

27 Let their I camp be I desolate:
  and let I no man I dwell · in their I tents.

28 For they persecute him whom I you have I stricken:
  and multiply the pain of I him whom I
    you have I wounded.

29 Let them have punishment up I on I punishment:
  let them I not re I ceive · your for I giveness.

† 30 Let them be blotted out of the I book · of the I living:
  let them not be written I down a I mong
    the I righteous.]

31 As for me I am I poor · and in I misery:
  O God let your de I liver·ance I lift me I up.

32 And I will praise the name of I God · in a I song:
  and I glori·fy I him with I thanksgiving.

33 And that will please the Lord I more · than an I ox:
  more than a bull with I horns and I cloven I hoof.

34 Consider this you that are I meek · and re I joice:
  seek God and I let your I heart be I glad.

35 For the Lord I listens · to the I poor:
  he does not despise his I servants I in cap I tivity.

36 Let the heavens and the ǀ earth ǀ praise him:
the ǀ seas and ǀ all that ǀ moves in them.

37 For God will ǀ save ǀ Zion:
he will reǀbuild the ǀ cities · of ǀ Judah.

38 His people shall live there and possess it
the seed of his servants ǀ shall inǀherit it:
and those who ǀ love his ǀ name shall ǀ dwell in it.

PSALM 70

1 O God be ǀ pleased · to deǀliver me:
O ǀ Lord make ǀ haste to ǀ help me.

2 Let them be put to shame and confounded who ǀ
seek my ǀ life:
let them be turned back and disǀgraced who ǀ
wish me ǀ evil.

3 Let them turn aǀway for ǀ shame:
who ǀ say to me · 'Aǀha aǀha!'

4 Let all who seek you be joyful and ǀ glad ‿
beǀcause of you:
let those who love your salvation say ǀ always ǀ
'God is ǀ great.'

5 As for me I am ǀ poor and ǀ needy:
O ǀ God be ǀ swift to ǀ save me.

6 You are my helper and ǀ my deǀliverer:
O ǀ Lord make ǀ no deǀlay.

PSALM 71

1 To you Lord have I ǀ come for ǀ shelter:
let me ǀ never · be ǀ put to ǀ shame.

2 In your righteousness rescue ǀ and deǀliver me:
incline your ǀ ear to ǀ me and ǀ save me.

3 Be for me a rock of refuge * a fortress ǀ to deǀfend me:
for you are my high ǀ rock ǀ and my ǀ stronghold.

4 Rescue me O my God from the | hand · of the | wicked:
   from the grasp of the | piti·less | and un|just.

5 For you Lord | are my | hope:
   you are my confidence O | God · from my |
   youth | upward.

6 On you have I | leaned · since my | birth:
   you are he that brought me out of my mother's womb
   and my | praise · is of | you con|tinually.

7 I have become as a fearful | warning · to | many:
   but | you are · my | strength · and my | refuge.

8 My mouth shall be | filled · with your | praises:
   I shall sing of your | glory | all the · day | long.

9 Cast me not away in the | time of · old | age:
   nor forsake me | when my | strength | fails.

10 For my enemies | speak a|gainst me:
   and those that watch for my life‿
   con|spire to|gether | saying,

†11 'God | has for|saken him:
    pursue him   take him   for | there is | none
    to | save him.'

12 Be not far | from me · O | God:
   my | God make | haste to | help me.

13 Let my adversaries be confounded and | put to | shame:
   let those who seek my hurt‿
   be | covered · with | scorn · and dis|grace.

14 As for me   I will wait in | hope con|tinually:
   and I will | praise you | more and | more.

15 My mouth shall speak of your righteousness |
   all the | day:
   and tell of your salvation | though it · ex|ceeds
   my | telling.

16 I will begin with the mighty acts of the | Lord
   my | God:
   and declare your righteous | dealing | yours a|lone.

17 O God you have taught me from my | youth | upward:
    and to this day I pro|claim your | marvel·lous | works.

18 Forsake me not O God in my old age   when I am |
    grey|headed:
        till I have shown the strength of your arm⌣
        to future generations * and your | might to |
        those that · come | after.

19 Your righteousness O God | reaches · to the | heavens:
    great are the things that you have done
    O | God | who is | like you?

20 You have burdened me with many and bitter troubles
    O | turn · and re|new me:
        and raise me up a|gain · from the | depths ·
        of the | earth.

21 Bless me beyond my | former | greatness:
    O | turn to me · a|gain and | comfort me.

22 Then will I praise you upon the lute⌣
    for your faithfulness | O my | God:
        and sing your praises to the harp O | Holy | One
        of | Israel.

23 My lips shall re|joice in · my | singing:
    and my soul | also · for | you have | ransomed me.

†24 My tongue shall speak of your righteous dealing |
    all the · day | long:
        for they shall be put to shame and disgraced⌣
        that | seek to | do me | evil.

PSALM 72

1 Give the king your | judgement · O | God:
    and your righteousness to the | son | of a | king,

2 that he may judge your | people | rightly:
    and the | poor · of the | land with | equity.

3 Let the mountains be laden with peace⌣
    be|cause of · his | righteousness:
        and the hills also with pros|per·ity | for his | people.

4   May he give justice to the poor a ˈmong the ˈ people:
    and rescue the children of the ˈ needy ·
    and ˈ crush · the opˈpressor.

5   May he live while the ˈ sun enˈdures:
    and while the moon gives light throughˈout
    all ˈ generˈations.

6   May he come down like rain upon the ˈ
    new-mown ˈ fields:
    and as ˈ showers · that ˈ water · the ˈ earth.

7   In his time shall ˈ righteous·ness ˈ flourish:
    and abundance of peace till the ˈ moon shall ˈ
    be no ˈ more.

8   His dominion shall stretch from ˈ sea to ˈ sea:
    from the Great ˈ River · to the ˈ ends · of the ˈ earth.

9   His adversaries shall bow ˈ down beˈfore him:
    and his ˈ enemies · shall ˈ lick the ˈ dust.

10 The kings of Tarshish and of the isles⌣
    shall ˈ bring ˈ tribute:
    the kings of Sheba and ˈ Seba · shall ˈ offer ˈ gifts.

†11 All kings shall fall ˈ down beˈfore him:
    and all ˈ nations ˈ do him ˈ service.

12 He will deliver the needy ˈ when they ˈ cry:
    and the ˈ poor man · that ˈ has no ˈ helper.

13 He will pity the helpless ˈ and the ˈ needy:
    and ˈ save the ˈ lives · of the ˈ poor.

†14 He will redeem them from opˈpression ·
    and ˈ violence:
    and their blood shall be ˈ precious ˈ in his ˈ sight.

15 Long may he live   and be given of the ˈ gold of ˈ Sheba:
    may prayer be made for him continually
    and men ˈ bless him ˈ every ˈ day.

16 Let there be abundance of ˈ wheat · in the ˈ land:
    let it ˈ flourish · on the ˈ tops · of the ˈ mountains;

† 17   let its ears grow fat like the ˈ grain of ˈ Lebanon:
       and its sheaves ˈ thicken · like the ˈ grass ·
       of the ˈ field.

18   Let his name ˈ live for ˈ ever:
       and en ˈdure as ˈ long · as the ˈ sun.

19   Let all peoples use his ˈ name in ˈ blessing:
       and all ˈ nations ˈ call him ˈ blessèd.

(20   Blessèd be the Lord God the ˈ God of ˈ Israel:
       who a ˈlone does ˈ great ˈ wonders.

21   Blessèd be his glorious ˈ name for ˈ ever:
       and let the whole earth be filled with his glory ˈ
       Amen ˈ A ˈmen.)

PSALM 73

1   God is indeed ˈ good to ˈ Israel:
       to ˈ those whose ˈ hearts are ˈ pure.

2   Nevertheless my feet were ˈ almost ˈ gone:
       my ˈ steps had ˈ well-nigh ˈ slipped.

3   For I was filled with envy ˈ at the ˈ boastful:
       when I saw the un ˈgodly · had ˈ such tran ˈquillity:

4   For they ˈ suffer · no ˈ pain:
       and their ˈ bodies · are ˈ hale and ˈ fat.

5   They come to no mis ˈfortune · like ˈ other folk:
       nor ˈ are they ˈ plagued like ˈ other men.

6   Therefore they put on ˈ pride · as a ˈ necklace:
       and clothe themselves in ˈ vio · lence ˈ as ·
       in a ˈ garment.

7   Their eyes shine from ˈ folds of ˈ fatness:
       and they have ˈ all that ˈ heart could ˈ wish.

8   Their talk is ˈ malice · and ˈ mockery:
       and they hand down ˈ slanders ˈ from on ˈ high.

9   Their mouths blas ˈpheme a · gainst ˈ heaven:
       and their tongues go ˈ to and ˈ fro on ˈ earth.

10   Therefore my ' people ' turn to them:
         and ' find in ⌈ them no ' fault.

11   They say ' 'How can · God ' know:
         is there under'standing · in the ' Most ' High?'

12   Behold ' these are · the un'godly:
         yet they ' prosper · and in'crease in ' riches.

13   Was it for nothing then that I ' cleansed my ' heart:
         and ' washed my ' hands in ' innocence?

14   Have I been stricken all day ' long in ' vain:
         and re'buked ' every ' morning?

†15   If I had said ' 'I will · speak ' thus':
         I should have betrayed the ' fami·ly '
         of your ' children.

16   Then I thought to under'stand ' this:
         but it ' was too ' hard ' for me,

17   till I went into the ' sanctuary · of ' God:
         and then I under'stood · what their ' end will ' be.

18   For you set them in ' slipper·y ' places:
         and cause them to ' fall · from their '
         treacher·ous ' footholds.

19   How suddenly they are ' laid ' waste:
         they come to an ⌈ end they ' perish · in ' terror.

†20   As with a dream when ' one a'wakes:
         so when you rouse yourself O Lord ' ‿
         you will · de'spise their ' image.

21   When my ' heart was ' soured:
         and I was ' wounded ' to the ' core,

22   I was but ' brutish · and ' ignorant:
         no ' better · than a ' beast be'fore you.

23   Nevertheless I am ' always ' with you:
         for you hold me ' by my ' right ⌈ hand.

24   You will guide me ' with your ' counsel:
         and afterwards ' you will ' lead me · to ' glory.

25 Whom have I in ˈ heaven · but ˈ you?
    and there is no one upon earth⌣
    that I deˈsire · in comˈparison · with ˈ you.

26 Though my flesh and my ˈ heart ˈ fail me:
    you O ˈ God · are my ˈ portion · for ˈ ever.

27 Behold those who forˈsake you · shall ˈ perish:
    and all who whore after other ˈ gods you ˈ will deˈstroy.

28 But it is good for me to draw ˈ near to ˈ God:
    I have made the Lord God my refuge
    and I will tell of ˈ all that ˈ you have ˈ done.

PSALM 74

1 O Lord our God   why cast us ˈ off so ˈ utterly:
    why does your anger burn aˈgainst the ˈ sheep of ·
    your ˈ pasture?

2 Remember your congregation * whom you took⌣
    to yourˈself of ˈ old:
    the people that you redeemed ⌣
    to be your own possession
    and Mount ˈ Zion · where ˈ you have ˈ dwelt.

3 Rouse yourself and go to the ˈ utter ˈ ruins:
    to all the harm that the ˈ enemy · has ˈ done ·
    in the ˈ sanctuary.

4 Your adversaries have made uproar
    in the place appointed ˈ for your ˈ praise:
    they have set ˈ up their ˈ standards · in ˈ triumph.

5 They have destroyed on ˈ every ˈ side:
    like those who take axes ˈ up · to a ˈ thicket · of ˈ trees.

6 All the carved woodwork they have ˈ broken ˈ down:
    and ˈ smashed it · with ˈ hammers · and ˈ hatchets.

7 They have set ˈ fire to · your ˈ sanctuary:
    and defiled to the ground the ˈ dwelling · place ˈ
    of your ˈ name.

8 They have said in their hearts   'Let us make I havoc I
of them':
   they have burned down
   all the holy I places · of I God · in the I land.

9 We see no signs* there is not one I prophet I left:
   there is none who knows how I long these I things
   shall I be.

10 How long shall the adversary I taunt you · O I God:
   shall the enemy blas I pheme your I name for I ever?

†11 Why do you hold I back your I hand:
   why do you keep your I right hand I in your I bosom?

12 Yet God is my I king · from of I old:
   who wrought de I liverance · up I on the I earth.

13 You divided the I sea · by your I might:
   you shattered the heads of the I dragons I
   in the I waters.

14 You crushed the I heads · of Le I viathan:
   and gave him as food to the I creatures ·
   of the I desert I waste.

15 You cleft open I spring and I fountain:
   you dried up the I ever I flowing I waters.

16 The days is yours* and so also I is the I night:
   you have es I tablished · the I moon · and the I sun.

17 You set all the boundaries I of the I earth:
   you cre I ated I winter · and I summer.

18 Remember O Lord the I taunts · of the I enemy:
   how a mindless I people · have blas I phemed
   your I name.

19 Do not give to the wild beasts the I soul that I
praises you:
   do not forget for ever the I life of I your af I flicted.

20 Look on all that I you have I made:
   for it is full of darkness
   and I violence · in I habits · the I earth.

21   Let not the oppressed and reviled turn a | way re | jected:
       but let the poor and | needy | praise your ⌐ name.

22   Arise O God * plead your | own | cause:
       remember how a mindless people | taunt you |
       all day | long.

23   Do not forget the | clamour · of your | adversaries:
       or how the shouting of your ⌐ enemies ·
       as | cends con | tinually.

PSALM 75

1   We give you thanks O God we | give you | thanks:
      we call upon your name
      and tell of all the | wonders | you have | done.

2   'I will surely ap | point a | time:
      when I the ⌐ Lord will | judge with | equity.

3   'Though the earth shake and | all who | dwell in it:
      it is ⌐ I · that have | founded · its | pillars.

4   'I will say to the boasters | "Boast no | more":
      and to the wicked | "Do not | flaunt your | horns;

†5   ' "do not flaunt your | horns so | high:
      or speak so | proud and | stiff | necked." '

6   For there is none from the east or | from the | west:
      or from the wilderness | who can | raise | up;

7   but it is God who | is the | judge:
      who puts down | one · and ex | alts an | other.

8   For there is a cup in the | Lord's | hand:
      and the wine | foams · and is | richly | mixed;

9   he gives it in turn to each of the | wicked · of the | earth:
      they drink it and | drain it | to the | dregs.

10   But I will sing praises to the | God of | Jacob:
      I will | glorify · his | name for | ever.

11   All the horns of the | wicked · I will | break:
      but the horns of the | righteous · shall be |
      lifted | high.

PSALM 76

1 In Judah ' God is ' known:
   his ' name is ' great in ' Israel.

2 At Salem ' is his ' tabernacle:
   and his ' dwelling ' is in ' Zion.

3 There he broke in pieces the flashing ' arrows ·
of the ' bow:
   the shield the ' sword · and the ' weapons · of ' battle.

4 Radiant in ' light are ' you:
   greater in majesty ' than · the e'ternal ' hills.

5 The valiant were dumbfounded   they ' sleep
their ' sleep:
   and all the men of ' war have ' lost their ' strength.

6 At the blast of your voice O ' God of ' Jacob:
   both horse and ' chariot · were ' cast a'sleep.

7 Terrible are ' you Lord ' God:
   and who may stand be'fore you · when '
you are ' angry?

8 You caused your sentence to be ' heard from ' heaven:
   the earth ' feared ' and was ' still,

9 when God a'rose to ' judgement:
   to ' save · all the ' meek · of the ' earth.

10 For you crushed the ' wrath of ' man:
   you bridled the ' remnant ' of the ' wrathful.

11 O make vows to the Lord your ' God and ' keep them:
   let all around him bring gifts
to him that is ' worthy ' to be ' feared.

12 For he cuts down the ' fury · of ' princes:
   and he is terrible to the ' kings ' of the ' earth.

PSALM 77

1 I call to my God   I cry ' out to'ward him:
   I call to my God   and ' surely ' he will ' answer.

2   In the day of my distress I seek the Lord
        I stretch out my hands to | him by | night:
           my soul is poured out without ceasing
           it re | fuses | all | comfort.

3   I think upon God and | groan a | loud:
        I | muse · and my | spirit | faints.

4   You hold my | eyelids | open:
        I am so | dazed · that I | cannot | flee.

5   I consider the | times · that are | past:
        I remember the | years of | long a | go.

6   At night I am | grieved · to the | heart:
        I ponder | and my | spirit · makes | search;

7   'Will the Lord cast us | off for | ever:
        will he | show us · his | favour · no | more?

8   'Is his mercy clean | gone for | ever:
        and his promise come to an | end for |
        all · gener | ations?

9   'Has God for | gotten · to be | gracious:
        has he shut up his | pity | in dis | pleasure?'

10   And I say * 'Has the right hand of the Most High |
        lost its | strength:
        has the | arm · of the | Lord | changed?'

11   I will declare the mighty | acts · of the | Lord:
        I will call to | mind your | wonders · of | old.

12   I will think on all that | you have | done:
        and | meditate · up | on your | works.

13   Your way O | God is | holy:
        who is so | great a | god as | our God?

14   You are the God that | works | wonders:
        you made known your | power a | mong the | nations;

15   by your mighty arm you re | deemed your | people:
        the | children · of | Jacob · and | Joseph.

16 The waters saw you O God
the waters saw you and | were a |fraid:
    the | depths ⌈also · were | troubled.

17 The clouds poured out water   the | heavens | spoke:
and your | arrows | darted | forth.

18 The voice of your thunder was | heard ·
in the | whirlwind:
    your lightnings lit the world
    the | earth | shuddered · and | quaked.

19 Your way was in the sea * your path in the |
great | waters:
    and your | footsteps | were not | seen.

20 You led your | people · like | sheep:
by the | hand of ⌈Moses · and | Aaron.

PSALM 78

1 Give heed to my teaching | O my | people:
incline your ⌈ears · to the | words of · my | mouth;

2 for I will open my | mouth · in a | parable:
and expound the | mysteries · of | former | times.

3 What we have | heard and | known:
what | our fore |fathers · have | told us,

4 we will not hide from their children
but declare to a generation | yet to | come:
    the praiseworthy acts of the Lord
    his ⌈mighty · and | wonder·ful | works.

5 He established a law in Jacob
and made a de |cree in | Israel:
    which he commanded our fore |fathers ·
    to | teach their | children,

6 that future generations might know
and the children | yet un |born:
    that they in turn might | teach it | to their | sons;

7   so that they might put their | confidence · in | God:
        and not forget his | works but | keep ·
        his com | mandments,

8   and not be as their forefathers
        a stubborn and re | bellious · gener | ation:
        a generation that did not set their heart aright
        whose spirit | was not | faithful · to | God.

9   The children of Ephraim | armed · with the | bow:
        turned | back · in the | day of | battle.

10   They did not keep God's covenant
        they refused to | walk in · his | law:
        they forgot what he had done
        and the | wonders | he had | shown them.

11   For he did marvellous things⏑
        in the | sight of · their | fathers:
        in the land of Egypt | in the | country · of | Zoan.

12   He divided the sea and | let them · pass | through:
        he made the | waters · stand | up · in a | heap.

13   In the daytime he | led them · with a | cloud:
        and all night | long · with the | light of | fire.

14   He cleft | rocks · in the | wilderness:
        and gave them drink in abundance | ⏑
        as from | springs of | water.

† 15   He brought streams | out of · the | rock:
        and caused the waters to | flow | down like | rivers.

16   But for all this they sinned yet | more a | gainst him:
        and rebelled against the Most | High | in the | desert.

17   They wilfully put | God · to the | test:
        and de | manded | food · for their | appetite.

18   They spoke against | God and | said:
        'Can God prepare a | table | in the | wilderness?

19   'He indeed struck the rock
      so that the waters gushed and the |
      streams · over|flowed:
          but can he also give bread
          or provide | meat | for his | people?'

20   When the Lord heard it he was angry
      and a fire was kindled a|gainst | Jacob:
          his wrath | blazed a|gainst | Israel.

21   For they put no | trust in | God:
          nor would they be|lieve his | power to | save.

† 22 Then he commanded the | clouds a|bove:
          and | opened · the | doors of | heaven.

23   He rained down manna for | them to | eat:
          and | gave them · the | grain of | heaven.

24   So men ate the | bread of | angels:
          and he | sent them | food · in a|bundance.

25   He stirred up the south east | wind · in the | heavens:
          and | guided · it | by his | power.

26   He rained down meat upon them | thick as | dust:
          and winged | birds · like the | sands · of the | sea.

27   He made them fall into the | midst of · their | camp:
          and | all a|bout their | tents.

28   So they ate and were | well|filled:
          for he had | given · them | what · they de|sired.

29   But before they had | satisfied · their | craving:
          while the | food was | still in · their | mouths,

30   the anger of God | blazed · up a|gainst them:
          and he slew their strongest men
          and laid | low the | youth of | Israel.

31   But for all this they | sinned yet | more:
          and | put no | faith · in his | wonders.

32   So he ended their | days · like a | breath:
          and their | years with | sudden | terror.

33 When he struck them down ⁞ then they ⁞ sought him:
　　they turned and ⁞ sought ⁞ eagerly · for ⁞ God.

34 They remembered that ⁞ God · was their ⁞ rock:
　　that God Most ⁞ High was ⁞ their re ⁞ deemer.

35 But they lied to him ⁞ with their ⁞ mouths:
　　and dis ⁞ sembled ⁞ with their ⁞ tongues;

36 for their hearts were not ⁞ fixed up ⁞ on him:
　　nor ⁞ were they ⁞ true to · his ⁞ covenant.

37 Yet he being merciful
　　forgave their iniquity and did ⁞ not de ⁞ stroy them:
　　many times he turned his anger aside
　　and would not ⁞ wholly · a ⁞ rouse his ⁞ fury.

38 He remembered that they ⁞ were but ⁞ flesh:
　　like a wind that passes ⁞ and does ⁞ not re ⁞ turn.

39 How often they rebelled against him ⁞ in the ⁞ wilderness:
　　and ⁞ grieved him ⁞ in the ⁞ desert!

40 Again and again they put ⁞ God · to the ⁞ test:
　　and provoked the ⁞ Holy ⁞ One of ⁞ Israel.

41 They did not re ⁞ member · his ⁞ power:
　　or the day when he re ⁞ deemed them ⁞
　　from the ⁞ enemy;

42 how he wrought his ⁞ signs in ⁞ Egypt:
　　his ⁞ wonders · in the ⁞ country · of ⁞ Zoan.

43 For he turned their ⁞ rivers · into ⁞ blood:
　　so that they ⁞ could not ⁞ drink · from the ⁞ streams.

44 He sent swarms of ⁞ flies · that de ⁞ voured them:
　　and ⁞ frogs that ⁞ laid them ⁞ waste.

45 He gave their ⁞ crops · to the ⁞ locust:
　　and the fruits of their ⁞ labour ⁞ to the ⁞ grasshopper.

46 He struck down their ⁞ vines with ⁞ hailstones:
　　and their ⁞ syco·more ⁞ trees with ⁞ frost.

47 He gave up their ⁞ cattle · to the ⁞ hail:
　　and their ⁞ flocks · to the ⁞ flash · of the ⁞ lightning.

48 He loosed on them the fierceness of his anger
his fury his indignation ˈ and disˈtress:
    and these were his ˈ messen·gers ˈ of deˈstruction.

49 He opened a ˈ path · for his ˈ fury:
he would not spare them from death
    but gave ˈ up their ˈ lives · to the ˈ pestilence.

50 He struck down the ˈ firstborn · of ˈ Egypt:
the first-fruits of their manhood ˈ ‿
    in the ˈ dwellings · of ˈ Ham.

51 As for his own people   he led them ˈ out like ˈ sheep:
    and guided them in the ˈ wilder·ness ˈ like a ˈ flock.

52 He led them in safety   and they were ˈ not a ˈ fraid:
    but the ˈ sea ˈ covered · their ˈ enemies.

53 He brought them to his ˈ holy ˈ land:
    to the mountains that his ˈ own right ˈ hand had ˈ won.

54 He drove out the nations before them
and apportioned their lands ˈ as a · posˈsession:
    and settled the tribes of ˈ Israel ˈ in their ˈ tents.

55 But they rebelled against God Most High‿
and ˈ put him · to the ˈ test:
    they would ˈ not oˈbey · his comˈmandments.

56 They turned back and dealt treacherously ˈ ‿
like their ˈ fathers:
    they turned aside ˈ slack · as an ˈ unstrung ˈ bow.

57 They provoked him to anger with their ˈ
heathen ˈ shrines:
    and moved him to jealousy ˈ with their ˈ
carved ˈ images.

58 God heard and was angry * he utterly reˈjected ˈ Israel:
    he forsook the tabernacle at Shiloh
    the ˈ tent · where he ˈ dwelt a·mong ˈ men.

59 He gave the ark of his might ˈ into · capˈtivity:
    and his glory ˈ into · the ˈ hands · of the ˈ enemy.

60 He delivered his ˈ people · to the ˈ sword:
    and was enraged aˈgainst his ˈ own posˈsession.

61 Fire de | voured the · young | men:
  there was | no one · to be | wail the | maidens;

62 their priests | fell · by the | sword:
  and there was | none to | mourn · for the | widows.

63 Then the Lord awoke like a | man · out of | sleep:
  like a warrior that had been | over | come with | wine.

64 He struck the backs of his enemies | as they | fled:
  and | put them · to per | petu·al | shame.

65 He rejected the | family · of | Joseph:
  he re | fused the | tribe of | Ephraim.

66 But he chose the | tribe of | Judah:
  and the hill of | Zion | which he | loved.

67 He built his sanctuary like the | heights of | heaven:
  like the earth which | he had | founded · for | ever.

68 He chose | David · his | servant:
  and | took him | from the | sheepfolds;

69 he brought him from | following · the | ewes:
  to be the shepherd of his people Jacob
  and of | Israel · his | own pos | session.

70 So he tended them with | upright | heart:
  and | guided them · with | skilful | hand.

PSALM 79

1 O God the heathen have | come in·to your | land:
  they have defiled your holy temple
  they have made Je | rusalem · a | heap of | stones.

2 They have given the dead bodies of your servants⌣
  as food to the | birds · of the | air:
  and the flesh of your faithful ones⌣
  to the wild | beasts | of the | earth.

3 Their blood they have spilt like water⌣
  on every | side · of Je | rusalem:
  and | there is | none to | bury them.

4 We have become a mockery ˈ to our ˈ neighbours:
   the scorn and ˈ laughing-stock · of ˈ those aˈbout us.

5 How long O Lord shall your anger be ˈ so exˈtreme:
   will your jealous ˈ fury ˈ burn like ˈ fire?

6 Pour out your wrath on the nations that ˈ
   do not ˈ know you:
   on the kingdoms that have not ˈ called
   upˈon your ˈ name.

7 For they have deˈvoured ˈ Jacob:
   and made his ˈ dwelling-place · a ˈ desoˈlation.

8 Do not remember against us the sin of ˈ former ˈ times:
   but let your compassion hasten to meet us
   for we are ˈ brought ˈ very ˈ low.

†9 Help us O God our saviour for the ˈ honour ·
   of your ˈ name:
   O deliver us and expiate our ˈ sins · for your ˈ
   name's ˈ sake.

[10 Why should the heathen say ˈ 'Where is · their ˈ God?'
   O let vengeance for the blood of your servants⌣
   that is shed
   be shown upon the ˈ nations ˈ in our ˈ sight.]

11 Let the sorrowful sighing of the prisoners ˈ come
   beˈfore you:
   and as your power is great   reprieve ˈ those
   conˈdemned to ˈ die.

[12 For the taunts with which our neighbours⌣
   have taunted ˈ you O ˈ Lord:
   repay them seven times ˈ over ˈ into · their ˈ bosoms.]

13 So we that are your people and the sheep of your pasture
   shall give you ˈ thanks for ˈ ever:
   we will declare your praise in ˈ every ˈ generˈation.

PSALM 80

1 Hear O Shepherd of Israel
you that led ˈ Joseph · like a ˈ flock:
   you that are enthroned upon the cherubim ˈ ‿
   shine ˈ out in ˈ glory;

2 before Ephraim Benjamin ˈ and Man ˈ asseh:
   stir up your ˈ power and ˈ come to ˈ save us.

†3 *Restore us again O ˈ Lord of ˈ hosts:*
   show us the light of your countenance ˈ ‿
   and we ˈ shall be ˈ saved.

4 O Lord ˈ God of ˈ hosts:
   how long will you be ˈ angry · at your ˈ
   people's ˈ prayer?

5 You have fed them with the ˈ bread of ˈ tears:
   and given them tears to ˈ drink in ˈ good ˈ measure.

6 You have made us the victim ˈ of our ˈ neighbours:
   and our ˈ ene · mies ˈ laugh us · to ˈ scorn.

7 *Restore us again O ˈ Lord of ˈ hosts:*
   show us the light of your countenance ˈ ‿
   and we ˈ shall be ˈ saved.

8 You brought a ˈ vine · out of ˈ Egypt:
   you drove out the ˈ nations · and ˈ planted · it ˈ in.

9 You cleared the ˈ ground be ˈ fore it:
   and it struck ˈ root and ˈ filled the ˈ land.

10 The hills were ˈ covered · with its ˈ shadow:
   and its boughs were like the ˈ boughs · of the ˈ
   great ˈ cedars.

11 It stretched out its ˈ branches · to the ˈ sea:
   and its tender ˈ shoots · to the ˈ Great ˈ River.

12 Why then have you broken ˈ down its ˈ walls:
   so that every passer ˈ by can ˈ pluck its ˈ fruit?

13 The wild boar out of the woods ˈ roots it ˈ up:
   and the locusts from the ˈ wild ˈ places · de ˈ vour it.

14   Turn to us again O **l** Lord of **l** hosts:
        look **l** down from **l** heaven · and **l** see.

15   Bestow your care up **l** on this **l** vine:
        the stock which your **l** own right **l** hand has **l** planted.

16   As for those that burn it with fire and **l** cut it **l** down:
        let them perish
        at the re **l** buke **l** of your **l** countenance.

17   Let your power rest on the man at your **l** right **l** hand:
        on that son of man whom you **l** made so **l**
        strong · for your **l** self.

18   And so we shall **l** not turn **l** back from you:
        give us life   and we will **l** call up **l** on your **l** name.

19   *Restore us again O* **l** *Lord of* **l** *hosts:*
        show us the light of your countenance **l**
        and we **l** *shall be* **l** *saved.*

PSALM 81

1   O sing joyfully to **l** God our **l** strength:
        shout in **l** triumph · to the **l** God of **l** Jacob.

2   Make music and **l** beat up · on the **l** drum:
        sound the **l** lute and · the mel **l** odi · ous **l** harp.

3   Blow the ram's horn at the **l** new **l** moon:
        and at the full moon **l** of our **l** day of **l** festival.

4   For this was a **l** statute · for **l** Israel:
        a com **l** mandment · of the **l** God of **l** Jacob,

✝5   which he laid on Joseph as a **l** solemn **l** charge:
        when he came **l** out of · the **l** land of **l** Egypt.

6   I heard a voice that I had not **l** known **l** saying:
        'I eased your shoulders of the burden
        and your **l** hands were **l** freed · from the **l** load.

7   'You called to me in trouble **l** and I **l** rescued you:
        I answered you from the secret place of my thunder
        I put you to the **l** test · at the **l** waters · of **l** Meribah.

8   'Listen my people and I I · will ad Imonish you:
       O Israel if I only I you would I hear me.

9   'There shall be no strange I god a Imong you:
       nor shall you bow I down · to an I ali·en I god.

✝10   'I am the Lord your God
       who brought you up from the I land of I Egypt:
       open wide your I mouth and I I will I fill it.

11   'But my people would not I listen · to my I voice:
       and I Israel I would have I none of me.

12   'So I left them to the stubbornness I of their I hearts:
       to walk ac Icording · to their I own de Isigns.

13   'If only my I people · would I listen:
       if Israel I would but I walk in · my I ways,

14   'I would soon put I down their I enemies:
       and turn my I hand a Igainst their I adversaries.

15   'Those that hate the Lord would I cringe be Ifore him:
       and their I punishment · would I last for I ever.

16   'But Israel I would feed with the I finest I wheat:
       and satisfy you with I honey I from the I rocks.'

PSALM 82

1   God has stood up in the I council · of I heaven:
       in the midst of the I gods I he gives I judgement.

2   'How long will you I judge un Ijustly:
       and I favour · the I cause · of the I wicked?

3   'Judge for the I poor and I fatherless:
       vindicate the af Iflicted I and op Ipressed.

4   'Rescue the I poor and I needy:
       and I save them · from the I hands · of the I wicked.

5   'They do not know   they do not understand
       they walk a Ibout in I darkness:
       and the found Iations · of the I earth are I shaken.

6   'Therefore I say | "Though · you are | gods:
       and all of you | sons · of the | Most | High,

7   ' "nevertheless you shall | die like | man:
       and | fall like | one of · the | princes." '

8   Arise O God and | judge the | earth:
       for you shall take all | nations · as | your pos | session.

PSALM 83

1   Hold not your | peace O | God:
       O God be not | silent | or un | moved.

2   See how your | enemies · make | uproar:
       how those that hate you have | lifted | up their | heads.

3   For they lay shrewd plots a | gainst your | people:
       they scheme against | those whom | you
       have | cherished.

4   'Come' they say 'let us destroy them
       that they may no | longer · be a | nation:
       that the very name of Israel may | be re | membered ·
       no | more.'

5   With one mind they con | spire to | gether:
       they | make al | liance · a | gainst you,

6   the tribes of Edom | and the | Ishmaelites:
       the people of | Moab | and the | Hagarites,

7   Gebal and | Ammon · and | Amalek:
       Philistia | and · the in | habitants · of | Tyre;

8   Asshur | also · is | joined with them:
       and lends a friendly | arm · to the | children · of | Lot.

9   Do to them as you | did to | Midian:
       as to Sisera and Jabin | at the | river · of | Kishon,

10   who were de | stroyed at | Endor:
       and be | came like | dung · for the | earth.

11   Make their leaders as | Oreb · and | Zeeb:
       and all their princes like | Zebah | and Zal | munna,

12   who said 'Let us | take pos|session:
       let us | seize the | pastures · of | God.'

13   Make them like | thistledown · my | God:
       or like chaff | blown be|fore the | wind.

14   As fire con|suming · a | thicket:
       or as flame that | sets the | hillsides · a|blaze,

15   pursue them | with your | tempest:
       and | terrify · them | with your | storm-wind.

16   Cover their faces with | shame O | Lord:
       that | they may | seek your | name.

[17   Let them be disgraced and dis|mayed for | ever:
       let them | be con|founded · and | perish,]

(†) 18   that they may know that you whose | name ·
       is the | Lord:
           are alone the Most | High · over | all the | earth.

PSALM 84

1   How lovely | is your | dwelling-place:
       O | Lord | God of | hosts!

2   My soul has a desire and longing⌣
       to enter the | courts · of the | Lord:
           my heart and my flesh re|joice · in the | living | God.

3   The sparrow has found her a home
       and the swallow a nest where she may | lay
       her | young:
           even your altar   O Lord of | hosts my | King · ⌣
           and my | God.

4   Blessèd are those who | dwell in · your | house:
       they will | always · be | praising | you.

5   Blessèd is the man whose | strength · is in | you:
       in whose | heart · are the | highways · to ⸢Zion;

6   who going through the valley of dryness
       finds there a spring from | which to | drink:
           till the autumn | rain shall | clothe it · with | blessings.

† 7   They go from ❘ strength to ❘ strength:
         they appear every one of them⌣
         before the ❘ God of ❘ gods in ❘ Zion.

8   O Lord God of hosts ❘ hear my ❘ prayer:
         give ❘ ear O ❘ God of ❘ Jacob.

9   Behold O God ❘ him who · reigns ❘ over us:
         and look upon the ❘ face of ⌐your a❘nointed.

10   One day in your courts is ❘ better · than a ❘ thousand:
         I would rather stand at the threshold of the house⌣
         of my God
         than ❘ dwell · in the ❘ tents of · un❘godliness.

11   For the Lord God is a rampart and a shield
         the Lord gives ❘ favour · and ❘ honour:
         and no good thing will he withhold ⌣
         from ❘ those who ❘ walk in ❘ innocence.

† 12   O Lord ❘ God of ❘ hosts:
         blessèd is the man who ❘ puts his ❘ trust in ❘ you.

PSALM 85

1   O Lord you were gracious ❘ to your ❘ land:
         you re❘stored the ❘ fortunes · of ❘ Jacob.

2   You forgave the iniquity ❘ of your ❘ people:
         and ❘ covered ❘ all their ❘ sin.

3   You put aside ❘ all your ❘ wrath:
         and turned away from your ❘ fierce ❘ indig❘nation.

4   Return to us again O ❘ God our ❘ saviour:
         and ❘ let your ❘ anger ❘ cease from us.

5   Will you be displeased with ❘ us for ❘ ever:
         will you stretch out your wrath
         from one gene❘ration ❘ to an❘other?

6   Will you not give us ❘ life a❘gain:
         that your ❘ people ❘ may re❘joice in you?

†7 Show us your | mercy · O | Lord:
and | grant us | your sal |vation.

8 I will hear what the Lord | God will | speak:
for he will speak peace to his people
to his faithful ones whose | hearts are |
turned to | him.

9 Truly his salvation is near to | those that | fear him:
and his | glory · shall | dwell · in our | land.

10 Mercy and truth are | met to |gether:
righteousness and | peace have | kissed each | other;

11 truth shall flourish | out of · the | earth:
and righteousness | shall look | down from | heaven.

12 The Lord will also give us | all · that is | good:
and our | land shall | yield its | plenty.

13 For righteousness shall | go be |fore him:
and tread the | path be |fore his | feet.

PSALM 86

1 Incline your ear to me O | God and | answer me:
for | I am | poor · and in | misery.

2 Preserve my life for | I am | faithful:
my God save your servant who | puts his |
trust in | you.

3 Be merciful to | me O | Lord:
for I | call to · you | all the · day | long.

4 O make glad the | soul of · your | servant:
for I put my | hope in | you O | Lord.

5 For you Lord are | good · and for |giving:
of great and continuing kindness⌣
to | all who | call up |on you.

6 Hear my | prayer O | Lord:
and give heed to the | voice · of my | suppli |cation.

† 7 In the day of my trouble I ᐧ call up ᐧon you:
       for ᐧ you will ᐧ surely ᐧ answer.

8   Among the gods there is none like ᐧ you O ᐧ Lord:
       nor are there ᐧ any ᐧ deeds like ᐧ yours.

9   All the nations you have made⌣
     shall come and ᐧ worship · be ᐧfore you:
       O Lord they shall ᐧ glori ᐧfy your ᐧ name.

10   For you are great and do ᐧ marvel·lous ᐧ things:
       and ᐧ you a ᐧlone are ᐧ God.

11   Show me your way O Lord   and I will ᐧ walk in ·
     your ᐧ truth:
       let my heart de ᐧlight to ᐧ fear your ᐧ name.

12   I will praise you O Lord my God with ᐧ all my ᐧ heart:
       and I will ᐧ glorify · your ᐧ name for ᐧ ever.

13   For great is your abiding ᐧ love to ᐧward me:
       and you have delivered my life⌣
       from the ᐧ lowest ᐧ depths · of the ᐧ grave.

14   Insolent men O God have ᐧ risen · a ᐧgainst me:
       a band of ruthless men seek my life
       they have not set ᐧ God be ᐧfore their ᐧ eyes.

15   But you Lord are a God ᐧ gracious · and com ᐧpassionate:
       slow to anger ᐧ full of ᐧ goodness · and ᐧ truth.

16   Turn to me and be merciful
     give your ᐧ strength · to your ᐧ servant:
       and ᐧ save the ᐧ son of · your ᐧ handmaid.

17   Show me some token ᐧ of your ᐧ goodness:
       that those who hate me may see it and be ashamed
       because you Lord are my ᐧ helper ᐧ and my ᐧ
       comforter.

PSALM 87

1   He has founded it upon a ᐧ holy ᐧ hill:
       and the Lord loves the gates of Zion⌣
       more than ᐧ all the ᐧ dwellings · of ᐧ Jacob.

2   Glorious things shall be | spoken · of | you:
    O Zion | city | of our | God.

3   I might speak of my kinsmen in Egypt | or in | Babylon:
    in Philistia Tyre or Nubia | where | each was | born.

4   But of Zion it | shall be | said:
    many were born in her
    he that is Most | High | has es|tablished her.

5   When the Lord draws up the record | of the | nations:
    he shall take note where | every | man was | born.

6   And the singers and the | dancers · to|gether:
    shall | make their | song · to your | name.

PSALM 88

1   O Lord my God   I call for | help by | day:
    and by night also I | cry | out be|fore you.

2   Let my prayer come | into · your | presence:
    and turn your | ear · to my | loud | crying.

†3 For my soul is | filled with | trouble:
    and my life has come | even · to the | brink ·
    of the | grave.

4   I am reckoned among those that go | down · to the | Pit:
    I am a | man that | has no | help.

5   I lie among the dead
    like the slain that | sleep · in the | grave:
    whom you remember no more
    who are cut | off | from your | power.

6   You have laid me in the | lowest | Pit:
    in darkness and | in the | water·y | depths.

7   Your wrath lies | heavy · up|on me:
    and all your | waves are | brought a|gainst me.

8   You have put my | friends far | from me:
    and made me to | be ab|horred | by them.

9   I am so fast in prison I | cannot · get | free:
    my eyes fail be|cause of | my af|fliction.

10   Lord I call to you | every | day:
       I stretch | out my | hands to | ward you.

11   Will you work | wonders · for the | dead:
       or will the shades rise | up a | gain to | praise you?

12   Shall your love be de | clared · in the | grave:
       or your faithfulness | in the | place · of de | struction?

13   Will your wonders be made | known · in the | dark:
       or your righteousness in the land ‿
       where | all things | are for | gotten?

14   But to you Lord | will I | cry:
       early in the morning my | prayer shall |
       come be | fore you.

15   O Lord why have | you re | jected me:
       why do you | hide your | face | from me?

16   I have been afflicted and wearied from my |
       youth | upward:
       I am tossed high and | low   I | cease to | be.

17   Your fierce anger has | over | whelmed me:
       and your | terrors · have | put me · to | silence.

18   They surround me like a flood | all the · day | long:
       they close up | on me · from | every | side.

19   Friend and acquaintance you have put | far | from me:
       and kept my com | panions | from my | sight.

PSALM 89

1   Lord I will sing for ever of your | loving | kindnesses:
       my mouth shall proclaim your faithfulness ‿
       through | out all | gener | ations.

2   I have said of your loving-kindness ‿
       that it is | built for | ever:
       you have established your | faithful · ness |
       in the | heavens.

3   The Lord said   'I have made a covenant Ι
     with my Ι chosen:
       I have sworn an Ι oath · to my Ι servant Ι David.

4   'I will establish your Ι line for Ι ever:
       and build up your Ι throne for Ι all · gener Ι ations.'

5   Let the heavens praise your Ι wonders · O Ι Lord:
       and let your faithfulness be sung⌣
       in the as Ι sembly Ι of the Ι holy ones.

6   For who amidst the clouds can be com Ι pared ·
     to the Ι Lord:
       or who is like the Lord a Ι mong the Ι sons of Ι heaven?

7   A God to be feared in the council Ι of the Ι holy ones:
       great and terrible above Ι all that Ι are a Ι round him.

8   O Lord God of hosts   Ι who is Ι like you?
       your power and your Ι faithfulness · are Ι
       all a Ι bout you.

9   You rule the Ι raging · of the Ι sea:
       when its Ι waves Ι surge you Ι still them.

10   You crushed Rahab Ι like a Ι carcase:
       you scattered your enemies Ι by your Ι mighty Ι arm.

11   The heavens are yours * so also Ι is the Ι earth:
       you founded the Ι world and Ι all · that is Ι in it.

12   You created the Ι north · and the Ι south:
       Tabor and Mount Ι Hermon · shall Ι sing of · your Ι
       name.

13   Mighty Ι is your Ι arm:
       strong is your hand * and your right Ι hand is Ι
       lifted Ι high.

14   Righteousness and justice are the foundation Ι
     of your Ι throne:
       loving-kindness and Ι faithfulness ·
       at Ι tend Ι your presence.

15 Happy the people who know the tri│umphal │ shout:
　　who walk O │ Lord · in the │ light of · your │
　　countenance.

16 They rejoice all the day long be│cause of · your │ name:
　　because of your │ righteousness · they │ are ex │alted.

17 For you are their glory │ and their │ strength:
　　and our heads are up │lifted │ by your │ favour.

18 Our king be│longs · to the │ Lord:
　　he that rules over us to the │ Holy │ One of │ Israel.

19 You spoke │ once · in a │ vision:
　　and │ said │ to your │ faithful one,

20 'I have set a youth a│bove a │ warrior:
　　I have exalted a │ young man │ out of · the │ people.

21 'I have found my │ servant │ David:
　　and anointed him │ with my │ holy │ oil.

22 'My hand │ shall up│hold him:
　　and my │ arm │ shall │ strengthen him.

23 'No enemy │ shall de│ceive him:
　　no │ evil │ man shall │ hurt him.

24 'I will crush his │ adversaries · be│fore him:
　　and │ strike down │ those that │ hate him.

25 'My faithfulness and loving-kindness │ shall be │
　　with him:
　　and through my name his │ head · shall be │
　　lifted │ high.

26 'I will set the hand of his dominion⌣
　　upon the │ Western │ Sea:
　　and his right hand shall stretch⌣
　　to the │ streams of │ Meso·po│tamia.

27 'He will call to me 　　│ "You · are my │ Father:
　　my God and the │ Rock of │ my sal│vation."

28 'I will make him my │ first-born │ son:
　　and highest a│mong the │ kings · of the │ earth.

29 'I will ever maintain my loving⎮kindness · to⎮ward him:
    and my covenant ⎮ with him · shall ⎮ stand ⎮ firm.

30 'I will establish his ⎮ line for ⎮ ever:
    and his ⎮ throne · like the ⎮ days of ⎮ heaven.

31 'If his children for⎮sake my ⎮ law:
    and ⎮ will not ⎮ walk in · my ⎮ judgements;

32 'if they pro⎮fane my ⎮ statutes:
    and ⎮ do not ⎮ keep · my com⎮mandments,

33 'then I will punish their re⎮bellion · with the ⎮ rod:
    and ⎮ their in⎮iquity · with ⎮ blows.

34 'But I will not cause my loving⎮kindness · to ⎮
    cease from him:
    nor will ⎮ I be⎮tray my ⎮ faithfulness.

35 'I will not pro⎮fane my ⎮ covenant:
    or alter ⎮ what has ⎮ passed from · my ⎮ lips.

36 'Once and for all I have ⎮ sworn · by my ⎮ holiness:
    I will ⎮ not prove ⎮ false to ⎮ David.

37 'His posterity shall en⎮dure for ⎮ ever:
    and his throne be ⎮ as the ⎮ sun be⎮fore me;

38 'like the moon that is es⎮tablished · for ⎮ ever:
    and stands in the ⎮ heavens · for ⎮ ever⎮more.'

39 Yet you have been enraged a⎮gainst · your an⎮ointed:
    you have ab⎮horred him ⎮ and re⎮jected him.

40 You have spurned the covenant ⎮ with your ⎮ servant:
    and de⎮filed his ⎮ crown · to the ⎮ dust.

41 You have broken down ⎮ all his ⎮ walls:
    and ⎮ made his ⎮ strongholds ⎮ desolate.

42 All that pass ⎮ by ⎮ plunder him:
    he has be⎮come the ⎮ scorn of · his ⎮ neighbours.

43 You have exalted the right hand ⎮ of his ⎮ adversaries:
    and ⎮ gladdened ⎮ all his ⎮ enemies.

44 His bright sword you have | turned | backward:
    you have not en|abled him · to | stand · in the | battle.

45 You have brought his | lustre · to an | end:
    you have | cast his | throne · to the | ground.

46 You have cut short the | days of · his | youth:
    and | clothed him | with dis|honour.

47 How long O Lord will you hide your|self so | utterly:
    how long shall your | fury | burn like | fire?

48 Remember how I draw to my e|ternal | end:
    have you created | all man|kind for | nothing?

49 Where is the man who can live and | not see | death:
    who can deliver his | life · from the | power ·
    of the | grave?

50 Where O Lord are your loving |kindnesses · of | old:
    which you have vowed to ⌐David | in your |
    faithfulness?

51 Remember O Lord how your servant | is re|viled:
    how I bear in my bosom the | onslaught |
    of the | peoples;

52 remember how your | ene·mies | taunt:
    how they mock the | footsteps · of | your an|ointed.

(†) (53 Blessèd be the | Lord for | ever:
    A|men and | A|men.)

PSALM 90

1 Lord you have | been our | refuge:
    from one gener|ation | to an|other.

2 Before the mountains were born
    or the earth and the world were | brought to | be:
    from eternity to e|terni·ty | you are ⌐God.

3 You turn man | back · into | dust:
    saying   'Return to | dust you | sons of | Adam.'

4   For a thousand years in your sight
    are like I yester·day I passing:
        or I like one I watch · of the I night.

5   You cut them I short · like a I dream:
    like the fresh I grass I of the I morning;

6   in the morning it is I green and I flourishes:
    at evening it is I withered · and I dried I up.

7   And we are con I sumed · by your I anger:
    because of your indig I nation · we I cease to I be.

8   You have brought our in I iquities · be I fore you:
    and our secret I sins · to the I light of ·
        your I countenance.

9   Our days decline be I neath your I wrath:
    and our years I pass a I way · like a I sigh.

10 The days of our life are three score years and ten
    or if we have I strength four I score:
        the pride of our labours is but toil and sorrow
        for it passes quickly a I way and I we are I gone.

11 Who can know the I power of · your I wrath:
    who can know your indig I nation · like I those
        that I fear you?

12 Teach us so to I number · our I days:
    that we may ap I ply our I hearts to I wisdom.

13 Relent O Lord * how long will I you be I angry?
    take I pity I on your I servants.

14 O satisfy us early I with your I mercy:
    that all our days we I may re I joice and I sing.

15 Give us joy for all the days you I have af I flicted us:
    for the I years · we have I suffered · ad I versity.

16 Show your I servants · your I work:
    and let their I children I see your I glory.

† 17   May the gracious favour of the Lord our |
        God · be up|on us:
           prosper the work of our hands
           O | prosper · the | work · of our | hands!

PSALM 91

1   He who dwells in the shelter of the | Most | High:
        who abides under the | shadow | of the · Al|mighty,

2   he will say to the Lord
        'You are my refuge | and my | stronghold:
          my | God in | whom I | trust.'

3   For he will deliver you from the | snare · of the | hunter:
        and | from the · de|stroying | curse.

4   He will cover you with his wings
        and you will be safe | under · his | feathers:
          his faithfulness will | be your | shield · and de|fence.

5   You shall not be afraid of any | terror · by | night:
        or of the | arrow · that | flies by | day,

6   of the pestilence that walks a|bout in | darkness:
        or the | plague · that de|stroys at | noonday.

7   A thousand may fall beside you
        and ten thousand at your | right | hand:
        but | you it | shall not | touch;

8   your own | eyes shall | see:
        and look on the re|ward | of the · un|godly.

9   The Lord him|self · is your | refuge:
        you have | made the · Most | High your | stronghold.

10   Therefore no | harm · will be|fall you:
        nor will any | scourge come | near your | tent.

11   For he will com|mand his | angels:
        to | keep you · in | all your | ways.

12   They will bear you | up · in their | hands:
        lest you dash your | foot a|gainst a | stone.

13   You will tread on the | lion · and the | adder:
        the young lion and the serpent
        you will | trample | under | foot.

14   'He has set his love upon me
    and therefore I | will de | liver him:
        I will lift him out of danger be | cause ·
        he has | known my | name.

15   'When he calls upon me | I will | answer him:
        I will be with him in trouble
        I will | rescue him · and | bring him · to | honour.

16   'With long | life · I will | satisfy him:
        and | fill him · with | my sal | vation.'

PSALM 92

1   How good to give | thanks · to the | Lord:
        to sing praises to your | name | O Most | High,

2   to declare your | love · in the | morning:
        and at | night to | sing of · your | faithfulness,

† 3   upon the lute   upon the lute of | ten | strings:
        and to the | melo·dy | of the | lyre.

4   For in all you have done O Lord you have |
    made me | glad:
        I will sing for joy be | cause of · the | works ·
        of your | hands.

5   Lord how glorious | are your | works:
        your | thoughts are | very | deep.

6   The brutish do | not con | sider:
        and the | fool · cannot | under | stand

7   that though the wicked | sprout like | grass:
        and | all wrong | doers | flourish,

8   they flourish to be de | stroyed · for | ever:
        but you Lord are ex | alted · for | ever | more.

9   For behold   your enemies O Lord ‿
     your | enemies · shall | perish:
       and all the workers of | wicked · ness |
       shall be | scattered.

10   You have lifted up my head
     like the horns of the | wild | oxen:
       I am an | ointed · with | fresh | oil;

11   my eyes have looked | down · on my | enemies:
       and my ears have heard the ruin ‿
       of | those who · rose | up a | gainst me.

12   The righteous shall | flourish · like the | palm tree:
       they shall spread a | broad · like a | cedar · in | Lebanon;

13   for they are planted in the | house · of the | Lord:
       and flourish in the | courts of | our | God.

14   In old age they shall be | full of | sap:
       they shall be | sturdy · and | laden · with | branches;

15   and they will say that the | Lord is | just:
       the Lord my Rock in | whom is | no un | righteousness.

PSALM 93

1   The Lord is King * and has put on | robes of | glory:
       the Lord has put on his glory
       he has | girded · him | self with | strength.

2   He has made the | world so | firm:
       that it | cannot | be | moved.

3   Your throne is es | tablished · from of | old:
       you | are from | ever | lasting.

4   The floods have lifted up O Lord
     the floods have lifted | up their | voice:
       the | floods lift | up their | pounding.

5   But mightier than the sound of many waters
     than the mighty waters or the | breakers · of the | sea:
       the | Lord on | high is | mighty.

6   Your decrees are | very | sure:
       and holiness O Lord a | dorns your | house for | ever.

PSALM 94

1 O Lord God to whom **|** vengeance · be **|** longs:
   O God to whom vengeance be **|** longs shine **|**
   out in **|** glory.

2 Arise **|** judge · of the **|** earth:
   and requite the **|** proud as **|** they de **|** serve.

3 Lord how **|** long · shall the **|** wicked:
   how **|** long · shall the **|** wicked **|** triumph?

4 How long shall all evildoers **|** pour out **|** words:
   how **|** long · shall they **|** boast and **|**
   flaunt themselves?

5 They crush your **|** people · O **|** Lord:
   they op **|** press your **|** own pos **|** session.

6 They murder the **|** widow · and the **|** alien:
   they **|** put the **|** fatherless · to **|** death.

7 And they say 'The **|** Lord · does not **|** see:
   nor does the **|** God of **|** Jacob · con **|** sider it.'

8 Consider this   you senseless a **|** mong the **|** people:
   fools **|** when · will you **|** under **|** stand?

9 He who planted the ear   does **|** he not **|** hear:
   he who formed the **|** eye   does **|** he not **|** see?

10 He who disciplines the nations will **|** he not **|** punish:
   has the **|** teacher · of man **|** kind no **|** knowledge?

†11 The Lord knows the **|** thoughts of **|** man:
   he **|** knows · that they **|** are mere **|** breath.

12 Blessèd is the man whom you **|** discipline · O **|** Lord:
   and **|** teach **|** from your **|** law,

13 giving him rest from **|** days of **|** misery:
   till a **|** pit is **|** dug · for the **|** wicked.

14 The Lord will not cast **|** off his **|** people:
   nor **|** will he · for **|** sake his **|** own.

15 For justice shall return to the ᛁ righteous ᛁ man:
   and with him to ᛁ all the ᛁ true of ᛁ heart.

16 Who will stand up for me aᛁgainst the ᛁ wicked:
   who will take my part aᛁgainst the ᛁ evil ᛁdoers?

17 If the Lord had not ᛁ been my ᛁ helper:
   I would soon have ᛁ dwelt · in the ᛁ land of ᛁ silence.

18 But when I said   'My ᛁ foot has ᛁ slipped':
   your ᛁ mercy · O ᛁ Lord was ᛁ holding me.

19 In all the ᛁ doubts · of my ᛁ heart:
   your consolᛁation · de ᛁlighted · my ᛁ soul.

20 Will you be any friend to the ᛁ court of ᛁ wickedness:
   that contrives ᛁ evil · by ᛁ means of ᛁ law?

21 They band together against the ᛁ life · of the ᛁ righteous:
   and con ᛁdemn ᛁ inno·cent ᛁ blood.

22 But the ᛁ Lord · is my ᛁ stronghold:
   my ᛁ God · is my ᛁ rock · and my ᛁ refuge.

23 Let him requite them for their wickedness
   and silence them ᛁ for their ᛁ evil:
   the ᛁ Lord our ᛁ God shall ᛁ silence them.

PSALM 95

1 O come let us sing ᛁ out · to the ᛁ Lord:
   let us shout in triumph to the ᛁ rock of ᛁ
   our salᛁvation.

2 Let us come before his ᛁ face with ᛁ thanksgiving:
   and cry ᛁ out to · him ᛁ joyfully · in ᛁ psalms.

3 For the Lord is a ᛁ great ᛁ God:
   and a great ᛁ king a·bove ᛁ all ᛁ gods.

4 In his hand are the ᛁ depths · of the ᛁ earth:
   and the peaks of the ᛁ mountains · are ᛁ his ᛁ also.

†5 The sea is his and ᛁ he ᛁ made it:
   his hands ᛁ moulded ᛁ dry ᛁ land.

6 Come let us worship and ᛁ bow ᛁ down:
   and kneel beᛁfore the ᛁ Lord our ᛁ maker.

7 For he is the ˈ Lord our ˈ God:
    we are his ˈ people · and the ˈ sheep of · his ˈ pasture.

8 Today if only you would hear his voice
    'Do not harden your ˈ hearts · as at ˈ Meribah:
    as on that day at ˈ Massah ˈ in the ˈ wilderness;

9 'when your ˈ fathers ˈ tested me:
    put me to proof though ˈ they had ˈ seen my ˈ works.

10 'Forty years long I loathed that generˈation · and ˈ said:
    "It is a people who err in their hearts
    for they ˈ do not ˈ know my ˈ ways";

11 'of whom I ˈ swore · in my ˈ wrath:
    "They ˈ shall not ˈ enter · my ˈ rest." '

PSALM 96

1 O sing to the Lord a ˈ new ˈ song:
    sing to the ˈ Lord ˈ all the ˈ earth.

2 Sing to the Lord and bless his ˈ holy ˈ name:
    proclaim the good news of his salˈvation · from ˈ
    day to ˈ day.

3 Declare his glory aˈmong the ˈ nations:
    and his ˈ wonders · aˈmong all ˈ peoples.

4 For great is the Lord and ˈ greatly · to be ˈ praised:
    he is more to be ˈ feared than ˈ all ˈ gods.

5 As for all the gods of the nations ˈ they are · mere ˈ
    idols:
    it is the ˈ Lord who ˈ made the ˈ heavens.

6 Majesty and ˈ glory · are beˈfore him:
    beauty and ˈ power are ˈ in his ˈ sanctuary.

7 Render to the Lord you families ˈ of the ˈ nations:
    render to the ˈ Lord ˈ glory · and ˈ might.

8 Render to the Lord the honour ˈ due · to his ˈ name:
    bring offerings and ˈ come inˈto his ˈ courts.

9 O worship the Lord in the beauty ˈ of his ˈ holiness:
    let the whole earth ˈ stand in ˈ awe of ˈ him.

10   Say among the nations that the | Lord is | king:
        he has made the world so firm that it can never⌣
        be moved
        and he shall | judge the | peoples · with | equity.

11   Let the heavens rejoice   and let the | earth be | glad:
        let the sea | roar and | all that | fills it;

12   let the fields rejoice and | every · thing | in them:
        then shall all the trees of the wood⌣
        shout with | joy be|fore the | Lord;

†13   for he comes   he comes to | judge the | earth:
        he shall judge the world with righteousness
        and the | peoples | with his | truth.

PSALM 97

1   The Lord is king   let the | earth re|joice:
        let the | multitude · of | islands · be | glad.

2   Clouds and darkness are | round a|bout him:
        righteousness and justice are the found|ation |
        of his | throne.

3   Fire | goes be|fore him:
        and burns up his | enemies · on | every | side.

4   His lightnings | light the | world:
        the | earth | sees it · and | quakes.

5   The mountains melt like wax be|fore his | face:
        from before the face of the | Lord of |
        all the | earth.

6   The heavens have pro|claimed his | righteousness:
        and all | peoples · have | seen his | glory.

7   They are ashamed * all those who serve idols⌣
        and glory in | mere | nothings:
        all | gods bow | down be|fore him.

8   Zion heard and was glad
        and the daughters of | Judah · re|joiced:
        be|cause of · your | judgements · O | God.

9 For you Lord are most high over ∣ all the ∣ earth:
   you are exalted ∣ far a·bove ∣ all ∣ gods.

10 The Lord loves ∣ those that · hate ∣ evil:
   the Lord guards the life of the faithful
   and delivers them from the ∣ hand of ∣ the un∣godly.

11 Light ∣ dawns · for the ∣ righteous:
   and ∣ joy · for the ∣ true of ∣ heart.

12 Rejoice in the ∣ Lord you ∣ righteous:
   and give ∣ thanks · to his ∣ holy ∣ name.

PSALM 98

1 O sing to the Lord a ∣ new ∣ song:
   for he has ∣ done ∣ marvel·lous ∣ things;

2 his right hand and his ∣ holy ∣ arm:
   they have ∣ got ∣ him the ∣ victory.

3 The Lord has made ∣ known · his sal∣vation:
   he has revealed his just de∣liverance · in the ∣
   sight of · the ∣ nations.

4 He has remembered his mercy and faithfulness‿
   towards the ∣ house of ∣ Israel:
   and all the ends of the earth‿
   have seen the sal∣vation ∣ of our ∣ God.

5 Shout with joy to the Lord ∣ all the ∣ earth:
   break into ∣ singing · and ∣ make ∣ melody.

6 Make melody to the Lord up∣on the ∣ harp:
   upon the harp and ∣ with the ∣ sounds of ∣ praise.

7 With trumpets ∣ and with ∣ horns:
   cry out in triumph be∣fore the ∣ Lord the ∣ king.

8 Let the sea roar and ∣ all that ∣ fills it:
   the good earth and ∣ those who ∣ live up∣on it.

9 Let the rivers ∣ clap their ∣ hands:
   and let the mountains ring out to∣gether ·
   be∣fore the ∣ Lord;

10   for he comes to ˡ judge the ˡ earth:
            he shall judge the world with righteousness
            and the ˡ peoples ˡ with ˡ equity.

PSALM 99

1   The Lord is king   let the ˡ nations ˡ tremble:
            he is enthroned upon the cherubim ˡ let the ˡ
            earth ˡ quake.

2   The Lord is ˡ great in ˡ Zion:
            he is ˡ high aˡbove all ˡ nations.

3   Let them praise your great and ˡ terri·ble ˡ name:
            for ˡ holy ˡ is the ˡ Lord.

4   The Mighty One is king and ˡ loves ˡ justice:
            you have established equity * you have dealt ˡ ⌣
            righteousness · and ˡ justice · in ˡ Jacob.

†5   *O exalt the ˡ Lord our ˡ God:*
            and bow down before his ˡ footstool · for ˡ he is ˡ holy.

6   Moses and Aaron among his priests
            and Samuel among those who call upˡon his ˡ name:
            they called to the ˡ Lord ˡ and he ˡ answered.

7   He spoke to them from the ˡ pillar · of ˡ cloud:
            they kept his teachings ˡ and the ˡ law ·
            that he ˡ gave them.

8   You answered them O ˡ Lord our ˡ God:
            you were a forgiving God to them
            and ˡ pardoned · their ˡ wrongˡdoing.

9   *O exalt the ˡ Lord our ˡ God:*
            and bow down towards his holy hill
            for the ˡ Lord our ˡ God is ˡ holy.

PSALM 100

1   O shout to the Lord in triumph ˡ all the ˡ earth:
            serve the Lord with gladness
            and come before his ˡ face with ˡ songs of ˡ joy.

2   Know that the Lord I he is I God:
       it is he who has made us and we are his
       we are his I people · and the I sheep of · his I pasture.

3   Come into his gates with thanksgiving
   and into his I courts with I praise:
       give thanks to him and I bless his I holy I name.

4   For the Lord is good * his loving mercy I is for I ever:
       his faithfulness through I out all I gener I ations.

PSALM 101

1   My song shall be of I steadfastness · and I justice:
       to I you Lord I will I I sing.

2   I will be wise in the I way of I innocence:
       O I when I will you I come to me?

3   I will walk with I in my I house:
       in I puri I ty of I heart.

4   I will set nothing evil be I fore my I eyes:
       I hate the sin of backsliders   it shall I get no I
       hold I on me.

†5   Crookedness of heart shall de I part I from me:
       I will I know I nothing · of I wickedness.

[6   The man who secretly slanders his neighbour I I
   will de I stroy:
       the proud look and the arrogant I heart ·
       I will I not en I dure.]

7   My eyes shall look to the faithful in the land
   and they shall I make their I home with me:
       one who walks in the way of innocence I
       he shall I minis · ter I to me.

8   No man who practises deceit shall I live in · my I house:
       no one who utters I lies shall I stand in · my I sight.

[9   Morning by morning I will destroy
   all the I wicked · of the I land:
       and cut off all evildoers
       from the I city I of the I Lord.]

PSALM 102

1   O Lord | hear my | prayer:
     and | let my | cry | come to you.

2   Do not hide your face from me in the | day of ·
     my | trouble:
       turn your ear to me
     and when I | call be | swift to | answer.

3   For my days pass a | way like | smoke:
     and my bones | burn as | in a | furnace.

4   My heart is scorched and | withered · like | grass:
     and I for | get to | eat my | bread.

5   I am weary with the | sound of · my | groaning:
     my | bones stick | fast to · my | skin.

6   I have become like an | owl · in the | wilderness:
     like a | screech-owl · a | mong the | ruins.

7   I keep watch   and | flit · to and | fro:
     like a | sparrow · up | on a | housetop.

8   My enemies taunt me | all day | long:
     and those who | rave at me · make | oaths a | gainst me.

9   Surely I have eaten | ashes · for | bread:
     and | mingled · my | drink with | tears,

10   because of your wrath and | indig | nation:
     for you have taken me | up and | tossed · me a | side.

†11   My days de | cline · like a | shadow:
     and I | wither · a | way like | grass.

12   But you Lord are en | throned for | ever:
     and your name shall be known
       through | out all | gener | ations.

13   You will arise and have | mercy up · on | Zion:
     for it is time to pity her   the ap | pointed |
     time has | come.

14   Your servants love | even · her | stones:
     and her | dust moves | them to | pity.

15 Then shall the nations fear your | name O | Lord:
and all the | kings · of the | earth your | glory,

16 when the Lord has | built up | Zion:
when he | shows him|self · in his | glory,

17 when he turns to the | prayer · of the | destitute:
and does not de|spise their | suppli|cation.

†18 Let this be written down for | those who · come | after:
and a people yet un|born will | praise the | Lord.

19 For the Lord has looked down from the | height ·
of his | holiness:
from heaven he has | looked up|on the | earth,

20 to hear the | groaning · of the | prisoner:
to deliver | those con|demned to | die;

21 that they may proclaim the name of the | Lord in | Zion:
and his | praises | in Je|rusalem,

22 when the nations are | gathered · to|gether:
and the | kingdoms · to | serve the | Lord.

23 He has broken my strength be|fore my | time:
he has | cut | short my | days.

24 Do not take me away O God in the | midst of · my | life:
you whose years ex|tend through | all · gener|ations.

25 In the beginning you laid the foun|dations ·
of the | earth:
and the | heavens · are the | work of · your | hands.

26 They shall perish   but | you · will en|dure:
they shall all grow old like a garment
like clothes you will change them and | they shall |
pass a|way.

27 But you are the | same for | ever:
and your | years will | never | fail.

28 The children of your servants shall | rest se|cure:
and their seed shall be es|tablished | in your | sight.

PSALM 103

1 Praise the Lord [|] O my [|] soul:
   and all that is within me [|] praise his [|] holy [|] name.

2 Praise the Lord [|] O my [|] soul:
   and for [|] get not [|] all his [|] benefits,

3 who forgives [|] all your [|] sin:
   and [|] heals [|] all · your in [|] firmities,

4 who redeems your [|] life · from the [|] Pit:
   and crowns you with [|] mercy [|] and com [|] passion;

†5 who satisfies your being with [|] good [|] things:
   so that your [|] youth · is re [|] newed · like an [|] eagle's.

6 The Lord [|] works [|] righteousness:
   and justice for [|] all who [|] are op [|] pressed.

7 He made known his [|] ways to [|] Moses:
   and his [|] works · to the [|] children · of [|] Israel.

8 The Lord is full of com [|] passion · and [|] mercy:
   slow to anger [|] and of [|] great [|] goodness.

9 He will not [|] always · be [|] chiding:
   nor will he [|] keep his [|] anger · for [|] ever.

10 He has not dealt with us ac [|] cording · to our [|] sins:
   nor rewarded us ac [|] cording [|] to our [|] wickedness.

11 For as the heavens are high a [|] bove the [|] earth:
   so great is his [|] mercy · over [|] those that [|] fear him;

12 as far as the east is [|] from the [|] west:
   so far has he [|] set our [|] sins [|] from us.

13 As a father is tender to [|] wards his [|] children:
   so is the Lord [|] tender · to [|] those that [|] fear him.

†14 For he knows of [|] what · we are [|] made:
   he re [|] members · that we [|] are but [|] dust.

15 The days of man are [|] but as [|] grass:
   he flourishes [|] like a [|] flower · of the [|] field;

16 when the wind goes over it | it is | gone:
    and its | place will | know it · no | more.

17 But the merciful goodness of the Lord
    endures for ever and ever toward | ⌣
    those that | fear him:
        and his righteousness up|on their | ⌣
        children's | children;

18 upon those who | keep his | covenant:
    and re|member · his com|mandments · to | do them.

19 The Lord has established his | throne in | heaven:
    and his | kingdom | rules · over | all.

20 Praise the Lord all you his angels
    you that ex|cel in | strength:
        you that fulfil his word
        and obey the | voice of | his com|mandment.

21 Praise the Lord all | you his | hosts:
    his | servants · who | do his | will.

22 Praise the Lord all his works
    in all places of | his do|minion:
        praise the | Lord | O my | soul!

PSALM 104

1 Bless the Lord | O my | soul:
    O Lord my | God how | great you | are!

2 Clothed with | majesty · and | honour:
    wrapped in | light as | in a | garment.

3 You have stretched out the | heavens ·
    like a | tent-cloth:
        and laid the beams of your | dwelling ·
        up|on their | waters;

4 you make the | clouds your | chariot:
    and | ride up·on the | wings · of the | wind;

5 you make the | winds your | messengers:
    and | flames of | fire your | ministers;

6   you have set the earth on | its foun | dations:
       so | that it · shall | never · be | moved.

7   The deep covered it | as · with a | mantle:
       the waters | stood a | bove the | hills.

8   At your re | buke they | fled:
       at the voice of your | thunder · they | hurried · a | way;

9   they went up to the mountains
    they went | down · by the | valleys:
       to the place which | you · had ap | pointed | for them.

10   You fixed a limit which they | may not | pass:
       they shall not return a | gain to | cover · the | earth.

11   You send springs | into · the | gullies:
       which | run be | tween the | hills;

12   they give drink to every | beast · of the | field:
       and the wild | asses | quench their | thirst.

13   Beside them the birds of the air | build their | nests:
       and | sing a | mong the | branches.

14   You water the mountains from your | dwelling ·
    on | high:
       and the earth is | filled · by the | fruits of · your | work.

15   You cause the grass to | grow · for the | cattle:
       and all green things for the | servants | of man | kind.

16   You bring food | out of · the | earth:
       and wine that makes | glad the | heart of | man,

17   oil to give him a | shining | countenance:
       and | bread to | strengthen · his | heart.

18   The trees of the Lord are | well | watered:
       the cedars of | Lebanon · that | he has | planted,

19   where the birds | build their | nests:
       and the stork | makes her | home · in the | pine-tops.

20   The high hills are a refuge for the | wild | goats:
       and the crags a | cover | for the | conies.

21   You created the moon to | mark the | seasons:
       and the sun | knows the | hour · of its | setting.

22 You make darkness ǀ and it · is ǀ night:
    in which all the beasts of the ǀ forest ǀ
    move by ǀ stealth.

23 The lions ǀ roar · for their ǀ prey:
    seek ǀ ing their ǀ food from ǀ God.

24 When the sun rises ǀ they re ǀ tire:
    and ǀ lay them · selves ǀ down · in their ǀ dens.

†25 Man goes ǀ out · to his ǀ work:
    and to his ǀ labour · un ǀ til the ǀ evening.

26 Lord how various ǀ are your ǀ works:
    in wisdom you have made them all
    and the ǀ earth is ǀ full of · your ǀ creatures.

27 There is the wide im ǀ measur · able ǀ sea:
    there move living things without ǀ number ǀ
    great and ǀ small;

28 there go the ships ǀ to and ǀ fro:
    and there is that Leviathan
    whom you ǀ formed to ǀ sport · in the ǀ deep.

29 These all ǀ look to ǀ you:
    to give them their ǀ food in ǀ due ǀ season.

30 When you give it to ǀ them they ǀ gather it:
    when you open your hand they are ǀ satisfied ·
    with ǀ good ǀ things.

31 When you hide your ǀ face · they are ǀ troubled:
    when you take away their breath
    they ǀ die · and re ǀ turn · to their ǀ dust.

†32 When you send forth your spirit they ǀ are cre ǀ ated:
    and you re ǀ new the ǀ face · of the ǀ earth.

33 May the glory of the Lord en ǀ dure for ǀ ever:
    may the ǀ Lord re ǀ joice · in his ǀ works.

34 If he look upon the ǀ earth · it shall ǀ tremble:
    if he but touch the ǀ mountains ǀ they shall ǀ smoke.

35 I will sing to the Lord as ǀ long as · I ǀ live:
    I will praise my ǀ God · while I ǀ have · any ǀ being.

36 May my meditation be ∣ pleasing ∣ to him:
     for my ∣ joy shall ∣ be · in the ∣ Lord.

†37 May sinners perish from the earth
     let the wicked ∣ be no ∣ more:
         bless the Lord O my soul
         O ∣ praise ∣ – the ∣ Lord.

PSALM 105

1   O give thanks to the Lord   and call up∣on his ∣ name:
     tell among the ∣ peoples · what ∣ things · he has ∣ done.

2   Sing to him O ∣ sing ∣ praises:
     and be telling of ∣ all his ∣ marvel·lous ∣ works.

3   Exult in his ∣ holy ∣ name:
     and let those that seek the ∣ Lord be ∣ joyful · in ∣ heart.

4   Seek the ∣ Lord · and his ∣ strength:
     O ∣ seek his ∣ face con∣tinually.

5   Call to mind what wonders ∣ he has ∣ done:
     his marvellous acts   and the ∣ judgements ∣
     of his ∣ mouth,

6   O seed of ∣ Abraham · his ∣ servant:
     O ∣ children · of ∣ Jacob · his ∣ chosen one.

7   For he is the ∣ Lord our ∣ God:
     and his judgements ∣ are in ∣ all the ∣ earth.

8   He has remembered his ∣ covenant · for ∣ ever:
     the word that he ordained for a ∣ thousand ∣
     gener∣ations,

9   the covenant that he ∣ made with ∣ Abraham:
     the ∣ oath · that he ∣ swore to ∣ Isaac,

10 and confirmed it to ∣ Jacob · as a ∣ statute:
     to Israel as an ∣ ever∣lasting ∣ covenant,

11 saying   'I will give you the ∣ land of ∣ Canaan:
     to be the ∣ portion · of ∣ your in∣heritance',

12 and that when they ∣ were but ∣ few:
     little in number   and ∣ ali·ens ∣ in the ∣ land.

13   They wandered from | nation · to | nation:
        from one people and | kingdom | to an | other.

14   He suffered no man to | do them | wrong:
        but re | proved · even | kings for · their | sake,

† 15   saying 'Touch not | my an | ointed:
        and | do my | prophets · no | harm.'

16   Then he called down a | famine · on the | land:
        and destroyed the | bread that | was their | stay.

17   But he had sent a | man a | head of them:
        Joseph | who was | sold · into | slavery,

18   whose feet they | fastened · with | fetters:
        and thrust his | neck in · to a | hoop of | iron.

19   Till the time that his | words proved | true:
        he was | tested · by the | Lord's com | mand.

20   Then the king | sent and | loosed him:
        the ruler of | nations | set him | free;

21   he made him master | of his | household:
        and ruler | over | all · his pos | sessions,

† 22   to rebuke his | officers · at | will:
        and to | teach his | counsel · lors | wisdom.

23   Then Israel | came · into | Egypt:
        and Jacob | dwelt · in the | land of | Ham.

24   There the Lord made his | people | fruitful:
        too | numer · ous | for their | enemies,

25   whose hearts he turned to | hate his | people:
        and to deal de | ceitful · ly | with his | servants.

26   Then he sent | Moses · his | servant:
        and | Aaron · whom | he had | chosen.

27   Through them he | manifested · his | signs:
        and his | wonders · in the | land of | Ham.

28   He sent darkness | and it · was | dark:
        yet they would | not o | bey · his com | mands.

29 He turned their | waters · into | blood:
   and | slew the | fish there |in.

30 Their country | swarmed with | frogs:
   even the inner | chambers | of their | kings.

31 He spoke the word   and there came great |
   swarms of | flies:
   and | gnats with·in | all their | borders.

32 He sent them | storms of | hail:
   and darts of | fire | into · their | land.

33 He struck their | vines · and their | fig-trees:
   and shattered the | trees with |in their | borders.

34 He commanded   and there | came | grasshoppers:
   and young | locusts · with |out | number.

35 They ate up every green thing | in the | land:
   and de |voured the | fruit · of the | soil.

36 He smote all the first-born | in their | land:
   the | first-fruits · of | all their | manhood.

37 He brought Israel out with silver | and with | gold:
   and not one among their | tribes was |
   seen to | stumble.

38 Egypt was | glad · at their | going:
   for dread of | Israel · had | fallen · up |on them.

39 He spread out a | cloud · for a | covering:
   and | fire to | lighten · the | night.

40 The people asked and he | brought them | quails:
   and satisfied them | with the | bread from | heaven.

41 He opened a rock so that the | waters | gushed:
   and ran in the parched | land | like a | river.

42 For he had remembered his | holy | word:
   that he gave to | Abra |ham his | servant.

43 So he led out his | people · with re |joicing:
   his | chosen ones · with | shouts of | joy;

44   he gave them the ^l land · of the ^l nations:
       and they took possession of the ^l fruit
       of ^l other · men's ^l toil,

† 45   so that they might ^l keep his ^l statutes:
       and faithfully obey his laws
       O ^l praise ^l – the ^l Lord.

PSALM 106

1   Praise the Lord.
      O give thanks to the Lord for ^l he is ^l good:
      and his ^l mercy · en ^l dures for ^l ever.

2   Who can express the mighty ^l acts · of the ^l Lord:
      or ^l fully ^l voice his ^l praise?

3   Blessèd are those who act ac ^l cording · to ^l justice:
      who at ^l all times ^l do the ^l right.

4   Remember me O Lord
      when you visit your people ^l with your ^l favour:
      and come to me ^l also · with ^l your sal ^l vation,

† 5   that I may see the prosperity ^l of your ^l chosen:
      that I may rejoice with the rejoicing of your people
      and exult with ^l those who ^l are your ^l own.

6   We have sinned ^l like our ^l fathers:
      we have acted per ^l versely · and ^l done ^l wrong.

7   Our fathers when they ^l were in ^l Egypt:
      took no ^l heed ^l of your ^l wonders;

8   they did not remember
      the multitude of your ^l loving ^l kindnesses:
      but they re ^l belled · at the ^l Red ^l Sea.

9   Nevertheless he saved them for his ^l name's ^l sake:
      that he ^l might make ^l known his ^l power.

10   He commanded the Red Sea and it ^l dried ^l up:
      and he led them through the ^l deep as ^l
      through a ^l desert.

11 He delivered them from the | hand ·
of their | adversary:
    and redeemed them | from the | power ·
    of the | enemy.

12 The waters closed over | their op|pressors:
    so that not | one was | left a|live.

13 Then they be|lieved his | words:
    and | sang him | songs of | praise.

14 But in a little while they forgot what | he had | done:
    and would | wait · for his | counsel · no | more.

15 Greed took hold of them | in the | desert:
    and they put | God · to the | test · in the | wilderness.

16 So he gave them that which | they de|sired:
    but sent a | wasting | sickness · a|mong them.

17 Then they grew envious of Moses | in the | camp:
    and of Aaron the | holy · one | of the | Lord;

18 whereupon the earth opened and | swallowed · up | Dathan:
    it closed over the | compan·y | of A|biram;

19 fire flared out a|gainst their | number:
    and | flame de|voured · the un | godly.

20 At Horeb they | made themselves · a | calf:
    and bowed down in | worship | to an | image.

21 And so they exchanged the | glory · of | God:
    for the likeness of an | ox that | eats | hay.

22 They forgot God who | was their | saviour:
    that had done such | great | things in | Egypt,

23 who had worked his wonders in the | land of | Ham:
    and his terrible | deeds · at the | Red | Sea.

†24 Therefore he | thought · to de|stroy them:
    had not Moses his servant stood before him⌣
    in the breach
    to turn a|way his | wrath · from de|stroying them.

25 Then they despised the | pleasant | land:
    and | put no | faith · in his | promise,

26 but murmured | in their | tents:
    and would not o|bey the | voice · of the | Lord.

27 So he lifted his hand to swear an | oath a|gainst them:
    that he would | strike them | down ·
    in the | wilderness,

28 and cast out their children a|mong the | nations:
    and | scatter them · through | all the | lands.

29 Then they joined themselves to the | Baal · of | Peor:
    and ate things sacrificed to | gods that | have no | life.

30 They provoked him to anger with their |
    wanton | deeds:
    and | plague broke | out a|mong them.

31 Then stood up Phinehas and | inter|posed:
    and | so the | plague was | ended;

32 and that was counted to | him for | righteousness:
    throughout all gener|ations · for | ever|more.

33 They angered God also at the | waters · of | Meribah:
    so that Moses | suffered · for | their mis|deeds;

34 for they had em|bittered · his | spirit:
    and he spoke | rashly | with his | lips.

35 They did not de|stroy the | peoples:
    as the Lord had com|manded | them to | do,

36 but they mingled themselves | with the | heathen:
    and | learned to | follow · their | ways.

37 They worshipped | foreign | idols:
    and | these be|came their | snare,

38 so that they | sacrificed · their | sons:
    and their | own | daughters · to | demons.

39 They shed | inno·cent | blood:
    even the blood of their | own | sons and | daughters,

40   whom they offered to the I idols · of I Canaan:
      and the ˥ land · was de I filed with I blood.

41   They made themselves I foul · by their I acts:
      and with wanton deeds I whored · after I
      strange I gods.

42   Then was the wrath of the Lord kindled ⌣
      a I gainst his I people:
      and he I loathed his I own pos I session;

43   he gave them into the I hands · of the I nations:
      and their I adver·saries I ruled I over them.

44   Their enemies be I came · their op I pressors:
      and they were brought into sub ˥ jection ·
      be I neath their I power.

45   Many a I time he I saved them:
      but they rebelled against him ⌣
      to follow their own designs
      and were brought I down I by their I wickedness.

46   Nevertheless he looked on I their dis I tress:
      when he I heard their I loud I crying.

47   He remembered his I coven·ant I with them:
      and relented   according to the a I bundance ·
      of his I loving I kindness.

48   And he caused them I to be I pitied:
      even by I those that I held them I captive.

(†) 49   Save us O Lord our God
      and gather us from a I mong the I nations:
      that we may give thanks to your holy name
      and I make our I boast · in your I praises.

(50   Blessèd be the Lord the God of Israel
      from everlasting to I ever I lasting:
      and let all the people say Amen I
      Praise I – the I Lord.)

PSALM 107

1   O give thanks to the Lord for | he is | good:
    for his loving | mercy | is for | ever.

2   Let the Lord's re | deemed | say so:
    whom he has redeemed from the |
    hand | of the | enemy,

† 3   and gathered in from every land
    from the east and | from the | west:
    from the | north and | from the | south.

4   Some went astray in the wilderness and | in the | desert:
    and found no ⌈ path to · an in | habit·ed | city;

5   they were | hungry · and | thirsty:
    and their | heart | fainted · with | in them.

6   Then they cried to the Lord in | their dis | tress:
    and he | took them | out of · their | trouble.

7   He led them by the | right | path:
    till they | came to · an in | habit·ed | city.

8   *Let them thank the | Lord · for his | goodness:*
    and for the wonders that he | does · for the |
    children · of | men;

9   *for he | satisfies · the | thirsty:*
    and fills the | hungry · with | good | things.

10   Some sat in darkness and in | deadly | shadow:
    bound | fast · in af | fliction · and | iron,

11   because they had rebelled against the | words of | God:
    and scorned the purposes | of the | Most | High.

12   So he bowed down their | hearts · with af | fliction:
    they tripped | headlong · with | none to | help them.

13   Then they cried to the Lord in | their dis | tress:
    and he | took them | out of · their | trouble.

† 14   He brought them out from darkness and |
       deadly | shadow:
          and | broke their | chains in | two.

15   *Let them thank the | Lord · for his | goodness:*
          and for the wonders that he | does · for the |
          children · of | men;

16   *for he shatters the | doors of | bronze:*
          and | cleaves the | bars of | iron.

17   Fools were far | gone · in trans | gression:
          and be | cause of · their | sins · were afflicted.

18   They sickened at | any | food:
          and had | come · to the | gates of | death.

19   Then they cried to the Lord in | their dis | tress:
          and he | took them | out of · their | trouble.

20   He sent his | word and | healed them:
          and | saved their | life · from the | Pit.

21   *Let them thank the | Lord · for his | goodness:*
          and for the wonders that he | does · for the |
          children · of | men;

22   *let them offer sacrifices of | thanks | giving:*
          and tell what he has | done with | shouts of | joy.

23   Those who go down to the | sea in | ships:
          and follow their | trade on | great | waters,

24   these men have seen the | works of | God:
          and his | wonders | in the | deep.

25   For he spoke and | raised the | storm-wind:
          and it lifted | high the | waves · of the | sea.

26   They go up to the sky   and down a | gain ·
       to the | depths:
          their courage melts a | way · in the | face ·
          of dis | aster.

27   They reel and stagger like | drunken | men:
          and are | at their | wits' | end.

28   Then they cried to the Lord in ˈ their disˈtress:
    and he ˈ took them ˈ out of · their ˈ trouble.

29   He calmed the ˈ storm · to a ˈ silence:
    and the ˈ waves · of the ˈ sea were ˈ stilled.

30   Then they were glad beˈcause · they were ˈ quiet:
    and he ˈ brought them · to the ˈ haven · they ˈ longed for.

31   *Let them thank the ˈ Lord · for his ˈ goodness:*
    and for the wonders that he ˈ does · for the ˈ children · of ˈ men;

32   *let them exalt him in the asˈsembly · of the ˈ people:*
    and ˈ praise him · in the ˈ council · of ˈ elders.

33   He turns the ˈ rivers · into ˈ desert:
    and springs of ˈ water · into ˈ thirsty ˈ ground.

34   He makes of a fruitful land a ˈ salty ˈ waste:
    beˈcause · its inˈhabitants · are ˈ evil.

35   He turns the wilderness into a ˈ pool of ˈ water:
    and parched ˈ ground · into ˈ flowing ˈ springs.

36   And there he ˈ settles · the ˈ hungry:
    and they ˈ build a ˈ city · to ˈ live in.

37   They sow fields and ˈ plant ˈ vineyards:
    which ˈ give them ˈ fruitful ˈ harvest.

38   He blesses them   and they ˈ multi·ply ˈ greatly:
    he does not ˈ let their ˈ cattle · dimˈinish.

39   But he pours conˈtempt up·on ˈ princes:
    and makes them ˈ stray · in the ˈ pathless ˈ desert;

40   they are weakened and ˈ brought ˈ low:
    through ˈ stress of · adˈversity · and ˈ sorrow.

41   But he lifts the ˈ poor · out of ˈ misery:
    and increases their ˈ families · like ˈ flocks of ˈ sheep.

42   The upright shall ˈ see it · and reˈjoice:
    and all ˈ wickedness · shall ˈ shut its ˈ mouth.

† 43   Whoever is wise   let him ob | serve these | things:
        and consider the loving | kindness | of the | Lord.

PSALM 108

1   My heart is fixed O God my | heart is | fixed:
       I will | sing and | make | melody.

2   Awake my soul   awake | lute and | harp:
       for | I · will a | waken · the | morning.

3   I will give you thanks O Lord a | mong the | peoples:
       I will sing your | praise a | mong the | nations.

4   For the greatness of your mercy | reaches ·
    to the | heavens:
       and your | faithful · ness | to the | clouds.

5   Be exalted O God a | bove the | heavens:
       and let your glory be | over | all the | earth;

6   that those whom you love may | be de | livered:
       O save us by | your right | hand and | answer me.

7   God has said in his | holy | place:
       'I will exult and divide Shechem
       I will parcel | out the | valley · of | Succoth.

8   'Gilead is mine and Man | asseh · is | mine:
       Ephraim is my helmet and | Judah · my |
    rod · of com | mand.

† 9   'Moab is my wash-bowl   over Edom will I |
    cast my | shoe:
       against Philistia | will I | shout in | triumph.'

10   Who will lead me into the | forti · fied | city:
       who will | bring me | into | Edom?

11   Have you not cast us | off O | God?
       you | go not | out · with our | armies.

12   Give us your help a | gainst the | enemy:
       for | vain · is the | help of | man.

13   By the power of our God we ˈ shall do ˈ valiantly:
       for it is he that ˈ will tread ˈ down our ˈ enemies.

PSALM 109

1   O God of my praise do ˈ not be ˈ silent:
       for evil and deceitful ˈ mouths are ˈ opened ·
       a ˈ gainst me.

2   They speak of me with ˈ lying ˈ tongues:
       they surround me with words of hatred
       they fight a ˈ gainst me · with ˈ out ˈ cause.

3   In return for my friendship ˈ they op ˈ pose me:
       and ˈ that for · no ˈ fault of ˈ mine.

4   They repay me ˈ evil · for ˈ good:
       and ˈ hatred · for ˈ my af ˈ fection.

[5   Appoint an evil man to ˈ stand a ˈ gainst him:
       and let an adversary ˈ be at · his ˈ right ˈ hand.

6   When he is judged   let him be ˈ found ˈ guilty:
       let his prayer for ˈ help be ˈ counted · as ˈ sin.

7   Let his ˈ days be ˈ few:
       and let another ˈ take what ˈ he has ˈ hoarded.

8   Let his children be ˈ made ˈ fatherless:
       and his ˈ wife be ˈ come a ˈ widow.

9   Let his children be ˈ vagabonds · and ˈ beggars:
       let them seek alms ˈ far · from their ˈ own ˈ homes.

10   Let the usurer exact ˈ all · that he ˈ has:
       and let strangers ˈ plunder · the ˈ fruit · of his ˈ toil.

11   Let no man be ˈ loyal · to ˈ him:
       and let no one have ˈ pity · on his ˈ
       father·less ˈ children.

12   Let his line be ˈ come ex ˈ tinct:
       in one generation let their ˈ name be ˈ blotted ˈ out.

13   Let the sins of his fathers be re ˈmembered ·
      by the ˈ Lord:
        and his mother's iniquity ˈ not be ˈ wiped aˈway.

14   Let their sins be constantly beˈfore the ˈ Lord:
        may he root out their ˈ memo·ry ˈ from the ˈ earth.

15   For he was a man that did not remember to ˈ
      show ˈ loyalty:
        but he persecuted the humble the poor and the⏝
        crushed in spirit
        and ˈ sought to ˈ put them · to ˈ death.

16   He loved to curse * let curses ˈ fall on ˈ him:
        he took no pleasure in blessing
        so let ˈ it be ˈ far from ˈ him.

17   He clothed himself in cursing ˈ like a ˈ garment:
        so let it seep like water into his body
        and like ˈ oil ˈ into · his ˈ bones.

18   Let it be as the clothes he ˈ wraps aˈbout him:
        or like the ˈ girdle · that he ˈ wears each ˈ day.

[†] 19   This is the Lord's recompense to ˈ those ·
      that opˈpose him:
        to ˈ those that · speak ˈ evil · aˈgainst me.]

20   Act for me O Lord my God for your ˈ name's ˈ sake:
        and deliver me   as your ˈ steadfast ˈ love is ˈ good.

21   For I am ˈ poor and ˈ needy:
        and my ˈ heart ˈ writhes withˈin me.

22   I fade like a ˈ lengthen·ing ˈ shadow:
        I am ˈ shaken ˈoff · like a ˈ locust.

23   My knees are ˈ weak from ˈ fasting:
        my ˈ flesh grows ˈ lean and ˈ shrunken.

†24   I have become the ˈ scorn of · my ˈ enemies:
        and when they see me they ˈ toss their ˈ
        heads · in deˈrision.

25   Help me O ˈ Lord my ˈ God:
        and save me ˈ for your ˈ mercy's ˈ sake,

26   that men may know it was | your | hand:
          that | you O | Lord have | done it.

27   Though they curse yet | give me · your | blessing:
          and those that come against me will be put to shame
          and your | servant | shall re|joice.

28   Let those that oppose me be | covered · with dis|grace:
          let them | wear their | shame · as a | garment.

29   And I will give the Lord great | thanks ·
      with my | mouth:
          and | praise him · in the | midst · of a | multitude.

30   For the Lord will stand at the right | hand ·
      of the | poor:
          to save him from | those that | would con|demn him.

PSALM 110

1   The Lord | said to | my lord:
          'Sit at my right hand
          until I | make your | enemies · your | footstool.'

2   The Lord commits to you the sceptre | of your | power:
          reign from | Zion · in the | midst of · your | enemies.

3   Noble are you * from the day of your birth⌣
      upon the | holy | hill:
          radiant are you even from the womb
          in the | morning | dew of · your | youth.

4   The Lord has sworn and will | not turn | back:
          'You are a priest for ever * after the | order |
          of Mel|chizedek.'

5   The king shall stand at your right | hand O | Lord:
          and shatter | kings · in the | day of · his | wrath.

6   Glorious in majesty * he shall judge a|mong
      the | nations:
          and shatter heads | over · a | wide | land.

†7   He shall slake his thirst from the brook⌣
      be|side the | way:
          therefore shall | he lift | up his | head.

PSALM 111

1 O praise the Lord.
  I will praise the Lord with my | whole | heart:
      in the company of the upright
      and a | mong the | congre | gation.

2 The works of the | Lord are | great:
      and studied by | all who | take de | light in them.

3 His deeds are ma | jestic · and | glorious:
      and his | righteous · ness | stands for | ever.

4 His marvellous acts have won him a name⏝
  to | be re | membered:
      the | Lord is | gracious · and | merciful.

5 He gives food to | those that | fear him:
      he re | members · his | covenant · for | ever.

6 He showed his people the | power · of his | acts:
      in giving them the | heri · tage | of the | heathen.

7 The works of his hands are | faithful · and | just:
      and | all · his com | mandments · are | sure;

8 they stand firm for | ever · and | ever:
      they are done in | faithful · ness | and in | truth.

9 He sent redemption to his people
  he ordained his | covenant · for | ever:
      holy is his name and | worthy | to be | feared.

10 The fear of the Lord is the beginning of wisdom
   and of good understanding are those⏝
   that | keep · his com | mandments:
       his | praise · shall en | dure for | ever.

PSALM 112

1 O praise the Lord.
  Blessèd is the man who | fears the | Lord:
      and greatly de | lights in | his com | mandments.

2 His children shall be | mighty · in the | land:
      a race of upright | men who | will be | blessed.

3   Riches and plenty shall be ˈ in his ˈ house:
     and his ˈ righteous·ness ˈ stands for ˈ ever.

4   Light arises in darkness ˈ for the ˈ upright:
     gracious and merciful ˈ is the ˈ righteous ˈ man.

5   It goes well with the man who acts ˈ generously ·
     and ˈ lends:
     who ˈ guides · his afˈfairs with ˈ justice.

6   Surely he shall ˈ never · be ˈ moved:
     the righteous shall be held in ˈ everˈlasting ·
     reˈmembrance.

7   He will not ˈ fear bad ˈ tidings:
     his heart is steadfast   ˈ trusting ˈ in the ˈ Lord.

8   His heart is confident and ˈ will not ˈ fear:
     he will see the ˈ downfall ˈ of his ˈ enemies.

9   He gives ˈ freely · to the ˈ poor:
     his righteousness stands for ever
     his ˈ head is · upˈlifted · in ˈ glory.

10   The wicked man shall see it ˈ and be ˈ angry:
     he shall gnash his teeth and consume away
     and the ˈ hope · of the ˈ wicked · shall ˈ fail.

PSALM 113

1   Praise the Lord.
     O sing praises you that ˈ are his ˈ servants:
     O ˈ praise the ˈ name · of the ˈ Lord.

2   Let the name of the ˈ Lord be ˈ blessed:
     from this time ˈ forward ˈ and for ˈ ever.

3   From the rising of the sun to its ˈ going ˈ down:
     let the ˈ name · of the ˈ Lord be ˈ praised.

4   The Lord is exalted over ˈ all the ˈ nations:
     and his ˈ glory · is aˈbove the ˈ heavens.

5   Who can be likened to the ˈ Lord our ˈ God:
     in ˈ heaven · or upˈon the ˈ earth,

6   who has his | dwelling · so | high:
     yet condescends to | look on | things be | neath?

7   He raises the | lowly · from the | dust:
     and lifts the | poor from | out of · the | dungheap;

8   he gives them a place a | mong the | princes:
     even among the | princes | of his | people.

†9   He causes the barren woman to | keep | house:
     and makes her a joyful mother of children |
     Praise | – the | Lord.

PSALM 114

1   When Israel came | out of | Egypt:
     and the house of Jacob from among a | people ·
     of an | alien | tongue,

2   Judah be | came his | sanctuary:
     and | Israel | his do | minion.

3   The sea saw | that and | fled:
     Jor | dan was | driven | back.

4   The mountains | skipped like | rams:
     and the little | hills like | young | sheep.

5   What ailed you O | sea · that you | fled:
     O Jordan that | you were | driven | back?

6   You mountains that you | skipped like | rams:
     and you little | hills like | young | sheep?

7   Tremble O earth at the | presence · of the | Lord:
     at the | presence · of the | God of | Jacob,

8   who turned the rock into a | pool of | water:
     and the flint-stone | into · a | welling | spring.

PSALM 115

1   Not to us O Lord not to us
     but to your name | give the | glory:
     for the sake of your faithfulness | and your |
     loving | kindness.

2 Why should the heathen say | 'Where is · their | God?'
   our God is in heaven   he | does what|ever · he | wills.

3 As for their idols   they are | silver · and | gold:
   the | work · of a | man's | hand.

4 They have | mouths but | speak not:
   they have | eyes · but they | cannot | see.

5 They have ears yet | hear | nothing:
   they have | noses · but | cannot | smell.

6 Hands they have but handle nothing
   feet but they | do not | walk:
   they | make no | sound · with their | throats.

†7 Those who make them | shall be | like them:
   so shall | everyone · that | trusts in | them.

8 O Israel | trust · in the | Lord:
   he is your | help | and your | shield.

9 O house of Aaron | trust · in the | Lord:
   he is your | help | and your | shield.

10 You that fear the Lord | trust · in the | Lord:
   he is your | help | and your | shield.

11 The Lord has remembered us and | he will | bless us:
   he will bless the house of Israel
   he will | bless the | house of | Aaron.

12 He will bless all those that | fear the | Lord:
   both | high and | low to|gether.

13 May the Lord in|crease you | greatly:
   you | and your | children | after you.

14 The blessing of the | Lord · be up|on you:
   he that | made | heaven · and | earth.

15 As for the heavens | they · are the | Lord's:
   but the earth he has | given · to the |
   children · of | men.

16 The dead do not | praise the | Lord:
   nor do | any · that go | down to | silence.

17   But we will ǀ bless the ǀ Lord:
       both now and for evermore
       O ǀ praise ǀ – the ǀ Lord.

PSALM 116

1   I love the Lord because he ǀ heard my ǀ voice:
      the ǀ voice of · my ǀ suppliǀcation;

2   because he inǀclined his ǀ ear to me:
      in the ǀ day ǀ that I ǀ called to him.

3   The cords of death encompassed me
      the snares of the ǀ grave took ǀ hold on me:
      I ǀ was in ǀ anguish · and ǀ sorrow.

4   Then I called upon the ǀ name · of the ǀ Lord:
      'O ǀ Lord · I beǀseech you · deǀliver me!'

5   Gracious and righteous ǀ is the ǀ Lord:
      full of comǀpassion ǀ is our ǀ God.

6   The Lord preǀserves the ǀ simple:
      when ǀ I was · brought ǀ low he ǀ saved me.

7   Return O my ǀ soul · to your ǀ rest:
      for the ǀ Lord ǀ has reǀwarded you.

8   For you O Lord have delivered my ǀ soul from ǀ death:
      my eyes from ǀ tears · and my ǀ feet from ǀ falling.

†9 I will walk beǀfore the ǀ Lord:
      in the ǀ land ǀ of the ǀ living.

10 I believed that I would perish   I was ǀ brought ·
      very ǀ low:
      I said in my haste ǀ 'All ǀ men are ǀ liars.'

11 How shall I reǀpay the ǀ Lord:
      for ǀ all his ǀ bene·fits ǀ to me?

12 I will take up the ǀ cup of · salǀvation:
      and ǀ call up·on the ǀ name · of the ǀ Lord.

13 I will pay my ǀ vows · to the ǀ Lord:
      in the ǀ presence · of ǀ all his ǀ people.

14 Grievous in the **|** sight · of the **|** Lord:
   is the **|** death **|** of his **|** faithful ones.

15 O Lord I am your servant
   your servant and the **|** son of · your **|** handmaid:
   you **|** have un **|** loosed my **|** bonds.

16 I will offer you a sacrifice of **|** thanks **|** giving:
   and **|** call up·on the **|** name · of the **|** Lord.

17 I will pay my **|** vows · to the **|** Lord:
   in the **|** presence · of **|** all his **|** people,

† 18 in the courts of the **|** house · of the **|** Lord:
   even in your midst O Jerusalem **|**
   Praise **|** – the **|** Lord.

PSALM 117

1 O praise the Lord **|** all you **|** nations:
   O **|** praise him **|** all you **|** peoples.

2 For great is his loving **|** kindness · to **|** ward us:
   and the faithfulness of the Lord endures for ever **|**
   Praise **|** – the **|** Lord.

PSALM 118

1 O give thanks to the Lord for **|** he is **|** good:
   his **|** mercy · en **|** dures for **|** ever.

2 Let Israel **|** now pro **|** claim:
   that his **|** mercy · en **|** dures for **|** ever.

3 Let the house of **|** Aaron · pro **|** claim:
   that his **|** mercy · en **|** dures for **|** ever.

4 Let those who fear the **|** Lord pro **|** claim:
   that his **|** mercy · en **|** dures for **|** ever.

5 In my danger I **|** called · to the **|** Lord:
   he **|** answered · and **|** set me **|** free.

6 The Lord is on my side   I **|** shall not **|** fear:
   what can **|** man **|** do to **|** me?

7   The Lord is at my side | as my | helper:
        I shall see the | downfall | of my | enemies.

8   It is better to take refuge | in the | Lord:
        than to | put your | trust in | man;

†9   it is better to take refuge | in the | Lord:
        than to | put your | trust in | princes.

10   All the | nations · sur|rounded me:
        but in the name of the | Lord I | drove them | back.

11   They surrounded   they surrounded me on |
    every | side:
        but in the name of the | Lord I | drove them | back.

12   They swarmed about me like bees
    they blazed like fire a|mong the | thorns:
        in the name of the | Lord I | drove them | back.

13   I was pressed so hard that I | almost | fell:
        but the | Lord | was my | helper.

†14 The Lord is my | strength · and my | song:
        and has be|come | my sal|vation.

15   The sounds of | joy · and de|liverance:
        are | in the | tents · of the | righteous.

16   The right hand of the Lord does | mighty | things:
        the right hand of the | Lord | raises | up.

17   I shall not | die but | live:
        and pro|claim the | works · of the | Lord.

18   The Lord has | disciplined · me | hard:
        but he has not | given · me | over · to | death.

19   Open me the | gates of | righteousness:
        and I will enter and give | thanks | to the | Lord.

20   This is the | gate · of the | Lord:
        the | righteous | shall | enter it.

21   I will praise you | for you | answered me:
        and have be|come | my sal|vation.

22   The stone that the | builders · re |jected:
      has be |come the | head · of the | corner.

23   This is the | Lord's | doing:
      and it is | marvel·lous | in our | eyes.

24   This is the day that the | Lord has | made:
      let us re |joice | and be | glad in it.

25   O Lord | save us · we | pray:
      O Lord | send | us pros |perity.

26   Blessèd is he who comes in the | name · of the | Lord:
      from the | house · of the | Lord we | bless you.

27   The Lord is God   and he has | given · us | light:
      guide the festal throng up to the | horns |
      of the | altar.

28   You are my God and | I will | praise you:
      you are my | God I | will ex |alt you.

†29   O give thanks to the Lord for | he is | good:
      and his | mercy · en |dures for | ever.

PSALM 119 (1)

1   Blessèd are those whose | way is | blameless:
     who | walk · in the | law · of the | Lord.

2   Blessèd are those who | keep · his com |mands:
     and seek him | with their | whole | heart;

3   those who | do no | wrong:
     but | walk · in the | ways of · our | God.

4   For you Lord | have com |manded us:
     to perse |vere in | all your | precepts.

5   If only my | ways · were un |erring:
     towards the | keeping | of your | statutes!

6   Then I should | not · be a |shamed:
     when I | looked on | all · your com |mandments.

7   I will praise you with sin |cerity · of | heart:
     as I | learn your | righteous | judgements.

8   I will ' keep your ' statutes:
       O for'sake me ' not ' utterly.

PSALM 119 *(2)*

9   How shall a young man's ' path be ' pure:
       un 'less he ' keep to · your ' word?

10   I have sought you with my ' whole ' heart:
       let me not ' stray from ' your com'mandments.

11   I have treasured your ' words · in my ' heart:
       that I ' might not ' sin a'gainst you.

12   Blessèd are ' you Lord ' God:
       O ' teach me ' your ' statutes.

13   With my lips I ' have been ' telling:
       all the ' judgements ' of your ' mouth;

14   and I find more joy in the way of ' your com'mands:
       than in ' all ' manner · of ' riches.

15   I will meditate ' on your ' precepts:
       and give ' heed ' to your ' ways;

16   for my delight is wholly ' in your ' statutes:
       and I will ' not for'get your ' word.

PSALM 119 *(3)*

17   O be bountiful to your servant that ' I may ' live:
       in o'bedi·ence ' to your ' word.

18   Take away the ' veil · from my ' eyes:
       that I may see the ' wonders ' of your ' law.

19   I am but a ' stranger · on the ' earth:
       do not ' hide · your com'mandments ' from me.

20   My soul is con'sumed with ' longing:
       for your ' judgements ' day and ' night.

21   You have re'buked the ' proud:
       and cursed are those who ' stray from '
       your com'mandments;

22   turn away from me their re|proach and | scorn:
      for | I have | kept · your com|mands.

23   Though princes sit and plot to|gether · a|gainst me:
      your servant shall | medi·tate | on your | statutes;

24   for your commands are | my de|light:
      and they are | counsellors · in | my de|fence.

PSALM 119 (4)

25   I am humbled | to the | dust:
      O give me life ac|cording | to your | word.

26   If I ex|amine · my | ways:
      surely you will answer me * O | teach me |
      your | statutes!

27   Make me to understand the | way of · your | precepts:
      and I shall meditate | on your ⌈ marvel·lous | works.

28   My soul pines a|way for | sorrow:
      O raise me up ac|cording | to your | word.

29   Keep me far from the | way of · de|ception:
      and | grant me · the | grace of · your | law.

30   I have chosen the | way of | truth:
      and have | set your ⌈ judgements · be|fore me.

31   I hold fast to | your com|mands:
      O Lord let me | never | be con|founded.

32   Let me run the way of | your com|mandments:
      for | you will | liberate · my | heart.

PSALM 119 (5)

33   Teach me O Lord the | way of · your | statutes:
      and I will | honour · it | to the | end.

34   Give me understanding   that I may | keep your | law:
      that I may keep it | with my | whole | heart.

35   Guide me in the path of | your com|mandments:
      for there |in is ⌈ my de|light.

36   Incline my heart to ⏐ your com⏐mands:
       and ⏐ not to ⏐ selfish ⏐ gain.

37   Turn away my eyes from ⏐ looking · on ⏐ vanities:
       as I walk in your ⏐ way ⏐ give me ⏐ life.

38   Make good your promise ⏐ to your ⏐ servant:
       the promise that en⏐dures for ⏐ all who ⏐ fear you.

39   Turn aside the ⏐ taunts · that I ⏐ dread:
       for your ⏐ judgements · are ⏐ very ⏐ good.

40   Lord I ⏐ long for · your ⏐ precepts:
       in your ⏐ righteous·ness ⏐ give me ⏐ life.

PSALM 119 *(6)*

41   Let your loving mercy come to ⏐ me O ⏐ Lord:
       and your salvation ac⏐cording ⏐ to your ⏐ word.

42   Then I shall have an answer for ⏐ those ·
who re⏐proach me:
       for I ⏐ trust ⏐ in your ⏐ word.

43   Do not take the word of truth utterly ⏐
out of · my ⏐ mouth:
       for in your ⏐ judgements ⏐ is my ⏐ hope.

44   Let me keep your ⏐ law con⏐tinually:
       O ⏐ let me ⏐ keep it · for ⏐ ever.

45   And so I shall ⏐ walk at ⏐ liberty:
       be⏐cause · I have ⏐ sought your ⏐ precepts.

46   I shall speak of your com⏐mands be·fore ⏐ kings:
       and shall ⏐ not be ⏐ put to ⏐ shame.

47   My delight shall be in ⏐ your com⏐mandments:
       which ⏐ I have ⏐ greatly ⏐ loved;

48   I shall worship you with ⏐ outstretched ⏐ hands:
       and I shall ⏐ medi·tate ⏐ on your ⏐ statutes.

PSALM 119 *(7)*

49   Remember your ⏐ word · to your ⏐ servant:
       on ⏐ which · you have ⏐ built my ⏐ hope.

50 This has been my comfort in ǀ my afǀfliction:
      for your ǀ word has ǀ brought me ǀ life.

51 Though the proud have ǀ laughed me · to ǀ scorn:
      I have not ǀ turned aǀside from · your ǀ law;

52 but I called to mind O Lord your ǀ judgements ·
      of ǀ old:
      and in ǀ them · I have ǀ found · consolǀation.

53 I am seized with indignation ǀ at the ǀ wicked:
      for ǀ they have · forǀsaken · your ǀ law.

54 But your statutes have beǀcome my ǀ songs:
      in the ǀ house ǀ of my ǀ pilgrimage.

55 I think on your name O ǀ Lord · in the ǀ night:
      and ǀ I obǀserve your ǀ law;

56 this has ǀ been · my reǀward:
      beǀcause · I have ǀ kept your ǀ precepts.

PSALM 119 *(8)*

57 The Lord ǀ is my ǀ portion:
      I have ǀ promised · to ǀ keep your ǀ words.

58 I have sought your favour with my ǀ whole ǀ heart:
      O be gracious to me acǀcording ǀ to your ǀ word.

59 I have taken ǀ stock of · my ǀ ways:
      and have turned back my ǀ feet to ǀ your comǀmands.

60 I made haste and did ǀ not deǀlay:
      to ǀ keep ǀ your comǀmandments.

61 The snares of the ǀ wicked · enǀcompassed me:
      but I did ǀ not forǀget your ǀ law;

62 at midnight I rise to ǀ give you ǀ thanks:
      for the ǀ righteous·ness ǀ of your ǀ judgements.

63 I am a friend to ǀ all who ǀ fear you:
      to ǀ those who ǀ keep your ǀ precepts.

64 The earth O Lord is full of your ǀ loving ǀ mercy:
      O ǀ teach me ǀ your ǀ statutes.

PSALM 119 *(9)*

65   Lord you have done ⎮ good to · your ⎮ servant:
      in ac⎮cordance ⎮ with your ⎮ word.

66   O teach me right ⎮ judgement · and ⎮ knowledge:
      for I ⎮ trust in ⎮ your com⎮mandments.

67   Before I was afflicted I ⎮ went a ⎮stray:
      but ⎮ now I ⎮ keep your ⎮ word.

68   You are good and you ⎮ do ⎮ good:
      O ⎮ teach me ⎮ your ⎮ statutes.

69   The proud have ⎮ smeared me · with ⎮ lies:
      but I will keep your precepts ⎮ with my ⎮
      whole ⎮ heart.

70   Their hearts are ⎮ gross like ⎮ fat:
      but my de⎮light is ⎮ in your ⎮ law.

71   It is good for me that ⎮ I was · af⎮flicted:
      so ⎮ I might ⎮ learn your ⎮ statutes.

72   The law of your mouth is ⎮ dearer · to ⎮ me:
      than a ⎮ wealth of ⎮ gold and ⎮ silver.

PSALM 119 *(10)*

73   Your hands have ⎮ made me · and ⎮ fashioned me:
      O give me understanding‿
      that ⎮ I may ⎮ learn · your com⎮mandments.

74   Those who fear you shall see me ⎮ and re⎮joice:
      for my ⎮ hope is ⎮ in your ⎮ word.

75   I know Lord that your ⎮ judgements · are ⎮ right:
      and that in ⎮ faithfulness · you ⎮ have af⎮flicted me.

76   Let your merciful kindness ⎮ be my ⎮ comfort:
      according to your ⎮ promise ⎮ to your ⎮ servant.

77   O let your mercy come to me that ⎮ I may ⎮ live:
      for your ⎮ law is ⎮ my de⎮light.

78   Let the proud be shamed
who steal my | rights · through their | lies:
     but I will | medi·tate | on your | precepts.

79   Let those who fear you | turn to | me:
     and | they shall | know · your com | mands.

80   O let my heart be | sound in · | your statutes:
     that I may | never · be | put to | shame.

PSALM 119 (11)

81   My soul languishes for | your sal | vation:
     but my | hope is | in your | word;

82   my eyes fail with | watching · for your | promise:
     saying 'O | when | will you | comfort me?'

83   I am parched as a wineskin | in the | smoke:
     yet I do | not for | get your | statutes.

84   How many are the | days of · your | servant:
     and | when · will you | judge my | persecutors?

85   The proud have dug | pitfalls | for me:
     in de | fiance | of your | law.

86   All your com | mandments · are | true:
     but they persecute me with lies * O | come |
     to my | help!

87   They have almost made an end of me | on the | earth:
     but I have | not for | saken · your | precepts.

88   In your merciful goodness | give me | life:
     that I may keep the com | mands | of your | mouth.

PSALM 119 (12)

89   Lord your | word · is for | ever:
     it stands | firm | in the | heavens.

90   Your faithfulness abides from one gener | ation ·
to an | other:
     firm as the | earth which | you have | made.

91 As for your judgements   they stand | fast this | day:
    for | all things | are your | servants.

92 If your law had not been | my de|light:
    I would have | perished · in | my af|fliction.

93 I will never for|get your | precepts:
    for by | them · you have | given · me | life.

94 I am | yours O | save me:
    for | I have | sought your | precepts.

95 The wicked have lain in wait for me | to de|stroy me:
    but I | think on | your com|mands.

96 I have seen that all perfection | comes · to an | end:
    only your com|mandment | has no | bounds.

PSALM 119 *(13)*

97 Lord how I | love your | law:
    it is my medi|tation | all the · day | long.

98 Your commandments have made me wiser |
  than my | enemies:
    for they re|main with | me for | ever.

99 I have more understanding than | all my | teachers:
    for I | study | your com|mands.

100 I am wiser | than the | agèd:
    be|cause · I have | kept your | precepts.

101 I have held back my feet from every | evil | path:
    that | I might | keep your | word;

102 I have not turned a|side from · your | judgements:
    for | you your|self are · my | teacher.

103 How sweet are your | words · to my | tongue:
    sweeter than | honey | to my | mouth.

104 Through your precepts I get | under|standing:
    therefore I | hate all | lying | ways.

PSALM 119 (14)

105 Your word is a lantern | to my | feet:
    and a | light | to my | path.

106 I have vowed and | sworn an | oath:
    to | keep your | righteous | judgements.

107 I have been afflicted be|yond | measure:
    Lord give me life ac|cording | to your | word.

108 Accept O Lord the freewill offerings | of my | mouth:
    and | teach me | your | judgements.

109 I take my life in my | hands con|tinually:
    yet I do | not for|get your | law.

110 The wicked have | laid a | snare for me:
    but I | have not | strayed from · your | precepts.

111 Your commands are my in|heritance · for | ever:
    they | are the | joy of · my | heart.

112 I have set my heart to ful|fil your | statutes:
    always | even | to the | end.

PSALM 119 (15)

113 I loathe those who are | double|minded:
    but your | law | do I | love.

114 You are my shelter | and my | shield:
    and in your | word | is my | hope.

115 Away from me all | you that · do | evil:
    I will keep the com|mandments | of my | God.

116 Be my stay according to your word that | I may | live:
    and do not disap|point me | in my | hope.

117 Hold me up and I | shall be | safe:
    and I will ever de|light | in your | statutes.

118 You scorn all those who | swerve from · your | statutes:
    for their | calumnies · a|gainst me · are | lies;

119 all the ungodly of the earth you | count as | dross:
    therefore I | love | your com|mands.

120　My flesh ∣ shrinks for ∣ fear of you:
　　　and I am a ∣fraid ∣ of your ∣ judgements.

PSALM 119 *(16)*

121　I have done what is ∣ just and ∣ right:
　　　O do not give me ∣ over · to ∣ my op∣pressors.

122　Stand surety for your ∣ servant's ∣ good:
　　　let ∣ not the ∣ proud op∣press me.

123　My eyes fall with watching for ∣ your sal∣vation:
　　　for the fulfilment ∣ of your ∣ righteous ∣ word.

124　O deal with your servant according to your ∣
　　　loving ∣ mercy:
　　　and ∣ teach me ∣ your ∣ statutes.

125　I am your servant　O give me ∣ under∣standing:
　　　that ∣ I may ∣ know · your com∣mands.

126　It is time for the ∣ Lord to ∣ act:
　　　for they ∣ vio·late ∣ your ∣ law.

127　Therefore I ∣ love · your com∣mandments:
　　　more than gold　∣ more · than the ∣ finest ∣ gold;

128　therefore I straighten my paths by ∣
　　　all your ∣ precepts:
　　　and I ∣ hate all ∣ lying ∣ ways.

PSALM 119 *(17)*

129　Wonderful are ∣ your com∣mands:
　　　and ∣ therefore · my ∣ soul ∣ keeps them.

130　The unfolding of your ∣ words gives ∣ light:
　　　it gives under∣standing ∣ to the ∣ simple.

131　I open my mouth and draw ∣ in my ∣ breath:
　　　for I ∣ yearn for ∣ your com∣mandments.

132　O turn to me and be ∣ merci·ful ∣ to me:
　　　as is your way with ∣ those who ∣ love your ∣ name.

133　Order my steps according ∣ to your ∣ word:
　　　that no evil ∣ may get ∣ master·y ∣ over me.

134 Deliver me from ' man's op'pression:
that ' I may ' keep your ' precepts.

135 Make your face shine up'on your ' servant:
and ' teach me ' your ' statutes.

136 My eyes gush out with ' streams of ' water:
because they ' pay no ' heed to · your ' law.

PSALM 119 *(18)*

137 Righteous are ' you Lord ' God:
and ' just are ' your ' judgements;

138 the commands that ' you · have com'manded:
are ex'ceeding·ly ' righteous · and ' true.

139 Zeal and indignation have ' choked my ' mouth:
because my enemies ' have for'gotten · your ' words.

140 Your word has been ' tried · in the ' fire:
and ' therefore · your ' servant ' loves it.

141 I am small and of ' no ac'count:
but I have ' not for'gotten · your ' precepts.

142 Your righteousness is an ever'lasting ' righteousness:
and your ' law ' is the ' truth.

143 Trouble and anguish have ' taken ' hold on me:
but your com'mandments · are ' my de'light.

144 The righteousness of your commands is ' ever'lasting:
O give me under'standing · and ' I shall ' live.

PSALM 119 *(19)*

145 I call with my ' whole ' heart:
hear me O Lord ' I will ' keep your ' statutes.

146 I cry out to ' you O ' save me:
and ' I will ' heed · your com'mands.

147 Before the morning light I ' rise · and I ' call:
for in your ' word ' is my ' hope.

148 Before the night watch my | eyes | wake:
   that I may | meditate · up | on your | words.

149 Hear my voice O Lord in your | loving | mercy:
   and according to your | judgements | give me | life.

150 They draw near to me who mal | icious·ly | persecute me:
   but | they are | far from · your | law.

151 You Lord are | close at | hand:
   and | all · your com | mandments · are | true.

152 I have known long since from | your com | mands:
   that you have | founded | them for | ever.

PSALM 119 *(20)*

153 Consider my affliction | and de | liver me:
   for I do | not for | get your | law.

154 Plead my cause and | set me | free:
   O give me life ac | cording | to your | word.

155 Salvation is | far · from the | wicked:
   for they | do not | seek your | statutes.

156 Numberless O Lord are your | tender | mercies:
   according to your | judgements | give me | life.

157 Many there are that persecute | me and | trouble me:
   but I have not | swerved from | your com | mands.

158 I am cut to the heart when I | see the | faithless:
   for they | do not | keep your | word.

159 Consider O Lord how I | love your | precepts:
   and in your | mercy | give me | life.

160 The sum of your | word is | truth:
   and all your righteous | judgements | stand for | ever.

PSALM 119 *(21)*

161 Princes have persecuted me with | out a | cause:
   but my heart | stands in | awe of · your | word.

162   I am as ' glad of · your ' word:
         as ' one who ' finds rich ' spoil.

163   Lies I ' hate · and ab'hor:
         but your ' law ' do I ' love.

164   Seven times a ' day I ' praise you:
         be'cause of · your ' righteous ' judgements.

165   Great is the peace of those who ' love your ' law:
         and ' nothing · shall ' make them ' stumble.

166   Lord I have waited for ' your sal'vation:
         and I have ' done ' your com'mandments.

167   My soul has heeded ' your com'mands:
         and I ' love them · be'yond ' measure.

168   I have kept your precepts ' and com'mands:
         for all my ' ways are ' open · be'fore you.

PSALM 119 (22)

169   Let my cry ' come to you · O ' Lord:
         O give me understanding ac'cording '
         to your ' word;

170   let my supplication ' come be'fore you:
         and deliver me ac'cording ' to your ' promise.

171   My lips shall pour ' forth your ' praise:
         be'cause you ' teach me · your ' statutes;

172   my tongue shall ' sing of · your ' word:
         for ' all · your com'mandments · are ' righteousness.

173   Let your hand be ' swift to ' help me:
         for ' I have ' chosen · your ' precepts.

174   Lord I have longed for ' your sal'vation:
         and your ' law is ' my de'light.

175   O let my soul live that ' I may ' praise you:
         and let your ' judgements ' be my ' help.

176   I have gone astray like a ' sheep · that is ' lost:
         O seek your servant
         for I do ' not for'get · your com'mandments.

PSALM 120

1   I call to the | Lord · in my | trouble:
    that | he may | answer | me.

2   O Lord deliver me from | lying | lips:
    and | from the | treacher·ous | tongue.

3   What will he do to you
    and what more will he do to you⌣
    O | treacher·ous | tongue?
    you are sharp as the arrows of a warrior
    that are | tempered · in | coals of | juniper.

4   Alas for me * I am like a | stranger · in | Meshech:
    like one who dwells a|midst the | tents of | Kedar.

5   My soul has | been too | long:
    among | those · who are | enemies · to | peace.

6   I am for peace   but | when I | speak of it:
    they | make them·selves | ready · for | war.

PSALM 121

1   I lift up my | eyes · to the | hills:
    but | where · shall I | find | help?

2   My help | comes · from the | Lord:
    who has | made | heaven · and | earth.

3   He will not suffer your | foot to | stumble:
    and he who watches | over · you | will not | sleep.

4   Be sure he who has | charge of | Israel:
    will | neither | slumber · nor | sleep.

5   The Lord him|self is · your | keeper:
    the Lord is your defence up|on your | right | hand;

6   the sun shall not | strike you · by | day:
    nor | shall the | moon by | night.

7   The Lord will defend you from | all | evil:
    it is | he · who will | guard your | life.

8   The Lord will defend your going out and your I
coming I in:
     from this time I forward · for I everImore.

PSALM 122

1   I was glad when they I said to I me:
     'Let us I go · to the I house · of the I Lord.'

2   And now our I feet are I standing:
     withIin your I gates · O JeIrusalem;

†3   Jerusalem which is I built · as a I city:
     where the I pilgrims I gather · in I unity.

4   There the tribes go up   the I tribes · of the I Lord:
     as he commanded Israel
     to give I thanks · to the I name · of the I Lord.

5   There are set I thrones of I judgement:
     the I thrones · of the I house of I David.

6   O pray for the I peace · of JeIrusalem:
     may I those who I love you I prosper.

7   Peace be withIin your I walls:
     and prosIperi·ty I in your I palaces.

8   For the sake of my brothers I and comIpanions:
     I will I pray that I peace be I with you.

9   For the sake of the house of the I Lord our I God:
     I will I seek I for your I good.

PSALM 123

1   To you I lift I up my I eyes:
     you who are enIthroned I in the I heavens.

2   As the eyes of servants look to the I hand of ·
their I master:
     or as the eyes of a maid toIward the I hand of ·
her I mistress,

†3   so our eyes look to the I Lord our I God:
     unItil he I show us · his I mercy.

4 Have mercy upon us O Lord have | mercy · up | on us:
   for we have | had our | fill · of de | rision.

5 Our souls overflow with the mockery of | those at | ease:
   and with the | contempt | of the | proud.

PSALM 124

1 If the Lord had not been on our side
   now may | Israel | say:
     if the Lord had not been on our side⌣
     when | men rose | up a | gainst us,

2 then they would have | swallowed us · a | live:
   when their | anger · was | kindled · a | gainst us.

3 Then the waters would have overwhelmed us
   and the | torrent · gone | over us:
     the raging waters | would have | gone clean | over us.

4 But praised | be the | Lord:
   who has not given us as a | prey | to their | teeth.

5 We have escaped like a bird from the | snare ·
   of the | fowler:
     the snare is | broken · and | we have · gone | free.

6 Our help is in the | name · of the | Lord:
   who has | made | heaven · and | earth.

PSALM 125

1 Those who put their trust in the Lord⌣
   shall | be as · Mount | Zion:
     which cannot be | shaken · but en | dures for | ever.

2 As the mountains stand about Jerusalem
   so stands the Lord a | bout his | people:
     from this time | forward · for | ever | more.

3 For the sceptre of wickedness shall have no sway
   over the land apportioned | to the | righteous:
     lest the righteous | set their | hands to · do | evil.

4 Do good O Lord to | those · who are | good:
   to | those · that are | upright · in | heart.

† 5 As for those who turn aside to crooked ways
    let the Lord lead them away with the | evil | doers:
        and in | Israel | let there · be | peace.

PSALM 126

1   When the Lord turned again the | fortunes · of | Zion:
        then were we like | men re | stored to | life.

2   Then was our mouth | filled with | laughter:
        and | our | tongue with | singing.

3   Then said they a | mong the | heathen:
        'The Lord has | done great | things for | them.'

4   Truly the Lord has done great | things for | us:
        and | therefore | we re | joiced.

5   Turn again our | fortunes · O | Lord:
        as the streams re | turn · to the | dry | south.

6   Those that | sow in | tears:
        shall | reap with | songs of | joy.

† 7 He who goes out weeping | bearing · the | seed:
    shall come again in gladness |⌣
        bringing · his | sheaves | with him.

PSALM 127

1   Unless the Lord | builds the | house:
        their labour | is but | lost that | build it.

2   Unless the Lord | keeps the | city:
        the | watchmen | watch in | vain.

3   It is in vain that you rise up early and go so late to rest
    eating the | bread of | toil:
        for the Lord bestows honour | and on | those ·
        whom he | loves.

4   Behold   children are a heritage | from the | Lord:
        and the | fruit · of the | womb is · his | gift.

5   Like arrows in the | hand · of a | warrior:
        are the | sons · of a | man's | youth.

6   Happy the man who has his | quiver | full of them:
       he will not be put to shame
       when he confronts his | enem·ies | at the | gate.

PSALM 128

1   Blessèd is everyone who | fears the | Lord:
       and walks in the | confine | of his | ways.

2   You will eat the | fruit of · your | labours:
       happy shall you | be and | all · shall go | well with you.

3   Your wife with | in your | house:
       shall | be · as a | fruitful | vine;

4   your children a | round your | table:
       like the fresh | shoots | of the | olive.

5   Behold thus shall the | man be | blessed:
       who | lives · in the | fear · of the | Lord.

6   May the Lord so | bless you · from | Zion:
       that you see Jerusalem in prosperity | ‿
       all the | days of · your | life.

†7   May you see your | children's | children:
       and in | Israel | let there · be | peace.

PSALM 129

1   Many a time from my youth upward have they |
       fought a | gainst me:
       now | may | Israel | say,

2   Many a time from my youth upward have they |
       fought a | gainst me:
       but | they have | not pre | vailed.

3   They have scored my back as | with a | ploughshare:
       they have | opened | long | furrows.

4   But the | Lord is | righteous:
       and he has cut me | free · from the | thongs ·
       of the | wicked.

5   They shall be confounded and ' turned ' backward:
    all ' those who ' hate ' Zion.

6   They shall be as the grass that grows up 'on
    the ' housetops:
       which withers before it ' comes to ' any ' good,

7   with which no reaper may ' fill his ' hand:
       nor the ' binder · of ' sheaves his ' bosom.

8   And none who pass by shall say to them
    'The blessing of the ' Lord · be up 'on you:
       we ' bless you · in the ' name · of the ' Lord.'

PSALM 130

1   Out of the depths have I called to ' you O ' Lord:
       Lord ' hear ' my ' voice;

2   O let your ears con 'sider ' well:
       the ' voice · of my ' suppli 'cation.

3   If you Lord should note what ' we do ' wrong:
       who ' then O ' Lord could ' stand?

4   But there is for 'giveness · with ' you:
       so that ' you ' shall be ' feared.

5   I wait for the Lord * my ' soul ' waits for him:
       and ' in his ' word · is my ' hope.

6   My soul ' looks · for the ' Lord:
       more than watchmen for the morning
       more I say than ' watchmen ' for the ' morning.

7   O Israel trust in the Lord * for with the ' Lord · ⌣
    there is ' mercy:
       and with ' him is ' ample · re 'demption.

8   He will re 'deem ' Israel:
       from the ' multi·tude ' of his ' sins.

PSALM 131

1   O Lord my ' heart is · not ' proud:
       nor ' are my ' eyes ' haughty.

2   I do not busy myself in ' great ' matters:
       or in ' things too ' wonder·ful ' for me.

3   But I have calmed and quieted my soul
       like a weaned child upon its ' mother's ' breast:
       like a child on its mother's breast ' ⌣
       is my ' soul with 'in me.

4   O Israel ' trust · in the ' Lord:
       from this time ' forward ' and for ' ever.

PSALM 132

1   Lord remember David and ' all his ' trouble:
       how he swore an oath to the Lord
       and vowed to the ' Mighty ' One of ' Jacob;

2   'I will not enter the ' shelter · of my ' house:
       nor climb into the ' comfort ' of my ' bed;

3   'I will not give ' sleep to · my ' eyes:
       or ' slumber ' to my ' eyelids,

4   'till I find out a place for the ' ark · of the ' Lord:
       a dwelling for the ' Mighty ' One of ' Jacob.'

5   Lo we ' heard of it · at ' Ephrathah:
       we ' found it · in the ' fields of ' Ja-ar.

6   Let us go to the ' place of · his ' dwelling:
       let us fall upon our ' knees be 'fore his ' footstool.

7   Arise O Lord ' into · your ' resting-place:
       you ' and the ' ark of · your ' might.

8   Let your priests be ' clothed with ' righteousness:
       and let your ' faithful · ones ' shout for ' joy.

†9 For the sake of ' David · your ' servant:
       do not turn away the ' face of ' your an 'ointed.

10 The Lord has ' sworn to ' David:
       an ' oath · which he ' will not ' break;

11   'One who is the ‖ fruit of · your ‖ body:
      I will ‖ set up ‖ on your ‖ throne.

12   'If your children will keep my covenant
      and the com‖mands · which I ‖ teach them:
          their children also shall sit up ‖ on your ‖ throne
          for ‖ ever.'

13   For the Lord has chosen ‖ Zion · for him‖self:
      he has de‖sired it · for his ‖ habi‖tation.

14   'This shall be my ‖ resting-place · for ‖ ever:
      here will I dwell   for ‖ my de‖light · is in ‖ her.

15   'I will bless her pro‖visions · with a‖bundance:
      I will ‖ satisfy · her ‖ poor with ‖ bread.

16   'I will clothe her ‖ priests with · sal‖vation:
      and her ‖ faithful ones · shall ‖ shout for ‖ joy.

17   'There will I make a horn to sprout⁀
      for the ‖ family · of ‖ David:
          I have prepared a ‖ lamp for ‖ my an‖ointed.

† 18   'As for his enemies   I will ‖ cover them · with ‖ shame:
      but upon his ‖ head · shall his ‖ crown be ‖ bright.'

PSALM 133

1   Behold how good and how ‖ lovely · it ‖ is:
      when brothers ‖ live to‖gether · in ‖ unity.

2   It is fragrant as oil upon the head
      that runs down ‖ over · the ‖ beard:
          fragrant as oil upon the beard of Aaron
          that ran down over the ‖ collar ‖ of his ‖ robe.

3   It is like a ‖ dew of ‖ Hermon:
      like the dew that falls up‖on the ‖ hill of ‖ Zion.

4   For there the Lord has com‖manded · his ‖ blessing:
      which is ‖ life for ‖ ever‖more.

PSALM 134

1 Come bless the Lord   all you ˡ servants · of the ˡ Lord:
     you that by night ˡ stand · in the ˡ house of ·
     our ˡ God.

2 Lift up your hands toward the holy place⌣
     and ˡ bless the ˡ Lord:
     may the Lord bless you from Zion
     the ˡ Lord who · made ˡ heaven · and ˡ earth.

PSALM 135

1 Praise the Lord.
     Praise the ˡ name · of the ˡ Lord:
     praise him you ˡ servants ˡ of the ˡ Lord,

2 who stand in the ˡ house · of the ˡ Lord:
     in the ˡ courts · of the ˡ house of · our ˡ God.

3 Praise the Lord for the ˡ Lord is ˡ gracious:
     sing praises to his ˡ name for ˡ it is ˡ good.

4 For the Lord has chosen Jacob ˡ for himˡself:
     and Israel ˡ as his ˡ own posˡsession.

5 I know that the ˡ Lord is ˡ great:
     and that our ˡ Lord · is aˡbove all ˡ gods.

6 He does whatever he wills* in heaven and
     upˡon the ˡ earth:
     in the seas and ˡ in the ˡ great ˡ depths.

7 He brings up clouds from the ˡ ends · of the ˡ earth:
     he makes lightning for the rain
     and brings the ˡ wind ˡ out of · his ˡ storehouses.

8 He struck down the ˡ firstborn · of ˡ Egypt:
     both ˡ man and ˡ beast aˡlike.

9 He sent signs and wonders into your ˡ midst O ˡ Egypt:
     against Pharaoh and aˡgainst ˡ all his ˡ servants.

10 He struck down ˡ great ˡ nations:
     and ˡ slew ˡ mighty ˡ kings,

11 Sihon king of the Amorites   and Og the |
    king of | Bashan:
       and | all the | princes · of | Canaan.

12 He made over their | land · as a | heritage:
       a | heritage · for | Israel · his | people.

13 O Lord your name shall en|dure for | ever:
       so shall your renown through|out all | gener|ations.

14 For the Lord will | vindicate · his | people:
       he will take | pity | on his | servants.

15 As for the idols of the nations
    they are but | silver · and | gold:
       the | work · of a | man's | hand.

16 They have | mouths but | speak not:
       they have | eyes · but they | cannot | see.

17 They have ears yet | hear | nothing:
       there is no | breath | in their | nostrils.

18 Those who make them | shall be | like them:
       so shall | every|one that | trusts in them.

19 Bless the Lord O | house of | Israel:
       bless the | Lord O | house of | Aaron.

20 Bless the Lord O | house of | Levi:
       you that | fear the · Lord | bless the | Lord.

†21 Blessèd be the | Lord from | Zion:
       he that dwells in Jerusalem |
       Praise | – the | Lord.

PSALM 136

1 O give thanks to the Lord for | he is | good:
      for his | mercy · en|dures for | ever.

2 O give thanks to the | God of | gods:
      for his | mercy · en|dures for | ever.

†3 O give thanks to the | Lord of | lords:
      for his | mercy · en|dures for | ever;

4   to him who alone does [|] great [|] wonders:
       for his [|] mercy · en [|] dures for [|] ever;

5   who by wisdom [|] made the [|] heavens:
       for his [|] mercy · en [|] dures for [|] ever;

6   who stretched out the earth up [|] on the [|] waters:
       for his [|] mercy · en [|] dures for [|] ever;

7   who made the [|] great [|] lights:
       for his [|] mercy · en [|] dures for [|] ever,

8   the sun to [|] rule the [|] day:
       for his [|] mercy · en [|] dures for [|] ever,

9   the moon and the stars to [|] govern · the [|] night:
       for his [|] mercy · en [|] dures for [|] ever;

10   who struck down Egypt [|] and its [|] firstborn:
       for his [|] mercy · en [|] dures for [|] ever;

11   who brought out Israel [|] from a [|] mong them:
       for his [|] mercy · en [|] dures for [|] ever,

†12   with a strong hand and with [|] outstretched [|] arm:
       for his [|] mercy · en [|] dures for [|] ever;

13   who divided the Red Sea into [|] two [|] parts:
       for his [|] mercy · en [|] dures for [|] ever,

14   and made Israel pass [|] through the [|] midst of it:
       for his [|] mercy · en [|] dures for [|] ever;

15   who cast off Pharaoh and his host into the [|] Red [|] Sea:
       for his [|] mercy · en [|] dures for [|] ever,

16   who led his people [|] through the [|] wilderness:
       for his [|] mercy · en [|] dures for [|] ever;

17   who struck down [|] great [|] kings:
       for his [|] mercy · en [|] dures for [|] ever,

18   who slew [|] mighty [|] kings:
       for his [|] mercy · en [|] dures for [|] ever,

19   Sihon [|] king · of the [|] Amorites:
       for his [|] mercy · en [|] dures for [|] ever,

20   and Og the ǀ king of ǀ Bashan:
        for his ǀ mercy · enǀdures for ǀ ever;

21   who made over their ǀ land · as a heritage:
        for his ǀ mercy · enǀdures for ǀ ever,

22   as a heritage for ǀ Israel · his ǀ servant:
        for his ǀ mercy · enǀdures for ǀ ever;

23   who remembered us in our huǀmiliǀation:
        for his ǀ mercy · enǀdures for ǀ ever;

24   and delivered us ǀ from our ǀ enemies:
        for his ǀ mercy · enǀdures for ǀ ever;

25   who gives food to ǀ all that ǀ lives:
        for his ǀ mercy · enǀdures for ǀ ever;

26   O give thanks to the ǀ God of ǀ heaven:
        for his ǀ mercy · enǀdures for ǀ ever.

PSALM 137

1   By the waters of Babylon we sat ǀ down and ǀ wept:
        when ǀ we reǀmembered ǀ Zion.

2   As for our harps we ǀ hung them ǀ up:
        upon the ǀ trees · that are ǀ in that ǀ land.

3   For there those who led us away captive
        reǀquired of us · a ǀ song:
            and those who had despoiled us demanded mirth
            saying 'Sing us ǀ one of · the ǀ songs of ǀ Zion.'

*4 How can we sing the Lord's ǀ song · in a ǀ strange ǀ land?

5   If I forget you ǀ O Jeǀrusalem:
        let my right ǀ hand forǀget its ǀ mastery.

6   Let my tongue cling to the ǀ roof of · my ǀ mouth:
        if I do not remember you
            if I do not prefer Jerusalem aǀbove my ǀ chief ǀ joy.

*sung to the last four bars of the chant.

[7　Remember O Lord against the Edomites‿
　　the ˡ day · of Je ˡrusalem:
　　　　how they said 'Down with it　　down with it ˡ
　　　　raze it · to ˡ its found ˡations.'

8　O daughter of Babylon　　ˡ you that · lay ˡ waste:
　　happy shall he be who serves ˡ you as ˡ you have ·
　　served ˡ us;

[†]9　happy shall he be who ˡ takes your ˡ little ones:
　　and ˡ dashes them · a ˡgainst the ˡ stones.]

PSALM 138

1　I will give you thanks O Lord with my ˡ whole ˡ heart:
　　even before the ˡ gods · will I ˡ sing your ˡ praises.

2　I will bow down toward your holy temple
　　and give ˡ thanks to · your ˡ name:
　　　　because of your faithfulness and your loving-kindness
　　　　for you have made your name and your ˡ word
　　　　su ˡpreme · over ˡ all things.

3　At a time when I called to you you ˡ gave me ˡ answer:
　　and put new ˡ strength with ˡin my ˡ soul.

4　All the kings of the earth shall ˡ praise you · O ˡ Lord:
　　for they have ˡ heard the ˡ words of · your ˡ mouth;

5　and they shall sing of the ˡ ways · of the ˡ Lord:
　　that the ˡ glory · of the ˡ Lord is ˡ great.

6　For though the Lord is exalted　　he looks up ˡon the ˡ
　　lowly:
　　but he ˡ humbles · the ˡ proud · from a ˡfar.

7　Though I walk in the midst of danger
　　yet will you pre ˡserve my ˡ life:
　　　　you will stretch out your hand‿
　　　　against the fury of my enemies
　　　　and ˡ your right ˡ hand shall ˡ save me.

8　The Lord will complete his ˡ purpose ˡ for me:
　　your loving-kindness O Lord endures for ever
　　do not forsake the ˡ work · of your ˡ own ˡ hands.

PSALM 139

1   O Lord you have searched me ^l out and ^l known me:
     you know when I sit or when I stand
     you comprehend my ^l thoughts ^l long be^lfore.

2   You discern my path   and the places ^l where I ^l rest:
     you are ac ^l quainted · with ^l all my ^l ways.

3   For there is not a ^l word · on my ^l tongue:
     but you Lord ^l know it ^l alto^lgether.

4   You have encompassed me be^lhind · and be^lfore:
     and have ^l laid your ^l hand up^lon me.

† 5   Such knowledge is too ^l wonder·ful ^l for me:
     so ^l high · that I ^l cannot · en^ldure it.

6   Where shall I ^l go · from your ^l spirit:
     or where shall I ^l flee ^l from your ^l presence?

7   If I ascend into heaven ^l you are ^l there:
     if I make my bed in the grave ^l you are ^l there ^l also.

8   If I spread out my wings to^lwards the ^l morning:
     or dwell in the ^l utter·most ^l parts · of the ^l sea,

9   even there your ^l hand shall ^l lead me:
     and ^l your right ^l hand shall ^l hold me.

10   If I say   'Surely the ^l darkness · will ^l cover me:
     and the ^l night ^l will en^lclose me',

11   the darkness is no darkness with you
     but the night is as ^l clear · as the ^l day:
     the darkness and the ^l light are ^l both a ^llike.

12   For you have created my ^l inward ^l parts:
     you knit me together ^l in my ^l mother's ^l womb.

13   I will praise you for ^l you are · to be ^l feared:
     fearful are your ^l acts and ^l wonderful · your ^l works.

14   You knew my soul * and my bones were not ǀ
hidden ǀ from you:
     when I was formed in secret
     and ǀ woven · in the ǀ depths · of the ǀ earth.

15   Your eyes saw my limbs when they were ǀ
yet imǀperfect:
     and in your book were ǀ all my ǀ members ǀ written;

†16   day by ǀ day · they were ǀ fashioned:
     and not ǀ one was ǀ late in ǀ growing.

17   How deep are your thoughts to ǀ me O ǀ God:
     and how ǀ great ǀ is the ǀ sum of them!

18   Were I to count them
they are more in number ǀ than the ǀ sand:
     were I to come to the ǀ end · I would ǀ still
     be ǀ with you.

[19   If only you would slay the ǀ wicked · O ǀ God:
     if only the men of ǀ blood · would deǀpart ǀ from me!

20   For they affront you ǀ by their ǀ evil:
     and your enemies exǀalt themǀselves aǀgainst you.

21   Do I not hate them O Lord that ǀ hate ǀ you:
     do I not loathe ǀ those · who reǀbel aǀgainst you?

22   I hate them with a ǀ perfect ǀ hatred:
     they ǀ have beǀcome my ǀ enemies.]

23   Search me out O God and ǀ know my ǀ heart:
     put me to the ǀ proof and ǀ know my ǀ thoughts.

24   Look well lest there be any way of ǀ wicked·ness ǀ in me:
     and lead me in the ǀ way · that is ǀ everǀlasting.

PSALM 140

1   Deliver me O Lord from ǀ evil ǀ men:
     and preǀserve me · from ǀ vio·lent ǀ men,

2   who devise mischief ǀ in their ǀ hearts:
     who stir up ǀ enmi·ty ǀ day by ǀ day.

3   They have sharpened their **|** tongues · like a **|** serpent's:
     and the venom of **|** asps is **|** under · their **|** lips.

4   Keep me O Lord from the **|** power · of the **|** wicked:
     preserve me from violent men
     who think to **|** thrust me **|** from my **|** course.

5   The arrogant have laid a snare for me
     and rogues have **|** stretched the **|** net:
     they have set **|** traps a**|**long my **|** way.

6   But I have said to the Lord **|** 'you are · my **|** God':
     hear O **|** Lord the **|** voice of · my **|** pleading.

7   O Lord my God and my **|** sure **|** stronghold:
     you have covered my **|** head · in the **|** day of **|** battle.

8   Do not fulfil O Lord the de**|**sire · of the **|** wicked:
     nor further the **|** evil · that he **|** has de**|**vised.

[9   Let not those that beset me **|** lift their **|** heads:
     but let the mischief that is **|** on their **|** lips **|**
     bury them.

10   Let hot burning coals be **|** poured up**|**on them:
     let them be plunged into that miry pit‿
     from **|** which · they shall **|** never · a**|**rise.

[†] 11 Let no man of evil tongue find **|** footing · in the **|** land:
     the evil   the violent man   let him be **|** hunted **|**
     to the **|** end.]

12   I know that the Lord will work justice **|**
     for · the op**|**pressed:
     and right **|** judgements **|** for the **|** poor.

13   Surely the righteous shall have cause to **|** praise
     your **|** name:
     and the **|** just shall **|** dwell in · your **|** sight.

PSALM 141

1   O Lord I call to you   make **|** haste to **|** help me:
     and **|** hear my **|** voice · when I **|** cry.

2   Let my prayer be as | incense · be|fore you:
      and the lifting up of my | hands · as the |
      evening | sacrifice.

3   Set a guard O | Lord · on my | mouth:
      and | keep the | door · of my | lips.

4   Let not my heart incline to evil speech
      to join in wickedness with | wrong|doers:
      let me not taste the | pleasures ⌐of their | table.

5   But let the righteous | man chas|tise me:
      and the | faithful | man re|buke me.

6   Let not the oil of the wicked an|oint my | head:
      for I pray to you | still a|gainst their | wickedness.

7   They shall be cast down⌣
      by that Mighty One who ⌐ is their | judge:
      and how pleasing shall my | words be | to them | then!

8   As when a farmer | breaks the | ground:
      so shall their bones lie | scattered · at the |
      mouth of | Sheol.

9   But my eyes look to you O | Lord my | God:
      to you I come for refuge | do not · pour |
      out my | life.

10   Keep me from the snare that | they have | laid for me:
      and from the | traps · of the | evil|doers.

†11 Let the wicked fall together into their | own | nets:
      whilst | I pass | safely | by.

PSALM 142

1   I call to the Lord with a | loud | voice:
      with loud | voice · I en|treat his | favour.

2   I pour out my com|plaint be|fore him:
      and | tell him | all my | trouble.

3   When my spirit is faint within me you | know my | path:
      in the way where I walk | ⌣
      they have | hidden · a | snare for me.

4   I look to my right ǀ hand and ǀ see:
        but ǀ no ǀ man will ǀ know me;

5   all esǀcape is ǀ gone:
        and ǀ there is ǀ no one · who ǀ cares for me.

6   I call to you O Lord   I say ǀ 'You are · my ǀ refuge:
        you are my ǀ portion · in the ǀ land · of the ǀ living.'

7   Heed my loud crying   for I am ǀ brought · very ǀ low:
        O save me from my persecutors ǀ ‿
        for they ǀ are too ǀ strong for me.

8   Bring me ǀ out of · the ǀ prison-house:
        that ǀ I may ǀ praise your ǀ name.

†9   When you have given me ǀ my re ǀ ward:
        then will the ǀ righteous ǀ gather · a ǀ bout me.

PSALM 143

1   Hear my ǀ prayer O ǀ Lord:
        in your faithfulness consider my petition
        and in your ǀ righteous·ness ǀ give me ǀ answer.

2   Bring not your servant ǀ into ǀ judgement:
        for in your sight can ǀ no man ǀ living · be ǀ justified.

3   For the enemy has pursued me
    he has crushed my ǀ life · to the ǀ ground:
        he has made me dwell in darkness‿
        like ǀ those for ǀ ever ǀ dead.

4   Therefore my ǀ spirit · grows ǀ faint:
        and my ǀ heart · is ap ǀ palled with ǀ in me.

5   I remember the days of old
    I think on all that ǀ you have ǀ done:
        I con ǀ sider · the ǀ works of · your ǀ hands.

6   I stretch out my ǀ hands to ǀ ward you:
        my soul yearns for you ǀ like a ǀ thirsty ǀ land.

7   Be swift to hear me O Lord   for my ǀ spirit ǀ fails:
        hide not your face from me
        lest I be like ǀ those who · go ǀ down · to the ǀ Pit.

8   O let me hear of your merciful kindness in the morning
     for my ǀ trust · is in ǀ you:
         show me the way that I should go
         for ǀ you ǀ are my ǀ hope.

9   Deliver me from my ǀ enemies · O ǀ Lord:
     for I ǀ run to ǀ you for ǀ shelter.

10   Teach me to do your will   for ǀ you are · my ǀ God:
     let your kindly spirit ǀ lead me · in an ǀ even ǀ path.

(†)11   For your name's sake O Lord pre ǀserve my ǀ life:
        and for the sake of your righteousness ǀ ⌣
        bring me ǀ out of ǀ trouble.

[12   In your merciful goodness slay my enemies
      and destroy all those that ǀ come a ǀgainst me:
          for ǀ truly · I ǀ am your ǀ servant.]

PSALM 144

1   Blessèd be the ǀ Lord my ǀ Rock:
     who teaches my hands to ǀ war ·
     and my ǀ fingers · to ǀ fight;

2   my strength and my stronghold
     my fortress and ǀ my de ǀliverer:
         my shield to whom I come for refuge
         who sub ǀdues the ǀ peoples ǀ under me.

3   Lord what is man   that you should be ǀ
     mindful ǀ of him:
         or the son of man   ǀ that you ǀ should
         con ǀsider him?

4   Man is but a ǀ breath of ǀ wind:
     his days are like a ǀ shadow · that ǀ passes · a ǀway.

5   Part the heavens O Lord and ǀ come ǀ down:
     touch the ǀ mountains · and ǀ they shall ǀ smoke.

6   Dart forth your lightnings
     and scatter them on ǀ every ǀ side:
         let loose your ǀ arrows · with the ǀ roar ·
         of the ǀ thunderbolt.

7   Reach down your hand from on high
rescue me   and pluck me out of the | great | waters:
    out of the | hands | of the | aliens,

8   whose | mouths speak | perjury:
    and their right hand | is a · right | hand of | falsehood.

9   I will sing you a new | song O | God:
    on the ten-stringed | lute · will I | sing your | praises.

10   You have given | victory · to | kings:
    and de|liverance · to | David · your | servant.

11   O save me from the | peril · of the | sword:
    pluck me out of the | hands | of the | aliens,

12   whose | mouths speak | perjury:
    and their right hand | is a · right | hand of | falsehood.

13   Our sons in their youth shall be like | sturdy | plants:
    and our daughters as the | carved | corners ·
    of | palaces.

14   Our barns shall be full   and give food of | every | kind:
    the sheep shall lamb in our fields
    in | thousands · and | tens of | thousands.

15   Our cattle shall be heavy with calf
there shall be no miscarriage or un|timely | birth:
    and no loud | crying | in our | streets.

16   Happy the people whose lot is | such as | this:
    happy that people who | have the | Lord for ·
    their | God!

PSALM 145

1   I will exalt you O | God my | king:
    I will bless your | name for | ever · and | ever.

2   Every | day · will I | bless you:
    and praise your | name for | ever · and | ever.

3   Great is the Lord * and wonderfully | worthy ·
to be | praised:
    his greatness is | past | searching | out.

4   One generation shall praise your ˈ works · to anˈother:
         and deˈclare your ˈ mighty ˈ acts.

5   As for me * I will be talking⌣
         of the glorious splendour ˈ of your ˈ majesty:
         I will tell the ˈ story · of your ˈ marvel·lous ˈ works.

6   Men shall recount the power of your ˈ terri·ble ˈ deeds:
         and ˈ I will · proˈclaim your ˈ greatness.

†7   Their lips shall flow⌣
         with the remembrance of your aˈbundant ˈ goodness:
         they shall ˈ shout for ˈ joy at · your ˈ righteousness.

8   The Lord is ˈ gracious · and comˈpassionate:
         slow to anger ˈ and of ˈ great ˈ goodness.

9   The Lord is ˈ loving · to ˈ every man:
         and his mercy is ˈ over ˈ all his ˈ works.

10   All creation ˈ praises you · O ˈ Lord:
         and your faithful ˈ servants ˈ bless your ˈ name.

11   They speak of the glory ˈ of your ˈ kingdom:
         and ˈ tell of · your ˈ great ˈ might,

†12   that all mankind may know your ˈ mighty ˈ acts:
         and the glorious ˈ splendour ˈ of your ˈ kingdom.

13   Your kingdom is an everˈlasting ˈ kingdom:
         and your dominion enˈdures through ˈ
         all · generˈations.

14   The Lord upholds all ˈ those who ˈ stumble:
         and raises up ˈ those · that are ˈ bowed ˈ down.

15   The eyes of all look to ˈ you in ˈ hope:
         and you give them their ˈ food in ˈ due ˈ season;

16   you open ˈ wide your ˈ hand:
         and fill all things ˈ living · with your ˈ bounte·ous ˈ gift.

17   The Lord is just in ˈ all his ˈ ways:
         and ˈ faithful · in ˈ all his ˈ dealings.

18   The Lord is near to all who ˈ call upˈon him:
         to all who ˈ call upˈon him · in ˈ truth.

19   He will fulfil the desire of ‖ those that ‖ fear him:
    he will ‖ hear their ‖ cry and ‖ save them.

20   The Lord preserves all ‖ those that ‖ love him:
    but the wicked ‖ he will ‖ utterly · de ‖ stroy.

†21   My mouth shall speak the ‖ praises · of the ‖ Lord:
    and let all flesh bless his holy ‖ name⌣
    for ‖ ever · and ‖ ever.

PSALM 146

1   Praise the Lord.
    Praise the Lord ‖ O my ‖ soul:
    while I ‖ live · I will ‖ praise the ‖ Lord;

2   while I ‖ have · any ‖ being:
    I will sing ‖ praises ‖ to my ‖ God.

3   Put not your ‖ trust in ‖ princes:
    nor in the sons of ‖ men who ‖ cannot ‖ save.

4   For when their breath goes from them
    they return a ‖ gain · to the ‖ earth:
    and on that day ‖ all their ‖ thoughts ‖ perish.

5   Blessèd is the man whose help is the ‖ God of ‖ Jacob:
    whose hope is ‖ in the ‖ Lord his ‖ God,

6   the God who made ‖ heaven · and ‖ earth:
    the sea and ‖ all ‖ that is ‖ in them,

†7   who keeps ‖ faith for ‖ ever:
    who deals justice to ‖ those that ‖ are op ‖ pressed.

8   The Lord gives ‖ food · to the ‖ hungry:
    and ‖ sets the ‖ captives ‖ free.

9   The Lord gives ‖ sight · to the ‖ blind:
    the Lord lifts up ‖ those · that are ‖ bowed ‖ down.

10   The Lord ‖ loves the ‖ righteous:
    the Lord cares for the ‖ stranger ‖ in the ‖ land.

11   He upholds the ‖ widow · and the ‖ fatherless:
    as for the way of the wicked he ‖ turns it ‖
    upside ‖ down.

† 12 The Lord shall be | king for | ever:
　　　your God O Zion shall reign through all **generations** |
　　　Praise | – the | Lord.

PSALM 147

1 O praise the Lord.
　　　For it is good to sing praises | to our | God:
　　　and to | praise him · is | joyful · and | right.

2 The Lord is re|building · Je|rusalem:
　　　he is gathering together⏝
　　　the | scattered | outcasts · of | Israel.

3 He heals the | broken · in | spirit:
　　　and | binds | up their | wounds.

4 He counts the | number · of the | stars:
　　　and | calls them | all by | name.

5 Great is our Lord and | great · is his | power:
　　　there is no | measuring · his | under|standing.

6 The Lord re|stores the | humble:
　　　but he brings down the | wicked | to the | dust.

7 O sing to the Lord a | song of | thanksgiving:
　　　sing praises to our | God up|on the | harp.

8 He covers the heavens with cloud
　　　and prepares | rain · for the | earth:
　　　and makes the grass to | sprout up|on the | mountains.

9 He gives the | cattle · their | food:
　　　and feeds the young | ravens · that | call | to him.

10 He takes no pleasure in the | strength · of a | horse:
　　　nor does he de|light in | any · man's | legs,

† 11 but the Lord's delight is in | those that | fear him:
　　　who | wait in | hope · for his | mercy.

12 Praise the | Lord · O Je|rusalem:
　　　sing | praises · to your | God O | Zion.

13 For he has strengthened the | bars of · your | gates:
　　　and | blessed your | children · with|in you.

14   He makes peace with | in your | borders:
      and satisfies you | with the | finest | wheat.

15   He sends his com | mand · to the | earth:
      and his | word runs | very | swiftly.

16   He gives | snow like | wool:
      and | scatters · the | hoar-frost | like | ashes.

17   He sprinkles his ice like | morsels · of | bread:
      and the waters | harden | at his | frost.

†18   He sends out his | word and | melts them:
      he blows with his | wind · and the | waters | flow.

19   He made his word | known to | Jacob:
      his | statutes · and | judgements · to | Israel.

20   He has not dealt so with any | other | nation:
      nor have they knowledge of his laws |
      Praise | – the | Lord.

PSALM 148

1   Praise the Lord.
    Praise the | Lord from | heaven:
      O | praise him | in the | heights.

2   Praise him | all his | angels:
      O | praise him | all his | host.

3   Praise him | sun and | moon:
      praise him | all you | stars of | light.

4   Praise him you | highest | heaven:
      and you waters that | are a | bove the | heavens.

5   Let them praise the | name · of the | Lord:
      for he com | manded · and | they were | made.

6   He established them for | ever · and | ever:
      he made an ordinance which | shall not | pass a | way.

7   O praise the | Lord · from the | earth:
      praise him you sea | monsters · and | all | deeps;

8   fire and hail ' mist and ' snow:
        and storm-wind ful'filling ' his com'mand;

9   mountains and ' all ' hills:
        fruiting ' trees and ' all ' cedars;

10   beasts of the wild and ' all ' cattle:
        creeping ' things and ' winged ' birds;

11   kings of the earth and ' all ' peoples:
        princes and all ' rulers ' of the ' world;

12   young ' men and ' maidens:
        old ' men and ' children · to'gether.

13   Let them praise the ' name · of the ' Lord:
        for ' his · name a'lone · is ex'alted.

14   His glory is above ' earth and ' heaven:
        and he has lifted ' high the ' horn · of his ' people.

†15 Therefore he is the praise of ' all his ' servants:
        of the children of Israel   a people that is near him '
        Praise ' – the ' Lord.

PSALM 149

1   O praise the Lord
    and sing to the Lord a ' new ' song:
        O praise him in the as'sembly ' of the ' faithful.

2   Let Israel rejoice in ' him that ' made him:
        let the children of Zion be ' joyful ' in their ' king.

3   Let them praise him ' in the ' dance:
        let them sing his praise with ' timbrel '
        and with ' harp.

4   For the Lord takes de'light · in his ' people:
        he adorns the ' meek with ' his sal'vation.

5   Let his faithful ones ex'ult · in his ' glory:
        let them sing for ' joy up'on their ' beds.

6   Let the high praises of God be ' in their ' mouths:
        and a ' two-edged ' sword · in their ' hands,

7   to execute vengeance ˈ on the ˈ nations:
         and ˈ chastisement · upˈon the ˈ peoples,

8   to bind their ˈ kings in ˈ chains:
         and their ˈ nobles · with ˈ fetters · of ˈ iron,

†9   to visit upon them the judgement that ˈ is deˈcreed:
         such honour belongs to all his faithful servants ˈ
         Praise ˈ – the ˈ Lord.

PSALM 150

1   Praise the Lord.
         O praise ˈ God · in his ˈ sanctuary:
         praise him in the ˈ firma·ment ˈ of his ˈ power.

2   Praise him for his ˈ mighty ˈ acts:
         praise him according to ˈ his aˈbundant ˈ goodness.

3   Praise him in the ˈ blast · of the ˈ ram's horn:
         praise him upˈon the ˈ lute and ˈ harp.

4   Praise him with the ˈ timbrel · and ˈ dances:
         praise him upˈon the ˈ strings and ˈ pipe.

5   Praise him on the ˈ high · sounding ˈ cymbals:
         praise him upˈon the ˈ loud ˈ cymbals.

6   Let everything that has breath ˈ praise the ˈ Lord:
         O ˈ praise ˈ – the ˈ Lord.

AUTHORIZATION

The Services of *The Alternative Service Book 1980*, together with the Calendar, Rules to Order the Service, and Lectionary, are authorized pursuant to Canon B2 of the Canons of the Church of England for use from the date of publication of The Alternative Service Book until 31 December 1990.

Decisions as to which of the authorized services are to be used (other than occasional offices) shall be taken jointly by the incumbent and the parochial church council; in the case of occasional offices (other than Confirmation and Ordination), the decision is to be made by the minister conducting the service, subject to the right of any of the persons concerned to object beforehand to its use; in the case of Confirmation and Ordination services, the decision lies with the confirming or presiding bishop.

The versions of the Psalter which have been authorized for use by the General Synod under Canons B1 and B2 are the Prayer Book Psalter, The Revised Psalter, and The Liturgical Psalter.

COPYRIGHT

ACKNOWLEDGEMENTS

Biblical passages are reproduced with permission from

The Revised Standard Version of the Bible (RSV), copyright 1946, 1952, © 1971, 1973 by The Division of Christian Education of the National Council of the Churches of Christ in the USA

The New English Bible (NEB), © 1961, 1970 Oxford and Cambridge University Presses

The Jerusalem Bible (JB), © 1966 by Darton, Longman & Todd Ltd and Doubleday and Company Inc.

Today's English Version (TEV), © American Bible Society 1966, 1971, 1976. British usage edition *Good News Bible* published 1976 by The Bible Societies and Collins.

The Liturgical Psalter (pp. 1095 ff) is published separately as *The Psalms: a new translation for worship*, © English text 1976, 1977, David L Frost, John A Emerton, Andrew A Macintosh, all rights reserved, © pointing 1976, 1977 William Collins Sons & Co Ltd. Psalms printed within the services follow the text and pointing of The Liturgical Psalter.

The texts of the Nicene Creed, the Gloria in Excelsis, the Sanctus and Benedictus, and the Agnus Dei, as they appear in Holy Communion Rite A, and the texts of the Apostles' Creed and the Canticles Benedictus, Te Deum, Magnificat, and Nunc Dimittis, as printed in Morning Prayer and Evening Prayer, are copyright © 1970, 1971, 1975 International Consultation on English Texts (ICET). The Lord's Prayer in its modern form is adapted from the ICET version.

The Book of Common Prayer is Crown copyright; material from the Prayer Book (some in adapted form) is reproduced with permission.

Table 4: A Daily Eucharistic lectionary derives, with some adaptation, from the *Ordo Lectionum Missae* of the Roman Catholic Church.

Thanks are also due to the following for permission to reproduce copyright material:

The Church of the Province of South Africa: The Song of Christ's Glory, from the South African Daily Office.

The Joint Liturgical Group (of Churches in Great Britain): Collects and prayers from *The Daily Office Revised*.

Oxford University Press: The hymn 'O gladsome light, O grace', translated by Robert Bridges (1844–1930), from the *Yattendon Hymnal*; Prayers (some in adapted form) from *The Book of Common Worship of the Church of South India*.